AN INTERNATIONAL
DICTIONARY
OF
THEATRE LANGUAGE

AN INTERNATIONAL DICTIONARY OF THEATRE LANGUAGE

JOEL TRAPIDO, *General Editor*

EDWARD A. LANGHANS,
Editor for Western Theatre
JAMES R. BRANDON,
Editor for Asian Theatre
June V. Gibson,
Assistant to the Editors

Greenwood Press
Westport, Connecticut · London, England

COPYRIGHT ACKNOWLEDGMENT

Grateful acknowledgment is made to the Dictionary Society of North America for permission to reprint portions of Joel Trapido's "Theatre Dictionaries: A View from Inside." This appeared in Number 2-3, 1980-81, of the Society's Journal, *Dictionaries*, edited by Richard W. Bailey.

Library of Congress Cataloging in Publication Data
Main entry under title:

An International dictionary of theatre language.

  Bibliography: p.
  1. Theater—Dictionaries.   I. Trapido, Joel.
II. Langhans, Edward A.   III. Brandon, James R.
PN2035.I5   1985   792'.03'21   83-22756
ISBN 0-313-22980-5 (lib. bdg.)

Library of Congress Catalog Card Number: 83-22756
ISBN: 0-313-22980-5

First published in 1985

Greenwood Press
A division of Congressional Information Service, Inc.
88 Post Road West
Westport, Connecticut 06881

Printed in the United States of America

The paper used in this book complies with the Permanent Paper Standard issued by the National Information Standards Organization (Z39.48-1984).

10 9 8 7 6 5 4 3 2 1

To the Memory of A. M. Drummond,
to Evelyn,
and
to all the others who helped.

CONTENTS

EDITORS

JOEL TRAPIDO, General Editor, is Emeritus Professor of Drama at the University of Hawaii at Manoa. His articles on theatre have appeared in the *Educational Theatre Journal, Theatre Design and Technology, Dictionaries,* and in other publications.

EDWARD A. LANGHANS, Editor for Western Theatre, is Professor of Drama and Theatre at the University of Hawaii at Manoa. He is co-author of the multivolume *A Biographical Dictionary of Actors, Actresses, Musicians, Dancers, Managers and Other Stage Personnel in London, 1660-1800* and author of *Restoration Promptbooks* and numerous articles published in *Theatre Notebook, Theatre Survey, On-stage Studies, Studies in Eighteenth Century Culture, Essays in Theatre,* and other scholarly journals and books.

JAMES R. BRANDON, Editor for Asian Theatre, is Professor of Drama and Theatre at the University of Hawaii at Manoa. He is the author of *Theater in Southeast Asia* and *Brandon's Guide to Asian Theatre* and translator-editor of *Kabuki: Five Classic Plays, On Thrones of Gold: Three Javanese Shadow Plays,* and *Sanskrit Drama in Performance,* among other works. He has contributed articles to the *Encyclopaedia Britannica, the New Grove Dictionary of Music and Musicians, Theatre Journal, The Drama Review,* and other scholarly journals.

CONTRIBUTING EDITORS

Contributing Editors gathered and defined the terms of the subject with which they are identified below. Their contribution is a major one, since they provided nearly 4,000 entries.

Cho, Oh-kon   **Korean Theatre**
B.A., M.A., Korea University; M.F.A., University of Oklahoma; Ph.D., Michigan State University. Associate Professor of Theatre, State University of New York College at Brockport. Author: *Korean Puppet Theatre: Kkoktu Kaksi.*

Gibson, June V.   **Stage Costume**
B.A., SUNY at Buffalo; M.A., University of Hawaii at Manoa. Information Specialist, College of Tropical Agriculture; and Human Resources, University of Hawaii at Manoa. Free-lance writer and researcher.

Long, Roger,   **Southeast Asian Theatre**
B.S., Southern Illinois University; M.A., Michigan State University; Ph.D., University of Hawaii at Manoa. Associate Professor of Drama and Theatre, University of Hawaii at Manoa. Author: *Javanese Wayang Kulit*, articles on Southeast Asian theatre.

Richmond, Farley   **Indian Theatre**
B.F.A., M.F.A., University of Oklahoma; Ph.D. Michigan State University. Professor and Chair, Department of Theatre, Michigan State University. Area Editor: *Asian Theatre Journal*. Drama Editor, *Journal of South Asian Literature*.

Wichmann, Elizabeth Ann   **Chinese Theatre**
B.A., University of Iowa; M.A., Ph.D., University of Hawaii at Manoa. Assistant Professor of Drama and Theatre, University of Hawaii at Manoa. Associate Editor: *The Asian Theatre Journal; Asian Theatre: A Study Guide and Annotated Bibliography.* Contributor: *Chinese Theatre: From its Origins to the Present Day.*

CONSULTANTS

Consultants examined some or all of the terms in the subjects with which they are identified below. They suggested additions and deletions and often provided new or corrected definitions. Except for some slight editing, we have printed their biographies as they supplied them.

Adedeji, Joel Adeyinka   **African Theatre**
M.A., New York University; Ph.D., University of Ibadan; Diploma Drama, Rose Bruford College; L.R.A.M. (Great Britain); F.R.S.A. (Great Britain). Professor and Head of Theatre Arts, University of Ibadan, Nigeria. Director of University Theatre Ensemble. Author: numerous articles on African drama and theatre. Editorial Member: *Theatre Research International*. Regional Editor, Africa: *Theatre Companies of the World*.

Aquino, Belinda A.   **Philippine Theatre**
B.A., University of the Philippines; M.A., University of Hawaii at Manoa; Ph.D., Cornell University. Assistant Professor of Political Science and Director of Philippine Studies, University of Hawaii at Manoa. Editor: *Philippine Studies Occasional Papers*. Consulting Editor: *Journal of Asian-Pacific and World Perspectives*.

Arnott, James Fullarton, 1914-1982   **Theatre History**
T.D., M.A., M.Litt., Oxon. First Professor of Drama, University of Glasgow, 1966-1979. Author: *English Theatrical Literature* (with J.W. Robinson), Sale Catalogues of Eminent Persons, vol. 12, *Actors*. Editor: *Theatre Research international*, 1964, 1981.

Arnott, Peter D.   **Greek and Roman Theatre**
B.A., Wales; B.A., Oxford; M.A., Wales; Ph.D., Wales; D.H.L., (Hon.) Suffolk. Professor of Drama, Tufts University. Author: *Greek Scenic Conventions*,

Greek and Roman Theatre, Introduction to the Greek Theatre, Theater in its Time.

Bailey, Richard W.   **Lexicography**
A.B., Dartmouth College; M.A. and Ph.D., University of Connecticut. Professor of English Language and Literature, The University of Michigan. Editor: *Dictionaries: Journal of the Dictionary Society of North America.* Author and Editor: *English Stylistics, Early Modern English, Stylistics and Style, Varieties of Present-Day English, English as a World Language, Computing in the Humanities, Literacy for Life.*

Bakshi, Sri Ram V.   **Indian Theatre**
B.A., M.A., Osmania University; Ph.D., University of Kansas. Associate Professor of Theatre, State University of New York at Brockport. Author: articles on Indian theatre and aesthetics. Editor: *Conversation on Indian Theatre.* Contributor: *Journal of South Asian Literature.*

Bellman, Willard F.   **Theatre Lighting, Scenography**
Ph.D., Northwestern University. Professor of Theatre, California State University-Northridge. Author: *Lighting the Stage, Art and Practice; Scene Design, Stage Lighting, Sound, Costume and Makeup, A Scenographic Approach.*

Bowman, Ned A.   **Technical Theatre**
Ph.D., Stanford University. General Manager, Rosco Laboratories. Author: *Handbook of Technical Practice for the Performing Arts, 1972-1975,* other titles.

Bowman, Walter P.   **Theatre Language, French**
B.A., Bowdoin College; Ph.D., Columbia University. Professor Emeritus of English and Comparative Literature, State University of New York at Brockport. Co-Author: *Theatre Language: A Dictionary of Terms in English,* and numerous articles and reviews.

Boyd, Mark A.   **Technical Theatre**
B.A., Macalester College; M.F.A., University of Hawaii at Manoa. Associate Professor of Drama and Theatre, University of Hawaii at Manoa.

Breneman, Lucille N.   **Readers Theatre**
B.A., Baylor University; M.A., University of Hawaii at Manoa. Emeritus Professor of Speech, University of Hawaii at Manoa. Co-Author: *Once Upon A Time: A Storytelling Handbook.* Contributor: *Readers Theatre Handbook.* Associate Editor: *Oral Interpretation of Literature.*

Burnim, Kalman A.   **Restoration,**
                                              18th, 19th C Theatre
B.A., Tufts University; M.A., Indiana University; Ph.D., Yale University.
Fletcher Professor of Oratory and Drama, Tufts University. Author: *David Garrick, Director*; articles on theatre history. Co-Author: *A Biographical Dictionary of Actors, Actresses, Musicians, Dancers, Managers, and Other Stage Personnel in London, 1660-1800.* Editor: *The Plays of George Colman the Elder.*

Burns, Alfred   **Greek and Latin**
B.A., M.A., Ph.D., University of Washington. Emeritus Professor of Classics, University of Hawaii at Manoa.

Caro, Warren   **Theatrical Production and Management**
B.A., J.D., Cornell University. Formerly: Executive Director, The Theatre Guild-American Theatre Society; Director of Theatre Operations, The Shubert Organization, Inc.; Vice President, American National Theatre and Academy (ANTA); Vice President and Chairman of the Board of Trustees, the Academy of Dramatic Art.

Carroll, W. Dennis   **Playwriting, Theory, Criticism**
B.A., M.A., Sydney University; M.F.A., University of Hawaii at Manoa; Ph.D., Northwestern University. Professor of Drama and Theatre, University of Hawaii at Manoa. Author: articles on Australian drama and theatre. Co-Author: articles on Finnish drama and theatre. Editor: *Kumu Kahua Plays.*

Chinoy, Helen Krich   **Acting and Directing**
B.A., M.A., New York University; Ph.D., Columbia University. Professor of Theatre, Smith College. Author: *Reunion: A Self-Portrait of the Group Theatre.* Co-Editor: *Actors on Acting, Directors on Directing, Women in American Theatre.*

Corson, Richard   **Stage Makeup**
B.A., DePauw University; M.A., Louisiana State University. Adjunct Professor, Southern Methodist University. Author: *Stage Makeup, Fashions in Hair, Fashions in Eyeglasses, Fashions in Makeup.*

Dissanayake, Wismal   **South Asian Theatre**
M.A., University of Pennsylvania; Ph.D. Cambridge University. Co-ordinator of the Humanities Forum, East-West Center, Honolulu. Author: many articles on drama and literature.

Donohue, Joseph   **18th-19th C. Theatre, Restoration**
Ph.D., Princeton University. Professor of English, University of Massachusetts, Amherst. Co-General Editor, *The London Stage 1800-1900: A Documentary Record and Calendar of Performances.* Author: *Dramatic Character in the*

English Romantic Age, Theatre in the Age of Kean. Advisory Editor: *Nineteenth Century Theatre Research.* Associate Editor: *Theatre Journal.*

Dukore, Bernard F.   **Playwriting, Theory, Criticism**
B.A., Brooklyn College; M.A., Ohio State University; Ph.D., University of Illinois. Professor of Drama and Theatre, University of Hawaii at Manoa. Author: *Harold Pinter; The Theatre of Peter Barnes; Bernard Shaw, Playwright; Bernard Shaw, Director.* Editor: *The Collected Screenplays of Bernard Shaw, Dramatic Theory and Criticism.*

Erickson, Mitchell   **Acting, Directing, Stage Management**
B.A., University of Hawaii at Manoa. Faculty, H.B. Studio, New York City. Production Stage Manager: Broadway; Kennedy Center, Washington, D.C. Actor, Director.

Falk, Heinrich R.   **Spanish**
B.A., Wittenberg University; Ph.D., University of Southern California. Professor of Theatre, California State University-Northridge.

Fernández, Doreen   **Philippine Theatre**
A.B., St. Scholastica College; M.A., Ph.D., Ateneo de Manila University. Chair: Department of English, Ateneo de Manila University. Author: *The Iloilo Zarzuela: 1903-1930; Contemporary Theatre Arts: Asia and the United States.*

Foley, Mary Kathleen   **Southeast Asian Theatre**
B.A., Rosemont College; M.A., University of Massachusetts; Ph.D., University of Hawaii at Manoa. Assistant Professor of Theater Arts, University of California at Santa Cruz. Editor and Contributor: publications on Southeast Asian theatre.

Frink, Peter H.   **Theatre Architecture**
B. Arch., Pennsylvania State University; M.S., Columbia University; M.F.A., Yale University. Principal/Partner, Frink and Beuchat: Architects; Assembly Places International. Editor: *Theatre Design '72.* Contributor: AIA Graphic Standards, Seventh Edition; Neufert-Architect's Data. Author: Miscellaneous articles on theatre architecture. Licensed Architect: Florida, New Jersey, New York, Pennsylvania, Virginia.

Gerould, Daniel C.   **Russian, Polish Theatre**
A.B., M.A., Ph.D., University of Chicago. Professor of Theatre and Comparative Literature, Graduate School, City University of New York. Author: *Witkacy.* Editor: *Melodrama, American Melodrama.* Translator: *Twentieth-Century Polish Avant-Garde Drama.*

Goldberg, Moses   **Children's Theatre**
B.S., Tulane University; M.A., Stanford University; M.A., University of Washington; Ph.D., University of Minnesota. Producing Director, Stage One: The Louisville Children's Theatre, Louisville, Kentucky. Vice Chairman, U.S. Center for ASSITEJ (International Association of Theatre for Young People). Author: *Children's Theatre: A Philosophy and a Method*, many plays for young audiences. 1980 Charlotte B. Chorpenning Cup for outstanding contributions to children's literature.

Graham-White, Anthony   **African Theatre**
A.B., Harvard University; Ph.D., Stanford University. Professor and Head, Department of Communication and Theatre, University of Illinois at Chicago. Author: *The Drama of Black Africa*.

Haskell, Phyllis A.   **Dance**
B.A., University of Arizona; M.F.A., University of Utah. Associate Professor of Drama and Theatre and Director of Dance, University of Hawaii at Manoa.

Hauch, Duane E.   **Vietnamese Theatre**
B.S., Northwestern University; M.S. University of Dayton; M.A., University of Hawaii at Manoa; Ph.D., Southern Illinois University. Author: *Theatre in the ESL Classroom*.

Hernandez, Tomas   **Philippine Theatre**
Ph.D., University of Santo Tomas; M.A., University of California-Santa Barbara; Ph.D., University of Hawaii at Manoa. Associate Professor of Theatre, Co-Director of Opera, Kansas State University. Author: *The Emergence of Modern Drama in the Philippines, (1898-1912)*.

Hewitt, Barnard   **Playwriting, Theory, and Criticism;**
                                    Restoration, 18th, 19th C Theatre
B.A., M.A., Ph.D., Cornell University. Professor of Theatre Emeritus, University of Illinois, Champaign-Urbana. Author: *Theatre U.S.A., History of the Theatre from 1800 to the present*. Editor: *The Renaissance Stage, Adolphe Appia's Music and the Art of the Theatre* and *The Work of Living Art*.

Hu, John Y.H.   **Chinese Theatre**
B.A., National Taiwan University; M.A., Baylor University; Ph.D., Indiana University. Professor of Theatre and Comparative Literature, National Taiwan University. Author: *Ts'ao Yu, In the Plum Song* (Chinese). Editor: Chung-Wai Literary Monthly.

Hunt, Tamara Robin   **Puppetry, Creative Drama**
B.A., M.F.A., Arizona State University; Ph.D., University of Southern Cali-

fornia. Professor of Drama and Theatre, University of Hawaii at Manoa. Co-Author: *Puppetry in Early Childhood Education, Pocketful of Puppets: Mother Goose.* Contributor: *The Puppetry Journal, Children Today, Continuum.*

Jit, Krishen   **Malaysian Theatre**
M.A., University of California at Berkeley. Professor of American History and Southeast Asian Theatre, University of Malaya. Director, actor, critic, author of many articles on traditional and contemporary theatre.

Leiter, Samuel L.   **Japanese Theatre**
B.A., Brooklyn College; M.F.A., University of Hawaii at Manoa; Ph.D., New York University. Professor of Theatre, Brooklyn College, CUNY. Author: *From Belasco to Brook: Great Stage Directors of the Century;* articles on Japanese theatre, American theatre history. Editor: *The Art of Kabuki: Famous Plays in Performance; Kabuki Encyclopedia; Encyclopedia of the New York Stage.*

Lo, Chin-T'ang   **Chinese Theatre**
B.A., M.A., Ph.D., National University of Taiwan; D. Litt, National Normal, Taiwan. Professor of Chinese Literature, University of Hawaii at Manoa. Author: (in English) *The History of Chinese Folk Literature.* (In Chinese) *The History of Chinese Short Songs; The Study of Synopses of Yuan Zaju Dramas; On Classical Chinese Drama; An Annotated Edition of Selected Ming and Qing Plays; A Comprehensive Bibliography of Chinese Drama; Short Songs of the Northern Style; Short Songs of the Southern Style.* Translator: (Chinese into English) *San Chu: Lyric Songs of the Yuan Dynasty.* (Japanese into Chinese) *A Study of the Dramatists of the Ming Dynasty.*

Loken-Kim, Christine   **Korean Theatre**
B.A., University of Michigan; M.A., UCLA; Ph.D. candidate, University of North Carolina-Chapel Hill. Author: articles on Korean dance and drama.

MacKay, Patricia   **Scenography**
Editor: *Theatre Crafts.* Co-Author: *The Shakespeare Complex.* Contributor: *Theatre Crafts Book of Costume,* other publications.

Mackerras, Colin P.   **Chinese Theatre**
B.A., Ph.D., The Australian National University; M. Litt., Cambridge. Chairman and Foundation Professor, School of Modern Asian Studies, Griffith University, Brisbane, Australia. Author: *The Rise of the Peking Opera, 1770-1870: Social Aspects of the Theatre in Manchu China; Amateur Theatre in China 1949-66; The Chinese Theatre in Modern Times: from 1840 to the Present Day; The Performing Arts in Contemporary China; Modern China: A Chronology.* Editor and Contributor: *Chinese Theater from its Origins to the Present Day.*

Matlaw, Myron   **20th C Drama**
M.A., Ph.D., University of Chicago. Professor of English, Queens College,
City University of New York. Author: *Modern World Drama* and other works.

Meserve, Walter J.   **Restoration, 18th, 19th C Theatre**
A.B., Bates College; M.A., Boston University; Ph.D., University of Washing-
ton. Professor of Theatre and Drama, Indiana University-Bloomington. Director:
Institute for American Theatre Studies. Author: *An Outline History of American
Drama, An Emerging Entertainment: Drama of the American People to 1828,
Robert E. Sherwood: Reluctant Moralist, American Drama to 1900.*

Morrison, Jack S.   **Theatre Administration and Management**
B.A., M.A., UCLA; Ed.D., University of Southern California. Executive Director Emeritus: American Theatre Association. Author: *The Rise of the Arts on
the American Campus* and miscellaneous articles.

Mullin, Donald   **Theatre Architecture**
A.B., A.M., State University of Iowa. Professor, University of Guelph, Canada.
Editor: *Essays in Theatre*. Author: *Development of the Playhouse, Victorian
Actors and Actresses in Review*. Contributor: *Encyclopedia Americana*.

Oda, Reiko T.   **Ballet**
B.A., University of Hawaii. Director, Oda Ballet School.

Oliver, William I.   **Spanish Theatre, Acting, Directing**
Ph.D., Cornell University. Professor of Theater, University of California at
Berkeley. Author: various articles and plays. Translator: French, Spanish, and
Latin-American drama. Director and Actor. Co-Editor: *Modern Drama: Essays
in Criticism*. Editor and Translator: *Voices of Change in the Spanish American
Theater*.

Ortolani, Benito   **Commedia dell'arte, Italian, German**
Ph.D., University of Vienna. Chairman, Department of Theatre, Brooklyn Col-
lege. Professor of Theatre, Brooklyn College and the Graduate Center of the
City University of New York; Director of the A.S.T.R. International Bibliog-
raphy of the Theatre and of the Theatre Research Data Center. Author: *Das
Kabukitheater, Kulturgeschichte der Anfaenge; Zenchiku's Aesthetics of the No
Theatre; Teatro No: Costumi e Maschere*. Author of articles on Japanese theatre,
on bibliography of the theatre, and on theatre education.

Rutnin, Mattani Mojdara   **Thai Theatre**
B.A., Wellesley College; M.A., Middlebury College-Sorbonne; Ph.D., University of London. Certificate in Acting and Directing, Royal Academy of Dramatic Art, London; Diplome des Études Françaises, Université de Paris. Professor

of Drama and Literature and Head, Drama Department, Thammasat University, Thailand. Author: *Development of Thai Drama*, textbooks and articles in drama and literature, playwright of numerous stage and television plays, film script writer. Editor: *The Siamese Theatre*. Director and Producer: traditional and modern plays.

Shattuck, Charles H.   **Acting, Directing, Popular Theatre**
A.B., M.A., Ph.D., University of Illinois. Professor of English Emeritus, University of Illinois. Author: *The Shakespeare Promptbooks, The Hamlet of Edwin Booth, Shakespeare on the American Stage*. Co-Editor: *Accent, A Quarterly of New Literature*.

Vaught, Raymond   **Music**
B.A., University of Idaho; M. Mus., Eastman School of Music, University of Rochester; Ph.D., Stanford University. Emeritus Professor of Music, University of Hawaii at Manoa.

Virulrak, Surapone   **Thai Theatre**
B.S., Chulalongkorn University; M.S., M.A., University of Washington; Ph.D., University of Hawaii at Manoa. Assistant Professor, Faculty of Communication Arts, Chulalongkorn University.

Wearing, J. P.   **Restoration, 18th, 19th C**
B.A., Ph.D., University of Wales; M.A., University of Saskatchewan. Associate Professor of English, University of Arizona. Author: *The Collected Letters of Sir Arthur Pinero; English Drama and Theatre, 1800-1900; American and British Theatrical Biography: A Directory; The London Stage 1900-1909: A Calendar of Plays and Players; The London Stage 1910-1919: A Calendar of Plays and Players*. Editor: *Nineteenth Century Theatre Research*.

Wehlburg, Albert F.C.   **Stage Lighting**
B.A.E., M.A., Ed.S., Ed.D, University of Florida. Instructor in Technical Theatre & Lighting Design, University of Florida. Author: *La Mordaza—The Vise* (translator) Literary Discoveries, 1966; "It is Better Upside Down," *Players Magazine*, 1974; *Theatre Lighting: An Illustrated Glossary, 1975*.

Wilmeth, Don Burton   **Popular Entertainment, Restoration, 18th, 19th C**
B.A., Abilene Christian University; M.A., University of Arkansas; Ph.D., University of Illinois. Professor of Theatre Arts and English, Chair, Department of Theatre Arts, Brown University. Author: *George Frederich Cooke: Machiavel of the Stage, The American Stage to World War I, American and English Popular Entertainment, The Language of American Popular Entertainment, Variety En-*

tertainment and Outdoor Amusements. Co-Editor: *Plays by William Gillette, Plays by Augustin Daly.*

Wolz, Carl   **Dance**
B.A., University of Chicago; M.A., University of Hawaii at Manoa. Dean of Dance, Hong Kong Academy for Performing Arts. Author: *Bugaku: Japanese Court Dance.*

Wright, Lin   **Children's Theatre**
B.S., M.A., Ph.D., University of Minnesota. Professor of Theatre, Arizona State University. President: Children's Theatre Association of America, 1982-83. Author: miscellaneous articles on child drama.

Yao, Hai-Hsing   **Chinese Theatre**
B.A., National Chen-chi University; M.A., University of Illinois at Champaign-Urbana. Director and actress.

CONTRIBUTORS

Contributors provided hundreds of descriptions of terms in the subjects with which they are identified below. These were of great value to the editors.

Finney, Sandra K.   **Stage Costume**
B.A., M.A., San Francisco State College. Associate Professor of Drama and Theatre, University of Hawaii at Manoa.

Tudiver, Lillian   **Popular Entertainment**
B.A., Brooklyn College, M.S. L.S. Columbia University. Emeritus Chief, Social Science Division, Brooklyn Public Library.

Many others have helped. The work could not have been completed without the many contributions in time and labor of the faculty, staff, and students of the University of Hawaii Department of Drama & Theatre. It is not possible to name them all, but Nancy Takei, a secretary without peer, is high on our list. Students Yukihiro Goto, Therese Moore, Sheila Turner, and Michiko Ueno have been helpful in various ways. So have faculty members Glenn Cannon, Terence Knapp, and Richard Mason. The staff of the University's Hamilton Library has assisted as only selfless professionals can; particular thanks go to Patricia Polanski, Annabelle Takahashi, and Susan Thompson. Administration, faculty, and staff elsewhere in the University have been cooperative in many ways: they include Mustapha K. Benouis, Leon Edel, James D. Ellsworth, Judith Gething Hughes, Robert J. Littman, Walter H. Maurer, Lawrence A. Reid, Paul A. Roth, and Richard K. Seymour. The University of Hawaii Foundation provided a grant that was most helpful in the later stages of work on the *Dictionary*. Outside the University, at various times we have had help ranging from encouragement or advice through providing assistance with certain specialized entries. Such aid has been given by Dan Anderson, Bernard Beckerman, L. W. Conolly, Walter Craver, Donald Doyle, Mary Jane Evans, Gene Fitzgerald, Frank Fuller, Jr., Roger Alan Hall, Errol G. Hill, Francis B. Hodge, Richard Hosley, Ken Kanter,

Gerald Kawaoka, George and Portia Kernodle, T. J. King, Hobe Morrison, the late Henry Alonzo Myers, Jock Purinton, A. C. Scott, James Sledd, Walter H. Stainton, Andrew T. Tsubaki, Zelma H. Weisfeld, Margaret B. Wilkerson, Melvin R. White, and Daniel S. P. Yang. For all this help we are most grateful.

PREFACE

This *Dictionary* began—was conceived is perhaps more accurate—in the early 1930s, when the General Editor, then a wide-eyed undergraduate, began to work in the Cornell University Theatre and found that many of the terms he heard backstage and in rehearsals, though clear enough in context, were not to be found in their theatre meanings in dictionaries. Having a long-standing interest in language, he began to make notes on theatre terms and meanings. Later, Professor Alexander M. Drummond was understanding enough to permit him to do a dissertation on the language of the classical and medieval theatres, and of the *Commedia dell'arte*. Since that time, a great deal of work has been done on theatre terminology. (Some had been done earlier. See the "Brief History of Theatre Glossaries and Dictionaries," later in these pages, for a treatment of this subject.) The laborers in the vineyard of the *Dictionary* could not have gone so far as they have without the fruits of their predecessors. The editors have a special debt to some of the major theatre dictionaries and glossaries: Walter P. Bowman and Robert H. Ball's *Theatre Language*, Don Wilmeth's *The Language of Popular Entertainment*, Albert Wehlburg's *An Illustrated Glossary of Stage Lighting*, and Wilfred Granville's *The Theater Dictionary*.

This Dictionary is designed to assist a wide variety of users. They include theatregoers, readers of plays and works about the theatre, undergraduate and graduate students, theatre people who work onstage or backstage or in the front of the house, amateurs and professionals, theatre faculties and scholars from related disciplines.

The *Dictionary* includes terms from theatre throughout the world, both historical and extant, as used in the English-speaking world. More specifically, the *Dictionary* enters some 10,000 English terms, as well as 5,000 from more than 60 foreign languages. The aim has been to find and define any theatre term which has been used by readers or speakers of English.

The *Dictionary* is the work of the Editors, the Contributing Editors, and more than 50 Consultants and Contributors. Editor Trapido wrote the entries for ancient Greece and Rome, stage lighting, creative drama, readers theatre, and some of the entries in various other subjects. Editor Langhans wrote most of the other entries for Western theatre, with Contributing Editor Gibson providing those for Western stage costume, many of the French entries, and some of those in various other subjects. Editor Brandon wrote the entries for Japanese theatre and worked closely with Contributing Editors Cho (Korea), Long (Southeast Asia), Richmond (India), and Wichmann (China). Except for a few definitions added in the final stages of preparing the *Dictionary*, all entries have been examined by specialists in their subjects. These consultants often suggested revisions or deletions and provided new meanings or entries, all of great value. The final responsibility for the definitions in the *Dictionary* rests, however, with the three editors.

Dictionary makers since before Samuel Johnson have relied on their predecessors, often using earlier definitions word for word. Where possible, we have avoided reproducing our predecessors, but the accuracy and cogency of many earlier definitions are such that some dozens of our entries are reproductions or near-reproductions of earlier definitions.

It is hardly possible to acknowledge adequately the volunteer assistance of June V. Gibson. Some of her contributions are noted elsewhere, but they do not indicate that for more than four years she has served the *Dictionary* as editorial, research, and administrative assistant, often after full-time work in other areas of the University of Hawaii. She also has prepared the bibliography and saw to the readying of the final manuscript. Editors Langhans, Brandon, and I, not to mention future users of the *Dictionary*, will be ever grateful for her devotion.

Inevitably, there will be corrections and comments. Any of the editors will be happy to receive them at the Department of Drama and Theatre, University of Hawaii at Manoa, Honolulu, Hawaii 96822.

Joel Trapido

GUIDE TO THE *DICTIONARY*

SCOPE

The *Dictionary* records the language of the theatre as used in books, articles, and conversations in English. The majority of the entries are, therefore, from the English of Britain and the United States, with Australian and Canadian terms entered when they differ from those in the United States and Britain. Also included are thousands of foreign terms used in English. The chronological coverage extends from the 6th Century BC to the present day, with the period when an older term was used ordinarily indicated in the definition.

The *Dictionary* covers the various aspects of production and drama. Included are such areas as acting, aesthetics, burlesque, children's theatre, costume, creative drama, criticism, dance, design, directing, dramatic literature, dramaturgy, lighting, makeup, musical theatre, opera, playwriting, puppetry, readers theatre, scenery, scenography, stage management, stage technology, theatre management, theatre architecture, theatre theory, variety, and vaudeville.

Various factors determined the extent of coverage devoted to any one subject, theatre form, or language. The number of practical theatre terms—production, staging, acting, technical theatre—is large, and this is reflected in the *Dictionary*. On the other hand, only a small fraction of the some 10,000 archaic Sanskrit theatre terms that appear in books in English are reported, in part because no clear understanding of the meaning comes down to us. Similarly, only a relatively small proportion of the terms used in such Western forms as musical theatre and opera are entered, in this instance because the *Dictionary* focuses on the theatrical rather than the musical aspects of these forms. In Asia, however, music and dance are integral to all traditional theatre; therefore a larger proportion of these terms will be found in the *Dictionary*. The small number of Russian, Lao, and Burmese terms reflects the relatively few words from these languages used in publications in English, while the larger number of Latin, French, Japanese, and Chinese terms reflects the opposite situation.

The *Dictionary* generally avoids proper nouns, trade names, or other terms with initial capitals. Some are entered because the evidence indicates that they are part of theatre language. Initial capitals are also used for foreign terms that are regularly capitalized in the original language, the obvious example being German nouns.

Inasmuch as the *Dictionary* deals with terms specific to the theatre and to drama, most standard implements and materials, however much used in the theatre, are excluded. So is most of the language of electricity, physics, various arts and crafts, and of the makers and manufacturers of theatre supplies and equipment. Thus, ceiling plate, a special piece of stage hardware, is included, but not strap hinge, caster, or other standard hardware.

The language of the mass media is excluded, as is the language of such forms of popular entertainment as the circus, night club, and magic acts (for which see Don Wilmeth's admirable *The Language of Popular Entertainment*). Excluded, too, are many of the terms in the multilingual glossaries (for which see below, in the Brief History of Theatre Glossaries and Dictionaries).

Foreign terms are included only if they appear in theatre publications in English in romanized form (for example, from languages such as Greek, Russian, Japanese, Chinese).

The bars to inclusion in the *Dictionary* are lowered for historic theatre. An example is 'gas bracket,' a non-theatrical term from the language of gaslighting, which was basic to theatre operations in the 19th Century. Entered, too, are many fashion terms much used in theatrical costume shops when preparing plays written or set before the early 20th Century. Similarly, a number of specialized materials and tools from crafts and arts outside the theatre are entered because, while important in the theatre now or in the past, they are not generally familiar and are usually found only in specialized glossaries; examples are angular liner, demet, and fitch.

Whether historic or not, terms adequately defined for our purposes in *Webster's New Collegiate Dictionary* are omitted unless their absence would create too obvious a gap in a theatre dictionary. For the same reason, we have sometimes included a lay meaning after one or more theatre meanings. An example is 'theatrics' as extravagant behavior, which appears after two theatre meanings.

The spelling of terms in foreign languages reflects their appearance in publications in English. Many—Russian, Chinese, Javanese, for example—have more than one transliteration. The most widespread recent spelling is the main entry; other usual spellings are noted there, and entered as cross-references. For example, the Library of Congress system is used for Russian; for Chinese, main entries are in *pinyin*, with Wade-Giles spelling noted and cross-referenced. Occasionally, a particular term appears in a number of spellings (as in *lakorn, lagon, lakhon*); the *Dictionary* attempts to include all variants that might be encountered with any frequency. When a Chinese term is defined in passing within another entry, its *pinyin* spelling is given first and its Wade-Giles spelling second, with 'or' separating the two. For instance, the definition of the term *wuchang* includes the information, "Also called gongs and drums (*luogu* or *lo ku*." These are not alternative Chinese spellings, but rather alternative romanizations of the same word; the entries for *luogo* and *lo ku* then simply refer the reader to *wuchang*.

METHOD OF ALPHABETIZING

Entries are in strict alphabetical order by letter, not word: dead blackout, deadline, dead pack. A few entries begin with an article in parentheses: (the) hail-hail; such entries are alphabetized by the letters after the article.

FORM OF ENTRIES

Entries begin with a headword (**ender,** *ikria*), followed by the language if not English. ('Chinese' means Mandarin Chinese, except for a very few terms in other regional Chinese dialects. 'Philippine' and 'Indonesian' identify terms from any of the Philippine and Indonesian languages.) A literal meaning of a foreign term, if given, usually follows immediately; occasionally, a literal meaning is dealt with as part of a discussion within an entry. A definition is next, sometimes followed by discussion, which may include a bit of encyclopedic information designed to enrich the meaning. If two or more meanings are given, they are usually numbered; but sometimes a range of meanings is discussed without numbering. The order of meanings is often by estimated frequency of use; but the sequence may be chronological, by category, or in some other way made clear in the definition. Entries may include synonyms, near-synonyms, cross-references, and citations.

Parts of speech are not given, since definitions are grammatically parallel to the headword:

end an act cold   To fail to get applause.

ender   The last act on a bill.

ikria (Greek)   Especially in the latter half of the 5th C BC, spectators' seats in a theatre.

Note that because *ikria* is plural, the definition is given in the plural.

Italics are used only for foreign terms. Both English and foreign theatre terms occur in many definitions; to avoid interrupting the reader, terms in English are generally unmarked in any way. Where this might be confusing, quotation marks enclose the term.

As part of the effort to make entries readable, abbreviations are kept to a minimum. They are such standard shortenings as i.e., e.g., and q.v., along with an occasional widely-used symbol such as OED for the *Oxford English Dictionary*. Beyond this, ordinal numbers and C indentify centuries: 18th C, 5th C BC; AD is occasionally used where its absence might be puzzling or misleading: "From the 4th C BC to the 1st C AD." For the shortenings used in bibliographical citations, please see Citations, below.

Such labels as slang, colloquial, argot, etc. are generally avoided. Often, however, various qualifiers locate a term: among lighting people, in box-office parlance, backstage, and other such guides to usage. Definitions place a term in time so far as our evidence permits: in the Renaissance, since the late 19th C, especially in the past, in medieval times, and other such indications of when a term was used. Ancient Latin terms are labelled Latin Roman after the headword; the time of other Latin terms is indicated in the definition. Greek terms apply to the classical theatre except for a very few identified in their definitions with later theatres.

A certain number of terms, almost all of which are historical fashion terms used in stage costume, are printed as English even though they appear to be foreign, often French. We have thought it preferable to include such terms rather than omit them because we were unable to verify their language; some are quite possibly coinages.

For terms in English, a cross-reference to an adjacent term is usually omitted; for foreign terms, such cross-references are usually entered.

CITATIONS

Many entries have citations. Some are merely to an example of use; some support part or all of the entry; some are to other definitions or brief explanations; and some are to material which goes well beyond the entry.

Citations consist of the surname(s) of the author(s) followed by a key word from the title. A number after the key word (or rarely, two words) identifies the page of the cited source; a date after the key word indicates that the citation is to a dated diary. The absence of a number or date means that the citation is to a glossary or dictionary. Here are examples.

Bellman SCENE 45

Bellman SCENE

Bowman/Ball THEATRE

Pepys DIARY 5 October 1667

Carlson "Inventory" 48

Bellman SCENE refers to Willard Bellman's *Scene Design, Stage Lighting, Sound, Costume & Makeup* in the bibliography. The first citation above is to page 45 in that work; the second citation is to the glossary in the book. Bowman/ Ball THEATRE refers to Walter Parker Bowman and Robert Hamilton Ball's *Theatre Language*, a dictionary. The citation to Pepys has no page because it the fullest separately published alphabetical treatment of backstage technical terminology: Warren C. Lounsbury's *Backstage From A to Z*. Lounsbury is really more than a glossary; it is a manual in alphabetical form, as is the latest revision, *Theatre Backstage From A to Z* (1972). Albert Wehlburg's *Theatre Lighting: An Illustrated Glossary* (1975) further expanded its subject from the valuable perspective of a man experienced in the academic, community, touring, and professional theatre.

Of a different sort are two other recent books. The earlier was *The Language of Show Biz* (1973) edited by Sherman Louis Sergel from contributions of twenty-one professionals (one anonymous!) in everything from ticket-brokerage to circus lingo. The definitions in *Show Biz* reflect its subject—vivid, informal, entertaining. A much fuller and more formal dictionary, Don Wilmeth's *The Language of Popular Entertainment*, reports the results of the author's extensive study of the literature of American popular entertainment from its beginnings and gives some attention to British popular entertainment. Wilmeth's fine work is much the best in its subject.

Different again are two works published in 1978 and 1979. Although Samuel Leiter's *Kabuki Encyclopedia* is, as its title indicates, neither glossary nor dictionary, it greatly enlarges the body of theatre language available in alphabetical form. An adaptation of a Japanese reference work, it enters kabuki terms at their place in the alphabet, thus producing the fullest treatment of the language of kabuki in any dictionary or encyclopedia in English. Jack Vaughn's useful *Drama A to Z* calls its vocabulary "A Dictionary of Terms and Concepts." The five hundred entries deal with dramatic literature, history, theory, and criticism; theatre history and production are excluded. Many of the entries are brief discussions, sometimes with suggestions for further reading. Perhaps Trapido's dissertation should be mentioned here: "An Encyclopaedic Glossary of the Classical and Mediaeval Theaters and of the *Commedia dell'Arte*," 1942. Covered are something less than one thousand terms, most of them in major foreign languages of Europe.

Two theatre dictionaries, one from Britain and one from the United States, are distinguished from everything else published in English. Neither of them is an encyclopedia, and neither confines itself to a limited discipline or group of disciplines within theatre or drama. The earlier, by Wilfred Granville, was called *A Dictionary of Theatrical Terms* in London and *The Theater Dictionary* in New York (both 1952). It is British, sometimes anecdotal, and emphasizes the theatre language of its time. Granville gives some attention to U.S. variants, but the U.S. work, *Theatre Language*, by Walter Parker Bowman and Robert Hamilton Ball, is naturally much fuller on that subject. Bowman and Ball is also considerably stronger in its treatment of backstage language and covers terminology in English from the Renaissance to the late 1950s. The authors, now emeriti, had careers in drama and language, while Granville's interest, as his dictionary and his other writings suggest, was in informal language. Both dictionaries have been reprinted, Granville's in 1970 and Bowman and Ball's as a 1976 paperback.

The latter has been the most important work in English treating general theatre language.

The *International Dictionary of Theatre Language* differs from all its predecessors. It has four times the number of entries of the fullest theatre dictionary in English. Its entries in foreign languages alone outnumber the total entries in any theatre dictionary in English. Its coverage of theatre language from most of the world, and its extensive use of citations are unique.

JT

AN INTERNATIONAL
DICTIONARY
OF
THEATRE LANGUAGE

A

A   See: A-lamp.

AA   See: acting area flood.

aar-kapar (Assamese)   A white cloth held by stage attendants which serves as a front curtain in an *ankiya nat* performance. (Neog SANKARADEVA 261, Mathur DRAMA 21)

AB   Asbestos curtain. (Lounsbury THEATRE)

ABA   In modern dance, two different themes in succession plus a return to the initial one, sometimes with variations. Equivalent to the ABA form in music. (Love DANCE 37)

abacot   A 14th C felt or beaver hat with an upturned brim, sharp peak in back and front, and a conical crown. Also called bycocket. (Walkup DRESSING 112)

abandon   In Britain in the 19th C, a performer's immersion in the emotional aspects of a role. (Bowman/Ball THEATRE)

abbara (Kannada)   Literally: noise, report. In *yaksagana*, a drum pattern played on the *maddale* and *cande*. (Ashton YAKSAGANA 61, 89)

abbé cape   A shoulder cape with three layers of graduated length attached to a long-sleeved abbot's cloak. (Wilcox DICTIONARY)

Abbot of Misrule   Master of the Revels in medieval times. Sometimes called the King or Lord of Misrule. Scottish: Abbot of Unreason. (Bowman/Ball THEATRE)

abduction   In dance, the muscular withdrawal of an arm, leg, or other part of the body from the vertical axis. See also: adduction.

abele spelen (Dutch)   Literally: beautiful or skillful plays. Dramatic productions with themes taken from chivalric romances. (Gassner/Quinn ENCYCLOPEDIA 193)

aberration   In stage lighting, a condition in which a lens or reflector produces rainbow effects, inadequate focus, spill light, or any combination of these. See also: chromatic aberration, spherical aberration. (Wehlburg GLOSSARY, Lounsbury THEATRE)

abhinaya (Sanskrit)   Literally: *abhi*, toward; *ni*, lead. 1. Acting. In Indian theatre acting consists of four component elements—decoration (*aharya*), movement (*angika*), truthful emotion (*sattvika*), and speech (*vachika*). (Bharata NATYASASTRA 150–151, Richmond in Baumer/Brandon SANSKRIT 90–102) 2. Mime. In dance, the imitation of human actions or the telling of a narrative through gesture and movement. (Vatsyayan in Baumer/Brandon SANSKRIT 63)

abhisarika (Sanskrit)   A type of heroine in classical Indian drama who is willing to meet her beloved in a tryst. (Keith SANSKRIT 309)

abhiyasam (Malayalam)   Dance training in *krishnanattam*. (Ranganathan ''Krsnanattam'' 284)

ablada (Philippine)   The spoken vocal style of *cenaculo*. Also spelled *hablada*. The sung vocal style is *cantada*. (Salazar in Cruz SHORT 97)

aboard   On stage.

abolla (Latin Roman)   A heavy woolen cloak, similar to the Greek *chlamys*. (Walkup DRESSING 54)

above   1. An upper performing area, especially in an Elizabethan theatre. Alternative term: aloft. 2. An appearance in such an area. 3. In acting, upstage, or upstage of something or someone. (Chambers ELIZABETHAN III 91, Bowman/Ball THEATRE)

Abregié (French)   In late medieval France, directors' copies.

abrocomus (Latin)   A word used in classic times of Dionysus. In medieval Byzantium, the term was applied to actors who supposedly preserved their hair in honor of Dionysus. (Tunison TRADITIONS 85)

absent treatment   Poor attendance.

abstract   In dance, to select and exaggerate essentials of movement, eliminate extraneous detail, and change details as required in emphasizing meaning or form. (Hayes DANCE 172)

abstract ballet   A ballet with no plot. (Grant TECHNICAL)

abstract dance   See: non-literal dance.

abstraction   In acting, observing an object and taking from it whatever qualities can be used in developing a character. (McGaw ACTING 80-82)

abstract movement   In dance, movement for its own sake, or movement expressive of mood. The opposite is movement used for the expression of a particular situation or subject. (Love DANCE 5)

abstract set, abstract setting   A stage design that does not attempt to represent actuality.

absurdism   See: theatre of the absurd.

A-bulb   See: A-type bulb.

academic drama, academical drama   See: educational drama.

academy   In 16th C Italy, a company of professional performers. The name was borrowed from the literary and social clubs that called themselves academies. There has been controversy over this meaning of academy. (Mantzius HISTORY II 269)

accelerando   In dance, an increase in speed. (Love DANCE)

accent   In dance, a sharper or stronger movement in a series. (Love DANCE)

accent light   1. An instrument, especially a spotlight, designed to emphasize an area or object, such as a doorway. 2. The illumination resulting from such lighting. Hence, accent lighting, a term which may have originated in the early years of television. (Bowman/Ball THEATRE)

access door   The portion of a lighting instrument which can be opened to expose its interior. The term has been used mainly of Fresnel and plano-convex spotlights. (Bowman MODERN)

accessoir (French)   See: *garçon d'accessoir*.

accessoire (French)   1. A minor role. Also called a *rôle accessoire*. 2. An employee added to the theatre staff on a supplementary basis, usually to help move scenery in spectacle plays. Also called a *garçon du théâtre*. 3. A stage property. (Moynet FRENCH 137)

accessory   1. Formerly, all but the housing of a stage lighting instrument. 2. Now, any device which adds to the capabilities of a lighting instrument but is not sold as normal equipment with the instrument; an example might be a special shutter, such as an iris diaphragm. 3. Any other than the leading character or characters in a play. 4. Said of a subordinate plot action.

accessory action   Vocal and pantomimic learned action, as opposed to impulsive, fundamental action. (Selden ACTING)

accommodage (French)   See: powdering.

ace   1. A one-night stand; a single performance on tour. 2. A member of a theatrical troupe (or anyone else) who is well-liked. (Wilmeth LANGUAGE)

ace draw   A featured attraction.

ace hit   An unusually successful show.

acetabulum (Latin Roman)   By Christian times, a juggler. Literally: a vessel for vinegar or sauce. Hence, the similar cup or goblet used by jugglers and ultimately the theatrical meaning. (Chambers MEDIAEVAL I 7)

achok (Malaysian)   Two plaited rattan mats that are tied together to form a storage and carrying case for Malaysian shadow puppets. Similar to *eblek* carrying cases in Indonesia. (Sheppard TAMAN 72)

achromatic lens   1. Strictly, a color-corrected lens, that is, a lens which does not separate light into its component colors. 2. Sometimes, a lens which is corrected for both color and distortion. Ideally, all lenses used in stage lighting instruments should be achromatic, but this is seldom feasible because of the cost. (Lounsbury THEATRE)

acoustical shell   See: orchestra shell.

acoustic space   A term used in readers theatre for the auditorium environment, including the imaginative space in the minds of the audience.

acroama, acroamata (Latin)   See: *akroama.*

acrobat   A pejorative term for a ballet dancer who is more interested in supposed virtuosity than in purity of line or dancing as an art. (Kersley/Sinclair BALLET)

acrylic   Clear sheet plastic (also available in other shapes and in colors) used in the theatre as a substitute for glass. (Gillett/Gillette SCENERY)

act   1. In Elizabethan times, when plays were not usually divided into acts, an interval or pause within a performance. See also: act pause, entr'acte. 2. The music that was played during such intervals. Also called the act music, act tune, or entr'acte music. 3. In 17th C promptbooks and later, a warning that the end of an act was near. 4. A note placed by prompters beside the name of a character who appears frequently during an act, to warn the performer to remain ready throughout the act. 5. A number or turn in a vaudeville or variety program. 6. To perform, to personate a character in a play. (Shattuck SHAKESPEARE 15, Rhodes FOLIO 120, Purdom PRODUCING) 7. Said in Britain of an actable play: it acts well. U.S. equivalent: it plays well. 8. A structural division in a play, as Act I, Act II, etc. (Bowman/Ball THEATRE)

acta (Latin)   Folk plays given in the Hippodrome, especially between games, toward the end of the Byzantine empire. (Tunison TRADITIONS 114)

actable   A way of describing a role which enables a performer to exercise acting skill. (Granville DICTIONARY)

act all over the place   Especially in the U.S., to overact.

act announcer   A device which indicates to an audience (at a vaudeville performance, for instance) which act is being performed.

act break   The interval between acts; intermission. The term is used more backstage than in the front of the house. More precisely, the term concerns the time when an act ends and the length of the intermission, as: the act breaks at 8:45, the act break is ten minutes.

act call   Short form: call. 1. A summons from the stage manager for performers to take their places for the beginning of an act, as: "On stage Act I!" or, "Places Please!" 2. A signal, such as the flicking of lobby lights or the ringing of a bell, to warn audience members that the act is about to begin.

act call bell   See: call bell.

act change   A shift of scenery during an intermission.

act curtain   See: house curtain.

act division   1. The separation of a play into acts. 2. The break created by such separation.

act drop   An alternate term for house curtain. But an act drop is sometimes a lighter, temporary, painted drop behind the house curtain. Also called an intermission drop. See also: drop scene, frontcloth. (Fay GLOSSARY)

act-drop scene   A scene at the end of which the act drop is lowered.

acte (French)   An act.

acted drama   See: acting drama.

acted prologue   A scene before a play, acted by two or more performers and usually providing the audience with background information. The prologues found in some Greek tragedies—in Sophocles' *Antigone*, for example—were dramatic episodes preceding the entrance of the chorus. Some Renaissance and Restoration prologues, instead of being solo addresses to the audience, were short acted scenes, sometimes called inductions. (Hennequin PLAYWRITING 101)

acteur (French)   1. Actor. 2. In medieval times, author.

act heading   1. The number of an act. 2. In rare instances, a title for an act, as in each of the three acts of Albee's *Who's Afraid of Virginia Woolf?*

acting   Impersonating a character in a play production.

acting area   1. The space used by actors when in view of the audience. Space outside that area would be considered offstage or backstage. The acting area in a proscenium theatre, even if its shape is not roughly rectangular, is often divided into nine sub-areas: downstage left, downstage center, downstage right, left center, center, right center, upstage left, upstage center, and upstage right (or slight variations on those terms). The terms are often abbreviated to DL, C, etc. In an arena stage the sub-areas are sometimes called by clock numbers, with the control room at six o'clock. In a production that uses auditorium aisles or other spaces for acting areas, directors often devise their own area designations. 2. In the U.S., one or more lighting instruments (often two or three) designated to light the performer in a single, specific area. 3. See: acting area flood. (Bellman SCENE, Bentham ART)

acting area flood   In Britain, a narrow-angle floodlight which reaches the acting area from directly overhead. Also called acting area or AA. (Bentham ART)

acting area instrument   1. A luminaire designed for lighting the acting area. 2. Any luminaire used to light the acting area. Both are U.S., the usual British term being acting area lantern, with acting area lamp a variant. (Rae/Southern INTERNATIONAL 18, Bowman/Ball THEATRE, Bentham ART 310)

acting area lamp, **acting area lantern**   See: acting area instrument.

acting area light   1. The light in the space used by performers when they are visible to the audience. 2. In the U.S., a spotlight in the auditorium, or on the bridge or first pipe, whose beam hits the performer's head at an angle of 30 to 45 degrees from both top and side. The angles do not really limit the term, since they are not always possible. 3. Any instrument used to light the acting area. (Bowman/Ball THEATRE) Meanings 1 and 3 are primarily U.S.

acting clothes   Costumes.

acting company   A group of performers and support personnel (stagehands, business officials, etc.) organized to present plays. Also called a company or dramatic company.

acting day   A day on which a Restoration theatrical company performed; only on such a day did rent have to be paid. (Van Lennep LONDON lii)

acting double   A practice dating from the 17th C of doubling (or at least increasing) ticket prices at the first performance of a new play. (Mongrédien MOLIÈRE 139)

acting drama   A piece or pieces intended to be produced on stage. Also called acted drama, acting play. (Bowman/Ball THEATRE)

acting edition   The published text of a play, usually based on the stage manager's production book or the playhouse prompt copy. An acting edition normally includes much more technical information than a reading edition: ground plans, property lists, sound cues, etc.

acting fee   1. In 16th-17th C England, fee payable to the Master of Revels for licensing a play for performance. 2. In 19th C England, a fee payable to the copyright holder for producing a dramatic work. (Bowman/Ball THEATRE)

acting lady   Especially in Britain, an incompetent actress. From the weak acting of society women who attempted the stage. (Partridge TO-DAY 226, Granville DICTIONARY)

acting level   An area above the stage floor (such as a platform) used for acting.

acting manager   1. In 17th and 18th C Britain, one whose duties encompassed directing, stage management, and business management. Later called a stage manager. 2. Now in Britain, business manager; the U.S. equivalent is company manager.

acting out   See: creative drama.

acting play   A piece which goes beyond being literary or affording effective lines to include acting possibilities for a performer. See also: actable, acting drama. (Granville DICTIONARY)

acting property   A hand property, such as a cigarette, book, or glass, used by a performer. See also: character property.

acting space   See: acting area.

acting text   See: acting edition.

acting time   The length of a performance, act, or scene.

acting version   1. An acting edition of a play, as opposed to a reading edition of it, which may differ somewhat. The term is also sometimes applied to a play based on a non-dramatic work. 2. A stage production based on an acting edition.

acting zone   That part of the stage which can be seen from any part of the auditorium. (Krows AMERICA 173)

act in one   See: in one.

act intermission, act interval   See: intermission.

actio (Latin)   In medieval times: 1. A play. 2. The performance of a play. (Chambers MEDIAEVAL II 105, Baxter/Johnson MEDIEVAL 5)

action   1. The physical movement of a performer on the stage, but sometimes, especially in the 18th C and earlier, the speaking of the lines as well; that is, acting. 2. Dramatic action: the movement or development of the plot or segment of the plot of a play. 3. See: *praxis*. (Bowman/Ball THEATRE)

action call   A curtain call with the actors remaining in character and playing a brief pantomime. (Nelms PRODUCTION)

action cue   1. A cue which must be taken from the physical action on stage rather than from a spoken line. A visual cue. (Halstead MANAGEMENT 29) 2. A cue calling for some specific action by the cast or crew. (Bowman/Ball THEATRE)

action dramatics   See: creative drama.

action mode   See: movement phrase.

action of a play   Especially in Britain, a series of speeches, movements, events, and dumb show. (Baker THEATRECRAFT)

action word   In prompting, a key word rather than the first words of a line an actor has forgotten. (Gruver/Hamilton STAGE)

active diameter   An occasional term for the effective diameter of a spotlight lens. Fuchs considered this to be about 1/4″ less than the actual diameter of the lens. (Fuchs LIGHTING 186)

activism   A form of expressionism with a realistic slant. (Bowman/Ball THEATRE)

activity   In Elizabethan times, acrobatic performance. (Bowman/Ball THEATRE)

act like a trouper   To perform like a veteran.

act music   In the Restoration theatre and later, music played between the acts. In promptbooks, the word ''act'' was used as a warning and ''ring'' as a cue for the act music.

acto (Spanish)   1. An act of a play. See also: *jornada*. 2. In 20th C California, a short political or social playlet. The term is associated with Chicano theatre, especially the Teatro Campesino. (Cameron/Gillespie ENJOYMENT)

acton   See: *pourpoint.*

actor   A person who plays a character in a dramatic production. Specifically, the term applies to a male, but the word has long been used to cover both men and women and to differentiate them from singers and dancers, even though singers and dancers often play characters in dramatic works. See also: actress.

actor (Latin Roman)   Literally: doer, performer. 1. A manager, usually an actor-manager, of a theatrical company. 2. An actor, especially when the word is part of a phrase. (Allen ANTIQUITIES 58, 131; Chambers MEDIAEVAL I 6)

actor-director   A performer who directs as well as acts in a play. (Krows AMERICA 59)

actor laddy   In late 19th C melodrama in Britain, a flamboyantly costumed actor who addressed his colleagues as "laddy." (Granville DICTIONARY)

actor list   A roster of the parts played by the performers in a play. (Bowman/Ball THEATRE)

actor manager, actor-manager   A performer who plays leading roles and manages his or her own company. The term has been used chiefly of the 19th C and earlier. Examples: Minnie Maddern Fiske, Sir Henry Irving, David Garrick, Molière.

actor mimicus (Latin Roman)   A mime actor. This phrase ultimately became more frequent than the original *mimus*. Also used were *actor mimi* and *actor mimarius*. (Nicoll MASKS 80, 83)

actor plot   A list of the characters in a play and the scenes in which they appear. (Gruver/Hamilton STAGE)

actor primarum (Latin Roman)   The head of a theatre company. The phrase is so used by Cicero. (O'Connor CHAPTERS 35)

actor primarum personarum (Latin Roman)   A protagonist. (Chambers MEDIAEVAL I 6)

actor proof, actor-proof   Said of a role or a play that is usually effective even if not well acted.

actor rep   A performer's representative.

actors' Bible   A publication which is read by most professional actors at any given time, such as *Variety*, or in Britain, *The Stage*. In the U.S., also called the Broadway Bible. (Bowman/Ball THEATRE)

actors' call   An act call or warning.

actors' check list   A sign-in sheet, usually posted when a production goes into dress rehearsals. The list often includes the names of crew members as well.

actor secundarum partium (Latin Roman)   Literally: actor of the secondary role. Especially in the mime, a secondary actor or deuteragonist. Beare notes that because the roles were foils to the chief actor, the term had the connotation of one who was very much a second fiddle. (Beare ROMAN 153)

actors file   A list kept by the stage manager of a company on tour. It names performers in areas of the country where the troupe will be playing, in case of emergency. (Gruver/Hamilton STAGE)

actor-sharer   See: shareholder.

actor's mask   A performer's face.

actor's preparation   A performer's feel and plan for the acting of a part as a single entity and as the part relates to the total play. (Granville DICTIONARY)

actor's rehearsal   A term used by Stanislavsky to describe a rehearsal in which he directed his energies toward individual performers who were in difficulty with some aspect of their craft. (Press "Stanislavsky" 265)

act-outline play   See: *mubiaoxi*.

act pause   The time interval between the acts of a play. Hence, entr'acte. In Renaissance times and later such pauses were very short or were taken up with entr'acte entertainment. Today, the intermission (U.S.) or interval (Britain) is longer and does not usually include entertainment. (Rhodes STAGERY 73)

actress   A female who impersonates a character in a play. See also: actor.

act time   The time between the acts of an Elizabethan play. (Rhodes STAGERY 73)

act tune   Entr'acte music. Sometimes shortened to act. (Wilmeth LANGUAGE)

actual curtain time   The time a performance begins, which is usually a few minutes after the advertised curtain time.

actual voltage   The voltage at which a lamp is burned or a circuit used; the voltage of a circuit when it is in use. A shortening of actual operating voltage. Compare: rated voltage. (Fuchs LIGHTING 160)

actus (Latin)   In medieval times: 1. A performer's gesture. 2. The production of a play.

act wait   See: intermission.

act warning   A warning or call given by the stage manager, usually at 30 minutes before curtain, then 15 minutes before, and then five minutes before. The final call is "Places, please!"

act-warning bell   Principally in Britain, a signal to audience members that curtain time is near.

acuchillados (Spanish)   See: slashings.

acus (Latin)   See: bodkin.

AD   1. Assistant to the director. 2. Act drop.

ada-ada (Indonesian)   A mood song (*suluk*) sung by the puppeteer (*dalang*) during a moment of strong emotion or action in a Javanese shadow play. (Brandon THRONES 55-56)

adage, adagio   From the Italian *ad agio*, at ease or leisure. In ballet: 1. A simple or complex exercise with slow and graceful movements. 2. The opening portion of a classical *pas de deux* (French). (Grant TECHNICAL)

Adam Sourguy   A backstage pessimist. (Berrey/Van den Bark SLANG 575)

adamuorisa (Yoruba)   In Nigeria, a ritual dramatic performance which involves masked actors in a rite of passage to honor the memory of distinguished sons and daughters of Lagos. (Adedeji glossary)

adaptable theatre   A theatre stressing flexibility. A multiple-use theatre. See also: flexible theatre.

adaptation   1. A play based on an earlier play or a narrative work, such as a novel. 2. The modification, abbreviation, or expansion of a play, sometimes for a particular audience or to permit twice-nightly performances. 3. A play altered in translation from one language to another (though such works are often called versions). (Purdom PRODUCING, Downs THEATRE II 1128) 4. In the Stanislavskian theory of acting, a performer's use of inner and outer phenomena to adjust to other performers within the play's context. (Bowman/Ball THEATRE)

adaptor, adapter   1. See: jumper. 2. A socket adaptor, a device which permits a lamp of one base size to be screwed into a receptacle designed for a larger base. An example is a medium to mogul adaptor, which permits a lamp with a medium base (household size) to be screwed into a mogul base. Also called a socket adaptor. 3. Any one-piece device that allows coupling of connectors that otherwise will not mate. (Lounsbury THEATRE, Wehlburg GLOSSARY, Bowman MODERN) 4. In Elizabethan times, one who corrected a playscript and prepared it for production. Such work was usually done by the prompter. (Massinger BELIEVE v-vi)

adauchimono (Japanese)   See: *katakiuchimono*.

adbhuta (Sanskrit)   Literally: wonder. One of the eight major sentiments (*rasa*) to be savored by the spectators of a classical Indian play. See also: *vismaya*. (Bharata NATYASASTRA 105–118)

ad captandum (Latin)   Something in a play having a catchy quality. The Latin is approximately 'in order to please.' (Krows PLAYWRITING 430)

ad curtain, ad drop   See: olio.

added attraction   In burlesque, a bait—such as a famous pugilist or cooch dancer—used to increase attendance. (Sobel BURLEYCUE 226–227)

additive color mixing   A system of mixing color stimuli by exposing the eye to stimuli from two or more visible wave lengths at the same time. In lighting this is usually done by using two or more sources, each producing a separate color, whose light strikes the same surface. For example, a red source and a green source striking a white surface will cause the sensation yellow. The term often refers to the blending of complementaries to produce colors or white. Both the process and the result are called additive lighting. Other similar terms: additive method, additive system, additive color, additive mixture, additive process. (Bellman LIGHTING 96–100)

additive primaries In lighting, red, green, and blue. See also: additive color mixing.

additive process See: additive color mixing.

additive secondaries In lighting, amber, magenta (purple), and blue-green (cyan). Despite the names, these are the yellow, red, and blue familiar as painters' primaries. See also: additive color mixing.

additive system See: additive color mixing.

ad drop See: olio.

adduction In dance, the muscular indrawing of an arm, leg, or other part of the body, toward the vertical axis. See also: abduction.

adegan (Indonesian) A generic term for a scene in classical drama. In Javanese *wayang kulit*, a minor scene. See also: *jejer, gapuran, perang kembang*. Brandon gives major types of *adegan* in THRONES 21–27.

Adelphi drama Melodramatic plays extravagantly acted. The term derived from the dramatic fare and acting at the old Adelphi Theatre in London. (Granville DICTIONARY)

adhibala (Sanskrit) In classical Indian theatre, "topping": one character vies with another for dominance in pitch and intensity of speech. (Keith SANSKRIT 329)

adhikara (Sanskrit) A section of a classical play in which the hero attains the object of his desire. (Keith SANSKRIT 297)

adhikari (Bengali) A stage manager/director of a *jatra* company. See: *sutradhara*.

adhikarika (Sanskrit) The principal plot or subject matter of a classical drama. See also: *vatsu*. (Keith SANSKRIT 297)

aditus maximus (Latin Roman) Literally: largest approach. One of the two main entrances to the orchestra and the lower rows of the auditorium (*cavea*). The *aditus maximi* lay between the ends of the auditorium and the scene building. They were usually large, vaulted passages in the position of the Greek *parodoi*. (Bieber HISTORY 187, 216, fig. 680)

adiutor (Latin Roman) Literally: helper, assistant. 1. A minor official associated with play production. He was one of a number of types of assistants who worked with a *procurator*, who appears to have been in charge of a kind of theatrical warehouse. 2. A subordinate actor. (Saunders COSTUME 21)

adiutor mimographorum (Latin Roman)   One who collaborated with the writers of mimes. (Nicoll MASKS 110)

adjoining cross-control   In some obsolete dimmer boards, a special mechanical interlocking system which permitted some dimmers in a single bank to be moved up while others in the same bank were moved down. (Fuchs LIGHTING 320)

adjustable brace   See: stage brace.

adjustable floor block   A grooved pulley or sheave housed in a wooden or metal frame secured to the stage floor at the side wall or on the fly gallery. A rope operating a counterweight passes down and around the sheave, and the sheave may be adjusted upward or downward to control the tautness of the rope. Called by some manufacturers an adjustable floor pulley.

adjustable lens tube   A lens housing which permits movement toward or away from the focal point of the lens. The phrase is sometimes applied to the movable (lens-holding) front section of ellipsoidal reflector spotlights.

adjustable proscenium   A proscenium opening capable of being changed in size and shape by such means as sliding, pivoting, or flying panels.

adjustable tip jack   See: tip jack.

adjustment   See: adaptation.

adjutant play   See: *canjunxi*.

ad lib, ad-lib   Short for *ad libitum* (Latin). Improvised speech; by extension, improvised action. Used as both noun and verb.

ad lip   Informally, an improvisation.

admish   Admission price.

ado (Japanese)   Literally: one who answers. The secondary role in a *kyogen* comedy. Analogous to the *waki* role in *no*. See also: *shite*. (Kenny GUIDE 12) *Ado za* (*ado*'s place) is upstage left on the stage, next to the flute pillar (*fue bashira*), where the *ado* sits when out of the action. (Berberich "Rapture" 64–65)

adorno (Spanish)   Stage furnishings. (Rennert SPANISH 17)

Adrienne   See: sack gown.

adulescens (Latin Roman)   Literally: young man or woman. The youthful lover in comedy. Also spelled *adolescens*. (Duckworth NATURE 237–242)

adult actor   In the Elizabethan theatre, a mature actor, as opposed to a boy actor.

adulterio (Latin Roman)   Literally: fornication, adultery. A traditional theme of the mime. Beare thinks the playwright Laberius "invented a set of technical terms" for this theme. They included *adulterio, adulteritas*, and *moechimonium*. (Beare ROMAN 156, 239)

adultery mime   An ancient Roman mime whose plot revolved around adultery. See also: *adulterio*.

advance   The number of tickets sold prior to the opening of a performance, or the money then collected. (Granville DICTIONARY)

advance agent   A person who travels on the road ahead of a touring company, making arrangements for transportation, publicity, accommodations, etc. Also called a forerunner or advance man. In Britain, advance manager. (Krows AMERICA 335)

advance booking   1. In Britain, seats for a production purchased in advance. An advance order. 2. In the U.S., the engagement of a coming attraction.

advanced money   Increased ticket prices in 18th C British theatres. (Stone LONDON xlviii)

advanced vaudeville   Vaudeville featuring major performers, some from the legitimate theatre. Also called refined or top-line vaudeville. (Wilmeth LANGUAGE)

advance man   See: advance agent.

advance manager   See: advance agent, advance stage manager.

advance notice   Publicity appearing before the first performance of a production.

advance order   A ticket or tickets reserved or purchased in advance of a performance.

advance sale   The sale of tickets in advance of a performance.

advance stage manager   A stage manager who works with a resident company preparing for the staging of a package show. (Bowman/Ball THEATRE)

adventurer   A sharer or investor in a theatrical company or theatre building. In the 17th C and later, the term was also used outside the theatre for any investor or speculator. (Cibber APOLOGY I 97)

advertised curtain time   The time at which a performance is scheduled to begin, usually a few minutes earlier than the actual curtain time. Both terms appear in the contracts of theatrical unions.

advertisement curtain   See: olio.

advice sheet, advice   On tour, a document usually issued by an advance agent concerning such matters as the scaling of the house, the free list, the contract with the transfer company, what the local manager will handle, etc. (Krows AMERICA 339)

aedes (Latin)   In medieval times, a *mansion* (French) or locale on stage. (Wickham EARLY I 158)

A-effect   See: *Verfremdungseffekt*.

aerial   In dance, a movement executed in the air. Also called *en l'air* (French).

aeroplane   A horizontal marionette control with cross pieces.

aesthetic attitude   A balance between a strong empathic response in the audience and its feeling of detachment (aesthetic distance). (Dolman ACTING 28)

aesthetic distance   Psychological, and usually physical, separation or detachment of an audience from the dramatic action. One of the effects of the raised stage, for example, is to assist in this detachment.

aetheroscope   See: Pepper's ghost.

affective memory   See: emotion memory.

afghani kulu (Urdu)   A conical cap worn by the *juthan mian* (Muslim character) in *bhavai* folk dramas in west India. A turban is generally tied around the cap, leaving tassels hanging on either side. (Vatsyayan TRADITIONAL 155)

a foro (Latin Roman)   Literally: from the forum. The stage entrance which led from the forum. (Duckworth NATURE 85, Pickard-Cambridge DIONYSUS 236–237)

after-beat Annie   A female dancer whose steps are late. (Berrey/Van den Bark SLANG 573)

afterdraft   In U.S. traveling repertory companies of the early 20th C, the ability of a production to bring patrons back to the theatre for a second or third time. (Schaffner in Matlaw AMERICAN 168)

after-money   In Restoration theatres and later, money taken in after the third act of the mainpiece; half price was the usual charge. (Avery LONDON xxxiv)

afterpiece, after-piece, aftershow   1. The second of two entertainments on a theatrical bill, normally a light work. 2. In a minstrel show, the second part of the performance, usually consisting of a brief farcical entertainment. 3. In early U.S. vaudeville, a brief sketch following an olio or scene 'in one.' (Hare MINSTREL 169, Wilmeth LANGUAGE)

after stage   See: inner stage.

ageha ogi (Japanese)   Literally: raised fan. In *no*, the standard gesture (*kata*) of raising an open fan overhead while taking three steps backward. (Keene NO 219)

agemaku (Japanese)   Literally: lift curtain. 1. A dark-colored curtain covering the exit from the runway (*hanamichi*) at the rear of the *kabuki* auditorium. (Leiter ENCYCLOPEDIA 8) 2. A five-colored curtain at the end of the bridgeway (*hashigakari*) of the *no* stage, lifted for entrances and exits by means of two bamboo poles attached to the bottom corners. (Shimazaki NOH 9)

agent   In the theatre world, a representative who performs such services as helping actors obtain engagements, helping dramatists find producers, etc. Hence, agency. See also: advance agent. (Bowman/Ball THEATRE) *age uta* (Japanese)   Literally: high song. A type of *no* song, in high pitch and regular rhythm (*hira nori*). One type of scene (*shodan*). (Hoff/Flindt "Structure" 225, Shimazaki NOH 45)

aging   See: breakdown.

agitator (Latin Roman)   Literally: driver. Charioteer. The usual term is *auriga*, plural: *-ae*. (Sandys COMPANION 508)

agit brigades   Travelling companies of performers which sprang up in Russia directly after the Revolution and were designed to carry the Soviet message to the peasants. These troupes performed at first in railroad stations and later in political clubs. Alternate names: shock troops, storm troops (or troupes), flying brigades. (Sobel NEW 624)

agitka (Russian)   Propaganda skits of the 1920s, based on Communist political issues. (Segal RUSSIAN 31)

agit-prop theatre   Agitation-propaganda theatre—theatrical productions designed to stir audiences to social protest. Clifford Odets' *Waiting for Lefty* in the 1930s is an example.

Agitstücke (German)   Plays performed by the *Agittruppen* or shock troupes of the German Communist party in the early 1930s for the purpose of spreading the Marxist doctrine. (Sobel HANDBOOK)

Agitstuecke (German)   See: *Agit-truppen*.

Agit-truppen (German)   Theatrical troupes in pre-Nazi Germany, formed about 1930 as branches of the German Communist Party. Their purpose was to spread the Marxist doctrine through their plays, called *Agitstuecke*. Also called shock troops (or troupes) or storm troops. (Sobel NEW)

agni-gad (Assamese)   Literally: fire-arc. A special bamboo archway with small lighted torches inserted along the top, at the entrance to the playing area of an *ankiya nat* performance. (Neog SANKARADEVA 261)

agoge (Greek)   A type of movement in the dithyramb. The dance or dance-like movement is thought to have been very rapid. (Pickard-Cambridge DITHYRAMB 14, 33)

agon (Greek), agon   1. In Greek drama, originally the contest between poets. 2. Later, also the contests between actors. 3. Still later, the conflict between characters in Old Comedy, now the principal meaning. Often "a farcical debate full of irrelevancy" (Arnott), the agon was ordinarily between an actor and a semi-chorous on one side and another actor and another semi-chorus on the other. 4. Sometimes, other conflicts in drama, especially in tragedy. An example is Francis Fergusson's use of agon (in *The Idea of Theater*) for the conflict between Oedipus and Teiresias in *Oedipus the King*. Greek *agon* (plural *agones*) was literally 'contest' and was used of athletic, musical, and other contests long before the emergence of drama. See also: antagonist, protagonist, synagonist. (Flickinger GREEK 41, 43–46, 49; Cornford ORIGIN 27–46; Arnott INTRODUCTION 27)

agonist   1. Chief actor, actor. Greek *agonistes*, contestant, was applied to participants in any of the many varieties of Greek contests. When used of actors, where its meaning tends to be protagonist, *agonistes* is almost invariably accompanied by some such adjective as the Greek for tragic or comic. Compare *synagonist*. (O'Connor CHAPTERS 27–28) 2. A dancer's contracting muscle, which is controlled by an opposing muscle.

agonothetes (Greek)   Literally: director of the contests. From the late 4th C BC until at least the 2nd C AD, the official who had charge of all contests at the City Dionysia. In bearing the contest costs, with some assistance from the state, the *agonothetes* replaced the individual *choregi*. U.S. English has agonothete, hence agonothetic. (Haigh ATTIC 54–55, Pickard-Cambridge DIONYSUS 167)

aharyabhinaya (Sanskrit)   Literally: spectacle. One of four elements of acting (*abhinaya*) in classical Indian theatre. It includes costumes, ornaments, properties and *sanjiva* (creatures). Abbreviated *aharya*. (Bharata NATYASASTRA 411–441, Raghavan in Baumer/Brandon SANSKRIT 23–24)

ahli cherita (Malaysian)   A professional story-teller in Pahang or Trengganu states. His stories may be sung or chanted, with or without drum accompaniment. (Sweeney in Malm/Sweeney STUDIES 53)

ahli lawak (Malaysian)   The principal comic characters in *bangsawan*, usually two, who engage in slapstick and act as intermediaries between the audience and the players. (Yassin in Osman TRADITIONAL 149)

aibiki (Japanese)   A stool on which a *kabuki* actor sits during a lengthy scene. Because it is tall, it gives the impression the character is standing.

aikata (Japanese)   1. A *shamisen* instrumental melody played as background music to a dialogue scene in *kabuki*. Leiter ENCYCLOPEDIA 76–91 lists numerous examples. 2. A *shamisen* instrumental interlude occurring between sung sections of a *kabuki* dance piece or a *bunraku* play (then also called *ai no te*). (Leiter ENCYCLOPEDIA 10, Malm in Brandon CHUSHINGURA 63–65)

ai kyogen (Japanese)   1. The expository interlude between the first and second parts (*ba*) of a *no* play, performed by one or more *kyogen* actors and occasionally by the secondary (*waki*) actor. See also: *hon kyogen*. 2. The *kyogen* actors in a *no* play. (Shimazaki NOH 6, 16; Berberich "Rapture" 4)

aimeiju, ai mei chü (Chinese)   A generic term for amateur performances of spoken drama (*huaju*) in the 1920s. Such performances were part of the movement to combat commercialism and improve the quality and educational value of theatre through emphasis upon scripts and a stringent rehearsal and performance system. *Aimei* is a transliteration of the French word *amateur* and literally means 'love beauty.'

ai no te (Japanese)   See: *aikata*.

aiorai (Greek)   The ropes used in a suspension machine (*mechane*). It is possible that, especially in Hellenistic times, *aiorai* referred to a lighter, more sophisticated version of the 5th C BC suspension device. It is, indeed, likely that even in that century ropes were sometimes fastened to an actor by means of a halter or bosun's seat. On this point, there may be significance in one of the meanings of the Greek singular, which is halter. (Pickard-Cambridge DIONYSUS 127, 236; Nicoll DEVELOPMENT 22)

air bisector   A high-kicking dancer. (Berrey/Van den Bark SLANG 573)

air dancing   Dances executed off the floor, using scaffolding, ropes, cords, wires, etc. as supports. (Carroll "Air" 5)

air de caractère (French)   A kind of *Leitmotif* (German, meaning signature tune) used in ballet, especially in the court of France, to announce the entry of a particular character. (Kersley/Sinclair BALLET)

airdome   In the early 20th C in the U.S., a type of open-air theatre surrounded by a temporary wall. (Wilmeth LANGUAGE)

airplane   To forget one's line.

aisle   An audience passageway (in Britain, gangway) between banks of seats in the auditorium. Hence, aisle seat, cross aisles, side aisles, radial aisles, longitudinal aisles, etc.

aisle and step lights   In theatre auditoriums, small shaded lights often built into the ends of rows, sometimes into steps.

aisle-sitter   A spectator with a seat on the aisle. Said of a reviewer who is given such a seat so as to be able to leave quickly to make a newspaper deadline.

aisvarya lila (Hindi)   A presentation of the deeds of Krishna that shows the heroic, masterly aspect of his character. One class of play (*lila*) in the *raslila* repertory. (Hein MIRACLE 282)

ajjuka (Sanskrit)   A courtesan, one female character-type, in classical Indian drama. (Keith SANSKRIT 314)

ajolokeloke (Yoruba)   Nigerian puppet theatre. The puppet shows usually served as comic interludes in *alarinjo* performances. Popularized by the Aiyelabola troupe, the puppets were made of carved wood and manipulated by actors concealed inside raffia masks. (Adedeji glossary)

AK   Antediluvian knight—an old trouper. (Berrey/Van den Bark SLANG 572)

akahime (Japanese)   Literally: red princess. 1. A role of a vivacious, high-ranking maiden in *kabuki*. She conventionally wears a red kimono and outer robe, hence the name. An example is Princess Sakura in *The Scarlet Princess of Edo* in Brandon CLASSIC 249–345. It is one type of princess (*hime*) role. (Gunji KABUKI 179) 2. The costume worn by that character. (Shaver COSTUME 165–166) *akasabhasita* (Sanskrit)   The classical acting technique of speaking to an imaginary person, followed by pretending to hear a reply and repeating the question aloud before answering it. (Keith SANSKRIT 305)

akhada (Sanskrit)   A consecrated performing area for *chhau* masked dance plays in northeast India. See also: *ranga*. (Vatsyayan TRADITIONAL 69)

akhara (Sanskrit)   1. A gymnasium used for acrobatics, dramatics, and dance. 2. A generic word for a company of performers. (Vatsyayan TRADITIONAL 165) 3. A school of acting. (Gargi FOLK 203) 4. An open space in between hillocks, where a fire is lighted, the orchestra takes its seat, and actors of *kariala* folk theatre appear. (Mathur DRAMA 15)

aki kyogen (Japanese)   Literally: autumn play. A *kabuki* play produced on the autumn bill. The program traditionally opened on the ninth day of the ninth lunar month (Chrysanthemum Day) and lasted until the tenth day of the tenth month. The term also applied to a *bon kyogen* performance that was delayed into the fall season. See also: *onagori kyogen*. (Leiter ENCYCLOPEDIA 20)

akitta kuttuka (Sanskrit)   In *kutiyattam*, preliminary songs invoking the Hindu deities Ganapati, Sarasvati, and Siva. Also called *gosthi*. (Vatsyayan TRADITIONAL 25)

akobujo (Japanese)   A mask worn by a human character or the spirit of a plant in the first part of a *no* play. (Shimazaki NOH 58)

akroama (Greek)   Literally: something heard. Liddell/Scott gives "pieces read, recited, played, or sung." At least by 100 AD, the word was used for all varieties of entertainment containing music, including some in which music was not primary. *Akroama* most often designated instrumental entertainment, especially by cithara or flute, but all forms containing music were apparently included; among these were New and Old Comedy, tragedy, and mime. For the plural, *akroamata*, Liddell/Scott gives "lecturers, singers, players." Latin adopted *acroama*, *-mata*. (Flickinger PLUTARCH 27, 30; Liddell/Scott LEXICON)

aksepiki dhruva (Sanskrit)   See: *dhruva*.

Akt (German)   An act.

aktër (Russian)   Actor.

Aktionsdrama (German)   A Bauhaus theatre term for physically active drama. (Schlemmer/Moholy-Nagy/Molnar BAUHAUS 49)

aktiory (Yiddish)   Actors. Presumably from Russian *aktër*.

aktrisa (Russian)   Actress.

akuba (Japanese)   Literally: evil woman. 1. A role of a female scoundrel in *kabuki*. An example is in Gunji KABUKI 185. It is one type of *onnagata* leading role. 2. An actor who plays this role.

akujo (Japanese)   A *no* mask of a fierce old man. It occurs in various types, such as 'large nostrils' (*hanakobu*) *akujo* worn by a mighty, aged god, and 'heavy' (*omoni*) *akujo* worn by the ghost of a vengeful old man. (Shimazaki NOH 58–59)

akunin, akuyaku (Japanese)   See: *katakiyaku*.

alabastine method   In Britain, a process for making hollow heads for puppets, using alabastine, water, and muslin as filler. (Philpott DICTIONARY)

alambana (Sanskrit)   The effect which the nature of the characters (primarily the hero and heroine) has on the expression of emotion (*bhava*) in a classical Indian play. Because character is constant and basic, the term is usually translated "fundamental determinant." It is one type of determinant (*vibhava*). (Keith SANSKRIT 315)

alamkara (Sanskrit)   1. Ornaments of poetic composition in classical Indian drama, for example, simile, metaphor, and alliteration. (Keith SANSKRIT 330–331) 2. Garlands, necklaces, and ornaments worn on different parts of the body and on the costume of an actor. Also spelled *alankara*. (Rangacharya NATYASASTRA 33, Richmond in Baumer/Brandon SANSKRIT 100)

A-lamp   A low-wattage lamp whose bulb varies from a short-necked pear to a pear whose neck has all but disappeared. The term is sometimes reduced to A, and sometimes lengthened to A-type lamp, which occasionally becomes A-type.

alankara (Sanskrit)   See: *alamkara*.

à l'antique (French)   Literally: in the old manner. Said of costumes for fanciful or mythological characters in *commedia dell'arte*. (Duchartre ITALIAN 264)

alapus (Latin Roman)   One of the names of the *stupidus* (mime fool). The term comes from *alapas*, blows, in situations in which the *stupidus* is beaten (as with straws). (Nicoll MASKS 89)

alarcca (Malayalam)   Non-verbal vocal sounds appropriate to particular characterizations in a *kathakali* dance-drama. (Jones/Jones KATHAKALI 106)

alarinjo (Yoruba)   Travelling Nigerian dance-theatre troupes which perform a variety of acts and sketches at the annual festivals of the Egungun society, within which the *alarinjo* developed in the 16th C. They are for hire on other occasions. See also: masque theatre. (Adedeji "Yoruba" 254)

alarm bell   Possibly a prompter's fire alarm bell in 18th C Dublin. (Hughes in Hume LONDON 132)

alarum, alarme, alarm   In Elizabethan plays and later, a stage direction for a call to arms by trumpets and drums. Sometimes a direction would call for alarums and excursions—the latter adding the running about of soldiers. (Bowman/Ball THEATRE)

alawada (Yoruba)   A comedian in Nigeria. The term has become an epithet for all comedians. The name was used for a comic theatre developed in the 1960s by Moses Adejumo Olaiya from the Concert Party troupe. (Adedeji glossary) *alazon* (Greek)   Literally: imposter, quack. An absurdly pretentious character in Old Comedy. Examples are the boastful soldier, politician, esthete, quack doctor—any character who takes himself too seriously. Among Aristophanic characters who suggest the *alazon* are Socrates in *Clouds* and Euripides in *Frogs*; the swaggering soldier of the *phlyakes* is another example. The ingenious philosopher in fragments of plays by Epicharmus is an *alazon sophos*. Some think the capitano of the *commedia dell'arte* a descendant of the *alazon*. Plural: *alazones*. (Pickard-Cambridge DITHYRAMB 174–178, 278; Cornford ORIGIN 115–146; Nicoll MASKS 246)

Albanian hat   Headgear with a raised front, high crown, and feather trim, seen in portraits of Henry IV. (Boucher FASHION)

alcove   See: inner stage.

aldabis (Philippine)   A term for a "cutting strike" used in battle scenes in *comedia*. (Mendoza COMEDIA 65)

alfalfa   A false beard.

alguaciles (Spanish)   In the 17th C, police officers usually stationed at the doors of a *corral* theatre and in the *alojería*. (Rennert SPANISH 116)

aliala (Philippine)   See: *carillo*.

alienation, alienation effect   See: *Verfremdungseffekt*.

alive   See: keep alive.

allah-udal (Hindi)   A form of ballad theatre found in Madhya Pradesh state, central India. (Vatsyayan TRADITIONAL 10)

allegory   The representation of an abstract theme through the symbolic use of character, action, and other concrete elements of a play. Allegory uses personification to present characters representing such abstract qualities as virtues and vices. The medieval morality play *Everyman* is an example.

allegro   In ballet, a bright and brisk movement. (Grant TECHNICAL)

all-electric dimmer system   In Britain, a system of lighting control which functions without mechanical connections. See also: remote control system. (Bentham ART 326, 336)

allemande (French)   A late 17th C fashionable court dance, developed from a German folk dance. (Perugini PAGEANT 109)

all'improvviso (Italian)   Literally: suddenly, on the spur of the moment. Improvised, as is the comic business and much of the dialogue in *commedia dell'arte*.

allongé (French)   Literally: lengthened. In dance, extended, outstretched. (Grant TECHNICAL)

all right on the night   Said of a show which will succeed despite problems during the rehearsal period. (Wilmeth LANGUAGE)

all-star   Especially in theatrical publicity, said of a production in which most or all roles are taken by star performers. Hence, all-star cast, all-star revival. (Bowman/Ball THEATRE)

almond oil   In the early 20th C, a substance used in removing makeup.

aloes (Indonesian)   See: *alus*.

aloft   An alternate term for 'above' in an Elizabethan theatre; an upper acting area. (Chambers ELIZABETHAN III 91)

alojería (Spanish)   In the 17th C, a room or tavern, probably at the rear of the *patio* of a *corral* theatre, where *aloja* (the drink metheglin) and other refreshments were sold. (Brockett HISTORY 234)

alone   In Elizabethan plays, a stage direction bringing a single character onstage. An alternate term is *solus* (Latin).

altacomedia (Spanish)   High comedy.

alternate   1. A performer who takes turns with another in a role. 2. An understudy. (Bowman/Ball THEATRE)

alternate stage   1. In Cheney, a wagon stage. 2. In Krows, an Elizabethan inner stage. (Cheney NEW 219, Krows AMERICA 148)

alternating cast   An alternate cast, that is, one which sometimes plays instead of the usual cast. (Bowman/Ball THEATRE)

alternative theatre   Anti-traditional theatre, usually experimental and politically or socially radical.

alto (Spanish)   Literally: high, above. The upper gallery of a *corral* theatre. (Shergold SPANISH)

alto del teatro (Spanish)   The rear portion of the stage in a *corral* theatre. (Sobel NEW)

"Altogether please!"   Especially in Britain in music hall entertainments, an invitation to the audience to join in singing. (Granville DICTIONARY)

aluminum powder   A substance sometimes still used to gray a performer's hair.

alus (Indonesian, Malaysian)   Literally: refined. 1. A refined male or female character, such as Arjuna or Sita, in Javanese and Balinese classical theatre. The refined male role is often played by a woman in dance plays. In Javanese dance, sub-types are *alus luruh* (refined modest) and *alus branyak* (refined proud). See also: *luruh, lanyap*. (Soedarsono DANCES 47–48) 2. In Bali, the manner of speaking and dancing a refined role. Also spelled *aloes*. Also called *manis* (sweet). (de Zoete/Spies DANCE 33–34) 3. In Sunda, a synonym for *lemes, lungguh,* and *luruh*. In Malaysian, spelled *halus*. See also: *gagah, kasar*.

Alzak   1. A widely used trade name of a patented electro-chemical process for anodizing, and hence protecting, aluminum. The process is owned and licensed by the Aluminum Corporation of America. 2. The resulting reflectors,

anya (Sanskrit)   In classical Indian drama, the role of a heroine, loved by the hero, who is the wife of another man. (Keith SANSKRIT 308)

anyein pwe (Burmese)   A variety entertainment featuring song, dance, clowns, and female dancers. Little dramatic content. (Sein/Withey GREAT 167)

aorigaeshi (Japanese)   Literally: flap change. An instantaneous scene change in *kabuki* accomplished by pivoting a hinged flat. (Leiter ENCYCLOPEDIA 14)

ap, AP   Ante proscenium.

apariencia (Spanish)   1. Appearance, discovery. 2. A theatrical machine. See also: *tramoya*. 3. In the 17th C, a system of wings and drops, usually painted in perspective, permitting rapid changes of scene. (Shergold SPANISH)

apart   Aside, but usually not a speech of an actor to the audience but rather to another character.

aparte (Philippine)   A verbal description of a scene in *comedia*. Also called *aside*. (Mendoza COMEDIA 52)

apati (Sanskrit)   See: *yavanika*.

ape   1. To steal the lines or business of another performer, especially in vaudeville. 2. A performer who so steals. (Bowman/Ball THEATRE)

apellatores (Latin)   Literally: callers. In medieval times, a play-like dialogue between two singing characters who introduce the prophets and comment on their predictions. (Chambers MEDIAEVAL II 53)

aperture   An opening situated on a plane at right angles to the optical axis of an optical device at or near the focal plane of an objective lens. The term is used especially of a slotlike opening in projectors and ellipsoidal reflector spotlights. In the former, the aperture is the opening where a slide (or film) is positioned; in an ellipsoidal reflector, it is the opening where a pattern, iris, or other beam-modifier may be inserted. For both types of instruments, gate is the usual term backstage. See also: gobo. (Bellman LIGHTING 84, 85, 449; Bellman SCENE; Wehlburg GLOSSARY)

aperture slide   A small piece of glass or other transparent non-flammable material. The slide is designed for insertion into the slot provided between lamp and lens in projection instruments and (sometimes) ellipsoidal reflector spotlights. The purpose is to control the size, shape, and color of the resulting light.

apeward   See: minstrel.

apiciosus (Latin Roman)   See: *stupidus*.

à plomb (French), **aplomb**   In dance, full control of the body and limbs, with the weight correctly centered during a movement. (Grant TECHNICAL)

aposento (Spanish)   Literally: a chamber or room. A theatre box. In a *corral* theatre of the 16th and 17th C, the boxes were in fact rooms in houses overlooking the central yard. There were upper and lower levels of boxes, called respectively *aposentos altos* and *aposentos bajos*. See also: *palco*. (Shergold SPANISH) *apparati* (Italian)   In the 17th C, such special stage devices as triumphal cars descending from above, wagons and carriages crossing the stage, etc. (Furttenbach in Hewitt RENAISSANCE 193)

apparent light source   A light source, such as a table lamp or the sun, which seems to the audience to illuminate a portion of the stage which is actually lighted primarily by stage lighting instruments. Compare: motivating light, which is essentially the same, and arbitrary light, which is the opposite. (Bowman MODERN)

apparition scene   A scene in which an apparently solid wall on stage disappears and the area behind it is revealed. The effect is managed by the use of scrim, which, when lit from the front, appears solid; when the area behind it is illuminated, the scrim becomes transparent. (Gillette/Gillette SCENERY 349–350)

appear   To perform, to make an appearance in a performance. Hence such phrases as stage appearance, in order of their appearance, to appear opposite (another performer), etc. (Bowman/Ball THEATRE)

appearance trap   A trap in the stage floor equipped with an elevator mechanism to make possible sudden appearances and disappearances. (Burris-Meyer/Cole SCENERY 288)

(to) appear opposite   See: appear, play opposite.

apples   A small salary.

appliance cap   See: cap.

apprentice   One who works in a theatre company without pay or for very little pay, in order to learn, usually, acting. (Bowman/Ball THEATRE)

apprentice school   In Britain, a reputable acting school or academy. (Granville DICTIONARY)

appuie (French)   Of a curtain, raised, flown. (Moynet FRENCH 26)

apretador (Spanish)   In the 17th C, a doorkeeper in a *corral* theatre. (Zabaleta in Nagler SOURCES 61)

apron   That portion of the stage extending into the auditorium beyond the proscenium arch (or, in some definitions, forward of the curtain). Also called an apron piece or apron stage, and sometimes used interchangeably with forestage. But forestage usually refers to an extensive apron, a usable acting area.

apron mates   A performing team.

apron piece   See: apron.

apron stage   In puppetry, an apron-costume worn by the puppeteer, with places in which to hide puppets and props until needed. It also serves as a kind of backdrop for the puppet action and a signal to children that puppetry time is near. See also: apron. (Hunt/Renfro PUPPETRY 61) *apsaras* (Khmer)   Heavenly dancing nymphs, of which bas reliefs carved on the temples at Angkor have served as models for classical dances recreated in recent times in *lokhon kbach boran* style. (Anonymous ROYAL 7, Brandon GUIDE 17)

apuntador (Philippine)   A prompter-director of a *comedia* performance who "dictates dialogue and directs movement from his box, called the *concha*." (Hernandez EMERGENCE 33)

apuntador (Spanish)   A prompter. *Apuntar* means to prompt. Also called a *consueta* or *soplador*. (Shergold SPANISH)

aqua drama, aquatic drama, aqua show   A spectacular 19th C entertainment staged in theatres equipped with water tanks, featuring sea battles and other aquatic events. Similar spectacles, staged in rivers, ponds, or theatres, date from ancient Rome. As aquashow the term is still used in Britain. Also called a nautical drama or tank spectacle. See also: *naumachia* (Latin Roman).

AR   Artist-in-Residence.

ara (Latin Roman)   Altar. In Roman comedy, an *ara*, commonly of Apollo, stood before one of the house fronts on the stage. (Duckworth NATURE 83–84)

arabesque   A posture in ballet in which the body is supported on one leg, straight or partially bent. The other leg is extended behind and at right angles to the body, and the arms are held in various harmonious positions to create a long line from fingertips to toes. (Grant TECHNICAL)

arabhati (Sanskrit)   Literally: violent. One of four styles (*vrtti*) of writing plot, characters, and sentiments in a classical Indian drama, derived, Bharata says, from the *Atharva Veda*. (Bharata NATYASASTRA 401–404)

aragoto (Japanese)   A bravura style of *kabuki* acting. The specialty of the Ichikawa Danjuro family of actors, *aragoto* is used for plays like *Narukami, the Thunder God* and *Wait a Moment*. (Brandon in Brandon/Malm/Shively STUDIES 68–71) *Aragotoshi* is an actor who plays roles of this type. (Gunji KABUKI 32)

araceli (Spanish)   In the medieval theatre, a cloud or 'glory' descending from above. (Shergold SPANISH)

arambha (Sanskrit)   1. "Desire to attain some end," the first stage in the development of dramatic action (*avastha*) of a classical Indian play. (Keith SANSKRIT 297) 2. Vocal warmup, the second stage in the preliminaries (*purvaranga*) that precede a classical play. (Keith SANSKRIT 339)

arannettam (Malayalam)   A debut performance of a dancer or actor.

arannu tali (Malayalam)   The ritualistic cleansing of the stage before a *kutiyattam* performance. (Raja KUTIYATTAM 12)

arati (Sanskrit)   Before a performance of *raslila*, *ramlila*, or *jhanki* in north India, a rite of worship to the god incarnated by a performer. (Hein MIRACLE 19–20)

Arbeitsgalerie (German)   Literally: work gallery. A fly gallery. (Fuchs LIGHTING 211, Rae/Southern INTERNATIONAL 42)

arbejdertaater (Danish)   Worker's theatre. (Marker/Marker "Thalia" 7)

arbitrary light   Unmotivated light which has no apparent source such as a table lamp, or a window in a daylight scene.

arbor   See: counterweight arbor.

arc   Usually, arc light. In the form 'arcing,' the word is used more generally of the sparking that may occur at a loose connection, a partial break, or a short circuit.

arc burner   The mechanism that holds the carbons in an arc light in position and moves them together as the carbon rods are consumed. See also: carbon arc.

arc cross   See: curved cross.

arc électrique (French) See: *arc votaïque*.

arc follow spot   A follow spotlight whose light source is a carbon arc. See also: arc light, carbon arc. (Bellman LIGHTING 111)

arch   1. Arch flat. 2. See: proscenium arch.

arch border   A border shaped like an arch.

arch flat, archway   A flat with an arched opening. The curve of the arch is called a sweep.

archimima (Latin Roman)   A female head, chief performer, and director of her own mime company. Plural: *archimimae*. (Nicoll MASKS 87, 241)

archimimus (Latin Roman)   Literally: chief mime. 1. In the developed mime of early Christian times, the chief performer. 2. The director and head of a mime company. This meaning derives from meaning 1, i.e., from the function of the *archimimus* as star; both meanings apply to the same person. Plural: *archimimi*. Also called an archmime, arch-mime (British), *magister mimariorum* (Latin). See also: *archimima*. (Nicoll MASKS 85–86, Allen ANTIQUITIES 85)

architecton (Greek)   Literally: master-builder, architect. By at least the 4th C BC, the lessee of a theatre. The returns from ticket sales were his. In exchange, he was obligated to keep the theatre in good repair. Also called a *theatrones*. (Allen ANTIQUITIES 40, Pickard-Cambridge FESTIVALS 47, 266)

architectural setting   A formal, sculptured setting, or one with massive buildings. (Bowman/Ball THEATRE)

archmime, arch-mime   See: *archimimus*.

archon (Greek), **archon**   From the early 7th C BC, any of nine magistrates among whom were divided the chief executive and judicial functions of Athens. In theatre literature, the term is often a convenient shortening for the *archon basileus* or (especially) *archon eponymos*, each of whom had major responsibilities for the festivals involving drama.

archon basileus (Greek)   The chief religious official in Athens and head of the Lenaea. With the help of others, including *epimeletai* (assistants), the *archon* conducted the festival procession (*pompe*). Aristotle notes that this *archon* was also in charge of the *agon*, this presumably later, in the 4th C BC. Also now printed archon *basileus*. See also: *archon*. (Pickard-Cambridge FESTIVALS 36, 40; Brockett HISTORY 25)

archon eponymos (Greek)   The official who controlled the City Dionysia; he was assisted by two *paredroi* and, for the procession, ten *epimeletai*. He appointed the *choregi* for tragedy and selected the poets who competed at the Dionysia and the Lenaea. Some of the duties of *archon* and *epimeletai* continued after the end of the choregic system. Also now printed archon *eponymos*, archon *eponymous*, or simply *archon* (q.v.). See also: *epimeletes*. (Pickard-Cambridge FESTIVALS 58, 75, 84, 86, 92, 95–97; Brockett HISTORY 25)

arc lamp, arc lantern   See: arc light.

arc light   1. The usual term for a luminaire, usually a spotlight or projector, whose light source is a carbon electric arc. Among many other terms: carbon arc, carbon electric arc, arc spot, arc lamp, arc spotlight, carbon spot, carbon, flaming arc, etc. Arc lantern is British, with arc light perhaps less frequent there. See also: carbon arc, Jablochkoff candle. 2. Occasionally, the light given by one or more arc lights. (Fuchs LIGHTING 43–45; Bellman SCENE 310–311, fig. 25–2, 580; Bellman LIGHTING 14–15; Lounsbury THEATRE 90–91; Bentham ART 336; Corry LIGHTING 56)

arc pocket   A name sometimes applied in the past to a high capacity stage receptacle which provided direct current for arc lights. (Fuchs LIGHTING 356–359)

arc rating   In an arc light, the number of amperes at which the carbons burn. See also: carbon arc.

arc spot, arc spotlight   See: arc light.

arc voltaïque (French)   Literally: voltaic arc. Arc light, carbon arc. Also called *arc*, *arc électrique* (the usual term in modern French). See also: arc light.

ardja (Indonesian)   See: *arja*.

area   In the 17th and 18th C, the forestage or apron. (Cibber APOLOGY II 84–85)

area lighting   The illumination of the acting place in a number of distinct areas which blend into each other to produce the final effect. Such lighting, usual in the modern theatre, often divides the visible stage into six, eight, or nine areas, each lighted by a group of two, three, or more spotlights.

areas   The divisions of a stage. On a proscenium or thrust stage, nine divisions are standard: center, down center, up center, left, down left, up left, right, down right, up right. The space can be further divided (left center, down left center, up left center, etc.) into 15 sections or into six rather than nine sections. An arena stage is subdivided like a clock, with 12 facing the control room. All 12 numbers may be needed in a large arena stage, with center (C) a thirteenth area, but for most arenas 12, 3, 6, 9, and C suffice. The clock layout can be superimposed on arena stages of any shape—rectangular, square, or ellipsoidal. (Lounsbury THEATRE, Dean/Carra FUNDAMENTALS 286–289)

arena (Latin Roman)   1. The walled performance area in amphitheatres and some theatres, particularly as used for gladiatorial combats, animal baitings, and similar entertainments. The word is properly *harena*, sand, by reference to the sand which often covered the *arena*, serving to absorb the blood of combatants. 2. This type of theatre itself. The Greeks sometimes used *konistra* and sometimes *orchestra* for *orchestras* converted into *arenas* (meaning 1); modern scholars also use English arena or orchestra. (Bieber HISTORY 215–219, 222, 252–253, figs. 662, 727; Flickinger GREEK 72–73)

arena   1. In an Elizabethan theatre, the pit or standing area partly surrounding the platform stage. 2. In Italy, an open-air theatre. 3. See: arena stage. (Mantzius HISTORY II 320, 329)

arena floodlight   An occasional British term for a wide-angle floodlight used in a hanging position. Also called an arena lantern. (Bowman/Ball THEATRE)

arena show   In Britain, a production in an enclosure seating 10,000 people or more. (Granville DICTIONARY)

arena stage, arena theatre   A central stage, with seating usually rising in tiers on all sides, and with no proscenium and usually no curtains. Hence, arena staging, central staging. Also called theatre-in-the-round, especially in England, and central stage, circle theatre, arena.

"Are you decent?"   An expression used at a dressing room door instead of "May I come in?" See also: be decent.

Argand burner, Argand lamp   1. A cylindrical wick for oil lamps, introduced in the late 18th C and soon used in the theatre. 2. An oil lamp with a cylindrical wick. 3. After the introduction of gas, a similar gas lamp. The lamp provided air both inside and outside the wick, resulting in a brighter, whiter light than had previously been available. The burner was named for its inventor, Aimé Argand; his younger brother added the glass chimney some years later. Strictly, the burner is the wick and base, and the lamp is the burner and chimney. Theatrical literature, however, often uses Argand burner for the lamp as a whole. Both the term and the device are now rare. Also called a patent lamp; in the U.S., sometimes round-flame burner or round burner. (Penzel LIGHTING 24, 89–92; Rees GAS 6, 7, 15 (illus.), 22, 206)

argentine   A shiny, thin metal alloy used in scenery to simulate window glass. (Bowman/Ball THEATRE)

argument   1. In Roman times, a summary of the action, spoken before the play. 2. In Elizabethan drama, a summary of the action, printed before an act, and perhaps not spoken in performance. The argument at the beginning of Jonson's *Volpone*, on the other hand, was clearly intended to be spoken to the audience.

argumentum (Latin Roman)   The plot of a play or a summary thereof. Some Greek and Roman plays used a prologue to present the *argumentum* to the audience. In published texts, the *argumentum* is often prefaced to the script—sometimes, in Roman comedy, in the form of an acrostic verse. English 'argument' is sometimes used. (Duckworth NATURE 61, 211; Vaughn DRAMA)

aria (Italian)   An elaborate air or song for a single voice.

aria da capo (Italian)   A song in two parts, the first of which is repeated, sometimes with embellishments to display the singer's virtuosity. The *aria da capo* was a feature of Baroque opera but remained popular into the 19th C.

arietta (Italian)   In opera, a solo song, shorter than an aria.

arisard   An 18th C Scottish woman's long, plaid, wraparound cloak. (Wilcox DICTIONARY)

aristerostatae (Greek)   Literally: men on the left. In the Greek tragic chorus, the first of the three files of chorus members. This file was nearest the audience and contained the best performers. (Haigh ATTIC 300)

Aristotelian theatre   Bertolt Brecht's term for the theatre of illusion which encourages the audience to identify with the characters on stage. (Fuegi BRECHT 18)

arja (Indonesian)   A secular Balinese dance-opera based on the Pañji tales, in which actresses play male roles and clown-servants (*penasar*) provide comedy. It dates from the 17th C and was formerly performed by all-male troupes. Also spelled *ardja*. (de Zoete/Spies DANCE 196–205, Soedarsono DANCES 178)

ark   A showboat.

arlecchino (Italian)   A harlequin, a merry andrew.

arlequin (French)   A harlequin, a merry andrew. See also: harlequin.

arlequinade (French)   A harlequinade, a buffoonery.

arm   See: hanger.

armazón (Spanish)   The framework or structure of any theatrical device or machine.

arm cyclorama   A drop with arms hinged to each end; when the drop is flown, the arms fold down to permit storage in a shallow space. When an arm cyclorama is in position, it encloses the acting area at the back and sides. Also called a traveling cyclorama.

armée (French)   The point at which bracing is put in stage scenery which must be flown. (Moynet FRENCH 111)

Armenian bole, bole   In the past, a red powder sometimes used by performers to make the skin appear sunburned. (Bowman/Ball THEATRE)

armet   A 15th-16th C helmet. (Wilcox DICTIONARY)

armiger   See: minstrel.

armil, armilla, armlet   A wraparound bronze, silver, or gold snake bracelet worn by Greek women and Roman men in the classical period. (Wilcox DICTIONARY)

armilausa   A medieval silk or linen cloak or cape worn over armor. (Wilcox DICTIONARY)

armlet   1. A very short, set-in sleeve. 2. See: armil. (Wilcox DICTIONARY)

arm puppet   Especially in Britain, a puppet which extends to full-arm length. Often a monster character such as a dragon or crocodile. (Philpott DICTIONARY)

arnis (Philippine)   An indigenous martial art used in duels and fight scenes in *comedia*. Four types of *arnis* combat are described by Mendoza in COMEDIA 59.

arqué (French)   In ballet, arched, bow-legged. Also called *cagneux*. See also: *jarreté*.

arras   In an Elizabethan theatre, a curtain or hanging. (Dekker in Nagler SOURCES 135)

arras setting   A stage set consisting of draperies.

arremedilhos (Portuguese)   Late 12th C imitations of animals and people. (Gassner/Quinn ENCYCLOPEDIA 675)

arrendador (Spanish)   The lessee of a theatre. (Shergold SPANISH)

arrendamiento (Spanish)   A lease. Also called an *arriendo*. (Shergold SPANISH)

(en) arrière (French)   In ballet, a command to move backward. (Grant TECHNICAL)

arsenic   A poor show.

arthadhari (Kannada)   Performers who sing the *tala maddale* version of *yaksagana*. See also: *veshadhari*. (Gargi FOLK 163)

arthaprakrti (Sanskrit)   In classical Indian dramatic theory, "elements of plot" of which there are five: *bija*, *bindu*, *pataka*, *prakari*, and *karya*. They occur in sequence in the construction of a plot (*vastu*). (Keith SANSKRIT 298) Byrski calls them five aspects of "subject matter" in Baumer/Brandon SANSKRIT 144. Kale calls them "meaning configurations" (THEATRIC 155–156).

arthopaksepaka (Sanskrit)   An explanatory scene that describes action which cannot be portrayed directly on stage in a classical Indian play. (Shastri LAWS 64–67, Keith SANSKRIT 301)

articles   Articles of agreement—regulations governing the affairs of a theatrical company, agreed to by the performers and the managers. (Nicoll HISTORY I 324)

articulated puppet   A puppet whose joints move. (Philpott DICTIONARY)

articulation   A dance term for a movement in a joint in the body. (Vincent DANCER'S)

artificial acting   An approach, not necessarily correct, to the acting of 17th and 18th C comedies of manners, based on the assumption that the high society of the time, and plays about that society, had an artificial code of behavior.

artificial comedy   See: comedy of manners.

artificial horizon   A cyclorama.

artificier (French)   A specialist in fire and fireworks. Essential to large French theatres of the 19th C performing spectacle or military plays. (Moynet FRENCH 124)

artist, artiste   In theatrical agreements and notices, the term used by managers of performers, especially performers in side shows, vaudeville, burlesque, etc. Also sometimes used by others, especially in the past.

artiste (French)   One who creates from simple material or no material at all.

artiste dramatique (French)   A performer, whether actor, actress, singer, or dancer.

artistic failure   A play which is unfavorably reviewed by theatre critics, though it may do well at the box office. (Granville DICTIONARY)

artist-in-residence, artist in residence   1. A trained theatre person who works in schools creating improvised theatre with children. See also: TIE. 2. A professional working with a non-professional group (such as a university theatre) for a period. Sometimes abbreviated to AR.

Artists of Dionysus   From the early 3rd C BC in Greece, the guild or union of theatre personnel. In addition to actors and such support personnel as stage managers and costumers, the guild included poets and every kind of musician. Also called Dionysiac Artists, Artists, *technitae*, or guild. (Pickard-Cambridge FESTIVALS 279–305; Bieber HISTORY 84, 86; Allen ANTIQUITIES 132)

artist's stump   A small roll of paper, somewhat pointed at one end, once used by performers for lining the face or body when making up. No longer in common use for makeup, but sometimes used by makeup artists for drawing. Also called an artist's paper stump, stump, stomp, lining stump, (rarely) pretzel.

artois   An 18th-19th C long cloth coat with three or four graduated capes extending to the waist. A favorite coachman's coat. (Wilcox DICTIONARY)

art theatre   Especially in the early 20th C, a term sometimes applied to U.S. theatres with an expressed interest in experimentation. (Bowman/Ball THEATRE)

art train   A proposed independent amateur theatre effort to bring Buenos Aires theatre to the Argentine countryside during the Juan Perón regime. Perón quashed the effort. (Karnis "Argentine" 309)

as   Playing the part of, as in 'Olivier as Hamlet.'

asan (Malayalam)   The honorific title of a master of *kathakali* acting, music, or costuming and makeup. (Jones/Jones KATHAKALI 106)

asar (Bengali)   A raised stage of a *jatra* theatre, circular in shape. (Sarkar "Jatra" 97)

asbestos, asbestos curtain, asbestos drop   See: fire curtain.

asbestos border   A short asbestos curtain sometimes seen directly downstage of a light pipe. The asbestos border is used mainly with the first light pipe, where it insulates the hot metal of lighting instruments from adjacent cloth hangings.

asbestos connector   Especially in the past, a pin connector with two holes at the end opposite the pins. Pin connectors normally have a single large hole for stage cable; the two smaller holes of the asbestos connector took the two asbestos wires which came from the lighting instrument. See also: asbestos leads. (Cornberg/Gebauer CREW 152–153, 272–273)

asbestos curtain   See: fire curtain.

"Asbestos going up!"   In a theatre required by law to have an asbestos fire curtain, a warning to cast and crew five minutes before performance time. The fire curtain must be raised in the presence of the audience.

"(The) asbestos is down."   1. Literally, "the fire curtain is in its lowered position." 2. In burlesque, a statement meaning that the audience is not responding to the comedians. (Wilmeth LANGUAGE)

asbestos leads, asbestos pigtails   Especially in the past, the asbestos-covered wires which led out of many lighting instruments. Asbestos has been replaced by other high-temperature insulation. Also called wire leads.

asbestos safety release line   See: fire curtain safety release line.

ascension   Chiefly in Britain, a term for forgetting one's lines or business, that is, making an ascension. See also: go up.

ashcan   1. Sometimes among British electricians, a unit of compartment footlights. The term may have come from motion pictures. (Granville DICTIONARY, Bowman/Ball THEATRE) 2. See: funnel.

ashi zukai (Japanese)   Literally: foot manipulator. The puppeteer in a three-man team who manipulates the visible feet of a male *bunraku* puppet or the skirt hems of the normally legless female puppet. (Adachi BUNRAKU 29–33)

aside   1. A dramatic convention in which a character is supposedly heard by the audience but not by any onstage character. 2. See: apart.

aside (Philippine)   See: *aparte*.

A-sign   Two panels back to back, set to form an A, like a sandwich board. Used in front of theatres to advertise a show. (Gilbert VAUDEVILLE)

askoliasmos (Greek)   In the Rural Dionysia, a tribute dance in which the performers jumped up and down on greased wineskins. (Lawler DANCE 116)

A.S.M., ASM   Especially in Britain, assistant stage manager.

asravana (Sanskrit)   The third stage of the preliminaries (*purvaranga*) to a classical Indian play, in which musicians tune their instruments. (Keith SANSKRIT 339)

assemblé (French)   In ballet, a step in which the working foot slides along the ground before being lifted into the air. (Grant TECHNICAL)

assembled text   In Elizabethan times, a printed text based on the playhouse 'plott' (or platt: scenario) and performers' parts or sides, instead of a text based on the promptbook. (Rhodes STAGERY 60)

Assembly, assembly   See: *ekklesia*.

assistant electrician   In some theatres or productions, an electrician's helper, especially an apprentice who assists the controlboard operator. In such arrangements, the assistant's duties include running the houselights and signalling such personnel as the house manager, the orchestra leader, and others as necessary. (Cornberg/Gebauer CREW 240)

assistant stage manager   The stage manager's helper, who often takes over such duties as prompting, checking properties, calling performers, etc. Often abbreviated A.S.M. or ASM, especially in Britain.

astamangalam (Sanskrit)   An auspicious offering of grain, fruit, flowers, etc. in a *kutiyattam* temple performance. (Vatsyayan TRADITIONAL 25)

astrophon   In Greek tragedy, the part of a choral ode (*stasimon*) outside the normal strophe and antistrophe. The term is from Greek *astrophos*, "without turning around," ultimately "without strophe." (Vaughn DRAMA, Liddell/Scott LEXICON)

ata (Kannada)   The generic term for a folk performance of a dance-drama. (Ranganath KARNATAK 12)

atakkam (Malayalam)   In *kathakali*, a choreographic passage added to a pure dance sequence (*kalasam*). (Jones/Jones KATHAKALI 72)

ataman (Yiddish)   An enthusiastic fan, often a claqueur or head of a claque. (Rosenfeld BRIGHT 24–25)

at back   See: backstage.

ATD   Short for autotransformer dimmer. (Bellman SCENE 353, 354)

ateburi (Japanese)   A mime technique in *kabuki* in which homonyms of the words being sung are danced, that is, a kind of punning through dance. See also: *furi*. (Brandon in Brandon/Malm/Shively STUDIES 81)

Atellan   1. See: *fabula Atellana*. 2. Farcical; hence, Atellan farce, Atellan play, etc. Also spelled Atellane. (Duckworth NATURE 10–13)

Atellanae (Latin Roman)   See: *fabula Atellana*.

Atellani (Latin Roman)   Performers in the *fabula Atellana*. (Beare ROMAN 142)

Atellaniolae (Latin Roman)   Literally: little Atellans. The word is one of the pieces of evidence that some, probably all, Atellan plays were brief. See also: *fabula Atellana.* (Beare ROMAN 141)

at full   See: full.

at half check   See: check.

Athenian Dionysia   A phrase sometimes used for the City Dionysia and the Lenaea of ancient Greece. (Allen ANTIQUITIES 49)

athletic droll   In Britain, a knockabout comedian. (Bowman/Ball THEATRE)

at liberty   Of a performer, unemployed. Also called at leisure, available, resting, between engagements, between plays, between shows. (Bowman/Ball THEATRE)

atmagatam (Sanskrit)   An aside in classical Indian drama. Also called *svagatam.* (Keith SANSKRIT 304)

atmosphere   The mood or feeling created by a play's events, locales, and situations and the representation of them on stage. See also: tone. (Brooks/Heilman UNDERSTANDING)

atmospheric scenery   A setting calculated to produce an emotional audience response. (Bowman/Ball THEATRE)

at quarter check   See: check.

at rise   What is seen on stage when the curtain rises.

ato za (Japanese)   Literally: rear seating place. That portion of the *no* stage, immediately behind the square main stage and connected to the *hashigakari,* on which musicians and stage assistants sit during performance. (Shimazaki NOH 11)

atsumori (Japanese)   A *no* mask worn by the ghost of a youthful warrior. The name is from the child warrior Taira no Atsumori, a historical figure who appears in several *no* plays. (Shimazaki NOH 59)

attachment plug   See: cap.

attack   See: inciting action.

attakatha (Malayalam)   Literally: acted story. A text of a *kathakali* play, written wholly in verse (*slokam*) and song (*padam*). (Jones/Jones KATHAKALI 71)

attaprakara (Malayalam)   A *kutiyattam* acting manual. It details techniques of acting and elaborates on the meaning of the verses, which are in Sanskrit. See also: *kramadipika.* (Vatsyayan TRADITIONAL 20, Enros in Baumer/Brandon SANSKRIT 276)

attendance register   Especially in Britain, a book used by the stage manager to keep track of performers as they arrive for rehearsals. (Bax MANAGEMENT 43)

attendee   A theatre patron. (Berrey/Van den Bark SLANG 574)

attifet   A 16th C woman's headdress consisting of an arc over each side of the forehead, covered by a veil. Favored in black for mourning. Also called a bongrace or widow's peak. See also: houppe. (Boucher FASHION, Wilcox DICTIONARY)

attiring house   See: tiring house.

attiring room   See: tiring room.

attitude   In ballet, a position similar to the arabesque, but with the raised leg bent at the knee at an angle of 90 degrees. (Grant TECHNICAL)

A-type bulb   1. Strictly, the glass portion of a low-wattage lamp with curved sides and inside frosting. Also called an A-bulb. 2. Loosely, the entire lamp.

aud   Auditorium.

audience dress, audience dress rehearsal   A performance before an invited (sometimes a paying) audience before a show has officially opened.

audience in his/her palm   Said of a performer who has manipulated the reactions of an audience. (Wilmeth LANGUAGE)

audience number   In 20th C U.S. burlesque, a scene in which the chorus leaves the stage to sit in the laps of the older patrons, amid squeals and ad-lib adjusting of skimpy costumes. (Allen in Matlaw AMERICAN 54)

audience-proof   Said of a play that is certain to please audiences.

audition   1. A tryout, usually competitive, of performers seeking roles in a production. Hence, to audition for, to be auditioned. Also known as a call. 2. A reading of a script to prospective investors. (Bowman/Ball THEATRE)

auditor   A playgoer.

auditorium (Latin Roman), **auditorium**   Literally: hearing-place. 1. The seating area of a theatre. See also: *cavea*, *theatron* (Greek). 2. The audience. (Sandys COMPANION 517–518, Flickinger GREEK 342) 3. A theatre building. 4. An assembly hall.

auditorium beams   See: beam lights.

auditorium lights   See: house lights.

auditorium main, auditorium master   A master electrical switch, relay control, or dimmer control for all lighting in the auditorium except emergency and aisle lighting.

auditory   1. From well before Shakespeare's time, the audience. 2. Auditorium.

audit stub   That portion of a theatre ticket retained by the theatre for later auditing. (Crampton HANDBOOK)

Aufführung (German)   Performance.

Aufklärung (German)   Literally: elucidation, enlightenment. An 18th C German literary movement that upheld French neoclassicism as the model for playwriting. (Roberts STAGE)

Aufstellung (German)   A stage setting.

Aufzug (German)   1. An act of a play. 2. A procession or pageant.

Augustan drama   British neoclassic drama, especially tragedies, of the late 17th and early 18th C. Named for the period of literary excellence in ancient Rome. (Bowman/Ball THEATRE)

aulaeum (Latin Roman)   The main curtain of a Roman theatre. There is no evidence for the introduction of such a curtain before the latter half of the 2nd C BC, but it was in use by 56 BC. This was evidently a roll curtain which rested in a long trough at the front of the stage. To raise it concealed the stage from view; to lower it revealed the stage. This arrangement was later reversed: probably by the 2nd C, and certainly by the 4th, the rise of the curtain revealed the stage, as in modern proscenium theatres. Plural: *aulaea*. (Beare ROMAN 267–274, plate VIII; Allen ANTIQUITIES 108–109, fig. 16; Duckworth NATURE 84–85)

aulaeum mittere (Latin Roman)   Literally: to lead down the curtain. To lower the curtain (and thus expose the stage to view). Also used was *aulaeum subducere*. See also: *aulaeum*. (Allen ANTIQUITIES 108, Sandys COMPANION 520)

aulaeum premere (Latin Roman)   1. To keep the curtain down. 2. To lower the curtain. Also spelled *aulaeum praemere*. See also: *aulaeum*. (Allen ANTIQUITIES 108, Sandys COMPANION 520)

aulaeum subducere (Latin Roman)   See: *aulaeum mittere*.

aulaeum tollere (Latin Roman)   To raise the curtain (the literal meaning) and thus hide the stage from view. See also: *aulaeum*. (Allen ANTIQUITIES 108, Sandys COMPANION 520)

aula regia (Latin Roman)   Literally: royal hall, royal residence. In the facade of a scene building, the entrance supposedly leading to the royal palace. The name, given by Vitruvius, is usually applied to the center door, which provided an impressive entrance for the leading actor. The term is commonly shortened to *regia*. (Bieber HISTORY 173, 187; Arnott ANCIENT 137)

auletike (Greek)   Flute music to accompany recitative. (Webster CHORUS 56)

aulos (Greek), **aulos**   An oboe-like instrument which accompanied recitative in Greek drama. Especially in the past, often referred to as a flute.

aumonière (French)   See: reticule.

auriga (Latin Roman)   A circus driver or charioteer. By the 5th C BC or earlier, the *auriga* was classed among *histriones* (actors). Also called an *agitator*. (Chambers MEDIAEVAL I 20)

Ausdruckskraft (German)   Force of expression, a concept central to the design theory of Adolphe Appia. The perpendicular setting, horizontal floor, moving three-dimensional performer, and lighted acting space were the primary elements in this expression.

Ausdruckstanz (German)   Expressive movement, especially as it related to the dance theory of Mary Wigman, a modern dance pioneer. (Odom "Wigman" 81)

Ausschreier (German)   The performer who concluded a medieval Shrovetide play, began the dancing, and sent the players on to the next street. (Mantzius HISTORY II 143)

Austrian knot   A black silk looped cord used on military dress; copied by Napoleon and used in the U.S. in the 19th C. See also: Brandenburg. (Wilcox DICTIONARY)

author-director   A playwright who directs his or her own play.

author's night   A benefit for the playwright. In Restoration times and later the author received the proceeds (probably after house charges had been subtracted) from the third, sixth, and ninth performances, and so on. For most playwrights, this was the only money they received for their work, and if a play received only one or two performances, they got nothing.

author's scene sketch   A playwright's production instructions for staging a scene. (Bowman/Ball THEATRE)

author's theatre   In Britain, a theatre whose production draws audiences by virtue of its playwright rather than its performers. (Bowman/Ball THEATRE)

auto   See: color boomerang.

auto (Spanish)   A one-act play, usually religious and often a morality. An *auto sacramental* in the 16th and 17th C was a short morality play dealing with a Holy Sacrament and performed annually on Corpus Christi Day. (Shergold SPANISH)

autofader   An electrical device for effecting a cross fade automatically. The time interval is pre-established and, once initiated, the fade runs by itself. (Bellman LIGHTING 220)

autografan, autograph fan   A theatre patron who collects performers' signatures. (Berrey/Van den Bark SLANG 574)

autokabdaloi (Greek)   Literally: improvisers. A variety of early (6th C BC) troupes of actors. Their performances were apparently improvised and non-choral, with the actors unmasked, ivy-crowned, and probably amateur. (Pickard-Cambridge DITHYRAMB 137–138 Stuart DRAMATIC 106)

automatic colour change   See: color boomerang.

automatic tension pulley   In counterweight systems, a grooved pulley in a wooden or metal frame. It automatically takes up and holds the operating rope line taut.

autor, autora (Spanish)   A theatre manager.

autor de comedias (Spanish)   The leader of a company of players; an actor-manager. (Rennert SPANISH 9)

auto sacramental (Spanish)   See: *auto*.

autos viejos (Spanish)   Transitional plays between the 15th and early 16th C farces and 17th C Eucharistic plays. (Rennert SPANISH)

autotransformer dimmer, ATD   An electromagnetic dimming device which operates by moving a sliding brush along an insulated coil of copper wire which surrounds an iron core; the slider changes the voltage which is permitted to reach a lamp. This dimmer may be seen in older installations. In Britain, sometimes called a choke dimmer. See also: dimmer, variable load dimmer. Illustrations are in all sources cited. (Bellman LIGHTING 177–184; Sellman/Lessley ESSENTIALS 125–126, fig. 8.6; Wehlburg GLOSSARY)

autumn tour   A theatrical tour, especially in Britain, made between late September or early October and Christmas. (Granville DICTIONARY)

auxiliary   In 19th C Britain, a visiting star in a provincial stock company. (Bowman/Ball THEATRE)

auxiliary switchboard   In the U.S., a small control board whose electrical supply is independent of the main control board. The British call this a special effects board. (Rae/Southern INTERNATIONAL 135)

avahana (Sanskrit)   In *tamasha*, the invocation to the god Ganesha, performed by musicians who have their backs to the audience. (Vatsyayan TRADITIONAL 172)

available   See: at liberty.

avalanche machine   A hexagonal wooden drum containing cannonballs or rocks. It is rotated to simulate the sound of an avalanche. (Collison SOUND 102)

avanis (Sanskrit)   The initial entrance of actors in *bhavai*. (Vatsyayan TRADITIONAL 172)

(en) avant (French)   In ballet, a command to move forward. (Grant TECHNICAL)

avant garde (French)   Literally: vanguard. Any fresh leadership or experimentation in drama and theatre; something ahead of its time in form or subject matter. In recent years, often printed as English (with hyphen).

avant scène (French)   Literally: in front of the scenic area. 1. The forestage or apron. 2. A box very close to the stage.

avanu (Sanskrit)   Literally: entry. Entrance music in *bhavai*, performed by musicians and singers. (Vatsyayan TRADITIONAL 152)

avastha (Sanskrit)   The five "stages of development" of the dramatic action or plot (*vastu*) of a Sanskrit play. The stages are *arambha, prayatna, praptyasa, niyatapti* and *phalagama*. (Keith SANSKRIT 297–298) Byrski says five "phases" of plot structure (*itivrtta*) in Baumer/Brandon SANSKRIT 143.

avatarana (Sanskrit)   The entry of performers in the preliminaries (*purvaranga*) that precede a classical Indian play. (Keith SANSKRIT 339)

aviary   In Britain, the chorus girls' dressing room. (Granville DICTIONARY)

a vista (Italian)   In view of the audience; said of a scene change made with the curtain up. The full term, not often found in English sources, is *cambiamento a vista*: change within sight.

awang batil, awang selampit (Malaysian)   See: *penglipur lara*.

awareness   In performing, a state of sensory alertness and preparedness to respond to sight, sound, taste, touch, and odor. (Selden ACTING)

ax   Any musical instrument. (Lees "Lexicon" 57)

axial lamp   A tungsten-halogen lamp designed for positioning along the axis of a spotlight.

axial mount   See: quartz ellipsoidal.

axial-mounted lamp   A lamp positioned along the axis of a spotlight.

axial movement   In modern dance, swinging, turning, beating, and similar movement which takes place around an axis or axes of the body, or of many dancers around a non-moving performer. The contrast is with locomotor motions in which one travels through space. (Love DANCE 8)

ayagiri (Japanese)   A *bugaku* mask used for a lovely woman. (Wolz BUGAKU 43)

ayakashi (Japanese)   A mask of an evil spirit of the sea used for a vengeful ghost in the second part of a demon *no* play. (Shimazaki NOH 60)

ayak kuklasi (Turkish)   In Turkestan, a foot puppet, similar to the French *marionnette à la planchette* (q.v.). (And KARAGÖZ 23)

ayang (Khmer)   A form of shadow theatre in which small, flat leather puppets are played against a white cloth illuminated by a single lamp. The plays are largely improvised comic depictions of peasant life. The word is probably derived from *wayang* (Java, Bali, and Malaysia). Also called *nang sbek touch* (small-hide puppet theatre), *nang kaloun* (from Thai *nang taloun*), or *nang trolung*. (Brunet in Osman TRADITIONAL 27–29, 52)

ayatsuri ningyo shibai (Japanese)   Literally: manipulation puppet play. A common term for commercial puppet theatre, 17th to early 20th C. Abbreviated *ningyo shibai* (puppet play), *ayatsuri shibai* (manipulation play). Today, commonly called *bunraku*. (Dunn EARLY 62, Kincaid KABUKI 144, Kawatake KABUKI 17, Scott KABUKI 56–57)

ayay (Khmer)   Popular songs, accompanied by simple dance movements, performed within the court dance tradition in the mid-19th C. (Anonymous ROYAL 10)

aynshrayer (Yiddish)   The crier in a Polish Purim play. (Kirshenblatt-Gim-blett "Contraband" 8)

ayoga (Sanskrit)   Literally: privation. In a classic Indian play, the circum-stance of lovers unable to unite. One sub-division of the erotic sentiment (*srngara rasa*). (Keith SANSKRIT 323)

ayuda de costa (Spanish)   A subsidy or advance sum; a guarantee for a 17th C acting company. (Rennert SPANISH 193)

ayukta (Sanskrit)   In classical Indian drama, the role of a chief attendant in a harem. (Keith SANSKRIT 312)

ayumi (Japanese)   A raised walkway in a *kabuki* theatre, 17th to 19th C, that connected the main and the temporary *hanamichi*. Audience, ushers, and actors would use it to pass from one side of the house to the other. (Leiter ENCY-CLOPEDIA 21) Also called *naka no ayumi* (middle walkway). (Pronko THEA-TER 141)

B

B 1. A letter sometimes used to designate low-wattage incandescent lamps whose bulbs contain a vacuum rather than one or more gases. Also called a B lamp or vacuum lamp. (Gassner/Barber PRODUCING 802) 2. Blank, as in a paper without writing, used as a property. (Shattuck SHAKESPEARE 14)

B.A., b.a., BA, ba See: bastard amber.

ba (Japanese) Literally: scene. 1. The dramaturgical unit of a scene within an act in *kabuki*, *bunraku*, and modern drama. Also called *bamen*. 2. In *bunraku*, sometimes a full act. 3. In *no*, the first or second part of a two-part play. (Hoff/Flindt "structure" 219)

baba (Japanese) Literally: old woman. A *bunraku* puppet head used for characters of virtuous old women. (Keene BUNRAKU 59, 239)

bāba (Arabic) A one-act shadow puppet play. (Gassner/Quinn ENCYCLO-PEDIA 22)

babad (Indonesian) See: *cerita babad*.

babayaku (Japanese) Literally: old woman role. 1. A role of an old woman in *kabuki*. One type of *kashagata* female role. (Dunn/Torigoe ANALECTS 168) 2. An actor who plays such a role. (Hamamura et al KABUKI 101)

babaylan (Philippine) A pre-Spanish term for actor. Also called *catalonan*. (Hernandez EMERGENCE 17)

bablas (Indonesian) To fall through the air after being struck, kicked, or thrown away. A movement technique in Javanese *wayang kulit*. Also called *kabur*, *kentas*. (Long JAVANESE 81)

babushka (Russian) Literally: grandmother. A triangularly folded kerchief for the head, or any head covering resembling it. Also called a *platok* or *shal'*.

Babu Yochne (Yiddish) The stock character of an old hag, always played by a man until after World War I. (Lifson YIDDISH 50–51)

baby 1. Informally, a name for anyone in show business. (Lees "Lexicon" 57) 2. Among lighting people, a frequent shortening of baby spotlight.

baby bullet   A 19th C U.S. spectacular production featuring children. (Wilmeth LANGUAGE)

baby lens   A rare early term for a baby spotlight. See also: lens. (Hartmann LIGHTING 68)

baby spot   A small lightweight spotlight, usually of 400 watts or less, with a plano-convex lens. Popular early in the 20th C, baby spots have been largely replaced by Fresnel spotlights. The term is now occasionally used of any relatively low-wattage spotlight. The phrase is a backstage shortening of baby spotlight, not much heard in the theatre; among lighting people, one is likely to hear simply 'baby.' (Lounsbury THEATRE 91, McCandless "Glossary" 633, Bellman SCENE)

bacinet   See: basinet.

back   1. To invest in a production. 2. Short for back stage, generally as 'in back.' 3. At back: against the back wall of the stage. 4. In rehearsals, a direction to repeat some of what has been done, usually as 'try back.' (Bowman/Ball THEATRE)

back batten   In Britain, the light pipe farthest upstage. The British also use sky batten, and number four batten. (Baker THEATRECRAFT 263, 264)

back cloth   See: back drop.

back-cloth star   Especially in Britain, a performer in a small role who is positioned upstage, near the back cloth (back drop). Frequently performers so called attempt, by means of byplay and other distractions, to draw attention to themselves. (Granville DICTIONARY)

back country   The provinces.

back drop, backdrop, back-drop   A large cloth hung upstage, usually painted to represent a landscape, sky, or other background. In Britain: back cloth, backcloth, back-cloth.

backed   Provided with a backing.

backflap   A pin hinge, usually measuring 2″ x 4″ when open, used for fixing two scenic units together. The pin may be loose (temporary) or tight (permanent).

back flat   A flat positioned upstage.

back focused   Of a light source, beyond the principal focal point of the lens. The term is used of a spotlight whose light source may be moved toward or away from its lens. Except for arc lights, modern instruments do not permit the light source to be moved into back focus, where they lose most of their light; this serves a purpose with arc lights, which cannot be dimmed by ordinary means. The term is also sometimes used of a lamp which is toward the rear of its travel, even though not in true back focus. (Fuchs LIGHTING 186, Bellman LIGHTING 76, Lounsbury THEATRE 60)

back-front box   See: basket box.

background scene   An expository segment of a play which provides information needed by the audience about the play. (Bowman/Ball THEATRE)

back-hair part   Especially in Britain, a role in which an actress has an opportunity to loosen her hair and let her tresses fall over her shoulders. (Partridge TO-DAY 226)

backing   1. The financing of a stage production. 2. A scenic piece set behind an opening, such as a door or window, to mask the offstage area and fill out the setting. Hence, exterior backing, sky backing, backing cloth, backing flat, door backing, window backing, etc. (Bowman/Ball THEATRE)

backing light   1. The illumination on scenic elements behind the main set. Typically, this is the lighting in a hall, through a window, etc. 2. An instrument used to produce backing light. 3. Sometimes, light which reaches the stage through an opening in the set. (Bowman/Ball THEATRE, Lounsbury THEATRE, Wehlburg GLOSSARY)

backing strip, backing striplight   A short strip of low-wattage lamps, usually in a metal housing, sometimes used to light a hallway or other background behind an opening in the set. Such a striplight is typically two or three feet long with four to six lamps. (Bellman SCENE)

back light, back lighting, backlighting   Light thrown at the performer from above and behind. The purpose is to provide plasticity by highlighting the top-rear of the head and shoulders and to separate the performer from the background. Back lighting is thought to have started in films. Also called rim lighting, since a ''rim'' of light appears around some of the performer's body.

back of the green   1. Behind the house curtain. 2. In Britain, behind the scenes. (Granville DICTIONARY)

back of the house   1. The rear of an auditorium. 2. Sometimes, the backstage area.

back-pack guide   In hanging stage curtains, a piece of hardware consisting of hanging chains and a metal plate which provide a sliding door effect and prevent a curtain from accumulating in gathers until the end of the curtain track is reached.

back painting   Painting the back of a scenic unit to make the cloth opaque or to eliminate wrinkles. (Lounsbury THEATRE)

back piece   A special wig worn on the back of the head. (Wilmeth LANGUAGE)

back pit   In the architect-designer Joseph Furttenbach's 17th C theatre, a cross-stage pit or trench upstage of the acting area.

back projection   An image thrown on a translucent screen from behind. Back projection was used with the first magic lanterns in the 17th C. Also called a rear projection. (Rees GAS 220)

back room   A stock kitchen interior drop carried by touring companies in the early 20th C. See also: front room, town, timber. (McNamara "Scenography" 20)

backscene, back-scene, back scene   1. Among some British writers, the facade providing the background of the Roman stage. (Beare ROMAN 124, 176–177) 2. In Restoration British theatres and later, the scenery, at first sliding back shutters (wide flats) but later a drop, closing off the prospect upstage, as in "the Garden in Tryphon as a Back Scene." (Southern CHANGEABLE 34, Boyle GUZMAN 37)

back shutters   See: backscene.

backstage, back stage   The parts of a theatre behind the proscenium arch or behind the stage setting, including the workshops, dressing rooms, and storage areas. Often called back, at back, in back, or behind. Sometimes called, confusingly, the back of the house. In an arena theatre, the backstage area may be behind or under portions of the seating area.

backstage cover   In Britain, a kind of blanket insurance policy covering performers' belongings and costumes where they are performing as well as in transit between engagements. Provided by British Actors' Equity. (Granville DICTIONARY)

backstage gossip   See: green room gossip.

backstage staff   Theatre workers behind the curtain, such as the stage carpenter, the technical director, stagehands, dressers, flymen, etc. Sometimes also called the company crew, especially on tour; the company crew may include the front-of-house personnel.

back wall   See: rear wall.

back-wall cyclorama   See: cyclorama.

backward   See: direction.

badagatittu (Kannada)   See: *yaksagana badagatittu bayalata.*

badchan (Hebrew)   A professional jester. (Zangwill GHETTO)

bad get in   In Britain, a theatre whose scene dock is so situated that moving in scenery is awkward, arduous, and time-consuming. Its opposite is good get in, a well-placed scene dock. (Granville DICTIONARY 86)

bad join   1. Said of two adjacent flats that do not quite meet. 2. Said of the front of a wig that is poorly painted into the forehead makeup.

badkhen, bodchin (Yiddish)   A topical rhymester-buffoon who performed at festivals and festive gatherings. The spirit of the *badkhen*, who was often the principal or sole entertainer at weddings, is said to have characterized early 20th C Yiddish theatre. Plural *badkhonim.* See also: *meshoyrerim.* (Lifson YIDDISH 126)

bad laugh   Unexpected laughter from an audience. Such laughter sometimes throws a performer, causing him to miss a cue or muddle a line.

bad quarto   In Elizabethan times, a pirated or corrupted edition of a play.

bad show town   See: show town.

badut (Indonesian)   See: *pelawak*.

baffle   A piece of suitable material which prevents light spill. In lighting instruments, especially spotlights, the baffle is usually a strip of lightweight metal behind the instrument's ventilation holes. Hence, baffled vent. Behind the scenery, the baffle is often any handy piece of opaque cloth. Also called a light baffle, especially in lighting instruments. (Bowman/Ball THEATRE, Lounsbury THEATRE, Granville DICTIONARY)

baffleboard   A board, usually ¾″ plywood, used to improve the tone of a loudspeaker. A hole is cut in the board to accommodate the speaker, which is attached with a rubber or cork gasket between the speaker rim and the board. (Lounsbury THEATRE)

baffled vent   See: baffle.

bag   1. A shortening of limelight bag or gas bag. 2. A sandbag. 3. To attach a sandbag to a line or set of lines.

bag a drop   To weight a drop with sand bags. (Berrey/Van den Bark SLANG 583)

bagattella   (Italian)   Literally: a trifle, a bauble. A term for a marionette in Renaissance Italy. Also called a *magatella*. (Kennard MASKS 105)

bag cheomji, bag czonm-zi (Korean)   See: *pak ch'omji*.

baggage man   In Britain, the theatre employee in charge of a company's property baskets, trunks, etc. In performances he helps with properties and scene changes and sometimes plays bit parts. In the U.S. professional theatre, his counterpart (a property man) would not be allowed to double as a performer. (Granville DICTIONARY)

bagging shoes   See: startups.

baggy-pants comic   A vaudevillian.

bag line   A pick-up or bull line to lift a sandbag while trimming or clewing a set of lines. (Parker/Smith DESIGN)

bagnolette   An 18th C hooded cloak, gathered at the neck and hem with fasteners, sometimes with a cape at the shoulders. (Boucher FASHION)

bag of tricks   A performer's stock of mannerisms and acting devices.

bag puppet   1. A stuffed paper-bag puppet made by children with the head and features glued on. Also called a sack puppet. 2. In China, a hand puppet. (Philpott DICTIONARY)

bags   Satin knee breeches, often black. (Chalmers CLOTHES 217)

bag sleeve   A medieval Flemish sleeve, soft and full, gathered into a simple, tight cuff. (Wilcox DICTIONARY)

bagwig   An 18th C powdered wig with ends encased in a black silk bag to prevent the powder from scattering on the wearer's coat. Sometimes worn with loosely rolled puffs of hair over the cheeks and ears, called pigeon's wings. Also called a *coiffure en bourse* (French). See also: campaign wig. (Wilcox DICTIONARY)

bahin (Philippine)   An act or scene in *zarzuela* (operetta). (Fernández ILO-ILO 100)

bai (Chinese)   See: *nianbai*.

bai (Vietnamese)   A recitative sung in *hat boi* that expresses character. Typically composed in two lines of seven syllables each. *Bai* comprise one of six major song categories. Also called *hat bai* (songs of particular characters). (Addiss "Theater" 141, Kim VIETNAMESE 13)

baigneuse (French)   An 18th C tucked bonnet originally worn in the bath and later in the street. (Boucher FASHION)

baignoires (French)   Literally: bath tubs. Boxes surrounding the *parterre* in 19th C French theatres. (Brockett HISTORY 498)

baiju, pai chü (Chinese)   A form of music-drama (*xiqu*) performed by the Bai nationality in Yunnan Province and some portions of Guizhou and Sichuan provinces. It is characterized by unaccompanied song (*chang*), with *suona* instrumental connectives (*guomen*); the percussion orchestra (*wuchang*) is that used in Bai folk music and dance. It developed in the 17th and 18th C, probably under the influence of *yiyangqiang* music-drama, and was later influenced by the *dianju* form. Called *chuichuiqiang* or *ch'ui ch'ui ch'iang* before 1949.

bailarine   (Spanish)   Dancer. (Rennert SPANISH 63)

baile, bayle (Spanish)   A dance or ballet with spoken and/or sung words, and music. Often used as a synonym for *entremes*. Considered morally questionable in the 16th C, such dances, accompanied by couplets, were presented at the end of the first act of a play in 17th C theatres. (Shergold SPANISH)

bails   Small brass balls set in sockets in the front edge of a scenic door to catch on the door frame and prevent the door from swinging open. (Bowman/Ball THEATRE)

baimian, pai mien (Chinese)   Literally: white face. A villainous, powerful, violent male role portrayed in predominantly white makeup; a major subcategory of the painted-face role (*jing*) in *kunqu* drama. Sometimes called assistant painted-face role (*fujing*). (Dolby HISTORY 105)

baisse (French)   1. The lowering of the ballet dancer's heel (or heels) to the stage floor. 2. The lowering of a ballerina to the stage floor by her partner after a lift. 3. The leaning forward of a ballet dancer. Also called *penché*. (Kersley/Sinclair BALLET)

baixi, pai hsi (Chinese)   Literally: hundred entertainments, hundred games. A type of spectacle similar to a circus, c. 3rd C BC-14th C AD, considered an important antecedent of Chinese drama. Composed of numerous acts, including tight-rope-walking, combat, pole-climbing, sword-swallowing, fire-eating, tumbling, equestrian acts, dances, and skits. See also: *sanyue, suyue*. (Dolby HISTORY 3, 15–16)

baja (Spanish)   A discount to a theatre lessee in recompense for such things as a performance at court. (Shergold SPANISH 315)

bajiaogu, pa chiao ku (Chinese)   Literally: eight-corner drum. 1. An octagonal, hand-held drum similar to a tambourine which is used in Manchu folk music and featured in some forms of storytelling (*quyi*). 2. See: *danxian*. 3. A form of storytelling popular in northeastern China and Mongolia in the 17th-19th C. It developed from Manchu folk singing, and was usually presented by seated performers.

bake a play   See: baking plays.

baked ceramic riser   See: black riser.

baking   A process of baking fabric in an oven at very low heat in order to create the effect of heavy linen or crinkled seersucker. (Barton COSTUME 14, 66)

baking plays   In the Yiddish theatre, rapidly turning out plays, often nearly indistinguishable from one another, usually by taking someone's play and giving it and its characters Yiddish names, then putting them in a Yiddish locale. Hence, bake plays, baked goods, bake a play. (Sandrow VAGABOND 105–108)

bakuya (Japanese)   A *bunraku* puppet head used for characters of bad old women. (Keene BUNRAKU 59)

balagnie cloak   A 17th C cape with a large collar secured by cords and draped over one or both shoulders. (Wilcox DICTIONARY)

balagtasan sa balitaw (Philippine)   A Sugbuanon folk performance which combines the debate (*duplo*) and the song (*balitaw*). (Ramas in Bresnahan CROSS-CULTURAL 218)

balance   In dance, the finely honed relationship maintained among the various parts of the body. (Rogers DANCE 183)

balancé (French)   In ballet, a fundamental *barre* exercise for the legs in which the foot is swung forward and back as the body sways forward (when the foot is at the back) and back (when the free foot is at the front). (Rogers DANCE 155)

balançoire (French)   In ballet, a front-and-back swinging motion. (Grant TECHNICAL)

balandran   A medieval-17th C rain cape. (Boucher FASHION)

balayeuse (French)   A 19th C petticoat or petticoat ruffle. Also called a streetsweeper or dust ruffle. (Barton COSTUME 510)

balcon (French)   1. A stage box in a 17th C French theatre. 2. In modern use, a balcony. (Nagler SOURCES 285)

balcony   1. An acting or seating area, usually above a door opening onto the forestage in 17th-18th C British theatres. Perhaps the same as a gallery box. (Avery LONDON xliv) 2. See: parade. 3. In U.S. theatres, a seating area above the ground floor or orchestra. In British theatres this area is usually called the dress circle, upper circle, or gallery. Indeed, in U.S. opera houses the British terminology is sometimes used. 4. In British theatres, the tier of seats above the dress circle and below the gallery, but see the British usage noted above. See also: gallery. (Granville DICTIONARY)

balcony box   In the U.S., an enclosure for spotlights at the front of a balcony. Such an enclosure is ordinarily on the face of the balcony and conceals the spotlights to greater or lesser degree. Sometimes called a balcony front box or balcony light box. In Britain, cage. (Bowman/Ball THEATRE)

balcony front lighting   Lighting which reaches the stage from the front of the balcony. Also called balcony lighting or balcony-face lighting. See also: balcony lights. (Fuchs LIGHTING 43)

balcony front spot   A spotlight located on the front of the balcony. (Granville DICTIONARY)

balcony lights   Spotlights whose beams reach the stage from positions on the face of the balcony. The phrase is used especially of older theatres (built before c. 1930), where better auditorium lighting positions are not available. Among other terms are the more formal balcony front lights and balcony front spots. Other phrases include balcony spots, balcony spotlights, balcony fronts, balcony rails, rail lights. See also: balcony front lighting. (Wehlburg GLOSSARY, Lounsbury THEATRE, Baker THEATRECRAFT)

balcony operator   A light crew member who works in the balcony. He usually changes gelatins or runs a follow spot. (Halstead MANAGEMENT 163–164)

balcony pan   See: balcony tray.

balcony rails   See: balcony lights.

balcony stage   In Elizabethan times, a balcony playing area. (Bowman/Ball THEATRE)

balcony stall   In British theatres, a seating position in the front rows of the dress circle. (Bowman/Ball THEATRE)

balcony tray   A protective pan under balcony lights. Also called a balcony pan. See also: tray. (Bowman/Ball THEATRE)

baldheaded row   The first row of seats in the orchestra, a row favored by aging playboys at girlie shows in the 1930s and earlier. (Bowman/Ball THEATRE)

bald wig   A wig which makes an actor appear to be bald.

balerie (French)   In medieval times, a light entertainment with songs and dances. (Frank MEDIEVAL 233, 236) *bali-balihan* (Indonesian)   Those secular forms of Balinese dance and theatre that can be performed for entertainment at any time. See also: *bebali, wali.* (Bandem/deBoer BALINESE 75–76)

baligtaran (Philippine)   Tumbling in fight sequences in *comedia*. (Mendoza COMEDIA 65)

balitaw (Philippine)   1. A general term for dance. 2. A Sugbuanon folk performance that is "a comic representation of the love chase and battle of the sexes," sung in verse dialogue and danced to the accompaniment of a harp or guitar. (Ramas in Bresnahan CROSS-CULTURAL 217)

ballabile (Italian)   A group dance, without solos. (Grant TECHNICAL)

balladeer   In U.S. minstrelsy, a singer (usually a tenor) of sentimental, melancholy songs. Often strikingly handsome, many balladeers became matinee idols. (Toll BLACKING 53–54)

ballad farce   A ballad opera with a farcical plot.

ballad opera   A musical theatre form popular in the 18th C. The music, interspersed in the spoken dialogue, was not usually original but was selected from existing tunes, usually ballads. The first and most popular ballad opera was Gay's *The Beggar's Opera* (1728).

ballantine   See: reticule.

ballast   A device which limits the flow of current in an electrical circuit. The principal stage use in the earlier decades of the 20th C was as a resistance in series with a carbon arc. More recently, an electromagnetic ballast has been used in AC applications. (Wehlburg GLOSSARY, Bellman SCENE)

ballatine   A ticket. A 15 November 1660 London agreement stated that receipts were to be taken in "by Ballatine, or Tickettes souled for all doores and boxes." The word is a variant spelling of bulletin. (Van Lennep LONDON lxxiii)

ball-bearing block   A head block (multiple sheaves or grooved pulleys in a wooden or metal frame) equipped with ball bearings.

ball carriers   Balls with hooks, riding in a channel. To the hooks, a traveler curtain is attached. Also called curtain balls or curtain carriers.

ballerina (Italian), **ballerina**   A principal female ballet dancer. Formerly, the specific rank of an outstanding female soloist. The French use *sujet.* (Chujoy/Manchester DANCE)

ballet   1. A dramatic dance which usually tells a story, performed with mime and musical accompaniment. See: movements in ballet and positions of the body. 2. A troupe of ballet dancers. 3. As a verb, to express through the medium of ballet (obsolete). 4. A ballad (obsolete).

ballet ambulatoire (French)   In the 15th C, an entertainment with several allegorical scenes called *entremets.* Jugglers and mountebanks often participated as well. (Perugini PAGEANT 48) *ballet blanc* (French)   Any ballet in which the performers wear the traditional long white costumes first used in *La Sylphide* in 1830. (Grant TECHNICAL)

ballet comique (French)   A 19th C French classical ballet danced by artists with slight builds. (Carlson FRENCH 40)

ballet d'action (French)   A dance which grows out of plot and character. Also called a narrative ballet.

ballet de cour (French)   A Renaissance court ballet performance. A song, dance, and spectacle entertainment in France parallel to Italian *intermezzi* and English masques. (Brockett HISTORY 246)

ballet divertissement (French)   See: *divertissement*.

ballet girl   An especially beautiful and vivacious 19th C chorus girl, often of equivocal virtue. (Parker/Parker CHORUS GIRL 21)

ballet master   1. See: *maître de ballet*. 2. A male ballet instructor responsible for the dancing in ballet, opera, musical comedy, or pantomime. (Fay GLOSSARY)

ballet mistress   1. See: *maître de ballet*. 2. A female ballet instructor responsible for the dancing in ballet, opera, musical comedy, or pantomime. (Fay GLOSSARY)

balletomane   A ballet enthusiast. Hence, balletomania, balletomaniac.

ballet shirt   A simple white cotton shirt with a fold-over collar, worn by members of the *corps de ballet* during rehearsals. Also called a chorus shirt. (Wilcox DICTIONARY)

balletto   The libretto or scenario for a ballet. (Berrey/Van den Bark SLANG 580)

ballim (Korean)   The technique of acting in *p'ansori*. (Korean KOREAN 27)

ballo (Italian)   Dance.

ballon (French)   A light, elastic jump in which a dancer bounds up, pauses a moment in the air, and descends lightly. (Grant TECHNICAL)

balloon   To forget lines or business in acting. In Britain, to make an ascension. (Bowman/Ball THEATRE)

balloon sleeve   An 1890s sleeve with fullness from shoulder to elbow and a close fit from elbow to wrist. Also called a melon sleeve. (Wilcox DICTIONARY)

balloon tire   In Britain, pouchiness under a performer's eyes. In the U. S., Columbus Circle. (Granville DICTIONARY)

ballotté (French)   A bright, tossing ballet step requiring a great deal of balance, in part because the body leans backward and forward with each change of weight. Also called a *pas ballotté* or *jeté bateau*. (Grant TECHNICAL, Wilson BALLET)

bally, ballyhoo   1. To perform outside a place of amusement to attract customers. 2. Such a performance outside a place of amusement. (Berrey/Van den Bark SLANG 586) 3. Advance publicity for a coming performance or performances.

balmoral   1. A 19th C tennis shoe. 2. A traditional Scottish flat, creased, blue-wool cap topped with a red or blue pompom and a ribbon cockade with a brooch or feather. A red and white checked band was sewn along its sides. Also called a Glengarry cap. (Wilcox DICTIONARY)

balmoral petticoat   A red and black striped wool underskirt of the late 19th C worn for walking. (Wilcox DICTIONARY)

balustrade, balustrade scene   A scenic unit with a balustrade painted on it, as opposed to a three-dimensional balustrade. (Fay GLOSSARY)

bambalinas (Spanish)   The flies. (Shergold SPANISH)

bamen (Japanese)   See: *ba*.

ban, pan (Chinese)   Literally: board. 1. A type of clapper consisting of two rectangular pieces of hardwood strung together loosely with a cord. It is featured in the percussion orchestra (*wuchang*) in many forms of music-drama (*xiqu*), including Beijing opera (*jingju*), where it is used by the orchestra conductor to mark accented beats. See also: *guban, bangzi*. (Scott CLASSICAL 47–48, 50; Wichmann ''Aural'' 442–443, 453–460) 2. See: *banyan*. 3. See: *banshi*.

banana   A burlesque comic. The best or senior comic was the top banana, the next the second banana, etc. (Wilmeth LANGUAGE)

bancos (Spanish)   Benches in the *patio* of a *corral* theatre. Behind them was a standing area. (Nagler SOURCES 60)

band   A group of chiefly wind and percussion instrumentalists. In the theatre, the orchestra was called a band until the 18th C, or it was sometimes referred to simply as the music (or musick).

banda stagnata (Italian)   A tin oil lamp with a small catch basin for overflow oil. Sabbattini calls attention to the term in describing a lamp used in the auditorium of Renaissance theatres. (Sabbattini in Hewitt RENAISSANCE 93)

band call   Especially in Britain, a rehearsal for the instrumentalists alone, usually the day before the first dress rehearsal of a musical theatre piece. (Bax MANAGEMENT 222)

band car   A wheeled platform carrying an orchestra—as at Radio City Music Hall, where the band car rolls downstage onto the forestage elevator and then is lowered.

bandeau   1. A narrow silk or velvet band for a hat. 2. See: brassiere.

bande de mer (French)   A long, low masking piece which represents water, set at the rear of the stage. (Carlson ''Inventory'' 48) *bande de toile* (French)   A painted border. (Moynet FRENCH 3)

banditti drama   A gangster play.

B. & O.   1. In vaudeville, an abbreviation for band and orchestra. 2. In touring groups, an abbreviation meaning that a player also performed in the band. See also: double in brass. (Wilmeth LANGUAGE)

band of blue   A 17th C sky border. (Larson "Evidence" 87)

band parts, band-parts   Especially in Britain, the copies of the orchestral music for each of the instruments. (Bax MANAGEMENT 254)

band room, band-room   Especially in Britain, a room in a theatre under the stage, where instrumentalists wait until they are needed in the orchestra pit. (Fay GLOSSARY)

B. & S.   In repertory companies, an indication that musicians acted and actors played musical instruments. See also: B. & O. (Wilmeth LANGUAGE)

band steel   Strap iron in flat metal strips.

band string   A 16th-17th C cord used to tie collars, ruffs, and bands. It ended in jewels, balls, and tassels. (Wilcox DICTIONARY)

bane   A medieval announcement, especially of a play; it was given by a herald and was a species of dialogue. (Ward LITERATURE I 77)

bang   A successful show.

bangdi (Chinese)   See: *di*.

banghu (Chinese)   See: *banhu*.

bangkitan (Malaysian)   Literally: invocation. A type of speech in *ma'yong* used to invoke the spirits. (Yousof "Kelantan" 114–116)

bangqiang, pang ch'iang (Chinese)   Choral singing in those forms of music-drama (*xiqu*) whose music is derived from the *gaoqiang* musical system. A chorus of singers, either on or off stage, joins with or replaces the principal performer in singing the final line or lines of a song. In some forms, performed by the members of the percussion orchestra (*wuchang*). Translated as "choral backing" (Dolby HISTORY 91, 282) and as "helping chorus" (Mackerras RISE 5, Mackerras "Growth" 70–71).

bangsawan (Malaysian)   Literally: noble people. A commercial theatre form that flourished c. 1880–1925. Growing out of all-male *wayang parsi*, it introduced actresses and 'modern' wing-and-drop scenery to Malaysia. Plays based on Arabic and Malay stories used local song and music styles. It is rarely performed today. (Yassim in Osman TRADITIONAL 143–153)

bang the BO's bull's-eye   To do good business at the box office.

bangu (Chinese)   See: *danpigu*.

bangumi (Japanese)   A theatre bill or program, that is, the order of events in a performance. See also: *puroguramu*.

bang up, bump up   Occasionally, in backstage language, to move a dimmer to full as briskly as possible. (Bowman MODERN)

bangzi, pang tzu (Chinese)   1. A type of clapper consisting of two unconnected pieces of hardwood, one cylindrical and one a rectangular solid. It is featured in the percussion orchestra (*wuchang*) in those forms of music-drama (*xiqu*) whose music is derived from the *bangziqiang* musical system. See also: *ban*. (Scott CLASSICAL 41) 2. Short form of *bangziqiang*.

bangziqiang, pang tzu ch'iang (Chinese)   A musical system (*shengqiang xitong*) characterized by the use of *banqiangti* musical structure and *bangzi* clapper rhythmic accompaniment. It arose c. 15th C from the folk songs of Shaanxi and Gansu provinces, probably first developing in the *qinqiang* form of music-drama (*xiqu*). In the 16th-18th C the influence of this musical system spread eastward and southward; later forms which derived from it include *puju*, Shanxi opera (*jinju*), Henan opera (*yuju*), Hebei *bangzi*, Shandong *bangzi*, and the *tanqiang* component of Sichuan opera (*chuanju*). Abbreviated *bangzi*. Often also called *qinqiang*, and in the 18th and 19th C, "jumbled plucking" (*luantan*). Often translated as "clapper opera." (Howard CONTEMPORARY 16–17, Mackerras MODERN 15–16, Mackerras RISE 7–10)

banhu, pan hu (Chinese)   Literally: board two-stringed spike fiddle. A two-stringed spike fiddle (*huqin*), the main instrument in the melodic orchestra (*wenchang*) in many forms of music-drama (*xiqu*) that use music from the *bangziqiang* musical system. Its body is a half hemisphere about 4″ in diameter and is made of bamboo, wood, or half a coconut shell; its head is a thin sheet of wooden board. It produces a loud and sonorous sound. In the past, also called *banghu* or *pang hu*. (Mackerras MODERN 22)

banjo torch   See: pan torch.

bank   1. A group of dimmers, usually in a horizontal row. 2. A row of lighting instruments. See also: battery of lights. 3. A section of seats in an auditorium, usually on a slope.

bankroll   To finance a stage production.

bankroller   1. A popular performer. 2. A financial backer.

banns, bans   In medieval times, public announcement of a forthcoming performance. (Bowman/Ball THEATRE)

banolan (Indonesian)   See: *banyolan*.

banqiang (Chinese)   See: *banshi*.

banqiangti, pan ch'iang t'i (Chinese)   Literally: accented-beat tune system. A type of musical structure in which music is composed to fit lyrics according to the specifications of such musical components as: melodic phrases (*qiang*), metrical-types (*banshi*), modes (*diaoshi*), and modal systems (*shengqiang xitong*). It is one of the major types of musical structure in music-drama (*xiqu*), where it is used in the *bangziqiang* and *pihuang* musical systems. See also: *lianquti*. (Wichmann "Aural" 273)

banshi, pan shih (Chinese)   Literally: accented-beat style. A pattern of meter, tempo, and characteristic melodic tendencies which is thought appropriate for certain dramatic situations; called "aria-type" or "metrical-type" in translation. Metrical-types are one of the principal components of *banqiangti* musical structure; a number of metrical-types are used in the music of each form of music-drama (*xiqu*) which follows this structure. Abbreviated *ban*, sometimes translated as meter. Also called song key (*qudiao* or *ch'ü tiao*) and accented-beat tune (*banqiang* or *pan ch'iang*). Metrical-types are divided into two main categories: regulated (*shangban*) and free metrical-types (*ziyouban*). (Pian in Crump/Malm CHINESE 65–79, Wichmann "Aural" 146–167)

banxi, pan hsi (Chinese)   The generic term for stage makeup in music-drama (*xiqu*). The distinctive makeups of each role category (*hangdang*) and major subcategory are described in detail in Halson PEKING 38–41 and Scott CLASSICAL 166–170. Also called *banzhuang* or *pan chuang*, *yibansanxiang* or *i pan san hsiang*, and *banxiang* or *pan hsiang*.

banxiang (Chinese)   See: *banxi*.

banyan, banian   1. An East Indian 18th C loose, full-sleeved, collarless man's leisure robe of velvet, cotton, silk, or brocade. (Chalmers CLOTHES 214) 2. An English knee-length linen jacket for informal home or town wear. (Boucher FASHION)

banyan, pan yen (Chinese)   The system of metrical organization followed in music-drama (*xiqu*). A *ban* (literally 'board') is an accented beat, and a *yan* (or *yen*, literally 'eye') is an unaccented beat. The three principal forms of metrical organization are one *ban* three *yan* (quadruple meter, 4/4 time), one *ban* one *yan* (duple meter, 2/4 time), and one *ban* no *yan* (single-beat meter, 1/4 time). See also: *shangban*. (Scott CLASSICAL 50–51)

banyol (Indonesian)   Literally: comedian. 1. Clowns or comic actors mentioned in Java in the 14th C. Also spelled *bonjol*. (Holt ART 286) 2. Joking by clowns. (Muljono in Osman TRADITIONAL 71) In Javanese: *lucu* or *lutju*. (Humardani in Osman TRADITIONAL 83)

banyolan (Indonesian)   A scene of joking by clowns in Sundanese rod-puppet theatre (*wayang golek*). (Foley "Sundanese" 113) In Java, spelled *banolan*, a general term for verbal joking. (van der Kroef "Roots" 318)

banzhuang (Chinese)   See: *banxi*.

banzuke (Japanese)   A printed playbill, usually including play and act titles, performers' names, and illustrations, published in the 17th-19th C for a *kabuki* or *bunraku* production. Usually a single sheet, but if a play synopsis was included, the playbill could run to several pages. (Kincaid KABUKI 178–179, Leiter ENCYCLOPEDIA 27–29)

baoer, pao erh (Chinese)   A middle-aged or elderly female role; a type of stock character in Song *zaju* and Jin *yuanben*. (Dolby HISTORY 26–27)

baotiao, pao t'iao (Chinese)   In the 19th C, a red paper poster announcing the day, time, and place of a performance by a particular troupe, posted at the door of the theatre itself, in markets, and along thoroughfares. (Dolby HISTORY 189–190)

baotou, pao t'ou (Chinese)   Literally: wrap-head. 1. In music-drama (*xiqu*), the generic name for hairdressing styles of all female roles (*dan*) except the old female (*laodan*). Such styles include big head (*dafa*), ancient costume head (*guzhuangtou*), and banner costume head (*qizhuangtou*). Most involve numerous pieces tied tightly on the head, the innermost of which raises the outer edges of the eyes and eyebrows. 2. A performer of a female role. (Mackerras RISE 97, Scott CLASSICAL 166)

baoxiang (Chinese)   See: *guanzuo*.

baoyi, pao i (Chinese)   A brightly-colored tunic which fastens on the right and has narrow cuffless sleeves; it is worn with loose pants of the same color by heroic, non-military fighters such as bandits in Beijing opera (*jingju*) and many other forms of music-drama (*xiqu*). Also called hero's clothes (*yingxiongyi* or *ying hsiung i*). (Scott CLASSICAL 156)

bapan (Indonesian)   1. The second section of a Balinese *baris* dance, of great power and energy. 2. A melody in *baris* and in *topeng* that introduces the clown-servant (*penasar*). (de Zoete/Spies DANCE 167–168, 185)

bar   1. In Britain, barrel. 2. See: toggle bar. 3. In 18th C theatres, apparently a device analogous to a turnstile. Fanny Burney in *Evelina* wrote of going to the King's theatre and obtaining tickets at "one of the doorkeeper's *bars*. . . ." (Hogan LONDON xxviii) 4. See: *barre*.

barba (Spanish)   See: *anciano*.

bar bell   In British theatres, warning bells in the front of the house to signal patrons that an act is about to begin. The term presumably stems from the fact that during intervals many playgoers go to one of the theatre's bars. Called in the U.S. an intermission bell.

barber shop   In the early 20th C U.S., a theatrical term for a discordant note. (Wilmeth LANGUAGE)

barbette (French)   A veil concealing a woman's chin and neck. From the 12th to the 15th C, the *barbette* was worn by old women and widows, and was compulsory for nuns, who retained it well into the 20th C. See also: chin scarf. (Boucher FASHION)

bar clamp, barrel clamp   In Britain, a pipe clamp.

Bard specialist   A performer who specializes in Shakespeare.

bare colored lamps   An occasional phrase for low-wattage lamps whose bulbs are of colored glass. (Gassner/Barber PRODUCING 795)

bare-stall family   In Britain, empty seats (or stalls). A poorly attended show. Also called wood family, plush family. (Granville DICTIONARY)

barillet (French)   In a limelight, the small, barrel-shaped chamber where oxygen and hydrogen were mixed before coming out of the jet.

baris (Indonesian)   In Bali, a semi-dramatic group dance by men displaying martial prowess in a ritualized form. (Soedarsono DANCES 161–162, Holt ART 110) De Zoete/Spies describe fifteen types of *baris*, including the 'dramatic *baris*,' in DANCE 57–65, 165–166, 262.

barn   A theatre that is too large.

Barnaby   In the early 20th C U.S., a theatrical term for a man who is subservient to his wife. (Wilmeth LANGUAGE)

barnacle   1. A man hanging around the stage door of a British music hall hoping to pick up a chorus girl. 2. Also in Britain, someone seeking theatrical employment. (Granville DICTIONARY)

barn doors   A type of beam modifier at the front of a spotlight. Early barn doors had a hinged leaf (flipper) at each side of the spotlight (and sliding cut-offs at top and bottom). Especially since the introduction of soft-edged Fresnel spotlights, four-leafed barn doors have appeared; these serve to reduce stray light, and can also modify the beam shape. Also called blinders.

barn-door shutters   In Britain, the preferred term for barn doors. (Rae/Southern INTERNATIONAL)

barnstorm   1. To perform successively in small towns, usually one-night stands and often in improvised spaces, as in barns. Hence, barnstorming, barn-stormer. 2. Formerly, in Britain, to ham, to rant. (Dolman ACTING, Bowman/Ball THEATRE)

barn theatre   A theatre set up in a barn or a barn-like building.

barong (Indonesian)   Literally: large. 1. The generic term for large animal masks used in certain Indonesian dances and dance dramas. In Bali, masks include: *bangkol* (boar), *gajah* (elephant), *kambing* (goat), *lembu* or *lemboe* (cow), *matjam* (tiger), *poe'oeh* (quail), *singa* (lion), and *tjitjing* (dog). (de Zoete/Spies DANCE 90) Also called *barongan*. (Holt ART 107) 2. The role of such an animal character in a dance or dance play. 3. A Balinese dance-drama which features a *barong*-masked character. The most important such drama is the 'ritual *barong*' in which a *barong kekek* battles the magically powerful witch *rangda* in an exorcistic confrontation. Villagers, men and women both, attempt to stab themselves with daggers (*kris*) while in a state of trance (*ngurek*), hence the drama's nicknames 'trance dance' and '*kris* dance.' (de Zoete/Spies DANCE 86–98, Moerdowo BALINESE II 82–88, Brandon SOUTHEAST 326)

barong keket (Indonesian)   In Bali, a playful but magically powerful mythological animal (often translated as 'lion' or 'dragon'), the Sovereign Lord of the Forest (Banaspati Raja). It is played by two men in a dance-play, the *barong*'s spirit possessing the performer wearing the large mask. Also called *barong ket*. See also: *rangda*. (Soedarsono DANCES 168, de Zoete/Spies DANCE 90)

barrack   In Britain, to jeer, deride, or boo a performance or performer. The term originated in Australian cricket and derives from a New Zealand word, *borak*, meaning derision. (Granville DICTIONARY)

barre (French), **bar**   A handrail used by ballet dancers to maintain balance while exercising. The *barre* is usually fastened to a wall about 42″ above the floor.

barrel   1. The British term for U.S. pipe batten or pipe. The word is often shortened to bar. Among various combinations: spot bar, spot barrel, bar clamp, barrel clamp, suspension barrel. A vertical bar or barrel at the side of the stage is a boom. (Bentham ART, Rae/Southern INTERNATIONAL) 2. A perforated pipe hanging above the stage, used to produce a rain or steam effect. Hence, bar, rain barrel, steam barrel. (Bowman/Ball THEATRE)

barrel clamp, barrel clip, barrel grip   In Britain, a device (such as a C-clamp) for fixing a lighting instrument to a pipe. (Bowman/Ball THEATRE, Rae/Southern INTERNATIONAL)

barrel filament   The earliest type of concentrated filament lamp, developed by 1920. See also: concentrated filament. (McCandless SYLLABUS 10)

barrel grip   See: pipe clamp.

barrel loft, barrel-loft   1. Formerly, the space above the gridiron. In the 19th C, fly lines were coiled on drums in the barrel loft. 2. In 20th C British theatres, the flies—where the barrels (battens) hang.

barrel skirt   See: peg-top skirt.

barrier   A Renaissance entertainment with a mock tournament accompanied by dialogue. (Bowman/Ball THEATRE)

barrister's wig   See: full-bottomed wig.

(en) bas (French)   Literally: below. In ballet, a low position of the arms.

bas de cotte (French)   In the late 17th C, the lower part of a petticoat. Also called a *bas de jupe* or a grand habit. (Boucher FASHION)

base   In lighting: 1. The device into which a lamp is inserted during use. The base provides mechanical support and electrical connections. Often called a socket. 2. That part of the lamp which fits into the base. 3. The heavy iron disc which serves as the bottom of a vertical pipe to which lighting instruments are attached. See also: light stand. (Wehlburg GLOSSARY) 4. In makeup, a foundation—such as greasepaint, creme makeup, cake makeup, or liquid makeup—used to color the skin.

base down, base down burning   In stage lighting, phrases used to indicate that a lamp should be used (burned) vertically base down, or not far from that position.

baselard A sword holder, triangular in shape, attached to a belt. (Chalmers CLOTHES 108)

base light See: fill light.

basement See: substage.

base up, base up burning Phrases used to indicate that a lamp should be used (burned) vertically base up, or not far from that position.

basic situation The problem from which a play arises, as in the rivalry between the families in *Romeo and Juliet.*

basinet In medieval times, a hood made of chain mail. Later, a light, un-seamed helmet of steel, with a cone-shaped helmet. Also called a bassanet. (Wilcox DICTIONARY)

basket In Britain, a storage box for properties. When a touring company did not make expenses, the baskets were left behind as security. When the company played to a full house, the 'baskets were in.' (Granville DICTIONARY)

basket box A box in late 18th C British theatres set behind a first tier box and separated from the first tier by a lattice or screen. Also called a back-front box—a box behind a front box. (SURVEY XXXV 52, Bowman/Ball THEATRE)

bassanet See: basinet.

basse danse (French) A 16th C court dance, the possible predecessor of modern ballet. (Perugini PAGEANT 69)

bastard amber A popular pinkish amber color medium used in stage light-ing. Often abbreviated to B.A., b.a., BA, or ba.

bastard prompt Especially in Australia: 1. A nickname for the prompter's corner when it is moved from its normal position to the opposite side of the stage, turning opposite prompt side (OP) into prompt side (PS). 2. The stage manager's backstage position when it is located opposite prompt side. (Win "Terms")

bastidor (Spanish) A flat, or canvas-covered wood frame; a wing. *El bastidor del foro* means back cloth. (Shergold SPANISH)

bat 1. Batten. 2. Harlequin's baton or wand in pantomime. French: *batte.*

batabata (Japanese) In *kabuki,* the onomatopoeic word for varied patterns of continuous beating of wooden clappers (*tsuke*), used to emphasize the action of running on or off stage. (Brandon in Brandon/Malm/Shively STUDIES 108, Leiter ENCYCLOPEDIA 30)

bâteleur (French) A juggler, buffoon, clown, fool, mountebank. Also called a *saltimbanque.*

batan (Japanese) In *kabuki,* the onomatopoeic word for the sound of a double beat of the wooden clappers (*tsuke*). The beat is used to emphasize sword strokes in battle scenes, falls, blows, and similar strong actions. (Brandon in Bran-don/Malm/Shively STUDIES 108)

batang pisang (Malaysian)   Literally: banana trunk. Either of the two banana trunks forming the stage of a shadow theatre and into which the support rods of puppets are stuck to hold them in place. See also: *debog*. (Yub in Osman TRADITIONAL 96)

batel (Indonesian)   A fast *gamelan* melody that accompanies battle scenes in Balinese *wayang kulit*. See also: *gender wayang*. (McPhee in Belo TRADITIONAL 180)

bâtiment (French)   See: *battement*.

batleika (Russian)   A late medieval Russian puppet-theatre folk drama. It consisted of a serious treatment of religious themes and comic interludes which depicted the folk life of the Byelorussian people. The form came from Poland and was popular into the early 20th C. (Seduro BYELORUSSIAN 10–20)

bato (Japanese)   A mask of a vengeful man in *bugaku*. The mask is bright red, with black or dark blue hair, a large beak-like nose, and plunging eyebrows. (Wolz BUGAKU 41)

batswing   See: batwing burner.

battant-l'oeil (French)   Literally: striking the eye. A headdress with wings projecting far enough in front of the temples and eyes to strike the latter when the wind blows toward the face. (Boucher FASHION)

battari (Japanese)   In *kabuki*, the onomatopoeic word for the sound of a double beat (Leiter ENCYCLOPEDIA 30) or a triple beat (Brandon in Brandon/Malm/Shively STUDIES 108) of the wooden clappers (*tsuke*). The beat is used to highlight a *mie* pose or a fighting movement.

batte (French)   See: bat, slapstick.

battement (French)   In ballet, a generic term for a number of movements which involve beating motions of the extended or bent leg. See Wilson BALLET and Grant TECHNICAL for the names and descriptions of many *battements*. Also called *bâtiment*.

batten   1. A long piece of wood used to reinforce a flat, to stiffen a drop, or to fasten flats together. Hence, battening, batten out, battening out, to batten. 2. A pipe (in Britain and Australia, a barrel, bar) or long piece of wood from which scenery, draperies, or lighting instruments are hung. Battens used for hanging are numbered from downstage to upstage; hence, first pipe or batten, second pipe or batten, etc., or number one batten, number two batten, etc. (Bowman/Ball THEATRE, National TECHNICAL) 3. In the U.S., sometimes a shortening of light batten. 4. In Britain, a compartment borderlight wired in two or more color circuits. (Bentham ART 318)

batten clamp   A metal clamp used for joining a fly line and a batten, to fasten a lighting instrument or scenic unit to a batten, or to fasten two battens together. (Bowman/Ball THEATRE)

batten connector strip   See: connector strip.

batten floodlight   In Britain, a floodlight hung on a pipe batten. (Bowman/Ball THEATRE)

batten hook   See: S-hook.

battening batten   A batten used to stiffen a flat.

batten light(s)   In Britain, a borderlight or striplight. (Fay GLOSSARY, Bowman/Ball THEATRE)

batten out   In Britain, to stretch canvas on battens, done by the stage manager on tour, or to fasten a piece of scenery to a batten. Hence, occasionally, the noun battening-out. (Granville DICTIONARY, Bowman/Ball THEATRE)

batten pocket   See: pocket.

batten ring   A ring with a set screw which, slipped over a batten, is used to fasten a trim (or trimming) chain to the batten. (Bowman/Ball THEATRE)

batten snatch chain, batten trim chain, batten trimming chain   A chain with a batten ring and snap, used to attach a scenic unit to a batten. Often shortened to snatch chain, trim chain, trimming chain. (Bowman/Ball THEATRE)

batterie (French)   In ballet, any movement in which a dancer's legs beat together or one leg beats against the other. The *grande batterie* requires a high elevation while the *petite batterie* is at a low elevation. (Grant TECHNICAL, Wilson BALLET)

battery   Rarely, a large compartment striplight such as might be used as part or all of a borderlight. (Bowman MODERN)

battery of lights   A sizable group of high-powered lights, often in two or more banks, as used in outdoor extravaganzas. (Lounsbury THEATRE, Wehlburg GLOSSARY)

battery system   In the U.S., an automatic emergency lighting system. In a loss of power, heavy duty batteries turn on special lights which permit those in the theatre to leave. (Bellman LIGHTING 168–169)

battle-scene   The scene of conflict in Old Comedy which often leads up to the agon. The term is borrowed from the French *scène de bataille*. (Pickard-Cambridge DITHYRAMB 201, 204, 205)

batts   1. 17th C utility oxfords worn in Europe and the American colonies. 2. Waddings of cotton or polyester used in quilting. (Wilcox DICTIONARY)

battu (French)   See: *pas battu*.

batwing   1. A man's bow tie. 2. A woman's sleeve style which is full under the arm, fitted on the arm top, and tapered to tightness at the wrist.

batwing burner   In 19th C Britain, a gas outlet which produced a wide, flat flame which gave more light than a number of individual jets. These burners were used in wing lights, gas battens, and auditorium chandeliers. Also called a batwing or, occasionally, a batswing. (Rees GAS 13, 14, 34, 39, 98)

bauble   See: zany.

Bauhaus   See: theatre of the Bauhaus.

bavette (French)   Literally: bib. A cloth flap which covers the bottom of a drop. The English equivalent is skirt.

bavolet (French)   1. 16th C headgear made of two yards of towel-like white fabric, fringed on the ends and pinned to a cap. Still worn in Italy, where it is called a *tovaglia*. 2. As revived in the 19th C, a deep ruffle on the back of a bonnet. (Wilcox DICTIONARY)

bawdeville   Bawdy vaudeville.

bayalata (Kannada)   See: *yaksagana badagatittu bayalata*.

bayang (Indonesian)   See: *wayang*.

bayani (Philippine)   An itinerant bard, or reciter of epics. (David in Cruz SHORT 27)

Bayes   The comic author-director character in the Duke of Buckingham's *The Rehearsal*. The play was very popular throughout the Restoration and 18th C and the name Bayes was often given to any theatre person who behaved ludicrously, as did Colley Cibber, or who tried to do everything in the theatre, as did David Garrick.

bayle (Spanish)   See: *baile*.

bayonet cap   The British equivalent of the U.S. bayonet base (a small smooth-sided lamp base). The two are not identical, however, since U.S. and European sizes differ. The shortening is, unsurprisingly, B.C. (Rae/Southern INTERNATIONAL)

bazi, pa tzu (Chinese)   Literally: handle. The generic term for stage weapons—knives, swords, and spears—in Beijing opera (*jingju*) and many other forms of music-drama (*xiqu*). Frequently used weapons are named and described in Halson PEKING 41 and Scott CLASSICAL 172. See also: *qiba*.

B.C.   See: bayonet cap.

BC play   A classical play.

be a gallery hit   To be a success with the uncritical. (Berrey/Van den Bark SLANG 584)

beam   1. The stream of light coming from an instrument such as a spotlight, projector, etc. 2. In the U.S. (by Illuminating Engineering Society standards), that part of the field of light coming from an instrument which includes all points having 50% or more of maximum brightness. This is usually expressed in degrees as the beam angle (q.v.). 3. A slot or recess in an auditorium ceiling where lighting instruments are placed to provide front lighting. Originally, a beam so used. Hence, beam light, beam spotlight, beam lighting, etc. 4. Timber placed horizontally to support a platform, the top of a temporary or false proscenium arch, etc.

beam angle   1. In U.S. technical language applied to theatre lighting, the angle within which a beam of light gives 50% or more of its maximum intensity.

In Britain, U.S. 50% becomes 10%. 2. An occasional shortening of beam-spread angle. (Corry PLANNING, Lounsbury THEATRE 169)

beam border   A hanging cloth border painted to represent a ceiling beam.

beam lights   1. Lighting instruments, usually spotlights, which illuminate the acting area from a beam in the ceiling of the auditorium or from a similar position. Hence, beams, beam spots, auditorium beams, beam front spots, beam front lights, and other combinations. 2. In the singular, the lighting which results from beam lights. Also called beam lighting. (Wehlburg GLOSSARY, Lounsbury THEATRE, Rae/Southern INTERNATIONAL 44, Baker THEATRECRAFT)

beam port   A ceiling port (q.v.).

beam projector   In the U.S., a high wattage parabolic reflector instrument which produces a very narrow beam of light. Projector is a frequent shortening of the name of this highly efficient fixed-focus instrument. Because a major use simulates sunlight, sun spot has also been used; and other terms include BP, projector unit, parabolic spotlight, projector spot, and washtub. (Bellman SCENE, Wehlburg GLOSSARY, Sellman/Lessley ESSENTIALS 189)

beam projector floodlight   An obsolete (and inaccurate) term for a beam projector. (Philippi STAGECRAFT)

beams   See: beam lights.

beam shaper   An occasional phrase for any device which alters the shape of a beam of light.

beam spots   See: beam lights.

beam spread, beam-spread angle   The angle at which light leaves the lens of a spotlight or projection instrument. Occasionally shortened by lighting personnel to 'spread.' Related terms: wide beam, medium beam, narrow beam, wide spread, medium spread; narrow spread is uncommon. See also: beam. (Fuchs LIGHTING 186–187)

Bearbeitung (German)   A reworking; a play based on an existing piece. (Fuegi BRECHT 3)

bearers   1. Battens placed on the bed of a truck, on which scenic units are laid. 2. Battens to which scenery may be tied. 3. Supernumerary performers playing spear bearers. 4. 16th C five-inch padded rolls worn by women at the back of the hip, to support a farthingale. (Bowman/Ball THEATRE, Chalmers CLOTHES 169)

bear merriment   A popular Russian entertainment of the 16th C, consisting of comic acts by trained bears, usually accompanied by a goat (or a buffoon disguised as a goat), trained dogs, and showmen. (Slonim RUSSIAN 15)

bear's paw   See: *solleret*.

bear the original   In medieval times, to prompt; to hold the manuscript of the play. (Chambers MEDIAEVAL II 361)

beat   1. A rhythmic unit in a play; sometimes called a motivational unit. 2. A momentary pause between speeches or actions. 'A beat and nine' (British) would mean a beat plus nine seconds. 3. In dance, the pulse or its principal divisions.

beat 'em down, beat 'em right down, beat 'em right down to the socks   To delight an audience. (Berrey/Van den Bark SLANG 584)

beating   See: *battement*.

beau   In the 17th and 18th C, a dandy or fop who frequented playhouses.

beau catcher   A spit curl.

beaver   1. A 14th C helmet visor. Also spelled bevor. 2. A felt fabric made from beaver pelts. (Wilcox DICTIONARY, Dreher HATMAKING, Chalmers CLOTHES 115) 3. A false beard.

bebali (Indonesian)   Within Balinese culture, 'ceremonial' theatre forms, occupying the middle ground between sacred (*wali*) performance and pure entertainment (*balibalihan*). They are dramatic and narrative and use many Hindu-Javanese story and performance elements. Examples: *gambuh*, *topeng*, *wayang wong*, *baris*, and *arja*. See also *kalangan*. (Bandem/deBoer BALINESE 28–29)

bebas (Indonesian)   Literally: free. 1. Movement determined by an actor, dancer, or puppeteer rather than being bound by a regular *gong* pattern. 2. In Sundanese rod puppet theatre, a contemporary ogre (*buta*) figure created by the puppeteer from his imagination. (Foley "Sundanese" 39, 159)

bec de gaz (French)   The jet of a 19th C gas lamp. By extension, gas lamp.

becket   See: saddle.

be cold   Not to applaud.

be decent   To be dressed.

bedolan (Indonesian)   Moving Javanese *wayang kulit* puppets off-screen after taking them from their fixed positions in the banana log stage (*debog*). One type of manipulation skill (*sabetan*). (Brandon THRONES 63)

bedroom farce   A risqué farce set in a bedroom or a room adjacent to a bedroom.

bedroom perfect   Uncertain of lines. Said of a performer who knew his/her lines at home but cannot remember them in rehearsal.

bee   An advance payment of salary. (Berrey/Van den Bark SLANG 593)

beef patron   A complaining theatre patron.

beef seats   Theatre seats for which tickets have not been printed, given to complaining patrons when no other seats are available.

beef trust   Formerly, a group of hefty burlesque girls, such as those assembled by entrepreneur Billy Watson in 1899. See also: big horse. (Sobel BURLEYCUE 124, Wilmeth LANGUAGE)

be fluffy   To forget one's lines.

before the lights   In British usage, performing on the stage. Said to mean 'in front of the footlights,' which suggests that the phrase is not recent. (Granville DICTIONARY)

beginners   The actors who appear in the opening scene of a performance. Thus, "Beginners, please!" is the warning to them to take their places.

beginner's play   A novice playwright's first offering. (Granville DICTIONARY)

beg-off speech   A thank-you speech to an audience, usually when a solo performer is too exhausted to continue.

beguin (French), **biggin, biggon**   A fine linen or coarse-woven cap of the 12-19th C. (Wilcox DICTIONARY)

behind   Back of the curtain or back of the stage setting; backstage.

behind-the-tent shows   Shows by small troupes playing one-night stands with shabby sets and costumes, and plenty of obscenity. (Green in Mayer/Richards WESTERN 160)

behuwa (Assamese)   A buffoon or jester in *ankiya nat*. (Vatsyayan TRADITIONAL 108)

(Die) Beiden Pathetiker (German)   In the Bauhaus theatre, two huge puppet figures, personifications of such concepts as Power and Courage, Truth and Beauty, or Law and Freedom. (Schlemmer/Moholy-Nagy/Molnar BAUHAUS 31)

beigong, pei kung (Chinese)   An aside spoken by a character in Beijing opera (*jingju*), usually as though to himself or herself.

Beijing opera, Beiping drama, Beiping opera   See: *jingju*.

beiqu (Chinese)   See: *qu*.

belahan (Indonesian)   The open space between the split section of a Javanese shadow puppet control rod. The hide puppet is inserted into the space, after which the rod is laced tightly to the puppet. (Long JAVANESE 14)

Belascoism   U.S. romantic naturalism. From the theatrical style of the early 20th C director-producer David Belasco. (Gorelik NEW)

belaying pin   A wooden or metal peg through a pin rail, around which rope lines are tied off. Also called a pin.

Beleuchter (German)   Electrician, lighting man. (Fuchs LIGHTING 368, Rae/Southern INTERNATIONAL 38)

Beleuchterlage (German)   Literally: electrician's place. The stage lighting control system in a German theatre. (Fuchs LIGHTING 368)

belian (Malaysian)   1. A danced ritual performed to protect villagers from wild animal attacks in newly cultivated areas, performed by a shaman, five young men, and five young women. 2. The role of the shaman in the ritual, assumed by a young girl. In trance, she imitates the actions of wild animals and begs them to forgive disturbances clearing the land may have caused them. (Sheppard TAMAN 88)

bell   Any bell (or buzzer), now often electric, used to signal spectators or theatre personnel. Hence, act call bell, bar bell, lobby bell, lounge bell, prompter's bell, bell board, bell and buzzer box, etc.

bell ringer   In vaudeville acts, one who pretends to chew tobacco and then spit into a cuspidor. A bell was rung when the spit hit the pan. (Wilmeth LANGUAGE)

belly buster   1. A comedian. 2. A funny joke.

belly dance   A dance emphasizing movements of the belly. Hence, belly dancer, also called a cooch dancer.

belly laff, belly laugh   1. A guffaw, especially from a theatre audience. 2. A joke which produces a guffaw. (Wilmeth LANGUAGE)

belly tickler, belly whopper   A funny joke.

belly wow   1. A funny joke. 2. A successful show. 3. Especially in vaudeville, riotous audience laughter. 4. To delight an audience.

belly wow 'em   To excite laughter.

below   1. Downstage, downstage of; as when a performer is downstage of another performer or object. 2. Elizabethan: beneath the stage.

below-stairs scene   See: feather-dusting scene.

bema (Greek)   1. In the classical Greek theatre, the wide lower step of the altar in the orchestra. The step was virtually a low platform, and wide enough to serve the flute players and perhaps also the actors. For the latter, it would have provided an occasionally useful elevation. 2. Sometimes, a similar step or platform elsewhere in a theatre. 3. In Roman times, the stage. 4. In Roman times, perhaps also the front wall of the stage. Both Latin and Greek have *bema* (plural *bemata*), whose literal meaning is step or platform. See also: *thymele*. (Miller DAEDALUS I 305; Bieber HISTORY 3, 18, 55; Pickard-Cambridge DIONYSUS 257–262, figs. 132, 135–138)

ben   A benefit; a benefit performance.

benang mentah (Malaysian)   The cotton wick of a shadow theatre oil lamp. (Sheppard TAMAN 70, 98)

bench act   A vaudeville song-and-dance turn which begins with a pair of performers seated on a park bench. (Wilmeth LANGUAGE)

bend   1. A fake 14th C version, in silk, of a gold band. (Chalmers CLOTHES 118) 2. To bow to an audience. 3. Such a bow.

bende (Indonesian)   See: *gamelan*.

bend rater   A successful show, one deserving curtain-call bows.

bends   Short for: do the bends, that is, bow to the audience. As a noun: bows.

benefit   Short form: ben. A theatrical performance, the profits from which are given to some person or persons (usually theatrical personnel) or some cause. Hence benefit night, benefit performance, benefit show. In the 17th C British theatre, the occasion was often called a person's day, as in the poet's day—the author's benefit. (Bowman/Ball THEATRE, Van Lennep LONDON lxxix, Chambers ELIZABETHAN I 370n)

Benesh Notation   See: movement notation.

Bengal fire, *flamme de Bengale* (French)   In Britain in the late 19th C (and perhaps earlier), a chemical substance which was lighted to produce the illusion of flames on stage. Compare: Bengal light. (Rosenfeld BRIGHT 199)

Bengal light   An open-flame gas burner introduced in Britain at the beginning of the 19th C and used for a time thereafter. (Rosenthal/Wertenbaker MAGIC 52)

bengbeng (Chinese)   1. See: *errenzhuan*. 2. See: *pingju*.

bengbengxi (Chinese)   See: *pingju*.

bengkong (Malaysian)   A folded sarong used as a waist-cloth in male roles in *ma'yong*. (Sheppard TAMAN 64)

bense, pen se (Chinese)   Literally: original color. Unadorned; a term of approbation in Chinese theatrical criticism. It indicates that a dramatic text is unaffected and natural, with dialogue and lyrics close to the language of everyday life; in such texts, literary allusions and parallelisms are used sparingly. (Dolby HISTORY 76)

benshi (Japanese)   Literally: speaker or explainer. During the silent film era, the live performer who narrated, spoke dialogue, and explained action during a public film showing.

bent foot iron   See: foot iron.

bentulan (Indonesian)   Literally: a small machete. A small, rounded nose of a *gagah* character in Javanese *wayang kulit*. (Long JAVANESE 70)

be on the gate   To take tickets.

be ready   An imperative warning found in early 17th C British promptbooks to alert performers, musicians, or stagehands.

bergerie (French)   See: *Schäferei*.

berjamu (Malaysian)   A ritual in which a puppet master (*dalang*) makes food offerings to spirits to protect a person or community. The ceremony blends *wayang kulit* ritual and shamanistic activities. Types of *berjamu* are *pelimau* (ritual bathing of pupils), *pelepas niat* (releasing from a vow), and *menyemah* (propitiation of spirits). (Sweeney MALAY 18, Sweeney RAMAYANA 275)

Berl Broder   In the late 19th C Yiddish theatre in eastern Europe, a Broder singer (q.v.). Berl Broder was the name of the first famous 19th C Broder singer; by the 1860s many performers called themselves Berl Broder. (Sandrow VA-GABOND 36–37)

berne   See: Sbernia.

berry   Short for raspberry.

berserk   A Viking expression for a tunic (called a serk) torn off by the wearer in the heat of combat. (Walkup DRESSING 75)

bertep (Byelorussian)   See: *szopka*.

bespeak, bespeak performance   1. A performance requested by an audience member or members—usually a local magnate or a group of influential people. 2. As a verb, to request a performance. (Troubridge BENEFIT 33)

best boy   Informally, in the parlance of the New York professional theatre, the chief assistant to the head electrician. The term may have begun in motion pictures (and is still much used there). (Berrey/Van den Bark SLANG 576)

bestiarii (Latin Roman)   Animal fighters in the *venationes*. Such performers were prisoners of war, condemned criminals, or men hired for the purpose. All were trained in special schools. Also called *venatores*, which is uncommon in theatre literature. Singular *bestiarius* is literally ''one who fights with wild beasts (in the shows).'' (Sandys COMPANION 509–510, Oxford LATIN)

besut (Indonesian)   A shortening of *ludruk besut*. See: *ludruk*.

Bethlehem dress   A Middle-East woman's ankle-length dress consisting of a long, close-fitting body of red or blue linen trimmed with beads, braid, and embroidery in varied soft colors. It is bloused over a wide cummerbund. A bolero jacket with wide, wrist-length sleeves is worn over it. Also called a khurkeh. (Wilcox DICTIONARY)

Betsie   A small collar or ruff made of rows of fluted lace, worn by Queen Elizabeth I. Called later, in Paris, a *cherusse* or *cherusque*. Also called a collarette. (Wilcox DICTIONARY)

between acts   See: entr'acte.

between engagements, between plays, between shows   Unemployed.

bevor   See: beaver.

Bewegungespiel (German)   In medieval Germany, a play marked by physical activity. (Nagler MEDIEVAL 69)

bhada (Sanskrit)   A professional singer, dancer, musician or actor who performs as part of a troupe, moving from one village to another. Also called *nat*, *gandharva*, *vairagi*, and *binkara*. (Vatsyayan TRADITIONAL 4)

bhagat (Hindi)   A folk theatre form in north India.

bhagavata (Kannada, Telugu, Tamil)   1. In central and south Indian regional dance dramas—especially *yaksagana*, *kuchipudi*, and *bhagavata mela nat-*

akam—a producer, director, and chief singer/narrator. In Kannada also called *bhagavatar* and in Telugu *bhagavatalu*. (Vatsyayan TRADITIONAL 38, 57; Gargi FOLK 191, 192) 2. The singer-narrator in puppet plays in many parts of India. Also spelled *bhagavat*. (ASIAN 18) See also: *sutradhara*.

bhagavata mela natakam (Tamil, Telugu)   A dance-drama in southern India, based on classical *bharata natyam* dance. Performed for religious festivals by an all-male cast. Abbreviated *bhagavata mela*. (Benegal PANORAMA 58, Gargi FOLK 193)

bhaint (Hindi)   A devotional song of invocation, sung by the stage manager (*ranga*) at the beginning of a *nautanki* performance. (Gargi FOLK 37, 47)

bhamakalapam (Telugu)   A dance-drama in Andhra Pradesh state, based on *kuchipudi*. Emphasis is on the theme of separation of the heroine from the god-hero, Krishna.

bhana (Sanskrit)   A type of classical Indian drama written as a monologue in one act and performed by one actor. One of ten major play types (*rupaka*). (Kale THEATRIC 166)

bhand (Hindi, Punjabi)   1. A clown or jester who appears in rural theatre forms such as *raslila*. See also: *vidusaka*. (Hein MIRACLE 170–171) 2. A roving band of singers and dancers. (Rangacharya INDIAN 89)

bhand pathar (Hindi)   A scroll play or folk drama performed by a travelling troupe (*bhand*) in Kashmir that mixes legend with contemporary social criticism. A performance is called *bhand jashna*. (Mathur DRAMA 55)

bhangi (Assamese)   A dance in *ankiya nat* known by the name of the character who performs it, for example, *krsna-bhangi* (dance of Krsna) and *gopi-bhangi* (dance of milk maidens). Rhythmic patterns and dance steps delineate a character's temperament and mood. (Richmond ''Vaisnava'' 159)

bhanika (Sanskrit)   A one-act form in classical Indian drama. One type of 'minor play'(*uparupaka*). (Keith SANSKRIT 268, 351)

bharata (Sanskrit)   1. An actor. The term is said to have derived from a tribe of the same name. 2. Capitalized, the reputed author of the *Natyasastra* (*The Art of Theatre*). Also called Bharata-muni, or the Sage Bharata. (Keith SANSKRIT 29–30)

bharata natyam (Sanskrit)   A classical dance form whose style influenced Indian dance-dramas. It is derived from ancient temple dances and is performed by a single female dancer. (Gargi FOLK 38-44)

bharatavakya (Sanskrit)   The benedictory verse that closes a classical Indian play. (Keith SANSKRIT 82, 83, 111, 265)

bharati (Sanskrit)   Literally: verbal. One of four styles (*vrtti*) of dramatic writing and presentation in classical Indian drama. It emphasizes rhetorical embellishment. (Keith SANSKRIT 326, 344) ''Improvisational'' style, according to Kale (THEATRIC 151). The style is derived, Bharata says, from the *Rig Veda* (NATYASASTRA 404).

bhav (Hindi)   See: *bhava*.

bhava (Sanskrit)   A human emotion or state of being. According to classical Indian dramatic theory the actor conveys *bhava* through acting (*abhinaya*) within the framework of the character and the play. Bharata describes eight fundamental emotions (*sthayibhava*)—*rati, hasa, soka, krodha, utsaha, bhaya, jugupsa,* and *vismaya*—and 33 transitory emotions or states (*vyabhicari bhava*) in NATYAS-ASTRA 119–149. *Santa* (tranquility), a ninth *bhava*, is added in later texts such as Dhanamjaya's *Dasarupa*. In Hindi, *bhav*. See also: *rasa*. (Jones/Jones KA-THAKALI 107, Raghavan in Baumer/Brandon SANSKRIT 21–22)

bhavai (Gujarati)   A folk drama with considerable satiric and humorous content performed by an all-male troupe in rural areas of Gujarat and Rajasthan, west India. The form originated in the 15th C. (Gargi FOLK 51–71)

bhavaiya (Gujarati)   A company of actors who perform *bhavai*.

bhawari yar nac (Assamese)   A special actor's dance in *angkiya nat* that precedes the drama but follows the introductions. (Richmond "Vaisnava" 159)

bhawariya (Assamese)   Literally: one who impersonates another. An *ankiya nat* actor. (Richmond "Vaisnava" 162)

bhaya (Sanskrit)   Literally: terror. One of the eight fundamental emotions (*sthayibhava*) expressed by actors of classical Indian plays. See also: *bhayanaka*. (Keith SANSKRIT 323)

bhayanaka (Sanskrit)   Literally: fear. One of the eight sentiments (*rasa*) to be experienced by spectators of classical Sanskrit plays. It is aroused by the enacted fundamental emotion (*sthayibhava*) of terror (*bhaya*). (Keith SANSKRIT 319, 324)

B'howery b'hoy   See: Mose the B'howery b'hoy.

bhungal (Gujarati)   A copper wind instrument played in *bhavai*. (Gargi FOLK 55–56, 61)

biandan, pien tan (Chinese)   Pole play, portable booth puppet. A puppet show performed by one puppeteer who manipulates the puppets, speaks and sometimes sings, and provides musical accompaniment. It is performed on a small stage mounted on a single vertical pole; the puppeteer uses the pole to carry the stage and puppets over his shoulder when moving from site to site. Also called *gulizi* or *ku li tzu*, literally "coolie show." (Foreign FOLK 53–54, Obraztsov CHINESE 9–16)

bianwen, pien wen (Chinese)   Literally: changed words. Popularizations of Buddhist sutras and other scriptures for oral proselytization, c. 7th-10th C; by the 10th C, many were entirely secular. *Bianwen* were often composed in a mixture of literary and vernacular styles, and probably influenced the development of drama in form as well as content. Sometimes translated as "Mandala texts'' (Dolby HISTORY 11–12, 39), and as ''popular Buddhist tracts'' (Mackerras RISE 254).

biaomu (Chinese)   See: *jiamen.*

bibboka (Sanskrit)   Affected indifference of a female character for her beloved. One of ''ten graces'' of a heroine in classical Indian drama. (Keith SANSKRIT 310)

bibhatsa (Sanskrit)   Literally: horror. One of the eight sentiments (*rasa*) to be experienced by the spectators of a Sanskrit play. It is aroused by the enacted fundamental emotion (*sthayibhava*) of disgust (*jugupsa*). (Keith SANSKRIT 319, 324; Bharata NATYASASTRA 116)

bibi (French)   A small, elegant, lace-decorated or otherwise festooned bonnet of the 19th C. (Boucher FASHION)

Bible   A program in magazine form.

bib puppet   A puppet whose head is that of the puppeteer. A small body, arms and legs are string-controlled and hung from the operator's neck. A curtain or screen masks the puppeteer's body from the audience. Also called a humanette or living marionette. (Philpott DICTIONARY)

bichele (Yiddish)   See: *buechel.*

bicycle bal(moral)   A kind of sneaker made of leather or canvas, with a low heel, worn by cyclists in the 19th C. (Wilcox DICTIONARY)

bidadari (Indonesian)   The character of a nymph in classical theatre. (Foley ''Sundanese'' 107)

Biegsameskabel (German)   Literally: flexible cable. Apparently an early term for stage cable. *Kabel* is now sometimes used; and *ummanteltes Kabel* is modern heavy-duty rubber-covered cable. (Fuchs LIGHTING 367, Rae/Southern INTERNATIONAL 24)

biff   A successful show.

big bills   See: great bills.

big-boat pilot   A wealthy person who invests in a theatrical venture. (Berrey/Van den Bark SLANG 574)

big butter-and-egger, big butter-and-egg-man   A wealthy person who invests in a theatrical venture. (Berrey/Van den Bark SLANG 574)

big click   A successful show.

big dance in Newark   A New York show business excuse for bad business. (Wilmeth LANGUAGE)

big flash   A featured attraction.

biggin, biggon   See: *beguin.*

big ham-and-egger, big ham-and-egg-man   A wealthy person who invests in a theatrical venture. (Berrey/Van den Bark SLANG 574)

big hand   Resounding applause.

big head, big-head   In Britain, a large mask covering a performer's head, or sometimes his whole body, often used to caricature a public figure. Usually made of papier maché, big heads were used in 19th C pantomimes.

big horse   Especially in early burlesque, a hefty chorus girl. Also called a hill horse. See also: beef trust. (Wilmeth LANGUAGE)

big noise   A featured attraction.

big sucker-and-egg-man   A wealthy person who invests in a theatrical venture. (Berrey/Van den Bark SLANG 574)

big time   In the heyday of vaudeville, theatres presenting two performances daily. By extension, highly successful professional theatres and people. Hence, in the big time, big-time performer, etc. See also: small time.

big-time hit, **big wow**   A successful show.

bija (Sanskrit)   Literally: germ, seed. The first of five elements of the plot (*arthaprakrti*) of a classical Indian play during which the object of the hero's desire is revealed. (Keith SANSKRIT 298)

bijou theatre   In Britain, a small-scale, modestly mounted theatre seating about 500 people. (Granville DICTIONARY)

bilangan (Malaysian)   1. In shadow theatre (*wayang kulit*), a memorized narrative section describing major characters or the scene of an action. Also called *ucap*. (Sweeney RAMAYANA 65–72) 2. The generic term for song lyrics in *ma'yong*. (Yousof "Kelantan" 116)

Bildprojektionsapparat (German)   An early term for a projector, now called a *Projektionsapparat*. (Fuchs LIGHTING 211)

biliment   A 16th C delicate, elaborate headdress of gold-threaded lace and jewels, ribbons, beads, and gauze. Sometimes embellished with a single feather. (Wilcox DICTIONARY)

bill   1. A playbill; a poster or handout listing the theatrical offerings at a given theatre on a given day. Used in England as early as the 1590s. 2. The structure or content of a program, such as a double bill. 3. A single play in the repertoire of a Toby show troupe. 4. The acts in a variety show; thus, the whole show. 5. The peak of a cap. (Chambers ELIZABETHAN II 113, Wilmeth LANGUAGE, Walkup DRESSING 114)

billboard, bill board   1. A board on which theatrical advertisements are displayed. 2. The advertisement itself. (Wilmeth LANGUAGE)

billboard pass   See: bill pass.

bill carrier   A theatre employee responsible for posting playbills. Also called a bill setter or bill sticker.

billet corporatif (French)   In the World War II Vichy government, a voucher enabling workers to buy theatre tickets scaled to their salaries. (Rosenberg "Vichy's" 132) *billet de faveur* (French)   In the World War II Vichy government, a free ticket to a performance. (Rosenberg "Vichy's" 132)

billet special (French)   In the World War II Vichy government, a ticket giving the holder a 50% discount on the price of admission. (Rosenberg "Vichy's" 132)

bill hook   In 19th C French theatres (and presumably elsewhere) a kind of sickle at the end of a pole, used by firemen in a theatre, probably for cutting down draperies or ropes. (Moynet FRENCH 21)

billing   1. The ranking or mention of a performer in advertisements, at a theatre, or in handouts. Hence, top billing, bottom billing, etc. 2. The advertisement itself. (Wilmeth LANGUAGE)

billing in a box   In a theatrical advertisement, the placement of an attraction or a performer's name in a box to draw attention to it. The box was also called a coffin. (Wilmeth LANGUAGE)

billing star   A performer whose name is given prominence on a playbill, sometimes illegitimately, as by a bribe. Not to be confused with star billing or box-office star. (Wilmeth LANGUAGE)

bill inspector   The person in early 19th C theatres overseeing those who posted the bills. (Hogan LONDON clxiv)

bill it like a circus   In the 19th C, to advertise a show on a grand scale. (Flint in Matlaw ENTERTAINMENT 190)

Bill Jonesing   Playing a character in an uncertain, loose, unfocused manner. (Golden/Shore STAGE-STRUCK 165–166)

bill of fare   A printed program.

bill pass, billboard pass, bill board pass   A free ticket given to a tradesman in exchange for displaying window playbills or posters in his shop. (Fay GLOSSARY)

bill setter, bill sticker   See: bill carrier.

billy, billy act   Especially in vaudeville, a southern mountaineer act.

billy block, billy   In Britain, a pair of double or triple pulleys with one rope reeved through. The rigging provides extra purchase. Also called a block and fall. (Corry PLANNING)

Bim-Bom   An improvisational Polish theatre form which borrows from the fine arts, circus, carnival, street fair, music hall, and film. (Gerould "Bim-Bom" 99)

bindu (Sanskrit)   Literally: drop. The second element of the plot (*arthaprakrti*) of a classical Indian play. Like a drop of oil spreading out on water, the plot expands. (Keith SANSKRIT 298) It indicates "continuity of action" according to Byrski (Baumer/Brandon SANSKRIT 144) and is a "point" according to Kale (THEATRIC 155).

binette (French)   See: full-bottomed wig.

binkara (Sanskrit)   See: *bhada*.

binten (Indonesian)   Fighting technique in Javanese shadow theatre in which characters repeatedly kick at one another's knees. (Long JAVANESE 63, 91)

bio-box   An old British term for U.S. projection booth, especially in the early years of film projection. (Granville DICTIONARY)

biologos (Greek)   Literally: speaker of life, a term which came to be almost equivalent to mime-player. Implied is a view of the mime as a reflection of life. See also: *ethologos*. (Nicoll MASKS 36)

bio-mechanics   The Russian director Vsevelod Meyerhold's production system. This used the actor as a puppet (a biological mechanism), fully controlled by the director, and limited the stage to the barest necessities. (Hartnoll COMPANION, Cameron/Hoffman GUIDE)

biplane filament   In spotlight lamps, a concentrated filament whose two sets of coils are parallel to each other without quite touching, and so placed that the spaces between the coils of one set are opposite the coils of the other set. See also: concentrated filament. (McCandless SYLLABUS 10)

bipost base   In U.S. spotlight lamps, a base with two relatively heavy round prongs. In Britain, such bases are limited to lamps of 2000 watts and up and, hence, to the U.S. mogul size. Like the prefocus base, the bipost forces the lamp into precise relation to a spotlight's reflector and lens system. Bipost is used in such other combinations as bipost lamp and bipost holder, the latter being British for U.S. bipost socket. (Wehlburg GLOSSARY; Bentham ART 77–78, fig. 42)

bird   Short for: getting the bird, that is, an unfavorable reception by the audience. The term originated with the shrill whistles sometimes used by gallery playgoers. In Britain, a faint sound of disapproval (a small bird) is called a linnet.

bird's-eye lamp, Birdseye lamp, Birdseye   See: reflector lamp.

bird's nest   A false beard made of crêpe wool. (Bowman/Ball THEATRE)

biretta (Italian)   1. A 13th-14th C man or woman's flat hood reaching to the shoulders. A more elaborate version was worn by the clergy. 2. A 16th C round cap which became square on top, giving it the shape still seen on the clergy. (Boucher FASHION)

Birmingham screwdriver   A hammer. A nickname devised in Britain when lazy stage carpenters hammered screws into wood, finishing off with a few turns of a screwdriver. (Granville DICTIONARY)

"Bis!" (French)   Literally: twice. A call for an encore. From Latin.

bisellia (Latin Roman)   The wide, throne-like seats of honor set on a broad step which followed the curve of the orchestra and amounted to the first row of seats. From *bi*, double, and *sella*, seat, since such seats were virtually wide enough for two spectators. Also called seats of honor. (Bieber HISTORY 173, 193, 194)

Bishop's revolving gridiron   See: revolving gridiron.

biscuit   A loudspeaker station on an intercommunication system.

bit   1. A minor speaking or silent role in a production. Hence, a bit player, bit part. 2. A small piece of dialogue. 3. A burlesque or vaudeville sketch. (Bowman/Ball THEATRE)

bite a cue   In acting: 1. To interrupt another performer's speech, that is, to cut the other's cue. Hence, to bite cues. In Britain, cut in. 2. To deliver one's own cue lines unemphatically. (Bowman/Ball THEATRE)

bit part, bit player   See: bit.

biwa hoshi (Japanese)   During the middle ages (c. 1200–1600), a blind 'priest' (*hoshi*) who chanted a historical epic, usually *The Tale of the Heike*, while playing a lute (*biwa*). See: *heikyoku*. (Ruch in Hall/Toyoda MUROMACHI 288)

biz   1. Stage business. 2. Show business. Hence, show biz. 3. Ticket sales.

biz man, biz rep   A performer's representative.

biz up   Improved box office business.

(the) black   In Britain, the apron, which used to be painted black. (Baker THEATRECRAFT)

Black aesthetic   As viewed by the Black Arts movement, an ethic which questions which reality is the more valid—the Black or the white—and how the ethical issues that question raises can be integrated into its theatre aesthetic. (Neal ''Black'' 30)

black and tan   A blackface vaudeville act. (Wilmeth LANGUAGE)

black and white artiste   In Britain, a music hall performer who quickly draws caricatures in black on a white surface or vice versa. (Granville DICTIONARY)

black box, blackbox   A name given to a flexible performance space—usually a sizable room (often painted flat black) in which any seating or performing arrangement can be set up. Hence, blackbox space.

black comedy, black farce   A form that both provokes and undercuts laughter by making audiences, as they laugh, perceive the bleakness of a character's situation or of his/her existence in an irrational universe. See also: theatre of the absurd.

blackface, black-face   Especially in 19th C minstrel shows and in vaudeville, black makeup on a white performer. The practice is centuries old: Morris dances in the middle ages, white actors playing such parts as Othello, etc.

black lamp   See: blacklight lamp.

black light   Invisible rays beyond the violet end of the spectrum. Such rays, which produce fluorescence in certain substances, have been used for many years on darkened stages to yield striking scenic, costume, and make-up effects. Also called ultraviolet light or UV light. (Bellman SCENE, Bowman MODERN)

blacklight lamp   In the U.S., a deep purple lamp which emits mainly ultraviolet light for use in fluorescent effects. The British equivalent is black lamp. The U.S. term is sometimes designated BLB (blacklight bulb) in stage lighting catalogues. (Corry LIGHTING 114–116)

blackout, black out, black-out, BO   1. A condition in which the stage is dark or (sometimes) nearly dark. The term usually means complete darkness, but it has been used for situations in which, for example, a performer switches off the lights in a room but some outside light remains; this meaning may be more common in Britain, where 'dead blackout' emphasizes complete darkness. 2. On some present control boards, off. 3. As a verb, to switch off lights suddenly and usually all at once. This use is as frequent as meaning 1, and parallel to it. 4. A skit or other short piece, as in a revue, which ends in a sudden blackout. Hence, blackout skit. (Bellman SCENE, Bellman LIGHTING 221, Sellman/Lessley ESSENTIALS, Bentham ART, Corry PLANNING)

blackout skit   See: blackout.

blackout switch, black-out switch   A single switch which controls all the light on stage. The switch is often labeled BO.

black powder   An explosive powder that gives a bright flash of light and much smoke. (Gillette/Gillette STAGE)

black riser   In some step lenses, the blackened plane which rises to each of the curved rings of the lens. The effect of these risers, which are ceramic, is to reduce stray light. Also called a riser, ceramic black riser, or, occasionally, baked ceramic riser.

blacks   A set of black curtains of velour, cotton velvet, or rep, at the sides and rear of the acting area. The black is a theatrical convention which signifies that artistically the curtains are invisible and so are to be ignored; indeed, when the stage is properly lit, the blacks may virtually disappear.

black technique   A puppetry style which uses manipulators dressed in black leotards and masks working before a black drape. Their hands are gloved in white—all that is visible as they manipulate their puppets. (Baird PUPPET 22)

black theatre   1. Especially in the U.S., theatre by and about black people. 2. One of the many ideas of the Czech director Alfred Radok, used with his Laterna Magika theatre form. The latter combined images and live stage action in poetic, innovative ways which influenced traditional staging in this century. Black theatre used black background and black or partially black costumes, creating a variety of illusions—objects moving in air or disappearing, people moving without legs, etc.

black up, blacken up   See: cork up.

black wax   A substance which is kneaded and then applied to the back and front of a performer's teeth to block them out.

bladder   1. An animal bladder (or imitation thereof) used by comics as a weapon. The tradition goes back at least to the Middle Ages, when bladders were used by court jesters. 2. An obsolete term for an intemperate and aging female trouper. (Wilmeth LANGUAGE)

blagorodnaia komediia (Russian)   Russian adaptations of French salon comedies. (Welsh RUSSIAN 60)

B lamp   See: B.

blank   1. An undecorated flat serving as a side wing in an exterior setting. (Bowman/Ball THEATRE) 2. A paper without writing, used as a property.

blanking paper   In Britain, blue paper pasted over bills advertising a play when the latter is withdrawn or a theatre is dark. (Granville DICTIONARY)

BLB   See: blacklight lamp.

bleachers   See: scaffold.

bleed   1. Said of paint when an undercoat shows through an overcoat. 2. Said of fabric color that is not fast when immersed in water. 3. Said of light when it can be seen through a scenic unit.

blencong (Indonesian)   A bronze oil lamp which hangs above the puppeteer's head and supplies illumination for a shadow theatre performance. Today, largely replaced by pressure lamps or electric light. Also spelled *blentjong*. (Long JAVANESE 17–18, Brandon THRONES 35–36) Called *damar* in Bali. (McPhee in Belo TRADITIONAL 147, Moerdowo BALINESE II 115)

blend   1. In using makeup, to smooth out, especially where differing colors meet. 2. In scene painting, to dry-brush in order to mix the edges of two colors. 3. In acting, to adjust body movement and voice to harmonize with other performers. 4. In lighting, to overlap lighting areas so that a performer crossing the stage will be evenly lit. (Bowman/Ball THEATRE)

blender   A flesh-colored band in the fore-part of a wig. It is made up to blend with the forehead.

blend in   In acting, to adjust body position so as to make a unified stage picture.

blending   The smoothing out of facial makeup, or the shading of one color into another so that the division between them is imperceptible.

blending light   Light which smoothes the illumination on the stage so that no marked differences are obvious as a performer moves from one area to another. The effect is usually to enhance realism, and it is in realistic lighting that the procedure is most common. See also: toning lights. (Bellman SCENE, Wehlburg GLOSSARY)

blending powder   A term, now seldom used, for theatrical face powder.

blentjong (Indonesian)   See: *blencong*.

blind   1. A shade for dimming stage lights in the 18th C. The Covent Garden theatre inventory of 1743, for example, lists "5 tin blinds to stage lamps" and "24 blinds to scene ladders . . . " 2. In 18th C theatres and later, a masking piece, such as a piece of scenery painted like a cloud, hiding a machine that brings characters down from above the stage. 3. See: house curtain. (Visser in Hume LONDON 101)

blind alley theme   A problem in a play that cannot be solved, or a problem whose solutions are unsatisfactory or undesirable. (Archer PLAY-MAKING 224)

blinder   1. In a beam projector, a small circular mirror or mask directly in front of the lamp. The purpose is to cut off or redirect light rays which would fall outside the main beam. 2. Any cutoff or framing device used in controlling a light beam. 3. See: barn doors. 4. In Britain, a curtain of light or light curtain, used to blind the audience during a scene shift. 5. Occasionally, any material used on the back of a flat to prevent light leaks. Meanings are primarily U.S. (Bowman MODERN, Wehlburg GLOSSARY, Lounsbury THEATRE, Bowman/Ball THEATRE)

blind recording   In memory lighting systems, a procedure which permits the operator to put cues into memory (or remove them) without altering the lighting currently on the stage. (Bellman LIGHTING 245)

blind seat   A box office term for an auditorium seat from which a spectator can see only part of the stage. Also called an obstructed view. (Bowman/Ball THEATRE)

blinker   1. A type of backstage signal which uses an on-off light. See also: cue light. (Lounsbury THEATRE) 2. See: flasher.

Blitz-gerät (German)   Literally: lightning-flash instrument. A lighting instrument designed to project forked lightning.

blitz-light   In Britain, a small hand-held projector whose light source is an electronic flash gun activated by a button. This German instrument is used with cutouts in the gate to project forked lightning. (Pilbrow LIGHTING 171)

Blk   Blank, as in a paper without writing used as a property. (Shattuck SHAKESPEARE 14)

blobby   Among British electricians, spotty. The word characterizes lighting which is uneven. Hence, blobbiness. The terms have also come into use among directors. (Granville DICTIONARY, Baker THEATRECRAFT)

block   1. A wooden or metal frame on the gridiron above the stage which contains one or more sheaves (pulley wheels) which take fly lines. Hence, head block, loft block, triple block, etc. 2. Especially in Australia, a 3″ to 4″ length of 1″ square wood screwed to the stile of a flat to serve as a stop, and ensure a tight join when two flats are set at an angle. 3. A group of seats for a show.

(Bowman/Ball THEATRE, National TECHNICAL) 4. To establish with performers their onstage movement in a play. See also: blocking, block out.

block and fall   See: billy block.

block booked   Said of a group of vaudeville acts—normally eight—hired for a series of theatres in succession. (Wilmeth LANGUAGE)

blocked butt joint   Two boards, as in a stage door frame, butted against one another and held at right angles by blocks of wood screwed or glued to the rear of the joint.

blocking   1. A written description, in words, symbols, or sketches, of performers' movements in a production. Also called blocking notes, blocking notation. 2. The process of setting such movements and positions.

blocking rehearsal   A rehearsal at which performers' movements are set.

block out, block   To plan or work out the principal movements, positions, and business of performers during rehearsals. (Bowman/Ball THEATRE) See also: blocking.

block shoe   A female ballet dancer's slipper, fashioned with a padded toe. Also called a toe shoe or *pointe* shoe (French-English). (Kersley/Sinclair BALLET)

blood and thunder   A term applied to sensational melodramas, usually of the 19th C.

blood tub   A Victorian theatre specializing in sensational melodramas. (Granville DICTIONARY)

blood vessel   A minor-circuit vaudeville theatre.

bloomer   An obsolete term for: 1. A town in which shows have not succeeded. 2. A theatrical failure. (Wilmeth LANGUAGE)

bloomer stand   An unprofitable engagement.

blow   1. In acting, to forget one's lines or business; to blow a scene, blow up, or, in British terminology, to make an ascension. Hence, blowing up. 2. To leave a cast during the run of a show, or break an engagement; to blow the show. (Bowman/Ball THEATRE)

blower   A fan for creating wind effects.

blow-off   1. The end of an act. 2. The final performance of a show.

blow-through jet   See: safety jet.

blue   Said of lines or business in vaudeville bordering on the obscene. In general use as lewd and lascivious about 1900. Hence, blue gags, blueology.

blue blouse   A club and factory entertainment given in Russia during the early years of the Revolution, to educate citizens in Socialism. The repertory consisted of scenes from plays, operettas, and vaudeville. (Markov SOVIET 139)

blued clout nail   See: clout nail.

blue gags, blueology   See: blue.

blues   1. A 19th C term for sky borders. (Roberts STAGE) 2. Bleacher seats in the traveling U.S. vaudeville tent shows of the early 20th C, often painted blue. (Ashby in Matlaw AMERICAN 143, Wilmeth LANGUAGE)

blue shirt lead   In a Toby show, a leading man who plays a rural character calling for the wearing of a blue shirt. (Wilmeth LANGUAGE)

blues shouter   A female singer whose loud singing could be heard for blocks. See also: throwing it from the velvet. (Hughes/Meltzer MAGIC 97, 99)

blue stuff   Risqué (often obscene) material. Blue as risqué, which may have originated in early vaudeville, occurs alone and in combinations both within and outside the theatre. (Wilmeth LANGUAGE, Wentworth/Flexner SLANG)

bluff   In actors' boarding houses in the days of vaudeville, a sandwich and a bottle of beer at night after the show, included in the price of the room. (Laurie VAUDEVILLE 276)

BM   Board measure. (Gassner/Barber PRODUCING 698)

BO, B.O.   1. Box office. By extension, the revenue taken in there. (Carrington THEATRICANA) 2. In stage lighting, blackout.

bo, po (Chinese)   Brass cymbals about six inches in diameter which are featured in the percussion orchestra (*wuchang*) in Beijing opera (*jingju*) and many other forms of music-drama (*xiqu*). Also called *naobo* or *nao po*. (Scott CLASSICAL 49–50; Wichmann ''Aural'' 447, 453–460)

BO ante   Admission fee.

BO appeal, BO drag, BO draw, BO pull   The commercial value of a show or performer.

board   1. A general term for the central control device for the stage lighting circuitry. It normally implies direct control, as opposed to 'console,' which denotes remote control apparatus, often computer assisted. The term is a shortened form of control board or, still older, switchboard. Major components include switches, dimmers, and fuses or circuit breakers. The following terms are usually followed by ''board'' to form more specific terms: ATD, autotransformer, bracket handle, deadface(d), dead front, dimmer, direct control, direct operated, five-scene-preset, fixed, house, live front, open front, package, packaged memory, piano, portable, preset, remote control, resistance, road, self-release, stage, touring, tracker wire, tube, two preset, etc. 2. A box-office ticket rack. 3. In 19th C Britain, a placard carried onstage to convey a notice or bit of dialogue and thus to avoid the Licensing Act. Similar to locality or title boards of earlier times and those in 20th C burlesque and variety shows. 4. Short for: call board, the notice board for performers. 5. A theatrical advertisement, such as a poster. 6. In the U.S., the policy-making body of a theatre, especially of a non-Broadway theatre and more especially of a non-professional theatre. (Bowman/Ball THEATRE)

board captain   An occasional term for the crew member in charge of the operation of a control board. (Bowman MODERN)

board fever   Stage ambition.

board hookup   See: hookup.

board light   In Britain, the small working light by which an electrician or other staff member reads his cue board. (Baker THEATRECRAFT, Granville DICTIONARY)

board man, board operator   A crew member who operates part or all of the light control board.

(the) boards   1. The stage floor, from the early days when a stage was boards set on trestles. Hence, to walk or tread the boards. 2. The stage generally. 3. The acting profession. 4. Tickets.

board set-up   See: set-up.

board shover   A scene shifter.

boat   In minstrelsy, a railroad train. (Wilmeth LANGUAGE)

(the) boat sails Tuesday   A stock remark by London managers in the early 20th C when an American act failed at the first performance. (Berrey/Van den Bark SLANG 585)

boat show   1. A river steamboat or cruise ship featuring theatrical entertainment. 2. The entertainment presented on such a boat. (Wilmeth LANGUAGE)

boatswain's chair, boatswain's stool   See: cradle.

BO attraction   See: BO draw.

boat truck   In Britain, a low, wheeled platform. (Southern CHANGEABLE 251)

bobbin   1. In Britain, a wooden runner on a curtain wire to which a curtain hook is attached. 2. In Australia, a sliding or wheeled carrier from which draw curtains are suspended. (Purdom PRODUCING, National TECHNICAL)

bobbinet, bobbinette   See: theatrical gauze.

BO blues   Poor box-office receipts.

bobo (Philippine)   A court fool in *comedia*. (Mendoza COMEDIA 99) See also: *pusong*.

bobo (Spanish)   A fool or buffoon. The word was used in 18th C plays and then replaced by *gracioso*. (Shergold SPANISH)

BO breeze   An attraction which draws a small audience.

bobtail piece   In Britain, a domestic play in a local setting. The reference is to ragtag and bobtail—common types of characters. (Granville DICTIONARY)

bob wig   An 18th C man and boy's everyday white wig; bushy, curly, and short. Favored by the clergy and the Quakers. (Wilcox DICTIONARY)

bodchin (Yiddish)   See: *badkhen*.

BO click   See: BO draw.

bodkin   1. A hairpin of metal or bone in the shape of a long, pointed pin. Worn in ancient Greece and Rome. Also called an *acus* (Latin). 2. A cloak fastening of the Saxons, who called it a hair needle. 3. A needle with a large eye and blunt end, used to draw elastic or ribbon through eyelets or a hem. (Wilcox DICTIONARY)

BO draft   A strong audience attraction at the box office.

BO draw   A successful show. Also called a BO attraction, BO click, BO fodder, BO success, BO timber, BO wow, etc. Sometimes expanded to box-office draw, etc. (Berrey/Van den Bark SLANG 584)

body   1. A show girl's term for a man. (Wilmeth LANGUAGE) 2. See: line connector.

body alignment   The direction in which a dancer stands in relation to the audience. (Grant TECHNICAL)

body movement   The movement of a performer's body without a change in stage position. (Bowman/Ball THEATRE)

body position   The performer's physical stance in relation to the audience, such as full front, profile, etc. (Canfield CRAFT)

body scene   In 20th C U.S. burlesque, a stock presentation which includes costumes, props, two comedians, a straight man, talking females, a character man, and possibly a juvenile. (Allen in Matlaw AMERICAN 48)

body take   See: take.

boek rong (Thai)   Preliminary offering dances which precede the performance of a traditional play (*khon* or *lakon*). See also: *praleng*. (Yupho in Rangthong SOUVENIR 86)

boemio (Spanish)   A 16th C knee-length man's cape. (Boucher FASHION)

boerden (Flemish)   See: *sotternyen*.

boeta (Indonesian)   See: *buta*.

bofeton (Spanish)   1. Stage decoration representing folding doors. 2. A scene door which revolves rapidly, revealing or removing a performer.

boff, boffo   1. Box office. By extension, box-office appeal or success; thus, a hit show. Also called boffola. 2. Formerly, poor business; box office 'off.' 3. A hearty laugh. 4. A comedian. See also: socko, whammo.

boffo   1. A comedian. 2. A very good performance that is also a box office success. 3. A laugh which virtually stops a show. See also: socko, whammo.

BO fodder   See: BO draw.

BO gag   A device to increase box-office receipts. (Berrey/Van den Bark SLANG 593)

bogen A joining of wings and a border to form a single piece. See also: leg drop. (Krows AMERICA 132)

Bogenlampe (German) Arc light. (Fuchs LIGHTING 209, Rae/Southern INTERNATIONAL 18)

bogie In Britain, a scenery wagon. (Bowman/Ball THEATRE)

bogus ducat A counterfeit ticket.

boilermaker's convention In vaudeville, a term for the audience. (Wilmeth LANGUAGE)

boîte conique, boîte conique à reflets (French) An apparently unique 19th C French floodlight which consisted of a gas burner at the narrow end of a long, four-sided reflective housing. Also called conical reflector box, conical reflector hood. (Penzel LIGHTING 99–100, figs. 37, 38)

bol (Malayalam, Hindi) In traditional Indian dance and theatre, rhythmic sound syllables recited by the leader of musicians to give the pattern for both drumming and dancing. (Ranganathan ''Krsnanattam'' 284, Swann ''Braj'' 22)

bolao, po lao (Chinese) An elderly male character, often a peasant; a type of stock character in Yuan *zaju*. (Dolby HISTORY 60)

bole See: Armenian bole.

boleta (Spanish) A ticket.

boleteria (Spanish) Ticket office.

boletero (Spanish) A ticket seller or ticket agent.

bolletini (Italian) Printed tickets in 18th C Venetian theatres. (Larson ''Venetian'' 452)

bomb 1. To fail in a performance. 2. A badly failed production. 3. In Britain, a production which scores a solid hit.

bombast 1. Padding used in Renaissance doublets. (Barton COSTUME 214) 2. Hyperbolic language.

bombazine, bombazeen See: fustian.

bomb tank A galvanized vessel with a wire mesh top; a small bomb is suspended within and detonated electrically to create an explosion effect. (Collison SOUND 100)

bommalatta, bommalattam (Kannada, Tamil, Telugu) A generic term for puppet plays in Andhra Pradesh and Mysore states, south India. (Mathur DRAMA 120–121)

bomoh (Malaysian) Literally: shaman. *Bomoh* are commonly members of theatrical troupes or shadow puppeteers (*dalang*) and are known for their spiritual powers. See also: *pawang*.

bomolochos (Greek) A buffoon, frequent in Old Comedy, who is sometimes an old rustic and sometimes a joking slave. He often makes a fool of boastful characters such as the *alazones*. (Pickard-Cambridge DITHYRAMB 174–178)

bona, pona (Korean)   Balancing and spinning of sieves and bowls on a long pole. One of six acts in *namsadang*. (Kim "Namsadang" 12, Sim/Kim KOREAN 23)

bonachebi (Korean)   The *bona* manipulator in a *namsadang* troupe. (Kim "Namsadang" 12)

bonang (Indonesian)   See: *gamelan*.

bon bon   In Britain, a spotlight focused on a performer's face. (Granville DICTIONARY)

bone   In the past, a Black or blackface actor. (Berrey/Van den Bark SLANG 573)

bone crusher   A comic acrobatic act popular in the early 20th C. See also: dumb act. (Leslie ACT 130–131)

bones   Small tickets made of ivory, issued to performers and engraved with their names; used for free admission to 18th C theatres. (Hogan LONDON xxxiv)

Bones, Brudder Bones   The nickname given the end man in a minstrel show who played rhythm clacker bones. Also called the pair of bones player. His partner at the other end of the semicircle of performers was called Tambo. See also: Rastus. (Wilmeth LANGUAGE, Brockett HISTORY 481, Toll BLACKING 54)

bone solo   In early vaudeville, an act in which the performer manipulated four pieces of bone, two in each hand, making clacking noises and imitating the sound of horses, a cobbler, etc. (Gilbert VAUDEVILLE 55–56)

boneyard, bone-yard   A storage house for scenery. The theatrical meaning probably stems from the 19th C use of boneyard to mean cemetery. (Bowman/Ball THEATRE)

bongrace   See: attifet.

bonjol (Indonesian)   See: *banyol*.

bon kyogen (Japanese)   Literally: *bon* plays. In *kabuki* of the 18th and 19th C, those plays performed in late summer during the *bon* season when spirits of the dead return to earth to be honored. Since the plays feature returned spirits, they are often referred to as ghost plays. (Gunji KABUKI 36, Leiter ENCYCLOPEDIA 31–32)

bonnet à bec (French)   Literally: a beaked cap. An 18th C bonnet extending over the forehead in a point. (Boucher FASHION)

boodle bag   See: grouch bag.

boogie man   A severe critic. (Berrey/Van den Bark SLANG 575)

book   1. The spoken text of a play or musical. Hence, a prompter is on the book or holds the book (the promptbook). 2. To engage or contract for a production, a theatre, or the services of a performing group or performer. Hence, booking, booked up (fully scheduled). 3. In Britain, to buy a theatre ticket or reserve a seat; to book a seat. Hence, a booking, a show that is booked up (sold out). 4. To hinge two flats so that they may be folded like a book. Hence, a book, a book or booked ceiling, flat, or wing. 5. To set such a piece in its open position. (Bowman/Ball THEATRE, Cameron/Gillespie ENJOYMENT)

book ceiling   A ceiling for a stage setting, built in two pieces and hinged to fold lengthwise (cross stage) for easy handling in the flies. Also called a two-leaf ceiling. (Bowman/Ball THEATRE)

booker   A booking agent.

book flat, book-flat, bookflat   Two flats hinged together. Also called a two-fold.

bookholder, book holder   A prompter.

bookie, booky   A booking agent.

booking   1. See: book. 2. In the plural in Britain, the number of seats sold in advance. (Bowman/Ball THEATRE)

booking agency   An office which makes arrangements for engaging performers, touring companies, etc. Also called a ticket agency or booking office.

booking manager   In vaudeville, one who engaged acts for theatres. (Wilmeth LANGUAGE)

booking office   See: booking agency.

bookkeeper, book-keeper   In a 17th C British theatre, the prompter, who not only prepared the promptbook and held it during performances, but kept the library of play copies and parts (sides).

book number   A dance or musical score advancing the action of a musical play, comedy, etc. (Bowman/Ball THEATRE)

book of the play   The script, text.

books down   Said of a rehearsal when performers are expected to work without their play texts in hand.

book show   A musical entertainment with a text, hence at least a minimal plot line, as opposed to a revue or series of musical sketches. (Bowman/Ball THEATRE)

book wing, book-wing, bookwing   In Britain: 1. A book flat or two-fold used as a side wing. 2. A wing, normally one of four, fixed to a spindle extending below the stage floor, where wheels and ropes rotate the wings for scene changes. Used in 19th C theatres. See also: *periaktoi*. (Bowman/Ball THEATRE)

boom   See: boomerang.

boom arm   A short pipe fastened horizontally to a vertical boom. Such arms support spotlights. Also called a side arm. (Bowman/Ball THEATRE, Corry PLANNING)

boomerang, boom   1. Especially in Britain, a vertical arrangement of lights, such as spotlights on a pipe in the wings. 2. In the U.S., a box-like metal color-changer usually attached to the front of a spotlight. The term, which now often means that the boom is remotely controlled, has also been used for manual color changers. Also called a color box. See also: color boomerang. 3. Occasionally in the U.S., a batten which runs horizontally across the stage. 4. Occasionally in the U.S., a light on a boom, i.e., on a vertical or horizontal pipe. Hence, boom flood, boom spot. 5. A movable platform with two or more levels upon which workers stand to paint drops or other scenic units. 6. Boom: Good business at the box office. (Bellman SCENE, Lounsbury THEATRE, Wehlburg GLOSSARY, Bentham ART, Bowman/Ball THEATRE)

boom flood   Especially in Britain, a floodlight on a boom.

boom spot   A spotlight hung on a boom or boom arm. Parallel in meaning are such combinations as boom flood and boom light. (Bowman/Ball THEATRE 36)

boone   To scout for new talent. (Berrey/Van den Bark SLANG 589)

boot   In Britain, an alternate term for sloat.

booth   1. Especially in theatres of recent decades, a room behind and above the seating area of a theatre, often near the ceiling. Booths have a clear view of the stage, and most are used for lighting: hence, projection booth and light booth, as well as such other phrases as booth spot and control booth. (Lounsbury THEATRE) 2. See: booth stage.

boother   A performer in a booth theatre. (Wilmeth LANGUAGE)

booth lights   Ordinarily, high-wattage spotlights which reach the acting area from a booth at the back of the auditorium. (Lounsbury THEATRE)

boot hose   17th C protective sheer white linen stocking worn over costly silk hose. Its lace frill folded over the top of a boot. (Wilcox DICTIONARY)

booth spot, booth spotlight   See: booth lights.

booth stage, booth theatre   A temporary theatre, often found at fairs in the 17th C and later. Sometimes these were simple platform stages outdoors, but often they were theatres inside other buildings, with scenes and machines. Often called simply booths. See also: fit-up.

boot rattler   A dancer. (Berrey/Van den Bark SLANG 573)

boots   A tragedian, from the buskins or boots worn by actors in tragedy in ancient times. See also: *kothornos* (Greek).

BO pay-off   Box-office receipts.

BO pickup   An improvement in business at the box office.

bordeor (French)   See: minstrel.

border   1. A short drop or scenic unit used to mask the flies. Borders are now usually neutral (black, brown, grey, tan) and made of velour, rep, etc., but in the past they were often painted cloths representing a ceiling, clouds, the sky, etc. Hence, ceiling border, cloud border, sky border, etc. Other types include chamber border, cloth border, curtain border, drapery border, festoon border, foliage border, frame or framed border, kitchen border, proscenium border, swag border, working border. Borders are numbered from downstage to upstage; hence, first border, second border, etc., or number one border, number 2 border, etc. See also: pelmet. (Corry PLANNING, Nicoll STUART 47) 2. See: borderlight.

border batten   A long piece of suspended lumber or pipe to which a shallow masking cloth or a borderlight is fastened. The phrase is now less frequent than early in the 20th C; when it occurs, it is more likely to refer to the masking cloth than the borderlight. See also: batten, borderlight.

border bell   A prompter's bell used to cue a change in the borders in 18th C theatres. (Hughes in Hume LONDON 131)

borderlight, border light, border   A long row of overhead lights in a metal container parallel to the proscenium. Often arranged in three or four color circuits, a border consists of one or more striplights totalling at least two-thirds the width of the proscenium. Especially among lighting people, border is more common than borderlight. Borders are numbered from downstage to upstage: first border, second border, etc., or (less often) number 1 border, number 2 border, etc.; very large stages, as in older opera houses, may have six or more borderlights. The first border is sometimes called the X-ray border or the concert border. In a compartment borderlight, a partition separates each lamp from its neighbor, while an open-trough borderlight has no partitions. A roundel (rondel) borderlight has a colored glass roundel in each compartment. A cyclorama borderlight is one specially designed to provide even light on a high cyclorama. Borderlights, occasionally referred to as toning lights, are now often limited to a first border and a "cyc" border. Britain sometimes uses batten, especially for a compartment border (hence, compartment batten), reserving border for scenic pieces. Louns-bury has illustrations. (Bellman LIGHTING 53–54, Lounsbury THEATRE 87–88)

borderlight batten   In the U.S., a long horizontal pipe (formerly sometimes timber) to which a borderlight is attached. (Fuchs LIGHTING 426–427)

borderlight cable   A multi-conductor stage cable containing a number of individually insulated wires. Such a cable carries current to borderlights, electric pipes, and other equipment with a number of circuits. The pairs of conductors for each circuit are often color-coded. Borderlight cable is sometimes called cable or, less often, stage cable. (Bellman SCENE)

borderlight section   See: section.

borderstrip, border striplight   1. A short, portable unit of borderlights. Such a unit can be used alone, or several may be mounted with other such units to form a borderlight. 2. Especially in the past, an occasional name for a bor-derlight. (McCandless "Glossary" 634, Bowman/Ball THEATRE)

Bordonis   Since the 1920s in Europe, multi-channel autotransformers used as theatre dimmer systems. The Bordoni, sometimes with forty-eight individual dimmer tracks, has been widely used in large theatres and opera houses. (Bentham ART 48, 123, 320–321)

bori (Hausa)   In Nigeria, the traditional Hausa dramatic performance, done both as ritual and as entertainment. The present form developed from pre-Islamic times. Also called *wasan bori*. (Adedeji glossary)

born in a trunk   Born into a theatrical family. Also called born in a dressing room or (in Britain) born in a property basket. (Wilmeth LANGUAGE, Granville DICTIONARY) See also: theatrical trunk babies.

borscht circuit   From shortly before World War II, the Catskill (New York) mountain region toured by vaudeville and burlesque troupes and entertainers. Borscht is a Russian beet soup popular with the many Jewish patrons.

boscaresqui (Italian)   A Renaissance term for plays on pastoral or mythological subjects. (Mantzius HISTORY II 345)

bosh lines   The violin strings a puppeteer uses to manipulate a marionette or puppet. From *bosh*, a Rumanian gypsy term for a fiddle. (Granville DICTIONARY)

boss carpenter   See: master carpenter.

boss flyman   The person in charge of the crew on the fly gallery. (Burris-Meyer/Cole SCENERY 370)

bossing out   Used of Renaissance scenery with built, three-dimensional elements, that is, embossed. (Serlio in Nagler SOURCES 75)

Boston version   A cleaned-up version of a production containing (originally) risqué material. See also: banned in Boston.

BO success   See: BO draw.

bosun's chair, bosun's stool   See: cradle.

bot (Thai)   Literally: dramatic text. The poetic text for a masked dance play (*khon*). *Bot lakon* is the text for a dance-drama with dialogue (*lakon*). (Rutnin ''Development'' 3)

bot (Vietnamese)   Literally: flour. Secondary roles in *hat boi* and *cai luong* which require only the simplest white 'flour' make-up. (Pham-Duy MUSICS 124)

bota (Malaysian)   See: *buta*.

BO timber   See: BO draw.

botou, po t'ou (Chinese)   A dance or play, and perhaps a form of theatre, which originated in Central Asia or India and was popular in the 6th C. It concerned a non-Chinese man who was eaten by a tiger and whose son pursued the beast and killed it. (Dolby HISTORY 5–6)

bottine   A 19th C woman's seamed fabric boot in beige with a black leather tip, first worn by Queen Victoria. It had elastic side gussets. Also called a jemima. (Wilcox DICTIONARY)

bottle   Informally in the U.S., an occasional backstage term for a lamp used in stage lighting. (Stern MANAGEMENT)

bottler   In Punch and Judy shows, a puppeteer's assistant who serves as a barker and a go-between from the fantasy puppet world to the audience world, and who collects coins from the spectators. Also called an interpreter, pardner, or front man. (Baird PUPPET 233, Philpott DICTIONARY, Speaight PUPPET 181, Wilmeth LANGUAGE)

bottom billing   See: billing.

bottom box   See: box.

bottom hanger iron   A piece of strap iron shaped like an L. It is attached to the bottom of a flat which is to be flown. Snatch lines from a batten are attached to top and bottom hanger irons to raise the flat. (Nelms PRIMER 130)

bottom lighting   In Britain, the instruments used to light the bottom of a setting, or, less often, the light which results. (Granville DICTIONARY, Baker THEATRECRAFT, Bowman/Ball THEATRE)

bottom rail   1. The bottom piece in the wood frame of a flat. It runs the full width of the flat and is attached to the upright stiles, usually by corner blocks. 2. See: trim rail.

boudoir cap   A softly-gathered and ruffled cap worn over curlers. (Wilcox DICTIONARY)

boudoir of the fairy baneful   In Britain, a name for a kind of fanciful stage setting common in 19th C plays. (Crampton HANDBOOK)

boukinkan   See: Buckingham.

boulevard drama   Especially in 19th C Paris, melodrama; now sometimes sophisticated comedy. The name came from the Boulevard du Crime, a street so named because the theatres on it regularly presented melodramas featuring crime and seduction. Hence, boulevard dramatist. (Barnet/Berman/Burto ASPECTS)

bounce drop   An opaque drop with a highly reflective front surface. In a typical use, light thrown upon it is cast forward to a painted or dyed scrim or other translucency (such as a very thin muslin). Also called a reflector drop.

bounce light   Light reflected from such surfaces as scenery or the stage floor. (Wehlburg GLOSSARY)

bound flow   In dance, restricted or tense movement (not necessarily undesirable). (Dell PRIMER 14)

bourdyour   See: minstrel.

bourgeois drama   Serious plays dealing with middle-class society, with an emphasis on pathos and morality. Especially popular in the 18th C.

bourrée (French)   See: *pas de bourrée*.

bourrelet (French)   A stuffed, cotton, sausage-like padding in dresses, hats, and trimmings. Also called a child's pudding, roll. (Boucher FASHION)

boutade (French)   A 17th C theatre form at the royal court of Sweden. It consisted of several impromptu scenes and was part ballet and part masquerade. (Carlson ''Scandinavia's'' 13)

bow   1. A first performance. 2. The performer's recognition of audience applause.

bowl   An amphitheatre.

bowl 'em, bowl 'em over   To delight an audience.

bow-off   1. The end of an act. 2. The final performance of a show.

BO wow   See: box-office draw.

bow snap line   A bowed stick of wood with a taut string attached to each end, used for marking lines on scenery to be painted. The string is rubbed with chalk, held against the surface to be painted, and snapped to leave a mark. See also: snap line.

bow teller   In Britain, a person (usually the stage manager) who listens to the applause at the end of a performance, and signals the cast whether or not to take another bow. (Granville DICTIONARY)

box   1. See: mansion. 2. A partly enclosed seating space in a theatre, usually more expensive and more private than other seating areas. In 1609 Dekker referred to the lords' rooms at a public theatre as boxes. Later 17th C theatres often had one or more levels of boxes, forming a U around the auditorium floor; many modern opera houses still follow this pattern, though boxes in most modern theatres are found, if at all, at the ends of a mezzanine and/or balcony, near the stage. The capacity of boxes now is usually four to six, with patrons sitting on chairs rather than fixed seats. In the 17th C some boxes could hold as many as 20 people, often on benches. 3. To mix paint by pouring it back and forth from one container to another. 4. In acting, to focus on a word, phrase, or sentence, usually by putting a pause before and after it. 5. Sometimes, as in limelight plots, shorthand for 'limelight.' Top box and bottom box refer to the relative positions, vertically, of a pair of limelights. 6. See: light booth.

box book   In 18th C theatres, a plan of the boxes, with patrons' seat assignments. (Hogan LONDON xxv)

box bookkeeper   The house servant in 18th C theatres and later who assigned places in the boxes and kept the box book. (Hogan LONDON xxiv)

box boom   Especially in an auditorium box or in a similar position, a ladder-like arrangement of pipes on which lights may be mounted; by extension, any vertical light pipe in the auditorium. The term is sometimes limited to vertical light pipes which are not floor-based.

boxcar   A chorus girl. (Berrey/Van den Bark SLANG 573)

boxed   Said of a box set—a stage setting consisting of a back wall, two side walls, and sometimes a ceiling—as opposed to an open set with a backscene and side wings.

boxes *en escalier* (English-French)   Side boxes which are stepped down from one another descending toward the proscenium, to provide better sight lines. (Mullin PLAYHOUSE 55)

box holder   1. In Shakespearean theatres, an employee who held the box into which admission money was put. (Chambers ELIZABETHAN I 356) 2. A theatre patron who subscribes for a box for the season.

boxiganga (Spanish)   A 16th C strolling troupe consisting of six or seven men, two women, and a boy. (Villandrando in Nagler SOURCES 58)

box inset   A scenic unit such as a fireplace, door, or window which is set into an opening in a flat.

box interior   See: box set.

box keepers   In 17th C British theatres and later, house servants in charge of the boxes and entrances to them. They also sold tickets for the boxes.

box light   A simple floodlight used for general illumination. The term is sometimes a shortening of open box light. (Wehlburg GLOSSARY, McCandless "Glossary" 633)

box lime   A limelight which reached the stage through a lens; a lime spotlight. The phrase is presumably from limelight box. See also: open lime. (Rees GAS 63, 202)

box lobby   An area where box patrons can lounge.

box office   1. The place in a theatre where tickets are reserved, sold, and distributed. Formerly, the office where tickets to the boxes could be obtained. Also called the BO or B.O. 2. Box-office receipts. 3. The price of tickets at the box office, as opposed to brokers' prices. 4. An attraction, such as a popular performer.

box-office appeal, box-office drag, box-office draw, box-office pull   The commercial value of a show or performer. Often shortened to BO appeal, BO drag, etc.

box-office card   In Britain, information about a play printed on stiff cardboard and displayed where tickets are sold. See also: window card. (Fay GLOSSARY)

box-office clerk   In Britain, one who sells and reserves seats at the box office of a theatre. (Fay GLOSSARY)

box-office draw   A successful show. Also called a box-office attraction, box-office click, box-office fodder, box-office success, box-office timber, box-office wow, etc. Often shortened to BO draw, etc.

box-office keeper   In 18th C British theatres and later, one who works in a box office.

box-office manager   The person in charge of all activity in a theatre's box office: ordering, printing, and selling tickets and keeping the accounts. In the professional theatre, the person is called the box-office treasurer. In some non-professional or regional theatres, the box-office manager is the theatre's business manager and may also oversee other front-of-house activities, such as publicity.

box-office name   A popular performer.

box-office order   A form exchangeable for a ticket when presented and paid for at the box office.

box-office plan   See: seating chart.

box-office poison   An author, performer, production, or play unable to attract audiences. (Bowman/Ball THEATRE)

box-office score   Box-office receipts.

box-office star   A major performer whose name in a cast can assure the success of a production. Not to be confused with billing star. (Wilmeth LANGUAGE)

box-office statement   A detailed report and inventory of ticket sales and related information on box-office activity.

box-office treasurer   See: box-office manager.

boxofficially   According to the box-office receipts.

box room   In 18th C Dublin theatres, a lounge outside the boxes where patrons could meet for conversation. See also: anti-room. (Oman GARRICK 52)

box scene   See: box set.

box screw   In 19th C British theatres, evidently a turning device to lock or unlock doors to the boxes: "door-keepers, by the box-screw, kept winding in their late arrivals. . . . " (Boaden JORDAN I 237)

box set   An interior stage setting made up of a back wall, two side walls, and sometimes a ceiling. The fourth wall, at the curtain line, is imaginary. Box sets came into use in the 1830s, but Italian designers used box sets as early as 1687, and possibly even a century earlier. Also called a box interior, box scene, a chamber set, a sealed set. Italian: *scena parapettata*. French: *scène en boîte*. (Cameron/Gillespie ENJOYMENT, Larson "Evidence" 79–90)

box teaser   An L-shaped teaser which holds and masks lights. The long horizontal bottom of the L holds a pipe and the lights affixed thereto, while the back of the L faces the audience and serves as masking. The bottom of the L is sometimes called the teaser thickness. (Dean/Carra FUNDAMENTALS 363, Bowman/Ball THEATRE)

boy   Apprentice actor, often playing female roles in the Elizabethan theatre. ". . . *Hart* was *Robinson's* Boy or Apprentice. . . . " (Wright HISTORIA 3) See also: principal boy.

boy company   In Elizabethan times, a performing troupe made up of boys.

boys   Ticket brokers. (Bowman/Ball THEATRE)

boys' *kabuki* (English-Japanese)   See: *wakashu kabuki*.

bozze (Italian)   Glass containers used as light sources or color modifiers during the Renaissance. As light sources they contained oil, or oil floating on water, and a wick. As color modifiers, they were filled with liquid of the desired color. The *bozze* varied somewhat in size and shape, but as color modifiers they were often rounded on one side and flat or convex on the other; the flat or convex side faced the light source. (Penzel LIGHTING 5–7, 11–13, fig. 2)

bozzeto (Italian)   An ensemble sketch.

BP   1. Theatre slang for the British public. 2. See: beam projector.

br   Bankroll: to finance a production.

bracae (Latin)   See: oxford bags.

(a) braccia (Latin)   Said of improvised or off-the-cuff comedy. (Oreglia COMMEDIA 1)

brace   See: corner brace, stage brace.

brace clamp   A clamp on a stage brace which allows for adjusting its length and securing it. (Bowman/Ball THEATRE)

brace cleat   A metal eye attached to the back of a flat. Into it the hook at the end of a stage brace can be fixed; the other end of the brace is secured to the stage floor. Also called a brace eye or bracing eye.

brace hook   The metal hook at the upper end of a stage brace.

brace jack   See: jack.

bracer, brace rail   See: corner brace.

brace weight   A weight or anchor, especially a notched iron counterweight, used to hold a stage brace on the floor and avoid use of a stage screw—a useful practice for fast scene shifts.

bracing eye   See: brace cleat.

bracket   1. Especially in Britain, a wall bracket (q.v.). 2. Primarily in Britain, a hanger similar to a U.S. yoke; Britain also uses fork, both terms sometimes preceded by 'tilting.' (Fay GLOSSARY; Bax MANAGEMENT 184, figs. 47, 48)

bracket clamp   A two-part clamp often used in fastening the yoke of a spotlight to a pipe; the clamp "brackets" the pipe. Since the device is most often used on light bridges, it is also called a bridge clamp. Another alternative is yoke clamp. (Lounsbury THEATRE)

bracket fixture   See: wall bracket.

bracket handle board   In Britain, a manually operated light control board which uses screw-in bracket handles to permit selective group dimming. (Corry PLANNING, Bowman/Ball THEATRE)

bracket light   See: wall bracket.

braconnière (French)   Formerly, a hip-length skirt of armor made of over-lapping steel plates. (Wilcox DICTIONARY)

Brady   A theatre seat reserved for a friend of the management; named after U.S. manager William Brady in the early 20th C. (Wilmeth LANGUAGE)

braggart captain   A frequent phrase (sometimes capitalized) for the *miles gloriosus*, a common type in Roman comedy. Also called a braggart warrior, braggart soldier, and similar terms. (Beare ROMAN 59)

braguette (French)   A codpiece. (Wilcox DICTIONARY)

braies (French)   Trunks worn by Germans, Gallo-Romans, and Romans, in varying materials and lengths. Also called: *petit draps*. (Boucher FASHION)

brail   1. See: contour curtain. 2. To attach a rope to a hanging piece of scenery or to a batten and pull it upstage, downstage, or to the side. Hence, a brail, brail line, brailing line, drag line, guide line, breast line, breasting line. See: breast. 3. To fasten a part of a scene to a batten with short pieces of ropes. (Bowman/Ball THEATRE, Fay GLOSSARY)

brail curtain   See: contour curtain.

brains   Informally, a playwright.

branc   A 15th C woman's smock. (Boucher FASHION)

branch circuit   1. The electrical path, usually the last, with the protective device (fuse or breaker) of lowest amperage. 2. An electrical path after the last fuse or circuit breaker. (Lounsbury THEATRE, Wehlburg GLOSSARY, Bowman MODERN)

branch-off connector   In lighting, a line (female) connector which can be fastened to a cable running through it, without cutting the cable; a number of connectors may be fixed to a continuous cable at different points. Sometimes called a tap-off. (Gassner/Barber PRODUCING 793)

Brandenburg   A braided loop and button fastener worn on military outerwear in the 17th C and later. See also: Austrian knot. (Wilcox DICTIONARY)

branle (French)   A lively, swaying 16th C dance. (Perugini PAGEANT 69)

bras, positions de (French)   See: *port de bras*.

brass   See: double in brass.

brasserole   A medieval camisole worn by little girls and by women after childbirth. (Wilcox DICTIONARY)

brassiere   1. A 14th-17th C short, sleeveless, fur-lined undershirt worn by women and men as nightwear. 2. According to Molière, a popular quilted jacket. 3. After 1912, a woman's undergarment to support the bosom. Sometimes called a bandeau. (Wilcox DICTIONARY)

brassiere sluffer   A strip-tease dancer.

bravura (Italian)   Literally: skill, bravery. A florid acting style. The term has been applied to the bragging soliloquies (*tirate*) of the captain in *commedia dell'arte*, but the concept also includes physical skill and the ability to speak rapidly. *Bravure* were called Italian if in the buffoonish mode, and Spanish if outrageously boastful.

brazill   In an early 17th C English translation of Sebastiano Serlio, the "virgin wax" used with other ingredients when wine was not available for color filters (bottles with colored liquid). A French translation published in the same year as the original Italian (1545) has *coppeaux de bresil*. The term is presumably related to brazil-wood, from which various red dyes have been made. (Serlio in Hewitt RENAISSANCE 33)

break   1. A pause in a rehearsal. Hence, "take a break." 2. In acting, the accidental omission of lines or business. Hence, make a break. 3. The end of an act, scene, or performance, or the interval between acts or scenes. See also: act break. Also used as a verb, as in "the show breaks at eleven." 4. To paint or roughen the surface of a property to make it look old or used. 5. To fold or unfold scenery. (Baker THEATRECRAFT, Parker/Smith DESIGN) 6. Of an electrical circuit, to interrupt the flow of current. Also, as a noun, a break in a circuit. (Bowman MODERN)

break a leg   The traditional wish of good luck among theatre people, probably deriving from the idea that a performer should give one's all in a performance. The phrase should never be directed at dancers, though it sometimes is.

break an act   To break up a partnership or team of performers.

breakaway   1. A property or piece of scenery built to break during the action of a play. In Britain: break-up, or collapse, used as either a verb or a noun. 2. A costume designed to fall off at the pull of a string, as in a Japanese *kabuki* performance (see *hikinuki*) or U.S. strip tease.

break character   In performing, to do anything not consistent with what one's character would do; to drop out of character.

breakdown   1. A fast dance popular in U.S. minstrel shows and 19th C British burlesque. 2. Later, in minstrelsy, sayings inserted in songs. 3. The process of treating costume fabrics to give the appearance of age. Also called aging, distressing. (Wilmeth LANGUAGE, Dryden FABRIC)

break down   To roughen or paint a piece of scenery, a property, or a costume to make it look used.

break-down scenery   See: demountable door frame.

breaker   Among stage technicians, a circuit breaker.

breaker magazine   See: magazine panel.

breaker switch   A circuit breaker. (Lounsbury THEATRE 148)

break-even   The point at which theatre income equals expenses. The production and the theatre each have their own break-even. In Britain, get out. (Bowman/Ball THEATRE)

breakfast food   A grass skirt. Also called a haystack or shredded wheat. (Berrey/Van den Bark SLANG 579)

break hibernation   To open a season.

break in   1. In the professional U.S. theatre, any performance before the official New York opening. 2. An obscure theatre where new vaudeville material was tested. 3. To open a show in a provincial town. By extension, a show which so opens. 4. To try out a vaudeville act or routine. 5. In Britain, to gain entrance to a theatre illegally, especially on a benefit night.

break-in act   A performance or series of performances designed to introduce a new performer.

breaking   The closing of a run of performances.

breaking point   The time in the run of a play when receipts and production costs are in balance and investors begin to receive a return on their money. See also: break-even. (Bowman/Ball THEATRE)

"Break it up!"   A command to stop routine dancing practice. (Berrey/Van den Bark SLANG 589)

break up   1. In scene design, to make a large area such as a wall or other bare space visually more interesting by dressing it with pictures, curtains, furniture, etc. 2. To make a battered sky cyclorama look acceptable by having it seen through a window or trees, or any cut-out scenic pieces that will prevent its being seen as a whole. 3. In scene painting, to use pointillage. (Nelms PRIMER 113) 4. Especially in Australia and Britain, a scenic unit or property designed to collapse. (National TECHNICAL) 5. In performing, to drop out of character and laugh at another performer's comic work. 6. To cause a fellow performer to drop character.

breast   To attach a rope to a hanging piece of scenery or to a batten which is then pulled upstage, downstage, or to one side. Hence, breasting, breasting line, breast line. Also called a drag or guide line. In Britain: brail.

breeches   1. From the 16th C in Britain, hose. Also called *grègues*, *trousses* (French), slops. See also: upper hose. 2. 17th-19th C short trousers fitting tightly below the knee. Also called *chausses*. (Barton COSTUME 216, Boucher FASHION, Walkup DRESSING 99, 111)

breeches part, breeches role   A role in which an actress dresses as a man, presumably adding sexual titillation to dramatic interest. Many of Shakespeare's characters such as Viola in *Twelfth Night* and Rosalind in *As You Like It*, though written for boy actors, became breeches parts after the Restoration. In the 18th C in England some roles written for men, such as Sir Harry Wildair in *The*

Constant Couple, were played by actresses. Also called a trousers part or trousers role.

bridge   1. The usual U.S. backstage term for a light bridge, a narrow platform on which stage lights are mounted. Most U.S. bridges hang from the grid in the first borderlight position, extend from wing to wing, and can be raised or lowered. They simplify the mounting and focusing of lights, as well as any necessary adjustments during a show. Also called a catwalk and sometimes fly bridge or flying bridge. In Britain: lighting bridge, which is occasionally used in the U.S. (Bellman SCENE, Wehlburg GLOSSARY, Lounsbury THEATRE, Bentham ART, Baker THEATRECRAFT) 2. A section of the stage floor, especially in Britain, which can be raised or lowered. 3. In a play, a transitional passage. 4. See: *hashigakari*. 5. In Britain, an orchestra pit platform with steps, used in rehearsals by the director. (Granville DICTIONARY) 6. A platform backstage in a puppet theatre, its height related to the height of the proscenium opening, where manipulators stand while working. They are hidden from view by a backdrop. See also: leaning rail, hanging rail. (Philpott DICTIONARY)

bridge clamp   See: bracket clamp.

bridge crew   In the U.S. non-professional theatre, an occasional term for crew members who work on the light bridge. Typically, they mount, focus, and gel the lighting equipment on the bridge.

bridge lights   Any stage lights mounted on a bridge. (Stern MANAGEMENT, Gassner/Barber PRODUCING 792)

bridge lines   Cables (from the gridiron) to which the light bridge is attached.

bridge operator   A crew member who works on the light bridge during a production. His duties may at times involve changing gels, running a follow spot, or even changing the focus or direction of one or more spotlights. (Halstead MANAGEMENT 163–164)

bridge position   The place of the first light batten upstage of the main curtain. Sometimes called the teaser position, since the teaser often masks the first light batten. (Cornberg/Gebauer CREW 272, Bowman/Ball THEATRE)

bridge spot   A spotlight on the light bridge. (Bowman/Ball THEATRE)

bridge trousers   Until World War II, sailor's trousers having a panel in front which fastened to the vest with three buttons, operating like a drawbridge. Also called a frontfall or broadfall. (Wilcox DICTIONARY)

bridgeway   See: *hashigakari*.

bridging   The explanatory words which a director, in rehearsal, inserts into the play's dialogue to make the meaning clearer to performers. (Bowman/Ball THEATRE)

bridging a fuse   Putting a piece of metal in place of a fuse. This is not just illegal but dangerous in the extreme: the protection not merely of equipment, but against fire, is voided. (Bellman LIGHTING 152)

bridle   See: saddle.

brief   In Britain, a free pass to a theatre.

bright lights   A theatrical district.

bring down the house   To draw an ovation from the audience.

bring 'em low   To delight an audience.

bring in   1. To lower, as a batten or some flown object. Also called: drop in, lower in. 2. To increase light intensity gradually, often imperceptibly.

bring the audience to its feet   To gain a wildly enthusiastic response.

bring up   In backstage lighting language, to increase brightness.

brisé (French)   In ballet, a small beating step in which the movement is broken. (Grant TECHNICAL)

bristle trap   In Britain, a hole in the stage floor through which a performer can rise or descend; bristles or twigs the same color as the floor project inward from the edge of the trap, making the appearance or disappearance more surprising. See also: star trap. Called in France a *trappe Anglaise* (English trap). (Bowman/Ball THEATRE, Crampton HANDBOOK)

British lounge coat   A black, braid-trimmed formal coat with a matching waistcoat, worn instead of a cutaway or morning coat. (Wilcox DICTIONARY)

broad   1. Lacking in subtlety. Usually applied to low comedy and low comedians—obvious, unrestrained, and often risqué. 2. An occasional term for a wide-angle floodlight. From film. (Wehlburg GLOSSARY)

broadfall   See: bridge trousers.

broadside   In the 17th C and later, a play announcement printed on one side of a sheet, though the more common and specific term for a theatre advertisement was a playbill or a bill. A broadside could as easily be a ballad, poem, or announcement having nothing to do with theatre. (Sobel NEW)

Broadway   The professional theatre in New York City, named for the main avenue running through the theatrical district.

Broadway Bible   See: actors' Bible.

Broadway swell   A stock minstrel show character, flashily attired in bad taste, with actions to match. He was a posturing, bold sport whose self-possession bordered on the preposterous. (Charters WILLIAMS 28)

brodequin (French)   1. Until the 16th C, a light boot derived from the *cothurnus* (Latin). 2. A shoe with a strap across the instep, worn inside boots during weapon practice. 3. An 18th C man's boot. 4. 19th C elegant footwear for women in fine linen or silk. (Boucher FASHION)

Broder singer   From about the 10th C, a wandering Jewish entertainer not unlike a troubadour. In addition to songs, often-improvised material included costumed impersonations, monologues, and, perhaps only later, playlets. The name, from 19th C descendants, means a singer from Brod (an eastern Polish city, then part of the Austro-Hungarian Empire), which produced the first famous 19th C performer of the type, Berl Broder. Also printed as Yiddish: *Di Broder Zinger*. (Sandrow VAGABOND 36–39, Sandrow in Matlaw MODERN 846)

Brodie, brodie   A theatrical failure. Named for Steve Brodie who, when found in the water below the Brooklyn Bridge in New York on 23 July 1886, said he had jumped from the bridge. Hence, to do or take a brodie. (Wilmeth LANGUAGE, Wentworth/Flexner SLANG)

broiler   See: cream puff.

broken color   Especially in scene painting, the slight varying of texture and color to make a surface more interesting. Also applicable to stage lighting and costumes.

broken medium   In Britain, a gelatine whose effect has been modified by a star-shaped hole cut in its center. (Goffin LIGHTING 63)

broken reed   A 19th C minstrel-show yodeler. (Paskman GENTLEMEN 16)

broken setting   See: divided setting.

broken speech   An interrupted speech.

broken wrist   In ballet, a fault in arm movement which causes the hand to droop or bend back, distracting from the movement as a whole. (Kersley/Sinclair BALLET)

broker   1. An agent. An intermediary who helps dramatists find producers, performers find jobs, producers find theatres, etc. 2. A ticket broker—one who sells theatre tickets at a premium.

broker's men   In Britain, a pair of comic roles in a pantomime. (Bowman/Ball THEATRE)

bronchial   In Britain, a spectator who coughs constantly during a performance and rattles the performers. (Granville DICTIONARY)

bronteion (Greek)   A thunder machine. At least three methods are thought to have been used. On the basis of Pollux' description, stones were poured from jars into a large brass container. Mantzius suggests leather bags filled with stones and beaten or thrown against metal. Haigh notes these methods and a third: lead balls dropped on a drum-tight leather surface. Under *bronteon*, the OED reports a method using heavy weights under the seating area. Also found as U.S. English bronteum. (Haigh ATTIC 218, Nicoll DEVELOPMENT 22, Mantzius HISTORY I 145, Pollux in Nagler SOURCES 9)

Bronx cheer   See: raspberry.

bronze powder   A metallic makeup used by some performers to give the effect of auburn-colored hair. A non-metallic makeup that looks metallic is safer.

broquette (French)   A tack used to attach cloth to a flat.

brother act   An act with two men.

brouhaha (French)   Molière's term for the exaggerated acting style of some of the French actors of the 17th C.

Brudder Bones   See: Bones.

Brudder Tambo   See: Tambo.

Brunetière's Law   "In drama or farce, what we ask of the theater, is the spectacle of a *will* striving towards a goal, and conscious of the means which it employs." The human will is strongly asserted and collides with contending desires or obstacles. (Brunetière in Clark/Popkin EUROPEAN 382)

brush   1. In the U.S., a sliding electrical contact, often graphite, in a dimmer. The brush alters light intensity by changing the effective voltage as it slides along the coils of the dimmer. Also called a shoe, slider, or electrical brush. (Wehlburg GLOSSARY, Lounsbury THEATRE, Bellman LIGHTING 183–184) 2. With the definite article, the provinces.

brush lining   In scene painting, a technique used when painting moldings, panels, and cornices to make them look three-dimensional.

brush-up rehearsal   A rehearsal, usually for lines only, called after a cast has had a few days between performances or has weakened during a long run. Also called a pick-up or touch-up rehearsal.

"Brush your teeth!"   A burlesque comedian's reply to a jeer from the audience. (Wilmeth LANGUAGE)

brutal   Said of slow ticket sales.

brutal brothers   In vaudeville, an act in which performers hit each other for laughs. (Wilmeth LANGUAGE)

bruton (Indonesian)   Literally: chicken tail. Descriptive term for the nose shape of the clown-servant Bagong in Javanese shadow theatre. (Long JAVANESE 71)

bubkas   The low price paid by management to a vaudevillian just breaking into the business. From Yiddish. Also called peanuts. (Smith VAUDEVILLIANS 34)

Bucco (Latin Roman)   One of the types of stock clowns of Atellan farce. He was a fool, but of what sort is uncertain. Latin *bucco* is a fool, a dolt. The name has been connected with *bucca*, for which Oxford LATIN gives "The lower part of the cheek(s) . . . (applied to persons who habitually puff out their cheeks)," quoting references in Juvenal to bombastic orators and trumpeters. See also: *fabula Atellana*. (Beare ROMAN 139, 143, 145)

buck   A hard-shoe tap dancing step, with movement from the hips down. (Davy "Burns" 346)

buck and wing   1. Originally, in minstrel shows, a clog dance with leg flings. 2. Later, a popular tap dance in vaudeville. (Wilmeth LANGUAGE)

buck a skull   A dollar admission fee.

Buckingham   A man's cap with a flat and a raised visor. Called a *montera* in Spain. Also called a boukinkan. (Boucher FASHION)

bucklebuster   A bit, such as a line, which draws a huge laugh in vaudeville or burlesque. (Wilmeth LANGUAGE)

bucksain   A 19th C man's padded overcoat with wide sleeves. (Boucher FASHION)

buddy puppet   A teaching aid, often a fuzzy, huggable animal with whom children may form a bond, who develops a personality and voice with which children may identify. Used to assist children in articulating their problems, and by the teacher to introduce concepts, maintain order, and tell stories. (Hunt/Renfro PUPPETRY 52–53)

Bude light   For a time in 19th C Britain, one of the names for a limelight. Sir Goldsworthy Gurney, who lived in Bude, Cornwall, invented the oxy-hydrogen blowpipe used in limelights. In 1839, when limelights had already been used in the theatre, a patent issued to Gurney and Frederick Rixon made clear that the Bude light used oxygen but not lime. Nevertheless, Gurney's partisans continued to use 'Bude light' for 'limelight' into the 1840s and beyond. (Rees GAS 64)

budger   In Britain, a comic whose skill can persuade (budge) spectators into laughter. (Granville DICTIONARY)

buechel (Yiddish)   Literally: book, small book. A literary play; a play better suited to the library than the stage. Such plays, not quite closet dramas, were occasionally performed, but even their producers sometimes viewed them with scorn. Also spelled *bichele*. (Lifson YIDDISH 174, 334)

buer, pu erh (Chinese)   An elderly female character; a type of stock character in Yuan *zaju*. (Dolby HISTORY 60)

buffcoat   A 16th-17th C buffalo-hide military coat. Officers' versions were richly trimmed with embroidery, lace, loops, buttons, and often precious metals. (Wilcox DICTIONARY)

buffo   A burlesque actor. From the Italian *buffa* (feminine), *buffo* (masculine), and *buffe*, *buffi* (plural) for singers of comic roles in opera.

buffoon   1. A clown type: an apparently stupid rustic. 2. In opera, a male singer specializing in comic roles (Italian: *buffo*); hence *opera buffa* (comic opera). (Wilmeth LANGUAGE)

bug (Korean)   See: *puk*.

bugaku (Japanese)   Literally: dance and music. Court dance, often masked, introduced from China and supported at the imperial court and major Shinto shrines since c. 8th C. The current repertory consists of 61 dances. See also: *gagaku, samai, umai*. (Wolz BUGAKU 1)

bug hole   In Britain, a second- or third-rate theatre. Also called a flea pit. (Granville DICTIONARY)

bughouse *Hamlet* A burlesque of *Hamlet*, popular in late 19th C variety halls. (Gilbert VAUDEVILLE 59–60)

buhat habagat (Philippine) The Western faction in fight sequences in *comedia*. (Mendoza COMEDIA 65)

Bühne (German) The stage.

Bühnenbild (German) A stage setting.

Bühnenfassade (German) Literally: stage facade, stage front. The scenic facade of the Graeco-Roman theatre. See also: *scaenae frons*. (Flickinger GREEK 61)

Bühnenplan (German) Floor plan of a stage.

Bühnenregulator (German) For a time between the two World Wars, and perhaps somewhat earlier and later, the group of handles which controlled dimmers. This was then distinct from the switchboard proper. Plural: adds *-en*. (Fuchs LIGHTING 367–370)

Bühnenreif (German) Literally: stage ripe. Said of a performer trained and ready to appear on stage.

Bühnensprache (German) Stage speech.

build 1. A show whose box office business is improving. 2. To increase intensity in acting, usually by quickening the tempo or raising the volume or both; to develop toward a climax. Hence, build it, build it up, build up. 3. To develop a character. 4. To increase the intensity of the stage lighting. 5. To construct scenery or costumes. (Bowman/Ball THEATRE, Wentworth/Flexner SLANG, Stern MANAGEMENT)

building See: scaffold.

building carpenter See: master carpenter.

building crew A crew consisting of carpenters, painters, electricians, flymen, and those in charge of properties and special effects. (Bowman/Ball THEATRE)

building on the stage Bleacher seating on stage, a common practice in 18th C French and British theatres in order to accommodate more playgoers. (Avery LONDON xlvi, Troubridge BENEFIT 142)

building sharers Investors in a theatre building (as opposed to investors in a theatrical company). The term and practice date from as early as Elizabethan times. (Nicoll HISTORY I 297)

build up 1. An audience consisting largely of pass-holders. 2. In playwriting, initial plot development. 3. To groom a performer for a leading part.

build-up Publicity for a performer or production. (Berrey/Van den Bark SLANG 571)

built   A scenic piece which is constructed in three dimensions rather than painted to so appear. Hence, built unit, built rock, built up, etc. See also: set piece.

built-in insurance   An element in a theatrical production that is thought to insure its success, such as a star performer, a play by an established playwright, etc.

built-out box   Especially in Britain, an extension to a stage box on a benefit night. (Troubridge BENEFIT 143)

buka (Japanese)   Literally: dance and song. In *no*, the technical skills of dancing and singing, as opposed to acting (*monomane*). (Tsubaki "Performing" 300)

buka panggung (Malaysian)   Literally: opening the stage. A ritual that begins a traditional theatre performance such as *ma'yong* or *wayang kulit* that is designed to insure a receptive audience and to call on the spirits for blessing. (Sweeney RAMAYANA 275) Yousof gives a detailed list of prayers, music, and songs that make up the ritual in *ma'yong*. ("Kelantan" 146–171)

bukkaeri (Japanese)   A costume technique developed in *kabuki* and also used in *bunraku*. The upper part of the kimono is dropped around the hips to reveal a different kimono beneath it. The changed costume indicates a significant alteration of personality or character, as when the gentle priest Narukami turns into the God of thunder in *Narukami, the Thunder God*. (Brandon in Brandon/Malm/Shively STUDIES 110)

bulb   1. The transparent envelope, usually glass or quartz, which surrounds the light-giving elements of an incandescent lamp. 2. Loosely, the entire lamp. This is essentially a lay meaning used by some theatre people but not by lighting technicians. (Bellman SCENE, Sellman/Lessley ESSENTIALS)

bulldog   An iron grip used to fasten one cable or line to another. Also called a line grip. See also: clew and sunday. (Bowman/Ball THEATRE)

bull frog   A melodrama performer with a deep voice. Hence, any actor so endowed. (Granville DICTIONARY)

bull line   A heavy, four-strand hemp rope used on a winch to raise units which are not counterweighted. (Parker/Smith DESIGN)

bull roar, bull roarer   A large metal can open at one end, with a cord running through a hole in the closed end; when the cord is held taut and rubbed with rosin, a variety of roaring sounds can be made. (Lounsbury THEATRE)

bull's-eye lantern   In 19th C theatres, a tin box holding a lamp, with a hole or holes in the side of the box, to which lenses were attached. (Mullin "London" 84)

bull switch   An occasional term for the stage main, or, sometimes, for a master switch which controls selected groups of circuits. See also: company switch. (Bellman LIGHTING 145, Bowman/Ball THEATRE)

bull wheel winch   A winch designed to operate a brail-type (contour) asbestos curtain where headroom is too limited for other types.

bululu (Spanish)   A single 17th C strolling player. (Villandrando in Nagler SOURCES 57)

bum   A third-rate chorus girl. (Berrey/Van den Bark SLANG 573)

bump   1. To drop a scenic unit to the floor forcefully, either in error or to help restore trim. 2. To increase or decrease the intensity of a lighting instrument suddenly: to bump up or down. 3. A sudden forward lunge of the pelvis by a stripper or exotic dancer. See: bumps and grinds. (Lounsbury THEATRE, Wilmeth LANGUAGE)

bumper   1. A stationary downstage platform against which moving platforms can bump. 2. A metal hoop attached to a batten carrying lighting instruments; the hoop protects the instruments from flown scenic units and scenic units from the hot instruments. (Parker/Smith DESIGN) 3. Especially in the 18th and 19th C, a night when a theatre is filled to capacity.

bumper house   In Britain, a sold-out performance. (Granville DICTIONARY)

bumper play   See: *zhengben daxi*.

bump in   In Australia, to put up a stage setting and lights.

bump on   To switch on. Occasionally, to be switched on, as in "Number 6 can bump on with the chandelier."

bump out   In Australia, to take down a stage setting and lights.

bumps and blackout drama   A burlesque show.

bumps and grinds   The provocative body movements, especially of the pelvis, made by strippers.

bump up, bang up   To increase light intensity as rapidly as possible. (Stern MANAGEMENT)

bunch   An old term for members of the chorus. (Wilmeth LANGUAGE)

bunched filament   See: concentrated filament.

bunch light, bunchlight, bunch   A floodlight consisting of a group of small light sources. The 19th C gas bunch light contained a number of flames inside a single reflector. In the early years of electricity, the flames gave way to carbon filament lamps, which were later replaced by low wattage tungsten lamps. With the development of high wattage incandescent lamps, the bunchlight has gradually disappeared. The last three citations below have illustrations. In Britain, gas standard was sometimes used for the early fixture. (Bellman SCENOGRAPHY 566; Fay GLOSSARY; McCandless "Glossary" 633; Fuchs LIGHTING 182; Hartmann LIGHTING 61–62; Rees GAS 41, figs. 21, 22)

bungakusei (Japanese)   See: *engekisei*.

bun no mai (Japanese)   'Civil' dance in *bugaku*. A graceful, elegant dance in which the dancers wear the dress of civil servants. Analogous to Chinese *wen* style performance. (Immoss/Mayer JAPANESE 50) See also: *bu no mai*.

bu no mai (Japanese)   'Martial' dance in *bugaku*. A heroic, virile dance in which the dancers carry a sword or halberd. Analogous to Chinese *wu* style performance. (Immoss/Mayer JAPANESE 50) See also: *bun no mai*. (Inoura HISTORY 36)

bunraku (Japanese)   Puppet theatre of the most sophisticated type, in which each puppet is manipulated by three puppeteers and the puppets move on a full-sized stage within built sets. In each scene of a multi-act play, one chanter (*tayu*) sings and speaks all narrative and dialogue passages, accompanied by one *shamisen* player. The term is from the name of the 19th C puppeteer, Bunrakuken (also Bunrakken). Also called *ayatsuri ningyo shibai*, *joruri*. See also: *gidayu*, *maruhon*.

bunshichi (Japanese)   A *bunraku* puppet head representing a virtuous middle-aged man, often a warrior tormented by secret grief. The most commonly used head in history plays (*jidaimono*). From the name of the puppet character Karigane Bunshichi. (Keene BUNRAKU 210)

bunya bushi (Japanese)   One of three early types of narrative music and chanting—*noroma* and *sekkyo bushi* being the others—preserved today mainly on Sado Island. (Keene BUNRAKU 56)

burag-je (Korean)   See: *sonang-je*.

burattino (Italian)   Literally: little dummy. A puppet or marionette.

burble   To mix up one's words.

burdash   An 18th C fringed sash tied around a man's waist. (Chalmers CLOTHES 212)

burla (Italian)   A practical joke in *commedia dell'arte*, similar to a *lazzo*. (Lea ITALIAN I 66, 186)

burlap ingenue   See: burlesque ingenue.

burlesque   1. A dramatic parody of a well-known play, person, or institution. Hence, to burlesque something or someone. 2. In the U.S., a variety show which stresses low comedy and undressed or undressing women who dance. (Hennequin PLAYWRITING 53)

burlesque comedy   A Russian play of the 1730s ridiculing ignorant physicians and attacking foreigners, especially the Dutch. (Varneke RUSSIAN 66)

burlesque ingenue   An incompetent female burlesque performer. Often pronounced 'burlap' ingenue. (Wilmeth LANGUAGE)

burlesque queen   A leading stripper.

burlesquerie   A burlesque theatre.

burlesque tragedy   A frequent rendering of Latin *hilarotragodia*.

burletta   Literally: a small joke. The word comes from the Italian—a diminutive of *burla*: a practical joke. 1. A form of musical comedy half-way between opera and comic opera. The form is Italian in origin but was popular in England in the 18th C, when it was sometimes used to evade the Licensing Act. A play in three acts with five or six songs, it continued into the 19th C. 2. In early 19th C London, a short piece in recitative, rhymed, with an orchestral accompaniment. 3. A short farce with a slight plot. (Bowman/Ball THEATRE, Murray "Elliston's" 99)

burleycue, burlycue, burlecue, burlicue, burley-q, burley, burleskue   Burlesque.

burley wheel   A burlesque circuit.

Burma circuit   See: kerosene circuit.

burn base   An occasional term for the usually removable socket assembly in an ellipsoidal reflector spotlight. (Bellman SCENE)

burner, gas burner   In 19th C gas lighting systems, a jet capable of delivering gas; 'burner' also means the jet and flame. Among the types of burners: Argand, rat tail, cockspur, cockscomb, batwing, and fishtail. (Rees GAS 7, 13–14, figs. 1, 2, 10)

burner light   Primarily in Britain, a cluster of lights on a pipe stand. The term is an apparent equivalent of 'bunch light.' (Purdom PRODUCING, Downs THEATRE II 1130, Bowman/Ball THEATRE)

burning position   The angle at which an incandescent lamp gives its best service. See also: base down burning, base up burning, universal burning. (Fuchs LIGHTING 156, 157, 161)

burn out   Formerly, to lighten gelatine colors by exposure to sunlight or to the light of the instruments in which the gelatines are to be used. Length of exposure varies with the color, but more than an hour or two is usually required. (Rubin/Watson LIGHTING 57)

burnt cork   Makeup used in the past by white minstrel performers to blacken their skin. Hence, cork up.

burnt sugar   A substance which, when mixed with water, frequently represents an onstage beverage. (Granville DICTIONARY)

burr-head   A minstrel performer; the term comes from the practice of white performers wearing furry wigs in minstrel shows. (Wilmeth LANGUAGE)

bury the show   To strike (take down and store) the scenery, properties, lights, costumes, etc.

bus, bus.   Stage business.

bus and truck house   An off-the-beaten-track theatre featuring touring companies traveling by bus, with their physical production traveling by truck. Hence bus and truck tour, bus and truck company, etc. (Wilmeth LANGUAGE)

(the) bush   The provinces.

bushes   A false beard.

business   1. Stage action as distinct from dialogue, such as lighting a cigarette, pouring a drink, handling a book, etc. 2. A sequence of such actions, forming a piece of business. 3. The theatrical profession—when he or she is in the business. 4. Attendance or theatrical income—whether business is good or bad. 5. See: line of business.

business cue   A cue, usually for lights, sound, or curtain, based on something a performer does rather than on a line of dialogue.

business manager   The person in charge of a theatre's or a producing company's business affairs. In the professional theatre, often called a general manager. In Britain: acting manager.

business property   A property used by a performer, as opposed to one on stage for decorative or other purposes.

business rehearsal   A rehearsal which focuses on stage business—as opposed to a line rehearsal.

busk   1. To perform on a street corner, vacant lot, or any location where passersby might stop. In Britain, to do so for a line at a theatre or outside a bar. A hat is passed for donations. 2. Especially in Britain, to tour with simple and scanty equipment. Hence, busker, busking. From buskin or boot. (Wilmeth LANGUAGE) Or from *busquer* (Old French), to seek one's fortune. (Granville DICTIONARY) 3. A piece of wood placed in a stomacher to produce the effect of a straight line (Russell COSTUME). 4. See: cuirass.

buskin   1. The boot of classical tragedy, which by the 2nd C BC acquired a thick sole. 2. Tragedy. 3. Acting, especially tragic acting. 4. Primarily in Britain, the profession of theatre. The source of the word is uncertain. Recent suggestions include old French *brousequin* or *broisequin*, middle Dutch *broseken* or *brosekin*, and Italian *borzachino*; these vary in meaning from small shoe to high boot; see also the OED. See also: *kothornos*, *soccus*, sock and buskin. (Barnet/Berman/Burto ASPECTS 255–256, Bowman/Ball THEATRE, Partridge ORIGINS, Granville DICTIONARY)

bust cold   See: open cold.

bust developer   One who croons offstage during a strip tease. (Wilmeth LANGUAGE)

bustling comedian   A performer who specializes in dashing, impudent parts. (Rowell in Donohue MANAGER 191)

busy body   A cooch dancer. (Berrey/Van den Bark SLANG 573)

buta (Indonesian, Malaysian)   From Sanskrit *bhuta* (evil being). An ogre figure in *wayang* and classical dance theatre. (Sweeney RAMAYANA 5) 1. In Sundanese *wayang golek*, grotesque monsters (*bebas*) and noble giants (*tetep*). (Foley "Sundanese" 32) 2. In Bali and Java, a non-human monster, as distinct from the more noble *raksasa*. (Holt ART 59, de Zoete/Spies DANCE 25) Also spelled *boeta* in Java and Bali and *bota* in Sunda. Also called *raksasa, danawa* or *denawa*. (Long JAVANESE 70)

butaca (Spanish)   A theatre seat with arms and a back. Also the term used in the Philippines in the early 20th C for an orchestra seat. (Hernandez EMERGENCE 182)

butai (Japanese)   A stage. The term is used for the main stage of all types of theatres: *kabuki, bunraku, no, kyogen,* and modern theatres. (Ernst KABUKI 32) In *no*, the term refers specifically to the square, roofed main stage (*hon butai*) and the attached rear stage (*ato za*) and side stage (*waki za*). It is on this stage area that the main action of the play occurs, and the musicians, stage assistants, and chorus members sit. The bridgeway (*hashigakari*) is considered a separate area, and not a part of the main stage. (Komparu NOH 128)

butaika (Japanese)   Literally: make stageworthy. To dramatize or make a theatre performance out of a novel or short story.

butai sochi (Japanese)   See: *dogu*.

buta-kala (Indonesian)   Demons in the retinue of the Balinese *barong keket* who possess the chorus of villagers in the *barong* dance-drama. (de Zoete/Spies DANCE 98)

butcher   A vendor of candy, literature, music, pictures, etc. at a burlesque or other variety house. Also called a candy butcher.

buttafuori (Italian)   A callboy.

butter-and-egg man   1. A wealthy patron who invests in a theatrical venture. (Berrey/Van den Bark SLANG 574) 2. In Britain, a no-talent performer who puts on some form of ''entertainment'' for money. Granville says, ''He might as well sell groceries.'' (Granville DICTIONARY)

butterfly dance   A non-dance performed by female vaudevillians in which they posed in diaphanous gowns while colored slides, giving a butterfly effect, were projected upon them. Two sticks were positioned on the hem of the gown, and the performer moved these to enhance the butterfly effect. (Laurie VAUDEVILLE 40)

button buster   A comedian.

buttons   A small salary.

buy   A block purchase of tickets, usually by a ticket agency or broker. When an agency makes such a purchase, they make a 'buy.' Such tickets are not returnable or exchangeable at the box office.

buyo (Japanese)   Literally: dance. A 20th C generic term for dance, whether Japanese or Western. See also: *nihon buyo*. (Gunji BUYO 75)

buyo geki (Japanese)   Literally: dance-drama. In *kabuki*, a dance play that includes dialogue, dramatic development, and conflict. See also: *shosagoto*. (Brandon CLASSIC 19)

buzzer   See: lobby bell.

bycocket   See: abacot.

by desire   By request.

byplay   Stage business that is not the main focus of attention but takes place while the main action is going on, as in Molière's *Tartuffe*, when Orgon reacts under the table while Tartuffe is trying to seduce his wife. (Cameron/Gillespie ENJOYMENT)

byrnie   See: hauberk.

Byron collar   A 19th C woman's wide, sailor-style collar. (Walkup DRESS-ING 322)

bytovaia komediia (Russian)   A satirical comedy of manners. Also called a *komediia nravov*. (Welsh RUSSIAN 102–108)

C

C   1. Center (of the stage). 2. See: C-lamp.

C (Latin Roman)   Probably an abbreviation of *canticum* (song). The letter appears in some manuscripts of Plautus at the beginnings of scenes or after the names of some characters. See also: *DV*. (Beare ROMAN 220, 229)

cabale (French)   A group of theatregoers who work together to bring about the rise or fall of a play or performer by means of shouts, jeers, shrieks, etc. See also: claque.

caban   A wide-sleeved, close-fitting, sometimes belted coat with unsewn side seams, of Arab origin. Fashionable from the 14th C to the present. Also called a gabardine. (Boucher FASHION)

cabasset   See: morion.

cabinet   In 18th C exterior and interior settings, a window and/or door flat placed between side wings. (Larson ''Evidence'' 89)

cabinet drawing   An oblique drawing with dimensions on the oblique angles reduced to one half. (Gillette/Gillette SCENERY)

cable   See: stage cable.

cable clamp   Usually a device for securing a cable such as a borderlight cable, ordinarily to a horizontal pipe batten. Other smaller types are sometimes used, as in attaching cable or wire to a wall or ceiling. (Bowman/Ball THEATRE, Lounsbury THEATRE 24)

cable connector   A female stage connector which has a single large hole (about a half-inch in diameter) for insertion of stage cable. See also: pin connector. (Cornberg/Gebauer CREW 152)

cable cradle   A curved metal cable holder used to suspend borderlight cable so that the cable is not damaged or kinked when a lifting line is attached. Also called a cradle support, cradle cable support, cable cradle support, cradle. Fuchs has an illustration. (Fuchs LIGHTING 173, 174)

cable hanger   See: cable hook.

cable hook   In stage lighting, a heavy, stiff wire U attached to a light stand so that excess cable can be coiled and hung from the stand. Lounsbury has an illustration. (Lounsbury THEATRE 70, Bowman MODERN)

cable slot   On a gridiron, the space between loft-block beams. (Burris-Meyer/Cole SCENERY 260)

cable support   A heavy bracket which prevents the weight of a borderlight cable from pulling at the borderlight. The cable support is fastened near the end of the pipe from which the borderlight is hung; the support is then also fastened securely to the borderlight cable. The support and the pipe, not the borderlight, thus bear the weight of the cable. Fuchs has an illustration. (Fuchs LIGHTING 173-174)

cable cradle support   See: cable cradle.

cabotinage (French)   1. A strolling player's life. 2. Bad acting.

cabriole (French)   1. A 16th-17th C leaping dance. 2. A caper. In ballet, a step of elevation in which the extended legs are beaten in the air. (Winter BALLET 7, Grant TECHNICAL)

cabriolet   See: *calèche*.

cabtyre cable, cabtyre, cab tyre   In Britain, rubber-covered stage cable. (Rae/Southern INTERNATIONAL, Bowman/Ball THEATRE, Baker THEATRECRAFT)

cache-folie (French)   An early 19th C small wig used to hide the short hair women often wore after the French Revolution. (Boucher FASHION)

cache-nez (French)   See: *touret*.

cackle   In Britain, a term for dialogue, especially meaningless patter spoken by a performer to cover forgotten lines or a missed entrance. Hence, cackle-chucker or cackle-thrower (prompter), cackler (performer), which is sometimes used in the U.S. (Bowman/Ball THEATRE, Granville DICTIONARY)

cacky   In burlesque, obscene or risqué. (Wilmeth LANGUAGE)

cacology   In Britain, a blanket term covering a performer's muddy articulation, fast-and-loose phonology, faulty diction, or errant pronunciation. (Granville DICTIONARY)

cadalso (Spanish)   A 17th C scaffold or temporary stage. Also found as *cadahalso*, *cadafal*, *cadaffal* and *cadafalch*. (Shergold SPANISH)

cadence   A 17th and 18th C rhetorical affectation involving the giving of emphasis to words (also called toning; see: tone). (Highfill in Hume LONDON 167)

çadir hayal (Turkish)   Literally: tent play. 1. In parts of central Asia and Turkestan, a puppet or marionette theatre. 2. In Turkestan, a string puppet or marionette. (And KARAGÖZ 22-23, 25) *cae el telon* (Spanish)   See: *telon*.

cage   1. See: balcony box. 2. Sometimes, an enclosure of heavy wire which separates a light control board from the surrounding area. 3. Any enclosure or partial enclosure which protects delicate (or valuable) theatre equipment or supplies, such as tickets, tools, or sound control equipment. (Bowman/Ball THEATRE, Lounsbury THEATRE)

cagneux (French)   See: *arqué*.

caichaxi, ts'ai ch'a hsi (Chinese)   Literally: tea-picking plays. A form of flower drum play (*huaguxi*) which developed from labor folk songs sung during tea harvests. (Dolby HISTORY 220)

caidan (Chinese)   See: *choudan*.

cai luong (Vietnamese)   Literally: reformed theatre. A scripted form of popular sung drama, usually melodramatic, that draws upon *hat boi, tuong tau*, and southern folk song traditions. Emotionally evocative melodies are its hallmark, with some forty to fifty numbers in a play. *Cai luong* developed in southern Vietnam in the 20th C, attained its highest popularity in the 1930s, and remained important in the south through the 1970s. Also called *hat cai luong* (sung reformed theatre). See also: *tuong Phat, tuong tau, tuong tien*. (Song VIETNAMESE 27-33, Brandon SOUTHEAST 76, Pham-Duy MUSICS 114-115, Addiss "Theater" 144)

Cain's   See: gone to Cain's.

cainsil   See: chainse.

caiqiao, ts'ai ch'iao (Chinese)   1. To walk on small wooden platform shoes in simulation of the gait of a woman with bound feet; a skill of female role (*dan*) performers, especially flower female (*huadan*) performers. Not used since 1949 in the People's Republic of China. 2. The shoes themselves. (Scott CLASSICAL 143-144)

cak (Indonesian)   See: *kecak*.

cakes   A small salary.

cakewalk   A lively, high-stepping dance, originally competitive and performed by U.S. Black couples. The winners received a cake; hence, take the cake. (Wilmeth LANGUAGE)

cakewalk wedding   A popular U.S. vaudeville dance act showing a couple's meeting, engagement, wedding, and honeymoon. (Charters WILLIAMS 351)

ca kich bai choi (Vietnamese)   Literally: hut-game theatre. One type of modern folk theatre (see: *kich*). The term comes from gambling games (*bai choi*) in which a man sings the names or numbers of the cards being played in order to attract more participants. (Pham-Duy MUSICS 149-152) Also called *hat bai choi* (Addiss "Theater" 149-150) and *san khau ca kich bai choi* (Pham-Duy MUSICS 149).

cakyar (Malayalam)   A sub-caste of temple servants in Kerala who are the hereditary actors of *kutiyattam*. Also spelled *chakkiar, cakkiyar, chakkyar*. (Enros in Baumer/Brandon SANSKRIT 275)

calash   See: *calèche*.

calcium   A spotlight. (Sobel HANDBOOK)

calcium light, calcium lime, calcium   See: limelight.

cale   1. A hood with double ribbons knotted under the chin. 2. A flat cap covering the top of the head. (Boucher FASHION)

calèche (French)   An 18th C high hood on a hooped folding frame, like a carriage roof. Also called a cabriolet, calash, caravan, Friends bonnet, Friends hood, Quaker bonnet, Thérèse. (Barton COSTUME 342, Wilcox DICTIONARY)

caliper stage   A proscenium stage with arm-like extensions on each side into the front of the auditorium. See also: side stage.

call   1. An audition. 2. A summons for a rehearsal. 3. A rehearsal. 4. A warning to performers that curtain time is approaching: a half-hour call, a five-minute call, etc. 5. A prompter's note to warn performers of coming entrances. Used also to warn music and other effects. See also: be ready. 6. A notice on the call board for cast or crew or both. Various combinations: rehearsal call, photo call, company call, train call, etc. 7. An appearance before the audience at the end of a performance: a curtain call. 8. See: swazzle.

call back   A tryout or audition for roles in a production in which the best possibilities for roles not already filled are brought together, usually for ensemble readings.

call beginners   The stage manager's direction to the call boy or an assistant to summon the performers needed for the opening scene.

call bell   1. A prompter's bell used to summon performers to their places. 2. A stage manager's signal to warn the audience that an act is about to begin. Sometimes called an act call bell.

call-board, callboard   A bulletin board backstage on which casting, rehearsal notices, costume appointments, etc. are posted.

call book   In the 18th C and later, a manuscript list used by the call boy or prompter's assistant to warn performers of forthcoming entrances.

call boy, call girl   A person who warns performers of their entrances. Also called a prompter's boy or prompter's girl.

call door   A proscenium door, used in the 19th C and earlier by actors taking bows. (Bowman/Ball THEATRE)

call girl   See: call boy.

callithumpian   Especially in Britain, music which is raucous and discordant or the player of such. (Granville DICTIONARY)

call man   A porter in an 18th C theatre in Britain who would go to performers' lodgings and give them their day's schedule. (Everard MEMOIRS 40)

call out   To demand a curtain speech, as when an audience refuses to stop applauding at the end of a performance, wanting a star to reappear and acknowledge the applause. (Granville DICTIONARY)

call over   In Britain, a telephone call from the box office to ticket agents to identify sold and unsold seats for that night's performance. (Fay GLOSSARY)

call sheet   For a company going on tour, an information sheet posted by the stage manager giving details about the move from one city to another, such as train times, baggage-pickup times, performance time, etc. (Gruver/Hamilton STAGE)

call the act   A direction from the stage manager to warn performers that an act is about to begin.

call time   To advise a cast how many minutes remain before curtain.

calonarang (Indonesian)   A Balinese dance-drama, created c. 1890, that provides a dramatic frame for the appearance of the magically powerful widow (*rangda*). It is given in a special performance area (*kalangan*), prepared at a graveyard or a cross-roads where danger lurks. Also spelled *chalonarang* or *tjalonarang*. See also: *barong, wayang calonarang*. (Bandem/deBoer BALINESE 131-142)

calotte, calot (French)   A skullcap. Also called a Juliet cap or a *zucchetto* (Italian). See also: caul.

calpac, calpack   See: *kolpak*.

calvi mimici (Latin Roman)   Bald-headed mimes. These mimes are sometimes identified with the *stupidus*, who is also a true fool, i.e., one who is deceived by all. Ancient references indicate that in early times these mimes used shaved heads, not wigs. *Mimus calvus* (singular) is sometimes seen for the same meaning. *Calvus* and a number of related Latin words have to do with baldness, but *calvor* means to deceive; according to an ancient commentator, this verb, notably in the form *calvitur* (he is deceived), comes from the bald-headed mime as *stupidus*. (Nicoll MASKS 87-88)

camaram (Malayalam)   Long false hair worn by *kathakali* actors. (Jones/Jones KATHAKALI 107)

cambaleo (Spanish)   A 17th C strolling troupe consisting of five men and a woman. (Villandrando in Nagler SOURCES 58)

cambiamento a vista (Italian)   See: *a vista*.

cambré (French)   Literally: bent. In ballet, bending the body from the waist. (Kersley/Sinclair BALLET)

came in to get warm   Said of an unresponsive audience, especially in vaudeville. Also called cold or cold house. (Wilmeth LANGUAGE)

camel driver A supernumerary, a spear bearer. (Cartmell HANDBOOK)

cameo A small but well-written role, sometimes played by a performer of some repute.

camisole 1. A 16th-17th C shirt or undershirt, sleeved or sleeveless. 2. The top half of a slip, worn under a sheer blouse. 3. A neckline characterized by shoulder straps holding up a bodice cut straight across. (Wilcox DICTIONARY)

camp Exaggerated mannerisms, often effeminate. Hence, campy, to camp it up.

campaign wig A military and traveling wig of the 17th-18th C, having a curly toupee in front and pigeon's wings over the ears. The back hair was held in a black silk bag. Also called a toupee wig. See also: bagwig. (Wilcox DICTIONARY)

campala (Indonesian) See: *cempala*.

camper A chorus boy. (Berrey/Van den Bark SLANG 573)

campo (Italian) See: *platea*.

Canadian wheel A vaudeville circuit in the northeastern U.S. and eastern Canada in the 1920s, traveled by U.S. entertainers.

canal (Spanish) A groove for sliding scenic units. (Shergold SPANISH)

canale (Italian) Literally: channel. A groove in which a scenic unit can slide. (Southern CHANGEABLE 344)

canang (Malaysian) See: *gamelan*.

canary 1. A singer in the chorus of a musical theatre piece. 2. A solo female vocalist. 3. A 16th C lively court dance.

canavaccio, canovaccio (Italian) See: scenario.

cancan A bawdy, spirited French dance of the late 19th C characterized by high kicks, rear views, and other anatomical revelations considered shocking in their day.

cande (Kannada, Malayalam) In *yaksagana*, *kathakali*, and *krishnanattan*, a cylindrical drum played with fingers or sticks that introduces special characters and battle scenes or emphasizes movements. Also spelled *chande*, *centa*, *chanta*. (Ashton/Christie YAKSAGANA 3, 4, 8, 49, 61, 90; Jones/Jones KATHAKALI 77-78)

candegara (Kannada) In *yaksagana*, a *cande* drummer. (Ashton/Christie YAKSAGANA 51)

candelabra, candelabra base The smallest lamp base ordinarily used on the U.S. stage. The candelabra is about two-thirds the diameter of the medium base, which is the standard household size. (Bellman LIGHTING fig. 2-3b, Wehlburg GLOSSARY)

candilejas (Spanish) Footlights.

candle hoop   In the 17th C and for a time after, a circular lighting fixture suspended above the heads of the actors; tallow candles were placed around the circle. Hoops were also used in the auditorium. Also called a corona or ring. (Fuchs LIGHTING 36, Bellman LIGHTING 122)

candle keeper, candle man   In 18th C theatres and earlier, a house servant responsible for the wax and tallow candles used around a theatre. He was a chandler and either served as a candle snuffer or was in charge of the candle snuffers. (Stone LONDON 817)

candy butcher   See: butcher.

canevas (French)   A plot outline or scenario used by Italian *commedia dell'arte* players to remind them of entrances, exits, and business—but not dialogue. The information was written on a piece of canvas hung backstage. (Perugini PAGEANT 113)

canggu (Chinese)   See: *canjunxi.*

cangklet-cengkah (Indonesian)   Javanese *wayang kulit* fighting technique in which two characters grasp each other at the waist and push one another back and forth across the screen. (Long JAVANESE 82)

cangtou (Chinese)   See: *canjunxi.*

canh tuong (Vietnamese)   A theatrical entertainment that evolved, during the 12th and 13th C, into *tuong.* Dancing, singing, and skits were presented as a kind of variety show. It may have contributed to the development of *hat boi.* (Pham-Duy MUSICS 113, Addiss "Theater" 136-137)

canion, canon   16th C short, shaped breeches of silk, often with slashings and worn with a codpiece. (Wilcox DICTIONARY)

canjun (Chinese)   See: *canjunxi.*

canjunxi, ts'an chün hsi (Chinese)   Literally: adjutant play. A type of play, and very likely a form of theatre, popular from the 7th to the 9th C. At least one version involved acting, speaking, singing, costume, and makeup. Such plays included two main roles, the butt (*canjunzhuang* or *ts'an chün chuang,* literally "adjutant pillar," abbreviated *canjun* or *ts'an chün*) and the knave (*canggu* or *ts'ang ku,* literally "gray hawk," also called *cangtou* or *ts'ang t'ou,* literally "gray head") by whom he was maltreated. Apparently, these two functions were on occasion reversed. (Dolby HISTORY 7, Liu INTRODUCTION 160)

canjunzhuang (Chinese)   See: *canjunxi.*

cannon   1. In the Restoration, a male's linen stocking with a beribboned flounce of attached lace extending over the breeches. 2. Possibly the flounce, worn without the stocking. (Barton COSTUME 280, 294)

canon   See: canion.

canopy   In Elizabethan times: 1. A term for the heavens (q.v.). 2. A curtained alcove. (Bowman/Ball THEATRE) *cantada* (Philippine)   Singing in *cenaculo*. (Salazar in Cruz SHORT 97)

cantant (Latin)   Literally: they sing. In Elizabethan drama, a stage direction for a song.

cantarina (Italian)   An actress who was in charge of singing *intermezzi* or short songs in the *commedia dell'arte*. (Duchartre ITALIAN 268)

cantat (Latin)   A stage direction in a medieval play indicating that a line is to be sung or chanted. (Chambers MEDIAEVAL II 90)

cantica (Latin Roman)   1. Broadly, all meters in comedy except the iambic senarius. 2. More narrowly, seven- and eight-footed iambs and trochees. 3. According to one ancient writer, monologues. *Canticum* is often rendered 'song,' and *cantica* were accompanied by the pipe (*tibicen*). The old view, based on an ancient anecdote, that the *cantica* were performed by a miming actor, a singer, and a flute player has been discarded; only actor and flutist were involved. Duckworth argues that 'lyric' *cantica* were sung and 'recitative' *cantica* were chanted. Beare accepts no such distinction: noting that ancient speech depended upon pitch rather than stress, he argues that speech and song were probably not very different from each other. See also: *diverbia*. (Duckworth NATURE 361-380, Beare ROMAN 219-230)

cantiga (Spanish)   In the 15th-16th C, a musical entertainment, often bawdy, usually performed at Christmas along with a *juego*.

canto   Informally, an act.

Cantonese opera   See: *yueju*, meaning 1.

cantor (Latin)   1. A singer, a poet. 2. In ancient Rome, an actor, especially one who pleaded for applause at the end of a performance.

can't touch the part   Of a performer in Britain, not sufficiently competent to play a particular role. (Granville DICTIONARY)

canvas   1. Linen or duck cloth used to cover flats and make drops. 2. To cover a flat. (Bowman/Ball THEATRE)

canvas and greasepaint   The theatre.

canvas knife   A knife used to cut and trim canvas in a scene shop.

canvassing bench   A scene shop bench on which flat frames are covered with canvas.

canvas theatre   In Britain, a large marquee or tent in which a theatrical entertainment is presented on a festive occasion. (Granville DICTIONARY)

cap   1. In the U.S., a term sometimes used for a male household connector, occasionally known as an Edison plug, appliance cap, or attachment plug. Such connectors are sometimes seen on stage on domestic equipment such as lamps, and occasionally in scene shops, box offices, or elsewhere in a theatre. The term can also be used of many male connectors. 2. In Britain, the metal bottom of a lamp; called a base in the U.S. (Lounsbury THEATRE 117, Bentham ART 77) 3. In acting, to do something well, to top one's part.

capa, cappa (Spanish)   Literally: cape, cloak. 1. A 16th-17th C full, hooded cloak worn in Spain and France. 2. A 19th C formal cloak for evening wear. Also called a *cape à l'Espagnole* (French). 3. An ecclesiastic or academic cloak. 4. A toreador's red cape. (Wilcox DICTIONARY, Boucher FASHION)

capacity   1. Seating capacity—the number of people a theatre auditorium will accommodate. Hence, capacity audience (a full house), capacity house (all tickets sold for a given performance). 2. The load an electrical circuit, dimmer, or other electrical equipment (sound, etc.) will take, usually expressed in amperes or watts. (Bowman/Ball THEATRE, McCandless SYLLABUS 49)

cap à pie (French), **cap-a-pie**   Dressed (usually in armor) from head to foot.

capa y espada (Spanish)   Cloak and dagger or cape and sword. In the 17th C, a romantic drama of gallantry and intrigue. Called in English a cape-and-dagger play, cape-and-sword play, cloak-and-dagger play, etc.

cape à l'Espagnole (French)   See: *capa.*

cape-and-dagger play, cape-and-sword play   See: *capa y espada.*

capeline   A skimmer; a hat of straw or felt with a wide, flat brim and a round crown. (Dreher HATMAKING)

capeng (Indonesian)   1. In Javanese *wayang kulit*, the action of adjusting arm decorations, dagger, and headdress, in preparation for departure or going into battle. (Long JAVANESE 22, 50) 2. In Sundanese *wayang golek*, a similar adjustment of the arm bands by the puppet, taken from classical Sundanese dance movement. When repeated, called *raras konda.* (Foley "Sundanese" 162)

capitan (Philippine)   A leader of an army in a *sayaw* folk play. (Mendoza COMEDIA 102)

capitano (Italian), **capitano**   A braggart-warrior type in *commedia dell'arte.* The character was usually given a blustering, swaggering name, such as Cardone (big thistle), Culonero (black-assed), Matamoros (Moor-killer), Sangre y Fuego (blood and fire), Spaccamonti (mountain splitter), Spavento (terror), Spezzafero (iron breaker), Terremoto (earthquake), etc. He was also named Coccodrillo, Cucurucu, Engoulevant, Fracasse, Fracasso, Horribilifibrax, Rinoceronte, Rodemont, Rodomonte, Taille-bras, etc. See also: braggart captain. (Oreglia COMMEDIA 101-103)

capocomico (Italian)   In 16th C Italy and later, the head of a company of performers. (Mantzius HISTORY II 269)

capot (French)   The prompter's partly-covered box located downstage center in an opera house. The term presumably derives from *capote*—a hood on a cloak. (Nalbach KING'S 33)

capote (French), **Capote**   1. An 18th C long, full, hooded overcoat with a large and a small collar, the latter capable of protecting the face. Favored by the military. Also called a greatcoat. (Boucher FASHION) 2. A medieval woman's cloak. 3. A mid-Victorian bonnet tied under the chin, with a deep ruffle at the back of the neck. Also called a coal-scuttle bonnet, *fanchon*, poke bonnet. (Wilcox DICTIONARY)

cappa (Spanish)   See: *capa.*

cappuccio (Italian)   See: *chaperon.*

caprine   Goat-like. Typically, satyrs were caprine and *sileni* equine, but the distinction appears to have been made only outside the theatre. See also: satyr. (Flickinger GREEK 24-25)

captatio benevolentia (Latin Roman)   An appeal for audience sympathy which occurs in the prologue of a number of classical plays. Literally, the phrase is approximately 'straining after friendship.' (Duckworth NATURE 61, 74-75)

capuchon (French)   A medieval short or long cape with a pointed hood, worn by men, women, children, and churchmen. See also: *chaperon.* (Wilcox DICTIONARY)

car   A flown unit capable of carrying people. Also called a machine. See also: pageant. (DAILY POST 2 October 1736)

ca ra bo (Vietnamese)   An early name for *cai luong*, c. 1917. (Addiss ''Theater'' 143)

caracalla   See: cassock.

caraco (French)   An 18th C hip-length, peasant-style jacket, fitted in front and loose in back. Also called a *pet-en-l'air*, *robe à la créole*, gown à la créole. See also: *casaquin.* (Boucher FASHION)

caractère (French)   1. Character. 2. See: *air de caractère.* 3. See: *danse-caractère.*

caranam, charanam (Telugu, Malayalam)   In many forms of traditional dance-drama, the verses of a song (*padam*) which follow the introductory lines (*pallavi* and *anupallavi*). (Jones/Jones KATHAKALI 71)

carangan (Indonesian)   See: *lakon.*

caratteri (Italian)   1. Characters, roles in a play. 2. Character masks in *commedia dell'arte.* (Oreglia COMMEDIA 125)

caravan   See: *calèche.*

carbon   1. The light-giving element in an arc light. 2. Among lighting technicians, an occasional term for an arc light.

carbon arc   The usual source of illumination in the most powerful stage lighting instruments, notably projectors and spotlights. Sometimes called carbon electric arc or arc, this light source consists basically of two sticks of carbon whose ends are separated by a small air gap (a fraction of a centimeter). When electric current is sent through the carbons, it arcs across the air gap; in so doing, it heats the ends to incandescence. The burning ends gradually vaporize, causing the carbons to shorten, and the gap between them to increase; since this ultimately extinguishes the arc, a device is needed to maintain a relatively constant gap. Among other disadvantages of the arc are that it may flicker and sputter, it can be noisy, its light is bluish, it produces poisonous carbon monoxide, and it can be dimmed only with an iris shutter which must ordinarily be hand-operated. The carbon arc is now being replaced by more powerful and more reliable enclosed arc sources such as HMI and xenon lamps. The most powerful theatre instruments are effective for some 400 feet—more than the length of a football field. See also: Jablochkoff candle. (Fuchs LIGHTING 152-154; Bellman LIGHTING 14-15, 111; Bellman SCENE 310-311)

carbon arc spotlight   See: lime.

carbon dimmer   A British term for an obsolete dimmer which mixed carbon dust and sand in a stoneware pot. When fully compressed, the mixture offered little resistance to electricity; as pressure was released, the resistance was increased and the light was dimmed. See also: carbon pile dimmer. (Corry PLANNING 98)

carbon electric arc   See: carbon arc, arc light.

carbon holder   The device which grips a carbon in a carbon arc spotlight. (Bowman/Ball THEATRE)

carbon pile dimmer   In the U.S., an obsolete resistance dimmer which consisted of a pile of thin carbon discs under pressure. When fully compressed by a kind of vise, the pile offered little resistance to the flow of electricity; as pressure was released, resistance was increased and the light in the circuit was dimmed. See also: carbon dimmer. (Fuchs LIGHTING 326)

carbon spot   See: arc light.

carburetted hydrogen   Coal gas, sometimes substituted for hydrogen in a limelight gas supply. The results were not equal to those of an oxy-hydrogen flame, and such limelights were used only in small halls. (Rees GAS 57)

carcaille (French)   The flaring collar of a 15th C *houppelande* or *pourpoint*, coming up to the ears. (Boucher FASHION)

card   A program, bill.

cardinal   See: French hood.

card reader   In the console of an infinite preset lighting control system, now obsolete, a device capable of acting on information fed to it. Such information could be in the form of a punched card or other type of program. Also called a card reading machine. (Bellman LIGHTING 219)

cari (Sanskrit)   Literally: gait. A walk appropriate to a character in classical Indian theatre. (Keith SANSKRIT 340, Bharata NATYASASTRA 216-241)

caricati (Italian)   In *commedia dell'arte*, less important roles such as noble parents and lovers, who were not masked and who provided background for the more important characters. (Mazzone-Clementi "*Commedia*" 59) *carillo* (Philippine)   A shadow play, possibly derived from Indonesian *way-ang kulit*, popular through the 19th C. It was performed solo by an itinerant puppeteer. (Salazar in Cruz SHORT 45-46, 97) There were various regional names: *aliala* in La Union, *gagalo* or *kikumut* in Pampanga and Tarlac, *titire* in Bataan and Zambales, and *titires* in Ilocos and the Visayans. Also spelled *car-rillo*. (Tonogbanua SURVEY 74)

cariyos (Indonesian)   Literally: to narrate. A short narrative section that con-nects minor scenes in Javanese shadow theatre. It usually describes a character's actions or emotions. Also spelled *tjarijos*. See also: *janturan*. (Brandon THRONES 29-30)

carmine   A 19th C red, chalky substance used to tint the cheeks. (Walkup DRESSING 292)

carp   An early 20th C nickname for a stage carpenter.

carpa (Spanish)   "A mobile Mexican popular theatre on the order of the Italian *commedia dell'arte*." (Gorelik NEW)

carpenter   1. Especially in the professional theatre, a stagehand who builds or repairs scenery. 2. To doctor or revise a play script, usually someone else's. See also: *Dramaturg*, play doctor. (Bowman/Ball THEATRE)

carpenter pipe, carpenter pipe batten   A batten with trim chains, used for flying scenery or for hanging lighting instruments. Also called a carpenter batten.

carpenter's drawing   In Britain, blueprint.

carpenter's room   Scenery workshop.

carpenter's scene   A short scene performed in front of a drop on a downstage plane of the stage, usually full of bustle, to cover the preparations for the next scene. Also called a scene in one.

carpet cut   Principally in Britain, a hinged board running along the setting line; it lifts to bind in position the edge of a carpet or stage cloth. (Granville DICTIONARY)

carpet-cut ring   In Britain, a ring inserted flush in a carpet cut to lift the cut. (Granville DICTIONARY)

carpet hoist   A modification of the regular counterweight system that makes it possible to lower a heavy scenic unit or such a property as a carpet, and detach it without removing any counterweights. A line is secured to the counterweight cradle to keep it in place until the scenery or property is reattached to the counterweighted lines.

carpet hoist cradle   A special counterweight cradle used for a carpet hoist operation when the weight of the flown object is especially heavy. A second counterweight cradle is used to counterbalance the first when the weight is taken off the lines from the first cradle.

carpet pin   A nail driven into the stage floor: to it and its fellows the grommets of a floor cloth are fixed.

carpet runner   See: runner.

carreta   In Lagos, Nigeria, a masked theatrical entertainment: masquerade music dramas based on character sketches. The term is a corruption of 'character.' The form was introduced to Lagos by Brazilian immigrants, and the shows are staged at Christmas and Easter. Similar masked pageants with elaborate costumes developed in the Gold Coast (Ghana). (Adedeji glossary)

carriage   1. See: counterweight arbor. 2. See: chariot-and-pole system. 3. A medieval pageant wagon.

carriage-and-frame system   See: chariot-and-pole system.

carrick   A 19th C man's driving overcoat of heavy fabric, double-breasted, with a deep collar. (Wilcox DICTIONARY, Boucher FASHION)

carriers   See: ball carriers.

carrillo (Philippine)   See: *carillo*.

carrillo (Spanish)   In the 17th C: 1. A small cart or wagon, undecorated, placed between two decorated carts to serve as a platform stage. 2. A tackle for hoisting light objects. (Shergold SPANISH)

carro (Spanish)   In the 17th C, a car, cart, wagon. A *carro triunfal* was a triumphal car, similar to medieval English pageant wagons. (Shergold SPANISH)

carry   To perform so that the voice is heard clearly in the house. (Bowman/Ball THEATRE)

carry a scene   Of a performer, to be the mainstay of a scene.

carry a spare   To have an understudy. (Berrey/Van den Bark SLANG 587)

carry-off   Offstage access steps leading to an entrance on a raised level.

carry one's own audience   Of a performer, to give tickets to friends for the sake of their applause. (Berrey/Van den Bark SLANG 593)

carry the comedy   1. To play a comedy role. 2. To be the outstanding performer in a comedy.

carry the heavy   To act as a heavy, usually a villain.

cartel (Spanish)   A poster.

cartridge fuse   A current-limiting device consisting of a fuse element enclosed in a fiber cylinder with brass ends. Smaller-capacity fuses (30-100 amps) use round brass ferrules; larger-capacity fuses (125 amps or more) use brass or copper blades.

cartridge pleat   1. A tubular rather than flat pleat. A much-used pleating in men's Renaissance and 18th-19th C gowns and in the upper sleeve and yoke of academic robes today. 2. In military dress, a small round pleat which held cartridges. (Wilcox DICTIONARY)

cartwheel   1. A 16th C man or woman's nine-inch ruff. (Chalmers CLOTHES 166) 2. A 16th C French hoop or farthingale, flat on top and up to 45" wide, with a shelf-like top. (Barton COSTUME 225) 3. A floppy felt or straw hat resembling a capeline but with a wider brim. (Dreher HATMAKING)

casa (Italian)   In medieval productions, a house or *mansion* (French)—a scenic unit representing some locale.

casa de comedias (Spanish)   A playhouse. (Rennert SPANISH 192)

casamenti merlati (Italian)   See: *castelli.*

casaque (French)   1. A short jacket worn over armor, and by civilians. 2. In the mid-16th C and after, an above-knee-length unbelted overcoat, open-sided, with short or long sleeves, heavily ornamented, worn for hunting and riding. 3. A 19th C woman's coat or overgown. 4. A 20th C blouse worn outside a skirt. 5. A French jockey's brilliantly-colored short silk jacket. (Wilcox DICTIONARY, Boucher FASHION)

casaquin (French)   An 18th C short negligee or dressing gown with a flaring back, worn at home with petticoats. See also: *caraco.* (Wilcox DICTIONARY, Boucher FASHION)

cascade (French)   A line or business added by performers.

cascata (Italian)   Literally: cascade. Uncalled-for lines or business in *commedia dell'arte*, in questionable taste. (Duchartre ITALIAN 73, 102)

casement   A frame for a stage door or window. Also called a casing.

case merlade (Italian)   See: *castelli.*

case money   One's last penny—an early 20th C U.S. theatrical term.

casing   1. Especially in Britain, the housing of a projector. 2. See: casement.

casnar (Latin Roman), **Casnar**   Among the ancient Romans, the name for the Pappus of the Atellan farce. See also: Pappus, *fabula Atellana.* (Beare ROMAN 138, 139)

cassette (French)   In the past, a groove in which slid the wood uprights supporting painted scenery. (Moynet FRENCH 39)

cassock   1. A 16th C unbelted overcoat, heavily ornamented. Called a caracalla by the Gauls. 2. A 17th C European foot-soldier's and cavalryman's overcoat. 3. A clergyman's straight, full-length semi-fitted coat, sometimes with a sash, buttoned down the front from neck to hem, for outdoor or indoor wear. Also called a *soutane* (French). (Wilcox DICTIONARY, Boucher FASHION)

cast   1. To assign or be assigned a performing role. Hence, casting. In 18th C Britain the term was sometimes used in the sense of throw: to cast a part to a performer. 2. In Britain in the 18th C, the type of character usually played by a particular performer; Thomas Death's "cast was the Smarts and Footmen." (Wilkinson WANDERING I 209) 3. The performers in a production. Hence, cast of characters, cast list.

cast case   A box on the wall of the green room for the posting of cast lists. The cast case has been replaced in recent times by a call-board. (Bowman/Ball THEATRE) *castelet* (French), *castello* (Italian), *castillo* (Spanish)   Literally: little castle. A traveling puppet booth dating from medieval times, used chiefly for hand puppets. It consisted of a crannied wall flanked by castle turrets. (Baird PUPPET 65, Jacobus "Puppets" 111)

castelli (Italian)   Literally: castles. Doorways at the rear of a 15th C stage, representing the houses of characters in the play. Probably the same as the doorways shown in pictures of Terence stages. Also called *casamenti merlati* or *case merlade* (battlemented houses). (Nicoll DEVELOPMENT 70)

castello (Italian)   See: *castelet*.

caster jack   See: lift jack.

caster piece   A wheeled scenic unit (such as a platform or steps).

caster plank   A long board fitted with casters. When two such boards are attached to the bottom of a large platform or other large scenic unit, the unit becomes a wagon.

caster stand   A term sometimes used for a light stand whose base rolls on casters. Such a base usually consists of three radial spokes with a caster at the end of each spoke. See also: light stand.

castillo (Spanish)   Literally: castle. 1. In the 17th C, a pageant wagon or float carried by several men. See also: *entremes*. (Shergold SPANISH) 2. See: *castelet*.

casting agent   A person who finds performers for a production. Often an actors' agent, who also finds employment for performers.

casting couch   A couch in a director's office upon which, if he is unscrupulous, he might seduce a starlet as a condition for giving her a part.

casting director   The person in charge of recruiting performers for plays or musical comedies. (Granville DICTIONARY)

casting office   An agency that puts actors in touch with producers or managers.

cast-iron comic   In Britain, a performer whose routines and technique bore sophisticated audiences by being outdated and belabored. (Granville DICTIONARY)

cast list   Cast. The list of performers and their roles. (Bowman/Ball THEATRE)

cast of characters   See: cast.

castor   A beaver hat. (Dreher HATMAKING, Chalmers CLOTHES 222)

castrato (Italian)   A male singer, especially popular in the 18th C, who was castrated before puberty in order to preserve the soprano or contralto range of his voice. A *castrato* had the power of a male singer and the flexibility of a female. Also called an *evirato*. (NEW GROVE)

castrum (Latin)   Literally: castle. A mansion or station in a medieval play production. (Sobel NEW)

cast to type   1. To cast a performer in the one kind of role he or she seems most suited for, often the character type the actor actually is or has played successfully. 2. Said of a performer so cast.

Catalan puppet   A five-finger-technique puppet (three fingers in the shoulders, two in the arms) from Catalonia, Spain. (Philpott DICTIONARY)

catalonan (Philippine)   See: *babaylan*.

cat-and-mouse dialogue   See: stichomythia.

catastasis   Of a dramatic work, its climax. (Bowman/Ball THEATRE)

catastrophe   1. Especially in serious plays, the final action which resolves the plot or precipitates the final resolution. Sometimes defined as the unravelling of the plot. 2. Especially in comedy, the dénouement.

catcall   1. A squeaking instrument or whistle used to hoot at poor performers. 2. The cry made by such an instrument or by the human voice.

catch   1. To see all or a part of a performance, usually for professional purposes and often getting to the theatre just in time to do so. Hence, to catch an act, to catch a particular performer's act. 2. To impress an audience.

catch a cold   In Britain, to fare badly at the box office in the provinces. When the term is applied, the usual reason for the failure is not the play itself but rather its negative connotations for a particular audience. (Granville DICTIONARY)

catch all tricks   In vaudeville and burlesque, the ability of a drummer in the band to coordinate his effects with performers' bumps, grinds, pratfalls, etc. Hence, catch the bumps. (Wilmeth LANGUAGE)

catch flies   To make distracting movements in a scene where the focus should be elsewhere, as in "He was catching flies during her big scene."

catch scene   In Britain, the penultimate scene in a harlequinade. Also called a cat scene. (Bowman/Ball THEATRE)

catch the bumps   See: catch all tricks.

catch word   In 18th C British acting, a cue word. (PUBLIC ADVERTISER 5 February 1784)

caterva (Latin Roman)   According to Mantzius HISTORY I 226, an occasional term for a theatrical company. The literal meaning is crowd, throng, mob. See also: *grex*.

catever   Formerly in Britain in temporary, traveling companies, a disaster which could be anything from low attendance to being stranded in the provinces (often multy catever). (Granville DICTIONARY)

catharsis   The accepted English form of Aristotle's *katharsis* (q.v.).

Catherine wheel   See: farthingale.

cat in the box   A bit of stage business in which a cat crawls from under a piece of furniture where it had been confined in a concealed box and stretches, on cue. David Belasco, in a late 19th C play, put a big cat in a small box, releasing it by means of a concealed wire at the appropriate moment. (Boyd "Checking" 25 May 1983)

catrik (Indonesian)   Literally: disciple. In Sunda, an apprentice puppeteer (*dalang*). (Foley "Sundanese" 69-74)

cat scene   See: catch scene.

cattle call   An open audition, often for the aspirants to the chorus.

caturasramadhya (Sanskrit)   Literally: square-middle. The preferred type of theatre structure in ancient India, square shaped and of medium-size. Abbreviated *caturasra*. (Gandhi in Baumer/Brandon SANSKRIT 115)

catwalk   1. A narrow walkway or bridge crossing above the stage or auditorium, providing access to scenery or lighting. 2. See: runway.

cauellera (Spanish)   A wig. See also: *peluca*. (Villandrando in Nagler SOURCES 57)

cauka (Kannada)   Literally: square. An open-air dressing room in *yaksagana*, enclosed on three sides and made of bamboo pole frames to which palm-frond matting is attached. Also spelled *cauki*, *chauki*. (Ashton/Christie YAKSAGANA 52-53, 84-85)

cauka abbara (Kannada)   Announcement of a performance of *yaksagana*. (Ashton "Ritual" 251)

cauki (Kannada)   See: *cauka*.

caul   A medieval headdress which concealed the hair in silk, attached to a heavy net cap of precious metal cord ornamented with spangles, pearls, and beads. Also called a crepin(e), crespinette, crestine, tressour, tressure. The cap alone is called a *calotte* (French). See also: dorelet. (Chalmers CLOTHES 18, Walkup DRESSING 118, Wilcox DICTIONARY)

cauldron trap   A trap, usually square, in the middle of the scenic area; it was used for sinking the cauldron in *Macbeth*, hence its name. (Southern CHANGEABLE 284)

cavalier boots   17th C bucket or funnel-top boots worn with hose folded over the boot cuff. (Wilcox DICTIONARY)

cavalier's hat   See: Swedish hat.

cavatina (Italian)   In opera, a simple air or song for a single voice. A *cavatina* is similar to an *aria* but simpler and shorter.

cavea (Latin Roman)   Literally: cavity, hollow. The auditorium of a theatre; hence, often the theatre itself, occasionally the spectators. Since *theatrum* (and Greek *theatron*), which had early meant auditorium, soon came to signify the whole theatre, *cavea* has been regularly used for the auditorium of either the Greek or the Roman theatre. The auditorium shape varied, but the Roman seating area was characteristically semi-circular, and the Greek somewhat fuller. The

Greeks also used *koilon* for the basic meaning 'auditorium.' See also: *maenianum primum*, *spectacula*, *theatron*. (Bieber HISTORY 194, Sandys COMPANION 518, Allen ANTIQUITIES 96, Flickinger GREEK 60)

caviar mob, caviar set   Snobbish theatregoers.

cazuela (Spanish)   Literally: stew-pan. 1. That part of a 17th C *corral* theatre reserved for unaccompanied women, most of whom were evidently prostitutes. The *cazuela* was normally at the rear of a theatre on an upper level. Some *corrales* had an upper and lower *cazuela*, called respectively *cazuela alta* and *cazuela baja*. 2. The uppermost gallery in a theatre. Also called the *paradiso*. (Shergold SPANISH)

CB   In old promptbooks, curtain bell. (Shattuck SHAKESPEARE 22)

C-clamp   1. A device for attaching a lighting instrument to a pipe. The name comes from the C-shaped working portion, which is bolted to the pipe. Sometimes called a pipe clamp. Lounsbury has illustrations. 2. A much larger C-shaped clamp used in scenery, as in fastening two platforms together. (Lounsbury THE-ATRE 24, Wehlburg GLOSSARY)

CD, C.D.   1. See: center door. 2. See: creative drama.

CE   See: center entrance.

ceiling   Anything serving as the ceiling of an interior stage setting. A ceiling may be one large framed piece, unframed cloth stretched across the top of a setting, two framed pieces hinged together, two or more framed pieces with spaces between them for lighting positions, or hanging borders painted to look like a ceiling and ceiling beams. See: book ceiling and roll ceiling, the two standard examples of ceilings that can be flown.

ceiling beam   1. A beam in the ceiling of an auditorium in which spotlights are concealed. (Stern MANAGEMENT) 2. See: ceiling flipper.

ceiling border   See: border.

ceiling bracket   A metal bracket designed to hold a curtain track and secure it to a ceiling.

ceiling cloth, ceiling piece   In Britain and Australia, a framed cloth resting on top of a set. (National TECHNICAL)

ceiling flipper   A long narrow flat attached to the downstage edge of a ceiling frame to mask the edge of the frame and the flies. Also called a ceiling beam.

ceiling iron   See: ceiling plate.

ceiling lights   An occasional term for spotlights which reach the acting area from the auditorium ceiling. The phrase, close to being a lay term, is used by theatre people but not ordinarily by lighting technicians. Ceiling spots is a variant, slightly more specific. See also: beam lights. (Bowman/Ball THEATRE, Dean/Carra FUNDAMENTALS 375, Wehlburg GLOSSARY)

ceiling piece   In the U.S., a framed cloth resting on top of a set.

ceiling plate   A metal plate with a ring, used to hold pieces of a ceiling together and provide a method of attaching the ceiling pieces to lines from above. Also called a ceiling iron.

ceiling port   An opening in the auditorium ceiling through which one or more spotlights may be directed to the stage.

ceiling set   A set of lines used to fly a ceiling or part of a ceiling (which may require two or three sets of lines).

ceiling slot   An opening in an auditorium ceiling, preferably running its full width, through which spotlights are focused onto the stage. See also: sidewall slot.

ceiling spots   See: ceiling lights.

Celastic   The trade name for a material used for making masks, small properties, moldings, etc. In dry form, it is in soft sheets not unlike felt; when a piece is dipped in acetone or a similar solvent, it can be modelled into any shape. When it dries it becomes hard and retains the modelled shape.

celempung (Indonesian)   A thirteen-stringed zither in a Javanese *gamelan* ensemble. Also spelled *chelempung*. (Malm MUSIC 30)

celestials   Gallery spectators.

cellar   In Britain, the space under the stage. (Granville DICTIONARY)

cell block theatre   A therapy program which seeks to teach prisoners via improvisation to pause in conflict situations and listen, hear, look, and verbalize feelings. (Ryan "Prison" 32)

cello   An actress with a contralto voice.

Cel-O-Cloth   The trade name for a thin sheet of cellophane with a backing of loosely-woven thread. Used to simulate glass. (Gillette/Gillette SCENERY)

Cel-O-Glass   The trade name for screen wire treated with a coating of cellophane to render it transparent. Used to simulate glass. (Gillette/Gillette SCENERY)

celosías (Spanish)   Window shutters. Hence, sometimes, the window itself. Also called *rejas*: the grilled windows serving as boxes, looking down on a 17th C *corral* theatre. (Rennert SPANISH 42)

cement mixer   A poor dancer. (Berrey/Van den Bark SLANG 573)

cempala (Indonesian)   A tapper which a *wayang* puppeteer strikes against the wooden puppet chest (*kothak*) or metal plates (*kepyak*) for dramatic effect or as a music cue. In Java, of wood or metal (Brandon THRONES 37), in Bali of wood only (McPhee MUSIC 202). Also spelled *chempala* or *tjempala*. In Sundanese, *campala*. (Foley "Sundanese" 51)

cempurit (Indonesian)   The collective term for the control rods of a Javanese shadow puppet, usually made of buffalo horn. They include the central stick (*gapit*) and two arm sticks (*tuding*). Also spelled *tjempurit*. (Long JAVANESE 13)

cenaculo (Philippine)   A dramatic performance of the passion and death of Jesus Christ presented during Lent. Introduced in the 18th C and still popular today. Texts are in octosyllabic verse, eight verses to the stanza. The crucifixion today is often extraordinarily realistic in portrayal. Also spelled *sinakulo*. See also: *ablada, cantada*. (Tonogbanua SURVEY 80-81, Salazar in Cruz SHORT 97)

cennalam (Malayalam)   An eight-inch bronze gong played by the lead singer (*ponnani*) in *kathakali*. (Jones/Jones KATHAKALI 77)

centa (Malayalam)   See: *cande*.

centage   In Britain, percentage—the division of the gross receipts between the theatre lessee and the proprietor of a touring company. (Fay GLOSSARY)

center, centre   1. A stage position in the middle of the acting area. Abbreviation: C. 2. See: center line. 3. To focus the mind on significant words while reading lines. (Bowman/Ball THEATRE)

center door   An entrance upstage center. Abbreviation: CD. (Bowman/Ball THEATRE)

center door fancy   An early 20th C term for a stage setting with a decorated entrance upstage center. Also called a front room set. (Krows AMERICA 121)

center entrance   An upstage center entrance in a setting. Abbreviation: CE.

centering   An actor's term for localization of the human energy sources in the body, usually in the abdomen. (Cameron/Gillespie ENJOYMENT)

center line   1. An imaginary or actual line running upstage-downstage at the center of a stage. On floor plans, rendered as CL or $\mathcal{C}_L$, sometimes C. In Britain: centre mark, centre line. 2. See: set of lines.

center of interest   The point in a stage picture upon which the audience should focus; it shifts with the movements of the performers and for other reasons, such as a change in the lighting. (Bowman/Ball THEATRE)

center opening   An entrance in the center of a stage setting, not necessarily a door.

center overlap   The overlapping of the two onstage edges of a traverse curtain.

center piece   A scenic unit placed in the center of the stage.

center practice   In ballet, exercises performed in the center of the room without the support of the *barre* (French); useful for developing balance and control. (Grant TECHNICAL)

center prompt box   A hooded prompter's position downstage center, a feature of opera houses more than of legitimate theatres, but common in 19th C French playhouses. (Granville DICTIONARY)

center stage   1. The middle of the acting area. 2. In Australia ('centre' stage), an arena stage. (National TECHNICAL)

center theatre   One of three theatrical circles in Russia in the mid-1920s, the other two being politically left and right. (Carter SPIRIT 115)

central loudspeaker system   A cluster of speakers mounted over the center of a proscenium arch, or above the center of an arena stage.

central stage, central staging   See: arena stage.

centre   See: center.

centrifugal   In dance, used of movement propelled outward from the top of a spiral, and then at the base. (Love DANCE)

centripetal   In dance, used of movement pulled inward. (Love DANCE)

centunculus (Latin Roman)   Literally: patchwork cloth. A garish, many-colored, harlequin-like jacket commonly worn by performers in mimes. (Beare ROMAN 155, Chambers MEDIAEVAL I 5)

cepak (Indonesian)   See: *wayang golek.*

ceraca (Thai)   Literally: dialogue or conversation. 1. Rhythmic passages declaimed by actors or narrators in masked-drama (*khon*) or shadow theatre (*nang yai*). Given in prose or verse, they are either part of the written text or are interpolated by the narrator. 2. See: *rai.* See also: *kampak.* (Yupho KHON 41, Dhaninivat/Yupho KHON 4)

ceramic black riser   See: black riser.

Cereales (Latin Roman)   See: *ludi Cereales.*

cerita (Indonesian, Malaysian)   Literally: story. 1. Shortened form of numerous story types in Southeast Asian theatre. For example, *cerita babad* are history stories that, especially in *ketoprak* and *sandiwara*, are based on local histories or chronicles. Other examples are *cerita rumahtangga* (contemporary domestic stories), *cerita pahlawan* (stories of legendary heroes), and *cerita revolusi* (stories of the Indonesian Revolution, 1945-1950). Also spelled *cherita* or *tjerita.* (Peacock RITES 104, Brandon SOUTHEAST 185)

cerita babad (Indonesian)   Literally: history story. In Java and Sunda, a local history or chronicle. By extension, especially in *ketoprak* and *sandiwara*, a play based on local history. Sometimes spelled *tjerita babad.* Also called *babad.* (Brandon SOUTHEAST 185)

cernui (Latin Roman)   See: *petauristae.*

ceruss   A cosmetic used to heighten cheek color in the 17th C. (Chalmers CLOTHES 190)

cesta (Sanskrit)   In classical Indian theatre, a movement involving the actor's whole body, such as walking or adopting sitting positions. One of three types of bodily expression (*angika*). See also: *mukhaja, sarira.* (Raghavan in Baumer/Brandon SANSKRIT 32-33) *ceta* (Sanskrit)   A servant or slave role in a classical Indian play. (Keith SANSKRIT 312)

cevippuvu (Malayalam)   Literally: ear flowers. Circular ornaments worn just above the ear for most male roles in *kathakali*, *kutiyattam*, and *krishnanattam*.

chachar (Gujarati)   A round earthen acting area marked out for a *bhavai* performance. Also called *paudh*. (Gargi FOLK 54-57)

ch'a ch'ien (Chinese)   See: *chaqian*.

chaconne (French)   1. A rondo-like fashionable court dance of the late 17th C. (Perugini PAGEANT 109) 2. A late 19th C ribbon tie or cravat.

chaconne compassée (French)   A dance component of the noble style of 18th C ballet. Characteristically it was the climactic point of the work. (Winter BALLET 139)

chaeim (Korean)   A male musician or entertainer of low caste. (Yi ''Mask'' 57)

chai bot (Thai)   See: *ti bot*.

chain anchor   A device for fixing a length of chain to the gridiron: a piece of 2″ x 4″ lumber with a hole drilled through its center is placed on the gridiron so that it bridges two channel irons; the chain is dropped through the hole in the 2″ x 4″ and fixed at its correct length by running a 12d nail through a link and letting it rest on the top of the lumber. The device is used when securing a fixed cyclorama pipe to the gridiron.

chaînes (French)   Literally: chains, links. In ballet, a series of rapid turns on *pointes* or *demi-pointes*, done in a straight line or in a circle. (Grant TECHNICAL)

chain hanger   An adjustable chain by which borderlights, and sometimes floodlights, are hung from a horizontal pipe. The verb 'chain hang' occurs occasionally. (McCandless SYLLABUS 28, Philippi STAGECRAFT)

chain pocket   A horizontal sleeve at the bottom of a drapery, into which a length of chain can be put.

chainse   A forerunner of the chemise. A straight-hanging tunic which in early times was in rough or fine fabric depending upon the social status of its wearer, who could be a man, woman, or child. Also called a cainsil. (Boucher FASHION, Wilcox DICTIONARY)

chain trimmer   See: trim chain.

chairman, chairwoman   See: master/mistress of ceremonies.

chair rail   A strip of lumber attached horizontally to a wall at a height which keeps the backs of chairs from scuffing the wall. (Lounsbury THEATRE)

chair warmer   A minor performer with little or no dialogue.

chakkiar, chakkyar (Malayalam)   See: *cakyar*.

chak lang (Thai)   A painted backdrop. (Virulrak "Likay" 134)

chak mun (Thai)   A diorama. (Virulrak "Likay" 136)

chakuto (Japanese)   Literally: arrival. Music played on drums and flute thirty minutes before curtain time in *kabuki*, to warn the audience and cast the play is about to begin. *Chakuto ita* (arrival board) is located at the backstage entrance. An actor puts a peg in the hole above his name to indicate he has arrived. (Leiter ENCYCLOPEDIA 37)

chali (Oriya)   Literally: walking. A walking movement or gait in east Indian *chhau* dance and dance-drama.

chalk a scene   To mark on the stage floor (or the floor of any rehearsal space) the positions of the scenery and properties.

chalk bag   See: pounce bag.

chalk line   A length of string which can be rubbed with chalk, stretched against the floor or a flat, and snapped. The result is a light, straight, chalk line to serve as a guide for the scene painter. See also: bow snap line, snap line.

chalonarang (Indonesian)   See: *calonarang*.

cha'long (Philippine)   A ritual drama in the Ifugao area which depicts a mythological battle between Bugan, the tribal ancestress played by a boy, and her husband and two sons. (Munoz in Manuud BROWN 658)

chalou, ch'a lou (Chinese)   See: *xiyuan*.

chalumeau (French)   The blowpipe apparatus in a limelight. (Moynet FRENCH 94)

'cham (Tibetan)   An early Buddhist dance and drama, the precursor of *mani-rimdu* masked dance-drama. (Jerstad MANI-RIMDU 61-73)

chamani (Greek)   Literally: Turkish bath. The body (or main division) of a 19th C Greek shadow puppet (*Karaghiöz*) theatre. See also: *Karagöz*. (Myrsiades "Karaghiözis" 53)

chamarre (French)   A fur-lined, heavily ornamented, floor-length coat with full sleeves and an open front, first seen in the late 15th C. See also: samare. (Boucher FASHION)

chambara (Japanese)   Sword fighting. Popular plays (as well as films and TV dramas) that feature sword fighting. The term probably comes from the sound of swords clashing (*chan-chan*). See also: *tate*.

chamber   1. In an Elizabethan theatre, a recessed, curtained acting area (also called an inner stage) at the rear of the platform stage. (But there has been controversy over the existence of the chamber; see: pavilion.) 2. A stock interior stage setting, also called a chamber scene or chamber set.

chamber batten   In Britain, the furthest downstage light pipe suspended from the gridiron, often used to light interior settings. Also called a concert batten, number one batten (No. 1 batten, #1 batten), or proscenium batten. (Bax MANAGEMENT 183)

chamber border   Formerly, a hanging, painted border, used to represent the ceiling of an interior setting. Two or three are usually needed to mask the flies.

chambermaid   1. The part of a female servant or of any soubrette. 2. An actress who plays such parts. (Bowman/Ball THEATRE)

chamber scene, chamber set   See: chamber.

chamber theatre   A form of readers theatre restricted to narrative fiction and requiring both presentational and representational performance.

chambre à quatre portes (French)   Literally: room with four doors. A typical setting for a 17th C French comedy. (Brockett HISTORY 274)

chambrée (French)   17th C French actors' term for their share of a performance or a day's receipts. (Mongrédien MOLIÈRE 143)

chamois stump   Formerly in makeup, a lining stick made of rolled-up chamois or tipped with chamois.

champ (French)   In medieval France, a term for the open acting area in front of the *mansions*. (Frank MEDIEVAL 148–149)

'cham-ra (Tibetan)   A stone courtyard which serves as the performance area for *mani-rimdu* masked dance-drama. (Jerstad MANI-RIMDU 84)

chanang (Malaysian)   See: *gamelan*.

chande (Kannada)   See: *cande*.

chandelier cloth   In Britain, a ceiling piece with a hole for an electrical cable. (Granville DICTIONARY)

chang, ch'ang (Chinese)   Literally: to sing. 1. The sung portions of a music-drama (*xiqu*) play, or any single sung passage. Described in Scott CLASSICAL 18, 53, 92-96 and Wichmann "Aural" 81-115. See also: *nianbai*. 2. Song; one of the four basic performance skills (*jiben gongfu*) in Beijing opera (*jingju*) and many other forms of music-drama. Described in Scott CLASSICAL 18, 53, 92-96 and Wichmann "Aural" 381-393, 410-425. See also: *nian, zuo, da, changbai*.

chang (Thai)   A theatre specialist, often technical crew (*chang chak*), electricians (*chang fai*), painters (*chang kien*), and carpenters (*chang mai*). In northern Thailand dancers are sometimes called *chang fon*.

changbai, ch'ang pai (Chinese)   Literally: to sing and read aloud. A general term for vocal technique in music-drama (*xiqu*); it usually includes both song (*chang*) and speech (*nian*). Important specific techniques are described in Scott CLASSICAL 18, 53, 92-96 and Wichmann "Aural" 81-126, 381-425.

ch'ang ch'iang (Chinese)   See: *changqiang*.

change   See: scene change.

change an act, change a set   To shift from one stage setting to another. See also: scene shift.

changement de pieds (French)   Literally: change of feet. In ballet, springing steps in the fifth position, the dancer changing feet in the air and alighting in the fifth position with the opposite foot in front. (Grant TECHNICAL)

change of fortune   See: *peripeteia*.

change-over   1. A period in which the put-out of one touring show overlaps with the take-in of another. 2. Especially in Australia, shifting from the setting for one production to the setting for another. (Burris-Meyer/Cole THEATRES 155, National TECHNICAL)

changgai (Malaysian)   Long, false fingernails worn in dance dramas and by heroic characters in shadow theatre (*wayang siam*). (Sheppard TAMAN 77)

ch'ang-geug (Korean)   See: *ch'ang-kug*.

changgo, changko, janggo (Korean)   In *namsadang*, masked plays, puppet plays, and other traditional theatre, a double-headed drum shaped like an hour-glass and made of paulownia wood. See: *samhyon yukkak*. (Kim ''Namsadang'' 11)

ch'ang hsi chü, ch'ang hsi wen hsi (Chinese)   See: *xiju*, meaning 2.

changkao, ch'ang k'ao (Chinese)   Literally: long armor. A role category which includes high ranking, dignified warriors dressed in full stage armor (*kao*) and features combat (*da*), dance-acting (*zuo*), and some song (*chang*) skill; a major subdivision of the martial male role (*wusheng*) in Beijing opera (*jingju*). (Dolby HISTORY 180, Scott CLASSICAL 66)

ch'ang-kug, ch'ang-geug (Korean)   Literally: song and drama. An operetta form that developed out of *p'ansori* in the early 1900s. (Korean KOREAN 49)

changmian, ch'ang mien (Chinese)   The collective name for the musical instruments played to accompany a performance of music-drama (*xiqu*). This orchestra consists of two sections, the civil orchestra (*wenchang*) and the martial orchestra (*wuchang*). Today also called *yuedui* or *yüeh tui*. (Scott CLASSICAL 41–50, Wichmann ''Aural'' 433–497, Zung SECRETS 31–34)

ch'ang pai (Chinese)   See: *changbai*.

changqiang, ch'ang ch'iang (Chinese)   Literally: sung tune. In music-drama (*xiqu*), a song passage composed of two or more melodic phrases (*qiang*). The term is most frequently used to refer to a series of melodic phrases which as a unit are characteristic of a particular form of music-drama or school (*liupai*) of performance. (Wichmann ''Aural'' 136–146)

chang t'ou k'uei lei (Chinese)   See: *zhangtou kuilei*.

changxiju, changxi wenxi (Chinese)   See: *xiju*, meaning 2.

channel   1. In memory lighting systems, a single dimmer or a group of dimmers which operate as a unit. (Bellman LIGHTING 242) 2. A single lighting circuit, complete with dimmer and independently controllable. (Bentham ART)

channel beam   See: channel iron.

channel drum   A circular channel under a revolving stage platform, into which the driving cable is set. (Gillette/Gillette SCENERY 308)

channel iron   A U-shaped iron, used extensively on theatre gridirons to form the grid floor. Also called a channel beam. (Lounsbury THEATRE)

channel mimic   See: mimic.

chanson de geste (French)   See: *geste*.

chansonnier (French)   A song writer who sings his own songs, usually ballads. Formerly, a writer and performer of satirical songs, monologues, and skits.

chanta (Kannada)   See: *cande*.

chante-fable (French)   In medieval France, a song-story (the literal meaning) designed for performance, but not a play in the usual sense. Sometimes said to be on the brink of dramatic comedy. (Frank MEDIEVAL 237–238)

chanter   A London street singer. (Orwell DOWN 174)

chanteur (French)   See: minstrel.

chanteuse (French)   A female singer. Often applied in show business to an incompetent singer and pronounced chantoozie.

chaoju, ch'ao chü (Chinese)   A form of music-drama (*xiqu*) popular in Chaozhou and the Shantou (i.e., Swatow) district of Guangdong Province and the southern portion of Fujian Province since the 17th C. Its music is derived from *yiyangqiang*; it uses a helping chorus (*bangqiang*), and a number of fixed-melodies (*qupai*) as the melodies for songs. (Mackerras MODERN 145)

chaophap (Thai)   A sponsor of a theatre performance, whether a person or an organization. See also: *ngan*. (Virulrak "Likay" 259)

chaopo (Thai)   The leader of a *likay* troupe. Also called *topho*. (Virulrak "Likay" 273)

chap, chappie   Especially in Britain, an actor.

chapeaugraphy   A kind of itinerant street entertainment in London about 1918 in which the performer used a circle of felt which was manipulated into typical hats befitting a bishop, a cowboy, an admiral, etc., for the crowds lined up for theatres. (McNamara "Press" 316)

chapeaux des fermes (French)   The cross-beams in a substage which support the traps. (Moynet FRENCH 32)

chaperon (French)   A 12th-16th C shoulder cape and attached hood. Developed from the *capuchon*, it added a long tail or liripipe. Also called a *collet*, *cappuccio* (Italian). (Barton COSTUME 131, Boucher FASHION, Wilcox DICTIONARY)

chapiao, ch'a p'iao (Chinese)   See: *chaqian*.

chappie   See: chap.

chapsaek (Korean)   A mimed skit performed as part of 'farmers' music' (*nongak*). (Chang "Farmer's" 29)

chaqian, ch'a ch'ien (Chinese)   Literally: tea money. Money paid for tea in a tea-house theatre (*xiyuan*) of the 17th-early 20th C; when performances were given, this fee was increased and included seating for the show. Also called tea ticket (*chapiao*). See also: *zuoerqian*. (Dolby HISTORY 191, Mackerras MODERN 87, Scott CLASSICAL 221-222)

char (French)   A 17th-18th C wagon (not a *chariot*) used to transport a performer through the air: a triumphal wagon. (Carlson "Inventory" 48)

chara-ch'um (Korean)   Literally: turtle dance. Bringing hands alternately in front of the face, a dance gesture used in masked plays of the Yangju area. (Yi "Mask" 46)

character   1. The second of Aristotle's six parts of a play, the first being plot—since plot reveals the qualities of the protagonist. 2. One of the *dramatis personae* (Latin) in a play. 3. The type of personality portrayed. Hence, stay in character. 4. A character actor. Hence, character juvenile, character man, character woman, etc. (Cameron/Gillespie ENJOYMENT, Bowman/Ball THEATRE)

character actor, character actress   A performer with the ability to portray personalities which differ considerably from his or her own, especially older or eccentric characters. Also called character man or character woman.

character comedy   In Britain, a series of thematic, extemporaneous speeches by performers around which a plot is drawn. Frequently seen in fit-up theatres. Also called a gag show. (Granville DICTIONARY)

character development   In playwriting, the gradual revelation of the nature of a character. (Archer PLAY-MAKING xxv)

characterization   1. Delineation by a dramatist of a role in a play. 2. The portrayal by a performer of a role on the stage; the art of interpreting a dramatic role in all aspects of human thought, feeling, and behavior. (Stern MANAGEMENT, Selden ACTING)

character juvenile   A performer of juveniles playing a part which is slightly older than the usual juvenile roles. (Granville DICTIONARY)

character lines, character makeup   Makeup applied by a younger performer to trace age lines and thus suggest an older appearance. (Granville DICTIONARY)

character man   1. See: character actor. 2. In Britain, one who played doctors, lawyers, and other professionals (as distinguished from the juvenile). (Granville DICTIONARY)

character old man   A young male actor who plays roles of old men, sometimes not very convincingly. (Granville DICTIONARY)

character old woman   1. An actress who specializes in playing elderly women. 2. A young actress who plays roles of older women, sometimes not very convincingly. (Granville DICTIONARY)

character part   A role in which peculiarities or eccentricities of character are stressed in acting and makeup. (Purdom PRODUCING)

character play   A play which has a particular character as the chief attraction, or a character with a vice or defect which the situations in the play reveal (as in Molière's *Tartuffe*). (Mantzius HISTORY II, 165)

character prop   A property—usually small—such as a pipe, comb, cane, etc.—used by a performer to aid characterization. See also: personal prop, hand prop.

character role   See: character part.

character woman   See: character actor.

charanam (Telugu, Malayalam)   See: *caranam*.

charcoal   Formerly, a Black or blackface actor. Now offensive. (Berrey/Van den Bark SLANG 573)

charcoal act   A blackface act. Now offensive.

charge   House charge; the fee charged by the theatre management at benefits to cover operating costs. Whatever income was left over went to the beneficiary.

chargé (French)   1. A dropped or lowered curtain. 2. A shutter. (Moynet FRENCH 26)

chari ba (Japanese)   Literally: comic scene. A scene in *bunraku*, where a comic puppet figure (*chari*) is the source of humor. (Leiter ENCYCLOPEDIA 37)

chariot (French)   In the past, a small wagon, supporting the *montant* (pole), running on tracks under the stage in the chariot-and-pole system. (Carlson "Inventory" 38, 42-43, 45, 48)

chariot-and-drop system   A 19th C scene-changing system using chariots and poles for the side wings and painted drops for the back scenes. (Mullin PLAYHOUSE 141)

chariot-and-pole system   A method of scene shifting developed in 17th C Italy. In the substage on tracks ran wheeled chariots or carriages at each wing and shutter position; they were moved onstage and off by ropes attached to a central winch or cylinder. Poles (masts) or ladders rose from each chariot through slots in the stage floor, and to them were attached the scenic wings and shutters. Two chariots at each position, one moving offstage and the other onstage, made for coordinated scene changes. Also called the pole-and-carriage system, the carriage-and-frame system, the pole-and-chariot system, etc.

chariot stage   An occasional term for a medieval wagon stage. Also occasionally called a wheeled stage. See: pageant. (Frank MEDIEVAL 165)

charity benefit   A theatrical performance whose profits are used for charitable purposes—for indigent performers, families in distress, churches, etc. (Troubridge BENEFIT 71)

Charleston   A lively dance, named after Charleston, South Carolina, in which the knees are twisted in and out and the heels swung sharply outward on each step.

charley   The beadle, policeman, or constable sent to arrest Punch in the Punch and Judy shows in 19th C England. (Speaight PUPPET 194)

Charlotte   A large 18th C hat for women. The brim was covered with a flounce and the crown was wide and tightly gathered. Somewhat simplified, this hat returned to popularity in the late 19th and early 20th C. (Boucher FASHION)

Charon's steps   In the Greek theatre, probably a step and trap door arrangement which permitted the entrance or exit of ghosts and spirits. The source is Pollux (see Flickinger). Such steps and openings have been found at either end of a tunnel going from the scene house to the center of the orchestra. Charon's steps cannot be dated earlier than the 4th C BC, and are not needed in any existing 5th C BC script. Also called Charonian staircase, Charonian steps, Charonic ladders, Charon's staircase, and no doubt other variants. See also: *anapiesma*. (Flickinger GREEK 106, 362-363, fig. 87; Bieber HISTORY 78, fig. 284; Arnott SCENIC 25; Haigh ATTIC 217-218)

chase   1. Choose or purchase. Charles Lamb in "My First Play" said that a fruitress in late 18th C London would call, "Chase some oranges, chase some numparels [chocolates], chase a bill of the play...." (Hogan LONDON xli) 2. See: chaser.

chase a kite   To forget one's line.

chase music   See: chaser.

chase play   A farce in which an object or person must be found by a certain time, on pain of a serio-comic disaster. (Bricker TODAY 223)

chaser   1. In the early 20th C, a baby spot (spotlight) used as a follow spot. Hence, at that time, sometimes any baby spot. (Hartmann LIGHTING 68, Krows AMERICA 206) 2. Lights which go on and off consecutively giving the illusion of movement along a line or within a pattern. Also called chaser lights. Originally used on theatre marquees but now often part of spectacle lighting on stage. (Wehlburg GLOSSARY) 3. The last act on a bill. 4. Music played as an audience leaves an auditorium. Sometimes called chase music or chase.

chaser lights   See: chaser.

chasing shadows   In a production using footlights, shadows (usually unwanted) which appear to follow each other on the setting as a performer moves. Such shadows appear on a back wall or backdrop.

chassé (French)   In ballet, a step in which one foot chases the other out of its position. From the 16th-17th C gliding dance step of the same name. (Grant TECHNICAL)

chassis (French)   In a 19th C device for moving gas wings on and off stage, the wheeled structure, just below the stage floor, which carried the gas wing.

The wing itself was a *faux chassis* (*faux* for ''false''), since it could be replaced by another wing or a three-dimensional piece. (Rees GAS 33, fig. 13)

chat (French)   See: *grand pas de chat.*

châtelaine (French)   A precious metal chain (or chains) worn around a lady's waist and fastened to the skirt. Used to carry a handkerchief, sewing notions, keys, mirror, smelling salts, etc. Also called a *troussoire.* See also: countenances, *sautoir.* (Barton COSTUME 520, Wilcox DICTIONARY)

chatouilleur (French)   Especially in the 19th and early 20th C, a member of a claque hired to keep an audience in good spirits by passing out candy, telling (sometimes ribald) stories, and distributing playbills. (Saxon ''Claque'' 19)

chatri (Thai)   See: *lakon jatri.*

chatsby   A British nonsense word used by a performer when the correct word is forgotten. (Granville DICTIONARY)

chauki (Kannada)   See: *cauka.*

chausse (French)   See: epitoga.

chausses (French)   See: breeches.

chausses en bourse (French)   Short, striped padded breeches of the 17th C, full at the bottom in a flat balloon shape. (Boucher FASHION)

chautauqua   A late 19th-early 20th C summer lecture circuit. Often working in tents, performers sometimes did vaudeville or dramatic sketches. The name comes from the permanent educational-entertainment institution on Lake Chautauqua in western New York State. (Wilmeth LANGUAGE)

chaya asobi (Japanese)   See: *keiseikai.*

chaya nataka (Sanskrit)   1. In ancient India, shadow theatre or plays. The puppets were cut-out figures, held between a semi-transparent screen and a light source. 2. A collection of dramas written in the 13th C by Subhata. (Sorensen ''Shadow'' 1-2)

chayna (Quechua)   A pre-Columbian flute made of cane and used to accompany love songs and elegies in Incan drama. See also: *pirutu.* (Karnis ''Pre-Columbian'' 42)

chayuan, ch'a yüan (Chinese)   See: *xiyuan.*

che (Chinese)   See: *zhe.*

cheat   1. To move a dimmer setting so that the change in lighting is not noticed by the audience. Also called sneak or steal. 2. Sometimes, to modify slightly the position of an area spotlight which, for example, creates an undesirable spill in a particular scene. (Bowman MODERN) 3. To make a small adjustment in body position on stage, usually in order to make more of one's face visible to the audience or to help balance the stage picture. Hence, cheat left, cheat right, cheat out, cheat front. 4. To leave out portions of an act.

check   1. Especially in the 18th C, a theatre employee hired to see that handlers of money did not cheat: to be a "Cheque on the Box Office-keeper." (Stone LONDON lxxxv) 2. In 18th C theatres and later, a small metal disc used as a ticket. Now called a gallery check. See also: silver tickets. (Hogan LONDON xxvi) 3. To reduce power, as when lighting instruments are dimmed. To 'check the house' is therefore to dim the house lights, ordinarily to blackout. 4. As a noun, any position on a dimmer between full and blackout; hence such phrases as 'at quarter check' and 'at half check.' The term, originally British, has come into some U.S. use. (Bentham ART, Downs THEATRE II 1130, Bowman/Ball THEATRE)

checkboard   An electric seat indicator.

check chain   A chain attached to the gridiron and to the top batten of the asbestos curtain, designed to check the fall of the curtain just as it reaches the stage floor. (Burris-Meyer/Cole THEATRES 248)

checker, check taker   In Britain, a ticket taker at a theatre.

checkout   1. Especially in the professional theatre, the electrician's test of his equipment, principally lamps and circuits, before each performance. Hence, dimmer check, instrument check, lamp check, etc. 2. As two words, to dim lights to blackout.

check returns   See: check.

check taker   In 18th C theatres and later, a ticket taker. (Hogan LONDON clxiv)

check the house   1. See: check, meaning 3. 2. To check box office records against ticket stubs. (Granville DICTIONARY)

check up   In Britain, to gain entrance to a full house by waiting until some audience member leaves during the performance. (Partridge TO-DAY 226)

cheesecake   Publicity photographs of female performers displaying their physical attractions. (Wilmeth LANGUAGE)

chef d'emploi (French)   The lead performer in a particular type of part. (Roberts STAGE)

cheguxi (Chinese)   See: *gezixi.*

ch'e hsi (Chinese)   See: *cherxi.*

cheironomia (Greek)   Pantomimic gesture and symbolic movement, especially important in *emmeleia*, the dance of tragedy. It was said that an able dancer could tell the entire story of a play without a word. (Lawler DANCE 12, 82)

che k'ou (Chinese)   See: *shisanzhe.*

ch'e ku hsi (Chinese)   See: *gezixi.*

chelempung (Indonesian)   See: *celempung.*

chemical etching   Applying chemicals to plastic or similar surfaces partially to dissolve the surface and produce a textured effect. (Bellman SCENOGRAPHY)

chemin de mer (French)   A sea lane. Used in 19th C naval scenes to suggest the movement of waves. A stage ship resting on four wheels moved along two roller coaster-like wooden lanes or tracks laid across the stage. (Moynet FRENCH 150)

chemise, *chemise* (French)   A descendant of the medieval chainse. By the 13th C it was a wool body garment; later a linen cloth was used. The garment hung straight from top to bottom, without an indented waistline. It is a recurring classic silhouette. Also called a sack, sacque, sheath, shift. (Wilcox DICTIONARY, Boucher FASHION)

chemise gown   See: gown à la lévite.

chemisette (French)   A 19th-early 20th C woman or girl's lawn and lace underbodice, long or short-sleeved. Also called a guimp(e), Swiss bodice. (Wilcox DICTIONARY)

chempala (Indonesian)   See: *cempala*.

ch'en chü (Chinese)   See: *chenzi*.

cheng ching (Chinese)   See: *zhengjing*.

cheng lou (Chinese)   See: *zhenglou*.

cheng mo (Chinese)   See: *zhengmo*.

cheng pen ta hsi (Chinese)   See: *zhengben daxi*.

cheng sheng (Chinese)   See: *zhengsheng*.

cheng tan (Chinese)   See: *zhengdan*.

cheng tiao, *cheng tiao shih* (Chinese)   See: *zheng diaoshi*.

chenju (Chinese)   See: *chenzi*.

chen sang tzu (Chinese)   See: *dasangzi*.

chenzi, *ch'en tzu* (Chinese)   Literally: padding written characters. One or more written characters added to a standard line of sung verse in those forms of music-drama (*xiqu*) in which the number of written characters within a line is regulated, e.g. Yuan *zaju*, *kunqu*, and Beijing opera (*jingju*). The padding written characters serve to clarify meaning and to make the verse more lively and colloquial. Sometimes also called padding lines (*chenju* or *ch'en chü*) and piled written characters (*duozi* or *tuo tzu*). (Dolby HISTORY 25, 56, 73-74, 101, 183)

cheo (Vietnamese)   Literally: satire. See: *hat cheo, phuong cheo boi*.

cheo san dinh (Vietnamese)   See: *phuong cheo boi*.

cheque   See: check.

cherita (Malaysian)   A play. When a classic play is meant, also called *lakon*. See also: *cerita*. (Sweeney RAMAYANA 54) *cherita ranting* (Malaysian)   Locally created shadow play stories (*cherita*) that branch from the trunk of the main *Ramayana* story line or from Javanese *Panji* stories. (Sweeney MALAY 57) The "more obscure" *ranting* plays are, by extension, called *cherita daun* (leaf stories) and *cherita bunga* (flower stories). (Sweeney RAMAYANA 269)

cherusse, cherusque (French)   See: Betsie.

cherxi, chexi, ch'e hsi (Chinese)   Literally: cart play. A form of flower drum play (*huaguxi*) which developed from popular songs sung during the Chinese New Year Lantern Festival. See also: *caichaxi, madengxi.* (Dolby HISTORY 220)

chesty   In early 20th C U.S., said of an actor who overrated his ability. (Wilmeth LANGUAGE)

che tzu (Chinese)   See: *xuezi.*

che tzu hsi (Chinese)   See: *zhezixi.*

cheval (French)   See: *pas de cheval.*

chew the scenery   To overact, especially in emotional scenes. Hence, scenery chewer. (Bowman/Ball THEATRE)

chexi (Chinese)   See: *cherxi.*

chhabi (Hindi)   Literally: picture. A tableau in a *raslila* performance. (Gargi FOLK 127)

chhau (Oriya)   A masked dance and dance-drama performed exclusively by men that occurs in related styles in contiguous regions of Orissa, Bihar, and Bengal states in east India. (Gargi FOLK 167-181)

chhing (Khmer)   A pair of small bronze cymbals used in the classical *pinpeat* musical ensemble. (Anonymous ROYAL 22, Brunet "Nang" 29)

chi (Chinese)   See: *chu.*

chia (Chinese)   See: *jia.*

chia kun (Chinese)   See: *gundiao.*

chia men (Chinese)   See: *jiamen.*

ch'iang (Chinese)   See: *qiang.*

ch'iang tiao (Chinese)   See: *diaoshi.*

chiao pan (Chinese)   See: *jiaoban.*

chiao se (Chinese)   See: *jiaose.*

chiao ti, chiao ti hsi (Chinese)   See: *jiaodi.*

chiaroscuro (Italian)   Light and shade in scene painting, used to create the effect of three dimensionality. The 18th C spelling was *chiaro obscuro.* (Algarotti in Nagler SOURCES 319)

chia sang tzu (Chinese)   See: *xiaosangzi.*

chia tzu hua lien (Chinese)   See: *fujing, erhualian*.

ch'i chuang t'ou (Chinese)   See: *qizhuangtou*.

chicken roost   The uppermost gallery.

chief   A head usher. Sometimes a head electrician or other crew head.

chief and state play   See: *Haupt-und-Staatsaktion*.

chief electrician   1. Especially in the U.S. professional theatre, the head of the crew which sets up and operates the stage lighting. Sometimes called the electrician. (Wehlburg GLOSSARY) 2. See: chief engineer.

chief engineer   In Britain, the person who maintains all the electrical equipment in a theatre. In addition to lighting, this includes everything from motors through wardrobe irons to heating or ventilating equipment. (Bax MANAGEMENT 56-58) See also: chief electrician.

chief illuminator   See: illuminator.

ch'ien chü (Chinese)   See: *qianju*.

chien i (Chinese)   See: *jianyi*.

ch'ien t'ai (Chinese)   See: *wutai*.

chien tzu (Chinese)   See: *jianzi*.

ch'ih (Chinese)   See: *chu*.

ch'ih hsin, ch'ih tzu (Chinese)   See: *chizi*.

chih wei (Chinese)   See: *zhiwei*.

chih wei sheng (Chinese)   See: *zhiweisheng*.

chikyu (Japanese)   A wooden, one-piece *bugaku* mask, perhaps of East European origin. The mask has a long pointed nose and a broad smile. (Wolz BUGAKU 45)

child drama   1. See: children's drama. 2. See: creative drama.

children of Thespis   See: thespian.

children's dance   See: creative movement.

children's drama   In the U.S., for many years the principal term for all forms of theatre by and for children, including children's theatre, creative drama, and recreational theatre. (Goldberg CHILDREN'S 4) The British equivalent, child drama, is now coming into use in the U.S. Also recently used has been theatre education.

children's theatre   1. All types of theatrical activity or performance involving children. This is the meaning approved by the Children's Theatre Association of America in the late 1970s. (Davis/Boehm ''Terminology'' 10) Sometimes abbreviated to C.T. or CT. 2. From at least the 1950s and often today, performances for children, whether by children or adults or both. (Viola ''Children'' 140, Goldberg CHILDREN'S 5) 3. Performances by adults for children. (Goldberg CHILDREN'S 5.)

child's pudding   A small sausage-like cloth hat providing protection to the head if a child should fall. See also: *bourrelet*. (Boucher FASHION)

chimney   1. A standard term for the glass which surrounded the flame of an oil or gas lamp in 19th C theatres. Also called a lamp glass, glass, or globe. (Rees GAS 6-7, 207) 2. Sometimes a term for the lamp housing on an ellipsoidal reflector spotlight.

chimney pot   A 19th C black felt top hat. (Wilcox DICTIONARY, Walkup DRESSING 264)

china circuit   The Pennsylvania towns of Pottstown, Pottsville, and Chambersburg, known for the chamberpots made there. By extension, any theatrical circuit consisting of relatively small and unsophisticated towns. (Wilmeth LANGUAGE)

china crash   See: glass crash.

china orange wench   A fruit vendor in a theatre. (Vincent in Nagler SOURCES 213)

chin armor   A false beard.

ch'in ch'iang (Chinese)   See: *qinqiang*.

chin chü (Chinese)   See: *jinju*.

Chinese shadows, Chinese shadow puppets   See: *ombres chinoises, piyingxi*.

ching (Chinese)   See: *jing*.

ching (Korean)   In masked-dance plays and *p'ungmul*, a large gong which is struck with a beater made of straw or cloth.

ching (Thai)   1. A small pair of bell-cymbals used to mark time in most types of theatre music. 2. An onomatopoeic word for the ringing sound of bell-cymbals. (Duriyanga in Rangthong SOUVENIR 259)

ch'ing ch'ang (Chinese)   See: *qingchang*.

ching ch'iang (Chinese)   See: *jingqiang*.

ching chü (Chinese)   See: *jingju*.

ch'ing chü (Chinese)   See: *qingju*.

ching chü che k'ou (Chinese)   See: *shisanzhe*.

ching hsi (Chinese)   See: *jingju*.

ch'ing hsi (Chinese)   See: *qingxi*.

ching hu (Chinese)   See: *jinghu*.

ch'ing i (Chinese)   See: *zhengdan*.

ch'ing ming hsi (Chinese)   See: *qingmingxi*.

ch'ing yang ch'iang (Chinese)   See: *qingyangqiang*.

ch'ing yang hsi (Chinese)   See: *qingju*.

chin piece   An artificial beard.

chin scarf A medieval, round, often open-crowned headcovering of stiff linen whose attached scarf-veil passed under its cap, then over the chin and neck. See also: *barbette*.

chin sheng (Chinese) See: *jinsheng*.

Chin yüan pen (Chinese) See: Song *zaju*.

chip Especially in Australia, to find fault with a theatre, a performer, an audience, etc. (Granville DICTIONARY)

ch'i pa (Chinese) See: *qiba*.

ch'i pao (Chinese) See: *qibao*.

chi pen kung, chi pen kung fu (Chinese) See: *jiben gongfu*.

chips Primarily in Britain, a nickname for a stage carpenter.

chiquetades (French) See: *slashings*.

chironomy The act of hand movements: gesture. (Granville DICTIONARY)

chirp In Britain, to heckle a performer or a play. Hence, chirper (a heckler). (Granville DICTIONARY)

chisel in To attend a performance without a ticket.

chiton (Greek), **chiton** The basic tunic worn by Greek men and women in ancient times. Used in both comedy and tragedy, the *chiton* might reach the ankles or stop above the knees; women generally wore a long *chiton*. The actor's *chiton* was usually sleeved, belted below the chest, highly colored, and elaborately trimmed. In Old Comedy and perhaps in New, the man's *chiton* was short so that the phallus would show. See also: *poikilon*. (Fuchs CLASSICS, Pickard-Cambridge FESTIVALS 331, Bieber HISTORY xii)

chiton chortaios (Greek) A tunic of coarse material always worn by Silenus, the father of the satyrs. Webster describes such a *chiton* as showing "pieces of wool representing white hair." Liddell/Scott says "a shaggy coat of skins worn by the actor who played Silenus." Also called a *chiton mallotos*. (Pickard-Cambridge FESTIVALS 238, Webster PRODUCTION 32, Liddell/Scott LEXICON)

chiton mallotos (Greek) See: *chiton chortaios*.

chitterling An 18th-19th C linen frill on a man's shirtfront. (Wilcox DICTIONARY, Chalmers CLOTHES 217)

chiu lung k'ou (Chinese) See: *jiulongkou*.

ch'iung chü (Chinese) See: *qiongju*.

ch'iung sheng (Chinese) See: *qiongsheng*.

chiusetta (Italian) A short strophe at the conclusion of a monologue or dialogue in *commedia dell'arte*.

chiu yin lo (Chinese) See: *yunluo*.

chixin (Chinese) See: *chizi*.

chizi, ch'ih tzu (Chinese)   Literally: pond. In a tea-house theatre (*xiyuan*) of the 17th-early 20th C, the portion of ground-floor seating extending from the stage to the center of the house. In some theatres this was inexpensive seating at tables. The area may at one time have been unroofed. Only the scattered seats (*sanzuo*) and the big wall (*daqiang*) seats were cheaper. Sometimes called *chixin* or *ch'ih hsin*. (Mackerras RISE 203, Dolby HISTORY 190-191)

chlaina (Greek)   A small cloak often worn thrown over the shoulders by satyrs and maenads. It is a variety of *himation*, at least in being an outer garment. (Bieber HISTORY 16, Fuchs CLASSICS)

chlamys (Greek), **chlamys**   A short cloak, often highly colored, usually pinned at the shoulder (occasionally in front). The *chlamys*, characteristic of such active wearers as young men, travelers, and soldiers, was often fastened at the right shoulder so as to leave the right arm free; it was also sometimes thrown over the shoulders. Also appears as Greek *chlamus* (rare), and clamus (rare). (Bieber HISTORY 154, fig. 399b; Fuchs CLASSICS; Nicoll DEVELOPMENT 27)

cho (Assamese)   An effigy (monkey, bear, horse, elephant) used in *ankiya nat*. Constructed of bamboo frames and covered with cloth or papier-mâché. *Cho-ghar* is a room for storing the effigies, and an actors' dressing room. (Richmond "Vaisnava" 155)

chobo (Japanese)   In *kabuki*, the duo of chanter (*tayu*) and *shamisen* player who perform in *gidayu* style narrative portions of plays adapted from the puppet theatre. See also: *yuka*. (Malm in Brandon/Malm/Shively STUDIES 139, Leiter ENCYCLOPEDIA 41)

chocolateer   Formerly, a black or blackface actor. Now offensive. (Berrey/Van den Bark SLANG 573)

cho-ghar (Assamese)   See: *cho*.

chok (Thai)   The major male clown role in *likay*. Other types are *chok ying* (female clown) and *chok kong* (clown villain). The term is probably derived from the English word 'joker.' (Virulrak "Likay" 190)

choke dimmer   In Britain, a term for an autotransformer dimmer. (Corry PLANNING 98)

choker   1. A rope or cable secured to the locking rail in a fly gallery and tied with a prusik knot to the onstage side of the operating line of an unbalanced counterweight arbor, to keep the arbor from lowering. The choker can be a block and tackle to allow for upward or downward adjustments to the arbor. 2. A comedy. 3. See: *katakeleusmos*.

chok kong, chok ying (Thai)   See: *chok*.

chondong (Indonesian)   See: *condong*.

ch'ongun (Korean)   Literally: heavenly lord. A ceremony of heaven-worship in which some participants wore masks, in the tribal state of Mahan (3rd C BC to 3rd C AD). (Cho "Yangju" 27)

chopines   16th-17th C wooden stilts on shoes to support heel and toe and to provide protection from mud and water. Used largely in southern Europe, especially Venice. Also called moiles. (Barton COSTUME 226, Wilcox DICTIONARY)

chops   Technique in a performer. (Lees "Lexicon" 57)

choragia (Latin Roman)   See: *choragium, itinera versurarum.*

choragium (Latin Roman)   Production materials and equipment. The word apparently included costumes, properties, and any other equipment needed. *Choragium* originally signified the training and production of a chorus; the OED calls *choragium* dancing-ground, and marks it foreign. Plural *choragia*; but see also *itinera versurarum.* (Saunders COSTUME 20-21)

choragus (Latin Roman)   A professional provider of costumes and properties. The *choragus* was apparently a theatrical supplier who, like his modern counterpart, appears also to have conducted business outside the theatre. One ancient source says he also functioned as stage manager. Also called *conductor.* See also: *choregus.* (Duckworth NATURE 74, 89; Saunders COSTUME 17-20; Allen ANTIQUITIES 58)

choral ode   See: *stasimon.*

choral reading   In readers theatre, multiple voices interpreting together.

choraules (Latin Roman)   A flute player who accompanied the chorus. Bieber's 1939 choraulet, later replaced by *choraules*, may have been an attempt to anglicize the Latin word. (Bieber HISTORY 305 n.23, 1939 Bieber HISTORY 413)

chord in "G"   In Britain in the past, a musical fanfare used in melodrama to emphasize an especially dramatic moment or line of dialogue. (Granville DICTIONARY)

chord on, chord off   1. At musical comedy rehearsals, a piano chord cuing a performer's entrance or exit. 2. In vaudeville, a fanfare announcing a performer's entrance. (Granville DICTIONARY)

choregein (Greek)   1. To pay for the chorus, to serve as *choregus.* 2. To provide. This meaning is late, after the choregic system had been replaced. See: *choregus.* (Flickinger GREEK 186)

choregia (Greek)   The service rendered by a wealthy citizen in bearing financial responsibility for a play or plays at one of the Dionysian festivals. Also appears as choregy, though rarely. See also: *choregus.* (Allen ANTIQUITIES 44, Flickinger GREEK 270-271)

choregic system, Choregic System   See: *choregus.*

choregus (Greek), **choregus**   Literally: chorus leader. 1. Early, the leader or trainer of the chorus. 2. In classic Greece, a wealthy citizen responsible for the cost of a play or group of plays produced at the City Dionysia. These expenses were borne as a state tax by some sixteen or eighteen *choregi* selected by the *archon* who headed the festival; this method (choregic system) of paying for play production probably dates from about 502 B.C. A given *choregus* might be concerned with one play (comedy), a group of three or four plays (trilogy or tetralogy), or simply a chorus (dithyramb). In comedy and tragedy, the *choregus'* responsibility apparently included chorus, leader, extra actors, and flutist—everything but the chief actors and matters pertaining to them. The choregic system ended late in the 4th C BC, when the *choregi* were replaced by a single *agonothetes*: he bore the cost of the festival with the help of state funds. Also spelled *choregos* (plural: *choregoi*), sometimes in the U.S., choragus. See also: *choragus*. (Allen ANTIQUITIES 44-46, Flickinger GREEK 270-271, Pickard-Cambridge DITHYRAMB 36-37, Arnott SCENIC 111)

choregy   See: *choregia*.

choreographer   An artist who notates or creates a dance. Sometimes called a choreographist. (Purdom PRODUCING)

choreography   The actual steps, groupings, and patterns of a ballet or dance composition. (Grant TECHNICAL)

choreutai, choreutae (Greek)   Members of the chorus. (Pickard-Cambridge FESTIVALS 74, 246; Allen ANTIQUITIES 37, 47)

chorikon, chorika (Greek)   See: *stasimon*.

chorister   A singer. In Britain, a term for a member of the chorus in a musical theatre production. (Bowman/Ball THEATRE)

choristka (Yiddish)   A chorus girl. Russian: *khoristka*.

chorodidaskalos (Greek)   Especially after the 5th C BC, the trainer or teacher of the chorus. (Earlier, the poet had trained the chorus himself.) Among his other duties, the chorus leader probably (with the protagonist) distributed the roles among the subordinate actors. Also printed *chorodidaskalus*. See also: *coryphaeus, didaskalos*. (Bieber HISTORY 81; 1939 Bieber HISTORY 150; Pickard-Cambridge FESTIVALS 76, 90-91)

chorolektes (Greek)   Probably an assistant to the *choregus* in the dithyramb. Haigh and Pickard-Cambridge seem to agree that he may have assembled the chorus without necessarily selecting them. Pickard-Cambridge also notes, however, that in context the word "seems to mean the leader of the chorus, who gave them the...starting note." Liddell/Scott gives "one who selected the chorus." (Haigh ATTIC 60, Pickard-Cambridge FESTIVALS 76, Liddell/Scott LEXICON)

choroscript   See: movement notation.

chorpodium (Greek)   Literally: chorus platform, chorus stage. According to some, a raised stage for the chorus, used in Aeschylean times. This view is widely opposed; Bieber and Pickard-Cambridge do not believe that such a stage ever existed. Also spelled *chor-podium*; German uses *Oberbühne*. (Bieber HISTORY 79, Pickard-Cambridge DIONYSUS 34)

chorus   1. A group of performers functioning as a unit. In ancient Greece, the dithyramb was almost completely choral, the satyr play somewhat less so. In early tragedy, the chorus was often more than half the play; much reduced by the end of the 5th C BC, it seems nevertheless to have persisted as long as the form did. The comic chorus, however, virtually disappeared with Old Comedy (early 4th C BC), becoming in New Comedy (late 4th C BC) essentially a between-scenes entertainment of dance and song. Division into semi-choruses sometimes occurred, perhaps more often in the satyr play and comedy than in tragedy; especially in comedy, the semi-choruses might be hostile to one another. Lines for individual members of the chorus were not unknown. The choruses were men masked as whatever the play required. The choral singing was in unison and the chorus was normally, but not always, on stage throughout the performance. For further detail on chorus members, see *aristerostatae, dexiostatae, kraspeditae, laurostatae*. 2. The material presented by such a unit, including lines, music, business, and movement. 3. In Elizabethan drama, the speaker of a prologue or epilogue who sometimes commented on the action. 4. A group of singers and dancers in a musical comedy or revue. Hence, chorus boy, chorus girl. 5. A group of singers who sing the choral parts of an opera, operetta, or oratorio. 6. A song or part of a song (especially a refrain) to be sung by more than one person.

chorus boy, chorus girl   Traditional terms for a member of the chorus of a musical theatre production.

chorus-room   In Britain, the chorus' dressing room. (Granville DICTIONARY)

chorus shirt   See: ballet shirt.

choryphaeus (Greek)   See: *coryphaeus*.

chottae (Korean)   In masked dance-drama, a transverse bamboo flute. See: *samhyon yukkak*. (Cho ''Ogwangdae'' 29)

cho tzu (Chinese)   See: *zhuozi*.

chou, ch'ou (Chinese)   Literally: ugly, scandalous. Clown role. A comic role, usually male and portrayed with a patch of white makeup in the center of the face, but also including comic, generally middle-aged female characters; a major role category (*hangdang*) in many forms of music-drama (*xiqu*). Clown role characters may be evil or mentally tortured as well as actually foolish or ribald. In *kunqu*, major subcategories of the clown role include assistant (*fu*) and small face (*xiaomian*); in Beijing opera, civil clown (*wenchou*), martial clown (*wuchou*), and clown female (*choudan*). Popularly called small flower face (*xiaohualian* or *hsiao hua lien*) and third flower face (*sanhualian* or *san hua lien*). (Dolby HISTORY 105-106, 181; Mackerras MODERN 25; Scott CLASSICAL 76-78; Scott INTRODUCTION 30–31)

choudan, ch'ou tan (Chinese)   Literally: clown female role. A comic or villainous female character whose portrayal parodies that of female roles (*dan*);

a major subcategory of the clown role (*chou*) in Beijing opera (*jingju*) and many other forms of music-drama (*xiqu*). In some forms, called rocking female role (*yaodan* or *yao tan*). Also called clown woman (*choupozi* or *ch'ou p'o tzu*) and colorful female role (*caidan* or *ts'ai tan*). Sometimes these latter two names are used to distinguish older from younger clown female characters respectively; the younger *caidan* characters are sometimes played by performers of the flower female role (*huadan*). (Scott CLASSICAL 74)

chou kun (Chinese)   See: *zhougun*.

ch'ou p'o tzu, choupozi, ch'ou tan (Chinese)   See: *choudan*.

chou tzu (Chinese)   See: *zhouzi*.

chowki (Kannada)   A dressing room in a *yaksagana* theatre.

Christmas pantomime   See: pantomime.

Christy   A nickname for E. P. Christy's minstrel show and its participants. The Christy minstrels performed in both the U.S. and Britain, and the term Christy was often used to mean minstrel, or, in the plural, blackface entertainers. (Leavitt MANAGEMENT 377)

chromatic aberration   A condition in which a lens breaks light into some or all of its component colors (approximately the colors of the rainbow). Onstage, this occurs typically at the edge of a beam cast by a plano-convex (PC) spotlight, or, less often, at the riser edges of a step lens. When a PC spotlight is focused down to its narrowest beam, the aberration appears as a rainbow-colored ring at the edge of the pool of light cast by the spotlight. Sometimes called a color aberration. (Bellman LIGHTING 72-73, Lounsbury THEATRE)

chronicle history play   A play, especially from Shakespeare's period, based on events in history, usually concerned with a particular monarch's reign. Such modern playwrights as August Strindberg and Maxwell Anderson have also used the form. Sometimes shortened to chronicle play, chronicle, history play, or history. (Bowman/Ball THEATRE)

chronométrage (French)   The precise timing of a performance. Vsevelod Meyerhold's way of controlling an actor's tempo and form. (Law "*Woe*" 91)

chu, ch'u (Chinese)   A scene in a *chuanqi* play; a single play consists of forty to fifty scenes. Sometimes also called *chi* or *ch'ih*, and *zhe* or *che*. See also: *zhezixi*. (Scott CLASSICAL 37)

chü (Chinese)   See: *ju*.

ch'ü (Chinese)   See: *qu*.

ch'uan ch'i (Chinese)   See: *chuanqi*.

ch'uan chü (Chinese)   See: *chuanju*.

chuang chü (Chinese)   See: *zhuangju*.

chuang ku (Chinese)   See: *zhuanggu*.

chuang tan (Chinese)   See: *zhuangdan*.

ch'uan hsi (Chinese)   See: *chuanju.*

chuanju, ch'uan chü (Chinese)   Sichuan (or Szechwan) opera, the principal form of music-drama (*xiqu*) in Sichuan Province; also popular in Yunnan and Guizhou provinces. It includes four musical systems which were introduced into Sichuan from outside the province, *gaoqiang, kunshanqiang, pihuang* (called *huqinqiang* in its Sichuan form), and *bangziqiang* (called *tanqiang* or *t'an ch'iang* in its Sichuan form), as well as indigenous Sichuanese lantern plays (*dengxi*). In the 18th C, these five came to be performed together, and by the 20th C the name *chuanju* was given to the combination, in which the influence of *gaoqiang* is predominant. Also called *chuanxi* or *ch'uan hsi.* (Dolby HISTORY 226-227, Howard CONTEMPORARY 17, Kalvodova/Vanis "Origin" 505-523, Mackerras MODERN 156-162)

chuanke, ch'uan k'e (Chinese)   See: *yongju.*

chuanqi, ch'uan ch'i (Chinese)   1. A type of script and performance prevalent in 14th-18th C which developed out of southern drama (*nanxi*). These plays were performed in *kunqu, yiyangqiang, qingyangqiang,* and numerous other forms of music-drama (*xiqu*). The plays are well-knit, regular in structure, and have complex plots and characters; most consist of a prologue (*jiamen*) and thirty to fifty scenes (*chu*) and are written for four main role categories (*hangdang*): male (*sheng*), female (*dan*), painted-face (*jing*), and clown (*chou*). Each play required one to three days to perform; from the 18th C, excerpted scenes (*zhezixi*) were usually presented instead. (Dolby HISTORY 71-78, 82-99; Liu INTRODUCTION 247-260) 2. See: Yuan *zaju.*

chuantongju, ch'uan t'ung chü (Chinese)   Literally: traditional play. Since 1949, a music-drama (*xiqu*) set in the 19th C or earlier and composed, choreographed, and refined by master performers before 1949. In performance, such plays exemplify traditional aesthetic principles, skills, and techniques. Also called *chuantongxi* or *ch'uan t'ung hsi* and history play (*lishiju* or *li shih chü*). See also: *xiandaiju, xinbiande lishiju.* (Mackerras ORIGINS 188)

chuantongxi, ch'uan t'ung chü, ch'uan t'ung hsi (Chinese)   See: *chuantongju.*

chuanxi (Chinese)   See: *chuanju.*

ch'u chü (Chinese)   See: *chuju.*

ch'ü chü (Chinese)   See: *quju.*

chucker out   In Britain, one who removes hecklers and other unruly spectators; a bouncer. (Granville DICTIONARY)

chuck the part   To give up a role.

chud (Thai)   Literally: set. 1. A set of puppets used in a performance of shadow theatre (*nang yai*). 2. By extension, a dramatic episode from the *Ramakien* (*Ramayana*) that makes up a day's performance in *nang yai* or *khon* and hence a 'play.' See also: *ton*. (Dhaninivat/Yupho KHON 16-17, Yupho KHON 52, Brandon SOUTHEAST 65)

chudiao (Chinese)   See: *hanju*.

chüeh se (Chinese)   See: *jiaose*.

ch'ü i (Chinese)   See: *quyi*.

ch'uibari (Korean)   See: *kkaeki-ch'um*.

ch'ui ch'iang (Chinese)   See: *chuiqiang*.

chuichuiqiang, ch'ui ch'ui ch'iang (Chinese)   See: *baiju*.

chuiqiang, ch'ui ch'iang (Chinese)   Literally: blown music. A musical mode (*diaoshi*) characterized by horizontal bamboo flute (*di*) accompaniment. It is one of the most important modes in *huiju*, and is also used in Beijing opera (*jingju*) and other forms of music-drama (*xiqu*). It developed in the 17th and 18th C from the influence of *kunqu* upon *sipingqiang*; it originally used *lianquti* musical structure, but later adopted *banqiangti*. Called *anqingdiao* or *an ch'ing tiao* in Hunan opera (*xiang-ju*), and *sanwuqi* or *san wu ch'i* in *wuju* and *shaoju*.

chuji (Korean)   Literally: lion. A lion-like figure, danced by two men, in the *pyolsin-kut* ritual masked dance of Hahoe village. See also: *saja*. (Korean MASKS 9)

chujo (Japanese)   A melancholy and elegant mask worn by the ghost of a young warrior in the second part (*nochi ba*) of a warrior *no* play. The term derives from *chujo*, a military rank which a number of these heroes (for example, Taira no Kiyotsune) held in real life. (Shimazaki NOH 59, Nippon Gakujutsu JAPANESE 61-73)

chuju, ch'u chü (Chinese)   A form of music-drama (*xiqu*) popular in Hubei Province. It developed c. 18th-early 19th C from folk songs and dances of the Huangpi and Xiaogan regions of Hubei and the influence of *yiyangqiang*. In the early 20th C it was influenced by *hanju* and Beijing opera (*jingju*), and in the 1950s it absorbed *qingxi* and was further influenced by the *gaoqiang* musical system. Called Huangpi and Xiaogan flower drum (*huangxiao huagu* or *huang hsiao hua ku*) and western road flower drum (*xilu huagu* or *hsi lu hua ku*) before 1926. (Dolby HISTORY 223-224, Mackerras MODERN 156)

chukpangul-patki (Korean)   See: *taegwangdae-p'ae*.

chu kung tiao (Chinese)   See: *zhugongdiao*.

ch'um (Korean)   A generic term for folk or popular dance, including masked dances and disco.

chump   A burlesque theatre patron. Originally, a person easily fooled. (Wilmeth LANGUAGE)

chump educator   A show business news publication; the term usually referred to *Variety* and *Billboard*, both of which 'educated' chumps (outsiders). (Wilmeth LANGUAGE) *chu'nanxi, ch'u nan hsi* (Chinese)   See: *qingju*.

chung (Korean)   See: *mokchung*.

chung chou tzu (Chinese)   See: *zhouzi*.

chung hsü (Chinese)   See: *daqu*.

chung lu pang tzu (Chinese)   See: *jinju*.

chu nikai (Japanese)   Literally: mid-second story. Dressing rooms located on the mezzanine, between the first and second stories of a *kabuki* theatre of the 18th and 19th C. The rooms were used by middle-ranking actors of female roles (*onnagata*). (Leiter ENCYCLOPEDIA 41-43)

ch'ün k'ou (Chinese)   See: *xiangsheng*.

chu nori (Japanese)   1. A *no* rhythm in which sixteen syllables of text are sung within an eight-beat musical measure. It is the fastest of the *hyoshi au* rhythms and is used for active dances. (Hoff/Flindt "Structure" 236) 2. Flying an actor in *kabuki* or a puppet in *bunraku* over the stage or the audience by means of wires and pulleys. Also called *chu zuri*. One type of *keren*. (Leiter "Spectacle" 177-179, Leiter ENCYCLOPEDIA 43)

ch'ü p'ai (Chinese)   See: *qupai*.

chupak (Indonesian)   See: *cupak*.

chü pen (Chinese)   See: *juben*.

ch'ü p'o (Chinese)   See: *qupo*.

ch'ü ti (Chinese)   See: *di*.

ch'u tiao (Chinese)   See: *hanju*.

ch'ü tiao (Chinese)   See: *banshi*.

ch'ü tzu hsi (Chinese)   See: *meihuju*.

chu zuri (Japanese)   See: *chu nori*.

ciarlatano (Italian)   A charlatan, a quack. Said of a *commedia dell'arte* or any other traveling performer.

cidamian (Chinese)   See: *zhengdan*.

cielo (Italian)   Literally: heaven, sky. In the theatre of the Renaissance, the painted borders hanging over the stage. (Nicoll DEVELOPMENT 89)

cinaedologi (Latin Roman)   Obscene performers, perhaps chanters-dancers, of ancient Greek times. (Duchartre ITALIAN 24)

cinq positions des pieds (French)   In ballet, the five positions of the feet. Every step or movement is begun and ended in one or another of these. For descriptions, see: first position, second position, etc. (Grant TECHNICAL)

circle   1. In the Stanislavsky system, an imaginary barrier a performer sets up about him or her to prevent distraction. Once in the circle, that is, in character, the performer stays within it throughout the acting time. 2. Chiefly in Britain, a seating area above the orchestra or main auditorium floor: the dress circle and, above it, the upper circle. The U.S. equivalents are mezzanine and balcony, or first balcony and second balcony. (Bowman/Ball THEATRE) In dance: 3. A smooth, unbroken arc or curved movement of the arms, legs, etc. 4. Movements in a circular path.

circle front spot   In Britain, a spotlight in a protective enclosure at the front of the dress circle. See also: balcony lights. (Granville DICTIONARY)

circle stock, circuit stock   A repertory arrangement in which a troupe does the same play for a few days, first in one town and then in another on a roughly circular path, before returning to the first town with a different play. (Wilmeth LANGUAGE, Ashby in Matlaw AMERICAN 139)

circle theatre   A synonym for arena theatre, especially when the stage and seating arrangement approach the circular form.

circuit   1. Any complete path of an electric current. In stage lighting, for example, a circuit may be the path from the stage main through the stage lighting equipment and back to the main, or it may be any smaller circuit from the control board through a dimmer, a load (such as a spotlight), and back to the controlboard; or it may be any other complete path. (Bellman SCENOGRAPHY, Wehlburg GLOSSARY, Bentham ART) 2. Theatres in various towns where touring companies perform. Usually the chain of theatres is under a single management. Hence, circuit booking, circuit stock, playing the circuit.

circuit stock   See: circle stock.

circular chorus   The translation of a Greek term which always means dithyramb (Pickard-Cambridge does not give the Greek term). It is thought that dithyrambic choruses danced and sang in a circle, rather than in the rectangular formation of dramatic choruses. (Pickard-Cambridge DITHYRAMB 32)

circular structure   In playwriting, organization in which the action shows little progression and ends much as it began. (Cassady/Cassady VIEW)

circular sweep   A piece of wood cut in an arc to form part of a circular object, such as a column or tree.

circulatores (Latin)   Itinerant troupes in the Dark Ages. (Nicoll MASKS 93)

circus   1. An entertainment consisting of elaborate spectacle, animal acts, clowns, acrobats, etc., stemming from 18th C equestrian shows. 2. A place where such entertainments are presented. 3. Said of a style of theatrical production, chiefly spectacular. 4. To turn a scenic unit around and reveal its other side.

circus games   See: *ludi circenses*.

circus job   A lavish publicity effort promoting a show, especially one that is in danger of failing. (Wilmeth LANGUAGE)

cishadan, tz'u sha tan (Chinese)   Literally: stabbing and killing female role. 1. A heroic, avenging young or middle-aged female role; a major subcategory of the female role (*dan*) in *kunqu* drama, and a subdivision of the principal female role (*zhengdan*) in Beijing opera (*jingju*). (Dolby HISTORY 105, Scott CLASSICAL 32) 2. A cruel, licentious female role which emphasizes dance-acting (*zuo*) skill; a subdivision of the flower female role (*huadan*) in Beijing opera.

ciseaux (French)   See: *pas ciseaux*.

citharistria (Latin Roman)   A female cithara player. Such musicians were among the mixed group of entertainers who performed alongside the mime players. (Nicoll MASKS 36)

citharoedi (Latin)   See: minstrel.

citrawara (Malaysian)   See: *drama moden*.

citronella circuit   Especially in the past in U.S., summer theatres in country areas (from the name of a then popular mosquito repellent). (Granville DICTIONARY 45)

citte (Kannada)   Literally: a dot. White thorn-like dots which are part of the makeup of demonic characters in *yaksagana*. (Karanth YAKSAGANA 105)

City Dionysia   In ancient Greece, the major Athenian festival in honor of Dionysus. By all odds the most important to drama of the Greek festivals, the City Dionysia was held from late March to early April, a time when Athens was filled with visitors. The first of the festival's five or six days was largely taken up with a great religious procession lasting several hours. Except during the Peloponnesian wars, the program normally consisted of three days given to tragedy and one day to five comedies; the order of these days is unknown. During the Peloponnesian wars, three tragedies, a satyr play, and a comedy were probably given on each of three days. Tragedy, the chief attraction until at least the 2nd C AD, was first given in 534 BC. Before the end of the 6th C BC the satyr play and then the dithyramb were introduced. Comedy was added early in the 5th C BC. Though both dithyramb and the satyr play were older than tragedy, not, apparently, until they had gained artistic and literary quality were they admitted to the festival. Also called the Dionysia, Great (sometimes Greater) Dionysia, occasionally Athenian Dionysia. See also: Dionysian festivals. (Pickard-Cambridge FESTIVALS 57-101; Bieber HISTORY 39, 52-53, 80; Haigh ATTIC 6-7)

city flat cap   A black wool knitted or felt courtier's beret up to the 17th C, when it became a favorite of the middle and lower classes. Also called a status cap, flat cap. (Barton COSTUME 212)

civic theatre   See: community theatre.

civilian   A vaudevillian's term for someone not in show business.

CL (often Ç)   Center line—a real or imaginary line marking the exact center of the stage, running upstage-downstage.

clambake   A poorly constructed or rehearsed program. (Wright UNDERSTANDING)

clamp   A wooden or metal device with jaws to hold two things together, such as two pieces of wood being glued, two flats that do not join evenly, a lighting instrument and a pipe batten, two or more rope lines, etc. See also: bracket clamp, C-clamp, pipe clamp.

C-lamp   An early designation of any gas-filled incandescent lamp. The term and its variants—Mazda C, C-type lamp, Type C, C-type, C—are now rarely heard. See also: gas-filled lamp. (Fuchs LIGHTING 110, Gassner/Barber PRODUCING 802)

clamus   See: *chlamys*.

Clancy, Clancy hook   See: picture frame hanger and socket.

Clapham Junction   In Britain, a botched makeup operation in which age lines are indiscriminately drawn with a few parallel lines on the forehead and nose-to-mouth. (Melvill MAKE-UP)

clapper   A sound effects device for simulating crackling fire. Two leather straps sewn together at one end are snapped together. (Bowman/Ball THEATRE)

(the) claps   Applause.

claptrap   1. A cheap device used by a performer, such as rhetorical delivery or over-sentimentalizing, to trap or catch applause. Hence, theatrical claptrap, claptrap sentiment, 2. Formerly, a noise-making device to stimulate applause. (Bowman/Ball THEATRE, Dolman ACTING)

claque   1. A group of hired applauders. There are indications that claques were employed by both actors and poets of the Greek theatre at least as early as Menander (born 342 BC). In Christian Roman times, claquers were familiar and vociferous—so vociferous, indeed, that opposing claques often caused riots in the theatre. Also called *fautores* and *theatrales operae*. In France, *claque*. (Haigh ATTIC 345, Mantzius HISTORY I 228, Sandys COMPANION 520) 2. In dance, a beating together of the heels or soles of the feet. (Rogers DANCE 244)

clarification   See: *katharsis*.

classic acting   An acting style marked by formality in presenting passion and by polished, stately speech and physical action. (Bowman/Ball THEATRE)

classical ballet   Dance in which pattern, movement, and form are of primary importance. (Kersley/Sinclair BALLET)

classical drama   Specifically, Greek drama and theatre from 534 to 336 BC, but classic or classical are terms often used to cover all of Greek and Roman drama from the 6th C BC to the 6th C AD. In later periods, when playwrights modelled their works on those of the ancient dramatists, the plays were categorized as neo-classic. But every language has its classical drama, as Shakespeare in English, Racine in French, etc. Hence, classic, classicism, the classics, classic play, classic theatre. (Cameron/Gillespie ENJOYMENT, Bowman/Ball THEATRE)

clatter crash   A device for simulating a crash. Odd pieces of timber are strung a foot or two apart on a long cord; the cord runs up to a pulley and down to a tie-off. When the cord is released, the pieces of wood clatter to the floor. (Collison SOUND 101)

clavilux   Early in the 20th C, an instrument which played upon a screen varying colors in essentially abstract patterns. The invention of Thomas Wilfred, the clavilux was an attempt to create with light and color a theatrical form analogous to music.

clay modelers   In vaudeville, an act in which a performer (often an accomplished sculptor) fashioned a quick replica of a famous personage. If the person was unpopular, he threw extra wads of clay at it. The same routine was followed for a replica of a mother-in-law. (Laurie VAUDEVILLE 212)

clean   See: clear.

clean house   A sold-out performance. Hence, the house has 'gone clean.' (Sobel NEW)

clean it up   A director's order for performers to rehearse a scene until it improves.

clear   Of a light controlboard, to move all controls to an off position, as in "Clear your board." Clean is an occasional synonym. Clear may be used in a more limited fashion, as in "Clear channels 7, 9, 11, and 12."

"Clear!"   A command by the stage manager to get stagehands and unneeded actors off the stage before the curtain rises. Also as: "Clear stage!" (Bowman/Ball THEATRE)

clearance   See: edge clearance.

clear benefit   A performer's benefit with all house charges or expenses paid by the management. Also called a free benefit. (Troubridge BENEFIT 19)

cleared   1. Moved off or taken away, as when a property is removed from the stage. 2. Said of a stage emptied of workers or performers before the rise of the curtain.

clearer   A stagehand who takes properties offstage or brings them on during a scene shift.

clearing house   A daily meeting of the stage manager and assistants. (Gruver/Hamilton STAGE 60)

clearing pole, clearing stick   A long piece of wood, sometimes with a crosspiece at the top end, used to untangle fouled lines or scenery. Also called a long arm. (Bowman/Ball THEATRE)

clear stage   A stage ready for a performance. See also: "Clear!"

cleat   1. A wooden or metal projection or hook to which a line can be tied or laced to keep scenery in position. Hence, brace cleat, lash cleat, tie-off cleat, etc. 2. To tie together two scenic units by such means. (In Australia, 'toggle' is used for both the above meanings.)

cleat bar   A term sometimes used for a fly rail. (Bowman/Ball THEATRE)

cleat line   See: lash line.

clench, clenching   See: clinch plate.

clerks' play   A medieval miracle play, so called because associations of clerks produced such plays. (Chambers MEDIAEVAL II 104)

clew   1. A metal clamp used for joining a single rope to a group of ropes so that the single rope may be used to operate the entire group. Hence, to clew, clewing, common clew, curtain clew, three-line clew, etc. Occasionally spelled clue. 2. To draw up the bottom half of a drop or drapery in order to halve its length and remove it from the audience's view. Also called trip. Hence, tripping. (Bowman/Ball THEATRE)

clichés in acting   Stereotyped mannerisms or properties which, because they have been so frequently repeated, would occur immediately to even an unimaginative mind. (McGaw ACTING)

cliché situation   In playwriting, a stereotyped situation, such as a last-minute rescue, which can get a stock response from an audience. (Brooks/Heilman UNDERSTANDING)

clicker   A complimentary ticket. (Wilmeth LANGUAGE)

client   A theatre patron.

climax   1. In playwriting, the scene or moment near the end of a play when tensions are the greatest and when the plot and theme are finally and fully revealed and resolved. See also: catastrophe. Such playwriting terms as climax are given different meanings by different people. 2. In vaudeville, the point of greatest interest in a sequence of words or events. (Wilmeth LANGUAGE) 3. The next to the last act in a play.

climax curtain   The curtain closing the next-to-last act. (Berrey/Van den Bark SLANG 578)

clinch plate, clinching plate   Especially in the recent past, a metal plate placed under a flat when corner blocks and keystones were being nailed to the framework; clout nails driven through the plywood blocks and framing pieces hit the plate and bent or clinched, gripping the front face of the frame. Also called a clinch, clinching iron, or clout plate; sometimes spelled clench or clenching.

clip   Especially in British usage, an alternate for clamp, as in barrel clip and hanging clip, both for U.S. pipe clamp. (Bowman/Ball THEATRE, Rae/Southern INTERNATIONAL)

clip a cue   To cut in on another performer's line before it is complete. See also: cue bite, step on a laugh, step on a line, overlap.

clip connectors   Clips which hold a cartridge fuse. (Bellman LIGHTING 150)

clip terminal   A spring fastener sometimes used onstage in making a temporary electrical connection. (Lounsbury THEATRE, Wehlburg GLOSSARY)

cloak-and-dagger play, cloak-and-sword play   See: *capa y espada.*

cloak-and-suiter   An early 20th C term for a wealthy person who invested in a theatrical venture. (Berrey/Van den Bark SLANG 574)

cloaths   Formerly, costumes.

clodhopper   A London street dancer. (Orwell DOWN 174)

(the) clods   The provinces.

clog dance   A lively dance in which the performer wears clogs or heavy shoes. (Wilmeth LANGUAGE)

close   1. To end the run of a show. 2. To draw the curtains together. 3. To turn the body away from the audience. 4. To be the last number on a variety program. 5. To sign a contract.

closed rehearsal   A rehearsal to which visitors are not admitted.

closed turn   A turn away from the audience by a performer. The opposite of an open turn. (Canfield CRAFT)

close in   1. To draw curtains or shutters together or to drop a curtain. 2. To turn the body toward the center of the stage. 3. When hyphenated, a flat used as a return at the side of a stage setting.

close-in curtain   A draw or traveler curtain.

close-in drop   An act drop or main curtain.

closer   The last act on a bill, as in vaudeville. Hence, to close the show, closing, closing spot, closing stanza.

closet drama   A play written to be read rather than produced on stage. See also: literary drama. (Brooks/Heilman UNDERSTANDING)

closing glee   See: opening glee.

closing notice   An announcement posted by the management on the callboard that a play's run will terminate following a specified performance on a specified date. Posted in the professional theatre by Equity rule, a week in advance. (Sobel NEW)

closing woman   In burlesque, the featured female performer.

cloth   1. A painted drop, such as a mountain cloth, sky cloth. 2. Material used to cover flat frames or serve as a curtain, drop, or floor covering. Hence, backcloth, cut cloth, floor cloth, front cloth, leg cloth, stage cloth, star cloth (a drop with small holes and lights behind them), etc. (Bowman/Ball THEATRE, Crampton HANDBOOK)

cloth border   See: border.

cloth cyclorama   See: cyclorama.

cloth dutchman   See: dutchman.

clothes   Costumes. Old spelling: cloaths.

clothes horse   See: show girl.

clothespin   In some types of interconnecting panels, a device resembling a clothespin used in making an electrical connection. (Bowman MODERN)

cloud bell   In the 18th C, a prompter's bell apparently used to cue cloud machines. There was a border bell to cue the movement of cloud borders. (Hughes in Hume LONDON 131)

cloud border   A hanging cloth border simulating the sky. Once called a clouding.

cloud cloth   See: umbrator.

Cloud Creator, cloud creator   See: Nebulator.

clouding   1. Formerly, a masking piece used to cover the junction of a border and wing or to serve as the front face of a flying rig. The Covent Garden Theatre inventory of 1743 implies that a clouding could be drawn off to the side when not needed. (Visser in Hume LONDON 84) 2. See: cloud border.

cloud machine, cloud projector   Any lighting instrument which shows clouds, usually on a sky drop or sky cyclorama. The modern cloud projector is a lens instrument with provision for one or more slides. Cloud machines vary greatly in their complexity and may include provision for moving clouds; such a projector is likely to be called an effect(s) machine or effect(s) projector. Cloud projector is primarily U.S., while cloud machine has long been used in both the U.S. and Britain. Sometimes called a cloud-effect machine. (Bowman/Ball THEATRE, Fuchs LIGHTING 212, Rae/Southern INTERNATIONAL)

clout   1. Formerly, a piece of cloth simulating a cloud. "They fly through Clouds [made] of Clouts...." (Fane LOVE N4r) 2. A 17th C working-class woman's chin scarf. (Chalmers CLOTHES 193)

clout nail   Full term: blued clout nail. A wedge-shaped nail formerly used to fasten corner blocks and keystones to scenic frames. The end of the nail is relatively soft, and when a clinch plate is placed under the pieces of wood to be nailed together, the clout nail goes through the wood and clinches. Also called a cut nail.

clout plate   See: clinch plate.

clown   1. In legitimate theatre, a buffoon, often a yokel; a rough, uncouth low comedy character. 2. A performer who plays such parts. 3. To act like a clown. Hence, clownish, clowning, clownage, clownade. A clown is sometimes described as a fool or jester, but those comic types are usually far more clever. (Bowman/Ball THEATRE, Dolman ACTING)

clown the come-in   To entertain an audience before the main attraction begins. (Berrey/Van den Bark SLANG 586)

clown white   An opaque white greasepaint used mainly as a foundation by harlequins and clowns.

club date   A private club or casino engagement for a performer, act, play, or company.

clue   See: clew.

cluster   See: central loudspeaker system.

clutch-type board   Especially in the past in Britain, a remote control panel which operated switches magnetically and dimmers by magnetic clutches and motors. (Corry PLANNING, Bowman/Ball THEATRE)

co (Vietnamese)   A two-stringed fiddle played in *cai luong* and *hat boi*. Also called *dan co*, *dan nhi*, *nhi*. (Addiss "Theater" 140, Brandon SOUTHEAST 128)

coach   1. A person, usually a specialist, who instructs others in some aspect of acting, as a voice coach. 2. Sometimes, more broadly, a director of acting, as in dramatic coach. 3. To provide such instruction. (Bowman/Ball THEATRE)

coal-oil Johnny   An early 20th C nickname for a wealthy person who invests in a theatrical venture. (Berrey/Van den Bark SLANG 574)

coal-scuttle bonnet   See: *capote*.

coast   To sponge off others until pay day.

coat of arms   1. An 11th-17th C long tunic reinforced with metal rings. After the advent of armor, it became a ceremonial garment worn over a coat of mail. 2. A heraldic symbol used to designate individual clans, families, royal houses, etc. (Boucher FASHION)

cobrador (Spanish)   One who collected the money in the 17th C public theatres. (Shergold SPANISH)

cockscomb burner   In 19th C Britain, a gas outlet with four or more jets. (Rees GAS 13)

cockspur burner   In 19th C Britain, a gas outlet which produced three separate flames from a single fitting. (Rees GAS 13, 15, fig. 1)

cocktail   A chorus girl. (Berrey/Van den Bark SLANG 573)

cocoon   A 20th C loose knee-length coat trimmed with fur at the hem, collar, or cuffs. The hem was narrower than the shoulders. (Geen COSTUME)

cod   In Britain, to fool a fellow artist. (Granville DICTIONARY)

coda   The concluding part of a dramatic work, dance, or piece of music.

(the) code, Code   In lighting contexts, that part of the National Electrical Code designed to provide for electrical safety. The code, which has a section on theatres, has no legal status, but much or all of it has been enacted into law in many cities and states. (Bellman LIGHTING 157-158, McCandless "Glossary" 628)

co-director   1. A theatre person who shares with another the directing of actors, decision-making about designs, publicity, etc. 2. More often, one who shares the governance of a production organization and sometimes directs a production.

codpiece   A padded male pouch-like crotch covering made of the same material as a jerkin or stockings and often elaborately decorated. It could also be fastened separately by ties or buckles. Worn in the 15th-16th C and considered a sign of virility. Used also to hold money and bonbons. Also called a *braguette*.

cod version   In Britain, a take-off on a famous play. (Granville DICTIONARY)

coffee-and-cake money   A small salary.

coffee-and-cake time   In show business, small time, very minor league. (Wilmeth LANGUAGE)

coffee grinder   A striptease act involving a very strenuous grind. (Wilmeth LANGUAGE)

coffin   See: billing in a box.

coffin corner   Seats located in the extreme front and side of an auditorium.

cofradías (Spanish)   In the 16th C, charitable organizations which controlled the Madrid theatres. (Brockett HISTORY 232)

coherence   In playwriting and play production, the logical consistency of the various elements. (Bowman/Ball THEATRE)

coif   1. A head-conforming piece of cloth worn under a helmet or hood in the 13th-15th C. 2. By extension, a nightcap or hat or wig lining. (Boucher FASHION) 3. Abbreviation for a coiffure. 4. As a verb, to fashion a hair-do.

coiffure en bouffons (French)   Louis XIII women's coiffure consisting of bunches of curled hair over the temples, the forehead being covered by a fringe called a *garcette*. (Boucher FASHION)

coiffure en bourse (French)   See: bagwig.

coiffure en cadenettes (French)   1. A 17th C hairstyle, with a lock of hair (called a *moustache*) on each side of the face, tied with bows. Worn by men and women. 2. In the 18th C, a male hairstyle with the two locks held back with a ribbon on the back of the head, sometimes untied and dangling. (Boucher FASHION)

coiffure en raquette (French)   A late 16th C women's coiffure, with hair brushed up around the face, puffed at the temples, and held by a hoop. (Boucher FASHION)

coincidence   In playwriting, the simultaneous occurrence of two events, such as two characters happening to come to the same place at the same time. Sometimes used for a comic or ironic effect, but sometimes a sign of inept handling of plot and character. (Brooks/Heilman UNDERSTANDING)

cointise, contoise   A medieval woman's headdress ornament or scarf, given to her champion for his jousting helmet at a tournament. Also called a volet. The scarf was also called a lambrequin, mantling, quintise. See also: gonfalon, *heaume* (French). (Wilcox DICTIONARY)

co kich phap dich (Vietnamese)   See: *kich.*

cold   1. To open cold; that is, to open a production without tryout performances. 2. An unresponsive audience.

cold audience   An unresponsive audience. Also called a cold house.

cold cream   See: theatrical cold cream.

cold curtain   Little or no applause at the curtain.

cold hand   Little or no applause.

cold house   See: cold audience.

cold mirror   In a "cool" lighting instrument, a surface which reflects visible rays and passes heat (infra-red) rays. Lounsbury has an illustration. See also: dichroic filter, dichroic reflector. (Lounsbury THEATRE 36-37, Bentham ART 92)

cold one   An unprofitable engagement.

cold patch   To plug a lamp or other load into an outlet which is without current (open, off, dead).

cold show   A show which opens on Broadway without a tryout.

cold side   In electrical equipment, the lighting instrument and cable coming from it. The contrast is with hot side, which comes from the power source.

cold-theatre audience   Spectators in a poorly-heated theatre in winter. In consequence, they may be unresponsive. (Krows AMERICA 390)

collapse   See: breakaway.

collarette   See: Betsie.

collar work   The sometimes herculean effort of a performer needed to engage an unresponsive audience. The reference is originally to the collar of a draught horse. (Granville DICTIONARY)

collective mystery, collective play   A medieval mystery play cycle. (Mantzius HISTORY II 29, 37)

college show   A revue or other entertainment about (usually American) college life, most often written and produced by students. (Granville DICTIONARY)

collegium (Latin Roman)   An association, club, guild. Most *collegia* were apparently non-theatrical, but the term was sometimes used of a company of actors (as in *collegium mimorum*, a mime troupe) and a *collegium poetarum*, a poets' association which included actors, was formed late in the 3rd C BC. (Duckworth NATURE 40, 62, 75; Nicoll MASKS 85)

collet (French)   See: *chaperon.*

colliyattam (Malayalam)   Literally: dancing words. In *kathakali*: 1. A *kalasam* dance sequence performed to song and having fixed choreography. 2. Rehearsal. (Jones/Jones KATHAKALI 72)

collodion   In flexible form, a makeup substance which can be painted over absorbent cotton to build up the neck and face. It is seldom used now, since liquid latex can serve the same purpose more effectively. In non-flexible form, the collodion is applied on dry skin to imitate scars. It can be removed by peeling off or by the use of acetone.

collodion paper   A paper chemically treated to give a flash effect.

colombier (French)   Literally: dovecote. The top gallery of a French theatre. Also called the *paradis* or *poulailler.* (Partridge TO-DAY 225)

Colonial clap   Cadenced, disapproving applause of a vaudeville act. From the behavior of audiences at the old New York Colonial Theatre. See also: slow clap. (Smith VAUDEVILLIANS 12)

color aberration   See: chromatic aberration.

colorator   See: illumiscope.

color bank   1. A group of controls for a single color, as in a color bank for the amber circuits in footlights or borderlights. Also called a color section. 2. A group of controls for all color circuits. (McCandless "Glossary" 636, Bowman/Ball THEATRE)

color boomerang   1. In the U.S., a box-like spotlight accessory with a number of color frames which can be moved into or out of the spotlight beam. Sometimes called a color magazine. 2. In the U.S., sometimes such a device only when remotely controlled. Also called a color boom, boomerang, remote color change(r), color box, or boom (rare). In Britain: auto, colour runners, colour-change lantern, pre-set spot. Britain also uses various modifiers of colour change; they include: auto, automatic, remotely-controlled, remotely operated. See also: color magazine, light tower. (Bowman/Ball THEATRE, McCandless "Glossary" 639, Bellman SCENE, Gassner/Barber PRODUCING 793)

color booth   Especially in the past, a name sometimes given to an enclosure in which fabrics and paint samples could be tested under lighting which duplicated the color(s) to be used on the stage. (Fuchs LIGHTING 131-132)

color box   See: color boomerang.

color cap   Formerly, in open-trough footlights and borderlights, a color medium which consisted of a natural-colored glass cap fastened to the lamp bulb. Fuchs has illustrations. Also called a glass color cap. (Fuchs LIGHTING 164-165, 172)

color circuit   An electrical path which controls a number of lights of the same color. The term has been used primarily of the circuits in borderlights and footlights. See also: color main.

color-dipped lamp   A low-wattage lamp whose color comes from lamp dip. Also called a dipped lamp (U.S.). See also: lamp dip. (Rae/Southern INTERNATIONAL)

colored glass plate   An occasional term for a color medium of glass. (Fuchs LIGHTING 414)

colored lacquer   See: lamp dip.

colored lamp dip   See: lamp dip.

color filter   See: color medium.

color frame   A metal (occasionally wood) holder or slide for a gelatine or other color medium. The color frame slides into a grooved color-frame holder at the front of a lighting instrument. Also called a gel frame, gelatine frame, color screen holder; in Britain, medium frame, colour frame, etc. (Wehlburg GLOSSARY, Lounsbury THEATRE)

color-frame holder   See: slide frame.

color grinder   In 18th C theatres and later, an employee who prepared paint for scenery, mixing various substances to achieve the desired colors. (Hogan LONDON clxiv)

coloring drum   See: illumiscope.

color magazine   See: color boomerang.

color main   Especially in older U.S. stage lighting installations, a circuit or switch which supplies current for two or more sub-mains, and thence for a number of sub-circuits. The term is from the design and operation of older switchboards, which at one time had footlight and borderlight circuits broken into such colors as red, green, blue, and amber. The term persisted even when, for example, the 'red color main' no longer had anything to do with red. Hence such terms as color circuit, color master, colour master switch (British); in Britain, a colour shaft is a bar which operates a row or other group of dimmers, and a colour master wheel operates a colour shaft. (Fuchs LIGHTING 62-64, Corry PLANNING 94)

color medium   Any material used to modify the color of light. Modern color media include various plastics, gelatine (sometimes gelatin), and glass; silk and other materials were much used in the past. Among other terms: color filter, filter, medium, color screen (occasional). Colour filter has been at least as common in Britain as colour medium; medium is also frequent there, perhaps somewhat less so in the U.S. (Bellman SCENE, Rae/Southern INTERNATIONAL)

color plate   In the past, an occasional term for a roundel. Among other such rare older phrases: glass plate, glass color plate, round glass color plate.

color roundel   See: roundel.

color screen   See: color medium.

color section   See: color bank.

color temperature   A temperature reading in degrees Kelvin that indicates the color content of near-white light. For example, a reading of 2400° K describes a warm white light; 6000° K describes a cold, bluish-white light. See also: Kelvin scale. (Bellman SCENE)

color wash   See: wash.

color wheel   1. A large disc with from four to seven openings for flexible color media such as gelatine. Each opening is the size of the lens in the spotlight to which the wheel may be attached. Whether hand-operated or motor-driven, the device permits rapid changes from one color to another. See also: effect wheel. 2. An arrangement of pigment colors in the form of a circle which usually summarizes the color relationships. (Bellman SCENE, Wehlburg GLOSSARY)

colour-change lantern   See: color boomerang.

colour master switch, colour master wheel   See: color main.

colour runners   See: color boomerang. (Rae/Southern INTERNATIONAL)

colour shaft   See: color main.

colouvred   A term used in Britain of Fresnel lenses with black risers. See also: black riser. (Bentham ART 312)

Columbia wheel   The first major U.S. burlesque circuit, begun in 1905. (Wilmeth LANGUAGE)

Columbus Circle   See: balloon tire.

combat reglé (French)   In ballet, a choreographed duel. (Winter BALLET 252)

combination   1. In the late 19th C, a U.S. touring company that carried with it everything needed for a performance. Hence, combination company, combination system, combination house, road combination. (Carroll MATINEE 11-12) 2. In dance, a prescribed sequence of movements.

combination box light   An obsolete floodlight which contained a cylindrical and two parabolic reflectors, any one of which could be used as the reflecting element in the floodlight. (Fuchs LIGHTING 180)

combination curtain   A curtain that can be either drawn or flown. (Burris-Meyer/Cole THEATRES 250)

combination floor block   See: floor block.

combination olivette   Formerly, a special type of floodlight which contained a mogul socket and two medium sockets. The purpose was to add to an instrument's usual capabilities: the olivette could provide a small quantity of light without using a dimmer. (Fuchs LIGHTING 180)

combination production   In the commercial theatre, according to Burris-Meyer and Cole, a system under which the various elements of a stage production are independent and are assembled only near the end of a rehearsal period—a standard practice in the commercial theatre today. According to Sobel, a system supposedly introduced by Joseph Jefferson in the 1860s, under which the old stock company system of production was abandoned and a completely new company was assembled for a given play. (1938 Burris-Meyer/Cole SCENERY 11, Sobel NEW)

combined chat   In Britain, a performer's lodging consisting of a bed-sitting room (studio). Possibly from the slang word for louse—chat—a sometime habitué of boarding houses and other performer lodgings. Also called a combined room. (Granville DICTIONARY)

combo   1. A combination stage-and-film presentation. Also called a pic-flesh or vaudfilm. (Berrey/Van den Bark SLANG 582) 2. A performing team.

comeback   1. A performer's return to the stage after retirement. 2. A performer's success following a failure. (Berrey/Van den Bark SLANG 585)

"Come back Tuesday"   An agent's typical statement to a performer for whom no engagement is available: "Ask again another day."

comedetta   In Britain, a one-act farce or short comedy sketch. (Granville DICTIONARY)

comedia (Philippine)   Originally a folk play performed at a saint's day fiesta, showing the victory of a Christian prince over a Muslim (Moor) prince (hence also called, disparagingly, *moro moro*) and marriage of the Christian hero to a Muslim princess. The first recorded performance, in Latin and Spanish, was in 1598. Vernacular language *comedia* were widely performed in commercial theatres in the 19th C. Also called Spanish *ensayo* (rehearsal). (Mabesa "Philippine" 15) Also spelled *komedya*, *kumedya*, or *kumidya*. In Sugbuanon, called *linambay*. (Ramas in Bresnahan CROSS-CULTURAL 219, Tonogbanua SURVEY 82-86, Mendoza COMEDIA 34-69)

comedia (Spanish)   A comedy. Also used as a general word for a play. (Shergold SPANISH)

comedia a fantasia (Spanish)   A full-length play with romantic subject matter. (Roberts STAGE)

comedia a lo divino (Spanish)   A sacred play. (Rennert SPANISH 265)

comedia a noticia (Spanish)   A full-length play using realistic subject matter. (Roberts STAGE)

comedia de capa y espada (Spanish)   See: *capa y espada*.

comedia de carácter (Spanish)   A play with emphasis on character portrayal.

comedia de costumbres (Spanish)   A comedy of manners.

comedia de cuerpo (Spanish)   A 17th C play in which rulers, noble persons, mythological characters, or saints are involved in actions in faraway places. Also called *ruido*. (Brockett HISTORY 229)

comedia de enredo (Spanish)   A play with emphasis on the complexity of the plot.

comedia de figurón (Spanish)   A 17th C comedy whose protagonist embodies some ridiculous vice or folly.

comedia de historias (Spanish)   An historical play.

comedia de magia (Spanish)   A play employing many *tramoyas* (stage machines) or effects.

comedia de repente (Spanish)   An improvised play. (Shergold SPANISH)

comedia de santos (Spanish)   In the 16th C, a play about the life of a saint. (Rennert SPANISH 145)

comedia de teatro (Spanish)   A play requiring much scenery, along with many properties and effects.

comedia de tramoyas (Spanish)   A play with machines. (Shergold SPANISH)

comedia heroica (Spanish)   A play focusing on high-ranking and heroic personages.

comedian   1. Strictly, an actor specializing in humorous roles, but sometimes used for a comic actress. See also: comedienne. 2. A playwright who writes comedies. 3. Formerly, a general term for any actor.

comediantes (Spanish)   Performers. Sometimes applied to the more distinguished players in a 17th C company who rode in coaches instead of carts. (Rennert SPANISH 155)

comedia palaciega (Spanish)   A play with scenes in a palace. (Sobel HANDBOOK 549)

comedia publica (Spanish)   A specially-authorized public performance to celebrate an unusual event or particular holiday.

comedia togada (Spanish)   A play based on classical Roman plots and subjects.

comédie (French)   Comedy.

comédie à ariettes (French)   18th C operetta; musical comedy. (Speaight PUPPET 139)

comédie à l'impromptu (French)   Improvised comedy. The usual name in France for *commedia dell'arte*. (Duchartre ITALIAN 19)

comédie ballet (French)   A 17th C French play in which dances related to the theme were presented between acts. (Hawkins ANNALS I 256, Arnott FRENCH 107)

comédie de moeurs (French)   See: comedy of manners.

comédie-en-vaudeville (French)   An 18th C play with songs set to popular tunes; performed at fairs. (Brockett HISTORY 372)

comédie improvisée (French)   Improvised comedy. A name in France for *commedia dell'arte*. Usually called *comédie à l'impromptu*. (Duchartre ITAL-IAN 19)

comédie larmoyante (French)   Tearful comedy, popular in France in the 18th C. (Brockett HISTORY 367)

comédie mixte (French)   In the 16th C and later in France and Italy, a play that was partly memorized and partly improvised. 2. A play using spoken dialogue, dance, singing, and spectacle. 3. A mixed-genre play, such as a tragical-comical-historical-pastoral piece. In Italian, *regiacomica*.

comédien, comédienne (French)   Actor, actress.

comedienne   An actress who specializes in humorous roles. See also: comedian.

comédie rosse, pièce rosse (French)   A late 19th C play in which the usual principles of morality are reversed. (Brockett HISTORY 550)

comedietta   A short, farcical comedy. In the 19th C, the term implied less frantic movement and more depth of characterization than was usually found in farce. (Sobel NEW, Hennequin PLAYWRITING 53)

comedist   In Britain, an author of comedies. (Granville DICTIONARY)

come down   1. To move toward the audience. 2. In lighting, to reduce intensity.

come down from the flies   In Britain, an admonition to a performer to ''come off it'' when overly self-impressed by a small success. (Granville DICTIONARY)

comedy   A genre of drama that usually deals with citizens and servants, not royalty; is in prose, not verse; and concerns love, money, and the affairs of daily life, not the problems of kings. Comedy has more depth of characterization than farce, though farce is sometimes thought of not as being different from comedy but as emphasizing certain aspects or devices of comedy—and farce can exist within a comedy. Comedy tends to rely on the mind more and to be more topical than tragedy; it can deal with serious social problems, though many comedies—such as those of Shakespeare—are non-didactic and celebratory. Indeed many comedies end in a wedding or similar celebration. The word is literally 'comus-song, song of the revelers,' from Greek *komos*, a band of Dionysian revelers, and *ode*, song. The literal meaning is not far from Aristotle's statement that comedy grew out of the activities of the leaders of the phallic revelry (the *komos*) performed in connection with the Dionysian cult. For information on the Greek origins of comedy, see Arnott INTRODUCTION 25-30 and Pickard-Cambridge DITHYRAMB 132-290.

comedy club   A club made of wire netting, padded and covered with cloth and painted; within the club is a strip of plywood and a spring-hinged wooden knocker to make a striking sound. (Collison SOUND 102)

comedyllion (Greek)   19th C Greek vaudeville with the Aegean Islands and their simple peasant population as the backdrop. (Gassner/Quinn ENCYCLO-PEDIA 395)

comedy merchant   A comedian.

comedy of art   See: *commedia dell'arte*.

comedy of character   Comedy which focuses on or derives from character, as in Molière's *Tartuffe* or *The Miser*.

comedy of humours   Comedy based on the humour or dominant trait or traits of a character. Popularized by Ben Jonson in Jacobean times and based on the notion that human bodies contained four fluids or humours: phlegm, yellow bile or choler, black bile, and blood. Humours comedy shows what happens when a character's traits or temperaments which derive from these fluids are out of balance and he becomes phlegmatic, choleric, melancholy, or sanguine in the extreme.

comedy of intrigue   Comedy that focuses on connivance and intrigue, usually amorous. Especially popular in Restoration and 18th C England. (Bowman/Ball THEATRE)

comedy of manners   A genre of comedy especially popular in the 17th C in England and France: witty, satirical (especially of the behavior of the upper classes), and artificial to a degree. Congreve's *The Way of the World* is an example. Comedy of manners is related to comedy of character, since much of the humor derives from the characters and their social relationships. Sometimes called artificial comedy, drawing-room comedy, high comedy, or old comedy in later periods. In French, *comédie de moeurs*; in Spanish, *comedia de costumbres*.

comedy of morals   Comedy which takes a judgmental stance toward deviations from a social code. (Bowman/Ball THEATRE)

comedy of sensibility   See: sentimental comedy.

comedy point of view   The objective attitude a performer sometimes takes toward a comic role. He/She stands, as it were, slightly outside the character and lets the audience sense his/her delight in some aspect of the character. (Seyler/Haggard CRAFT 10)

comedy quartette   In vaudeville, an act consisting of a straight man, a sissy boy, the number one comic, and a tramp. The comedy was rough and tumble. (Laurie VAUDEVILLE 75)

comedy team   In vaudeville and burlesque, a pair of comic actors, one usually the comedian and the other the straight man. (Wilmeth LANGUAGE)

come-in   An incoming audience. (Berrey/Van den Bark SLANG 574)

come on   To make an entrance.

comica accesa (Italian)   An alternate term for the young female lover in *commedia dell'arte*, a serious character. More often called the *innamorata* or *amorosa*. (Mantzius HISTORY II 266)

comic epilogue   A witty speech, normally in verse, closing productions of 17th C and later comedies. Such epilogues often contained contemporary social commentary. (Bowman/Ball THEATRE)

comicer   The comedian in a comedy team; his partner is the straight man. (Sobel NEW) Presumably from Yiddish, where it is pronounced comiker. (Weinrich YIDDISH 58)

comic irony   Comedy or a comic scene which provides ironic relief. The porter's scene in *Macbeth* and much of the gravediggers' scene in *Hamlet* are examples. See also: comic relief.

comic muse   Thalia, the Greek muse of comedy.

comico (Italian)   Literally: comic. A comedian—that is, a performer.

comico acceso (Italian)   An alternate term for the young male lover in *commedia dell'arte*. More often called the *innamorato* or *amoroso*. (Mantzius HISTORY II 264)

comic opera   1. In the 18th C, sentimental stories set to music; later, light opera with some roles spoken and some sung, with a happy ending. Occasionally used as synonymous with musical comedy. Also called *opéra bouffe* or *opéra comique* (French) and *opera buffa* (Italian). (Cameron/Gillespie ENJOYMENT, Bowman/Ball THEATRE) 2. In late 19th and early 20th C U.S., a type of musical imitative of European operettas. Also called a light opera. (Wilmeth LANGUAGE)

comic relief   1. An amusing scene inserted into a tragedy or serious drama to relieve the emotional tension. Also called light relief. See also: comic irony. 2. A comic character similarly used.

comic's skull   See: take.

comic up in all   1. A comic in a Toby or tent show who could help put up and take down the tent. 2. An actor who could act secondary roles, play a musical instrument, or assist a show in some other way. (Wilmeth LANGUAGE)

comisarios de comedias (Spanish)   In the 17th C, commissioners for plays. (Shergold SPANISH)

comito (Italian)   A 16th C long, wide-sleeved gown worn by young lovers from age 20. (Chalmers CLOTHES 174)

commande (French)   A strong rope operating a *tambour* on which a curtain, a *ferme*, or an illumination batten is rigged. (Moynet FRENCH 45)

command performance   In Britain, a performance given at the request of the royal family.

commedia all'improvviso (Italian)   See: *commedia dell'arte*.

commedia a soggeto (Italian)   A comedy developed from a plot, theme or subject, performed by *commedia dell'arte* troupes. (Brockett HISTORY 178)

commedia dell'arte (Italian)   Improvised professional comedy, popular in Europe from the 16th to the 18th C. Also called *commedia dell'arte all'improvviso*, *commedia all'improvviso* (with one *v*, Venetian), *commedia a soggeto*, etc. It has sometimes been called comedy of art. *Commedia* was characterized by the use of stock character types (young lovers, clever servants, braggarts, lecherous old men, etc.) and improvisation based on a scenario.

commedia erudita (Italian)   A memorized, erudite play based on neo-classical ideals, performed at courts and academies in Renaissance Italy, often by *commedia dell'arte* troupes. Also called *commedia sostenuta* (literally, sustained, in two meanings: leaning upon a text, and of an elevated tone, as opposed to improvised and popular).

commediante (Italian)   Player, comedian; figuratively, hypocrite.

commedianti (Italian)   Comedians.

commedia sostenuta (Italian)   See: *commedia erudita*.

commentator   1. A master of ceremonies, expositor, or narrator, such as the Stage Manager in Thornton Wilder's *Our Town*. 2. Formerly, a Master of Revels, a Lord of Misrule, etc. (Bowman/Ball THEATRE)

(the) commercial, (the) commersh   A commercial backer of a performance. (Berrey/Van den Bark SLANG 576)

commercial olio   See: olio.

commercial play   A drama without artistic pretensions, presented solely for its promise of making money. (Granville DICTIONARY)

commercial theatre   Professional, tax-paying, non-subsidized theatre, usually operated for a profit.

commissionaire   See: linkman.

commode   A late 17th-early 18th C wire or wicker frame, covered in silk and supporting a coiffure piled high off the forehead in curl clusters. Also called a palisade. See also: Fontanges. (Wilcox DICTIONARY)

common clew   See: clew.

common flat   See: flat.

common meter   See: dry meter.

commonwealth   A British sharing system in which, after production expenses are paid, the performers share in the profits.

commune (Latin Roman)   Literally: a state, a community; hence, a group treated as a unit. A term sometimes used of a company of actors, as in *commune mimorum*. See also: *grex*. (Nicoll MASKS 85) *commune mimorum* (Latin Roman)   Literally: a community of mimes. A mime company. (Nicoll MASKS 85)

communion   Part of the Stanislavsky system of actor training: listening, hearing, responding. See also: contact.

community drama   Especially in Britain, plays suitable for acting in a community theatre. (Purdom PRODUCING)

community theatre   1. A theatre operated by and for members of a particular community. Usually using amateur (unpaid) participants, some community theatres have paid directors, designer-technicians, and business managers. 2. Such theatre as a type. In Britain, civic theatre. See also: recreational drama.

commus (Latin Roman)   See: *kommos*.

comoedus (Latin)   A rendering of the Greek *komoidos* (*komodos*). The Latin word is used of both Greek and Roman comedy. See also: *tragoidos*, whose various meanings are parallel to those of *komoidos*. (Allen ANTIQUITIES 131-132)

comos   See: *komos*.

comp   1. A complimentary ticket; a pass. 2. By extension, a person using a pass.

compagnie des fous (French)   A medieval fool company or society performing short secular plays. Also called a *confrérie des fous*. (Roberts STAGE)

compagnie joyeuse (French)   A medieval fool company or society specializing in comedies. Also called a *confrérie joyeuse* or *société joyeuse*. (Chambers MEDIAEVAL II 91, Brockett HISTORY 137)

compañía (Spanish)   In the 17th C, the largest of the various strolling troupes, consisting of 16 performers and support personnel. (Villandrando in Nagler SOURCES 59)

compañía de gira (Spanish)   A touring company.

compañía de la legua (Spanish)   In the 17th C, an illegal or unlicensed acting company. (Rennert SPANISH 146)

compañía de parte (Spanish)   In the past, a company in which the performers owned shares and lived not on salaries but on their portion of the profits.

compañía real o de título (Spanish)   An authorized or licensed acting company.

company   A group of performers (actors, dancers, etc.) and support personnel (stagehands, business officials, etc.) organized to present theatrical productions, especially on tour. Hence, acting company, dance company, dramatic company, theatrical company, etc.

company call   1. A curtain call in which the full cast bows. 2. A rehearsal involving both cast and orchestra. 3. A gathering of a company for any purpose.

company crew   See: backstage staff.

company list   A list of the names, addresses, and telephone numbers of all members of a theatrical company. The performers are identified also by the roles they play. (Bax MANAGEMENT 39)

company manager   Especially on tour, the person responsible for a company's business and administrative affairs. Called in Britain an acting manager. Typical duties include payroll, expenses, accounting for ticket sales, extra performance arrangements, rehearsal calls, etc. (Krows AMERICA 290)

company picture call   A notice for performers (and any necessary support personnel) to assemble for photographing scenes from a production.

company rehearsal   A rehearsal involving the full theatrical company, especially when on tour, or during a run, to keep performances functioning well. (Bowman/Ball THEATRE)

company switch   A large-capacity electrical power source backstage for connecting portable dimmer boards. The ''company'' is the electric supply company. Also called a bull switch.

company treasurer   The paymaster of a performing company. (Bowman/Ball THEATRE)

comparse (French)   A non-speaking character. From the Italian *comparsa*.

compartment   1. In striplights, an individual lamp and its reflector, partitioned off from its neighbor. Typical phrases include compartment strip, compartment border, compartment foots. Many compartments, especially in footlights and borderlights, contain or make provision for color media. Britain sometimes uses magazine for compartment. (McCandless ''Glossary'' 634, Bowman/Ball THEATRE) 2. An occasional term for one of the acts on a variety or vaudeville bill. (McNamara ''Scenography'' 19)

compartment batten   In Britain, a borderlight with separate compartments for each lamp and reflector. The phrase has also been used to mean compartment strip, whether for footlights or borderlights. (Rae/Southern INTERNATIONAL, Baker THEATRECRAFT)

compartment borderlights, compartment footlights, compartment striplights   See: compartment.

compensating strip   See: tumbler.

compère (French)   See: waistcoat.

compiled script   See: script.

complementary-tint system   Coloring the acting area light by a scheme descended from Stanley McCandless' method. The actor is lit from either side at the usual 45° angles with complementary tints which additively come close to white. See also: single-color system. (Bellman LIGHTING 116-118)

complexion veil   A 19th C gauze veil in white or grey overlaid with patterns of fine black thread. (Chalmers CLOTHES 248)

complication   In playwriting, a plot twist or development that usually intensifies the conflict or sends it in a new direction. The main body of a play is normally made up of a series of complications, leading to their resolution. (Cameron/Gillespie ENJOYMENT)

complimentary   1. In Britain, a benefit performance. 2. See: courtesy. (Granville DICTIONARY)

composite   Several pictures in a performer's resumé showing him or her in various costumes and poses. (Stern MANAGEMENT)

composition   See: choreography.

compostura (Spanish)   Makeup, or any substance or device that alters a performer's personal appearance. See also: *postizo*.

compound parabolic-spherical-parabolic reflector   A floodlight reflector of the shape indicated by its name. The parabola at the front of the reflector has a short focal length, while that at the rear has a long focal length. The reflector as a whole gathers some 240° of the light coming from the lamp. (McCandless SYLLABUS 19, Bowman/Ball THEATRE)

compulsive action   In a performance, vocal or pantomimic action on stage which invites kinesthetic participation or an empathic response from an audience. (Selden ACTING)

computer-assisted lighting system   A lighting control system in which the operator is assisted by computer technology. Cue data and fade times, both linear and non-linear, are stored in the computer's memory and recalled for control by the operator as needed. Computer devices are also used for the organization of data, timing of manual fades, and many other functions. The rhythm and final operation of the lighting are, however, under human control. Sometimes called a memory lighting system, computer lighting system, stage lighting computer, or computer. See also: memory lighting system. (Bellman SCENE 364-366; Sellman/Lessley ESSENTIALS 135-144, fig. 8.12; Pilbrow LIGHTING 152)

computer lighting system   See: computer-assisted lighting system.

comus (Latin Roman)   See: *komos*.

con   To learn a role by heart, to memorize.

concealing the skeleton   In playwriting, skillful handling of the plot so that its framework is not obvious. (Gallaway CONSTRUCTING 116)

conceit   1. A fanciful idea or elaborate metaphor in a dramatic character's speech. 2. In the Italian *commedia dell'arte*, a memorized set speech (*concetto*) of a similar kind.

concentrated filament   A general term for the compact filament used in spotlight lamps. Called bunched filament in Britain. Among the shapes: barrel filament, monoplane filament, biplane filament. See also: point source. (Bellman LIGHTING 19-20, Bellman SCENE, Wehlburg GLOSSARY, Goffin LIGHTING 29)

concentration   1. In playwriting, the effect of compactness and intensity, as in Sophocles' *Oedipus the King*. (Brooks/Heilman UNDERSTANDING) 2. In the Stanislavsky system, the total absorption of a performer in the created world of a scene.

concert   1. A special entertainment presented after the main performance of a Toby show. It was usually brief, consisting of vaudeville acts or a short farce. Tickets for it were sold during the last intermission in the main show. (Wilmeth LANGUAGE) 2. Since the late 19th C in West Africa, a variety show of songs, dances, and sketches. Like vaudeville and music hall, the term came to be used for any type of variety show. (Adedeji glossary)

concertare (Italian)   Literally: to adjust, to plan, to hatch a plot. To rehearse a *commedia dell'arte* scenario. (Perrucci in Nagler SOURCES 257)

concertatore (Italian)   See: *corago*.

concert batten   In Britain, the first light pipe upstage of the proscenium. Also called the number one (No. 1, #1) batten. (Baker THEATRECRAFT)

concert border, concert border light   1. The first borderlight upstage of the proscenium. The source of the name is the instrument's use to light the downstage area, in which concerts often take place. Also called the first border, X-ray border, X-rays, number one (No. 1, #1) border. 2. A cloth border masking such lights.

concert formula   A ruse used after the Licensing Act of 1737 in London: minor theatres offered musical concerts in two parts, with a play offered free between the two halves. (Scouten LONDON 855)

concert garden   See: concert saloon.

concert hall   In 19th C U.S., the name given to some small-town theatres to give them an air of respectability. They were not necessarily used for concerts. Sometimes called an opera house or town hall. (Wilmeth LANGUAGE)

concertmaster   See: leader.

concert meeting   A performance by actors and opera singers in Russia after the 1917 Revolution. The presentations were interrupted by political speeches, frequently delivered by spectators from their places in the auditorium. (Gorchakov RUSSIA 99)

concert party   1. A traditional British seaside entertainment, using sketches, dances, comic songs, etc. Sometimes shortened to C.P. 2. In Ghana, both a theatre form and one of many popular acting troupes consisting of three performers (hence the alternative name, trios). The sketches, presented in the Akan language, are comic and often moralistic. 3. In Nigeria, a popular musical comedy form.

concert reading   See: readers theatre.

concert saloon   During the 1850s in the U.S., a place where a patron could smoke, drink, and be entertained by a variety of specialty acts and skits. Also called a concert garden, concert room, music hall. (Zellers "Saloon" 578)

concert set   See: orchestra shell.

concetto (Italian)   In *commedia dell' arte*, a memorized speech, usually a fanciful idea or elaborate metaphor. A set speech. Plural: *concetti*.

conch   In the 16th-17th C, especially in France and England, a gauze hat, shaped like a shell, draped on a tin frame and worn by widows. (Boucher FASHION)

concha (Philippine)   A prompter's box in *comedia*. (Hernandez EMERGENCE 33)

conclusion   The denouement or final scene in a play, when all the loose ends of the plot are tied up.

concrete   In acting, expression by means of actions and words that are characteristic and significant, that is, specific and original rather than stereotyped and conventional. (Brooks/Heilman UNDERSTANDING)

condenser spotlight   In the U.S., a term sometimes used for a plano-convex spotlight. (Bentham ART 312)

condensing lens, condenser   A lens used in such a manner that it converges a beam of light but does not bring it to a focus. The lenses in Fresnel and plano-convex spotlights operate as condensers. (Bellman LIGHTING 76)

condensing system   A pair or more of lenses used to gather and concentrate light on the slide in a projection system. (Bowman MODERN)

conditionalism   In Russia, the activity or spirit attributed to something, such as joy in *A Midsummer Night's Dream*; everything in a stage production should be conditioned by that spirit. (Carter SPIRIT 55)

condong (Indonesian)   The role of a female servant to the refined princess or queen in Balinese *arja*, *topeng*, *wayang wong*, and other dance-dramas. Also spelled *chondong* or *tjondong*. (de Zoete/Spies DANCE 34)

conductor (Latin Roman)   Literally: contractor. A supplier of costumes, sometimes also properties and perhaps stage management. See also: *choragus*.

confidant, confidante   In playwriting, a (usually) minor character paired with a major one, who shares confidences that provide expository information and help develop the plot and reveal characters.

conflict   In playwriting, a struggle. A conflict can be between two or more persons, between different ideologies or actions, etc. In some plays, as in *Hamlet*, there are multiple external conflicts, as well as an internal conflict within the hero.

confrère (French)   A member of a *confrérie*. (Frank MEDIEVAL 167) *confrérie* (French)   A medieval organization producing religious plays. (Frank MEDIEVAL 166-168, Roberts STAGE)

confrérie des fous (French)   See: *compagnie des fous*.

confrérie joyeuse (French)   See: *compagnie joyeuse*.

confrérie pieuse (French)   A troupe of actors in medieval France, organized to perform mystery plays. (Sobel HANDBOOK 32)

con gran aparato (Spanish)   A 16th C production with elaborate scenery. (Rennert SPANISH 23)

conical reflector box, conical reflector hood   See: *boîte conique*.

conistra   See: *konistra*.

conjunction   The moment when the image and the personality of a performer become one. Hence, conjunctive theatre, especially in Africa.

connector   A device for joining electrical equipment and a source of current. Most connectors used in the theatre consist of a small block or cylinder of hard insulating material which contains metal projections or sleeves. Among the characteristic names and types, all followed by the word connector: branch-off, cable, multiple, pin, prong, slip, stage, Twist-lock. Other terms widely used in the theatre, also as modifiers of connector: female, house, line, load, male. (Bellman SCENE)

connector box   See: plugging box.

connector strip   A metal housing containing a row of stage connectors, often at the ends of pigtails. Sometimes called a batten connector strip. A similar row of connectors without pigtails is occasionally called a plugging strip.

connuttati (Malayalam)   See: *cukannattati*.

conquistores (Latin Roman)   Officials who saw that order was kept in the theatres. It is not clear whether or not such personnel were normally part of the theatre staff. The word is ultimately from *conquiro*, to seek out, to search out. (Beare ROMAN 169)

console, light console   A desk-like arrangement of lighting control devices. Ideally, the arrangement facilitates ease of operation. The word console is derived from the resemblance of early units to a pipe organ console (from which one early light console was adapted). Similar arrangements of sound control devices are used for controlling sound; hence, sound console. Especially in Britain, sometimes control desk. Consoles are normally remote control devices. See also: control board, board. (Bellman LIGHTING 207-218, Wehlburg GLOSSARY, Bentham ART)

console unit   See: package board.

constant-rise floor slope   An architect's term for an auditorium floor profile in which the rise per row is constant.

construction   1. In playwriting, the building of the plot of the play. Construction is dramatic architecture, involving the careful arrangement of actions to create strong and believable conflicts and tensions. (Archer PLAY-MAKING 125) 2. In 18th C British and French theatres, bleacher-type seating on stage at special performances, usually benefits. Also called building on the stage. 3. Design that uses different levels, ladders, platforms, ramps, steps, etc., as in a constructivist setting. 4. The building of stage settings, properties, costumes, curtains, etc.

constructivism   A non-realistic style of design promoted by Vsevelod Meyerhold after World War I; the style used ramps, platforms, steps, and other skeletal structures as performance spaces.

consueta (Spanish)   1. A theatrical production given regularly or customarily. 2. In some places in Spain, a prompter. See also: *apuntador*. (Shergold SPANISH)

contact   1. In acting, playing with another performer: responding, giving, taking. See also: communion. 2. In acting, performing so that the audience can see a performer's eyes, that is, not appearing to look over the heads of spectators. Even in realistic acting, a good actor, even though not appearing to recognize the existence of the audience, often creates eye contact with it.

contact improvisation   A dance form whose emphasis is upon two or more human bodies interacting in concert with the laws of momentum, inertia, gravity, and mass. (HONOLULU ADVERTISER "Visiting" 10 April 1980, B1, 3)

contactor   An electromagnetically operated switch used in some systems for remote control of stage lighting equipment. Since contactors are bulky and noisy, they are usually placed in a basement or other area distant from the stage and auditorium. Also called a relay or magnet(ic) switch. An assembly of such switches is sometimes called a contactor switchboard; its small control switches on or in view of the stage make up the pilot board. Fuchs has illustrations. In a modern system the contactors may be controlled by computer instead of switches. (Bellman SCENE, Sellman/Lessley ESSENTIALS, Fuchs LIGHTING 334-335, Corry PLANNING 95)

contactor switchboard   See: contactor.

contadura (Spanish)   The counting house; the theatre business and ticket office. (Shergold SPANISH)

contaminatio (Latin Roman), **contamination**   The practice of using material from more than one Greek play in writing a Latin comedy. Terence said he did so, and noted that he was following earlier Roman practice, including that of Plautus. Contamination, which refers to 'spoiling' the Greek original, has been used to explain supposed errors, such as inconsistencies and repetitions, in Latin plays on Greek subjects. In the early decades of the 20th C, detailed analyses of Latin plays called *contaminatio* the source of every imaginable imperfection in Plautus and Terence. By the middle of the century, however, this extreme position produced a strong reaction. The recent view is that while Roman playwrights sometimes used parts of more than one play, their own comic invention was the source of the essential character of their plays and of much of the detail therein. See also: *retractatio*. (Duckworth NATURE 191, 197, 202-208; Beare ROMAN 310-313)

contest   In the literature of the classical theatre, the usual English for Greek *agon* (q.v.).

continental cyclorama   See: rolling cyclorama.

continental parallel   See: parallel.

continental seating   A U.S. term for a seating plan in which the rows are spaced far enough apart to allow the elimination of radial or longitudinal aisles, as at the Wagner Festspielhaus at Bayreuth, Germany. Also called continuous-row seating. See also: modified continental seating, multiple-aisle seating.

continuity   1. In playwriting or production, the cohesive sequence of events. 2. A link between scenes. (Bowman/Ball THEATRE)

continuously rated dimmer   Formerly, a term for a dimmer which could function continuously at its maximum rated load without overheating or damage. (Bowman/Ball THEATRE)

continuous-row seating   See: continental seating.

continuous vaudeville   A vaudeville show that is repeated several times, as opposed to two-, three-, or four-a-day shows. In Britain: continuous or nonstop variety. See also: family time. (Wilmeth LANGUAGE)

contoise   See: cointise.

contortionist   A performer, usually double-jointed, who specializes in un-natural body positions. Also called a posturer, posture maker, or posture master.

contouche   See: kontush.

contour curtain   An act curtain with individually controlled lines dropping through evenly-spaced rings on the back of the curtain to ties at the bottom. As the lines are raised, the curtain is gathered upward. Since the lines can be controlled individually, designs or contours can be made. Also called a brail curtain, festoon, or French curtain. (Lounsbury THEATRE 32, Burris-Meyer/Cole SCENERY 285)

contour piece   A ground row made of profile board or some other stiff material cut to the appropriate shape (such as distant rolling hills). (Bowman/Ball THEATRE)

contraction-release   In dance, the tightening and relaxing of muscles, similar to inhalation and exhalation in breathing.

contrapposto (Italian)   Literally: opposite. In dance, a spiral or twisting movement. (Love DANCE)

contrasto (Italian)   A crude farce (dramatized debate) performed on street stages in medieval Italy. (Smith COMMEDIA 37, 53) *contretemps* (French)   Counter-beating. In dance, a compound step used for traveling to the side. The second half of the step is called a *demi-contretemps*. (Grant TECHNICAL)

contrivance   In playwriting, the implausible manipulation of actions and characters. See also: *deus ex machina* (Latin). (Gassner in Archer PLAY-MAK-ING xviii)

control   1. In puppetry, the device—including the human hand—used to manipulate marionettes. Also called a crutch or a perch. (Philpott DIC-TIONARY) 2. Sometimes in Britain, a control board or control system. (Pilbrow LIGHTING 150-151) 3. In dance, the basic concept by which movement is initiated and stopped and by which the body is held in an upright position or allowed to fall.

control board   The device which controls the distribution of electricity to stage lighting instruments, and sometimes to the house. The basic elements are switches, dimmers, and fuses or circuit breakers within a metal housing. The term is often limited to direct control boards, as distinct from consoles, which normally provide remote control. Sometimes spelled controlboard. Often called board, light control board, sometimes switchboard. (Bellman SCENE, Wehlburg GLOSSARY, McCandless "Glossary" 636)

control board operator   The crew member who runs the light controls for a production. Often shortened to board operator, or simply operator. Switchboard operator is now used only occasionally and primarily in older installations. (Sellman/Lessley ESSENTIALS 188)

control booth, control room   The control center for lighting and sound. Ideally, it overlooks the stage. It may also serve as the stage manager's post, especially in an arena theatre. Sometimes, depending on its use, called the light booth, sound booth, projection booth.

control circuit   A circuit, usually low voltage, which operates a dimmer, contactor, or other such device.

control console, control desk   See: console.

controller   A small, manually operated device, usually a resistance, which activates a remotely controlled dimmer. Its main electrical part is usually a potentiometer (q.v.), a name sometimes applied to the entire control. (Bellman LIGHTING 222, McCandless SYLLABUS 50)

control room   See: control booth.

control system   See: control.

control voltage   The voltage or signal applied to a silicon controlled rectifier dimmer, or similar device, which causes the device to function.

convenience outlet   The common domestic wall outlet seen in dressing rooms and elsewhere in theatres. For stage lighting, it is a metal box which contains such an outlet for use with domestic equipment such as table lamps and floor lamps. A double convenience outlet is a similar metal box with two such outlets; but simple "convenience outlet" is sometimes used for the double. Also called a utility outlet, with handy box an occasional backstage name. (Bowman MODERN, Lounsbury THEATRE)

convention   1. A way of doing things on stage that is agreed upon by an unstated contract between spectators and theatre artists (an agreed-upon lie, as Thornton Wilder said). In musical comedy, for example, it is an accepted convention that characters will sing rather than speak their most important feelings. 2. A style of production stressing the artificiality of the stage rather than attempting a reproduction of real life. Hence, conventional, theatrical convention. See also: presentational. (Cameron/Gillespie ENJOYMENT, Bowman/Ball THEATRE)

conversation piece   A play containing much talk and little physical action. (Stern MANAGEMENT)

conversation play   See: drama of conversation.

conversion   A change of will or sentiment by a main character near the end of a play which disentangles the plot and leads to a logical conclusion. (Archer PLAY-MAKING 218–223)

convertible set   See: unit set.

convertible top   A wig.

convex glass roundel   See: roundel.

conveyour   In medieval England, a stage manager.

cooch, cooch dancing   A precursor of the striptease, combining bumps, grinds, exposure, erotic movements, teasing, etc. Also called hoochie-coochie (or hootchy-cootchy). Hence, coocher, cooch dancer, hoochie-coochie dancer.

cookie   Especially in the past among professional electricians, a metal cut-out such as is inserted in the gate of an ellipsoidal reflector spotlight to cast a pattern of light on the scene. Sometimes called a template. The term is thought to have come from cucaloris (cuckaloris and other spellings), sometimes shortened to cuke; the original source may be a Yiddish word meaning unusual scene. Gobo is and has been used for such pattern cut-outs, but see that entry. Wehlburg has an illustration. (Wehlburg GLOSSARY, Bowman/Ball THEATRE)

cooking   Performing with great fervor. (Lees "Lexicon" 57)

cool   Of lights or pigment, having the psychological effect of reducing apparent temperature. Colors ranging from blue-purple through blue-green are normally "cool."

cool color   See: cool.

cooling   Unemployed.

cool key   Key light (strongly directional) in one or more cool colors. (Bellman LIGHTING 228)

coon 1. A now obsolete, offensive term for a Black minstrel or a white man in blackface. 2. In Britain, a performer having a droll personality. (Granville DICTIONARY)

coordination In dance, body wholeness as a result of the balance of the mental and the physical. (Rogers DANCE 183)

cop big In Britain, to garner wide, enthusiastic audience favor. (Granville DICTIONARY)

cope 1. Before the 15th C, a hooded rain cloak or ceremonial garment for both sexes. 2. Later, a clerical ceremonial garment, sleeveless, hoodless, and richly decorated. 3. In the 19th and 20th C, a clerical robe closely resembling the earliest style. (Boucher FASHION)

copiste (French) In the 17th C and later, the prompter, historian, and copyist of a French acting company. (Roberts STAGE)

coppeaux de bresil (French) See: brazill.

copper tickets Especially in 18th C theatres, metal checks issued to a playgoer in return for his paper ticket (usually for a benefit) or because his name was on the free list. See also: silver tickets. (Hogan LONDON xxvii)

copper toe In Britain, a copper strip attached to the bottom of a flat to facilitate sliding (running) the flat along the floor. See also: saddle. (Granville DICTIONARY)

cop the curtain To be applauded so strongly that the curtain is raised for a bow or for more bows than usual. (Partridge TO-DAY 227, Granville DICTIONARY)

cop the laughs To excite laughter.

copyist In the 17th C and later, the prompter, or someone working under him, who prepared parts or sides and made copies of a full play script. See also: music copyist. (Chappuzeau in Nagler SOURCES 184)

copyright performance In 19th C Britain, a performance, usually without scenery or costumes, given to secure stage copyright under the Dramatic Copyright Act of 1833. (Bowman/Ball THEATRE)

coq, coque The feathers of a rooster, long, iridescent, and black or dark green, used on hats. Those of the Spanish rooster are the most highly desired. (Dreher HATMAKING)

corago (Italian) The manager of a *commedia dell'arte* troupe—usually the leading performer. Also called a *concertatore*. (Perrucci in Nagler SOURCES 257)

coranto (Italian) See: *volta*.

cord In the U.S., a pair of insulated electrical conductors made into a single bundle by enclosing them in an outer wrapper.

cordax (Latin Roman), **cordax** See: *kordax*.

cord connector body   See: socket.

'core   In Britain, a contraction of encore. (Granville DICTIONARY)

corker   In Britain, an actor who ruins a play. Also called a dead stick. (Sobel NEW)

cork opera, cork op'ry   A minstrel show in which white performers blackened their faces with burnt cork. (Wilmeth LANGUAGE)

cork popper   A bicycle pump with the end removed and replaced by a cork. Used to simulate the sound of a cork popping. (Collison SOUND 102)

cork up   To put on black makeup, originally with burnt cork. The term is apparently 20th C, although alternatives to burnt cork have been used for many years. Also called black up or blacken up. The 19th C used black up.

corn   In writing, directing, or performing, doing something that is trite, to please the crowd. Hence, corny. Probably from rural corn-belt performances in the early days. (Wilmeth LANGUAGE)

(the) corner   1. In Britain, the prompter's corner of the stage. (Baker THEATRECRAFT) 2. See: take the corner.

corner block   A triangular piece of 1/4'' plywood used to strap together the vertical and horizontal members of a flat frame at the corners. Also called, in Australia, a cornerstone. (National TECHNICAL)

corner boy   See: end man.

corner brace   In the construction of a flat or parallel, a diagonal supporting piece used to keep the unit rigid. Also called a bracer or brace rail.

corner iron   See: angle iron.

corner man   See: end man.

corner plate   An L-shaped metal plate used in place of or (on tour) in addition to a corner block to strap together vertical and horizontal members of a flat.

cornerstone   See: corner block.

corner trap   A trap downstage and to the right or left, usually about two feet square.

cornet   A medieval headdress of muslin and/or lace, in many styles. Modern nurse's and chef's cap styles are based on it. Also called an escoffion, horned cap, horned headdress. (Wilcox DICTIONARY)

cornet hat   A Directoire period hat with a narrow brim and gathered crown.

Cornish round   In medieval times, a mound of earth in a circular form in Cornwall where plays were performed. The acting took place in the middle of the circle, with the audience and most of the settings on the perimeter.

coro (Italian)   Chorus.

corona   In the 17th and 18th C in England, a hoop, often of wood, containing some thirty candles. Coronas gradually replaced chandeliers for stage lighting. Also called a ring.

corporeal mime   The portrayal of emotion by means of body movement in three dimensions: rotation, inclination, or translation. The body is divided into parts closely analogous to a musician's division of sounds into notes, thus making the body capable of imitation of all things. (Anonymous "Names" 7)

corps (French)   Literally: body. In the 17th C, a bodice of stiff fabric. (Boucher FASHION)

corps à baleine (French)   See: *corps piqué.*

corps de ballet (French), **corps de ballet**   Dancers who do not appear as soloists. (Grant TECHNICAL)

corps dramatique (French)   A theatrical company.

corpse   1. Especially in Britain, to collapse with laughter when performing. 2. To forget one's lines or business or to spoil another performer's lines or business by bad timing.

corps piqué (French)   1. A 16th-17th C stiffened, quilted, sleeveless under-bodice. 2. A 17th-18th C tightly-laced whalebone underbodice. Also called a *corps à baleine.* (Boucher FASHION)

corpus (Latin Roman)   Literally: body. Sometimes, a company of actors. See: *grex*, the principal Latin term. (Nicoll MASKS 85)

Corpus Christi play   A medieval religious play presented in England on the Thursday after Trinity Sunday—the traditional time for the performing of cycle plays.

corral (Spanish)   Literally: courtyard. A theatre, a playhouse. Spanish theatres of the 16th and 17th C were set up in open-air courtyards within a square building complex. (Nagler SOURCES 60)

corredor (Spanish)   In the 17th C, a theatre gallery with windowed or railed hallways overlooking a *patio*. (Shergold SPANISH)

corredor de las mugeres (Spanish)   In the 17th C, an alternate term for the *cazuela* or women's gallery at the rear of a *corral* theatre. (Brockett HISTORY 234)

corrido (Spanish)   The ballad form in Chicano drama, derived less from the story than from the music. It often dramatizes a folk ballad. (Copelin "Chicano" 74)

corridor   A stage setting painted on a downstage drop and representing a hallway. Used for a shallow scene during which a more elaborate setting can be arranged backstage.

corridor (French)   Fly gallery.

corset   1. A medieval short or long overcoat with or without sleeves. 2. Later, a woman's robe laced in front and fur-lined in winter. 3. In the 17th C, a relatively unboned bodice for women. 4. In the 19th C, an undergarment varying from very rigid to lightly-boned, according to the dictates of contours and fashion. (Boucher FASHION)

Corsican trap   A mechanism operated through a stage cut, consisting of a small truck on an inclined railway. It lifts a performer from below to full visibility at stage level as it moves across the stage. Named for *The Corsican Brothers*, a popular 19th C melodrama in which such a device was used. Also called a ghost glide.

coryphaeus (Greek), **coryphaeus**   From about the time of Sophocles, the leader of the chorus. The *coryphaeus'* two assistants, the *parastatai*, were added at the same time as the *coryphaeus* himself. The leader's responsibilities were considerable: he led the choral odes and dances, frequently had recitative passages of his own, and participated in the episodes. As there was no contest for *coryphaei*, their names were not listed in official records of victories. *Coryphaeus*, the usual transliteration of the Greek, appears to have been the chief 5th C BC term for the chorus leader in the regular drama, the earlier word having been *choregus*. *Chorodidaskalos* and *orchestrodidaskalos* are post-5th C BC, and represent a division of the functions of the *coryphaeus*. *Coryphaios* is an occasional transliteration of the Greek, while *choryphaeus* and *choryphaios* are simply versions. (Haigh ATTIC 301, Allen ANTIQUITIES 127, Arnott ANCIENT 12, Pickard-Cambridge FESTIVALS 348, Roberts STAGE)

coryphaios (Greek)   See: *coryphaeus*.

coryphée (French)   The leader of the *corps de ballet*. (Grant TECHNICAL)

cossack cap   See: *kolpak*.

co-star   1. To share star billing with another performer. Hence, co-starring. 2. One who shares star billing. (Bowman/Ball THEATRE)

costière (French)   A slit in a stage floor, parallel to the curtain line, through which is thrust a pole based on a carriage in the substage. See: chariot-and-pole system. (Southern CHANGEABLE 371)

costumbrismo (Spanish)   Latin-American regional comedy of manners. (Matlaw MODERN 167)

costume   1. The clothing an actor wears on stage. Also called a stage costume, theatrical costume, dress, habit, shape. 2. To make and/or design such clothing. (Bowman/Ball THEATRE)

costume actor   See: costume play.

costume à l'antique (French)   A 19th C very low-cut gown with a very high (Empire) waistline, worn by Mme. Recamier. Also called an Empire dress. (Walkup DRESSING 251)

costume crew   The theatre workers who make and/or maintain stage clothing.

costume designer   The person responsible, in concert with the director, for the planning and execution of clothing and personal properties to be worn and used by actors in a production. Sometimes called a costumer, *costumier*, *costumière* (French), theatrical costumer.

costume fitting   A try-on of a costume by a performer so that it can be judged (and altered, if necessary) for fit and appearance. Also called a fitting, tryout. (Bowman/Ball THEATRE)

costume mistress, costume master   See: wardrobe keeper.

costume parade   See: dress parade.

costume part   See: costume play.

costume play   A play in which actors appear in historical, classical, or other non-contemporary costumes. Hence, costume actor, costume part. (Purdom PRODUCING)

costume plot   A list of all the characters in a play and their costumes, sometimes scene by scene. Also called a dress plot.

costume prop, costume property   An accessory such as gloves, a fan, a cane, or a walking stick, used by an actor in a play. (McGaw ACTING 201)

costumer   1. See: costume designer. 2. One who supplies costumes commercially. Also called a *costumier*, *costumière* (French), theatrical costumer.

costume rehearsal   A rehearsal which focuses on costumes.

costume shop   The area in a theatre where costumes are prepared, usually adjacent to the wardrobe, where costumes are stored.

costumier, *costumière* (French)   See: costume designer, costumer.

côte, cotte (French)   A 13th C loosely-cut coat with sleeves and body in one piece. The top of the garment was frequently wider than the bottom. Now called a dolman. (Barton COSTUME 132)

(de) côté (French)   In ballet, a term used to indicate that a step is to be made to the side. (Grant TECHNICAL)

côte cour (French)   Literally: court side. The post-Revolutionary name for stage left (toward the Court of the Carrousel monument in Paris). See also: *côte de la reine*, *côte du roi*, *côte jardin*. (Moynet FRENCH 17)

côte de la reine (French)   Literally: queen's side. The pre-Revolutionary name for the left side of the forestage, where the box used by the queen was placed. See also: *côte cour*, *côte du roi*, *côte jardin*.

côte du roi (French)   Literally: king's side. The pre-Revolutionary name for the right side of the forestage, where the box of the king was placed. See also: *côte cour*, *côte de la reine*, *côte jardin*.

côtehardie (French)   A medieval garment described variously as an overcoat with split sides and a buttoned front, a sort of dressing gown, a man's short gown, a short over-garment worn by jesters after the 15th C, a high-buttoned woman's coat with long, tight sleeves and circular skirt, and a beltless princess-style coat flared at the bottom. (Barton COSTUME 135, 160; Boucher FASHION; Walkup DRESSING 115-116)

côte jardin (French)   Literally: garden side. The post-Revolutionary term for stage right (toward the Tuileries gardens in Paris). See also: *côte cour*, *côte de la reine*, *côte du roi*. (Moynet FRENCH 17)

coterie theatre   Theatre (or a theatre) designed for a private or special audience. See also: private performance. (Bowman/Ball THEATRE)

cothurn   See: *kothornos*.

cothurnus (Latin Roman), **cothurnus**.   See: *kothornos*.

cotton rep   See: rep.

cou-de-pied (French)   In ballet, the part of the foot between the ankle and the base of the calf—the 'neck' of the foot. (Grant TECHNICAL)

cough and a spit   In Britain, a very small part. Also called two lines and a spit. (Granville DICTIONARY)

coulisse, *coulisse* (French)   Literally: wing. 1. In the classical Greek theatre, a movable panel or screen. Bieber uses the term for both the *pinax* (Greek) and the *scaena ductilis* (Latin). (Bieber HISTORY 74, 116) 2. A wing flat. 3. A groove in which a wing flat slides. 4. The space between wing flats. 5. Any backstage space. 6. Movable scenery. 7. A screen serving as a background or side decoration. (Bowman/Ball THEATRE, Bieber HISTORY 74, 116, 129)

countenances   In the 16th-17th C, a pin cushion, a small mirror, and small scissors, each individually suspended by a ribbon from a lady's waist. See also: *châtelaine* (French).

counter   In acting, to move in the opposite direction from a move made by another performer, usually to avoid masking or to balance the stage picture. Hence, countercross, countering. (Canfield CRAFT, Bowman/Ball THEATRE)

counterbalance, counterpiece   See: counterweight.

countercross   See: counter.

counterfoil   The British equivalent of the U.S. ticket stub.

counter focus   In directing, the arrangement of performers on stage in such a way as to focus the attention of the spectator on one figure or group but provide a secondary focus on another figure or group.

counter-marque   Especially in 17th C French theatres, a ticket marked with the place where the holder was entitled to sit, given to the playgoer after reaching the inner door of a playhouse. (Riccoboni in Nagler SOURCES 287)

counterpiece   See: counterweight.

counterplay   Those portions of a play when the protagonist is acted upon. (MacEwan FREYTAG'S 105, 107-109)

counter player   A character in the subordinate action of the plot of a play. (MacEwan FREYTAG'S 162)

counterplot   A subplot that helps emphasize and enhance the main plot through contrast. (Sobel NEW)

counterpoint lighting   A way of conceptualizing lighting in terms of patterns of light, a number of which are constantly changing in synchronization with the rhythm of the play, usually as expressed by actor movement. Analogous to musical counterpoint, hence the name. Discrete lighting is its opposite: it emphasizes a particular "look" or fixed state of lighting which may be altered to another fixed state. Pattern control describes an arrangement of a lighting console that makes counterpoint lighting easily operable. (Bellman LIGHTING 213, 232-235, figs. 10-5a, b, c, d; Bellman SCENE 357-358)

counterpoise   Counterweight.

countertext   See: fore-text.

counterweight   A metal weight used in a carriage or arbor rigged to balance the weight of a flown object. The principal type, the slip counterweight, is slotted at each end so that it readily slips into the bars of the counterweight carriage. Hence, counterweight system, counterweight house. Also called a counterbalance, counterpiece, counterpoise. Counterweights are also used to hold down objects. Hence, brace weight, stage weight.

counterweight arbor   A carriage in a counterweight system used to hold metal weights. Also called a counterweight carriage or cradle, or simply arbor.

counterweight cradle   See: carpet hoist.

counterweight house   A theatre with a flying system using wire ropes and counterweights in arbors, as opposed to a rope or hemp house.

counterweight set   A group of lines (usually from three to five) running from a counterweight arbor to a batten. (Burris-Meyer/Cole THEATRES 237)

counterweight system   A stage rigging arrangement designed to fly heavy scenic units or draperies hung on battens. Wire ropes from a batten run upward to loft blocks on the gridiron over the stage, then across to head blocks at the side wall of the stage house, and then down to a counterweight arbor. Metal weights in the arbors balance the weight of the flown units and can be pulled up and down by operating lines. Sometimes called a counterbalance system.

counterweight track   A metal track which runs up the side wall of a stage house and serves as a guide for a counterweight arbor.

(the) country   In Britain, the provinces; anywhere outside London. In the U.S., the road, the provinces, the sticks, etc. (Granville DICTIONARY)

count the box   To count the stubs in the ticket box. (Wilmeth LANGUAGE)

count the house   1. To scan the audience before a performance begins to obtain a rough estimate of the attendance. 2. To look at the audience while performing, out of character. (Bowman/Ball THEATRE)

count the rack   To count the unsold tickets. (Wilmeth LANGUAGE)

count-up   1. A box-office record of each performance. 2. To prepare such a record. (Bowman/Ball THEATRE)

count-up room   A room where ticket stubs are audited.

coup de théâtre (French), **coup de theatre**   1. A successful play, a "hit." 2. A showy, often sensational scene/machine segment, often with more clever stagecraft than relevance to the play. 3. An unexpected but frequently logical turn of the plot in a play. (Arnott SCENIC 79, Bowman/Ball THEATRE, Sobel NEW, Stuart DRAMATIC 50)

coupé (French)   In ballet, a small intermediary step in preparation for, or as the impetus for, some other step. (Grant TECHNICAL)

couple-of-coughs-and-a-spit   In Britain, a very small role. (Marsh COLOUR 82)

couple of flats   1. A pair of shutters (flats) sliding on from each side of the stage and joining at the center to form a prospect. 2. In Britain, two bad performers. (Partridge TO-DAY 227)

courante (French)   A 16th-17th C dance characterized by a running or gliding step, as distinguished from leaping steps. (Perugini PAGEANT 69)

courtesy   1. Courtesy of the profession—free admission to a theatre, primarily for a member of the theatrical profession. In Britain: on one's card. 2. In the plural, complimentary tickets. (Bowman/Ball THEATRE)

court masque   See: masque.

court patches   See: patches.

court-pie (French)   A 14th C man's knee-length, circular cloak in two colors, with a hole cut for the head. (Walkup DRESSING 111)

court plasters   See: patches.

court theatre   A theatre at the court of a monarch, operated for the pleasure of the ruler and the court circle. Productions sometimes involved courtiers and their ladies as participants. The heyday of court theatres in Europe was from the 16th to the late 18th C.

couru (French)   See: *pas couru*.

couvre-chef (French)   See: wimple.

cove lighting   Concealed lighting, often indirect, from a recess in public areas of a theatre, such as a lobby or auditorium. When used for stage lighting, usually of the downstage acting areas, cove lighting consists of lamps concealed in auditorium side walls or ceiling. Hence, cove light.

cover   1. To hide another performer from the view of the audience by standing in front of him. 2. To serve as an understudy, thus covering another performer. 3. To canvas, usually a flat. Hence, covering. 4. A property man stationed in the wings to fire a cover gun. 5. In an Elizabethan theatre, the partial roof over the stage; the heavens. (Baker THEATRECRAFT, Bowman/Ball THEATRE)

coverchief   See: wimple.

cover flat   A canvas-covered frame used to mask the supporting structure of a platform or step unit. Also called a cover piece. (Nelms PRIMER 94)

cover gun   A pistol with blank cartridges, kept in readiness backstage in case an onstage gun fails to fire.

cover piece   See: cover flat.

cover scene   A scene in a play which allows time for offstage action by a character (such as answering a doorbell) or time for a scenery or costume change. (Gallaway CONSTRUCTING 179)

cover spot   A rare term for a spotlight which provides light for (i.e., covers) a special area.

cover the theatre   To review a performance.

cover up   In burlesque, to conceal a lapse in the lines; to cover up a mistake. (Wilmeth LANGUAGE)

cowshed circuit   Summer stock. (1938 Burris-Meyer/Cole SCENERY 40)

C.P.   In Britain, short for concert party. (Granville DICTIONARY)

crab one's act, crab one's lines   To spoil another performer's effect. (Berrey/Van den Bark SLANG 587)

crab the turn   To spoil another performer's act. (Berrey/Van den Bark SLANG 587)

crack a chestnut   To tell a trite joke. (Berrey/Van den Bark SLANG 587)

cracowe   A 14th C man's or woman's wooden sole with a raised area under the ball of the foot and a projecting point which supported the shoe's long toe. (Chalmers CLOTHES 16)

cradle   1. See: counterweight arbor. 2. A boatswain's (or bosun's) chair or stool. 3. A see-saw or rocking device used to create snow or wave effects. 4. A sling in the flies for storing battens and drops. 5. Abbreviation for spotlight cradle: a horizontal pipe to which a small number of spotlights are fixed. 6. In Britain, a cyclorama floodlight on casters. (Bowman/Ball THEATRE, Cornberg/Gebauer CREW 268)

cradle support   See: cable cradle.

cramignole   A 15th-16th C man's cap, originally made of velvet and trimmed with pompoms and feathers; the brim was turned up and cut all around. (Boucher FASHION)

cramp   In the 18th C and later, fast memorization. A "part very considerable, and difficult cramp study..." (Wilkinson WANDERING I 174)

crane   In the Greek and Roman theatre, a hoisting device. But English crane is also used for a supposed arm of the Greek *mechane* (q.v.). (Gascoigne WORLD 29; Bieber HISTORY 67, 77)

crash   See: glass crash.

crash box   A container in which glass, china, etc. is smashed offstage to simulate a crash sound.

crash cold   See: open cold.

crash machine   A rotating drum with protruding pins. Hardwood slats pressed against the drum are raised and snapped back, making a crashing sound. (Lounsbury THEATRE)

crash onto the stage   To become a performer.

cravat   A neckcloth or necktie dating from the 17th C, normally wide and of some length. It could be folded and tied in many ways, from simple to intricate. Also called a focal or stock. See also: *chaconne*. (Boucher FASHION, Wilcox DICTIONARY)

crawler   A performer who evades rehearsals.

crazy act   A comedy act.

cream puff   1. A small chorus girl in a troupe, usually put in the front row of the ensemble. Also called a broiler or pony. (Carrington THEATRICANA) 2. A chorus boy.

create   Of a performer, to be the first to play a part. (Granville DICTIONARY)

creative dance   See: creative movement.

creative drama, creative dramatics   1. The use of drama when working with young children, stimulating their imaginations by encouraging them to develop their own acted-out stories. The form is improvised, with emphasis on the process, not on exhibition of the results. Creative dramatics, the principal U.S. term for many years, is falling into disuse. Other terms found in the literature include acting out, action dramatics, C.D., CD, child drama, creative play acting, developmental drama, dramatic education, drama with children, educational drama, educational dramatics, improvisational drama, informal drama, interpretive dramatics, playmaking, and story dramatization. See also: drama in education, dramakinetics, dramatic play, theatre games. (Davis/Behm "Terminology" 10-11; Goldberg CHILDREN'S 5-6, 8-9) 2. More specifically, the U.S. method of story dramatization (q.v.).

creative if   In the Stanislavsky system of acting, "the imagined truth which the actor can believe as sincerely and with greater enthusiasm than he believes practical truth.... From the moment of the appearance of *if* the actor passes from the plane of actual reality into the plane of another life, created and imagined by himself." (Stanislavsky in Cole/Chinoy ACTING 495)

creative mood   In the Stanislavsky system of acting, a physical and spiritual condition favorable for the creation of inspiration in a performer. (Stanislavsky in Cole/Chinoy ACTING 492)

creative movement   A dance experience that explores the concepts of time, space, shape, energy, and motion by using the body in imaginative and innovative ways. The process is improvisational, with emphasis on the experimental aspects rather than exhibition of the results. Often used in work with children, the term has been particularly in favor when "dance" is unsuitable, particularly in public education. Children's dance, creative dance, and creative rhythmic movement also occur in the literature.

creative play acting   See: creative drama.

creative rhythmic movement   See: creative movement.

crèche parlante (French)   Literally: talking crib. A medieval five-level, raked puppet stage upon which rod-controlled marionettes of various sizes performed Nativity plays. Related to the Polish *szopka*. (Malkin PUPPETS 21)

credit list   Acknowledgements in a theatre program to firms who have supplied or lent theatre properties, equipment, etc. for use in a production. (Granville DICTIONARY)

credits   1. A listing in a theatre program of the previous work of a performer, director, designer, producer, etc. 2. See: credit list.

creme makeup   A tinted oil- (sometimes water-) based foundation or makeup base.

créole, gown à la   See: *caraco*.

crepe   A short artificial beard. (Berrey/Van den Bark SLANG 580)

crepe hair   In plaited form, a wool or wool substitute used in making up, especially for beards. It is available in many colors.

crepida (Latin Roman)   A Greek open shoe or sandal, probably often with a heavy sole, connected sometimes with tragedy and sometimes with comedy. Oxford LATIN says "a kind of footwear consisting of a thick sole attached by straps to the feet, characteristically worn by Greeks and usually regarded as an affectation when worn by Romans." Since *crepidae* were worn in everyday life (and over a long period of years), it is likely that they varied in both appearance and use. Beare argues that as everyday wear they would connect with comedy rather than tragedy. See also: *fabula crepidata*. (Beare ROMAN 265-266; Bieber HISTORY 239, 242; Pickard-Cambridge DIONYSUS 77; Pickard-Cambridge FESTIVALS 205)

crepidata (Latin Roman)   See: *fabula crepidata*.

crepin(e)   See: caul.

crescendo   In dance, an increase in force. (Love DANCE)

crespinette, crestine   See: caul.

crevés (French)   See: slashings.

crew   See: backstage staff.

cri (French)   A medieval announcement of a play. Also spelled *cry*. (Nicoll DEVELOPMENT 65)

crick   A critic.

cri du sang (French)   See: *voix du sang*.

crieur (French)   In medieval times, the speaker of the prologue. (Mantzius HISTORY II 143)

crisis   A turning point in the dramatic action of a play.

crisotan (Philippine)   A type of drama in the Pampango area in the early 20th C, named after the writer Crisostomo Sotto. (Cruz SHORT 226)

crispin   A 19th C collarless one-piece coat worn by actresses in drafty theatre wings as they awaited their cues. Later adopted by men, other women, and children. (Boucher FASHION)

crit   In Britain, short for a review of a new play; its notices. (Granville DICTIONARY)

criticism   Ideally, the careful, systematic, and imaginative analysis and/or evaluation of dramatic works or theatrical productions (or any form of art). Hence, critic. See also: reviewer. (Cameron/Gillespie ENJOYMENT)

crix   Slang for critics. (Sobel HANDBOOK)

CRO   See: crotch row.

crocus (Latin Roman)   From about the 1st C AD, a spray of saffron sometimes used to cool and scent an auditorium. See also: *sparsiones*. (Sandys COMPANION 518-519)

croisé (French)   In ballet, crossing the legs, with the body placed at an oblique angle to the audience. (Grant TECHNICAL)

croisé devant, croisé derrière (French)   See: positions of the body.

cropped-hair play   See: *zangirimono*.

cross   1. Movement from one area of the stage to another; hence, a cross left, cross right, cross down, etc. 2. To so move. Abbreviation: X. See: cross light.

crossbar interconnection panel   See: interconnecting panel.

cross batten   In the construction of a roll ceiling or other large flat, a 1'' x 3'' piece of lumber serving as a stretcher between the downstage and upstage frames. Also called a spreader.

cross-connect(ing) panel, cross-connect unit   See: interconnecting panel.

cross control   In lighting control boards of the early 20th C, a form of master interlocking in which one group of dimmers could be brought up at the same time as another was brought down. See also: cross fade. (McCandless "Glossary" 636)

cross fade   To dim one light or a group of lights up as another light or group is being faded out, but not necessarily at the same speed. The two fades normally constitute a single cue. Also called cross dim. As a noun, the term is sometimes hyphenated. See also: cross control. (Bowman MODERN)

cross fader   An electrical or mechanical device for effecting a cross fade. See also: dipless cross fader, autofader.

crossfire   In Britain, two comedians' rapid exchange of wisecracks. See also: stichomythia. (Granville DICTIONARY)

cross in   To move toward the center of the stage.

cross-light, cross light   1. To angle lights (usually spotlights) so that their beams reach an area from two sides, often meeting at an angle near 90 degrees. Also called cross. 2. To throw light across part or all of the stage, as from a wing. As a noun, the result (either meaning) is often called cross-lighting, sometimes cross-light. Illustrations are in Wehlburg and Hewitt. (Bowman/Ball THEATRE; Wehlburg GLOSSARY; Hewitt ART 237-238, 244)

crossover   1. A passageway from one side of the stage to the other, behind the stage setting. 2. A lateral aisle in the auditorium, permitting audience members to move from one side to the other.

cross-over beard   A disguise for an actor who doubles parts. The actor, wearing a beard, crosses the stage and exits; he then re-enters, unbearded, as his second character. The ruse is used when there is no backstage crossover. (Granville DICTIONARY)

cross stringer   See: stringer.

crosstalk comedians   In Britain in a vaudeville act, a leading performer and the feed (q.v.). (Granville DICTIONARY)

crotch row   Especially in a burlesque theatre, the second row of seats, behind 'baldheaded row.' So named because a spectator's eye level was even with a performer's crotch. Tickets for this row were marked CRO. (Wilmeth LANGUAGE)

crowd   1. Supernumeraries hired for crowd scenes. 2. The audience. 3. Especially in Britain, a theatrical company. (Granville DICTIONARY)

cruelty   See: theatre of cruelty.

crutch   See: control.

crux   A play's central issue or problem. (Granville DICTIONARY)

cry (French)   See: *cri*.

crypta (Latin Roman)   A curved corridor, vaulted or otherwise roofed, within an auditorium. In Augustan times, such a corridor lay between the second and third galleries of a large Pompeiian theatre; six doors (*vomitoria*) led to the stairways which divided and gave access to the sections (*cunei*) of the second gallery.

CT, C.T.   See: children's theatre.

C-type, C-type lamp   See: C-lamp.

cuadros (Philippine)   Literally: frame. A change of scenery in *zarzuela*. (Fernández ILOILO 100)

cubism   A movement in theatre related to cubism in painting, popular in the post-World War I period. Stage productions presented nature in geometric forms—in the scenery, lighting, and even the acting.

cucalorus, cuckaloris   See: cookie.

cue   A signal in dialogue, action, or music for a performer's action or speech or a technician's duty backstage. (Stern MANAGEMENT)

cue bite   To begin one's line too soon and spoil the effect of the previous speech. Hence, cue biter. See also: clip a cue, step on a line, step on a laugh.

cue board   In Britain, the stage manager's desk. (Rae/Southern INTERNATIONAL)

cue bound   See: cue struck.

cue capacity   In memory lighting systems, the maximum number of presets (cues) which the system can store. Modern data recording systems such as floppy disks have made this concept obsolete. (Bellman LIGHTING 241)

cue card   A card containing the scene shift assignments of a stagehand.

cue feeder   See: feeder.

cueing   See: cuing.

cue insertion   In memory lighting systems, a procedure by which an additional cue can be placed in memory in its proper sequence. For example, new cue 14a can be inserted between existing cues 14 and 15. (Bellman LIGHTING 244, 253)

cue light   A light used as a signal to a crew member or, occasionally, a performer. In one popular arrangement, a green light is a warning signal and a red light is the signal to execute the cue. The green-red scheme is often referred to in the plural: cue lights. (Baker THEATRECRAFT, Bax MANAGEMENT, Bowman/Ball THEATRE)

cue lines   1. Lines which provide a cue. 2. In Britain, sometimes electric cables which terminate in cue lights. (Granville DICTIONARY)

cue list   In Britain, a record of all cues maintained by prop men, electricians, and others who work with stage effects. In the U.S., cue card, when used by the stage manager. (Granville DICTIONARY)

cuerpo (Spanish)   See: *comedia de cuerpo*.

cue sheet   Broadly, a list of signals for actions by crew members. The term is perhaps most often used for the list or chart of changes made by the operator(s) of the light control board. But there are cue sheets for sound control, scenery and property changes, and sometimes costume or other changes. And a stage manager may have a cue sheet which combines all of these. (Bellman SCENE, Wehlburg GLOSSARY, Lounsbury THEATRE, Sellman ESSENTIALS)

cue struck   Said of a performer who delays words or action by waiting for the cue in full. Also called cue bound. (Bowman/Ball THEATRE)

cue tape   A length of nonrecording tape spliced between sections of sound tape to serve as a cue. It can also be used as a leader or end tape, and is sometimes called a leader or timing tape.

cuff   To let someone into a performance free of charge. Hence, cuffo, cuffola—on the cuff or for free. (Wilmeth LANGUAGE)

cuff-shooter   A performer who, after telling a joke, pulls down his shirt cuff. (Laurie VAUDEVILLE 87)

cuing, cueing   Reading cues to a performer to assist in line memorization.

cuirass   A medieval warrior's breastplate made of leather. Later, a soldier wore a metal cuirass, also called a busk or plastron. Breastplates are still worn by some European cavalrymen. (Wilcox DICTIONARY, Chalmers CLOTHES 115, Walkup DRESSING 130)

cukannattati (Malayalam)   Literally: red beard. In *kathakali*, a demonic and villainous anti-hero or an animal character who wears a red beard. One type of bearded (*tati*) character. Also spelled *cuvannattati, connuttati*. (Jones/Jones KATHAKALI 29)

cuke   See: cookie.

culika (Sanskrit)   An offstage voice in a classical Indian play that narrates events which have occurred between acts. (Keith SANSKRIT 302)

culottes   1. 16th-19th C breeches for men, varying in tightness and length according to the fashion of the time. 2. In modern times, a woman's tailored pant-skirt. (Boucher FASHION, Wilcox DICTIONARY)

cum farsura (Latin)   Literally: with stuffing. Said of parts of a medieval church Mass to which a trope had been added. Also called *farsa* (Italian, stuffed). (Frere WINCHESTER ix)

cumulative form   In modern dance, a tenet related to increase in intensity or in tempo: fast and slow movement accelerated in a succeeding movement, a single dancer's movement picked up by the remainder of the company, or a single dancer's beginning a phrase with one part of the body, followed by other parts of the body. (Love DANCE 20)

cundapoo (Malayalam)   See: *cuntappuva*.

cunei (Latin Roman)   Literally: wedges. 1. The wedge-shaped divisions of a theatre auditorium. 2. Hence, spectators. Singular: *cuneus*. Both singular and plural occur in U.S. English. See also: *kerkides* (Greek). (Haigh ATTIC 98; Bieber HISTORY 70, fig. 477)

cuntappuva (Malayalam)   A plant seed placed in the eye of a *kathakali* actor to induce a rose-like coloring of the white of the eye. Also spelled *cundapoo*. (Jones/Jones KATHAKALI 20) *cupak* (Indonesian)   A Balinese dance-drama depicting conflicts between two brother princes, Cupak and Grantang. See also: *wayang cupak*. Also spelled *chupak* or *tjoepak*. (de Zoete/Spies DANCE 143-149, Soedarsono DANCES 175-178)

cup-and-saucer   A nickname given to some of the drawing-room plays of the mid-19th C, especially works by Thomas Robertson and their productions by the Bancrofts. The plays had little stage activity and were marked by the serving of tea, during which social problems were discussed. Hence, cup-and-saucer drama, comedy, role, etc. (Bowman/Ball THEATRE)

cupola   See: *Kuppelhorizont* (German).

curb   A single step (riser and tread) in a step unit.

curricle   A 19th C knee-length woman's lace overskirt. (Chalmers CLOTHES 229)

curse   The edge of a piece of lumber or a flat which tends to splinter.

curtain   1. A movable, usually suspended barrier or screen of cloth or other material in a proscenium theatre, sometimes used to conceal the stage from the audience until an act begins and sometimes to provide a scenic effect. Some productions use a main curtain which rises at the beginning of a play and descends at the end, with an act or scene curtain dropping between the structural divisions of the play. 2. The cue to move such a curtain. 3. The end of an act or scene; the last piece of action before the fall of the curtain. 4. A theatrical effect, solution, or line at the end of an act or performance. Hence, strong curtain. 5. A curtain call. (Bowman/Ball THEATRE)

curtain balls   See: ball carriers.

curtain bell   In 18th C theatres and later, a prompter's bell used to cue the rise or fall of a curtain. Abbreviation: CB. (Hughes in Hume LONDON 131)

curtain border   A short horizontal drapery matching a curtain and hung just in front of it.

curtain call   Short form: call. Performers coming before an audience to acknowledge the applause with a bow.

curtain carriers   See: ball carriers.

curtain check   See: check chain.

curtain clamp   A piece of stage hardware for shortening a drop by clamping a rolled portion of it on a batten. Also called a roll drop hook. (Carrington THEATRICANA)

curtain clew   See: clew.

curtain cue   1. A signal given to the technician operating a curtain to raise, lower, or draw it. 2. The lines or business which serve as the cue. (Bowman/Ball THEATRE)

curtain cut   See: cut.

curtain cyclorama   See: drapery.

"Curtain down!," curtain down   1. A stage manager's command to lower the curtain. 2. A notation in the stage manager's time sheet indicating what time the curtain fell at the end of an act or scene.

"Curtain going up!"   The stage manager's warning that the act is about to begin.

curtain grip   A stagehand who operates the curtain.

curtain guides   Spools or rings attached to the sides of a drop curtain. Vertical guide wires run through the guides to keep the curtain from swaying. (Bowman/Ball THEATRE)

curtain line   1. The usually imaginary line where a curtain touches the stage floor. 2. In dialogue, the last line of a scene, at which the curtain falls. 3. A rope or cable for moving a curtain; a curtain pull. (Bowman/Ball THEATRE)

curtain man, curtain operator   The stagehand in charge of operating a curtain. (Bowman/Ball THEATRE)

curtain music   Music played just before the curtain rises.

curtain of light   See: blinder, light curtain.

curtain plot   A list of cues for the curtain to be raised or lowered.

curtain pole   1. A stick used in scene shifting. 2. A curtain rod. (Bowman/Ball THEATRE)

curtain pole hanger   See: hanger.

curtain pull   The operating line for raising and lowering, or opening and closing a curtain. Also called a curtain line or curtain rope.

curtain raiser   1. The opening act of a vaudeville show. 2. In a performance consisting of more than one entertainment, the first event. See also: front piece, mainpiece, afterpiece.

curtain rehearsal   A rehearsal concentrating on curtain cues and speeches. (Belasco DOOR 82-83)

curtain roller   Small wheels with a curtain carrier hanging from them, rolling in a curtain track or channel, used to operate a traveler curtain. See also: ball carriers.

curtain rope   See: curtain pull.

curtain routine   The sequence of curtain and lighting cues at the opening or closing of the curtain.

curtain runner   1. A curtain track or channel. 2. A stagehand who helps open and close a traveler curtain by guiding its onstage end. (Bowman/Ball THEATRE)

curtain scene   See: act-drop scene.

curtain set   A stage setting made up of draperies or mainly draperies, with a single insert of flats or a set piece. Also called a drapery setting. See also: cyclorama set. (National TECHNICAL)

curtain shutter   A shaping device in or on a spotlight which moves down from the top of the beam in the manner of a drop curtain.

curtain speech   1. Words spoken before or after a performance by some member of the company to the audience, announcing a change in cast, acknowledging applause, advertising the next production, etc. 2. A speech at the end of an act or play. (Granville DICTIONARY)

curtain stacking area, curtain storage area   Space at the offstage end of a traveler curtain to accommodate the curtain when it is gathered in the off position.

curtain taker   In Britain, a conceited performer; one who takes excessive curtain calls and makes too many curtain speeches. See also: milk. (Granville DICTIONARY)

curtain time   1. See: actual curtain time. 2. See: curtain tune.

curtain track   A hanging channel containing balls or rollers to which a traveler curtain can be attached. Also called a traveler track.

curtain track bracket   A wall fixture fastened at the bottom of a counterweight track when the latter does not rest on the stage floor. It stops falling weights. Also called a track bracket.

curtain tune   In Restoration and 18th C British theatres, the third of three sets of tunes preceding the beginning of a performance. The curtain tune was occasionally called the curtain time.

"Curtain up!"   A stage manager's command to take up the curtain.

curtain warmers   FOH (front-of-the-house) lights used to illuminate the act curtain. Also called warmers.

curved approach   See: curved cross.

curved backcloth   A cyclorama or a substitute for it.

curved cross   The movement of a performer in a curved rather than a straight line. Also called an arc cross or curved approach.

curved path traverse wagon   A mechanized wagon stage on tracks that form a splayed U around the proscenium opening. Burris-Meyer/Cole have an illustration. (Burris-Meyer/Cole THEATRES 206)

cush   An early 20th C U.S. term for money. (Wilmeth LANGUAGE)

cushion time   Hours or days into which scenery construction work is not scheduled but may overflow if necessary. (Burris-Meyer/Cole SCENERY 70)

customers   In Britain, especially in music halls, the audience. (Granville DICTIONARY)

cut   1. In a set of grooves in a 17th C theatre in Britain, one of the channels in which a wing or shutter slid. 2. Short for stage cut or slider cut, a narrow transverse section of the stage floor that can be opened and through which persons or scenic units can be raised from below or into which a curtain can be rolled. Hence, staircase cut, curtain cut, etc. Also called a runner. See also: sloat. 3. To remove, usually intentionally, or to omit lines or business. 4. Such an omission. Hence, cutting. 5. Said of a border, drop, or leg when it includes a cut-out, or has been cut irregularly, e.g., so as to represent foliage. (Purdom PRODUCING, Bowman/Ball THEATRE) 6. In stage lighting in the U.S., to open a circuit. By the 1920s, a direction to break the flow of current, as to a spotlight. Cut implies a near-instantaneous breaking of the circuit as opposed to dimming. (McCandless "Glossary" 628) 7. In dance, to transfer weight quickly from one foot to the other by a sharp downward movement of the leg. (Rogers DANCE 244)

cut and flash   In playwrighting, cutting the main action just before it grows dull, and filling the gap with material from a subplot. (Krows PLAYWRITING 140)

cut-and-parry dialogue, cut-and-thrust dialogue   See: stichomythia.

cut a pigeon wing, cut the pigeon's wing   To execute a fancy step in which a dancer jumps and strikes the legs together. (Berrey/Van den Bark SLANG 589)

cutaway   A man's formal, single-breasted coat, cut away at the waist and extending to knee-height in tapered panels at the back. Also called a frac or morning coat. See also: British lounge coat, frock coat, lounge suit. (Wilcox DICTIONARY)

cut border   See: cut cloth.

cut bridge   In Britain, a stage elevator. (Rae/Southern INTERNATIONAL)

cut cloth   Any cloth (a border, drop, leg, etc.) cut to represent pillars, trees, shrubs, etc. Hence, cut border, cut drop, cut flat scene, cut wood. Cut cloths are numbered, beginning downstage with one. See also: cut out.

cut-down scenery, cut-down set   Scenic units usually no more than eight or ten feet high, standing in front of black draperies. Sometimes called a vignette.

cut drop, cut flat scene, cut foliage border   See: cut cloth.

cut frost   See: frost.

cut heavens   A sky border in Renaissance theatres that was cut to allow a flying rig to make a character disappear into the flies. See also: entire heavens.

cuticle, cutie   A chorus girl. (Berrey/Van den Bark SLANG 573)

cut in   See: bite a cue.

cut line   A rope holding the asbestos fire curtain in the raised position; when cut, the rope releases the asbestos, sealing off the stage area from the auditorium.

Also called an asbestos curtain safety release line, emergency rope, fire curtain safety release line.

cut nail   See: clout nail.

cutoff, cut-off   1. Any device which shapes a spotlight beam or reduces its spill. Cutoffs, often used at the front of spotlights, include funnels, mats, irises, and other beam modifiers. Sometimes called a cut out. 2. The edge, especially the hard edge, of a light beam. (Lounsbury THEATRE, Bowman MODERN, Bowman/Ball THEATRE, McCandless "Glossary" 639)

cut of the gate   A percentage of the box-office receipts.

cut out   1. A profiled ground row or other scenic piece with portions cut out. Hence, cut-out ground row, cut-out piece, cut-out scenery, cut-out setting, etc. In Britain, cut-out or fret piece. See also: cut cloth, profile. 2. See: cutoff.

cut-out mask   See: mask.

cut-out setting   A setting divided by a partial wall, so that action can be seen better. See also: open scene. (Bowman/Ball THEATRE)

cut-out switch   A term sometimes used in Britain for a simple on-off switch. (Goffin LIGHTING 47, 56)

cut plug   Among professional lighting crews, a stage plug which has been cut so that it will accept large capacity cable (#6 or better).

cut scene   See: open scene.

cut step   In dance, a movement in which one foot is moved out in order to change the body's weight. (Rogers DANCE 151)

cut the buck   To dance a buck and wing.

cutti (Malayalam)   In *kathakali*, the unique white paper and paste border that frames an actor's face. (Jones/Jones KATHAKALI 108)

cuttikaranamar (Malayalam)   A makeup artist in *krishnanattam*. (Ranganathan "Krsnanattam" 285)

cutting list   A list of the dimensions of the pieces of wood needed for the scenery, properties, etc. of a production.

cut to the seagulls   To shorten a scene to the utmost. (Berrey/Van den Bark SLANG 583)

cut wood   See: cut cloth.

cuvannattati (Malayalam)   See: *cukannattati*.

cyc   The usual backstage term for cyclorama. Cyc is often combined with other terms, particularly lighting terms, producing such combinations as cyc foots, cyc borders, cyc lights. The same is true of cyclorama, but the shorter combinations are usual among backstage people. Cyke and cyclo are variants.

cyclas   A 13th C warrior's tunic or cloak worn over armor, dating from ancient Greece and Rome. (Barton COSTUME 137, Wilcox DICTIONARY)

cycle   A series of medieval plays dramatizing biblical episodes (such as the Abraham and Isaac story, the Deluge, the Annunciation, the Nativity, the raising of Lazarus, the Last Supper, the Crucifixion, the Resurrection), the whole forming a cosmic drama. Some cycles took many days to perform, a portion being presented each day (usually during Lent) on pageant wagons or on a stage with several settings. Hence, cyclic or cyclical drama.

cyclo   In Britain, short for cyclorama. (Granville DICTIONARY)

cyclorama   Short forms: cyc, cyke, cyclo. A surrounding scenic curtain or permanent wall used to represent the sky or open space. Also called an artificial horizon. A cloth cyclorama is fabric attached to a U frame curving around the back and sides of the acting area. A permanent cyclorama is a similarly-shaped wall made of wood, steel, mesh, etc. and plastered (German: *Rundhorizont*). When dome-shaped, such a wall is called a horizon, dome horizon, plaster dome, sky dome, dome, plaster cyclorama (German: *Kuppelhorizont, Horizont*). See also: sky drop, drapery cyclorama.

cyclorama arms   Extensions of a cyclorama, running downstage on each side.

cyclorama base   See: cyclorama light pit.

cyclorama borderlight   See: borderlight.

cyclorama floods   Floodlights used in the position of a cyclorama borderlight. (Bowman MODERN)

cyclorama footlights   Striplights placed at the foot of a cyclorama to illuminate its lower half.

cyclorama horizon light   An occasional term for cyclorama footlight(s). (Bowman/Ball THEATRE)

cyclorama knuckle   Hardware for attaching the side arms of a cyclorama to the main cyclorama batten.

cyclorama light batten   Any batten upon which cyclorama lights are mounted. While these would normally be the cyclorama borderlights, other lights, such as scoops, are sometimes used. (Fuchs LIGHTING 427)

cyclorama light pit   A long, narrow trough in the stage floor in front of the cyclorama. Such a pit contains the cyclorama footlights, and is often covered with traps when the footlights are not wanted. Fuchs has drawings. Also called a cyclorama pit, cyclorama base, cyclorama trough, and, in Britain, light pit. (Fuchs LIGHTING 424, 425, 427; Bowman/Ball THEATRE)

cyclorama lights   Lighting instruments used to light a cyclorama. This is one of many combinations of cyclorama and a lighting term. Other frequent phrases are cyclorama footlights and cyclorama borderlights, the two instruments most often used to light a cyclorama. Compare: cyc. (Gassner/Barber PRODUCING, Bellman SCENE, McCandless ''Glossary'' 630)

cyclorama overheads   Lights hung above the stage, usually striplights, which illuminate a sky cyclorama. (Bowman/Ball THEATRE)

cyclorama pit   See: cyclorama light pit.

cyclorama set   A stage setting made up of a drapery cyclorama and drapery wings and borders. See also: curtain set.

cyclorama trough   See: cyclorama light pit.

cyke   See: cyc.

cyprus   A 16th-17th C black crepe fabric used for hatbands and mourning veils. (Dreher HATMAKING, Wilcox DICTIONARY)

czardas   A Hungarian dance in duple time, with the dancers beginning slowly and finishing with a fast whirl.

D

D   Downstage.

da, ta (Chinese)   Literally: to fight. Combat; one of the four basic perform-ance skills (*jiben gongfu*) in Beijing opera (*jingju*) and many other forms of music-drama (*xiqu*). See also: *dongzuo*.

dab   See: efforts.

dabiki   A 15th C fabric named after its Egyptian point of origin and used for robes and turbans. The material was so light that 50 yards of it could be used for one turban. (Boucher FASHION)

dabo-dabo (Hausa)   A puppet of southern Nigeria. (Malkin PUPPETS 66)

dabola (Hausa)   A puppeteer of southern Nigeria. (Malkin PUPPETS 66)

da capo (Italian)   See: *aria da capo*.

dadaiko (Japanese)   A large, two-headed, barrel-shaped drum used in *ga-gaku*. (Wolz BUGAKU 18)

dadaism   A movement in art that penetrated the theatre but not deeply or for long. The dada theory rejected artistic values, rationalism, and the idea of meaning in art. The dadaists, wishing to shock the Establishment, went against both realism on the one hand and expressionism on the other. Dadaism flourished during World War I and shortly thereafter. (Rowe HEAD 212)

daddy   In Britain, a nickname for: 1. An actor-manager, especially in the provinces. 2. A director. 3. A repertory company performer who specializes in elderly roles in comedy. (Partridge TO-DAY 224, Granville DICTIONARY)

dado   The front of a box in an 18th C auditorium.

daejabi, taejabi (Korean)   Literally: rod holder. The chief puppeteer of a traditional puppet troupe or of the *tolmi* puppet pieces in *namsadang*. See: *kkoktu kaksi*. (Kim "Namsadang" 16) *Daejabido* is an assistant puppeteer. (Sim/Kim KOREAN 66)

daf (Marathi)   A drum played in *tamasha*.

dafa (Chinese)   See: *datou*.

daga (Philippine)   A ritual dramatic dance to exorcise evil spirits, performed in Iloilo City before the Spanish regime. (Cruz SHORT 245)

dagelan (Indonesian)   1. A generic term for clown or clown-servant roles in *ketoprak, ludruk*, and the shadow play (*wayang kulit*) in Java. See also: *pawongan, penasar, punakawan*. (Long JAVANESE 71) 2. A travelling troupe in Central or East Java made up of four or five clown actors and the improvised comedies they perform. (Brandon SOUTHEAST 289) 3. In *ludruk*, a comic prologue to the main play, performed by clown actors (*pelawak*). Also spelled *dhagelan*. (Peacock RITES 81)

dagged   A garment edge cut in the shape of leaves. (Chalmers CLOTHES 17)

dagu, ta ku (Chinese)   Literally: big drum. 1. A type of storytelling (*quyi*) which arose in the 17th and 18th C in Shandong and Hebei Provinces. Currently at least ten different forms of big drum are popular throughout northern China as well as in areas bordering the Changjiang (Yangtze) and Zhujiang (Pearl) rivers. Most forms include one singer-drummer, and one or more players of the three-string lute (*sanxian*) and/or other accompanying instruments. (Howard CONTEMPORARY 30, Scott LITERATURE 62) 2. See: *tanggu*.

daguomen (Chinese)   See: *guomen*.

dahualian, ta hua lien (Chinese)   Literally: large flower face. A painted-face role (*jing*), usually a character of fairly high social status, which emphasizes song (*chang*) skill; a major subcategory of the painted-face role in Beijing opera (*jingju*) and many other forms of music-drama (*xiqu*). (Scott CLASSICAL 75–76)

daicho (Japanese)   See: *daihon*.

daihon (Japanese)   Literally: basic book. A handwritten script of a *kabuki* play. Also called: *daicho* (basic book), *seihon* (true book), and in Kyoto-Osaka *nehon* (root book). See also: *shohon, kyakuhon*. (Gunji KABUKI 33, Leiter ENCYCLOPEDIA 366)

daijin bashira (Japanese)   Literally: minister's pillar. 1. In *no*, the downstage left pillar, so named because the secondary character (*waki*) who normally sits there is often a minister (*daijin*). Also called *waki bashira* (*waki* pillar). 2. The downstage left pillar in early 17th C *kakubi* adaptations of the *no* stage. (Gunji KABUKI 232, Ernst KABUKI 32) 3. In contemporary *kabuki* theatres, the two pillars, stage left and stage right, of the inner-proscenium; they mark the extremes of usable stage space. (Leiter ENCYCLOPEDIA 46)

daijo (Japanese)   In *bunraku*, the opening act or prologue of a full-length history play. (Malm in Brandon CHUSHINGURA 75, 79)

daikon (Japanese)   Literally: large white horseradish. In *kabuki*, an epithet for a poor actor. A spectator who doesn't like some bit of acting may shout out *daikon* or *daikon yakusha* (radish actor). (Leiter ENCYCLOPEDIA 47) *daimyo kyogen* (Japanese)   Literally: lord play. A *no-kyogen* play in which the leading role (*shite*) is that of a *daimyo*, a large land owner. (Berberich "Rapture" 21)

daisho mae (Japanese): The area on a *no* stage directly in front (*mae*) of the large and small hand drums (*daisho*), that is, upstage center.

daisy   In Britain, a term of approval for a favorite performer. Equivalent of "She's a honey." (Granville DICTIONARY)

daksina (Sanskrit)   A courteous heroic character in classical Indian drama. (Keith SANSKRIT 307)

dalan (Indonesian)   See: *dalang*.

dalang (Indonesian, Malaysian)   The master puppeteer who speaks dialogue, chants narration, sings mood songs, directs the musical ensemble, and manipulates the puppets in a *wayang* puppet performance. Also spelled *dalan, dhalang*. (McPhee in Belo TRADITIONAL 147, Long JAVANESE 6–7, Foley "Sundanese" 67, Sweeney RAMAYANA 53) In dance-drama (*wayang wong*), the *dalang* sings mood songs and chants short narrative passages only. (Brandon "Types" 52–53)

dalang budak (Malaysian)   Literally: child puppeteer. A child who performs with home-made puppets. (Sweeney RAMAYANA 41)

dalang muda (Malaysian)   Literally: young puppeteer. An apprentice shadow play puppeteer who assists the master *dalang* and usually performs the prologue of the play. (Sweeney RAMAYANA 43)

dalang tajali (Malaysian)   Literally: puppeteer by revelation. A puppeteer whose talents and performance knowledge are obtained by revelation. Often the same as *dalang tiru*. (Sweeney RAMAYANA 41)

dalang tiru (Malaysian)   Literally: puppeteer by imitation. A semi-professional or amateur shadow puppeteer who has learned to perform by observing others instead of studying with an established teacher. (Sweeney RAMAYANA 41)

daluo, ta lo (Chinese)   Literally: large gong. A brass gong about a foot in diameter which is held by a rope handle and struck with a padded stick. It is featured in the percussion orchestra (*wuchang*) in Beijing opera (*jingju*) and many other forms of music-drama (*xiqu*). (Scott CLASSICAL 48, 50; Wichmann "Aural" 445–446, 453–460)

dama (Spanish)   Actress.

damager   In Britain, manager. Presumably coined because of the power to hurt plays'—and performers'—prospects. (Granville DICTIONARY)

damar (Indonesian)   See: *blencong*.

dame   1. In Britain, the part of a comic old woman—a dame part—usually played by a man and usually in a pantomime. But see also: grande dame. 2. A music hall male entertainer, popularized at Drury Lane Theatre by Augustus Harris in the late 19th C. (Bowman/Ball THEATRE, Brockett HISTORY 501)

damian, ta mien (Chinese)   Literally: big face. An upright, imposing, ferocious male role, such as a mighty general, which is portrayed with colorful, non-realistic full-face makeup; a major subcategory of the painted-face role (*jing*) in *kunqu* drama. Also called principal painted-face role (*zhengjing*), abbreviated *jing*. (Dolby HISTORY 105)

dan, tan (Chinese)   Female role, a major role category (*hangdang*) in many forms of music-drama (*xiqu*). In Yuan *zaju*, major subcategories of the female role included principal female (*zhengdan*), supporting female (*waidan*), young female (*xiaodan*), and old female (*laodan*). In *kunqu*, major subcategories include old female (*laodan*), principal female (*zhengdan*), action female (*zuodan*), stabbing and killing female (*cishadan*), boudoir door female (*guimendan*), and secondary female (*tiedan*); in Beijing opera (*jingju*), old female (*laodan*), principal female (*zhengdan*), flower female (*huadan*), boudoir door female (*guimendan*), martial female (*wudan*), sword and horse female (*daomadan*), and flower tunic (*huashan*). In both *kunqu* and Beijing opera, performers of all subcategories except the old female speak and sing in falsetto voice (*xiaosangzi*) and wear stylized, white and pink makeup; old female performers use the "natural" voice (*dasangzi*) and wear almost no makeup. (Dolby HISTORY 60, 105, 180–181; Scott CLASSICAL 31–32, 68–74)

dan (Japanese)   1. A French scene within the first or second part (*ba*) of a *no* play. (Hoff/Flindt "Structure" 219) 2. An act in a *bunraku* play. History plays (*jidaimono*) are written in five *dan*, domestic plays (*sewamono*) in three. 3. Less often, a scene within an act of a *bunraku* play. (Malm in Brandon CHUSHINGURA 74–76, Dunn EARLY 104–105)

danawa (Indonesian)   A giant, ogre, or demon in Indonesian theatre. Frequently a foreigner as well. Also called *raksasa* or *buta*. (Long JAVANESE 70)

dan ca kich (Vietnamese)   See: *kich*.

dance-a-thon   A dance marathon. Sometimes printed dancathon.

dance company   A group of dancers and support personnel (stagehands, business officials, etc.) organized to present dance productions. Also called simply a company.

dance director   The person who has charge of the dancers' performance patterns and rehearsals in musical comedy. (Granville DICTIONARY)

dance drama   A story whose plot unfolds through the medium of dance. For related Asian terms, see *bhagavata mela, buyo geki, kathakali, kuchipudi, kutiyattam, lakon, ma'yong, wayang wong, wuju,* and *yaksagana*.

dancing doll   1. A marionette. 2. A 19th C lay term to describe any kind of puppet performance. (Philpott DICTIONARY)

dancing mat   A portable section of floor carried by vaudeville tap dancers. (Gilbert VAUDEVILLE 164)

dan co (Vietnamese)   See: *co*.

dandakam (Malayalam)   1. One form of metre used in Sanskrit dramatic compositions. (Keith SANSKRIT 132, 187) 2. A type of metre and verse, used as an introduction or interlude, in *kathakali* texts. (Jones/Jones KATHAKALI 108)

dan gao (Vietnamese)   See: *gao*.

dangiri (Japanese)   See: *kiri*.

dangziban, tang tzu pan (Chinese)   The generic term for small groups of traveling storytellers (*quyi*) in the 17th–19th C who primarily performed *shibuxian* and *danxian*. Their performances involved the same plots and characters as those of the music-drama (*xiqu*) companies, but were much simpler; they were the most frequent performers in variety houses (*zashuaguan*), and also played in private homes. (Mackerras RISE 200, 210)

dan kiku sa (Japanese)   A colloquialism for the *kabuki* era, c. 1877–1902, dominated by the star actors Ichikawa Danjuro IX, Onoe Kikugoro V, and Ichikawa Sandanji I. The word is made up of the first ideograph of each actor's given name. (Tsubouchi/Yamamoto KABUKI 70, Leiter ENCYCLOPEDIA 50)

dankou (Chinese)   See: *xiangsheng*.

danmari (Japanese)   A *kabuki* pantomime scene, set in the dark, in which possession of a treasured object passes from hand to hand. A *danmari* is performed in slow-motion to instrumental music, without song or dialogue. (Gunji KABUKI 39)

dan nhi (Vietnamese)   See: *co*.

danpigu, tan p'i ku (Chinese)   Literally: single-skin drum. A drum consisting of a solid piece of wood with a hole bored through the center and a single head made of skin. It is featured in the percussion orchestra (*wuchang*) in many forms of music-drama (*xiqu*), including Beijing opera (*jingju*). Also called accented-beat drum (*bangu* or *pan ku*), and small drum (*xiaogu* or *hsiao ku*). See also: *guban*. (Scott CLASSICAL 46–47, 50; Wichmann "Aural" 443–444, 452–460)

danse (French)   Dance.

danse-caractère (French)   A character dance. In ballet, any traditional, national, or folk dance, or a dance using gestures or movements that establish the character of a role. (Grant TECHNICAL)

danseur, danseuse (French)   A male/female ballet dancer.

danseuse coryphée (French)   A female ballet dancer who is not a prima ballerina but who dances in small groups. Classified in the Imperial Russian ballet as between the soloist and the company as a whole. Sometimes (incorrectly) designated as a minor soloist. (Kersley/Sinclair BALLET)

danshichi (Japanese)   A *bunraku* puppet head used for the character of a rough middle-aged man. The term is from the name of the puppet character Danshichi Kurobei. (Keene BUNRAKU 217)

danxian, tan hsien (Chinese)   Literally: single string. A form of story-telling (*quyi*) popular in Beijing, Tianjin, and northeastern China involving three or more performers; it developed in the 17th and 18th C. Its music mainly follows *lianquti* musical structure, and features an octagonal drum (*bajiaogu*) and a three-string lute (*sanxian*). In the 17th–19th C, *dangziban* storytellers frequently gave *danxian* performances which included a great deal of buffoonery. Also called *bajiaogu* and *paiziqu* or *p'ai tzu ch'ü*. See also: *shibuxian, kuaishu*. (Howard CONTEMPORARY 30, Mackerras RISE 200)

danza (Italian)   Dance.

danza (Spanish)   Dance, as in *danza de espadas* or sword dance. (Shergold SPANISH)

danzante (Spanish)   A dancer. *Danzantes* were evidently lesser members of a 17th C touring group; they rode in carts rather than coaches. (Rennert SPANISH 155)

dao (Vietnamese)   An actress in Vietnamese theatre. (Pham-Duy MUSICS 124)

daoban, tao pan (Chinese)   Literally: lead-in meter, or, written with a different initial character, collapsed meter. A free meter (*ziyouban*) metrical-type (*banshi*) used in the songs of many forms of music-drama (*xiqu*) for an outpouring of emotions, and for offstage singing which precedes an entrance. In Beijing opera (*jingju*), it is used in both the *xipi* and *erhuang* modes (*diaoshi*), often for only the first line of the first couplet (*lian*) in a multi-couplet song. See also: *huilong*. (Wichmann "Aural" 160–164)

daoguanzuo, tao kuan tso (Chinese)   Literally: backwards officials' seats. In a teahouse theatre (*xiyuan*) of the 17th–early 20th C, the portion of second-floor veranda seating on either side of the stage, facing the back of the auditorium. This seating was usually for actors' relatives and friends. (Dolby HISTORY 190, Scott CLASSICAL 222)

daomadan, tao ma tan (Chinese)   Literally: sword and horse female role. A fairly young female role which features martial arts and combat (*da*) skill but also emphasizes song (*chang*) and dance-acting (*zuo*) skills as well; a major subcategory of the female role (*dan*) in Beijing opera (*jingju*) and many other forms of music-drama (*xiqu*). (Dolby HISTORY 180, Scott CLASSICAL 73)

daoqixi (Chinese)   See: *luju*.

daqiang, ta ch'iang (Chinese)   Literally: big wall. A 19th and early 20th C name for the cheapest seats in a teahouse theatre (*xiyuan*): ground-floor seating on two raised brick benches, one located on each side of the auditorium, under the veranda behind the scattered seats (*sanzuo*). (Scott CLASSICAL 222, Dolby HISTORY 191)

daqu, ta ch'ü (Chinese)   Literally: big song. A large-scale song and dance form performed at palace feasts in the 7th–13th C. Most pieces are believed to have been divided into three sections: an initial introductory section (*sanxu* or *san hsü*), a central section (*zhongxu* or *chung hsü, paixu* or *p'ai hsü*) which featured ten or more songs and included dance, and a final section (*po* or *p'o*) performed at a more rapid tempo which included song but featured dance. The big song was an important predecessor of Yuan *zaju*, and possibly influenced the development of Japanese *no* as well. Sometimes also called *qupo*. (Liu INTRODUCTION 165)

dara maku (Japanese)   See: *hon maku.*

darat (Malaysian)   Literally: hinterland. A shadow puppeteer whose performance is considered crude or countrified in speech, manipulation, music, or the puppets he uses. (Sweeney RAMAYANA 288–289)

daring buffoonery   16th and 17th C Russian entertainments—songs, dances, puppet shows—performed by traveling players. (Varneke RUSSIAN 7–10)

dark   Said of a theatre at which no performance is being presented. Hence, a dark house, a dark night.

dark change   In late 19th C British light plots, a scene change with the curtain up and the stage dark. The stage would not have been completely dark, since house lights were ordinarily kept at a low level during acts. (Hughes "Irving's" 254)

dark house   See: dark.

dark juvenile   See: light juvenile.

Darktown strut   Formerly, a strutting style of dancing originated by Black dancers. Hence, Darktown strutter. (Berrey/Van den Bark SLANG 588)

"Darling"   A common theatrical greeting used by or in speaking to an actress. (Bowman/Ball THEATRE)

daru (Sanskrit)   In many forms of traditional Indian theatre, a song having a specific dramatic function. See also: *dhruva.* (Gargi FOLK 193–194, Vatsyayan TRADITIONAL 61)

darza pather (Hindi)   A topic, taken from daily life, that forms the theme of a play among the strolling players (*bhand*) of Kashmir. (Rangacharya INDIAN 89)

dasa (Kannada)   A professional actor, in Mysore state, south India. (Ranganath KARNATAK 39)

dasangzi, ta sang tzu (Chinese)   Literally: large voice. "Natural" voice, as opposed to falsetto (*xiaosangzi*); one of two basic types of vocal production in many forms of music-drama (*xiqu*). Also called "true voice" (*zhensangzi* or *chen sang tzu*). In Beijing opera (*jingju*), it is used for painted-face (*jing*), clown (*chou*), and old female roles (*laodan*), and for all male roles (*sheng*) except young male (*xiaosheng*). See also: *xiaosangzi.*

dasantong, ta san t'ung (Chinese)   Literally: beat three times. Traditionally, instrumental music played by the percussion orchestra (*wuchang*) and the *suona* before a performance of music-drama (*xiqu*) to notify the audience that the performance was about to begin and warn the actors to be ready for their calls. (Scott CLASSICAL 49) It was played in three sections, separated by intervals of silence. Today it is much shorter, and the term is rarely used. Abbreviated *datong* or *ta t'ung*.

dasavatara (Sanskrit)   A dance or drama that depicts ten incarnations of the god Vishnu, found, for example, in folk theatre of Maharashtra state and Goa. Also spelled *dashavatar*. (Varadpande TRADITIONS 76, Vatsyayan TRADITIONAL 171)

dashavatar (Sanskrit)   See: *dasavatara*.

date   A playing engagement.

date book   A book showing a touring company's route.

dates   The days on which a performer or a company has engagements. (Fay GLOSSARY)

date sheet   On posters prepared to advertise touring companies, a sheet containing time and place of performances, changed from town to town. (Krows AMERICA 326)

datong (Chinese)   See: *dasantong*.

datou, ta t'ou (Chinese)   Literally: big head. The most frequently used traditional female hairdressing style (*baotou*) in Beijing opera (*jingju*) and many other forms of music-drama (*xiqu*). It includes a large, flat bun at the upper back of the head and nine curls encircling the face, and is considered appropriate for most traditional young and middle-aged female roles regardless of social position. Also called *dafa* or *ta fa*. (Halson PEKING 37, Scott CLASSICAL 164–166)

Davidrama   The 117 plays produced by the "factory" of Owen David and Al Woods in the late 19th and early 20th C. (Goff "Factory" 202)

daxi, ta hsi (Chinese)   Literally: large theatre. 1. Any form of music-drama (*xiqu*) which has a complete complement of role categories—male (*sheng*), female (*dan*), painted-face (*jing*), and clown (*chou*); a large repertoire of plays on national, historical, and local topics; and a full complement of performance skills—song (*chang*), speech (*nian*), dance-acting (*zuo*), and combat (*da*). Such forms are performed throughout a large region, in some instances all or most of the country. Often translated "large-scale theatre form," as opposed to small-scale folk theatre form (*xiaoxi*). *Kunqu,* Beijing opera (*jingju*), *qinqiang, hanju, chuju, minju,* and *chuanju* are all large-scale theatre forms. Also called *daxing xiqu* or *ta hsing hsi chü*. (Dolby HISTORY 222–229) 2. A full-length music-drama play, as opposed to a one-act play (*xiaoxi*). 3. A serious music-drama play, as opposed to a light play (*xiaoxi*).

daxing xiqu (Chinese)   See: *daxi*.

day   Especially in Restoration theatres, a benefit, as in the author's 'day.' (Van Lennep LONDON lxxxi)

day bill   See: window card.

dayi (Chinese)   See: *yixiang*.

dayingxi, ta ying hsi (Chinese)   Literally: great shadow theatre. A type of 12th–13th C shadow theatre performed by human actors rather than puppets. (Dolby HISTORY 34, Liu INTRODUCTION 164–165)

dayixiang (Chinese)   See: *yixiang*.

day man   A stagehand who works daytimes.

day of play   In Britain, the first performance, chaotic and full of nervous performers. (Granville DICTIONARY)

day set   A stage setting for the opening scene in a play, prepared during the daytime. (Bowman/Ball THEATRE)

Daytshmerish (Yiddish)   A Germanized Yiddish, especially in pronunciation, sometimes used in the theatre in Russia in the late 19th C and after, and in the U.S. in the early 20th C. The original purpose was to avoid a Russian ban on Yiddish theatre; later, the language variation, which included some German words, was thought suitable for characters above the common run. Also spelled *Deitchmeirish*. (Sandrow VAGABOND 25, 57–58, 128; Lifson YIDDISH 34, 56)

dazhang, ta chang (Chinese)   Literally: big curtain. A large embroidered curtain hung between the entrance door (*shangchangmen*) and exit door (*xiachangmen*) on the back wall of a traditional stage, especially in 17th-early 20th C teahouse theatres (*xiyuan*). Designs on such curtains were decorative, rather than representational of locales. Also called hall curtain (*tangmu* or *t'ang mu*). Today referred to as *shoujiu* or *shou chiu*, literally "the old observance." (Scott CLASSICAL 221)

dazhouzi (Chinese)   See: *zhouzi*.

DBO, D.B.O.   See: dead blackout.

DC   Down center.

ddunsoe (Korean)   See: *ttunsoe*.

de (Japanese)   Literally: entrance. 1. In *no*, the entrance of a character. 2. A scene in *kabuki* set on the runway (*hanamichi*) featuring the first appearance of a major character. The function is to introduce the personality of a character through movement and dialogue. If in a dance play, it is also called *deha*. (Brandon in Brandon/Malm/Shively STUDIES 93–98)

dead   1. In a theatrical production, anything no longer needed. 2. In Britain, to trim or make level a flown scenic unit. Hence, to dead, on its dead, on the dead, high dead, low dead. 3. Said of an unsuccessful production. 4. Formerly said of a very bad actor. 5. Said of a circuit without electrical current. (Bowman/Ball THEATRE, National TECHNICAL, Wilkinson WANDERING I 182)

dead act   A poorly-received act, as in vaudeville, or a lifelessly performed act in a play.

dead area   A relatively dark portion of the stage. See also: dead spot. (Bowman/Ball THEATRE)

dead audience   An unresponsive audience.

dead blackout   Complete blackness on the stage as seen from the audience. Often shortened to DBO (D.B.O.), especially in light plots. Apparently British originally, and perhaps still primarily so. The term is more emphatic than blackout, and not necessarily redundant: see blackout. (Bentham ART 337, Granville DICTIONARY, Bowman/Ball THEATRE)

dead cue   A precise cue.

dead-face(d) board   See: dead front board.

dead fold   A free-falling draped effect created by the absence of underlying stiffness which would hold fabric away from the body. (Barton COSTUME 64)

dead front board   A control board which has no current-carrying parts on its face. Such boards have for some decades been required by law in most areas. Also called a dead-face(d) board. (Bellman LIGHTING 168, Bowman MODERN, Corry PLANNING, McCandless "Glossary" 637)

deadhead   1. A person with a free ticket to a performance. Possibly derived from the ancient Roman custom which gave free admission "tickets" which were actually small death heads carved from ivory. (Broadbent PANTOMIME 57) 2. An unresponsive spectator.

dead hoofer   Slang for a poor dancer.

dead house   1. An auditorium with a relatively short reverberation time. 2. An unresponsive audience.

dead hung   Said of something permanently hung from the gridiron and not capable of being raised or lowered.

"Dead it!"   1. An order to a stagehand to remove something from the stage. 2. An order to fasten something at a given height or length. (Bowman/Ball THEATRE)

deadline, dead line   1. In a theatre auditorium, an imaginary line beyond which the view of the stage is impaired. (Bowman/Ball THEATRE) 2. In the flies, a line or set of lines dead-tied and thus not capable of being used to raise or lower anything.

dead man switch   A safety device requiring an operator to maintain constant pressure on an electrical switch for it to continue operating.

dead march   Especially in Elizabethan plays, a dirge.

dead pack, dead stack   Scenic units no longer needed.

dead pan   1. An expressionless face, generally assumed for comic effect but occasionally inadvertent among unskilled performers. 2. An actor whose face is expressionless. (Cartmell HANDBOOK 100, Bowman/Ball THEATRE)

dead season   See: off season.

dead sell   Primarily in Britain, a successful show or act. (Wilmeth LANGUAGE)

dead share   In a sharing system, a share paid to the manager to cover his expenses for costumes, scenery, etc. (Bowman/Ball THEATRE)

dead spot   A portion of the stage which is darker than it should be. The term is usually used of the acting area. Occasionally called a light pocket. (Wehlburg GLOSSARY)

dead stage   1. A stage floor with no resilience, unsuitable for dancing. (Gilbert VAUDEVILLE 164) 2. An empty stage.

dead stick   See: corker.

dead theatre   A theatre at which no show is being given.

dead tied   See: deadline.

deadwood   Unsold theatre tickets returned by agencies.

dea ex machina (Latin)   Literally: goddess from the machine. An occasional term for a female parallel of the *deus ex machina*. (Frank MEDIEVAL 120)

death trail   A vaudeville circuit in the northwestern U.S. consisting of widely scattered small towns. (Gilbert VAUDEVILLE 220)

death watch   Drama critics. (Berrey/Van den Bark SLANG 575)

débat (French)   In the Dark Ages, a dialogue without much action between two allegorical characters, such as Summer and Winter or Good and Evil.

debayashi (Japanese)   Literally: onstage ensemble. In *kabuki* dance plays, the *nagauta* ensemble of musicians and singers that sits onstage in view of the audience at the rear of the acting area. See also: *degatari*. Examples are in *The Subscription List* and *The Zen Substitute* in Brandon TRADITIONAL 211–236, 241–272. (Leiter ENCYCLOPEDIA 55)

debog (Indonesian)   Two horizontal banana trunks into which the central rod (*gapit*) of a Javanese *wayang* puppet is placed, to hold the puppet figure in position during static scenes. Also called *gedebog*. (Long JAVANESE 18–19) Called *gebog* in Sundanese *wayang golek* (Foley "Sundanese" 48) and *gedebong* in Balinese *wayang kulit* (McPhee in Belo TRADITIONAL 147, Moerdowo II BALINESE 121).

debut   A performer's first appearance, either on a professional stage, in a new production, or in a new place. (Bowman/Ball THEATRE)

decay'd musicians   An 18th C British term for indigent and usually retired theatre musicians.

decencies   An obsolete term for pads worn by an actor to give him a better figure. (Partridge TO-DAY 227)

decent   See: "Are you decent?"

deck   Originally U.S., the stage floor. From the language of the sea. (Granville DICTIONARY, Bowman/Ball THEATRE)

deckhand, deck hand   A stagehand.

declaim   To deliver one's lines in a highly formal, rhetorical manner. The word is often used to indicate bombast and rant, but only in a period when a realistic acting style is dominant. (Bowman/Ball THEATRE)

declamatory   In a rhetorical manner.

décor (French)   Stage decoration or design. The term embraces scenery and furnishings.

decorador (Philippine)   A scene painter or designer in *zarzuela*. (Fernández ILOILO 130)

décorateur (French)   A stage designer, a scene painter.

decorations   1. In 17th C France, the visual aspects of a stage production. 2. In 18th C London, properties and accessories. 3. In 18th C London, the interior features of the auditorium. (d'Aubignac, Ménestrier in Nagler SOURCES 172, 187; Hogan LONDON 580)

decorator   In 17th C French theatres, the scene painter, who was responsible for painting the scenery, maintaining order backstage, and overseeing the candle snuffers. (Chappuzeau in Nagler SOURCES 185)

décor multiple, décor simultané (French)   Multiple, simultaneous staging— a medieval system of having several locales represented on stage at the same time, with action moving from one to another (Nicoll DEVELOPMENT 94).

decorum   In neoclassic theory, the behavior of a dramatic character in keeping with the character's status, age, sex, and occupation. Also the maintenance of purity and taste in language, characterization, and action, especially in tragedy. (Cameron/Gillespie ENJOYMENT, Bowman/Ball THEATRE)

decrescendo   In dance, a decrease in force. (Love DANCE)

(en) dedans (French)   Literally: inward. In ballet, a term indicating that the leg moves in a circular direction, counterclockwise from back to front. (Grant TECHNICAL)

ded-balagur (Russian)   Literally: gag grandfathers. In Russian 18th and 19th C comedies, grandfather characters who cracked jokes about everyday life. (Yershov SOVIET 7)

deerstalker   See: fore and aft.

deficiency   Especially in 18th C theatres, the loss suffered by performers at a benefit that did not bring in enough income to pay the house charges. (Hogan LONDON clxxxviii)

dégagé (French)   In ballet, pointing the foot in an open position to pass from one position of the feet to another. Also called *pas dégagé*. Wilson BALLET has an illustration. (Grant TECHNICAL)

degatari (Japanese)   Literally: onstage narrative. In *kabuki* dance plays, the ensemble of onstage musicians and singers who perform narrative (*joruri*) style music. See also: *debayashi*. (Leiter ENCYCLOPEDIA 55)

degrees   Stepped seats in Renaissance theatres. (Nicoll STUART 38)

degrees Kelvin   See: Kelvin scale.

deha (Japanese)   See: *de*.

(en) dehors (French)   Literally: outside. In ballet, a term indicating that the leg moves in a circular direction, clockwise. (Grant TECHNICAL)

deigan (Japanese)   A *no* mask with golden eyes, representing a woman transformed into a powerful spirit, sometimes a dragon goddess and sometimes a jealous spirit. (Shimazaki NOH 61)

deikelistai (Greek)   Small, early companies of comic actors, probably masked and perhaps connected with the development of the mime and of Old Comedy. Thought to be from *deikelon* (plural *deikela*), mask, or perhaps representation or imitation in the sense of performance. (Pickard-Cambridge DITHYRAMB 134–136, 163; Beare ROMAN 149, 150; Webster PRODUCTION 128–129)

deikelon (Greek)   Literally: likeness, imitation. 1. A performance (i.e., a performance viewed as an imitation of an action). 2. Mask. Plural *deikela*. (Pickard-Cambridge DITHYRAMB 135, Beare ROMAN 150)

deikterias (Greek)   A female mime player of a special type. Little is known of this performer beyond the suspected conection with the earlier *deikelistai* suggested by the name. (Nicoll MASKS 50)

deĭstvovat' (Russian)   To act.

deĭstvuiushchee litso (Russian)   Literally: acting personage. A dramatic persona—a character in a play. (Senelick RUSSIAN 183n)

deistvuiuschiĭ (Russian)   Acting.

Deitchmeirish (Yiddish)   See. *Daytshmerish*.

delivery   The manner in which a performer speaks his lines.

Delsarte system   A highly codified, precise system of action, gesture, vocal tone, and inflection developed by François Delsarte in the 19th C in France. (Dolman ACTING 240)

deluge curtain   A device above a house curtain to soak the curtain with water in case of fire. See also: water curtain.

delusor (Latin)   See: minstrel.

de Medici ruff   See: ruff.

demet   A material used in Britain for making stage window curtains. (Fay GLOSSARY)

demi-amphithéâtre (French)   Literally: semi-amphitheatre. In partly Romanized Western Europe, including northern France, a theatre intended for both amphitheatrical and theatrical use. Also called *théâtre mixte*. (Bieber HISTORY 202)

demi-caractère (French)   A 19th C French classic ballet having a dancer with an average build who performed a wide range of roles using many techniques. (Carlson FRENCH 39)

demi-contretemps (French)   See: *contretemps*.

demi-plié (French)   In ballet, half or slight bending of the knees outward.

demi-pointes (French)   In ballet, the balls of the feet, usually part of a direction to stand in that position. Also called half toes.

demon play   See: *kiri no*.

demountable door frame, demountable window frame   Frames for doors or windows that can be placed into openings in flats, kept in place with strap hinges, and easily removed. Also called breakdown scenery. (Cornberg/Gebauer CREW 268)

denawa (Indonesian)   See: *danawa*.

dendenmono (Japanese)   See: *maruhonmono*.

dengaku (Japanese)   Literally: field entertainment. Originally, ritual and folk dances performed at rice-planting and harvest ceremonies. By the 14th C *dengaku* included juggling, singing, dancing, and plays arranged in a variety format. It was popular in Kyoto and other cities and competed vigorously with *no* for audiences. (Bowers JAPANESE 11, Inoura HISTORY 71–76, Tsubaki ''Performing'' 306)

dengakugaeshi (Japanese)   Literally: skewer change. A technique of pivoting a flat on a horizontal or vertical axis to produce a sudden change of scenery. The device, often used in ghost scenes, originated in 1789 in *bunraku* and was later adopted for use in *kabuki*. (Ernst KABUKI 55, Leiter ENCYCLOPEDIA 56)

dengxi, teng hsi (Chinese)   Literally: lantern plays, lantern theatre. A Sichuan Province small-scale folk theatre form (*xiaoxi*) which probably originated with exorcistic and celebratory shamanistic performances. It was originally presented by three performers on bare ground or on a mat, with lanterns used to light evening shows. It was formally incorporated into the repertory of professional Sichuan opera (*chuanju*) troupes in the early 20th C. (Dolby HISTORY 226; Mackerras MODERN 156, 158)

denouement, *dénouement* (French)   The unravelling of the plot in the final scene in a play. In a tragedy, this portion of the play is sometimes called the catastrophe. Also called the resolution. (Bowman/Ball THEATRE)

dent the lid   In Britain, to applaud enthusiastically. (Granville DICTIONARY)

deportment   Especially in Britain, a performer's movement, repose, carriage, and general bearing on stage. (Granville DICTIONARY)

depot billing   In the days of touring, advertising a show in the vicinity of the railroad station at which a company would arrive.

depth stage   A stage whose settings and acting area are behind the proscenium, rather than one in which the forestage is important. (Gorelik NEW)

derby   An occasional term for a small floodlight whose shape resembles that of a derby hat. (Bowman MODERN)

derma wax   A soft substance useful in altering a performer's features.

(à) derrière (French)   Literally: behind, back. In ballet, a movement, step, or placing of a limb in back of the body. (Grant TECHNICAL)

desembocadura (Spanish)   See: *embocadura*.

designator (Latin Roman)   See: *dissignator*.

(au) dessous (French)   Literally: under. In ballet, a term indicating that the working foot passes behind the supporting foot. (Grant TECHNICAL)

(le) dessous (French)   1. The substage. (Moynet FRENCH 32) 2. The subtext; the underlying motives of the characters in a play.

(au) dessus (French)   Literally: over. In ballet, a term indicating that the working foot passes in front of the supporting foot. (Grant TECHNICAL)

desván (Spanish)   Literally: an attic or loft. In the 17th C., a third-level box overlooking the *patio* in a *corral* theatre.

detail   1. A box office statement that analyzes the number of seats sold in all parts of the theatre and the money taken in. 2. In scene painting, definition and fine work through lining, texturing, and stencilling. (Baker THEATRE-CRAFT, Parker/Smith DESIGN 263)

détiré (French)   In ballet, drawing out or stretching the leg, usually at the *barre*. (Grant TECHNICAL)

détourné (French)   In ballet, a backward turn in the direction of the back foot which reverses the position of the feet. (Grant TECHNICAL)

deuce   1. In vaudeville, a two-night stand. (Wilmeth LANGUAGE) 2. A performing team of two. 3. A flat two feet wide.

deuce act, deuce spot   In vaudeville, the second act on a bill—not considered a desirable position. Hence, deucing it, to deuce it. (Wilmeth LANGUAGE)

deuce week   A second week's engagement. (Berrey/Van den Bark SLANG 589)

deuchi (Japanese)   Literally: onstage beating. In *kabuki*, an old custom of having a stage assistant strike the *hyoshigi* in full view of the audience. The technique is rarely used today, except in revivals of old plays. (Leiter ENCYCLOPEDIA 56–57)

deverbium (Latin Roman)   See: *diverbia*.

deus (Latin)   See: *deus ex machina*.

deus ex machina (Latin)   Literally: god out of (from) the machine. The phrase originated in Greek times from the use of the *mechane* (Greek) (*machina*) to lower gods to the stage. From this use came its literal meaning and its figurative senses. Primary among the latter is a god appearing near the end of a play in a climactic scene which resolves the problems of the characters. Less directly, the phrase is used of any dramatic character, incident, or device which brings the play to an unmotivated close. According to Aristotle (*Poetics*), the *deus* was properly usable only for exposition by a god or gods of events not falling within the plot of the play, but related to it and taking place before or after it; the *deus* should not, thus, be used to explain anything otherwise irrational. The phrase is ordinarily pejorative, but the device has been defended, for example, as theatrically effective, as suitable to comedy, and even as permitting Euripides to cover in one play events that formerly required a trilogy. Sometimes shortened to *deus* by writers in English. See also: *mechane*. (Stuart DRAMATIC 52–53, 96–97; Butcher ARISTOTLE'S 55–57; Vaughn DRAMA; Flickinger GREEK 294)

deuteragonist   When used of the classical theatre, a second actor, an actor of secondary roles. Ancient Greek *deuteragonistes* is literally second contestant; the only surviving uses of the Greek word which certainly apply to actors are in early Christian times, but the English word has long been used for the second actor of all periods of the Greek theatre. Compare: *actor secundarum partium*. See also: protagonist, tritagonist. (Allen ANTIQUITIES 138–139, O'Connor CHAPTERS 31–36)

devanadera (Spanish)   A turning scenic element in two parts: when half open it could reveal the scene behind it, and when fully rotated it displayed yet another scene painted on its back surface.

devantière   A 17th C woman's riding habit, split at the back. (Boucher FASHION)

development   1. In playwriting, the main body of the play, following the exposition and inciting action, and leading ultimately to the climax. Also called the complication section, since the plot increases in complexity and intensity. 2. In acting, an expansion and change of character traits as the play develops. (Bowman/Ball THEATRE)

developmental drama   1. A method of improvisation with youth, first developed in England, in which participants engage in theatre games (q.v.) rather than story dramatization. 2. The study of developmental patterns in human enactment. (Courtney THOUGHT 5) See also: creative drama.

développé (French)   In ballet, a movement in which the working leg is drawn up, slowly extended to an open position, and held there with perfect control. (Grant TECHNICAL)

device   A medieval emblem, often embroidered on clothes. Also called a motto. (Boucher FASHION)

devozioni (Italian)   The earliest type of Italian liturgical play, dating from the 14th C. (Chambers MEDIAEVAL II 92) *dewa* (Malaysian)   In shadow theatre, a puppet character of a god or demi-god. (Sweeney MALAY 83, Sweeney RAMAYANA 55)

dexiostatae (Greek)   Literally: men on the right. In the Greek tragic chorus, the last (and second best) of the three files of chorus members. Though much of the time farthest from the audience, the last file was fully visible when the chorus pivoted and hence consisted of better performers than the middle file. (Haigh ATTIC 300)

dezukai (Japanese)   Literally: onstage manipulation. In *bunraku*: 1. Broadly, the usual manipulation technique seen today in which puppeteers appear onstage in view of the audience, as opposed to the practice before the early 17th C of concealing puppeteers beneath the stage. (Dunn EARLY 63) 2. More narrowly, the appearance of the chief puppeteer of a three-man team, bare-faced, without the black hood which usually hides his face. (Adachi BUNRAKU 146)

DF   In 18th C theatres and later, a door flat: a flat with a door built into it. (Shattuck SHAKESPEARE 17)

dhagelan (Indonesian)   See: *dagelan.*

dhalang (Indonesian, Malaysian)   See: *dalang.*

dhanasi (Malayalam)   A concluding danced benediction in *kathakali.* (Jones/Jones KATHAKALI 108)

dharana (Sanskrit)   A stance of a character in *mayurbhanj chhau.* (Vatsyayan TRADITIONAL 79)

dhawah (Indonesian)   A term used in Javanese shadow puppet battles to describe falling to the ground without losing consciousness. Variations include: *dhawah kantep* (falling on one's hip), *dhawah kongsep* and *dhawah krungkep* (falling on one's face), *dhawah klumah* (falling on one's back), *dhawah mengker noleh* (fall landing on one's feet and returning to battle), *dhawah ngglundhung* (fall and roll), and *dhawah njempalik* (fall spinning in the air). (Long JAVANESE 66–67)

dhemali (Assamese)   Preliminaries of music, dance and introduction of characters that precede an *ankiya nat* performance.

dhira (Sanskrit)   Literally: self-controlled. An attribute of a hero in a classical Indian play. (Keith SANSKRIT 305)

dhol (Hindi)   A drum played with the palm and fingers of the left hand and a blunt stick in the right. Used as musical accompaniment in many rural Indian theatre forms.

dholki (Hindi)   A percussion instrument used in *tamasha* folk theatre.

dholki bari (Marathi)   See: *tamasha*

dhruva (Sanskrit)   In a classical Indian play, a song written in Prakrit language that has a specific dramatic function: entrance (*pravesiki*), departure (*naiskramiki*), to convey mood (*prasadiki*), to alter the situation (*aksepiki*), or to cover a mishap to an actor (*antara*). (Raghavan in Baumer/Brandon SANSKRIT 37)

dhvani (Sanskrit)   The poetic device of suggestion, used by authors of classical Sanskrit drama.

di, ti (Chinese)   A horizontal bamboo flute, sometimes called *dizi* or *ti tzu*; there are two main types. The *qudi* or *ch'ü ti* is large and produces a mellow, rich sound; it is the main instrument in the melodic orchestra (*wenchang*) in *kunqu* and is also used in Beijing opera (*jingju*). The *bangdi* or *pang ti* is small and higher in pitch, and produces a clear, melodious sound; it is featured in most forms of music-drama (*xiqu*) which use music derived from the *bangziqiang* musical system. (Scott CLASSICAL 46; Wichmann "Aural" 440, 451–452)

dialect   An idiosyncrasy of speech pertaining to a certain section of a country or its people. Hence, dialect part, dialect play. (Carrington THEATRICANA)

dialect comedy act   A vaudeville act, usually involving two comedians, in which ethnic humor and foreign dialects were used. Irish, Jewish, Italian, and German dialects were most common. Dialect comedy was most popular from 1890 to 1920 in the U.S., the period of the major immigrations. (Wilmeth LANGUAGE)

dialogian   A playwright.

dialogue   1. The words of a play, as written by the playwright but also as spoken on stage by performers, usually two or more, though technically a dialogue is conversation between two people, no more and no less. 2. A song with alternating parts to be sung by different performers. Hence, a dialogued song. 3. To break a song into such parts. (Bowman/Ball THEATRE)

dial plate   1. See: gas plate. 2. A calibrated disc at the back of a rotating control knob.

diamanté (French)   Literally: diamonded. Powdered glass used to sparkle scenery and costumes. (Bowman/Ball THEATRE)

diamond horseshoe   The dress circle.

dianju, tien chü (Chinese)   Yunnan opera, a form of music-drama (*xiqu*), the largest in scale of the forms popular in Yunnan Province; also prevalent in portions of Sichuan and Guizhou provinces. Its 17th and 18th C development was influenced by forms popular in other provinces, probably including *qinqiang, hanju,* and *huiju*, which were brought to Yunnan by traveling troupes. *Dianju* uses three musical systems (*shengqiang xitong*), including a version of *pihuang* called *huqinqiang,* and a version of *bangziqiang*.

dianoia (Greek)   Thought (also the literal meaning), the third in order of importance in Aristotle's elements of tragedy in the *Poetics*. As he uses the word, it means intellectual capacity or skill. Myers viewed *dianoia* as tragedy's "... most important contribution to a philosophy of value, the unique conception of justice latent in the dianoetic background of tragic art.''(Meyers VIEW 24, 33; Butcher ARISTOTLE'S 334ff)

diaochang, tiao ch'ang (Chinese)   Literally: hanging (suspending) the scene. 1. In *chuanqi* drama, a short performance piece relatively independent of the plot which was presented at the end of a scene by two or more characters who remained on stage after the scene proper was concluded. 2. In 19th and 20th C music-drama (*xiqu*), a recapitulation speech. Such speeches are most prevalent in scenes excerpted from longer plays and performed as independent pieces (*zhezixi*); they are usually delivered by secondary characters, and serve to remind the audience of the plot developments preceeding the excerpted piece.

diaoshi, tiao shih (Chinese)   Literally: tune style, key style. A set of pre-scribed patterns of written character placement within metrical organization, song structure, melodic contour, melodic construction, key, and cadence; per-ceived as producing a particular atmosphere. Usually translated ''mode.'' Modes are one of the principal musical components of *banqiangti* musical structure; several modes are used in the music of each form of music-drama (*xiqu*) which follows such structure, and several specific metrical-types (*banshi*) are used with every mode. Also called tune key (*qiangdiao* or *ch'iang tiao*). See also: *zheng-diaoshi, fandiaoshi*. (Wichmann ''Aural'' 167–261)

diaoyutai, tiao yü t'ai (Chinese)   Literally: fishing platform. In a tea-house theatre (*xiyuan*) of the 17th-early 20th C, the portion of ground-floor seating on either side of the stage. That near the stage exit (*xiachangmen*) was the most expensive ground floor seating; that near the stage entrance (*shangchangmen*) was less expensive because of its proximity to the orchestra. Also called small pond (*xiaochizi* or *hsiao ch'ih tzu*). (Dolby HISTORY 190–191, Mackerras RISE 203, Scott CLASSICAL 221–222)

diaphragm   See: iris.

diapositive   In Britain, a slide used for a projection. The British term, with such slight variations as German *Diapositiv* and Italian *diapositiva*, is used in most Western European languages. (Rae/Southern INTERNATIONAL)

diaulion (Greek)   Instrumental music used for special effect in Old Comedy, as in the imitation on a flute of the nightingale's song in Aristophanes' *Birds*. Such effects were also called *mesaulion*. (Pickard-Cambridge FESTIVALS 262)

diazoma (Greek), **diazoma**   In ancient Greece, a passageway across a theatre auditorium that usually separated its tiers from each other. Thus, an auditorium in three tiers would have two such *diazomata*. One might be wider than another (as in the Theatre of Dionysus in Athens) if connecting directly with a road, or if for any other reason it was designed to be used by a greater number of spectators. Pickard-Cambridge says that the passageway at the Theatre of Dio-nysus is the only road *diazoma* whose existence is proved. The word, which was originally Hellenistic Greek, is literally girdle, belt. Haigh says that the tiers of seats rather than the passageways were the girdles. Compare Latin *praecinctio*. (Pickard-Cambridge DIONYSUS 138–139; Allen ANTIQUITIES 65, 93–94; Haigh ATTIC 98–99)

Di Broder Zinger (Yiddish)   See: Broder singer.

dicho (Philippine)   A stylized manner of delivering lines of verse dialogue in *comedia*. Also called *loa*. See also: *tagulaylay*. (Mendoza COMEDIA 45)

dichroic filter   A coating applied to glass surfaces which selectively reflects certain bands of wave lengths and transmits others. As used in the theatre, dichroic filters are applied to lenses, reflectors, and occasionally glass plates to sort infrared (heat) wave lengths from visible light, making the visible light beam cooler and allowing removal of the heat energy of the infrared in a harmless manner. See also: dichroic lens, cold mirror, hot mirror. (Lounsbury THEATRE, Bentham ART 91–92)

dichroic lens   A spotlight lens whose flat back has been treated with the dichroic process. See also: dichroic filter.

dichroic reflector   A glass reflector whose surface has been treated by the dichroic process. See also: dichroic filter.

dicit (Latin)   A stage direction in a medieval play indicating that a line is to be spoken rather than sung or chanted. (Chambers MEDIAEVAL II 90)

dicky bird   Especially in Britain, a performer who can both act and sing.

dictador (Philippine)   A prompter-director.

diction   1. In Aristotle's *Poetics*, ''one of the six parts of a play; the formal cause of music, the material of thought; the words of a play.'' 2. In acting, the manner in which words are spoken. (Cameron/Gillespie ENJOYMENT, Purdom PRODUCING)

did a Brodie   See: Brodie.

didactic drama   1. A play with ideas or a message that the playwright wishes to impress upon the audience. Often propagandistic, but not so militant or political as an agit-prop play. Most of Aristophanes' and Bernard Shaw's plays are didactic. 2. Such plays as a group. (Cameron/Hoffman GUIDE, Shaw in Cole/Chinoy PLAYWRITING 199)

didactic interlude   A late medieval form of the morality play. (Pollard MIRACLE lxvii)

didascalos (Greek), **didascalos**   See: *didaskalos*.

didaskalia, didascalia (Greek)   Literally: a teaching. 1. The training of a chorus. Compare *didaskalos*. 2. The record of contests in drama. Such documentation at various times included the names of *choregi*, tribes, authors, and chorus trainers; some records were inscribed on stone. There were other records, especially victors' lists, but the distinction between them and the *didaskalia* is not always made by writers in English. *Didaskalia* also appears in English as didascaly. 3. Sometimes, production information at the beginning of a play script.

4. A group of three tragedies and a satyr play. Meanings 2 and 4 suggest that the plays were seen as results of the teaching, perhaps also that the plays were viewed as teaching the populace. Plurals -*iae* (for both spellings) and *didaskaliai*. Attributive: didascalic. (Flickinger GREEK 198, 318–326; Pickard-Cambridge FESTIVALS 71–73, 108–111, 124–125)

didaskalos (Greek)   Teacher or trainer of the chorus. In the 6th C BC and for a time afterward, *didaskaloi* were usually the poets themselves, and sometimes actors. Hence, the term is sometimes rendered 'director.' The rise of the separate chorus-teacher is thought to have resulted from the performance of plays whose authors were no longer living. Variant spellings include *didascalos* and *didascalus*, the former also accepted in U.S. English. *Hypodidaskalos* was used at times and, after the 5th C BC, *chorodidaskalos*. (Haigh ATTIC 61–62; Flickinger GREEK 318; Allen ANTIQUITIES 45; Pickard-Cambridge DITHYRAMB 56; Arnott ANCIENT 39, 114)

die   To fail to get applause or other audience response. Hence, die standing up, died.

diezi (Chinese)   See: *xuezi*.

difangxi, ti fang hsi (Chinese)   Any form of music-drama (*xiqu*) that is specific to one region. Such forms differ from one another primarily in music and dialect, rather than in subject matter and basic performance style. They began developing in the 10th C; Yuan *zaju*, southern drama (*nanxi*), *kunqu*, and Beijing opera (*jingju*) all originated as regional theatre forms. Apart from those which developed from *kunqu*, the great majority of regional theatre forms were and are popular theatre. Today there are more than three hundred different forms of regional theatre, including both large-scale theatre forms (*daxi*) and small-scale folk theatre forms (*xiaoxi*). (Dolby HISTORY 219–229, Mackerras RISE 4–11, Mackerras "Growth" 58–91

differential dimming   See: proportional dimming.

diffuse(d)   1. Of stage lighting generally, spread and softened. The word is used in various forms and combinations, as are related words: diffusing, diffusion, diffused light, etc. (Bowman/Ball THEATRE) 2. Of reflectors, a surface each point of which reflects light equally in every direction. See also: diffuse reflection.

diffuser   A filter which spreads and softens a beam of light. Some diffusers also modify the shape of the beam. Among other terms: diffusing screen, diffusing medium, diffusion medium. See also: frost. (McCandless "Glossary" 639, Bowman/Ball THEATRE)

diffuse reflection   Reflection which is non-directional; reflection which spreads in all directions.

diffusing screen, diffusing medium   See: diffuser.

diffusion filter   A medium which combines the effects of filtering (altering wave-length content) of light and causing the light to spread in a diffuse manner. See also: diffuser, frost.

diffusion medium   See: diffuser.

dig   To sell tickets on the street.

digger   See: ticket scalper.

dikay (Thai)   See: *likay*.

dikpalastuti (Sanskrit)   A song praising the world guardians in the preliminaries (*purvaranga*) before a classical theatre performance. (Keith SANSKRIT 369)

dilly Nell   A dilatory chorus girl—one who is always late for rehearsals. (Berrey/Van den Bark SLANG 573)

dim   To alter the brightness of light either upward or downward. Older definitions sometimes limited the meaning to lowering the brightness, particularly in Britain.

dima (Sanskrit)   One of the ten major types of drama (*rupaka*) in ancient India. It was composed in four acts, based on a well-known story, and had gods and demons as characters. (Keith SANSKRIT 266–267, 295–296)

di man dritta (Italian)   Up center stage in *commedia dell'arte*, though the phrase means, literally, on the right hand. (Mantzius HISTORY II 215)

dim down   To decrease light intensity by appropriate adjustment of one or more dimmers. (Hewitt/Foster/Wolle PLAY)

dime museum   1. In the late 19th and early 20th C in the U.S., a place of entertainment which might have provided anything from freak shows, wax figures, and jugglers to dioramas, comedians, and musicians. 2. A bad play. (Wilmeth LANGUAGE, Partridge TO-DAY 227)

dimer   In the early 20th C in the U.S., a theatre with a 10 cent admission charge. (Berrey/Van den Bark SLANG 577)

dim in   To increase light gradually, often imperceptibly.

dimmer   Any device which gradually alters the brightness of one or more lights. The following list includes the principal names used of theatre dimmers, and most of the names used less frequently. Entries for those starred contain information on most of the others: ATD, ★autotransformer dimmer, ★carbon, carbon pile, choke dimmer, disk (disc) dimmer, dual rated dimmer, electronic tube dimmer, flexible dimmer, ★grand master, interlocking plate dimmer, liquid dimmer, liquid pot dimmer, magamp, magnetic amplifier, master dimmer, metallic dimmer, multi-capacity (resistance) dimmer, ★plate dimmer, pot dimmer, radial arm dimmer, ★reactance dimmer, reactor dimmer, rectangular plate dimmer, ★remote control dimmer, ★resistance dimmer, resistor dimmer, rheostat, round plate dimmer, ★salt water dimmer, saturable choke, saturable core dimmer, saturable reactor dimmer, ★silicon controlled rectifier (SCR) dimmer, ★slide (slider) dimmer, slide resistance dimmer, spotlight dimmer, thyratron dimmer, ★thyratron tube dimmer, thyrister, thyristor dimmer, Triac, tube dimmer, variable dimmer, ★variable load dimmer, water dimmer, water-barrel dimmer, water resistance dimmer, wire dimmer, wire resistance dimmer.

dimmer bank   1. In stage lighting, a metal enclosure containing remote control dimmers and their associated circuitry. 2. A group of dimmers, especially in a horizontal or vertical row. 3. See: dimmer board.

dimmer board   In lighting, especially in the past, a framework or container which houses dimmers. The term was sometimes used of boards which included both dimmers and switches. Sometimes called a dimmer bank.

dimmer channel   See: channel.

dimmer check   See: checkout.

dimmer pack   See: package board.

dimmer rack   In modern remote control lighting systems, a heavy steel rack on which the dimmers and their appurtenances are mounted. (Bellman LIGHTING 218)

dimmer room   In modern remote control dimmer systems, a special room in which dimmers and their appurtenances are isolated. (Bellman LIGHTING 218)

dimmer way   A control channel or circuit which includes a dimmer. (Bellman LIGHTING 284)

dimming curve   The relation of the light output to the scale, usually 1 to 10 or 1 to 100, which notes dimmer settings.

dim out   To reduce light to blackout gradually, often imperceptibly.

"Dim the house"   See: house lights.

dim up   To increase light intensity by appropriate adjustment of one or more dimmers. (Hewitt/Foster/Wolle PLAY)

dinding dunia (Malaysian)   See: *kelir*.

dingchangbai, ting ch'ang pai (Chinese)   Literally: set-the-scene speech. A prose speech in which the character states his or her full name, place of origin, salient life experiences, and current situation; a type of self-introductory material (*zibao jiamen*) in Beijing opera (*jingju*) and many other forms of music-drama (*xiqu*). Such speeches are spoken by a major character after a set-the-scene poem (*dingchangshi*), and vary greatly in length. Also called *zuochangbai* or *tso ch'ang pai*; sometimes called *tongming*. See also: *shangchangbai*. (Scott CLASSICAL 93–94)

dingchangshi, ting ch'ang shih (Chinese)   Literally: set-the-scene poem. A verse consisting of one to four couplets which describes the basic situation of the scene to follow, and conveys the general state of mind of the character speaking; a type of self-introductory material (*zibao jiamen*) in Beijing opera (*jingju*) and many other forms of music-drama (*xiqu*). Such poems are spoken by a major character after a lead-in poem (*yinzi*), and are followed by a set-the-scene speech (*dingchangbai*); they ususally consist of two couplets (*lian*), though one or four may also be used. Also called *zuochangshi* or *tso ch'ang shih*. See also: *shangchangbai*. (Scott CLASSICAL 93, Scott TRADITIONAL I 150)

dinner theatre   A restaurant offering light entertainment, sometimes plays or musicals. Also called showroom theatre or theatre restaurant.

Dionysia   See: City Dionysia, Dionysian Festivals.

Dionysiac Artists   See: Artists of Dionysus.

Dionysian festivals   In ancient Greece, joyous religious observances in honor of the god Dionysus. The festivals closely related to the origin and growth of the Greek theatre were the Rural Dionysia (lesser Dionysia), the Lenaea (Lenaean festival, Lenaean games, etc.), and the City Dionysia (Great Dionysia, Dionysia). They were held, in the order given, from late December to April. See the individual entries for each festival for further information. Also called Dionysiac festivals. See also: (the) Anthesteria. (Pickard-Cambridge FESTIVALS 1–103, Bieber HISTORY 51–53)

diorama   1. A backcloth that unrolls from a vertical cylinder at one side of the stage and rolls onto another on the opposite side. Also called a panorama, moving panorama, rolling backcloth. 2. A scenic view seen through a cutout drop, a translucency, or a transparency. (Burris-Meyer/Cole SCENERY 74, Cameron/Gillespie ENJOYMENT)

diorama à double effet (French)   A diorama with some details painted on the front and some on the back of a transparent cloth. (Brockett HISTORY 447)

dip   1. In Britain, a stage floor pocket, usually beneath a small hinged trap. Also called a trap box. 2. In the U.S., a momentary partial decrease in the light on stage. 3. In the 19th C British water joint for gas pockets, the pipe which was "dipped" into the water joint. See also: water joint slide. 4. Also in 19th C Britain, a candle which had been made by repeated dipping of a wick into wax. 5. See: lamp dip. 6. To color a low-wattage lamp by immersing it briefly in lamp dip. (Bentham ART; Bellman LIGHTING 220, 225; Bowman/Ball THEATRE; Granville DICTIONARY; Rees GAS 6) 7. Slang for an advance agent.

diphtheritis (Greek)   Literally: clad in a leather frock. According to Pollux, as noted by Nicoll, a mask without a headdress, worn by a not-quite middle-aged woman dressed in leather. (Nicoll DEVELOPMENT 30)

dipless cross fader   An electrical device that effects a cross fade (q.v.) without causing a lamp common to both the up and down fade at the same reading to vary in intensity. The device may be either manual or automatic.

dipped lamp   See: color-dipped lamp.

diptarasa (Sanskrit)   The sentiment (*rasa*) of excitement (*dipta*), found in a play of the minor type (*uparupaka*). (Keith SANSKRIT 265)

dire   In Britain, a performer's word for a colleague's bad performance. (Granville DICTIONARY)

direct   To serve as a stage director, integrating an entire production and coaching the performers.

direct beam projection   Casting a shadow or shape by lensless equipment, such as a Linnebach projector. (Lounsbury THEATRE, Wehlburg GLOSSARY)

direct beam projector   A term sometimes used for a lensless projector. See also: Linnebach projector. (Lounsbury THEATRE 122)

direct control   In U.S. stage lighting, any mechanical arrangement in which the operator moves dimmers or switches directly rather than by a relay or other electrical device. Hence, direct-control dimmer. See also: direct-control switchboard.

direct-control switchboard   Especially in U.S. lighting systems, a control-board whose switches and dimmers carry all of the current used by the lamps. Such a board has no remote control devices (e.g., potentiometers). 'Direct-operated' replaces 'direct-control' in Britain, and is sometimes used in the U.S., as is 'manual.' (Bowman/Ball THEATRE; Bellman LIGHTING fig. 11-1d; Bentham ART 338)

direct emphasis   In directing, arranging performers on stage so that spectators focus on a particular character or group of characters, as opposed to an arrangement that leads the spectator's eye from one spot to another. Also called direct focus.

directeur (French)   See: director.

direct exposition   In playwriting, background information presented directly to the audience through a narrative device (as in Tennessee Williams' *The Glass Menagerie*) or a soliloquy (as in Shakespeare's *Richard III*).

direct focus   See: direct emphasis.

direction   1. In the context of a dancer's stance, pelvis-front position, one of eight places in space which can be recognized in movement. The directions are high, low, up, down, right side, left side, forward, and backward. See also: positions of the body. (Dell PRIMER 72) 2. A dancer's body alignment in relation to the audience. (Grant TECHNICAL) 3. The work of a stage director. 4. A playwright's instructions concerning stage action or other production matters. (Bowman/Ball THEATRE)

directional frost   See: frost.

directional light   Light whose direction is obvious, usually because it produces sharp shadows. The term is older than key light, whose meaning is similar. (Bellman LIGHTING 327, Wehlburg GLOSSARY)

directional lighting   1. Directional light. 2. Lighting of a relatively small, well-defined portion of the stage. (Bowman/Ball THEATRE)

directional lighting unit   A lighting instrument, usually a spotlight or beam projector, designed to produce directional lighting. (Bowman/Ball THEATRE)

directions of the body   See: direction.

direct-operated switchboard   See: direct-control switchboard.

director   1. The person responsible for the integration of an entire stage production, especially the coaching of the performers. The British equivalent, producer, gave way to director after World War II. The French equivalent is *metteur en scène* or *régisseur*, the latter often used in English. 2. The head of a theatre.

director's holiday   A play which is a joy to direct. (Bowman/Ball THEATRE)

direct profile position   Two performers face to face, their profiles to the audience.

dirty heavy   1. A villain character. 2. A performer who plays such parts.

disappearance trap   See: appearance trap.

disappearing footlights   Footlights which may be sunk below the level of the stage floor when not in use. An occasional alternate, flush footlights, emphasizes the continuity of the floor when the footlights are not in use. (McCandless "Glossary" 634, Fuchs LIGHTING 167–168)

disappoint   To fail to appear for a performance.

disappointment act   An act in which one performer substitutes for another, disappointing the audience. (George Burns on the Johnny Carson TV show 1980)

discharge a part   To act a role.

discharge lamp   See: lamp.

disc   A visual effects device which, when turned in front of a light source, shows pictures. (Bowman/Ball THEATRE)

disc makeup   In Britain, a creme foundation in skin tones, applied to the face and body. (Melvill MAKE-UP)

discours (French)   In the Italian *commedia dell'arte*, a long set speech with rhetorical and stylistic flourishes. (Scott in Mayer/Richards WESTERN 24)

discovered, discovered at rise   Whatever and whoever is on the stage when the curtain goes up.

discovery   1. In playwriting, the revelation of information about the characters. This is often linked with recognition, when a character learns a truth about himself, as in Aristotle's *anagnorisis* (Greek). Hence, discovery scene. (Hatlen ORIENTATION). 2. In Renaissance theatres and later, a pre-set scene revealed by the opening of a curtain or shutters or the raising of a curtain or drop. Hence, a character is 'discovered.'

discovery space   In an Elizabethan theatre, a recessed ("inner") stage or a pavilion set against the tiring house wall. (Weiner Review 238)

discrete cue   A cue which establishes an entire "look" or stage lighting picture which is considered by the designer to be a constant until changed to produce another picture by a second discrete cue. Discrete cues are often operated as presets on lighting consoles. Hence, discrete lighting. See also: counterpoint lighting. (Bellman LIGHTING 213)

disc stage   See: revolving stage.

diseur, diseuse (French)   An actor/actress delivering poetry or prose with musical accompaniment but no scenery or costume. Both words are sometimes treated as English. (Armstrong KEMBLE 305, Carrington THEATRICANA)

disguise   1. To conceal one's identity or assume the identity of another character. 2. A costume or mask used to make such a change.

disguising   A popular diversion at court in Elizabethan England, usually a masked ball or entertainment. Disguisings developed into the court masques of the 17th C. Also called a mumming. (Ward/Waller CAMBRIDGE VI 331)

dished floor   An auditorium floor which combines a slope of either constant rise or iscidomal (equal seeing) with some degree of encirclement.

disk dimmer, disc dimmer   See: plate dimmer.

dismissed   Performance cancelled; audience dismissed. (Troubridge BENEFIT 56)

disour   A medieval term for a professional story teller, a jester.

disputation   A medieval semi-dramatic form; a dialogue. (Ward HISTORY I 25)

dissecting skeleton, skeleton   A marionette made of bones which can come apart and be reassembled in performance onstage. Used especially with more macabre theatrical material such as graveyard scenes. Very popular with audiences in Britain. (Philpott DICTIONARY)

dissignator (Latin Roman)   An usher, perhaps a head usher. According to Beare, "usher," probably before the use of theatre tickets in early Christian times. Sandys says that tickets "were marked so as to indicate the place of the seats," and the *dissignatores* saw that "people took their proper places." Oxford LATIN defines the word as "an official who assigned seats in the theatre," which suggests a head usher or perhaps a box-office official. Also spelled *designator*. (Beare ROMAN 169, 173; Sandys COMPANION 519)

dissolve   1. In scenic projection, to change slowly from one image (or set of images) to another by causing the second image to appear over the other as the first fades out. May be effected mechanically or electrically. 2. To change the color of stage lighting gradually, as in going from sunset to twilight. 3. See: dissolving view. (Downs THEATRE II 1132, Bowman/Ball THEATRE)

dissolving view, dissolve   In the early 19th C, a cross-fade with magic lanterns. The two lanterns that produced a dissolve were replaced later in the century by a single lantern with two or three complete optical systems, one above the other; each contained limelight, slide holder, and lens system. A late 19th C patented version with three systems was called a tri-unial lantern or triple lantern.

distancing   See: *Verfremdungseffekt*.

distegia (Greek)   Literally: second story. Pollux, the source, seems to describe the *distegia* as a special structure atop the scene building, but this has been doubted. The word may refer to the roof of the scene building, usually called the *theologeion*, or possibly to the second story of the scene building. Compare *episkenion*. (Arnott SCENIC 42–43, Haigh ATTIC 186–188)

distressing   See: breakdown.

distributed loudspeaker system   An arrangement in which speakers are placed throughout an auditorium.

distribution   In stage lighting, the way in which light is spread about the visible stage. The term is also applied to the way in which the rays of a beam are spread within the beam or, occasionally, to where the beam of an instrument is placed. Also called light distribution. (Sellman/Lessley ESSENTIALS 4, Bowman/Ball THEATRE)

distribution vault   See: intake.

dithyramb   1. By the 7th C BC, a choral song presenting events in the life of Dionysus to the accompaniment of dancing and flute-playing. 2. Later, any similar choral song.

On the authority of Plato, the dithyramb was originally a song celebrating the birth of Dionysus. In what may have been a typical subject, Dionysus, captured by pirates, is rescued by his satyrs, who batter the pirates and throw them into the sea; there they become dolphins. Subjects were not always Dionysian, however; great heroes, such as some from Homer, were often treated.

Some scholars derive tragedy from the dithyramb by way of the satyr play. Pickard-Cambridge, among others, argues that tragedy and satyr drama originated separately. Flickinger and others believe tragedy and the satyr play grew out of the dithyramb, but did so independently.

The earliest example of the word is from the 7th C BC, but the form, and probably the word, are older. The literal meaning was long thought to be ''twice-born,'' from the legend of Dionysus' having been produced from Zeus' thigh. This is now rarely suggested, the view being that the source of the word is unknown. (Pickard-Cambridge DITHYRAMB 5–148, Flickinger GREEK 1–35, Bieber HISTORY 6–9)

diva (Italian)   Literally: goddess. A female opera star. The word is widely used as English.

diverbia (Latin Roman)   Literally: of words. The spoken dialogue of comedy (by contrast with recitative or song) accompanied by the *tibicen*. *Diverbia* was used regularly for exposition and often before songs. Singular *-ium*. Compare *cantica*. Oxford LATIN prefers *deuerbium, -ia*. (Duckworth NATURE 362–363, 373–374; Beare ROMAN 219–223)

diversified emphasis   In directing, arranging the performers on stage so as to place equal importance on three or more characters or groups of characters.

diversion   A shortening of 'for his own diversion'—said of a performer who acts without asking a salary. (Scouten LONDON 1204)

divertisement, divertissement   Especially in the past, a short entertainment, usually presented between the acts of a play.

divertissement (French)   1. In contemporary ballet, a piece without story line or mood which exploits to the best advantage the talents of the dancer. 2. In ballet, a group of dances (*entrées*) unrelated to a ballet, but inserted in it to display the talents of individuals or groups. Also called a *ballet divertissement*. (Kersley/Sinclair BALLET, Grant TECHNICAL)

divided setting   A setting, portions of which can be revealed by removing—or partially removing—barriers. Also called a broken setting. (Bowman/Ball THEATRE)

divided stage   Especially in Australia, a setting that combines two scenes, such as an interior and exterior of a house, or two rooms in a house. (National TECHNICAL)

division   See: *mansion*.

divot   A wig.

divyant (Sanskrit)   In classical Indian drama, the role of a gambler. (Keith SANSKRIT 336)

dizi (Chinese)   See: *di*.

djanger (Indonesian)   See: *janger*.

djanturan (Indonesian)   See: *janturan*.

djaoek (Indonesian)   See: *jauk*.

djauk (Indonesian)   See: *jauk*.

djedjer (Indonesian)   See: *jejer*.

DL   Down left.

DLC   Down left center.

do a Brodie   See: Brodie

do a fold, do a fold-up   1. To fail. 2. To close a show because of poor attendance. (Berrey/Van den Bark SLANG 585)

do a Houdini   In vaudeville, to escape, to disappear. (Laurie VAUDEVILLE 113)

do a Joe Jefferson   To have a long sleep. Named after the 19th C actor who played Rip Van Winkle over a period of years. (Wilmeth LANGUAGE 145)

do a Whistler   To kick over a bucket of paint. Named for Howard Whistler, a scene painter of the 1920s who did so.

do black   In vaudeville, acting in blackface.

dock   1. Scene dock—a storage bay for scenery. 2. The space under a stage, or any theatre space used for storage.

dock doors   Doors leading to the scene dock—in some theatres, from the street.

doctor   1. An expositor. 2. To revise a play script. 3. One who revises a play script. 4. A ridiculous physician character. 5. In some medieval plays, a stock character who comments on the action.

documentary theatre   Drama and theatre which attempt to portray events with the appearance of authenticity, as in the Federal Theatre's living newspaper productions. Also called theatre of fact.

doddata (Kannada)   See: *yaksagana badagatittu bayalata*.

dodger   A small theatrical handbill. (Wilmeth LANGUAGE)

dodogan (Indonesian)   In wayang, rapping on the wooden box (*kothak*) with the tapper (*cempala*). (Humardani in Osman TRADITIONAL 83, Muljono in Osman TRADITIONAL 70).

dog   1. A screw used to fasten a brace to the stage floor. 2. Someone, usually a performer with a small role, who serves as a call boy and does other chores around a theatre. 3. An unsuccessful production. 4. An unsophisticated audience. Hence, to try it on the dog, that is, to try out a production in a secondary theatre or town. Obsolete. 5. Rarely, a stage manager. (Bowman/Ball THEATRE)

dogaline   A medieval and 16th C Venetian man or woman's loose, straight gown with wide sleeves drawn up to the shoulder, revealing the sleeve of an undergown. Briefly revived in France in the 19th C. (Boucher FASHION)

doghouse   A theatre used for testing a show.

dog show   A show which opens in a provincial or 'dog' town or in a 'doghouse.'

dog's letter   See: *littera canina*.

dog town   Formerly, a provincial town where plays were tried out. Hence, try it on the dog. (Bowman/Ball THEATRE 405)

dogu (Japanese)   In *kabuki* and *bunraku*, scenery. See also: *kodogu*, *tsukurimono*.

dogugawari (Japanese)   Literally: scenery change. In *kabuki* and *bunraku* a single clack of the clappers (*hyoshigi*) that signals a scenery change.

dogu kata (Japanese)   Literally: scenery person. A stagehand.

dogu maku (Japanese)   Literally: scenery curtain. A painted front curtain which falls away to reveal the main set behind it. (Leiter ENCYCLOPEDIA 57)

doji (Japanese)   A *no* mask worn by a deity or a spirit who appears as a boy in the first part (*mae ba*) of a warrior or god play. (Shimazaki NOH 59)

dokeyaku (Japanese)   Literally: comic role. 1. The general term for a comic role in *kabuki*. Abbreviated: *doke*. (Gunji KABUKI 32, Dunn/Torigoe ANALECTS 164) 2. An actor who plays such a role. Also called *dokegata, dokeshi*. (Hamamura et al KABUKI 101, Leiter ENCYCLOPEDIA 57–59)

dokuhaku (Japanese)   A monologue, especially in *kabuki*. One type of dialogue (*serifu*). See also: *taihaku*. (Scott KABUKI 117)

doliman   See: stambouline.

dolium (Latin)   Literally: a large cask. In medieval stage productions, a barrel or something similar used to represent a mountain or other high place.

doll matinée   In the late 19th C, a Christmas-season matinée at which dolls were given to child patrons. (Zellers PASTOR 72)

dolly   1. An alternate term for scenery wagon. 2. Any stage device with wheels. (Carrington THEATRICANA)

dolman   See: *côte*.

dolmi (Korean)   See: *tolmi*.

doma (Japanese)   Literally: ground space. The open pit area in a *kabuki* theatre before the 20th C. From the mid-18th C, the open pit was gradually replaced by enclosed areas (*masu*). Also called *kiriotoshi*. (Ernst KABUKI 48, Leiter ENCYCLOPEDIA 59, 395)

dome   1. See: cyclorama. 2. Ceiling lights in an auditorium. By extension, the ceiling concealing such lights. (Bowman/Ball THEATRE)

dome (Japanese)   See: *tome*.

dome horizon   See: cyclorama.

dome lights   Especially in Britain, lights which reach the stage from the auditorium ceiling. Also called dome spotlights. Hence, dome lighting. See also: beam lights. (Baker THEATRECRAFT, Bowman/Ball THEATRE)

domestic drama   18th C plays dealing with the middle class and its everyday problems. Plots tended to be contrived, with a tendency toward pathos, servants were shown sympathetically, and the aristocracy was the villain. Hence, domestic tragedy. These plays enjoyed enormous popularity with middle-class patrons, many of whom were new to theatregoing. In French: *drame*. Also called bourgeois drama or homiletic (drama) tragedy.

domestic play   See: *sewamono*.

domestic twisted flex   See: flex.

domi (Latin)   See: houses.

dominate a scene   In acting, to take a strong position on the stage or in some other way to capture the audience's attention.

domino   In Britain, a wrong note played on a piano. (Granville DICTIONARY)

dominus (Latin Roman)   See: *dominus gregis*.

dominus gregis (Latin Roman)   Literally: master of the company. The actor-manager of a theatrical company. He secured the play, hired the actors and other personnel, took the risks, and was usually the chief actor. Also called an *actor, dominus, princeps gregis,* or *rex gregis.* (Duckworth NATURE 73–75, Arnott ANCIENT 111)

domus (Latin)   See: *mansion.*

don (Thai)   Improvisation, especially in *likay.* (Virulrak "Likay" 210)

dongxiao (Chinese)   See: *xiao.*

dongzuo, tung tso (Chinese)   Literally: movement, action. The generic term for stage movement and gesture in Beijing opera (*jingju*) and many other forms of music-drama (*xiqu*); includes both dance-acting (*zuo*) and combat (*da*) skills. Major types of movements—including sleeve, hand, finger, foot and steps, leg, arm, waist, pheasant feather (*zhiwei*), and beard (*rankou*)—are described in detail in Scott CLASSICAL 96–137 and Zung SECRETS 77–133. Conventional actions are described in Halson PEKING 44–51, Scott CLASSICAL 176–178, and Zung SECRETS 135–148.

donkey   An electric winch. (Parker/Smith DESIGN)

donut   In lighting, a drop-in mask with a circular opening smaller than the diameter of the lens, placed in the front of an ellipsoidal reflector spotlight. Used with a gobo, the donut improves the focus of the pattern.

door backing   See: backing.

door button   A thumbscrew, used to hold a door shut or keep flats in line.

door count   The actual attendance at a performance, arrived at by counting the ticket stubs collected by the ticket taker. The count can also be arrived at by the counter on a turnstile, if the theatre is so equipped.

door flat   A flat with an opening for a door unit. Sometimes abbreviated to DF.

door frame   A solid wood door frame, with thickness, built to fit into the opening in a door flat. Also called a door frame unit, door unit, or door.

door furniture   The hardware used on a stage door, such as latches, bolts, handles, etc. (Fay GLOSSARY)

door iron   See: foot iron.

doorkeeper   In Elizabethan theatres and later, an employee who took money from patrons at the door. He was often named more specifically: lobby doorkeeper, pit doorkeeper, gallery office doorkeeper, etc.

doorknocker   See: Psyche knot.

door list   A record of persons to receive free admission passes. Also called a house list.

doorman   A theatre employee who opens and closes theatre doors, serves as a porter, and sometimes takes tickets. Also called a house doorman. See also: linkman.

door mat   A wig.

door opposite prompt   See: DOP.

door saddle   See: saddle iron.

doors of entrance   In 18th C theatres in Britain and the U.S., proscenium doors opening onto the stage. (Cibber APOLOGY II 85)

door space   Especially in Britain, the place in a flat wherein a door frame is set. (Granville DICTIONARY)

door stop   A molding attached to a door jamb to prevent the door from swinging through the opening.

door unit   See: door frame.

DOP   Door opposite prompt side. (Shattuck SHAKESPEARE 16)

dope   1. See: lamp dip. 2. An adhesive for fastening canvas to the frame of a flat before it is nailed or tacked. (Bowman/Ball THEATRE)

dorelet   A 14th C caul with an attached net into which all the hair could be tucked. (Chalmers CLOTHES 121)

dos amigos (Philippine)   Literally: two friends. A festival dance performed as a part of a *comedia* play. (Aquino PHILIPPINE 11)

dos Anglais (French)   See: English back.

Dossenus   One of the types of stock clowns in Atellan farce. Some have connected the name with *dorsum*, back, and thought the type a hunchback and hence a wise fool; but there is no evidence for this. One doubtful interpretation of a Latin passage calls Dossenus another name for Manducus. See also: *fabula Atellana*. (Beare ROMAN 139, 140, 143–144)

dos veces (Philippine)   In *zarzuela*, to repeat a line in a song. (Fernández ILOILO xiii)

do the agents   In Britain, to go the rounds of agents in search of employment as a performer.

do the bends   To take bows before an audience.

dottore (Italian)   The doctor, a stock old man character in *commedia dell'arte*, often named Bombarda, Francolin, Graziano, Lembron, Partesana, Spacca Strumolo (goitre burster), but most often named Doctor Baloardo or Doctor Balanzone. Typically, he was a Bolognese. (Oreglia COMMEDIA 84–86)

double   1. An understudy; a performer who substitutes for another. 2. To serve as an understudy. 3. A performer who plays two or more parts in one production. 4. To play two or more parts in the same production. Hence, doubling. 5. To perform two different engagements on the same evening. 6. A team act. 7. To use the same properties in different scenes by changing their appearance. 8. In Britain, the same theatre seat sold to two different persons. Also called a duplicate. (Troubridge BENEFIT 110)

(the) double   In the dramatic theory of Antonin Artaud, life itself—the double of theatre.

double act   In vaudeville in Britain, two comedians, singers, dancers, etc. in a single act. Also called double turn. (Granville DICTIONARY)

double action   A plot with a main and a subordinate action or plot. Also called a double plot. See also: multiple plot. (MacEwan FREYTAG'S 44)

double audience   A vaudeville audience consisting of both men and women. Tony Pastor in 1881 in New York began presenting clean performances for family audiences. (Gilbert VAUDEVILLE 125)

double bell box   A box containing batteries capable of activating either of two doorbells attached to the outside of the box. Push buttons on the box ring the bells, or sockets may be provided to allow for remote control. (Collison SOUND 101)

double benefit   A benefit performance, the profits of which are shared by two recipients. (Troubridge BENEFIT 24)

double bill   An entertainment made up of two separate works.

double boards   A pair of boards used in compressing a limelight's oxygen and hydrogen bags simultaneously. Because the bags sometimes slipped from between the boards, a third board (or a piece of stiff cloth) was sometimes added between the top and bottom boards. See also: limelight bag.

double booking   Booking two shows into a provincial theatre on the same date, a practice used by early 20th C U.S. managers and owners to protect themselves from canceled attractions. The show that arrived in town first got the date. Sometimes three shows were booked for the same date and town. (Wilmeth LANGUAGE)

double boxes   Oversize boxes. According to the accounts at Drury Lane Theatre in November 1714, each of the double boxes held 20 persons. (Avery LONDON xxiv)

double cast   To cast two performers in a role, each taking turns or one serving as an understudy. Hence, double casting.

double charges   Twice-normal ticket prices for special events. (Van Lennep LONDON lxxi)

double connector   See: twofer.

double convenience outlet   See: convenience outlet.

double crown   See: sheet.

double-deck drop   A tall drop with two scenes painted on it, one above the other. The drop moves up and down through a cut in the stage floor. (Krows AMERICA 113)

double end   See: lamp base.

double hang   To place and focus spotlights so that an area of the stage is lit by a warm and a cool beam from each side. Hence, double hung. See also: double McCandless method.

double in brass   To perform an acting role and also play a musical instrument in the band, or to play two roles in one production. Also called double pit.

double joint   In late 19th C British theatres, a V-shaped attachment to the gas supply. Each arm of the V could carry a tip or burner. (Rees GAS 204)

double luff   Ropes and pulleys arranged to give a mechanical advantage of four to one. Also called a double whip. (Gillette/Gillette SCENERY 429)

double McCandless method   A lighting arrangement in which each segment of the acting area is lit not merely by a warm color from one side and a cool color from the other, but by a warm and cool from each side. Named after the lighting specialist Stanley McCandless. (Lounsbury THEATRE 84) See also: double hang.

double pit   To work in more than one theatrical capacity—such as playing in the pit band and serving elsewhere in a production. Also called double in brass. (Wilmeth LANGUAGE)

double plot   See: double action.

double proscenium   Two permanent proscenia, as at Richard Wagner's theatre at Bayreuth, Germany. The effect Wagner wanted was of a mystic chasm or gulf separating the real world in the auditorium from the ideal world of the stage.

double purchase   Counterweight rigging which has the load balanced by double its own weight; the weight travels half the distance of the load. (Bax MANAGEMENT 92)

double-row footlights   See: single-row footlights.

double stage   An elevator stage with two levels, so that one stage setting may be made ready while another is in view, as in Steele Mackaye's Madison Square Theatre in New York in the 19th C. Also called a drop stage, elevator stage.

double stars   Two performers with equally important roles, such as Othello and Iago or Brutus and Cassius.

doublet   A 14th–16th C jacket, originally of two layers of fabric, often with padding between the layers. A short skirt or ruffle extended to a depth of three or four inches below the waist, which dipped to a deep point in front. (Chalmers CLOTHES 163, Walkup DRESSING 109)

double take   A delayed reaction that seems to come in two stages: one expression followed by a pause, then a second reaction.

double theatre   An amphitheatre. The phrase is sometimes used of the Roman *amphitheatrum*. (Sandys COMPANION 518)

double turn   See: double act.

double up   To perform as a team.

double whip   See: double luff.

double Willie   A stagehand who works through lunch and dinner and is paid double. (Wilmeth LANGUAGE)

double work   See: partnering.

doughnut   A wealthy person who invests in a theatrical venture. (Berrey/Van den Bark SLANG 574)

douse   To close a theatre.

douser, dowser   A built-in circular metal cutoff which can take an arc light or follow spot to instant blackout by cutting the beam between light source and lens. (Lounsbury THEATRE, Wehlburg GLOSSARY, Bowman MODERN)

douter   Formerly, a scissorslike tool with flat ends used to extinguish candles. MAGIC has an illustration. See also: snuffer. (Rosenthal/Wertenbaker MAGIC 46)

down   1. Downstage; at or toward the front of the stage. 2. Of an actor or a performance, lacking energy. 3. In stage lighting, below full intensity. 4. Sometimes, out. Thus, "The house is down" usually means the houselights are out.

down center   Abbreviation: DC. A stage position or area in the middle of the stage and toward the front.

down fade   In memory systems, a change in stage lighting which involves only channels whose intensity is to be reduced.

down front   1. The auditorium of a theatre. 2. In the front of a theatre auditorium.

down in one   Downstage, on the first plane.

down left   Abbreviation: DL. A stage position or area to the performer's left and toward the front of the stage.

down left center   Abbreviation: DLC. A stage position or area to the performer's left of the center line of the stage and toward the front, but not to the far left of the stage.

downlight, down light   1. A lighting instrument or fixture whose light is directed straight down from above. 2. The effect of such lighting, also called down lighting. Spotlights serve for downlighting in the acting area; built-in fixtures, often recessed, are so used in auditoriums, lobbies, and elsewhere. Rosenthal/Wertenbaker have illustrations. (Wehlburg GLOSSARY, Rosenthal/Wertenbaker MAGIC 146)

downlighting   See: downlight.

down on the bill   A good position on a variety program, toward the end of the second half. (Berrey/Van den Bark SLANG 590)

down right   Abbreviation: DR. A stage position or area to the performer's right and toward the front of the stage.

down right center   Abbreviation, DRC. A stage position or area to the performer's right of the center line of the stage and toward the front, but not to the far right of the stage.

downstage   1. Toward the front of the stage. The term derives from the days when stage floors were raked (slanted) downward toward the front of the stage. 2. Friendly. (Berrey/Van den Bark SLANG 594)

downstage left, downstage right   See: down left, down right.

downtowner   A downtown theatre.

dowser   See: douser.

DR   Down right.

drag cues   In acting, to fail to deliver spoken cues on time.

dragging   1. See: dry brushing. 2. Said of a scene whose tempo is slow.

drag line   See: breast.

drama   1. Dramatic literature. A literary work, usually intended for stage production. Works not intended for production are called closet dramas. 2. A serious play that is not a tragedy. 3. In the 18th C, a serious play (in French, *drame*) dealing with domestic problems of the middle class, as opposed to the traditional neoclassic tragedy or heroic drama. 4. The literary component of a performance: the play, as opposed to the theatrical production of it. Hence the frequent distinction: drama and theatre. 5. Conflict, tension, emotional intensity. 6. A stage performance. 7. An all-encompassing term embracing any legitimate stage production. (Cameron/Gillespie ENJOYMENT, Bowman/Ball THEATRE, Carrington THEATRICANA) 8. The generic term for the process of theatre with children, i.e., moving children from unsupervised play to improvised performance. 9. The spontaneous human process of identifying with and impersonating others. (Courtney RE-PLAY 3)

drama (Philippine)   A prose play, first written in the 19th C, in contrast to earlier musical plays in verse (*comedia* and *zarzuela*). (Fernández ILOILO 28)

drama balitaw (Philippine)   Sugbuanon folk theatre that developed from *balitaw* (dance). The story line is composed by weaving together at least two *balitaw* sequences. (Ramas in Bresnahan CROSS-CULTURAL 217)

drama den   In Britain: 1. In the past, a theatre in the provinces showing heavy drama. 2. At present, a broken-down theatre where performers of questionable merit hold forth. (Granville DICTIONARY)

drama house   In Britain, a theatre whose presentations are a bit more professional than those of a drama den (q.v.). (Granville DICTIONARY)

drama in education   1. The term used by the Library of Congress in cataloguing the literature of creative drama. 2. Any form of theatrical or dramatic activity by or for children or young people. 3. A method of improvisation with youth, developed in England in the 1960s, in which participants create roles and scenarios based on subjects important to the group. Excludes story dramatization and theatre games. See also: creative drama.

dramakinetics   A variety of creative drama which focuses on movement and gesture. See also: creative drama.

dramalogue   A dramatic reading.

drama man   Especially in Britain, an actor in a stock company. (Granville DICTIONARY)

drama masyarakat (Malaysian)   Literally: social drama. A play of social consciousness in the *drama moden* movement.

drama moden (Malaysian)   Literally: modern drama. Realistic drama, based on 20th C Western models, that became important in Malaysia in the 1960s. An earlier term (c. 1950s) is *citrawara* (story representation). See also: *drama masyarakat*.

drama moderen (Indonesian)   Literally: modern drama. Contemporary Indonesian spoken drama, based on Western models, performed by amateur groups, especially in East Java. See also: *komedie*. (Peacock RITES 57)

drama of conversation   1. Especially in the past, a play containing much rapid repartee, as opposed to one with long set speeches. (Hamilton THEORY 81) 2. Now, usually a play dependent on dialogue rather than physical action. In German: *Konversationsstück*, which is the analogue of drawing-room comedy.

drama of development   Especially in Britain, a piece whose beginning presents the conflict rather than a drama whose plot proceeds to a conflict. (Granville DICTIONARY)

drama of fate   See: *Schicksalstragödie*.

drama of ideas   See: social drama.

drama of illusion   Drama (and the production of it) which attempt to create an illusion of reality on stage through the use of natural speech and actions, everyday characters and plots, etc.

drama of indirection   A term frequently applied to the plays of Anton Chekov and describing dramaturgy which is both "oblique and inferential." The playwright "works indirectly through appearance to reality." (Corrigan "Chekov's" 108)

drama of rhetoric   In the Elizabethan period, a play containing stately speeches and high-sounding terms, performed on a platform stage. (Hamilton THEORY 77)

drama of sensibility   Sentimental drama, popular in the 18th C.

drama sejarah (Malaysian)   See: *purbawara*.

dramatic   1. Pertaining to stage productions or works written for the stage, as: dramatic action, dramatic author, dramatic criticism, a dramatic performance. 2. Emotionally intense, as: dramatic lighting, a dramatic romance. 3. Having to do with a straight play, as opposed to a musical theatre work or a film. Hence, a dramatic actor, as opposed to a film actor. 4. Now obsolete: a dramatist. (Bowman/Ball THEATRE)

dramatic action   The movement of the plot of a play or an incident in that movement. (Bowman/Ball THEATRE)

dramatic agent   A theatrical agent; one who helps find employment for performers. Hence, dramatic agency.

dramatic art   The arts and skills used in dramatic representation, particularly playwriting and acting. (Bowman/Ball THEATRE)

dramatic company   See: acting company.

dramatic composition   1. A play. 2. Playwriting.

dramatic conflict   A struggle of opposing external forces or those within an individual or individuals from which the action in a play develops. (Bowman/Ball THEATRE)

dramatic critic, dramatic criticism   See: criticism.

dramatic education   See: creative drama.

dramatic end tent   In early 20th C U.S., a tent designed for dramatic shows, with the center pole replaced by two side poles. (Wilmeth LANGUAGE)

dramatic evenings   In late 19th C Russia, private gatherings featuring theatrical entertainments. (Brockett HISTORY 532)

dramatic foreshadowing   See: foreshadowing.

dramatic idyll   A 19th C Greek theatre form using song and dance against the backdrop of life in mountain areas. (Gassner/Quinn ENCYCLOPEDIA 395)

dramatic image   See: dramatic metaphor.

dramatic irony   1. A condition that is the reverse of what was expected, or a statement whose intended application is different from its literal or intended sense, as when Oedipus says he will seek the killer of King Laius as though Laius had been his father—which he was. 2. A character's failure to realize a truth evident to the audience, or his lack of awareness of a hidden truth in his own statement, which the audience understands.

dramaticism   An occasional term for the quality of being dramatic. (Bowman/Ball THEATRE)

dramatic lighting   Stage lighting which is theatrical in effect, often at the expense of realism. Characteristic of dramatic lighting, which is designed to underline emotions, are sharp shadows in sharply defined areas of light. (Bowman/Ball THEATRE)

dramatic line   Especially in Britain, a term describing the classic dramatic progression from initial incident through rising action to denouement and conclusion. (Granville DICTIONARY)

dramatic literature   1. Plays. 2. Plays deemed to have some substance.

dramatic metaphor   A central idea, theme, concept, or image in a play (such as disease in *Hamlet* or blindness in *Oedipus the King*) which can be conveyed visually to the audience, especially through the scene design. Also called a dramatic, graphic, master, or scenic image.

dramatic opera   1. In Restoration England, a spectacular stage piece using spoken dialogue with some song and music. 2. In musical theatre, a serious opera, as opposed to a comic opera.

dramatic play   1. A play written for stage production, as opposed to film, television, musical theatre, etc. (Bowman/Ball THEATRE) 2. From at least the 1950s, a form of creative drama in which children relive familiar experiences or create improvisations based on a rhythm, a poem, a piece of literature, etc. (Viola ''Children'' 140) 3. See: spontaneous drama.

dramatic poem   A play in verse; a poem in dramatic form. Hence, dramatic poetry. The implication of the term is literary rather than theatrical: Such a work as Goethe's *Faust*, which is difficult to stage, or such a closet drama as Milton's *Samson Agonistes*. Yet for centuries, playwrights who wrote producible plays employing verse were called dramatic poets.

dramatic preparation   See: foreshadowing.

dramatic question   See: inciting action.

dramatic reader   One who reads plays in public, solo or with others. Hence, a dramatic reading, dramatic recital. (Bowman/Ball THEATRE)

dramatic recital   A performance consisting of sketches and excerpts from plays, presented by one or more actors, usually without costumes, scenery, and other elements of full stage productions. (Bowman/Ball THEATRE)

dramatic reversal   In playwriting, a change in the expectations of the characters or of the audience, or both, as in *Oedipus the King*, when Oedipus learns that Polybus was not his father. In Greek, *peripeteia*.

dramatic review   See: review.

dramatic rights   The option of a copyright holder to grant or refuse permission to have a work adapted or performed. (Bowman/Ball THEATRE)

dramatic romance   A romantic play with serious overtones, rapidly changing emotions, adventure, and sometimes fantasy. (Bowman/Ball THEATRE)

dramatics   The study and practice of theatre and drama. Applied especially to the lower schools and to amateurs.

dramatic situation   1. The character relationships in a play and the forces operating on them under a given set of conditions. 2. A point in a plot when the action crystalizes significantly. 3. In Britain, the physical positions of the actors at a significant moment in the play. Often called situation. (Bowman/Ball THEATRE)

dramatic structure   In playwriting, the arrangement of the plot (usually) into exposition, inciting action (or point of attack), complication, climax, and denouement. (Bowman/Ball THEATRE)

dramatic suspense   In playwriting, the uncertainty as to the outcome of the plot or a portion of the plot. (Bowman/Ball THEATRE)

dramatic technique   In playwriting, the manner in which an author handles plot, character, and ideas.

dramatic tension   In playwriting and directing, emotional or intellectual intensity which rivets an audience's attention.

dramatic theory   A clear system of general principles by which a work of art may be evaluated (Senelick Review 272).

dramatic time   The amount of time represented in a play. (Cassady/Cassady VIEW)

dramatic unity   Coherence. In playwriting, but also in play production, the bringing together of all elements into an artistic whole. See also: unity.

dramatic version   A play derived from a non-dramatic work. (Bowman/Ball THEATRE)

dramatic writer   A playwright.

dramatis personae (Latin)   The cast of characters in a play.

dramatist   A writer of plays, a playwright.

dramatize   To take material from a non-dramatic source and make it into a play. Hence, dramatization, dramatizer. (Bowman/Ball THEATRE)

Dramaturg (German)   A combination play reader and play doctor who sometimes directs productions. In English, dramaturge.

dramaturgy   The art or technique of playwriting. Hence, *Dramaturg* (German), dramaturge, dramaturgist, dramaturgic, dramaturgical. (Bowman/Ball THEATRE)

drama with children   See: creative drama.

drame (French)   A serious play, neither tragic nor comic, which deals with contemporary middle-class problems. The term dates from the 18th C. (Hatlen ORIENTATION)

drame à clef (French)   Literally: play with a key. A play whose characters and situations are such that at least some of the characters can be identified with real people. The Duke of Buckinghmam's *The Rehearsal* and Arthur Miller's *After the Fall* are examples.

drame bourgeois (French)   A drama whose subject is the middle class.

Dramen (Yiddish)   Serious plays, dramas. (Lifson YIDDISH 51)

dramma per musica (Italian)   Literally: drama with music. An early term for opera.

drammer   A corruption of drama; more precisely, melodrama. The term is often used lightly.

drammer dammer   A critic who adversely reviews a play.

dran (Greek)   A word applied in ancient Greece to tragedy and satyric drama. The term has the sense of doing (rather than, for example, narrating). (Pickard-Cambridge DITHYRAMB 109–110)

drapery   Soft, usually heavy curtain material hung in gathers and used as part of a stage setting. Hence, drapery border, drapery cyclorama, drapes, etc. (Bowman/Ball THEATRE)

drapery border   See: border.

drapery cyclorama   A curved curtain, usually on a traveler track, partly enclosing the acting area.

drapery hanger   See: hanger.

drapery rake   An implement used to push a drapery along its track or batten, or to adjust the position of a pivoting batten.

drapery setting   See: curtain set.

drape shaping   A technique for forming plastic: a plastic sheet is softened by heating and allowed to sag into or over a mold. (Bellman SCENOGRAPHY)

draw   1. Attendance. 2. Box-office receipts. 3. To attract an audience. 4. A production or performer able to attract the public. Hence, drawing card. 5. A dance step in which one foot is brought up to the other by drawing it along the floor. (Rogers DANCE 243)

draw a big house, draw big   To attract a sizable audience.

draw curtain   A traveler or traverse curtain; the two halves of the curtain overlap at center and can be pulled off to each side. In Britain: tabs, draw tabs, French tabs, running tabs.

drawer   A popular performer.

drawing card   See: draw.

drawing-room comedy   See: comedy of manners.

drawing-room drama   A play that usually takes place in a drawing room and deals with high society. The genre is similar to comedy of manners, but is associated more with the 19th C than the Restoration and 18th C.

draw line   The operating line for a draw or traveler curtain. Also called a curtain line, curtain pull, curtain rope.

draw off, draw on   In 17th C theatres and later, to slide painted shutters offstage and onstage.

draw tabs   See: draw curtain.

DRC   Down right center.

dream play   See: *mugen no*.

Drehbühne (German)   A revolving stage.

drencher, drencher pipe   In Britain, a sprinkler pipe placed just upstage or downstage of a fire curtain.

dress   1. To costume a play; hence, dressing, overdress, etc. 2. In the 18th C, a costume. 3. Short for dress rehearsal. 4. In acting, to countercross. (Canfield CRAFT, Bowman/Ball THEATRE) 5. To put the finishing touches on a stage setting: to dress the stage.

dress box   A box just above the pit or stalls in a British theatre. The whole tier of dress boxes is called the dress circle. (Donohue KEAN 151)

dress circle   In British theatres, the seating area just above the pit or stalls; also called the grand circle or the royal circle. Patrons sitting in the dress circle are often fashionably dressed, hence the term. The term is also used for the corresponding space in U.S. opera houses. (Bowman/Ball THEATRE).

dress double   In acting, to wear one costume over another, in order to make a quick change. (Bowman/Ball THEATRE)

dresser   1. A member of the costume department who helps performers don, doff, and change their costumes. A dresser sometimes assists a particular performer, also cleaning, pressing, and maintaining the costumes. See also: tireman. (Crampton HANDBOOK, Bax MANAGEMENT 210, Rae/Southern INTERNATIONAL) 2. In Britain, a well-dressed, attractive walker-on (who helps to dress the stage). (Granville DICTIONARY)

dress form   See: dummy.

dressing   Stage properties and furnishings that complete a stage setting but are not actually used during a performance.

dressing room   A backstage room where a performer can put on a costume and makeup. Many theatres have individual dressing rooms for star performers and larger ones (chorus dressing rooms) for minor performers.

dressing-room actor   A boastful performer whose posing in the dressing room is not matched by ability on stage.

dressing-room list   A record of which performer is assigned to which dressing room.

dressing the stage   See: dress the stage.

dress parade   In advance of a dress rehearsal, a non-acting walk-through for the director, to check the performers in their costumes, makeup, wigs, etc., sometimes with lights and scenery. Also called a costume parade.

dress plot   A costume plot.

dress rehearsal   A rehearsal with all visual and aural elements; virtually an actual performance, but without an audience. At an audience dress rehearsal, spectators are present, usually by invitation but sometimes as paying patrons, although the show has not officially opened.

dress room   Formerly, a dressing room.

dress stall   In Britain, an alternate term for orchestra stall, a seat in the front rows of the stalls.

dress the house   1. To paper the house; to help fill the theatre by giving away complimentary tickets. 2. To make an auditorium appear to be fuller than it really is by the skillful distribution of ticket locations, thereby leaving scattered unsold seats and spreading out the audience.

dress the part   Especially in Britain, to be costumed appropriately for a role. (Granville DICTIONARY)

dress the stage   1. In acting, to adjust one's position in order to avoid blocking another performer from the view of the audience, or to improve the stage picture. 2. In staging, to complete the stage picture by adding (to an interior setting, for instance) draperies, pictures, vases, and other items not necessarily required by the performers.

dried   Forgot a line.

droll   1. A short farce, sometimes drawn from an existing play, popular at the late summer fairs in Restoration and 18th C London. (Nagler SOURCES 157) 2. A puppet show. 3. A comedy performance. 4. A clown or comedian. (Philpott DICTIONARY)

drop   1. A drop curtain. 2. A large, flown, painted canvas scenic unit, a back drop. 3. To lower a curtain. 4. To purposely slow down the action in a scene. 5. To omit a line of dialogue. 6. To lower the voice and fail to project.

drop box   See: drop pocket.

drop ceiling   A light-colored band painted around the top of a box set. (Buerki STAGECRAFT)

drop clamp   A device for securing the bottom batten of a drop to the stage. It is a metal strap with a claw to hold the batten, and a hole through which a stage screw can be put into the floor. Also called a floor stay.

drop cloth   See: drop curtain.

drop cloth bell   In 18th C theatres and later, a prompter's bell used to cue the movement up or down of a painted drop. (Hughes in Hume LONDON 131)

drop curtain   A curtain which can be raised and lowered, as opposed to a draw or traveler curtain which pulls off to each side. Also called a fly curtain, guillotine curtain. In Britain: drop cloth.

drop dead dress   A very expensive gown. (Smith VAUDEVILLIANS 186)

drop hanger, drop holder   See: batten clamp.

drop in   See: bring in.

drop off   Especially among professional stage electricians, a dimming technique in some older switchboards in which the operator unlocks a dimmer handle during a long fade. The effect is to leave the unlocked dimmer at the setting it has then reached. The phrase also serves as a verb, as in "Drop off numbers 7 and 9 at 4."

drop pocket   A metal box containing receptacles into which electrical cables can be plugged. It hangs from the gridiron and is used for lighting instruments mounted on light pipes above the stage. Also called a drop box or hanging pocket.

drop scene   1. A curtain or painted drop that can be lowered and raised, in front of which a scene can be played while a setting is being changed behind it. Sometimes called a scene in one, an olio, a drop, or an act drop. 2. The last scene in a play. 3. A scene acted in a lower emotional key than the previous one. (Bowman/Ball THEATRE, Southern CHANGEABLE 170)

drop stage   See: double stage, elevator stage.

drugget   In Britain, a carpet runner laid behind a stage setting to dampen footsteps of stagehands or offstage performers.

drugget pin   An easily removable nail with a flat, brass head to secure druggets. (Granville DICTIONARY)

drum and shaft   The substage cylinder onto which lines from carriages in the chariot-and-pole system wind. Also called shaft and drum.

drum beater   An agent who beats the drum—literally or figuratively—for a show. The tradition goes back at least to the Middle Ages. (Wilmeth LANGUAGE)

Drummond light   One of the names for the limelight. Lieutenant Thomas Drummond, a Scot trained in mathematics and engineering, created a limelight instrument in 1825 in connection with his work on a survey of Great Britain. The brilliance of incandescent lime was apparently known as early as 1816, but Drummond developed its practical uses, and is usually said to have invented the limelight. At some time before his limelight, Drummond had tried magnesium oxide and zinc oxide; both were far brighter than the Argand lamp, but lime was better than either. See also: limelight. (Rees GAS 42, Fuchs LIGHTING 42, Penzel LIGHTING 56–57)

drum roll   A kind of musical fanfare used to create an atmosphere of fear and/or anticipation. (Granville DICTIONARY)

Drury Lane melodrama   In 19th C Britain, sensational and spectacular melodramas, named for the Drury Lane theatre, whose elaborate facilities housed many such plays.

dry   1. A forgetting of lines by a performer, as in "a dry in the first act." 2. To forget one's lines. See also: go dry, dry up.

dry brushing   A painting technique using a partially dry brush. Also called dragging.

dry color   Colored powder from which scene paint is made by mixing it with water and glue. (Buerki STAGECRAFT)

dry meter   From about the mid-19th C, the preferred type of gas meter for use in theatres. The alternative, the wet meter (sometimes referred to as the common meter), required water and servicing and was both less reliable and less safe. (Penzel LIGHTING 82–83, 84–85)

dry up   1. To forget one's lines. 2. To lose popularity.

dry-up company   A touring group whose management is not altogether reliable; it is consequently likely to find itself stranded. (Granville DICTIONARY)

DS   Downstage.

DSM   Deputy stage manager.

dua dalok (Lao)   A clown or comic role in a *mohlam* play. (Miller "Kaen" 222)

dua gong (Lao)   See: *poo rai*.

dual-capacity dimmer   See: dual rated dimmer.

dual-issue ending   A play ending with good rewarded and evil punished. See also: poetic justice. The term usually applies to melodrama. (Cameron/Gillespie ENJOYMENT)

dual-rated dimmer   An obsolete type of resistance dimmer which was effective with a range of different loads. Also called a dual capacity dimmer or multicapacity (resistance) dimmer. (Bowman/Ball THEATRE, Heffner/Selden/Sellman MODERN 495–496)

dual role   Two parts in a production played by the same performer.

duanda, tuan ta (Chinese)   Literally: short fighting. A role category which includes bandits and fighters from the ordinary populace, such as swordsmen and fist-fighters, and features combat (*da*) and dance-acting (*zuo*) skills; a major subdivision of the martial male role (*wusheng*) in Beijing opera (*jingju*). (Dolby HISTORY 180, Scott CLASSICAL 66)

DuBarry Pink   In stage lighting, a delicate pink color medium. The name is from the successful use of this tint by David Belasco in the early 20th C in his production of *DuBarry*. The reason for the special color was the brilliant red hair and unusual complexion of the star, Mrs. Leslie Carter. (Belasco DOOR 174–175)

ducat, ducket, dukie   1. A ticket. 2. Admission fee.

ducater, ducat snatcher   Ticket collector. (Berrey/Van den Bark SLANG 576)

ducat hustler   A ticket seller. (Berrey/Van den Bark SLANG 576)

duck   A poor dancer. (Berrey/Van den Bark SLANG 573)

duckbill shoe   A late 15th-early 16th C shoe with an extra wide upper, successor to the *poulaine* (French). (Boucher FASHION, Walkup DRESSING 144)

ducket   Ticket.

dud   In Britain, a flop.

dudahan (Indonesian)   See: *wayang dudahan*.

dude   A fop, especially a comedian in the Victorian "silly ass" tradition. (Granville DICTIONARY)

duègne (French)   An 18th C aged female comic character. (Roberts STAGE)

duikou (Chinese)   See: *xiangsheng*.

duilian, tui lien (Chinese)   A single couplet (*lian*) of poetry, consisting of two related lines, frequently used in music-drama (*xiqu*). When recited after an entrance, called an entrance (*shangchang* or *shang ch'ang*) *duilian*, and when recited before an exit called an exit (*xiachang* or *hsia ch'ang*) *duilian*. The latter is used somewhat more frequently, and usually concludes the relevant scene or act.

dukey   A penny theatre—a 19th C London neighborhood theatre.

dukie   Ticket.

dumb act   A vaudeville turn with no dialogue, as an acrobatic or juggling act. It was often the first act in the show, since latecomers would not disturb it. Also called a sight act. See also: bone crusher. (Smith VAUDEVILLIANS)

dumb it down   To make a play, production, or performance less subtle. (Berrey/Van den Bark SLANG 583, Granville DICTIONARY)

dumb show   A story acted in pantomime, often as a prologue to the play that will contain the story in full, as in the pantomime that precedes the play-within-the-play in *Hamlet*.

dummy   1. A minor performer with little or no dialogue. (Berrey/Van den Bark SLANG 572) 2. A costumer's dress form.

dump   At an agency, to sell tickets at a discount, just as a performance is about to begin. (Wilmeth LANGUAGE)

dumps   Unsold tickets returned to the box office by an agency. (Wilmeth LANGUAGE)

dung-chen (Tibetan)   A ten-foot long brass or copper trumpet that accompanies *mani-rimdu* masked dance-drama. (Jerstad MANI-RIMDU 85–88)

dungeon   The cellar of a British theatre, generally used for storage. (Granville DICTIONARY)

duodrama   A play for two characters. An early form of melodrama, with music accompanying the performers. Also called a two hander.

duo emphasis   In directing, arranging performers on stage so as to give equal emphasis to two characters or two groups of characters.

duologue   1. A scene or play involving only two performers. 2. A scene or portion of a scene in which two performers converse but others on stage, by convention, do not overhear them. (Bowman/Ball THEATRE)

duozi (Chinese)   See: *chenzi*.

duplicate   See: double.

duplo (Philippine)   Literally: double. An extemporized debate in verse, consisting of accusations and defense, by male and female groups. Pre-Spanish in origin and a possible precursor of Philippine drama. (Tonogbanua SURVEY 75–80, Hernandez EMERGENCE 5–6)

durmallika (Sanskrit)   One of the minor forms of drama (*uparupaka*) mentioned by ancient theorists. No example survives. Said to have been composed in four acts about a hero of low rank. (Keith SANSKRIT 351)

dusta (Sanskrit)   In classical Indian drama, the role of a rogue. (Keith SANSKRIT 84)

dust ruffle   See: *balayeuse*.

duta (Sanskrit)   The role of a messenger in classical Indian drama. (Keith SANSKRIT 311–312)

Dutch doll   Since the 1920s, a wooden doll sometimes used as a marionette. The doll has jointed limbs, but the head, neck, and body are usually in one piece. The head can be made movable. (Philpott DICTIONARY)

Dutch jacket   See: samare.

dutchman   1. A strip of canvas used to cover a crack between two flats and present the appearance of a solid wall. Also called a stripper or wart. 2. To apply such a strip. 3. A scab or mending cleat. 4. See: tumbler. 5. A wedge used to level a flat on a raked floor. Also called a fox wedge. 6. A second condensing lens on an effect machine. 7. A performer who specializes in gradually disrobing. 8. To apply a stiffener to the back of two or more flats. (Bowman/Ball THEATRE, Nelms PRODUCTION, Parker/Smith DESIGN)

DV (Latin Roman)   Probably an abbreviation of *diverbium* (spoken dialogue). The letters appear in some manuscripts of Plautus at the beginnings of scenes or after the names of some characters. See also: *C*. (Beare ROMAN 220, 229)

dynamics   In dance, contrast in energy.

dynamiter   A scene stealer. (Berrey/Van den Bark SLANG 573)

Dziady (Polish)   Literally: old men, beggars, bumblers, vagabonds. A rural dramatic tradition dating from antiquity; a calling-forth of the ghosts of the dead. (Young ''Polish'' 16)

E

E   Entrance. Also printed Ent.

early doors   In Britain, entrances to cheaper seats, opened before those to the more expensive sections of a theatre. (Granville DICTIONARY)

early turner   An inferior music-hall performer, forced to play one of the early acts on the bill. (Partridge TO-DAY 227)

earth   A standard electrical term, primarily British, for the usual U.S. 'ground.' The words are used both nominally and verbally. (Bentham ART, Wehlburg GLOSSARY, Rae/Southern INTERNATIONAL)

eat a play   Of an audience, to eat it up, to enjoy a play thoroughly. (Granville DICTIONARY)

eat 'em   When one is a broker, to keep unsold tickets.

eat the ginger   Of a performer, to play a part as a lead and/or with opportunity to speak good dialogue and show off acting ability. (Granville DICTIONARY)

eat up   See: gobble up.

eblek (Indonesian)   A plaited bamboo carrying case for *wayang* shadow puppets.

écarté (French)   1. In ballet, a movement in which the dancer faces either one of the two front corners of a proscenium stage, and the leg nearer the audience is pointed on the floor or raised in the air with the torso straight and the arm raised on the same side as the extended leg. (Grant TECHNICAL) 2. See: positions of the body.

écart en l'air (French)   See: *pas ciseaux*.

eccentric comedian   A comic performer who uses such tricks as special makeup and personal idiosyncrasies to gain effects; a funnyman, as opposed to a straight performer. (Sobel NEW)

eccentric dancer   A performer of dances in a grotesque or contortionistic fashion—ordinarily in a revue or musical comedy. (Granville DICTIONARY)

eccentrism   From the 1920s to the mid-1930s in Russia, an acting technique borrowed from clowns and side-show entertainers. The performer selected, exaggerated, and eventually exhausted the illogical, unexpected, and ludicrous possibilities of a given situation, then moved on to another, which was performed differently, but with equal zeal. (Gerould "Wiseman" 71–72)

Ecclesia (Greek)   See: *ekklesia*.

eccyclema   See: *ekkyklema*.

ecdysiste   A fancy word for a stripper, probably from ecdysiast (coined by H.L. Mencken) and artiste. The ultimate source is Greek *ekdysis*, a getting out.

échappé (French)   In ballet, a level opening of both feet from a closed to an open position, with both feet traveling an equal distance from the original center of gravity. (Grant TECHNICAL)

echo   In playwriting, the antonym of foreshadowing—a line or action that reminds one of something earlier in the play.

éclairages à la rampe (French)   Footlights. *Rampe* alone is also used. Compare that entry, and German *Rampe*.

eclecticism   In the early 20th C, the idea that each play calls for its own production style. (Cameron/Gillespie ENJOYMENT)

école de bon sens (French)   A 19th C French theatre movement emphasizing regular structure, simple and natural situations, and an unaffected tone. (Carlson FRENCH 93)

écriteau (French)   In 17th and 18th C France, a large card or scroll suspended above the stage containing plot information. Used by pantomime actors when dialogue was forbidden by law. (Scott "Pantomime" 126, Smith COMMEDIA 221)

ecstasis   In word/line delivery, pronouncing a short vowel as a long one. (Granville DICTIONARY)

edge, edged   See: hard edge(d), soft edge(d).

edge clearance   The distance between the edge of a flat and any corner blocks, keystones, or hardware. This permits another flat to fit snugly at a right angle at the back of the flat.

edge up   See: walk up.

edifizio (Italian)   See: pageant.

Edison base   In U.S. lighting, the medium screw base common in household use. (Wehlburg GLOSSARY)

Edison connector   A term sometimes used for connectors of household size, whether screw base and socket, or plug and outlet. Compare: cap, convenience outlet. (Bowman MODERN)

Edison plug   An occasional term (and an old one) for a standard household connector such as that used on a table lamp. (Lounsbury THEATRE 117–118)

Edison Screw   In lighting, the British term for a U.S. medium screw base. Often reduced to E.S. (Bentham ART 74, Corry LIGHTING pl. I)

edition   A revue based on a formula or concept found in similar revues but different from the original version. (Wilmeth LANGUAGE)

Edo *sanza* (Japanese)   Literally: Edo's (Tokyo's) three theatres. Three theatres were licensed to perform *kabuki* in Edo during the 18th and 19th C: the Nakamuraza, the Ichimuraza, and the Moritaza. Before 1714, the city had four licensed *kabuki* theatres but in that year the Yamamuraza was permanently closed by the government. (Leiter ENCYCLOPEDIA 61–62)

educational drama, educational dramatics   1. See: creative drama. 2. Any form of theatrical or dramatic activity by or for children or young people. The term is also sometimes applied to production and course work in colleges. Also called academic drama, academical drama.

educational puppetry   1. Puppet performances aimed at developing an audience's cultural and social awareness. 2. The use of puppetry as a developmental tool in schools, colleges, continuing education courses, and youth organizations. 3. Occupational and psychotherapeutic use of puppets. (Philpott DICTIONARY)

educational theatre   Theatre maintained by an educational institution to enrich its student body and community and for training students in drama and theatre. The tradition goes back at least to the early Renaissance, when plays were presented in academies. (Bowman/Ball THEATRE)

effacé (French)   In ballet: 1. One of the directions of *épaulement* (shoulder placement) in which a dancer stands at an oblique angle to the audience; part of the body is taken back and almost hidden from view. 2. A pose in which the legs are open (not crossed). (Grant TECHNICAL)

effect   1. An impression made on the spectator by a performer's action, a bit of music, a change in lighting, etc. 2. An aural or visual occurrence in a performance, such as the sound of rain, a flash of lightning, etc. Often called a special effect or stage effect.

effect head   An accessory for special effects, designed for use at the front of a suitable spotlight.

effect lantern, effects lantern   In Britain, an alternate for effect(s) projector. (Bowman/Ball THEATRE)

effect machine, effects machine   1. Among theatre people generally, any equipment which produces visual or auditory stage effects, sometimes even olfactory. (Barnet/Berman/Burto ASPECTS, Downs THEATRE II 1132) 2. Any lighting equipment which produces visual effects. Also called a scenic effect machine. (Canfield CRAFT, Bowman/Ball THEATRE) 3. Among lighting people, any equipment which produces visual effects in motion. Examples are moving clouds, rippling water, and rain. Also called a scenic effect machine or sciopticon. (McCandless "Glossary" 365, Bowman MODERN, Sellman/Lessley ESSENTIALS) See also: effect projector.

effect projector, effects projector Primarily in Britain, a projection machine capable of throwing still or moving effects on a scene. Compare: effect machine. (Downs THEATRE II 1132, Rae/Southern INTERNATIONAL)

effects man A specialist in creating stage effects. (Bowman/Ball THEATRE)

effect wheel In Britain, a circular housing used at the front of a spotlight to produce special effects. Typical are the colour wheel and the flicker wheel. (Bax MANAGEMENT 188)

effort In dance, the concentrating of exertion involved in movement. See also: shape. (Dell PRIMER 6, 59)

efforts In dance as seen by Rudolph von Laban, there are eight efforts or combinations of the elements of weight, space, and time: the dab (a direct, light, quick movement); the flick (an indirect, light, quick movement); float (an indirect, light, slow movement); glide (a direct, light, slow movement); press (a direct, strong, slow movement); punch (a direct, strong, quick movement); slash (an indirect, strong, quick movement); and wring (an indirect, strong, slow movement).

e-flat revue A second-rate touring revue. (Granville DICTIONARY)

egg 1. To throw eggs at a performer. 2. A theatrical failure.

egg-shaped auditorium See: horeshoe-shaped auditorium.

egloga (Spanish) A 15th C pastoral play.

egnsteater (Danish) Neighborhood collective theatre in Denmark, subsidized by national and municipal sources and dealing with contemporary social issues. (Marker/Marker ''Thalia'' 10)

ehon kyogen bon (Japanese) See: *eiri kyogen bon*.

Ehrenhold, Einschreier (German) In medieval Shrovetide plays, the speaker of the prologue—the herald. (Mantzius HISTORY II 131, 149)

Eidophusikon Jacques de Loutherbourg's late 18th C miniature, moving scenes of nature, such as Niagara Falls, a storm and shipwreck, Satan arraying his troops, etc., on a stage 6' wide and 8' deep. A major element was an atmosphere produced in large part by unusual lighting. De Loutherbourg's work had considerable influence on the scenery of his time and after. (Nicoll DEVELOPMENT 199, Bowman/Ball THEATRE, Highfill/Burnim/Langhans BIOGRAPHICAL IV 308–309)

eighteen favorite plays See: *juhachiban*.

Einfühlung (German) Empathy.

eiri kyogen bon (Japanese) Literally: illustrated play book. An illustrated script or scenario of a *kabuki* play, sold at the theatre and to the general public beginning in the 1690s. Also called *kyogen bon* (play book), *ehon kyogen bon* (picture play book). (Brandon CLASSIC 3, Leiter ENCYCLOPEDIA 63) *eiskyklema* (Greek)   A word used by the 2nd C AD grammarian Pollux, who says this is what the *ekkyklema* (a rolling platform) is called when "[it] is wheeled in." See also: *ekkyklema*. (Pollux in Arnott SCENIC 79)

eisodoi (Greek)   Literally: entrances. The approaches and entrances to the acting place in an ancient Greek theatre. The term, so used in Aristophanes, was an early word for the *parodoi* and did not long persist. Singular *eisodos*; variant plural *eisodi*. See also: *parodos* (Allen ANTIQUITIES 61–62, Flickinger PLUTARCH 53, Pickard-Cambridge DIONYSUS 21)

ekanban, ekamban (Japanese)   See: *shibai e*.

ekkadigaru (Kannada)   In *yaksagana*: 1. Broadly, musicians. 2. A school of musicians mentioned in the 16th C by Ratwakara Varni. (Ashton/Christie YAKSAGANA 21, 91)

ekklesia (Greek)   An official assembly held in the theatre after the City Dionysia. Improper actions during the festival were punished and certain awards given. Bieber's language suggests that all prizes and awards were bestowed at this assembly. The term also appears as *Ecclesia*, Assembly. (Pickard-Cambridge FESTIVALS 64, 67, 68–70; Bieber HISTORY 53)

ekkyklema (Greek), **eccyclema**   A stage machine probably used for showing interiors, especially those containing dead bodies or other prepared tableaux. The word is literally 'that which is rolled out,' from *ek*, out, and *kyklein*, to wheel. The verb *ekkyklein* is often used to mean reveal or display. An ancient writer (Pollux, 2nd C AD) describes the *ekkyklema* as ". . . a high platform on posts, on which stands a throne. It shows the dreadful things done indoors, behind the *skene*." Some scholars think the machine was a wheeled, semicircular platform which revolved about a pivot; others think it a wheeled platform which was simply pushed or trundled forward; a third group believes the pivoting *ekkyklema* was used before about 430 BC and the rolling *ekkyklema* thereafter. Among the last group, there is a tendency to identify the eccyclema as the earlier, pivoting device, the *exostra* as the later, rolling one. There is also some opinion that the two were identical, and some that the *ekkyklema* was used in tragedy and the *exostra* in comedy. Arnott and most writers before him believe the device came into use in the 5th C BC. Pickard-Cambridge's examination of the evidence convinces him that the 5th C BC use of the machine is very doubtful. Also spelled *ekkuklema*. Compare: *exostra*. (Arnott SCENIC 78–88, Pickard-Cambridge DIONYSUS 100–122)

ek-tara (Hindi)   A one-stringed musical instrument used to accompany *tamasha* performances.

EL   Entrance left. The entrances between the wings were formerly numbered 1, 2, 3, etc. from downstage to upstage. Entrance designations were also given as L1, L1E, L2, L2E, etc.

élancer (French)   See: movements in ballet.

electric   1. In Britain, having to do with lighting, as in electric bar (U.S. light batten, light pipe). As a noun, the term has come into U.S. use, as in first electric (the first light pipe upstage of the proscenium), second electric, etc. 2. In Britain, any property or effect which makes use of electricity. (Wehlburg GLOSSARY, Bellman SCENE)

electrical arc   See: carbon arc, arc light.

electrical brush   See: brush.

electric ballet   See: electric scene.

electric batten   In Britain, a borderlight using electric lamps. The term is used even of the earliest of these, in the 1880s. (Rees GAS 173, 179, fig. 87).

electric carbon arc   See: arc light.

electrician   1. One who sets up and operates stage lighting equipment. Also called a gaffer, juicer, juice, juiceman, juice hand, or lamp man. 2. The chief of the lighting crew, i.e., the chief electrician. 3. The member of the lighting crew who operates the control board. Meanings 1 and 2 are used especially in the professional theatre. (Bellman SCENE, Lounsbury THEATRE)

electrician's knot   1. Especially before the widespread use of connectors which lock, an overhand knot often tied in stage cable where connectors are joined. The knot prevents the connectors from being kicked or pulled apart inadvertently. (Bowman MODERN) 2. A knot tied in an electric cable just before it goes into a connector, to prevent the cable from pulling loose. Also called an underwriter's knot.

electrician's plot   See: light plot.

electric lead   British for stage cable or other electric conductor. Often shortened to lead. (Rae/Southern INTERNATIONAL 50)

electric light   A term sometimes used in mid-19th C Britain for a carbon arc light. See also: electric limelight. (Rees GAS 141–142)

electric limelight   In Britain in the middle and late 1860s, a carbon arc spotlight. ''Limelight' was likely to be used for any bright spotlight, but the carbon arc light was also at times separately identified in such phrases as ''powerful electric light.'' (Rees GAS 75)

electric room   In Britain, a name sometimes given to the room in which lighting equipment and supplies are stored. The phrase was also used of 19th C rooms in which the lighting materials had to do in part with gas. (Rees GAS 59, fig. 37; 60, fig. 38)

electrics   1. An occasional term for stage lighting, the stage lighting installation, or some part of either. 2. As ''Electrics,'' a call to an electrician. (Granville DICTIONARY 20, Bowman/Ball THEATRE)

electric scene   In late 19th C Britain, a scene which depended on the effect of a large number of lighted electric bulbs. A picture of such a scene in a pantomime of the early 1880s shows five light bulbs crowning the heads of each of a number of ladies, and more than 150 bulbs in two large scenic arches in the dark background. Such scenes were for a time also popular in ballet. Hence, electric ballet. (Rees GAS 182–184, fig. 88)

electric spark lighter   In the late 19th C, any of various devices which produced a spark used in lighting gas jets. (Penzel LIGHTING 108–109)

electric sticks   See: lightning sticks.

electronic tube dimmer   See: thyratron tube dimmer.

electronic winch system   A stage rigging system in which each line runs to a separate, electronically-controlled winch (hoist) on the gridiron.

element   In acting, a portion of a play, usually shorter than a scene, dominated by one emotion or attitude on the part of a performer. The changes between elements are beats, though the words are sometimes used interchangeably. (Rosenstein/Haydon/Sparrow ACTING 101)

eleos (Greek)   Supposedly a table on which a single performer answered the chorus. This was said to have occurred before Thespis, and is thought a likely predecessor of a platform or raised area for performers. (Pickard-Cambridge DITHYRAMB 86–87)

élévant (French)   Of a stage, raked. (Moynet FRENCH 3)

élévation (French)   In ballet, the ability to attain height in dancing; the height attained in springing steps. The dancer jumps with a graceful elasticity, like the bouncing movement of a rubber ball which touches the ground a moment and then rebounds into the air. (Grant TECHNICAL)

elevation sight line   See: vertical sight line.

elevator forestage   A forestage capable of rising and descending in one section or several. It can serve as an extension of the stage, an extension of the auditorium floor, an orchestra pit, or a freight elevator—often all of these. Also called a forestage elevator, forestage lift, orchestra pit lift, pit lift.

elevator stage   1. A stage or portion of a stage that can be raised or lowered. Also called a stage elevator or (especially in Britain) a bridge, lift, lifting stage, sinking stage. 2. See: double stage. See also: modular lift system.

eleven forty-five   A tall silk hat used by minstrel performers in early 20th C U.S. The minstrels donned the hats at 11:45 for a street parade. By extension, the parade itself. Also called a Hi Henry or an Oscar Hammerstein. (Wilmeth LANGUAGE)

eleven o'clock song, 11 o'clock song   On Broadway, a play doctor's device for reviving a weary audience by putting a noisy song into the final act of a play.

ELH   Entrance left hand. See also: EL.

Elizabethan theme   An extemporaneous entertainment which often followed the performance of a play in an Elizabethan theatre, consisting of improvisations in verse on a theme or topic suggested by a member of the audience. (Sobel HANDBOOK)

el kuklasi (Turkish)   A hand or glove puppet. Also called *Kol Korçak*. (And KARAGÖZ 24)

Ellipsenspiegel-Linsenscheinwerfer (German)   Ellipsoidal reflector spotlight. The term is literally 'elliptical-mirror lens-light-thrower.' (Bentham ART 313)

ellipsoidal   See: ellipsoidal reflector spotlight.

ellipsoidal flood   A floodlight in the shape of one end of an ellipsoid. See also: scoop. (Bellman LIGHTING 52–53, 60–63, fig. 3–3b)

ellipsoidal reflector floodlight   A floodlight which consists essentially of an ellipsoidal reflector. Many scoops (q.v.) are of this sort. ERF is a backstage shortening. (Bellman LIGHTING 52–53, Parker/Smith DESIGN 453, 594, fig. 17–7b)

ellipsoidal reflector spotlight   A highly efficient instrument which has a light source mounted at one focal point of an elliptical reflector and a lens system to focus the light. Beam-shaping devices (shutters, iris, gobo) are located at the conjugate focal point of the reflector. Shortenings include ellipsoidal, ellipsoidal spotlight, and ERS. See also: Lekolite.

elocution   The practice and art of public address. It includes articulation, inflection, pronunciation, pitch, rhythm, etc. (Granville DICTIONARY)

'em, 'em out front   Them, the audience.

embas (Greek)   In the 5th C BC and probably for a time thereafter, a soft shoe or half-boot. The word was evidently used of a variety of footwear, though especially that of old men, and may also have been applied to the footwear of actors and chorus members. The identification of the *embas* with the *soccus* of later comedy is true to this extent. By the 2nd C AD, and perhaps somewhat earlier, the term was equivalent to the *kothornos* of the time: Bieber notes that the Greek satirist Lucian used the plural *embates* for the thick-soled shoes or clogs of tragedy. (Pickard-Cambridge FESTIVALS 205, 207; Bieber HISTORY 239, 242; Allen ANTIQUITIES 141)

embocadura (Spanish)   The front of the stage, whether it has a proscenium or not. Also called a *desembocadura*. See also: *proscenio*.

emboîté (French)   Literally: fitted together. In ballet, from *demi-plié*, a spring from two feet to one foot, landing with one foot tightly fitted in front of the other ankle.

emboliaria (Latin Roman)   By the 1st C BC, one of the terms for an actress in mime. The literal meaning approximates 'a female performer in an *embolium*.' See also: *emboliarius*. (Nicoll MASKS 101) *emboliarius* (Latin Roman)   One of the words for a male actor in the mime. The term is from *embolium*, intermission entertainment, a function the mimes served by the 1st C BC. See also: *emboliaria*. (Nicoll MASKS 101)

embolima (Greek)   Literally: things thrown in. Especially in the late 5th C BC and after, irrelevant but entertaining additions to the choral odes, often stock choral interludes. Aristotle, unhappy about the *embolima*, asks in the *Poetics* that the chorus be as much a part of the plot as one of the actors. Compare *embolium*. (Lawler DANCE 85; Arnott ANCIENT 78; Pickard-Cambridge FESTIVALS 233, 238)

embolium (Latin Roman)   An interlude, an intermission entertainment. The term is used of various types of performance. An example is the so-called pyrrhic dance. See: *embolima*. (Nicoll MASKS 101, Chambers MEDIAEVAL I 7)

embrouillement (French)   In playwriting, complication. (Chapelain in Clark/Popkin EUROPEAN 91)

embryo, embryo spot   A very small Fresnel spotlight, usually designed for a lamp of 100 or 150 watts. The housing can be contained within one hand; as this suggests, the embryo is particularly adapted to cramped quarters. Also called an inky (possibly a diminutive of incandescent). (Lounsbury THEATRE 93, Wehlburg GLOSSARY)

emcee, emsee   Master or mistress of ceremonies. Also printed MC, M.C.

emergency door   In Britain, a fire exit from an auditorium or an escape door from a stage setting. (Bowman/Ball THEATRE)

emergency lights   In a power outage or similar emergency in the U.S., lights for the auditorium and exits and sometimes the stage. For obvious reasons, such lights are often fed and controlled separately from the normal electrical service. Hence, emergency lighting. The British equivalent is secondary lighting. See also: panic lights. (McCandless "Glossary" 637, Dean/Carra FUNDAMENTALS 368)

emergency rope   See: cut line, fire curtain safety release line.

emmeleia (Greek)   The dance of tragedy. Literally: harmony, originally an abstract word used, for example, of a graceful oratorical style. Much discussed has been whether *emmeleia* applies only to the "formal tetragonal, march-like" (Lawler) dance of the choral odes or to all dancing in tragedy. If the latter, the meaning would be broad, since the tragedies call for not only semi-religious processions, but also wedding dances and ". . . even the old ecstatic, Dionysiac dance itself, with wild running, shouting, tossing of hair, of *thyrsi*, and of torches, and [the] ultimate collapse of the dancers" (Lawler). (Lawler DANCE 83, Pickard-Cambridge FESTIVALS 253–254)

emotional memory, emotional recall   See: emotion memory.

emotional truth   1. In acting, believable communicated feelings. 2. In children's theatre, the director's objective in insisting that actors portray authentic, dimensionalized characters, rather than condescending emotionally to a child's supposed lack of understanding. (Goldberg CHILDREN'S 138)

emotion memory   In the Stanislavsky system of acting, remembered emotions or actions. McGaw says that physical action memory is a more appropriate designation of what Stanislavsky called emotion memory or affective memory. A performer has an experience, retains the memory of it, recalls the sensory and physical details, and uses the recollection to create a believable situation in performance. See also: sense memory. (McGaw ACTING 102, Stanislavski ACTOR 175–181)

'em out front   See: 'em.

empathy   A spectator's participation in the feelings of one or more characters or situations on stage. In German: *Einfühlung*.

empereur de la basoche (French)   Head of a *basoche*—an association of medieval clerks who put on plays.

emphatic curtain   An ending to a scene or act that has a significant piece of business or an effective final line. (Bowman/Ball THEATRE)

Empire dress   See: *costume à l'antique*.

emploi (French)   Stereotyping in casting performers, limiting them to roles they are supposedly able to fill: thus the labels eccentric comedian, low comedian, soubrette, etc. Also called line of business. (Archer in Matthews PAPERS 96)

empresario (Spanish)   A producer, a theatrical director. Spelled *impresario* in the 17th C.

emsee   Master or mistress of ceremonies.

enchaînement (French)   In ballet, two or more steps put together to form a phrase. (Kersley/Sinclair BALLET)

encirclement   A term used by architects to describe the seating arrangement in a theatre. Zero encirclement describes a proscenium or end stage, 180 to 270 degree encirclement a Greek or Elizabethan public theatre, and 360 degree encirclement an arena theatre. (Ramsey/Sleeper ARCHITECTURAL 20)

encore   1. Primarily in musical theatre, a repetition, usually of a song or dance. (The practice is also common at recitals and concerts.) 2. A call by an audience for a performer to appear again and, usually, repeat what was just done.

end   In an Elizabethan theatre, a side entrance. Chambers takes it that stage directions calling for an entrance from the end of the stage meant from the side. (Chambers ELIZABETHAN III 74)

end an act cold   To fail to get applause.

ender   The last act on a bill.

endha (Indonesian)   Javanese shadow puppet term for dodging a blow or an attack without moving off-screen. (Long JAVANESE 65)

endless line   See: operating line.

endless runner   See: treadmill.

end line   See: set of lines.

end man   In a minstrel show, a comedian at either end of the seated semicircle of performers. In Britain, corner man or corner boy. See also: Bones, Tambo.

end stage   A stage at one end of an auditorium or other enclosed space, with no proscenium in evidence.

energy   In dance, the degree of force the body releases to accomplish a given movement or movements.

enfarinée (French)   In white face; from *farine* (flour). (Scott in Mayer/Richards WESTERN 24)

(l')enfer (French)   See: hellmouth.

engageantes (French)   17th-18th C two- or three-tiered ruffled lace cuffs, for men's or women's sleeves. (Boucher FASHION, Chalmers CLOTHES 18)

engaged   Especially of performers, working.

engagement   1. The period of a company's stay at a theatre. 2. A performer's employment, or the duration thereof.

engei (Japanese)   Variety entertainments—storytelling, narratives, songs, vaudeville, juggling—performed today in commercial, urban variety theatres (*yose*). Also called *kei engeki* (light entertainment). (Kawatake KABUKI 66)

engeki (Japanese)   A modern term derived from Western theatre: 1. The generic term for theatre arts. 2. More narrowly, a play or drama. 3. In *kabuki*, a dialogue play, as distinguished from a dance play (*shosagoto*). In this meaning, also called *ji gei, ji kyogen*. (Kawatake KABUKI 21)

engekisei (Japanese)   Literally: theatrical nature. In modern dramatic criticism, the theatrical aspects of a play or drama, as distinct from its literary (*bungakusei*) or philosophic (*kannensei*) aspects. (Ortolani in Shively MODERNIZATION 491–493)

engi (Japanese)   Acting. *Engisei* (acting nature), indicates 'acting or show elements' of a play, as opposed to literary elements. (Berberich ''Rapture'' 10–11)

engine   In Restoration theatres and later, a device, such as a winch, for making something else move (as opposed to a machine, which is the moving thing itself). But engine had been used in the early 17th C to mean a machine or special effect, and in time it covered all devices effecting movement upon the stage. (Southern CHANGEABLE 121–122, Nagler SOURCES 143)

engineer   A shortening of British chief engineer. (Bowman/Ball THEATRE)

engisei (Japanese)   See: *engi*.

English   See: stage English.

English back   In 19th C Britain, and later in France (where it was literally translated as *dos Anglais*), an acting device in which, when the play demanded it, the performer turned his or her full back to the audience. This represented a departure from the dogma of neo-classic acting. (Carlson "*Hernani's*" 26)

English gown   See: gown à l'Anglaise.

English trap   A kind of bristle trap in the stage floor or in a wall, consisting of twigs or steel teeth covered with painted canvas. It is spring or counterweight loaded so that a performer may appear instantaneously. Used in 19th C British pantomimes. (Bowman/Ball THEATRE)

en l'air (French)   In dance, a movement executed in the air. Also called an aerial.

enlèvement (French)   In ballet, the lifting of a dancer into the air by a partner. (Kersley/Sinclair BALLET)

en muette (French)   In mime.

ennen no (Japanese)   The concluding and most important part of an *ennen* program (Buddhist services and Shinto ceremonies for longevity), consisting of a song and dance drama accompanied by music that included recitation (*kaiko*) and comic scenes. Masks, simplified costumes, props and settings were used. Established in the 12th C, and a precursor of present-day *no*. (Inoura HISTORY 52–62)

ensayo (Spanish)   A rehearsal. An *ensayo general* is a dress rehearsal. (Shergold SPANISH)

ensayo (Philippine)   See: *comedia*.

ensemble   1. A performing group. 2. Acting that emphasizes unity, cohesion; hence, ensemble acting. 3. The general look of the stage picture.

Ensemblespiel (German)   Ensemble playing.

ensemble theatre   Theatre (or theatres) whose performers are hired by the year rather than for one play. (Bowman/Ball THEATRE)

en sourdine (French)   Muted music played as background for a love scene or a quiet segment of a performance. (Granville DICTIONARY)

Ent   See: E.

enter   To come onstage.

enter above   In Elizabethan theatre and later, a stage direction indicating that a performer should appear in an upper acting area, such as a balcony over a stage entrance door.

enterlude, entrelude   See: interlude.

entertainment   1. In Elizabethan times, a brief, light amusement with music and lyrics, usually performed as a welcome for royal visitors; a simple masque. It probably developed from the medieval reception or royal entry. (Chambers

MEDIAEVAL II 176) 2. In the 18th C, an afterpiece, or whatever followed the mainpiece. (Avery LONDON lviii)

entire heavens   In Renaissance theatres, a sky border with no cuts, made of cloth stretched over a frame. See also: cut heavens. (Sobel HANDBOOK 503)

entr'acte (French), **entr'acte**   1. An intermission; the interval between the acts of a play. Also called an inter-act. 2. Any entertainment performed during an intermission. (Flickinger GREEK 193, 194, 309)

entr'acte music   See: act.

entrada general (Philippine)   General admission. (Fernández ILOILO 132)

entrailles (French)   In acting, the ability to move an audience emotionally by being moved oneself. (Hawkins ANNALS II 5)

entramés, entrameso (Spanish)   See: *entremés*.

entrance   1. A place on stage where a performer can appear. Sometimes E, or entrance door. 2. A performer's appearance on stage, especially the first, as well as the manner of appearance.

entrance cue   The signal for a performer to come on stage; usually a word or piece of business.

entrance left   See: EL.

entrance left hand   See: ELH.

entrance light   An occasional term for a light provided at a point of entrance to or exit from a setting. Hence, entrance lighting. (Bowman/Ball THEATRE)

entrance line   The first words a character speaks when coming on stage, often a speech which helps establish character or state of mind.

entrance money   In 17th C theatres, money taken from patrons at the door.

entrance right, entrance right hand   See: ER, ERH.

entrance round   Applause at the first entrance of a favorite player.

entrances   The spaces between grooved wing positions in 18th C theatres. (Shattuck KEMBLE I xix)

entrance strip   A striplight used to light an entrance or its backing. (McCandless "Glossary" 634)

entrechat (French)   In ballet, a spring into the air in which the legs crisscross rapidly. (Wilson BALLET)

entrée (French)   Literally: entrance. 1. The arrival of a dancer or group of dancers who perform a number in a *divertissement*. 2. See: *divertissement*. 3. The beginning of a *grand pas de deux* in which the male and female dancers enter. (Grant TECHNICAL)

entrelude   See: interlude.

entreme (Philippine)   See: *sainete*.

entremés (Spanish)   1. A pageant wagon, float, or cart in early Corpus Christi and other processions, including pageantry at banquets. Also spelled *entramés* and *entrameso*. 2. In the early 17th C, an interlude or short topical sketch, sometimes sung, performed between acts of plays. See also: *castillo, roca, sainete*. (Shergold SPANISH, Brockett HISTORY 230).

entremet (French)   A performance similar to an English disguising of the 15th C. (Chambers ELIZABETHAN I 152)

entretoise (French)   In the 19th C: 1. A trestle upon which a tiny stage was supported in salon theatre performances. (Moynet FRENCH 189) 2. Metal pieces which supported traps and kept beams in square. (Carlson "Inventory" 43, 48–49)

entry   1. Occasionally in the past, an act. The five acts of *The Siege of Rhodes* are labelled entries. 2. An entrance by a performer. 3. An entranceway. 4. Formerly, a dance. (Southern CHANGEABLE 111, FLYING POST 2–4 July 1700)

envelope   The bulb of a lamp, usually transparent glass or quartz. The term seems to be an improvement on the older 'bulb': bulbs are not always bulbous, bulb is often used for lamp, and bulbs envelop the filament and its appurtenances. (Wehlburg GLOSSARY)

environmental theatre   Theatre whose performance space is the audience's environment, so that the performance surrounds some or all of the spectators, and the line between audience space and performance space is crossed. Environmental theatre does not normally use traditional theatre space, but rather found or created space, the features of which help shape the production. (Cameron/Gillespie ENJOYMENT)

eorema (Greek)   According to Suidas' lexicon (10th C), a synonym for *mechane* (hoisting device). The term is a special form related to words having to do with suspension and swinging. (Nicoll DEVELOPMENT 22)

épaulé (French)   See: positions of the body.

épaulement (French)   In ballet, the placement of the shoulders. *Épaulement* gives the finishing artistic touch to every movement and is a characteristic feature of the modern classical style compared to the old French style, which has little *épaulement*. (Grant TECHNICAL)

epeisodion (Greek)   Literally: episode. In classic Greek tragedy, all of the portion of the play between two choral odes; the histrionic portion of the play. In early times, the choral odes were the important parts of the production: hence the term *epeisodion*, connoting an interruption. Though it was the episodes that became the heart of the play in the developed tragedy, the term was never replaced. The episodes were normally in dialogue and varied in length from some thirty lines to nearly 500. Plural *epeisodia*. (Allen ANTIQUITIES 120, Bieber HISTORY 29)

epic   1. Said of drama with a vast historical sweep. 2. Said of a play or a production, often anti-naturalistic, concerned with social propaganda, especially during the 1920s and early 1930s. Also called panoramic drama. See also: epic theatre, living newspaper. (Bowman/Ball THEATRE)

epic realism   In Bertolt Brecht's epic theatre theory, the presentation of an aspect of social reality.

epic theatre   A term created by Erwin Piscator to describe a kind of drama and theatre where the audience response (ideally) is objective, not subjective; which is panoramic, not compact; and in which such devices as film projections and titles are used. Popularized by Bertolt Brecht, the typical epic theatre play is set back in time or the events are played as historical (see: historification). It often draws an audience into the play and then jolts it into an objective state by a sudden change in style, a shift to song, the use of projections, etc. (the *Verfremdungseffekt*: distancing). Epic theatre is regularly anti-illusionistic and didactic yet usually open-ended, its purpose being to stir spectators to consider and then take social action.

epilogue   A scene or speech, normally in verse, following a play, usually a direct address to the audience and sometimes a plea for applause. Epilogues were especially popular in the 17th and 18th C and, like prologues, contained topical comment.

epimeletes (Greek)   Literally: one who has charge, manager. An official who assisted at times in the management of dramatic festivals. He and the *archon basileus* directed the procession at the Lenaea, and he worked with that *archon* at the Rural Dionysia. *Epimeletai* also assisted the *archon eponymos* at the City Dionysia in various ways, including selection of *choregi*. The term may also have been used of a guild official connected with financial management. (Pickard-Cambridge DIONYSUS 36, 51, 58, 70; Mantzius HISTORY I 179)

episkenion (Greek)   Literally: upon the *skene*. A second story of the *skene* (scene house), sometimes called the *theologeion* or *distegia*. Also spelled *episcenium* or *episcaenium*. (Allen ANTIQUITIES 67, 83; Flickinger GREEK 59, 106–109, 361; Pickard-Cambridge DIONYSUS 61, 157)

episode   1. See: *epeisodion*. 2. An incident, unit, or action within a play. A play in which the episodes are not causally united is called episodic—normally a weakness in play structure. But Bertolt Brecht, as in *The Private Life of the Master Race*, used an episodic structure purposely to keep the spectators' attention on each episode rather than on the play's outcome.

epitasis   The part of a play in which the main action takes place. (Bowman/Ball THEATRE)

epitoga   1. In classical times, a wide, bell-sleeved unbelted cloak worn over a toga. 2. In medieval times (especially 13th C), academic dress. 3. A ceremonial shoulder-length hood worn by heads of state for ceremonial occasions. Also called an épomine or *chausse* (French). (Boucher FASHION)

equally divided scene   A scene in a play in which two characters have equal prominence.

equestrian drama   A spectacular entertainment involving horses (and sometimes other trained animals), music, and actors. The horses were trained to dance, play dead, rescue women and children, etc. The form developed in Britain in the late 18th C and continued popular there and in the U.S. in the 19th C. The spectacles were performed in equestrian amphitheatres and sometimes in converted legitimate theatres. Also called a hippodrama. (Wilmeth LANGUAGE, Saxon "Circus" 301)

equipment ground   In a three-wire electrical system, the grounding wire often required in cable used with portable lighting equipment. (Bellman LIGHTING 167)

ER, ERH   Entrance right, entrance right hand. The entrances between the wings were normally numbered 1, 2, 3, etc. from downstage to upstage. Entrance designations were also given as R1, R1E, R2, R2E, etc.

eradaneya (Kannada)   Literally: second. In *yaksagana*, the star dancer of a troupe, who performs heroic roles such as Rama, Arjuna, Bhima, Dharmaraya, and Duryodhana. (Ashton/Christie YAKSAGANA 49, 51, 91)

ERF   A backstage term for an ellipsoidal reflector floodlight. (Parker/Smith DESIGN)

erh hu (Chinese)   See: *erhu.*

erh hua lien (Chinese)   See: *erhualian.*

erh huang (Chinese)   See: *erhuang.*

erh huang p'ing pan (Chinese)   See: *sipingdiao.*

erh i, erh i hsiang (Chinese)   See: *yixiang.*

erh jen chuan (Chinese)   See: *errenzhuan.*

erh jen t'ai (Chinese)   See: *errentai.*

erh liu, erh liu pan (Chinese)   See: *erliuban.*

erh mien (Chinese)   See: *fu.*

erhu, erh hu (Chinese)   Literally: second two-stringed spike fiddle. A two-stringed spike fiddle (*huqin*) which is featured in the melodic orchestra (*wenchang*) in many forms of music-drama (*xiqu*), and is also used in many forms of storytelling (*quyi*). It has a cylindrical bamboo or wooden body about 3″ to 3½″ in diameter and a snakeskin head; it is very expressive, with a low, gentle tone quality. (Scott CLASSICAL 42–44, 50; Wichmann "Aural" 436–437, 450)

erhualian, erh hua lien (Chinese)   Literally: second flower face. A painted-face role (*jing*) which emphasizes dance-acting (*zuo*) and speech (*nian*) skills; a major subcategory of the painted-face role in Beijing opera (*jingju*) and many other forms of music-drama (*xiqu*). Also called posture painted-face role (*jiazihualian* or *chia tzu hua lien*). (Scott CLASSICAL 75–76)

erhuang, erh huang (Chinese)   In music-drama (*xiqu*), the musical mode (*diaoshi*) considered best suited for expressing grief, remembrance, and lyricism. It may have originated in Jiangxi Province in the late 16th and early 17th C; in the 17th C it was further developed through combination with *chuiqiang* and *gaobozi*. It is now one of the two principal modes (*zheng diaoshi*) in the *pihuang* musical system (*shengqiang xitong*). See also: *xipi*. (Mackerras MODERN 19, Mackerras "Growth" 84–90, Wichmann "Aural" 167–227)

erhuang pingban (Chinese)   See: *sipingdiao*.

erliuban, erh liu pan (Chinese)   Literally: two-flowing meter or, written with a different central character, two-six meter. A duple meter regulated (*shangban*) metrical-type (*banshi*), faster than primary meter (*yuanban*), which is used in the songs of many forms of music-drama (*xiqu*) for situations such as reasoning aloud, and emotionally expressive sung dialogue. In Beijing opera (*jingju*) it is used primarily in the *xipi* mode (*diaoshi*). Abbreviated *erliu* or *erh liu*. See also: *banyan*. (Wichmann "Aural" 153–156)

ermian (Chinese)   See: *fu*.

***erregende* moment** (German-English)   In playwriting, the inciting action, when the equilibrium of the play is destroyed and the plot goes into motion. (Archer PLAY-MAKING 126)

errentai, erh jen t'ai (Chinese)   Literally: two people stage. A form of small-scale folk theatre (*xiaoxi*) popular in the Inner Mongolian Autonomous Region, northern Shanxi Province, and parts of Hebei Province. It was originally played by only two performers, one of male and one of female roles, but later came to have one performer for each character in a given play. It arose in the 19th C from a number of sources including local Mongolian and Han Chinese folksongs and dances, and was influenced somewhat by *jinju*. Also called *shuangwanyier* or *shuang wan i erh*, literally "double amusement intention."

errenzhuan, erh jen chuan (Chinese)   Literally: two people transmit. A form of story-telling (*quyi*) that developed in the 18th C and is popular today throughout northeast China. It is usually presented by two performers, one of male and one of female roles. Also called *bengbeng* or *peng peng*, literally "bouncing," and *shuangwanyier* or *shuang wan i erh*, literally "double amusement art."

ERS   See: ellipsoidal reflector spotlight.

Erstevorstellung (German)   First performance.

erudite theatre   Any theatre whose audience is upper class and intellectual, whose organization is not usually professional, and whose aim is often the imitation of earlier forms, such as the court theatre of James I in England. (Cameron/Hoffman GUIDE)

eryi, eryixiang (Chinese)   See: *yixiang*.

E.S.   See: Edison Screw.

esbatement (French)   A frolicsome, dance-like entertainment performed, like the *mômerie*, in the halls of the medieval nobility. (Frank MEDIEVAL 160)

esbatementen (Dutch)   Literally: beautiful (or skillful) plays. Dramatic productions with themes taken from chivalric romances. (Gassner/Quinn ENCYCLOPEDIA 193)

escaffignon   1. A 12th C light shoe of rich fabric. 2. A 16th C flimsy, flat-heeled shoe, often slashed on its uppers. Also called an eschapin. (Boucher FASHION)

escape door   See: fire exit.

escape ramp   A sloping exit to offstage, usually from an onstage level higher than the permanent flooring.

escaramosa (Philippine)   A display of skill and grace in using weapons in *comedia*. The term may be from Scaramouche, implying showing off. (Mendoza COMEDIA 54–55)

escarelle   A pouch attached to a belt, frequently used to hold a knife. (Russell COSTUME)

escena (Spanish)   The scene; what is represented on stage.

escenario (Spanish)   A stage.

eschapin   See: escaffignon. (Boucher FASHION)

escoffion   A 14th–15th C elaborate headdress with two horn-like protrusions from its crown. See also: cornet, hennin. (Wilcox DICTIONARY)

escotillón, escutillón (Spanish)   A trap door. (Shergold SPANISH)

esempio (Italian)   Literally: example. A medieval mystery play. (Mantzius HISTORY II 2)

esprit   A 19th C egret plume used as a hair or hat ornament. (Boucher FASHION)

establish   In playwriting or production, to make character, locale, mood, etc. clear to the audience. (Bowman/Ball THEATRE)

estal (French)   See: *mansion*.

estar de suplente (Spanish)   To be an understudy. See also: *suplente*.

estates   Seating sections in 18th C London theatres. (Stone/Kahrl GARRICK 81)

esthetic distance   See: aesthetic distance.

estival (French)   See: *stivale*.

estocado (Philippine)   The main fighting scene in a *sayaw* folk play. (Mendoza COMEDIA 103)

estrif (French)   See: flyting.

établir le plan (French)   To set up the scenario or plot. (Diderot in Clark/Popkin EUROPEAN 244) *étendre* (French)   See: movements in ballet.

ethelontai (Greek)   Literally: volunteers. Possibly a variety of early amateur mime performers. Compare *sophistai*. (Nicoll MASKS 26–27, Pickard-Cambridge DITHYRAMB 137)

Ethiopian delineator   In the early 19th C, a white performer in blackface. Such performers claimed they were giving authentic depictions of American Blacks. When minstrel shows became popular, the phrase fell out of use. (Toll in Matlaw AMERICAN 22, 23; Wilmeth LANGUAGE)

Ethiopian minstrelsy, Ethiopian opera   Early names for minstrel shows. (Wilmeth LANGUAGE)

Ethiopian paradise   Formerly, the uppermost gallery in a theatre.

ethologos (Greek)   Literally: character-speaker. Used by Cicero, among others, the word came to be almost equivalent to mime-player. Nicoll suggests the implication is that the mime was viewed as an imitation of life. See also: *biologos*. (Nicoll MASKS 36)

ethos (Greek), **ethos**   Character, the second of the six qualities of tragedy discussed by Aristotle in the *Poetics*. By character, Aristotle meant the tendencies which determine the behavior of a human being. He put *ethos* second in importance to plot because he felt character showed itself in the events of a well-constructed plot. (Butcher ARISTOTLE'S 337–361, Vaughn DRAMA 27–28)

eth-oxo limelight   Near the end of the 19th C in Britain, a limelight which used ether in place of hydrogen or coal gas. This limelight came into some use in small theatres in the provinces. (Rees GAS 57–58, figs. 35–36)

études (French)   Literally: studies. In the Moscow Art Theatre, improvisations; exercises based on action, from which early 20th C director Eugene Vakhtangov believed the performer's emotion arose.

etui, *étui* (French)   An 18th C ornamental case worn at the waist and containing scissors, thimble, scent bottle, and other notions. (Walkup DRESSING 236)

Eugénie hat   A small hat with a point in front, ornamented with a feather sweeping gracefully down in back. (Walkup DRESSING 360)

eurhythmics   Émile-Jaques Dalcroze's system of gymnastics (hygienic, athletic, vocal, mental, and rhythmic, among others) aimed at the simultaneous development of body and mind. Less concretely, the system seeks (among other goals) to establish equilibrium between will and motion and character and temperament, and freedom of mind and body from cramping motor habits. (Rogers DANCE 269)

eutony   In acting, the control and direction of bodily tension and elimination of excess strain. (Feldenkrais "Restoration" 121)

every-other-row vision   In theatre architecture, an auditorium floor profile which permits seated spectators to see over the spectators two rows ahead and between spectators in the row directly ahead. Also called second-row vision.

every-row vision   In theatre architecture, an auditorium floor profile which permits seated spectators to see over the heads of spectators in the row directly in front.

evirato (Italian)   See: *castrato*.

Evraiski aktiory (Yiddish)   Jewish actors. The phrase, which is literally Hebrew actors, was used in Russian-Jewish areas in the late 19th C. In Russian, *Evreĭskiĭ aktëry*.

exarchon (Greek)   Literally: leader. Especially in early times, the leader of a dithyramb. Plural *exarchontes*. Bieber believes the *exarchon* evolved from the satyr play when the leader, though still masked as a satyr, was costumed as a god or a hero such as Dionysus, Hermes, or Silenus. She suggests that he next discarded the satyr mask and donned that of the god or hero; having come this far, he could then have stepped out of the chorus. Pickard-Cambridge notes that Aristotle apparently looked on the *exarchon* as the first actor; Kitto feels that Aristotle's remarks mean that tragedy developed from the *exarchon*. Sometimes seen as *exarchos,* plural *exarchoi.* (Bieber HISTORY 6, 15, 18–19; Pickard-Cambridge DITHYRAMB 89–91; Kitto GREEK 7)

excess baggage   1. In vaudeville, a wife or other woman traveling with a male performer but not working in the show. 2. An old term for a poor performer. (Wilmeth LANGUAGE)

excitant determinant   See: *uddipana* .

exciting force   The dramatic element from which springs the action of a play. It may precede the play itself. See also: inciting action. (Bowman/Ball THEATRE)

excursions   Especially in the Elizabethan theatre, the busy stage movement of soldiers in battle scenes. Typical stage directions read: alarums and excursions.

exercising   Formerly, performing: exercising one's lungs, exercising plays. (Lord Mayor in Nagler SOURCES 113)

exeunt, exeunt omnes (Latin)   Literally: they go out, they all go out. A stage direction for more than one character leaving the stage. Singular, *exit* (also English). When characters leave the stage by different exitways, the direction reads '*exeunt* severally.' The terms are fairly common in Elizabethan plays.

exhaustra (Greek)   See: *exostra*.

exhibitionism   A performer's display of superficial skill rather than a serious projection of character and situation.

exhibition room   An early term for a theatre in the U.S., used to avoid legal problems or censorship. Also called a lecture room or lecture hall. (Wilmeth LANGUAGE)

exit   1. A door or other place through which a performer can leave the stage or the audience leave a theatre. 2. To leave. See: *exeunt.*

exit cue   A line, action, or effect which takes a performer off the stage.

exit door   A door leading to the exterior of a theatre.

exit lights   Lights over exits from a theatre. Usually red or green, such lights are required by law nearly everywhere, and must be lit during performances. (Carrington THEATRICANA, Baker THEATRECRAFT)

exit line   The last speech of a character before leaving the stage.

exit without lines   1. Of a performer, to leave the stage without speaking a line or lines. 2. Such an exit. (Bowman/Ball THEATRE)

exodiarius (Latin Roman)   An actor in an *exodium* (concluding piece). The term was used especially of the actors in an Atellan farce when it served as the *exodium* for a tragedy, and later of mime actors when the mime replaced the Atellan as an afterpiece. Plural *exodiarii*. Also called an exodiary (obsolete). Compare *emboliarius*. (Nicoll MASKS 67, 99; Bieber HISTORY 160)

exodium (Latin Roman)   A concluding piece. See also: *exodiarius*. (Bieber HISTORY 160, Nicoll MASKS 67)

exodos (Greek)   1. The final song of the chorus in Greek drama. 2. The exit of the performers in Greek drama. 3. The last scene in a Greek drama. 4. A way out of a Greek theatre. (Bieber HISTORY xii, 29)

exostra (Greek)   Literally: that which is thrust forth. A staging device which may have been similar to the *ekkyklema* (a rolling platform). The 2nd C AD writer Pollux and some others have considered the two identical. Pickard-Cambridge thinks the *exostra* was, as he puts it, "a contrivance on the upper story" of the stage building. Occasionally spelled *exhaustra*. (Pickard-Cambridge DIONYSUS 100, 103, 118; Allen ANTIQUITIES 111; Arnott SCENIC 80)

exotic dancer   A modern term for a stripper. Much used by these performers, the phrase may have been created by them. (Wilmeth LANGUAGE)

expense money   Money paid to a performer during a rehearsal period. (Bowman/Ball THEATRE)

experimental theatre   A 20th C term for dramatic literature or theatrical production that breaks from tradition.

explicator   See: *mystère mimé.*

explicit (Latin)   In some Elizabethan and Jacobean plays, a word added to stage directions indicating the end of an act or play. The word had been used by scribes in medieval times to end a book or a unit within a book.

exploded box set   A stage setting in which the side walls do not meet the back wall and the ceiling is suspended above the tops of the walls. A favorite of German designer Caspar Neher. (Cole "Trends" 30–31)

exposition   In playwriting, the revelation of necessary background information, usually but not exclusively set forth in the opening section of a play.

expositor   From the 14th to the 16th C, a performer who commented on the action and, at the end of a morality play, pointed the moral. (Bowman/Ball THEATRE)

expressionism   1. Especially in Europe in the early 20th C, a movement in the arts which was critical of realism and naturalism. It focused on the subjective struggle for spiritual renewal rather than on outer reality. In drama, this inner, psychological focus led to episodic scenes which were thematic rather than the result of cause and effect. Characters were usually abstractly named. Acting was often stylized, emotionally-charged, urgent, and replete with rhythmic posturing and movement. Staging tended to be cubistic, surrealistic, and simple. August Strindberg's *A Dream Play* is perhaps the most famous example of expressionist drama. 2. A kind of highly subjective, emotional modern dance. (Love DANCE)

extemp   Extemporaneous speaking or acting.

extempore acting   Improvised performing, without a script.

extended control   In stage lighting, a term sometimes used for an arrangement by which some of the light may be controlled from a position not on, or even near, the control board. Sometimes called foreign control. (McCandless SYLLABUS 51, Bowman MODERN)

extended stage   See: multi-proscenium stage.

extending brace, extension brace   See: stage brace.

extension (French)   In ballet, a dancer's ability to raise and hold the leg extended in air. (Grant TECHNICAL)

extension pipe stand, extension stand   A telescoping light stand. Also called a light stand.

exterior backing   See: backing.

exterior scene   1. Scenery depicting the out-of-doors. 2. A scene in a play which takes place out of doors.

extra   A supernumerary; a performer hired to play walk-on parts.

extra man, extra woman   In vaudeville, a performer used for non-speaking roles; not a regular member of the troupe. (Wilmeth LANGUAGE)

extravaganza   A spectacular theatre piece, usually a musical with a light and improbable plot and exaggerated characters. By extension, any extravagant, exaggerated entertainment. (O'Hara/Bro INVITATION, Bowman/Ball THEATRE)

eyebrow pencil   See: makeup pencil.

eye-fixing pillar   See: *metsuke bashira*.

eye level   In performing, keeping the chin up and eyes on a level with spectators in a low balcony or mezzanine.

F

---

fable   In Aristotelian criticism, the plot, the planned action or intrigue of a play. (Sobel HANDBOOK 624)

fabliau   Fable; a medieval minstrel entertainment.

fabu (Chinese)   See: *faqu*.

fabula (Latin Roman)   Literally: story, narrative, play. This meaning may be almost as old as 'story,' since the word was early attached to a variety of play types. The Romans named the various *fabulae* according to the characteristic clothing or footwear worn by the actors. (Beare ROMAN 264)

fabula Atellana (Latin Roman)   A form of rustic southern Italian farce thought to have been masked and improvised. Surviving fragments suggest that the Atellan was boisterous in the extreme, with a number of coarse, greedy clowns as stock characters: Pappus, Maccus, Bucco, and Dossenus, the last perhaps another name for Manducus. Attempts to call these figures direct ancestors of similar clowns in the *commedia dell'arte* are unproved. There is also no evidence that more than one or two appeared in any given playlet.

The Atellan was short, serving often as an afterpiece (*exodium*) to tragedy. During its life in Rome, the Atellan was for a time "literary," but it soon returned to improvisation. Surviving titles and other evidence suggest that plots often involved disguises and mistaken identity. Probably under the influence at Rome of Greek New Comedy, the plays added mythological burlesque and parody of tragedy to the raucous rural farce. The *Atellanae* were evidently developed originally by the Oscans (in Campania, north of Naples), and are thought to have reached Rome from Atella, a Campanian town. Unsurprisingly, the literature shows a variety of names in both Latin and English: *Atellana*, the plurals *ludi Osci* and *Atellaniolae, Oscum ludicrum*; Atellan(e), Atellan farce, Atellan play, Oscan play, Oscan farce. (Beare ROMAN 137–148)

fabula crepidata (Latin Roman)   A Latin comedy on a Greek subject. The phrase is thought to have been an alternative for *fabula palliata*, the more frequent term for such comedy. The source is *crepida*, a Greek open shoe. Plural *fabulae crepidatae*. Also appears as *crepidata*. (Beare ROMAN 264–266)

fabula duplex (Latin Roman)   Literally: double story. 1. Double plot, double action. 2. A play containing such a plot. Plural *fabulae duplices*. (Stuart DRAMATIC 143)

fabulae satyricae (Latin Roman)   Perhaps, Atellan plays. Bieber believes that after the Atellan plays had been rewritten from Oscan into Latin and had replaced the *fabula satura* and satyr play as concluding pieces, they may have been called *fabulae satyricae*. See also: *fabula Atellana*. (Bieber HISTORY 148)

fabula palliata (Latin Roman)   A Latin comedy on a Greek subject. Not merely subjects, but characters and costumes were modeled after Greek New Comedy. Probably created in the 3rd C BC, the form lasted about 200 years. The extant plays of Plautus and Terence are *fabulae palliatae*. *Palliata* is from *pallium*, the Latin word for the Greek cloak (*himation*). Also called *palliata* or *crepidata*. (Beare ROMAN 264–266; Bieber HISTORY 92, 149, 154.

fabula praetexta (Latin Roman)   In early Christian times, a modified form of tragedy written in Latin on a Roman subject. Usually historical, *praetextae* may have been performed in conjunction with Roman triumphs or funeral processions. The name is from the striped, purple toga of the patricians, the *toga praetexta*, worn by the actors. Plural *fabulae praetextae*. Also called *praetexta*. (Beare ROMAN 41–44, 235–236, 264; Bieber HISTORY 149, 156)

fabula Rhinthonica (Latin Roman)   The literary *hilarotragodia* (burlesque tragedy). From Rhinthon of Tarentum (3rd C BC), believed to have been the first to give literary form to these plays. Also called *Rhinthonica*. (Beare ROMAN 25, Bieber HISTORY 131, 146, 151)

fabula riciniata (Latin Roman)   The mime. The term derives from the *ricinium* (or *recinium*) worn by the actors. This is described by Beare as ''apparently a square hood which could either be thrown back or drawn forward so as to conceal the head....'' Plural *fabulae riciniatae*. See also: mime. (Beare ROMAN 153)

fabula saltica (Latin Roman)   1. From late in the 1st C BC, the script of a form of pantomime in which a solo actor-dancer was supported by an orchestra and chorus. The performer used masks in presenting a variety of characters. 2. The performance itself. The term is sometimes used as a synonym for the Roman pantomime. *Saltica* is related to *salto*, to dance, especially with the gestures of pantomime. (Bieber HISTORY 236, Allen ANTIQUITIES 28)

fabula satura (Latin Roman)   A loosely-constructed comic entertainment of early Roman times combining dance, music, pantomime, and dialogue. The earliest known stage in Rome, a temporary one, was built for these plays, first performed in the Circus Maximus before the middle of the 4th C BC. Like the Greek satyr play, the *fabula satura*, also called *satura*, served for a time as an afterpiece to tragedy. Latin *satura*, literally 'mixture, medley,' was used in various contexts, e.g., of a dish of mixed fruit or a collection of poems. Modern scholars doubt that there was ever a Roman dramatic form called *satura*; the word was merely a description of an entertainment which probably contained various types of meter, music, and dance. (Beare ROMAN 16–19, 231; Duckworth NATURE 5–7, 8–10; Bieber HISTORY 148)

fabula tabernaria (Latin Roman)   See: *fabula togata.*

fabula togata (Latin Roman)   From the late 2nd or early 1st C BC, a type of Latin comedy modeled on Greek New Comedy but treating an everyday Roman subject. Both the *fabula togata* and the *fabula tabernaria* refer to native Latin comedy. Some think the terms synonymous, while Bieber and others believe the *tabernaria* dealt with lower class life and grew out of the *togata*; note that *taberna* usually means a tavern, or a shed or stall where something is sold. Since the Romans regularly named their plays for the characteristic dress of the performers, the likelihood is that the *tabernariae* showed few or no togas. Plurals *fabulae togatae* and *fabulae tabernariae*. Also called *togata* or *tabernaria*. (Beare ROMAN 264, 266; Duckworth NATURE 68; Bieber HISTORY 160)

(the) fabulous invalid   The theatre; which seems to maintain strong, pulsing life despite chronic indispositions. (Bowman/Ball THEATRE)

facade   See: *scaenae frons.*

facchino (Italian)   Literally: porter. A rough servant type in *commedia dell'arte*. (Lea ITALIAN I 61)

face   A mask. So used as early as the 16th C. In the plural, a Directoire-period dandy's flat hair locks framing the face. (Boucher FASHION)

face (French)   Forestage. (Moynet FRENCH 25)

face lace   A false beard.

face-showing performance   See: *kaomise kogyo.*

fa ch'ü (Chinese)   See: *faqu.*

(the) factory   To a performer, the theatre.

fade   1. To decrease light by dimming gradually, sometimes imperceptibly. 2. Sometimes, to increase or decrease gradually. (Bowman MODERN)

fade in   To increase the amount of light or sound gradually, sometimes imperceptibly. (Lounsbury THEATRE, Wehlburg GLOSSARY)

fadeout   A gradual and complete reduction in light or sound. (Bowman/Ball THEATRE)

fade out   To decrease light or sound gradually and completely. (Lounsbury THEATRE)

fader   In many modern dimming systems, a device which controls the current to one or more groups of dimmers, i.e., presets. In a typical arrangement, a fader will dim down one preset as it dims up another. The term came into stage lighting from sound systems. (Bellman LIGHTING 220, Wehlburg GLOSSARY, Bentham ART)

fade rate   In stage lighting, the speed at which brightness is increased or decreased.

fader wheel   See: manual takeover.

fahrbahre Scheinwerferbrücken (German)   Literally: transportable spotlight bridges. Movable enclosures which permit unusual positions for projectors. (Fuchs LIGHTING 211)

failli (French)   Literally: failed. In ballet, a step done on one count, involving a leap and a turn in the air. (Grant TECHNICAL, Wilson BALLET)

faincte (French)   1. An invented allegorical character, as opposed to one drawn from life. (De la Taille in Clark/Popkin EUROPEAN 56) 2. A medieval special effect. (Mantzius HISTORY II 75)

fair copy   Especially in Elizabethan times, a clean, usually final manuscript of a play. By contrast, foul papers are earlier messier drafts, often by the playwright.

faire les tiroirs (French)   In ballet, to cross and then recross the stage. Performed by two or more lines of dancers opposite each other. (Kersley/Sinclair BALLET)

fair theatre   See: booth stage.

fairy godfather   A theatrical sponsor or backer.

fake   1. An old term for a complimentary ticket. 2. To cover a mistake by improvising lines or business. 3. To omit lines or business or execute business in less time than would be required in real life. 4. To convey the impression of doing something without actually doing it. (Cartmell HANDBOOK, Dolman ACTING, Bowman/Ball THEATRE)

fake a curtain   To force an encore or take an unmerited curtain call. (Berrey/Van den Bark SLANG 591)

fake map   A mask. (Berrey/Van den Bark SLANG 579)

fake up   To make up.

falbalas   See: furbelows.

faldetta   See: huke.

fal-fals   See: furbelows.

Fallen (German)   Joseph Furttenbach's 17th C term for a trap door. (Furttenbach in Hewitt RENAISSANCE 228)

falling action   Dramatic action directly following a climax. (Bowman/Ball THEATRE)

falling band   A white lawn collar with a lace edge. Much worn by the subjects of painter Anthony Van Dyck (16th–17th C). Also called a Van Dyck. See also: rabat(o). (Wilcox DICTIONARY)

falling flap   Especially in the 18th and 19th C, a hinged flat, painted on both sides, whose upper half showed a new scene when dropped over its lower half. (Bowman/Ball THEATRE)

falling ruff   During the reign of Henry IV, an unstarched ruff which fell in tiers on the shoulders. Also called a *fraise à la confusion* (French). (Boucher FASHION).

fall-recovery   In modern dance, the synthesis which comes from the inter-relation of body balance and unbalance; the move away from and return to center. From the Humphrey-Weidman technique. (Love DANCE 35)

Fally Markus   In vaudeville, a date on which performers tried out new material. (Fally Markus was a small-time theatre booker who paid low salaries.) (Wilmeth LANGUAGE)

false blackout   A brief blackout within a scene, usually to denote the passage of time. The term is rare. (Stern MANAGEMENT)

false calves   See: symmetricals.

false gown   An 18th C fashion (borrowed from little girls) with a tight bodice, gathered skirt, and ribbon belt. So called because it was in one piece rather than having an overgown and a petticoat. (Boucher FASHION)

false masque   See: antimasque.

false proscenium   See: inner proscenium.

false sleeve   A 14th C panel sewn to a sleeve, often falling to the ankle. (Boucher FASHION)

false stage   A stage built above the actual stage. (Bowman/Ball THEATRE)

Familienkatastrophe (German)   Family tragedy. Popular in Germany in the last half of the 19th C with the rise of naturalism. (Sobel NEW)

family box   A box for family parties. (Bowman/Ball THEATRE)

family circle   Formerly a seating area in a balcony, in some theatres the topmost gallery. In Britain, the seating area behind or above the dress circle. (Bowman/Ball THEATRE)

family pass, family ticket   A free admission pass for an entire family. (Granville DICTIONARY)

family reunion   In 19th C Russia, a gathering at which amateur theatrical entertainments were presented. Also called a dramatic evening. (Brockett HISTORY 532)

family theatre, family play, family production   A play which appeals to a wide range of ages, from elementary school children to adults. *Peter Pan* is an example. (Goldberg CHILDREN'S 109–110, 144–146)

family ticket   See: family pass.

family time   In vaudeville, a theatre where performances were given three or more times a day. See also: continuous vaudeville. (Carrington THEATRICANA)

fan and deluge system   A fire safety system that eliminates a fire curtain and uses instead a deluge water curtain at the proscenium opening and a powerful fan system to remove smoke.

fanchon (French)   See: capote.

fan dance   A dance in which an exotic dancer teasingly uses two large ostrich plumes to conceal and reveal her body. Hence, fan dancer, fanner. Popularized by Sally Rand at the Chicago World's Fair in 1933. Bubbles were sometimes also used. (Wilmeth LANGUAGE)

fandiao (Chinese)   See: *fandiaoshi.*

fandiaoshi, fan tiao shih (Chinese)   Literally: inverse mode. In Beijing opera (*jingju*), the generic name for modes (*diaoshi*) which are based upon principal modes (*zheng diaoshi*) but are pitched a fourth higher, and often sung at a somewhat slower tempo. They are considered more tragic than their respective principal modes, and have fewer associated metrical-types (*banshi*). Beijing opera includes three inverse modes: *fanxipi* or *fan hsi p'i, fanerhuang* or *fan erh huang,* and *fansipingdiao* or *fan ssu p'ing tiao.* Often referred to simply as *fandiao* or *fan tiao.* (Scott CLASSICAL 51; Wichmann "Aural" 228–236, 244)

fan effect   In the past, a sudden scene-changing device achieved by a segmented back scene which collapsed like two folding fans. (Bowman/Ball THEATRE)

fanerhuang, fan erh huang (Chinese)   See: *fandiaoshi.*

fanfare   1. A flourish of trumpets. 2. Theatrical news.

fan hsi p'i (Chinese)   See: *fandiaoshi.*

fanner   A fan dancer.

fanny shaker, fanny wobbler   A hip dancer.

fansipingdiao, fan ssu p'ing tiao (Chinese)   See: *fandiaoshi.*

Fantasiestück (German)   See: *Phantasiestück.*

fantastic realism   A feature of Eugene Vakhtangov's theatre c. 1920 in Russia. The performer was required to work for truth of emotions but to bring them to the audience in augmented, exaggerated form. (Slonim RUSSIAN 266–267)

fantasy   A play unrestricted by literal and realistic theatrical inventions; a romantic representation of the unlikely, the whimsical, and the grotesque. (Stern MANAGEMENT, O'Hara/Bro INVITATION)

fantasy makeup   Makeup which transforms a human face into that of an animal, gnome, monster, etc.

fantesca (Italian)   See: *servetta.*

fan tiao, fan tiao shih (Chinese)   See: *fandiaoshi*.

fantoccini, *fantoccini* (Italian)   1. Figures manipulated by means of hidden strings or wires attached to machinery. Usually associated with trick puppets. 2. Shows which employ this type of puppet. (Bowman/Ball THEATRE, Philpott DICTIONARY)

fanxipi (Chinese)   See: *fandiaoshi*.

fa pu (Chinese)   See: *faqu*.

faqu, fa ch'ü (Chinese)   Literally: dharma song. A kind of song accompanied by small and large cymbals (*naobo*), bells, chimestones, vertical bamboo flutes (*xiao*), and lutes (*pipa*). Originally used in Buddhist ceremonies, such songs developed out of the combination of indigenous and Central Asian music and instruments during the 4th–6th C and reached their zenith in the 7th-10th C when they were taught in the Pear Garden (Liyuan). Originally called *fayue* or *fa yüeh*; later called *fabu* or *fa pu*. (Dolby HISTORY 11, 20–21)

farándula (Spanish)   A 17th C strolling troupe next in size to a full company, consisting of a number of men and three women. Now, strolling players generally; the acting profession. (Villandrando in Nagler SOURCES 59)

Farbscheiben (German)   Color media. Among other German terms used for 'color medium' (singular) are *Farbfilter* 2nd *Filter-Scheibe*. (Fuchs LIGHTING 370, Band-Kuzmany GLOSSARY 17, Luterkort THEATRE 24)

farce   Fast-paced, broad comedy written to excite laughter, often with little regard for logic in plot or depth of characterization, but with plenty of physical action, notably mishaps, surprises, and reversals.

farce (French)   A farce. The word has been used in many combinations, including the *farce de bande* (farce for a regular company), the *farce de collège* (school farce), and the *farce de noces* (wedding farce). Medieval spellings include *farsse* and *farse*. (Frank MEDIEVAL 150, 250)

farce à un personnage   A farcical monologue. (Frank MEDIEVAL 246–247)

farce-comedy   A dramatic form mingling comedy characters and farcical situations. (O'Hara/Bro INVITATION)

farcette   A short farcical sketch, as in a revue. (Granville DICTIONARY) In 19th C Britain, farcetta. (Bowman/Ball THEATRE)

farceur (French), **farceur**   A farce author or actor.

farceuse (French)   A farce actress.

farcir (French)   Literally: to stuff. In the 14th C, to pack comic sequences into the heavily sermonized plots of the drama of the time. Hence, farce, from this practice. (Gassner/Quinn ENCYCLOPEDIA 282)

farsa (Latin)   See: *cum farsura*.

farsa (Italian)   In medieval times, a play.

farsa (Spanish)   Originally, a play. In the 19th C the term acquired its generic connotation of a farce.

farse, farsse (French)   See: *farce*.

farthingale   16th–17th C stuffed rolls formed into hoops, one resting on each hip. Worn under petticoats to hold outer skirts away from the body. Also called a Catherine wheel, guard-infanta, hoop, verdingale, vertugadin. See also: pannier, patent tilter. (Barton COSTUME 225, Boucher FASHION, Wilcox DICTIONARY)

fascia   Especially in Australia, a covering for the face or sides of steps or platforms, to conceal the construction. (National TECHNICAL)

Fassung (German)   Socket, lamp holder. Plural *-en*. (Fuchs LIGHTING 367, Rae/Southern INTERNATIONAL 50)

fast curtain, quick curtain.   A curtain lowered or closed quickly at the end of an act or scene.

Fastl (Turkish)   A series of episodes comprising the plot of a Turkish shadow puppet play. (Gassner/Quinn ENCYCLOPEDIA 865)

Fastnachtspiel (German)   Literally: Shrovetide play. A ribald secular play popular at German fairs in the 1500s; a carnival play.

fat   1. Said of effective stage business or lines. 2. Said of a role with good acting opportunities.

fate tragedy   See: *Schicksalstragödie*.

fatten up   To enrich a role.

fauteuil (French)   Literally: armchair. In a British theatre, a seat with arms, usually in the front of the stalls. (Bowman/Ball THEATRE)

fautores (Latin Roman)   A claque. Plural of *fautor*: supporter, one who favors. Also called *theatrales operae*. (Sandys COMPANION 520)

faux bon rôle (French)   A false good part; a part in a play which appears to be meaty and effective but is neither. Ordinarily there is a trickiness about the character which the audience recognizes as not ringing true. (Hamilton THEORY 116)

faux chassis (French)   See: *chassis*.

favola in musica (Italiana)   Literally: musical fable. An early term for opera.

favola pastorale (Italian)   An Italian Renaissance pastoral play whose theme came from classical mythological poetry. A forerunner of opera. (Gassner/Quinn ENCYCLOPEDIA 477)

fayue, fa yüeh (Chinese)   See: *faqu*.

Feast of Fools   A medieval village festival in which the lower orders of the clergy made fun of the upper orders. In Latin: *festum stultorum*. In French, *Fête des fous*.

Feast of Misrule   A medieval parody on chuch ritual, led by a mock bishop. (Arnott FRENCH 147)

Feast of the Ass   A medieval festival burlesquing religious ceremonies with comedy, satire, and homely realism. (Cole/Chinoy ACTING 35)

Feast of the Boy Bishop   A medieval village festival in which a boy was made a kind of king for a day, and elders were mocked. Performed by choir boys, but outside the church.

feather dusting   A painting technique using a feather duster, to produce a mottled effect. (Buerki STAGECRAFT)

feather-dusting scene   An expository scene at the beginning of old dramas, usually involving two servants ("below stairs" employees) talking about their employers while dusting furniture. Also called a below-stairs scene. (McGraw-Hill ENCYCLOPEDIA V 221)

featherman   An 18th C theatre employee responsible for a company's collection of plumes, which were standard features on the helmets of tragic heroes. See also: heroic feathers. (Stone LONDON 817)

feature   To give a performer a billing second only to that of the star of a show, though the term feature player is sometimes used to describe a performer who appears only in starring roles. Hence, featured performer, featured player, featuring, etc. (Bowman/Ball THEATRE, Purdom PRODUCING)

featurette   A short act in a variety show or vaudeville.

Federal Theatre Project   A U.S. government-supported theatre project in the 1930s, designed to put unemployed theatre people to work and encourage regional theatre. Often referred to simply as the Federal Theatre.

feed   1. To play up to the leading performer in a scene, especially in comedy, where the straight man feeds lines to the leading comedian. 2. The straight man who feeds such lines. Hence, feeder. 3. The part of a feeder. 4. The line delivered by the feeder. 5. To prompt. (Bowman/Ball THEATRE, Purdom PRODUCING) 6. A standard electrical term for a conductor which carries potential, i.e., which comes from a source of electricity. Also called a feed line.

feeder   1. A straight man in a comic duo. 2. See: feeder cable.

feeder cable, feed cable, feeder   A heavy cable which connects a switchboard to a main source of electrical supply. (Wehlburg GLOSSARY, Bowman MODERN)

feeder line   Cue line.

feed line   See: feed.

feel   1. To be emotionally affected by performing before an audience, as in feeling the audience. 2. To bury oneself in a role, to feel a part. 3. To test the tautness of a rope line above the tie-off rail. (Bowman/Ball THEATRE)

feel a draft   Especially in show business, to feel unwelcome. Originally the phrase meant to feel racial prejudice. (Lees "Lexicon" 57)

feel of the house   A performer's perception of the sympathetic impact (or the lack of it) his or her performance is generating in the audience. (Granville DICTIONARY)

feel the part   To act by imagining oneself as the character. (Berrey/Van den Bark SLANG 587)

féerie (French)   A fairy tale play.

feintes, feyntes (French)   A medieval term, variously spelled, for stage machines or tricks. Also called *secrets* or *ingegni* (Italian). See also: *truc*. (Mantzius HISTORY II 73, 339)

feirdig soubrettin (Yiddish)   A fiery soubrette. (Picon/Grillo MOLLY 24)

female, female connector   See: line connector.

female heavy   1. An actress specializing in powerful, dominant, sometimes villainous roles. 2. Such a role.

female impersonator   A male who plays the part of a woman. The term refers chiefly to night-club acts and early 20th C plays rather than to the boy actors of Elizabethan times or the male specialists in female characters (*onnagata*) in the *kabuki* theatre in Japan and (*nandan*) in Chinese music-drama.

female plug   See: line connector.

férie (French)   A spectacular stage presentation characterized by showy scenery, furnishings, and parades. Also called a Christmas pantomime. (Hennequin PLAYWRITING 49)

ferme (French)   1. A shutter. 2. The backscene. (Gassner/Allen THEATRE I 402; Moynet FRENCH 24, 41, 43)

fermé (French)   Literally: closed. In ballet, the closing of a dancer's feet, either both together or one foot to the other. (Kersley/Sinclair BALLET)

ferme Américaine (French)   A 19th C specially-rigged set of lines used in staging glories. (Moynet FRENCH 56)

Ferris waist   A late 19th C blouse made without bones. It gave the wearer a somewhat shapeless look. (Chalmers CLOTHES 248)

ferris wheel   A late 19th C continuous performance. (Zellers PASTOR 96)

ferronière (French)   A small jewel attached to a chain and worn in the middle of the forehead. See also: frontlet. (Boucher FASHION)

Fescennine verses   About the 5th C BC, primitive pre-dramatic exchanges in verse, probably often obscene. The Fescennines, which occurred at wedding and harvest celebrations, are thought not to have been dramatic for some time. Beare says, "In the Fescennine verses, the bantering dialogue of clowns at the harvest-home, the Romans found the germ of their own drama." Ancient writers said the name came from Fescennium, the Etruscan town where the verses were believed to have begun, or from the Latin Roman *fascinum* (enchantment, witchcraft); it was thought the ribaldry warded off the witchcraft. Modern scholarship favors Fescennium as the source, but Beare finds the other interesting. Also called *versus Fescennini* (Latin), Fescennines (occasionally). (Beare ROMAN 11–16, Duckworth NATURE 7–8)

festa (Italian)   A medieval mystery play. (Mantzius HISTORY II 2)

festaiolo (Italian)   1. Master of the Revels, a reveller. 2. In medieval times, the leader of a troupe of performers. (Roberts STAGE)

festival theatre   1. In Africa, a communal celebration which contains a reenactment of a familiar story about a mythical, legendary, or historical figure or event. The performance involves masquerade performers, chiefs, priests, and citizens. The dramatic conflict occurs in a series of episodes using improvisation and audience participation in dance, music, ritual, dialogue, and games in sketches. An example is the *Play of Moremi* in the Edi festival in Nigeria. (Adedeji glossary) 2. A theatre devoted to the production of opera or classical plays, such as the Bayreuth (Wagner) opera house or the Shakespeare Memorial Theatre at Stratford-upon-Avon. (Granville DICTIONARY)

festoon   1. A hanging border of cords, flowers, leaves, etc. Also called a festoon border. 2. A curtain that can be looped up to hang in folds. Also called a French or contour curtain. 3. To loop a curtain or other fabric in folds. 4. Strings of lights hung in loops for decoration. (Corry PLANNING, Baker THEATRECRAFT)

Festspielhaus (German)   A theatre devoted especially to the performance of operas such as those of Wolfgang Amadeus Mozart or Richard Wagner. See also: festival theatre. (Granville DICTIONARY)

festum stultorum (Latin)   See: Feast of Fools.

Fête des fous (French)   See: Feast of Fools.

feu(x) (French)   1. In the 19th C, a candle made of tallow, used to light dressing rooms. 2. Metaphorically, money received over and above the salary of a performer. (Moynet FRENCH 155)

(à) feuilles, (à) feuillets (French)   Two-fold or doubled, when referring to a pair of stage wings. (Visser "Garrick's" 109)

Fev   Abbreviation for French enamel varnish. (Parker/Smith DESIGN)

fiaba (Italian)   Literally: a fable, fairy tale, fib, story. Satiric fairy tales written by Carlo Gozzi for *commedia dell'arte* performers in the 18th C, though the term had been in use for centuries. (Brockett HISTORY 364)

ficelle (French)   1. A 19th C manipulative device, usually in a fairy play, used as a way to rescue heroes so that persecuted innocence could triumph. 2. A stage trick. (Moynet FRENCH 158)

field angle   Especially in describing spotlight performance, the angle within which the beam produces 10% or more of its maximum intensity.

field diameter   Especially in describing spotlight performance, the diameter of the beam at a stated distance from the spotlight. The beam diameter depends in part on the distance of the light source from the lens; in some spotlights, this distance is adjustable.

field music   See: *dengaku.*

fiery furnace show   In Russia from the 16th to the 18th C, the presentation before Christmas in church of the story of Nebuchadnezzar casting the Israelite men into the fiery furnace. (Varneke RUSSIAN 10–11)

fifteen minutes   A warning call to performers before the beginning of an act or scene. In Britain: quarter of an hour.

fifth business   1. In old repertory companies, a minor role essential to the plot. 2. By extension, the performer given such a role. (Davies FIFTH [iii])

fifth business man, fifth business woman   A utility actor or actress.

fifth position   In dance, the crossing of the feet inward so that the heel of one foot touches the toe of the other. (Rogers DANCE 259)

fig-branch   Possibly a twitting or otherwise comic name for the Greek *mechane*. Compare *krade*, whose literal meaning is fig-branch. Also spelled Fig-branch. (Haigh ATTIC 210)

figurant, figurante (French)   1. A male/female dancer who performs in a group. 2. A performer who plays a role with no lines, a supernumerary. (Bowman/Ball THEATRE) See also: *marcheur.*

figure   A string puppet.

figurer (French)   To play an extra, especially a non-speaking role.

filament image   A sharply focused reproduction on the setting of a spotlight's hot wire source (lamp filament). (Lounsbury THEATRE, Wehlburg GLOSSARY)

fill   1. To improvise lines or business in order to cover a mistake in a performance. (Cartmell HANDBOOK) 2. See: fill light.

fillet   In Britain, a segment of the stage floor between cuts. (Bowman/Ball THEATRE)

fill-in-date   A performance by a road company to take up the slack on unbooked days. (Granville DICTIONARY)

filling   See: slider.

filling-station town   See: tank.

fill light   Light which softens the shadows created by strongly directional lighting. The term comes from photography. Also called a base light or fill. See also: key light. (Bellman LIGHTING 327–329, Bellman SCENE, Wehlburg GLOSSARY)

filter   See: color medium.

filter frame   A color frame. (Baker THEATRECRAFT)

filter holder   A color frame. (Bowman/Ball THEATRE)

final   The last place on a variety bill.

final bends   Bows to the audience at the end of a show.

finale   The conclusion of a show—the last scene or final number, especially in a musical theatre work.

finale bend   Old term for a curtain call at the end of a show.

finaletto   In a musical play, the ending of Act I. (Bowman/Ball THEATRE)

fin de fiesta (Spanish)   A playlet presented after a mainpiece to round off an entertainment. (Shergold SPANISH)

fine-box   In Britain, a stage manager's container for collecting assessments from performers guilty of breach of theatre discipline. Also called a forfeit-box. (Granville DICTIONARY)

finesse   In 18th C acting, supplemental byplay. (Stone/Kahrl GARRICK 563)

finger flash   A flash effect produced by rubbing collodion paper. (Bowman/Ball THEATRE)

finger plays   Short chants, rhymes, or songs acted out by children as they recite them. "Itsy Bitsy Spider" is a favorite example. (Heinig/Stillwell CREATIVE 23)

fingerposting   See: foreshadowing.

finger puppet   A small puppet which fits on or around a finger. Small animals or tiny people are usually portrayed.

finger wringer   A performer who acts emotionally.

firdöndü (Turkish)   Literally: swivel. In the shadow theatre, a device which permits the operator to flip a puppet so that it turns 180°. (And KARAGÖZ 31)

fire a trap   To put a trap mechanism in motion. (Bowman/Ball THEATRE)

fire box   In the 19th C, an iron container for colored fire. Used for stage conflagrations, fire boxes varied in size and shape; the inside, in which the fire powder was sometimes spread loosely, may often have been white to increase reflection. (Rees GAS 151)

fire curtain   A fireproof safety curtain made of asbestos on a fine metal mesh, or sometimes of iron or steel. It is located in front of the theatre's main curtain and is designed to close the proscenium opening automatically in case of fire. Also called the asbestos, asbestos curtain, asbestos drop, fireproof curtain, green curtain, iron, iron curtain, safety curtain. (Krows AMERICA 82, Burris-Meyer/Cole SCENERY 279–281)

fire curtain safety release line   A formal term for a rope that secures an asbestos curtain in the raised position. It is fitted with a fusible link which will melt in case of fire, releasing the rope and lowering the asbestos. Also called the asbestos curtain safety release line, cut line, emergency rope.

fire exit   Any auditorium door through which members of an audience may escape in case of fire. Also called an escape door. In Britain: emergency door. (Bowman/Ball THEATRE)

fireman drama   In the 19th C U.S., popular drama dealing with the activities of volunteer firemen, especially Mose the "firebouy." (Wilmeth LANGUAGE)

fireplace backing   A small scenic unit, usually a three-fold, set behind a fireplace opening in a flat.

fireplace flat   A flat with an opening for a fireplace.

fireplace unit   A three-dimensional unit of scenic materials imitating a fireplace, including the mantel. It may be free-standing or made to fit into the opening in a fireplace flat.

fireproof curtain   See: fire curtain.

fire screen   In the 19th C, a large fan used by women. (Walkup DRESSING 314)

firing step   In Britain, a platform in the flies for storing slack ropes. (Bowman/Ball THEATRE)

first   In stage equipment numbered in relation to the proscenium, the piece which is furthest downstage. Hence, first pipe, first border, first electric, etc., the next being second, third, etc. No. 1, No. 2, etc. are primarily British.

first account   The money taken in at 18th C theatres for full-price tickets, that is, money received up to the end of the third act of the mainpiece. That income was entered in the books; after the third act, half price was charged, and that income was entered on the second account. (Hogan LONDON xxxix)

first act   A warning call to performers about five minutes before curtain time. See also: overture.

first balcony   In the U.S., the first seating area above the auditorium floor, unless there is an intervening mezzanine. In Britain, usually dress circle. 'First' balcony implies one or more above it.

first billing   The advertising given to a star, usually a listing before the title of the production, such as: Laurence Olivier in *Hamlet*.

first border, first borderlight, second border, etc.   See: border, borderlight.

first circle   The uppermost seating area, above the dress or royal circle in British (and formerly in U.S.) theatres. The term is rarely used today. (Bowman/Ball THEATRE)

first day man   In Britain, a theatre employee who works during the day as the chief assistant to a department head, such as the stage carpenter, the property master, the electrician, etc. (Fay GLOSSARY)

first door   The place where Restoration playgoers received their tickets. From that point, they went to the door leading to that section of the theatre (the pit, the gallery, etc.) for which they had paid. There a doorkeeper would take their ticket. (Van Lennep LONDON lxxii)

first electric   The light pipe furthest downstage. Sometimes called the first pipe or teaser batten. (Rubin/Watson LIGHTING 30)

first entrance   1. The furthest downstage entrance to the stage. See also: in one. 2. A performer's first appearance on stage. (Bowman/Ball THEATRE)

first flies   Especially in 18th C theatres, the lower of two or more fly floors or backstage galleries at the sides of the stage, from which flown scenic units or machines were operated. (Public Record Office C 11/2662/1)

first gallery, second gallery, etc.   See: gallery.

first groove, second groove, etc.   Designations in old theatres for the grooves parallel to the front of the stage in which wings and shutters slid. In effect, the grooves divided the stage into planes, the first groove and plane being nearest the footlights. The entranceways between the grooves took their number from the grooves—presumably the grooves upstage of the entrance. (Hogan LONDON lvii)

firstie   A minstrel-show novice. (Wilmeth LANGUAGE)

first man, first woman   Principal singers in 18th C and later theatrical companies. (Hogan LONDON ci)

first-money guarantee   A producer's assurance that the expenses of the theatre owner will be met before gate and ticket presale receipts are distributed to other creditors. (Bowman/Ball THEATRE)

first music   In Restoration and 18th C British theatres, the first of three sets of tunes played before the beginning of a performance.

first night   The opening performance of a production. Hence, first nighter— one who attends an opening, or one who attends openings frequently.

first-night list   A record of those who will receive free admission passes for an opening night performance.

first-night wreckers   In late 19th C Britain, gangs of hoodlums who came to first-night performances with the intention of rattling the performers by heckling and cat calling. (Granville DICTIONARY)

first of May   Said of an amateur performer. The hidden meaning is sap. (Berrey/Van den Bark SLANG 571)

first old man, first old woman   Especially in the past, the most important elderly characters in a play calling for more than one. (Hennequin PLAY-WRITING 76)

first-part ladies   Female minstrels who opened early variety shows, sitting in the ensemble; later they sold drinks to spectators in the boxes. (Wilmeth LANGUAGE).

first pipe, second pipe, etc.   Hanging pipes (battens) numbered from downstage to upstage, to which are attached borders, scenic elements, or lighting instruments. See also: first electric.

first position   In dance, the placement of the feet outward in a line, heels touching.

first spot   The first act on a bill.

first whistle, second whistle, etc.   In Restoration theatres and later, a signal to scene shifters to prepare for a change; a whistle was blown at the shift. The second whistle signalled the second change in the act.

fish   1. A poor show. 2. Slang for a theatre patron.

fish and chip tour   In Britain, a tour which offers just enough salary for a performer to eat fish and chips, and not much else. Also called a Woolworth circuit. (Granville DICTIONARY)

fish face   A performer who maintains an expressionless face.

fishing   Said of a performer struggling to remember his lines.

fish puppet   See: glove puppet.

fishtail burner   In the 19th C, a gas outlet in which two jets met each other so that the resulting flame resembled a fish tail. In the theatre, the fishtail is known to have been used in footlights and wing lights. In the U.S., also called a union jet or union burner. (Rees GAS 13, 14, 34)

fitch   A small brush used in scene painting, varying in width from 1/4'' to 1/2''.

fitting   1. In Britain, an apparent light source in a setting. Examples include a table lamp or wall bracket. (Bentham ART 241–245, 248–249; Fay GLOSSARY) 2. See: costume fitting.

fit-up   In Britain: 1. A temporary stage and its equipment, formerly often carried by touring companies. Hence, fit-up theatre, fit-up stage. See also: booth stage. 2. A company using such a stage. (Bowman/Ball THEATRE) 3. In the plural, small touring engagements of one to three nights. See also: one-night stand. In the U.S., hideaway.

fit-up tour   In Britain, a tour using a temporary or fit-up stage.

"Five minutes!"   A warning to performers five minutes before curtain. Sometimes defined as an act call and often elongated to "Five minutes to curtain!"

five-scene preset   See: preset.

fixed board   A built-in light board which usually controls little more than the auditorium lights. The term has been used as an equivalent of house board. (McCandless "Glossary" 637)

fixed focus light   A stage lighting instrument which cannot be focused. The term is used of such fixtures as a beam projector or a PAR lamp. (Lounsbury THEATRE 94–95)

fixed grooves   In 18th C theatres, permanent channels in which wings or shutters slid. See also: loose grooves. (Southern CHANGEABLE 245)

fixed points   In a dance practice room or on a stage, the corners and the centers of each side of the area, numbered to help a dancer keep a sense of direction. (Grant TECHNICAL)

fixer   A booking agent.

fixing iron   See: hanger iron.

fixture   A lighting instrument, a luminaire. The term is from industry and is used by experienced theatre technicians primarily when dealing with industry, as when discussing rentals or purchases. The word is probably an example of an established general term (e.g., for wall brackets) which has crept into theatre use because the manufacturers of household fixtures began to manufacture stage lighting "fixtures." The general use of the word may, indeed, go back to 19th C gas lighting fixtures. See also: lighting instrument. (Wehlburg GLOSSARY, Bellman LIGHTING 163)

fizzer   In Britain, a production or performance certain to succeed.

flack   See: press agent.

flag   1. A curtain. 2. A small piece of cloth attached to the operating line in a counterweight system, to serve as a trim mark or a warning. (Stern MANAGEMENT, Parker/Smith DESIGN) Occasionally in the U.S.: 3. A cutoff placed in front of a lighting instrument to mask spill light. The term is apparently from film and TV and the name from its frequently rectangular shape. (Gobo, q.v., has been widely used in these media for this meaning but may be going out of use there; the reason perhaps lies in the widespread theatre use of gobo in another meaning.) 4. To swing a hand in front of (for example) a spotlight lens, so that the area covered by the light can be seen.

flag waver   A performer who seeks easy applause with something other than talent.

flaming arc   See: arc light.

flamme de Bengale (French)   See: Bengal fire.

flandan   See: pinner.

flannel mouth   In vaudeville and burlesque: 1. A straight man with false teeth. 2. A performer (straight man) who feeds lines to a comic. 3. A performer who is mushy-mouthed because of drinking too much. (Wilmeth LANGUAGE)

flap   1. A hinged cover for a long, narrow, upstage opening in a stage floor. 2. The opening itself, named for its cover. In 19th C theatres, flat scenes were raised through the opening. Also called a cut. See also: slider. 3. In 18th C theatres, a hinged portion of an auditorium bench. Since there were no aisles within the seating area, and since the benches were backless, the lift-up flap provided a bit of temporary aisle and access to the bench behind; when lowered, the flap was part of the bench and provided extra seating. 4. See: falling flap. (Southern CHANGEABLE 284; Hogan LONDON xlix; Leacroft DEVELOPMENT 144, 197, figs. 93, 121; Leacroft/Leacroft THEATRE 40)

flare   In Britain, to place and regulate sound and light apparatus. (Bowman/Ball THEATRE)

flash.   1. A star performer. 2. A showy or well-dressed performer. 3. An act that has a good appearance. 4. A featured attraction. 5. The collection of all performers for a closing number. 6. In striptease, to uncover any part of the body briefly. (Wilmeth LANGUAGE, Berrey/Van den Bark SLANG 582) 7. In lighting, to switch on and off, as in a lighting designer's direction to "Flash number 16, please." The term is used in checking lights for coverage, blending, and similar characteristics.

flash act   1. In vaudeville, an act consisting of a good single performer backed by a singing and dancing chorus and attractive scenery. A flash act sometimes had its own conductor. 2. A man and woman act with a line of girl (and/or boy) singers and dancers, who have their own limited scenery (only enough to fit in a trunk) and often their own conductor. (Smith VAUDEVILLIANS)

flash back   In vaudeville, a straight man's turn of a comic's laugh into a laugh for himself. (Wilmeth LANGUAGE)

flash box   A device for producing lightning or other flash effects on stage. In a 19th C form, a bellows was fastened to a tin box with a perforated lid on which sat a lighted candle. The flash was produced when the bellows blew lycopodium powder from the box through its lid. Powdered resin or magnesium were sometimes substituted for lycopodium. Also called a flash pot. Sebastiano Serlio's 16th C version (in Nagler SOURCES 80) was similar. (Rees GAS 144, Bax MANAGEMENT 78)

flash buttons   On 19th C gas tables, controls which gave short bursts of flame, as in simulated scenic fires. (Rosenthal/Wertenbaker MAGIC 51–52)

flash effect   Any special effect which provides a flash—using powders, flash-bulbs, strobe lights, etc. (Gillette/Gillette SCENERY)

flasher   In memory lighting systems, a special circuit which, if put into a channel control, causes its dimmer(s) to skip to full or, if at full, to go off. In some arrangements, the channel continues to flash until turned off. Also called a blinker. (Bellman LIGHTING 244)

flashes   Short street theatre plays of the Living Theatre collective in the 1970s. (Ryan "Living" 16)

flash light, flash burner   In the early 20th C in Britain, a system of lighting a number of gas jets by a single faucet-like stopcock at a control center; more specifically, the core of that system. A flash burner for a borderlight (for which the system may have been invented) had three parallel pipes. The lowest pipe had three or four permanently lit pilot lights. The next pipe had a greater number of burners, while the top pipe was the working borderlight. A small turn of the stopcock at the control station admitted gas to the middle pipe, whose burners were then lit by the pilot lights; with a further turn of the stopcock, gas reached the top pipe, whose burners ignited immediately. The middle pipe was the heart of the flash light. (Rees GAS 38, fig. 20; 39, 212, 213)

flash portrait   A picture in front of a theatre. (Berrey/Van den Bark SLANG 594)

flash pot   1. See: flash box. 2. A ceramic or other fireproof pot used for electrically-produced flash or smoke effects. (Lounsbury THEATRE 138, Bowman MODERN)

flash powder   Lycopodium. A smoke powder ignited by passing an electric current through it. (Baker THEATRECRAFT)

flash torch   A 19th C U.S. device used to produce brief bursts of flame in stage fires. (Rees GAS 150)

flat   1. A cloth-covered wooden frame, painted to serve as a scenic unit. A common, standard flat is rectangular, but there are also special units: door flat, fireplace flat, narrow flat (a jog), window flat, etc. 2. In the commercial theatre, the stiffening of two or more hinged wings into a plane or wall. (Parker/Smith DESIGN) 3. When used of lighting: shadowless, producing a two-dimensional effect, as in "The light down left is a little flat." See also: flat lighting. (Goffin LIGHTING 74)

flat cap   See: city flat cap.

flat cleat   See: stop cleat.

flat figure   A two-dimensional puppet which can be manipulated from below the stage with strings or rods, or by horizontal rods from the side. (Speaight PUPPET 22)

flat-flame burner   19th C U.S. gas jets whose flames were flat—the fishtail and the batwing; the contrast is with the Argand burner, sometimes called the round-flame burner. (Penzel LIGHTING 89–92)

flat foot iron   See: foot iron.

flat frame   A basic scenic unit used by Sebastiano Serlio in 1545. The 1611 English edition of Serlio described flats as "spars, or rafters or lathes, covered with linnin cloth." (Serlio in Hewitt RENAISSANCE 26n, 29)

flat lighting   Relatively even, shadowless illumination. In the modern theatre, the term is usually pejorative when used of the lighting of performers and three-dimensional objects. The opposite is plastic lighting.

flat man   See: grip.

flat marking   Stencilled or painted identification marks on the back of a flat to facilitate its being stacked in order of its use onstage or its being packed efficiently while on tour. (Granville DICTIONARY)

flat scene   A pair of shutters—canvas-covered wooden frames—sliding in a cross-stage groove; the shutters could slide onstage, meeting at the center line of the stage to form the prospect. The practice began in the Renaissance. The term was used as early as the late 17th C and in time was shortened to flat. Also (later) called a pair of flats. See also: front scenes. (Southern CHANGEABLE 196, 244–245; Hogan LONDON lvii)

flatted ellipsoidal reflector, flattened ellipsoidal reflector, flatted reflector   An ellipsoidal reflector whose surface consists of many small plane reflectors. The purpose is to smooth the beam produced by the spotlight. (Bellman LIGHTING 62, Wehlburg GLOSSARY)

flat ticket   An individually-printed or computerized ticket, as opposed to roll tickets, which are often used for theatrical performances with unreserved seating.

flat wing   A flat at the side of the stage, usually parallel with the curtain line, serving to mask the offstage area. A series of wings on each side of the stage, with hanging borders above, and shutters or a drop at the back, all painted in perspective, formed the standard wing-and-drop stage settings in proscenium theatres from the Renaissance into the 19th C.

flaw   See: *hamartia*.

flea pit   See: bug hole.

flesh   Live. Hence, flesh actor, flesh show. (Bowman/Ball THEATRE)

flesh diversion   See: leg piece.

fleshings, fleshing tights   Flesh-colored tights, often worn to make a performer appear naked. (Wilmeth LANGUAGE)

flesh peddler   A performer's agent.

flesh show   A performance by live actors.

flex   In Britain: 1. Stage cable, usually with conductors consisting of stranded copper wire. Also called flexible cable, flexible, and stage flex. 2. Any flexible electric cord with conductors of stranded copper wire. Workshop flex is somewhat lighter than stage cable. Domestic twisted flex, often shortened to flex is household electric cord. (Bentham ART, Bowman/Ball THEATRE 137, Rae/Southern INTERNATIONAL)

flexible   1. See: flex. 2. In 19th C Britain, a lighting man's term for a short length of gas tubing. See also: length. (Rees GAS 204)

flexible cable   See: flex.

flexible control   In stage lighting, an arrangement in which some or all lights are not permanently connected to particular circuits. The term is used for installations with very limited flexibility and, at the other extreme, for modern control systems in which any load or combination of loads may be connected to any outlet, so long as the circuit is not overloaded. Hence, flexible control board.

flexible dimmer   Especially in the past, a term for a dimmer which was effective with varying loads. (Bowman/Ball THEATRE, Halstead MANAGEMENT 234)

flexible load cord   See: interconnecting panel.

flexible set   See: unit set.

flexible theatre   A theatre space capable of more than one stage and audience arrangement. See also: adaptable theatre and multiple-use theatre. (Burris-Meyer/Cole THEATRES 135)

flexion   In dance, the bending of a part of the body. (Rogers DANCE 155)

flick   See: efforts.

flickers, flicker (wheel)   See: lobsterscope.

flied   See: flown.

flies   1. In 18th C theatres and later, the fly floors or galleries above and at the sides of the stage. A 1743 inventory of Covent Garden Theatre scenes and machines includes "Flats in the Top Flies. . . " and "Painted pieces in first flies. . . ." Sometimes spelled flys in Britain. (Southern CHANGEABLE 200–201, Bentham ART) 2. The space above the stage between the top of the proscenium arch and the gridiron, where scenery, lighting, and other equipment hangs out of sight of the audience until needed. Also called fly loft, fly space, flying space, hanging loft, hanging space, loft, rigging loft, stage loft, etc. Bowman and Ball define fly loft as the upper part of the flies, and they call the fly space the part of the flies above the acting area. (Bowman/Ball THEATRE, Cornberg/Gebauer CREW, Hewitt/Foster/Wolle PLAY)

flipper   1. In the early 20th C, a scenic unit with an irregular edge extending outward upon the stage from a brace attached to the lower rail of the fly gallery—a cut wing. 2. A narrow flat hinged to a wider flat so that the pair may be set at an angle. 3. A scenic unit or part of the stage floor that can be flipped quickly into position. (Bowman/Ball THEATRE, Krows AMERICA 129) 4. See: flipper shutter.

flipper act   In vaudeville, an act by a man and a trained seal. (Davy "Burns" 347)

flipper shutter, flipper   In lighting, a hinged leaf on barn doors. (Bowman MODERN)

flip puppet   A puppet which can be turned inside out to reveal another puppet character.

flirtation scene   In early 20th C U.S. burlesque, a short, risqué, one-joke scene with a straight man, a comic, and a girl or two. (Allen in Matlaw AMERICAN 46)

flivved   Flopped.

float   1. In Britain, a footlight. Before the use of electricity and gaslight in theatres, light was provided by a wick floating in oil. 2. In Britain, a truck for transporting scenery. 3. A pageant wagon. 4. To lower a flat to the stage floor by holding one's foot against the bottom rail and allowing the air to cushion the flat's fall. 5. To give advance money to a stage manager or other theatre personnel to cover small purchases or other expenses. (Bowman/Ball THEATRE, National TECHNICAL) 6. See: efforts.

floating floor   A floor that is separated from the building structure by resilient mounts.

floating stage   1. A stage in a floating (showboat) theatre. 2. The floating theatre itself. 3. A stage on supports which is moved up and off to a backstage area by a motor, and then replaced by another stage. Similar to a wagon stage. 4. A dance floor. (Bowman/Ball THEATRE)

floating theatre   Any theatre floating on water, such as a showboat. (Bowman/Ball THEATRE)

float lamp   A former light source which consisted of a saucer-like container with a wick in oil floating on water. More sophisticated versions, used in theatres until well after the Renaissance, were the source of the British term float. Sometimes called a floating lamp or floating wick oil lamp.

float spot   Especially in the recent past in Britain, a simple plano-convex spotlight whose lens was three inches in diameter. This was the instrument of choice for use in the float (footlights), and the term is now used similarly: any spotlight small enough to be used in the footlights, as well as any spot used there. (Bentham ART 311, Baker THEATRECRAFT, Bax MANAGEMENT)

flocket   A 16th C old woman's loose, wide-sleeved gown. (Chalmers CLOTHES 160–162)

flog   To beat dust or charcoal or chalk sketch lines from a flat by whipping the flat with a flogger—canvas strips attached to a handle. (Fay GLOSSARY)

flood   1. The usual backstage term for a floodlight. 2. As a verb, to enlarge or 'flood' the beam of a lighting fixture. This use occurs primarily with such spotlights as the Fresnel and the plano-convex; the effect appears when the lamp is moved toward the lens. 'Flood out' has the same meaning. When a lamp is as close to its lens as it can go, it is said to be in flood focus. Moving the lamp is sometimes known as focal adjustment.

flood bar   In Britain, a horizontal pipe containing a number of floodlights. Such a pipe is sometimes used in a borderlight position to light a drop. Sometimes called a flood batten. (Baker THEATRECRAFT)

flood batten   See: flood bar.

flood focus   See: flood.

flood lantern, flooding lantern   British terms for floodlight. (Bowman/Ball THEATRE 139)

floodlight   A lighting unit whose basic components are a high-wattage lamp and a reflective housing with an open front, often with provision for a color frame. The usual shapes are ellipsoidal, and box-like with slanted sides. Flood is the usual backstage term. The form 'flood light' is seen occasionally, mainly in the U.S. through the early decades of the 20th C. See also: scoop. (Corry PLANNING 99)

floodlight projector   One of the names for a beam projector (q.v.). The virtue of this term is that the beam projector, unlike nearly all other projectors, is really a floodlight. (Sellman/Lessley ESSENTIALS 189)

flood out   See: flood.

floor block   A sheave (pulley) in a frame fastened to the floor or weighted. Around the sheave passes an operating line such as that for a traveler curtain. A combination floor block has a sleeve above the block, with a rope lock. See also: take-up block.

floor box   See: floor pocket.

floor cloth   A covering for the stage floor, usually painted and sometimes padded. It can be secured on the downstage edge in a carpet cut and on the other three edges by tacks. The painting on a floor cloth varies according to the requirements of a production; it can be neutral (often a dark brown) or painted to represent a pavement, flooring, grass, etc. Also called a ground cloth or, in Britain, a stage cloth.

floor electrician   Especially in the professional theatre, any member of a lighting crew who works on the stage floor. The term covers both control board and floor equipment personnel.

floor hook   A hook used to fasten guy wires or ropes to the stage floor. (Carrington THEATRICANA)

floor iron   See: sill iron.

floor mopper   An acrobatic dancer. (Granville DICTIONARY)

floor operator   The light crew member who makes any necessary changes during a show in lighting equipment on the stage floor or readily reachable therefrom. This includes, for example, fixtures used in or on an interior setting. (Halstead MANAGEMENT 162–163)

floor pattern   In dance, the ground path traced by the body's base as it changes from one place to another. (Eshkol/Wachmann NOTATION 157)

floor peg   See: stage screw.

floor plan   1. A diagram (orthographic projection) of a stage setting, as seen from above, showing doorways, windows, step units, furniture, backings, trees, benches, etc. Also called a ground plan or scene plan. 2. In dance, a description of a ground space to be occupied by dancers, giving their starting places relative to each other and the space in which they will be dancing. (Eshkol/Wachmann NOTATION 157)

floor plate   A metal device on the floor of a stage, to which the lower end of a stage brace is attached, eliminating the need for a stage screw. Typically a small square or oblong whose middle has an eye or ring.

floor plug   See: stage plug.

floor pocket   Electrical outlets in a metal box sunk into the stage floor. A pocket ordinarily contains two or more outlets protected by the metal box and its floor-level hinged top. Pockets are usually offstage, and sometimes also upstage, of the acting area. Also called a stage (floor) pocket, pocket, or floor box (U.S., occasional). British: dip. Lounsbury has illustrations. See also: wall pocket. (Bellman SCENE, Wehlburg GLOSSARY, Lounsbury THEATRE)

floor sleeve   A metal tube on a stage floor, through which a line can be passed.

floor stand   Especially in Britain, a phrase sometimes used for light stand. (Baker THEATRECRAFT)

floor stay   See: drop clamp.

floor work   In modern dance, movement designed to explore and develop the body's ability to move freely on the ground with the same facility as it does in midspace or in air. (Stodelle HUMPHREY 103ff)

flop   1. A failure. 2. To fail. See also: Brodie. 3. To stay in a town overnight.

flop sweat   Perspiration on a nervous performer who is doing badly in a performance. (Smith VAUDEVILLIANS 12)

Floralia   See: *ludi Florales*.

Florentine roller   In scene painting, a round wooden roller with a covering of rubber or leather, used to produce patterns.

flounce   In theatre makeup, a lower eyelash liner which brings out the eye in the harsh glare of stage lighting. (Granville DICTIONARY)

flourish   A trumpet call or fanfare to herald the entrance of an important character in Renaissance plays and later.

flow   In dance, the quality of tension in movement: its continual changing from free to bound. (Dell PRIMER 11, 16)

flower   See: *hana*.

flower path   See: *hanamichi*.

flower pot   See: stambouline.

flower way   See: *hanamichi*.

flown   Said of anything which has been raised into the flies above the stage. Also called flied.

flow pattern   A path described by a dancer moving along the ground. (Nahumck DANCE 47)

fluff   1. An imperfectly delivered line. 2. To deliver a line imperfectly. Hence, a fluffed line or—in Britain—fluffy (uncertain of one's lines). (Granville DICTIONARY)

flunkie   A stagehand. (Berrey/Van den Bark SLANG 576)

fluorescent lamp, fluorescent tube   See: lamp.

flush footlights   See: disappearing footlights.

flute pillar   See: *fue bashira*.

fly   To raise something into the flies above the stage.

fly bridge   See: bridge.

fly catching   Movement (especially of the hands and arms), business, or sound made by a performer to attract attention when emphasis should be elsewhere. (Wright UNDERSTANDING)

fly control side   The side of the stage where the rigging system is operated.

fly curtain   See: drop curtain.

fly dip   In Britain, an electrical receptacle (socket) in the flies. (Bentham ART 338)

flyed   Variant of flied; flown.

fly floor   1. See: fly gallery. 2. The floor of a fly gallery.

fly gallery   A narrow platform projecting from the side wall of a stage, running from front to back, usually some distance above the stage floor; from it are operated the lines used for flying scenery, lighting instruments, etc. Also called an operating gallery. Some theatres have no fly gallery, and lines are operated from floor level; some theatres have two or more fly galleries, in which case the lower one is sometimes called the fly floor.

fly grooves   In theatres in Britain in the 18th C and later, presumably the upper grooves, attached to the first fly floor and used to steady the tops of sliding wings and shutters. (Southern CHANGEABLE 238)

flying   1. Raising lighting instruments, scenic units etc., into the space above the stage. 2. Creating the illusion of flight by performers or properties by means of concealed wires. (Cameron/Gillespie ENJOYMENT)

flying balcony   A seating balcony that is separated from the rear wall of the auditorium so that more of the reverberant sound energy can reach the seating below.

flying bridge   See: bridge.

flying brigades   See: agit brigades.

flying equipment   1. Apparatus associated with the raising of scenery into the flies—lines, counterweights, etc. 2. Rigging used to fly a performer—harness, special lines, hook-up devices, etc.

flying gown   See: gown à la Polonaise.

flying iron   See: hanging iron.

flying machine   See: *mechane*.

flying perch   In 19th C vaudeville shows, a trapeze artist's platform located in front of the proscenium arch, above the audience. (Gilbert VAUDEVILLE)

flying rig   In old theatres, a scenic unit—such as a cloud or chariot—which is seen moving through the air during a performance.

flyings   1. An 18th C Dublin term used for both a flying effect and the flying device: "There is prepar'd two new Flyings for the Witches to fly with . . . " (*Reilly's* in Southern CHANGEABLE 214) 2. Flyable scenic units. (Granville DICTIONARY)

flying space   See: flies.

flying wall of canvas   An early 20th C term for the front curtain. (Krows AMERICA 233)

"Fly it."   A command to a stagehand to raise scenery or other items into the flies.

fly ladder   A ladder attached to the wall of the stage leading from the stage floor to the fly gallery. The ladder usually continues up to the gridiron.

fly line   See: line.

fly loft   See: flies.

flyman   A stagehand who raises and lowers flown scenic units, light battens, etc. Sometimes called a rigger.

fly plot   See: hanging plot.

fly plug   In Britain, an electrical outlet in a fly gallery. (Baker THEATRECRAFT)

fly posting   See: sniper.

fly rail   See: pinrail.

fly rail cleat   In Australia, a wood or metal pin to which rope lines are tied off at the pinrail. (National TECHNICAL)

fly rope lines   Ropes from the gridiron for raising and lowering battens or other items.

flys   1. In theatres in Britain in the 18th C and later, hinged sections of upper grooves, working like drawbridges, to extend the grooves further out over the stage. 2. Especially in Britain, a spelling of flies. (Bentham ART)

fly space   See: flies.

flyting   An early medieval playlet consisting of a scolding match between a husband and wife or between two rustic gossips. Also called an *estrif* or *strif* (French). (Archer PLAY-MAKING 22)

fly tower   Primarily in proscenium theatres, the portion of the building which rises above the stage area. The fly tower encloses the space, scenery, and devices above the stage.

focal   A Roman legionnaire's square fabric tie used for handkerchief and towel. Precursor of the cravat. (Wilcox DICTIONARY)

focal adjustment   See: flood.

focus   1. The point to which parallel rays of light converge after passing through a lens. 2. The direction in which a lighting instrument is aimed. 3. The adjustment of the size or shape of a light beam. 4. The invisible pointing by a director of moments of special significance in a play. 5. The point or object that draws the eyes of the audience to a part of the stage picture. 6. See: point of focus. (Parker/Smith SCENE, Heffner et al MODERN, Crampton HANDBOOK, Cameron/Gillespie ENJOYMENT). In dance: 7. The spatial projection of a movement's direction or intensity. (Turner/Grauert/Zallman DANCE 29) 8. The direction of a dancer's eyes.

focus a light   1. To sharpen the beam of light, such as an ellipsoidal reflector spotlight. 2. Especially with Fresnel and plano-convex spotlights, to set the lamp in relation to its lens. 3. See: focus lights.

focus lamp, focus lantern   In Britain, a plano-convex spotlight. The terms were used especially in the heyday of such instruments early in the 20th C. An alternate term was half-watt spotlight, since many of these instruments had 500-watt lamps. Britain has used float spot for a small plano-convex spot in the footlight position, and lens spot for the German *Linsenscheinwerfer*, a much larger plano-convex (to 3000 watts). Also called a focussing lamp or focussing lantern. (Bentham ART 311–312, Goffin LIGHTING 21, 23–25)

focus lights   To set the direction and beam spread of spotlights and occasionally of other lighting instruments. The term is not ordinarily used when floodlights or striplights are positioned. (Lounsbury THEATRE)

focussed   In Britain, with a lens. In discussions of the earliest spotlights, Rees uses the word in such phrases as "*focussed* lime-light" and "*focussed* arc light," as well as the more general "*focussed* light." (Rees GAS 52, 72, 140)

focussing lamp, focussing lantern   See: focus lamp.

fog machine   Any device for creating a fog or smoke effect onstage. The two common methods are the use of dry ice plunged into hot water, and passing mineral oil vapor over a heating element. (Gillette/Gillette SCENERY)

FOH   See: front of house, FOH lighting.

FOH control   See: FOH inhibitor.

FOH controller   In memory lighting systems, the controller which operates front-of-house lights. (Bellman LIGHTING 246)

FOH inhibitor   In memory lighting systems, a device which removes front-of-house lights from memory control. Also called FOH control. (Bellman LIGHTING 246)

FOH intake   See: intake.

FOH (F.O.H.) lighting   Front-of-house lighting: lighting which reaches the acting area from lighting instruments on the auditorium side of the main curtain. Footlights are not ordinarily included in the meaning of the term, which really refers to spotlights. The phrase is British, but has been coming into U.S. use for some years. (Baker THEATRECRAFT)

foil   1. A performer or character who enhances the qualities of another. See also: stooge. (Bowman/Ball THEATRE) 2. See: antimasque.

fol (French)   See: *sot.*

fold, fold up   1. To fail. 2. To close because of poor attendance. 3. See: trip.

folded paper puppet   An adaptation of Japanese *origami* (paper-folding) to the making of a puppet. (Philpott DICTIONARY)

foldee   1. A theatre that is closed because of poor attendance. 2. A show that has closed. (Berrey/Van den Bark SLANG 577)

folding batten   See: tumbler.

folding jack   A triangular wooden frame used to support scenery; it is hinged to the back of the scenery and can be folded flat against it when not in use. Sometimes called a hinged jack. (Gillette/Gillette SCENERY)

foliage   A false beard.

foliage border   A border hanging above the stage, cut out and painted to simulate tree branches and leaves. Also called a wood border.

folk play   A play using folklore material, often regional and traditional, usually presented by the people themselves. Hence, folk drama, folk theatre, etc. (Bowman/Ball THEATRE)

follies   In early 20th C U.S., lavish revues featuring chorus girls, songs, dances, elaborate costumes, etc.

follow   To keep a performer in a spotlight as he/she moves about the stage. (McCandless "Glossary" 629, Baker THEATRECRAFT)

follow cue   1. A cue (as in lighting) coming so quickly after another cue that it is not given a separate number. (Parker/Smith DESIGN) 2. After a light change, the main cue: an additional slow change not perceptible to the audience. 3. The signal for such a change.

following spot   In Britain, a follow spot. (Bowman/Ball THEATRE 143)

follow spot   A movable spotlight which keeps a performer in its beam.

follow spotter   An electrician who operates a follow spot. Also called a follow spot man. (Bellman LIGHTING 112)

follow the animated (cartoon)   To have the first place on a live variety bill at an old movie house.

follow through   See: continuity.

fondu (French)   Literally: melted, dissolved. In ballet, a method of completing a movement slowly: a soft landing rather than a sharp return to the stage floor. (Kersley/Sinclair BALLET)

Fontanges   1. A cap of several tiers of pleated ruffles, lace, and ribbons. See also: commode. 2. A coiffure made in that style. Also called a tower headdress. Named after the Duchesse de Fontanges. (Boucher FASHION, Chalmers CLOTHES 18, Wilcox DICTIONARY)

fool   See: jester.

fool actor   Especially in medieval times, an actor who played the role of a fool.

fool company   See: *compagnie joyeuse.*

fool king   In medieval times, especially in France, the head of a *compagnie joyeuse.* (Mantzius HISTORY II 181)

fool society   See: *compagnie joyeuse.*

foot   To hold the bottom rail of a large flat or framed drop in place with one's foot while someone else raises it to a vertical position or while it is allowed to fall to the floor.

foot iron   1. A right-angle metal brace screwed to the bottom of a scenic unit and secured to the stage floor with a stage screw. Also called a bent foot iron. Some foot irons are hinged to avoid snagging when a unit is flown. Hence, hinged foot iron. And some foot irons are not bent; hence, flat or straight foot iron. 2. A length of strap iron screwed to the bottom of a door flat to give it rigidity. Also called a door iron, but the usual alternate terms are saddle or sill iron. The sill may be a wood threshold.

foot-lamps   In 19th C Britain, a term for footlights. (Rees GAS 11)

footlight   1. A popular performer. 2. To perform. 3. Occasionally, footlights.

footlight baby   See: footlight spot.

footlighter   A performer.

footlight Fanny   A girl in the back row of the chorus who thrusts herself to the front, the better to be seen. (Granville DICTIONARY)

footlight it   To perform.

footlighting   Performing.

footlight lady   An actress.

footlights   1. In Renaissance theatres and later, oil lamps at the front of the stage, shielded from the audience by a board. Oil lamps were replaced by gas in the early 19th C and gas by electricity in the late 19th C. Footlights were popular as toning lights in the early 20th C but have for some time been out of fashion. Throughout the centuries there has been controversy over their use, since they illuminate performers from an unnatural angle. The shortening 'foots' is usual among theatre people. The term appears in many combinations: disappearing footlights, open-trough footlights, compartment footlights, footlight baby, etc. See also: float. 2. The line between the performer and the audience, whether actual footlights are used or not. (Wilmeth LANGUAGE) 3. The acting profession.

footlight section   See: section.

footlight spot   Especially in the U.S., the usual backstage term for a compact baby spotlight used in the footlights or in the footlight position. Sometimes called a footlight baby. In Britain: float spot. (Bowman/Ball THEATRE)

footlight strip   An occasional term for a striplight used for footlighting, or designed for such use. (McCandless "Glossary" 634–635)

footlight trap   A long metal trough at the front of an 18th C stage, filled with oil, on which floated small rectangular saucers holding two candles each, fed by the oil. The trough could be lowered to reduce the illumination. (Hogan LONDON lxvi)

footlight trough   A long recess in the stage floor near the front of the stage or in front of a sky drop or cyclorama, containing footlights. In Britain, footlight well.

footlight well   See: footlight trough.

footmen's gallery   The uppermost gallery in Restoration and 18th C theatres, where servants and other poor folk sat.

foot piece   A ground row. (Southern CHANGEABLE 259)

foots   Since at least the 19th C in Britain, (perhaps) later in U.S., a standard backstage shortening of footlights.

fop alley, fop corner, fop's alley   In Restoration theatres, the place near the front of the stage where the fops or young idlers congregated to show off their finery. The place may have been on the forestage itself. (Davenant MAN'S 77)

forain, théâtre forain (French)   An 18th C traveling company which performed at fairs. The performers (*forains*) were primarily acrobats who also sang, acted, performed as puppeteers, mimed, and danced. (Winter PRE-ROMANTIC 34, Duchartre ITALIAN 109)

fore and aft   A 19th C traveling and sport cap of plaid wool, with earflaps. Somewhat reminiscent of the Sherlock Holmes deerstalker. (Barton COSTUME 464, Wilcox DICTIONARY)

foreground action and reaction   Action and reaction on stage that commands the attention of the audience.

foreign control   See: extended control.

fore-play   A performing device developed by the Russian director Vsevelod Meyerhold in the early 20th C: before delivering a speech a performer used mimicry and gesture to inform the audience of his position and the struggle of his spiritual experiences. (Orlovsky in Bradshaw SOVIET 45)

forerunner   See: advance agent.

foreshadowing   In dialogue or business, to hint at action to come later. Also called fingerposting, dramatic foreshadowing, dramatic preparation, preparation. See also: pointer.

forestage   Often, apron. Some sources note that a forestage is larger than an apron and is an acting area in its own right. Forestage is often used today for the extensive acting area in front of the curtain line in 17th C theatres and later. See also: thrust stage. (Bentham ART)

forestage canopy   A scenic or architectural element over a forestage, thrust stage, or apron. It can incorporate sound reflecting surfaces, lighting positions, loudspeakers, etc.

forestage elevator, forestage lift   See: elevator forestage.

forestage gridiron   A gridiron above a forestage, thrust stage, or apron for handling flown scenic elements and stage lighting.

forestage lift   See: elevator forestage.

fore-text   In the early 20th C, the Russian director Vsevelod Meyerhold's answer to Constantin Stanislavsky's concept of subtext. To express the subtext Meyerhold's performers used mimicry and gesture. See also: fore-play. Meyerhold also called his concept a countertext. (Marshall RUSSIAN 133)

foreworks   Henrik Ibsen's term for the scenarios and drafts preceding the final scripts of his plays. (Archer PLAY-MAKING 35)

forfeit-box   See: fine-box.

for his own diversion   See: diversion.

fork   1. In Britain, a device to guide the tops of sliding flats or allow for the pivoting of wings. (Southern CHANGEABLE 393) 2. See: bracket.

form   1. The total organization of materials: in playwriting, the arrangement of characters, ideas, scenes, situations, etc.; in stage production, the shape and style of the lighting, performers, properties, setting, etc. 2. In Restoration theatres, a bench, usually backless. (Pepys DIARY 8 January 1663) 3. A variety of theatre, such as the Italian *commedia dell'arte*, the Japanese *kabuki*, vaudeville, Restoration comedy, etc.

formal   Said of a simple and non-specific stage setting which serves as a relatively permanent background, sometimes usable for different plays. Hence, formal stage. Examples are Jacques Copeau's Théâtre du Vieux Colombier in Paris in the early 20th C and the festival theatre at Stratford, Ontario, Canada.

formal balancing   In directing, a symmetrical balancing of the stage picture through the arrangement of performers.

formalism   1. In scene design, the use of non-representational shapes and forms or the use of a formal, generalized stage setting suitable for different plays. Hence, formal setting, formal stage. 2. An early 20th C Russian critical movement put into practice in the theatre by director Vsevelod Meyerhold and others. The theory emphasized exterior symbolism over inner truth and involved training of actors to make them ''puppets'' of the director. It was ultimately rejected by the Soviets as incompatible with socialist realism. (Hartnoll COMPANION, Matlaw MODERN)

formal stage   A stage consisting usually of a simple and generalized pattern of platforms, steps, and entrances, usable for a variety of plays with little change and minimal use of furniture or scenery. An example is Jacques Copeau's Théâtre du Vieux Colombier in Paris in the early 20th C.

formations   In dance, group shapes and relationships of dancers to each other in the performing space.

form-revealing light   See: *gestaltendes Licht*.

form toggle   A crosspiece at the top of a door opening or top and bottom of a window opening, which determines the vertical dimension of the opening.

fornices (Latin)   From *fornicatus*—arched, vaulted. The vaults below a Terence stage, as shown in the Lyons *Terence* of 1493. The vaults were an imitation of the arrangement in Roman theatres, notorious as a place where prostitutes gathered.

foro (Spanish)   The background or rear part of the stage. (Shergold SPANISH)

forredner (Yiddish)   The announcer in a Polish Purim play. (Kirshenblatt-Gimblett ''Contraband'' 10)

Forrestonian   A reference to the style of the 19th C actor Edwin Forrest, who tended toward bombast.

(the) Forties   In New York City, the theatrical district.

Fortuny lighting (system)   A much discussed but little used method of stage lighting resulting from experiments begun by Italian scene designer Mariano Fortuny in Germany in the early 20th C. Fortuny evolved a complicated scheme of indirect lighting primarily for cycloramas but also applicable to footlighting. He used powerful arc lights, mainly on colored silk (sometimes velvet or other fabric). The bands of silk were on rollers, each connected to a remotely controlled electric motor. Though the system produced remarkable effects of natural lighting and was tried for a time in Germany, the bulk, cost, and inefficiency of the method resulted in its virtual abandonment before 1930. The system produced such terms as Fortuny firmament and Fortuny heaven for Fortuny's cupola-like cyclorama, and Fortuny banners and Fortuny reflectors for the silk bands. (Fuchs LIGHTING 50, 401–402; Hartmann LIGHTING 116)

forum (Latin Roman)   The stage left entrance to the acting area. This led to the forum or anywhere else in the city. (Beare ROMAN 258–260)

fou (French)   1. See: *sot*. 2. A member of a medieval fool company or *compagnie joyeuse*.

fouetté (French)   In ballet, a short, whipped movement of the raised foot as it passes rapidly by the supporting foot, or a sharp turn of the body. (Grant TECHNICAL)

foul   To tangle or snag ropes, scenic units, or lighting units in the flies.

fouling pole   A long stick used to free fouled scenery in the flies. An extended stage brace is sometimes used as a substitute. (Lounsbury THEATRE)

foul papers, foul sheets   Especially in Elizabethan times, early, often messy, manuscript drafts of a play, often in the playwright's hand, with corrections. By contrast, a fair copy is a clean, usually final, draft.

found space.   A space not normally used for theatrical productions but, in an environmental theatre performance, used for such, usually without much adaptation and with little attempt to turn it into a theatre.

four   1. The fourth plane of the stage. 2. See: in one.

four-act   A vaudeville act with four performers. (Gilbert VAUDEVILLE 301–302)

four-a-day   An act or production presented four times daily, as in small-time vaudeville (whereas big-time vaudeville performed only twice a day). (Lewis BETHEL 207)

four and three   Four men and three women, a typical cast of a Toby show. (Wilmeth LANGUAGE)

fourberia della scena (Italian)   See: *furberia della scena*.

fourberie (French)   Literally: knavery. Especially in the Italian *commedia dell'arte*, a bit of trickery. (Scott in Mayer/Richards WESTERN 24)

four-light system   See: three-light system.

fourreau (French)   Literally: sheath. A large hem at the bottom and often at the top of a drop. A thin batten slides into the hem and is used to help raise and lower the drop and keep it flat and smooth.

fourth position   In dance, the placement of the feet with one forward of the other and approximately one foot-length apart.

fourth wall   The name given to the hypothetical wall that separates the stage and the audience in a proscenium theatre. When the curtain rises, the 'fourth wall' of a typical realistic box set is not there. The fourth wall is sometimes thought of as located at the back of the auditorium rather than at the curtain line. (Stern MANAGEMENT, Canfield CRAFT)

four walls   Said of a theatre rented to a producer for a fixed sum instead of a percentage of the profits. The producer assumes operating expenses. (Bowman/Ball THEATRE)

four-way   See: two-way.

fox   To criticize another's performance.

fox-hole circuit   A Caribbean circuit of 13,000 miles, later extended to Newfoundland, the Arctic, and other areas, toured by USO camp shows from 1941 on. (Matson ''Armed Forces'' 2)

fox wedge   See: dutchman.

foyer   The area in a theatre where ticket windows are located; from there patrons go through the ticket barrier to the lobby. But some sources identify the foyer as the lobby, or suggest that foyer is the British equivalent of the U.S. lobby. In any case, it is an outer, or first, entrance hall. (Burris-Meyer/Cole THEATRES 50–51)

(le) foyer des artistes (French)   The green room.

frac   An 18th C man's wide coat without pockets, for informal wear. In the 19th C, it became narrower and shorter, a formal dress coat, cut away in front. See also: cutaway. (Boucher FASHION)

fraise à la confusion (French)   See: falling ruff.

frame   1. In the Restoration period, the wooden structure upon which cloth was attached to form flats. 2. By the end of the 18th C, the structures in a chariot-and-pole system thrusting up through slots in the stage floor; scenic units (wings, for example) were attached to the frames. (Adams HERBERT 98, Leacroft DEVELOPMENT 154) 3. In lighting: a color frame. 4. The shutter frame on an ellipsoidal reflector spotlight. 5. One's place on a variety bill.

frame a show   To assemble or plan a show.

frame brace   See: jack.

framed border   A fabric border stretched on a wooden frame, like a flat.

framed drop   A fabric drop made rigid by being fastened to a wooden frame.

frame piece   A flat.

framing shutter   Any of a number of devices in or on a spotlight which modify the shape of its beam.

Française, gown à la   See: gown à la Française.

free   Said of scenery that is not fouled or tangled in the flies. (Lounsbury THEATRE)

free benefit   See: clear benefit.

free chorus   In early 20th C U.S., a chorus girl who was paid by her friends rather than by a producer. (Wilmeth LANGUAGE)

free list   In 18th C theatres and later, a list of people to whom complimentary tickets (actually, signed cards) were issued. The list consisted chiefly of friends of the theatre proprietors. (Hogan LONDON xxxv)

freeloader   One who goes to a show free.

free plantation   Placement of scenic units anywhere on stage, as opposed to wings and shutters standing in grooves at the sides and back of old stages. (Brockett HISTORY 512)

free theatre movement   A people's theatre, free of political and social restraints. Examples in the late 19th C were André Antoine's Théâtre Libre in France, Otto Brahm's Freie Bühne in Germany, and J.T. Grein's Independent Theatre in England.

freeze   To remain motionless on stage, especially for comic effect or while an audience is laughing.

French action   An Australian term for a traveler curtain or its track. The term is used, for example, at the Sydney Opera.

French brace   See: jack.

French curtain   See: contour curtain.

French enamel varnish   A shellac-alcohol mixture which can be painted or sprayed on costumes. Abbreviation: Fev. (Dryden FABRIC)

French farce   Fast-paced comic plays dating back at least to the 15th C in France. Endless variations on the eternal triangle—wife, deceived husband, and successful lover—made a fairly standard formula which paid little attention to what was probable. Though not improvised, French farce was not unlike the Italian *commedia dell' arte*, with French names for similar stock comic characters.

French flat   A back wall consisting of a large flat or series of flats battened together and flown, complete with practical doors and windows.

French frock   See: frock coat.

French gown   See: gown à la Francaise.

French hood   A 14th–18th C headgear of silk or velvet, tied under the chin and worn over a sheer white cap. Later worn by Quakers. Also called a cardinal, venerable hood. (Chalmers CLOTHES 153, Wilcox DICTIONARY)

French hoop   See: cartwheel.

French scene   In playwriting, beginning a new scene at each entrance or exit of a character, as in French neo-classic drama. See also: structural scene.

(the) French system   See: public rehearsal.

French tabs   1. See: draw curtain. 2. A single curtain drawn across the stage. Also called a trailer. (Corry PLANNING 106)

Fresnel lens   A plano-convex lens thinned by reducing the convex side to a series of concentric rings of approximately the same focal length. As used in the theatre, the surface of the flat side of the lens is broken up, so that the light beam is smooth and soft-edged. Hence, Fresnel light, Fresnel spotlight; often called simply Fresnel. The name is from Augustin Fresnel (pronounced fruh-'nell), a French physicist who created the lens early in the 19th C. See also: step lens. (Bellmen LIGHTING 79, 81, fig. 4–5; Lounsbury THEATRE 82; Wehlburg Glossary)

fret piece   See: profile

Freytag's pyramid   Gustav Freytag's diagram—shaped like a pyramid—of a dramatic plot. The action rises to a peak and then falls (though audience interest, theoretically, is not lost).

Friends bonnet, Friends hood   See: *calèche*.

fright wig   A wig with a string which, when pulled by the actor, gives the appearance of the hair standing on end. Also called a scare wig, fright hair. (Bowman/Ball THEATRE)

fringe   A decoration on a stripper's panties or G-string.

friponne (French)   Literally: a cheat. The middle skirt worn with a farthingale. Also called a hussy.

frise du manteau d'Arlequin (French)   The first proscenium border (teaser).

frock coat   A 19th C formal daytime coat for men. Made in grey, beige, or black, it was closely-fitted with a slight bottom flare, single or double-breasted, and frequently collared in velvet. Coats resembling it were seen as early as the 17th C. Also called a French frock, Prince Albert, walking coat. See also: cutaway. (Boucher FASHION)

Frohman   Formerly, the name given to the manager of a country theatre or opera house; from the late 19th and early 20th C New York manager Charles Frohman. (Wilmeth LANGUAGE)

frolic   An entertainer's term for a performance when it was one of several per day.

from hunger   Not employed.

Fronleichnamsspiele (German)   Medieval German Corpus Christi plays. (Nagler MEDIEVAL 69)

frons scaenae (Latin Roman)   See: *scaenae frons*.

front   1. See: front of house. 2. Downstage.

front and back, timber and town   The types of backdrops usually found in small-town theatres for the use of visiting companies: a parlor, kitchen, woods, and street. (Wilmeth LANGUAGE)

front box   In a 17th C British theatre and later, a box facing the stage, at the back of the auditorium rather than at the side. (Bowman/Ball THEATRE)

frontcloth   Especially in Australia, a show curtain, hung well downstage. Also called a show cloth. (National TECHNICAL)

front curtain   See: house curtain.

frontfall   See: bridge trousers.

frontier drama   A U.S. version of the French *drame*; a play with a fast-moving plot and much sentimentality, set in the West. (Hennequin PLAYWRITING 44)

frontispiece   A temporary frame for a stage, through which one views the scenic area. The term dates from the 17th C in England, though the use of such a frame goes back to the early 16th C. By 1778 the term frontispiece meant the face of the proscenium wall. (Southern CHANGEABLE 34, SURVEY XXXV 33)

frontlet   A 15th C woman's forehead pendant attached to a *calotte* (French) worn under a hennin or escoffion. When the pendant was of gold rather than silk or velvet, it indicated an income of ten pounds per year or more. See also: *feronnière*. (Wilcox DICTIONARY)

front lighting   1. See: front lights. 2. The effect of front lights. (Parker/Smith DESIGN)

front lights   Especially in the U.S., lights which reach the acting area from positions in the auditorium. The term signifies spotlights almost always, footlights being identified as foots. The term front lights came into use about 1930. Hence, front lighting. Other terms: front-of-house lights, fronts, front spotlights. See also FOH lighting, which has come into increasing use in the U.S.

front liner   A star performer.

front loge   In some theatres, the section of a horseshoe-shaped balcony nearest the proscenium, separated somewhat from the rest of the balcony and furnished with fancier seats.

front man   See: bottler.

front of house, front of the house   Often abbreviated to FOH. 1. That part of a theatre in front of the curtain—the auditorium but (usually) also the lobby, business offices, lighting positions in the auditorium, etc. Sometimes called the front. 2. All of the activity which takes place in those areas. 3. The auditorium itself, that is, the house. Also called out front or (in Britain) in front.

front-of-house lighting   See: FOH lighting.

front piece   A curtain raiser—a short play performed before the mainpiece. (Purdom PRODUCING)

front pipe   An occasional term for the first light pipe upstage of the main curtain. Hence, front pipe lighting. (Bowman/Ball THEATRE)

front playing   Playing toward the audience. (Canfield CRAFT)

front room   A stock interior drop carried by touring companies in the early 20th C. See also: back room, town, and timber. (McNamara "Scenography" 20)

front room set   See: center door fancy.

front row   1. The first line of a chorus. 2. The row of audience seats nearest the stage. (Wilmeth LANGUAGE)

fronts   See: front lights.

front scene   A scene set as far downstage as possible in order to allow the next scene to be set behind it.

front scenes   1. In 18th C theatres, apparently shutters or a drop downstage, in front of which a scene could be acted. 2. Scenes performed in this area. (Burnim GARRICK 92)

front set line   See: set line.

front stage   The forepart of the stage—the apron or forestage.

frost   1. A translucent white filter which diffuses light. The term now applies almost always to flexible plastic or gelatine, but it has in the past been used of glass. 'Diffuser' is similar but broader, since it may, for example, be used of a frosted bulb. A star frost is a frost whose center has been cut out in a jagged pattern so that the edge of the beam is diffused, but not the center. A directional frost is one which modifies the shape of the beam. Among other terms: frosted medium, frost gelatine, frosted gelatine (whether the frost is gelatine or plastic). (Lounsbury THEATRE, Wehlburg GLOSSARY) 2. Lacquer. 3. An unsuccessful play, performance, costume, set, etc. 4. An unresponsive audience. 5. To simulate snow by decorating a setting with glittering white material. Hence, frosting. (Bowman/Ball THEATRE, Wilmeth LANGUAGE, Berrey/Van den Bark SLANG 574)

frosted gelatine   See: frost.

frosted light   An occasional term for a fixture, such as a spotlight, which has a frosted gelatine. Sometimes called a frosted spot. (Lounsbury THEATRE)

frosted medium   See: frost.

frottola (Italian)   In medieval times, a comic, dramatized dialogue, mostly a disputation. (Ward LITERATURE I 227)

fruitress   A concessionaire in an 18th C London theatre. She sold fruits, copies of songs, musical pieces, playbills, etc. (Hogan LONDON xli)

fu (Chinese)   Literally: assistant. A sly, sinister or villainous comic character; a major subcategory of the clown role (*chou*) in *kunqu* drama. Also called second face (*ermian* or *erh mien*). (Dolby HISTORY 105)

fu ching (Chinese)   See: *fujing*.

fu chou hsi (Chinese)   See: *minju*.

fue (Japanese)   Side-blown bamboo flutes of various sizes used in *bugaku*, *no*, and *kabuki*. See also: *nokan*.

fue bashira (Japanese)   Literally: flute pillar. The upstage left pillar of a *no* stage, so called because the flute player sits beside it. (Shimazaki NOH 10)

fuguiyi, fu kuei i (Chinese)   Literally: garment of honor and wealth. A type of traditional costume, made of multicolored silk patches on a black robe, which is worn by a performer portraying a poverty-stricken scholar who eventually will gain honor and/or wealth in Beijing opera (*jingju*) and many other forms of music-drama (*xiqu*). (Scott CLASSICAL 144, Zung SECRETS 22)

Fujian opera   See: *minju*.

Fujima *ryu* (Japanese)   Literally: Fujima school. The most important school and style of *kabuki* dancing and choreography. Founded by Fujima Kambei in the early 19th C. (Gunji BUYO 184)

fujing, fu ching (Chinese)   Assistant painted-face role. 1. A powerful, often villainous male role which features dance-acting (*zuo*) and speech (*nian*) skills;

a major subcategory of the painted-face role (*jing*) in Beijing opera (*jingju*) and many other forms of music-drama (*xiqu*). Also called posture painted-face role (*jiazihualian* or *chia tzu hua lien*). (Dolby HISTORY 181, Scott CLASSICAL 75–76) 2. A male clown role portrayed with a painted face in Song *zaju* and Jin *yuanben*; a major role category (*hangdang*) in those forms. Abbreviated *jing*. (Dolby HISTORY 26) 3. See: *baimian*.

fukai (Japanese)   A *no* mask of a middle-aged woman. Also called *shakumi*. (Shimazaki NOH 61)

fukeoyama (Japanese)   1. A *bunraku* puppet head used for a loyal middle-aged heroine. The eyes are movable and a small pin attached to the side of the mouth catches a sleeve or hand towel to make the conventionalized gesture of weeping. (Keene *Bunraku* 60, 229) 2. A role of an older woman in *kabuki*. See: *kashagata*.

Fukien opera   See: *minju*.

fu kuei i (Chinese)   See: *fuguiyi*.

full   In stage lighting, at maximum intensity. Thus, a spotlight or a group of lights might be said to be 'full'; the phrase at full is sometimes used, as is full up. The latter has been used in Britain since at least the late 19th C. (Rees GAS 198, 200–201)

full back   In acting, to face directly upstage.

full-bottomed wig   A late 17th C light wig with three hair locks, created for Louis XIV. Also called a barrister's wig or *binette* (French). (Boucher FASHION)

full check   A capacity house.

full drop   Any drop curtain except a cut drop.

full front   In acting, facing directly downstage.

full house   A U.S. expression for an auditorium filled to capacity. Also called a full check or sold out. In Britain: house full.

fullness   The degree to which fabric is gathered, as in dresses or curtains. In theatre draperies this is given in percentages: 50% fullness means one and one-half times the fabric needed just to cover the opening.

full of larceny   Said of an act with stolen gags. (Berrey/Van den Bark SLANG 594)

full on   In British stage lighting, at maximum brightness. (Bentham ART 323)

full price   At 18th C theatres and later, the price charged patrons who arrived before the end of the third act (typically, of five) of the mainpiece. On special occasions, full price was charged no matter when a patron arrived. (Hogan LONDON xxxvii)

full set   1. A stage setting in 19th C British theatres using more than the first four planes of the stage. (Rees GAS 198) 2. A setting whose walls define the acting area.

full stage   The entire acting and setting area; all four planes of the stage, i.e., its full depth.

full up   See: full.

fumo, fu mo (Chinese)   1. A secondary performer who recited and sang a plot summary before the performance proper in southern drama (*nanxi*, 10th–14th C) and *chuanqi* drama (14th–19th C). (Dolby HISTORY 102, Scott CLASSICAL 31) 2. A dominant, fairly serious male role in Song *zaju* and Jin *yuanben*; a major role category (*hangdang*) in those forms. (Dolby HISTORY 26) 3. See: *mo*.

funambulist   See: *funambulus*.

funambulus (Latin Roman)   Especially from the late 1st C BC, a rope-walker, rope-dancer. Various English synonyms and related words have been used since the Renaissance; funambulist and funambulism are examples of forms still occasionally met; see the OED and Webster. See also: *schoenobates*. (Chambers MEDIAEVAL I 70, Duchartre ITALIAN 24)

functionalism   An aesthetic or artistic method that focuses on the function of objects (such as properties or scenery) instead of on decorativeness. (Cameron/Gillespie ENJOYMENT)

functional movement   1. Generally in modern dance, movement with overtones of expression and meaning. 2. Specifically in modern dance, all movement related to the performance of a given work. (Love DANCE 38)

functional prop   See: prop.

functioneer   A master or mistress of ceremonies.

fund   In 18th C London, a form of pension established by theatrical companies. Active performers contributed to it; after they retired, they could draw upon it. (Hogan LONDON cxxxiv)

fundamental determinant   See: *alambana*.

fundamental emotion   See: *sthayibhava*.

funeral games   See: *ludi funebres*.

funnel   Usually a light metal cylinder designed to control the spread, and sometimes the shape, of a beam of light; some funnels are square in section rather than circular. A square frame at one end of the funnel permits it to be slipped into a color frame slot at the front of an appropriate spotlight. Also called a top hat, high hat, hat, stovepipe, hood, snoot, ash can, Ted Lewis, snout, or tin hat (British). 'Hood' is sometimes used to distinguish the square from the circular funnel. (Bellman SCENE, Sellman/Lessley ESSENTIALS, Wehlburg GLOSSARY)

funny, funnyboner, funny man   A comedian.

funny old gal   The U.S. counterpart of the British "dame" in pantomime—a part played in dresses by end men in a minstrel show. (Wilmeth LANGUAGE) *funzione* (Italian)   A medieval mystery play. (Mantzius HISTORY II 2)

furbelows   18th C ornate pleating, ruching, lace ruffles, or flounces. Also called: falbalas, fal-fals.

furberia della scena (Italian)   The knavery or trickish part of a play. Spelled in some 18th C sources *fourberia della scena*. (1711 *Spectator* in Nagler SOURCES 245)

furi (Japanese)   Realistic mime-like movements—crying, eating, sewing, etc.—performed either by actors in *kabuki* dance scenes or by puppets in *bunraku* plays. See also: *kata*. (Brandon in Brandon/Malm/Shively STUDIES 76, 78; Gunji BUYO 76–77)

furidake (Japanese)   See: *furiotoshi*.

furigoto (Japanese)   See: *shosagoto*.

furikabuse (Japanese)   See: *furiotoshi*.

furiotoshi (Japanese)   In *kabuki*, a technique of suddenly releasing a light-weight curtain and allowing it to fall to the stage floor to reveal a new setting. The curtain is hung from pegs on a bamboo batten (*furidake*) that is rotated by pulling on an attached rope (*hikisen*) to release the curtain. When only the bottom of the curtain is allowed to fall, thus dropping in to hide a scene, the technique is called *furikabuse*. (Leiter ENCYCLOPEDIA 69)

furitsuke (Japanese)   Choreography, in *kabuki* dance plays, ballet, modern dance, and musicals. *Furitsukeshi* is a choreographer. See also: *tate*.

furniture plot   A record of all furniture items needed in a production, with notes on their location on the stage.

furniture store   A room in a theatre for storing stage furniture. (Bowman/Ball THEATRE)

furyu (Japanese)   1. An urban, elegantly costumed dance and mime accompanied by *hayashi* music and performed at the imperial court in Medieval times. (Inoura HISTORY 46–47) 2. In the 16th and 17th C, a fancy-dress procession or group dancing, often by townsmen, in the city streets. (Gunji KABUKI 19, Tsubaki "Performing" 307)

furyu no (Japanese)   A *no* play that emphasizes showy and spectacular effects, as opposed to human emotions. Nakamura NOH 33 says "refined" style plays. *Benkei in the Boat* in Nippon Gakujutsu JAPANESE 167–182 is an example. See also: *geki no*. (Hoff/Flindt "Structure" 214)

fuse   See: tape fuse.

fuse magazine   See: magazine panel.

fushi (Japanese)   Literally: melody. 1. Broadly, a melodic passage in a theatre text. A theatre musician will "chant a *fushi* passage." (Dunn/Torigoe ANALECTS 78) 2. In *no*, melodic singing of a song passage (*utai*). Such passages are marked with musical notation in texts and contrast with prose passages (*kotoba*), which are not sung or so marked. See also: *tsuyogin, yowagin.* (Malm MUSIC 128, Hoff/Flindt "Structure" 234) 3. A specific melodic pattern in *gidayu* music. (Malm in Brandon CHUSHINGURA 68, 80)

fusible link   A metal link that will melt at a low temperature. In a counterweight system it is inserted in a wire line or to a rope holding the asbestos fire curtain in its raised position. In case of fire, the link will melt, releasing the appropriate counterweight(s) and lowering the curtain, opening smoke hatches, etc.

Fussrampe (German)   Among backstage people, footlights. *Fuss* is literally 'foot.' Compare German *Rampe.* (Rae/Southern INTERNATIONAL 44)

fustian   1. Especially in early 20th C melodrama, a bombastic, ranting style of performing. (Granville DICTIONARY) 2. A strong cotton pile fabric formerly used in stage costumes. Also called bombazine (bombazeen).

futatateme (Japanese)   Literally: second piece. The second curtain-raiser (see also: *jobiraki*) on an all-day *kabuki* program. Performed in the early morning. The main play (*hon kyogen*) followed. Also called *futatsume.* (Leiter ENCYCLOPEDIA 70)

futurism   An artistic and theatrical movement in the early 20th C, founded by Filippo Marinetti, which rejected the past and glorified the speed and energy of the machine age. Productions mingled performer and spectator, and exploited modern technology and multimedia. A precursor of surrealism. (Brockett HISTORY 610–611)

fuzhouxi (Chinese)   See: *minju.*

G

G   1. A globe-shaped lamp used in stage lighting. Though now not common, the G-lamp was early in the 20th C the principal—for a time the sole—lamp for use in spotlights designed for wattages of 400 and above. Often called a G lamp, G-type, G-type lamp, and other variants; occasionally called a globular lamp. (Philippi STAGECRAFT 398, Lounsbury THEATRE 80, Fuchs LIGHTING 162) 2. A groove (in which slides a wing or shutter).

gabahan (Indonesian)   Eye shape of the most refined Javanese shadow puppets. The eye is thin and narrow, resembling a grain of rice. (Long JAVANESE 70)

gabardine   1. A medieval cloak or gown worn by Jews, usually made of black silk. It was ankle-length and buttoned to the waist in front. 2. See: caban. 3. A durable, twill-like fabric used especially in men's suits and women's informal wear. (Boucher FASHION, Wilcox DICTIONARY)

gabber   See: minstrel.

gabbing act   In vaudeville, a talking act. (Wilmeth LANGUAGE)

gable   A 16th C diamond-shaped, hood-like headdress with attached wimple and gorget, worn by older women. Although severe and hair-concealing, it was ornamented. Also called a kennel or pedimental headress.

gadget   On a stripper, a G-string.

gaff   See: penny gaff.

gaffer   1. The head of any of the stage crews. 2. The head of the lighting crew. 3. A member of the lighting crew, perhaps especially in the absence of the chief electrician. All uses originated in motion pictures. (Lounsbury THEATRE, Berrey/Van den Bark SLANG 576)

Gaff Street   Shaftesbury Avenue in London, or any street with a number of theatres. (Granville DICTIONARY)

gag   1. A joke or amusing piece of stage business or dialogue. 2. An interpolation by a performer. 3. To improvise, to introduce extemporaneous lines into a performance, usually comic and often topical. 4. To tell a joke. Hence, gagger, gaggist, gagman, gagster, gagging, gag line. See also: sight gag. (Bowman/Ball THEATRE)

gagah (Indonesian)   1. In puppet theatre and dance-drama, a robust, muscular character type such as Bima. (Long JAVANESE 70, Brandon THRONES 48-49) In Javanese dance plays, two sub-types are *gagah kambeng* (strong and humble) and *gagah kalang kinantang* (strong and proud). (Soedarsono DANCES 47-48) For two sub-types in Sundanese *wayang golek*, see: *angkara murka* and *punggawa*. (Foley "Sundanese" 32) 2. The style of dance and voice used to enact such characters. (Holt ART 159-160) See also: *kasar*.

gagaku (Japanese)   Literally: graceful music or entertainment. From the early 8th C, the official music and dance of the Imperial court, as opposed to *gigaku*, the music and dance of Buddhist temples. *Gagaku* consists of music (*kangen*) and dance (*bugaku*). See also: *togaku*, *komagaku*. (Inoura HISTORY 31, Togi GAGAKU 6)

gagalo (Philippine)   See: *carillo*.

gageki (Japanese)   Literally: music-drama. Western-style opera.

gagger   1. A London street performer or beggar. (Orwell DOWN 174) 2. See: gag.

gagging   Comedy crossfire. See also: gag.

gagist   See: gag.

gagiste (French)   1. A minor comic in an Italian *commedia dell'arte* troupe. 2. A supernumerary.

gag line   The punch line in a bit of joking dialogue.

gag man   See: gag.

gag piece   A play in which comic interpolations are easily made. (Berrey/Van den Bark SLANG 581)

gag show   A sketchily-plotted piece without set dialogue. The latter is provided by a leading performer in many long set speeches backed up by the company, which fills in. (Granville DICTIONARY)

gagsi (Korean)   See: *kaksi*.

gagster   See: gag.

gag tossing   Comedy crossfire.

gaku (Japanese)   Literally: music, entertainment. In *no*, a graceful and dignified simulation of *bugaku* dance. (Araki BALLAD 45)

gaku biwa (Japanese)   A pear-shaped lute with four strings and four frets, played with a plectrum, used in *gagaku*. (Wolz BUGAKU 19)

gakubuchi (Japanese)   Literally: picture frame. The proscenium arch in modern theatres.

gakugeki (Japanese)   A direct translation of Richard Wagner's term 'music-drama,' applied specifically to his operas.

gaku so (Japanese)   A thirteen-stringed, plucked zither used in *gagaku*. (Wolz BUGAKU 19)

gakuto (Japanese)   The "person appointed to organize the entertainment at any particular festival," especially of *no* or *dengaku* in the 12th and 13th C. (O'Neill EARLY 67)

gakuya (Japanese)   Dressing and work rooms backstage.

gakuya guchi (Japanese)   Literally: stage door, and this is its meaning. For *kabuki*, see also: *ura kido*.

gala, gala performance   Often the first or the final performance of a show, frequently a benefit, held in a festive atmosphere.

gal and tune show   A musical comedy.

galanes (Spanish)   In 17th C plays, young male or gallant roles. The word still indicates young male leading roles, or actors who play such roles. (Rennert SPANISH 323)

galanty show   1. A primitive 19th C British street version of Chinese shadow puppets. 2. Sometimes, the magic lantern slide shows of the same period. (Speaight PUPPET 236-237)

(the) galaxy   The theatrical district.

galearia (Latin Roman)   See: *galeri*.

galeong (Indonesian)   See: *ngibing*.

galeri (Latin Roman)   Wigs, which were thought in the past to have been used in Roman drama before the introduction of masks. Present opinion favors the view that the wigs were attached to the masks, which covered the whole head. The word means helmet-like head coverings. Also called *galearia*. (Bieber HISTORY 154-155, Beare ROMAN 389, Sandys COMPANION 521)

gallant   A 17th C small ribbon for the hair or clothes. (Boucher FASHION)

gallery   1. An upper stage in an Elizabethan theatre. 2. The uppermost balcony in early 20th C U.S. theatres, usually steeply raked and with wooden seats. 3. A seating area on an upper level at the rear and sometimes along the sides of an auditorium, not divided into boxes. This use is chiefly British; the modern U.S. equivalent is balcony. Galleries are usually called lower and upper or first, second, etc. Spectators in galleries are galleryites (or 'the gallery'), a term sometimes suggesting lack of taste, sophistication, or manners. See also: gods. 4. See: fly gallery.

gallery birds   Gallery spectators.

gallery box   In 18th C London theatres, a seating area over a proscenium door on the gallery level. (Avery LONDON xliv).

gallery check   See: check.

gallery commoner   In an Elizabethan theatre, a playgoer sitting in the top gallery (for a penny). (Dekker in Nagler SOURCES 133)

gallery draw   A performer popular with those who usually sit in gallery seats.

gallery gods   See: gods.

gallery hit   A success with the uncritical. (Berrey/Van den Bark SLANG 584)

galleryites   Gallery spectators.

gallery line   A line of dialogue delivered so as to reach the gallery and call forth applause. (Granville DICTIONARY)

gallery office keeper   In 18th C theatres and later, an employee in charge of a gallery office and accounts. There was an office keeper for each gallery. (Stone LONDON 817)

gallery wag   A gallery spectator who comes to boo or heckle a play or performance. (Berrey/Van den Bark SLANG 575)

galliard   A 16th C quick, lively dance in a masque, in which partners were selected from the audience.

gallop, gallup, *galop* (French)   1. In dance, a compound locomotor step consisting of a step plus a leap, the step needing twice the time of the leap. (Hayes DANCE 48) 2. A lively dance in duple measure.

gally breeches   16th C wide trunks striped by bands of vertical fabric, with another color in quilting showing between. By the 17th C they were known as Gally-Gascoignes. (Chalmers CLOTHES 164)

galur (Indonesian)   A standard, or classic play (*lakon*) in the Sundanese *wayang golek* repertory. (Foley ''Sundanese'' 108)

gamache   See: housse.

gamashes   17th C leggings of cotton or velvet, worn with shoes and boots against mud and water damage. Peasants wore them in linen for centuries. By the 19th-20th C, shortened and of heavy broadcloth or suede (winter) or linen (summer), they were considered very dapper over pumps or oxfords. Then also called spatterdashes or spats. (Wilcox DICTIONARY)

gambang (Indonesian)   See: *gamelan*.

gambeson   See: *pourpoint*.

gambhirya (Sanskrit)   Emotional stability—one of eight special attributes of a hero in a classical Indian play. (Keith SANSKRIT 307)

gamboeh (Indonesian)   See: *gambuh*.

gambuh (Indonesian)   The oldest (c. 14th C) and most formal dance-drama in Bali and the progenitor of most ceremonial (*bebali*) dance-dramas. It retains strong Javanese influence: Javanese Panji stories, archaic Balinese language based on Kawi (Old Javanese), and clown-servant characters (Semar and his sons) from Javanese *wayang kulit*. Also spelled *gamboeh*. (de Zoete/Spies DANCE 134-143, Soedarsono DANCES 175, Bandem/deBoer BALINESE 29-48)

game   A medieval term for an entertainment. (Wickham EARLY II, pt. 1, 361)

game book   In medieval times, the authoritative text of a play. (Chambers MEDIAEVAL II 143)

gamehouse   A multipurpose London building of the late 16th C which was easily convertible into a theatre. The Theatre, The Curtain, The Rose, and The Swan may have been such buildings. (Wickham EARLY II, pt. 2, 4)

gamelan (Indonesian, Malaysian)   The generic term for musical ensembles, of varied size (four to forty instruments), that accompany traditional theatre performances. 1. In Indonesia, most instruments are common to Bali, Java, and Sunda: metallophones of heavy bronze bars (*saron*), inverted bronze bowl or 'gong chime' sets (*bonang* in Java, Sunda; *reong* and *trompong* in Bali), wooden xylophones (*gambang*), large hanging gongs (*gong* in Java, Bali; *goong* in Sunda), smaller hanging gongs (*kempul* in Java, Sunda; *kempur* and *bende* in Bali), small horizontal punctuating gongs (*kenong* and *ketuk* in Java; *kenong* in Sunda; *kempli* and *kelenang* in Bali), a two-stringed fiddle (*rebab*), horizontal drums beaten with the hands (*kendang*), flutes (*suling*), and, with the exception of Sundanese ensembles, pairs of bronze xylophones (*gender*). Ensembles in each area include other instruments as well. In Bali, also called *gong*. (McPhee MUSIC 28-35, Foley "Sundanese" 53-54, Brandon SOUTHEAST 127) 2. In Malaysia, *gamelan* and *gamelan* derived ensembles accompany shadow theatre and various dance-dramas. Principal instruments are the spike fiddle (*rebab*), oboe (*serunai*), drums (*gendang*, *geduk*, and *gedombak*), tuned bronze bowls (*canang* or *chanang*), cymbals (*kesi*), and gongs. (Yub in Osman TRADITIONAL 107-111)

gamelan gong (Indonesian)   The most important type of Balinese *gamelan*. It consists of about twenty-five instruments and accompanies ceremonies as well as performances of *topeng*, *baris*, and some *wayang* plays. *Gamelan gong gede* includes large (*gede*) gongs. With about forty instruments, it is the largest musical ensemble used in Balinese theatre. Abbreviated *gong gede*. (McPhee MUSIC 63-112) *Gamelan gong kebyar* is a modernized version, played for *baris*, *topeng*, and other dance plays. Abbreviated *gong kebyar*. (McPhee MUSIC 329)

gamelan pelegongan (Indonesian)   A delicate sounding version of the Balinese *gamelan gong*, played for *barong* and *calonarang* performances and for the *legong* dance. (McPhee MUSIC 307–327)

gamelan suara (Indonesian)   Literally: voice orchestra. In Balinese *kecak* dance-drama, vocal reproduction of the rhythm and sound of a *gamelan* ensemble. Also spelled *gamelan soera*. (de Zoete/Spies DANCE 81)

gamurra   See: *ropa*.

gana (Kannada)   See: *yaksagana*.

gander the gams   To attend a chorus show (in order to look at the girls' legs). Wilmeth has an interesting history of the term gams. (Berrey/Van den Bark SLANG 591, Wilmeth LANGUAGE)

gandharva (Sanskrit)   See: *bhada*.

gandogaeshi (Japanese)   A scene change technique in *kabuki* in which a roof or entire building is hinged or pivoted backward to reveal a new setting. (Ernst KABUKI 53, Leiter ENCYCLOPEDIA 73)

gang   In lighting, to put two or more fixtures on the same circuit, or two or more dimmers or circuits on a single control. Also called tie. (Lounsbury THE-ATRE, Bowman MODERN)

gangarilla (Spanish)   In the 17th C, a strolling troupe consisting of four or five male performers. (Villandrando in Nagler SOURCES 57) Now, any company of touring players.

ganging   A group of two or more dimmers, switches, or circuits, as in a lighting designer's direction: "Put number 12 at the same reading as the rest of the ganging."

gangway   1. In Britain, an aisle. 2. In Britain, the passageway from the foyer into the auditorium.

ganju, *kan chü* (Chinese)   Jiangxi (or Kiangsi) opera; a form of music-drama (*xiqu*) popular in northeastern Jiangxi Province which developed between the late 14th and early 17th C. It includes music from the *gaoqiang*, *kunshan-qiang*, *bangziqiang*, and *pihuang* musical systems (*shengqiang xitong*), though *pihuang* has dominated somewhat in recent years.

gao (Vietnamese)   A two-stringed fiddle, with a coconut-shell sounding box, played in *hat boi* and *cai luong*. Also called *dan gao*. (Addiss "Theater" 140)

gaobozi, *kao po tzu* (Chinese)   Literally: high stirring. A musical mode (*diaoshi*) in the music of *huiju* and Beijing opera (*jingju*) expressive of indignant grief. It developed c. 17th C in Anhui Province from the combination of *qinqiang* and local folk music. (Wichmann "Aural" 253-259)

gaofang (Chinese)   See: *guanxue*.

gaoqiang, *kao ch'iang* (Chinese)   A musical system (*shengqiang xitong*) characterized by the use of *lianquti* musical structure, solo singing supported by offstage choral backing (*bangqiang*) on the closing line(s) of songs, and musical accompaniment composed entirely of percussion instruments. It arose in the 16th C through the influence of *yiyangqiang* music-drama, and is used today in Hunan opera (*xiangju*), Jiangxi opera (*ganju*), Sichuan opera (*chuanju*), and *wuju*. Sometimes called *yiyangqiang*. See also: *qingxi*, *jingqiang*. (Mackerras RISE 5)

gapit (Indonesian)   See: *cempurit*.

gapuran (Indonesian)   Literally: gate. A short scene at the gateway to the inner palace, usually the second scene in a *wayang* play. A shortening of *adegan gapuran*. (Brandon THRONES 93-94)

gara-gara (Indonesian)   A scene of 'world upheaval,' caused by the intense meditation of a hero. It begins the second part (*patet sanga*) of a Javanese *wayang* play. (Brandon THRONES 115-123, Holt ART 135, 145)

garaguz (Arabic)   Literally: the black eye. Performances in the Near East in which hand puppets were metaphors for human character types. See also: *Karagöz* (Turkish). (Gassner/Quinn ENCYCLOPEDIA 22)

garbha (Sanskrit)   The third of five "junctures" (*sandhi*) in the development of the plot of a classical Indian drama, in which partial attainment of the hero's goal is reached. (Keith SANSKRIT 299) Translated "womb span" by Byrski in Baumer/Brandon SANSKRIT 145.

garbhanka (Sanskrit)   In classical Indian dramaturgy, a play-within-a-play. (Keith SANSKRIT 303)

garcette (French)   See: *coiffure en bouffons*.

garcio (Latin)   See: minstrel.

garçon d'accessoir (French)   A 19th C property boy, gofer, and special effects operator.

garçon du théâtre (French)   Literally: theatre boy. A stagehand.

garde-corps (French)   A medieval overcoat. See also: hérigaute. (Boucher FASHION)

garden border   See: foliage border.

garden cloth   In Britain, a drop or cut drop representing a garden scene. (Granville DICTIONARY)

garden theatre   An open-air theatre using hedges and other vegetation for some or all of its masking. (Bowman/Ball THEATRE)

gargouillade (French)   A ballet movement consisting of a jump and bending of the legs up under the dancer while making small circles in the air. (Kersley/Sinclair BALLET)

garnacha (Spanish)   In the 17th C, a strolling troupe consisting of five or six men, a woman for leading female roles, and a boy for secondary female roles. (Villandrando in Nagler SOURCES 58) Now, any company of touring players.

gasalier   A name sometimes used in Britain for the gas chandelier which was a major source of auditorium lighting in 19th C theatres. The spelling varied, but that given appears to have been usual. (Rees GAS 94, 102-214)

gas bag   A closed sack used in collecting and feeding gas to a limelight. See also: limelight bag.

gas batten   From shortly before the middle of the 19th C in Britain, the horizontal gas pipe suspended above the stage, usually parallel to the proscenium. Even by mid-century, holes in the pipe served as burners; only later were the pipes supplied with jets. A gas batten had as many as seventy lights, and some theatres had five such borderlights. (Rees GAS 34-41)

gas bracket   A gas jet or gas burner. The typical gas bracket was a single burner ending in an Argand lamp or other type of flame, with or without a lamp glass. (Rees GAS 15, fig. 1; 94)

gas burner   A gas jet. See also: burner.

gas dial   See: gas table.

gas discharge lamp   See: lamp.

gaseous discharge lamp   See: lamp.

gas-filled lamp   Incandescent lamps whose bulbs are filled with gas, now usually nitrogen and argon. Since all lamps above 60 watts are gas-filled, these lamps are the large majority and by far the most important of those used in stage lighting. See also: C-lamp. (Bellman LIGHTING 18-19, Goffin LIGHTING 28)

gas float   In 19th C Britain, gas footlights. Note the use of the singular, and compare 'float.' (Rees GAS 26-27)

gas holder   In 19th C Britain, a gasometer. The term was used as both noun and adjective in such phrases as oxy-hydrogen gas-holders and gas-holder tanks. (Rees GAS 61)

gas-indicating plate   See: gas plate.

gas key   In 19th C theatres, an opening or operating key used at the gas table for certain sub-controls in the lighting system. (Rees GAS 206)

gas ladders   Especially in 19th C Britain, wing lights supplied by gas, with the lights reachable by built-in ladders. (Rees GAS 31, 33, fig. 14)

gas length   In the 19th C, a strip of gaslights used vertically behind a wing or the side of the proscenium. See also: length. (Bowman/Ball THEATRE).

gas man   In much of the 19th C, the man in charge of lighting. Especially in the earlier days of gas lighting, the gas man was likely to be a plumber; he was experienced with flow, with pipes and pipe fittings, and with control by faucets or cocks. (Rees GAS 14, Hartmann LIGHTING 9)

gas mantle   See: Welsbach burner.

gas meter   See: gasometer.

gasometer   A gas holder. In the 19th C, a cylindrical tank which stored oxygen or hydrogen for the limelight at low pressure. Confusingly, the phrase gas meter was used occasionally. Limelight tank appears to be a modern phrase for gasometer. (Rees GAS 58-60, Penzel LIGHTING 78-80)

gas plate   By the late 19th C, the official British term for the control center of a gas lighting system, analagous to an electrical control board. Other terms used in British theatres from the mid-19th C: regulation plate, dial plate, index plate, gas-indicating plate, large brass plate. See also: gas table.

Gassenbühne (German)   Literally: street stage. A theatre with painted wing-and-drop scenery. (Sobel HANDBOOK 424)

gas service   See: service.

gas standard   See: bunch light.

Gast (German)   Literally: guest. Usually, a guest star.

gas table   In 19th C U.S., the usual term for the gas control center in a theatre. Such a center, usually on stage on the prompt side, controlled the stage lights; it might also control such other backstage lights as those in property and dressing rooms, and major auditorium lights. Late in the 19th C, 'keyboard' came into use, perhaps under the influence of electricity. Occasionally called a gas dial or stage regulator. See also: gas plate, *jeu d'orgue*. (Penzel LIGHTING 85-87, figs. 18-23; Rees GAS 104-105; Bowman/Ball THEATRE; Fuchs LIGHTING 39-40)

gastieren (German)   To star as a guest performer.

Gastrolle (German)   A starring role as a guest performer.

Gastspiel (German)   A performance by a visiting star or company.

Gastspielreise (German)   A tour.

gas wings   Especially in 19th C Britain, wing lights supplied by gas. (Rees GAS 31, 34, figs. 12, 15, 16)

gate   1. Among lighting technicians, the usual term for the aperture in projectors and sometimes in certain spotlights. 2. In a silicon controlled rectifier (SCR) dimmer, a device which controls the voltage reaching a lamp and, thus, the amount of light it gives. (Bellman LIGHTING 193, fig. 10-1; Wehlburg GLOSSARY) 3. Attendance, box office receipts. See also: gross. 4. Admission fee.

gate-appealer   A popular performer.

gate batten   Especially in Australia, two barrels (battens), one above the other, joined by a number of cross members. Used for flying heavy or awkward scenic units requiring additional support. (National TECHNICAL)

gate cut   A percentage of the box-office receipts.

gate man   Ticket collector.

gatherer   In Elizabethan theatres and later, a collector of money. Gatherers were stationed at the entrances to the principal seating areas: the pit, galleries, and boxes. (Brockett HISTORY 215)

gathering   In dance, a shaping movement toward the body. See also: scattering. (Dell PRIMER 56)

gati (Sanskrit)   Literally: gait. The manner of moving or walking on stage. See also: *cari*. (Raghavan in Baumer/Brandon SANSKRIT 34)

gati pracharas (Sanskrit)   Face-to-face battle movements in *yaksagana*.

gaucho drama   Native Latin-American folk melodrama with guitars accompanying songs and dances. The type originated in Argentina and Uruguay in the late 19th C. The protagonist in these dramas is a highborn outlaw. (Matlaw MODERN 282)

gaugalâri (Old High German)   See: minstrel.

gaulle   See: gown à la lévite.

gauze   See: theatrical gauze.

gavotte   A dance of French peasant origin in moderately quick 4/4 time, marked by the raising rather than the sliding of the feet.

gayana-vayana (Assamese)   Literally: singers and drummers. The musicians who accompany an *ankiya nat* performance. (Richmond ''Vaisnava'' 157)

gay corners   A theatrical district.

gay white way   A theatrical district.

gazel (Turkish)   A song sung in the prologue of a Turkish shadow puppet play. It is somewhat mystical in character. (Gassner/Quinn ENCYCLOPEDIA 865)

gazin-shpil (Yiddish)   See: *royberbande-shpil*.

gazomètre (French)   Gasometer. (Rees GAS fig. 37)

G-bulb   A lamp bulb of globular shape. The term is sometimes used to mean the entire lamp. See also: G.

gebog, gedebog, gedebong (Indonesian)   See: *debog*.

gedig (Indonesian)   See: *ngibing*.

gedog (Indonesian)   See: *wayang gedog*.

gedombak (Malaysian)   See: *gamelan*.

geduk (Malaysian)   See: *gamelan*.

gedut (Indonesian)   See: *ngibing*.

geinin (Japanese)   Literally: art-person. A performer: actor, dancer, singer, or musician.

geino (Japanese)   Literally: art-skill. The performing arts. One of the oldest terms used in writings on Japanese theatre, *geino* encompasses all arts which use the performer's body as their medium of communication. (Hayashiya ''Ancient'' 1-2) When applied to such traditional forms as *no*, *kyogen*, and *kabuki*, the word implies that the performer, not the text, is the origin and basis of theatrical art.

geju, ko chü (Chinese)   Literally: song drama. A type of theatrical performance which features song but is not performed exclusively in the style of music-drama (*xiqu*). Such a performance may consist of an original Chinese composition or of a piece from one of the various forms of Western opera. Performances of this type originated in the 1930s, were much encouraged in the 1950s and early 1960s, and are now being actively developed. See also: *xingeju, xiju*. (Mackerras MODERN 201-204, Mackerras PERFORMING 107-112)

geki (Japanese)   Literally: a drama, a play. *Gekiteki*: dramatic. See also: *engeki*.

geki bushi (Japanese)   A masculine style of *joruri* music and chanting. First used in the puppet theatre, the style was later absorbed into *kabuki*'s *nagauta* music. (Leiter ENCYCLOPEDIA 73-74)

gekidan (Japanese)   Literally: theatre troupe. This is a contemporary term, which has partly supplanted the older *za*. (Ernst KABUKI 5)

gekijo (Japanese)   Literally: theatre place. Theatre building. The term came into use in the late 19th C, following contact with the West. (Gunji KABUKI 43)

geki no (Japanese)   Literally: dramatic *no*. A *no* play which emphasizes personal emotions, as opposed to one that is showy and spectacular (*furyu no*). *Kiyotsune* in Nippon Gakujutsu JAPANESE 61-73 is an example. (Hoff/Flindt "Structure" 214, Tsubaki "Performing" 300-301)

gel   1. The usual backstage shortening of gelatine. But gel is regularly used for any flexible color medium, including plastic; and it is often used still more broadly to mean any color medium, including glass. The meaning of gelly is similar, as is the occasional variant, jell. (Wehlburg GLOSSARY, Lounsbury THEATRE) 2. To place frames with gel in lighting instruments, as in "Let's gel," or "Gel that flood."

gelanggang (Malaysian)   Literally: arena. The central acting area of a *ma'yong* stage. (Yousof "Kelantan" 74)

gelatine, gelatin   1. A thin, flexible, transparent color medium whose basic element is animal jelly. Mixed with aniline dyes, gelatine provides a great variety of colors used in modifying the hues of light beams. The British often use the term medium for gelatine. (Wehlburg GLOSSARY, Bellman, SCENE) 2. A color frame and its gelatine. Sometimes called a gelatine slide. Writers on theatre have generally preferred the spelling gelatine, but the shorter form also occurs. See also: gel.

gelatine frame   See: color frame.

gelatine slide   An occasional term for color frame, with or without gelatine.

gelernte chorus (German-English)   Trained performers who as a group were used to introduce "uninitiated" performers to the reading-rehearsal of certain texts of the Brechtian *Lehrstücke*. (Wirth "Experiments" 59)

gel frame   See: color frame.

gellie   In Britain, short for gelatine.

gelling   Placing a color medium in a stage lighting instrument. The term is used whether or not the medium is gelatine, and whether or not it replaces an earlier medium. But compare regelling, often used when a gelatine is replaced. (Bellman LIGHTING 34)

gelly A color medium, or a color frame with medium. See also: gelatine, gel.

gelotopoios (Greek) A jokester, buffoon. The word is used by ancient writers for "mimes and buffoons." Ultimately from *gelos*, laughter. (Nicoll MASKS 36, Liddell/Scott LEXICON)

gel-up To replace a faded gelatine. (Bowman/Ball THEATRE 155)

geming xiandai geju, ke ming hsien tai ko chü (Chinese) Literally: revolutionary modern song drama. A song drama (*geju*) with a contemporary, revolutionary theme and characters. During the Cultural Revolution period (1966 to 1976) these were the only song dramas performed. (Dolby HISTORY 250-255)

geming xiandai jingju, ke ming hsien tai ching chü (Chinese) Literally: revolutionary modern Beijing opera. A contemporary play (*xiandaiju*) with a revolutionary theme and characters performed in Beijing opera (*jingju*). During the Cultural Revolution period (1966 to 1976), these were the only Beijing opera plays performed publicly. See also: *yangbanxi*. (Dolby HISTORY 250-255)

geming xiandai wuju, ke ming hsien tai wu chü (Chinese) Literally: revolutionary modern dance drama. A dance drama (*wuju*) with a contemporary, revolutionary theme and characters; in translation, often termed revolutionary modern ballets. During the Cultural Revolution period (1966 to 1976), these were the only dance dramas performed. See also: *yangbanxi*. (Dolby HISTORY 250-255)

gendai geki (Japanese) Literally: modern drama. Broadly, all plays in modern theatre (*shingeki*, films, television) which are set in post-Tokugawa times (1868 to the present). See also: *jidai geki*. (Cobin "Traditional" 158)

gendang (Malaysian) See: *gamelan*.

gendang keling (Malaysian) A five piece orchestra—oboe (*serunai*), two hand drums (*gendang*), and a pair of gongs—that accompanies a *selampit* performance. (Sweeney in Malm/Sweeney STUDIES 54)

gender (Indonesian) See: *gamelan*.

gender wayang (Indonesian) A *slendro*-tuned group of four *gender* that accompanies *Mahabharata* plays performed in Balinese shadow theatre or *wayang wong* dance-drama. When *Ramayana* plays are performed in the shadow theatre, other instruments are added and the ensemble is called *gender wayang batel*. (McPhee MUSIC 201-202)

gending (Indonesian) 1. In Bali and Java, a generic term for major instrumental compositions played by the *gamelan* ensemble to accompany *wayang* plays and classical dance-drama. Brandon gives names of 99 *gending* used in Surakarta-style *wayang* and their usage in THRONES 361-366. (Hood THEME

14-15) 2. More broadly, music in general. (Holt ART 132) 3. Instrumental melodies used in Sundanese *wayang golek*. For example, *gending perang*, 'battle gending,' are *gending* used in a battle scene. See also: *lagu*. (Foley "Sundanese" 150)

gendombak (Malaysian)   See: *gamelan*.

general business   Said of a performer who can play whatever is required.

general illumination, general lighting   Relatively shadowless light which floods a large area. The term was much used early in the 20th C for the light produced by borderlights and footlights; these and other striplights came to be called general instruments (sometimes general lights). The contrasting term was specific illumination (sometimes called specific lighting, occasionally localized illumination), which identified the shadow-producing light of spotlights; and spotlights were called specific instruments (sometimes specific lights). All these terms are now uncommon. Compare: key light, now usual for shadow-producing light, and fill light, the usual term for soft, shadowless light. (Bellman LIGHTING 108-109, 326-327; Sellman/Lessley ESSENTIALS 3; Wehlburg GLOSSARY)

general inspector   In 18th C theatres, the supervisor in charge of those employees who set candles and lamps and guarded against fire. (CRAFTSMAN 4 November 1727)

general instrument   See: general illumination.

general lighting   See: general illumination.

General Lighting Service lamp   The British term for U.S. general service lamp, a phrase sometimes also used in Britain. Such lamps are pear-shaped in the larger sizes, do not have concentrated filaments, and are often used for floodlighting. The standard shortening is G.L.S. (Bentham ART 74, fig. 40; Corry LIGHTING pl. I.)

general manager   Especially in the U.S., the business manager of a theatrical company.

general service lamp   See: General Lighting Service lamp.

general understudy   A performer engaged to perform, if necessary, in a number of roles in a given play. (Granville DICTIONARY)

general utility   See: utility.

género chico (Spanish, Philippine)   A short play, often farcical and with music. See also: *zarzuela*.

género ínfimo (Spanish)   A kind of vaudeville revue. (Sobel NEW)

genjoraku (Japanese)   A three-piece *bugaku* mask with Mongolian features. This is the most technically complicated of all *bugaku* masks. (Wolz BUGAKU 45)

genre   1. In Western dramatic criticism, a category of plays, such as tragedy, comedy, melodrama, farce, tragic-comedy, etc. (Cameron/Gillespie ENJOY-

MENT) 2. In English writings about Asian performances, a type of theatre, distinguished by a unique constellation of music, dance, acting, and play forms and techniques. For example, in Japan, *kabuki, no, bunraku,* and *kagura* are separate genres. Almost without exception a given troupe will perform in only one genre.

genre noble (French)   A 19th C French ballet of first importance, requiring tall, imposing dancers and stressing majesty and elegance. (Carlson FRENCH 39-40)

genta (Japanese)   A *bunraku* puppet head used for the character of a virtuous young man. The word comes from the name of the original character, Kajiwara Genta. (Keene BUNRAKU 202, 214)

genteel comedy   Polite comedy, a cross between the Restoration comedy of manners and the sentimental comedy of 18th C Britain.

gentlemen's rooms   See: lord's rooms.

gentlemen supers   See: walking gentlemen.

genzaimono (Japanese)   Literally: present-time play. One of the two major play classifications in *no*. A play which features an unmasked (*hitamen*) living protagonist (*shite*); hence the play takes place in the present time. *Ataka* in Nippon Gakujutsu NOH III is an example. Also translated 'present *no*.' See also: *mugen no*. (Nakamura NOH 32, Inoura HISTORY 121)

geometric marionette   A type of marionette showing the influence of cubism, with triangles and other angles predominating in its design. (Philpott DICTIONARY)

George Spelvin   A fictitious name used in a theatre program by an actor whose name has already appeared, that is, when an actor doubles. If the character dies in the course of the play, George X. Spelvin is sometimes used. The name has been reported as dating from about 1886 (Bowman/Ball) or 1907 (Stern). The female equivalent is Georgia or Georgiana Spelvin. Among other fictitious names are Harry Selby and, in Britain, Walter Plinge. (Bowman/Ball THEATRE, Stern MANAGEMENT)

geranos (Greek)   The *mechane* (a hoisting device) or possibly a similar machine used for such special purposes as moving dead bodies; perhaps the *geranos* moved more rapidly than the *mechane*. Since the word originally meant crane (the bird), and its theatre use appears to be late, it may refer to a *mechane* more crane-like in appearance than the original Greek machines. Also called a crane. See also: *mechane*. (Arnott SCENIC 78, Gascoigne WORLD 29, Pickard-Cambridge DIONYSUS 68, 266; Nicoll DEVELOPMENT 22)

gerong (Indonesian)   In Java, group singing of male *gamelan* musicians (*niyaga*) during the playing of an instrumental melody (*gending*) in a *wayang* performance. (Muljono in Osman TRADITIONAL 71, Brandon THRONES 54-55)

gertak perkakas (Malaysian)   Rattling or intermittent sounds of the musical instruments that punctuate action or speech of a character or provide a break for the puppeteer in the shadow theatre (*wayang kulit*). (Sweeney RAMAYANA 57)

G.E.S.   The standard British shortening of Goliath Edison Screw, their term for U.S. mogul base. (Bentham ART 74, Corry LIGHTING pl. I)

Gesamtbühnenaktion (German)   In the Bauhaus school of theatre, the totality of the stage action. (Schlemmer/Moholy-Nagy/Molnar BAUHAUS 62)

Gesamtkunstwerk (German)   Literally: total art work. The music-drama masterpiece resulting from the unifying synthesis of the master author-composer— as advocated by Richard Wagner in the 19th C.

Gesangpiesen (Yiddish)   Operettas. (Lifson YIDDISH 51)

gestaltendes Licht (German)   Literally: formative light, forming light. Adolphe Appia's form-revealing light, later often called specific illumination. Thus, shadow-producing light, which brings out the three-dimensionality of objects or people. The phrase has also been translated 'living light.' (Sellman/Lessley ESSENTIALS 2)

geste (French)   Literally: deed. In the 11-12th C, a *chanson de geste* (song of deed) which told of a brave act or acts of a knight. It was part of the oral tradition transmitted by the troubadours of the Middle Ages.

gesticulator (Latin)   A medieval performer, a buffoon. (Gascoigne WORLD 97)

gesture   1. A movement, usually of the hands, arms, head, or shoulders, to express a thought or feeling or to punctuate an idea. 2. To make such a movement. (Canfield CRAFT, Cameron/Gillespie ENJOYMENT)

gestus (Latin)   In Bertolt Brecht's epic theatre theory, the clear expression, through bodily stance or movement, of the social attitude of one person toward another or others.

"Gesundheit!" (German)   A comic response in burlesque to a Bronx cheer or heckle.

get   Especially in setting the positions of lights, to strike with a beam of light. A lighting designer onstage may say to an assistant, "Get me with number 6."

get a cold curtain, get a cold hand   To fail to get applause.

get across   In acting, successfully to project a character or situation to the audience; that is, to get across the footlights to the audience.

get across with a bang   In vaudeville, to be a rousing success. (Wilmeth LANGUAGE)

getaway night   1. In early 20th C U.S., the final night of a run in a vaudeville tent show. (Ashby in Matlaw AMERICAN 146) 2. The night a touring company gives its final performance in a particular theatre. (Bowman/Ball THEATRE)

get hot   To dance faster and more dynamically.

get in   1. In Britain, to bring a company's equipment to a theatre. Also called take in, haul in, load in. 2. When hyphenated, a noun meaning the process of bringing a show into a theatre.

get out   In Britain, to take a company's equipment out of a theatre. Hence, the amount of money required to cover the expenses of a performance; the break-even point. Also called haul out or take out.

get over   To make a role or a production successful; to succeed, get it over the footlights.

get the axe in the Ioways   To be banned by rural censors. (Berrey/Van den Bark SLANG 584)

get the bird, get the big bird   To be hissed or jeered by an audience.

get the hook   See: hook.

get the needle   To get stage fright.

get the show on the road   1. To go on tour. 2. Of a show in disarray, to pull things together. 3. To get going, to begin, as a rehearsal or performance.

get the spot   To be the center of attention on stage, to get the spotlight.

getting in, getting out   Alternate terms for get in, get out.

get up   In 18th C theatres, to produce, prepare, learn lines. Hence, getting up, got up. As in: to get up a part, get up a play. The use still occurs. (Milhous/Hume COKE'S 17)

get up the nut   To collect enough money to cover expenses. (Wilmeth LANGUAGE)

geusa (Korean)   See: *kosa*.

gewuju, ko wu chü (Chinese)   Literally: song-and-dance drama. A type of theatrical performance which features song and dance but is not performed exclusively in the style of music-drama (*xiqu*). Such a performance may consist of an original Chinese composition, or of a minority nationality or non-Chinese piece. Performances of this type were much encouraged in the 1950s and early 1960s, and are now being actively developed. See also: *xiju*.

geza (Japanese)   Literally: lower place. 1. Background music in *kabuki* which is played by *nagauta* musicians offstage to accompany dialogue scenes and action. See also: *debayashi*. Musical examples are in Leiter ENCYCLOPEDIA 76-91, Malm in Brandon/Malm/Shively STUDIES 140-170, and Brandon CLASSIC 44. 2. An offstage enclosed room in which the *geza* musicians sit when they perform. The room is built into the inner proscenium of a *kabuki* theatre, originally stage left, the 'lower' side of the stage, hence the name. The room moved to stage right in the late 19th C. Also called *hayashibeya* (music room). (Ernst KABUKI 52) 3. In *bunraku*, offstage percussion music, and the place where the percussion musicians play. (Adachi BUNRAKU 58)

gezixi, ko tzu hsi (Chinese)   A form of music-drama (*xiqu*) performed in Taiwan, southern Fujian, and overseas Chinese communities in Southeast Asia. It developed out of 17th and 18th C Taiwanese and Fujianese labor and folk songs, and was later influenced by Taiwanese storytelling (*shuochang*) and Beijing opera (*jingju*). Also called cart drum plays (*cheguxi* or *ch'e ku hsi*). (Dolby HISTORY 283)

ggogdu-gagsi (Korean)   See: *kkoktu kaksi*.

ghost   1. A company treasurer. Hence, payday is the day the ghost walks or ghost-walking day; to get one's salary is to see the ghost walk. When the ghost doesn't walk, one does not get paid. The pay window is the ghost window. The term is thought to have come from a performance of *Hamlet*, when the actor playing the ghost said he would not walk (perform) until he was paid. 2. In lighting, stray light resulting from an imperfection in the lens system of a spotlight. 3. The glow of a filament when a lamp has been dimmed to presumable blackout. (Bowman/Ball THEATRE, Granville DICTIONARY, Bellman SCENOGRAPHY) 4. In playwriting, to write someone else's play. Hence, ghost writer.

ghost a color   Especially in U.S. professional parlance, to cut out the center of a color medium and replace it with another color.

ghost doesn't walk   See: ghost.

ghost glide   See: Corsican trap.

ghost light   Especially in the professional theatre, the single light left burning in center stage when the theatre is empty. The source of the term is the superstition that a ghost will move in if the theatre is left completely dark. Pilot light and night light are frequent, though less colorful, alternates. (Wehlburg GLOSSARY)

ghost load   See: phantom load.

ghost play   A play in which ghosts appear. (Sobel NEW)

ghost's window, ghost window   The theatrical pay window. (Wilmeth LANGUAGE)

ghost trap   A trap door in the stage floor, named for the Ghost in *Hamlet*. Through it apparitions appear and disappear.

ghost-walking day   See: ghost.

ghost walks   See: ghost.

ghost writer   See: ghost.

ghunghru (Hindi)   In many Indian theatre forms, bands of small round bells, worn around a dancer's ankles, that give musical reinforcement to the beating of the dancer's feet.

gi-ag (Korean)   See: *kiak*.

gibus   See: opera hat.

gidayu bushi (Japanese)   The form of *joruri* narrative music used in *bunraku* puppet theatre. The term is from the name of its creator, the chanter Takemoto Gidayu (1651-1714). Abbreviated *gidayu*. See also: *takemoto*. (Malm MUSIC 199)

gidayu kyogen (Japanese)   See: *maruhonmono*.

gift shows   Performances in 19th C New England at which door prizes were given, usually at performances featuring minstrels, magicians, or musical entertainers. (Leavitt MANAGEMENT)

gigaku (Japanese)   Literally: skillful music or entertainment. A Buddhist performing art formerly given in temples on Buddha's birthday and other occasions. Imported from South China in the early 7th C, a typical program consisted of a sequence of ritual music and Buddhist prayers, a masked procession accompanied by music, dramatic sketches based on Buddhist precepts, and, as a finale, a parade of dancers. Performances ceased after about the 12th C. (Inoura HISTORY 23-29)

gig show   A minstrel show.

gigue (French)   Jig. A late 17th C fashionable court dance. (Perugini PAGEANT 109)

gikyoku (Japanese)   A play text, usually in published form. See also: *kyakuhon*, *shohon*.

gila mlajar kawon (Indonesian)   Literally: crazed running after being defeated. In Javanese shadow theatre, movement of a character who has been driven crazy by the incessant attack of his opponent. Usually the result of being bitten and clawed by a frenzied ape. (Long JAVANESE 105)

gilet   A 19th C man's white or light-colored undervest, worn with a waistcoat. (Barton COSTUME 430)

gimp   1. A kind of cloth braid used in trimming. 2. See: guimpe. (Barton COSTUME 203)

gin and fog   A juicy hoarseness in an actor's voice.

ginem (Indonesian)   See: *antawatjana*.

gineman wayang (Indonesian)   See: *pemungkah*.

ginger   From about 1900, said of risqué lines. (Bowman/Ball THEATRE, Wilmeth LANGUAGE)

giocolatore (Italian)   In medieval Italy, an entertainer, especially a juggler.

gipcière (French)   A 14th C man's purse worn at the waist, made of velvet or leather. (Chalmers CLOTHES 120)

gipon, gippon   A medieval undergarment to which breeches were attached. By the 14th C it looked almost like a doublet. See also: *jupe* (French). (Boucher FASHION)

gipsy   See: gypsy.

gira (Spanish)   A tour.

giraffe   An occasional term for a tall light stand.

girandole   In 19th C British theatres, a gas bracket with two or more branches. Such branched fixtures, sometimes much ornamented, were used in many places, including the fronts of the circles of boxes in theatre auditoriums. The word was earlier used of similar fixtures with candles. Though ultimately from Latin through Italian *girandola*, the term reached English from French *girandol*, where one meaning was a candleholder with several branches. (Rees GAS 10, 95, fig. 59)

giratorio (Spanish)   A revolving stage or scenic piece.

girdle *à la victime* (English-French)   A vividly-colored 19th C shoulder and waist sash. (Boucher FASHION)

girl and music show   A musical comedy.

girlie show, girly show, girly-girly show   Any show featuring attractive women, usually with a good deal of bare skin. (Wilmeth LANGUAGE)

giro (Indonesian)   In Javanese *wayang*, a series of twisting, spinning, and falling movements used for ogres when they run amok in battle or in excited anticipation of a violent encounter. (Long JAVANESE 101)

Gironée (French)   See: *robe Gironée*.

give   In acting, to move so as to leave another performer in a stronger position on stage. Hence, to give a scene, to give stage, giver, given position. (Bowman/Ball THEATRE)

giveaway   A complimentary ticket.

giveaways   Premiums to attract attendance on weak nights.

give cards   See: give the ticket.

give extra curtains   To give unwarranted curtain calls.

give him the skull   Do a take. Hence, to skull a line. (Wilmeth LANGUAGE)

"Give it a drink!"   A shout by an audience member deriding a performer with a poor voice or, sometimes, deriding a bad play or music-hall turn. (Partridge TO-DAY 227)

give it mouth   To speak up.

give it to' em   To perform.

given circumstances   In the Stanislavsky system of acting, the dramatic elements of character, plot, dialogue, and locale upon which a performer can draw to arrive at an appropriate physical action or sequence of physical actions. (McGaw ACTING 12, Stanislavski CREATING 201)

given position   A performer's position on stage, usually turned partly away from the audience, that helps the spectator focus attention on another character or object.

give out   In 18th C theatres and later, to announce the following day's bill.

give stage   See: give.

give the goose   To hiss.

give the horse-cough   To express derision by coughing during a performance. (Berrey/Van den Bark SLANG 592)

give the ticket   In the U.S., to fire a performer. In Britain, give cards. (Granville DICTIONARY)

give the word   To prompt.

G.K.P. projector   Gayling, Kann and Planer of Vienna visual effects apparatus used to throw scenic effects on a cyclorama. (Bowman/Ball THEATRE)

G lamp   See: G.

glance-lighting   Cyclorama lighting in which light from cyclorama borders and foots is reflected from the surface of the cyc; the light "glances" off the surface of the cyc. (Watson "Color" 257)

glare   1. In stage lighting, an onstage reflection or light source which is bright enough to be distracting or to cause discomfort to the viewer. (Sellman/Lessley ESSENTIALS, Lounsbury THEATRE) 2. Limelight, prominence.

glass   1. See: chimney. 2. The glass color filter used on limelights in late 19th C Britain. (Rees GAS 62-63, 207)

glass bracket   In 19th C theatres, the backstage storage rack for lamp glasses (chimneys). This was a piece of timber with a number of wooden pegs resembling those on an old-fashioned hat rack. (Rees GAS 206)

glass color cap   See: color cap.

glass color plate   See: color plate.

glass crash   A sound effect made by dropping pieces of glass on an appropriate surface. A china crash is similarly produced. Now usually a recorded effect.

glasses   Mirrors in 18th C theatres, especially in the auditorium, set behind lights to increase illumination. (Stone LONDON clxxxviii)

glass medium   Since at least the 19th C in Britain, a color filter of glass.

glass plate   See: color plate.

glawng (Thai)   See: *klong*.

gleeman   See: minstrel.

Glengarry cap   See: balmoral.

glide   See: efforts.

gligmon   See: minstrel.

glissade (French)   In ballet, a glide or traveling step with the working foot, with the other foot closing to it. (Grant TECHNICAL)

glisser (French)   See: movements in ballet.

glitch   1. Informally, among electricians, a brief but powerful surge of current. Such a surge, sometimes dangerous to lighting equipment, can result from turning on one or more large lamps or a large motor. (Bellman SCENE 463) 2. A brief fault in a control board or computer. 3. A brief fluctuation in the lights.

globe   1. See: chimney. 2. In U.S. theatres, an occasional term for lamp, a usage common in film practice. (Rees GAS 207, Lounsbury THEATRE 79)

globular lamp   See: G.

gloire (French)   See: glory.

glong (Thai)   See: *klong*.

gloria (Spanish)   Formerly, a cloud machine or glory that descended from above the stage, after the French and Italian tradition.

glory   1. In the Renaissance theatre, a flown scenic unit representing a cloud or sunburst, usually with a performer or performers playing deities. 2. In the Restoration theatre, a frame covered with taffeta, lit from behind and used to provide a glow behind a performer representing a deity. (Cameron/Gillespie ENJOYMENT, Bowman/Ball THEATRE)

glory grabber   A scene stealer.

glove puppet   A hollow cloth figure fitting over the hand, the head and hands moved by the puppeteer's fingers. Also called a hand or fist puppet. (Wilmeth LANGUAGE)

glow lamp   In Britain, an occasional term for an incandescent lamp. (Corry PLANNING 180)

G.L.S.   See: General Lighting Service lamp.

glue size   Powdered glue which, when heated and mixed with water and sometimes some white paint, is used for priming scenery. Also called size, size water, sizing. (Win "Terms")

Glühlampe (German)   Literally: glowing light. An incandescent lamp.

go   1. To work, to be effective, as in "That'll go," or to "go across the footlights." 2. Backstage, a signal to perform, e.g., to shift scenery, flash lightning, roll the thunder, etc.

goat song   See: *tragoidia*.

go back   1. To repeat, to rehearse again. In Britain, go back on. 2. To go backstage. In Britain, go behind, go round. (Bowman/Ball THEATRE)

gobanmemono (Japanese)   See: *kiri no*.

gobble up   To like enormously, as in "The audience gobbled it up." Also called eat up.

go behind   See: go back.

gobo   1. A projection slide, usually cut out of metal and used in the gate of an ellipsoidal spotlight. The term apparently originated in U.S. TV in mid-20th C and came into U.S. theatres some years later. By the late 1960s, it was used in Britain but also referred to as a U.S. term. Also called a pattern. 2. Especially among U.S. professional electricians, a mask at or near the front of a fixture to cut off light spill; some of these technicians have used 'cookie' for the drop-in cutout. As might be expected, these usages have led some theatre people to use either term for the drop-in cutout; at present and recently, the theatre has preferred gobo. See also: cookie, flag. (Bellman SCENE 442, 446, 458, fig. 39.10; Parker/Smith DESIGN; 1968 Bentham ART 335, 391; Bentham ART 279, 312; Lounsbury THEATRE 96, 170; Wehlburg GLOSSARY)

gochushin (Japanese)   1. In *kabuki*, the role of a messenger who arrives and delivers a long narrative, usually about a battle, with accompanying gestures. (Scott KABUKI 115) 2. The knee-length costume worn in that role. See also: *yoten*.

go clean   To sell all seats for a performance. See also: clean house.

go dark   Of a theatre, to be closed.

"God bless you both!"   A comic's *sotto voce*, sarcastic aside when a good joke is unappreciated by an audience. When a similar fate is met by an actor or actress, the aside is "It must be the landlady!" (Granville DICTIONARY)

godeg (Indonesian)   See: *ngibing*.

god out of the machine, god from the machine   See: *deus ex machina*.

go down   1. To move downstage. 2. To dim the lights. (Bowman/Ball THEATRE)

god play   See: *kami no*.

go dry   To forget one's lines.

gods   1. The top gallery. 2. Audience members sitting in the top gallery in old theatres. (Hogan LONDON cxcix)

gofer, gopher   A production assistant whose title stems from his frequently having to go for something, such as coffee. (Stern MANAGEMENT)

go for   In Britain, to attack a performer or performance in the press. Also called (to) slate. (Granville DICTIONARY)

Gogolian assortment   Décor used for Russian plays whose action is set in the first half of the 19th C. (Gorchakov RUSSIA 15)

go in   Exit.

going on cold   1. Performing without the benefit of rehearsal. 2. Auditioning without having read the script. (National TECHNICAL)

"Going up!"   A warning to performers that the curtain is about to rise. (Baker THEATRECRAFT)

gold brick   A star of the legitimate stage who gave readings or performed in one-act dramas on the vaudeville stage, lured there by a huge salary. (Zellers PASTOR 93-94)

goldfish   A wealthy person who invests in a theatrical venture. (Berrey/Van den Bark SLANG 574)

gold powder   A substance used to give light blonde or golden highlights to a performer's hair. Applied with a brush. See also: metallic powders.

gold tickets   In late 18th C London theatres, special admission checks given to important playgoers. The usual checks were copper. Also called guinea tickets. (Hogan LONDON xxvii)

go legit   1. To produce legitimate drama. 2. To become a performer in legitimate drama.

golek (Indonesian)   Literally: doll. 1. A graceful Javanese court dance performed solo by a young girl. (Holt ART 113) 2. In Javanese *wayang kulit*, a dance by a *golek* puppet which ends a performance. (Holt ART 113) 3. Abbreviation for *wayang golek* in Java and Sunda.

goliard   See: minstrel.

Goliath Edison Screw   The British term for U.S. mogul base. Often reduced to G.E.S. See also: lamp base. (Bentham ART 84, Corry LIGHTING pl. I)

golilla (Spanish)   A somewhat narrower version of the Elizabethan ruff. See also: gran gola. (Boucher FASHION, Russell COSTUME)

gombeyatta (Kannada)   A string puppet theatre form in Mysore state, south India, that performs plays from the dance-drama repertory of *yaksagana*. (ASIAN 11)

gom mu (Korean)   See: *kommu*.

gone clean   See: clean house.

gonelle   A Roman and pre-medieval man or woman's long tunic, also worn by monks and knights. The word relates to the English gown and the Italian *gonellone*, which meant cassock. (Boucher FASHION)

gone to Cain's   Said of a production that has closed. Cain's was a storage company in New York which sold or rented scenery to touring companies. It closed in the 1930s. (Bowman/Ball THEATRE 159)

gonfalon, gonfanon   A pennant or flag worn on a medieval warrior's lance. See also: cointise. (Walkup DRESSING 96)

gong (Indonesian)   See: *gamelan*.

gong (Thai)   The generic term for bronze gong sets played in theatre music. *Gong wong* is an instrument consisting of sixteen tuned bronze bowls arranged in a semi-circular frame. The classical *pi phat* ensemble contains a *gong wong yai* (large *gong wong*) and a *gong wong lek* (small *gong wong*). Also spelled *khawng*, *khong*, and *kong*. (Duriyanga THAI 21-23, Morton TRADITIONAL

50-52) *Gong hooi* is a set of 3, 5, or 7 small hanging gongs played in *khon*. (Duriyanga in Rangthong SOUVENIR 258)

gongfu (Chinese)   See: *jiben gongfu.*

gong gede (Indonesian)   See: *gamelan gong.*

gong hooi (Thai)   See: *gong.*

gong kebyar (Indonesian)   See: *gamelan gong.*

gong wong (Thai)   See: *gong.*

gonk   See: hokum.

good box office   1. Said of a popular performer. 2. Substantial ticket sales.

good date   A desirable engagement.

good get in   See: bad get in.

good join   A carpenter's term for two scenic units attached to one another smoothly and tightly.

good show town   See: show town.

good take   Good ticket sales.

good theatre   A term applied to an action, speech, scene, play, etc. which works effectively. (Sobel NEW)

go off   1. To exit. 2. Hyphenated, an exit. 3. Especially in Australia, to miss a performance for a good reason. (National TECHNICAL)

go on   1. To enter. 2. Hyphenated, an entrance. 3. To appear in place of a scheduled performer, as when an understudy performs.

go on a hamburger diet, go on a starvation diet   To play one-night stands on a percentage basis. (Berrey/Van den Bark SLANG 590)

goong (Indonesian)   See: *gamelan.*

go on the boards   To become a performer.

go on the road   To tour.

goose   1. Especially in vaudeville, a Hebrew or Jewish impersonator. Also called a Yid. See also: Hebe comic. (Wilmeth LANGUAGE) 2. To hiss a performance. 3. Any sound of derision, as in 'to give the goose.'

gooser   A performance that fails.

go out   To exit.

go over   1. To rehearse, to repeat, especially difficult lines or business. (Baker THEATRECRAFT) 2. To delight an audience. Hence, go over big, go over strong, etc. 3. Hyphenated, a successful show.

go over bits   To rehearse tricky cues, monosyllabic speeches, and scraps of dialogue likely to trip up a performer during a play. (Granville DICTIONARY)

go over with the gods   To be successful with the uncritical. (Berrey/Van den Bark SLANG 584) *gopa lila* (Oriya)   A hand puppet theatre form in Orissa state, east India. (ASIAN 11)

gopher   See: gofer.

goraku (Japanese)   A light or entertaining performance or play, in contrast to serious drama. *No* is not *goraku*; *kabuki* and musical comedy are.

gorger   A manager.

gorget, *gorgerette* (French)   1. A medieval neck covering trimmed with wool, linen, fur, or silk. See also: gable. Also called a *touret de col* (French). 2. Medieval armor: a protector for the neck and upper chest. 3. A 17th C silk or linen neckerchief. 4. An 18th C ribbon or tulle pleated edging for a square neckline. (Barton COSTUME 140, Boucher FASHION)

gorgias   1. 15th C gauze masking the low décolletage of gowns. 2. Hence, the neckline itself. Related to English gorgeous. (Boucher FASHION)

go round   See: go back.

goryu sanyaku (Japanese)   A composite term—'five schools' (of *shite* actors) and 'three roles' (*waki* and *kyogen* actors and musicians)—meaning an ensemble of all *no* performers. (Komparu NOH 157)

göstermelik (Turkish)   A set figure, sometimes a composite, shown on the screen during the overture to a shadow play. Similar to the *kayon* of Javanese shadow theatre. (And KARAGÖZ 30)

gosthi (Sanskrit)   1. A type of minor drama (*uparupaka*) in ancient India, possibly a pantomime with song, dance and music. (Keith SANSKRIT 351) 2. See: *akitta kuttuka*.

go tab   1. To condense plays. 2. To present condensed plays, that is, tabloids.

go the rounds   To go from one agent to another in search of employment. In Britain, do the agents. (Bowman/Ball THEATRE)

go to Cain's   See: gone to Cain's.

go to one's seat   In medieval English productions, to exit. The performer's usual method of exit was to a seat in his 'house.' (Davidson STUDIES 70)

go turkey   To work on a percentage basis. (Berrey/Van den Bark SLANG 593)

goukelaere (Middle High German)   See: minstrel.

got up   See: get up.

goulan, kou lan (Chinese)   Literally: hook balustrade. A type of 10th-14th C public theatre structure, located in an amusement quarter, in which both hundred entertainment (*baixi*) spectacles and *zaju* plays were performed. Audiences were seated on three sides of a raised stage which was enclosed by a low balustrade. Also called *gousi* or *kou ssu*, *kanpeng* or *k'an p'eng*, and *peng* or *p'eng*. (Dolby HISTORY 17, Mackerras RISE 193-194)

gousi (Chinese)   See: *goulan*.

go up   1. To move upstage. 2. To forget one's lines. (Bowman/Ball THEATRE)

go uphill   To forget one's lines.

go vaude   To become a vaudevillian.

go west   To fail.

gown à la créole   See: *caraco*.

gown à la Française   An 18th C long dress with a fitted top, train, and ornamented stomacher. Two large box pleats, called Watteau pleats, fell from the collar at the back. Also called a sack back, French gown, *robe à la Française* (French). See also: kontush, *petits bonshommes*, Watteau pleat. (Barton COSTUME 313, Boucher FASHION)

gown à la lévite   An 18th C long dress with wrist-length fitted sleeves and a full skirt draped over another skirt. The overskirt was free-falling, without hoops or puffs. Also called a chemise gown or gaulle. (Walkup DRESSING 225, Boucher FASHION)

gown à l'Anglaise   A late 18th C long gown, beloved of the artist Thomas Gainsborough for his female subjects. It was usually heavy satin of simple design: a fitted, unboned bodice closed over a vest, a full skirt split at the sides to reveal a usually matching petticoat, sheer sleeves, and a scarf, worn with a wide-brimmed velvet hat and ostrich plumes. Also called an English gown. See also: gown à la Française, Watteau gown. (Boucher FASHION)

gown à la Polonaise   In the late 18th C, a long dress whose bodice resembled the gown à l'Anglaise. The skirt had three panniers drawn up on cords which could be released to make a flying gown or *trollopée* (French). Later the panniers were sewn into position and the cords were ornamental. Also called a Polonaise gown, Polish gown, slammerkin. (Boucher FASHION, Chalmers CLOTHES 216)

gown à la sultane   An 18th C long dress, opening in front to reveal an underskirt of another color. (Boucher FASHION)

gown à la Turque   At the end of the 18th C, a long dress with a tight top, flaring sleeves, flat collar, and a draped bow at one hip. Also called a Turkish gown. (Boucher FASHION)

gown à l'insurgente   A gown à l'Anglaise with wide sleeves, inspired by the American Revolutionary war. (Boucher Fashion)

gr   Groove.

graciosa, gracioso (Spanish)   A simpleton or clown, often a servant, a popular character in 16th C and later plays. Also called a *jocosa* or *jocoso*. See also: *bobo*. (Brockett HISTORY 230, Falk ''Census'' 85)

graciosa de cantar (Spanish)   In 18th C provincial Spain, a singing comic actress. (Falk ''Census'' 85) *graciosa de versos* (Spanish)   In 18th C provincial Spain, a comic actress. (Falk "Census" 85)

gradas (Spanish)   Backless benches along the sides of the *patio* in a *corral* theatre, graduated in height. The term is still used for theatre seats. (Roberts STAGE)

gradi (Italian)   Literally: steps. Stepped seating or bleachers in Renaissance theatres. (Nagler SOURCES 81)

gradus (Latin Roman)   A step. *Gradi* were banks of seats for spectators. See also: *subsellia*.

grain   In the Stanislavsky system: 1. The essence of even the tiniest role; its basic drive or spine. 2. A play's main idea, which embodies the germ of its meaning.

graining   In scene painting, a technique which simulates the grain of wood by using a partially dry brush.

grallator (Latin Roman)   Especially from the late 1st C BC, stilt-walker, which is the literal meaning. This is one of the "lesser performers" included by Chambers among *scenici* (actors) and by Nicoll among performers attached to the mime. (Chambers MEDIAEVAL I 7, Nicoll MASKS 85)

grand   See: house curtain.

grand batterie (French)   See: *batterie*.

grand circle   In Britain, an occasional alternate for dress circle. (Bowman/Ball THEATRE)

grand drape   A grand drapery or grand drapery border. Sometimes the term is synonymous with teaser (a border which normally hangs upstage of the house curtain and sets the height of the proscenium opening). It is also used to mean a valance—a border, sometimes ornamented, hanging in front of the act curtain— or the act curtain itself. See also: teaser.

grand écart (French)   A split; often used by Italian *commedia dell'arte* actors as an acrobatic trick when a performance was dragging. (Duchartre ITALIAN 36)

grand coquette (French)   A 19th C French female comedy role, apparently almost equal to lead roles in its importance. (Carlson FRENCH 27)

grande dame (French)   An actress who plays queens and aristocratic old ladies. (Fay GLOSSARY)

Grand Guignol   1. See: Guignol. 2. The Paris theatre which specialized in short, sensational horror plays. By extension, such a play. Hence, Grand Guignol style, Grand Guignol elements, etc. (Bowman/Ball THEATRE)

grand habit (French)   See: *bas de cotte*.

grand jury   The occupants of the gallery.

grand master   A switch or dimmer which overrides all other switches or dimmers. A group master or sub-master operates a portion of the switches or dimmers. Master control applies either to the process or to the controller (such as a handle or button) which the board operator uses. Hence such terms as master handle, master dimmer, master switch, master dimmer wheel (which the British have used), and other combinations. Simple master is often used by lighting people for any of these terms except sub-master and group master. Also called the main. (Sellman/Lessley ESSENTIALS, Wehlburg GLOSSARY, Rae/Southern INTERNATIONAL)

grandmaster board   Especially in Britain, a type of older light control board with a large handle or wheel which can control all dimmers simultaneously.

grand opera   The term generally applied to the large-scale, usually serious operas of the 19th C, such as those of Richard Wagner and Giuseppe Verdi.

grand pas de chat (French)   Literally: large cat's step. In ballet, a step like a cat's leap. (Grant TECHNICAL 73)

grand pas de deux (French)   A structured *pas de deux* which generally contains an entry, an adagio, variations for a male and a female dancer, and a coda in which the dancers perform together. (Grant TECHNICAL 75)

grandstand   To seek applause.

grandstand play   An act or piece of business designed to obtain applause.

grand tab   See: house curtain.

grand tier   Especially in opera houses, a term sometimes applied to a large first balcony.

Grand Turk   One of the traditional come-apart marionettes inherited from the Italian *fantoccini*. The figure turns into six smaller figures derived from the hands, arms, legs, and body. So called because its only manifestation for many years was a Turkish marionette. See also: trick puppet.

gran gola   A 17th C wide ruff. See also: *golilla*.

granthika (Sanskrit)   A narrator, often working with a dancer-actor (*sobhanika*), who performed "dance-sketches" about Krishna as early as the 2nd C B.C., perhaps marking the beginning of Krishna plays (*raslila*) in India. (Hein MIRACLE 246-254)

graphic image   See: dramatic metaphor.

graphic score   See: visual scenario.

grass cloth, grass mat   A stage floor covering simulating grass.

grave trap   A rectangular trap near the front of the stage, named after its use in the graveyard scene in *Hamlet*.

gravy   1. Theatrical hokum. Sometimes called oakum. 2. Especially in Britain, racy lines. (Bowman/Ball THEATRE)

grease   Greasepaint.

greaseball   In the 1930s and later, a performer who used too much makeup.

greasepaint   In makeup, a foundation paint available in white, black, grey, and several hundred colors. Formerly it was a mixture of wax, oil, and lard (or spermaceti).

greasepaint and canvas   The stage, the theatre. (Rosenstein/Haydon/Sparrow ACTING 107)

greasepaint English   Theatrical jargon. (Berrey/Van den Bark SLANG 594)

grease pusher   A makeup artist.

grease rag   In Britain, a cloth used to remove makeup.

great bills   Oversize playbills, measuring about 14'' by 31'', usually printed in black and red, posted in 18th C London. Also called big bills or large bills.

greatcoat   1. Any heavy overcoat. 2. See: capote. (Wilcox DICTIONARY)

Great Dionysia, Greater Dionysia   See: City Dionysia.

great divider   Wrinkles.

great scene   In a well-made play (q.v.), the segment containing the climax. (Bowman/Ball THEATRE)

Great White Way   Broadway.

Grecian bend   In the early 20th C, the forward tipping of the female figure as a result of wearing high-heeled shoes. It served to emphasize a well-proportioned derrière. See also: kangaroo bend. (Barton COSTUME 462)

Greek it   On a stage sign or poster, to make bogus lettering which has no meaning. (Parker/Smith DESIGN)

green   1. Especially in vaudeville, the stage. A performer is said to be 'on the green' when performing. 2. An old term for the front curtain, which was usually green. Also called the green baize or green curtain. 3. A green baize stage carpet used in the 19th C and earlier in the closing scene of a tragedy to protect the performers' costumes when falling to the ground. (Bowman/Ball THEATRE)

greenback   See: green coat.

green baize   See: green.

green boxes   In 18th C London theatres and later, the boxes nearest the stage in the top tier. Sometimes called slips. (Hogan LONDON xv, xlvii)

green carpet   See: green.

green coat, green-coat man   In Restoration times, a stagehand dressed in green. Also called a greenback. (Bowman/Ball THEATRE)

green curtain   1. Evidently the standard color of the house curtain in 18th C theatres and later. (Irving in Nagler SOURCES 532) 2. See: fire curtain.

green fat   In Britain, a performer's role having comic business, good lines, and jokes. (Granville DICTIONARY)

"Green lime, please!"   A line which savors of old melodramas. From the practice of spotlighting the villain of a melodrama in a green limelight at the moment he indicated his vile intent. (Granville DICTIONARY)

green rag   Especially in Britain, the stage curtain. (Granville DICTIONARY)

green room   An offstage lounge for performers, and a place where they can receive visitors. The term was used as early as the 18th C. It may have derived from 'scene room,' a place mentioned by Samuel Pepys, where Restoration actors studied their lines, but green has long been associated with the stage. Hence, green-room gossip, to talk green room (i.e., to gossip about theatre matters), etc.

green-room actor   A performer who boasts of his talent in the actors' lounge but who is unsuccessful on stage.

green-room gossip   Especially in Britain, theatrical shop talk. Also called backstage gossip. (Granville DICTIONARY)

greget (Indonesian)   In *wayang kulit*, a feeling of intense emotion expressed by a puppet character. (Humardani in Osman TRADITIONAL 84) *Greget saut* is an angry mood. (Muljono in Osman TRADITIONAL 71)

grègues (French)   See: breeches.

grex (Latin Roman)   Literally: flock, group. The usual term for a theatrical company. Also called a *caterva* (occasionally) or *commune* (rare). (Duckworth NATURE 75, Allen ANTIQUITIES 58, Sandys COMPANION 519).

grid, gridiron   An open framework of beams over a stage, below the roof but with working room between the grid and the roof, used principally for the suspension of draperies, scenery, and lighting instruments by means of a rigging system. (Bowman/Ball THEATRE)

grid block   See: loft block.

grid connector   In Britain, a plugging box on the gridiron. (Corry PLANNING 97)

gridiron   See: grid.

grid plan, grid plot   See: hanging plot.

grid well   An opening in the gridiron running perpendicular to the curtain line, designed for the placement of loft blocks. The opening is created by the spacing of loft block beams. Also called a loft well.

grid winch   An electric winch located on the gridiron of a theatre, used for hauling a single line. Several winches can be synchronized and used as a replacement for a counterweight set.

gril, grille (French)   Gridiron, grid.

grim (Russian)   Makeup. The term is also Yiddish.

grind   1. A stripteaser's circular gyrations of the pelvic area. See also: coffee grinder, grind on the floor, bumps and grinds. 2. To so dance. 3. A show that runs continuously, without intermissions. Hence, grind house. 4. A full day of performing. 5. A tiresome engagement. (Wilmeth LANGUAGE)

grind house   See: grind.

grind on the floor   A burlesque term for a belly dance executed by a girl lying supine on the floor. (Sobel BURLEYCUE 13)

griot (Wolof, Fulani, Songhai)   A West African professional troubadour, a specialist in the spoken word who acts as a story-teller, clown, mime, dancer, herald, genealogist, musician, oral reporter, or paid flatterer or insulter at courts or important family functions. (Balandier/Maquet AFRICAN, Adedeji glossary)

grip   1. A stagehand. Also called a flat man, grip hand, scene shifter, or stage grip. 2. See: pipe clamp. 3. A U-shaped bolt used to hold two cables together; also called a bulldog, line grip, wire grip. (Corry PLANNING, Bowman/Ball THEATRE, Granville DICTIONARY)

gripping   1. Working as a stagehand or grip. 2. Running scenery along the floor by grasping the leading edge of the unit, lifting it slightly, and sliding it forward.

gro   Groove.

grommet   A metal eyelet or reinforcement for a small hole in the edge of a drop or curtain; a short piece of sash cord passes through the grommet and is tied to a batten. By extension, the pieces of sash cord are sometimes called grommets. Grommets are also used at the edges of floor cloths. In Britain: grummet.

groove   1. A wooden channel on the stage floor in which flat wings and shutters slid in 17th through 19th C theatres, especially in England. Grooves were numbered from the front of the stage to the back, the spaces between wings serving as entrances. The grooves on the stage floor were called the lower grooves; upper grooves steadied the tops of the wings and shutters. Upper grooves were hinged and could be drawn up and out of the way, hence groove arm. Floor grooves were sometimes fixed in position, sometimes loose and removable. Abbreviations: G, gr, gro. 2. A channel fixed to the front of a lighting unit to receive a color frame. 3. A channel in winch drums, sheaves, and pulleys.

gross   The total income from ticket sales before deductions for any purpose. Royalties of playwrights and salaries of stars, directors, and others are usually predicated upon percentages of the gross. Sometimes called the gate, though that term is usually used for sports events.

grosser   A production that brings in healthy financial returns.

Grossewolkenapparat (German)   A large cloud machine.

grotesque comedy, grotesque theatre   See: theatre of the grotesque.

grotesque dancing   An 18th C category of dance that consisted of representations of persons, passions, and manners—actions that in earlier stage productions had been sung or spoken. (Avery LONDON cxxxi-cxxxii) *grotteschi* (Italian)   Dancers of the 17th-19th C who played comic action through pantomime. The emphasis was on the pastoral, peasant, local color, and *commedia dell'arte* characterization and style. (Winter BALLET 150, 151)

grouch bag   A purse which performers used to pin to their underclothes. Also called a boodle bag.

ground   See: earth.

ground batten   Occasionally in Britain, a striplight (not usually the foot-lights) used on the stage floor. Also called a length. (Ridge/Aldred LIGHTING 2)

ground cloth   See: floor cloth.

ground lights   In late 19th C Britain, an occasional term for a ground row. This is evidently the meaning in a long 1882 description of the installation of carbon filament lamps at the new Savoy theatre in London. (Rees GAS 173)

ground line   1. In 19th C Britain, the gas supply line for a striplight used as a ground row. 2. Sometimes, the ground row strip itself. (Rees GAS 40)

groundling   1. A spectator at a medieval production. 2. A playgoer in an Elizabethan theatre, standing in the pit (ground level) around the stage platform. (Peter CORNISH 26, Dekker in Nagler SOURCES 133)

ground plan   See: floor plan.

ground row   1. A low piece of scenery, usually representing a wall, distant hills, ground foliage, etc., placed on the stage floor, freestanding. Also called a foot piece. Often used to help mask the bottom of a sky cyclorama or the cyclorama footlights. 2. In Britain and sometimes in the U.S., a strip of lights (in Britain, length) which illuminates the lower portion of a sky drop or cy-clorama. Originally, in the 19th C, a gas striplight. (Bentham ART, Rees GAS 40, Stern MANAGEMENT)

ground row strip   In the U.S., a striplight which illuminates a scenic ground row from below. (Dean/Carra FUNDAMENTALS 380, Bowman MODERN, Bricker TODAY 321)

group   1. In 18th C theatres, a straight lineup of performers facing the footlights at the end of a performance. (Hogan LONDON lxxxix) 2. A number of dimmers under a single control. (McCandless SYLLABUS 51)

grouping   Placing the cast about the stage. (Stern MANAGEMENT)

group master   A dimmer which controls some of the dimmers on a control board. Also called a sub-master. (Sellman/Lessley ESSENTIALS, Bentham LIGHTING)

group reading   See: readers theatre.

group scene   A scene involving several performers.

grove   Groove (q.v.).

gru (Thai)   See: *kru*.

grummet   1. In Britain, a grommet. 2. A rope bridle, the two ends of which are tied to a batten. 3. In Britain, a metal eye attached to the back of scenery, near the top, to which a throw (lash) line can be tied. Called in the U.S. a lash line eye. (Baker THEATRECRAFT)

Gruppenzielstücke (German)   Pressure-group plays. Politically oriented, didactic plays put on by workers' collectives in mid-20th C Germany. (Calandra "Terror" 115)

gruppi di base (Italian)   Community theatres.

G-string   A thin strip of cloth passed between the legs of a striptease dancer and supported by a waist cord. The term may be an analogy to the G-string of a violin. (Wilmeth LANGUAGE, Granville DICTIONARY)

G-type, G-type lamp   See: G.

gu, ku (Chinese)   A minister or high official; a type of stock character in Yuan *zaju*. (Dolby HISTORY 60)

gua (Philippine)   A French scene in *zarzuela*. (Fernández ILOILO 101)

guan, kuan (Chinese)   A wood-bodied, double or single reed instrument used in the melodic orchestra (*wenchang*) in *kunqu*, Beijing opera (*jingju*), and many other forms of music-drama (*xiqu*). (Mackerras RISE 7; Wichmann "Aural" 441, 452)

guanben zaju, kuan pen tsa chü (Chinese)   Literally: official-text variety drama. A listing of 280 titles of Song *zaju* plays which may have been written for the government.

Guangdong opera   See: *yueju*, meaning 1.

Guangxi opera   See: *guiju*.

guansheng, kuan sheng (Chinese)   Literally: headdress male role. A role category which includes young male characters of high social status such as well-to-do young scholars and lovers; a major subdivision of the young male role (*xiaosheng*) in *kunqu* drama. (Dolby HISTORY 105, Scott CLASSICAL 31)

guanxue, kuan hsüeh (Chinese)   Literally: official's boot. A square-toed boot with a thick white sole worn to enhance the dignity and height of many male role (*sheng*) and painted-face role (*jing*) actors in numerous forms of music-drama (*xiqu*). Also called high square (*gaofang* or *kao fang*) and thick-soled boot (*houdixue* or *hou ti hsüeh*). (Halson PEKING 37, Scott CLASSICAL 159)

guanyi, kuan i (Chinese)   Literally: official clothing. A round-necked robe which is plain except for a single square embroidered panel on the chest. It is worn on festive occasions by characters of high social status in Beijing opera (*jingju*) and many other forms of music-drama (*xiqu*). The male version is full-length, while the female is ¾ length and worn over a skirt. (Halson PEKING 21, Scott CLASSICAL 147-148) *guanzuo, kuan tso* (Chinese)   Literally: officials' seats. The most comfortable and expensive seating available in a tea-house theatre (*xiyuan*) of the 17th-early 20th C: the portion of second-floor veranda seating near the stage at the sides of the auditorium. These two areas were partitioned, and served as boxes for officials and wealthy men, and later on for women as well. Popularly called enclosing/hired side-rooms (*baoxiang* or *pao hsiang*). (Mackerras RISE 201-202, Scott CLASSICAL 222)

guaranteed benefit   In Britain, a benefit for a person or a group in which the amount of money for the beneficiary or beneficiaries is guaranteed by the management in advance. (Troubridge BENEFIT 28)

guardarropa (Spanish)   In the 17th C and later: 1. A wardrobe. 2. The person in charge of the wardrobe. (Shergold SPANISH)

guarded   In the 16th C, ornamented on the edges with gold and silver lace. (Chalmers CLOTHES 172, Dreher HATMAKING)

guard-infanta   See: farthingale.

guare (Cornish)   A medieval play. (Peter CORNISH 11)

guban, ku pan (Chinese)   Literally: drum-and-clapper. The collective term for the single-skin drum (*danpigu*) and the *ban* clapper played by the orchestra conductor when leading the orchestra (*changmian*) in many forms of music-drama (*xiqu*), including Beijing opera (*jingju*). (Wichmann "Aural" 442-444, 452-460)

guéridons (French)   Large hoops taped together to form a pannier. (Boucher FASHION)

guerilla theatre   See: street theatre.

guest   To appear as a guest artist.

guest artist   1. A visiting performer working with a repertory or stock company. 2. A professional performer working with amateurs or with a regional, university, or community theatre. Sometimes called a guest star or guest actor/actress.

guest-direct   To direct a production by invitation, in the place of the usual director. Hence, guest director. (Bowman/Ball THEATRE)

guest star   See: guest artist.

gugug, guguk (Korean)   See: *kuguk*.

gugunungan (Indonesian)   See: *kayon*.

guide lines   A pair of vertical steel lines behind the proscenium which guide a curtain up and down. (Granville DICTIONARY)

Guignol   A French puppet show stock character dating from the 18th C. The shows in which he appeared were often gruesome; by extension, plays of that nature were called "Grand Guignol." (Sobel HANDBOOK) *guignol* (French)   1. Puppet show. 2. Sometimes, a hand puppet. Also called a *marionnette à gaine* (Philpott DICTIONARY) 3. A quick-change room.

guiju, kuei chü (Chinese)   Guangxi (Kuangsi) opera, a form of music-drama (*xiqu*) popular in the northern and eastern portions of the Guangxi Zhuang Autonomous Region, and in southern Hunan Province. It developed in the 17th C under the influence of *kunqu* and *yiyangqiang*, and currently uses music from five musical systems (*shengqiang xitong*), including *kunshanqiang* and *gaoqiang*.

guild   See: Artists of Dionysius.

guilds   Medieval craft organizations; they produced liturgical plays appropriate to their craft, such as the boatwrights presenting a Noah play.

guillotine curtain   A curtain that raises and lowers; a drop curtain. Often shortened to guillotine.

guimendan, kuei men tan (Chinese)   Literally: boudoir door female role. A refined, aristocratic, unmarried young female role; one of the main subdivisions of the female role (*dan*) in many forms of music-drama (*xiqu*). Similar to but younger and more vivacious than the principal female role (*zhengdan*). In *kunqu*, also called fifth female role (*wudan* or *wu tan*) and young female role (*xiaodan*). (Dolby HISTORY 105, 180; Scott CLASSICAL 32, 74)

guimp(e)   1. A medieval veil covering the neck and chest and surrounding the face; worn especially by nuns and widows. See also: wimple. 2. A 16th-19th C filling for the décolletage of a bodice, usually of a fabric different from it. See also: modesty. The late 19th C version, with long or short sleeves attached, was called a chemisette. Also called a partlet or gimp. (Barton COSTUME 224, Boucher FASHION, Wilcox DICTIONARY)

guinea-pig circuit   Cities where an act is tried out before bringing it to New York, such as Boston, New Haven, Philadelphia, Washington, etc.

guinea tickets   See: gold tickets.

guise dancer   In Britain, a mummer, masquer, disguiser. Hence, guiser, guisard.

Guizhou opera   See: *qianju*.

gulabo-sitabo (Hindi)   A hand puppet theatre form in north India. (ASIAN 11)

guleron   The shoulder portion of a *chaperon* (French). Also called a patte. (Boucher FASHION)

gulizi (Chinese)   See: *biandan*.

gulong (Philippine)   A 'roll' fighting movement in *comedia*. (Mendoza CO-MEDIA 65)

gummat (Marathi)   A troupe of *tamasha* folk drama players. (Gargi FOLK 82) *gundiao, kun tiao* (Chinese)   A passage of song or speech added between the lines of original song lyrics to clarify meaning and create colloquial immediacy in adapting plays from earlier forms of music-drama (*xiqu*) for performance in *yiyangqiang* and later in various other regional forms of the 14th-17th C. To add a passage with a sense different from what had just been sung as further explanation was called *jiagun* or *chia kun*; to repeat the meaning of a section of song in simpler and more comprehensible style was called *hegun* or *ho kun*. The term *gundiao* is sometimes used to refer solely to *jiagun*. See also: *chenzi, duozi*. (Dolby HISTORY 101, Mackerras "Growth" 71-74)

gunongan (Malaysian)   See: *pohon beringin*.

guntai (Japanese)   See: *santai*.

gunungan (Indonesian)   See: *kayon*.

guoju (Chinese)   See: *jingju*.

guomen, kuo men (Chinese)   Literally: through the door. An instrumental passage or "connective" played as a prelude to a song and as an interlude between songs in many forms of music-drama (*xiqu*) and storytelling (*quyi*), including Beijing opera (*jingju*). The main types of instrumental connectives include large (*daguomen* or *ta kuo men*) and small (*xiaoguomen* or *hsiao kuo men*). (Scott CLASSICAL 54; Scott TRADITIONAL I 13; Wichmann "Aural" 177-181, 186-187, 200-201, 468-472; Zung SECRETS 34)

gusen (Indonesian)   Literally: gums. A character type in Javanese *wayang*. *Gusen* characters have muscular bodies, round eyes and noses, and constant grins that show their gums. They are loyal, powerful in battle, and may be extremely slow witted. (Long JAVANESE 70)

gushi (Chinese)   See: *sigu*.

gut (Korean)   See: *kut*.

guts and spinach   Among scene painters, roccoco or baroque ornamentation in a stage setting. The phrase is scene painters' argot.

Guttenburg   1. Formerly, a good-looking secondhand costume, named after the New York secondhand theatrical costumer. (Wilmeth LANGUAGE) 2. A performer's wardrobe. (Berrey/Van den Bark SLANG 579)

gutter   See: wire way.

guy   To improvise, especially in order to spoil a scene.

(the) guy's from Dixie   Said of a burlesque performer who is no good. (Wilmeth LANGUAGE)

guzhuangtou, ku chuang t'ou (Chinese)   Literally: ancient costume head. A soft, fairly loose female hairdressing style (*batou*) in Beijing opera (*jingju*) and many other forms of music-drama (*xiqu*). Created from historical models by the master actor Mei Lanfang in the first half of the 20th C. (Scott CLASSICAL 166)

guzici, ku tzu tz'u (Chinese)   Literally: drum lyrics. A form of storytelling (*shuochang*) which arose c. 11th C. It was made up of suites of tunes in mode groupings. See also: *zhugongdiao*. (Dolby EIGHT 10)

gwangdae (Korean)   See: *kwangdae*.

gyp   See: ticket scalper.

gypsies of the stage   Strolling players. (Ralph TASTE 223)

gypsy   A chorus member or dancer who is prepared to move quickly, from show to show or town to town, usually with other choristers, much like a gypsy group. (Wilmeth LANGUAGE)

H

habergeon   A 15th C cavalryman's hip-length tunic with a high neck, long sleeves, and a leather belt holding a sword. Worn over a cloth tunic, the habergeon was made of chain or ring mail. Also spelled haubergeon. See also: hauberk. (Wilcox DICTIONARY)

habima (Hebrew)   The stage.

habit   1. In the plural, garments in general. 2. A 17th C costume. Also called a shape or dress. 3. Also in the 17th C, a man's doublet, or doublet and mantle, or doublet, mantle, and breeches. (Boucher FASHION, Bowman/Ball THEATRE, Jonson in Nagler SOURCES 145). 4. Clothes used for a particular purpose, such as a court habit, riding habit, etc. (Boucher FASHION)

habit à la Française (French)   1. A light *justaucorps* (jacket). 2. A 20th C style of livery. (Boucher FASHION)

habit à la Romaine (French)   A 17th C adaptation of Roman armor; tunic and boots combined with a full-bottomed wig and plumed headdress. (Brockett HISTORY 271)

hablada (Philippine)   See: *ablada*.

hablada (Spanish)   A slow, deliberate style of line delivery in the *cenaculo* (q.v.). See also *cantada*. (Mendoza "Lenten" 24)

habutai (Japanese)   In *kabuki*, a silk cloth stretched tightly over the actor's head as a base for a wig. Now also used in films and television. (Shaver COSTUMES 308, Leiter ENCYCLOPEDIA 102)

hacer prueba (Spanish)   To try out for a role.

hacer teatro (Spanish)   Literally: to make theatre. To perform.

hack   An obsolete term for a play doctor (q.v.).

haegum (Korean)   In masked-dance plays, a two-stringed fiddle which is held vertically on the knee. See: *samhyon yukkak*. (Cho "Yangju" 31)

haik   See: huke.

(the) hail-hail   Two claps in unison by an audience. (Berrey/Van den Bark SLANG 591)

hainanxi, hai nan hsi (Chinese)   See: *qiongju*.

haincelin   A medieval short houppelande with two embroidered sleeves. (Boucher FASHION)

hairneedle   See: bodkin.

hair powder   Powder used on hair and wigs in the 18th C.

haiyanqiang, hai yen ch'iang (Chinese)   1. A form of music-drama (*xiqu*) native to Haiyan in northeastern Zhejiang Province which originated in the 10th-12th C and was quite popular in the 13th-14th C. It was a blend of northern *qu* music and the music then prevalent in Haiyan, perhaps that of southern drama (*nanxi*). The principal instruments in the orchestra were the lute (*pipa*), moon guitar (*yueqin*), and the *xiangban* clapper. 2. A musical system (*shengqiang xitong*) characterized by *lianquti* musical structure which arose in Zhejiang and Jiangsu Provinces in the 14th C through the influence of *haiyanqiang* music-drama. It was overshadowed and ultimately replaced by the *gaoqiang* and *kunshanqiang* musical systems, but certain of its elements are believed to be preserved today in at least one form of music-drama and one form of shadow theatre (*piyingxi*) in Zhejiang Province.

haiyu (Japanese)   An actor or actress, chiefly in modern drama but also in *kabuki*. The term came into use following contact with the West in 1868. See also: *yakusha*.

hakama (Japanese)   The generic term for wide, split trousers, like culottes, worn over a kimono in *no, kyogen, kabuki* and *bunraku*. Primarily, but not exclusively, a male costume. See also: *kamishimo*.

haki butai (Japanese)   Literally: swept stage. A stage empty of characters, typically at the beginning of an act in *kabuki*. Also called *kara butai* (empty stage). (Brandon in Brandon/Malm/Shively STUDIES 118)

Hako   A Pawnee Indian performance event consisting of interrelated rituals elaborated with songs and acts, in sequence, which establish and reinforce bonds among different tribes. (Jenkins/Wapp ''Native'' 7)

hakobi (Japanese)   The standard walk of a *no* actor in which the flattened foot slides across the floor. See also: *suri ashi*. Illustrated in Keene NO 219.

half   The half hour immediately preceding the curtain—the warning to a company that the curtain will rise in 30 minutes. (Baker THEATRECRAFT)

half a hand   Weak applause.

half-beaver   A 17th-18th C hat whose fabric was made of an equal combination of beaver and some other fur. (Boucher FASHION)

half benefit   In 18th C theatres in Britain and later, a performer's benefit with the house charges shared by the performer and the management. Also called a half-clear benefit. (Troubridge BENEFIT 19)

half-crown brigade   Formerly in Britain, out-of-work performers who try to borrow money from friends and acquaintances. (Granville DICTIONARY)

half-fool   An 18th C Purim play cast member, dressed as harlequin on one half of his body and as a "civilian" on the other half. (Sandrow VAGABOND 1)

half hour   A warning to performers 30 minutes before curtain.

half leg drop   A leg drop attached to a tree trunk, column, etc. It does not reach the floor.

half mask   A mask covering only the upper portion of the face, usually only the nose and eyes, as in some *commedia dell'arte* masks. See also: loo mask.

half-plug, half plug   A stage plug half as thick as a standard stage plug. The purpose was to permit two such plugs to fit into a single receptacle. Also called a split plug, which was more common among professional stage electricians than half-plug. The receptacle, because it was so large and open, was dangerous. Stage plugs are now obsolete. (Lounsbury THEATRE 118)

half price   The entrance charge made to 18th C (and later) playgoers who arrived at the theatre after the third act of the mainpiece (at "half time"). Also called second price. See also: second account. (Hogan LONDON xxxvi)

half-price deal   An arrangement by which tickets are sold for half the sum printed on the ticket, usually to a club or other organization. Also called a two-for-one deal.

half time   See: half price.

half toes   In dance, a position of the foot in which the heel is raised until the weight rests on the ball of the foot. Also called *demi-pointes* (French). (Rogers DANCE 153-154)

half-up   In British lighting parlance, at half brightness. (Baker THEATRE-CRAFT)

half value   At late 18th C theatre benefits for minor employees, the share of the income distributed to the beneficiaries. The management kept the other half. (Hogan LONDON clxxxix)

half-watt spotlight   See: focus lamp.

halgi (Marathi)   A drum with a fierce sound, used in *tamasha*. (Gargi FOLK 76)

hall backing   A scenic unit representing a hall seen through a doorway.

hall keeper   In Britain: the stage door attendant. In the U.S., stage doorman. (Fay GLOSSARY)

(the) halls   In Britain, short for music halls; vaudeville theatres, as opposed to legitimate houses. (Granville DICTIONARY)

hall show   A legitimate theatre performance. (Berrey/Van den Bark SLANG 580) *halmi* (Korean)   The character and mask of an old woman in various types of masked dance-plays. Also called *miyal halmi*. (Korean MASKS 11, 14)

halo   A band placed inside a hat which is too large, to make it fit more closely to the head. (Dreher HATMAKING)

halogen lamp   See: tungsten-halogen lamp.

halus (Malaysian)   See: *alus*.

ham   1. A bad performer, especially one who overacts. 2. To act badly or overact. Hence, ham acting, hambone, hammy, hamfatter. Also called am. (Dolman ACTING)

ham-and-egger, ham-and-egg man   A wealthy person who invests in a theatrical venture. (Berrey/Van den Bark SLANG 574)

hamartia (Greek)   In Aristotle's *Poetics*, a word usually rendered flaw, error, or fault, and often referred to as tragic flaw. Error or fault are now the preferred renderings of Aristotle's meaning in discussing the misapprehension which is partly responsible for a tragic character's downfall. See the cited works for two somewhat different discussions of the term. (Lucas ARISTOTLE 299-307, Vaughn DRAMA)

hamatsa (Kwakiutl)   In the winter ritual ceremonies of the Kwakiutl Indians of Canada, the cannibal dance. (Turner/Turner ''Ethnography'' 41)

hambalos (Philippine)   A 'blow' fighting movement in *comedia*. (Mendoza COMEDIA 65)

hambone   1. An unconvincing blackface dialectician. (Berrey/Van den Bark SLANG 573) 2. See: ham.

ham chewer   An inferior or amateur actor.

hamfatter   See: ham.

hammy   1. Acting that is overdone. 2. Said of old-fashioned stage business. (Carrington THEATRICANA)

hana (Japanese)   Literally: flower. The central concept of *no* performance according to Zeami Motokiyo (1363-1443), defined as ''an effect resulting from an excellent performance.'' The seed or basis of flower is *yugen*. (Konishi ''Approaches'' 24) 'Flower' is the freshness, variety, and uniqueness of a great actor's performance to which the audience instinctively responds. (Pronko PERSPECTIVES 80, Inoura HISTORY 88, Shimazaki NOH 1-2)

hanamichi (Japanese)   Literally: flower path. The runway leading from the right side of the *kabuki* stage through the audience to a curtained exit at the rear of the auditorium. Inspired by, but different in effect from, the bridgeway (*hashigakari*) of *no*, it is used for processions and for major entrances and exits. Sometimes also used in *bunraku*. See also: *hon hanamichi*. (Ernst KABUKI 92-104, Keene BUNRAKU 61) *hanare kyogen* (Japanese)   Literally: separate play. A short, independent play on an early 17th C *kabuki* program. Only after 1664 were long, multi-act *kabuki* plays written. See also: *tsuzuki kyogen*. (Leiter ENCYCLOPEDIA 305)

Hanayagi ryu (Japanese)   An important school and style of *kabuki*-style dance founded by Hanayagi Jusuke I in the mid-19th C. (Gunji BUYO 184)

hanayoten (Japanese)   See: *yoten*.

han chü (Chinese)   See: *hanju*.

hand, hand exercise   Applause.

hand and rod puppet   A puppet operated from below the stage. One of the puppeteer's hands controls the movements of the puppet's head, and the other hand holds rods which operate the arms and legs. Or rods may be used to manipulate the head. (Philpott DICTIONARY)

hand ballet   A dance in which the performer is the gloved hand of a puppeteer. (Philpott DICTIONARY)

handbill   A printed announcement, smaller than a double-crown poster and used as a flyer or handout for a forthcoming production.

handcuffed   Said of an audience that does not applaud. (Sobel HANDBOOK)

hand exercise   Applause.

handiao (Chinese)   See: *hanju*.

handle   A word not in the script but added by a performer to the beginning of a line, such as ''Oh'' or ''Well.'' (Stern MANAGEMENT)

handle puppet   Especially in the Polish *szopka*, a small figure operated by short wires or sticks which rise through slots in the stage floor. (Philpott DICTIONARY)

handler   A performer's agent.

handling line   See: operating line.

hand prop   A hand property. A small object which performers may handle, such as a teacup, letter, or book. The term is sometimes restricted to those properties (also called personal props) carried on or off stage by performers, the other small properties on stage being considered decorative. See also: character prop, personal prop. (McGaw ACTING, Roberts STAGE)

hand puppet   See: glove puppet.

Handscheinwerfer (German)   Literally: hand spotlight. A very small hand-held spotlight. (Fuchs LIGHTING 210)

hand-to-hand music   Applause.

hand-worked house   See: hemp house.

handy box   A small, open-faced metal box which contains a single electrical outlet or occasionally a switch. Also called a convenience outlet.

hang   To suspend, e.g. scenic units, curtains, lighting instruments, etc.

hang a show   To set up the scenery (from the days when most scenery was hung). (Lounsbury THEATRE)

hangdang, hang tang (Chinese)   The generic term for role categories in all forms of music-drama (*xiqu*). In Song *zaju* and Jin *yuanben*, the major role categories were male clown (*fujing*) and dominant male (*fumo*); in Yuan *zaju*, male (*mo*), female (*dan*), and clown or villain (*jing*). In *kunqu* and Beijing opera (*jingju*), there are four major role categories: male (*sheng*), female (*dan*), painted-face (*jing*), and clown (*chou*). Many contemporary forms also include a fifth category, supporting older male (*mo*); some, such as *hanju* and southern *yueju*, have a total of ten basic role categories. (Dolby HISTORY 8-9, 26-27, 60, 105-106, 180-181; Scott CLASSICAL 31-32, 60-77)

hang 'em on the chandeliers, hang 'em on the rafters   To attract an overflow audience. (Berrey/Van den Bark SLANG 584)

hanger   1. In stage lighting, a short length of metal, usually pipe, used in hanging lighting instruments. Typical are the pipes fastened at one end to a light batten and at the other end to a spotlight. The term is also used of the short horizontal pipes which often form arms on vertical light towers. Sometimes called arm, pipe arm, or suspension arm. 2. A U-shaped yoke used in hanging spotlights. (Lounsbury THEATRE, Wehlburg GLOSSARY, McCandless SYLLABUS 26) 3. Any of several devices for suspending draperies, scenery, lighting instruments, etc. Hence, hanger iron, curtain-pole hanger, drapery hanger, picture-frame hanger, etc. (Bowman/Ball THEATRE)

hanger iron   A short length of iron with screw holes and a ring, attached to the back of a scenic unit for flying purposes. Also called a hanging iron. The hanger iron at the bottom of a flat is usually turned up to hook under the rail of the flat. Hence, hook hanger iron, hook hanging iron. A rope is tied to the bottom hanger iron, run through the ring in the top hanger iron, and run up to the batten from which the scenic unit is hung. Also called a fixing iron. Parker and Smith have an illustration. (Baker THEATRECRAFT, Parker/Smith DESIGN 302)

hangguan (Chinese)   See: *huiguan*.

hanging   A curtain. In Elizabethan times, also called an arras. In Restoration times, a hanging was a curtain other than the main one. (Dekker in Nagler SOURCES 135, Digby ELVIRA 21)

hanging clip   See: pipe clamp.

hanging iron   See: hanger iron.

hanging length   See: length.

hanging loft   See: flies.

hanging piece   A flown scenic unit.

hanging plan and section   Scale drawings showing how the rigging system is laid out. See also: hanging plot.

hanging plot   A diagram (plan and section) of what has been attached to each batten and what the fly crew's duties are. Also called a fly plot, grid plan or plot, line plot, rigging plan or plot.

hanging pocket   See: drop pocket.

hanging rail   In a puppet theatre, a backstage device located near the bridge and used for storing puppets until they are needed onstage.

hanging ropes   See: flies.

hanging scene   In 19th C theatres, a border. Also called a top scene. (Southern CHANGEABLE 324)

hanging unit   Scenic elements joined and suspended as a single piece. (Bowman/Ball THEATRE)

hanging wing   A side wing suspended from a track rather than sliding in a groove or riding on a pole.

hang kuan (Chinese)   See: *huiguan*.

hangover   One who stays to see a performance a second time. (Berrey/Van den Bark SLANG 574)

hang tang (Chinese)   See: *hangdang*.

hangyuan, hang yüan (Chinese)   See *lingren*.

hanju, han chü (Chinese)   One of the chief forms of music-drama (*xiqu*) in Hubei Province, also popular in Henan, Shaanxi, Hunan, Guangdong, and Fujian Provinces. It probably derived initially from the *gaoqiang* musical system during the 14th-17th C; it adopted music from the *pihuang* musical system in the 18th C, before the ascendance of Beijing opera (*jingju*). Also called *handiao* or *han tiao*, and in the 17th-19th C, *chudiao* or *ch'u tiao*. (Dolby HISTORY 223; Mackerras MODERN 34, 154-156)

han maku (Japanese)   To quickly raise and then lower the curtain (*maku*) of a *no* theatre half way (*han*) to allow the audience a tantalizing glimpse of a character before he or she has actually entered. (Komparu NOH 147)

hannya (Japanese)   A two-horned *no* mask with angry eyes and gaping mouth. The mask is worn by a female demon or a woman transformed into a demoness because of jealousy. (Shimazaki NOH 62)

han tiao (Chinese)   See: *hanju*.

hanumanayaka (Sanskrit)   A clown or buffoon in *yaksagana* folk theatre. He speaks in rustic prose. See also: *vidusaka*. (Gargi FOLK 5, 147-148)

happening   A theatrical event with no script, with as much as possible left to chance, and with opportunities for audience involvement.

happy idea   The basic premise on which Greek Old Comedy was based. For example, in Aristophanes' *Lysistrata*, the happy idea is that women can stop war by withholding sex from their men. (Cameron/Gillespie ENJOYMENT) *haradashi* (Japanese)   Literally: bulging stomach. In *kabuki*, minor villains identified by strong red makeup and comically protruding bellies. They serve as foils for the hero. (Leiter ENCYCLOPEDIA 110)

hara gei (Japanese)   Literally: stomach art. The art of deeply truthful psychological acting in *kabuki*, created by Ichikawa Danjuro IX in the latter part of the 19th C for serious roles, such as Yuranosuke in *Chushingura*. (Komiya MEIJI 37)

harake (Kannada)   Literally: benediction. In *yaksagana*, a devotional song to a god. (Ashton/Christie YAKSAGANA 61, 91)

hard   See: inner proscenium.

hard edge(d)   With a sharply defined border. The term is used primarily of the beams of certain spotlights. (Bellman SCENE)

hard light   1. A light which casts sharp shadows. 2. A light with a sharply defined beam. (Lounsbury THEATRE 170, Wehlburg GLOSSARY)

hard scenery   1. Scenery with a surface hard to the touch (not fabric). It often has acoustic properties approaching those of structural walls. 2. Formerly, any scenery that could not be folded, rolled, etc. A flat was once considered hard scenery.

hard ticket   1. A scarce ticket for a highly successful production. 2. A show for which tickets are difficult to acquire.

hard ticketer   A theatre presenting two shows daily on a reserved-seat basis. (Lees "Lexicon" 57)

hardware   In stage costume, jewelry.

hardware cloth   A coarse metal screen used in building set pieces, such as trees. (Buerki STAGECRAFT)

hardwood   A substitute for a regular ticket, priced as marked by the box-office manager or treasurer—often a a ticket for standing room.

harena (Latin Roman)   See: *arena*.

hare's foot   A good-luck amulet once used by performers in applying powder and rouge. Also called a rabbit's foot. It has now been largely replaced by powder puffs and powder rouge brushes.

harikatha (Sanskrit)   A monodrama that uses no stage, no scenery, and no makeup. Usually performed in a temple yard or in a rich man's house. (Rangacharya INDIAN 54)

harlequin   1. A generic term for the most popular of *commedia dell'arte* characters, Arlecchino (Italian) or Arlequin (French)—the clever servant with the Bergamo dialect and motley costume. (Oreglia COMMEDIA 56-57) 2. A costume derived from *commedia dell'arte*, consisting of a one-piece, closely-fitting garment in a diamond pattern and brightly colored, with white hose and black slippers, a tight stocking cap to simulate a shaved head, a half-mask, and a sword. 3. As an adjective, parti-colored (Wilcox DICTIONARY)

harlequinade   The traditional second part of a British pantomime: a short play in dumb show featuring Harlequin, Pantaloon, Columbine, and a Clown. (Bowman/Ball THEATRE)

Harlequin's cloak   See: teaser.

harlot   See: minstrel.

harness   A device which a below-stage puppeteer wears to support a large rod puppet or a prop used by a puppet. (Philpott DICTIONARY)

harp   In the early 20th C U.S., one who played Irish roles or was an Irish comedian. (Wilmeth LANGUAGE)

harpax (Greek)   A hook in the *mechane* (hoisting device), perhaps at the top of whatever pulley arrangement was used. The source is Pollux. Among the meanings in Liddell/Scott LEXICON is "grappling iron, used in sea fights." Also called an *ankuris*. (Pickard-Cambridge DIONYSUS 127)

Harry Selby   1. A mythical American actor of great versatility whose name was written into play casts for luck. 2. A name used in a program for an actor who doubles in a second part. See also: George Spelvin. (Sobel THEATRE)

hasa (Sanskrit)   Literally: mirth. One of eight fundamental emotions (*sthay-ibhava*) depicted by the actors in classical Indian theatre. See also: *hasya*. (Keith SANSKRIT 323)

Hasait   A trade name for a special cyclorama, named after its inventor, Max Hasait. (Bowman/Ball THEATRE)

Hasait cloth   See: horizon lamp.

hashigakari (Japanese)   The raised wooden passageway or bridge that connects the stage (*butai*) and the dressing room (*gakuya*) in a *no* theatre. Characters enter and usually exit along this bridge. The idea of a passageway along which a god or spirit would travel from the sacred world to the world of men apparently originated in Shinto *kagura* performances in prehistoric times. In the 12th and 13th C the *hashigakari* could join a *sarugaku no* stage at various places; its present position, upstage right and angled away from the audience at approximately twenty degrees, became standard in the 17th C. The bridge is 25 to 40 feet long, is roofed, and sometimes has a back wall. (Ernst KABUKI 32, Shimazaki NOH 8, 10-11, Komparu NOH 136–138)

hassen (Japanese)   A one-piece mask of a crane used in *bugaku*. It is a lacquered dark green and has a small bell hanging from a beak-like nose. (Wolz BUGAKU 44)

hasta (Sanskrit)   Literally: hand. A hand gesture, in classical Indian theatre and dance, and in most forms of regional theatre. Bharata describes and cites uses of 24 single-hand and 13 double-hand gestures that convey emotion in mime sequences (*abhinaya*) and 30 gestures used in pure dance (*nrtta*) for decoration and beauty (NATYASASTRA 172-193). Also called *hasta mudra* (hand sign). In *kathakali*, called *mudra* (sign). In *ankiya nat* called *hat* (hand gesture). (Jones/ Jones KATHAKALI 85-90, Vatsyayan TRADITIONAL 107)

hasya (Sanskrit)   Literally: comic. One of the eight major sentiments (*rasa*) to be experienced by the audience of a classical play. It is aroused by the enacted emotion (*sthayibhava*) of mirth (*hasa*). (Keith SANSKRIT 323)

hasyagara (Sanskrit)   In *yaksagana*, the role of a narrator and jokester. (Rangacharya INDIAN 79)

hat   See: funnel.

hat (Assamese)   See: *hasta*.

hatarakigoto (Japanese)   In *no*: 1. Broadly, one of three categories of dance (*mai*). *Hatarakigoto* are performed to instrumental accompaniment. They are active, rhythmic dances that carry forward the action of the protagonist (*shite*) and usually occur in the second part (*nochi ba*) of the play. The dances include the sub-types *kakeri*, *iroe*, *tachimawari*, *mai bataraki*, *kirikumi*, and *inori*. 2. Narrowly, the dance of a demon in a play of the fifth group. Common abbreviation: *hataraki*. Also called *mai bataraki*. (Shimazaki NOH 37, Inoura HISTORY 118)

hat bac (Vietnamese)   Literally: song of the north. A musical genre of songs used in action scenes, both in *hat boi* and *cai luong*.

hat bai (Vietnamese)   See: *bai*.

hat bai choi (Vietnamese)   See: *ca kich bai choi*.

hat bo (Vietnamese)   See *hat boi*.

hat boi (Vietnamese)   Literally: song and gesture or pose. Classical sung drama or opera. Originated through contact with Chinese opera troupes, between the 11th and 14th C, and at first called *tuong* or *tuong tau*. It developed content, make-up and costume styles, music, and staging techniques related to, yet distinct from, Chinese models. The term is used primarily in the south. Also commonly called *hat tuong* (sung play) in northern Vietnam and *hat bo* in central and northern Vietnam. Pham-Duy describes eight types of *hat boi* in MUSICS 112-117. (Song VIETNAMESE 18-25, Hauch "Study" 5, Brandon SOUTHEAST 73-74)

hat cai luong (Vietnamese)   See: *cai luong*.

hat cheo (Vietnamese)   Literally: sung satirical drama. A satirical folk play of northern Vietnam which combines song, dance, and slapstick comedy. Evolved from early ceremonial entertainments, it reached its greatest popularity in the late 18th C. It remains a staple entertainment today. (Addiss "Theater" 131-136) Kim calls it a "simplified form of the *hat boi*." (VIETNAMESE 19) Pham-Duy gives five types of *hat cheo* and describes 60 styles of declamation and singing (MUSICS 126–139).

hat khach (Vietnamese)   Literally: song of strangers (that is, Chinese). A *hat boi* song using the pentatonic scale and usually composed in a seven-syllable line. It is performed in a syncopated rhythm and is used for active or joyful scenes. In Addiss it is one of six major song categories ("Theater" 141) and in Hauch one of three ("Study" 73). Four types of *hat khach* are listed in Hauch "Study" 73-74 and Pham-Duy MUSICS 119-120.

hat nam (Vietnamese)   Literally: song of the south. A gentle, melancholy southern-style song used in *hat boi* and *cai luong*. In Addiss it is one of six major song categories ("Theater" 140, 141) and in Hauch one of three ("Study" 74-77). Hauch lists six types of *hat nam* ("Study" 51).

hat nieu (Vietnamese)   A miscellaneous category of songs used in *hat boi*. Included are regional songs, love songs, songs of sacrifice, and students' songs. One of six major song categories. (Addiss "Theater" 142)

hatsu haru kyogen (Japanese)   Literally: first Spring play. In Edo (Tokyo) the second production in the *kabuki* season, opening in the first lunar month (February), when the first Spring flowers would appear; hence the name. Also called *hatsu shibai* (first play). See also: *ni no kawari*. (Leiter ENCYCLOPEDIA 272-273)

hat tuong (Vietnamese)   See: *hat boi*.

haubergeon   See: habergeon.

hauberk   A medieval Northern European soldier's knee-length coat of chain mail. Also called a byrnie or jupon. See also: habergeon. (Barton COSTUME 137, Boucher FASHION, Wilcox DICTIONARY)

haul in   See: get in.

hauling line   See: operating line.

haul out   See: get out.

Hauptaktion (German)   Mainpiece. The second part of a typical 18th C German bill was a *Nachspiel*—a comic afterpiece. (Sobel NEW)

Haupt-und-Staatsaktion (German)   A chief-and-state play: an 18th C mainpiece dealing seriously or comically with state affairs. (Brockett HISTORY 391)

(en) haut (French)   Literally: on high. In ballet, a high position of the hands. (Grant TECHNICAL)

hautbois, hautboy, hoboye   Early spellings of oboe, a common theatre instrument.

(à la) hauteur (French)   In ballet, a position in which one leg is at right angles to the hip. (Grant TECHNICAL)

hava (Sanskrit)   The awakening of love in the heroine of a classical Indian play, expressed by eye and brow movements. One of "ten excellences" ascribed to a heroine. (Keith SANSKRIT 309)

have the needle   Especially in Britain, to be on pins and needles; to experience pre-performance jitters or stage fright. (Granville DICTIONARY)

hawsa (Burmese)   Story-telling or dramatic recitation in verse form by a solo performer. (Aung DRAMA 42, 47)

hay   A round dance of Elizabethan times. Possibly a chain dance, similar to the more recent Paul Jones. (Perugini PAGEANT 62)

hayagawari (Japanese)   A quick change of a *kabuki* costume. Often several costumes are worn one over the other, the outer costume being whisked off to reveal one beneath it. Through *hayagawari*, an actor may play a half-dozen roles in one act. See also: *bukkaeri, hikinuki*. (Leiter "Spectacle" 179-180, Ernst KABUKI 186)

hayal (Arabic)   A word used in Turkey for both the shadow and the puppet theatre. (And KARAGÖZ 22)

hayal ağaci (Turkish)   Literally: puppet tree, shadow tree. In the shadow theatre, a Y-shaped device which permits the puppeteer to control a number of puppets at once (most of them stationary). (And KARAGÖZ 30-31)

hayaldji (Turkish)   *Karagöz* puppeteers. Also called *karagötsci*. (Malkin PUPPETS 54)

hayali zil, hayal-i zill (Turkish)   Literally: shadow phantoms. Especially in older Turkish texts, shadow theatre. Also printed *zill-i hayal*. (And KARAGÖZ 23, 33; Hartnoll COMPANION 842)

hayashi (Japanese)   1. Broadly, any ensemble of percussion (drums, gongs, bells) and wind instruments (flutes) that accompany theatrical performances, including *kagura*, festival dances, *furyu, dengaku, no, kyogen*, and *kabuki*. 2. More narrowly, the *no* ensemble of three drums (*otsuzumi, kotsuzumi*, and *taiko*) and one flute (*fue* or *nokan*). Also this ensemble when it functions within *kabuki* musical groupings. (Komparu NOH 178–180) 3. By extension, the group of musicians who play these instruments. Also called *hayashi kata* (*hayashi* person). (Inoura HISTORY 22, 47)

hayashi beya (Japanese)   Literally: musicians' room. 1. The *geza* musicians' dressing room in a *kabuki* theatre. (Leiter ENCYCLOPEDIA 113) 2. A synonym for *geza* room. (Ernst KABUKI 52)

hayashi kata (Japanese)   See: *hayashi*.

hayashimono (Japanese)   Literally: musical item. 1. A section of a *no* play in which drum rhythm is unusually important. 2. A cheerful, auspicious chant and dance section in a *no-kyogen* play.

hayashi za (Japanese)   Literally: musicians' place. The upstage area of a *no* stage where the musicians sit. (Shimazaki NOH 10-11)

hayloft   A small-town theatre.

haystack   See: breakfast food.

hazzarai (Yiddish)   A show business term for trashy theatre. From *hazzar* (pig). (Wouk YOUNGBLOOD 69)

head   1. A block in the shape of a head and neck, covered with linen or canvas and used to shape hats. (Dreher HATMAKING) 2. In the U.S., an occasional term for the serrated end of a hanger or pipe stand—the end which fastens to a spotlight or other lighting instrument. (Lounsbury THEATRE) 3. The chief of a crew (e.g., a lighting crew). (Bowman/Ball THEATRE)

headacher   1. A director. 2. A performer's agent.

head block   A metal frame containing three or more grooved wheels (sheaves) over which lines pass from the gridiron down to a counterweight arbor. Also called a lead block. (Stern MANAGEMENT) More strictly, a head block is one in which the grooved wheels are alongside each other on a single axle, while a lead block (tandem lead block) has its wheels one above the other in a frame. Illustrations in both sources. (Lounsbury THEATRE, Parker/Smith DESIGN 294-295)

head block beam   A double I-beam on the gridiron above the pinrail. Attached to the beam are the head blocks for all the sets of lines. Also called a strong back.

head carpenter   See: master carpenter.

head clearance   The vertical distance between the eye level of a seated spectator and the sightline from the row directly behind.

head electrician   Especially in professional parlance, the chief of a lighting crew. See also: head. (Bowman/Ball THEATRE 170)

header   1. A small flat used to fill in the space above a door or window when a door or window flat is not used. 2. A framed border flown from the gridiron and attached to side flats to form a false proscenium. (Carrington THEATRICANA, Baker THEATRECRAFT)

head inspection, head verification scene   See: *kubi jikken.*

headline   Especially in vaudeville, to get, or have, star billing. Hence, headliner, headlined, headlining, headline system. In Britain, to top the bill. Hence, top liner. (Bowman/Ball THEATRE)

head of the supers   See: super master.

headrail   An 11th C woman's veil of silk or linen worn over the head and sometimes wound also under the chin and over the shoulder. See also: wimple. (Walkup DRESSING 83)

head rail   See: top rail.

head spot   1. A beam of light not much wider than a performer's head. 2. A spotlight which produces such a beam. The head spot is an application of the pin spot.

head verification scene   See: *kubi jikken.*

heart act   An act with two romantic roles. Hence, heart team.

hearts   1. Padding used in tights worn by performers. 2. Falsies. See also: symmetricals. (Wilmeth LANGUAGE)

heat   In vaudeville, a performance. (Wilmeth LANGUAGE)

heat gun   A hand tool consisting of an electrically-powered heater and fan, used in the theatre to heat plastics, dry objects, etc. (Bellman SCENOGRAPHY)

heat up   Of a light, to turn on.

heaume (French)   A large medieval helmet worn in tournaments and pageants. Festooned with a leather or silk scarf. See also: cointise. (Wilcox DICTIONARY)

heaven   1. A standard scenic locale in many medieval productions using multiple simultaneous staging. The representation of the heavenly paradise was usually situated at the opposite end of the stage platform or acting area from the representation of hell. 2. A *Kuppelhorizont* (German) or dome horizon, a kind of plastered cyclorama.

heavenly body   A female star.

(the) heavens   1. In Elizabethan theatres, the underside of the roof that extended over the stage; also called the shadow, cover, stage cover, or *testa* (Latin). 2. In 17th C theatres, borders. 3. In 19th C theatres and later, the highest gallery in the auditorium. Also called the gods, paradise, peanut gallery, and nigger heaven (obsolete and offensive). (Sabbattini in Hewitt RENAISSANCE 47, Chambers ELIZABETHAN II 544, Cameron/Gillespie ENJOYMENT, Bowman/Ball THEATRE) 4. Theatrical stardom. 5. The world of star performers.

heavy   1. One who plays a serious or villainous role. 2. Often short for heavy lead, heavy man, and sometimes heavy woman. 3. A serious, solemn, or villainous role. 4. Said of a comic part whose effects require a pretense of seriousness. 5. Said of a very serious drama. (Bowman/Ball THEATRE)

heavy hinge pin   A pin used temporarily to join two halves of a heavy strap hinge. (Carrington THEATRICANA)

heavy lead, heavy man, heavy woman   1. A solemn leading character, sometimes a villainous one. 2. One who performs such a role. (Bowman/Ball THEATRE)

heavy merchant   An actor who takes, or specializes in, serious or villainous roles.

heavy name   A major performer. Hence, heavy name show. (Berrey/Van den Bark SLANG 572)

heavy properties   Stage furniture, such as tables, chairs, sofas, etc., as opposed to small hand properties. See also: prop.

heavy rain machine   A device for simulating the sound of rain. One type consists of a revolving drum with staggered protruding tabs; attached to an adjacent platform are strips of leather which are lifted and let fall by the tabs when the drum is rotated. (Collison SOUND 100)

Hebe comic   A show business term for a Jewish comedian. See also: goose, Yid. (Wilmeth LANGUAGE)

Hebei *bangzi*, Hopei *pang tzu* (Chinese)   A form of music-drama (*xiqu*) popular in Hebei, Liaoning, Jilin, and Heilongjiang Provinces and the Inner Mongolian Autonomous Region. The form arose in the 18th C through the influence of *qinqiang* and Shanxi opera (*jinju*). It features music from the *bangziqiang* musical system. (Halson PEKING 65)

Hebel (German)   A dimmer control handle or lever. (Fuchs LIGHTING 368-370)

Hebelkopf (German)   Literally: dimmer handle stand. In post World-War I German light control, a special device on dimmer handles in a complicated remote control interlocking scheme. The *Hebelkopf* on each dimmer handle permitted three different lock and unlock arrangements. (Fuchs LIGHTING 368-369)

hedge   A false beard.

hedolia (Greek)   1. Seats, especially the wooden benches in a 5th C BC theatre. 2. According to one ancient source, a semi-circle of such benches. Older references to stone seats in connection with *hedolia* seem to be without recent support. See also: *ikria*, the usual word for the seats in a 5th C BC theatre. (Mantzius HISTORY I 148)

heel and toe   A vaudeville dance derived from folk dancing. (Wilmeth LANGUAGE)

heel bar   The part of a marionette control device which enables the marionette to step backward. (Philpott DICTIONARY)

heel beater   A vaudeville dancer.

heel rapper   A tap dancer.

hefty   1. The character of a villain. 2. A performer who plays such parts.

hegun (Chinese)   See: *gundiao*.

heida (Japanese)   A mask worn by the ghost of a brave warrior in the second part of a warrior *no* play. (Shimazaki NOH 59)

heikyoku (Japanese)   Literally: Heike singing. A solo epic recitation, popular in the 14th-16th C, of *The Tale of the Heike*. See also: *biwa hoshi*. (Ando BUNRAKU 96)

Heimkehrerdrama (German)   Drama of a homecoming soldier. One of the types of Brechtian *Lehrstücke* (q.v.). (Wirth "Experiments" 58)

"Heist the rag!"   The cry of gallery spectators to raise the curtain. Sometimes printed "Histe the rag!" (Wilmeth LANGUAGE 131)

hell   The substage in an Elizabethan theatre.

Hellenike Epitheorisis (Greek)   A 19th C Greek revue; a satirical spectacle which took place outdoors and dealt with the political issues of the day as well as Greece's extramural enemies. It is still in existence. (Gassner/Quinn ENCYCLOPEDIA 395)

Hellenistic theatre   A Greek theatre built between c. 336 and c. 100 BC. (Cameron/Gillespie ENJOYMENT 284)

Helligkeit (German)   Literally: light. In the work of Adolphe Appia, general illumination or diffused illumination as Appia knew it, i.e., as produced by footlights and borderlights. (Sellman/Lessley ESSENTIALS 2)

hellmouth   A scenic representation of hell in a medieval production; the standard depiction was of a gaping monster's mouth. Hell was usually situated at the opposite end of the stage platform or acting area from the representation of heaven. Also called hell, *Höll* (German), *l'enfer* (French). (Nicoll DEVELOPMENT 56, 57, fig. 59)

hello frame   The first place on a variety bill.

hemp house   A theatre with a flying system using rope lines and sandbags. Also called a hand-worked house or rope house. See also: counterweight system.

hemp line   A fiber rope line.

hemp system   A flying system using ropes and sandbags rather than wire cables and iron counterweights in arbors. Also called a rope set or a rope or rope-line system.

Henan *bangzi* (Chinese), **Henan opera**   See: *yuju.*

hench-men   Late 16th and 17th C male dancers (men and boys) who performed Morris dances at court as part of a masque or disguising. (Perugini PAGEANT 78)

hengemono (Japanese)   Literally: transformation piece. A *kabuki* dance play that features the transformation of a major character by means of costume (and often makeup) changes. An actor may play four, six, seven, nine, or even twelve roles in one play. (Scott KABUKI 87, Leiter ENCYCLOPEDIA 406)

hennin   A possibly pejorative term for a 14th-15th C headdress of antique Oriental origin. Variously described as a pointed cone with an upturned face brim and a gauze veil wound around the cone and floating from its top (Barton); a skullcap with attached veil and frontlet (Wilcox); or simply a tall cornet (Boucher). Also called a steeple headdress. See also: escoffion. (Barton COSTUME 166, Boucher FASHION, Wilcox DICTIONARY)

hen roost   The gallery in a music hall. In France, *poulailler.*

herald   1. The speaker of the prologue in many medieval German Shrovetide plays. (Mantzius HISTORY II 131) 2. A single octavo sheet containing information on a forthcoming attraction, distributed through the mail, as a handout or as a program insert. (Carrington THEATRICANA)

hérigaute   A medieval garment similar to the housse or *garde-corps* (French), open at the sides. (Boucher FASHION)

hero, heroine   The central male and female figures in a dramatic work. (Bowman/Ball THEATRE)

heroic acting   A style popular in the 19th C emphasizing physical force and passion rather than sensitivity, intellectuality, or wit. Popularized by the U.S. actor Edwin Forrest. Also then called the American style. (Brockett HISTORY 477, Bowman/Ball THEATRE)

heroic drama   A form of drama popular in the late 17th C in England, often involving a conflict between love and honor. The main characters were noble or larger-than-life, and the language was high-flown and bombastic. Hence, heroic comedy, heroic tragedy. (Brooks/Heilman UNDERSTANDING)

heroic feathers   In the 17th and 18th C, plumes on the headgear of actors to connote an aristocratic or heroic character. (Roberts STAGE)

heroine   See: hero.

herse (French)   In the 19th C, an overhead borderlight. (Moynet FRENCH 82)

Hessian boot   In the 18th C and after, calf-high footwear, lower in back than in front, where it dipped and was ornamented by a tassel. Also called a hussar boot, Souvaroff boot. (Walkup DRESSING 248, Wilcox DICTIONARY)

heuze   A 9th-15th C thick-soled leather boot, the end of which often left part of the foot uncovered. Its height varied from calf to thigh. Frequently confused with a gaiter or legging. Also called a *housseau* (French). (Boucher FASHION)

HI   See: sob stuff.

hichiriki (Japanese)   A small double-reed wind instrument played in *gagaku*. (Wolz BUGAKU 18)

hick act   A rustic act.

hick stand   1. A provincial town. 2. A small-town theatre.

hidarizukai (Japanese)   Literally: left-manipulation. The puppeteer on a three-man team who manipulates the left arm of a *bunraku* puppet. (Adachi BUNRAKU 29-33)

hideaway   See: fit-up.

hideout   A false beard.

hierarchy of expression   Adolphe Appia's theory of unifying the elements of theatrical expression in word-tone drama. Music expresses the soul of the drama, but the drama seeks and gains substance through the performer, who, submitting voice and body to the music, through movement creates the setting—the musical space. Light, like music, is expressive in time but lacking in substance, and therefore can express the drama directly. Moreover, light has the unique capability of uniting actor and setting for the eye by emphasizing their three-dimensionality. (Appia MUSIC 26ff)

hiereus (Greek)   The head of a theatrical guild. The *hiereus* was a priest (the word's basic meaning) who was also usually a performer. The term appears in the provinces in the 4th C BC, but the first known mention in Athens is five centuries later. (Pickard-Cambridge FESTIVALS 303, Mantzius HISTORY I 179)

higashi (Japanese)   Literally: east. Stage left in *kabuki*. So called because major theatres in Edo (Tokyo) faced south in the 18th and 19th C, putting stage left to the east. Also called *kamite* (upper hand). (Leiter ENCYCLOPEDIA 116)

higashi fu (Japanese)   Literally: eastern style. In *bunraku* music, a chanting style made popular at the Toyotake Puppet Theatre, located on the east side of Dotombori Canal in Osaka. See also: *nishi*. (Malm in Brandon CHUSHINGURA 85)

higeki (Japanese)   Literally: tragic drama. A direct translation of 'tragedy.'

high boot   See: *kothornos*.

high-brow stuff   Serious drama.

high C   A minstrel term for a cornetist. (Wilmeth LANGUAGE)

high comedy   Comedy of intellect and language, emphasizing upper-class characters and concerns, and evoking thoughtful laughter. See also: comedy of manners. (Cameron/Gillespie ENJOYMENT, Bowman/Ball THEATRE)

high dead   See: dead.

high hat   See: funnel.

high-hatters   Formerly, silk-hat theatre patrons.

highlight   Light-colored makeup used to bring out the performer's bone structure and, in conjunction with dark-colored makeup, to create the illusion of wrinkles and sagging flesh.

(the) high part   In Irish theatres, the gallery or upper circle. (Granville DICTIONARY)

high *shund* (English-Yiddish)   See: *shund*.

high spot   A principal number on a variety bill.

high trim   The height of a flown piece when in the out or up position.

highway circuit   Summer stock. (1938 Burris-Meyer/Cole SCENERY 40)

hi Henry   See: eleven forty-five.

hiiki (Japanese)   A fan or patron, either of a theatre or of an actor, especially in *kabuki*. (Leiter ENCYCLOPEDIA 116, Gunji KABUKI 50)

hikae yagura (Japanese)   Literally: transferred tower or license. Transferral from one theatre to another, by renting or leasing, of a license to perform *kabuki*, the public sign of which was a tower (*yagura*) over the theatre entrance. See also: *yagura*. (Kumakura "Traditional" 55, Leiter ENCYCLOPEDIA 116)

hiki (Japanese)   Literally: to pull. A word used in various compounds for *kabuki* technical terms. *Hiki dai* (pulled platform) is a small platform pulled onstage. *Hiki dogu* (pulled scenery) is scenery capable of being pulled or rolled on and off stage. *Hiki maku* (pulled curtain) is the standard front curtain that is pushed open or pulled closed from one side of the proscenium arch to the other. *Hiki sen* (pulled cord) is the line that is pulled to drop a curtain in *furiotoshi* technique. (Leiter ENCYCLOPEDIA 116-117)

hikinuki (Japanese)   Literally: pulling out. In *bunraku* and *kabuki*, a technique for quickly changing a costume in view of the audience. An outer kimono is first detached from an inner kimono by pulling out basting threads, and then it is whisked off to reveal the costume beneath it. (Shaver COSTUMES 351-355)

hikkomi (Japanese)   Literally: withdrawal. In *kabuki*, the exit of a major character, usually down the *hanamichi*. (Brandon in Brandon/Malm/Shively STUDIES 93, Leiter ENCYCLOPEDIA 118)

hilarious tragedy   See: *hilarotragodia*.

hilarodia (Greek)   Burlesque tragedy, one of the varieties of early lyric mime grouped under the general heading of *mimodia*. The *hilarodia* may have been an early precursor of the *hilarotragodia*. (Nicoll MASKS 34)

hilarodos (Greek)   According to an ancient writer, a singer of lewd and funny songs. Thought to have been dressed in white, the *hilarodos* presumably performed in the *hilarodia* (burlesque tragedy). Plural: *hilarodi*. (Nicoll MASKS 34, Duchartre ITALIAN 24)

hilarotragodia (Latin Roman)   A type of *phlyax* farce which burlesqued mythology. Sometimes called tragicomedy, each such play probably used both comic and serious masks. These farces are thought to have parodied such figures as Heracles, Odysseus, and even Zeus. Also called burlesque tragedy, hilarious tragedy (the literal meaning), or *tragicomoedia*; sometimes spelled *hilarotragoedia*. (Bieber HISTORY 129-131, Duckworth NATURE 13, Nicoll MASKS 63)

hilir (Malaysian)   Literally: down river. Down river suggests the civilized lowlands, hence a shadow puppeteer who is respected for high performance standards. (Sweeney RAMAYANA 288-289)

hill horse   See: big horse.

himation (Greek), **himation**   A cloak often worn in comedy and tragedy by both actors and chorus. A large cloth rectangle, the *himation* could be draped in various ways or carried on the arm. The Roman equivalent of the *himation* was the *pallium* for men and the *palla* for women. Plural *himatia*. (Pickard-Cambridge FESTIVALS 180-185, 211-213, 215, 230; Bieber HISTORY xii, 92; Boucher FASHION; Brockett HISTORY 32) *hime* (Japanese)   Literally: princess. The role of a princess or young daughter of a court noble in *kabuki*. It is one type of *onnagata* role. See also: *aka hime*. (Gunji KABUKI 179)

hina dan (Japanese)   Literally: doll steps. In *kabuki*, a red-covered platform upstage, usually in two levels, on which the *nagauta* orchestra sits during a dance play. The *hina dan* is named for its resemblance to the traditional stepped-platform of the same name on which dolls are displayed during the Girls' Festival. See also: *debayashi*. (Leiter ENCYCLOPEDIA 118)

hindere Graben (German)   Joseph Furttenbach's 17th C term for a rear pit—a trough cutting across the stage, upstage of the acting area. From the German *hinter* (behind) and *Graben* (ditch, trench). (Furttenbach in Hewitt RENAISSANCE 211)

hinged foot iron   See: foot iron.

hinged jack   See: folding jack.

Hinterbühne (German)   See: rear stage.

hinter den Kulissen (German)   Back stage, behind the scenes.

hinterland mobs   Provincial audiences.

hip dance   In burlesque, a grind, a rotation of the hips. Hence, hip dancer.

hip flinger   A recent term for a cooch dancer. (Wilmeth LANGUAGE)

hippodrama   See: equestrian drama.

hip swinger   A chorus girl.

hira-gasy (Malagasy)   Literally: Malagasy song. Players in Madagascar who combine dances with dramatic elements borrowed from French music-hall entertainment and either long traditional moral songs or, in more westernized troupes, short plays. (Gerard ''Madagascar'' 365)

hiraki (Japanese)   Literally: open. A standard gesture (*kata*) in *no*, in which the arms are spread open. Illustrated in Keene NO 220.

Hiram   A young rube or unsophisticated person. (Carrington THEATRICANA)

hira nori (Japanese)   Literally: ordinary rhythm. The standard rhythmic pattern for singing (*utai*) poetic passages in *no* that are composed of seven and five syllables per line (for example, *age uta*, *sageuta*, *shidai*). Each line fits into an eight-beat musical measure. See also: *hyoshi au*. (Shimazaki NOH 44, Komparu NOH 195–197)

hireling   In Elizabethan and Restoration theatres, a performer on a salary rather than in a sharing capacity. See also: journeymen. (Van Lennep LONDON xcviii)

hister (Etruscan)   See: *histrio*.

''Histe the rag!''   See: ''Heist the rag!''

histoire (French)   1. A medieval historical play. 2. A medieval mystery play. (Mantzius HISTORY II 2)

historia (Latin)   See: liturgical drama.

historical play   A play based on historical events, often nationalistic in import and episodic in structure.

historification   A Brechtian epic theatre device of setting events back in time, of playing the events of a play as historical events in such a way as to emphasize the similarities between the earlier epoch and the contemporary one.

history   A medieval mystery play. (Mantzius HISTORY II 2)

history play   See: chronicle history play, *jidaimono, xinbiande, lishiju.*

histrio (Latin Roman)   Ultimately, the principal Latin term for actor. The word is from Etruscan *hister* (or *ister*), performer, perhaps originally, dancer. *Hister* was Latinized to *histrio* not later than the 3rd C BC. The meaning soon broadened so that in the 1st C BC, Cicero used *cantor, histrio,* and *actor* of the same performers. By early Christian times, *histrio* seems to have included performers of all kinds, including mimes and pantomimes, and even *aurigae* (circus drivers). The plural, *histriones,* is at least as frequent among writers in English as *histrio. Ludius* (a player) is an occasional alternate. See also: *cantor, actor.* (Chambers MEDIAEVAL I 6; Beare ROMAN 16, 229; Duckworth NATURE 5-6; Nicoll MASKS 83)

histrio (Latin)   1. One of the four general terms for a medieval minstrel. See: minstrel. 2. An actor.

histriones (Latin Roman)   See: *histrio.*

histrionic   1. Theatrical. 2. Of or pertaining to performing and performers.

histrionics   1. Stage shows. 2. Extravagant performing.

hit   1. A successful production. 2. To be successful. 3. In backstage lighting parlance, to strike with a beam of light, as in "Hit the bottom of the tree with number 12."

hitamenmono, shitamenmono (Japanese)   Literally: bareface play. A *no* play in which the protagonist (*shite*) is unmasked throughout the play. The ideographs can also be read *hitaomotemono.* See: *genzaimono.* (Zeami KADENSHO 22)

hitomakumono (Japanese)   A one-act play, which is also the literal meaning.

hitori shibai (Japanese)   Literally: one-man play. A monodrama.

hit the back of the house   To make one's voice and action carry to the rear of an auditorium. (Berrey/Van den Bark SLANG 586)

hit the boards   Of a show, to be produced on stage. Of a performer, to appear on stage.

hit the ceiling   To forget one's lines.

hit the grid   To forget one's lines.

hit the highway, hit the road, hit the tanks   To tour.

hit the hot spots   To perform in large cities.

hit the nut   To cover production expenses, usually by ticket sales.

hit the road   To tour, or begin a tour.

hit the stand   To arrive at a place of engagement.

hit the tanks   To tour small towns.

HMI lamp   See: short-arc lamp.

hne (Burmese)   A double-reed, oboe-like instrument used in traditional Burmese theatre performances. (Sein/Withey GREAT 47, Brandon SOUTHEAST 127)

HO   See: holdover.

hoarser   Prompter.

hobble skirt   An early 20th C woman's garment gathered into a bottom band of 28 inches or less, causing the gait which gave the skirt its name. (Barton COSTUME 551)

hoboye   See: hautbois.

Hoftheater (German)   Court theatre.

hog the act, hog the limelight, hog the spotlight, hog the stage   To steal the center of attention.

hoist   1. See: sloat. 2. A winch.

hojok (Korean)   See: *t'aep'yongso*.

hoke   1. Devices in playwriting which have proven successful. Also called pat stuff, sure-fire stuff, tried-and-true claptrap. (Berrey/Van den Bark SLANG 581) 2. To overplay, usually to get a sentimental response from the audience. Hence, to hoke it up. See also: hokum.

hokum   1. A time-worn gag, speech, situation, piece of business, etc. that can get a predictable response from an audience—usually applause or tears. Also called hoke or gonk. (Wilmeth LANGUAGE) 2. In late 19th C vaudeville, broad, low, off-color humor. (Senelick "Gagbooks" 8) 3. See also: hoke.

ho kun (Chinese)   See: *gundiao*.

hold   1. A pause in acting, either intentional, for effect, or unintentional. 2. To take such a pause. 3. To capture and keep the audience's attention. 4. To freeze during a laugh. 5. To stop the action in a rehearsal for directorial comments. 6. To stay in position on stage at the end of an act in order for a photograph to be taken. 7. Said of a stage action that, though exaggerated, will be accepted by the audience—action that will 'hold.' (Stern MANAGEMENT, Bowman/Ball THEATRE, Cartmell HANDBOOK 100, Granville DICTIONARY)

hold a scene   To stay in one's position on stage at the end of a scene, forming a tableau, as for a photograph. (Granville DICTIONARY)

holder   British for U.S. socket or receptacle: the metal fitting which "holds" the base of a lamp. (Bentham ART 87)

holdover   A production that is retained for a longer run than originally announced. Hence, to hold over. Abbreviation: HO. (Berrey/Van den Bark SLANG 580)

hold the boards   See: hold the stage.

hold (the) book   To serve as prompter.

hold the stage   To continue to be presented, to remain popular. Also called hold the boards.

"Hold the picture!"   Stay in position.

hold up the backdrop, hold up the scenery   1. To appear on stage merely to show off one's clothes or body, as in the case of showgirls. 2. To have a very small part. (Sobel NEW)

hold up the exits   To receive many encores. (Berrey/Van den Bark SLANG 586)

Höll (German)   See: hellmouth.

holy actor   The Polish director Jerzy Grotowski's term for the performer in his system: the actor is trained to free his body from every resistance to any psychic impulse, to sacrifice his body and thus come close to holiness. (Grotowski POOR 34-36)

homester   A local performer.

homiletic tragedy   See: domestic drama.

homme du théâtre (French)   Literally: man of the theatre. An encomium reserved for the most accomplished, most versatile, most creative, and most influential of theatre practitioners.

hon ame (Japanese)   Literally: real rain. One of two types of water scene (*hon mizu*) in *kabuki*. An actor is drenched with water that falls like rain from holes in bamboo pipes suspended over the stage. (Leiter ENCYCLOPEDIA 13)

Honan opera, Honan *pang tzu* (Chinese)   See: *yuju*.

hon butai (Japanese)   The main stage (also the literal meaning), distinguished from adjacent acting areas such as the *hanamichi* in *kabuki* or the *ato za* and *hashigakari* in *no*. (Ernst KABUKI 34-35, Komparu NOH 128)

hongjing, hung ching (Chinese)   Literally: red painted-face role. A loyal painted-face role (*jing*) in Beijing opera (*jingju*) and many other forms of music-drama (*xiqu*) that is characterized by red, full-face makeup and features dance-acting (*zuo*) skill; usually a portrayal of the historical figure Guan Yu of the 3rd C. See also: *hongsheng*.

hongreline   A 17th C woman's jacket, predecessor of the 19th C *jaquette* (French). (Boucher FASHION)

hongsheng, hung sheng (Chinese)   Literally: red male role. A loyal older male role (*laosheng*) in Beijing opera (*jingju*) and many other forms of music-drama (*xiqu*) that is characterized by red, full-face makeup and features song (*chang*) skill; usually a portrayal of the historical figure Guan Yu of the 3rd C. See also: *hongjing*.

hon hanamichi (Japanese)   Literally: main runway. The fixed runway stage in a *kabuki* theatre. It joins the main stage, stage right, as opposed to the now rarely used temporary (*kari*) runway stage left. See: *hanamichi*. (Ernst KABUKI 35, Hamamura et al KABUKI 57)

hon kyogen (Japanese)   Literally: main, or true play. 1. An independent *kyogen* play that appears between *no* plays on a *nogaku* program. It is comic and felicitous, as opposed to serious *no* plays and is performed entirely by *kyogen* actors (*kyogen kata*). See also: *ai kyogen*. (Berberich "Rapture" 4) 2. In *kabuki* of the 18th and 19th C, the main play on a program, written in four or more acts, usually beginning at dawn and continuing until dusk. (Brandon CLASSIC 24-25)

honky tonk   1. A saloon in which burlesque performances were given. 2. A cheap, small-town theatre.

hon maku (Japanese)   1. In *kabuki*, a rhythmic sound pattern, made by striking together hard wooden clappers (*hyoshigi*), that accompanies the opening or closing of the *kabuki* curtain. Beats, at first slow and loud, gradually accelerate and diminish in loudness. Also called *dara maku*. Abbreviated *maku*. (Brandon CLASSIC 352) 2. Also in *kabuki*, a front curtain, divided in the center, used in theatres in Kyoto and Osaka. (Leiter ENCYCLOPEDIA 124) 3. In *no*, to raise the curtain at the bridgeway (*hashigakari*) high in the air for the entrance of a character. (Komparu NOH 146)

hon mizu (Japanese)   Literally: real water. The staging technique of using real water in certain *kabuki* scenes, rather than conventionally indicating water with a blue cloth (*mizu nuno*). See also: *hon ame*, *mizu iri*. Diagrams and illustrations are in Leiter "Spectacle" 184-187. (Leiter ENCYCLOPEDIA 124)

hon tsurigane (Japanese)   Literally: real bell. In *kabuki* offstage music (*geza*), a large, thick, bronze temple bell which tolls to create atmosphere in night scenes. (Malm MUSIC 226)

hoochie-coochie   See: cooch.

hoofer   Originally, a dancer in minstrel shows. Later, a dancer in vaudeville or on a tour of second-rate theatres; ultimately, any performer on tour. Now, any stage dancer. Hence, hoof it, hoofer act, etc.

hoofery   1. A theatre featuring dancers. 2. A dance hall.

hoofology   Tap dancing. (Sobel HANDBOOK)

hook   A hook on a pole, used in 19th C vaudeville to pull a failing performer offstage on amateur night. Hence, get the hook, to be hooked. In Britain, wooden arm. (Bowman/Ball THEATRE)

hook hanger iron, hook hanging iron   See: hanging iron.

hookup, board hookup   Especially in the U.S. professional theatre, a listing of which circuits have which lights, where the light fixtures are, where their light falls, and their color. MAGIC has an extended example. (Rosenthal/Wertenbaker MAGIC 159, 161-166)

hook up   1. In budgeting, to compare the costs of production and operations. 2. Such a comparison. (Bowman/Ball THEATRE) 3. To connect electrically. 4. To be engaged to perform.

hoop   1. See: candle hoop. 2. See: farthingale.

ho'opa'a (Hawaiian)   One of the musicians of the *hula ki'i*, who assisted the puppeteer, serving as both drummer and (sometimes) as interlocutor. (Malkin PUPPETS 158)

hoop-petticoat   In 18th C Britain, a pannier. (Boucher FASHION)

hoop skirt   A skirt stiffened with hoops or made to look so.

hoosier   An out-of-town theatre patron.

hootchy-kootchy   See: cooch.

hop   1. In dance, a simple locomotor step in which weight moves away from one foot and back to the same foot. (Hayes DANCE 47) 2. In touring, a journey from one stand to another. 3. To make such a journey.

Hopei *pang tzu* (Chinese)   See: Hebei *bangzi*.

hoqueton (French)   A padded, fitted Renaissance tunic, frequently ornamented with precious metal and stones. See also: journade, *pourpoint*, saie. (Boucher FASHION)

horizon   1. In a Renaissance theatre, apparently the height of the vanishing point in the perspective scenery. (Serlio in Hewitt RENAISSANCE 21) 2. In 17th C theatres, the shutters closing off the prospect.

horizon cloth   A cyclorama.

horizon flood   In Britain, a floodlight used to light the cyclorama, or designed for such use.

horizon lamp   In Britain, a special cylindrical floodlight used vertically in lighting cycloramas. This was a German instrument (Schwabe-Hasait Company) which lit the Hasait cloth, a full cyc of cylindrical shape. Also called a *Horizontleuchte* (German). (Bentham ART 319)

horizon light   A cyclorama footlight or other fixture which illuminates the cyc from below. (Bowman/Ball THEATRE).

horizon pit   A trough in front of a sky cyclorama or *Kuppelhorizont* (German) to house footlights.

horizon row   A ground row in front of a cyclorama.

Horizont (German)   See: *Kuppelhorizont*.

Horizontbeleuchtung (German)   Cyclorama lighting. (Fuchs LIGHTING 370, Rae/Southern INTERNATIONAL 34)

Horizontlaternen (German)   Instruments used to light the cyclorama. (Fuchs LIGHTING 209, 211-212)

Horizontleuchte (German)   Literally: horizon light, cyclorama light. A floodlight of cylindrical shape designed for lighting cycloramas. See: horizon lamp. (Bentham ART 319)

horizontal sight line   An imaginary line drawn from the auditorium seats farthest from the center line of the house to the sides of the proscenium opening and onto the stage. The purpose is to determine what portions of the stage can be seen from those seats and what masking will be needed.

horn butting   See: *jiaodi*.

horned cap, horned headdress   See: cornet.

horror tragedy   A form of drama popular in the early 17th C in England, characterized by a decadent mood and scenes of torture. John Ford's *The Broken Heart* is an example. (Sobel NEW 682)

horse opera   A nickname for melodrama. The term may derive from the equestrian shows of the 18th C and later. It is now used chiefly of Hollywood westerns.

horseshoe   The dress circle.

horseshoe runway   In a burlesque theatre, a runway for strippers which went around the orchestra pit. (Wilmeth LANGUAGE)

horseshoe-shaped auditorium   An auditorium shape that was especially popular in the 18th C and often supplanted the U-Shape found in many 17th C theatres. Also called an ovoid or egg-shaped auditorium. A good example is the Teatro di Torina of 1740. (Mullin PLAYHOUSE 56-57)

hortensia   In ballet, a step in which the dancer jumps into the air with legs drawn up, one in front of the other, then reverses their position in the air several times before landing with feet apart. The legs do not beat. (Grant TECHNICAL)

hortus (Latin Roman)   Literally: garden. On floor plans suggested by Beare for certain comedies, the unseen garden of a house whose front is onstage in view of the audience. (Beare ROMAN 258-260)

hose   1. To enclose a cable. 2. A heavy electrical cable. 3. A fire hose. 4. Stockings.

hoshi (Japanese)   Literally: Buddhist priest. A performer in the 11th-16th C who, because he was associated with a Buddhist temple, was loosely identified as a 'priest.' Performers of *dengaku* and *sarugaku* were often called *dengaku hoshi* and *sarugaku hoshi*.

Hosho *ryu* (Japanese)   Literally: style of Hosho. 1. One of the five styles of acting *no* drama, characterized by restrained expression. Established at least by the 14th C, the style has continued as an unbroken tradition to the present time. 2. The troupe or association of *no* actors who perform in this style. This is a contemporary usage. Before the 20th C, the term Hosho *za* (Hosho troupe) identified the performers. For other styles see also: Kanze, Kita, Kongo, Komparu. (Inoura HISTORY 108, Shimazaki NOH 84, Keene NO 68)

hospitalia (Latin Roman)   Literally: guest chambers. In the facade of a scene building, the doors supposedly leading to guest chambers on either side of the central door. (Bieber HISTORY 173, 182)

hot   1. Of an electrical circuit or some portion of it, such as a socket: on, live, with current flowing or ready to flow. 2. Of the appearance of light on the stage: bright, usually with the connotation of "too bright." See some of the following entries for common terms in which these meanings are used. 3. Said of a performer much in demand, or a show that is highly successful. Hence, a hot ticket, the hottest ticket in town.

hot chocolate   Formerly, a Black female performer. Now offensive. (Berrey/ Van den Bark SLANG 573)

hot circuit   A live electrical circuit, an electrical circuit with current. Also called a hot or live line.

hôtellerie (French)   See: *Vårdskap.*

hot front   Said of a controlboard with live parts on its surface. Such boards are rare, unsafe, and illegal. (Wehlburg GLOSSARY)

hot line   See: hot circuit.

hot mirror   In a "cool" lighting instrument, a surface which passes visible rays and reflects heat (infra-red) rays. Lounsbury has an illustration. See also: dichroic filter, dichroic lens. (Lounsbury THEATRE 36-37, Bentham ART 92)

hot number   A good act.

hotokemawari (Japanese)   Literally: Buddha turning. A puppet entertainment of the late 16th C which was associated with Buddhist temples. A solo performer operated eighteen-inch puppets while he chanted Buddhist texts and sermons.

hot patching   Plugging a lamp into a circuit when the circuit is live. Also called hot plugging. Both phrases occur in other forms, such as hot plugged.

hot plugging   See: hot patching.

hot side   See: cold side.

hot spot   1. A small area of the stage which is lit brightly, usually too brightly, as in "There's a hot spot left of the sofa." 2. Similarly, an over-bright part of a spotlight beam resulting from irregularities in the relationship between lamp, reflector, and lens.

hot ticket   A successful show for which a ticket is hard to get.

hot-water play   A farce.

hot-wire cutter   An electric tool used for cutting foamed plastics, such as styrofoam; the hot wire on the tool can be shaped to make complicated cuts, such as moldings. (Bellman SCENOGRAPHY)

houdixue (Chinese)   See: *guanxue.*

houppe, *houppe* (French)   A 16th C short headdress of the Low Countries worn under a shawl and peeking out from it. See also: attifet. Also called an *huppette.* (Wilcox DICTIONARY)

houppelande, *houppelande* (French)   1. A 14th-15th C man or woman's long, full, generally ornate outer robe, buttoned from neck to knees, where it swept backward to the floor. It had wide sleeves (only one of which was embroidered) and a *carcaille* (flaring collar). 2. A 17th C loose riding coat buttoned down the front and at the sides. 3. Occasionally, a man or woman's full overcoat. See also: haincelin. (Boucher FASHION, Chalmers CLOTHES 111-112)

hourd, hourdement, hourt (French)   A stage: a platform occupied by medieval performers (and occasionally spectators). (Gascoigne WORLD 80)

house   1. Playhouse. Hence, house servants—such employees as dressers, sweepers, doorkeepers, etc. 2. The audience seating area in a theatre. 3. The areas of a theatre in front of the curtain, also called the front of the house or FOH. 4. An audience. 5. In a Renaissance court theatre, a scenic unit representing a building or other locale. 6. The management of a theatre being used temporarily by a troupe. (Van Lennep LONDON 214, Chambers ELIZABETHAN I 78, Crampton HANDBOOK, Bowman/Ball THEATRE)

"House!"   A command to the operator of the house lights to perform the next scheduled operation. Thus, the meaning at the end of a scene is "Raise the house lights part way," to a previously planned setting. The meaning at the beginning of the play, or an act, is "Lower the house lights to blackout." Other terms used in these situations include "House up" and "House down."

houseau (French)   See: heuze.

house author   A playwright or play doctor employed by a theatre. The practice was common during the heyday of the stock company at the end of the 19th C. Now virtually obsolete. (Granville DICTIONARY)

house board   1. A posting place for theatre advertisements, outside the theatre but next to it or on its walls—a display case. 2. An electrical switchboard, usually controlling only the auditorium lights but sometimes work lights and, in older theatres, footlights and borderlights; part of the permanently installed lighting equipment. (Bowman/Ball THEATRE)

house border   1. Especially in speaking of a theatre used by a touring company, a borderlight which is part of the theatre's equipment. 2. See: teaser.

house carpenter   A stage carpenter in attendance in a professional theatre even when a show is not in production (i.e., when the house is dark). Under union rules, he must be there whenever scenic equipment is used or handled.

house charge   In 18th and 19th C theatres, the fee charged by the management at benefits; whatever income was left after the house charge went to the beneficiary. (Hogan LONDON clxxxv)

house count   Attendance figures for a performance.

house crew   1. A theatre staff: the stage carpenter, electrician, property man, stagehands, front-of-house personnel, etc. 2. The front-of-house personnel in a theatre.

house curtain   The main front curtain in a U.S. theatre. Also called an act curtain, act drop, the blind, front curtain, the grand, the grand tab or house tab (if rigged as a tableau curtain), the main or main curtain, the rag, tab, tableau, working curtain. The house curtain is located behind the asbestos curtain and the grand drapery (if the theatre has one). Lounsbury distinguishes between an act curtain and a theatre's main curtain, calling the former a curtain designed for a specific production; such a special curtain is usually called a show curtain. (Bowman/Ball THEATRE, Lounsbury THEATRE, Burris-Meyer/Cole THEATRES 248)

house doorman   See: doorman.

"House down!"   A direction to dim the house lights, usually to blackout.

house dramatist   A playwright who is a member of a producing company and tailors plays to the talents of the troupe. Shakespeare was a house dramatist, his 'house' being the Globe Theatre and its players. (Krows PLAYWRITING 445)

house equipment   See: house installation.

house full   See: full house.

house full board   In Britain, an announcement board outside a theatre indicating that a show is sold out. (Granville DICTIONARY)

household connector   A standard home plug such as that used at the end of a cord on a table lamp. Also called an Edison plug or just plain plug, among other names. See also: cap.

householder   In Elizabethan times and later, a member of a theatrical company who owned a share of the theatre building. (Cameron/Gillespie ENJOYMENT)

house installation   The electrical wiring and especially the lighting equipment permanently set into a theatre. House equipment is a somewhat more specific phrase for essentially the same meaning. (Fuchs LIGHTING 14)

housekeeper   1. In Elizabethan times, a theatre owner, proprietor, or controller, in whole or in part, who received a part or share of the admission receipts and was responsible for the building. 2. A theatre custodian who cleans or supervises the cleaning of the building. (Bowman/Ball THEATRE)

house lights   1. The main auditorium lights. The term does not ordinarily include the exit lights or other lights required by law (in some areas, for example, aisle lights). 2. The switches and/or dimmers which control the auditorium lights. 3. Sometimes, the auditorium lights and the lobby or other lights in the front areas of the theatre. The term is often shortened to house, as in "Dim the house" or "House down." The single word houselights is seen occasionally.

house list   See: door list.

houseman   A flyman temporarily employed during preparation for a production, to ensure that the trimming of scenery is accurate. (Bowman/Ball THEATRE)

house manager   The person responsible for the front-of-the-house operation during a performance. The house manager may also be the theatre's general manager or a deputy.

house of amusement   In 17th C Russia, the forerunner of the theatres built by Czar Mikhail. In the 17th C the term for amusement also meant theatre. (Marshall RUSSIAN 2)

houses   Scenic structures in a medieval production. Also called *mansions* (French), *domi, loci, sedes* (Latin).

house seats   A limited number of seats in good locations held in reserve in the box office for the use of the theatre, producer, director, designer, leading performers, and certain others. The right to have house seats reserved in the professional theatre is usually written into one's contract. Hence, personal house seat. House seats can also be used by the box-office manager or treasurer to redress errors in ticketing.

house servants   In Restoration theatres and later, non-performing theatre employees such as dressers, sweepers, doorkeepers, etc.

house spot   A spotlight in the auditorium. (Cornberg/Gebauer CREW 273)

house tab   See: house curtain.

housetop backing   A drop painted to represent the tops of roofs of buildings. Used for scenes taking place on the upper floor of a building or on a rooftop. (Carrington THEATRICANA)

"House up!"   A direction to raise the house lights, usually from blackout.

housing   In stage lighting, the metal container which serves as support and protection for such electrical, optical, and mechanical elements as a lighting instrument requires. The housing is essentially a necessary shell for the spotlight, floodlight, striplight, or other instrument. In Britain: casing.

housse   An outer garment of various lengths, with wide short sleeves (which formed a pelerine or short cape) and two small neck tabs. A tabless version was called a gamache. See also: hérigaute. (Boucher FASHION)

houtai, hou t'ai (Chinese)   Literally: rear platform. Backstage; the area behind the stage used by actors for makeup, dressing, and awaiting entrance. In a hook balustrade (*goulan*) theatre of the 10th-14th C it usually consisted of a single large rectangular room; in a tea-house theatre (*xiyuan*) of the 17th-early 20th C, it was often divided into three rooms. In a proscenium theatre today, it is similar to backstage areas in the West. Also called theatrical room (*xifang* or *hsi fang*). (Dolby HISTORY 191-192, Mackerras RISE 194, 196)

hou ti hsüeh (Chinese)   See: *guanxue*.

hsi (Chinese)   See: *xi*.

hsia ch'ang (Chinese)   See: *xiachang*.

hsia ch'ang men (Chinese)   See: *xiachangmen*.

hsia ch'ang tui lien (Chinese)   See: *duilian*.

hsia chü (Chinese)   See: *lian*.

hsiang chü (Chinese)   See: *xiangju*.

hsiang pan (Chinese)   See: *xiangban*.

hsiang sheng (Chinese)   See: *xiangsheng*.

hsiao (Chinese)   See: *xiao*.

hsiao ch'ih tzu (Chinese)   See: *diaoyutai*.

hsiao ch'ou (Chinese)   See: *xiaochou*.

hsiao chou tzu (Chinese)   See: *zhouzi*.

hsiao hsi (Chinese)   See: *xiaoxi*.

hsiao hsing to yang (Chinese)   See: *xiaoxing duoyang*.

hsiao hua lien (Chinese)   See: *chou*.

hsiao ku (Chinese)   See: *danpigu*.

hsiao kuo men (Chinese)   See: *guomen*.

hsiao lo (Chinese)   See: *xiaoluo*.

hsiao mien (Chinese)   See: *xiaomian*.

hsiao mo (Chinese)   See: *xiaomo*.

hsiao sang tzu (Chinese)   See: *xiaosangzi*.

hsiao sheng (Chinese)   See: *xiaosheng*.

hsiao tan (Chinese)   See: *xiaodan*.

hsia wu se (Chinese)   See: *xiawuse*.

hsi chü (Chinese)   See: *xiju*.

hsi ch'ü (Chinese)   See: *xiqu*.

hsi chuang (Chinese)   See: *xizhuang*.

hsieh erh (Chinese)   See: *xiezi*.

hsieh p'i sheng (Chinese)   See: *xiepisheng*.

hsieh tzu (Chinese)   See: *xiezi*.

hsien sheng (Chinese)   See: *jiamen*.

hsien tai chü, hsien tai hsi (Chinese)   See: *xiandaiju*.

hsien tzu (Chinese)   See: *sanxian*.

hsien tzu hsi (Chinese)   1. See: *meihuju*. 2. See: *liuzixi*.

hsi fang (Chinese)   See: *houtai*.

hsi lou (Chinese)   See: *xiyuan*.

hsi lu hua ku (Chinese)   See: *chuju*.

hsin chü (Chinese)   See: *xinxi*.

hsing t'ou (Chinese)   See: *xingtou*.

hsin hsi (Chinese)   See: *xinxi*.

hsin ko chü (Chinese)   See: *xingeju*.

hsin pien te li shih chü (Chinese)   See: *xinbiande lishiju*.

hsi p'i (Chinese)   See: *xipi*.

hsi t'ai (Chinese)   See: *wutai*.

hsi wen (Chinese)   See: *nanxi*.

hsi yüan (Chinese)   See: *xiyuan*.

hsüan ssu k'uei lei (Chinese)   See: *mu'ou*.

hsüeh tzu (Chinese)   See: *xuezi*.

hsü sheng (Chinese)   See: *laosheng*.

hto zat (Burmese)   Literally: made-up *zat*. A *zat* play using non-*Jataka* (Buddha's birth) dramatic materials. (Aung DRAMA 35)

hua (Philippine)   See: *loa*.

huabai (Chinese)   See: *nianbai*.

huabu, hua pu (Chinese)   Literally: flower part. An 18th C term for all then-contemporary forms of music-drama (*xiqu*) other than the classical *kunqu* drama. See also: *yabu, luantan*. (Dolby HISTORY 274; Mackerras MODERN 20; Mackerras RISE 6-7, 53–54)

hua chi hsi (Chinese)   See: *huajixi*.

hua chü (Chinese)   See: *huaju*.

huadan, hua tan (Chinese)   Literally: flower female role. 1. A vivacious, flirtatious principal young female role that features dance-acting (*zuo*) and speech (*nian*) skills. A major subcategory of the female role (*dan*) in Beijing opera (*jingju*) and many other forms of music-drama (*xiqu*). Called secondary female role (*tiedan* or *t'ieh tan*) in some forms including *hanju* and southern *yueju*. (Dolby HISTORY 180, Scott CLASSICAL 73) 2. A general term for female roles other than the old female (*laodan*) and clown female (*choudan*) in some forms of music-drama.

huadengxi, hua teng hsi (Chinese)   Literally: flower lantern play. The generic term for many forms of small-scale folk theatre (*xiaoxi*) in central and southern China which developed from folk songs and dances. (Dolby HISTORY 220)

huaguxi, hua ku hsi (Chinese)   Literally: flower drum play, theatre. The generic term for a number of similar forms of small-scale folk theatre (*xiaoxi*) popular in Hunan, Hubei, Jiangxi, and Anhui Provinces. Major forms include tea-picking plays (*caichaxi*), cart plays (*cherxi*), and horse-lantern plays (*madengxi*). (Howard CONTEMPORARY 17, Dolby HISTORY 220, Foreign FOLK 36)

huai chü (Chinese)   See: *huaiju*.

huaihaixi, huai hai hsi (Chinese)   A form of small-scale folk theatre (*xiaoxi*) popular in many areas of Jiangsu Province which developed in the 19th C. Originally it was performed on the ground, informally; later it developed into a stage art. Accompanied by the *ban* clapper and the three-string lute (*sanxian*). See also: *lahunqiang*.

huaiju, huai chü (Chinese)   A form of music-drama (*xiqu*) that originated in Jiangsu Province c. 18th-19th C and is popular today in Shanghai, Jiangsu Province, and parts of Anhui Province. It developed through the combination of local folk music, religious performances, and *huiju*.

huajixi, hua chi hsi (Chinese)   Literally: farce. A form of music-drama (*xiqu*) popular in Shanghai and parts of Jiangsu and Zhejiang Provinces. It developed from Shanghai storytelling (*quyi*), and emphasizes comedy and farce; regional dialects from all over China are used liberally, often in parody, as is music from Beijing opera (*jingju*) and numerous regional forms of music-drama popular in Jiangsu and Zhejiang.

huaju, hua chü (Chinese)   Literally: spoken drama. Modern or Western-style drama in which the spoken word is primary; imported to China via Japan in the late 19th and early 20th C. Spoken drama scripts include translations of Western plays, adaptations of Western novels and plays, translations of Japanese *shinpa* and *shingeki* plays, and original Chinese plays. Performances emphasize realism, rather than the stylization of music-drama (*xiqu*). The term itself was popularized in the 1920s; previously such plays were referred to as new plays (*xinxi*) and civilized plays (*wenmingxi*). See also: *xiju*. (Dolby HISTORY 202-215, Howard CONTEMPORARY 17-18, Hu TS'AU 15-21)

hua ku hsi (Chinese)   See: *huaguxi*.

hualian, hua lien (Chinese)   See: *jing*.

huamian, hua mien (Chinese)   See: *jing*.

huang hsiao hua ku (Chinese)   See: *chuju*.

huangmeidiao, huang mei hsi, huang mei tiao (Chinese)   See: *huangmeixi*.

huangmeixi, huang mei hsi (Chinese)   A form of music-drama (*xiqu*) popular in Anhui Province and parts of Jiangxi and Hubei Provinces which originated in the tea-picking plays (*caichaxi*) of the Huangmei region of Hubei in the early

19th C. Later influenced by the music and performance techniques of *qing-yangqiang* and *huiju*, and by folk music. Formerly called *huangmeidiao* or *huang mei tiao*.

huangxiao huagu (Chinese)   See: *chuju*.

hua pai (Chinese)   See: *nianbai*.

hua pu (Chinese)   See: *huabu*.

huashan, hua shan (Chinese)   Literally: flower tunic. A young female role which combines the characteristics and performance skills of the principal female role (*zhengdan*), flower female role (*huadan*), and sword and horse female role (*daomadan*), and therefore features four basic performance skills: song (*chang*), speech (*nian*), dance-acting (*zuo*), and combat (*da*). It was developed in the late 19th and early 20th C by the master performer Mei Lanfang, and is now a major subcategory of the female role (*dan*) in Beijing opera (*jingju*). (Scott CLASSICAL 73-74)

hua tan (Chinese)   See: *huadan*.

hua teng hsi (Chinese)   See: *huadengxi*.

hubris, hybris (Greek)   In dramatic criticism, the self-will, overconfidence, or pride which marks some characters, especially in tragedy. Pride has been a frequent rendering, but the original meaning in Greek is closer to wanton violence arising from pride of strength. (Vaughn DRAMA, Barnet/Berman/Burto ASPECTS 266, Liddell/Scott LEXICON)

hu ch'in (Chinese)   See: *huqin*.

hu ch'in ch'iang (Chinese)   See: *huqinqiang*.

hu chü (Chinese)   See: *huju*.

hug the spotlight   To steal the center of attention.

huiban, hui pan (Chinese)   Literally: Anhui troupes. The generic name for music-drama (*xiqu*) troupes which performed music in the *erhuang* musical mode (*diaoshi*) in the 17th-early 19th C; Anhui was regarded as the foremost center of *erhuang*. Many troupes went to Beijing in 1790 to perform for the celebration of Emperor Qianlong's birthday, and led the way in developing Beijing opera (*jingju*) in the 19th C. (Dolby HISTORY 149; Mackerras RISE 11, 124-129)

hui chü (Chinese)   See: *huiju*.

huidiao (Chinese)   See: *huiju*.

huiguan, hui kuan (Chinese)   A guild in the 17th-19th C. An actors' guild defended its members against people outside the profession, enforced rules of the trade, organized charitable work, and often maintained a private stage. Also called *hangguan* or *hang kuan*. See also: *huishou*. (Mackerras RISE 224-230)

hui hsi (Chinese)   See: *huiju*.

huiju, hui chü (Chinese)   A form of music-drama (*xiqu*) popular throughout southern China which originated in Anhui Province. It arose out of the combination of a number of forms including *qingyangqiang, sipingqiang, kunqu*, and *qinqiang* in the 17th and 18th C, and is regarded as having been the primary source of development for the *erhuang, chuiqiang*, and *gaobozi* musical modes (*diaoshi*). It was influential in the development of many southern theatre forms, and instrumental in the rise of Beijing opera (*jingju*). Also called *huixi* or *hui hsi* and *huidiao* or *hui tiao* at various times in its history.

huik   See: huke.

hui kuan (Chinese)   See: *huiguan.*

huilong, hui lung (Chinese)   Literally: returning dragon. A quadruple or duple meter regulated (*shangban*) metrical-type (*banshi*) used in the songs of Beijing opera (*jingju*) to express intense, unexpected and usually unhappy emotions. It always begins with the second line of a couplet (*lian*), following a first line sung in lead-in meter (*daoban*). Also called *huilongqiang* or *hui lung ch'iang*. See also: *banyan*. (Wichmann "Aural" 161-164)

huilongqiang, hui lung, hui lung ch'iang (Chinese)   See: *huilong.*

hui pan (Chinese)   See: *huiban.*

huishou, hui shou (Chinese)   The leader of an actors' guild (*huiguan*) from the 17th to the 19th C.

hui tiao, huixi (Chinese)   See: *huiju.*

huju, hu chü (Chinese)   Shanghai opera, a form of music-drama (*xiqu*) popular in Shanghai and parts of Jiangsu and Zhejiang Provinces. It originated in folk songs popular in the Shanghai region. In the 19th C, these developed into Shanghai *tanhuang* storytelling, which was later influenced by Suzhou *tanhuang* and by civilized plays (*wenmingxi*), and given the name *huju* in the late 1940s. It uses *banqiangti* musical structure.

huke   An 11th-17th C heavy black wool cloak which survives in North Africa, Spain, and Ireland. Also called a faldetta, haik, huik, huque. (Boucher FASHION, Wilcox DICTIONARY)

hula ki'i (Hawaiian)   1. Until about the 1880s, an indigenous puppet of Hawaii. About one-third life size, these were wood and cloth hand puppets whose performances were often satirical, gossipy, and hard-hitting at personal and social evils. 2. The name given to this puppetry form. (Malkin PUPPETS 157, 158)

hulubalang (Malaysian)   Literally: warrior. In *awang batil*: 1. The character of a captain. 2. The mask worn by the storyteller when portraying this character. (Sweeney in Malm/Sweeney STUDIES 54-55)

human drama   See: developmental drama.

humanette   See: bib puppet.

human interest, human interest stuff   See: sob stuff.

humanist drama   Especially in the Renaissance, drama based on classical models.

humour   See: comedy of humours.

hun (Thai)   Literally: mannequin. The generic name for doll puppets. *Hun luang*, royal puppets, is a marionette theatre using string puppets operated from below. A physically smaller version is called *hun krom phra ratchawang bowon* or "deputy king's puppets." *Hun krabok* or *hun krabawk* is a rod-puppet form.

Hunan opera   See: *xiangju*.

hunch   In Britain, stage dancing.

hundred entertainments, hundred games   See: *baixi*.

hung (Vietnamese)   A hero role in *hat boi* or *cai luong*.

hung ching (Chinese)   See: *hongjing*.

hunger-hooting   A festival in Ghana which celebrates a bumper harvest and no worries about food shortages. (Lokko "Ghana" 43)

hung sheng (Chinese)   See: *hongsheng*.

hung up   Said of a performer left without a cue.

huppette (French)   See: houppe.

huqin, hu ch'in (Chinese)   1. The generic term for the numerous kinds of two-stringed spike fiddles which are featured in the melodic orchestra (*wenchang*) in many forms of music-drama (*xiqu*). Most have a long, thin neck and a small, round body, and are played with a bamboo bow strung with horsehair. Three of the most important are the *jinghu*, *erhu*, and *banhu*. (Mackerras PERFORMING 154; Scott CLASSICAL 42-44, 50) 2. See: *jinghu*.

huqinqiang, hu ch'in ch'iang (Chinese)   The name for music and plays of the *pihuang* musical system incorporated into Sichuan opera (*chuanju*), and Yunnan opera (*dianju*). (Dolby HISTORY 227, Mackerras MODERN 157)

huque   See: huke.

hurluburlu, hurlupe   A late 17th C woman's hair style consisting of a head full of short curls. (Boucher FASHION)

hurry door   See: *kirido guchi*.

hurry music   Music with a fast tempo, played to enhance the rapid action of a melodrama. (Wilmeth LANGUAGE)

hussar boot   See: Hessian boot.

hussy   See: *friponne*.

hut   The superstructure in an Elizabethan theatre, on top of the roof over the stage and backstage. It served as a storage area and a place where sound effects and descents from "heaven" could be made.

hutch   See: thunder run.

huwina kolu (Kannada)   Literally: flower decorated stick. The presentation, by a *yaksagana* student, of his knowledge of dialogue following his training. (Ashton/Christie YAKSAGANA 49)

hyang-ag O-gi (Korean)   Literally: five styles of mask play. One of several general types of masked drama in the Silla Kingdom (57 BC to 935 AD). (Gassner/Quinn ENCYCLOPEDIA 510)

hybris (Greek)   See: *hubris*.

hydraulic joint   See: water joint.

hygerium metallic iodide lamp   See: short-arc lamp.

hyobanki (Japanese)   See: *yakusha hyobanki*.

hyoshi au (Japanese)   Literally: congruent rhythm. In *no* theatre, a generic term for sung passages (*utai*) which match the rhythm of instrumental (*hayashi*) music. Lyrics are sung in one of three regular meters: *hira nori*, *o nori*, or *chu nori*. See also: *hyoshi awazu*.

hyoshi awazu (Japanese)   Literally: non-congruent rhythm. Declaimed passages (for example, *kotoba*, *issei*, *sashi*) in *no* whose musical accompaniment, if any, is not in a regular beat. See also: *hyoshi au*. (Shimazaki NOH 44, 47-48)

hyoshigi (Japanese)   Two hardwood sticks that are struck together to produce various rhythmic and signaling sound patterns in *bunraku* and, especially, *kabuki*. Commonly abbreviated: *ki*. See also: *dara maku*, *hyoshi maku*. Brandon CLASSIC 351-352 describes a number of patterns.

hyoshi maku (Japanese)   In *kabuki*, a *hyoshigi* sound pattern, first swelling, then tapering off in volume. The pattern is played at the end of a scene or act in a domestic play (*sewamono*) to accompany the closing of the curtain. (Brandon CLASSIC 352)

hyper-extension   The pushing or extension of a joint beyond its anatomically correct position. (Schurman/Clark DANCE)

hypocrites (Greek)   See: *hypokrites*.

hypodidaskalos (Greek)   Literally: under-teacher. The term might at times have been used of chorus trainers hired by playwrights. By the 4th C BC and after, these trainers, perhaps by then professionals, might often have dropped the *hypo*. Compare *didaskalos*. (O'Connor CHAPTERS 69; Pickard-Cambridge FESTIVALS 76, 90-91, 303-304)

hypokrites (Greek)   From the later 5th C BC on, the chief word for 'actor.' *Hypokrites* was used for the one, two, or three performers who played principal roles—that is, who took part in the dialogue—not for chorus members or even their leader, nor for non-speaking players. The word is usually said to come from *hypokrinesthai*, to interpret, to answer. Pickard-Cambridge and others favor an etymological meaning of 'one who answers.' Bywater and others favor a meaning of 'interpreter of the poet's text.' It seems at present impossible to say whether answer or interpret is the source of the meaning. The term is the obvious source of English hypocrite, especially in the sense of pretending. Also (occasionally) spelled *hypocrites*. (Pickard-Cambridge DIONYSUS 110, 127; Haigh

ATTIC 226; Flickinger GREEK 340; Allen ANTIQUITIES 131; Bywater AR-
ISTOTLE 136)

hyporcheme (Greek)   To the older grammarians, "a song accompanied by
dance" in tragedy (Dale). Liddell/Scott LEXICON would add pantomimic action
to this description. Webster notes that "one meaning of the difficult word *hyporcheme* is certainly lively dance." Also spelled *hyporchema*; plural *hypor-
chemata*. All three words have long been accepted in U.S. English, as has
hyporchesis, the choral dance done to the *hyporcheme*. (Dale PAPERS 38-40;
Webster CHORUS 63, 95, 133; Pickard-Cambridge DITHYRAMB 20)

hyporchesis   See: *hyporcheme.*

hyposcenium (Latin Roman)   Literally: understage. 1. By early Christian
Roman times and perhaps a century earlier, the space under the stage (*pulpitum*).
2. At the same time, the front wall of the *pulpitum*. Also seen as *hyposcaenium*
or *hyposkenion* (Greek); U.S. hyposcenium has a similar meaning. (Flickinger
GREEK 60-61, 74, 84, 100-101, fig. 24; Pickard-Cambridge DIONYSUS 70,
116)

hyposkenion (Greek)   See: *hyposcenium.*

hypothesis (Greek)   In Hellenistic times and perhaps earlier, the argument
of a play, the plot of a play. The term is used especially of the mime, where it
is also sometimes the name of a play when the name suggests the subject. Plural
hypotheses. Latin uses the same word. (Beare ROMAN 150, 319; Bieber HIS-
TORY 107; Flickinger GREEK 330)

I

ibersetzungen (Yiddish)   Adaptations, as of Shakespeare, Goethe, Tolstoy, etc. (Lifson YIDDISH 61)

ical (Indonesian)   To evade a blow by exiting off-screen. A standard battle movement in Javanese shadow theatre. (Long JAVANESE 65-66)

ice   A premium paid by a ticket broker for a theatre ticket intended to be sold for yet a higher price. Hence, iceman. The practice goes back at least to the middle of the 19th C.

icebreaker   The opening number in a musical comedy, designed to put the audience in the proper mood, usually by bringing on the chorus girls to lively music. (Jablonski/Stewart GERSHWIN 105)

ichibanmemono (Japanese)   Literally: first part or piece. The first main play of a *kabuki* program (in Kyoto-Osaka) or the first section of an all-day play (in Edo, now Tokyo), usually in four acts. It is invariably a history (*jidai*) piece. Commonly abbreviated *ichibanme* (first). Also called *ichibanme kyogen* (first play). See also: *hon kyogen, nibanmemono.* (Brandon CLASSIC 241, Leiter ENCYCLOPEDIA 147)

ichimonji (Japanese)   The black cloth masking borders upstage of the proscenium in modern *kabuki* theatres. (Leiter ENCYCLOPEDIA 134)

ichi no matsu (Japanese)   Literally: first pine. 1. The first (and nearest to the stage) of three small pine trees that stand in front of the *no* bridgeway (*hashigakari*). (Komparu NOH illus. 129) 2. The acting area on the bridgeway marked by the first pine. (Berberich ''Rapture'' 64)

ichiyazuke (Japanese)   Literally: one-night pickles. Derisive slang of the 17th and 18th C for a topical play based on a scandalous event, usually in *kabuki* but also in *bunraku*. Also called *kiwamono* (topical piece). (Brandon CLASSIC 4, Leiter ENCYCLOPEDIA 137)

ID   Inside diameter. The term is used of pipes to which stage lighting instruments are fastened. OD (outside diameter) is occasionally used instead.

idea   In Aristotelian criticism, the meaning of a play or performance. See also: drama of ideas. (Cameron/Gillespie ENJOYMENT)

identification   1. The recognition by an audience member of elements of him or herself in a dramatic character and identification with the character—a theory not accepted by all. 2. The immersion of a performer into a character. (Cameron/Gillespie ENJOYMENT)

idler   See: take-up block.

idler sandbag   A weight attached to an idler or take-up block to create tension on the operating line and thereby take up the slack.

idolitis   Infatuation of late 19th C young girls with matinee idols. (Carroll MATINEE 15)

ie no gei (Japanese)   Literally: family art. In *kabuki*, a unique style of acting associated with a family of actors, such as the bravura (*aragoto*) style of the Ichikawa Danjuro acting family. (Leiter ART 277)

iemoto (Japanese)   The master of an artistic school. *Iemoto seido* (*iemoto system*) is the traditional master-to-pupil system for teaching and preserving family acting traditions in *no*, *kyogen*, theatre music and dance, and, in modified form, in *kabuki*. (Immoss/Mayer JAPANESE 75, Ortolani ''Iemoto'' 297-306)

igel-igel bojog (Indonesian)   In Bali, to dance in monkey style. Also spelled *igel-igel bodjog*. (de Zoete/Spies DANCE 25)

igel sambiran (Indonesian)   The character Rama's opening dance in Balinese *wayang wong*. (de Zoete/Spies DANCE 22)

iguse (Japanese)   See: *kuse*.

''I hope it keeps fine for you.''   In Britain, a call boy's good luck wish to a performer. (Bowman/Ball THEATRE)

''I hope it rains today.''   In burlesque, a remark indicative of a poor show that depends on bad weather driving customers into the theatre. (Wilmeth LANGUAGE)

''I hope the gentleman sits on it.''   A vaudeville comic's response to a heckler, especially to a Bronx cheer, in the audience. (Wilmeth LANGUAGE)

''I hope you break a leg.''   See: break a leg.

i hsiang (Chinese)   See: *yixiang*.

ikria (Greek)   Especially in the latter half of the 5th C BC, the spectators' seats in a theatre. These wooden seats have been referred to in English as scaffolding, planks, benches, and bleachers. Compare *hedolia*, *spectacula*. (Beare ROMAN 244-247; Pickard-Cambridge DIONYSUS 10-15, 19)

ilakiyattam (Malayalam)   In *kathakali*: 1. A mimed sequence, of fixed choreography, that an actor may interpolate into a performance. It is not accompanied by song. 2. A short mime interpolation within a song (*padam*). 3. Prescribed dance movements that accompany certain gestures. See also: *manodharmma*. (Jones/Jones KATHAKALI 74)

ilattalam (Malayalam)   See: *sankiti*.

illegitimate humor   Lines of dialogue which elicit laughter when they are not designed to do so. Usually they are the result of pent-up nervous tension in the audience caused by high or over-acted drama or outdated dialogue. "Bring in the bier" (*Richard III*) often causes titters in an audience. (Granville DICTIONARY)

illegitimate theatre   Performances in the late 19th C which combined farce, tragedy, opera, and whatever else appealed to the author or producer. (Sobel HANDBOOK)

"I'll send you the birdseed next week."   A burlesque comic's reply to a Bronx cheer in the audience. (Wilmeth LANGUAGE)

illuminator   The chief of the lighting crew when oil lamps were used in 19th C theatres. Sometimes called the chief illuminator. (Rees GAS 7-8)

illumiscope   In Steele Mackaye's descriptions of some of his inventions, a pair of curved reflectors within a coloring drum he called a colorator. The reflectors were independently movable, and thus controlled the direction of the reflected light. The colorator's surface was transparent or translucent as required, and permitted tinted light to be thrown upon scenery representing a landscape or sky. (The pages cited below, which contain illustrations, are in the Addenda.) (Mackaye EPOCH lxxxiv-xc)

illusion   In stage production, the attempt to simulate real life, or the result of such an attempt. Hence, illusionary, illusionism, illusion of reality, illusion-istic theatre, etc. (Bowman/Ball THEATRE)

illusion of the first time   A phrase of the actor William Gillette: "When the spectators have the sense that this particular time, when they are present, is the first time the story has unfolded itself...." (Krows PLAYWRITING 30)

"I love you darling, but the season's closed."   The goodbye when lovers in a troupe break up as the season ends. (Wilmeth LANGUAGE)

iltamat (Finnish)   Evening programs involving large numbers of people, often taking place in meeting halls and consisting of speeches and poetry recitations followed by drinking and dancing. (Carroll/Carroll "Finnish" 36)

ima cavea (Latin Roman)   See: *maenianum primum*.

imagery   Communication by means of concrete and particular meanings through the use of metaphors, similes, and clusters of words relating to sensory impressions. From a study of the imagery in a play, a designer often arrives at a dramatic metaphor which will underlie the design. (Hatlen ORIENTATION)

imaginative play   See: spontaneous drama.

imitation   See: *mimesis*.

imitative setting   A realistic stage picture. (Bowman/Ball THEATRE)

impares (Latin Roman)   See: *pares*.

impersonate   To assume a character, to act. Hence, impersonation, impersonator.

implied scenery   An impressionistic stage setting designed to create a mood rather than to depict a place. (Wright UNDERSTANDING 154)

impracticable, impractical   Of a scenic piece, not usable—such as a stage window that looks real but is not built to work.

impresario   A producer of operas, concerts, and ballets; but the name is sometimes used for a producer of any theatrical event. (Carrington THEATRICANA)

impresario (Spanish)   A 17th C theatre director; the modern spelling is *empresario*. (Rennert SPANISH 33)

impressionism   An artistic movement in the early 20th C which aimed at the evocative rather than the boldly expressive. In drama, Maurice Maeterlinck was one of the proponents. Impressionism was more successful in painting and music than in the theatre, where its moody and mysterious quality was too static and its implications a puzzle to audiences. More often called symbolism.

improvisation   1. In the Stanislavsky system, the acting out of scenes not in a script but invented by a performer as practice for a role in a play. 2. Spontaneous invention by performers of actions, dialogues, and characters, built on a basic idea or situation. Used in actor training but often turned into theatrical performances. (Bowman/Ball THEATRE, Hatlen ORIENTATION) 3. In dance, a complex process of creative exploration in responding to a stimulus, which provides varied movement experiences and forswears intellectual planning (choreography). It involves practice in creating and discarding dances and phrases, experiencing them kinesthetically, and responding to other dancers' movements. (Turner/Grauert/Zallman DANCE 33-34)

improvisational drama   See: creative drama.

improvisator   A performer who improvises, acts extempore.

improvise   To ad lib speech or action.

impulse   In dance, a precipitating action which induces motion.

in   1. Toward the center of the stage. 2. Down, as when a piece of flown scenery or a flown curtain is brought 'in' to position. 3. Said of a performer playing a character, as "Olivier in Othello."

in a front cloth   The British equivalent of the U.S. 'in one.'

in Áirithe (Gaelic)   Reserved seat. The expression is still used on white cards at the Abbey Theatre in Dublin. (Pettet "Irish"110)

inaka shibai (Japanese)   See: *ji kyogen*.

inang (Malaysian)   Literally: chaperon. The role of a female attendant in *ma'yong*. (Yousof "Kelantan" 99-100)

in back   See: back.

in bocca al luppo (Italian)   Literally: in the mouth of the wolf. Among performers, a wish for good luck. See also: break a leg. (Winters SHELLEY 459)

incan   Especially in lamp lists in stage supply catalogues, a shortening of incandescent. The contrast is with quartz, though that is also an incandescent lamp.

incandescent burner   See: Welsbach burner.

incandescent ellipsoidal   Especially in the recent past, an occasional term for an ellipsoidal reflector spotlight which uses an incandescent lamp; the lamp may have either a glass or quartz bulb.

incandescent lamp   Strictly, a light source whose illumination comes from the luminosity of its heated filament. This includes the filament in a glass envelope as well as the filament with the more recent quartz envelope. Perhaps because 'incandescent' referred to the glass-enclosed lamp for so many decades, the term is sometimes limited to its long-time meaning.

incident   An event within the dramatic action of a play.

incidental music   Music played during a dramatic performance and usually written especially for a specific play. Grieg's music for Ibsen's *Peer Gynt* or Mendelssohn's for *A Midsummer Night's Dream* are examples.

inciting action, inciting incident, inciting moment   The instant at which some overt act upsets the equilibrium that opened the play and moves the plot forward, as when Oedipus commits himself to the finding of the killer of King Laius, or when Hamlet swears to revenge his father's murder. Also called the dramatic question, the point of attack, *erregende* moment (German-English). (O'Hara/Bro INVITATION)

incline   Especially in the past, the rake or slant of a stage floor; hence the terms upstage and downstage.

incongruity   In comic theory, an imbalance ranging from simple disharmony to outright absurdity. The incongruity exists between what the audience might expect and what it actually sees on stage.

independent   A dimmer channel that is electrically independent from the master or sub-master control. See also: non-dim.

independent theatre movement   A movement in London in the 1890s involving the establishment by J. T. Grein of the Independent Theatre and the promotion of plays by the new social dramatists, especially Henrik Ibsen and George Bernard Shaw. Grein's work was patterned after that of André Antoine at the Théâtre Libre in Paris and Otto Brahm at the Freie Bühne in Berlin.

index plate   See: gas plate.

index striplight   In a rope system for hanging scenery, a striplight which illuminates the numbers which identify the various sets of lines. (Bowman/Ball THEATRE)

India rubber man   A 19th C stretchable trick marionette. (Philpott DICTIONARY)

indiennes   A 17th-18th C term for all fabrics of Eastern origin, printed or painted. (Boucher FASHION)

indirect exposition   Facts about incidents which occurred before the beginning of a play, conveyed obliquely in some way—for example, under a major plot event, through stage business or activity, or through symbols or other visual details in the *mise en scène*.

indirect focus   An arrangement of performers on stage that directs the spectator's attention to one character or group of characters but then redirects it to another character or group.

indirect footlights   Footlights which depend entirely upon reflected light. Such footlights, necessarily inefficient, have not been common. See also: Fortuny lighting (system). (Fuchs LIGHTING 168-169, McCandless METHOD 82, Ridge/ Aldred LIGHTING 29-30)

individual select/record   See: manual takeover.

induction   Especially in the past, an expository part of a play, such as a prologue. 17th C English playwrights sometimes used inductions, calling the speaker of the induction the presenter. (Bowman/Ball THEATRE)

indulto (Spanish)   A tax paid on imports into Spain in the 18th C. By extension, a tax levied in London on leading actors' profits received from benefits in which they appeared. (Milhous/Hume ''Silencing'' 433)

in escrow   Unemployed.

inevitability   A feeling of irreversible impending tragedy created by a playwright in an audience by arranging character and plot so that the outcome seems unavoidable.

in exostra (Latin Roman)   On stage and in view of the audience. Compare *exostra*. (Beare ROMAN 270)

infamis (Latin Roman)   Under the stigma of *infamia*, a legal status in which certain civil rights were denied. Most professional actors were *infames* (plural). (Chambers MEDIAEVAL I 8-9, Allen ANTIQUITIES 134-135)

infernum (Latin)   An alternative term for hell in medieval theatre. (Tydeman THEATRE)

infinite preset   In U.S. light control, any system which theoretically permits an unlimited number of dimmer or 'scene' settings to be reproduced on cue.

The term has been used primarily of card systems, now obsolete. (Bellman LIGHTING 224-225, Bentham ART 330)

inflection   The raising or lowering of the pitch of a performer's voice, such as an upward or downward inflection at the end of a line of dialogue, to clarify the meaning.

informal balancing   A balanced but assymetrical stage picture created by a director.

informal drama   See: creative drama.

in four   See: in one.

in front   See: front of house.

ingegni (Italian)   Medieval stage machines. (Nagler SOURCES 41)

ingenue   1. The stage role of a young woman, usually naive. 2. An actress who plays such roles. 3. In burlesque, the chief female performer. (Roberts STAGE, Sandberg ''Mills'' 341) 4. An old term for a shade of makeup used by actresses playing youthful roles.

inggahaken (Indonesian)   In Javanese shadow theatre, a biting technique in which giants grasp their opponents in their mouths and attempt to crush them to death. (Long JAVANESE 102)

ingong (Philippine)   A ritual revenge dance, of the Negritos, in which a warrior, armed with arrows and *bolo*, enacts the killing and beheading of his opponent. (Alejandro SAYAW 28)

ingressus (Latin)   Stairways in an Elizabethan theatre. (Gascoigne WORLD 117)

inhyong (Korean)   A modern term for puppet. See also: *kkoktu*. (Cho KOREAN 185)

initial   To have the first place on a variety bill.

initial canto   The first act on a bill.

initial incident   The incident in a plot which first changes the existing dramatic situation. See also: inciting action. (Bowman/Ball THEATRE)

initial situation   The status quo when a play begins.

initial stanza   1. The first week of a run. 2. The first act on a bill.

inky   See: embryo.

in medias res (Latin)   Literally: into the midst of things. In playwriting, said of a play which begins after the actual story is somewhat advanced.

innamorata (Italian)   The female young lover in *commedia dell'arte*; also called the *amorosa*, *prima donna* (first woman), or *comica accesa*. The character was often named Isabella, but also Ardelia, Aurelia, Camilla, Flaminia, Lavinia, Ortensia, Rosaura, Silvia, Vittoria, etc. (Brockett HISTORY 183, Oreglia COMMEDIA 116) *innamorato* (Italian)   The male young lover in *commedia dell' arte*; also called the *amoroso* or *comico acceso*. The character was given such names as Aurelio, Cinzio, Fabrizio, Flavio, Florindo, Leandro, Lelio, Lindoro, Orazio, Ottavio, etc. (Brockett HISTORY 183, Oreglia COMMEDIA 116)

inner biography   The philosophical idea in a play, shown through social and psychological characters. To show that idea was one of the main purposes of the Moscow Art Theatre in the early 20th C. (Markov SOVIET 62)

inner drama   According to the designer Adolphe Appia, the innermost material of a drama, from which theatre as a unified work of art must grow. (Bellman ''Aesthetics'' 119)

inner proscenium   A second or false proscenium behind the permanent proscenium opening, made of flats or drapes and used to change the size and/or shape of the opening and serve as a scenic frame. Referred to as hard when built of flats, soft when made of cloth. Also called a portal.

inner proscenium batten   A pipe batten fastened to the back of the horizontal part of an inner proscenium or hanging just upstage of it. Spotlights are mounted on the batten.

inner stage, inner below, inner above   According to one theory, an inset, curtained acting area in a Shakespearean theatre, located at the back of the platform stage on stage level and one story above. Also called an alcove, chamber, discovery space, study, or after stage. But the inner stage theory has been challenged; see: pavilion. See also: rear stage. (Rhodes STAGERY 19-20, Bowman/Ball THEATRE)

inn theatre   1. In Elizabethan times, a simple trestle stage set up in an innyard. 2. An inn turned into a theatre. (Bowman/Ball THEATRE)

in one   1. The stage area downstage of the first set of wings (the furthest downstage plane of the stage). A scene 'in two' is played in the area downstage of the second wings, 'in three' downstage of the third wings, 'in four' downstage of the fourth wings. Hence, act in one, working in one, scene in two, etc. Comics in vaudeville often work 'in one,' in front of a curtain or drop, while the next scene or act is being set up. Also called a carpenter's scene. 2. Said of an act with no scene changes.

in order of appearance   The manner in which characters are usually listed in a theatre program.

inori (Japanese)   Literally: prayer. A scene in *no* in which a demon is subdued by means of a Buddhist prayer. One type of *hatarakigoto*. (Keene NO 81, Shimazaki NOH 38)

in person   1. Said of a performer such as a film or television star who appears in a stage production. (Bowman/Ball THEATRE) 2. Hyphenated, used of such a performance—an in-person appearance.

in rep   Said of a performer working in a repertory company.

in role   In improvisation with children and young people, the taking of a role by the leader in order to help the participants maintain focus or guide them to a more sophisticated level.

insakut (Korean)   See: *p'ungmul.*

in scaena (Latin Roman)   On the stage. Compare *scaena.* (Flickinger GREEK 77)

in scene   See: out of scene.

inset scene   A small setting inside a larger one. (Granville DICTIONARY)

inside   In dance, a turn which goes in the same direction as the leg upon which the body is moving: e.g., a turn to the right on the right leg. (Stodelle HUMPHREY 227)

inside frost   A translucent surface on the inside of a bulb.

inside talker   A kind of barker who introduced and lavishly praised the "live art" acts in the dime museums of the early 20th C. (Frick/Johnson "Coney" 132)

instant puppet   A puppet made from such found materials as tin cans, socks, boxes, etc. (Philpott DICTIONARY)

instant theatre   Improvised scenes whose content is suggested by an audience and performed by an acting ensemble. (Davis/Evans CHILDREN'S 38)

instauratio (Latin Roman)   From at least the 3rd C BC, the repetition of a festival, usually for religious reasons. Evidently not much more than a missed cue in a play was necessary for a festival to be deemed improperly performed. Repetitions may often have been due to the popularity of the plays: an audience disturbance, for example, would have been enough to require redoing a festival. Three or four repetitions of the same festival in one year were not uncommon; the Plebian Games were repeated seven or eight times on two occasions (about 205 BC and 195 BC). Plural *instaurationes.*

instrument   1. A performer's voice and body. (Cameron/Gillespie ENJOYMENT 300) 2. See: lighting instrument.

instrumenta (Latin Roman)   Stage equipment. The term includes, for example, the *siparium* (small curtain) of the mime players. The word is literally apparatus, instruments; hence, equipment. (Beare ROMAN 170)

instrument check   See: checkout.

instrument schedule   A multi-columned table which lists necessary information about the instruments used to light a production. Such a schedule typically includes the type of instrument and its location, color medium, use, circuit, and dimmer; columns for wattage, notes, and other facts are also sometimes included. (Bellman LIGHTING 386-387, Rubin/Watson LIGHTING 17-20)

insurgente, gown à l'   See: gown à l'insurgente.

inszenieren (German)   To direct a play.

Inszenierung (German)   Staging, production. In French, *mise en scène*.

intake, intake room   In Britain, the room or other enclosure which houses the main electrical supply and its appurtenances. The stage intake and the FOH (front of house) intake are sometimes separately identified. Called in the U.S. a transformer vault or distribution vault (or room). (Bentham ART, Bax MANAGEMENT 175)

integrated arts   In schools, art works melded into other subject matter, as in studying history by enacting scenes, learning geography by drawing maps, etc.

Intendant (German)   The director or manager of a theatre. (Lucas GERMAN)

intensity   1. In sound transmission, the principal physical factor controlling the sensation of loudness, measured in decibels. (Burris-Meyer/Mallory SOUND 1) 2. Brightness, amount of light, in footcandles (the light thrown on a surface a foot away from a standard candle). (Bellman SCENE)

inter-act   A variant of entr'acte. 1. The time between acts; an intermission or (in Britain) interval. 2. An entertainment provided during such time. (Bowman/Ball THEATRE)

interconnecting panel   In lighting, a collection of electrical receptacles and plugs that permits any plug to be connected to any receptacle. A common type inserts each load (a plug) into the line (a jack) selected; such arrangements are often called patch boards, patch bays (this term from similar arrangements in radio), or patch panels; the flexible load cord is a patch cord, and a record of what load is connected to what dimmer and when, is sometimes called a patch sheet. Patch boards, which resemble old-fashioned telephone switchboards, are sometimes referred to as telephone board interconnectors, telephone-type interconnecting systems, and similar phrases. A version in which the plug cords are withdrawn into the board when not in use is a retractable-cord (interconnect) system. A slider (or crossbar) interconnec(tion) panel is a matrix of bars: a long panel contains a slider for each load, and any slider may be clipped to any dimmer's output bar (enclosed in the panel). Still another type, used in direct control boards, uses a rotary switch to connect dimmers and loads. Other names sometimes used for any of these arrangements are interconnect(ion) panel, plugging or interplugging panel, cross-connect or cross-connecting panel or unit, and programming panel. A pin matrix has been used recently to perform a similar function at control voltages. See: matrix interconnection panel. (Bellman LIGHTING 277-281, figs. 11-1a, b, c, d, e; Wehlburg GLOSSARY; Sellman/Lessley ESSENTIALS 117-120, figs. 8-1, 8-2)

interior monologue (or **dialogue**)   A modern version of the soliloquy and the aside, devices borrowed from the stream-of-consciousness technique of novelist James Joyce. Eugene O'Neill used the technique in *Strange Interlude*, allowing the audience to hear the thoughts of the characters. (Sobel NEW)

interior scene   1. Scenery depicting an indoor locale. 2. A scene in a play which takes place indoors.

interlocking plate dimmer   See: plate dimmer.

interlocking resistance dimmer   A resistance dimmer whose control can be slipped into a notched shaft, where the control remains. A master control moves the shaft and all dimmers locked into it.

interlocutor   In a minstrel show, the straight man, seated at the center of the semicircle and serving as a kind of master of ceremonies. Also called the middleman.

interlocutores (Latin)   Cast of characters.

interlocutori (Italian)   Cast of characters.

interlude, enterlude, entrelude   1. A dramatic entertainment presented between other events, such as the courses of a banquet in medieval and Renaissance times. (Cameron/Gillespie ENJOYMENT) 2. A short dramatic work, performed independently or as part of a longer work in late 16th C England. Sometimes the term seems to be an equivalent of play. 3. Today, any short entertainment, especially during an intermission. (Bowman/Ball THEATRE, Greg HENSLOWE'S II 148)

interludens (Latin)   An actor. (Chambers MEDIAEVAL II 233)

interludium (Latin)   In medieval times, an interlude.

interlusor (Latin)   An actor. (Chambers MEDIAEVAL II 233)

intermède (French)   1. An interlude. 2. A one-act play.

intermède rustique (French)   A bucolic interlude between plays or acts of a play, often in dance, song, or pantomime or some combination thereof. (Frank MEDIEVAL 231)

intermedii (Italian)   In Renaissance Italy, elaborate song-and-dance spectacles performed between the acts of revived classical plays. Singular: *intermedio*. Not to be confused with *intermezzi*.

intermezzi (Italian)   Literally: intervals. 1. In the early 18th C, one-act comic operas, usually for two singers and a pantomime player, performed between the acts of an *opera seria*. Singular: *intermezzo*. Since there were two intermissions, the plots of the two *intermezzi* were often related. The most famous was Giovanni Battista Pergolesi's *La Serva Padrona*. The terms *intermedii* and *intermezzi* are sometimes confused. 2. Short songs in *commedia dell'arte*. See also: *intermedii*.

intermission   The time or wait between acts. Also called an act wait. In Britain: interval. When entertainment is offered, such as instrumental music, songs, or dances, the period is usually called an entr'acte.

intermission bell   See: bar bell.

intermission drop   See: act drop.

interplugging panel   See: interconnecting panel.

interpolation   Dialogue or business inserted in a play, often by a performer, ad lib. Hence, interpolate, interpolator.

interpreter   In puppet performances, the operator or the operator's assistant. The interpreter explains the action to the audience. Often he or she interacts with the puppets and collects coins from the spectators. See also: bottler, pardner. (Philpott DICTIONARY)

interpreters theatre   See: readers theatre.

interpretive dance   1. In contemporary dance usage, a translation of what is heard into what is seen: music is made into movement. Hence, interpretive dancer. 2. The interpretation in movement of ideas and things: natural phenomena, colors, etc. (Love DANCE 47)

interpretive dancer   1. See: interpretive dance. 2. A euphemism for a stripper or cooch dancer. (Wilmeth LANGUAGE)

interpretive dramatics   See: creative drama.

interruption scene   In 20th C U.S. burlesque, a stock presentation in which a supposedly "cultured" straight man is interrupted and gradually driven to distraction by comic interference with his routine. (Allen in Matlaw AMERICAN 55-56)

interval   See: intermission.

in the aisles   Said of spectators figuratively (or even literally) falling out of their seats with laughter. Hence, knock 'em in the aisles, lay 'em in the aisles.

in the round   1. A term applied to arena or central staging, where the performance is seen, as it were, from all around. Hence, theatre in the round, to play in the round, etc. 2. Said of a three-dimensional scenic unit, such as a rock.

in the test tube   Said of a theatrical production in tryout.

in three   See: in one.

intimate theatre   1. A small playhouse with a limited seating capacity. 2. A production with a small cast, fostering a sophisticated intimacy between spectators and the performance. Hence, intimate play, intimate revue, etc. (Bowman/Ball THEATRE)

intrat   Enter. Used by some Elizabethan playwrights.

intrigue comedy   Comedy of situation, usually concerned with amorous matters and stressing stratagems and conspiracies. (Brooks/Heilman UNDERSTANDING)

in trim   See: trim.

introductive speeches   Formerly, cues. "Mr. Wilks used to read the introductive Speeches" for Richards. (Chetwood HISTORY 231)

introito (Spanish)   See: *introyto*.

intro number   A short preliminary performance or act.

introyto, introito (Spanish)   A prologue, an introduction; a *loa* (dramatic sketch). The term probably derived from the Latin *introit*, the opening part of a Mass. (Chambers MEDIAEVAL II 8)

in two   See: in one.

invención (Spanish)   A device, clever effect, or conceit, particularly in connection with the pageantry of tournaments. (Shergold SPANISH)

inverse square law   The standard U.S. term for a physical phenomenon of particular importance to stage lighting. The intensity of light on an object is inversely proportional to the square of the object's distance from the light source. An object ten feet from a light will therefore have 1/4 (not 1/2) the light provided by the same source at five feet. Also called the law of squares and law of inverse squares in Britain. (Bellman LIGHTING 48, Goffin LIGHTING 58)

inverted float, inverted Argand   In late 19th C Britain, footlights in which Argand lamps were burned upside down. In order to achieve this, the manufacturer (Strode Engineering) provided a strong draft in the lamp chimney which connected with an exhaust pipe: heat and smoke were thus drawn off beneath the stage as a health/safety measure. These inverted floats were installed in a number of British theatres in the 1860s and 1870s; a similar footlight went into the new Paris Opera in 1875. Also called a Strode float or siphon light. (Rees GAS 28-29, fig. 11)

ioculator (Latin)   One of the four general terms for a medieval minstrel. See: minstrel.

iocus (Latin)   In medieval England, a play. (Chambers MEDIAEVAL II 138)

i pan san hsiang (Chinese)   See: *banxi*.

ipli kukla (Turkish)   A string-controlled marionette. (And KARAGÖZ 24)

ippon choshi (Japanese)   Literally: single-line pattern. Machine-gun-like delivery of a long, complex passage in a bravura style male monologue in *kabuki*. (Brandon CLASSIC 71)

ippon guma, ippon kuma (Japanese)   Literally: single-line shading. One type of stylized *kumadori* makeup used in *kabuki*. One broad line of black and one of red outline the cheek. (Scott KABUKI 124-125)

iris, iris shutter   Primarily in the U.S., a device used in or at the front of a spotlight to change the diameter of the beam of light, sometimes to blackout. The iris, a large version of the iris shutter on a camera, is most used on follow spots and arc spots; on the latter it often serves to narrow and dim the beam to blackout. The British prefer iris diaphragm or diaphragm, though iris is not unknown. (Bax MANAGEMENT 187)

iris curtain   A novelty theatre curtain designed in semi-circular rigid strips, in layers, capable of closing in the proscenium opening from all directions at once, much like the iris on a camera or spotlight. (Krows AMERICA 85)

iris diaphragm   See: iris.

iris out   To dim a spotlight to blackout by closing the iris all the way.

Irish justice   A burlesque turn in which a judge hits a defendant with a rubber bladder. (Wilmeth LANGUAGE)

Irish nightingale   In vaudeville, a tenor or countertenor who sang Irish ballads, using an Irish accent. (Wilmeth LANGUAGE)

iro (Japanese)   Literally: color. A 'parlando' or song-speech passage in a *bunraku* or *kyogen* play. In *bunraku*, also called *ji iro* (musicalized speech). (Malm in Brandon CHUSHINGURA 71, Berberich "Rapture" 151)

iroe (Japanese)   Literally: color added. A circling movement by a female character in *no*, performed as a prelude to a major dance. One type of *hatarakigoto*. (Keene NO 81, Shimazaki NOH 37)

iroko (Japanese)   Literally: sex child. An adolescent boy who acted in early *kabuki*. So called because offstage he was a catamite. (Shively in Brandon/Malm/Shively STUDIES 37, Tsubouchi/Yamamoto KABUKI 188)

iron, iron curtain   See: fire curtain.

irony   See: dramatic irony.

irradiation   Stanislavsky's term for in- and out-going energy from an actor in the process of performing. (Stanislavsky ACTOR 199-206)

iscidomal floor slope   An architectural term for an auditorium floor profile incorporating a variable rise per row to provide equal hearing and equal seeing from all seats.

isho (Japanese)   Costumes in all theatre forms. Illustrations of *no* and *kyogen* costumes are in Keene NO 299-302. Descriptions of *no* costumes are in Nippon Gakujutsu JAPANESE ix-xiii and Shimazaki NOH 66-81. Illustrations of 200 *kabuki* costumes are in Shaver COSTUMES. In *no*, also called *shozoku*. (Bethe/Brazell NO 124) *Isho kata* (costume person) or *ishoya* (costume proprietor) is a costumer. (Hamamura et al KABUKI 112)

iskemle kuklasi (Turkish)   A jigging puppet, string-controlled by street showmen. (And KARAGÖZ 24)

isolation   In dance, the movement of single or related body parts so as to use those parts independently.

issei (Japanese)   1. The introductory song of the protagonist (*shite*) in *no*, in the fixed form of twenty-nine syllables in three lines (5 + 7, 5 + 7, 5) sung in a high register and in free rhythm by the *shite* and the chorus, or by the chorus alone. (Shimazaki NOH 47, Keene NO 76, Inoura HISTORY 116) 2. A similar song in a *kyogen* play. (Berberich "Rapture" 47, 172)

isshi soden (Japanese)   Literally: one-son inheritance. Special secrets of *no* performance that are transmitted only from father to son. See: *kuden*. (Konishi "Approaches" 1) *ister* (Etruscan)   See: *histrio*.

istrio (Latin)   Actor. A variant of *histrio*. (Duchartre ITALIAN 78)

Italian mimes   See: *phlyakes*.

"I think I'll phone in the act today."   A remark used by a vaudeville performer when he was sick, drunk, or hung over. (Wilmeth LANGUAGE)

ithyphalloi (Greek)   Literally: straight phalluses. Early performers, masked as drunkards and wreathed, possibly connected with Dionysus and perhaps Thespis. (Pickard-Cambridge DITHYRAMB 137, 139-141; Webster PRODUCTION 36)

itinera (Latin Roman)   See: *itinera versurarum*.

itinera versurarum (Latin Roman)   The enclosed vaulted side entrances to a theatre or stage. The term sometimes refers to the side entrances to the stage, analogous to the *paraskenia* entrances to a Greek stage, and sometimes to the adjacent side entrances to the seating area, counterpart of the Greek *parodoi*. Also appears as *itinera* and *choragia* (Vitruvius). (Bieber HISTORY 172, 187, figs. 656, 657)

itivrtta (Sanskrit)   See: *vastu*.

"It must be the landlady!"   See: "God bless you both!"

ito ni noru (Japanese)   See: *nori*.

"It will be all right on the night."   See: "All right on the night."

"I've gone."   "I've forgotten my line."

iwato kagura (Japanese)   Literally: heavenly cave dance. A sacred Shinto dance (*kagura*), performed by shamans (*miko*, priestesses who are traditionally considered descendants of the Goddess Ame-no-Uzume). The dance represents the myhological origins of performing arts in Japan. (Inoura HISTORY 19)

i yang ch'iang (Chinese)   See: *yiyangqiang*.

Izenour dimmer   See: thyratron tube dimmer.

Izenour switchboard   A trade name for a light control board using thyratron tube dimmers (q.v.). The inventor was George Izenour. (Lounsbury THEATRE, Bellman LIGHTING 192-194)

Izumi *ryu* (Japanese)   One of two extant schools of *kyogen* actors. Originated in the 15th C. See also: Okura.

J

jabisen (Japanese)   See: *shamisen*.

Jablochkoff candle   An electric arc light in which two parallel sticks of carbon are separated by an insulating material. The carbons and the insulator vaporize at the same rate; the Jablochkoff resembles a candle in general shape and in shortening as it burns. Invented in the middle 1870s, the Jablochkoff came into some theatre use, but not for long: three years after its appearance, Edison in the U.S. and Swan in England demonstrated the electric incandescent lamp. Fuchs has an illustration. See also: arc light, carbon arc. (Fuchs LIGHTING 45)

jack   1. A brace jack: a frame, usually triangular, attached at right angles to the back of a scenic unit, such as a ground row, to hold it upright. In Britain, it is called a French or frame brace. See also: lift jack, tip jack. 2. A tool used to raise a heavy object. 3. In stage lighting and sound, a receptacle for the insertion of a plug, but the term is sometimes used for the plug itself.

jackal   In 17th C England, a name given a theatrical underling who advertised the time and place of performances, especially surreptitious performances during the Commonwealth (1649-1660). (Wright HISTORIA 9)

jacketed lamp   A tungsten-halogen lamp whose quartz tube is inside an outer bulb. (Sellman/Lessley ESSENTIALS 67)

jackknife stage   A wagon stage or rolling platform pivoted at the downstage-offstage corner to swing in an arc onstage and off. Hence, jackknife set. Also called a swing or swinging stage and a scissor stage. See also: wagon stage.

jack roller   See: lift jack.

Jack's come home   1. British slang for a slapdash, overly-carefree attitude toward a performance. 2. In Australia, a theatrical lodging house, usually providing rooms of indifferent quality. (Marsh VINTAGE 150, 160; Granville DICTIONARY) *janger* (Indonesian)   Literally: humming. A Balinese female group dance and play which developed out of the vocal accompaniment to the trance dance (*sanghyang*). Also spelled *djanger*. (de Zoete/Spies DANCE 211-217, Soedarsono DANCES 182)

janggo (Korean)   See: *changgo*.

jangler   See: minstrel.

jan k'ou (Chinese)   See: *rankou*.

janome mawashi (Japanese)   Literally: bull's-eye revolve. In 18th and 19th C *kabuki*, two revolving stages, one set inside the other, that could turn in either the same or opposite directions. Today some musical comedy stages are equipped with *janome mawashi*, but no present day *kabuki* theatre is. Also called *janome butai* (bull's-eye stage). (Leiter ENCYCLOPEDIA 147, Scott KABUKI 282-283)

janseniste (French)   See: pannier.

janturan (Indonesian)   1. In Sundanese *wayang golek*, a row of puppets set up as a decorative arrangement on either side of the playing area. See also: *simpingan*. (Foley "Sundanese"49) 2. In Javanese *wayang*, narration which introduces and describes a major scene, accompanied by *gamelan* music. Also spelled *djanturan*. See also: *cariyos*, *peretitala*. (Muljono in Osman TRADITIONAL 70, Brandon THRONES 29-30)

januam (Latin Roman)   See: *prothyron*.

jape   Literally: joke, gag. Improvised dialogue and horseplay, popular in medieval times and earlier.

japer   See: minstrel.

jaquette (French)   1. A 14th-16th C male peasant blouse, rather closely fitted. 2. Later, a small boy's garment, forerunner of the jacket. 3. A 19th C woman's jacket. See also: hongreline. (Boucher FASHION)

jarjara (Sanskrit)   Literally: one who crushes. (Rangacharya INDIAN 41) The god Indra's flagstaff, which was used to drive away evil sprits in the first dramatic production in the heavens. Its appearance on stage became an essential element of stage preliminaries (*purvaranga*). (Keith SANSKRIT 41, 369; Gargi FOLK 204, Vatsyayan in Baumer/Brandon SANSKRIT 52)

jarreté (French)   In ballet, close-legged, knock-kneed. See also: *aigué*. (Grant TECHNICAL)

jasbo   See: jazbo.

Jasper   In Britain, a traditional name for the villain in a melodrama.

jatra (Bengali, Oriya, Assamese)   Literally: to go in a procession. An extremely popular theatre form in northeast India that emphasizes singing and bravura acting and is normally performed in the round in a temporary stage area. The travelling troupes of professional actors and musicians who perform *jatra* are highly commercial in organization. Also spelled *yatra*. (Sarkar ''Jatra'' 87-94)

jatri (Thai)   See: *lakon jatri*.

jauk (Indonesian)   1. A Balinese masked dance-drama dating from the 18th C in which episodes from the *Ramayana* and the *Mahabharata* are enacted; now rarely performed. Also spelled *djaoek*. (Soedarsono DANCES 180, de Zoete/Spies DANCE 174-177) 2. A demon follower of the *barong* in the Balinese *barong* play. Also called *omang*. (de Zoete/Spies DANCE 99)

jaulipinde (Kannada)   A member of a *yaksagana* troupe who is responsible for carrying and caring for costumes and for holding the curtain during performance. (Ashton/Christie YAKSAGANA 53, 91)

javanika (Sanskrit)   See: *yavanika*.

jay   A patron of an out-of-town theatre.

jay town   In the early 20th C U.S., a theatrical term for a small town visited by a touring company, the implication being that the townsfolk were simple-minded and unsophisticated. (Wilmeth LANGUAGE)

jazbo, jazzbo, jasbo   1. A vulgar comic bit. 2. A Black performer in a minstrel show. (Wilmeth LANGUAGE)

jazz dance   Popular, commercial entertainment; a style of dance seen in film, Broadway musicals, and on television. Performed to popular, rock, or jazz music.

jazz-vaudeville drama   In the 1920s, a type of experimental drama written by left-wing playwrights in the U.S. which attempted to use the vigor and originality of jazz and vaudeville to provide a rhythm and tempo for their criticism of American society. (Turner ''Jazz'' 110)

Jean de Bry   A 19th C evening coat with very long tails, reminiscent of the coat worn by ''Uncle Sam.'' (Walkup DRESSING 259)

jeblosan (Indonesian)   Fighting movement in Javanese shadow theatre when both characters simultaneously lunge past each other, then repeat the movement as they return to their original positions. (Long JAVANESE 62)

jeblosan linton (Indonesian)   Javanese shadow theatre (*wayang kulit*) technique in which the puppeteer releases both puppets as he performs the *jeblosan* movement. The puppets are caught in mid-air, turned, and thrown back again to complete the movement. (Long JAVANESE 62)

jejer (Indonesian)   Literally: array. An 'array' of puppets which begins a scene in Javanese shadow theatre; hence, by extension, a major act or scene in a *wayang* play. (Holt ART 136) Each of the seven major scenes in Yogyakarta-style *wayang* is a *jejer* (Long JAVANESE 7); only the first scene of the play is a *jejer* in Surakarta-style *wayang*. Also spelled *djedjer*. (Brandon THRONES 20) See also: *adegan*.

jejer pandita (Indonesian)   See: *pandita*.

jejer putri (Indonesian)   See: *putri*.

jell   See: gel.

jelly roll, jelly wobble   A shimmy dance. (Berrey/Van den Bark SLANG 589)

jemima   See: bottine.

Jenny   A chorus girl. (Berrey/Van den Bark SLANG 573)

jen wu (Chinese)   See: *jiaose*.

jerk   1. To remove or discontinue a show or act. Also called pull or yank. (Berrey/Van den Bark SLANG 584) 2. In burlesque in the plural, the audience. (Wilmeth LANGUAGE)

jerkin   1. A 16th-17th C outer doublet with or without sleeves. When made of leather, its sleeves were of a rich fabric. (Boucher FASHION) 2. A kind of hip-length, square-necked, fitted jumper worn over a shirt or blouse.

jerkwater town   See: tank.

Jessnertreppen (German)   Steps of varying shapes and sizes, used to create a stage composition. Developed by the Berlin director Leopold Jessner after World War I. (Sobel NEW)

jester   A comic entertainer in medieval times and earlier, usually found at court and given to jokes and riddles. Also called a fool. Both terms name types and characters in Elizabethan plays.

jeté, pas jeté (French)   Literally: thrown step. In ballet, a spring from one foot to the other in which the working leg appears to be thrown. Many kinds of *jetés* are entered and described in Grant. (Grant TECHNICAL, Wilson BALLET)

jeté bateau (French)   See: *ballotté*.

jeu (French)   1. Especially in the Italian *commedia dell'arte*, a completely structured comedy unit with a beginning, middle, and end. (Scott in Mayer/Richards WESTERN 24) 2. Of a performer, style of acting. 3. Since medieval times, a play, a dramatic amusement, or the text thereof. 4. The presentation of a play.

jeu de scène (French)   Stage action dependent upon the setting. (Duchartre ITALIAN 60)

jeu de théâtre (French)   See: *jeu muet*.

jeu d'orgue (French)   The gas control center for the stage lighting system in a 19th C French theatre. Compare: gas table. (Rees GAS 106-107, fig. 66; Penzel LIGHTING 85-86, fig. 18)

jeu muet (French)   Dumb show, stage business. Also called *jeu de théâtre*.

jeune premier, jeune première (French)   Juvenile lead (male, female). The terms are used for the stock characters as well as the performers who play them.

jeux-partis (French)   See: *tensons*.

jhanki (Hindi)   1. The opening tableau of a *raslila* performance in which Krishna is seated on his throne with Radha on his left. (Swann "Braj" 22) 2. A sacred performance in north India, in which devotional songs are sung before the deities Rama and Krishna, played by boys, posed in a tableau vivant. (Hein MIRACLE 18-20)

ji (Japanese)   1. The seated chorus in *no*, usually consisting of eight or ten men, who sing portions of the text in unison, often taking over lines of the protagonist (*shite*) and occasionally of the secondary character (*waki*). Also called *ji utai*, *ji utai kata* (chorus singers). (Shimazaki NOH 44) 2. Those portions of a *no* play that are sung by the chorus. Also called *ji utai* (chorus song). (Nippon Gakujutsu JAPANESE 100-101, Komparu NOH 162) 3. In *bunraku*, those portions of text that are sung, as opposed to spoken portions (*kotoba*) and parlando sections (*iro*). Also called *jiai*, *fushi*. (Malm in Brandon CHUSHINGURA 66-68)

jia, chia (Chinese)   An emperor or monarch; a type of stock character in Yuan *zaju* (13th-14th C). (Dolby HISTORY 60)

jiagun (Chinese)   See: *gundiao*.

jiai (Japanese)   See: *ji*.

jiamen, chia men (Chinese)   Literally: background. A short, one-act prologue delivered by a secondary performer (*fumo*) at the beginning of southern drama (*nanxi*) and *chuanqi* plays. It acquainted the audience with the playwright's intention and the spirit in which he hoped the play would be taken, summarized the plot, and raised audience interest. Also called points and purposes (*biaomu* or *piao mu*), performance opening (*kaichang* or *k'ai ch'ang*), opening purpose (*kaizong* or *k'ai tsung*), summary (*tonglüe* or *t'ung lüeh*), and harbinger (*xiansheng* or *hsien sheng*). See also: *zibao jiamen*. (Dolby HISTORY 84)

Jiangxi opera   See: *ganju*.

jianyi, chien i (Chinese)   Literally: arrow clothing. A round-necked tunic with narrow cuffed sleeves which is slit to the waist at center front and back and drawn in with a wide, stiff sash. It is worn by male characters to indicate travelling, and as a fighting garment when stage armor (*kao*) is not worn, in Beijing opera (*jingju*) and many other forms of music-drama (*xiqu*). (Halson PEKING 24, Scott CLASSICAL 157)

jianzi, chien tzu (Chinese)   Literally: pointed written-character. A sound whose pronunciation requires that the tongue be pointed directly out against the back of the upper teeth; such sounds are particularly stressed in Beijing opera (*jingju*). See also: *tuanzi*. (Wichmann "Aural" 363-370)

jiaoban, chiao pan (Chinese)   Literally: asking for the beat. In music-drama (*xiqu*), a performer's signal to the orchestra conductor (*sigu*) indicating readiness to begin singing. The cue may be a drawn-out word, a sigh, crying, laughter, or a movement. (Scott CLASSICAL 94, Zung SECRETS 79) *jiaodi, chiao ti* (Chinese)   Literally: horned resistance. 1. Wrestling or 'horn butting' often included in performances of the hundred entertainments (*baixi*) in the 3rd C BC–3rd C AD. (Dolby HISTORY 3) 2. A generic term for all types of music, dance, and acrobatic performances in the 1st-3rd C AD. Also called horned resistance entertainments (*jiaodixi* or *chiao ti hsi*).

jiaose, chiao se (Chinese)   Literally: role, part. 1. A specific character in a specific play. Also called *renwu* or *jen wu*. 2. More generally, a type of character, such as a leading man, an old woman, a buffoon. 3. See: *hangdang*. Sometimes pronounced and romanized *juese* or *chüeh se*.

jiasangzi (Chinese)   See: *xiaosangzi*.

jiazihualian (Chinese)   See: *fujing, erhualian*.

jiben gongfu, chi pen kung fu (Chinese)   Literally: basic skill. The generic term for basic performance skills. In Beijing opera (*jingju*), these include song (*chang*), speech (*nian*), dance-acting (*zuo*), and combat (*da*). Abbreviated *jibengong* or *chi pen kung*. Also called the four skills (*sigong* or *ssu kung*).

jidai geki (Japanese)   Literally: period drama. A history play (or a film or television drama) outside traditional genres. See also: *jidaimono, gendai geki*. (Cobin ''Traditional'' 158)

jidai joruri (Japanese)   See: *jidaimono*.

jidai kyogen (Japanese)   See: *jidaimono*.

jidaimono (Japanese)   Literally: history play. 1. Broadly, in *kabuki* and *bunraku*, any non-dance play set in the historical or legendary past and dealing with samurai, aristocratic, or legendary characters. Also called *jidai kyogen* (history play) in *kabuki* and *jidai joruri* (history play) in *bunraku*. Sub-categories are *ochomono, oiemono*. (Kawatake KABUKI 18, Scott KABUKI 202) 2. More narrowly, in *bunraku*, a sub-category of history plays set in the period of feudal wars, c. 12th C, and dealing primarily with members of the defeated Heike clan. *Chronicle of the Battle of Ichinotani* in Brandon CLASSIC 171-211 is an example. Abbreviated *jidai*. See also: *ichibanme, juhachiban, katsureki geki, sewamono*. (Brandon CLASSIC 15-16, 165-211; Kawatake HISTORY 26-29, 35-39)

jidaisewamono (Japanese)   Literally: history-domestic play. In *kabuki* and *bunraku*, an all-day play that includes history and domestic acts, in that order. Examples are *The Forty-seven Loyal Retainers* in *bunraku* (Takeda/Miyoshi/ Namiki CHUSHINGURA) and *The Scarlet Princess of Edo* in *kabuki* (Brandon CLASSIC 245-349). Abbreviated *jidaisewa*. In *bunraku* also called *jidaisewa joruri* (history-domestic play). (Leiter ENCYCLOPEDIA 148)

jidori (Japanese)   The last two lines of a *shidai* section of a *no* play, softly sung by the chorus (*ji*). One type of *shodan*. (Shimazaki NOH 46)

jig   1. A sprightly dance, or a song accompanied by such a dance, in triple rhythm. 2. A comic afterpiece in the Elizabethan theatre consisting of often ribald songs and dances. Jigs have been compared to the *lazzi* in Italian *commedia dell'arte* performances. Jigs were used in minstrel shows in the 19th C. 3. By extension, a derogatory term for a Black man. Now offensive. Hence, formerly, jig band, jig show, etc. (Bowman/Ball THEATRE, Duchartre ITALIAN 310)

jigasuri (Japanese)   Literally: earth dyed. A ground cloth in *kabuki*. The cloth may be painted earth tones, grey for rocks, grained for a floor, white for snow (*yuki nuno*, snow cloth), or blue for ocean waves (*nami nuno*, wave cloth) or water (*mizu nuno*, water cloth). (Leiter ENCYCLOPEDIA 148; Ernst KABUKI 92, 128)

ji gei (Japanese)   See: *ji kyogen*.

jigger   1. A tap dancer. (Smith VAUDEVILLIANS 253) 2. See: tumbler.

jigging puppet   See: *marionnette à la planchette*.

jig opry, jig show   Formerly, a minstrel show. Offensive.

jijiyaku (Japanese)   Literally: old man role. 1. A role of an old man in *kabuki*. 2. An actor who plays the role. (Hamamura et al KABUKI 101)

ji kyogen (Japanese)   1. A dialogue play in 17th C *kabuki*, in contrast to a dance play (*shosagoto*). Also called *ji gei* (basic art). (Dunn/Torigoe ANALECTS 6) Ernst KABUKI 218 gives the opposite meaning. 2. A later meaning is an amateur *kabuki* performance by farmers usually given in mid-winter at a shrine or temple festival for a local audience. Also called *ji shibai* (regional play), *inaka shibai* (country play), *mura shibai* (village play). (Gunji KABUKI 27, Dunn/Torigoe ANALECTS 165)

Jim Crow   A figure in 19th C British Punch and Judy shows. He was a black, bearded servant whose dialogue was usually confined to the single word "shallaballa," probably gibberish. (Speaight PUPPET 193)

Jim Crow song and dance   A routine developed by Thomas D. Rice in the U.S. about 1830, based on a catchy song and dance he saw a crippled black stableman performing as he worked. Rice performed in blackface, and his routine led to the development of minstrel shows in the 1840s. Also called jump Jim Crow (offensive). (Wilson AMERICAN 38)

jin (Malaysian)   The character of a genie or ogre in *bangsawan* (Yassin in Osman TRADITIONAL 149) or *ma'yong* (Yousof "Kelantan" 104).

jing, ching (Chinese)   1. Painted-face role. A forceful male role, often a general, warrior, or powerful villain, portrayed with colorful, non-realistic full-face makeup (*lianpu*); a major role category (*hangdang*) in many forms of music-drama (*xiqu*). Popularly called flower face (*hualian* or *hua lien*, *huamian* or *hua mien*). In *kunqu*, major subcategories of the painted-face role include big face (*damian*) and white face (*baimian*). In Beijing opera (*jingju*), there are two main systems of subcategorization; one includes principal painted-face (*zhengjing*), assistant painted face (*fujing*), and martial painted-face (*wujing*), and the other large flower face (*dahualian*) and second flower face (*erhualian*). (Dolby HIS-

TORY 105, 181; Scott CLASSICAL 74-75) 2. A clown or villain role, or a combination of the two; a major role category in Yuan *zaju* and southern drama (*nanxi*). (Dolby HISTORY 60)

jinghu, ching hu (Chinese)   Literally: Beijing opera two-stringed spike fiddle. A two-stringed spike fiddle (*huqin*) which is the main instrument in the melodic orchestra (*wenchang*) in Beijing opera (*jingju*) and is also used in a number of other forms of music-drama (*xiqu*). It has a cylindrical bamboo body about 2″ in diameter and a snakeskin head; it produces a piercing, high-register sound. Sometimes called *huqin*. (Scott CLASSICAL 42-44, 50; Wichmann "Aural" 436, 449-452)

jingju, ching chü (Chinese)   Literally: capital drama. Beijing (Peking) opera, the most important and widespread form of music-drama (*xiqu*) since the early 19th C; it is performed throughout China. It began its development in Beijing in 1790 with the arrival of the Anhui troupes (*huiban*) for the celebration of Emperor Qianlong's 80th birthday; development occurred through the mutual influence of a number of forms including *hanju*, *huiju*, *kunqu*, and *qinqiang*. Beijing opera music is predominantly of the *pihuang* musical system (*shengqiang xitong*); in the 19th and early 20th C, the term *pihuang* frequently referred solely to Beijing opera. Also called capital theatre (*jingxi* or *ching hsi*), national drama (*guoju* or *kuo chü*), and Beiping (or Peiping) drama (*pingju* or *p'ing chü*); in the 18th and 19th C, sometimes referred to as "jumbled plucking" (*luantan*). (Scott CLASSICAL, Mackerras RISE, Wichmann "Aural")

jingju zhekou (Chinese)   See: *shisanzhe*.

jingqiang, ching ch'iang (Chinese)   Literally: capital tunes. A form of music drama (*xiqu*) which developed out of *yiyangqiang* in Beijing; it was very popular in the late 17th and 18th C, but died out after the introduction of *qinqiang* and the Anhui troupes (*huiban*) to Beijing in the late 18th C. It featured music of the *gaoqiang* musical system. (Mackerras MODERN 28-34; Mackerras RISE 5, 89-91)

jingxi (Chinese)   See: *jingju*.

jinju, chin chü (Chinese)   Shanxi (or Shansi) opera, a form of music-drama (*xiqu*) popular in central Shanxi Province, and in certain areas of Hebei and Shaanxi Provinces and the Inner Mongolian Autonomous Region. It developed out of *puju* and central Shanxi folk songs and dances, including *yangge*, in the early 19th C, and uses music from the *bangziqiang* musical system (*shengqiang xitong*). Sometimes called central road *bangzi* (*zhonglu bangzi* or *chung lu pang tzu*) and Shanxi *bangzi* or Shansi *pang tzu*. (Halson PEKING 65-66)

jinsheng, chin sheng (Chinese)   Literally: cloth-cap male role. A young scholar role, often a male romantic lead of lower social status than a headdress male role (*guansheng*); a major subdivision of the young male role (*xiaosheng*) in *kunqu* and many other forms of music-drama (*xiqu*). It is essentially the same as the fan male role (*shanzisheng*) in Beijing opera (*jingju*), and is sometimes called by that name. (Dolby HISTORY 105)

Jin *yuanben* (Chinese)   See: Song *zaju*.

ji shibai (Japanese)   See: *ji kyogen*.

jitney spot   In the early 20th C in the U.S., a theatre with a five-cent admission charge. (Berrey/Van den Bark SLANG 577)

jitsuaku (Japanese)   Literally: true villain. 1. A heavy villain role in *kabuki*, traditionally played by the head actor of a troupe. It is one type of *katakiyaku* role. An example is in Gunji KABUKI 181. 2. An actor who plays this role.

jitsugoto (Japanese)   1. The role of a courageous, reserved, mature hero in *kabuki*. It is one type of *tachiyaku* role. An example is Yuranosuke in *Chushingura*. (Gunji KABUKI 182) 2. An actor who plays this role. Also called *jitsugotoshi*.

jitte (Japanese)   A foot-long metal rod carried by a policeman as a restraining weapon in *kabuki* fight scenes. (Leiter ART 268)

jiulongkou, chiu lung k'ou (Chinese)   Mouth of the nine dragons. A position upstage right in the performance of music-drama (*xiqu*); on a traditional stage, it was several steps onstage from the entrance door (*shangchangmen*). When entering, major characters frequently pause at this position and display their costume, makeup, and basic nature, often performing a *liangxiang*. (Scott TRADITIONAL I 33)

ji utai (Japanese)   See: *ji*.

jiuyinluo (Chinese)   See: *yunluo*.

jo (Japanese)   1. A slow introductory section in music or theatre performance. In *bugaku*, this is a free rhythmic section in which dancers move onto the stage. In *no*, it is the first section of the play and introduces the secondary (*waki*) character. 2. Also in *no*, the first, or god, play in a five-play program. See: *jo ha kyu*. (Inoura HISTORY 122)

Joan   Before the 19th C, the name for Judy in a Punch and Judy show. Also called Mozzy. (Bowman/Ball THEATRE)

jobber   1. Especially in the recent past in the U.S., a performer not given a regular engagement but hired for a particular role, usually minor and often in a summer or touring stock company. Hence, job in, to be jobbed in, jobbing. 2. Formerly, a performer unable to find regular employment (a job actor).

jobbing   Of an actor: 1. Unemployed. 2. Taking isolated engagements.

jobiraki (Japanese)   The second of three short practice pieces staged before the main play (*hon kyogen*) in 18th and 19th C *kabuki*. It lasted about thirty minutes and gave apprentice writers and actors an opportunity to develop their skills. See also: *waki kyogen, futatateme*. (Leiter ENCYCLOPEDIA 149; Brandon CLASSIC 24, 30) *joch* (Spanish)   The Catalán equivalent of *juego*; game, sport. (Shergold SPANISH)

jockey   1. A 19th C top hat. (Speaight PUPPET 226) 2. A 19th C epaulette formed by a flounce and sewn at a sleeve top. Also called a jokey. (Boucher FASHION)

jocosa, jocoso (Spanish)   See: *graciosa*.

joculator (Latin)   See: minstrel.

jodata (Kannada)   Literally: a pair of plays. In *yaksagana*, a competition between two troupes, in which they are judged for dancing ability and quickness of costume and makeup change. (Ashton/Christie YAKSAGANA 84, 91)

Joe Jefferson   See: do a Joe Jefferson.

Joe Miller   An old joke. Named after the 18th C English comedian Josias Miller. Hence, to Joe Millerize, or tell an old joke. (Wilmeth LANGUAGE)

Joe Morgan   In burlesque, the drunk. (Wilmeth LANGUAGE)

Joe Personality   A master of ceremonies.

Joe Public   The audience.

Joey   A clown. Named after the late 18th and early 19th C English comedian Joe Grimaldi, who played the clown in pantomimes.

jog   1. A narrow flat used to make an offset or jog in a scenic wall. Hence, any narrow flat. In Britain: return piece or narrow flat. 2. To put up such a flat.

jogala (Kannada)   Literally: lullaby. In *yaksagana*, a folk-song which does not use a traditional musical scale (*raga*). (Ashton/Christie YAKSAGANA 61, 91)

jogelour   See: minstrel.

joglar, jogleor (French)   See: minstrel.

jogo (Portuguese)   See: *juego*.

jo ha kyu (Japanese)   Literally: introduction, breaking, speeding-up. An aesthetic concept in Japanese traditional theatre that defines performance as a three-part sequence of changing tempos and emotional intensities. Introduced from China via *bugaku* in the 7th C. In *no*, each unit of performance—the day's program, the parts of a play (*dan* and *shodan*), and individual movements and vocal phrases—is regulated by *jo ha kyu*. (O'Neill EARLY 120-123, Inoura HISTORY 116) In *kyogen*, Berberich defines the sequence as "introduction, elaboration, and completion by soaring" through a state of "rapture." (Berberich "Rapture" 193)

John, Johnny   See: stage-door Johnny.

Johnny collar   See: mandarin collar.

Johnny in the stalls   In Britain, a stage-door Johnny.

Johnny Newcomer   An amateur actor.

Johnny Sap   1. An amateur actor. 2. A first-season actor, especially in vaudeville. (Wilmeth LANGUAGE)

join   1. To fasten two scenic units together. The joint created is often called a join. Hence, good join, bad join. 2. Similarly, to blend the front of a wig into the forehead with makeup.

joint benefit   A benefit performance, the profits of which are shared by two or more beneficiaries. (Troubridge BENEFIT 19)

jokey   See: jockey.

jomaku (Japanese)   Literally: opening act. In *kabuki*: 1. The first act of an all-day play (*hon kyogen*). 2. The first act of the second play (*nibanmemono*). (Brandon CLASSIC 241, Leiter ENCYCLOPEDIA 149)

jong dondang (Malaysian)   The female singing chorus in *ma'yong*. (Yousof "Kelantan" 74)

jongleur (French)   1. When used to describe medieval performers, a minstrel. 2. When used of contemporary performers, a juggler.

jo no mai (Japanese)   One type of dance (*mai*) in *no* performed by the protagonist (*shite*) to instrumental music. An elegant and slow dance, it often occurs in god and woman plays. (Shimazaki NOH 35)

jornada (Spanish)   From medieval times, an act of a comedy. Still used interchangeably with *acto*. (Rennert SPANISH 286)

jornet   A 16th C man's loose travelling cloak. (Chalmers CLOTHES 164)

joruri (Japanese)   1. The generic term for a number of related musical styles of dramatic narrative accompanied by *shamisen* music. Included are *gidayu* in *bunraku*, and *takemoto*, *tokiwazu*, *kiyomoto*, and *tomimoto* in *kabuki*. (Malm MUSIC 188) 2. A puppet play accompanied by *joruri* style music. (Malm in Brandon CHUSHINGURA 59) 3. A *kabuki* dance play that uses *joruri* music. (Brandon CLASSIC 15-19)

joshiki maku (Japanese)   Literally: conventional curtain. In *kabuki*, and later in *bunraku*, the main act curtain, of alternating black, green, and rust stripes. The curtain is pushed open or pulled closed by a stage assistant who runs from one side of the proscenium to the other holding the curtain's leading edge. Also called *hiki maku* (pull curtain). (Ernst KABUKI 26-27, Gunji KABUKI 210)

joueur (French)   A performer, a player.

joueur de farces, joueur de farses (French)   A medieval farce player.

joueur de personnages (French)   A medieval actor. (Chambers MEDIAEVAL II 198)

joueurs de basteaulx (French)   Medieval marionette operators.

jouglere (French)   See: minstrel.

jou k'uei lei (Chinese)   See: *roukuilei*.

journade   A 15th-16th C garment, probably for display or parades, resembling a cassock, but with wide, slit sleeves. Frequently confused with the *paletot*, *hoqueton* (French), and manteline. (Boucher FASHION)

journée (French)   Literally: daytime. A portion of a medieval play. The portion might well take a full day to perform. (Brockett HISTORY 130)

journeymen   Actors in an Elizabethan company who were employed by the shareholders to perform minor roles. See also: hireling.

jours ordinaires (French)   In the 17th C French theatre, the days when plays were normally presented (Tuesdays, Fridays, and Sundays). (Arnott FRENCH 36)

joya (Spanish)   Literally: jewel. The word came to mean the prize given annually to the acting troupe that performed the best *autos* (short plays) on Corpus Christi Day. By the 17th C the prize was always money, but on some occasions previously it had been a length of cloth. (Shergold SPANISH)

joyeux (French)   A *compagnie joyeuse* or fool company in medieval France.

joy plank   See: runway.

joy stick   A control device used in memory lighting systems. See: manual takeover.

joy-stick focus   A method of mounting a lamp socket which allows the lamp to be correctly positioned (focused) in the reflector by moving the socket in any direction.

joza (Japanese)   See: *nanori*.

ju, chü (Chinese)   A play, a drama, a theatrical work.

juan (Chinese)   See: *ruan*.

juba   A dance involving slapping or patting, used in minstrel and pre-minstrel shows. Also called patting juba. (Wilmeth LANGUAGE)

jubang (Malaysian)   See: *penglipur lara*.

juben, chü pen (Chinese)   Playscript.

jubón (Spanish)   Literally: jerkin. A 16th-17th C long-sleeved shirt, frequently paneled and buttoned down the front. Worn in Spain by women under certain gowns and by men under a doublet. (Boucher FASHION)

Judy   In Punch and Judy puppet shows, Punch's wife. Until the 19th C, called Joan or Mozzy. (Bowman/Ball THEATRE)

juego (Spanish)   From the 13th C, a game, a sport. 1. In the early period the word seems to have been used to mean a play. 2. In the 16th C, the festivities associated with the Corpus Christi festivals. In Catalán: *joch*; in Portuguese: *jogo*. (Shergold SPANISH, Hesler "Lope de Rueda" 50)

juegos de escarnios (Spanish)   13th C farces. (Rennert SPANISH 252)

juese (Chinese)   See: *jiaose*.

juggling puppet   A trick marionette fitted with strings controlling balls which are pulled up and land on the hands or head of the doll. (Philpott DICTIONARY)

juglar (Spanish)   Formerly, a troubadour, clown. The Spanish equivalent of the French *jongleur*.

jugupsa (Sanskrit)   Literally: disgust. One of eight fundamental emotions (*stayibhava*) expressed by actors to produce a corresponding response (*rasa*) in the audience. See also: *bibhatsa*. (Keith SANSKRIT 323)

juhachiban (Japanese)   Literally: the eighteen. A collection of eighteen favorite *kabuki* plays of the Ichikawa Danjuro family that exemplify bravura (*aragoto*) acting. All but one are history plays (*jidaimono*). Named by Danjuro VII in the mid-19th C. The earliest, *The Scabbard Crossing*, dates from 1680; the last is *The Subscription List*, 1840. A complete list is in Leiter ENCYCLOPEDIA 152-154 and Scott KABUKI 209-211.

juice   1. Among those who work with stage lighting, electric current. The use goes back in Britain to at least the 1920s. 2. A name for a stage electrician. This meaning occurred early in the 20th C in the U.S., when it tended to be capitalized. 3. Especially among professionals, a member of a lighting crew. Also called a juicer, juiceman, or juice hand. Hence, juice gang for the lighting crew. (Fay GLOSSARY, Krows AMERICA 232, Lounsbury THEATRE, Bowman/Ball THEATRE, Berrey/Van den Bark SLANG 576)

juicer   1. An occasional term for the member of the stage lighting crew who operates the control board. 2. Any member of the lighting crew. See also: juice. (Lounsbury THEATRE 49, 75)

juicy part   A role containing rich acting opportunities. (Bowman/Ball THEATRE)

Juive (French)   See: tunic à la mameluck.

Juliet cap   See: *calotte*.

Juliets   Large, floppy shoes worn especially by clowns and burlesque comics. (Wilmeth LANGUAGE)

ju lin, ju lin pan (Chinese)   See: *rulin*.

jumble   A mixture of tragedy, opera, and farce devised in England by George Colman (1762-1831).

jump   1. A one-night stand. 2. The distance traveled between one-night stands. 3. To make such a journey. 4. To omit a line or lines and thus jump ahead in the script. 5. To begin one's speech before another performer has completed his or hers; hence, to jump a cue. (Bowman/Ball THEATRE) 6. In dance, a simple locomotor step in which weight is moved from both feet to both feet or from one foot to both feet. (Hayes DANCE 47)

jump a rail   In Britain, to add an extra horizontal wooden member (rail, toggle rail, or bar) to the back of a flat so that a picture or lighting fixture can be attached to the front of the flat at that height. (Baker THEATRECRAFT)

jumper   Any short length of wire or cable used to make a temporary electrical connection. Jumpers usually have a connector at each end, typically a male on one end and a female on the other; the connectors may differ in size or design or both. The usual stage use is to join two cables whose connectors do not match. Sometimes called an adaptor. (McCandless SYLLABUS 52, Bowman MODERN)

jumping jack   Especially in the 18th C, a wood or cardboard two-dimensional single-string painted puppet. In French, *pantin*. See also: *marionnette à la planchette*. (Philpott DICTIONARY)

jumping-off place   A provincial town.

jump Jim Crow   See: Jim Crow song and dance.

jump lines   To speak dialogue several lines ahead of what is called for in the script, thus rattling fellow players, changing meanings, and mixing up cues. (Granville DICTIONARY)

juncture   See: *sandhi*.

juniors   Children's tickets.

junk   A monologue. Also called a string of talk. (Wilmeth LANGUAGE)

junsui kabuki (Japanese)   Literally: pure *kabuki*. A play originally created for *kabuki*, as opposed to one adapted from a *bunraku*, *no*, or *kyogen* play. Examples (*Sukeroku: The Flower of Edo*, *Narukami the Thunder God*, *Benten the Thief*, *The Scarlet Princess of Edo*) can be found in Brandon CLASSIC and Leiter ART. Abbreviated *jun kabuki*.

jupe (French)   Literally: skirt. 1. A medieval to 17th C woman's jacket. See also: gipon. 2. From the late 17th C to the present, a woman's skirt. (Boucher FASHION)

jupon (French)   1. A petticoat. 2. See: hauberk. See also: *jubón*.

juponnage (French)   Literally: skirting. An ankle-length tutu. (Kersley/Sinclair BALLET)

juri (Bengali)   Literally: double. A singer in *jatra* who sings portions of a song on behalf of an actor. The practice began in the middle of the 19th C. Also called *mukhtyar*. (Gargi FOLK 26-27)

juru dalang (Indonesian)   An ordinary Balinese *dalang* before he becomes a priest-puppeteer (*pemangku dalang*). (McPhee in Belo TRADITIONAL 152)

juru gender (Indonesian)   The musicians who play the *gender wayang* ensemble for the Balinese shadow play. (McPhee in Belo TRADITIONAL 147)

juru tandak (Indonesian)   In Bali: 1. The lead singer in *gambuh*. 2. The story teller in *sanghyang* trance performance. (de Zoete/Spies DANCE 73)

jury   A first-night audience. (Sobel NEW)

justaucorps (French)   1. A medieval linen shirt or jacket. 2. A 17th-18th C body coat, forerunner of the jacket. Also called a serte. See also: *habit à la Française*. (Walkup DRESSING 94, Wilcox DICTIONARY)

justification   Motivation for a character's lines or actions.

juve   A juvenile.

juve femme   A female juvenile.

juvenile   1. A young male character, usually a pleasant accessory to the plot. 2. Especially in Britain, juvenile lead. 3. One who plays such characters. 4. A sometime term for a young female character, though she is usually called an ingenue. 5. In burlesque, a young singer or dancer who can also double as a second straight man or woman and serve as a general utility performer. (Wilmeth LANGUAGE)

juvenile drama   Regency and Victorian British toy theatre. (Philpott DICTIONARY)

juvenile lead   The principal young male role in a play.

juve trade   Young theatre patrons.

K

K   The symbol for Kelvin, used in stating color temperature. See: Kelvin scale.

k., k.w., kw   A thousand watts (one kilowatt). Lamps used in stage lighting are often so designated among lighting personnel, as in a direction involving a 2000-watt lamp: ''Get a 2 kw.'' (Lounsbury THEATRE 76) The most common of the three abbreviations today is k.

kaba (Malaysian)   See: *penglipur lara*.

Kabel (German)   See: *Biegsameskabel*.

kabogelan (Indonesian)   To cut short a Javanese shadow performance before its usual conclusion at dawn. (Brandon THRONES 68)

kabu isshin (Japanese)   Literally: song-dance one-heart. A major theory of *no* aesthetics propounded by Komparu Zenchiku (1405-c. 1470), Zeami's son-in-law. It asserts the unity of the poetic text with its danced performance. (Ortolani ZENCHIKU'S 3-6)

kabuki (Japanese)   A spectacular commercial theatre form performed by all-male troupes in the major cities of Japan. All-day plays (or programs of several plays) incorporate history (*jidai*), domestic (*sewa*), and dance (*shosa*) sections and are performed by actors who speak prose dialogue (*serifu*), or dance, accompanied by various types of music and sound effects. The term *kabuki* was probably first used in 1603 to describe a modern dance (*kabuki odori*) performed by the female entertainer Okuni in a small, outdoor theatre in Kyoto. The word derives from the verb *kabuku* (to incline) and signifies behavior that is new, unorthodox, faddish. About 1620-1630, *kabuki* was written with Chinese characters meaning song, dance, and prostitute, indicating that troupes were then chiefly composed of performer-prostitutes. *Kabuki* is at present written with characters meaning song, dance, and skill.

kabuki zoshi, kabuki soshi (Japanese)   A scroll or printed booklet depicting *kabuki* of the earliest period (1600-1620). The illustrations, in particular, provide unique information about early *kabuki* performance. (Malm in Brandon/Malm/ Shively STUDIES 134)

kabur (Indonesian)   See: *bablas*.

kadatonan (Indonesian)   See: *kedatonan*.

kaebokch'ung (Korean)   Literally: costume change hall. A temporary costume room for masked-dance performers. (Cho "Yangju" 29)

kaen (Lao)   See: *khaen*.

kaffiyeh, keffiyeh   An Arab headgear of linen, silk, or cotton, striped or plain, folded into a triangle and held to the head by thick cords of wool or goat hair. (Wilcox DICTIONARY)

kagami ita (Japanese)   Literally: mirror board. The wooden, permanent back wall of a *no* stage on which is painted a gnarled pine tree, symbolizing a sacred tree through which the spirit of the first *no* performance is supposed to have descended to earth. The origin of the term is unclear.

kagami no ma (Japanese)   Literally: mirror room. A portion of the dressing room of a *no* theatre adjacent to the bridge (*hashigakari*) equipped with a full-length mirror. The *shite* actor looks into the mirror while he puts on his mask, to enter into the character of the mask. (Shimazaki NOH 8-9, Komparu NOH 126-127)

kageki (Japanese)   Literally: song-drama. Western-style opera.

kagekiyo (Japanese)   A powerful, melancholy *no* mask used for the warrior Kagekiyo, the leading role in a play of that name. (Shimazaki NOH 64)

kage o utsu (Japanese)   See: *tsuke*.

kage shibai (Japanese)   Shadow theatre, which is also the literal meaning.

kagura (Japanese)   Literally: god-entertainment. A sacred dance or acted performance dedicated to a native Shinto diety. *Kagura* is the oldest type of performing art in Japan. See also: *mi kagura*, *sato kagura*. (Inoura HISTORY 16-17, Sadler "O-Kagura" 275)

kaguraden (Japanese)   Literally: *kagura* hall. A square, raised, wooden-floored dancing stage in the precincts of a Shinto shrine used for *kagura* performances. (Sadler "O-Kagura" 279, Komparu NOH illus. 112)

kaichang, k'ai ch'ang (Chinese)   See: *jiamen*.

kaidanmono (Japanese)   Literally: ghost play. A sub-category of *kabuki* domestic play (*sewamono*) popularized by Tsuruya Namboku IV in the mid-19th C and featuring scenes of bloody vengeance by the ghost of a wronged dead person. (Scott KABUKI 206)

kaimingxi, k'ai ming hsi (Chinese)   See: *wenmingxi*.

kaisiki (Sanskrit)   Literally: graceful. One of the four styles (*vrtti*) of writing and of acting classical Sanskrit drama. (Keith SANSKRIT 326-327, Gandhi in

Baumer/Brandon SANSKRIT 128) It is appropriate to plays devoted to the erotic sentiment (*srngara rasa*) and is derived, Bharata says, from the *Sama Veda*. (NATYASASTRA 404)

kai waing (Burmese)   See: *saing waing*.

kaizong, k'ai tsung (Chinese)   See: *jiamen*.

kajon (Indonesian)   See: *kayon*.

kakawin (Indonesian)   1. A type of mood song sung in Javanese *wayang kulit*. See also: *sendon*, *suluk*. 2. Spelled *kakawen* in Sundanese, a mood song sung in archaic language by the puppeteer (*dalang*) in Sundanese *wayang golek*. Some lyrics are directly drawn from epic poems (*kakawin*), especially sections of the *Mahabharata*, written in Old Javanese (Kawi). Analagous to Javanese *suluk*. See also: *sebrakan*, *sendon*, *sisinderan*. (Foley "Sundanese" 203-215)

kakeai (Japanese)   Literally: alternation. 1. In a *kabuki* play, alternation between two or more types of music. 2. In *no*, a rapid exchange of dialogue in verse form, usually between the protagonist (*shite*) and the secondary character (*waki*).

kakegoe (Japanese)   Literally: calling out. 1. A spectator's shout of appreciation in the theatre, especially in *kabuki*, during performance. (Shively in Brandon/Malm/Shively STUDIES 20) 2. Standardized calls by stage musicians that function as cues or indicate tempo, in *no*, *kabuki*, and *bunraku*. (Malm MUSIC 125, Keene NO 78) Originally the purpose of the calls was to cajole the gods to descend during a performance. (Immoss/Mayer JAPANESE 34)

kakeri (Japanese)   Literally: flight. 1. One type of *hatarakimono* dance in *no*. It is usually performed in the first or the last play on a program. It consists of flowing movements accompanied by instrumental music. (Shimazaki NOH 37) 2. In *kyogen*, a mime sequence accompanied by a song in *no* style. (Berberich "Rapture" 184)

kakikae (Japanese)   Literally: rewrite. The process of rewriting well-known play materials into new plays, especially in 19th and 20th C *kabuki*. (Gunji KABUKI 35)

kakinuki (Japanese)   Literally: writing extraction. 1. The process of a playwright writing an actor's lines into a side. (Immoss/Mayer JAPANESE 151) 2. The excerpted script or side. (Hamamura et al KABUKI 73, 102; Leiter ENCYCLOPEDIA 162)

kakko (Japanese)   A small two-headed, lashed, barrel-shaped drum used in *gagaku*. (Wolz BUGAKU 18)

kakra (Gujarati)   A torch brandished by female characters when they enter and dance in *bhavai* folk theatre. (Gargi FOLK 63-64)

kaksi, gagsi (Korean)   Literally: virgin, young girl. 1. A generic term for puppet. See also: *kkoktu kaksi*. (Choe STUDY 51) 2. A mask of a young girl in masked dance-plays. (Korean MASKS 5) *kaksyavibhaga* (Sanskrit)   In classical Indian theatre, the division of the acting area of a stage into different zones, by conventional usage, rather than by scenic representation. Also shortened to *kaksya*. (Gandhi in Baumer/Brandon SANSKRIT 119)

kalangan (Indonesian)   The playing space for a Balinese dance-drama, usually marked out on the ground by a low fence, palm fronds, or banners and umbrellas and located according to the sacredness of the genre being performed. See: *bebali*, *wali*. (Bandem/deBoer BALINESE 31-33)

kalari (Malayalam)   A *kathakali* training space. (Jones/Jones KATHAKALI 109)

kalasam (Malayalam)   In *kathakali*: 1. A decorative dance sequence which generally comes after a line of a song (*padam*). 2. A dance sequence used for an entrance. 3. Percussion music which functions as an actor's cue. *Iratti* (doubled) *kalasam* is graceful and dignified; *valiya* (big) *kalasam* is danced by a male character; *vattam vaccu* (circling) *kalasam* is slow and emotional. (Jones/ Jones KATHAKALI 72-73)

kali vilakku (Malayalam)   A large, standing oil lamp of bronze that lights a *kathakali* performance. (Jones/Jones KATHAKALI 109)

kal sadhakam (Malayalam)   Rhythmic exercises for the legs and feet used in *kathakali* training routines. (Jones/Jones KATHAKALI 109)

kamae (Japanese)   The standard, feet-together, 'at rest' body position or stance from which a *no* or *kabuki* actor moves, especially in dance. (Komparu NOH 216)

Kamakura *sarugaku* (Japanese)   One of several early and now extinct types of *sarugaku no*, named for the Kamakura period (1192-1333). It featured tricks, juggling, and sleight-of-hand. (Inoura HISTORY 67)

kamban (Japanese)   See: *kanban*.

kamengeki (Japanese)   Literally: masked play. A generic term for masked drama of all types.

kamigakari za (Japanese)   Literally: upper troupes. Among the five schools of *no*, the Kanze and Hosho troupes were based in Kyoto. Kyoto is north of Nara, where the other troupes were based; hence Kyoto troupes were the 'upper troupes.' See also: *shimogari za*. (Inoura HISTORY 108, Shimazaki NOH 84)

kamigata kyogen (Japanese)   A *kabuki* play (*kyogen*) written and produced in the *kamigata* (Kyoto-Osaka) area. The typical play was a *keiseikai* romantic comedy acted in soft (*wagoto*) style. (Leiter ENCYCLOPEDIA 163)

kamiko (Japanese)   Literally: paper kimono. A kimono designed to look as if it was patched together from love letters, worn by a young lover in a prostitute-buying *kabuki* play. An example is in *Love Letter From the Licensed Quarter* in Brandon CLASSIC 220. (Tsubouchi/Yamamoto KABUKI 265)

kami mai (Japanese)   Literally: god dance. 1. A dance in quick tempo performed by a young god in a god *no* play. See also: *mai*. (Shimazaki NOH 34, Inoura HISTORY 118) 2. A type of sacred Shinto dance (*kagura*). (Hoff SONG 204)

kami no (Japanese)   Literally: god *no*. A *no* play in which the protagonist (*shite*) is usually a Shinto deity (*kami*). An example is *Takasago* in Nippon Gakujutsu JAPANESE 2-17. Also called *shodanmemono* (first place play) because it is the first in the regular series of five plays in a day's program, or *waki no* (beside *no*) because it appears after, or 'beside,' the ceremonial *Okina* that sometimes precedes the five-play series. (Shimazaki NOH 23, 87-101)

kami shibai (Japanese)   Literally: paper theatre. A play for children using pictures on large cards to tell a story. A solo performer narrates and changes the pictures. For portability, the small stage is often mounted on a bicycle. (Ernst KABUKI 116)

kamishimo (Japanese)   Literally: top and bottom. A stiff winged vest (*kataginu*) and a divided skirt (*hakama*) worn over a kimono (*kitsuke*). It is a common costume for samurai characters in *kabuki* and *bunraku* and is also worn by onstage musicians in *no*, *kabuki*, and *bunraku*. (Shaver COSTUMES 129-134)

kamite (Japanese)   Literally: upper hand. Stage left. Also called *higashi*. See also: *shimote*. (Ernst KABUKI 52)

Kammerspiele (German)   Intimate theatre.

kampak (Thai)   Literally: narrative text. The generic term for verse sections of *khon* and *nang yai* texts that are chanted by one or more narrators (*kon pak*). Also spelled *khampak, khamphak*. See also: *ceraca*. (Dhaninivat/Yupho KHON 3-4)

kanban, kamban (Japanese)   Literally: billboard. A signboard publicizing a theatrical performance, especially in *kabuki* and *bunraku*, posted in front of a theatre. This form of publicity began in the 17th C and continues today. Leiter lists types of signboards according to content—play title, actors' and musicians' names, play synopsis, etc.—in ENCYCLOPEDIA 171. See also: *shibai e*. (Kincaid KABUKI 178-179)

kanchaliya (Gujarati)   In west India, a female dancer in *bhavai*, so called because she wears a *kanchali* (blouse). (Gargi FOLK 63-64, 69-70)

kan chü (Chinese)   See: *ganju*.

kancukin (Sanskrit)   In classical Indian drama, the role of a king's chamberlain, an old Brahmin, who conveys royal orders within the palace. (Keith SANSKRIT 313)

kandys (Greek)   A relatively short, decorated *chiton*, often sleeved, which may have been worn for a time in Greek tragedy. (Pickard-Cambridge FESTIVALS 201-202)

kaneru yakusha (Japanese)   Literally: combination actor. In *kabuki*, an actor capable of performing any type of role. The designation is ultimate praise, since the technical demands of *kabuki* acting restrict most performers to a narrow range of role types. (Leiter ENCYCLOPEDIA 172)

kangaroo bend   An early 1900s female standing attitude in which the bust led, the abdomen followed, and the hips and derrière curved "opulently." See also: Grecian bend. (Barton COSTUME 546)

kangen (Japanese)   The instrumental selections that precede *bugaku* dances in a *gagaku* performance.

kanguan, k'an kuan (Chinese)   Literally: looking officials. A polite name for the audience at *yuanben* and Yuan *zaju* performances in the 13th-15th C. (Dolby HISTORY 65)

kanjin (Japanese)   Literally: subscription. A special public performance requiring paid admission ('subscription'), as opposed to a private, sponsored production. *Kanjin no* and *kanjin dengaku* performances were common, 14th-19th C, and lasted from several days to one or two weeks. (O'Neill EARLY 73-78, Inoura HISTORY 75, Keene NO 47-48) *Kanjin hijiri* is the organizer of a *kanjin* performance.

kanji shitsu (Japanese)   Literally: supervisor's room. A backstage room in modern theatres used by the director, playwright, stage manager, and other supervisory staff members. (Leiter ENCYCLOPEDIA 174)

k'an kuan (Chinese)   See: *kanguan*.

kannensei (Japanese)   See: *engekisei*.

kanpeng, k'an p'eng (Chinese)   See: *goulan*.

kantan otoko (Japanese)   A *no* mask used for the role of a god or a young Chinese man. Originally it was created for the play *Kantan*, hence its name. (Shimazaki NOH 59)

Kanze *ryu* (Japanese)   Literally: style of Kanze. 1. The most influential and widely performed of the five styles of acting *no* drama, characterized by delicacy and nuance of expression. The name is said to be a compound of the first syllables of the names of Kannami Kiyotsugu and his son, Zeami Motokiyo, who founded the style in the 14th and 15th C. 2. The troupe or association of *no* actors who perform in this style. This is a contemporary usage. Before the 20th C, the term Kanze *za* (Kanze troupe) identified the performers. For other styles see also: Hosho, Kita, Kongo, Konparu. (Inoura HISTORY 108, Shimazaki NOH 84, Keene NO 68)

kao, k'ao (Chinese)   A stiff, embroidered outer garment consisting of two large front and back panels and two smaller and shorter side panels. It represents armor and is often worn by male and female warriors and generals in Beijing opera (*jingju*) and many other forms of music-drama (*xiqu*), often with four or eight triangular pennants strapped to the back. (Halson PEKING 23, Scott CLAS-SICAL 154-156, Zung SECRETS 21-22)

kao awase (Japanese)   Literally: face-to-face meeting. The ceremonial first meeting of members of a *kabuki* troupe to start a new theatre season, held about one month before the season's first production. (Hamamura et al KABUKI 101-102)

kao ch'iang (Chinese)   See: *gaoqiang*.

kao fang (Chinese)   See: *guanxue*.

kaomise kogyo (Japanese)   Literally: face-showing performance. In 18th and 19th C *kabuki*, the first production of the theatre season. Scheduled during the eleventh lunar month, the production introduced audiences to the acting company that would be playing at the theatre over the next twelve months. Although annual contracts are no longer customary, each *kabuki* theatre today has an annual *kaomise* performance featuring an all-star cast. Abbreviated: *kaomise*. *Kaomise kyogen* is a play produced during this production. (Leiter ENCYCLO-PEDIA 174-175; Scott KABUKI 203, 206; Shively in Brandon/Malm/Shively STUDIES 22-23)

kao po tzu (Chinese)   See: *gaobozi*.

kapa   The Yugoslavian national headgear for men: a small pillbox. An unmarried female wears a kapa of black velvet with a red top; a married woman wears an all-black kapa. (Wilcox DICTIONARY)

Kapellmeister (German)   Literally: chapel master. An opera orchestra conductor. (Granville DICTIONARY)

kara butai (Japanese)   See: *haki butai*.

karagatan (Philippine)   Literally: open sea. A quasi-dramatic extemporized verse debate, in which a princess' ring is sought in the sea. (Hernandez EMERG-ENCE 5-6)

Karaghiöz (Greek)   A shadow puppet. More widely known as the Turkish *Karagöz*.

Karagiosis (Greek)   A shadow play, or such plays collectively. The name is from the original character, still the principal. See also: *Karaghiöz*. (Spatharis SCREEN 95ff)

karagoto (Japanese)   A *no* play (*goto*) based on a Chinese (*kara*) source. (Komparu NOH 43)

karagotsci (Turkish)   See: *hayaldji*.

Karagöz (Turkish)   Literally: dark eye. 1. A shadow puppet: a beloved if misshapen clown, and the chief theatrical "star" of the Ottoman Empire. The classical comic challenger of authority, he may have been an ancestor of Punch, whom he resembles in character. 2. A Turkish shadow play, or such plays as a form. The form dates back to the 14th C. Also spelled *Karagoz*. See also: *garaguz*, *chamani*, *zenna*.

karahinan (Indonesian)   To continue a Javanese shadow performance past dawn. (Brandon THRONES 68)

karakuri (Japanese)   Literally: a contrivance. A commercial show featuring mechanical dolls moved by water power or a clockwork mechanism. They were popularized by Takeda Izumo in Osaka in the late 17th C.

karana (Sanskrit)   A unit of non-mimetic, pure dance (*nirtta*), consisting of a bodily pose, hand gesture (*hasta*), and often movement, used in classical Indian theatre for its beauty of form. Bharata describes 108 by name (NATYASASTRA 48-60). Several *karana* are linked together to form larger dance units (*angahara*).

karangan (Indonesian)   See: *lakon*.

kari (Malayalam)   In *kathakali*, the role of a demoness, "comic, satiric, and grotesque." One type of bearded (*tati*) character. (Jones/Jones KATHAKALI 32)

kariala (Hindi)   See: *karyala*.

kariginu (Japanese)   Literally: hunting clothes. Especially in *no* and *kabuki*, an informal, outdoor costume of a court noble, distinguished by its round neck opening and hanging front panel. (Shaver COSTUMES 27)

kari hanamichi (Japanese)   In *kabuki*, a temporary (*kari*) runway (*hanamichi*) joining the stage at stage left, as opposed to the permanent runway (*hon hanamichi*) stage right. See also: *hanamichi*. (Ernst KABUKI 35, Hamamura et al KABUKI 117)

karre   A variant medieval English term for a pageant.

kartala (Indonesian)   The second of two clown-attendants to a king or prince in Balinese dance plays. He is foolish and simple-minded and is considered the 'younger brother' of the *penasar* clown-attendant. (de Zoete/Spies DANCE 35-37)

karuna (Sanskrit)   Literally: pathos. One of the eight dominant sentiments (*rasa*) experienced by the audience seeing a Sanskrit play. It is aroused by the enacted fundamental emotion (*sthayibhava*) of sorrow (*soka*). (Keith SANSKRIT 324-325)

karuttatati (Malayalam)   Literally: black beard. A demonic character type in *kathakali*. Only the color of the beard (*tati*) distinguishes the role from the red-bearded demonic type (*cukannattati*). (Jones/Jones KATHAKALI 30)

karya (Sanskrit)   Denouement. The last of five elements of plot (*arthaprakrti*) in classical Indian dramaturgy, in which the action leads to the attainment of the super objective of the play or the desire of the protagonist. (Keith SANSKRIT 298) The element of "action," according to Byrski (in Baumer/Brandon SANSKRIT 144) or "activity" according to Kale THEATRIC 155.

karyala (Hindi)   A form of folk theatre in Himachal Pradesh, north central India. Also spelled *kariala*.

kasaejin (Korean)   See: *p'ungmul*.

kasal (Philippine)   A wedding scene in *comedia*. (Mendoza COMEDIA 107)

kasar (Indonesian, Malaysian)   Literally: rough. An unrefined character, usually an ogre or demon (*raksasa*), or the acting style of such a character. Contrasted to *alus*. In Bali, also called *kras* (rough). (Holt ART 160, de Zoete/Spies DANCE 155) In Malaysia, the term applies to *wayang kulit* puppet types. (Sweeney RAMAYANA 56) See also: *gagah*.

kasaveck   A 19th C woman's fitted, waist-length jacket of wool with wide sleeves. (Walkup DRESSING 271)

kashagata (Japanese)   A generic term for middle-aged and old woman roles in *kabuki*, especially in the 17th C. Now these roles are called *fuke oyama*. (Dunn/Torigoe ANALECTS 166)

kashira (Japanese)   Literally: head. 1. The generic term for puppet head. In *bunraku* a head is often given a name based on its features, sex, age, or the character it was first created for. See Keene BUNRAKU 209-247 for illustrations of 65 head types. 2. A large, mane-like wig worn by a demon or deity character in *no*. (Komparu NOH 248)

Kassettenklappen (German)   Hinged flaps closing cuts in the stage floor. (Krows AMERICA 113)

kasshiki (Japanese)   A *no* mask worn by a Zen acolyte (*kasshiki*). (Shimazaki NOH 59-60)

kasumi no ogi (Japanese)   Literally: mist fan. The standard gesture (*kata*) in *no*, open fan extended horizontally in front of the body, used to indicate mist, a waterfall, or wind in the mountains. Illustrated in Keene NO 220.

kata (Japanese)   Literally: form, model. 1. In general, traditional styles or patterns of performing handed down from generation to generation in *no*, *kyogen*, *kabuki*, and *bunraku*. 2. Narrowly defined, especially in *nogaku*, the actor's patterns of movement and voice. The standard repertory of *no* movements is given in Shimazaki NOH 29-33 and Wolz "Spririt" 57-58 and is illustrated in Keene NO 219-222. *Kyogen* movement *kata* are illustrated in Keene NO 223-226. 3. Broadly defined, especially in *kabuki*, acting patterns plus costume, makeup, music, and staging forms that support them. (Brandon in Brandon/Malm/Shively STUDIES 65-126, Leiter ART xvi-xxi) 4. In *bunraku*, one of two types of movement. *Kata* are non-mimetic movements and spectacular poses intended to be appreciated for their beauty. See also: *furi*. (Keene BUNRAKU 65-66)

katabainein (Greek)   Literally: to descend. Of an actor, to exit. See also: *anabainein*.

katablemata (Greek)   Movable scenery, or other materials which suggest a change of scene. The usual view is that such changes were made on the *periaktoi* by fastening thereto painted curtains or boards. Some think such materials were sometimes "attached to the wall at the back of the stage." (Haigh) Liddell/Scott LEXICON gives the meaning "curtain of a theatre." Also spelled *katablemmata* (rare). (Pickard-Cambridge DIONYSUS 235; Haigh ATTIC 186; Bieber HISTORY 74, 75, 337)

kataginu (Japanese)   See: *kamishimo*.

katahazushi (Japanese)   In *kabuki*, the role of a high-ranking samurai wife or a noble woman. It is one type of *onnagata* role. The name is from the off-center (*hazushi*) topknot of the wig worn by the character. (Gunji KABUKI 32)

katakeleusmos (Greek)   After an opening half-chorus in the debate (*agon*) of Old Comedy, a pair of spirited lines of recitative in which the chorus leader encourages the first speaker to present his case. He does so, ending with breath-taking speed (the *pnigos*, or choker). The process is repeated with the leader of the opposing half-chorus encouraging (*antikatakeleusmos*) the second speaker, who also finishes with a breath-takingly rapid appeal (*antipnigos*). The chorus' decision is the *sphragis* (seal). (Harsh HANDB00K 260)

katakiuchimono (Japanese)   Literally: revenge play. A *kabuki* or *bunraku* history play (*jidaimono*), especially popular in the early 19th C, featuring a scene in which faithful samurai gain vengeance against a villain. An example is *Chushingura: the Treasury of Loyal Retainers*. (Takeda/Miyoshi/Namiki CHU-SHINGURA 29-180) Also called *adauichimono* (revenge piece) and *adauchi kyogen* (revenge play).

katakiyaku (Japanese)   Literally: enemy role. 1. A villain role in *kabuki* or *bunraku*. Includes sub-types: *jitsuaku*, *kugeaku*, *tedai gataki* among others. Also called *akunin* (evil person), *akuyaku* (evil role). 2. A *kabuki* actor who plays villain roles. (Dunn/Torigoe ANALECTS 108-109, 166; Gunji KABUKI 32, Leiter ENCYCLOPEDIA 179-180)

kataloge (Greek)   See: *parakataloge*.

kata maku (Japanese)   To hold aside one side (*kata*) of the *no* curtain (*maku*) to allow the musicians to enter the bridgeway (*hashigakari*) and cross to the stage. (Komparu NOH 147)

katari (Japanese)   Literally: narrative. 1. Storytelling, usually of a lengthy work. (Yamashita "Structure" 48) 2. In *no* and in *kyogen*, a narrative of a past event spoken in prose (*kotoba*), usually by the protagonist (*shite*). (Shimazaki NOH 49, Berberich "Rapture" 122) 3. A narrative summary of a *kabuki* play posted in front of a theatre or included in a printed program. (Leiter ENCY-CLOPEDIA 183) 4. See: *monogatari*.

katarimono (Japanese)   Literally: narrative piece. 1. Broadly, all types of narrative performing arts, such as *heikyoku* and *joruri*. Generally synonomous with *monogatari*. (Yamashita "Structure" 67, Malm in Brandon CHUSHIN-GURA 59) 2. In *kabuki* music, a play or dance piece in narrative style (for example, *takemoto*, *tokiwazu*, *kiyomoto*), as distinguished from one in lyric style (*utaimono*). (Malm MUSIC 188-189)

katari te (Japanese) Literally: narrator. A storyteller or reciter. (Horiguchi "Literature" 15)

katatome (Greek) Literally: cutting, incision. The word is used of the theatre of Dionysus in Athens, which has a substantial cutting away of the cliff at the rear of the seating area. This hollowed-out area contained a choregic monument, and probably also the uppermost bank of seats. (Bieber HISTORY 64, 70; Pickard-Cambridge DIONYSUS 138, 169)

katatsuke (Japanese) Literally: set-down *kata*. Stage directions written into a *no* text (*utaibon*) by the head of a *no* school. (Konishi "Approaches" 14)

kathakali (Malayalam) A dynamic, pantomimic dance-drama in Kerala state, southwest India, dating from the 17th C. Actors mime and dance a verse accompanied by singing and instrumental music provided by four musicians. Many plays are based on the epics the *Ramayana* and the *Mahabharata*. Costume and makeup are exceptionally elaborate. (Jones/Jones KATHAKALI 8-22)

katharsis (Greek), **catharsis** An Aristotelian term in the *Poetics*, used in three senses by the Greeks: purgation, purification, and clarification. Dramatic criticism has long used the first two, with some recent criticism favoring clarification as closer to Aristotle's scientific method and thought. Among the controversies associated with *katharsis* is the precise meaning of its relation to pity and fear, particularly in the extent to which *katharsis* applies to the audience, the characters, and the action of the play. (Vaughn DRAMA 26-27; Lucas ARISTOTLE 273-290; Golden/Hardison ARISTOTLE'S 112-118, 133-137; Else ARISTOTLE'S 224-232, 423-427)

kathodghata (Sanskrit) Literally: caught up. A transitional sequence in classical Indian theatre that leads from the prologue, delivered by the stage manager, into the body of a drama. The first character then enters, repeating or paraphrasing these remarks. (Keith SANSKRIT 340)

kathputli (Hindi) Literally: wooden doll. String puppets used in theatre performances in Rajasthan state, northwest India. (ASIAN 11)

kat khru (Thai) Literally: proclaim the teacher. The prayer of invocation sung before many types of traditional theatre performance, principally *lakon jatri* and *nang talung*. See also: *prakat khum khru*. (Ginsberg in Rutnin SIAMESE 66)

kato bushi (Japanese) One type of narrative music (*katarimono*) used in a small number of *kabuki* plays, of which *Sukeroku: Flower of Edo* in Brandon CLASSIC 55-92 is the best known. (Leiter ENCYCLOPEDIA 183)

katongan (Indonesian) In *wayang* theatre, the generic term for king roles. (Muljono in Osman TRADITIONAL 62)

katsura, kazura (Japanese) A wig. Major types of *kabuki* wigs are given in Leiter ENCYCLOPEDIA 531-532, and Shaver COSTUMES 305-333 has 60 illustrations. Descriptions of *no* wigs are in Nippon Gakujutsu JAPANESE II xiii-xv. *Katsura boshi* (wig-hat) is a cloth that is draped over the head of a female character in *kyogen*; it takes the place of a wig. *Katsuraya* (wig proprietor) is a wig maker.

katsuramono (Japanese)   See: *kazuramono*.

katsureki geki (Japanese)   Literally: living-history play. A late 19th C, new-style *kabuki* history play, influenced by Western realism and sticking close to historical facts. These plays were written primarily for the actor Ichikawa Danjuro IX. (Hamamura et al KABUKI 85-86; Leiter ENCYCLOPEDIA 218; Kincaid KABUKI 3, 4, 8)

kattalan (Malayalam)   Literally: forest man. In *kathakali*, the role of an aborigine hunter or jungle dweller. (Jones/Jones KATHAKALI 109)

kattalatti (Malayalam)   Literally: forest woman. In *kathakali*, the wife of a *kattalan* character. (Jones/Jones KATHAKALI 109)

katti (Malayalam)   Literally: knife. A green-faced role in *kathakali*, both noble and demonic. Examples are the evil kings Duryodhana and Ravana. (Jones/Jones KATHAKALI 27)

kattiakaran (Tamil)   A herald who maintains order. In *therukoothu* folk theatre in southeast India, a stage manager and director. See: *sutradhara*. (Gargi FOLK 133)

katuttatati (Malayalam)   In *kathakali*, the role of a male comic demon, equivalent to the female *kari* role. (Jones/Jones KATHAKALI 32)

kaunakai (Greek)   Thick woolen cloaks worn by performers in the Dionysian revels. See also: *phallophoroi*. (Webster CHORUS 69)

kavya (Sanskrit)   In ancient India, a one-act play. A minor play type (*uparupaka*). (Keith SANSKRIT 351)

kawara kojiki (Japanese)   Literally: riverbed beggar. Throughout *kabuki* history, a derogatory term for a *kabuki* actor. Early itinerant troupes set up theatres in dry riverbeds, land which was unowned and untaxed, hence the term. Also called *kawaramono* (riverbed creature). (Shively in Brandon/Malm/Shively STUDIES 3, Bowers JAPANESE 39)

kawih (Indonesian)   A song in Sundanese *wayang golek* that has an eight-beat structure and is accompanied by the full *gamelan* music ensemble. It is usually sung by female singers (*pasinden*). See also: *tembang*. (Foley "Sundanese" 153-156)

kayala (Hindi)   See: *khyal*.

kayol (Korean)   Literally: joining the ranks. Young performers in a *namsadang* troupe. (Kim "Namsadang" 10)

kayon (Indonesian, Malaysian)   In shadow theatre (*wayang kulit*), a large leather puppet usually identified as the 'tree-of-life' (Muljono in Osman TRADITIONAL 79), although Rassers disputes this interpretation (PANJI 172-195).

It is used as a scene divider and to represent mountains, the sky, rocks, clouds, trees, jails, magic powers, fire, blood, etc. Performance begins and ends with the *kayon* in the center of the screen (*kelir*). Also spelled *kajon, kekayon*. Also called *gunungan* in Java and Sunda, and additionally in Sunda, *gugunungan*, both words meaning 'mountain,' indicating its shape. See also: *göstermelik*. (Moerdowo BALINESE II 119, Long JAVANESE 7, Holt ART 134-135, Foley "Sundanese" 44-45)

kazura (Japanese)   See: *katsura*.

kazuramono, katsuramono (Japanese)   Literally: wig play. A *no* play in which the protagonist (*shite*) plays a woman and hence is wigged. Also called *sanbanmemono* (third place play) because it appears third on a five-play program. (Nippon Gakujutsu JAPANESE xiv, Shimazaki NOH 24)

keban, k'o pan (Chinese)   A training school or class for music-drama (*xiqu*) performers in the 18th-early 19th C; most were attached to professional troupes. See also: *piaoyou*. (Mackerras RISE 148, Scott CLASSICAL 59)

kecak (Indonesian)   1. A male chorus, derived from the Balinese ritual trance dance (*sanghyang*), that uses monkey-like sounds (*kecak*) as accompaniment. Abbreviated: *cak, tjak*. 2. A choral dance-drama in Bali that grew out of this male chorus in the 1930s. Episodes from the *Ramayana* and other epics are danced within a circle formed by 100-150 chanting chorus members seated on the ground. (de Zoete/Spies DANCE 81-85, Soedarsono DANCES 173-174, Brandon GUIDE 70)

kechopong (Malaysian)   The high, decorative crown worn by shadow puppets of Rama and Laksmana, patterned after crowns used in traditional Cambodian and Thai dance drama. (Sheppard TAMAN 76)

kecrek (Indonesian)   See: *kepyak*.

kedatonan (Indonesian)   Literally: inside the palace. 1. The second or third scene in a Javanese *wayang* play, set in the personal quarters of the king, that is, the inner palace. (Brandon THRONES 21) 2. Spelled *kadatonan* in Sundanese, the opening scene of a rod-puppet play (*wayang golek*), set in a king or prince's palace. (Foley "Sundanese" 111)

kedelen (Indonesian)   A character type in Javanese *wayang kulit* distinguished by a soy-bean shaped eye and a mixture of refined and robust physical traits. Also spelled *kedhelen*.

keelu bomma (Telugu)   Literally: moving dolls. Opaque doll marionettes, operated by strings attached to the doll's joints. See also: *bommalata*. (Sorensen "Shadow" 1)

keep alive   To store scenery or properties so that they are readily available, as opposed to putting them in dead storage. Hence, alive, live.

keeper hook, keeper   In the U.S., a piece of strap iron shaped somewhat like a flattened S. Two or more are used when attaching a stiffener, usually to the back of hinged or other adjacent flats. Also called a batten hook or latch keeper; often in the past, and sometimes today, called an S-hook. Lounsbury has an illustration. (Lounsbury THEATRE 70, Philippi STAGECRAFT 400, fig. 49)

keeping places   Holding seats for playgoers. In Restoration and 18th C theatres servants were sometimes sent to the theatre early to occupy seats for their employers. (Hogan LONDON xxxii)

keep the stage   To remain popular. Said of a play that has remained popular and, by extension, of a playwright whose works are still performed long after his death.

keffiyeh   See: kaffiyeh.

kegua, k'o kua (Chinese)   Literally: knocking gourd. A stage property used for raining comic blows in 7th-10th C adjutant plays (*canjunxi*). It was probably used most often by the gray hawk (*canggu*) to beat the adjutant pillar (*canjunzhuang*). (Dolby HISTORY 9, 26, 265)

kei engeki (Japanese)   See: *engei*.

keigoto (Japanese)   Literally: show piece. 1. A dance scene, usually a travel dance (*michiyuki*), in a *bunraku* play or a *kabuki* version of it. (Kawatake HISTORY 84) 2. The Kyoto-Osaka term for a *kabuki* dance scene or play, synonymous with *shosagoto*. (Tsubouchi/Yamamoto KABUKI 164, Leiter ENCYCLOPEDIA 187-188)

keiko (Japanese)   Rehearsal. See also: *hon yomi, tachi geiko, yomi awase*.

keisei (Japanese)   Literally: courtesan. 1. The role of a common prostitute in *kabuki*, especially in the 17th C. See also: *tayu*. (Dunn/Torigoe ANALECTS 6, 102-103) 2. A *bunraku* puppet head used for the character of a prostitute. (Keene BUNRAKU 59, 230)

keiseigai (Japanese)   Literally: prostitute buying. A type of *kabuki* play especially popular in Kyoto-Osaka that recounts the wooing of a courtesan by a young man-about-town. The earliest plays of this type were called *chaya asobi* (brothel playing). They were acted by the actress Okuni in the first recorded *kabuki* performances (c. 1603) and later developed by the Kyoto actor Sakata Tojuro, between 1678 and 1709. Also called *keiseigoto* (prostitute piece) and *keiseimono* (prostitute play). See also: *wagoto*. (Brandon CLASSIC 2, 6; Scott KABUKI 202; Ernst KABUKI 216)

keiseigoto, keiseimono (Japanese)   See: *keiseigai*.

kekayon (Indonesian)   See: *kayon*.

kelenang (Indonesian)   See: *gamelan*.

kelir (Indonesian, Malaysian)   The white cloth screen against which flat hide puppets are played in Indonesian and Malaysian *wayang kulit*. Balinese and Malaysian screens stretch from the floor to the ceiling of the stage (*panggung*) opening and incline toward the audience at the top. In Malaysia, also called *dinding dunia* (wall of the world). In Bali, also spelled *klir*. Javanese screens are wider, are raised about two feet from the floor, and are held in a free-standing frame which can be moved to any desired location. (Yub in Osman TRADITIONAL 96, Brandon THRONES 35, Muljono in Osman TRADITIONAL 60-61, McPhee in Belo TRADITIONAL 147)

Kelvin scale, Kelvin color temperature scale   A measure of color which identifies the whiteness of nearly white light. The scale uses centigrade (Celsius) degrees and begins at absolute zero. Fahrenheit 0° is therefore 273° Kelvin (shortened to K), while 1000° Fahrenheit is 1273° K. Noon sunlight registers about 5250° K, a daylight fluorescent lamp about 6500° K. Ordinary incandescent lamps used on stage are slightly under 3000° K. Lord Kelvin was a widely known British physicist. (Bellman LIGHTING 16-18, pl. VIII; Bellman SCENE)

ke ming hsien tai ching chü (Chinese)   See: *geming xiandai jingju*.

ke ming hsien tai ko chü (Chinese)   See: *geming xiandai geju*.

ke ming hsien tai wu chü (Chinese)   See: *geming xiandai wuju*.

kempli, kempul, kempur (Indonesian)   See: *gamelan*.

ken (Vietnamese)   An oboe-like reed instrument played in *hat cheo* and *hat boi*. Called a *sona* by Addiss. Also called *ken dam, ken tau*. (Addiss ''Theater'' 140)

kendang (Indonesian)   See: *gamelan*.

kenduri (Malaysian)   Offerings and invocations at the beginning of a ritual performance of *wayang kulit, main puteri*, or other ritual form. (Sweeney RAMAYANA 274)

kennel   See: gable.

kenong (Indonesian)   See: *gamelan*.

kensho (Japanese)   Literally: seeing place. The auditorium or seating area for a *no* audience. (Komparu NOH 140)

kentas (Indonesian)   See: *bablas*.

ken tau (Vietnamese)   See: *ken*.

kep (Vietnamese)   The male actor in classical Vietnamese theatre. (Pham-Duy MUSICS 124)

kepjak (Indonesian)   See: *kepyak*.

keprak (Indonesian)   In Java, a hollow wooden box on which a dance master raps cues and rhythms during classical dance rehearsal and performance. See also: *kepyak*. (Holt ART 113, 165)

kepyak (Indonesian)   Three small metal plates which are struck with a metal or wooden mallet (*cempala*) to separate speeches, to emphasize fight movements, or to cue musicians in theatre performances that use a *gamelan*. Also spelled *kepjak*. Also called *keprak* and *kecrek* or *ketjrek*. (Brandon THRONES 37)

Kepyakan is striking the plates. (Humardani in Osman TRADITIONAL 83, Muljono in Osman TRADITIONAL 70, Foley "Sundanese" 51)

keraunoskopeion (Greek)   A device mentioned by the 2nd C AD grammarian Pollux, who said it was designed to represent lightning. It has been suggested that the effect may have been achieved by means of a rapidly revolving *periaktos* with a lightning flash painted on its panels. But Liddell/Scott LEXICON gives "machine for making thunder on the stage." (Arnott SCENIC 89, Haigh ATTIC 218)

keren (Japanese)   In *kabuki*, and less often in *bunraku*, acting techniques that depend upon spectacular effects, such as acrobatics, quick costume changes, or the sudden appearance of a ghost. The term is often pejorative, in contrast to serious *hara gei*. (Leiter "Spectacle" 175-188)

kerkides (Greek)   The wedge-shaped divisions of an ancient theatre auditorium. Singular *kerkis*, wedge, from its resemblance to the shuttle, a tapered tool used in weaving. See also: *cunei* (Latin Roman). (Bieber HISTORY 70-71, Pickard-Cambridge DIONYSUS 139)

kerosene circuit   Especially in the past, a circuit of towns with poorly-equipped theatres using kerosene instead of gas or electric lighting. Also called a Burma circuit. (Wilmeth LANGUAGE)

kesabhara kiritam (Malayalam)   Literally: jewelled crown. The crown worn by divine, noble, or royal characters (*pacca*, *katti*), which has a huge nimbus-like circular attachment at the back. (Jones/Jones KATHAKALI 25)

keshimaku (Japanese)   Literally: disappearance curtain. A *kabuki* curtain, usually black, held up by a stage assistant; an actor playing a person just killed can exit behind it without being seen. (Leiter ENCYCLOPEDIA 190)

kesho (Japanese)   Makeup. See also: *kumadori*.

kesi (Malaysian)   See: *gamelan*.

kethoprak (Indonesian)   See: *ketoprak*.

ketjak (Indonesian)   See: *kecak*.

ketjrek (Indonesian)   See: *kepyak*.

ketoprak (Indonesian)   A commercial, spoken drama performed since 1914, primarily in central Java. Historical plays and Arabic romances are improvised by actors and actresses performing on a proscenium stage with wing-and-drop scenery and accompanied by *gamelan* music. Also spelled *kethoprak*. (Brandon SOUTHEAST 47-49)

ketuk (Indonesian)   See: *gamelan*.

keupat (Indonesian)   See: *ngibing*.

Kevenhüller (German)   See: *androsmane*.

key   1. See: key light. 2. Admission fee.

keyboard   1. An occasional term for a special type of control board, ordinarily with controls like those on slider dimmers. (Lounsbury THEATRE) 2. See: gas table.

key city   A town outside New York, such as Chicago, Boston, or Philadelphia, which presents world premières or important shows. (Sobel NEW)

key-fill contrast   The differences between directional and non-directional light at a particular moment or in a particular light setting. (Bellman LIGHTING 332)

key-fill ratio   The relation between directional and non-directional light. (Bellman LIGHTING 336)

key grip   A head stagehand.

key light   1. Strongly directional light. 2. An instrument which produces such light. Originally a term used in photography, the phrase probably reached the theatre through television. The first meaning is sometimes reduced to key, or referred to as key lighting. Compare: directional light, fill light. (Bellman LIGHTING 327-328, Wehlburg GLOSSARY)

key puppet   A puppet of the rod type controlled by an intricate harness, lever, and pedal arrangement. (Philpott DICTIONARY)

key set   See: unit set.

keystone   A piece of 1/4" plywood usually cut in the shape of a wedge (roughly resembling a keystone) and used to strap together members of a flat frame, especially toggles to stiles. In Britain: plate.

khaen (Lao)   A wind instrument consisting of from six to sixteen bamboo pipes joined at the end or center by a wind chamber. Used to accompany *mohlam* and *mohlam luong*. Also spelled *kaen*. (Malm CULTURES 95)

khaen (Thai)   See: *mohlam*.

khampak, khamphak (Thai)   See: *kampak*.

khana (Thai)   The generic term for a group of *khon*, *lakhon*, or *likay* actors who perform together. A temporary and fluctuating troupe. (Virulrak "Likay" 269)

khanikar (Assamese)   A monastery initiate in charge of masks for *ankiya nat* performance. (Vatsyayan TRADITIONAL 108)

khanjani (Oriya)   A type of small tambourine cymbal used by the leader of a shadow theatre troupe in Orissa, east India.

khawng (Thai)   See: *gong*.

kheimeh shab bazi (Iranian)   The traditional Iranian puppet theatre form. (P.R.R. "Ru-howzi" 114)

khel (Hindi)   See: *khyal*.

khlong hong (Thai)   Literally: noosing the bird. Enactment of part of the *manora* repertory as a ritual of initiation for a young performer. (Ginsberg in Rutnin SIAMESE 73)

khol (Assamese)   A horizontal drum played in *ankiya nat* folk theatre.

khon (Thai)   Classical masked ballet primarily of *Ramakien* (*Ramayana*) episodes, danced by a male cast to chanted narrative and *pi phat* musical accompaniment. *Khon* originated in the 16th C or earlier. *Khon luang* (royal *khon*) was supported at the king's court in the 17th C. *Khon klan klang plaeng* (open-air *khon*) emphasizes battles and recitation (*kampak*). In *khon rong nai* ('inner' or palace *khon*) songs are drawn from *lakon fai nai* and actresses perform roles of women (for example, Sida/Sita) and refined men (for example, Rama). *Khon na cho, khon na jaw* (*khon*-before-a-screen) is a version in which the dancer-actors are silhouetted against a white cloth screen. (Dhaninivat/Yupho KHON 17-19, Yupho KHON 3, Rutnin "Development" 5-6, Brandon SOUTHEAST 65-66)

khon bawk bot (Thai)   A prompter in classical dance-drama. (Ingersoll in Rama SANG 31)

khong (Thai)   See: *gong.*

khon phak (Thai)   See: *kon pak.*

khon ruang (Thai)   Literally: story-teller. The actor or troupe head in *likay* who chooses the story to be performed and directs actors during performance. (Virulrak "Likay" 274)

khoristka (Russian)   See: *choristka.*

khru (Thai)   See: *kru.*

khruang ha (Thai)   See: *pi phat khruang ha.*

khurkeh   See: Bethlehem dress.

khyal (Hindi)   An operatic folk drama of Rajasthan, north India. The term is from Urdu *khyal*, meaning imagination, or is a corruption of Hindi *khel*, meaning a play. Also spelled: *kayala.* (Gargi FOLK 47-48, Vatsyayan TRADITIONAL 160)

ki (Japanese)   See: *hyoshigi.*

kiak, gi-ag (Korean)   Literally: skilled music. A formal Buddhist masked-dance and drama accompanied by music, c. 7th C, in the kingdom of Paekche. It is the probable source of present-day folk masked plays in Korea. See also: *gigaku.* (Yi "Mask" 37, Gassner/Quinn ENCYCLOPEDIA 510)

Kiangsi opera   See: *ganju.*

kich (Vietnamese)   1. The generic term for modern, 20th C drama, influenced by Western models. *Kich* play types include: *kich tho* (poetic plays), *nhac kich* (musical plays), and *dan ca kich* (folk plays). (Pham-Duy MUSICS 115) 2. Specifically, spoken drama modeled on modern realistic Western drama that depicts contemporary themes and situations. (Brandon SOUTHEAST 76) It is primarily a southern term; in northern Vietnam *kich noi* (talking plays) is more common. (Song VIETNAMESE 34-36) *Co kich phap dich* are classic French plays in translation. (Pham-Duy MUSICS 115)

kich tho (Vietnamese)   See: *kich.*

kick in the head   To start a performance.

kid   A well-liked chorus girl. (Berrey/Van den Bark SLANG 573)

kido (Japanese)   Literally: gateway. 1. A spectators' entrance to a *kabuki* or *bunraku* theatre. See: *nezumi kido.* 2. Abbreviation of *kido guchi*, a small, standing gateway in a *kabuki* stage set which can be removed during a scene when not needed. Scott KABUKI 153 and Leiter ENCYCLOPEDIA 191 list subtypes.

kido geisha (Japanese)   Literally: entrance entertainer. A barker or entertainer who performed in front of a *kabuki* theatre in the 18th and 19th C to attract an audience. (Shively in Brandon/Malm/Shively STUDIES 12)

kigeki (Japanese)   Literally: joyful drama. The Japanese translation of the English term comedy.

kikimut (Philippine)   See: *carillo.*

kilim arasi (Turkish)   Literally: between carpets. An improvised puppet stage consisting of a folded carpet held by two assistants masking the puppeteer from view. (Philpott DICTIONARY)

kill   1. To deliver a comic line so badly that no one laughs, or an heroic or triumphant line so badly that no one applauds. Hence, to kill a laugh, kill a hand. 2. To begin speaking during an audience response and hence dampen or cut off the response. 3. In lighting, to turn off (one or more lights). 4. Backstage generally, to remove, temporarily or permanently (lights, scenery, etc.).

kill a baby   To remove a baby spotlight, e.g., from a lighting plot.

kill an actor   To spoil another performer's effect. (Berrey/Van den Bark SLANG 587)

kill a shadow   To remove the hard line of a spotlight, e.g., by frosting it or using a floodlight. (Granville DICTIONARY)

kille kettas (Kannada)   A nomadic shadow theatre troupe in Mysore state, south India. (Sorensen "Shadow" 11)

kilnori (Korean)   Literally: road play. In a masked dance-play, a procession of the performers from the village well to the playing area. (Yi "Mask" 47, Cho "Suyong" 36)

kim (Vietnamese)   See: *nguyet.*

kimari (Japanese)   A pose taken by a gentle character, male or female, in a *kabuki* play. It is a softer version of a *mie*, without eye-crossing (*nirami*) or sound effects (*tsuke*). (Brandon in Brandon/Malm/Shively STUDIES 108) *kimpira joruri* (Japanese)　　See: *kinpira joruri*.

kinesiology　The science and study of movement, basic to dancers.

kinesphere　Rudolph Laban's term for dancers' personal spheres which surround them and in which they constantly move. This space is delimited by the dancer's reach into space without taking a step or changing place. (Preston-Dunlop DANCE 22, Dell PRIMER 69)

kinesthesia　See: kinesthetic sense.

kinesthetic　In dance, the type of sensory experience derived from the sense organs in muscles, tendons, and joints when they are stimulated by body movement.

kinesthetic memory　In dance, a sensory memory of motional experience derived from the proprioceptors (sense organs) in the muscles, tendons, and joints stimulated by body movement.

kinesthetic sense　A dancer's awareness of the time, energy, and space inherent in the movement of his or her body. Sometimes called kinesthesia. (Hayes DANCE 66-67)

kinetic　In dance, of or pertaining to motion with potential, such as kinetic energy: the dynamic interplay of forces related to changing motion.

Kinetography/Laban　See: movement notation.

king-game　A medieval entertainment and folk custom involving the election of a "mock Saturnian ruler." It later became a part of the 16th C court masque. (Suvin "Happenings" 136)

kingkin (Indonesian)　In Javanese *wayang*, an arm position denoting grief. The front hand of the character is placed over the rear shoulder while the rear arm hangs straight down. (Long JAVANESE 47)

King of Misrule, Lord of Misrule, Abbot of Misrule　Master of the Revels. In Scotland: the Abbot of Unreason. A medieval term. (Bowman/Ball THEATRE)

king's box　See: royal box.

kinpira joruri, kimpira joruri (Japanese)　A 17th C style of puppet performance, first seen in Kyoto and later in Edo, that dramatized superhuman events in the life of the legendary hero Kinpira (Kimpira). This vigorous, even violent, puppet performing style was superseded by the more refined *gidayu joruri* in the 18th C. (Dunn EARLY 84-95)

kinshu (Japanese)　A financial backer of a *kabuki* theatre, especially in 17th C Kyoto-Osaka. (Dunn/Torigoe ANALECTS 16)

kipataken (Indonesian)　To spit an opponent out of one's mouth. Used by ogres in Javanese shadow theatre (*wayang kulit*) after attempting to bite their opponents to death. (Long JAVANESE 102)

Kirby Flying System　A safety-harness, piano-wire, weight, pulley, and rope arrangement of exceptional strength, enabling performers to appear to fly. (Granville DICTIONARY) *kiri* (Japanese)   Literally: cutting off. 1. In general, the concluding section of a performance. 2. In *bunraku*, the final section of an act (*dan*). Also called *dangiri*. (Ando BUNRAKU 79) 3. In *no*, the final section of one play. (Shimazaki NOH 43) See also: *kiri kyogen, kiri no*.

kiri ago (Japanese)   See: *okina*.

kirido guchi (Japanese)   A small, sliding door in the upstage left corner of a *no* stage, used by the chorus and stage assistants. Abbreviated: *kirido*. Also called *okubyo guchi* (coward's door) or hurry door. (Keene NO 25, Shimazaki NOH 9, Komparu NOH 143-144))

kirikumi (Japanese)   In *no*, fighting with swords. One type of *hatarikigoto*. (Shimazaki NOH 37)

kiri kyogen (Japanese)   Literally: concluding play. 1. The final *kyogen* comedy on a *nogaku* program. It immediately precedes the final (*kiri*) *no* play. 2. In *kabuki*, the final play or act of a day's program. Broadly, the entire domestic play (*sewamono*) that makes up the second half (*nibanme*) of a program. (Gunji KABUKI 23, Brandon CLASSIC 29, Ernst KABUKI 209) More narrowly, either the final dance scene of the domestic play, or an independent dance play at the end of the program, then also called *ogiri* (big conclusion). (Leiter ENCYCLO-PEDIA 195, 285; Gunji KABUKI 35; Brandon CLASSIC 19, 21)

kiri no (Japanese)   Literally: concluding *no*. The concluding *no* play on an all-day program. It features spectacle and vigorous dancing by the protagonist (*shite*), who is a demon. Also called *gobanmemono* (fifth place play) because it is the fifth play on the five-play program. (Nippon Gakujutsu JAPANESE xxxiv; Shimazaki NOH 26, 35)

kiriotoshi (Japanese)   See: *doma*.

kirit (Hindi)   Literally: crown. A headdress or halo indicating royal or godly rank in regional Indian dance-dramas. Also spelled *kirita* (Kannada), *kiritam* (Malayalam, Telegu). (Ashton/Christie YAKSAGANA 54, 92; Jones/Jones KA-THAKALI 25; Ranganathan "Krsnanattam" 282; Hein MIRACLE 29)

kirttaniya (Hindi)   1. A performer of Krishna's deeds in the 16th C, a predecessor of the modern *raslila* actor (*rasdhari*). (Hein MIRACLE 231-232) 2. An actor today in Bihar state, north India. 3. In Bengal state, any singer of religious songs.

kiss-kiss   A kissing scene.

kiss-me-quick   1. A 19th C sunbonnet. 2. A small curl or ringlet in front of the ear. (Walkup DRESSING 326)

kit   See: *pochette*.

Kita ryu (Japanese)   Literally: style of *Kita*. 1. The newest of the five styles of acting *no* drama. It was founded in the early 17th C as an offshoot of the Kongo style and is noted for its strong, martial quality, especially in movement. 2. The troupe or association of *no* actors who perform in this style. For other styles see: Hosho, Kanze, Kongo, Komparu. (Inoura HISTORY 108, Shimazaki NOH 84)

kitchen border   See: border.

kitoku (Japanese)   A mask of a noble used in *bugaku*. Two different versions exist: *jimmen* with scowling expression and *koiguchimen* with startled expression. (Wolz BUGAKU 44)

kitsuke (Japanese)   1. The basic kimono worn by male and female characters in *no* and *kabuki* and by *bunraku* puppets. (Nippon Gakujutsu JAPANESE II x, Leiter ENCYCLOPEDIA 196) 2. More narrowly, a kimono in *kabuki* which is worn under overgarments. (Shaver COSTUMES 124) See also: *isho*.

kiva (Hopi Indian)   A house or hut erected in multiples by Hopi Indians for the drama of the Great Serpent. (Roberts STAGE 11)

kiwamono (Japanese)   See: *ichiyazuke*.

kiyomoto bushi (Japanese)   One style of narrative (*katarimono*) singing and *shamisen* music which accompanies a *kabuki* dance play. Created in 1814 by Kiyomoto Enjudayu. Abbreviated: *kiyomoto*. (Malm MUSIC 199)

kizahashi (Japanese)   A three-step unit at the front of a *no* stage that leads down to the audience area. Also called *shirasu hashigo* (white-pebble ladder). (Berberich "Rapture" 5; Komparu NOH 143)

kizami (Japanese)   1. In *no* and *nagauta* music, a stick drum (*taiko*) pattern of regular beats. 2. In *kabuki*, a rapid beating of wooden clappers (*hyoshigi*) that accompanies the opening or closing of the main curtain. (Leiter ENCYCLOPEDIA 197)

kizewamono (Japanese)   Literally: raw domestic play. A type of domestic play (*sewamono*) in *kabuki* featuring gangsters and scenes of stylized violence. The playwrights Tsuruya Namboku IV and Kawatake Mokuami established and refined the form in the 19th C. (Ernst KABUKI 232, Brandon CLASSIC 21-24)

kkach'i ch'um (Korean)   Literally: magpie step. In masked dance-plays, a skipping step accompanied by waving arm gestures, used for exits. (Yi "Mask" 53)

kkaeki-ch'um (Korean)   In masked plays, a category of dance which is light, gay and quick. It is usually danced to *t'aryong* or *kutkori* rhythms, often by the character of the prodigal (*ch'uibari*). Abbreviated: *kkaeki*. (Cho "Suyong" 31; Yi "Mask" 47, 53)

kkoksoe (Korean)   The character of a servant to a nobleman (*yangban*) in the lion dance of the Pukch'ong area. (Yi "Mask" 75, Korean MASKS 35)

kkoktu kaksi, ggodu gagsi (Korean)   1. An old, generic term for puppet. The etymology of the word has not been established, but see Choe STUDY 14-17 for a discussion. Abbreviated: *kkoktu, kkoktouk*. See also: *inhyong*. 2. The puppet character of the wife of *pak ch'omji*. (Choe STUDY 18) 3. A traditional puppet play using figures of humans and animals. Largely humorous and a folk art, it deals with the corruption of Buddhist monks, domestic problems, and the immorality of the nobility and government officials. See also: *tolmi*. (Cho "Traditional" 27)

kkoktusoe (Korean)   The elected head of a *namsadang* troupe, chosen from the ranks of the fourteen veterans (*ttunsoe*). (Kim "Namsadang" 10)

kkopch'u, kopch'u (Korean)   The character and mask of a female hunchback in masked dance-plays of the Pukch'ong area. (Yi "Mask" 75)

kkwaenggwari, kkwaengkwari (Korean)   In traditional theatre and in *namsadang*, a small gong which is struck with a small wooden club or stick. (Cho "Traditional" 32, Kim "Namsadang" 11)

klaft   The sphinx' headdress, also worn by pharaohs. A striped cloth fitting over the temples and falling in folds over the ears. (Boucher FASHION)

klana topeng (Indonesian)   See: *wayang topeng*.

kleig light   See: Klieglight.

Kleine Kunst (Yiddish)   See: *kleynkunst*.

klepsiambos (Greek)   A harp-like instrument which sometimes accompanied recitative. Haigh believes the harp was used "originally," and Pickard-Cambridge says that it was used "later," after the flute. (Haigh ATTIC 269-271, Pickard-Cambridge FESTIVALS 157-158)

kleynkunst (Yiddish)   1. An irreverent, witty, sophisticated cabaret revue in vogue among Polish Yiddish-speaking audiences in the 1920s and earlier. Also spelled *Kleine Kunst*. 2. The Yiddish division of the Federal Theatre Project (1930s), whose productions resembled those of the 1920s, though with political, topical emphases. (Sandrow VAGABOND 284, 285, 323-324; Lifson YIDDISH 193)

klezmorim (Yiddish)   Instrumentalists in rural Poland from as early as the 16th C. One of a small group of entertainers who eked out a modest living from performing. Since 1975, there has been a revival of activity by *klezmorim* in New York City. See also: *meshoyrerim*, *badkhen*. (Kirshenblatt-Gimblett "Contraband" 7, Ferraro "Klezmer" 54-57)

klieg   A bright light. See also: Klieglight. (Parker/Smith DESIGN, Bellman SCENE 459)

Klieglight   Trademark of the Kliegl Bros. ellipsoidal reflector spotlight since its first appearance well before World War II. But 'klieg light' and 'kleig light' (sic) have been entered in large general dictionaries for some fifty years as a carbon arc light used in film making. The -ei- spelling does not occur in writers on theatre (nor, of course, in Kliegl catalogues). See also: klieg. (Bellman SCENE, Bentham ART)

klir (Indonesian)   See: *kelir*.

klong (Thai)   The generic term for drum. *Klong thad* or *klong that* is a large barrel-drum, beaten with two sticks, that is played in pairs or threes in a classical *pi phat* musical ensemble. Over a dozen drum types are used in Thai dance drama to signal, among other things, the nationality of various characters in the plays. Also spelled *glawng*, *glong*. (Duriyanga THAI 32, Morton TRADITIONAL 74-75)

klon pat (Thai)   A four-line verse form with complex internal rhyme schemes, used for songs in classical dance-drama (*lakon*). (Virulrak "Likay" 203-205)

kluchten (Flemish)   See: *sotternyen*.

knife   1. A steel rudder for a wagon stage guided in a slot in the stage floor. 2. A curtain which runs up and down. Also called a guillotine or drop curtain. 3. To cut a play or speech.

knockabout   Said of comedy or farce with much physical business. Hence, knockabout comedians, knockabout business. Also called slapstick or slap-around comedy, pie-throwing humor, etc. (Berrey/Van den Bark SLANG 581)

knock 'em bowlegged   To overwhelm an audience.

knock 'em cold, knock 'em dead, etc.   To delight an audience. (Berrey/ Van den Bark SLANG 584)

knock 'em in the aisles   See: in the aisles.

knockout   A highly successful production.

knocks herself out   Said of a stripper who works very hard. (Wilmeth LANGUAGE)

knuckle   A joint formed where two flats are secured with a cleat.

knuckle buster   1. A metal clamp fastened to a counterweight operating line to mark the trim. Also called a stop or trimmer. 2. An open-end wrench likely to slip off bolts.

koado (Japanese)   Literally: small *ado*. A second supporting character (*ado*) in a *kyogen* play. (Berberich "Rapture" 54)

kobeshimi (Japanese)   A *no* mask with a tight-lipped, fierce expression. It is worn by a deity in the second part of a god play, or by the King of Hell in the second part of a demon play. (Shimazaki NOH 62)

kobold   1. A 12th-14th C central European glove puppet found in the bag of tricks of the wandering minstrel. 2. A medieval earth-sprite puppet. Also called a tatterman. (Baird PUPPET 65-66, Crothers PUPPETEER'S 82, Malkin PUPPETS 182)

kobyoshi (Japanese)   Literally: small rhythm. In *kyogen*, a type of speech characterized by strong rhythm and rapid tempo. (Berberich "Rapture" 127-128)

ko chü (Chinese)   See: *geju*.

kodan (Japanese)   A solo storytelling form. Didactic tales from war epics and heroic narratives make up the large repertory. It is performed in variety theatres (*yose*) today. *Kodanshi* (*kodan* person) is the performer. (Ernst KABUKI 116, Brandon GUIDE 88)

kodangi (Kannada)   Literally: buffoon. In *yaksagana*, an apprentice actor-dancer who portrays minor characters. (Ashton/Christie YAKSAGANA 48, 54, 85, 92)

kodogu (Japanese)   Literally: small articles. Small properties in *no*, *kabuki*, *bunraku*, and *shingeki*. Types of *no* props are described in Nippon Gakujutsu JAPANESE xxv-xxvi. Leiter ENCYCLOPEDIA 307 gives sub-categories of *kabuki* hand props, foot props, and animal costumes. See also: *tsukurimono*. (Scott KABUKI 143-152)

kodogu beya (Japanese)   Literally: property room. A property storage room and green room for property men in a *kabuki* or *bunraku* theatre. (Leiter ENCYCLOPEDIA 198)

kodurum-ch'um (Korean)   In masked plays, a category of dance that features slow, heavy, and gentle movements and is accompanied by the six-beat *yombul* rhythm. Abbreviated *kodurum*. (Yi "Mask" 47, Korean TRADITIONAL 47)

koiguchimen (Japanese)   See: *kitoku*.

koilon (Greek)   A hollow; hence, an auditorium. Bieber uses this word for the seating area after *theatron* had come to mean the entire theatre. Compare *theatron*, *cavea*. (1939 Bieber HISTORY 114, Bieber HISTORY 282 note 6)

kojō (Japanese)   A *no* mask of a comely and noble old man. It is worn by a deity in a god (*kami*) play. Also called *koujijo* or *koushijo*. (Shimazaki NOH 58)

kōjō (Japanese)   Literally: a speech. In *kabuki*, an announcement made directly to the audience by a star actor or, in his place, by a minor actor or assistant stage manager (*todori* or *kojo yaku*). Examples are in Brandon CLASSIC 55, 248. See: *shumei*. (Leiter ENCYCLOPEDIA 199-200, Shively in Brandon/Malm/ Shively STUDIES 18-20)

kojoruri (Japanese)   Literally: old *joruri*. Various types of early and crude *joruri* narrative performance (for example, *kinpira joruri*). They were superseded in the early 18th C by the new *gidayu bushi* musical style of Takemoto Gidayu (1651-1714) and the new puppet plays of Chikamatsu Monzaemon (1653-1725). (Dunn EARLY 7)

kojo yaku (Japanese)   See: *kōjō*.

kokata (Japanese)   Literally: child performer. 1. A child role in *no*. 2. The adult or child actor playing the role. See also: *koyaku*.

koken (Japanese)   Literally: behind-watching. A stage assistant to an actor, normally an actor himself. He brings and removes props, adjusts the actor's costume or wig, and resolves any problem that might interfere with the actor's performance. The term is from his usual position upstage of the actor. A *koken* wears standard stage dress (*kamishimo*) in *no* and *kyogen*. He is usually hooded and dressed in black to be 'invisible' in *bunraku* and *kabuki*, except that in a *kabuki* dance play he wears formal dress and in a snow scene is hooded and dressed in white. See also: *kurogo*. (Ernst KABUKI 106-111)

kokoshnik (Russian)   A woman's tiara or diadem-style headdress. (Boucher FASHION)

k'o kua (Chinese)   See: *kegua*.

kokyu (Japanese)   A Chinese-derived, bowed, stringed instrument which may accompany a scene of pathos in a *bunraku* or puppet-derived *kabuki* play. (Keene BUNRAKU 54)

kolam penglipurlara (Malaysian)   The oil-containing section of the lamp used in Malaysian shadow theatre. (Yub in Osman TRADITIONAL 98)

Kol Korçak (Turkish)   A glove or hand puppet. Also called *el kuklasi*. (And KARAGÖZ 24-25)

kolpak (Russian)   Literally: dunce cap. A traditional cap of astrakhan fur worn by cossack officers. Also called a cossack cap. Alternate spellings: calpac, calpack. See also: *papakha*.

kolpoma (Greek)   In tragedy, a special short padded *chiton* (tunic) worn over the regular *chiton* by kings. The purpose was to increase the king's size. (Nicoll DEVELOPMENT 27, Haigh ATTIC 252 note 2, Pickard-Cambridge FESTIVALS 203)

komachi (Japanese)   The mask used for Ono no Komachi, a celebrated beauty and court poetess who appears in three important *no* plays. (Shimazaki NOH 65)

komagaku (Japanese)   In *bugaku*, music (*gaku*) which is derived from Koma (Korea). It accompanies dances of the right (*umai*). (Togi GAGAKU 6)

ko mai (Japanese)   Literally: small dance. A short independent dance sequence in *kyogen*, usually interpreting the lyrics of a song (*ko utai*). (Hoff SONG 134, Berberich "Rapture" 154-157)

komali (Tamil)   A clown role in south Indian *therukoothu* folk theatre. See also: *vidusaka*. (Karanth YAKSAGANA 11)

komedia rybałtowska (Polish)   The comedies performed by *rybałts*—16th C wandering minstrels. (Gassner/Quinn ENCYCLOPEDIA 665)

Komedias (Yiddish)   Comedies. (Lifson YIDDISH 51)

komedie (Indonesian)   Modern spoken drama, drawing on Western dramatic materials, performed in Bandung in the late 19th C. See also: *drama moderen*. (Brandon SOUTHEAST 50)

komediia (Russian)   Comedy.

komediia nravov (Russian)   See: *bytovaia komediia*.

komedya (Philippine)   See: *comedia*.

komedyantchik (Yiddish)   A buffoon, a low comedian. (Rosenfeld BRIGHT 17)

komei (Japanese)   A *bunraku* puppet head used for characters of good middle-aged men. From the name of the character Shokatsu Komei. (Keene BUNRAKU 213)

kommos (Greek)   Literally: an unrestrained lament. Originally, in tragedy and perhaps earlier, a lyrical lament exchanged between chorus leader and chorus; later, such an exchange between actor or actors and chorus. Also spelled *commus*. Compare *komos*. (Flickinger GREEK 96, 169; Allen ANTIQUITIES 119-120)

kommu, gom mu (Korean)   Literally: sword and dance. A masked-dance play of the Silla Kingdom (57 BC to 935 AD). It probably originated in a war or hunting dance that used swords and spears. Today it exists in two forms: classical female dances and women's folk dances. (Kim/Heyman "Chinju" 51, Cho "Yangju" 27, Gassner/Quinn ENCYCLOPEDIA 510)

komoidos (Greek)   See: *tragoidos*.

komos (Greek)   Literally: revel, carousal. 1. A procession of Dionysian revelers. 2. The revelry of the participants. *Komoi*, which were of many varieties, were characteristically boisterous, unrestrained, phallic. The word is commonly applied to the joyous revelry at the close of Old Comedy (it is also used of the supposed revel which was a source of a portion of Old Comedy). Pickard-Cambridge (among others) suggests that the scenes in Old Comedy which came from a *komos* were those between the chorus entry and the end of the *parabasis*. He postulates a *komos* consisting of a choral entry or *parodos*, followed by a debate (*agon*), and ending in an address to the audience (the *parabasis*). Plural *komoi*, occasionally *komai*. *Comus*, a Latinized form, is about as frequent as *komos; comos* is less so. *Exodos* is sometimes used for the final scene of rejoicing. (Pickard-Cambridge DITHYRAMB 132-162; Allen ANTIQUITIES 7, 35; Flickinger GREEK 36, 42-46)

Komparu *ryu* (Japanese)   Literally: style of Komparu. 1. One of the five styles of acting *no* drama. Also spelled Konparu. Called 'old style' or orthodox, in all likelihood it is the oldest of *no* performing styles, dating from the early 14th C. 2. The troupe or association of *no* actors who perform in this style. This is a contemporary term. Before the 20th C, Komparu *za* (Komparu troupe) was the common term. For other styles see Hosho, Kanze, Kita, Kongo. (Inoura HISTORY 108, Shimazaki NOH 84, Keene NO 68)

kong (Khmer)   A set of bronze gongs used in the classical *pinpeat* musical ensemble. The *kong touch* is high-pitched and set in a circular configuration. The *kong thom* consists of 17 low-pitched gongs. (Brunet in Osman TRADI-TIONAL 216, Brandon SOUTHEAST 127)

kong (Thai)   1. See: *gong*. 2. *Tua kong* is a villain role in *likay*. (Virulrak "Likay" 189)

Kongo *ryu* (Japanese)   Literally: style of Kongo. 1. One of five styles of acting *no* drama. It is noted for vigorous, even acrobatic dance. Established at least by the 14th C, it has continued as an unbroken tradition to the present time. 2. The troupe or association of *no* actors who perform in this style. This is a contemporary usage. Before the 20th C, the term Kongo *za* (Kongo troupe) identified the performers. For other styles see: Hosho, Kanze, Kita, Komparu. (Inoura HISTORY 108, Shimazaki NOH 84, Keene NO 68)

kong thom, kong touch (Khmer)   See: *kong*.

konistra (Greek)   Rarely and in late Greek times, the *orchestra*. *Konistra*, literally 'a place covered with dust,' is equivalent to the Latin *arena*. A major view is that the word may have come into use after the *orchestra* had been walled to protect spectators at gladiatorial combats. Sometimes spelled conistra, perhaps an attempt to anglicize the term. (Bieber HISTORY 214; Haigh ATTIC 101-102; Flickinger GREEK 72n, 73; Pickard-Cambridge DIONYSUS 258n)

konju (Japanese)   A mask of a Mongolian man used in *bugaku*. (Wolz BU-GAKU 38)

konkoba (Kankan)   In Guinea, a masquerade variety show with troubadours, dancers, and musicians. (Adedeji glossary)

kono-donkili (Bambara)   A puppet show developed by touring mask-performers in west Africa. The puppets are manipulated by strings and dance to vocal accompaniment. (Adedeji glossary)

kon pak (Thai)   A reciter or narrator in *khon* or *nang yai*. Also spelled *khon phak* or *kon phak*. (Dhaninivat/Yupho KHON 3-4, Yupho KHON 41)

Konparu (Japanese)   See: Komparu.

kon phak (Thai)   See: *kon pak*.

kontush   1. A Polish full-cut cloak. 2. An 18th C German or Nordic gown à la Française. Also spelled contouche. (Boucher FASHION)

Konversationsstücke (German)   See: drama of conversation.

ko omote (Japanese)   Literally: little mask. A *no* mask used to portray young women, primarily in the Kita and Komparu schools. (Shimazaki NOH 60)

Kooney-Lemels (Yiddish)   See: *Kuni-Lemls*.

koothadis (Tamil)   An ancient community of actors in Tamil Nadu state, south India. (Rangacharya INDIAN 88)

koothumadam (Malayalam)   A temple stage in Kerala state, southwest India, that can be used as a puppet stage. (ASIAN 21)

k'o pan (Chinese)   See: *keban*.

kopch'u (Korean)   See: *kkopch'u*.

kopsawi-ch'um (Korean)   One type of *kkaeki* dance step, in which each arm is alternately circled around the head and shoulders on each step. Abbreviated: *kopsawi*. (Cho "Yangju" 51, Yi "Mask" 53)

kordax (Greek)   The characteristic dance of Old Comedy, marked by drunkenness and vulgarity. Pickard-Cambridge remarks that "Its exact nature is (perhaps fortunately) undiscoverable...''; he finds that since Old Comedy had more than one kind of vulgar dance, attempts to describe the *kordax* on the basis of vase paintings are unconvincing. See Lawler and Bieber for such descriptions. Compare *mothon*. Also seen as Latin *cordax*, U.S. cordax. (Pickard-Cambridge DITHYRAMB 164, 167-169; Lawler DANCE 87, 88, 133, 135; Bieber HISTORY 43)

kori (Korean)   In *namsadang*, a scene. (Sim/Kim KOREAN 3)

koro (Philippine)   A chorus in operetta (*zarzuela*). (Fernandez ILOILO 117)

koroshiba (Japanese)   Literally: murder scene. A scene in a *kabuki* domestic play (*sewamono*) emphasizing the grisly death of a major character. An example is in *The Scarlet Princess of Edo* in Brandon CLASSIC 328-330. (Hamamura et al KABUKI 75-76)

kosa, geusa (Korean)   1. A communally based, all-male singing and dancing troupe. See also: *sadang*. (Cho KOREAN 11) 2. A pre-play rite, performed in front of the masks to be worn during a masked play. (Yi "Mask" 40)

ko shibai (Japanese)   Literally: small theatre. 1. In *kabuki*, 17th to 19th C, small unlicensed theatres as opposed to the nine—sometimes ten—major, government-licensed *kabuki* houses. (Gunji KABUKI 53) 2. Today, small theatres where pseudo-*kabuki* and sword plays are performed by marginal travelling troupes. Also called *koya* (small shack), *shibai goya* (small theatre). See also: *gekijo*.

kotak (Indonesian)   1. A storage box for *wayang* puppets. During performance the box is placed at the *dalang*'s left and is struck for sound effects. Also spelled *kothak*. (Long JAVANESE 19, Foley "Sundanese" 49) In Balinese, *kropak* or *gedog*. (McPhee in Belo TRADITIONAL 147, Moerdowo BALINESE II 121) 2. By extension, a set of puppets. (Holt ART 133, 145) 3. In Javanese *wayang wong*, a dressing room for dancers. (Holt ART 158)

koteba (Bambara)   In Senegal and Mali, farcical comedies traditionally performed by young men's societies. (Meillasoux "Koteba" 28-62)

kothak (Indonesian)   See: *kotak*.

kothornos (Greek)   1. A loose-fitting, soft boot identifiable in Greece in the late 7th C BC, and early connected with Dionysus. Such footwear, sometimes laced and sometimes with cuffs, was evidently widespread in daily life by the 5th C BC. Decorative in varying degrees, it may well have been used in tragedy. The extent to which the term, sometimes translated "the Grecian shoe," specifically designated the footwear of 5th C tragedy, is less clear. Pickard-Cambridge, for example, finds no evidence that the word was so used in the 5th C BC. 2. In late Greek tragedy and in Roman tragedy based on Greek originals, a high-soled boot, possibly of varying colors according to the character. Recent scholarship finds that the high sole cannot be dated earlier than the 2nd C BC. 3. By association, tragedy.

The forms of the word are a minor morass. Recent scholarship prefers *kothornos*, but *kothurnos* is also seen. Latin *cothurnus* is frequent, and has been accepted in U.S. English for many years; cothurn is an occasional variant. Most plurals are in -*i*, but the Greek forms sometimes appear in Roman type with an -oi plural. "Buskin" has long been a favorite synonym. "High boot" is sometimes the high boot of meaning 1, and sometimes the high-soled boot of meaning 2. Compare *fabula crepidata*. (Pickard-Cambridge FESTIVALS 204-208; Webster PRODUCTION 37-38, 44; Bieber HISTORY 26, 34, 157)

kotoba (Japanese)   Literally: word. In *no*, *bunraku*, or *kowakamai*, a prose passage, usually dialogue, in contrast to a sung verse passage (*utai* or *ji*). (Nippon Gakujutsu JAPANESE xii, Malm in Brandon CHUSHINGURA 64-65, Araki BALLAD 10)

kotobide (Japanese)   A *no* mask worn by an active but minor god, such as a fox deity. (Shimazaki NOH 62)

kotsuzumi (Japanese)   A small, hour-glass shaped drum used in *no* and *kabuki*. It is held at shoulder level and struck with the fingers. See also: *hayashi*.

ko tzu hsi (Chinese)   See: *gezixi*.

koujijo (Japanese)   See: *kojō*.

kou lan (Chinese)   See: *goulan*.

koumian, k'ou mien (Chinese)   See: *rankou*.

koushijo (Japanese)   See: *kojō*.

kou ssu (Chinese)   See: *goulan*.

ko uta (Japanese)   Literally: small song. 1. A generic term for short, popular songs prior to the 20th C. 2. In *no*, most songs (*utai*), except for the *kuse*. (Konishi "Approaches" 7) 3. In *kyogen*, a popular song of the 15th or 16th C, sung in free rhythm and with rich vocal ornamentation. See also: *ko utai*. (Berberich "Rapture" 54) 4. Written with different ideographs, in the 18th and 19th C, a short song accompanied by *shamisen* music. (Berberich "Rapture" 102-103)

ko utai (Japanese)   Literally: small song. A short character song or chant performed in *kyogen*. See also: *ko uta*. (Berberich "Rapture" 72)

kowakamai (Japanese)   A male dance, narrated and sung, popular among the samurai class during the 15th C. *Kowakamai* contributed dance and musical elements to the formation of *no*. Today remnants of the repertory are preserved in performance in a few villages in western Japan. Abbreviated: *kowaka*. (Araki BALLAD 71-79, Inoura HISTORY 15)

ko wu chü (Chinese)   See: *gewuju*.

koya (Japanese)   See: *koshibai*.

koyaku (Japanese)　　Literally: child role. 1. A child's role in *kabuki*. 2. A child actor who performs such a role, usually the son of a star. See also: *kokata*. (Leiter ENCYCLOPEDIA 39)

krade (Greek)　　Probably another name for the *mechane* (a hoisting device). The literal meaning is "branch" or "fig-branch." The 2nd C grammarian Pollux speaks of the *krade* as the counterpart in comedy of the *mechane*, but modern scholarship thinks this unlikely and tends to include *krade* among other names for the *mechane*. (Pickard-Cambridge DIONYSUS 68, 127; Flickinger GREEK 298)

kramadipika (Malayalam)　　A staging manual used by actors of *kutiyattam*. It gives regulations and procedures for staging plays and for treatment of songs, dances, and music. See also: *attaprakara*. (Vatsyayan TRADITIONAL 20, Enros in Baumer/Brandon SANSKRIT 276)

kras (Indonesian)　　See: *kasar*.

kraspeditae (Greek)　　Literally: men on the fringe. In the tragic chorus, the six men forming the two end ranks of the normal choral arrangement. Singular: *kraspedites*. See also chorus. (Haigh ATTIC 299, fig. 31, 300; Pickard-Cambridge FESTIVALS 241)

kris (Indonesian)　　See: *barong*, *nyuduk*, trance-dance.

krisasvin (Sanskrit)　　A term for actor used in India as early as the 5th C B.C. See also: *nata*. (Hein MIRACLE 258, Raghavan in Baumer/Brandon SANSKRIT 10)

krishnalila (Sanskrit)　　Literally: Krishna's sport. Any literary or dramatic presentation of incidents in the life of the god Krishna. (Hein MIRACLE 289)

krishnanattam (Malayalam)　　A dance-drama, closely related in performing style to *kathakali*, in which legends of Krishna are enacted through elaborate movement and song. Only one company exists, that of Guruvayur Temple, south India. (Ranganathan "Krsnanattam" 275-283)

krishnasvarup (Hindi)　　In *krishnalila*, the actor portraying the god Krishna and in whom the deity becomes incarnate. (Hein MIRACLE 289)

krodha (Sanskrit)　　Literally: anger. One of the eight major emotions (*sthayibhava*) expressed by actors in classical Indian theatre. See also: *raudra*. (Keith SANSKRIT 323)

kropak (Indonesian)　　See: *kotak*.

kru (Khmer)　　Literally: master. A narrator in shadow theatre, who chants the epic text while other performers move the puppets. There are two *kru* in *nang sbek* and five or six in *ayang*. From Sanskrit, *guru*. (Sheppard "Khmer" 200-201)

kru (Thai)　　A teacher or master of an artistic discipline. From Sanskrit *guru*. See also: *wai kru*.

ku (Chinese)   See: *gu.*

k'ua i (Chinese)   See: *kuayi.*

kuaiban, k'uai pan (Chinese)   Literally: fast meter. The fastest regulated (*shangban*) metrical-type (*banshi*) used in the songs of Beijing opera (*jingju*). It is in single-beat meter and is used in the *xipi* mode (*diaoshi*) for intense situations, such as excited or anxious debate. See also: *banyan.* (Wichmann "Aural" 150-151)

kuaibanshu, k'uai pan shu (Chinese)   Literally: fast clapper book. A form of storytelling (*quyi*) popular in northern China, presented by a single performer who speaks, sings, and plays two types of clappers, one held in each hand. Performances consist of a number of short pieces. (Howard CONTEMPORARY 23, 30)

k'uai pan (Chinese)   See: *kuaiban.*

k'uai pan shu (Chinese)   See: *kuaibanshu.*

kuaisanyan, k'uai san yen (Chinese)   Literally: fast-three-unaccented beats. A quadruple meter regulated (*shangban*) metrical-type (*banshi*), slower than primary meter (*yuanban*), used in the songs of many forms of music-drama (*xiqu*) for both introspective and relatively straightforward situations. In Beijing opera (*jingju*), it is used in both the *xipi* and *erhuang* modes (*diaoshi*). See also: *banyan.* (Wichmann "Aural" 151-153)

kuaishu, k'uai shu (Chinese)   Literally: fast book. A type of *danxian* storytelling (*quyi*) performance characterized by a swiftly moving rhythm. (Howard CONTEMPORARY 30, Mackerras RISE 200)

kuan (Chinese)   See: *guan.*

Kuangsi opera   See: *guiju.*

kuan hsüeh (Chinese)   See: *guanxue.*

kuan i (Chinese)   See: *guanyi.*

kuan pen tsa chü (Chinese)   See: *guanben zaju.*

kuan sheng (Chinese)   See: *guansheng.*

kuan tso (Chinese)   See: *guanzuo.*

kuayi, k'ua i (Chinese)   A round-necked jacket with narrow cuffless sleeves which is usually plain and black and is decorated down the center front and the two sides with a narrow criss-cross pattern. It is worn by lower-class, non-military male fighters in Beijing opera (*jingju*) and many other forms of music-drama (*xiqu*). (Halson PEKING 26, Scott CLASSICAL 157)

kubi jikken (Japanese)   A scene in a *bunraku* history play, especially of the mid-18th C, in which a head (*kubi*) of a relative is identified (*jikken*) incorrectly as a ruse to save someone's life. The conflict of emotions within the examiner—duty vs. human feelings—creates a deeply moving scene. Examples are in Ernst

THREE 124-125, Keene BUNRAKU 173-177, and Brandon CLASSIC 200-202. (Scott KABUKI 114-115)

kubi oke (Japanese)   Literally: head cask. The carrying case for a head in a *kabuki* or *bunraku* scene of a head identification (*kubi jikken*). (Scott KABUKI 114)

kubol (Philippine)   The prompter's box for the prompter-director (*diktador*) of *comedia*. It is located downstage. (Mendoza COMEDIA 62)

kuchiake (Japanese)   See: *mitateme*.

kuchidate (Japanese)   Literally: made-by-improvisation. 1. In *kyogen*, training and performing through improvisation. (Inoura HISTORY 110) 2. In early 17th C *kabuki*, the practice of improvising a whole play. From about 1680, improvisation was replaced by a written play script (*kyakuhon*) composed first by actors and then by playwright specialists. (Gunji KABUKI 34, Scott KABUKI 200)

kuchipudi (Telugu)   1. A dance-drama in which song, dance, narrative, and dialogue are fused. Performed today by a troupe of Brahmin males, in the village of Kuchipudi, Andhra Pradesh state, southeast India. The repertory consists of Krishna devotional plays. (Vatsyayan TRADITIONAL 63-64) 2. A classical solo dance style derived from the dance-drama, which is performed on the concert stage by women.

ku chuang t'ou (Chinese)   See: *guzhuangtou*.

kudaragaku (Japanese)   In *gagaku*, music (*gaku*) of Kudara (the Korean kingdom of Paekche). One of two sub-types of *komagaku* music. (Inoura HISTORY 31)

kuden (Japanese)   Literally: oral transmission. In *no*, secret knowledge which is held by the master (*iemoto*) of a school or troupe and transmitted only to favored pupils, either orally or through a closely guarded secret treatise (for example, Zeami Motokiyo's *The Way of the Flower*). See also: *isshi soden*. (Konishi "Approaches" 1)

kudoki (Japanese)   A scene of lamentation within a musical context, performed by a female character: 1. In *kabuki*, a dance or mime scene accompanied by plaintive *shamisen* melodies. (Malm in Brandon/Malm/Shively STUDIES 143-159) 2. In *bunraku*, a major scene in which a puppet character mimes her grief, while a chanter sings her unspoken feelings and thoughts. There are examples in Keene BUNRAKU 178-181 and Brandon CLASSIC 202-204. 3. The expression of grief within a *sashi* unit of a *no* play. (Shimazaki NOH 48)

Kueichow opera   See: *qianju*.

kuei chü (Chinese)   See: *guiju*.

k'uei lei (Chinese)   See: *kuilei*.

k'uei lei hsi (Chinese)   See: *kuileixi*.

kuei men tan (Chinese)   See: *guimendan*.

k'uei t'ou (Chinese)   See: *kuitou*.

kugeaku (Japanese)   Literally: noble villain. 1. The role of a powerful, villainous court noble in *kabuki*. One type of *katakiyaku*. An example is Prince Hayakumo in *Saint Narukami and the God Fudo* in Brandon CLASSIC 101-104. 2. An actor of such a role. (Gunji KABUKI 32)

kuguk, gu guk, gugug (Korean)   Literally: old play. A musical drama based on a traditional story, popular in the 19th C. (Gassner/Quinn ENCYCLOPEDIA 511, Kardoss OUTLINE 12)

kugutsu (Japanese)   Simple, hand-held puppets dating from the 8th C. Early puppet performances (*kugutsu mawashi*) were connected with Shinto worship and probably consisted of crude sword-play, wrestling, and short improvised playlets. (Keene BUNRAKU 25, 55)

kuilei, k'uei lei (Chinese)   Puppet.

kuileixi, k'uei lei hsi (Chinese)   The generic term for all types of puppet theatre. See also: *mu'ouxi, piyingxi, zhangtou kuilei, dayingxi, roukuilei, shuikuilei, yaokuilei, xiju*. (Liu INTRODUCTION 163-165, Obraztsov CHINESE 27, Scott LITERATURE 56-60)

kuitou, k'uei t'ou (Chinese)   The generic term for hats, helmets, and headdresses worn in music-drama (*xiqu*). Important types are described in detail in Halson PEKING 31-36 and Scott CLASSICAL 160-166.

kukla (Turkish)   1. A puppet. 2. A shadow puppet show. Also called a *hayali zil*. (And KARAGÖZ 24, Matlaw MODERN 777)

kulintang (Philippine)   A set of tuned bronze bowls used in Muslim performances on Mindanao. Analagous to Indonesian *bonang*. (Alejandro PHILIPPINE 29)

Kulisse (German)   A wing, side scene, backdrop. Hence, *hinter den Kulissen* (back stage, behind the stage), *Kulissen fieber* (stage fright), *Kulissenmaler* (scene painter), *Kulissenreisserie* (playing to the gallery), *Kulissenschieber* (scene shifter), *Kulissentür* (stage door), etc.

ku li tzu (Chinese)   See: *biandan*.

kuma (Japanese)   See: *kumadori*.

kumadori (Japanese)   In *kabuki*, highly stylized and colorful makeup of face, torso, and limbs expressing exaggerated strength in *aragoto* style plays. Red indicates bravery, blue or grey evil, black power. There are a dozen named patterns. This type of makeup was first worn by Ichikawa Danjuro I in playing the mythological superman, Kintoki, in 1673. Abbreviated: *kuma*. Illustrations are in Brandon CLASSIC frontispiece, Gunji KABUKI 194, and Shaver COSTUMES 339-340. (Scott KABUKI 124, Leiter ENCYCLOPEDIA 209)

kumedya (Philippine)   See: *comedia*.

kumiawase (Japanese)　　Literally: assemblage. In *no*, the arrangement or sequence of movement patterns (*kata*) in a performance. (Wolz "Spirit" 56)

kumidya (Philippine)　　See: *comedia*.

kumis (Indonesian)　　See: *ngibing*.

kumo no ogi (Japanese)　　Literally: cloud fan. In *no* dance, the standard gesture (*kata*) to indicate looking at a cloud. Extended arms are spread open, while the actor looks upward. Illustrated in Keene NO 220.

k'un ch'iang (Chinese)　　See: *kunshanqiang*.

k'un chü, k'un ch'ü (Chinese)　　See: *kunqu*.

kundhei nata (Oriya)　　See: *gopa lila*.

kungdungi ch'um (Korean)　　A dance step used by an old wife or midwife in various types of masked plays. Characterized by swinging the buttocks from side to side. Also called *ongdongi ch'um*. (Yi "Mask" 47, 53)

kung fu (Chinese)　　See: *jiben gongfu*.

Kuni-Lemls (Yiddish)　　Idiotic, loutish clowns. The word entered the language from the 19th C play *The Two Kuni-Lemls*, one of various titles. Also spelled *Kuny-lemels*, *Kooney-Lemels*, and *Kuni-Lemmels*. (Sandrow VAGABOND 47, 49, 433; Lifson YIDDISH 50, 355; Rosenfeld BRIGHT 48, 108, 111)

kunju (Chinese)　　See: *kunqu*.

kunqiang (Chinese)　　See: *kunshanqiang*.

kunqu, k'un ch'ü (Chinese)　　Literally: Kunshan songs. The most important and widespread form of music-drama (*xiqu*) in China, 17th-early 19th C; it is still performed today. The music of *kunqu*, sometimes called "water polished music" (*shuimodiao* or *shui mo tiao*) because of the care taken in its composition, was created by Wei Liangfu and others c. 1540-1566 in Kunshan, Jiangsu Province, under the influence of *haiyanqiang*, *yiyangqiang*, southern and northern *qu* singing, and the music of local plays. It uses *lianquti* musical structure, and is accompanied by a horizontal bamboo flute (*di*). The theatrical form was born c. 1579, when Liang Chenyu wrote the first *chuanqi* play to suit this music. During the 16th-17th C, regional forms of *kunqu* developed throughout China, giving rise to one of the principal musical systems (*shengqiang xitong*) in music-drama, called *kunshanqiang*. Popular with the educated elite until the mid-19th C, *kunqu* was ultimately overshadowed by various regional theatre forms, especially Beijing opera (*jingju*). It was partially incorporated in a number of them, and is still independently performed today. Also called Kunshan drama (*kunju* or *k'un chü*), and "the elegant part" (*yabu*). (Dolby HISTORY 91-130; Mackerras MODERN 15-22; Scott TRADITIONAL I 4, 7-10; Scott TRADITIONAL II 3-10; Yao "Rise" 63-84)

kunshanqiang, k'un shan ch'iang (Chinese)　　A musical system (*shengqiang xitong*) characterized by the use of *lianquti* musical structure and horizontal bamboo flute (*di*) accompaniment. It arose through the influence of *kunqu* drama in the 16th-17th C. In addition to *kunqu*, contemporary forms of music-drama (*xiqu*) which feature music from the *kunshanqiang* musical system include Beijing opera (*jingju*), Hunan opera (*xiangju*) and *huiju*. Also called *kunqiang* or *k'un chiang*.

Kunstfigur (German)   Artificial figure. The use of marionettes so as to achieve total control and integration of figure, sound, and light. Vsevelod Meyerhold, Gordon Craig, and Oskar Schlemmer were all interested in this idea of an *Übermarionette* (super puppet) to replace the performer. (O1f "Debate" 491)

kun tiao (Chinese)   See: *gundiao*.

Kuny-Lemels (Yiddish)   See: *Kuni-Lemls*.

kuo chü (Chinese)   See: *jingju*.

kuo men (Chinese)   See: *guomen*.

ku pan (Chinese)   See: *guban*.

kuplét (Yiddish)   A comic patter song. Hence, *kupletists*, performers of such songs. (Sandrow VAGABOND 126-127, 390-391)

Kuppelhorizont (German)   Short form: *Horizont*, horizont. A cupola-shaped plaster cyclorama designed to provide, when lit, the effect of infinite space. Also called a cupola, heaven, sometimes *Rundhorizont*. (Brockett HISTORY 588)

Kupplung (German)   See: *Stecherkupplungen*.

kurai (Japanese)   Literally: rank. *No* and *kyogen* plays are ranked according to difficulty and refinement. Higher ranked plays are performed at a slower tempo. (Komparu NOH 192-193)

kuravanji (Tamil)   A form of drama in south India using *bharata natyam* classical dance style, in which a gypsy is the chief character.

kuri (Japanese)   A short, high-pitched, melodious section (*shodan*) of a *no* play sung in free rhythm (*hyoshi awazu*). (Shimazaki NOH 47)

kuriage (Japanese)   Literally: raise up. In *kabuki*, a vocal and writing technique in which the repeated and rapid exchange of a word or phrase by opposing characters sharply raises the emotional tension of a scene. Examples are in Leiter ART 26 and Brandon CLASSIC 322, 328. (Leiter ENCYCLOPEDIA 212)

kurogo (Japanese)   Literally: black costume (variant writing: black child). 1. A black costume, consisting of a long wrap, leggings, hood, and often gloves, worn onstage by a stage assistant in *kabuki* and *bunraku*. 2. A stage assistant who wears this costume onstage in view of the audience. In *kabuki*, he may be either an acting assistant (*koken*) or a stagehand (*kyogen kata*), depending upon the play and stage function. The slang form is *kurombo, kuronbo*. See also: *namiko, yukiko*. (Scott KABUKI 111, Ernst KABUKI 106-111)

kurohige (Japanese)   Literally: black beard. A *no* mask painted with a black beard, used for dragon gods. (Shimazaki NOH 62)

kurombo, kuronbo (Japanese)   See: *kurogo*.

kuro yoten (Japanese)   Literally: black-costumed *yoten*. See: *yoten*.

kurumkuzhal (Malayalam)   A small wind instrument used in *kutiyattam*.

kuse (Japanese)   A long narrative song recalling past events that forms the core of a *no* performance. It may occur in the first or the second part (*ba*) of a play. It is sung by the chorus (*ji*) on behalf of the protagonist (*shite*). There are two types: *maiguse* (danced *kuse*), in which the protagonist dances the story being sung, and *iguse* (sitting *kuse*), in which he does not dance. Respective examples are in the plays *Takasago* and *Izutsu* in Nippon Gakujutsu JAPANESE 5-17 and 95-105. (Shimazaki NOH 46; Inoura HISTORY 89-90, 116)

kusemai (Japanese)   Literally: unconventional dance. 1. A narrative song in irregular rhythm, usually danced, of the 14th and 15th C. Kannami Kiyotsugu introduced it into *no*, where it became the *kuse*. (O'Neill EARLY 53-57) 2. Sometimes synonymous with *kowakamai*. (Araki BALLAD 73)

kusheng, k'u sheng (Chinese)   See: *xiepisheng*.

ku shih (Chinese)   See: *sigu*.

kushilava (Sanskrit)   See: *nata*.

kuski (Russian)   An act of a play divided into smaller units of varying length, each unit being a *kusok*. (Houghton MOSCOW 70)

kusok (Russian)   Literally: piece. A small unit or scene within an act of a play. A *kusok* can vary from a few lines to several pages, the length being indicated by the unity of the thought being expressed. (Houghton MOSCOW 70)

kut, gut (Korean)   1. Originally, a shamanic ritual. 2. An exorcistic play or drama. (Korean KOREAN 34)

kutambalam (Malayalam)   A theatre building attached to a temple in Kerala, south India, and designed for performances of *kutiyattam*. (Enros in Baumer/Brandon SANSKRIT 286-287)

kutapa (Sanskrit)   The orchestra that accompanies a performance in classical Indian theatre. (Gandhi in Baumer/Brandon SANSKRIT 117)

kutchung p'ae (Korean)   A shaman ritual performance that includes dancing and singing. (Yi "Mask" 76)

kutiyattam (Malayalam)   Literally: combined acting. A dance-drama in Kerala, south India, that strongly influenced *kathakali*. Originated in the 10th or 11th C. It is the oldest living theatre form in which classical Sanskrit plays are still performed. (Enros in Baumer/Brandon SANSKRIT 275-276)

kutkori (Korean)   In masked dance-plays, a 12/8 rhythm derived from farmer's music (*p'ungmul*) of Kyonggi Province. (Yi "Mask" 46, Cho "Hwanghae" 42)

kuttu (Malayalam)   A performance in Kerala, south India, in which the clown or jester (*vidusaka*) expounds on Puranic stories and takes the roles of various characters while accompanied by a drummer.

ku tzu tz'u (Chinese)   See: *guzici*.

kuzetsu (Japanese)   Literally: lovers' quarrel. A scene in a *kabuki* prostitute-buying play (*keiseikai*) in which lovers have a humorous quarrel. An example is in Brandon CLASSIC 232-233.

kwagh-hir (Tiv)   In Nigeria, a traditional story-telling puppet theatre which became popular during the 1960s. Usually staged at night by itinerant troupes, the string puppets are carved images or dolls manipulated from inside a screened enclosure. "The show includes huge animal mask figures, a chorus of singers and dancers who enliven the acts of the storyteller." (Adedeji glossary)

kwangdae, kwangtae, gwangdae (Korean)   Literally: broad and large. A male performer of puppetry, masked dance-plays, tumbling, or *p'ansori*. (Cho KOREAN 11, Choe "Yangju" 3)

Kwangtung opera   See: *yueju*, meaning 1.

kyakuhon (Japanese)   A play script or text for *kabuki*, *bunraku*, and modern drama (as well as television or films). See also: *daihon*.

kyakusha (Japanese)   Spectator, audience member.

kybisteter (Greek)   Tumbler, acrobat. Such performers influenced the early Greek mime. (Nicoll MASKS 35)

kyi waing (Burmese)   See: *saing waing*.

kyogen (Japanese)   Literally: enraptured words. 1. "Extraordinary language, uttered in fun," in ancient times (c. 8th C). Later, by extension, the term was applied to short, comic plays that alternate with *no* plays on a *nogaku* program. (Berberich "Rapture" 34-36) The plays are performed entirely by *kyogen* actors (*kyogen kata*). They are mostly in prose dialogue, but music, songs, and masks are used in about half the 200-plus plays in the repertory. Also called, more formally, *no-kyogen*. 2. The generic term in *kabuki* for a play or drama. A modern equivalent is *engeki*. See also: *hon kyogen*.

kyogen bon (Japanese)   See: *eiri kyogen bon*.

kyogen kata (Japanese)   Literally: *kyogen* person. 1. The actors who perform all roles in a *kyogen* play (see: *kyogen*, meaning 1) and specified *kyogen* roles within a *no* play. 2. In *kabuki*, low ranking playwrights or dramaturgs responsible for copying sides, prompting, helping with rehearsals, and cuing performances with signals of the clappers (*hyoshigi*). Robed and hooded in black, they are part of the black costume group of stage functionaries (*kurogo*). Also called *kyogen sakusha* (play writer). See also: *tate zakusha*. (Gunji KABUKI 205, Leiter ENCYCLOPEDIA 216)

kyogen sakusha (Japanese)   Literally: playwright. See: *tate zakusha*.

kyogen za (Japanese)   Literally: *kyogen* seat. The place at the end of the bridge (*hashigakari*) adjoining the *no* stage, where a *kyogen* actor sits during a *no* play when he is not taking part in a scene. (Komparu NOH 130)

kyokugei (Japanese)   Acrobatics and juggling.

kyoranmono (Japanese)   Literally: deranged-person play. In *no*: 1. Broadly, a play appearing fourth on a bill of five plays, even though it may not be about a deranged person. Also called *yonbanmemono* (fourth place play), *zatsumono* (miscellaneous play) or *zatsu no* (miscellaneous *no*) because it may be of a variety of types. (Nippon Gakujutsu JAPANESE xxiv, Shimazaki NOH 24) 2. Narrowly, a play of the fourth group in which the protagonist (*shite*), usually a woman, has been driven insane by grief. (Shimazaki NOH 24-25)

kyu (Japanese)   Literally: fast. 1. The third and fastest section within a unit of a performance according to the *jo ha kyu* aesthetic principle. 2. In *bugaku*, an extended coda. (Wolz BUGAKU 20) 3. In *no*, the last play, a demon (*kiri*) play, in a five-play program. (Nippon Gakujutsu JAPANESE xxvi) 4. The final section of a *no* play featuring a fast dance. (Bowers JAPANESE 9, Inoura HISTORY 122)

kyzykchi (Russian)   19th C traveling performer-clowns in Uzbek, Russia. They used a combination of prepared and improvised material. (Macleod VOLGA 174)

L

L 1. Left—the left half of a proscenium stage. 2. At or toward stage left. All references to L or left are from the performer's point of view.

L1, L1E, L2, L2E, etc. Left first entrance (q.v.), left second entrance, etc.

laban (Philippine) 1. A battle sequence in *comedia*. (Mendoza COMEDIA 65) 2. Music played during such a sequence. (Mendoza in Cruz SHORT 115)

Labanotation See: movement notation.

label A highly ornamented strip used profusely on Elizabethan costumes at the shoulder and waist to create a look of much decorated complexity. (Russell "Shakespearean" 109)

laboratory theatre See: studio theatre.

labor drama Drama dealing with working class issues in a capitalistic society. Often produced by working people.

lace See: lash.

lacon (Thai) A French transliteration of *lakon* used in Thailand.

lacopodium An apparent error for lycopodium. See: podium.

lacquer See: lamp dip.

ladak (Indonesian) A refined but haughty puppet figure in Sundanese *wayang golek*, such as the young Kresna (Krishna). One type of refined (*lemes*) character. See also: *luruh*. (Foley "Sundanese" 34)

ladder In 18th C theatres, a vertical structure behind each wing, to which lights were attached. See also: ladder lights, scene frame. (Brockett HISTORY 340)

ladder dancing In the 18th C and later, entertainment presumably consisting of acrobatic feats involving ladders. (Dennis in Nagler SOURCES 252)

ladder lights Lights on a vertical ladder-like arrangement of pipes; when just upstage of the proscenium, often called a proscenium ladder or proscenium lights. The ladder to which the lights are attached is called in the U.S. a light ladder, in Britain a ladder. (Downs THEATRE II 1135, Fay GLOSSARY 23, Bowman/Ball THEATRE)

ladder of clouds   A vertical chain of scenic units painted to represent clouds, individually controlled so that each could be pulled up or down. (Visser in Hume LONDON 102)

lady   Especially in the past, walking lady: a player of minor female roles.

Lady Macbeth   A nickname for a tragic actress. (Berrey/Van den Bark SLANG 572)

lagor (Thai)   A spelling of *lakon* rarely seen today, but used by King Rama VI in 1911. (Vajiravudh in Rutnin SIAMESE 7)

lagor talok (Thai)   A comic dance-drama performed by a company of actors and actresses. (Vajiravudh in Rutnin SIAMESE 8)

lagu (Indonesian, Malaysian)   Literally: song. The generic term for *wayang* instrumental melodies in Malaysia and West Java (Sunda). For Malaysian *wayang siam*, Sweeney lists twenty-five standard melodies and their appropriate use (RAMAYANA 57-58, 62). In Sundanese *wayang golek*, the terms *lagu gede* (large tune), *lagu sedang* (medium tune), and *lagu leutik* (small tune) indicate length and hence appropriate theatrical use. *Lagu perang* is a battle melody, *lagu jalan* is travelling music. See also: *gending*. (Foley "Sundanese" 144, 150)

lah-de-dah show   A musical.

lahunqiang, la hun ch'iang (Chinese)   Literally: soul-pulling tunes. Until 1949, the collective name for three closely related forms of music drama (*xiqu*) in east central China: *liuqinxi*, *huaihaixi*, and *sizhouxi*.

laid an egg   See: lay an egg.

laisse-tout-faire (French)   A 17th-18th C apron, elevated into a fashion accessory of gold or silver lace, without a bib. (Boucher FASHION)

lake liner   Crimson makeup pigment used to draw age lines.

lakhon (Thai)   See: *lakon*.

lakhorn (Thai)   See: *lakon*.

lakhorn phut (Thai)   See: *lakon pud*.

lakon (Indonesian, Khmer, Malaysian, Thai)   1. In Indonesia and Malaysia, a generic term for a classical play, scripted or in scenario or narrative form. See: *pakem, cerita, lampahan*. (Holt ART 136; Foley "Sundanese" 110; Brandon THRONES 10, 33-34; Sweeney RAMAYANA 54) 2. The relation of a play to its epic or chronicle source, indicated by combining *lakon* with modifiers. Javanese *lakon pokok* (trunk play) is a play based closely on an epic source. Also called *lakon dapur, lakon jejer, lakon lajer, lakon lugu*, and in Sundanese, *lakon galur*. In contrast, a wholly or partially invented play in Java is *lakon carangan* or *lakon tjarangan* (branch play), and in Sunda *lakon karangan* (created play). Also called *lakon sempalan* (detached play). (Holt ART 138, Foley "Sundanese" 108, Brandon THRONES 13-14) 3. In Thailand, the generic term for unmasked classical dance plays in which songs sung by a seated chorus play an integral part, as distinct from masked *khon*. In this meaning, an abbreviation for *lakon ram* dance-drama. Also spelled *lakhon, lakhorn, lokhon*. See also: *lakon pud*. (Yupho KHON 75, Vajiravudh in Rutnin SIAMESE 7-8) 4. For Khmer usage see *lokhon bassac, lokhon kbach boran, lokhon khol*.

lakon bassac (Khmer)   See: *lokhon bassac*.

lakon chatri (Thai)   See: *lakon jatri*.

lakon dukdamban (Thai)   Literally: ancient *lakon*. A type of classical dance-drama developed from *lakon fai nai* in the 19th C. Male actor-dancers sing and speak lines. There is no off-stage chorus, nor are there elaborate descriptive passages as in *lakon fai nai*.

lakon fai nai (Thai)   Literally: inner court *lakon*. A dance-drama, originally performed by the women of a king's or prince's court and hence a drama 'inside' the palace. Plays are based on the *Inao* (*Panji*) and *Ramakien* stories and feature graceful dance and singing appropriate to female performers. Accompanied by *pi phat* music and a singing chorus. Often abbreviated *lakon nai* (inner *lakon*). Also called *lakon phuying*. (Yupho KHON 75, 231; Rutnin "Development" 6)

lakon jatri (Thai)   Literally: shaman's play. In southern Thailand, a professional dance-drama based on the legend of Manora, a half-bird, half-human princess. In the 20th C, it is performed by either men or women, performers of both sexes being credited with shamanic powers of healing and exorcism. (Ginsberg in Rutnin SIAMESE 64-69, Brandon SOUTHEAST 328) In central Thailand it has absorbed elements of *lakon nok*. Also called *manora jatri, manora, lakon nora*, or simply *nora*, after the heroine's name. Abbreviated *jatri*. Also spelled *lakhon chatri*. See also: *nora*.

lakon kawl (Khmer)   See: *lokhon khol*.

lakon kbach boran (Khmer)   See: *lokhon kbach boran*.

lakon lek (Thai)   A production using both rod and string puppets. See also: *hun*.

lakon luang (Thai)   Literally: court *lakon*. A troupe of female palace dancers formed by the king in the 19th C. They performed primarily in *lakon fai nai* style. (Rutnin "Development" 6)

lakon nai (Thai)   See: *lakon fai nai*.

lakon nok (Thai)   Literally: outside drama. A commercial, urban style of play and performance that emphasizes dialogue scenes, action, and comedy. A performance will include some classical dance and *pi phat* music as well. Plays are based on tales of Buddha's birth (*jataka*), local history, and legend. The term was used as early as the 17th C. Also spelled *lakhon nok*. (Ingersoll in Rama SANG 24-25; Yupho KHON 93, 231; Brandon SOUTHEAST 349)

lakon nora (Thai)   See: *lakon jatri*.

lakon phanthang (Thai)   Literally: drama with one thousand directions. A modified dance-drama that deviated from the rigid rules and repetitive plots of *lakon nok*. Stories are drawn from historical legends, and foreign characters use Thai stereotypes of the character's national costume, dance, and music. (Yupho KHON 75)

lakon phleng (Thai)   Literally: song drama. An operatic play accompanied by a Western musical ensemble. Developed in the 1930s. Also spelled *lakon pleng*.

lakon phuying (Thai)   See: *lakon fai nai*.

lakon pleng (Thai)   See: *lakon phleng*.

lakon pud (Thai)   Spoken drama, introduced to Thailand c. 1879 from the West. Also spelled *lakhorn phut*. (Yupho KHON 75)

lakon ram (Thai)   Literally: dance play. The generic term for classical dance plays. (Rutnin "Development" 8) Categories of songs, dances, and music in *lakon ram* are in Virulrak "Likay" 170-175, 179-188. See: *lakon*.

lalita (Sanskrit)   1. In classical Indian dramaturgy, a light-hearted or gay hero (*nayaka*), usually a king. (Keith SANSKRIT 305) 2. A type of folk drama of Maharashtra state, west India. (Hein MIRACLE 2)

lambrequin   See: cointise.

lam luong, lam mu (Lao)   See: *mohlam luong*.

lamp   1. A light-producing element such as a glass or quartz envelope (bulb), its contents, and its base. The incandescent lamp, including the tungsten-halogen version, remains the chief light source in the theatre. (Such alternate names as bulb, globe, light globe, and simple 'light' are lay terms.) Other types of lamps include gaseous discharge lamps and short-arc lamps. The gaseous discharge lamp (also called a gas discharge lamp or discharge lamp), though not called an incandescent lamp, produces light on similar principles: electric current causes a gas (argon, sodium, or many others) to glow. The short-arc lamp is a specialized version of the gaseous discharge lamp which produces a highly concentrated light source used in certain projection applications. See also: incandescent lamp, short-arc lamp, tungsten-halogen lamp. 2. As a verb, to provide a spotlight or other lighting instrument with a lamp. 3. Sometimes, a lighting instrument and its light source. The British often use lantern for this meaning. (Bellman SCENE 309, 311, fig. 303; Wehlburg GLOSSARY; Bowman MODERN)

lampadion (Greek)   According to Pollux, one of the masks for the character of a courtesan. The *lampadion* represents the youngest of the courtesans, and perhaps the one who is ultimately discovered to be of noble birth and hence is not a courtesan. The word means 'little torch,' for the mask's coiffure: the hair-ends come to a point resembling a torch. (Bieber HISTORY 98, fig. 366; Nicoll DEVELOPMENT 36-37)

lampahan (Indonesian)   1. In Bali, a play. "Many *dalang* specialize in either one or the other group of *lampahan*." See: *lakon*. (McPhee in Belo TRADI-TIONAL 150) 2. In Java, the generic term for basic walking and sitting move-ments of *wayang kulit* shadow puppets. It is one type of movement technique (*sabetan*). (Brandon THRONES 63) Long describes in detail: *lampah dhodhak* (squatting walk), *lampah jogetan* (dancing walk), *lampah lembehan* (swinging-arm walk), *lampah mboten lembehan* (walking without swinging arms), *lampah njepengiwiron* (joined hands walk) in JAVANESE 49-55, 71.

lamp base   The metal bottom of a lamp. The base—to which the term is usually reduced—fastens into a socket (technically, a receptacle) in a lighting instrument. The base sizes most frequent in the theatre are the medium and the mogul (large); less common is the smaller candelabra. The principal base types in the theatre are the prefocus base and the bipost base. Hence, such combinations as large prefocus (Britain), mogul prefocus (U.S.), etc. For continuous glass tube types, the terms single end and double end are current. (Bellman LIGHTING 21, 25, figs. 2-2, 2-3b; Bentham ART 77; Corry LIGHTING pl. I)

lamp chamber   In a spotlight, an occasional phrase for the space surrounding the lamp.

lamp check   See: checkout.

lamp cord   See: zip cord.

lamp data   The characteristics of a lamp, such as bulb shape and size, base type and size, filament type, wattage, and rated voltage. Such data often appear in stage lighting catalogues. (Bowman MODERN)

lamp dip   A lacquer used in coloring low wattage lamps such as those used in some striplights. The lamp—vacuum (B), and not above 50 watts—is dipped briefly into the colored lacquer and then lit to dry the lacquer. A number of colors are available and they can be mixed. Lamp dip is also sometimes used for painting projection slides. Sometimes called in the U.S. lacquer, colored lacquer, light dip, theatrical lamp dip, colored lamp dip, dip, stage dip. British: dope. (Bellman SCENOGRAPHY, Wehlburg GLOSSARY, Bax MANAGE-MENT)

lamp down   To replace a lamp with one of lower wattage.

lamp glass   See: chimney.

lampholder   The socket in a lighting instrument. In Britain, often hyphenated. (Bowman MODERN, Rae/Southern INTERNATIONAL)

lamp housing   See: housing.

lampiste (French)   A 19th C lighting technician. (Moynet FRENCH 84)

lamp man, lampman   Especially in the professional theatre, any member of the lighting crew. The term derives from the 18th C use of oil lamps. See also: candle man. (Rees GAS 7, Berrey/Van den Bark SLANG 576)

lamps   In 18th C theatres, footlights, though the term seems also to have been used for lights behind wings. (Hogan LONDON lvi)

lamp schedule   A listing of lamps to be used in a production. Such a schedule contains considerable lamp data—wattage, base type and size, filament type, burning position, etc. See also: lamp data.

land a spot   To be engaged to perform.

land of make-believe   The world of the theatre.

landrine   A Louis XIII calf-high boot with a widely flared top of soft fabric which could be folded up for riding. Also called a *lazarine* (French). (Boucher FASHION)

landscape   A drop painted with an exterior vista.

Landschaft (German)   A painted scene showing a landscape.

land the nod   To be engaged to perform.

landtschap   A variant Elizabethan spelling of landscape (in a stage setting). (Campbell SCENES 166)

langak (Indonesian)   The high, upturned gaze of giants and "gummed" (*gusen*) characters, and some of the larger, muscular puppets in Javanese *wayang kulit*. The gaze usually denotes a character who is somewhat scatter-brained. (Long JAVANESE 70)

langen driya (Indonesian)   Literally: entertainment of the heart. An elegant court dance-opera, created in central Java in the 19th C. Plays were based on *Damar Wulan* stories, and dialogue in *tembang* lyrics was sung. (Holt ART 128) Later dance-opera forms, *langen asmara* (entertainment of love), *langen pranasmara* (entertainment of the heart and love), and *langen mandra wanara* (entertainment of beautiful apes) dramatized *Menak*, *Panji*, and *Ramayana* stories respectively. (Soedarsono DANCES 44-46)

lang rong (Thai)   See: *nai rong*.

lanjapan (Indonesian)   See: *lanyap*.

lantern   1. In Britain, a light source in a housing. The term is equivalent to U.S. lighting instrument or fixture, as well as illuminating engineers' luminaire. Britain often uses lantern as U.S. would use light: spot lantern is spotlight, flood lantern is floodlight, etc. 2. Especially in the past, short for magic lantern. 3. See: smoke hatch. (Bentham ART 310-311; Bax MANAGEMENT 184, 186-187, figs. 45-51; Bowman/Ball THEATRE)

lantern light   See: smoke hatch.

lantern slide   1. A glass slide used in a magic lantern. 2. Rarely, a glass slide used in any projection device. (Bowman/Ball THEATRE)

lanyap (Indonesian)   1. In Javanese *wayang*, a straightforward gaze, allowing direct eye contact. 2. A small, refined *wayang* puppet with a *lanyap* gaze and an aggressive personality. (Long JAVANESE 75-86) Also called *lanyapan* or *lanjapan*. (Brandon THRONES 49) See also: *ladak*. (Foley "Sundanese" 32)

lao (Vietnamese)   The old man role in Vietnamese classical theatre. (Pham-Duy MUSICS 124)

laodan, lao tan (Chinese)   Old female role. A dignified, elderly female role which features song (*chang*), speech (*nian*), and dance-acting (*zuo*) skills. A major subcategory of the female role (*dan*) in many forms of music-drama (*xiqu*). See also: *dan*. (Dolby HISTORY 60, 105, 180; Scott CLASSICAL 32, 74)

laolao, lao lao (Chinese)   Literally: mumble-mumble. A local name given to the performance of *kunqu* and *huiju* popular in Fujian Province in the 18th and 19th C, presumably because they were not in the local dialect and were therefore difficult to understand. Such performances were absorbed by the developing *minju* drama in the early 20th C. (Dolby HISTORY 225)

laomo, lao mo (Chinese)   An older, supporting male role; a major subcategory of the male role (*mo*) in Yuan *zaju*. (Dolby HISTORY 60)

laosheng, lao sheng (Chinese)   Older male role. A dignified, middle-aged or elderly bearded male role; a major subcategory of the male role (*sheng*) in many forms of music-drama (*xiqu*). The main subdivisions of the older male role in Beijing opera (*jingju*) include civil older male (*wenlaosheng*) and martial older male (*wulaosheng*); in both Beijing opera and *kunqu*, supporting older male roles include the *wai* and the *mo*. Older male roles in these two forms are spoken and sung in the "natural" voice (*dasangzi*). Sometimes also called bearded male role (*xusheng* or *hsü sheng*). (Dolby HISTORY 105, 180; Scott CLASSICAL 31, 66-67)

lao tan (Chinese)   See: *laodan*.

lao tzu (Chinese)   See: *lianhualao*.

laowai, lao wai (Chinese)   See: *wai*.

laozi (Chinese)   See: *lianhualao*.

lap dissolve   A film term occasionally used in theatres in the past for a crossfade in which the first light setting remains on for a time after the second setting is faded in. (1967 Bellman LIGHTING 175)

lappet   1. A 14th C man or woman's sleeve trimming, worn on the *côte-hardie* (French): a velvet, fur, or other contrasting fabric band, fastened above the elbow. (Chalmers CLOTHES 107) 2. A lace or other fabric flap or fold falling down the back or sides of a headdress. (Dreher HATMAKING)

lapse of time curtain   A one- to two-second lowering of the stage curtain to indicate the passage of time in a play. (Granville DICTIONARY) *lapsus memoriae* (Latin)   Literally: lapse of memory. In Britain, to dry up on stage. (Granville DICTIONARY)

large bell   In 18th C theatres, a bell used to imitate a church bell. (Hughes in Hume LONDON 132)

large bills   See: great bills.

large brass plate   See: gas plate.

large prefocus   See: lamp base.

lash   To tighten the joint of two flats by lacing a sash cord over cleats on the inner edges of the stiles. Hence, lash lines, lash cleats, etc. In Britain: to lace with throw lines or cleat lines.

lash cleat   A metal spur extending past the inside edge of the stile of a flat, around which a lash line can be laced to pull the edges of two flats together. Also called a lash line cleat.

lash knot   An easily-untied knot used to bind a lash line to a flat.

lash line   Sash cord attached to a flat near the top and used to lace it to an adjoining flat. In Britain: throw line or cleat line.

lash line cleat   See: lash cleat.

lash line eye   A metal eye attached to the inside of a stile on a flat, near the top, to which a lash line is tied. In Britain: a grummet.

lash line hook   A metal hook attached to a stile, especially when the use of a lash cleat is not feasible.

lash screw   A substitute for a lash or a tie-off cleat: a screw partially embedded in the inside edge of the stile of a flat.

last line   1. See: tag line. 2. A request from a performer for the repetition of a cue line not heard or understood. Short for "give me the last line." See also: "Line please."

lasya (Sanskrit)   The graceful or sensuous style of dance and drama. Often described as feminine, in contrast to masculine (*tandava*) style. (Benegal PANORAMA 56)

latch keeper   See: keeper hook.

latent business   Minor physical action not indicated in the script of a play but created by a performer or director. (Bowman/Ball THEATRE)

laterna magika (Czech)   A type of theatre combining live performers and projected images. Developed by Josef Svoboda and first shown publicly in the late 1950s, the form uses actors, singers, dancers, and musicians along with slide and film projections on several mobile screens. (Burian SVOBODA 80, 83-89, figs. 80-83)

Laterne (German)   Lighting instrument, lighting fixture. See also: instrument. (Bentham ART 310)

latex   A liquid rubber material that sets when exposed to the air. Used in makeup, especially for the creation of false noses, chins, etc., and to make molds for casting. Latex is also used in paints as a binder. (Bellman SCENE)

latter account   See: second account.

lattice   See: private box.

lattice box, lettice box   Especially in 18th C European theatres, a private box separated from other seating areas by a screen or lattice. (Bowman/Ball THEATRE)

lattice track guide   In a counterweight rigging system, a latticed guide in which a counterweight arbor runs.

laugh assignment   A comedy part.

laugh biz, laugh business   A comic routine.

laugh giver, laugh hander, laugh star   A comedian.

laughing comedy   English comedy of the late 18th C: light, amusing, and not sentimental. (Cameron/Gillespie ENJOYMENT)

laugh team   Comic performers, usually working as a pair.

laundry list tunes   In the lyrics of Cole Porter, tunes whose rhymes were essentially lists of people or places comically juxtaposed. (Bordman MUSICAL 522)

laurostatae (Greek)   Literally: men in the alley. In the ancient tragic chorus, the second of the three files of chorus members: since this middle file was least seen, it contained the weakest performers. See also: chorus. (Haigh ATTIC 299-300, fig. 31; Pickard-Cambridge FESTIVALS 241)

lavani (Kannada, Marathi)   A type of theatre song. 1. In *yaksagana*, a ballad, sung to a rustic tune. (Ashton/Christie YAKSAGANA 61, 92) 2. See: *tamasha*.

lavender boy   A chorus boy. (Berrey/Van den Bark SLANG 573)

law of inverse squares, law of squares   See: inverse square law.

lay a bomb, lay an egg, lay an omelet   To fail notably. See also: Brodie.

lay'em in the aisles, lay 'em low, lay 'em out, etc.   To delight an audience.

laying down iron   Tap dancing. (O'Connor Cagney)

lay off   An unemployed performer. Presumably a theatrical coinage from the verb. (Wilmeth LANGUAGE)

layoff lane   In New York City, 47th Street and Broadway, the heart of the performers' world. (Berrey/Van den Bark SLANG 576)

layout   A drawing showing the floor plan of a stage setting or the position of the lighting instruments.

layover   A period on the road when a performer has no engagement.

lay the skids   To spoil another performer's effect. (Berrey/Van den Bark SLANG 587) *lazarine* (French)   See: landrine.

lazzo (Italian)   In *commedia dell'arte*, comic stage business or jests in mime, words, song, or dance. Plural: *lazzi*.

LC   Left center.

LCE   Left center entrance.

LCL   Light center length. The distance from the base of a lamp to the center of its filament. (The measuring point on the base varies with the type of base.) The LCL is crucial because the center of the filament must be on the optical axis of a spotlight—a line from the center of the reflector to the center of the lens system. (Wehlburg GLOSSARY)

LDOP, LDPS   Lower door opposite prompt, lower door prompt side. Found in some 18th C promptbooks to indicate which proscenium door or wing passageway was to be used for an entrance.

lead   1. A principal role in a play. With *the*, the principal role. Also called a lead role or leading role. 2. A performer who plays such roles. Hence, heavy lead, juvenile lead, female lead, leading actor, etc. 3. A cue; a line that leads into another line. (Bowman/Ball THEATRE) 4. The short length of wire, often asbestos-covered, which protrudes from many stage lighting instruments. Such leads, sometimes called asbestos leads or pigtails, ordinarily end in a male connector. Sometimes called lead conductors or lead cable. 5. Cable with a male connector at one end and a female connector at the other. In Britain, 'lead' is cable or wire. Compare: jumper, electric lead. (McCandless "Glossary" 629, Rae/Southern INTERNATIONAL, Goffin LIGHTING 39)

lead block   See: head block.

lead cable, lead conductors   See: lead.

leader   Since the early 19th C, a term for the concertmaster (first violinist) in a British orchestra—the second in command to the conductor.

leader of the band   In 18th and 19th C theatres in Britain and the U.S., the conductor of the orchestra.

leader tape   See: cue tape.

leading business   Leading roles.

leading lady, leading man   1. A performer who plays principal roles. 2. Old terms for shades of makeup used by performers playing those stock roles.

leading strings   1. 17th-18th C long pieces of fabric sewn to the shoulders of small children's garments to enable their elders to hold on to them when they began to walk. Also called *tatas* (French). 2. 18th C vestiges of the 17th-18th C strings worn as dress decorations by young girls until their marriage. (Boucher FASHION)

lead sheet   1. A set of cues to guide a musical director. (Sobel NEW) 2. An outline of a vaudeville song.

leaf   A framed section of a scenery ceiling in two or more parts, as in a two-leaf ceiling.

leak   1. See: light leak. 2. As a verb, to escape, as in to leak light.

leaning rail   In a puppet theatre, a device located along the front of the bridge. The operator can rest on the rail as the puppets are manipulated. (Philpott DICTIONARY)

leap   In dance, a simple locomotor step in which weight is transferred from one foot to another as in a run, but with greater energy and height or distance. (Hayes DANCE 47)

leaptick   1. A mattress on which vaudeville comics could fall. 2. The stuffing used to fatten a vaudeville comic's belly. (Wilmeth LANGUAGE)

learning plays   See: *Lehrstücke*.

learn up   An old phrase meaning to memorize. (Milhous/Hume COKE'S 17)

Leblanged   Formerly in the U.S., said of a production supported by ticket sales through cut-rate agencies in New York City such as (in the early 20th C) Joe Leblang's. Hence, to Leblang. (Bowman/Ball THEATRE)

lecheor (French)   See: minstrel.

leçon (French)   Lesson—the class taken daily by dancers as long as they remain active. (Grant TECHNICAL)

lecture room, lecture hall   Like exhibition room, 18th and 19th C terms for a theatre, used to avoid censorship. Barnum's American Museum in New York in the 1840s had a theatre called a lecture room. (Leavitt MANAGEMENT 13-14)

LED   Light-emitting diode. A tiny battery-powered light recently used in stage areas where there is not enough light for glowtape to be seen. An example is the end of an offstage exit ramp. Also appears as L.E.D. Illustrations in Johnson "LEDs" 35, 38.

left   1. The left half of a proscenium stage. 2. In or toward stage left. All references to L or left are from the performer's point of view.

left center   The area about half way between the center line and the far left side of a proscenium stage, from the performer's point of view. Abbreviation: LC.

left center entrance   In the past, an entrance half way upstage and to the left, from the performer's point of view. Abbreviation: LCE.

left dance   See: *samai*.

left first entrance, left second entrance, etc.   Entrances on the left side of a proscenium stage, from the performer's point of view, numbered from the farthest downstage to the farthest upstage. Abbreviations: L1, L1E, L2, L2E, etc.

left hand   See: LH.

left hand door   See: LHD.

left hand upper entrance   See: LHUE.

left-legged pony   A short chorus girl with little dancing talent.

left second entrance   See: left first entrance.

left stage   The left side of a proscenium stage, from the performer's point of view. More often called stage left.

left theatre   One of three theatrical circles in Russia in the mid-1920s, the others being politically center and right. The leading figure in the left theatre was Vsevelod Meyerhold. (Carter SPIRIT 115)

left upper entrance   The farthest upstage entrance on the left side of a proscenium stage, from the performer's point of view. Abbreviation: LUE.

leg   1. A tall, relatively narrow drape or cloth hanging at the side of the stage, usually paired with another on the opposite side, and matched by a horizontal border. Two legs and a border tend to form a kind of inner proscenium and are modern versions of the older side wings and borders. A typical stage will have at least two sets of legs and borders, backed by a drop which closes off the stage. Also called a leg piece or, in Britain, a leg cloth or tail. 2. A drape or cloth, as above, used to simulate a tree trunk or column. 3. An upright platform support.

legato   In dance, connected, as opposed to staccato (disconnected) movement.

leg bar   In puppetry, part of the string control mechanism used to manipulate a puppet's leg(s). (Philpott DICTIONARY)

leg cloth   The British term for a leg or leg drop. Also called a tail.

leg drop   A drop cut to form a wide inverted U, resembling a pair of legs and a border, but in one piece. In Britain, leg curtain. See also: bogen, leg.

legend   A sign, caption, statement, or screen projection that comments on the action, gives a title to a scene, explains what will happen next, etc. Used especially by Bertolt Brecht and Erwin Piscator.

legit, legitimate, legit man, legit woman   A performer in legitimate drama.

legitimate drama, legitimate theatre   Short form: legit. Usually, plays, as opposed to such other entertainments as vaudeville, pantomime, television, film, opera, etc. Hence, legitimate actor/actress. The term originally helped distinguish the dramatic fare of the patent theatres in England from entertainments at the minor theatres, which usually included music, though now musical theatre entertainments are often considered legitimate theatre. (Bowman/Ball THEATRE)

leg lady   A chorus girl.

legmania   1. A passion for dancing. 2. Used in combination with 'dancer' for a performer with superior acrobatic talent. Also spelled leg mania, called legomania. (Bowman/Ball THEATRE)

leg piece   1. A show featuring women showing off their bodies, as in burlesque and revues. Also called a leg show. In Britain, flesh diversion. 2. A leg or leg drop.

Lehrstücke (German)   Learning plays, plays with a pedagogical intent. Bertolt Brecht's *Lehrstücke* were meant to teach the new Marxist ethic.

(at) leisure   Of actors, unemployed.

Leitmotiv (German)   A signature tune used by composers, usually in operas, to identify a character, idea, or object, as in the music dramas of Richard Wagner. English: leitmotif, leitmotiv.

Leitungsanlage (German)   Wiring, wiring layout. (Fuchs LIGHTING 367)

Lekolite   The registered trade name of Strand-Century for an ellipsoidal reflector spotlight of its manufacture. Perhaps because of the early and widespread use of these products, the trade name has sometimes been used as if it were a synonym for ellipsoidal reflector spotlight. So, too, the frequent shortening, Leko. The name is from Levy and Kook, the creators of the spotlight.

lemes (Indonesian)   Literally: smooth. 1. The generic term for refined puppet figures in Sundanese *wayang golek*. They are divided into two sub-types: modest (*luruh*) and aggressive (*ladak*). (Foley "Sundanese" 32) 2. Refined dance style in Javanese *ludruk*. (Peacock RITES 168)

lemon stand   An unprofitable theatrical engagement.

Lenaea   The lesser of the Athenian festivals important to drama, held in January. It is almost certain that contests in comedy and tragedy were not part of the Lenaea until the middle of the 5th C BC. Comedy was primary, perhaps from the beginning. Very little is known of the rites or the early content of the festivals. The source of the term was long thought to be its presumed connection with the wine press, *lenos* (Greek). The more recent view derives the term from Greek *lenai*, maenads. Pickard-Cambridge views the source of the word as unproved. Also appears as *Lenaia* and Lenaean festival. (Pickard-Cambridge FESTIVALS 29-42)

length   1. A page of a performer's lines (usually 42 lines maximum); also called a side. The size of a role was determined by the number of lengths required: "twenty lengths, a part very considerable . . ." (Wilkinson WANDERING I 174) 2. In Britain, a short row of low wattage lamps: striplights in a casing. In major uses, strips have been hung behind such openings as doors or windows to light backings (hence, hanging length, proscenium length). Lengths go back at least to 19th C gas lights. The word was then also used occasionally for the pieces of flexible tubing which carried gas to the jets; such lengths varied from a foot or two to six feet or more. 3. A batten used on the stage floor. Also called a ground batten. (Bentham ART; Bax MANAGEMENT 186; Rees GAS 40, 200, 204-205; Bowman/Ball THEATRE; Ridge/Aldred LIGHTING 2)

lengthwise battens   The outside members that extend the full length of a roll or book ceiling. (Gillette/Gillette SCENERY) *leng trot* (Khmer)   A ceremonial dance used to encourage the coming of the monsoon rains. It portrays hunters and prey through a combination of folk and classical dance steps and is accompanied by a chorus. (Steinberg CAMBODIA 265)

lens   In the early decades of this century, a spotlight—i.e., a lighting instrument with a lens. Hence, baby lens, 25-amp. lens, etc. (Hartmann LIGHTING 68)

lens box   Early in the 20th C, a term occasionally used for a spotlight housing. (Hartmann LIGHTING 23)

lens holder   Any device for holding a lens in place in a lighting instrument.

lens hood   An occasional term, now uncommon, for a spotlight.

lens lamp   A term sometimes used in the past for a spotlight. (Hartmann LIGHTING 23)

lensless projector   See: Linnebach projector.

lens light   An occasional term for a spotlight.

lens projection   An image produced by a lens projector. (Burris-Meyer/Cole THEATRES 191)

lens projector   A projector, usually for scenic slides, typically with condensing and objective lenses, a relatively high wattage lamp, and appropriate cooling arrangements. Often called simply a projector, but see that entry. (Sellman/Lessley ESSENTIALS)

lens spot   In Britain, a high-wattage plano-convex spotlight. See also: focus lamp. (Bentham ART 311-312)

lens unit   A stage lighting fixture with a lens; a spotlight. (Bowman/Ball THEATRE)

lenyap (Indonesian)   See: *luruh*.

leotard   A thin, skin-tight garment worn by dancers and acrobats, named for the inventor of the flying trapeze act, Jules Leotard. (Wilmeth LANGUAGE)

lerog (Indonesian)   See: *ludruk*.

Les Girls   The chorus. (Berrey/Van den Bark SLANG 573)

lesser Dionysia   See: Rural Dionysia.

lesson   Formerly, a set of pieces often composed for a single instrument, such as a harpsichord, and used occasionally in plays or as an entr'acte entertainment. The meaning goes back at least to Elizabethan times.

let in   To lower a flown batten, scenic piece, drop, etc.

lets (Hebrew)   See: *nar*.

letter perfect   Said of a performer who knows his or her lines exactly. In Britain, dead letter perfect or up in the part.

levées (French)   Spaces under a 19th C stage floor (offstage right and left) into which disappeared each half of a trap opened at the middle of the stage, by sliding the halves under the floor. *Levées* enabled the stage floor to open almost to its entire width. See also: *tiroir*. (Moynet FRENCH 28)

level   1. In acting, volume, loudness. 2. A platform. 3. Height, especially of the stage floor, from which most other heights are measured. 4. The strength of a sound signal. 5. The intensity of a light setting.

level guide   A short strip of wood (one of several) screwed into a ceiling batten to keep it in trim when two single-leaf ceilings are flown.

level speaking   The speaking quality used in the 18th C for less important passages in a play (as opposed to the more vehement style used for high points). (Brockett HISTORY 347)

lévite, gown à la   See: gown à la lévite.

leyak (Indonesian)   In Bali, the role of a "hobgoblin" (de Zoete/Spies DANCE 336), a "spook," a "vampire-spirit" (Holt ART 183, 348) in a dance or shadow play. The character is usually in the retinue of the widow-witch (*rangda*). (McPhee in Belo TRADITIONAL 182)

LH   Left hand, an old term for stage left.

LHD   Left hand door.

LHUE   Left hand upper entrance.

liaison des scènes (French)   1. In playwriting, seamless continuity of ideas. 2. Act and scene divisions, especially in French neo-classic theatre, stressing continuous action within acts of a play, with a new scene number each time a character enters or exits. Hence, a French scene. (Krows PLAYWRITING 150)

lian, lien (Chinese)   A couplet, the basic structural unit for song lyrics in Beijing opera (*jingju*) and many other forms of music-drama (*xiqu*). Each couplet consists of two lines of equal length: a first line (*shangju* or *shang chü*) and a second line (*xiaju* or *hsia chü*). The standard line length of seven or ten written characters may be varied by adding 'padding written characters' (*chenzi*). (Wichmann "Aural" 91-100)

liangbatou (Chinese)   See: *qizhuangtou*.

liang hsiang (Chinese)   See: *liangxiang*.

lianglang, liang lang (Chinese)   See: *sanzuo*.

liang pa t'ou (Chinese)   See: *qizhuangtou*.

liangxiang, liang hsiang (Chinese)   Literally: bright appearance. In music-drama (*xiqu*), a brief pause in which, through movement into a statue-like posture, the essence of a character's nature and state of being is concentrated and displayed. It may be performed after a section of movement (*dongzuo*) has been completed, upon entrance (*shangchang*), or just before an exit (*xiachang*) by a single performer, or by two or more simultaneously.

lianhualao, lien hua lao (Chinese)   Literally: lotus flower falling. The generic name for a number of forms of storytelling (*quyi*) popular throughout China which began developing c. 11th C; most combine regional dialects with folk songs. Originally such forms had only one or two singers who accompanied themselves with a bamboo clapper; a number of contemporary forms now have stringed instrument accompaniment as well. Also called lotus flower music (*lianhuayue* or *lien hua yüeh*), and *laozi* or *lao tzu*; sometimes pronounced and romanized *lianhualuo* or *lien hua lo*. (Dolby HISTORY 163-164, Foreign FOLK 38-40)

lianhualuo, lianhuayue (Chinese)   See: *lianhualao*.

lianpu, lien p'u (Chinese)   Literally: face chart. Full-face makeup in bright colors and non-realistic designs worn by performers of the painted-face role (*jing*) in Beijing opera (*jingju*) and many other forms of music-drama (*xiqu*). Each color and type of design used is indicative of character; the principles of *lianpu* makeup and several specific designs are described in Halson PEKING 39-41 and Scott CLASSICAL 167-170.

lianquti, lien ch'ü t'i (Chinese)   Literally: joined song system. A type of musical structure characterized by a large number of specific, fixed-melodies (*qupai*) to which lyrics are written for individual plays. It is one of the major types of musical structure in music-drama (*xiqu*), and is used in the *kunshanqiang* and *gaoqiang* musical systems (*shengqiang xitong*). See also: *banqiangti*. (Wichmann "Aural" 273)

(at) liberty   Of actors, unemployed.

liberty cap   See: Phrygian bonnet.

library   In Britain, a ticket agency, a booking office. (Bowman/Ball THEATRE)

librettist   The author of the text of an opera or other musical theatre piece, the text itself being the libretto.

libretto (Italian), **libretto**   Literally: small book. The text of an extended musical work, such as an opera.

license   In 17th and 18th C England, permission granted by the Lord Chamberlain to operate a theatre. A license was temporary (as opposed to a patent), but by the end of the 18th C a license and patent were considered the same. (Hogan LONDON cxxviii)

licensee   In the 19th and early 20th C in Britain, the owner of a theatre license. He was previously called a proprietor, but that term came to mean the owner of a theatre.

lid   1. See: tip. 2. Slang for hat.

lie down to rest   Of a production, to fail.

lien (Chinese)   See: *lian*.

lien ch'ü t'i (Chinese)   See: *lianquti*.

lienco (Spanish)   A canvas hanging separating the dressing room from the stage in a *corral* theatre. (Rennert SPANISH 93)

lien hua lao, lien hua lo, lien hua yüeh (Chinese)   See: *lianhualao*.

lien p'u (Chinese)   See: *lianpu*.

lieu, liu (French)   A locale or *mansion* in a medieval production. Plural *lieux*. (Wickham EARLY I 158)

lieux communes (French)   See: *robe generiche*.

lift   1. An elevator, such as an orchestra lift or, in Britain, a bridge or section of the stage that can be raised or lowered. 2. In playwriting, to plagiarize. 3. To raise flown equipment, such as a curtain, scenery, or draperies. 4. In acting, to put more spirit into one's part. Hence, lift it. 5. A movement used in partnering work when one or more dancers (usually males) support other dancers (usually females) in the air.

lifting jack   See: lift jack.

lifting stage   In the early 20th C, a combination of a sliding wagon stage and an elevator stage, according to Krows. The stage is lowered and slid off to one side, making way for another stage, already containing a setting, to be slid on from the opposite side and then raised into position. But Bowman and Ball call a lifting stage a simple elevator stage. (Krows AMERICA 189, Bowman/ Ball THEATRE)

lift jack   A wooden lever hinged to the bottom of a piece of scenery; on its bottom surface, near the scenery, is attached a caster. By depressing the lever an inch or so and locking it into position, the scenery is raised and can be rolled on the caster. Also called a caster jack, lifting jack, or jack roller. Lounsbury has an illustration. (Lounsbury THEATRE 131-132)

lift stage   See: elevator stage, lifting stage.

ligeh lao (Lao)   See: *mohlam luong*.

light and shade   The nuances of modulation, inflection, and intonation in a performer's reading of a part.

light area   Especially in area lighting, one of a specific number of stage spaces which is, or is to be, lit. See also: area lighting. (Dean/Carra FUNDA- MENTALS 373)

light baffle   See: baffle.

light batten   A pipe (or, in some old theatres, a length of wood) to which lights are attached. Lighting batten is the usual British term.

light board   A control board for stage lighting. Usually shortened to board.

light boom   See: boomerang.

light booth   A room or enclosure which usually provides a clear view of the stage and control of some or all of the stage lighting. Especially in Britain, often called a lighting booth or box. Occasionally called a light(ing) control booth. The room usually serves also for sound control and sometimes stage management. Often shortened to booth.

light border   Occasionally, a border which masks lights. (Bowman/Ball THEATRE)

light box, light-box   1. An occasional term for the housing of a light, especially of a spotlight. (Bowman/Ball THEATRE) 2. See: light booth.

light bridge   A flying catwalk just behind the main curtain, usually operated by an electric winch. Lighting units are attached to the bridge. (Gillette/Gillette SCENERY)

light center length   See: LCL.

light check   In Britain, a cue at which lights are dimmed. See also: check. (Baker THEATRECRAFT)

light comedian   A comic actor whose forte is wit rather than physical business.

light comedy   A play with pleasant characters and situations, amusing dialogue, but no depth of feeling or three-dimensional characterization. (O'Hara/ Bro INVITATION)

light console   See: console.

light control board   See: control board.

light control booth   See: light booth.

light cue   1. A signal to begin a planned change in the lighting. 2. The change itself. (Bowman/Ball THEATRE)

light cue sheet   A sequential list of changes in the stage lighting. Such a listing, often chart-like, notes when each change occurs, what it consists of, and any other necessary information. Often reduced to cue-sheet, sometimes called a lighting cue sheet.

light curtain   1. Especially in U.S. open-air theatres, lights in front of the stage directed toward the audience. The lights are intended to have the effect of a closed curtain. The British term is blinder. See also: Luxauleator. (Rubin/ Watson LIGHTING 68, Rae/Southern INTERNATIONAL 22) 2. A bank of narrow-angle, very high-intensity lamps or fixtures arranged in a line. They illuminate dust in the air and give the appearance of a substantial wall. Jules Fisher's design for *Pippin* is an example.

light designer   In the U.S., the person in charge of the design and execution of the lights for a production. The term dates from the late 1930s, before which time a separate designer of lighting was not so designated, even when there was such a person. Theatre programs often use the phrase "lighting by," and lighting designer also occurs. Sometimes called the lighting director. (Bowman MODERN, Sellman/Lessley ESSENTIALS 146, 148)

light dip   See: lamp dip.

light distribution   See: distribution.

lighten it   1. To make a speech less emphatic. (Cartmell HANDBOOK 100) 2. To make a speech brighter.

lighter's room   Evidently a room used by the lampman in 18th C theatres. (Hogan LONDON clx)

light ground row   Striplights placed on the stage floor to illuminate a sky drop, cyclorama, or other scenic unit.

lighting batten   Primarily in Britain, a pipe batten used for lighting. Light batten is the same. (Purdom PRODUCING, Bowman/Ball THEATRE)

lighting booth, lighting box   See: light booth.

lighting bridge   See: bridge.

lighting by   See: light designer.

lighting by chorus   Bentham's term for full-stage lighting which often uses two hundred spotlights on battens above the acting area, booms at the sides of the stage, and backlights which include backdrops lit as transparencies. The spotlights "constitute a great choir sometimes all shining together in unison and, at other times, in lesser combinations as altos, basses, or whatever." Hence, spotlight chorus. (Bentham ART 262-263, fig. 148)

lighting control booth   See: light booth.

lighting crew   See: lights.

lighting cue sheet   See: light cue sheet.

lighting designer, lighting director   See: light designer.

lighting flies   In Britain, a gallery used for lighting a portion of the visible stage. Such galleries are ordinarily in a wing, and at right angles to the proscenium wall. (Corry PLANNING 99)

lighting instrument   A device which gives light, such as a spotlight, flood-light, or striplight. Commonly called simply an instrument, sometimes a fixture (q.v.), occasionally a luminaire (Illuminating Engineering Society term). Bentham notes that the term is not used in Britain. (Selden/Sellman SCENERY 228, 370; Bentham ART 310)

lighting layout, lighting plot   See: light plot.

lighting rehearsal   See: light rehearsal.

lighting unit   A spotlight, floodlight, or other lighting instrument. Sometimes shortened to unit.

light juvenile   An old term for a shade of makeup used by actors playing youthful characters. An alternate shade was called dark juvenile.

light ladder   See: ladder lights.

light layout   See: light plot.

light leak   A sliver or point of unwanted light, usually showing through scenery.

light man   Especially in the past, one who works on stage lighting. (Bowman/ Ball THEATRE)

lightning box   An occasional term for a box-like device intended to produce the effect of lightning. The essential elements are a high wattage lamp in a box whose front can be opened and shut rapidly, thus producing the effect of lightning on the area which the light hits. (Rose EFFECTS 26-28, fig. 20)

lightning calls   Rapid curtain calls taken by a greedy performer.

lightning change artist   See: quick-change artist.

lightning effect   1. The appearance of lightning on part or all of a setting. 2. Any device which produces such an effect. (Bowman/Ball THEATRE, Lounsbury THEATRE)

lightning lantern   See: lightning-striker.

lightning sticks, electric sticks   Primarily in Britain, an electrical device consisting of a pair of carbon rods with wooden handles. When the rods are briefly brought together, a flash results. A 19th C creation, the sticks have been used in Britain in the 20th C. (Fay GLOSSARY, Melvill THEATRECRAFT, Bowman/Ball THEATRE)

lightning-striker   A remotely controlled electro-magnetic device which uses a carbon arc to produce a flash. Sometimes called a lightning lantern. (Bowman/ Ball THEATRE)

light opera   Comic, usually romantic, opera.

light operator   Especially in the professional theatre, the person in charge of the lighting system in a theatre. (Bowman/Ball THEATRE)

light pan   In 19th C Britain, a hand-held contrivance used in stage fires. This evidently resembled a dust pan with metal sides; the fire burned in a small cylinder within the pan. (Rees GAS 151)

light pipe   See: pipe batten.

light pit   1. Any opening in the stage floor from which a lighting instrument can be directed toward acting or scenic areas. 2. Especially in Britain, the cyclorama light pit. (McCandless "Glossary" 630, Bax MANAGEMENT 186)

light plot   Primarily in the U.S., a complete plan for the lighting of a production. A typical plot shows the floor plan of each setting, together with the kind, wattage, placement, and color of each lighting instrument and the area of the stage it strikes. Stage electricians are likely to call it simply the plot, or, in the professional theatre, electrician's plot. Especially in the U.S., light layout and lighting layout are alternatives. Lighting plot, the usual British term, has come into U.S. use. (Bellman LIGHTING 375-394, figs. 18-1b, c, d; Sellman/ Lessley ESSENTIALS 157-177, figs. 9.3-5, 9.7-9; Wehlburg GLOSSARY)

light pocket   See: dead spot.

light portal   A vertical slot in the proscenium or the side walls of the auditorium. If the latter, the portals are usually near the front of the auditorium. Sometimes called a portal, port, or sidewall slot. (Lounsbury THEATRE 119, Wehlburg GLOSSARY)

light pylon   A towerlike structure sometimes used for mounting lights in outdoor theatres. See also: light tower. (Rubin/Watson LIGHTING 70)

light rain machine   A rotating drum with wire-mesh sides containing stiff paper fragments; paddles within the drum stir up the paper when the drum is rotated, simulating the sound of light rain. (Collison SOUND 100)

light rehearsal   In the U.S., a rehearsal of light changes and cues, sometimes without actors. Called a lighting rehearsal in Britain. (Rae/Southern INTERNATIONAL)

light relief   See: comic relief.

light run through   In Britain, a rehearsal for words only, with no emphasis on acting or movement. In the U.S., line rehearsal. (Granville DICTIONARY)

lights   Especially in academic and other non-professional theatres in the U.S., the lighting crew, the lighting, or a crew member.

"Lights!"   Especially in non-professional theatres in the U.S., a call to the lighting crew or any member thereof.

light script   A script (or the necessary parts thereof) in which light cues are recorded. (Bowman MODERN)

light slot   In some modern theatres, a long opening in the auditorium ceiling, or in a side wall, through which spotlights may be directed toward the stage. Also called a ceiling slot or sidewall slot.

light stand, stand   A support for stage lights set up mainly in the wings, but sometimes elsewhere backstage. The usual stand consists of a heavy round iron base in the center of which is a pipe four or five feet high. Inside the pipe is an iron rod which can be fixed at any desired height up to seven or eight feet. A spotlight or floodlight is normally fastened to a fitting at the top of the inner pipe. Also called, mainly in the U.S., an extension pipe stand, light tree, pipe stand, portable extension pipe stand, standard, or telescopic pipe stand. 'Stand' is the usual term among lighting personnel. In Britain: floor stand, pillar stand (19th C). Compare: base. (Sellman/Lessley ESSENTIALS, Bowman/Ball THEATRE)

light-tight   Showing no light, permitting no light to be seen. The term is used of the housings of some lighting instruments and sometimes of scenic areas, such as the place where two flats meet.

light tormentor   Especially in the past, an occasional term for a tormentor so constructed that lights can be mounted on its upstage side, usually on a built-in vertical pipe.

light tower   A vertical pipe or structure to which stage lights, usually spot-lights, are attached. The term is used of a simple pipe, often with horizontal arms, as well as of a tower-like metal structure, often on casters and with a built-in ladder and working platform. The vertical pipe with arms is sometimes called a tree or light tree; but these terms are occasionally applied to any light tower. Simple 'tower' is also used, especially among lighting personnel. Other terms are boomerang and its shortening, boom. (Lounsbury THEATRE, Wehlburg GLOSSARY, Bowman/Ball THEATRE)

light tree   A light tower. The term is especially appropriate for towers with horizontal arms, and is often restricted to such towers. See: light tower. (Wehlburg GLOSSARY, Lounsbury THEATRE 96)

light up   The point where the lights come on in a brief burlesque scene that begins in the dark and is suddenly lighted, usually for the punch line. (Wilmeth LANGUAGE)

ligne (French)   Literally: line. The outline of a ballet dancer while dancing. The line is made out of head, body, legs, and arms. (Grant TECHNICAL)

lijepan (Indonesian)   See: *luruh*.

likay (Thai)   Popular, commercial 'opera' that utilizes many elements derived from classical dance-drama (*lakon*), including dance, singing, and *pi phat* music. Originated, in part, from Muslim prayer songs (*dikay*, Thai pronunciation *yikay*, hence the term *likay*) of Malay immigrants. In central Thailand often called *yikay*, *yeekay*. Also spelled *like*. (Virulrak "Likay" 26-27, 110, 114, 248; Brandon SOUTHEAST 329)

likay lao (Lao)   See: *mohlam luong*.

like   Especially in Elizabethan plays, dressed or disguised as. As in "Enter Scudmore, like a serving-man. . . ."

like (Thai)   See: *likay*.

lila (Sanskrit)   Literally: play. 1. A play, as in *raslila* (the play of *ras*) or *ramlila* (the play of Rama). (Hawley KRISHNA 315) 2. The second part of a *raslila* performance in which the earthly career of Krishna is enacted through dialogue, song, and sometimes dance. In a given performance one of the hundred or so existing episodes is staged. (Swann "Braj" 21)

Lilliputians   See: stage children.

limbo   Occasionally, a background on stage with no visible detail, usually black or nearly black. (Wehlburg GLOSSARY)

lime   1. Especially in the 19th C, a shortening of limelight. 2. From about 1865 in Britain, a limelight or a carbon arc spotlight. 3. In modern Britain, any lighting unit, but especially a spotlight, and more especially a follow spot directed at center stage. (Bentham ART, Fay GLOSSARY, Bowman/Ball THEATRE)

lime box   See: limelight box.

lime boy   In 19th and early 20th C Britain, a man who operated an arc light from a perch (an off-the-floor platform in the tormentor position). (Melvill THEATRECRAFT)

limelight, lime-light, lime light   1. A brilliant light produced by heating lime to incandescence with an oxygen-hydrogen flame. Lieutenant Thomas Drummond first demonstrated its use in connection with his work as surveyor in November 1825. The light emitted is often described as brilliantly white, but it may have had a faintly greenish cast; the development of color media apparently offset that. The term also meant the lighting instrument. The limelight continued to be used into the 20th C, since the quality of its light was better than that of the carbon electric arc, and it was more brilliant than any early incandescent lamp.

Lenses were used with the light, making it the first spotlight; the earliest recorded theatre use was 1837. Its great disadvantages were that it required two cylinders of compressed gas and the constant attendance of an operator. Cylinders and light were sometimes strapped to the operator, who was then free to direct the light from any position he could reach. Also called a calcium light, Drummond light, calcium lime, calcium, oxy-hydrogen light, oxy-calcium lamp, or Bude light. Sometimes shortened to lime; hence, the 'limes.' Citations include illustrations. (Rees GAS 42-64; Fuchs LIGHTING 42-43, 74; Penzel LIGHTING 56-60; Hartmann LIGHTING 8, 9) 2. In Britain, any bright spotlight, especially one directed down center. 3. By extension, any well-lighted position, especially down center. (Bowman/Ball THEATRE)

limelight bag, gas bag   In the 19th C, a closed sack which held the oxygen or hydrogen used in a limelight. Bags were of rubberized material (though occasionally leather) which, when compressed, forced the gas through a rubber tube. Pressure boards enabled the gas to be fed evenly; the later development of double boards forced the gas out of both bags simultaneously. Also called a bag. (Rees GAS 46-52, figs. 24-29)

limelight box   The housing of a limelight. Until the beginning of the 20th C, the housing was a square wooden box. Also called a lime box. (Rees GAS 61-62, fig. 27)

limelight master   A term used by Rees of Walter Kerr, evidently the most eminent of 19th C limelight men—lighting men, one might say, since they were also sometimes responsible for electric light. (Rees GAS 127-128, 231)

limelight tank   A large cylinder for storing one of the gases used in a limelight. (Rees GAS 61)

limited engagement   Said of a production or a performer advertised for a specific number of performances.

linambay (Philippine)   See: *comedia*.

line   1. Anything used on stage for tying, lashing, hanging, etc. Hence, brail line, fly line, guide line, set of lines, short line, long line, center line, cleat line, lash line, throw line, tracker line, trick line, working line, etc. 2. A speech in a play—a line of dialogue. 3. A performer's specialty. Also called line of business. 4. "Line!" is a request by a performer for a prompt.

linear plot   A plot organized in chronological order, with a carefully articulated sequence of actions, often linked through a pattern of cause and effect. (Hatlen ORIENTATION)

line-bitter   A performer who plays bit parts hoping to be noticed for a leading role. (Berrey/Van den Bark SLANG 572)

line connector   A device which feeds current from a source of electricity. Such a connector has holes rather than pins or hooks. Often called a female connector, female, body, sometimes (imprecisely) female plug or line plug. (Bellman SCENE, Wehlburg GLOSSARY 24)

line cue   A spoken cue.

line grip   See: bulldog.

line of business   The parts in which a performer specializes. Also called line.

line of lamps   In the first half of the 18th C, a term sometimes used for footlights. (Penzel LIGHTING 18)

"Line, please."   A request from a performer for assistance from a prompter. See also: last line.

line plot   See: hanging plot.

line plug   See: line connector.

liner   A makeup pencil used to create wrinkle and other lines on the face.

line rehearsal   A rehearsal of dialogue but not of physical action.

lines   Words spoken by a performer in a play.

line set   See: set of lines.

line side   1. See: live. 2. Especially where cable is joined by connectors, the side electrically nearer the current source. (Bowman MODERN)

lines of sight   See: sight lines.

line tosser   A jokester.

ling (Thai)   A role of a monkey played by a male dancer in masked ballet (*khon*). (Rutnin "Development" 13)

ling jen (Chinese)   See: *lingren*.

linglun, *ling lun* (Chinese)   See: *lingren*.

lingren, *ling jen* (Chinese)   Literally: musician. A performer of *yuanben* and Yuan *zaju*, c. 14th-15th C. Also called bywayman (*luqiren*, abbreviated *luqi* or *lu ch'i*), music official (*yueguan* or *yüeh kuan*), sing-song house player (*hangyuan* or *hang yüan*), and *linglun* or *ling lun*, the name of a mythical music master, Ling Lun.

ling tzu (Chinese)   See: *zhiwei*.

ling tzu sheng (Chinese)   See: *zhiweisheng*.

lingzi (Chinese)   See: *zhiwei*.

lingzisheng (Chinese)   See: *zhiweisheng*.

lining   1. Using a straight edge and a lining brush to paint architectural details on scenery. 2. In makeup, to rim the eyes, continue the eyebrow line, emphasize wrinkles, etc. 3. An inner cloth in a costume to make it easier to put on and to improve its hang. (Sobel NEW)

lining colors   See: shading colors.

lining stick   See: chamois stump.

lining stump   See: artist's stump.

linkman   An attendant at the front of a theatre in Britain in the 19th C (and earlier) who helped patrons from their carriages when they arrived and called for their conveyances when the play was over. The attendant carried a lighted torch or link. Also called a commissionaire. (Fay GLOSSARY)

Linnebach projector, Linnebach lantern   A simple projection device whose essential elements are a concentrated light source such as a spotlight lamp, and a slide or cut-out whose shadow is thrown on a screen. The light source is in a dull black housing; the slide may be painted; and the screen is often a sky drop or cyclorama. The principles are the same as those in which a child holds his fingers in front of a light and casts a shadow on a wall. Adolph Linnebach was technical director of the Munich Opera early in the 20th C when he introduced the shadow projector. Linnebach lantern, the early name, may derive from the British use of 'lantern,' or by analogy to the magic lantern. Other terms: shadow projector, shadow-box projector, shadowgraph projector, scene projector, square law projector, lensless projector, direct beam projector. Curiously, the term Linnebach projector is not used in Germany, where the usual choice is *Schattenbildapparat*, shadow picture machine. (McCandless "Glossary" 635; Bellman SCENE 435)

linnet   See: bird.

Linsenscheinwerfer (German)   A high-wattage plano-convex spotlight. The term is literally 'lens light-thrower.' (Bentham ART 311-312)

linty   In Britain, a kind of goblin blamed for untoward incidents in a theatre. From the Scottish *lintie* (linnet) a bad-luck bird. (Granville DICTIONARY)

lip   1. A strip of thin wood overhanging the vertical edge of a flat so that it covers the join with the adjacent flat. 2. The nose or overhang of a tread on a stair.

liquid dimmer   See: salt water dimmer.

liquid makeup   A water- (sometimes oil-) based foundation or makeup base.

liquid pot dimmer   See: salt water dimmer.

liripipe   The tail of a *chaperon* (French). (Barton COSTUME 157)

lishiju, li shih chü (Chinese)   See: *chuantongju*.

literalism   Naturalism. The principle of making an exact stage replica of a subject. (Gorelik NEW)

literarische piesen (Yiddish)   Literally: literary pieces, literary plays. In the U.S. Yiddish theatre of the early 20th C, serious plays which were thought better or more artistic than the usual sentimental melodrama of popular theatre. (Lifson YIDDISH 339, 484-485)

literary drama   Plays of literary value. Some literary drama of the past was not intended for stage production. Such works are called closet dramas.

literary montage   In the 1920s in Russia, a dramatic form of the propaganda theatre which mixed a variety of texts and visual genres and applied them to the stage. (Gorchakov RUSSIA 144)

literary revue   Since the late 19th C, especially in Europe, short satiric scenes, with songs and dances.

literary theatre   1. Drama that has value as literature. 2. Sometimes, drama that is more literary than theatrical.

literatátnik (Yiddish)   Especially among commercial theatre people, a mildly ironic term for an actor, playwright, or critic fond of literary or intellectual plays. Also called a *literatchnik*. (Sandrow VAGABOND 263, Lifson YIDDISH 339)

litho   See: sheet.

littera canina (Italian)   Literally: dog's letter. In Britain, a performer's trilled ''R'' resembling a dog's growl. (Granville DICTIONARY)

little looking glass   Playwright Jerzy Szaniawski's term for the naturalistic theatre. (Szydtowski POLAND 41)

little Mary   The Mary figure in the medieval Nativity stories told via puppet shows. The word marionette (little Mary) evolved from this close association of puppets with Nativity plays. (Baird PUPPET 67)

little name   Minor performer.

little Russian plays   A term applied to Ukrainian plays at the end of the 19th C. (Macleod VOLGA 50)

little theatre   1. In Britain, a repertory theatre. 2. In the U.S., amateur (usually) theatre in the first half of the 20th C. In both countries, little theatres were normally small operations, but some lasted many years and turned out professional performers, technicians, and playwrights.

little timer   1. See: small timer. 2. A minor-circuit vaudeville theatre.

liturgical drama   Sacred plays drawing upon the Bible for plots and characters. Such plays were widely performed in medieval times (and well into the Renaissance), at first within Roman Catholic churches by members of the clergy but in time, in some places, outside the church, often by townspeople. Various medieval manuscripts call the plays *historia, ludus, miraculum, misterium, officium, ordo, processio, repraesentatio*, and *similitudo*, all Latin.

liu (French)   See: *lieu*.

liu ch'in hsi (Chinese)   See: *liuqinxi*.

liupai, liu p'ai (Chinese)   A school or style of performance in music-drama (*xiqu*); many were developed by master actors and are identified by their surnames. Abbreviated *pai* or *p'ai*. (Scott CLASSICAL 52-53)

liuqinxi, liu ch'in hsi (Chinese)   A form of music-drama (*xiqu*) especially noted for the ornamentation in its female singing; popular in parts of Jiangsu, Shandong, and Anhui Provinces. It uses *banqiangti* musical structure, and is accompanied by the *liuyueqin*. See also: *lahunqiang, sizhouxi*.

liushui, liu shui (Chinese)   See: *liushuiban*.

liushuiban, liu shui pan (Chinese)   Literally: flowing-water meter. A single-beat meter regulated (*shangban*) metrical-type (*banshi*), faster than two-flowing meter (*erliuban*), used in the songs of Beijing opera (*jingju*) for expressing light, relaxed pleasure or excited indignation. It is used in both the *xipi* and *erhuang* modes (*diaoshi*). Abbreviated *liushui*. See also: *banyan*. (Wichmann "Aural" 153-156)

liu tzu hsi (Chinese)   See: *liuzixi*.

liuyeqin, liu yeh ch'in (Chinese)   See: *liuyueqin*.

liuyueqin, liu yüeh ch'in (Chinese)   A four-stringed plucked instrument, similar to but smaller than the lute (*pipa*), used to accompany *liuqinxi*. Also called *liuyeqin* or *liu yeh ch'in*.

liuzixi, liu tzu hsi (Chinese)   A form of music-drama (*xiqu*) popular in Shandong Province and parts of Jiangsu and Henan Provinces which developed out of songs popular in Henan and Shandong, c. 17th C. Its principal musical accompaniment is provided by the three-string lute (*sanxian*), the mouth-organ (*sheng*), and the horizontal bamboo flute (*di*).

live   1. Performed for and in the presence of an audience. Hence, live actor, live theatre, living theatre. 2. Said of a property or scenic unit which will be used again during a performance. Hence, keep alive (Bowman/Ball THEATRE) 3. Containing electric current. See: hot. 4. In an electrical circuit, the wire which carries current to the load. Also called the feed line or line side.

live art   In the early 20th C, acts performed on elevated platforms which were interspersed with inanimate objects in dime museums. These acts could be freaks, exhibitions of strength, magic, monologues, etc. They were performed up to 20 times daily. (Frick/Johnson "Coney" 132)

live-front board   A switchboard with exposed current-carrying parts. The term is historic in aura, if not in use: such boards have long been illegal. Also called an open-front board. (Bellman LIGHTING 171)

live house   An auditorium with a relatively long reverberation time and thus better suited to music than to speech.

live line   See: circuit.

liver-head   A burlesque performer who has trouble learning dialogue or business. (Wilmeth LANGUAGE)

live stage   A stage with scenery.

living curtain   A proscenium opening filled with gorgeously-dressed showgirls, created in the early 20th C by Erté, the Russian-born Parisian designer for the Folies-Bergère. (Leslie ACT 205)

living history play   See: *katsureki geki*.

living light   See: *gestaltendes Licht*.

living marionette   See: bib puppet.

living newspaper   1. A documentary work given at clubs and factories in Russia during the first years of the Revolution to educate socialist citizens. Such works were constructed like a newspaper, treating topics of the day. (Markov SOVIET 139) 2. From the 1930s in the U.S. Federal Theatre Project until about the end of World War II, a stage production conceived in documentary style. These productions frequently resembled motion pictures in their short, rapidly-paced scenes portraying problems of modern life and ways of solving them. Used as a propaganda tool by the U.S. armed forces in World War II, and as an adult education program in Britain in the same period. (Hartnoll COMPANION)

living panoramas   Open-air propaganda performances given by the Communist Party in Russia following the Revolution of 1917. Casts ran into the thousands. (Slonim RUSSIAN 232-233)

living person play   See: *genziamono*.

living statue   See: *pose plastique*.

living theatre   Live performers playing before a live audience.

livret de mise en scène (French)   A promptbook. (Carlson "*Hernani's*" 10)

livret scénique (French)   In 19th C France, a promptbook. (Brockett HISTORY 449)

liyepan (Indonesian)   See: *luruh*.

liyuan, li yüan (Chinese)   Literally: pear garden, pear orchard. 1. An academy for stage performers, primarily dancers and musicians, founded in the 8th C by Emperor Minghuang. (Dolby HISTORY 10-11, Mackerras RISE 223) 2. A music-drama (*xiqu*) troupe or company. So called because the 8th C Pear Garden academy came to represent the theatrical profession.

liyuan dizi, li yüan ti tzu (Chinese)   Literally: child of the pear garden. A music-drama performer. See also: *liyuan*.

li yüan hsi (Chinese)   See: *liyuanxi*.

li yüan ti tzu (Chinese)   See: *liyuan dizi*.

liyuanxi, li yüan hsi (Chinese)   A form of music-drama (*xiqu*) popular in southern Fujian Province. It dates from at least the 16th C, and still contains elements deriving from 10th-15th C southern drama (*nanxi*). Its music appears to be distinct from the principal musical systems (*shengqiang xitong*) of music-drama, and its performances have many similarities with puppet theatre. (Mackerras MODERN 125-127)

loa (Spanish, Philippine)   Literally: compliment. 1. In Spain in the 16th C and later, a form of monologue or dramatic sketch. The subject matter varied and was not always relevant to the play that followed. Also called *introito*. (Brockett HISTORY 229-230, Shergold SPANISH, Karnis "Hispanic" 105) 2. In 18th C Argentina, a short dramatic piece often written on the spur of the moment for a special occasion, usually in honor of someone. It was often copied from a classical model with names and places changed to meet the local situation. 3. In the Philippines, the first type of dramatic presentation introduced by the Spanish from Mexico. It consisted of dancing and declamation performed inside a church during a festival. *Loante* is a reciter of *loa*. (Jocano in Manuud BROWN 320) 4. The prologue of a Philippine *comedia* play. It includes songs and prayers to the Saints or the Virgin Mary asking for guidance during performance. Also spelled *loas*. Also called *lua* or *hua*. (Mendoza in Cruz SHORT 106) 5. See: *dicho*. (Hernandez EMERGENCE 152)

load   1. The equipment (e.g., a spotlight) to which electric current is supplied, or the amount of current in a circuit (or a group of circuits). Sometimes called the resistance. 2. For a show on tour, the amount of theatrical goods, such as properties and scenery, that can be carried by an average-sized truck. (Bax MANAGEMENT 253)

load connector   In electricity, a connector which comes from equipment (e.g., a spotlight) rather than from the electrical supply. Also called a load plug, male, male connector, male plug, plug, or prong connector (occasional).

loader   See: phantom load.

load in   See: get in.

load independent   A phrase used of dimmers which can dim to black any load up to their rated capacity. (Bentham ART 328)

loading   The placing of strain on an actor by the rapid succession of emotionally-charged scenes demanding great energy, with few pauses for rest between them. (Tynan "Olivier" 87)

loading bridge, loading flies, loading floor, loading gallery   See: loading platform.

loading platform   A narrow gallery next to the counterweight lines just below the gridiron, from which counterweights are loaded into the cradles or arbors. This work can be done from the fly gallery if there is a means, such as a winch, of pulling the cradle down to that level. The loading platform is also called a loading bridge, loading floor, loading gallery, and, in Britain, loading flies.

load of hay   A group of spectators seeing a show free.

load out   See: get out.

load plug   See: load connector.

load range   In describing a dimmer, the load variation within which the dimming curve will not be noticeably affected. (Bowman/Ball THEATRE)

load sensitive   Of dimmers, operating according to the load. The classic example is the resistance dimmer, where a 1,000-watt dimmer, for example, will have very little effect on, say, a 100-watt load. The problem is solved by adding a phantom load. (Bellman SCENE)

load side   Especially where a cable is joined by connectors, the side nearer the load (e.g., the spotlight); the opposite is line side.

loante (Philippine)   See: *loa*.

lo' bat bazi (Persian)   Oral, folkloric marionette plays dating back to the 11th C. (Gassner/Quinn ENCYCLOPEDIA 647)

lobby   The distribution area in a theatre, usually reached after passing through the ticket barrier. From there audience members move to entrances leading to the section of the auditorium where their seats are located. But some sources identify the foyer as the lobby or suggest that foyer is the British equivalent of U.S. lobby. In any case, it is an entrance hall. (Burris-Meyer/Cole THEATRES 51)

lobby bell   A bell (sometimes a buzzer) used to signal theatregoers that an act is about to begin.

lobby doorkeeper   In an 18th C theatre, an attendant at one of the doors leading to the lobby. (Stone LONDON 817)

lobby frame   A frame, often glassed, for displaying a poster, enlarged copy of a review, etc. (Bowman/Ball THEATRE)

lobster alley   In New York City, the theatrical district. (Berrey/Van den Bark SLANG 576)

lobsterscope   A spotlight with an attachment which produces a flickering effect. The usual attachment fits into the color frame grooves at the front of the spotlight. It resembles a color wheel in size and general shape but is pierced by four or more slots; depending upon the speed with which it is rotated, it produces a more or less rapid flicker. British: flickers, flicker (wheel). (Lounsbury THEATRE; Bax MANAGEMENT 188, fig. 54; Fay GLOSSARY; Wehlburg GLOSSARY)

loca (Latin)   A locale or 'house' in a medieval production. (Chambers MEDIAEVAL II 83)

local control   See: remote control system.

locality board   A sign displayed on or near the stage of an Elizabethan theatre to indicate the locus of the scene. Also called a title board. There is some question about the regularity of its use. (Greg DRAMATIC xi)

localized illumination   See: general illumination.

location   A complimentary ticket, a free seat.

loci (Latin)   See: houses.

lock off   To close the lock of a counterweight unit, binding the operating line and holding the set of lines in position.

lock rail, locking rail   A rail near the bottom of a counterweight system. Clamps lock the rope lines of the system in place.

locomotor movement   A physical component of dance movement inherent in the natural structure of a dancer's body and characterized by jumping, walking, running, leaping, hopping, and traveling through space. (Turner/Grauert/Zallman DANCE 28)

lodier   A 17th C short-lived quilted and padded wrap used for a roll to increase the bulk of the hips. (Boucher FASHION)

loft   1. The space between the gridiron and the roof of a theatre. 2. See: flies.

loft block   A metal frame holding a grooved wheel (sheave). The frame is attached to the gridiron, and through it passes a line from the headblock down to a batten or other flown object. Also called a grid block or, in a rope system, a rope sheave.

loft block beams   Two steel or wood beams on the gridiron, running upstage-downstage. On them the loft blocks are mounted. A single beam is used for an underhung system.

loft well   See: grid well.

log   A printed program.

loge   1. A box or stall. 2. Sometimes the front section of a mezzanine or balcony.

loge (French)   1. A medieval structure occupied by performers as their *mansion*. 2. A box in a French theatre. 3. A performer's dressing room.

loge à salon (French)   A sitting room in a 19th C theatre. (Brockett HISTORY 498)

logeion (Greek), *logeion*   1. Before the 4th C BC in some Greek theatres, probably the roof of the columned *proskenion* thought to have stood before the first story of the *skene*. As the literal meaning (speaking place, from *legein*, to speak) suggests, the *logeion* was then presumably the acting-place. 2. Later, the *pulpitum*, the Roman stage (about five feet high). 3. Sometimes, in late writers, the *orchestra*. Also appears as Latin *logium* or occasionally *logeum*.

(Pickard-Cambridge DIONYSUS 206-210, 212; Arnott SCENIC 19; Bieber HISTORY 111, 114-115)

logeis (French)   See: *mansion*.

logeum (Latin Roman)   See: *logeion*.

loghê (French)   Fake stage jewelry, made from tinfoil. (Moynet FRENCH 104)

logium (Latin Roman)   See: *logeion*.

loi (Vietnamese)   See: *noi loi*.

lointain (French)   Literally: far off. The back wall of the stage. (Moynet FRENCH 25)

lokadharmi (Sanskrit)   In classical Indian theatre, the naturalistic style of production, where it is permissible to be representational and to use scenic properties. See also: *natyadharmi*. (Gandhi in Baumer/Brandon SANSKRIT 122-123)

lokhon bassac (Khmer)   Literally: theatre of the Bassac region. Spoken popular drama incorporating dance and music. It developed in the late 19th and early 20th C and melds Cambodian and Vietnamese elements. Also spelled: *lakon bassac*. (Brandon SOUTHEAST 60-61)

lokhon kbach boran (Khmer)   Usually translated 'Cambodian Royal Ballet.' Classical court dance-drama, unmasked and performed by women. Episodes from the *Panji* tales (called *Inao* in Khmer) and local romances are danced and acted to the accompaniment of classical *pinpeat* music. Also spelled *lakon kbach boran*. (Brandon GUIDE 17-18)

lokhon khol (Khmer)   A masked, all-male pantomimed dance-drama using *Ream Ker* (*Ramayana*) stories as subject matter. A classical court theatre form, it is similar in performance style to Thai *khon*. Also spelled *lakon kawl*. (Brunet in Osman TRADITIONAL 53, Brandon SOUTHEAST 60)

lo ku (Chinese)   See: *wuchang*.

lo lo ch'iang (Chinese)   See: *luoluoqiang*.

long arm   See: clearing pole.

long carry   An expression describing a long, by-hand trek of stagehands carrying (humping) scenery. Also called a long hump. (Granville DICTIONARY)

long center line   See: set of lines.

long hump   See: long carry.

long line   See: set of lines.

long load   Scenery over 16' long, requiring a special truck for transportation. (Bowman/Ball THEATRE)

long run   A production that performs night after night for a long period—as opposed to the repertory system, in which the production changes from night to night.

long scene   Formerly, a stage set at full depth.

longtao, lung t'ao (Chinese)   Literally: dragon set. A group of male soldiers, servants, or court attendants in music-drama (*xiqu*) who move and speak in unison. Usually each group is composed of four performers, and two groups are on stage simultaneously; additional groups are added in pairs. (Scott CLASSICAL 178)

long throw   See: throw.

longueur (French)   A dull segment in a play. (Granville DICTIONARY)

loo mask   A woman's half-mask of velvet, linen, or silk, worn as sun protection while riding. Popular in 18th C U.S. Also called a *loup* (French). See also: *touret*. (Wilcox DICTIONARY)

loose grid   A rigging system using rope ties at the pin rail.

loose grooves   In 18th C theatres, removable channels in which wings or shutters slid. See also: fixed grooves. (Southern CHANGEABLE 245)

loose legs   Said of a chorus girl who is not in step. (Berrey/Van den Bark SLANG 573)

loose line   See: spot line.

loose pin backflap, loose pin hinge   See: backflap.

loose set   A set of lines in a hemp system (q.v.). (Cornberg/Gebauer CREW 189)

Lord of Misrule   See: King of Misrule.

lords' rooms   The highest-priced seating areas in an Elizabethan theatre, situated next to the stage platform on each side. Also called the gentlemen's rooms or twelve-penny rooms. (Fortune contract in Nagler SOURCES 119, Brockett HISTORY 203)

lose   1. To forget, as in to lose a line. 2. De-emphasize, as when a performer fails to point a line. 3. Of a light, to take out, to remove.

loudness   In sound transmission, the subjective measure of the intensity of a sound. (Burris-Meyer/Mallory SOUND 1)

lounge   1. A relaxing area, usually off the lobby, for use of the audience before a show or during intermissions. See also: green room. (Burris-Meyer/Cole THEATRES 61) 2. A 19th C jacket for informal wear, single or double-breasted. Also called a sakkos. See also: sack coat. (Wilcox DICTIONARY)

lounge bell   A bell (sometimes a buzzer) in the relaxing area for theatregoers, rung to indicate that an act is about to begin.

loungers   Spectators on the stage in 18th C theatres. (Stone/Kahrl GARRICK 152)

lounge suit   World War I term for formal wear for men. See also: cutaway. (Geen COSTUME 108) *loup* (French)   See: loo mask.

louvers, louvres   See: spill rings.

louvered ceiling, louvred ceiling   1. In a stage setting, ceiling pieces, each hung on two sets of lines with the downstage edge higher than the upstage edge. The result is a ceiling with gaps through which light can be projected. 2. An occasional phrase for an auditorium ceiling with slanted openings for spotlights.

love suicide play   See: *shinjumono*.

love team   A couple playing romantic roles.

low comedian   A performer specializing in obvious, slapstick, knockabout comedy.

low comedy   Elementary, obvious comic business and lines. Hence, low comedy part.

low dead   See: dead.

lower door opposite prompt, lower door prompt side   See: LDOP, LDPS.

lower gallery   The first gallery in a two-gallery theatre or the lowest in a three-gallery theatre.

lower grooves   In 17th C theatres and later, channels on the stage floor in which wings and shutters could slide. See also: upper grooves.

lower in, lower out   See: bring in.

lower *paraskenia* (English-Greek)   See: *paraskenia*.

lower perch   See: perch.

lower stocks   See: netherstocks.

lower the asbestos   To close a theatre.

lowest *cavea* (English-Latin Roman)   See: *maenianum primum*.

low-life farce   Popular 19th C U.S. knockabout drama, often using lower-class situations. (Wilmeth LANGUAGE)

low light, lowlight   In makeup, to simulate a hollow in the face by using darker makeup.

low trim   The height of a flown piece when it is in its working or down position.

lre   Letter; a hand prop. The abbreviation is found in some old promptbooks. (Shattuck SHAKESPEARE 14)

LSE   Left second entrance. See: left first entrance.

lua (Philippine)   See: *loa*.

luantan, luan t'an (Chinese)   Literally: jumbled plucking. 1. During the 18th and 19th C, a generic term for all forms of music-drama (*xiqu*) outside of the *kunshanqiang* musical system, or of both the *kunshanqiang* and the *gaoqiang* musical systems. See also: *huabu*. (Dolby HISTORY 170, 195) 2. See: *bang-*

ziqiang and *qinqiang*. 3. A mode (*diaoshi*) derived from the *bangziqiang* musical system. 4. See: *jingju*.

lubang nyawa pelita (Malaysian)   A hole cut in the reflector of the lamp used in shadow theatre to allow the puppeteer to view the puppets as he manipulates them. (Yub in Osman TRADITIONAL 98-99)

lubki (Russian)   Popular short skits produced in small theatres in Russia during and after the Revolution, consisting of crude entertainment, political messages, folk verses, songs, etc. (Yershov SOVIET 3-4)

lubyet (Burmese)   A clown role in traditional theatre. (Aung DRAMA 8)

lucar (Latin Roman)   1. The money paid by the state for theatrical production expenses. 2. The (usually small) pay received by actors. (Beare ROMAN 164, Allen ANTIQUITIES 134, Sandys COMPANION 506)

lu ch'i, lu ch'i jen (Chinese)   See: *luqiren*.

lu chü (Chinese)   See: *luju*.

lü chü (Chinese)   See: *lüju*.

lucu (Javanese)   See: *banyol*.

ludentes (Latin)   Medieval actors. (Chambers MEDIAEVAL II 185)

ludi (Latin Roman)   Games, plays. The singular, *ludus*, is infrequent in theatre literature. The meaning is broad, and may include almost any kind of sport, game, play, or play-like entertainment, exercise, or similar diversion.
All *ludi* grew out of religious festivals, and most retained at least a nominal connection with one of the gods. Early *ludi* of a broadly theatrical kind, which go back in Etruria north of Rome to the 6th C BC or earlier, were circus-like: chariot races and other races and games (*ludi circenses*). Sandys notes that the gladiatorial activities are "more properly, *munera*, and athletic and musical contests, *agones*..." i.e., not *ludi*. (Allen ANTIQUITIES 50-60, Duckworth NATURE 76-79, Sandys COMPANION 501-512)

ludi Apollinares (Latin Roman)   From 212 BC, a July festival in honor of Apollo. These games had at least two days of plays; the building of a theatre near the temple of Apollo in 179 BC has been thought to suggest the importance of plays at the festival. See also: *ludi extraordinarii*. (Duckworth NATURE 76)

ludi Cereales (Latin Roman)   From at least 202 BC, an April festival in honor of Ceres. By the end of the 1st C BC, seven days were given to plays; there is some opinion that there were at least two days of dramatic entertainment in the preceding century. Also called *Cereales*. (Duckworth NATURE 77, Allen ANTIQUITIES 54, Sandys COMPANION 502)

ludi circenses (Latin Roman)   Chariot races and other Roman circus entertainments, including boxing, wrestling, and horse racing. Also called circus games, the literal meaning. See also: *ludicrum*. (Allen ANTIQUITIES 52, Brockett HISTORY 74, Sandys COMPANION 508)

ludicrum (Latin Roman)   Literally: sport, game, show. The term is given by Duckworth in reporting Livy's comments on early 6th C BC circus games. See also: *ludi circenses*. (Duckworth NATURE 79)

ludi extraordinarii (Latin Roman)   Extraordinary games, that is, public games usually given only once; but such special games, often including plays, were sometimes made annual later. Thus, the *ludi Apollinares*, first given in 212 BC, became annual four years later. The *ludi Florales* were extraordinary about 240 BC, but did not become annual for nearly 70 years. (Sandys COMPANION 503)

ludi Florales (Latin Roman)   From 173 BC, a festival given in late April and early May in honor of the goddess Flora. Allen's reference to these games as "a sort of Bacchanalian carnival" is probably no exaggeration: mimes were the chief dramatic entertainment. Also called Floralia. See also: *ludi extraordinarii*. (Duckworth NATURE 77; Allen ANTIQUITIES 54; Bieber HISTORY 159, 238)

ludi funebres (Latin Roman)   Literally: funeral games. Such games, usually at the funerals of public figures, included scenes from tragedies, and even comedies. Sometimes called *ludi funerales*. (Bieber HISTORY 152, 227)

ludi Graeci, ludi Graeci astici (Latin Roman)   From 240 BC, plays translated or adapted from Greek originals. The term came into use to distinguish such plays from *ludi Latini*, at which plays of Latin origin were presented. (Sandys COMPANION 507) Earlier in the 3rd C, the *ludus Graecus* (singular) may have been done in Greek. (Beare ROMAN 151)

ludi Graeci thymelici (Latin Roman)   Musical performances consisting largely of singing and dancing. (Allen ANTIQUITIES 57)

ludi honorarii (Latin Roman)   Games given by private citizens, such as magistrates, to gain public favor. Such games often included plays. (Allen ANTIQUITIES 51-52)

ludi Latini (Latin Roman)   Probably performances of *praetextae* (serious Latin dramas), *togatae* (native Latin comedies), and perhaps other theatrical entertainments of Roman origin. (Allen ANTIQUITIES 56)

ludi magni (Latin Roman)   Literally: great games. 1. Special votive games to Jupiter, given occasionally, which may have included plays. 2. See: *ludi Romani*. Compare *ludi votivi*. (Duckworth NATURE 77, Sandys COMPANION 504)

ludi Megalenses (Latin Roman)   At least from the early 2nd C BC, a festival given in April in honor of Cybele, the *Magna Mater*. By the end of the next century and perhaps much earlier, six days were given to plays. Among those produced were a number by Terence. Also called *Megalesia*. (Duckworth NATURE 77, Sandys COMPANION 502)

ludiones (Latin Roman)   Players, pantomimists. The term is used of the mid-4th C BC Etruscan performers. Singular *ludio*, from *ludus*, game, play. (Allen ANTIQUITIES 22, 53) *ludi Osci* (Latin Roman)   Literally: Oscan games. Oscan farces, so-called for the Oscans through whom the plays reached Rome; these farces had been *phlyakes* when farther south (the Naples area and below) in Italy. As taken up and modified by the Oscans, they were known chiefly as *fabulae Atellanae*. The Oscans were early inhabitants of Campania, an area in the region of modern Naples. Also called Oscan plays. See also: *fabula Atellana*.

ludi Plebeii (Latin Roman)   From at least 220 BC, the plebeian games (the literal meaning), a festival at which a Plautus play is known to have been given twenty years later. During the next century, at least three days were given to plays. (Duckworth NATURE 76)

ludi privati (Latin Roman)   Games organized, funded, and usually managed by private citizens. Among them were the public *ludi funebres*, *votivi*, and *honorarii* and private exhibitions such as those given by emperors. Whether plays were included or not, *ludi privati* were ordinarily one-time affairs. (Allen ANTIQUITIES 50-51, Sandys COMPANION 503)

ludi publici (Latin)   Public religious festivals, public games (the literal meaning). This was the general term for state-supported games. It was at a number of these, such as the *ludi Romani* and the *ludi Apollinares*, that plays were regularly performed. Compare *ludi*. (Allen ANTIQUITIES 50-51)

ludi Romani (Latin Roman)   The first public games in Rome with drama (from 364 BC). Tragedies and comedies translated from the Greek were introduced in 240 BC. Twenty-six years later, four days were given to drama. Productions included a number of plays by Terence. Also called the Roman games, sometimes *ludi magni*. Compare: *ludi votivi*. (Allen ANTIQUITIES 52-53, Duckworth NATURE 76-77)

ludi saeculares (Latin Roman)   Secular games, first certainly held in 249 BC and theoretically every hundred years thereafter. The records of the third games (17 BC) show a great deal of drama. A *saeculum* was the longest span of human life, taken to be about one hundred years. Also called *ludi Tarentini* or *Terentini* (from Tarentum, supposedly the area where the games were held), *saeculares ludi*, or secular games. (Allen ANTIQUITIES 55-56, Sandys COMPANION 111-112, Seyffert DICTIONARY 554)

ludi scaenici (Latin Roman)   Literally: scenic games. *Ludi scaenici* (which may go back to the first half of the 4th C BC) are not so much games given to plays, as games which include plays or play-like entertainments. Whether plays were dominant or peripheral, the games or portions of them were likely to be referred to as *ludi scaenici*. During most of Roman history, plays were given or were predominant at well over half of the *ludi* of all types. Compare *ludi*. (Duckworth NATURE 76-79; Allen ANTIQUITIES 51, 53-57)

ludi sollemnes (Latin Roman)   Annual public games, by contrast with *ludi extraordinarii*, usually given only once. Most annual games, however, began as extraordinary games. Before the end of the 1st C BC, of the 76 days given to the annual games, 55 provided drama. (Allen ANTIQUITIES 51, Sandys COMPANION 503)

ludi stativi (Latin Roman)   Literally: stationary festivals. Regularly recurring festivals. The *ludi Romani* and the *ludi Apollinares* are examples of many which included plays. (Sandys COMPANION 502)

ludi Tarentini, ludi Terentini (Latin Roman)   See: *ludi saeculares*.

ludi theatrales (Latin)   Medieval entertainments such as the Feast of Fools, involving clergy or choir boys. (Chambers MEDIAEVAL II 100)

ludius (Latin Roman)   See: *histrio*.

ludi Victoriae Caesaris (Latin Roman)   The games instituted by Julius Caesar in 46 BC at the dedication of the temple to Venus Genetrix (hence also called *ludi Veneris Genetricis*). They were among the games which gave emphasis to plays. (Allen ANTIQUITIES 51, 54-55)

ludi Victoriae Sullanae (Latin Roman)   Games instituted by Sulla in 82 BC in memory of his victory at the Colline Hill. These games are among those which emphasized drama. (Allen ANTIQUITIES 54-55, Sandys COMPANION 505)

ludi votivi (Latin Roman)   From before the 4th C BC, privately supported games on the occasion of dedications or triumphs. The *votivi* often included plays; there has, indeed, been some opinion that the *ludi Romani* developed from these celebrations. Also called votive games (the literal meaning). Compare: *ludi magni*. (Allen ANTIQUITIES 50-52, Bieber HISTORY 152)

ludruk (Indonesian)   A contemporary professional theatre form in Java, incorporating *gamelan* music, a clown (*dagelan*) scene, song and dance interludes (*selingan*) performed by transvestites (*taledek*), and a spoken main play (*cerita*). Performed primarily in East Java. *Ludruk bandan* or *bendang* and *ludruk lyrok* or *lerog* were exorcistic dance-plays reputed to have existed as early as the 13th C. Modern *ludruk* is descended from *ludruk besut*, created in the 1920s by a clown actor named Besut. (Peacock RITES 29-30, Brandon SOUTHEAST 48)

ludus (Latin)   A medieval play, entertainment, amusement. (Chambers MEDIAEVAL II 104). See also: *ludi*.

ludus matutinus (Latin Roman)   An animal show. The phrase was also used of the school for training the animal fighters. The literal meaning, morning game, suggests that the animal shows were held in the morning, with the gladiatorial combats in the afternoon. (Sandys COMPANION 509-510)

LUE   Left upper entrance.

luju, lu chü (Chinese)   A form of music-drama (*xiqu*) popular in parts of Anhui Province which developed in the late 18th C. It originated in labor and folk songs, later absorbing several forms of small-scale folk theatre (*xiaoxi*), and was influenced by Beijing opera (*jingju*) and *huiju*. Before 1949, called *daoqixi* or *tao ch'i hsi*.

lüju, lü chü (Chinese)   A form of music-drama (*xiqu*) popular in Shandong Province and parts of Jiangsu, Anhui, and Henan Provinces which developed out of a form of storytelling (*shuochang*), and was later influenced by several forms of small-scale folk theatre (*xiaoxi*). Performed on stage since 1900, it uses *banqiangti* musical structure, and accompaniment which includes the three-string lute (*sanxian*) and the lute (*pipa*).

luk thung (Thai)   A 20th C variety show, including popular songs and comedy acts. (Ginsberg in Rutnin SIAMESE 65)

lumber-buster   A wooden-shoe dancer in a minstrel show. (Wilmeth LANGUAGE)

lum glawn (Lao)   See: *mohlam*.

luminaire   A lighting instrument. 'Luminaire' appears to emphasize the functional completeness of the unit (e.g., with lamp), while 'instrument' does not. Originally a term used in architectural lighting, perhaps first by illuminating engineers, the word moved into television and has come into some theatre use among technicians. (Lounsbury THEATRE, Wehlburg GLOSSARY, Bentham ART 310)

lum luang, lum moo (Lao)   See: *mohlam luong*.

lump   In the professional theatre, a term occasionally used by designers for an overly bright place in the lighting.

lum plun (Lao)   See: *mohlam luong*.

lunetas (Spanish)   Semicircular rows of benches near the stage in a *corral* theatre of the late 17th C. (Brockett HISTORY 233-234)

lunge   In dance, a full-length pace in any direction, keeping the heel on the floor and bending the knee. The non-moving leg may be straight or bent slightly. (Stodelle HUMPHREY 34)

lungguh (Indonesian)   See: *luruh*.

lung t'ao (Chinese)   See: *longtao*.

luoghi deputati (Italian)   Locales or 'houses,' especially those used in medieval plays presented inside a church. (Chambers MEDIAEVAL II 92)

luogu (Chinese)   See: *wuchang*.

luoluoqiang, lo lo ch'iang (Chinese)   1. A form of music-drama (*xiqu*) initially popular in Hubei and Jiangxi Provinces and later in parts of Jiangsu Province in the late 17th and 18th C. Its music was light and lively, very close to that of folk songs. It was for the most part absorbed by Beijing opera (*jingju*) and other forms in the 19th C, but descendants of *luoluoqiang* are still performed in Shanxi Province. (Mackerras RISE 60, 75) 2. A musical system (*shengqiang xitong*) currently prevalent in Shanxi Province; it consists of several forms of music-drama which are descended from the 18th C form.

lup (Thai)   A pair of scenery wings. (Virulrak ''Likay'' 134)

luqi (Chinese)   See: *lingren.*

luqiren, lu ch'i jen (Chinese)   Literally: byway man. 1. A folk performer in the 10th-14th C. 2. See: *lingren.*

lurah sekar (Indonesian)   Literally: song leader. The musician in a Sundanese *gamelan* ensemble who acts as an interlocutor, speaking with comic puppets and commenting on the story. (Foley "Sundanese" 76)

luruh (Indonesian)   1. The downcast gaze of a refined character. 2. The most refined character type in Javanese shadow and Sundanese puppet theatres, distinguished by a downcast gaze, small, refined physical features, and gentle behavior. (Long JAVANESE 71-75) In Java, also called *liyepan* or *lijepan.* (Brandon THRONES 49) In Sunda, also called *lungguh* or *lenyep.* (Foley "Sundanese" 34) See also: *alus.*

lusiator (Latin)   A medieval actor. (Chambers MEDIAEVAL II 186)

lusor (Latin)   A medieval entertainer. (Wickham EARLY I 183)

lustres   Lights in 18th C theatres. (Scouten LONDON lxvii, Hogan LONDON li)

lutju (Indonesian)   See: *banyol.*

Luxauleator   Steele Mackaye's name for a light curtain which he patented in 1893. The invention, designed to avoid lowering the curtain for scene shifts, consisted of bordering the auditorium side of the proscenium with lights directed toward the audience. See also: light curtain. The citation below, which includes illustrations, is in Mackaye's Addenda. (Mackaye EPOCH II lxxiv-lxxvi)

lycopodium A flash powder used for stage effects since at least the 19th C. Often shortened to podium.

lycopodium flash box   A 19th C device which simulated lightning by exploding lycopodium powder. The modern British version is called a lycopodium pot. (Rees GAS 148, Rae/Southern INTERNATIONAL)

lycopodium pipe   In the early 20th C in the U.S., a blowpipe used to simulate lightning by moving flammable powder, often lycopodium, into a flame. The magnesium gun used magnesium in the same way for the same purpose. (Krows AMERICA 221)

lycopodium pot   See: lycopodium flash box.

lyric   1. Said of drama that is not spoken but sung. Hence, lyric drama, lyric stage, lyric theatre, lyric role. 2. In the plural, the words of a song. Hence, lyricist (in opera: librettist). (Bowman/Ball THEATRE)

lyristae (Latin)   See: minstrel.

lysiodi (Greek)   Early mime singers who played women. (Duchartre ITALIAN 24)

lysiodia (Greek)   A form of early lyric mime thought to be one of the varieties of *mimodia* (operatic mime). From Lysius, a mythic Dionysus-like god, or Lysis, who made *magodia* (primitive farce-operas) literary and gave them his name. (Nicoll MASKS 34, Liddell/Scott LEXICON)

lystspil (Norwegian)   Comedy.

M

M   Music. (Shattuck SHAKESPEARE 22)

ma (Japanese)   Literally: pause or interval. A moment between two units of action in which neither movement or speech occurs. This crucial pause is found in all traditional Japanese performing arts. Malm defines *ma* in *joruri* music in Brandon CHUSHINGURA 66-67. In *kabuki* the *ma* is a silent motionless moment, alive and expressive and sustained by controlling the breath (*ki*). An example is the *mie* pose. (Brandon CHUSHINGURA 128, Gunji BUYO 72-73) In *no*, a *ma* functions both in space and time. (Komparu NOH 71)

maanch (Hindi)   A lyrical drama of the Malwa region in Madhya Pradesh, central India. The word is from *manch*, meaning stage. (Gargi FOLK 48-49)

mabian (Chinese)   See: *tangma*.

macaroni   An 18th-19th C bizarre dressing style affected by young members of the club of the same name in London. This foppish style included polka dot hose, swords hanging down to the heels, and small cocked hats. (Walkup DRESSING 220)

Macbeth trap   A small trap with an elevator, named for the appearances and disappearances of the witches.

macchietta (Italian)   Literally: little spot, eccentric. 1. In *commedia dell'arte*, a cameo role. (Mazzone-Clementi "Commedia" 59) 2. A comic act popular in Italian music halls in which performers improvise scenes to music. (Leslie ACT 75) 3. A solo character sketch.

macchiettista (Italian)   A type of 19th C vaudeville comedian descended from the *commedia dell'arte* who specialized in satirizing social stereotypes. (Sogliuzzo "Notes" 68)

Maccus (Latin Roman)   One of the types of stock clowns in Atellan plays. The names of the clowns (compare *fabula Atellana*) are frequent in the more than 100 surviving titles, and Maccus occurs more than any other. The name has been related to words suggesting stupidity and perhaps blandness. It may be that Maccus was a good-natured gull. (Beare ROMAN 139-141, 143-144)

maceria (Latin Roman)   An unseen wall supposedly separating the gardens of two houses whose fronts are onstage in view of the audience. (Beare ROMAN 260)

machina (Latin Roman)   See: *mechane*.

machina versatilis (Latin)   In the early 17th C English theatre, changeable scenery. (Nicoll STUART 68)

machine   1. When used of Greece and Rome, usually the *mechane* (hoisting device), but sometimes any other stage device or instrument. In the latter sense, the use is broad: machine may refer, for example, to the *ekkyklema*, the *exostra*, the *eorema*, the *bronteion*, or even the *periaktoi*. See: *mechane*. (Nicoll DEVELOPMENT 21-22) 2. A device or machinery for special effects, such as a moving cloud or waves. Ben Jonson used the term as early as 1606. (Jonson in Nagler SOURCES 146)

machinee (Japanese)   The Japanese pronunciation of 'matinee,' with the same meaning.

machine for (the) gods   See: *mechane*.

machine for theatre   In design, the idea that a stage setting is a machine which functions during the period of a performance, serving the actors and the script. (Gorelik NEW)

machine play   A play calling for spectacular effects, often a melodrama or opera in the 17th C and later. (Chappuzeau in Nagler SOURCES 183)

machine theatre   Said of a theatre equipped with elaborate stage machinery.

machine-made   Said of mechanical acting, with no individual style. (Granville DICTIONARY)

machinery   See: stage machinery.

machinist   In 17th C theatres and later, the stage technician responsible for the scenery and machinery. (Wilson ''Player's'' 28)

machiniste (French)   In the 17th C, a maker of scenery. Later, a kind of major-domo stagehand responsible for shifting scenery and sets. (Roberts STAGE)

machi utai (Japanese)   Literally: waiting song. A brief song at the beginning of the second part (*nochi ba*) of a *no* play, in which the supporting character (*waki*) waits for the reappearance of the protagonist (*shite*). (Shimazaki NOH 47)

(a) Macready   In acting, a marked pause and catching of the breath before certain words. Named after the English 19th C actor William Charles Macready. (Wilmeth LANGUAGE)

madah (Malaysian)   A formal invitation to spirits to attend a feast. In *wayang kulit*, the invitation may consist of brief invocations or it may be the entire drama. (Sweeney RAMAYANA 276) *madang* (Korean)   Literally: playing ground. 1. An open space or a courtyard in front of a house used for performance. 2. An act or scene of a masked play. (Korean MASKS 9)

maddale (Kannada)   A small two-headed, barrel-shaped drum played with the hands and fingers. It is used in *yaksagana* and other south Indian traditional theatre forms. *Maddlegara* is a player of the *maddale*. (Ashton/Christie YAK-SAGANA 61, 92)

madengxi, ma teng hsi (Chinese)   Literally: horse-lantern play. A form of flower drum play (*huaguxi*) which developed from popular songs sung during the Chinese New Year Lantern Festival. (Dolby HISTORY 220)

made the nut   See: nut.

made the play   Said of something—a performer, usually—who saved a poor play from failure. (Granville DICTIONARY 120)

madhurya (Sanskrit)   Literally: amiability. In classical Indian dramaturgy, one of eight "special excellences" of a hero. (Keith SANSKRIT 307)

madhya (Sanskrit)   Literally: medium. In classical Indian plays, the role of a heroine (*nayika*) who is "moderately" experienced in love. (Keith SANSKRIT 308)

mado buta (Japanese)   Literally: window cover. In a *kabuki* theatre of the 18th and 19th C, the shutters that covered the high windows over the boxes (*sajiki*) on both sides of the auditorium. Because performances were in the day time, the amount of light reaching the stage was regulated by opening and closing the shutters. (Leiter ENCYCLOPEDIA 221)

madrigal comedy   *Commedia dell' arte* in madrigal form. It developed as early as the late 16th C in Italy, and was later used in marionette productions in Britain. (Philpott DICTIONARY)

mae (Thai)   See: *nang*.

mae ba (Japanese)   Literally: front scene. The first part of a two-part *no* play. See also: *ba*. (Hoff/Flindt "Structure" 219)

mae bot (Thai)   Literally: mother of lessons; hence, alphabet of dance. The vocabulary of standard movements and gestures (*tha ram*) of classical dance-drama (*lakon*) that is taught beginning dancers. (Yupho in Rangthong SOU-VENIR 149, 151) Two alphabets of choreographic patterns are used: one of 18 sequences taken from the dance treatise of the late 18th C King Rama I (Yupho CLASSICAL 73-74), and one of 65 sequences composed by Prince Damrong in the 20th C (Yupho PRELIMINARY 15-16, Yupho in Rangthong SOUVENIR 35-38). See also: *tamra fon ram*.

mae jite, mae shite (Japanese)   Literally: front *shite*. The protagonist (*shite*) who appears in the first (*mae*) part of a two-part *no* play. See also: *nochi jite*. (Shimazaki NOH 23)

maen (Indonesian)   See: *main*.

maenads   In the classical theatre, the characters of ecstatic female followers of Dionysus. (Pickard-Cambridge DITHYRAMB 80-81, 128-129)

maenianum primum (Latin Roman)   Literally: first balcony. In large theatres, the rows of seats between the orchestra and the first semicircular corridor (*praecinctio*). Above the corridor might be a second tier of rows called the *maenianum medium*, or *media cavea*, separated by a second corridor from a third tier, called the *maenianum summum*, or *summa cavea*. The *maenianum primum* is also referred to as the *maenianum imum*, the first *maenianum*, *ima cavea*, the lowest *cavea*, and other combinations. (Bieber HISTORY 194, Sandys COMPANION 518)

mae payah (Lao)   The role of an older woman, mother, or queen in a *mohlam* play. (Miller "Kaen" 222)

mae yok (Thai)   A female patron of a *likay* actor. (Virulrak "Likay" 255)

mafors   A 6th-11th C woman's long, narrow veil, usually covering the head and draping over the shoulders. (Boucher FASHION)

mag   A magazine-style playbill.

magak (Indonesian)   Holding grip for a medium-sized *wayang* puppet. The main control rod is grasped by the fingers with the thumb extended upwards against the rod for stability. (Long JAVANESE 24)

magamp   See: reactance dimmer.

magatelli (Italian)   Marionettes; also called *bagattelli*. (Kennard MASKS 105)

magazine   1. In Britain, a compartment. Typical terms: magazine batten, magazine footlights. But compartment is also used. 2. See: magazine panel. (Bowman/Ball THEATRE, Rae/Southern INTERNATIONAL)

magazine footlights   In Britain, footlights in which each lamp is in its own compartment. (Corry PLANNING 100)

magazine panel   A steel box or small cabinet, often embedded in the wall near the main switch supplying electricity to the theatre or stage. On stage, such a panel box contains the fuses or breakers which protect the control-board circuits. Among other terms: magazine, panel box, breaker magazine, fuse magazine. (Fuchs LIGHTING 326-329; Bellman LIGHTING 154, fig. 11-1a)

magic if   See: scenic truth.

magic lantern   The name of an early form of projector which came into theatre use early in the 19th C. Though seen mainly in increasingly sophisticated showings of slides, it was used in regular drama by 1820 and for scenic projection in the next few years. (Rees GAS 81-85)

magischer Realismus (German)   Literally: magical realism. A post-expressionistic German dramatic style which was matter-of-fact, unsentimental, practical, and non-visionary yet was often marked by a certain religiosity or belief in the divine wellsprings of reality. (Gassner/Quinn ENCYCLOPEDIA 351) *magister mimariorum* (Latin Roman)   Literally: chief of the mimes. See also: *archimimus*. (Nicoll MASKS 86)

magnesium gun   See: lycopodium pipe.

magnesium lamp   In late 19th C Britain, a lighting instrument which produced a brilliant bluish-white beam of light by burning a ribbon (or wire) of magnesium at the focus of a parabolic reflector. The magnesium lamp was used in the theatre for a time, but its difficulties were such that it was never a real rival to the limelight or the arc light. (Rees GAS 78-80, fig. 51)

magnetic amplifier dimmer, magamp   See: reactance dimmer.

magnetic switch, magnet switch   See: contactor.

magnifico (Italian)   In *commedia dell'arte*, a wealthy and usually lecherous old man, the best-known example of which is Pantalone (Pantaloon in English), the (usually) Venetian merchant. In English Renaissance comedy an example of the type is Ben Jonson's creation, Volpone. (Nicoll HARLEQUIN 50)

magnifying lens   A lay phrase sometimes used for a lens added to a projector to enlarge the image it throws. (Bowman/Ball THEATRE)

magnitude   The elevation of spirit that Aristotle said characterized tragedy. (Hatlen ORIENTATION)

magodia (Greek)   In one ancient writer, a rude pantomime. On the basis of modern analyses of other ancient references, thought to be a form of lyric mime akin to a primitive farce opera. See also: *mimodia*. (Nicoll MASKS 34)

magojiro (Japanese)   A *no* mask of a young woman used by the Kongo school. (Shimazaki NOH 60

magtugi (Korean)   See: *malttugi*.

mahanataka (Sanskrit)   See: *nataka*.

maharas (Hindi)   1. In Puranic legend, the final and fullest form of the *rasa* dance that the god Krishna performed with his milkmaid devotees. 2. The dramatic re-enactment of this dance. Also called: *maharas lila*. (Hein MIRACLE 265)

mahattara (Sanskrit)   The minor role of a governess in classical Indian drama. (Keith SANSKRIT 313)

mahkota (Malaysian)   Literally: crown. A velvet head-dress that peaks in front, worn by a hero (*pa'yong*) in *ma'yong* dance-drama. (Sheppard TAMAN 64)

mai (Japanese)   1. A generic term for many forms of dance, classical and folk, especially those from the medieval period (c. 1100-1500), in which circling or pivoting is a central feature. (Gunji BUYO 74) 2. Broadly, all types of dance in *no*. (Shimazaki NOH 34) 3. More narrowly in *no*, those dances which are performed to instrumental music and do not have sung accompaniment, including *kami mai* (god dance), *jo no mai* (slow dance), *chu no mai* (medium-tempo dance), *ha no mai* (middle dance), and others. They are distinguished by the elegance and restraint of movement and gesture. See also: *hatarakimono, shimai*. (Shimazaki NOH 34-36) 4. *No*-style dance sequences in *kabuki* dance. (Gunji BUYO 74-75)

mai bataraki (Japanese)   A dance of felicitation in a god *kyogen* play. (Berberich "Rapture" 173)

mai guse (Japanese)   See: *kuse*.

mai kyogen (Japanese)   Literally: dance *kyogen*. A *kyogen* play that follows *no* dramatic structure and includes dance and song. (Berberich "Rapture" 60)

main   1. A switch which controls all, or a major portion, of a lighting installation. Hence, house main—the switch controlling the auditorium lights, stage main—the switch controlling the stage lights. A shortening of main switch; also called a grand master. 2. A shortening of main line, which is a major cable such as a borderlight cable. (Fuchs LIGHTING 173) 3. See: house curtain.

main (Indonesian, Malaysian)   To perform: to act, dance, or play music. Also spelled *maen*.

main action   In a play with multiple plots, the most important one.

main bertewas (Malaysian)   Literally: competitive performance. In *wayang kulit*, two performances given simultaneously and in competition. The performer drawing the larger audience is the winner. (Sweeney RAMAYANA 290)

main curtain   See: house curtain.

main deck   A 19th C term for the stage floor visible to the public.

main line   See: main.

main pajak (Malaysian)   A commercial performance of Malaysian *wayang kulit*. (Sweeney RAMAYANA 27)

main peri (Malaysian)   A free (*peri*) performance in Malaysia. (Sweeney RAMAYANA 26)

mainpiece   In 18th C theatres and later, the chief offering on a theatrical bill, normally a comedy or tragedy.

main puteri (Malaysian)   Literally: female performance. In shadow theatre (*wayang kulit*) and *ma'yong* dance-drama, a ritual performance in which a shaman (*bomoh*) communicates with spirits and heroic gods to heal an illness. Possession, dance, music, and scenic enactments may occur. (Sheppard in Osman TRADITIONAL 141, Yousof "Kelantan" 146-151)

main service   See: service.

Main Stem   Broadway. The term is used as either noun or adjective. (Sobel HANDBOOK 662)

Main Street   The provinces.

main switch   See: main.

maison (French)   A *mansion* or locale in a medieval production.

maitakhap (Thai)   A split bamboo slapstick used by clowns in *likay* and other theatre forms. (Virulrak "Likay" 144)

maître de ballet, maîtresse de ballet   A ballet master or mistress. The person responsible for training the dancers in a company and conducting rehearsals. (Grant TECHNICAL)

maître des feintes, maître des secrets (French)   In medieval times, a master of stage machinery. Sometimes called a master of secrets (special effects). (Mantzius HISTORY II 73)

maître du jeu (French)   A director or organizer of a medieval play or, more often, a group of plays such as a mystery cycle. The *maître* was likely to be everything from actor trainer to technician and performer to play doctor. (Frank MEDIEVAL 170).

maize country   The provinces.

makata (Philippine)   A local or village poet. Also a playwright, since most vernacular *comedia* were written by *makata*. (Mabesa "Philippine" 5)

make   1. Of an electrical circuit, to close (as with a switch) so that current flows. (Lounsbury THEATRE 148, Bowman MODERN) 2. To be hired by a traveling show, such as a Toby show. (Wilmeth LANGUAGE)

make a break   See: break.

make a comeback   1. To return to the stage. 2. To be successful after two or three failures.

make an ascension   Especially in Britain, to forget one's lines.

make and break connection   A phrase for any arrangement which permits an electrical circuit to be closed and opened with dispatch. Switches and interconnecting panels are major examples. (Bowman MODERN)

make an entrance   To come on stage, especially with authority.

make a set, make a setup   To put up the scenery.

make a sleeper jump   To take a train to the next engagement immediately following an evening's performance. Also called take the owl.

make a spot   To be engaged to perform.

make fast   To tie off, e.g., a line.

make off   In Britain: 1. To tie off a line. 2. The downstage flat on either side that joins a setting to the proscenium or tormentor. (Fay GLOSSARY)

make one's bow, make one's debut   To appear for the first time as a performer.

make the rounds   To go from one agent or producer to another in search of theatrical employment.

makeup   1. All the accoutrements (paints, liners, powder, wigs, putty, crepe hair, rouge, etc.) used by a performer to change his or her appearance and to compensate for undesirable changes in appearance produced by artificial light on the stage. 2. The finished product. 3. To use makeup.

makeup artist, makeup man, makeup woman   One who puts makeup on performers.

makeup box   A container for the appurtenances used in preparing a performer's face and body.

makeup man   See: makeup artist.

makeup morgue   A file of newspaper, magazine, and other clippings containing photographs—unretouched—of men and women of various ages and types. Used by performers as a reference in duplicating makeup and wig styles as required by a role. The morgue often includes makeup catalogues, price lists, and other miscellaneous makeup data. (Corson MAKEUP 54)

makeup pencil   A wooden pencil with a hard greasepaint center. Available in a variety of colors. When used for making up the eyebrows, it is usually referred to as an eyebrow pencil.

makeup prosthetics   Three-dimensional devices such as artificial jowls, noses, humps, etc. used to alter the appearance of a performer's face or body.

makeup woman   See: makeup artist.

makidhupuh (Indonesian)   A kneeling position for Javanese puppets, used by characters showing respect. The character is lowered and leaned forward to represent a semi-reclining position, and the hands are placed at ground level directly in front of the puppet. (Long JAVANESE 34)

Makishi   A kind of secret cult ritual designed to uphold the social and economic customs of its geographical area. It is practiced in Africa from Zaire to Zimbabwe and in some areas of Angola and Zambia. Masked characters are important, appearing on specific occasions associated with the initiation ceremonies of boys. Masks include an old fisherman (symbol of happiness and self-confidence), a spirited young woman (symbol of fertility), etc. (Gründ-Khaznadar "Ritual" 31)

maku (Japanese)   1. A stage curtain in most forms of theatre. See: *doncho, hiki, joshiki.* (Leiter ENCYCLOPEDIA 45). 2. An act of a play marked by the opening and the closing of a curtain. This is a modern usage derived from western theatre. (Gunji KABUKI 47) 3. See: *hon maku.*

maku ai (Japanese)   Literally: act interval. An intermission between acts or between plays. (Leiter ENCYCLOPEDIA 141)

maku gire (Japanese)   Literally: act end. The moment just before the curtain is closed, in which a scene or play reaches a climax.

maku guchi (Japanese)   Literally: curtain entrance. The far end of the *no* bridgeway (*hashigakari*), separated from the dressing room (*kagami no ma*) by a lift-curtain (*agemaku*).

maku soto (Japanese)   Literally: outside the curtain. In *kabuki*, action that takes place on the runway (*hanamichi*) in front of the closed act curtain. (Brandon in Brandon/Malm/Shively STUDIES 118-119)

makuta (Indonesian)   See: *ngibing*.

maku uchi (Japanese)   Literally: inside the curtain. The backstage 'world,' actors and crew, as distinguished from front-of-the-house staff (*omote kata*).

mak yong (Malaysian)   See: *ma'yong*.

malang kadhak (Indonesian)   In Javanese *wayang kulit*, a puppet arm position in which the elbows are bent to the rear and away from the body. (Long JAVANESE 32–34)

malangkah kaping kalih (Indonesian)   Literally: leap over two times. A Javanese *wayang* fighting technique in which the attacking character leaps completely past his opponent, then leaps past again after the other character has turned to face him. (Long JAVANESE 62)

malang kerik (Indonesian)   A Javanese puppet arm position in which the character's elbows are turned outward. The front hand is placed at the waist and the rear hand either overlaps the front or is held away from the body. Used for a variety of fighting, flying, and walking movements. (Long JAVANESE 34)

male, male connector   See: load connector.

malé divadla (Czech)   The small theatres of Prague which broke away from the repertory system of traditional theatre to work with anecdotes, dialogue, mime, poetry, songs, and stories. (Burian "Prague" 232)

malefit   A poorly attended benefit performance, according to John O'Keeffe in 1764. (Troubridge BENEFIT 54)

male impersonator   A female who specializes in male roles. Popular in British music halls and to some extent in vaudeville. Not to be confused with women who played breeches parts. (Wilmeth LANGUAGE)

male plug   See: load connector.

mali (Latin Roman)   Literally: poles, masts. The masts at the top of some large theatres. They held the awnings which protected the spectators from sun and rain. See also: *velum*. (Sandys COMPANION 518)

maline   A very thin, almost transparent material used by strippers for bras and nipple caps. (Wilmeth LANGUAGE)

malita (Assamese)   A short song-poem that precedes a performance of *ankiya nat*. (Richmond "Vaisnava" 157)

malttugi, magtugi (Korean)   Literally: a pole to which a horse is tied. The character and mask of a nobleman's groom in various types of masked play. (Korean MASKS 6, 13, 21) *mamandapan baksa* (Indonesian)   See: *ngibing*.

mameluke, tunic à la   See: tunic à la mameluck.

mammy   In burlesque, a dresser for strippers who also stood in the wings to catch clothing as a stripper disrobed. (Wilmeth LANGUAGE)

man (Latin)   See: *manet*.

manager   1. A theatre official overseeing some important aspect of production. A business manager handles money, accounts, contracts, etc. A company manager runs a touring company. A house manager oversees the auditorium and ushers (though the term is sometimes used for the person who looks after the theatre building). A personal manager serves as a representative or agent for a playwright, composer, performer, etc. 2. In Britain, a producer. (Stern MANAGEMENT)

manban, man pan (Chinese)   Literally: slow meter. A quadruple meter regulated (*shangban*) metrical-type (*banshi*) used in the songs of many forms of music-drama (*xiqu*) for relatively peaceful, introspective situations. In Beijing opera it is the slowest regulated metrical-type, and is used in both the *xipi* and *erhuang* modes (*diaoshi*). See also: *banyan*. (Wichmann ''Aural'' 148-150)

manch (Hindi)   A stage.

mancheron (French)   A 16th C half-sleeve, probably either from shoulder to elbow or from elbow to wrist, which showed through or under the slit sleeve of a doublet or houppelande. (Boucher FASHION)

manche-volante (French)   Literally: flying sleeve. A 16th C richly-lined fur or contrasted fabric oversleeve, fastened by points. (Walkup DRESSING 149)

mandala (Sanskrit)   A movement sequence made up of a succession of movements through space (*cari*), to represent a fight or battle in classical Indian theatre. (Rangacharya NATYASASTRA 30)

Mandala texts   See: *bianwen*.

mandali (Hindi)   Literally: a circle. A troupe of actors. (Hein MIRACLE 290)

mandapa (Sanskrit)   1. Broadly, an acting area. 2. More narrowly, a hall or pavilion in a temple complex, used for dance as well as rituals. (Kale THEATRIC 14)

mandarin collar   A narrow standing collar attached to a close-fitting jacket, blouse, or dress. Also called a Johnny collar or Nehru collar. (Wilcox DICTIONARY)

mandorla (Italian)   In the 15th C, an almond-shaped machine resembling a glory. (Bergman LIGHTING 33)

Manducus (Latin Roman)   One of the types of stock clowns in Atellan plays. A number of ancient references make it certain that Manducus was ogre-like with a large mouth; his teeth and jaws evidently sometimes chattered and sometimes crunched. His name has been connected with various words related to eating: *mando* (chew) and *manducare* (crunch) are among them. See also: *fabula Atellana*. (Beare ROMAN 139-146)

(en) manège (French)   In ballet, the travelling of a dancer around the stage in a circle while performing. The term is from the circus. (Grant TECHNICAL, Wilson BALLET)

maneki ogi (Japanese)   Literally: inviting fan. A standard gesture (*kata*) in *no*, in which a horizontal, open fan is waved overhead to beckon or indicate affection. Illustrated in Keene NO 221.

manet (Latin)   Remain; stay on stage. Plural: *manent*. Sometimes occurs as *man*.

mang (Chinese)   A round-necked robe which is covered with complex patterns signifying social rank. It is worn on formal occasions by characters of high social status in Beijing opera (*jingju*) and many other forms of music-drama (*xiqu*). The male version is full-length, while the female is three-quarter and worn over a skirt. (Halson PEKING 20, Scott CLASSICAL 144-147, Zung SECRETS 19)

mangala (Kannada)   The closing song, a benedictory verse, of a dramatic or musical performance. Also spelled *mangalam* (Telugu).

mangalacaran (Hindi)   A song of praise offered to Radha and Krishna to invoke their blessing at the beginning of a *raslila* performance. It is the first part of the *ras* portion of a performance. In it Krishna dances with the milk-maidens (*gopi*). (Hein MIRACLE 143-144)

mangalam (Telugu)   See: *mangala*.

mangal-kavya (Bengali)   A propitious poem in Bengali literature which provided the structure of *jatra* drama. (Sarker ''Jatra'' 87)

manifold set   A 17th C French stage partitioned into four or five components, each representing a different locale. (Mongrédien MOLIÈRE 124)

manikin   An occasional term, especially in Britain, for marionette. (Purdom PRODUCING)

mani-rimdu (Tibetan)   A masked dance-drama performed in Sherpa villages in Tibet and Nepal. Its religious function is to commemorate the triumph of Buddhism over the primitive Bon religion. The dances performed in its thirteen acts are described in Jerstad MANI-RIMDU 107-164.

manis (Indonesian)   See: *alus*.

mannerism   A personal, highly individual style devoted to obtaining striking effects. (Russell ''Mannerism'' 325)

manners comedy   See: comedy of manners.

manodharmma (Malayalam)   Literally: imagination. In *kathakali*, a freely improvised passage of mime interpolated into a performance by an actor. It is accompanied by instrumental music, but not song. See also: *ilakiyattam*. (Jones/Jones KATHAKALI 74)

man of parts   A versatile actor. (Granville DICTIONARY)

manora, manora jatri (Thai)   See: *lakon jatri*.

man pan (Chinese)   See: *manban*.

man-seog-jung, mansog-zung (Korean)   A type of folk puppet play performed in mime on the eighth day of the fourth lunar month (Buddha's birthday). See: *kkoktu kaksi*. (Gassner/Quinn ENCYCLOPEDIA 511, Choe STUDY 3-4)

mansion (French), **mansion**   A scenic representation of a locale in a medieval production. Also called a box, *casa* (Italian), *castrum* (Latin), division, *domus* (Latin), *estage, estal* (French), house, *lieu* (French), *loca* (Latin), *logeis* (French plural), *luoghi deputati* (Italian plural), *maison* (French), players' house, *pulpitum* (Latin), room, *sedes* (Latin plural), *siège* (French), stall, and *tenti* (Latin plural). See also: *platea*.

manta (Spanish)   Literally: shawl, poncho, blanket. 1. An ankle length square of coarse black cotton draped over the head and then falling from the shoulders, secured by a pin at the chest. 2. A short cape worn by a Spaniard over a bolero. 3. A black lace shawl-like headdress for an aristocratic lady. 4. A black alpaca or cashmere headdress for a not-so-aristocratic lady. (Wilcox DICTIONARY)

manteau (French)   1. A 17th C overdress, or just its bodice, with an attached train which draped over a bustle. 2. An 18th C term for the old male comic role. 3. A modern term for cape or overcoat. (Boucher FASHION, Chalmers CLOTHES 187, Roberts STAGE)

manteau d'Arlequin (French)   See: teaser.

mantelet (French)   An 18th C woman's silk or taffeta scarf, narrow in front and wide in back. The ends were often crossed at the waist. Usually of black or a dark color. (Barton COSTUME 346)

manteline   A 15th-16th C short ceremonial tunic, generally highly ornamented, sometimes with a hood. See also: journade. (Boucher FASHION)

mantenedor (Philippine)   In a tournament scene in *comedia*, the umpire who pairs opponents and, with a banner, starts and stops duels. (Mendozoa COMEDIA 40-41)

mantling   See: cointise.

mantrin (Sanskrit)   See: *amatya*.

manual   In a memory lighting system, the manual bank of controllers. The manual-record (e.g., a button) sends into the memory whatever is on the manual bank; manual record also occurs without hyphen, and similar phrases are sometimes used. (Bellman LIGHTING 243, 250)

manual bank   In a light console, a row of controllers, each of which operates one dimmer path. The controllers are analogous to the dimmer handles on a manually-operated switchboard. (Bellman LIGHTING 219)

manual control   See: remote control system.

manual-record, manual record   See: manual.

manual switchboard   See: direct-control switchboard.

manual takeover, individual select/record, solo   In a memory lighting system, removing a channel from memory and operating it manually. A fader wheel is a specific device for doing so: a hand-operated wheel. A joy stick is another such device, this one being a small vertical shaft which is moved to either side. A rocker switch is a third device, a switch whose three positions leave the channel in memory, move it up, or move it down. (Bellman LIGHTING 244, 245)

manuscript   A written or typed play, often the text used in rehearsal for a play or musical. The usual theatre term is script.

manzai (Japanese)   1. Literally: ten-thousand years. A felicitous dance performed in court- and shrine-related dance presentations to assure long life. 2. Written with other ideographs, literally: comic skill. A comic vaudeville duo and the type of comic patter they perform, especially popular in Osaka in the 20th C. (Sadler "O-Kagura" 289, Brandon GUIDE 88)

ma pien (Chinese)   See: *tangma*

maple massager   A dancer, especially a tap dancer. Hence, maple massaging. (Berrey/van den Bark SLANG 573)

maquette (French)   A stage design in miniature; a model of a set. (Moynet FRENCH 96)

maquillage (French)   Stage makeup. Also called *peinture*.

maquillar (Spanish)   To make up. Hence, *maquillaje*, makeup.

maquinista (Spanish)   See: *tramoyista*.

marcar (Spanish)   To coach an actor.

marcha (Philippine)   Music in a slow, dignified tempo used for a processional entrance or exit in *comedia*. (Mendoza COMEDIA 53, 56)

Märchenlustspiel (German)   A romantic, fairy-tale comedy. (Meyer IBSEN 95)

marcheur, marcheuse (French)   A ballet dancer. See also: *figurant(e)*.

marescallus (Latin)   See: minstrel.

Marienklage (German)   An early form of liturgical drama dealing with the Crucifixion. (Davidson STUDIES 20)

Marienspiel (German)   See: Mary play.

Marie Tempest   A metal hinge with a screw lever adjustment to make doors on raked stages remain in their open position; named after the early 20th C English actress who asked for such hinges.

marionette, *marionnette* (French), ***marionetta*** (Italian)   Literally: little Mary—a small figure of the Virgin Mary. A string puppet. *Marionette* is also the Italian plural. (Kennard MASKS 105)

marionette control   See: control.

marionette theatre   See: *mu'ouxi, yokthe pwe*.

marionettist   The manipulator of a string puppet.

marionnette à fil (French)   A string-controlled marionette. (Philpott DICTIONARY)

marionnette à gaine (French)   A glove or hand puppet. Also called a *guignol* and sometimes a *marionnette à main*. (Philpott DICTIONARY)

marionnette à la planchette (French)   A 19th C jointed figure through which a piece of looped string was threaded and attached to a short piece of flat wood. The puppeteer placed the wood on the ground, his foot on the wood, and the loop around his leg, causing the figure to dance as he jiggled his leg. Similar to the Turkish *ayak kuklasi*. Also called a jigging puppet. (McNamara "Press" 322)

marionnette à main (French)   See: *marionnette à gaine*.

marionnette à tige (French)   A rod puppet controlled from below the stage.

marionnette à tringle (French)   A single-rod puppet controlled from above the stage. (Philpott DICTIONARY)

market drama   Plays written, mostly in English, for consumption in Nigeria. The plays are in dialogue but are not intended to be produced on stage. They are paperbound tracts which deal with history, politics, etiquette, male-female relationships, and personal advice. (Gassner/Quinn ENCYCLOPEDIA 8)

marking up   The first costume fitting and its corrections. (Geen COSTUME 16)

mark it   In setting the intensity of light or sound, to record the level of the controller(s). (Lounsbury THEATRE)

marks (Yiddish), **marks**   Shares. Especially in late 19th and early 20th C Yiddish theatre, a common financial arrangement in which receipts were divided, often into 100 shares, with each member of a company receiving one or more shares. But theatre owners, stagehands, and other fixed costs were paid before the division into shares, and stars had many shares. Often called the mark system. (Rosenfeld BRIGHT 81, Sandrow VAGABOND 55, Lifson YIDDISH 128)

markstitch   Needle-and-thread marking for a first costume fitting. (Geen COSTUME 16) *marlota* (Spanish)   Literally: a Moorish gown. A kind of coat worn for bull-fights and other tournaments. (Boucher FASHION)

marlotte (French)   See: *ropa*.

maroon   A British term for a sound effect simulating an explosion. (Rae/ Southern INTERNATIONAL)

marot, marotte (French)   1. At first, the sceptre or stick of the medieval fool, adorned at one end by a small head with cap and bells. 2. Much later, a rod puppet. (Philpott DICTIONARY, Malkin PUPPETS 18)

marquee   A canopy or roof projecting over the entrance to a theatre, usually with a display, illuminated at night, advertising the current production. (Bowman/ Ball THEATRE)

marshelik (Yiddish)   Literally: jester. An entertainer and master of cere-monies at Purim plays and other festivities. Not given to low comedy, he was likely to use complex wordplay and disputation. (Sandrow VAGABOND 1, 11)

martingale breeches   16th C breeches with a panel between the legs, secured to the belt with points and buttons. (Boucher FASHION)

maruhon (Japanese)   Literally: whole text. The text of a *bunraku* puppet play (*gidayu kyogen*). The term comes from the fact that the full play was written in one bound book, in contrast to *kabuki* where only sides were written out. Also called *shohon*. (Malm in Brandon CHUSHINGURA 61-62)

maruhonmono (Japanese)   A *kabuki* play which is adapted from a *bunraku* play, and hence utilizes the *joruri* style of chanted narrative and the heavy *shamisen* of the puppet theatre. Also called *gidayu kyogen* (*gidayu* play) and slang *dendenmono*, from the twanging sound of the *shamisen*. (Brandon CLAS-SIC 14, Gunji KABUKI 25, 34)

marvel   A medieval miracle play. (Ward LITERATURE I 57)

Mary play   A medieval miracle play in which a miracle is performed by the Virgin Mary. In German: *Marienspiel*. (Mantzius HISTORY II 16, 26)

Mary Queen of Scots cap   A heart-shaped linen hood with a peak pointed over the forehead. Frequently worn with a veil hanging behind. (Walkup DRESS-ING 163)

masamune (Japanese)   The head of a *bunraku* puppet used for characters of virtuous old men. (Keene BUNRAKU 225)

máscara (Spanish)   1. A mask. 2. A masquerade.

mascherata (Italian)   A masquerade.

maschere (Italian)   *Commedia dell'arte* masked actors. (Philpott DICTIONARY)

mask   1. To hide from view, such as offstage space masked from the au-dience's view by flats or draperies. Hence, masking, masking border, masking piece, to mask in, to mask off. 2. In acting, to take a position which covers another performer and spoils the view of the audience. 3. Short for masking control—a diaphragm or other device which shapes a beam of light coming from an instrument. Also called a cut-off, mat, or cut-out mask. See also: gobo. (Sellman/Lessley ESSENTIALS 68, Stern MANAGEMENT) 4. A full or partial face covering or disguise. 5. To put on such a covering. 6. A variant spelling of masque. (Bowman/Ball THEATRE) 7. In Britain, an undesirable effect in makeup created by failure to continue color on the face to a point well under the jaw and chin line. This creates an unwanted contrast in color between face and neck. (Melvill MAKE-UP 9)

mask and flipper   In lighting, a term sometimes used for barn-door shutters with two hinged leaves and two sliding cut-offs. See also: barn doors.

masked comedy   Usually, *commedia dell'arte*.

masked play   See: *barong, bugaku, chhau, gigaku, khon, lokhon khol, manirimdu, no, parwa, sandae, sato kagura, topeng, wayang wong.*

masker   See: masquer.

maskhara (Kashmiri)   A clown or jester in *bhand pathar*, a folk theatre in Kashmir, north India. See also: *vidusaka*. (Mathur DRAMA 44)

masking   See: masking piece.

masking control, mask   A diaphragm, cut-off, or other means of modifying the size or shape of a beam of light. (Bowman/Ball THEATRE)

masking piece   A scenic unit (flat, border, backing, etc.) used to conceal part of the stage from the view of the audience.

maskinmester (Danish)   Stage manager. (Marker/Marker "Bloch" 91)

masque, mask   A spectacular private theatrical entertainment (masquerade) which developed in Renaissance Italy and spread to the courts of France and England. Usually intended for a single performance, a masque combined elaborate costumes, music, poetry, and spectacular staging effects. It was a social event in which members of the court acted as both spectators and performers.

masque (French)   1. Before the 19th C, a mask; especially in comedy and tragedy, a mask which served as a voice amplifier. 2. An exercise in improvisation for performers, used by director Jacques Copeau in the early 20th C, in which the face was covered by a neutral mask and voice use was forbidden. The object was to train the performer's body to emulate and support what the voice would ordinarily impart. (Angotti/Herr "Decroux" 2)

masquer, masker   A performer in a masque.

masque theatre   African dramatic performances of masqueraders, mummers, and masked actors in masques (character sketches, revues, acrobatics, and dances) before general audiences. The term was popularized by Joel Adedeji in his description of the African theatre of the *alarinjo* (Yoruba); the purpose was to distinguish masque theatre from masquerade displays realized for purely ritualistic functions. Like the English masques of the 17th C, the *alarinjo* originated at court—the court of Alaafin Ogbolu Abipa, King of the Yoruba kingdom of Oyo toward the end of the 16th C. The king's staff bearer organized a variety entertainment of six masked actors as part of a banquet ceremony. Later the masque became a traveling theatre. (Adedeji glossary)

masque tragedy   A performance of tragedy in which the players wear masks, as in Greek tragedy.

mass   1. In scene design, the sense of size and weight. 2. In directing, the grouping of performers to create a sense of size and weight.

mass actions   Open-air, propagandistic Russian presentations in the early 20th C. Also called mass performances or mass plays. They dealt with historical and Revolutionary themes and used audience participation. (Orlovsky in Bradshaw SOVIET 24-25, Gorchakov RUSSIA 148)

mass drama   A play focusing on groups of characters rather than individuals.

mass performances, mass plays   See: mass actions.

mass spectacles   1. Communist demonstrations presented in Russia in the early 20th C using theatrical decor, properties, costumes and makeup. Political allegories and caricatures were presented. 2. Russian historical re-enactments with thousands of performers. (Gorchakov RUSSIA 146-151)

mass theatre   Open-air representations of past political and military events, presented in Russia after the Revolution of 1917. Also called militant theatre. Evidently similar to or the same as mass actions. (Carter SPIRIT 66).

mast   See: chariot-and-pole system.

master   1. Especially among backstage technicians, a master control or master switch. See also: grand master. 2. Especially in the 17th C, the leader or manager of a theatrical company. 3. In the early 17th C, the leader of a children's troupe. (Bowman/Ball THEATRE)

master art work   See: *Gesamtkunstwerk*.

master carpenter   Especially in the professional theatre, the stage employee in charge of scenery and the scenery crew. His duties may extend to maintenance of the stage, flies, gridiron, safety curtain, and non-electrical machinery. Also called the boss carpenter, building carpenter, head carpenter, stage carpenter, or scene-shop foreman. A comparable position in the non-commercial theatre is that of technical director. (Bax MANAGEMENT, Gillette/Gillette SCENERY 7)

master control   See: grand master.

master controller   See: preset.

master crew   During the rehearsal period of a Broadway production, the chief (or master) carpenter, electrician, and prop man. (Gibson SEASAW 26)

master dimmer, master dimmer wheel   See: grand master.

master electrician   The person in charge of the stage lighting and its crew.

master fader   See: preset.

master handle   See: grand master.

master image   See: dramatic metaphor.

master of ceremonies, mistress of ceremonies   Chiefly in vaudeville, an announcer, commentator, introducer, and director. Often abbreviated to MC, M.C., emcee, or emsee. Called in Britain the chairman or chairwoman, though the term master of ceremonies was used in 18th C Bath to designate the arranger of entertainments.

master of costumes   See: wardrobe keeper.

master of secrets   See: *maître des feintes*.

Master of the Revels   1. A court official in Renaissance England, in charge of court entertainments. In time he became the censor of plays presented by public theatre companies; that responsibility was later taken over by the Lord Chamberlain. 2. An old term for master of ceremonies. (Bowman/Ball THEATRE)

master property man   See: property master.

master switch   See: grand master.

master of the music   In Restoration theatres and later, the leader of the band of instrumentalists.

masu (Japanese)   Literally: measuring box. A reserved seating area in the pit (*doma*) of a traditional *kabuki, bunraku*, and rarely, *no* theatre, marked out by wooden partitions. Each *masu* was four to five feet square and held five to seven kneeling spectators. Between 1766 and c. 1880 the whole pit area of a *kabuki* theatre was converted into *masu*. With rare exceptions theatres of all types changed to Western-style seating after the 1923 Tokyo earthquake. (Ernst KABUKI 48, Leiter ENCYCLOPEDIA 225-226)

masugami (Japanese)   A *no* mask of a young woman, worn by a priestess or an agitated woman. (Shimazaki NOH 61)

mat   1. Short for matinee. 2. A cutoff used to shape a beam of light coming from a lighting instrument; often a piece of metal in a frame at the front of a spotlight. Also called a mask. 3. A grass mat. (Bowman/Ball THEATRE)

mât (French)   Mast; an upright pole that supports a wing flat (*chassis*). (Moynet FRENCH 19, 26–27) Also called an *âme* or *sablière*.

matahei (Japanese)   The head of a *bunraku* puppet used for "good" comic characters. (Keene BUNRAKU 220)

ma teng hsi (Chinese)   See: *madengxi*.

mathentheng (Indonesian)   The standard arm position for somewhat aggressive Javanese *wayang* characters. The rear arm is placed on the hip, a stance of defiance in Java, and the front arm hangs straight down. (Long JAVANESE 32-33) *mati-akhara* (Assamese)   Basic dance exercises in *ankiya nat* folk theatre. (Vatsyayan TRADITIONAL 107)

matinee, matinée   An afternoon performance. Short form: mat. From the French *matin*, morning. Hence, matinee idol—a star actor who appealed to the young women who frequented matinees in the late 19th and early 20th C. Hence, matinee girl, matinee hat, matinee madame, matinee mama, matineer, etc. (Carroll MATINEE 10)

matinee call   A notice to performers and crews of an afternoon performance.

matinee feeling   In performers, a lax attitude toward matinee performances, and hence, toward any performance.

matinee idol   See: matinee.

matinée inédite (French)   One of several types of 19th C French experimental theatre productions designed to bring talented but unknown playwrights to the attention of the theatregoing public. (Carlson FRENCH 180)

matraca (Spanish)   A rattle often used to summon an audience.

matrix interconnection panel   In stage lighting, an interconnecting device which encloses current-carrying crossbars. The visible surface of the device, sometimes called a pin matrix, contains many holes into which pin plugs can be inserted to make appropriate electrical connections between the horizontal and vertical crossbars.

matrona (Latin Roman)   Wife. Along with the courtesan, one of the important female roles in Roman comedy. Plural *matronae*. (Duckworth NATURE 255-257)

matsubamemono (Japanese)   Literally: pine-board play. A *kabuki* dance play based on a *no* or a *kyogen* play and played in a setting that reproduces the traditional *nogaku* stage of a pine tree painted on a wooden back wall. The first such play was *The Subscription List*, 1840; in Brandon TRADITIONAL 211-236. Also called *matsubame kyogen* (pine-board play). (Ernst KABUKI 137-138)

mattatore (Italian)   Italian slang incorporating 'to kill' and 'actor'—hence, actor killer: a performer who hogs the stage to the extent that fellow cast members are forgotten. (Longman "Duse's" 169)

mattavarani, mattavarini (Sanskrit)   A pillared area of the stage in a classical Indian theatre. It constitutes "one of the riddles of the *Natyasastra*" but it may have been a "ritual sanctuary" for performers. (Kale THEATRIC 23) Other interpretations of Bharata's vague description are: side stages, verandas of the main stage, or elephants on a frieze. (Richmond in Baumer/Brandon SANSKRIT 78)

mattress   A heavy false beard.

mawari butai (Japanese)   Literally: revolving stage. The first large permanent revolving stage, flush with the stage proper, was installed in *kabuki* in 1793. Since that time it has become a standard feature of all *kabuki* theatres. Temporary revolves, built on top of the main stage and intended to move only actors or a small unit of scenery, were used in *bunraku* as early as 1758. (Ernst KABUKI 53)

mawayang (Indonesian)   Literally: perform *wayang*. One of the earliest terms indicating Javanese *wayang* performance, inscribed on a copper plate dated 907. (Holt ART 282)

mawlam (Thai)   See: *mohlam*.

mawlum (Lao)   See: *mohlam*.

mawlum moo (Lao)   See: *mohlam luong*.

ma'yong (Malaysian)   Literally: queen. A court dance drama performed principally by women. Males play clown and secondary roles. Flourished in the 1920s and revived in the 1970s. The name comes from the important role of the queen in the play. (Sheppard in Osman TRADITIONAL 133-142) Also spelled *mak yong*. (Yousof "Kelantan" 92-93)

maximum overall length   See: MOL.

mazarine   See: mezzanine.

Mazda   The General Electric Company's trade name for its lamps. Earlier in this century, the term was loosely used for nearly all tungsten filament incandescent lamps in the U.S. The word is now rare in the theatre. (Fuchs LIGHTING 110, 155-156)

Mazda C   See: C-lamp.

Mazda lane   Formerly, Broadway.

mazurka   A Polish folk dance in moderate triple measure.

MB   Music bell; formerly, a prompter's cue to signal musicians to play. (Shattuck SHAKESPEARE 22)

mbanjut (Indonesian)   To lift an enemy's "spirit," rendering him unconscious. A fighting technique used primarily by the gods in Javanese shadow theatre (*wayang kulit*). (Long JAVANESE 86)

mbanting (Indonesian)   A violent fighting movement in Javanese shadow theatre (*wayang kulit*). An opponent is lifted high in the air and smashed to the ground. (Long JAVANESE 58)

mbanting-binanting (Indonesian)   A Javanese shadow theatre (*wayang kulit*) fighting technique. Two characters alternately throw each other to the ground. (Long JAVANESE 58)

mboguo (Akan)   In Ghana, the musical choral parts of *anansegoro* (story theatre). These parts are sometimes used as interludes and sometimes as accompaniment. (Adedeji glossary)

mbucal (Indonesian)   A Javanese shadow theatre (*wayang kulit*) battle technique in which an opponent is thrown off-screen. (Long JAVANESE 82-83)

M.C., MC   Master or mistress of ceremonies.

McCandless method   A lighting arrangement in which paired spotlights (from right and left) illuminate each portion of the acting area in a proscenium stage. The upstage areas are lit from the first pipe and the downstage areas from an auditorium ceiling position such as the first beam. Ideally, each pair of spotlights hits its area at an angle of about 45°; the spotlights are, however, separated from each other so that they meet at a horizontal angle of about 60° or very little more. In addition, the lights from one side are gelled slightly cool, and from the other, slightly warm. See also: double McCandless. (McCandless METHOD 33-65, Lounsbury THEATRE 84)

MD   1. Musical director. 2. Middle door.

MDOP, MDPS   Middle door opposite prompt, middle door prompt side. Found in some 18th C London promptbooks to indicate which proscenium door or wing passageway was to be used for an entrance.

meal ticket   A theatrical sponsor or backer.

measure   In dance, the grouping of beats by means of accent.

meat show   A production with strippers.

mechane (Greek)   A hoisting device in use on the stage by the late 5th C BC. Designed to suspend characters in mid-air or to move them through the air, the *mechane* consisted essentially of a fixed and a movable pulley. The fixed pulley, perhaps sometimes with a crane-like arm, was attached at or near the top of the *skene* (scene house), while the movable pulley was fastened to a basket or other device containing the character or characters to be suspended or moved.

The spelling *mekane* and the plural *mechanai* are uncommon. *Machina* is the Latin, machine (the literal meaning) the English. Similarly or identically used are Greek *eorema*, *krade*, and *geranos*, and English crane, flying machine (especially by Bieber), and machine for (the) gods. Fig-branch may have been a common twitting name for the *mechane* or some part of it. From the use of the machine to suspend or introduce gods came the English deus ex machina; originally the Latin for god from the machine, the phrase has been widely used in figurative senses. See also: *deus ex machina*. (Arnott SCENIC 52, 72-78, 90, 114; Pickard-Cambridge DIONYSUS 23, 55-56, 127-128, 236, 282; Gascoigne WORLD 29; Bieber HISTORY 76, figs. 281, 282)

mechanic   In 17th C theatres and later, the stage worker responsible for the stage machinery. (Anonymous COMPARISON 21) See also: machinist.

mechanical dimmer   A term sometimes used for a device which reduces the brightness of a light mechanically rather than electrically. The classical example is the use of an iris shutter on an arc light. (Bowman/Ball THEATRE)

mechanical interlock   Especially on older resistance and auto-transformer control boards, an arrangement which permits a number of dimmers to be tied together mechanically. The effect is that the movement of one of the interlocked dimmers moves all of them. (Bellman SCENE, Bellman LIGHTING 176)

mechanics   Blocking; the stage movements planned by a director for the performers.

medallion   A rug on the floor in a 'front room' or 'center door fancy' stage setting.

media cavea (Latin Roman)   See: *maenianum primum*.

mediated tragedy   A 19th C term for a play that tends toward tragedy but ends happily. The more common term now (and often in the past) is tragicomedy. (Hennequin PLAYWRITING 41)

Medici collar   See: ruff.

medium   1. In Britain, from at least the mid-19th C, the usual term for any filter which modifies the color of light. Plural media, sometimes mediums. A shortening of color medium, the term has been used in the U.S. for many decades, but appears to be used less often than in Britain; the closest U.S. analogue is probably gel. Academically, medium is sometimes used in the U.S. in its optical sense in discussions of the behavior of light: any material which transmits light to any degree. Since this includes, for example, air and clear glass, the stage use is a specific narrowing of the optical meaning. (Baker THEATRECRAFT; Rees GAS 30, 36, 37; Bellman LIGHTING 66) 2. The binder in a transparent coating such as lamp dip or slide-painting lacquer. Typically cellulose nitrate, cellulose acetate, or (currently) any of a variety of copolymers. 3. A medium-sized show girl, usually a dancer. (Carrington THEATRICANA)

medium base   A lamp base of standard household size. Of other bases used in the theatre, the mogul is larger and the candelabra smaller. See also: lamp base.

medium curtain   A curtain raised or lowered (especially lowered) at a moderate speed.

medium frame   See: color frame.

medium light   Early in the 19th C, the name given a magic lantern with a color wheel. The ''unearthly'' effects of the irregularly-turning color wheel in the storm scene of Edmund Kean's *King Lear* at Drury Lane were the first known use of the magic lantern in legitimate drama. (Rees GAS 84-85).

medium throw   See: throw.

med opera   A melodrama dealing with medicine.

medvezhatnik (Russian)   A bear trainer in Russia in the 18th and 19th C— a trouper descended from the *skomorokhi* (strolling players) of earlier centuries. (Yershov SOVIET 7)

Megalesia (Latin Roman)   See: *ludi Megalenses*.

megger   Theatre slang for a director. (Sobel HANDBOOK)

megile (Yiddish)   The Biblical story of Esther, the basis of Purim plays. In Hebrew: *Megillah*. See also: *Purimshpiln*. (Sandrow VAGABOND 2, Rosten JOYS 295)

mehossi (Korean)   A clown in the *bona* and *salp'an* sections of a *namsadang* performance. (Kim "Namsadang" 12)

mei hsiang (Chinese)   See: *meixiang*.

mei hu chü, mei hu hsi (Chinese)   See: *meihuju*.

meihuju, mei hu chü (Chinese)   A form of music-drama (*xiqu*) that originated in what are now Mei and Hu counties in Shaanxi Province; popular today throughout Shaanxi and in parts of other north central and northwestern provinces. It is closely related to northern and southern *qu*; it uses *lianquti* musical structure, with more than 100 fixed-melodies (*qupai*), and musical accompaniment which features the three-string lute (*sanxian*). Also called Mei and Hu County theatre (*meihuxi* or *mei hu hsi*), song theatre (*quzixi* or *ch'ü tzu hsi*), three-string lute theatre (*xianzixi* or *hsien tzu hsi*), and enchanting theatre (*mihuxi* or *mi hu hsi*).

meihuxi (Chinese)   See: *meihuju*.

meixiang, mei hsiang (Chinese)   Literally: plum-blossom fragrance. A soubrette; a type of stock character in Yuan *zaju*. (Dolby HISTORY 60)

mekane (Greek)   See: *mechane*.

mek mulong (Malaysian)   A program of song, dance, and comic interludes, the latter featuring interplay between the main character, often a king, and two or more masked clown figures. Performed in northwestern Malaysia and in southern Thailand. (Skeat MALAY 519)

mela (Sanskrit)   A folk performing troupe. (Gargi FOLK 205)

meller, mellerdrama, mellerdrammer, melo   Melodrama.

melocution   Mellifluous elocution, characteristic of old-fashioned villains. (Granville DICTIONARY)

melodram (German)   A musical work or part of it in which the orchestra plays a commentary on dialogue as it is spoken.

melodrama   A play designed to thrill spectators, with a stock set of characters (hero, heroine, villain, etc.), rapid turns in the dramatic action, a simplistic moral universe, and an ending with evil punished and virtue rewarded. The form has existed for centuries, and 'tragedies' with an emphasis on plot at the expense of character are sometimes called melodramas. The term derives from the Italian *melodramma*, which meant opera. Melodramas in England in the early 19th C, when the term began to be used, employed music to circumvent restrictions on the staging of plays in minor theatres (hence the word: literally, music drama). Eventually, serious plays with plots that thrilled, whether using music or not, were classed as melodramas. The form remains popular and is most frequently found in films and television. (Cameron/Gillespie ENJOYMENT, Cameron/Hoffman GUIDE, Millett/Bentley ART 12)

mélodrame (French)   Pantomimic action by a character, with accompanying music to express emotions. Jean Jacques Rousseau is credited with inventing *mélodrame* in the 18th C. By the 19th C the term began to be applied to thrillers, such as those by Guilbert Pixérécourt, and meant essentially the same as the English term melodrama. (Hartnoll COMPANION) Also called *tragédie du peuple*.

melodramma (Italian)   Opera, or drama with music. A descendant of the *favola pastorale* (pastoral drama). The term was used as early as the 16th C, and is related to the English melodrama, the French *mélodrame*, and the German *melodram*, though the French and German carry almost opposite meanings. Opera *libretti*, especially those for serious operas, often have many of the characteristics of melodrama: stock characters, thrilling plots, etc.

melody   One of Aristotle's six parts of a play; also translated as music.

melon sleeve   See: balloon sleeve.

melos   An operatic song.

melukat (Indonesian)   A purification ceremony in Bali in which either *wayang kulit* or dance-drama is an integral part. See also: *wayang lemah*. (Moerdowo BALINESE II 2)

member   A performer belonging to an acting troupe, especially a stock company. In Elizabethan times, the term distinguished a regular member of a troupe from a hired man (hireling) and from an apprentice. (Bowman/Ball THEATRE)

memoria de apariencias (Spanish)   A signed set of instructions, provided by a playwright, describing the scenery to be built for his play. Almost exclusively connected with *autos*. (Shergold SPANISH)

memorial book   In the past, a book, like a promptbook, written up during or after a production by one wishing to preserve an account of the scenery, business, acting, etc. (Shattuck SHAKESPEARE 5)

memorized fade time   In a memory lighting system, a fade whose duration has been put into memory, whence it may be started by the operator and run by an autofader. (Bellman LIGHTING 244)

memory lighting system   A light control system in which a console stores light intensity settings and the duration of fades, recalling either or both as desired. Such systems, some of which include computer elements, are sometimes called computer lighting systems. See also: computer-assisted lighting system. (Bellman LIGHTING 239-272, Pilbrow LIGHTING 152-157, Sellman/Lessley ESSENTIALS 135)

men (Japanese)   Literally: face. A generic term for masks in *bugaku, gigaku,* and many folk theatre forms. *Gigaku* and *bugaku* masks are illustrated in Togi GAGAKU pl. 58-69, 99-101 and Noma MASKS pl. 2-25. Also called *kamen*. Masks in *no* are commonly called *omote* (*men* and *omote* are alternative readings of the same ideograph). *Men* also appears in compounds, as in *nomen* (*no* mask). (Komparu NOH 226–228)

menace   1. The character or role of a villain. 2. A performer who plays such parts.

menagerie   A nickname given by performers to a theatre orchestra. (Downs THEATRE II 1136)

men aside   In Britain, stage workers offstage on each side, helping to run a performance (Baker THEATRECRAFT)

mending batten   A batten used to hold flats together temporarily.

mending cleat   See: dutchman.

mending plate   A flat metal plate used to strengthen scenery at a joint. (Bowman/Ball THEATRE)

mendu (Malaysian)   A late 19th C form of theatre in which Malay stories were enacted by a cast of twenty to fifty performers. Actors were dressed in Chinese costume. Also called *wayang makau*. (Skeat MALAY 520)

menek (Indonesian)   To climb into the branches of a tree. A movement used exclusively by monkey characters in Javanese shadow theatre (*wayang kulit*) performances. (Long JAVANESE 105)

ménestrel (French), **menestrel**   See: minstrel.

ménestrie (French)   Medieval minstrelsy. (Chambers MEDIAEVAL II 105)

ménestrier (French)   See: minstrel.

meneur, meneuse (French)   A star performer in a French music-hall show. (Leslie ACT 127)

mengadap rebab (Malaysian)   Literally: paying respect to the *rebab*. The opening ceremonial dance in *ma'yong* in which female performers slowly circle the stage. (Malm in Osman TRADITIONAL 339)

menghantar (Malaysian)   To send home, by reciting invocations, spirits that have attended a ritual feast. A ritual cleansing of the environment, used in most ritual theatre ceremonies. (Sweeney RAMAYANA 278)

mengker (Indonesian)   Literally: to turn. In Java, a movement used frequently in shadow theatre battle scenes when a character turns his back on an opponent. The movement may be part of a series of avoiding movements, or it may be used as an act of defiance of one's enemy. (Long JAVANESE 81)

menu   A printed program.

ménu-plaisir (French)   A light entertainment at the court of Louis XIV. (Moynet FRENCH 18, 191–192)

menus propos (French)   Rapid, glib speech like that of a barker or vaude-villian. The medieval *sot* is thought to have combined such patter with his clowning. (Frank MEDIEVAL 245)

menyemah (Malaysia)   See: *berjamu*.

mercury vapor lamp   A gaseous discharge lamp which produces blue-green light (and considerable ultraviolet) by the action of electric current on mercury vapor. (Wehlburg GLOSSARY, Bellman SCENE) *merde* (French)   The dancer's equivalent—best left untranslated—of the actor's "Break a leg" or "Have a good show," said by one dancer to another before going on stage.

mère folle (French)   The head of a medieval provincial fool company or *compagnie joyeuse*. The person was male, despite the name. (Chambers MEDIAEVAL I 374)

mère sotte (French)   The second in command in a fool company or *compagnie joyeuse*. The person was male, despite the name. (Chambers MEDIAEVAL I 376)

meretrix (Latin Roman)   Courtesan. Important among the female roles in Roman comedy, the type shows a number of variations in the plays of Plautus and Terence. Plural *meretrices*. (Duckworth NATURE 258-261)

meriyasu (Japanese)   1. In *kabuki*, a type of plaintive *shamisen* melody played offstage during a melancholy mime scene. (Leiter ENCYCLOPEDIA 231) 2. In *bunraku*, a type of emotion-tinged instrumental melody played as background to a dialogue scene or a battle. It is analogous to *aikata* offstage music in *kabuki*. (Malm in Brandon CHUSHINGURA 65-66)

merken   A material that looks like fuzz; it is used under a G-string by a stripper to create the effect of pubic hair. (Wilmeth LANGUAGE)

merry andrew, merry Andrew, Merry Andrew   A clown.

merry-merry   The chorus. (Sobel NEW)

Merry Widow hat   A 20th C feathered, wide-brimmed hat worn high on the coiffure front. (Chalmers CLOTHES 250)

mesaulion (Greek)   See: *diaulion*.

meshchanskaia komediia, meshchanskaia tragediia (Russian)   See: *slëznaia drama*.

meshoyrerim (Yiddish)   Cantors' assistants in rural Poland about 1900. One of a small group of entertainers who eked out a modest living from performing. See also: *klezmorim, badkhen*. (Kirshenblatt-Gimblett "Contraband" 7)

message play   A drama which espouses a cause, a play with a thesis.

metabasis (Greek)   Change of fortune. This is one of the terms used by Aristotle in the *Poetics* in discussing the necessary qualities of the "complex" tragic plot. In translation, there is danger of confusing it with *peripeteia*, often rendered "reversal of fortune."

metakinesis   The psychic aspect of movement, the latter being purposeful and to some extent functional. Modern dance distinguishes itself from other dance forms by virtue of its recognition of this purposefulness and emphasis on function. (Love DANCE 54)

metallic dimmer   In Britain, a dimmer which uses resistance wire. The term presumably dates from the early 20th C, by contrast with the liquid dimmer, a British term for the water resistance dimmer. (Bowman/Ball THEATRE)

metallic powders   Metal-based substances used by performers to create special hair and beard effects. A non-metallic makeup which gives a metallic look can be used on the body as well as on the hair and is now preferred for metallic effects.

metatheatre   1. Plays that deal with the theatre and theatricality. 2. Such a play.

meter   1. In dance, the time between pulses, divided regularly and arithmetically. 2. In music, the scheme of regularly recurring accents indicated by a time signature.

(the) Method   The best-known U.S. version of the Stanislavsky System of acting, stressing inner truth and realism. Associated with the Actors' Studio in New York City.

métier (French)   A medieval mystery play. (Mantzius HISTORY II 3)

metrical-type   See: *banshi*.

metsuke bashira (Japanese)   Literally: eye-fixing pillar. The downstage right pillar of a *no* stage. So named because the masked *shite* actor looks at it to orient his position on stage. (Nippon Gakujutsu JAPANESE xiii)

metteur en scène (French)   The director of a play. See also: *régisseur*.

mewinten dalang (Indonesian)   The ceremony at which a Balinese shadow play puppeteer (*dalang*) is consecrated as a priest-performer (*pemangku dalang, amangku dalang*). With this spiritual power he can perform ritual *wayang lemah* or *wayang sudamala*. (McPhee in Belo TRADITIONAL 152, Moerdowo BALINESE II 117-118)

Meydan Oyunu (Turkish)   An early form of Turkish theatre in which the audience was seated around the performance. (And KARAGÖZ 12)

mezzanine   1. A seating area just above or behind the main auditorium seating, or the forward part of such a mezzanine; the first balcony. The equivalent British term is dress circle, or sometimes grand circle or royal circle. A mezzanine may be overhung by a balcony and thus have a low ceiling, making it an intimate area. 2. The space under the stage where traps, sliders, elevators, and the like are operated. Old spellings of mezzanine include mazarine and mezzonine.

mezzanine (French)   In the 19th C, a partial floor or stage, stored in the basement below the stage floor. (Moynet FRENCH 32)

Michael Feeney   A hard-boiled director or stage manager. (Berrey/Van den Bark SLANG 576)

michiyuki (Japanese)   Literally: a journey. A travel scene: 1. In *no*, a sung section in the first part of a play in which the secondary character (*waki*) describes travelling to the present place of action. (Inoura HISTORY 58, 59) 2. In *kyogen*, a similar scene at the beginning of the play. (Berberich "Rapture" 60) 3. In *kabuki*, a dance-act showing a journey, often by lovers and usually in a gentle, melancholy mood. Originally one act in a longer play; by the late 19th C independent *michiyuki* were also composed. An example is in *The Forty-Seven Samurai* in Brandon CHUSHINGURA 179-186. (Scott KABUKI 98-99, Bowers JAPANESE 167-168) 4. The final scene of a three-act *bunraku* domestic play (*sewamono*) in which young lovers travel to a famous temple where they kill themselves to escape from intolerable circumstances. See also: *shinjumono*. (Keene CHIKAMATSU 24-25)

Middle Comedy   A transitional comic form of 4th C BC Greece. Middle Comedy, of which little is known, was essentially a bridge between Old Comedy and New Comedy. It may be dated from the late 5th C BC to about the time of Alexander the Great—say 330 BC—when it was succeeded by New Comedy. Its spirit was neither so exuberant nor so biting as that of Old Comedy, and its content parodied serious literature and drama along with certain social types; because of the defeats of the Peloponnesian Wars, there was no further interest in political lampoon. Some have felt that Middle Comedy never existed at all. The occurrence of a form which reflected Old Comedy and pointed toward New Comedy is, however, nowhere denied. (Norwood GREEK 37-58, Vaughn DRAMA)

middle door, middle door opposite prompt, middle door prompt side   See: MD, MDOP, MDPS.

middle gallery, mid gallery   Formerly, in Britain, the second of three balconies.

middle line   1. The center line of a stage—an imaginary line at center from downstage to upstage, dividing the area into two halves. 2. In stage rigging, the second of three or the third of five in a set of lines.

middleman   The interlocutor in a minstrel show.

midimu   One of the danced and masked ceremonies of the Makonde people of Tanzania. The ceremony's principal function is to celebrate the end of the initiation period of the male and female into man and womanhood. In the ceremony a performer appears wearing a mask of an old man, representing the ancestors of the initiates. (Gründ-Khaznader "Ritual" 25-26)

midnight matinee   Especially in Britain, a benefit, usually charitable, scheduled after all shows in town have ended, thus making it possible for participants in other shows to attend. See also: professional matinee. (Troubridge BENEFIT 84)

mie (Japanese)   A pose by one or more characters in *kabuki*. Motion and sound cease in order to emphasize a high point in a scene. The torso is set, limbs lock into position, the head snaps front, and eyes glare intensely. Two or three beats of the wooden clappers (*tsuke*) accent the pose. In the strongest *mie* one eye crosses over the other (*nirami*). *Mie* are frequently used by strong male characters in *aragoto* style plays and in fighting scenes (*tachimawari*). They are rarely performed by female or gentle male characters. See also: *kimari, ma, omoiire*. (Brandon in Brandon/Malm/Shively STUDIES 84-85, Leiter ENCY-CLOPEDIA 232-234)

migawari (Japanese)   Literally: body substitution. A *bunraku* scene in which a child is sacrificed, so that his or her body can be substituted for another person and thus save that person's life. An example is Kumagai killing his son in *Kumagai's Battle Camp* in Brandon CLASSIC 180-182. Called by Hamamura et al, a "scapegoat" scene (KABUKI 25).

mihuxi, mi hu hsi (Chinese)   See: *meihuju*.

mi kagura (Japanese)   A serious dance or dance-play connected to the Shinto religion and often performed as a ceremony in the Imperial court. (Inoura HISTORY 16-17)

miko mai (Japanese)   Literally: priestess dance. A ritual dance performed by a young Shinto priestess (*miko*). See also: *kagura*. (Hoff SONG 153)

Milan bonnet   A 16th C gold or cloth cap of German origin, worn on one side of the head, with a caul underneath. (Chalmers CLOTHES 18)

miles (Latin Roman)   Literally: soldier. An occasional shortening of *miles gloriosus*. (Duckworth NATURE 264, 265)

miles gloriosus (Latin Roman)   The swaggering soldier, especially of Plautine comedy. Often cowardly and gullible, he is similar to the *capitano* of the Italian *commedia dell'arte*, who is often said to be a descendant. Also called a braggart soldier, boastful soldier, swaggering soldier, braggart captain, captain, braggart warrior, and similar terms. (Nicoll MASKS 43, 246; Duchartre ITALIAN 29; Vaughn DRAMA)

militant theatre   See: mass theatre.

milk   To try to get more laughs or tears out of a line, piece of business, or scene than it deserves. Hence, milk a scene, milk it dry, milk the audience, milk man. See also: play for a round, curtain taker.

milk jump   1. A trip by a performing troupe to a small town accessible only by a milk train—an early-morning train that stops at all stations. 2. A one-night stand in such a town.

milkmen's matinee   In theatres in early western U.S. mining camps, a variety show that ran until four in the morning. (Wilmeth LANGUAGE)

milky way   A theatrical district.

Miller   See: Joe Miller.

Millie   A late 19th C corruption of the French Mlle. (*mademoiselle*), preceding the name of a belly dancer. (Sobel BURLEYCUE 227)

mimad   An actress, especially in the mimes of the Eastern Roman Empire, in early Christian times. Rare. (Tunison TRADITIONS 28)

mimae (Latin Roman)   Female performers in the mime. Singular *mima*. Both singular and plural occur, though rarely, in U.S. English. (Allen ANTIQUITIES 26)

mime   1. In Greece and Rome, a form of popular farce, usually improvised, which used dialogue, song and dance. 2. A performer in such a piece. 3. A performance of such a piece.

The ancient mime varied a good deal during its thousand-year history but was built on dance, facial expression, and gesture-movement which often involved the whole body: physical skills were of the essence. Subjects mocked might involve any aspect of life, including the life of the gods. City scenes were apparently usual. In the Roman mime, a favorite theme was adultery, but stupidity of all kinds in all classes was a constant subject of ridicule.

The mimes were short, often phallic, usually plotless, and unmasked. During much of their history, they were mainly intermission entertainments or afterpieces. By early Christian times, the mimes were the most popular kind of Roman theatre; by the end of antiquity they had supplanted other forms almost completely. Though often denounced as coarse and vulgar, they are regarded by modern scholars as neither moral nor immoral. Allen's characterization of them as ". . . a combination of ballet and harlequinade" may be the most complimentary modern comment; but Seneca saw redeeming social value; he complained that the mime neglected some of society's evils.

Among the Greek terms for mime performers were *mimos, moros, mimodos, mimologoi* (plural). *Deikelistai* (plural) may be related. Latin has *planipes* and *mimologi* (plural) as well as *mimus* and *mima*, used mainly in such phrases as *actor mimi, actor mimicus*, and *actor mimarius*. *Exodiarius* and *exodiaria, emboliarius* and *emboliaria* are used of the mime performer in *exodia* and *embolima* respectively. An early term was *saltator* and a late one *histrio*. The *archimimus* or *archimima* was the leading performer. For meanings 1 and 3, Greek has *mimos* and *mimodia*, the latter plural, while Latin uses *mimus, planipedia*, and *fabula riciniata; paegnia* and *hypotheses* are, respectively, mimes with and without plots. For the performer, U.S. English has mimologist and mima, both rare. Further information can be found in the individual entries. (Nicoll MASKS 80-130; Beare ROMAN 149-158, 239-240, 316-319; Allen ANTIQUITIES 24-26) 4. Now, one who specializes in wordless performances. 5. A play enacted without words. 6. To act, especially in a pantomime or other dramatic form, without words. Hence, mimer, miming, mimester, mimology. (Crampton HANDBOOK, Bowman/Ball THEATRE)

mimed mystery   In the early 14th C, a kind of dramatic pantomime celebrating a national victory or the entry of an important personage into a town. Evidently similar to a *tableau vivant* (French). (Sobel HANDBOOK)

mimesis (Greek)   Literally: imitation. This is the word used by Aristotle in the *Poetics* for the method common to poetry, music, dancing, painting, and sculpture. He does not define the term, and it has been variously interpreted. The meaning is broad and does not indicate reproduction of reality in any literal sense. English mimesis is often used in dealing with Aristotle.

mimesis   1. Acting by visual means, without words. Hence, mimetic. (Bowman/Ball THEATRE) 2. See: *mimesis*.

mimetic instinct   A natural tendency of human beings to imitate, to act.

mimic   1. One who imitates another. 2. To impersonate. Hence, mimicry. 3. In memory lighting systems, any arrangement which provides the operator with specific channel information at any given moment. Sometimes called channel mimic in Britain. (Bellman LIGHTING 244, Pilbrow LIGHTING 152)

mimic fool   In the ancient mime, a bald-headed fool. A number of bronze and terra cotta figures are thought to represent this clown. Along with the bald head, they show large ears and thick lips and often a broad or hooked nose. See also: secondary mime, *stupidus*. (Nicoll MASKS 47–49; 87–88, figs. 31–36)

mimi scriptor (Latin Roman)   A writer of mimes. Also called a *mimographus* or *mimorum scriptor*. See also: mimologist, mimographer. (Nicoll MASKS 110)

mimodia (Greek)   Lyric mime, operatic mime. A general term for this meaning, the word is thought to have included a number of varieties of early musical mime. See also: *magodia, hilarodia, simodia, lysiodia*. (Nicoll MASKS 34)

mimodos (Greek)   Literally: mime-singer. From *mimos* and *ode*. It is possible that the *mimus* (mime-actor, mime-speaker) and the *mimodos* were often the same person. (Nicoll MASKS 34)

mimo-drama   A pantomimed, serious, artistic entertainment. (Bowman/Ball THEATRE)

mimodrame (French)   A 19th C play in which (by statute) only one actor was allowed to speak. The others responded to him via signs (miming); their lines were delivered by a person behind the scenes in synchronization with the gestures.

mimodrame militaire (French)   After 1830, a form in which, to add variety and dialogue to a theatrical spectacle, a troupe of cavalry was joined with the actors. Battle charges, military music, and the enemy, were represented on stage, in a circus ring, and at its entrances. (Moynet FRENCH 172)

mimographer   A writer of mimes. The OED reports the synonym mimograph obsolete, as it does mimology (a mime performance) and both mimologer and mimologist, terms for a mime-player.

mimographus (Latin Roman)   See: *mimi scriptor*.

mimologeo (Greek)   To speak a mime, to act in a mime. The source, *mimologos* (mime actor), suggests the wide currency of that word and the popularity of the performances. (Nicoll MASKS 46)

mimologist   In the U.S., a mime-player. See also: mimographer.

mimologoi (Greek)   From at least the 3rd C BC, actors in a mime. The Latin is *mimologi*. (Bieber HISTORY 107; Beare ROMAN 151, 153)

mimorum aedes (Latin)   Literally: house of the actors. An Elizabethan theatre. (Gascoigne WORLD 118)

mimorum scriptor (Latin Roman)   See: *mimi scriptor*.

mimos (Greek)   1. The ancient mime. 2. A player in such a mime. Also called a *mimus* (Latin). See also: mime. (Chambers MEDIAEVAL I 2)

mimus (Latin Roman)   1. The mime. 2. A mime-player. Plural *mimi*. (English uses mimus for an ornithological genus which includes the mockingbird.) Greek: *mimos*. See also: mime. (Chambers MEDIAEVAL I 5, Beare ROMAN 150)

mimus (Latin)   One of the four general terms for a medieval minstrel. See: minstrel.

mimus albus (Latin Roman)   Literally: a white mime, apparently so named from the color of his costume (or face makeup?). He has been identified with the comic character Maccus in the *fabula Atellana*. Some think Pulcinella of the Italian *commedia dell' arte* a descendant. (Duchartre ITALIAN 29)

mimus calvus (Latin Roman)   See: *calvi mimici*.

mi narai (Japanese)   Literally: looking-learning. 1. An apprentice playwright in *kabuki*, so called because he learns by watching. (Kawatake KABUKI 44) 2. More generally, learning by observation, rather than by formal instruction.

min chien hsiao hsi (Chinese)   See: *xiaoxi*.

min chü (Chinese)   See: *minju*.

mincid (Indonesian)   See: *ngibing*.

minduk (Malaysian)   The assistant to an entranced *dalang* or shaman who is communicating with spirits. Especially important in *main puteri*. The *minduk*, who is a spiked fiddle (*rebab*) player, guides the conversation with the shaman while playing musical accompaniment. (Sweeney RAMAYANA 278)

minimum basic agreement   In the U.S., a standard agreement a producer signs to gain the right to produce a play by a Dramatists Guild member.

minimum call   Especially in the professional theatre, an agreed-upon minimum amount of time per day stagehands or orchestra members will work. The minimum call for union members is usually four hours, not including the performance.

ministeriales (French)   See: minstrel.

ministrallus (Latin)   One of the four general terms for a medieval minstrel. See: minstrel.

minjian xiaoxi (Chinese)   See: *xiaoxi*.

minju, min chü (Chinese)   Fujian (or Fukien) opera, a form of music-drama (*xiqu*) popular in Fujian Province which arose after 1911. It consists of elements from several 18th and 19th C forms including *pingjiang, rulin*, and *laolao*, and has been influenced by Beijing opera (*jingju*). Also called Fuzhou opera (*fuzhouxi* or *fu chou hsi*). (Dolby HISTORY 224-226; Mackerras MODERN 127-128, 145) *minkan kagura* (Japanese)   Literally: people's shrine dance. A contemporary term deliberately created to replace the usual term, *sato kagura* (village *kagura*), now considered derogatory. (Hoff SONG 147)

Minnie P. play   A late 19th and early 20th C nickname for a play involving a little maid who sings, dances, plays tricks, and wears short dresses. After Minnie Palmer, who acted such parts. (Partridge TO-DAY 228)

minnie revue   A miniature revue.

minnow   A small part. (Granville DICTIONARY)

minor business   Stage action of secondary importance.

minor theatre   A non-patent theatre in 18th and 19th C London.

minstrel   1. A medieval entertainer. The term was used broadly, and though minstrels were chiefly singers and musicians, the term was sometimes applied to dancers, mountebanks, reciters, and performers generally. Chambers found four general terms for minstrels: *ministrallus, ioculator, mimus*, and *histrio*—all Latin. Among the many variations in different languages: menestrel, *mynstral, ménestrel, ménestrier*, and *ministeriales* (French, the last plural); *joglar, jogleor, jongleur, jouglere* (French); *gaugalâri, goukelaere* (Old High and Middle High German respectively), and *joculator* (Latin); such abusive or derisive terms as bourdyour, gabber, harlot, jangler, japer, jogeleur, *ribaud* (French); *delusor, garcio, nebulo, saccularis*, and *scurra* (Latin); and such assorted terms as ape-ward, gleeman, gligmon, *bordeor, chanteur, lecheor, pantonnier*, and *trouvère* (French). A chief or leading minstrel was called an armiger, *marescallus, rex* (Latin), *roy* (French); Byzantine minstrels were called *citharoedi* or *lyristae* (Latin); and a goliard was a wandering minstrel, satirical and possibly scholarly, who commented on current events, often using Latin quotations. (Chambers MEDIAEVAL II 231-233, 238-239; Chadwick PLOWMAN 72-73; Tunison TRADITIONS 106; Nicoll DEVELOPMENT 48) 2. A 19th-20th C U.S. performer in a minstrel show. Hence, minstrelsy.

minstrel black   See: burnt cork.

minstrel show, minstrelsy   A U.S. entertainment form that developed in the 1840s, became immensely popular, but faded toward the end of the 19th C. Most of the performers were white men in blackface, and the entertainment consisted of three parts: repartee between the interlocutor (or middleman) and the end men (Bones and Tambo), a variety show, and a skit. The performers sat in a semicircle on the stage when not doing a routine.

minstrelsy   See: minstrel show.

mintha (Burmese)   Literally: prince. The leading actor of a *zat* troupe.

minthami (Burmese)   Literally: princess. A female solo dancer in traditional theatre.

minuet   A graceful, stately dance in 3/4 time, popular in the 17th-18th C.

minukku (Malayalam)   Literally: shining. In *kathakali*, a makeup type, basically matte yellow in color, used for naturalistic characters such as women, sages, Brahmans, and royal messengers. (Jones/Jones KATHAKALI 34)

minzoku geino (Japanese)   Literally: folk performing arts. The most common generic term for folk dance, music, and theatre. (Hoff SONG 142)

miracle play   A medieval religious play dealing with the lives of the saints. Compare: mystery play.

miraculum (Latin)   A medieval religious play dealing with a saint; the term in time came to mean any religious play, especially in England. (Chambers MEDIAEVAL II 104)

mirror arc   In Britain, a carbon arc light with a mirrored glass reflector and special lenses. (Bowman/Ball THEATRE)

mirror dancer   A pejorative description of a ballet dancer who has become overly accustomed to watching him or herself in the mirrors of practice rooms. This results, in performance, in a vacant or lost expression as the dancer tries to find—in the audience—the absent mirror. Mirror dancers lack eye contact with each other in love scenes, severely straining their emotional credibility. (Kersley/Sinclair BALLET)

mirror exercise   In acting training, an exercise in which two people face each other, one reflecting or copying the movements of the other as if he or she were a mirror.

mirror room   See: *kagami no ma*.

mirror spot   In Britain, a spotlight with an ellipsoidal reflector.

miscast   1. Said of a performer given an unsuitable part. 2. To cast a performer in such a part.

miscue   1. A slip of the tongue. 2. To deliver an incorrect cue line. 3. To miss a cue. Possibly derived from billiards.

miseba (Japanese)   Literally: show scene. A major scene in a *kabuki* or *bunraku* play. These took on standardized form during the 19th C. Examples are *michiyuki, koroshiba, nureba, monogatari, kubi jikken, yusuriba*, and *migawari*, among others. (Hamamura et al KABUKI 75-76)

misemono (Japanese)   A freak or side show.

mise en scène (French)   The arrangement of all the elements in a stage picture, either at a given moment or dynamically throughout the performance.

Misrule   See: King of Misrule.

miss a cue   1. Of a performer, to fail to hear a cue spoken on stage and thus be late for an entrance. Said also of anyone who does not carry out his/her duty at the proper moment, as by missing a light or curtain cue. 2. To miss the point of a story. (Granville DICTIONARY)

missed entrance   Said of a performer's failure to enter on cue.

mistère, misterie (French)   A medieval mystery play.

misterio (Italian)   A medieval mystery play. (Mantzius HISTORY II 3)

misterium (Latin)   See: *mysterium*.

mistress of costumes   See: wardrobe keeper.

Mitarbeiter (German)   Literally: collaborator, assistant. A co-worker on a play script. (Fuegi BRECHT 187–188).

mitate (Japanese)   In *kabuki* playwriting, characters and situations from the past brought up to date in a kind of parody of past plays and performances. Historic and contemporary worlds (*sekai*) are thereby brought togoether. An example is *Sukeroku: the Flower of Edo* in Brandon CLASSIC 55-92. (Gunji KABUKI 16-17)

mitateme (Japanese)   Literally: third. The third piece of an all-day *kabuki* program. It was the first act of the four-act main play (*hon kyogen*). Also called *mitsume, mitatsume* (third) and in Kyoto-Osaka *kuchiake* (opening). (Brandon CLASSIC 30, 99; Leiter ENCYCLOPEDIA 238-239)

miter, mitre   1. A liturgical headdress (tiara) worn over the forehead and shaped somewhat like a gothic arch. 2. A woman's evening headdress (tiara) usually of diamonds or semi-precious stones, worn over the forehead. (Boucher FASHION, Wilcox DICTIONARY)

miton (French)   See: *moufle*.

mitra   1. An Asia Minor, draped headgear: a scarf with ties at the ends, covering the head and framing the chin. See also: wimple. 2. An Asian wool cap with a turned-down point, fastened under the chin. (Boucher FASHION)

mitre   See: miter.

mitt   To applaud.

mitt 'em   To acknowledge applause by clasping one's hands above the head.

mixed bill   A program with two or more acts or numbers.

mixed jet   In a 19th C limelight apparatus, a jet with a single aperture which expelled gases previously mixed in a small chamber below the jet. (Rees GAS 56, figs. 32, 36)

mixed media performance   An experimental production often involving all of the arts and using such technical equipment as tapes, films, slides, etc. (Hatlen ORIENTATION)

mixed notices   Opposed reviews of a production. (Bowman/Ball THEATRE)

mixed play   Sometimes used for a medieval play that does not belong to any of the standard types, that is, not classifiable as a morality play, mystery play, etc. (Ward LITERATURE I 114)

miyaji shibai (Japanese)   Literally: shrine-grounds play. A temporary theatre building for *kabuki* or other popular theatre form, set up in the grounds of a shrine or temple for a festival. (Kumakura "Traditional" 56) *miyal halmi* (Korean)   See: *halmi*.

mizhavu (Malayalam)   A very large pot-shaped drum used in *kutiyattam*. One or two instruments may be used. (Raja KUTIYATTAM 9)

mizu iri (Japanese)   Literally: entering water. One of two types of *kabuki* scenes using real water (*hon mizu*); for example, an actor plunges into a vat of water. An example is the hero in the final scene of *Sukeroku: Flower of Edo* in Brandon CLASSIC 90-91. See also: *hon ame*. (Leiter ENCYCLOPEDIA 241)

mizu nuno (Japanese)   See: *hon mizu, jigasuri*.

mlumah (Indonesian)   To lie on one's back and look up at an opponent. Used most often by monkey characters during battle scenes in Javanese shadow theatre (*wayang kulit*). (Long JAVANESE 105)

MMC (Latin Roman)   According to a late Roman writer, a mark appearing on some *cantica* (the meters used in comedy). The letters, presumably the initials of *mutatis modis canticum*, may have designated a particular kind of song ('changing melody'?); or perhaps the letters distinguished song from other types of delivery used by performers. (Beare ROMAN 221)

m'michila (Nyasa)   In a tribal language of Malawi (formerly Nyasaland), the master of ceremonies in certain ritual enactments. (Kirby "Indigenous" 24)

mo (Chinese)   1. Male role; a major role category (*hangdang*) in Yuan *zaju* (13th and 14th C). Major subcategories included principal male (*zhengmo*), supporting male (*waimo*), young male (*xiaomo*), and older male (*laomo*). (Dolby HISTORY 60) 2. A supporting older male role (*laosheng*), often an elderly household steward or the presenter of a prologue, in many forms of music-drama (*xiqu*), including *kunqu* and Beijing opera (*jingju*). Similar to *wai*. In *kunqu*, also called *fumo*. (Dolby HISTORY 105, 180)

mob   The audience. (Berrey/Van den Bark SLANG 574)

mochok (Malaysian)   The main control rod of a shadow puppet. (Sweeney RAMAYANA 58-59)

mock-up   1. A model of a costume or accessory in a fabric other than that to be used in performance, used to test a pattern. Also called a muslin fitting, muslin mock-up, muslin model, toile, tryout. 2. Rehearsal scenery, usually skeletal but workable. (Burris-Meyer/Cole SCENERY 38)

modeling   The three-dimensionality of a performer (sometimes an object), often marked by light and shadow on the face. (Lounsbury THEATRE, Wehlburg GLOSSARY)

Modellbuch (German)   A production book of a play which attempts to capture the production for posterity. (Fuegi BRECHT 188)

modern drama   See: *drama moden, drama moderen, huaju, shingeki, shinpa, sinpa*.

modern dress   A production costumed in today's fashions, as opposed to period costuming.

modesty   1. A piece of gauzy fabric used to fill in the low necklines of 18th C gowns. Also called a modesty bit, modesty piece, *modiste* (French); souffle, tacker, tucker. See also: guimp(e). 2. A 17th C top skirt worn over several others. It was caught up in festoons by chains, bows, ribbons, or pins (Walkup DRESSING 194)

modification   In ballet, any term (such as *en l'air, fermé*) which indicates to a dancer in what direction or in what way a step or position is to be performed. Grant has illustrations. (Grant TECHNICAL)

modified continental seating   A hybrid seating pattern combining features of multiple-aisle seating and continental seating.

modiste (French)   1. A milliner, a hat-maker. 2. See: modesty.

modoki (Japanese)   1. A modification of an existing play or situation, often as comic parody. A common structural device of Japanese performing arts is to follow a serious, traditional piece with a lighter piece which turns the first upside down. Examples are *kyogen* comedies following serious *no* plays, and many scenes in *kabuki*. (Inoura HISTORY 19, 27, Brandon CLASSIC 23) 2. A comic character in *sato kagura*. (Sadler "O-Kagura" 281—282)

modular-lift system   An elevator system which can raise and lower a stage or auditorium floor in segments about 3' or 4' square. Hence, modular seating, modular stage.

moechimonium (Latin Roman)   See: *adulterio*.

moeurs populaires (French)   A dramatic genre in naturalistic style, dealing with popular manners and customs. A specialty of the Grand Guignol in the late 19th C, it dealt with undramatic, static subjects in the lives of the lowest strata of society. (Deák "Guignol" 35)

moghul breeches   Trousers worn in Hindustan. Also called pajamas or pyjamas. (Boucher FASHION)

mogul base   The large base in common use in the theatre on most lamps of 1000 watts and above. See also: lamp base.

mogul prefocus   See: lamp base.

mohlam (Thai)   Literally: expert singer. The generic term for popular northeastern Thai folk songs and drama. *Mohlam* singers are accompanied by the *khaen*, a mouth-blown reed organ. Also spelled *mawlam*.

mohlam (Lao)   1. Originally, epic tales or bawdy songs sung by a male singer accompanied by a *khaen* player. 2. Narrowly today, two or more singers singing in competition to *khaen* accompaniment. Also *mawlum glawn*, or abbreviated *lum glawn*. 3. Broadly, any of some eighteen types of dramatic forms, epic recitations, and song forms accompanied by *khaen* music and performed in Laos or the Lao-speaking area of northeast Thailand. Also spelled *mawlum*. (Miller "Kaen" 121-122, Brandon SOUTHEAST 69)

mohlam luong (Lao)   Literally: story *mohlam*. The major popular theatre form in Laos and Lao-speaking northeast Thailand. Begun as a Lao adaptation of Thai *likay* using *mohlam* music and singing, it was first called *likay lao* or *ligeh lao*. The influence of Thai-style staging, costuming, and story content remains strong. Described by Miller as "a spoken play with singing" ("Kaen" 243). Also known as *mohlam mu, mawlum moo*, and abbreviated *lam mu, lum moo* (group *mohlam*). Somewhat less common is the term *lam luong, lum luang* (sung story). A closely related dramatic form is *lum plun*. (Miller "Kaen" 209, 221; Brandon SOUTHEAST 70)

mohlam mu (Lao)   See: *mohlam luong*.

mohori (Khmer)   1. A style of light, popular theatre music. 2. The ensemble of string, wind, and percussion instruments that play it. (Osman TRADITIONAL 197-207)

moiles   See: chopines.

Moishe (Yiddish)   See: *Moyshe*.

moist rouge   A creamy coloring for the lips and cheeks.

mokador   A 16th C handkerchief. (Chalmers CLOTHES 170)

mokchung (Korean)   The character and mask of a Buddhist monk in various masked dance-plays. Abbreviated: *chung*. (Yi "Mask" 36; Korean MASKS 14, 19, 21)

moko   In scene painting in Britain, a special oil paint which produces an imitation of high gloss. (Granville DICTIONARY)

mokugyo (Japanese)   A hollowed wooden musical instrument, struck with a padded mallet. Borrowed from Buddhist religious music, it is one of the offstage musical instruments (*geza*) played in *kabuki*. (Malm MUSIC 69-70)

MOL   Maximum overall length. The length of a lamp from the tip of its base to the top of its bulb. This is not quite descriptive of lamps with a base at each end: it is then the distance from one base to the other. Compare: LCL. (Wehlburg GLOSSARY 38)

momer   An old variant spelling of mummer.

mômerie, mommerie (French)   Mummery. Popular in the 16th C.

momo (Spanish)   Buffoonery.

momos phalakros   The Greek term for the ancient bald-headed mime. Compare *stupidus*. (Nicoll MASKS 47)

Momus   A clown. From Momus, the Greek god of ridicule, often censorious. (Bowman/Ball THEATRE)

Mondapparat (German)   Literally: moon apparatus. A special effects machine for creating a moon. That in use after World War I was a large spotlight set in a solidly constructed sliding frame. (Fuchs LIGHTING 212) *mondo* (Japanese)   Literally: question and answer. A prose dialogue section of a *no* play in which the traveler (*waki*) questions the protagonist (*shite*) about events from the past. One type of *shodan*. (Shimazaki NOH 49)

money   In 18th C theatres in Britain, the amount of cash taken in at the door for all seats other than those in the boxes. On benefit nights the house charge was deducted from this amount. (Hogan LONDON xv)

money guy   The owner of a burlesque theatre. (Wilmeth LANGUAGE)

money player   A performer who is negligent in rehearsal but does well when there is a paying audience.

money-spinner   A successful performance, performer, or production. (Granville DICTIONARY)

money star   A popular performer.

money taker   In early 19th C theatres, an employee who presumably worked in a pay box, selling tickets (checks) to one section of the theatre. (Folger MS T.6.1)

mongsokmari-ch'um (Korean)   Literally: rug-rolling dance. A dance in masked plays in which the dancer moves forward as though rolling a rug. Abbreviated: *mongsokmari*. (Cho "Yangju" 31)

moni, mo ni (Chinese)   1. The actor-director in Song *zaju* and Jin *yuanben*. He sang and danced in the prologue and "may have played an increasingly active part in the play itself." (Dolby HISTORY 19, 22, 26-27) 2. See: *zhengmo*.

monitor system   A broadcasting system in a theatre which picks up the sound of the performance in the auditorium and carries it to speakers in rooms elsewhere in the theatre, such as dressing rooms, the green room, box office, etc.

monkey clothes, monkey suit   Dress clothes or a uniform. (Berrey/Van den Bark SLANG 579)

monkey music   See: *sarugaku*.

monkey pole   In Britain, a stick with a hole in the end, through which a throw (lash) line is drawn; used to guide the line when flats are laced together. (Baker THEATRECRAFT)

monkey suit   See: monkey clothes.

monkey-tail   An 18th C train looped about a foot from the floor and then allowed to drape freely. (Chalmers CLOTHES 216)

monobit   A monologue.

monodrama   1. A short piece for one performer, with musical accompaniment and a silent chorus. Popularized in Germany in the 1770's by the actor Johann Christian Brandes. See also: duodrama. 2. A theory of totally subjective theatre promoted by the Russian playwright Nikolai Evreinov in the early 20th C: the character becomes the ego and the spectator the alter ego. (Hartnoll COMPANION, Marshall RUSSIAN 50) *monogatari* (Japanese)   1. Generally, a spoken or chanted narrative, although sometimes synonymous with *katari*. (Yamashita "Structure" 61) 2. A scene in *bunraku* in which a male character tells of a past event, often a friend's or relative's death, through emotional language and gesture. An example is in *Kumagai's Battle Camp* in Brandon CLASSIC 194-196. 3. In *kabuki*, either a narrative scene taken over into *kabuki* from *bunraku*, or a narrative scene within a *joruri* dance play. See also: *katari*. (Malm in Brandon/Malm/Shively STUDIES 143, Leiter ENCYCLOPEDIA 244, Scott KABUKI 80, 113-114)

monogurui mono (Japanese)   See: *kyoranmono*.

monologist, monologuist   A performer who delivers a solo speech. The tradition probably derived from the speakers of prologues in ancient times; by the 18th C entire entertainments were given by single performers, leading to the stand-up comic routines of the 20th C.

monologue   1. An entertainment presented by one person; hence, monologist, monologuist. 2. The script of such an entertainment. 3. A soliloquy. (Bowman/Ball THEATRE)

monomane (Japanese)   Literally: imitation or acting. In *no*: 1. Broadly, skill in acting as opposed to techniques of singing and dancing (*buka*). 2. More specifically, truthful representation of character and human emotion, a goal first propounded by Kannami Kiyotsugu in the 15th C. At its highest level, imitation is of the essence of character, rather than of externals. Ortolani ("Zeami's" 111-112) notes the contrary needs of the actor to identify with a role and to beautify unsightly reality. See also: *yugen*. (Immoss/Mayer JAPANESE 70-71, Keene NO 31, Inoura HISTORY 86)

monomane kyogen zukushi (Japanese)   Literally: acted-play-fully. One year after *kabuki* was banned in 1652, the government allowed adult males to perform provided they staged 'fully acted plays,' rather than the previous variety programs of unrelated dances, songs, and sketches. (Dunn/Torigoe ANALECTS 41, Gunji KABUKI 21, Brandon CLASSIC 2)

monophobia   The fear of being alone on stage. (Granville DICTIONARY)

monoplane filament   In spotlight lamps, a concentrated filament in a single plane. (McCandless SYLLABUS 10)

monopolylogue   An entertainment by a solo performer doing impersonations. (Granville DICTIONARY)

monstre (French)   See: *montre*.

montant, montan (French)   A wooden scaffold rising from a chariot in the substage and protruding through the stage floor. It supported movable wings in the Torelli chariot-and-pole scene-shifting system.

montera (Spanish)   See: Buckingham.

monter sur les tréteaux (French)   To go on the stage; to tread the boards.

monthly rep   A repertory troupe performing the same play for a month. (Granville DICTIONARY)

montre (French)   A parade by actors in costume, serving to promote a forthcoming performance. In medieval times, sometimes spelled *monstre*.

moocher   A holder of a pass to a theatre.

mooch in, mouch in   To attend a performance without a ticket.

mood   The atmosphere or feeling created, usually, by the scenery and lighting; but the language of a play, the manner in which it is spoken, and the rhythm and tempo of the action can also create a mood.

mood lighting   Light designed primarily to enhance the emotional tone of a scene, act, play, dance, etc. Sometimes called psychological lighting. (Bowman MODERN, Sellman/Lessley ESSENTIALS 9)

mood piece   Any play that relies on mood and atmosphere rather than action.

moon box   From at least the early 19th C, a container with a light and a round hole covered with cloth, used to create a moon effect on stage. The container was often box-like; the light, oil, gas, or limelight; and the cloth, white linen. Also called a moonbox or moon, now often moon special. (Rees GAS 130-131, 206, figs. 74, 75)

moon burner   The gas jet in a moon box. (Rees GAS 206)

moon effect   Any lighting arrangement which creates an apparent moon on the stage. An example is the moon box. (Carrington THEATRICANA)

moon guitar   See: *yueqin.*

moonlight effect   A night scene which appears to be lit by moonlight.

moon special   A moon box or other arrangement which simulates the moon.

Moorish dance   See: Morris dance.

moral   See: morality play.

moral interlude   An English medieval play similar to a morality play but shorter. (Chambers MEDIAEVAL II 199)

moralité (French)   A medieval morality play. (Chambers MEDIAEVAL II 153)

morality play   A medieval secular, didactic, allegorical play. Often shortened to moral or morality, sometimes to moral play. (Brockett HISTORY 139)

moral lecture   A term used in the U.S. in the 18th C to describe a dramatic performance or reading in order to avoid censorship, a classic example being the advertisement of a production of *Othello* in Providence, Rhode Island, in 1761 as a series of moral dialogues.

moral play   See: morality play.

morgue   1. A theatre doing poor business. 2. A theatre's collection of press cuttings, programs, production records, etc. (Bowman/Ball THEATRE) See also: makeup morgue.

morion   A 16th C brimmed metal helmet often seen on Spanish *conquistadores*. A smaller version was called the cabasset. (Barton COSTUME 223; Wilcox DICTIONARY)

Moriones (Philippine)   A ritual reenactment of the conversion and beheading (*pugutan*) of the Roman centurion, Longinus, who participated in the crucifixion of Christ. A Lenten festival, Mexican in origin, unique to the Filipino province of Marinduque, a small island off southern Luzon. (The morion was the characteristic headgear of the Spanish *conquistadores* in Mexico.) (Mendoza "Lenten" 29, Salazar in Cruz SHORT 91-92)

Moriscoes   Morris (Moorish) dancers. (Serlio in Nagler SOURCES 79)

morning coat   See: cutaway.

morning game   See: *ludus matutinus*.

moro-moro (Philippine)   See: *comedia*.

moros (Greek)   Literally: dull, foolish, silly. The general term for a mime fool. (Nicoll MASKS 27-28)

morris bells   Bells worn by Renaissance jesters on ribbon-trimmed garters just below the knee. (Barton COSTUME 221)

Morris dance   1. A Moorish dance. A medieval village festival performance in which dancers blackened their faces. (Dekker in Nagler SOURCES 136) 2. A general 16th C term for theatrical dancing.

Mose the B'howery b'hoy   On the 19th C U.S. stage, a strutting, macho character, sentimental and chivalrous at heart, combining heroic deeds as a firefighter with brawling bravado and heroic defense of the underdog. (Toll BLACKING 15-16)

moshav letsim (Hebrew)   Literally: seat of scoffers. Theatre. A Talmudic term accompanied by condemnation of the theatre, often similar to Puritan and other religious attitudes. (Sandrow VAGABOND 16)

moshi awase (Japanese)   A rehearsal of major sections of a *no* play. (Nakamura NOH 157)

mosqueteros (Spanish)   Members of audiences in 17th C *corral* theatres, usually the dandies standing in the *patio* behind the row of benches. (Nagler SOURCES 64)

mostly paper   Said of an audience most of whom have complimentary tickets.

mot d'auteur (French)   A witticism in the dialogue of a play which can be uttered out of context. (Archer PLAY-MAKING 254)

mot de la fin (French)   A word or phrase at the end of a play, intended to wind it up emphatically. Important to the 19th C exponents of the well-made play; less important today. (Archer PLAY-MAKING 40)

mother powder   A hypothetical substance for whose actualization vaudevillian Ned Wayburn offered a substantial prize. The substance would be sprinkled on a 'stage mother,' causing either her demise or disappearance. The prize was never awarded. (Laurie VAUDEVILLE 145)

mothol (Indonesian)   A killing technique in Javanese shadow puppet theatre. An opponent's head is grasped between two hands and twisted sharply, snapping or severing the neck. The movement is used almost exclusively by the character Gathutkaca. (Long JAVANESE 93)

mothon (Greek)   A primitive Peloponnesian dance sometimes used in Old Comedy. The *mothon* is thought, partly on the basis of ancient statements, to have been as indecent as the *kordax*. Plural *mothones*. (Pickard-Cambridge DITHYRAMB 169)

motif   1. In scene design, a visual element appropriate to the play, repeated to give style and unity to the design. (Bellman SCENOGRAPHY) 2. In dance, a briefly stated but comprehensive design unit. (Nahumck DANCE 72) See also: *Leitmotiv.*

motion   1. A medieval term for a puppet play. 2. An Elizabethan term for a shadow or puppet play. 3. An Elizabethan term for a pantomime performed by masquers. (Chambers MEDIAEVAL II 158) 4. In dance, action in a time-space complex. (Turner/Grauert/Zallman DANCE 24)

motion choir   In modern dance, a lay as opposed to professional dancers' group. Also called a movement choir.

motion man   An Elizabethan puppeteer. (Baird PUPPET 68)

motion master   A 17th C puppeteer. (Philpott DICTIONARY 116)

motivated light   Especially in a realistic setting, light for which there appears to be a "real" source, such as a window or lighted lamp. Such an apparent light source is a motivating light. (Lounsbury THEATRE 85, Bowman/Ball THEATRE)

motivating light   See: motivated light.

motivation   The reason behind stage action and speech. Hence, a motivational unit is a scene unit defined by the beginning and end of a motivation. (Stern MANAGEMENT, Hatlen ORIENTATION, Cameron/Hoffman GUIDE)

motivieren (German)   In playwriting, to provide motivation.

motor-driven autotransformer   An autotransformer dimmer with a motor. Both are remotely positioned and controlled by the board operator, typically with a switch. The motor-positioned autotransformer is the same device, but controlled by a potentiometer. (Bowman/Ball THEATRE)

motor-positioned autotransformer   See: motor-driven autotransformer.

motto   See: device.

motto singer   In late 19th C vaudeville, a singer specializing in songs based on aphorisms.

mouches dans le lait (French)   See: patches.

mouchetures (French)   See: slashings.

moufle (French)   1. A Merovingian glove or mitten worn to hunt and for rough work. Also called a *miton*. 2. A 14th-15th C sleeve extension which covered the hand. (Boucher FASHION)

mount   To produce a play, especially the scenery, costumes, and properties.

mountebank   A seller of quack medicines. Mountebanks were a variety of minstrel in medieval times.

mounting   1. The staging of a production. 2. The equipment to which a lighting instrument may be attached, such as a vertical pipe or tree. 3. A device, such as a yoke, for attaching an instrument to a pipe or tree. (Bowman/Ball THEATRE)

mourning band   A black crepe broad band worn on the left sleeve to indicate that the wearer has had a death in the family. Largely given up in the U.S. after World War II, but seen in Europe and worn by officers at state funerals. The wearing of mourning bands goes back at least to the early 17th C. See also: cyprus. (Dreher HATMAKING, Wilcox DICTIONARY)

mousquetaire collar   A woman's capelike collar—the depth varies—usually made of lace or linen. Revived intermittently since the 18th C. Also called a palatine. (Boucher FASHION, Wilcox DICTIONARY)

mousquetaire glove   A 17th C musketeer's gauntlet.

moustache (French)   See: *coiffure en cadenettes.*

mouth the lines   1. To declaim bombastically. 2. To speak indistinctly. 3. To form words with the lips soundlessly.

movement   1. Stage movement. See also: blocking. 2. In dance, the fact of bodily action.

movement choir   See: motion choir.

movement imagery   In dance, the formation/visualization of images as a result of or in response to feeling; images remembered as a result of moving or seeing movement. A movement metaphor.

movement notation   In dance, any system which records and describes dancers' movements quantitatively and/or qualitatively. It is roughly analogous to music notation. Labanotation and Benesh Notation are the two systems most in use today. Kinetography/Laban is similar to Labanotation; stenochoreography is not in wide use. Alwin Nikolai's note-symbol system results in a 'choroscript.' Yet another system was developed by Eshkol and Wachmann.

movement phrase   The modern dance equivalent of a combination (q.v.). Also called an action mode. (Love DANCE 6)

movement quality   A physical component of dance movement inherent in the natural structure of a dancer's body, characterized as percussive, sustained, swinging, or vibratory. (Turner/Grauert/Zallman DANCE 28)

movements in ballet   The seven movements in French: *élancer* (to dart), *étendre* (to stretch), *glisser* (to glide or slide), *plier* (to bend), *relever* (to raise), *sauter* (to jump), and *tourner* (to turn around). (Grant TECHNICAL)

move off   To walk away from the center of the stage, often off the stage.

move on   To come on stage or move toward the center of the stage.

moves   In Britain: 1. Stage movement. 2. The performers' movements as arranged by the director. (Baker THEATRECRAFT)

moving panorama   See: diorama.

moving tracks   See: treadmill.

Moyshe (Yiddish)   Literally: Moses. The audience. The sense is that the audience is the performer's master, and yet the audience is often simple, a yokel whom the actor feels obligated to educate. Also spelled *Moishe*. (Sandrow VA-GABOND 94, Lifson YIDDISH 94-95)

mozos de comedias, mozos de corrales (Spanish)   In the 17th C and later, stagehands and odd-job men. (Shergold SPANISH)

mozzy   Punch's wife in a Punch and Judy show. Also called Joan. (Partridge TO-DAY 538)

mrdangam, mridangam (Sanskrit)   A large double-headed horizontal drum widely played in theatre music throughout south India.

Mr. Griffin   A cheap theatre patron. From the phrase, "Mr. Griffin he's stiffin." (Berrey/Van den Bark SLANG 574)

mridangam (Sanskrit)   See: *mrdangam*.

mua (Vietnamese)   One of three Vietnamese words used for dance. Used as the generic term for character dances in *hat cheo, hat boi*, and *cai luong*. Pham-Duy lists eight examples in MUSICS 136.

mua roi (Vietnamese)   Marionette theatre. There are two major types, *mui roi can*, "inland" or land marionettes, and *mua roi nuoc*, water puppets. Water puppets are one to three feet high and are played by puppeteers standing in a pool of water. A complex system of rods and strings allows the puppeteers to manipulate the figures while standing three to ten yards away from them. (Pham-Duy MUSICS 114, Tilakasiri PUPPET 48)

mubiaoxi, mu piao hsi (Chinese)   Literally: act-outline play. A performance sketched in outline but never fully written out; a type of 20th C Western-style performance (*wenmingxi*). (Dolby HISTORY 203)

much'on (Korean)   Literally: dance to the sky. A ceremony of heaven-worship that used masks in the ancient tribal state of Yae (3rd C BC to 3rd C AD). (Cho "Yangju" 27)

muck   Greasepaint, especially clown white. (Berrey/Van den Bark SLANG 580) *mucuk* (Indonesian)   The grip used to hold small, light Javanese shadow puppets. The puppet is held gently by the tips of the fingers, with the index finger placed in the indentation of the main control rod for added stability. (Long JAVANESE 23-24)

mud hole   A provincial town.

mudong (Korean)   Literally: dancing boy. A child who dances on the shoulders of an adult in a masked-dance play (*taegwangdae-p'ae*) or in the farmers' music (*p'ungmul*) section of *namsadang*. *Mudong-ch'um* or *mudong-nori* is the dance. (Cho "Ogwangdae" 27, Kim "Namsadang" 12)

mudra (Sanskrit)   See: *hasta*.

muestra (Spanish)   Literally: sample. In the 17th C and later, usually a dress rehearsal of an *auto* before Corpus Christi Day, presented to members of the town council and their wives to display a company's abilities. (Shergold SPANISH)

muff   A false beard.

muff a line   To deliver a line incorrectly or to cut it by mistake.

muff one's cue   To miss a cue.

mug   1. A villain character. 2. A performer who plays such a part. 3. To overact with the face. Hence, mugger, mugging.

mugdha (Sanskrit)   Inexperienced. In classical Indian dramaturgy, the role of a heroine (*nayika*) who is young and inexperienced. (Keith SANSKRIT 308)

mugen no (Japanese)   Literally: dream or vision *no*. A *no* play in which the protagonist (*shite*) is a spirit—a god, a demon, or the ghost of a long-dead human. The name is from the dream in which the visiting priest (*waki*) summons the spirit to appear. Also translated "phantasmal *no*" (Nakamura NOH 30). Examples are *Kiyotsune* and *Izutsu* in Nippon Gakujutsu JAPANESE 61-73, 95-105. See also: *genzaimono*.

mug up   To put on makeup.

mug up the lines   To study one's part. (Berrey/Van den Bark SLANG 587)

muhavere (Turkish)   Dialogue in a Turkish shadow puppet play. (Gassner/ Quinn ENCYCLOPEDIA 865)

mukaddeme (Turkish)   An introduction or prologue to a Turkish shadow-puppet play. (Gassner/Quinn ENCYCLOPEDIA 865)

mukha (Sanskrit)   Literally: face. 1. The opening or beginning of the drama. The first of five junctures (*sandhi*) of the dramatic action of a classical drama. (Keith SANSKRIT 298) 2. A face mask in *ankiya nat*, such as that depicting Ravana, the ten-headed demon. (Richmond "Vaisnava" 155)

mukhabhinaya (Sanskrit)   See: *mukhaja*.

mukhaja (Sanskrit)   The portrayal of emotions through facial expression. One of three major sub-divisions of movement (*angika*) in classical Indian theatre described by Bharata (NATYASASTRA 151). In *kathakali*, called *mukhabhinaya* (facial acting). (Jones/Jones KATHAKALI 111)

mukhavina (Sanskrit)   A small woodwind, similar to an oboe, played in theatre music ensembles throughout the Indian subcontinent.

mukhtyar (Bengali)   See: *juri*.

mukhya strivesa (Kannada)   Literally: most excellent. A *yaksagana* actor with delicate features who portrays leading female characters such as Draupadi and Sita. (Ashton/Christie YAKSAGANA 49)

muko onna kyogen (Japanese)   Literally: bridegroom and woman play. A *kyogen* play in which the main character is either a naive, blundering bridegroom or an aggressive wife. (Inoura HISTORY 128)

muktaya (Kannada)   Literally: conclusion. In *yaksagana*, introductory and concluding dance sequences performed while the narrator (*bhagavata*) sings. (Ashton/Christie YAKSAGANA 62, 92)

mula araw (Philippine)   Literally: from the sun. A fighting movement used in *comedia* battle sequences. (Mendoza COMEDIA 65)

muling block   A metal frame with a grooved wheel (sheave) fastened horizontally to the gridiron and used to change the horizontal direction of a line.

mull muslin   A very soft, stretchable kind of muslin used in millinery, and much prized by costumers for its ease of smoothing over a hat foundation without wrinkling.

multicapacity (resistance) dimmer   See: dual-rated dimmer.

multiconductor cable   Stage cable, such as borderlight cable, which contains a number of conductors. Also called a multicore cable.

multicore cable   A flexible electrical cable with several insulated cores protected by an outside covering.

multiform theatre   A theatre in which the orientation of the audience to the stage may be altered from production to production or even within a performance. Hence, multiform staging. See also: arena, thrust, proscenium staging.

multi-parts   In readers theatre, a term indicating that readers (including the narrator) may be cast in more than one role.

multiplate   See: uniplate.

multiple   In lighting: 1. See: twofer. 2. See: multiple connector.

multiple-aisle seating   See: American-plan seating.

multiple circuit   In electricity, a parallel circuit, i.e., one in which current can flow in two or more paths. Such circuitry is characteristic of stage lighting. Also called a shunt circuit. (Sellman/Lessley ESSENTIALS)

multiple connector   In stage lighting, a relatively large female connector which will accept up to three pin connectors. Also called a branch-off connector, multiple, multiple-pin connector, triple connector, or spider. (Cornberg/Gebauer CREW 153, fig. 229; Lounsbury THEATRE 118)

multiple control   A device enabling a single puppeteer to operate groups of marionettes from above or below. (Philpott DICTIONARY)

multiple costume   A huge garment created by the Russian-born Erté, designer for the Folies Bergère, worn by as many as a dozen show girls and covering as much as a quarter of the stage. (Leslie ACT 205)

multiple marionette   A five-headed marionette. (Philpott DICTIONARY)

multiple-pin connector   See: multiple connector.

multiple plot   In playwriting, a plot with more than a single action. See also: subplot.

multiple reading   See: readers theatre.

multiple setting, multiple simultaneous staging   A medieval staging system with several different locales represented scenically at the same time. Also called a simultaneous setting; in France: *décor simultané.*

multiple simultaneous staging   The representation on stage of more than one locale, as in medieval productions.

multiple-slider dimmer, multislider dimmer   In the U.S., a special type of autotransformer dimmer based on European patents available after WWII. This dimmer uses a single coil (typically with a capacity of 6,000 or 12,000 watts) from which a number of sliders can serve the same number of circuits—whose total, however, cannot exceed about two-thirds of the capacity of the coil. Also called the multiple-slider system, sometimes a Davis dimmer (for the Ariel Davis Manufacturing Co., now Electro Controls). (Bellman LIGHTING 185; Sellman/Lessley ESSENTIALS 125-126, fig. 8.6)

multiple-use theatre   An adaptable theatre that can be used for two or more purposes, such as drama, dance, opera, concerts, assemblies, etc. See also: flexible theatre.

multiple wing floods   In Britain, several floodlights mounted on a trolley. (Granville DICTIONARY)

multi-proscenium stage   A conventional proscenium stage plus side stages. Also called an extended stage. (Burris-Meyer/Cole THEATRES 130)

multiscened   Said of a play with a variety of locales.

multislider dimmer   See: multiple-slider dimmer.

mum, mumm   To act, especially in a mummers' play, masque, or disguising. Hence, mummer, mummery, mumming. (Bowman/Ball THEATRE)

mumchance   A kind of masquerade in the 14th C—a dicing game played in masks from house to house, usually at Christmas. (Ward/Waller CAMBRIDGE VI 332)

mummer   1. A clown or buffoon, in disguise, in a mummers' play, masque, or disguising. 2. A performer. Hence, mummery.

mummersetshire   In Britain, actors' (mummers') dialect, a light-hearted name for the speech used by many British performers for a number of regional dialects. (Granville DICTIONARY)

mummers' play   In medieval Britain, a folk drama with stock characters played by village amateurs, dealing with death and resurrection. The pieces were sometimes played in dumb show and involved the use of masks or disguises. Sometimes called a mumming or mumming play. (Bowman/Ball THEATRE)

mummery   A performance by mummers.

mumming   At medieval courts and noble houses, a series of costumed appearances, sometimes danced, possibly accompanied by a dumb show. Also called a disguising.

mundasu (Kannada)   Literally: turban. A towering headdress worn by a heroic character in *yaksagana*. (Gargi FOLK 155)

muñeco (Spanish)   See: *titere*.

mu'ou, mu ou (Chinese)   Literally: wood image. 1. A marionette. Also called string puppet (*xuansi kuilei* or *hsüan ssu k'uei lei*). (Dolby HISTORY 33) 2. Hand puppet. 3. Sometimes used as a generic term for puppet. See also: *kuileixi*.

mu'ouxi, mu ou hsi (Chinese)   Literally: wood image theatre, wood image plays. 1. Marionette theatre. 2. Hand puppet theatre. 3. Sometimes used as a generic term for puppet theatre. See also: *kuileixi*. (Obraztsov CHINESE 23-24)

mu piao hsi (Chinese)   See: *mubiaoxi*.

muqaadam (Arabic)   A puppeteer of the *bāba*. (Gassner/Quinn ENCYCLOPEDIA 22)

muraneya (Kannada)   Literally: third. In a *yaksagana* troupe, *muraneya vesa* is the third male character actor and *muraneya strivesa* is the third female character actor. (Ashton/Christie YAKSAGANA 51, 92)

murata (Kannada)   A performing competition among three *yaksagana badagatittu bayalata* troupes. (Ashton/Christie YAKSAGANA 83-85)

murder   A potent market for theatre tickets. (Wilmeth LANGUAGE)

murwa (Indonesian)   In Sundanese *wayang golek*, the long opening narrative (*nyandra*) that describes the setting of the opening scene. (Foley "Sundanese" 195-196)

muscular memory   Konstantin Stanislavsky's term for playing the outer characteristics without experiencing the emotions that lead to them. (Edward STANISLAVSKY 86)

muses   Greek goddesses associated with the arts and sciences. Melpomene was the muse of tragedy, Thalia of comedy, and Terpsichore of dance.

museum   A term sometimes used in the 19th C for a theatre, to give it respectability.

mushin (Japanese)   According to Zeami, the 'sublime' level of performance, the ultimate goal a *no* actor can achieve. See also: *hana, yugen.* (Ortolani "Zeami's" 114)

mushroom   See: reflector lamp.

mushroom star   A performer who gains stardom quickly. (Berrey/Van den Bark SLANG 572)

mush worker   A performer who plays emotions through facial expressions. (Berrey/Van den Bark SLANG 571)

music   1. One of Aristotle's six parts of a play; also translated as melody. (Cameron/Gillespie ENJOYMENT) 2. An art form of (usually) structured and expressive sound, often a part of stage productions. Hence, musical, musical comedy, music drama, musical theatre, musician, etc. 3. A band of musicians. In Elizabethan and Restoration theatres the band was often referred to as the musique or the musick. 4. Short for act music or curtain music. (Bowman/Ball THEATRE)

musical   See: musical comedy.

musical adaptation   A straight play turned into a musical theatre piece. Examples range from interpretations which are strict or close, as in *Where's Charley?* (from *Charley's Aunt*) to loose or free, as in *West Side Story* (from *Romeo and Juliet*).

musical comedy   1. A play which carries its story by spoken dialogue interspersed with songs and dances. The plot is generally light (even thin) and comic, sometimes sentimental. Musicals with more serious plots are sometimes categorized as musical theatre rather than musical comedy. Also called a musical, musical show, music show, musicomedy. (O'Hara/Bro INVITATION) 2. In Russia, a play with songs that do not advance the plot but are used only as diversions. (Bowers ENTERTAINMENT 65)

musical conductor   In opera and any theatrical entertainment involving an orchestra, the conductor of the instrumentalists. He or she may conduct the orchestra in performances and be the musical director (counterpart of the stage director) who is in charge of all the musical aspects of the production.

musical director   The person in charge of all musical aspects of a musical theatre production. He or she may or may not conduct the orchestra during performances.

musical drama   In the late 19th C, a play entirely or partly in verse; the verse was set to music, the prose spoken. Musical dramas had rather simple, slow-moving plots. (Hennequin PLAYWRITING 49)

musicalize   To turn a straight play into a musical. (Bowman/Ball THEATRE)

musical mokes   A blackface musical act featuring the playing of a variety of musical instruments. Now offensive. (Wilmeth LANGUAGE)

musical play   A play with music added; a more substantial form than musical comedy. Also called a play with music.

musical show   A musical comedy.

musical tab   A brief musical show—a tabloid musical.

musical tent theatre   A theatre under a tent, featuring musicals.

musical theatre   A broad category covering opera, operetta, musical comedy, lyric theatre—any entertainment in which music and lyrics (and often dance) play an integral part.

musical version   A play turned into a musical.

musica parlante (Italian)   In opera, recitative—words half-spoken, half-sung (Allen ANTIQUITIES 121)

music circus   A type of summer theatre in which operettas are performed in a circus tent, using arena staging.

music copyist   In the 18th C and later, one who wrote out the parts for members of a theatre band. (Folger MS T.6.1)

music cue   1. A note in a promptbook to indicate where music is to be used. 2. A signal for such music. (Fay GLOSSARY)

music drama   An opera in which drama and music are integrated, as in the works of Richard Wagner. (O'Hara/Bro INVITATION) See also: *xiqu*.

music exploitation man   A song plugger. (Wilmeth LANGUAGE)

music hall   1. In Britain, a vaudeville theatre, featuring variety entertainment. In the 19th C, music halls seated spectators at supper tables. The term was used not only for the building but also for the entertainment. Also called a hall. 2. A movie theatre with vaudeville entertainment between showings. (Bowman/Ball THEATRE)

music house   An old term for music hall or music room. (Bowman/Ball THEATRE)

musick   An old spelling of music. The term meant not only the music itself but the instrumentalists who played it.

musico (Spanish)   A musician.

musicomedy   A musical comedy.

music plot   A list of the musical numbers in a production, with cues. (Bowman/Ball THEATRE)

music room   1. In Elizabethan and Restoration theatres, the musicians' location. The word 'room' in the 17th C was often used in the sense of 'place' rather than a literal room. 2. A room in an 18th C tavern or other establishment in Britain where concerts were presented. (Chambers ELIZABETHAN III 96,

Pepys DIARY 7 November 1667, Brockett HISTORY 502) 3. A room in a theatre given over to musicians, instruments, etc.

music show   A musical comedy.

music visualization   An early attempt to formally structure modern dance by the systematic, orderly, and scientific translation of rhythm, melody, and harmony in a musical work into bodily action by the dancer. A term used by the dancer Ruth St. Denis. (Love DANCE 63)

music wire   See: piano wire.

musique   In Britain, the old spelling of music, taken from the French. In both instances the word meant music or the band of instrumentalists.

muslin fitting, muslin mock-up, muslin model   A sample of a costume design, sewn in muslin, for fitting purposes. Frequently used as the cutting pattern for a costume. Also called a mock-up, toile, tryout.

musume (Japanese)   Literally: maiden. 1. In *kabuki*, the role of an innocent maiden. It is one type of *onnagata* role. (Gunji KABUKI 32) 2. In *bunraku*, the puppet head used for a maiden. (Keene BUNRAKU 59, 231)

mutación (Spanish)   A change of scenery.

mutto (Thai)   An improvised verse in traditional theatre. (Ginsberg in Rutnin SIAMESE 66)

muttung ch'um (Korean)   The 'dance of the eight monks,' a standard scene in masked dance-plays, especially of the Pongsan region. (Yi "Mask" 53)

mutual wheel   A burlesque circuit in the U.S., from coast to coast, which in the 1920s and early 1930s was unusually permissive. (Wilmeth LANGUAGE)

mynstral   See: minstrel.

myraclis   A medieval miracle play. (Chambers MEDIAEVAL II 104)

mystère (French)   A medieval mystery play.

mystère mimé (French)   A medieval mystery play in tableaux, presented at great festivals or for royal visitors. Performers were sometimes the citizens of a town. Some pantomime was used and, occasionally, dialogue. (Frank MEDIEVAL 165–166)

mystère profane (French)   A 15th C secular mystery play. (Nicoll DEVELOPMENT 93)

mystère sacré (French)   A 15th C sacred mystery play. (Nicoll DEVELOPMENT 93)

mysterium, misterium (Latin)   Action. The word was used of certain liturgical plays. (Chambers MEDIAEVAL II 65)

mystery cycle   A series of medieval mystery plays, loosely linked and episodic, making up one long play. Performances of a complete cycle sometimes took many days. Sometimes called a mystery, cycle, or cycle mystery.

mystery play   Short form: mystery. 1. A medieval play dealing with the life of Christ, though the term is sometimes used more broadly to cover any play with Biblical subject matter. In French, *mistère* or *mystère*, sometimes *misterie*. In Italian, *misterio*. In Latin, *misterium* or *mysterium* (meaning action), the probable original for the medieval terms. See also: *sacra rappresentazione*. 2. Now, sometimes, a modern play dealing with a crime and its solution.

mystery stage   A stage upon which medieval mystery plays were performed.

mystic chasm   The physical and psychological gulf separating the real world in the auditorium from the ideal world on stage in the composer Richard Wagner's theatre at Bayreuth. Accomplished partly by means of a double proscenium arch. Also called the mystic gulf. (Brockett HISTORY 542)

N

N New, as in such newly constructed and painted stage settings as a new chamber, new town, new forest. Found in 18th C British promptbooks. (Hughes in Hume LONDON 127)

Nachspiel (German)   Literally: epilogue. A comic afterpiece, popular in the 18th C. (Brockett HISTORY 391)

nadai (Japanese)   Literally: famous. 1. In Kyoto-Osaka *kabuki*, the manager of a theatre. See: *zamoto*. (Dunn/Torigoe ANALECTS 16, Leiter ENCYCLO-PEDIA 251) 2. Written with different ideographs, a star actor in *kabuki*. A shortening of *nadai haiyu, nadai yakusha* (star actor). Also called *onadai*. (Gunji KABUKI 31) 3. The overall title of a *kabuki* or *bunraku* play. Also called *onadai*. (Leiter ENCYCLOPEDIA 291) *Nadai shita* (beneath *nadai*) is an actor of low rank.(Kawatake KABUKI 33)

nagabakama (Japanese)   Literally: long trousers. Very long training trousers worn over a kimono as formal dress for a character in *no, kyogen,* and *kabuki*.

nagara (Sanskrit)   A large hemispherical drum played with two thin sticks. It accompanies *chhau, nautanki, bhagat* and other north Indian folk theatre forms. (Gargi FOLK 37, 47)

nagaraka (Sanskrit)   The role of a man-about-town in classical Indian drama. (Keith SANSKRIT 285)

nagauta (Japanese)   Literally: long song. 1. A lyric style of *shamisen* music (*utaimono*) that originated in and is unique to *kabuki*. It is the major style of music that plays offstage (*geza*) during dialogue scenes and one of the possible styles of onstage music (*debayashi*) that may accompany a dance scene. See also: *katarimono*. 2. An ensemble that plays this music, consisting of a number of singers, several *shamisen* players, and musicians who play the *no*-derived flute and three drums (*hayashi*). (Malm MUSIC 205-220, Malm NAGAUTA 15-19) *naik* (Gujarati)   The director of a *bhavai* performance. See also: *sutradhara*. (Gargi FOLK 69)

nailed-up drama   In 19th C Britain, a drama depending heavily on elaborate scenery. (Partridge TO-DAY 228)

naimaze (Japanese)   In *kabuki*, the weaving together of two or more distinct 'worlds' of characters and historical periods (*sekai*) in one plot (*shuko*). See also: *mitate*. (Brandon CLASSIC 242, Leiter ENCYCLOPEDIA 253)

nai nang (Thai)   Literally: puppet master. A puppeteer in *nang talung* shadow theatre. (Smithies/Kerdchouay in Rutnin SIAMESE 132)

nai rong (Thai)   Backstage in a *likay* theatre. Also called *lang rong* (backstage). (Virulrak "Likay" 122)

naiskramiki dhruva (Sanskrit)   See: *dhruva*.

naka iri (Japanese)   Literally: going inside. The middle section of a *no* or *kyogen* play, during which the major actor (*shite*) is offstage, normally to change costume for the second entrance. (Berberich "Rapture" 60, Komparu NOH 77–78)

naka maku (Japanese)   Literally: middle act. A dance play, or a dance act from a longer play, placed between the history (*jidai*) and the domestic (*sewa*) parts of a *kabuki* program of unrelated plays, especially during the late 19th and 20th C. (Leiter ENCYCLOPEDIA 253, Brandon TRADITIONAL 201, Kincaid KABUKI 255)

naka no ayumi (Japanese)   See: *ayumi*.

naka shomen (Japanese)   Mid-front seating in a modern *no* theatre. The seats face the downstage right pillar of the stage and thus are not very desirable. (Komparu NOH 140)

naked drama   The mass display of ladies' legs on stage in the mid-19th C. (Green in Mayer/Richards WESTERN 158)

nalgaep'yogi-ch'um (Korean)   Literally: wing flapping dance. A dance in masked dance-drama, in which the dancer opens and closes his arms. Abbreviated: *nalgaep'yogi*. (Cho "Yangju" 51)

nallari, nalnari (Korean)   See: *t'aep'yongso*.

nam (Vietnamese)   See: *hat nam*.

namaghara (Assamese)   See: *rabha*.

nambyar (Malayalam)   In *kutiyattam*, a drummer, a member of a sub-caste of temple musicians. (Enros in Baumer/Brandon SANSKRIT 275)

name actor, name performer, name star   A performer whose reputation should attract an audience. Hence, name act, name billing. (Bowman/Ball THEATRE)

name-announcing speech   See: *nanori*.

name bill   A variety program featuring well-known players.

name part   A title role, such as Hamlet, Macbeth, King Lear.

name-saying speech   See: *nanori*.

nami ita (Japanese)   Literally: wave board. In *kabuki*, a low scenic piece on which waves are painted, representing the water's edge. (Ernst KABUKI 135)

namiko (Japanese)   Literally: wave costume. A blue costume and hood worn by a *kabuki* stage assistant in a water scene. See also: *koken*.

nami nuno (Japanese)   See: *jigasuri*.

namsadang, namsatang (Korean)   Literally: male-female performers. 1. A popular itinerant variety troupe of approximately fifty single male performers. Troupes existed until c. 1920. 2. A performance by such a troupe. It consisted of six items: *p'ungmul, bona, salp'an, orum, totbegi*, and *tolmi*. See: *sadang*. (Cho KOREAN 11, Sim/Kim KOREAN 23)

nanbangzi, nan pang tzu (Chinese)   Literally: southern *bangzi*. A musical mode (*diaoshi*) in Beijing opera (*jingju*) used for calm or happy sentiments, meditation, and thought by female (*dan*) and young male (*xiaosheng*) characters. (Wichmann "Aural" 236-244, Zung SECRETS 64)

nance   A female impersonator. Derogatory. (Berrey/Van den Bark SLANG 573)

nan ch'ü (Chinese)   See: *qu*.

nandan, nantan (Chinese)   A male performer of female roles (*dan*) in Beijing opera (*jingju*) and many other forms of music-drama (*xiqu*). Since 1949, only women have been trained to perform female roles, but *nandan* trained before 1949 who still perform today are highly prized.

nandi (Sanskrit)   The benediction at the beginning of a classical Indian theatre performance. One item of the preliminaries (*purvaranga*). (Keith SANSKRIT 339-342)

nandi-sutradhara (Sanskrit)   Literally: benediction-stage manager. In *kutiyattam*, the person who recites the benediction. He is the chief of the two drummers (*nambyar*). (Enros in Baumer/Brandon SANSKRIT 278)

nan dwin zat (Burmese)   Literally: palace *zat*. A term created in the mid-18th C to distinguish Thai-derived non-*Jataka* dance-dramas from orthodox *zat*. (Aung DRAMA 35)

nang (Thai)   1. Literally: leather. By extension a shadow puppet play, hence a common abbreviation of *nang yai* or *nang talung*. Also, today, movies, since they, like shadow plays, use a white screen. (Dhaninivat NANG 6–7) 2. Literally: woman. A second pronunciation of *nang* (and hence a different meaning) is used for a female role in traditional theatre. *Nang ek* is a heroine. (Yupho PRELIMINARY 4, Rutnin "Development" 13) In *likay*, other female roles are *nang rong* (minor female role), and *mae* (mother). (Virulrak "Likay" 189)

nang ek (Lao)   A leading female role, or princess, in a *mohlam* play. (Miller "Kaen" 222)

nang ek (Thai)   See: *nang*.

nang kaloun (Khmer)   See: *ayang*.

nangkis (Indonesian)   In Javanese shadow theatre, to block an opponent's blows or weapons, using the hands or elbows. (Long JAVANESE 66)

nang rabam (Thai)   Literally: dance puppet. A variety of shadow-play (*nang yai*) performed by dancing puppeteers during the day, rather than at night. Also called *nang ram*. (Dhaninivat NANG 14)

nang ram (Thai)   See: *nang raban*.

nang rawng (Lao)   A secondary female role in a *mohlam* play. (Miller "Kaen" 222)

nang re (Thai)   A travelling shadow play troupe or film show. (Virulrak "Likay" 248)

nang rong (Thai)   See: *nang*.

nang sbek (Khmer)   Literally: leather puppets. A major classical and folk theatre form in which large, non-articulated, flat hide puppets representing characters and scenes from the *Ream Ker* (*Ramayana*) are paraded alternately in front of and behind a wide, white screen, thus creating either silhouettes or shadows. Two narrators (*kru*) recite episodes from the epic while puppet manipulators/dancers, using traditional *lokhon khol* dance steps, manipulate the puppets above their heads as they dance. Also called *sbek thom* (large puppet), *nang sbek luong* (royal *nang sbek*), *robam nang sbek* (danced *nang sbek*). (Brunet in Osman TRADITIONAL 47-57, Tilakasiri PUPPET 44)

nang sbek luong (Khmer)   See: *nang sbek*.

nang sbek touch (Khmer)   See: *ayang*.

nang talung (Thai)   Literally: Pattalung shadow play. A type of shadow theatre (*nang*) supposed to have originated in the southern Thai city of Pattalung. Small leather puppets are manipulated by one puppeteer (*nai nang*) before a cloth screen to the accompaniment of a modified *pi phat* musical ensemble. (Smithies/Kerdchouay in Rutnin SIAMESE 129-133, Brandon SOUTHEAST 68, 330)

nang trolung (Khmer)   A corruption of Thai *nang talung*. See: *ayang*.

nang yai (Thai)   Literally: large leather. A shadow and silhouette play performed with large (*yai*), flat, incised leather puppets (*nang*) moved in front of and behind a wide cloth screen by dancing puppeteers. Two narrators (*kon pak*) recite an episode from the *Ramakien* (*Ramayana*) to the accompaniment of *pi phat* music. The earliest reference to *nang yai* is in the 16th C, but the term is certainly much older. Abbreviated *nang*. See also: *nang rabam, nang sbek, sbek thom*. (Dhaninivat NANG 6, Brandon GUIDE 148-149) *nan hsi* (Chinese)   See: *nanxi*.

naniwabushi (Japanese)   A highly emotional form of storytelling, performed by a team of singer and *shamisen* player. It began in the 18th C and is widely popular today in concert. Also called *rokyoku*.

nannyar (Malayalam)   A female singer and actress in *kutiyattam*, a member of a caste of traditional temple servants. Also spelled *nanyar*. (Enros in Baumer/ Brandon SANSKRIT 275)

nanori (Japanese)   Literally: name announcing. 1. In a *no* play, the passage in which the secondary character (*waki*), arriving at the end of a journey, announces who he is and why he has come to that particular place. 2. A name-announcing passage in a *kyogen* play. (Berberich ''Rapture'' 60) *Nanori za* (name-announcing place) is the position on the *no* stage, just left of the *shite* pillar (*shite bashira*), where the speech is delivered. Also called *jo za* (standard place) and *shite za* (*shite*'s place), because the principal actor (*shite*) stands there on his first entrance. (Nippon Gakujutsu JAPANESE xii) 3. A bravura speech in *kabuki*, in which a major character proudly boasts of his lineage and marvelous qualities. Examples are in Brandon CLASSIC 71-72 and Leiter ART 41-42. *Nanoridai* (name-announcing platform) was a small platform jutting into the audience from the runaway (*hanamichi*) in a mid-18th C *kabuki* theatre from which a name-announcing speech was delivered. A diagram is in Ernst KABUKI 35.

nan pang tzu (Chinese)   See: *nanbangzi*.

nanqu (Chinese)   See: *qu*.

nan tan (Chinese)   See: *nandan*.

nan tsa chü (Chinese)   See: *nanzaju*.

nanxi, nan hsi (Chinese)   Literally: southern drama. A type of script and performance which developed c. 10th C out of Song *zaju*, storytelling (*shuochang*), and other types of entertainment in a district of Zhejiang Province known at various times as Wenzhou and Yongjia. From the late 14th-15th C, it was the most important and widespread script and performance type in China. It used southern *qu* for its songs and lyric patterns, and included solos, duets, and ensemble singing. Plays typically contained forty or more scenes and a prologue, and were written for four major role categories (*hangdang*): male (*sheng*), female (*dan*), painted-face (*jing*), and clown (*chou*). Also called play text (*xiwen* or *hsi wen*), Wenzhou *zaju* or Wenchow *tsa chü*, and Yongjia *zaju* or Yungchia *tsa chü*. (Dolby HISTORY 27, 38, 71-78, 83-86; Liu INTRODUCTION 166-168; Liu SIX 13)

nanyar (Malayalam)   See: *nannyar*.

nanzaju, nan tsa chü (Chinese)   Literally: southern variety drama. A type of script and performance, 15th-17th C, that principally used southern *qu* for melodies and lyric patterns. The plays included solo, duet, and ensemble singing, and usually consisted of from one to ten or more acts (*zhe*).

naobo, nao po (Chinese)   See: *bo*.

naphat (Thai)   Special musical tunes for specific actions of characters in Thai classical dance-drama. In *likay*, a turn or scene by an actor or character, marked by his entrance and exit. (Virulrak "Likay" 227)

napuk (Indonesian)   Light slaps used by female characters to temporarily deter an enemy's attack in Javanese shadow play (*wayang kulit*) battle scenes. (Long JAVANESE 86)

naqal, naqqal (Punjabi)   A short farce, performed by a troupe of two or three comedians (*bhand*), in Punjab, north India. (Gargi FOLK 183)

ñaque (Spanish)   A strolling troupe consisting of two players. (Villandrando in Nagler SOURCES 57)

nar (Yiddish)   Literally: fool (in German and Yiddish). Originally in 18th C Purim plays, a clown who might do pratfalls, spew out nonsense, and hit others with an inflated bladder. Later, any similar fool. Also called a *lets* (Hebrew). (Sandrow VAGABOND 1, 10)

narae, narye (Korean)   Literally: ceremony of expelling evil spirits. An ancient court exorcism play. Hideous-looking masks were worn on New Year's Eve to expel demons and misfortunes of the old year. See: *sandaeguk*. (Cho "Yangju" 28, Gassner/Quinn ENCYCLOPEDIA 510)

naraku (Japanese)   Literally: hell. The pit beneath the *kabuki* stage and runway (*hanamichi*) where stage hands worked at winches that moved the revolving stage and traplifts. (Ernst KABUKI 54) The term continues in use today. (Hamamura et al KABUKI 113)

narimono (Japanese)   Primarily a *kabuki* term. 1. The approximately thirty percussion and wind instruments in the offstage ensemble (*geza*) that plays background music during performance. Instrument lists are in Leiter ENCYCLOPEDIA 267-269 and Malm MUSIC 225-227. 2. Melodies and rhythmic patterns played by these instruments. A list of patterns is in Leiter ENCYCLOPEDIA 78-91. Malm in Brandon/Malm/Shively STUDIES 144-170 discusses their use.

na rong (Thai)   See: *rong*.

narrative ballet   See: *ballet d'action*.

narrator   A performer who serves as a commentator on the play being presented and is often, like Tom in *The Glass Menagerie*, a character in the play.

narrow-beam projector spot   See: beam projector.

narrow flat   See: jog.

nartaka (Sanskrit)   A male dancer in ancient India, mentioned in the *Ramayana* epic. (Hein MIRACLE 115)

nartaki (Sanskrit)   A female dancer.

narye (Korean)   See: *narae*.

nasori (Japanese)   In *bugaku*, a complicated dragon mask with movable parts. (Wolz BUGAKU 44-45)

nat (Sanskrit)   See: *bhada*.

nata (Sanskrit)   In ancient Indian theatre, the most common term for actor, pantomimist, or dancer. Also called: *bharata, sailusa, kusilava*, and other terms as well. (Keith SANSKRIT 25, 28, 31, 36, 45, 49, 50, 67)

natadontri (Thai)   Literally: dance-music. A term created by the Thai government, 1942-1944, to describe music-dance-drama forms such as *likay*, as distinguished from sung drama or opera (*uparakon*) or spoken drama (*natakam*). (Virulrak "Likay" 91)

natagamani (Sanskrit)   See: *sutradhara*.

natak (Hindi)   A contemporary, generic term for a play written in prose dialogue and having formal scene divisions. (Hein MIRACLE 291)

nataka (Sanskrit)   The most important of the ten major play types (*rupaka*) of classical Indian drama. It should be in four to ten acts, have a legendary figure as a hero, and the dominant sentiment (*rasa*) should be the erotic (*srngara*) or heroic (*vira*). An example is *Shakuntala*. If in ten acts, then also called *mahanataka* (large *nataka*). (Keith SANSKRIT 345)

natakam (Thai)   See: *natadontri*.

nataksala (Sanskrit)   A temple theatre used for performances of plays designed to please the deities. (Varadpande TRADITIONS 48)

nata mandir (Sanskrit)   Literally: actors' hall. In India, a performance space attached to a Hindu temple; used for either dance or drama. (Varadpande KRISHNA 13)

nati (Sanskrit)   1. Actress. In classical Indian theatre, the wife of the troupe director (*sutradhara*). (Keith SANSKRIT 51, 66, 361) 2. See: *natika*.

natika (Sanskrit)   A romantic drama which combines features of the heroic play (*nataka*) and the social play (*prakarana*). Also called *nati*. An example is *Ratnavali* in Lal SANSKRIT 339–376. (Kale THEATRIC 163, Keith SANSKRIT 349-350)

National Electrical Code   See: code.

national theatre   A theatre subsidized by a national government.

native air opera   A development of the cantata in the early 1930s in Lagos, Nigeria, using Yoruba music and songs and dramatized biblical stories. (Adedeji glossary)

natives   Provincial audiences.

Nativity play   A play about the birth of Christ.

natkadaw (Burmese)   See: *nat pwe*.

nat pwe (Burmese)   A shaman dance performance by a professional dance-medium (*natkadaw*). (Brandon SOUTHEAST 71)

natsu kyogen (Japanese)   Literally: summer play. 1. A *kabuki* play performed during the dog days of summer. It is light and entertaining, and often contains spectacular effects (*keren*). The term sometimes encompasses plays performed in the sixth lunar month (July) as well as 'ghost' plays performed during the All-Souls period (*bon*) in the seventh and eighth lunar months (August-September). (Kawatake KABUKI 25, Leiter ENCYCLOPEDIA 31-33, 381). Gunji includes only those plays performed during the sixth month, putting the later plays in the category of *bon kyogen*. (Gunji KABUKI 36). Also called *natsu shibai* (summer play). 2. The summer program on which such plays are performed.

natucni (Marathi)   An actress in *tamasha*. (Vatsyayan TRADITIONAL 175)

natural   1. Said of a role ideally suited to a particular performer. 2. Said of a production that cannot fail. (Granville DICTIONARY)

natural color(ed)   Especially in the past in stage lighting, used of lamps or filters whose glass had been colored during manufacture. Examples: natural-color lamp, natural-colored glass. (McCandless "Glossary" 640, Bowman MODERN)

naturalism   In general, an extreme form of realism which seeks to demonstrate that heredity and environment determine character. Naturalist drama is tough, bleak, often sordid, and its themes are often oriented toward social problems. Its characters are frequently at the bottom of the social or economic ladder and are either in despair or apathetic about the prospects of rising above their situation. Naturalism's major practitioners were Émile Zola, André Antoine, and Maxim Gorki. The term is also applied to slice-of-life acting.

natya (Sanskrit)   1. In classical Indian dramatic theory, dramatic art, as distinguished from rhythmic dance (*nrtta*) and mimetic art (*nrtya*). Its essential characteristic is its ability to arouse or evoke sentiments (*rasa*) in the spectator. (Keith SANSKRIT 295-296) 2. Dance-drama, in which dancers enact a story through hand gestures (*hasta*) and acting (*abhinaya*). Music, songs, and occasionally dialogue are elements of performance. 3. More broadly, "all theatrical activity." (Kale THEATRIC 10)

natyacarya (Sanskrit)   See: *sutradhara*.

natyadharmi (Sanskrit)   The stylized or conventional style of production in ancient Indian theatre. In it suggestive gesture by the actor replaces props or other scenic aids. See also: *lokadharmi*. (Gandhi in Baumer/Brandon SANSKRIT 122-123)

natya guda (Oriya)   A rod puppet theatre form in Orissa state, northeast India. (ASIAN 11)

natyakara (Sanskrit)   A playwright.

natyamandapa (Sanskrit)   Literally: theatre pavilion. In ancient India, a public theatre, either permanent, as a hall in a temple, or a temporary structure for special performances. Also called *natyavesma* (playhouse). See also: *natyasala*. (Kale THEATRIC 14-15) *natyasala* (Sanskrit)   Literally: theatre hall. A private theatre, in a king's palace or a rich man's mansion. Also called *rangasala* (theatre hall). See also: *natyamandapa*. (Kale THEATRIC 14)

natyavesma (Sanskrit)   See: *natyamandapa*.

naumachia (Latin Roman), **naumachia, naumachy**   From the 1st C BC, a staged naval battle representing a historic occasion. Most *naumachiae* took place in artificial basins deep enough to float the triremes often used; one such basin measured 400 by 600 yards. The combatants, dressed as Athenians, Persians, or whatever group they represented, were condemned criminals or other prisoners who fought until all those on one side were dead or the emperor signalled an end to the battle. Combatants numbered in the hundreds or low thousands; one contest is said to have involved 19,000 men. The combatants were *naumachiarii*. (Sandys COMPANION 510-511, Bieber HISTORY 253)

nautanki (Hindi)   A folk theatre in north India that evolved out of ballad singing and now blends Hindu and Muslim stories and performance styles. Performed by itinerant all-male troupes. (Varadpande TRADITIONS 86, Gargi FOLK 36-49, Vatsyayan TRADITIONAL 163-167)

nautical drama   In the 19th C, British melodrama that featured sailors, ships, and stage tanks filled with real water. Also called an aqua drama. (Baker, THEATRECRAFT 353, 364-365)

nayaga (Indonesian)   In Sunda, a musician in a *gamelan* musical ensemble. (Foley "Sundanese" 76) In Javanese, *niyaga* or *nijaga*.

nayaka (Sanskrit)   1. Hero. The major role type in classical Indian drama. Sub-types are: *lalita, santa, udatta*, and *uddhata*. 2. The hero role in various forms of rural theatre in India today. (Keith SANSKRIT 84-85, 305-307)

nayanabhinaya (Malayalam)   Eye exercises rigorously practiced by a *kathakali* actor to develop emotional expressiveness. (Kothari "Kathakali" 56)

nayika (Sanskrit)   Heroine. The major female role in classical Indian drama and in rural forms of theatre. She is a lover or wife of the hero (*nayaka*) and can be categorized, according to Bharata, by experience (three types, see: *madya, mugdha, pragalba*), relation to hero (eight types), excellences of nature (ten types), feminine graces (ten types), etc. for 384 possible types of heroine. (Keith SANSKRIT 308-310)

ndamu (Indonesian)   In Javanese shadow theatre, a light puff of air, used primarily by refined gods in battle to blow their enemies away. (Long JAVANESE 86)

ndugang (Indonesian)   A kicking movement in Javanese shadow theatre. A puppet is tilted backwards as it directs a blow at its opponent's head. (Long JAVANESE 63, 92)

near the bone   Said of a risqué play or line. (Granville DICTIONARY)

neat drunk   In vaudeville, an actor who impersonates a slightly tipsy character, immaculately dressed, non-staggering, and not blubbering. (Laurie VAUDEVILLE 181)

Nebulator, nebulator   A patented (1893) lighting instrument designed to cast shadows of moving clouds. Strictly, Nebulator is the alternate name ("Cloud Creator or Nebulator") under which the patent was issued, while nebulator is the word used by inventor Steele Mackaye for the complex arrangement which amounted to the heart of the instrument. This was essentially a partly opaque cloth ('cloud cloth') on movable rollers, the whole in a sliding frame which, in addition to side-to-side movement, could approach or recede from the light source above it, thus increasing or decreasing the size of the moving clouds. The word, related to nebula and -ator, was apparently a creation of the inventive Mackaye; it can be rendered cloud maker. (The pages cited below, which contain illustrations, are part of Mackaye's Addenda.) (Mackaye EPOCH II lxxvii-lxxxi)

nebulo (Latin)   See: minstrel.

neck roll   An accidental sensation created by burlesque performer Harry K. Morton. While he was performing a practice handstand, a violent back cramp caused him to lower himself to the floor by degrees. He then dropped on his ear, lifted his leg, and twisted himself out of the cramp. (Sobel BURLEYCUE 229)

Nedervolt-Spiegelscheinwerfer (German)   See *Niedervolt-Spiegelscheinwerfer*.

needle points   In late 19th C gas borderlights in Britain, fine-pointed gas jets separated by only a small fraction of an inch. This was an innovation in which the lighting of one jet caused the flame to run along the entire row of jets. (Penzel LIGHTING 107-108)

nehon (Japanese)   See: *daihon*.

Nehru collar   See: mandarin collar.

nempiling (Indonesian)   A striking movement in Javanese shadow theatre: a light, slapping blow to an opponent's head. (Long JAVANESE 62, 83)

nendhang (Indonesian)   A short, chopping kick delivered to a fallen enemy's head or body in Javanese puppet theatre and dance drama. (Long JAVANESE 63)

neoclassic, neoclassical   1. A style in drama and theatre imitative of Greek and Roman models, popular from the 16th to the 18th C in Europe. 2. A school of criticism based on rigid and sometimes misinterpreted Aristotelian tenets. The school had its greatest influence in 17th C France. Hence, neoclassicism.

neo-realistic theatre   Alexander Tairov's approach to theatre in Russia in the 1920s. He aimed not for the illusion of actual life, but at providing rhythmic and plastic aids to acting—volume, cubes, and a variety of other solid geometric forms. (Carter SPIRIT 84)

neo-romanticism   A style in playwriting and production popular in the late 19th C that tried to recapture the idealism of the romantic theatre. Neo-romanticism was one of several reactions against realism and naturalism. *Cyrano de Bergerac* is an example. (Cameron/Gillespie ENJOYMENT)

nepathyagraha (Sanskrit)   A dressing room in a classical Indian theatre. Separated from the stage by a curtain. (Keith SANSKRIT 54, 359-360)

nepreryvnaia liniia (Russian)   Konstantin Stanislavsky's '"unbroken line' of significant and unrelated expression...." (Hobgood "Stanislavski's" 156)

nepszinmü (Hungarian)   A 19th C Hungarian folk play depicting village life in a highly idealized manner and combining folklore, music, and dance. (Gassner/Quinn ENCYCLOPEDIA 440, Matlaw MODERN 371)

net   See: theatrical net.

netherstocks   17th C men's stockings, shaped to the leg, reaching a bit above the knee, and held in place by garters. Also called netherhose or lower stocks.

netrabhinaya (Sanskrit)   In *kutiyattam*, conventionalized eye movements. (Vatsyayan TRADITIONAL 28)

netting   See: scrim.

netting compound   A glue used to fix cut-out foliage to a net.

neue Sachlichkeit (German)   Literally: new matter-of-factness. A post-expressionist German dramatic style, neo-realistic, pragmatic, and anti-emotional, yet often marked by a belief in the divine origins of reality. Bertolt Brecht is a prime exponent of the style. (Gassner/Quinn ENCYCLOPEDIA 351)

neuma, pneuma (Latin)   A wordless melody, or vowel sounds for melodies, added to the church service; part of a trope. Also spelled *neupma*. (Chambers MEDIAEVAL II 7)

neurobatae (Latin Roman)   Rope walkers, rope dancers. From the late 1st C BC, one of the types of performers who played in the mime in theatres. The usual Latin term is *funambuli*. (Nicoll MASKS 84)

neutral density filter   A grey-appearing gel which reduces all visible frequencies proportionally. Used as a dimmer occasionally in theatres (regularly in television and film) to avoid the red-richening effect of lowered power to a lamp. In current practice, polarizing filters are used for lesser density reductions. (Wehlburg GLOSSARY)

neutral drop   A cloth drop of neutral color, such as grey or tan.

neutral stage   A stage, such as in Shakespeare's Globe or the Stratford, Ontario, Festival Theatre, usually a simple performance space with a relatively plain facade behind it.

new dance   A 1920s term for dance which was performed as a reaction to classic ballet. Hence, an early designation of modern dance, still used occasionally. (Love DANCE 68)

new electric light   The phrase used for the carbon arc light upon its introduction to the English theatre in the middle of the 19th C. See also: arc light. (Rees GAS 65)

new stagecraft   See: new theatre.

new theatre   1. A theatre movement in the late 19th and early 20th C aiming for a unity of all production elements. The movement included such innovations as expressionism and theatricalism. Also called the new stagecraft. 2. A term applied to those theatre practices in the 1960s which emphasized ritual, the creation of a bond between audience and performer, and a serious and even spiritual theatre experience. (Bowman/Ball THEATRE)

next-to-closing, next-to-shut   The next-to-last position on a vaudeville bill, normally reserved for the star of the show. (Smith VAUDEVILLIANS)

next week *East Lynne*   By the early 20th C, a phrase used to indicate that a U.S. touring company was in trouble. A performance of *East Lynne*, a very popular show, was considered a remedy in the late 19th C. (Wilmeth LANGUAGE)

nezumi kido (Japanese)   Literally: mouse door. A pit entrance in a *kabuki* theatre of the 18th and 19th C. The nickname is from the high threshold and low lintel; they made it difficult to enter without paying. Abbreviated *kido*. (Shively in Brandon/Malm/Shively STUDIES 12, Toita KABUKI plate 76)

ngajengaken (Indonesian)   To turn around and face an opponent. A common fighting movement in Javanese shadow theatre. (Long JAVANESE 81)

ngan (Thai)   Literally: job, work. A shortening for *ngan pit wik* or *ngan plik*.

ngan pit wik (Thai)   A performance in an enclosed theatre, permanent or temporary, where admission is charged. (Virulrak "Likay" 240-244)

ngan plik (Thai)   A performance of popular theatre paid for by a sponsor (*chaophap*); the public attends without charge. (Virulrak "Likay" 240-244)

ngantem (Indonesian)   Striking movement in which a character strikes his opponent with an outstretched forearm. Used extensively in Javanese shadow theatre. (Long JAVANESE 61)

ngasta jemparing (Indonesian)   The action of shooting an arrow in Javanese shadow theatre. (Long JAVANESE 64-65)

ngelogi (Indonesian)   To jump or drop down on an opponent. A Javanese shadow theatre movement used mostly by monkey characters. (Long JAVANESE 105)

ngepok (Indonesian)   Holding grip used for large puppets in Javanese shadow theatre. The hand envelops the upper part of the body control rod, and the thumb extends up the rod until it is at or beyond the lower edge of the puppet. (Long JAVANESE 25) *ngepruk* (Indonesian)   A Javanese shadow puppet movement in which both arms are released as a character strikes at his opponent. (Long JAVANESE 61, 91-92)

nges (Indonesian)   In a *wayang* play, the emotion of romance (Muljono in Osman TRADITIONAL 71) or an atmosphere of distress (Humardani in Osman TRADITIONAL 83).

nggetak (Indonesian)   A powerful burst of air from the mouth of a giant in Javanese shadow theatre. Used as a fighting technique to blow an opponent off-screen. (Long JAVANESE 67)

ngibing (Indonesian)   1. In Java, a dance style used by a man when dancing with a professional female dancer (*taledek*). (Holt ART 111) 2. In Sundanese *wayang golek*, movement sequences of a puppet which are based on classical Sundanese dance and which follow the rhythmic cadences of *gamelan* music. Movement types include walking (*gedig, gedut, keupat, mincid*), turning (*galeong*), swiveling the head (*godeg*), scarf movements (*sampur, sapak soder*), grooming (*capeng, kumis, makuta, raras konda*), obeisances (*sembah, mamandapan baksa*) and others. See also: *bebas*. (Foley "Sundanese" 159-162)

nglarak (Indonesian)   A Javanese *wayang* fighting technique in which an opponent is yanked forward or to the ground before being struck and kicked. (Long JAVANESE 58, 83)

ngoerek (Indonesian)   See: *nguruk*.

ngo gyin (Burmese)   The climactic song, a lament, that occurs at the end of a *zat* play.

ngoma (Swahili)   Recently developed dramatized dances of Tanzania which show aspects of folk life. (Adedeji glossary)

ngremo (Indonesian)   Literally: rapture dance. The opening dance in Javanese *ludruk*, performed by a man dressed as a woman. Adapted from a classical lovemaking dance. (Peacock RITES 61-62)

ngruwatan (Indonesian)   See: *ruwatan*.

ngulungaken sirah (Indonesian)   A defiant movement in Javanese shadow theatre in which a character offers his unprotected head to be struck by the opponent. The movement is typically executed by comic and somewhat addle-brained characters. (Long JAVANESE 97)

ngundhamana (Indonesian)   Shaking a fist in an opponent's face. Used frequently by the less refined characters in Javanese *wayang kulit*. (Long JAVANESE 81)

ngurek (Indonesian)   Literally: be pierced. 1. To be in a state of trance, possessed by the spirit of a demon (*buta-kala*) in the retinue of the *barong* in the Balinese *barong* play. 2. A person in this state of trance during a performance. Also spelled *ngoerek*. (de Zoete/Spies DANCE 68, 98, 274) *nguyet* (Vietnamese)   A two-stringed moon-lute played in *cai luong* and *hat boi*. Also called *kim*. (Addiss "Theater" 140, Brandon SOUTHEAST 128)

nhac kich (Vietnamese)   See: *kich*.

nhip (Vietnamese)   Rhythms used in *hat cheo* music. Among various types are *nhip cach*, an irregular rhythm; *nhip cho*, a slow, regular beat; *nhip duoi*, a rapid rhythm in which phrases echo and overlap the melody; and *nhip sap*, a regular, quick rhythm. (Pham-Duy MUSICS 124, 127; Addiss "Theater" 132)

niais (French)   In 19th C French melodramatic bourgeois comedy, a fourth standard character; a simpleton, allied to the hero. He spoke in a low, vulgar dialect, far removed from the artificial but noble expressions of the hero, heroine, and villain. (Carlson FRENCH 43)

nian, nien (Chinese)   Literally: read aloud. Speech, one of the basic performance skills (*jiben gongfu*) in Beijing opera (*jingju*) and many other forms of music-drama (*xiqu*). Described in Scott CLASSICAL 18, 92-96, and Wichmann "Aural" 393-425.

nianbai, nien pai (Chinese)   The spoken portion of a play in Chinese traditional theatre (*xiqu*), or any single spoken passage. Abbreviated *bai* or *pai*. Also called *huabai* or *hua pai*. Described in Scott CLASSICAL 18, 92-96, and Wichmann "Aural" 115-126. See also: *chang*.

nibanmemono (Japanese)   Literally: second piece or play. 1. In *no*, the second, or warrior, play on a five-play program. See: *shuramono*. (Shimazaki NOH 23) 2. In Edo (Tokyo) style *kabuki*, the second or domestic (*sewamono*) part of a main play (*hon kyogen*), usually consisting of two acts. (Brandon CLASSIC 241) 3. In Kyoto-Osaka style *kabuki*, an independent domestic play, appearing second on the program after an independent history play (*jidaimono*). (Gunji KABUKI 23, Kincaid KABUKI 255) Abbreviated *nibanme*, which Dunn/Torigoe suggest meant second preliminary piece in 17th C Kyoto-Osaka (i.e.: *futatateme*), although this may be a misinterpretation. (Dunn/Torigoe ANALECTS 167)

nibhatkhin (Burmese)   A pageant utilizing dialogue, action, and comic elements, depicting events from the life of Buddha. As early as the 14th C, actors performed in scenes set on carts that were moved to various parts of the city. (Aung DRAMA 7)

nibs   In 19th C Britain, the gas man's term for the burners in gas battens, and perhaps in other places as well. Nibs was the word no matter what the shape of the burners. (Rees GAS 37)

nibusei (Japanese)   Literally: two-part system. A system of staging two performances a day, for 25 successive days each month. The matinee and evening programs may be the same or different. Common in commercial theatres (*kabuki, bunraku, shinpa*, popular theatre) since the Tokyo earthquake of 1923. (Leiter ENCYCLOPEDIA 273)

nice people   Among vaudeville agents, performers who gave them more than the usual ten percent commission. (Wilmeth LANGUAGE)

niche   One's place on a variety bill.

Niedervolt-Spiegelscheinwerfer (German)   Literally: low-voltage mirror-spotlight. Primarily in Germany, a low-voltage autotransformer spotlight designed around its reflector (*Spiegel*), but sometimes with a lens system. The first word is sometimes spelled *Nedervolt*. (Bentham ART 319)

nien (Chinese)   See: *nian*.

nien pai (Chinese)   See: *nianbai*.

nifty   1. A clever piece of stage business. 2. A joke, a wisecrack. 3. The punch line of a joke. 4. To tell a joke. (Bowman/Ball THEATRE. Berrey/Van den Bark SLANG 587)

nigger head   An obsolete and now offensive term for a portable power motor and winch used to raise a heavy object before counterweighted lines were attached.

nigger heaven   An obsolete and offensive term for the uppermost gallery in a theatre. (Bowman/Ball THEATRE)

nigger minstrel, nigger show   An obsolete and offensive U.S. term for a 19th C minstrel show. (Wilmeth LANGUAGE)

night   A benefit performance; a performer's 'night.' (Troubridge BENEFIT 11)

(the) night   Opening night.

night light   See: ghost light.

night man   A theatre employee hired for duty at night and receiving extra pay if asked to work during the day.

night piece   In Renaissance and Baroque theatres, possibly a skit or scene with the scenery representing the stars and clouds at night. (Campbell SCENES 168)

night rail   1. A 17th C woman's nightgown. 2. By the 18th C, a shoulder-length street wrap resembling a bed jacket. (Barton COSTUME 285, Walkup DRESSING 159)

night stand   One-night stand.

nihon buyo (Japanese)   Literally: Japanese dance. A term that came into use between c. 1912 and 1926 to distinguish *kabuki*-based dance from imported Western ballet and modern dance. Refers to *kabuki*-style dance performed in concert by members of dance schools (Fujima, Hanayagi, Nishikawa, etc.) and not to dance performed by *kabuki* actors in professional theatres. (Gunji BUYO 74-75)

nijaga (Indonesian)   See: *niyaga*.

niju butai (Japanese)   Literally: double stage. In *kabuki*, a platform, about two feet high, on which an interior set is placed. Abbreviated *niju*. (Scott KABUKI 153)

nimaime (Japanese)   1. The role of a gentle, handsome young lover in *kabuki*. It is one type of *tachiyaku* role. An example is Izaemon in *Love Letter from the Licensed Quarter* in Brandon CLASSIC 217-237. (Tsubouchi/Yamamoto KABUKI 266) 2. An actor who plays that role. The actor's name was written on the 'second position' (*nimaime*) advertising board posted in front of a theatre; hence the term. See also: *kanban*. (Gunji KABUKI 186, Leiter ENCYCLOPEDIA 275-276)

nimaime sakusha (Japanese)   Literally: second playwright. The second ranking playwright on a *kabuki* theatre staff in the 18th and 19th C. He wrote specific acts or scenes assigned by the chief playwright (*tate zakusha*). (Leiter ENCYCLOPEDIA 276, Ernst KABUKI 214)

ningyo (Japanese)   Puppet.

ningyoburi (Japanese)   Literally: puppet movement. A *kabuki* movement sequence, usually in a dance play, in which an actor moves as if he were a *bunraku* puppet. Two or three stage assistants pretend to be puppeteers manipulating him. See also: *ningyomi*. (Ernst KABUKI 168, Brandon in Brandon/Malm/Shively STUDIES 76-77)

ningyo joruri (Japanese)   Literally: puppet-narrative music. 1. From the early 17th C, a generic term for any type of puppet (*ningyo*) performance using sung narrative (*joruri*). (Kawatake HISTORY 15) 2. More narrowly today, the special form of puppet theatre commonly called *bunraku*. See also: *ayatsuri ningyo shibai*. (Kawatake KABUKI 17)

ningyomi (Japanese)   Literally: body of a puppet. A *kabuki* acting technique, largely in female roles, in which an actor copies a specific, identifiable *bunraku* puppet movement. See also: *ningyoburi*. (Brandon in Brandon/Malm/Shively STUDIES 76-77)

ningyo shibai (Japanese)   See: *ayatsuri ningyo shibai*.

ningyo zukai, ningyo tsukai (Japanese)   Literally: puppet handler. In *bunraku*, a puppeteer. Manipulation terminology is given in Adachi BUNRAKU 29. See also: *omo zukai*. (Scott KABUKI 62)

ninh (Vietnamese)   A villain role.

ni no kawari (Japanese)   Literally: second change. In Kyoto-Osaka, the second production of the *kabuki* season. See also: *hatsu haru kyogen*. (Dunn/Torigoe ANALECTS 19)

ni no matsu (Japanese)   Literally: second pine. 1. The second of three small pine trees in front of the *no* bridgeway (*hashigakari*). 2. The mid-spot on the bridgeway marked by the second pine. (Berberich ''Rapture'' 64, Komparu NOH 129) *nirami* (Japanese)   In *kabuki*, to cross one eye while holding the other straight, during a strong pose (*mie*). (Brandon in Brandon/Malm/Shively STUDIES 85)

nirmunda (Sanskrit)   See: *varsadhara*.

nirvahana (Sanskrit)   1. Conclusion. The fifth and last juncture (*sandhi*) of action in a classical Indian play. (Keith SANSKRIT 299) 2. In *kutiyattam*, exposition of events that precede the play, by one actor playing many roles. (Enros in Baumer/Brandon SANSKRIT 280-281)

nishi (Japanese)   Literally: west. Stage right, since a *kabuki* theatre traditionally faced south. More commonly called *shimote*. (Leiter ENCYCLOPEDIA 279)

nishi fu (Japanese)   Literally: Western style. The style of bunraku music developed at the Takemoto Puppet Theatre, located on the west side of Dotombori Canal in Osaka. See also: *higashi fu*.

nitrogen spot   1. Formerly, a term used for a spotlight lamp containing nitrogen. 2. Formerly, a spotlight using such a lamp. (McCandless ''Glossary'' 630, Bowman/Ball THEATRE)

nityakriya (Sanskrit)   During the preliminaries (*purvaranga*) in *kutiyattam*, dance sequences directed toward the deities. (Enros in Baumer/Brandon SANSKRIT 279)

nitya ras (Hindi)   The first part of a *raslila* performance, that presents a ritualized representation of the love-making of Radha and Krishna in the eternal, divine realm. (Swann ''Braj'' 21)

nix   To ban—as a play closed by the authorities.

niyaga (Indonesian)   In Java, a musician in a *gamelan* ensemble. Also spelled *nijaga* in Java, *nayaga* in Sunda. (Muljono in Osman TRADITIONAL 70, Brandon THRONES 37)

niyatapti (Sanskrit)   Certainty of success. The fourth of five stages of plot development (*avastha*) of a classical Indian play. (Keith SANSKRIT 297)

njagal (Indonesian)   A grip used to hold the largest of Javanese *wayang kulit* puppets. Animals, carriages, demonic gods, and other heavy puppets are held high on the main control rod (*gapit*). (Long JAVANESE 26)

njempalik (Indonesian)   Somersaulting movements used by apes and ogres in Javanese shadow theatre. (Long JAVANESE 67)

njunjung (Indonesian)   A Javanese shadow puppet technique in which an opponent is lifted high into the air during battle. (Long JAVANESE 58)

no, noh (Japanese)   Literally: skill. 1. Today, the usual term for the masked dance-drama form created out of *sarugaku no* (or *sarugaku*) by the actors Kannami Kiyotsugu (1333-1384) and his son Zeami Motokiyo (1363-1443). It became the official performing art (*shiki gaku*) of the samurai government during the Tokugawa period (1600-1868). Approximately 240 plays in the current repertory combine song (*fushi* or *utai*) and dialogue (*kotoba*) with music (*hayashi*) and dance (*mai*). The term *no* indicates that the actor's art is the focus of the theatre. A play centers on a protagonist (*shite*), and other roles are of minor importance. See also: *nogaku*. 2. Before Kannami's time, short dramatic pieces that were included in the variety-show repertory of a number of theatre forms, such as *sarugaku no, dengaku no,* and *ennen no.*

no butai (Japanese)   Literally: *no* stage. The working areas of a *no* theatre, consisting of the stage (*butai*), bridgeway (*hashigakari*), and dressing room (*kagami no ma*). (Komparu NOH 128)

nochi ba (Japanese)   Literally: later scene. The second part (*ba*) of a two-part *no* play. In it the protagonist (*nochi jite*) appears in his or her true form. (Hoff/Flindt "Structure" 219)

nochi jite, nochi shite (Japanese)   Literally: later protagonist. The protagonist (*shite*) who appears in the second part (*nochi ba*) of a two-part *no* play in his true identity, having been in disguise in part one. Costume and mask are usually changed during the interlude (*ai*). (Inoura HISTORY 116, Shimazaki NOH 23)

nod   1. A bow. 2. To bow, to take a bow. 3. See also: land the nod.

noeud (French)   Literally: knot. A plot complication which keeps the spectators in suspense. It is resolved by the *dénouement*; literally, the unravelling.

nogaku (Japanese)   The combined art of serious *no* and comic *kyogen*. Plays of both forms alternate on a single program and are performed on the same stage. (Inoura HISTORY 9)

nogakudo (Japanese)   Literally: *no* hall. A modern *no* theatre, consisting of a stage (*no butai*) and auditorium within an enclosing structure. (Komparu NOH 114)

noh (Japanese)   See: *no.*

noi loi (Vietnamese)   A generic term for the declamations or recitatives in *hat boi* and *cai luong*. Common situations are self-introduction, insulting the enemy, showing anger, and preparing for death. Major types are listed in Addiss "Theater" 143, 148, and Hauch "Study" 77.

noises off   Sounds made offstage to further the stage illusion, such as the sounds of battles, crowds, horses, thunder, etc.

noi su (Vietnamese)   A generic term for recitative sections in *hat cheo*. Addiss gives five types in "Theater" 133.

noi vat (Vietnamese)   A section of spoken dialogue in *hat cheo*. (Addiss "Theater" 133)

nojang (Korean)   The character and the mask of an old monk in various types of masked dance-play. (Yi "Mask" 36)

nokan (Japanese)   A small bamboo flute (*fue*) used in *no* and *kyogen*. See also: *hayashi*. (Malm MUSIC 119)

nokku (Malayalam)   Literally: look. Lowering the hand curtain (*tirassila*) in *kathakali* and related theatre forms so that the audience has a partial view of an actor before his first full appearance. See also: *tiranokku*. (Jones/Jones KA-THAKALI 76)

no-kyogen (Japanese)   See: *kyogen*.

nom de théâtre (French)   Stage name.

non-commercial   Said of a theatre, professional or amateur, not operated to make a profit.

non-dim   A marking used on some U.S. control boards to indicate that the marked circuit has no dimmer. The British parallel is 'switched only.' (Bentham ART)

nondirectional light, non-directional light   Light whose shadows, if any, are not apparent to the audience. (Bellman LIGHTING 326-327, Wehlburg GLOSSARY)

nongak (Korean)   See: *p'ungmul*.

non-lens spotlight   An occasional term for a floodlight, i.e., a light source and reflector. (Wehlburg GLOSSARY)

non-literal dance   Movement which creates non-verbal, aesthetic, sense experience through illusions in motion. Its value to the viewer lies in how it affects him or her overall, not by a traditional meaning, moral, or message. Also called abstract dance. See also: *nritta, rabam*. (Turner/Grauert/Zallman DANCE 3, 5)

non-practical   A scenic unit that appears to be workable—such as a door or window—but is not.

non-stop variety   See: continuous vaudeville.

nora (Thai)   1. Today, a spoken drama with traditional and *luk thung* style music. Actors and actresses perform modern stories in modern costume. 2. A version of *lakon jatri* dance drama based on the Princess Manora story.

noreum (Korean)   See: *norum*.

nori (Japanese)   Literally: riding. 1. In general, the manner in which a sung or spoken line 'rides' or is regulated by the rhythm of the music. 2. In *no*, any of three rhythmic patterns: *hira nori, o nori*, and *chu nori*, syncopated, fast, and very-fast rhythm. (Hoff/Flindt "Structure" 235-237) 3. In *bunraku*, short vocal passages or movement units that are precisely timed to the rhythm of their *shamisen* accompaniment. Also called *ito ni noru* (riding the strings) and *noru* (ride). 4. In *kabuki*, a sequence of *nori* borrowed from *bunraku* or a similar sequence, often comic, created within *kabuki*. An example is Bannai's challenge to Kampei in Brandon CHUSHINGURA 181. (Leiter ENCYCLOPEDIA 279-280)

nori (Korean)   See: *norum*.

nori dogu (Japanese)   In *no*, an abstractly constructed frame of a vehicle—boat or carriage—in which a character rides. One type of set prop (*tsukurimono*). (Komparu NOH 255)

nori-pan (Korean)   Literally: play-space. The playing area or stage, normally outdoors, for a folk play. See also: *norum*.

normal, normal line   A line perpendicular to a reflective surface; especially a line perpendicular to a curved surface (such as a lens) at a point of tangency. In stage lighting, sometimes applied to the point of incidence and reflection of a ray of light. (Bellman LIGHTING 50, Wehlburg GLOSSARY)

noroma (Japanese)   One of three old types of *joruri*—the other two, *bunya bushi* and *sekkyo bushi*—preserved today on Sado Island.

noru (Japanese)   See: *nori*.

norum, noreum, nori (Korean)   1. A play. 2. To play or perform. (Cho KOREAN 17, Choe STUDY 14)

nose   The portion of a step tread which projects beyond the step riser. Also called a lip or overhang. (Buerki STAGECRAFT)

nose out   In the U.S., to discover a play or performer. (Granville DICTIONARY)

nose paste   In makeup, nose putty.

nose putty   See: putty.

not according to the script   Extraneous, improvised. Also called not in the book.

not a hand   No applause.

notation   See: movement notation.

notation film   A film which records the choreography of a dance.

notice   1. A published review of a stage production. 2. A performer's or producer's notification of intent to end an engagement. 3. An announcement on a theatre's call board. (Bowman/Ball THEATRE)

notice board   1. A theatre call (bulletin) board. 2. A display board used onstage in 19th C unlicensed British theatres to provide the audience with information which could not legally be spoken. (Bowman/Ball THEATRE)

noticed   Recognized by the press.

not in the book   See: not according to the script.

no treasury   In Britain, said of a show that cannot pay the company members at the end of a week's run. (Partridge TO-DAY 224)

novelty act   A vaudeville routine with a new wrinkle.

nozoki mi (Japanese)   Literally: peek and see. The standard gesture (*kata*) in *kyogen* for peering around an object or through an opening. The open fan is held at arm's length before the face. Illustrated in Keene NO 223.

nritta, nrtta (Sanskrit)   Literally: pure dance. Non-mimetic dance that emphasizes rhythmic foot work, body movement, and hand gesture (*hasta*) for their beauty of form. Its function in classical theatre is minutely described by Bharata in NATYASASTRA 45-75. (Vatsyayan in Baumer/Brandon SANSKRIT 54)

nritya, nrtya (Sanskrit)   In Indian theatre, emotion-laden or story-telling dance in which the words of a song are expressed through a fusion of pantomime, facial expression, rhythmic foot-work, and active bodily movement. (Benegal PANORAMA 14, Keith SANSKRIT 275)

nrtta (Sanskrit)   See: *nritta*.

nrtya (Sanskrit)   See: *nritya*.

nubruk (Indonesian)   An unsuccessful striking movement frequently used in Javanese shadow theatre. A character leaps at his opponent with an outstretched arm but fails to hit him. (Long JAVANESE 62)

nude drama, nude theatre   Plays and productions featuring performers in scanty costumes or no clothes at all, as in *The Black Crook* in the 19th C and *Oh! Calcutta!* in the 20th.

nudie   1. A show which includes female nudity. 2. A performer in such an act. (Wilmeth LANGUAGE)

nudnick (Yiddish)   Literally, and as used in popular theatre, a bore or pest.

nuigurumi (Japanese)   Literally: sewed covering. A costume or construction worn by a *kabuki* actor when impersonating a bird or animal. (Leiter ENCYCLOPEDIA 281)

nujun (Malaysian)   1. The character of an astrologer. 2. The mask worn by the storyteller in *awang batil* when portraying that character. (Sweeney in Malm/Sweeney STUDIES 54-55)

number   In a variety show or musical, a specific song, dance, comedy routine, etc.

numberer   In 17th C theatres and for some time later, an employee who counted the number of spectators to see if they corresponded to the number of tickets distributed. (Hogan LONDON xvi)

number four batten   See: back batten.

number one   The rating in Britain of a sizable city outside London, such as Manchester, Birmingham, Edinburgh, etc., and also important London suburbs, such as Golder's Green or Streatham. (Granville DICTIONARY)

number one act, number one spot   The first act on a vaudeville bill.

number one batten, No. 1 batten, #1 batten   In Britain, the first borderlight or the first pipe batten upstage of the proscenium. Battens are numbered from downstage to upstage. Hence, number two batten, number three batten, etc. and number one border, number two border, etc.

number one boom, No. 1 boom, #1 boom   A boom in the farthest down-stage position in the wings. See also: boomerang.

number one border, No. 1 border, #1 border   See: number one batten.

number one comic   The leading comedian in a burlesque or vaudeville company. Also called the top banana.

number three   The rating in Britain of rural, industrial, or mining towns. Also known as thirds. (Granville DICTIONARY)

number three act, number three spot   The third act in a vaudeville bill, usually played 'in three' or on an almost full stage. (Carrington THEATRICANA)

number two   The rating in Britain of seaside resorts, cathedral towns, or small industrial cities. Also called seconds. (Granville DICTIONARY)

number two act, number two spot   The second act on a vaudeville bill, usually not an important one. (Wilmeth LANGUAGE)

number two company   A troupe which tours while the original company continues its run. (Bowman/Ball THEATRE)

numérotage (French)   In the argot of the 18th C French stage, the sequential ordering or planning of the scenes in a play, so as to ensure its moving forward to attain its goal. (Legouvé in Matthews PAPERS 258)

nuoc (Vietnamese)   See: *mua roi.*

nure ba (Japanese)   Literally: wet scene. A love scene. The term was first used in prostitute-buying plays (*keiseikai*) of early *kabuki* for the obligatory scene of lovers meeting in the licensed quarter. An example is in Brandon CLASSIC 231-237. See also: *kuzetsu, kudoki.* (Gunji KABUKI 167)

nuregoto (Japanese)   Literally: moist business. A romantic, comic style of playing a love scene. Also called *wagoto* (soft style). (Dunn/Torigoe ANALECTS 97, Hamamura et al KABUKI 76-77)

nursery   A training theatre for young performers in Restoration London: "...a Nursery erects it head, / Where Queens are formed, and future Hero's bred...." (Dryden MACFLECKNOE lines 74-75)

nut   1. Operating expense. A show making a profit is said to be off the nut, or it made the nut, though Berry/Van den Bark define off the nut as breaking even. If money set aside for overhead is drawn upon, the show is operating on the nut. (Bowman/Ball THEATRE, Berrey/Van den Bark SLANG 534). 2. See: nut act.

nut act   A comic vaudeville turn in which the script was less important than the coughs, squeaks, mugging, and spontaneous business of the performers. Hence, nut, nut along. (Gilbert VAUDEVILLE 134)

nut along   To improvise.

nut comic   An eccentric comedian.

nut foundry   A place of entertainment also used to get backers for a show—to provide the 'nut.' (Berrey/Van den Bark SLANG 577)

nut *Hamlet*   A burlesque of *Hamlet*, popular in late 19th C variety halls. (Gilbert VAUDEVILLE 59-60)

nut number   A novelty act.

nuts job   A desirable engagement.

nuvola (Italian)   A scenic cloud used in medieval productions.

nyakot (Indonesian)   A biting movement in Javanese puppet theatre, used mostly by ogre and monkey characters. *Nyakot resah* (repeated biting) is frenzied biting of an enemy by a monkey character. See also: *gila mlajar kawon*. (Long JAVANESE 102, 105)

nyamber (Indonesian)   A flying kick delivered by a character to an opponent's head while soaring through the air. Used regularly by Gathutkaca in Javanese shadow theatre (*wayang kulit*). (Long JAVANESE 63, 93)

nyandra (Indonesian)   A narrative section of a *wayang golek* performance. See also: *murwa*. (Foley "Sundanese" 195)

nyau   A masked African ritual dramatic performance designed to uphold the social and economic customs of its geographical area, which includes eastern Zambia and parts of Malawi and Mozambique. It is performed in song and dance by the Chews people. Masks and costumes used include a giraffe (symbol of grace), an elephant (symbol of dignity and power), etc. Some of these require two or more men to operate—the elephant, four. (Gründ-Khaznader "Ritual" 31, Adedeji glossary)

nyaut (Indonesian)   A striking technique in which a puppet's forearm is released and thrown forward as the character lunges at his opponent. (Long JAVANESE 61)

nyembur (Indonesian)   Spitting poison in an opponent's eyes. In Javanese shadow theatre (*wayang kulit*), used primarily by the character Antareja. (Long JAVANESE 65)

nyepeng (Indonesian)   Literally: to grasp or hold. In a Javanese shadow theatre (*wayang kulit*) battle, *nyepeng jaya* is to grasp an opponent by the chest, *nyepeng sirah* is to grasp an opponent's head, and *nyepeng tangan* is to hold or grasp an opponent by the hand. (Long JAVANESE 58-59)

nyikep (Indonesian)   A bear-hug. A fighting technique in Javanese shadow theatre (*wayang kulit*). (Long JAVANESE 58–59)

nyinden (Indonesian)   See: *sinden*.

nyledet (Indonesian)   Expressive movements of the eyes and eyebrows in Balinese dance and dance-drama. (Soedarsono DANCES 141)

nyobo (Japanese)   Literally: wife. 1. The role of a long-suffering wife in a *kabuki* domestic play (*sewamono*). An example is Osan in *The Love Suicides at*

Amijima in Keene CHIKAMATSU 387-425. 2. An actor who plays this role. (Gunji KABUKI 185)

nyotai (Japanese)   See: *santai*.

nyuduk (Indonesian)   In Javanese shadow theatre, stabbing an opponent with a dagger (*keris*). (Long JAVANESE 63-64)

O

(the) oak   1. The stage. 2. The stage floor—though stage floors are not normally made of a hard wood.

Oakley   See: Annie Oakley.

Oakley holder   The holder of a pass to a theatre. A free ticket was called, among other things, an Annie Oakley or Oakley. (Berrey/Van den Bark SLANG 574)

oakum   Minstrel jokes from the past. Also called gravy. (Wilmeth LANGUAGE)

oan (Vietnamese)   In *hat boi* and *cai luong*, a type of song written in lines of seven syllables. (Addiss "Theater" 141)

obangjin (Korean)   See: *p'ungmul*.

obbo   A 7th C cap worn by married women. (Walkup DRESSING 74)

Oberbühne (German)   1. The *chorpodium* (Greek) or stage for the chorus in an ancient Greek theatre. 2. A gallery in an Elizabethan theatre. 3. The upper floor of a double elevator stage. 4. The flies—the area above the stage in a proscenium theatre.

Oberlicht (German)   Literally: overlight, skylight. A simple borderlight or pipe batten. The plural adds *-e*. (Fuchs LIGHTING 209, 210; Rae/Southern INTERNATIONAL 20; Unruh THEATERTECHNIK 123)

obeshimi (Japanese)   A fierce *no* mask with a large compressed mouth, worn by a goblin (*tengu*). See also: *kobeshimi*.

obeya (Japanese)   Literally: large room. A communal dressing room used by low ranking actors, especially in *kabuki*. (Gunji KABUKI 52)

Obie   Annual awards to off-Broadway performers, playwrights, designers, and productions. The name is an abbreviation of Off-Broadway. (Cameron/Gillespie ENJOYMENT)

objective   1. In the Stanislavsky system, a character's goal within a motivational unit. (Cameron/Hoffman GUIDE) 2. See: objective lens.

objective lens   1. A transparent material such as glass which causes light rays to converge, especially so as to form a sharp image. 2. In a lens system, the lens (or lens combination) nearest the image, which serves to focus the projection slide sharply. Also called objective. (Bellman SCENE, Bentham ART, Lounsbury THEATRE 82, Wehlburg GLOSSARY) 3. Sometimes, in an effects projector, any and all lenses between slide and screen. (Bowman/Ball THEATRE)

obligatory scene   A scene the audience has come to expect and which a good playwright will include in his play. The scene in *Oedipus the King* between Oedipus and the herdsman is an example. Also called a plot scene or *scène à faire* (French), the latter much used in English.

oblique   1. Any piece of scenery set at an angle to the center line of the stage. 2. A type of mechanical drawing similar to isometric projection but with one face at right angles to the observer's sight line. See also: cabinet drawing. (Parker/Smith DESIGN 126–127)

oblique scene   In 18th C theatres, a scenic unit, usually a wing, standing at an angle instead of parallel to the curtain line. (Visser in Hume LONDON 75)

obraz (Russian)   The image of the character an actor creates. (Houghton MOSCOW 128)

obstacle   In playwriting, anything which prevents a character from achieving a goal. Obstacles create complications and conflict, both essential to many types of drama.

obstructed view   See: blind seat.

ochomono (Japanese)   See: *odaimono*.

OD   Outside diameter. The term is used of pipes to which stage lighting instruments are fastened, though ID (inside diameter) is the measurement often used. (Wehlburg GLOSSARY 44)

odaiko (Japanese)   The large barrel drum used in offstage *kabuki* music (*geza*) to create atmospheric effects and to accompany fighting scenes. (Malm MUSIC 223-224)

odaimono (Japanese)   Literally: court play. A *bunraku* or *kabuki* play set in the imperial court in ancient times (through the 12th C). Examples are *The House of Sugawara* in Ernst THREE 53-128 and *Saint Narukami and the God Fudo* in Brandon CLASSIC 99-164. It is one type of history play (*jidaimono*). Also called *ochomono* (dynasty play) and less often *ojidai* (great history). (Brandon CLASSIC 9-10)

odanshichi (Japanese)   Literally: large *danshichi*. The head of a *bunraku* puppet used for warriors who have a violent temper. The eyebrows and mouth are movable and the eyes move from side to side. (Keene BUNRAKU 217, 250)

odd money   In 18th C theatres, money entered in the accounts on benefit nights. It consisted of last-minute income not recorded in the original computation of the house charges. (Hogan LONDON xvi)

oddolaga (Kannada)   Literally: a royal court. In *yaksagana*, a ceremonial presentation in dance of the main characters at the beginning of a performance (Karanth YAKSAGANA 31-34)

ode   See: *stasimon.*

odeion (Greek), *odeum* (Latin), **odeum**   In ancient Greece and Rome, a music theatre, sometimes small and roofed. At the City Dionysia, the *odeion* of Pericles was used for the procession of play personnel which directly preceded the plays. (Bieber HISTORY 220-222, figs. 745–751) Now, when spelled odeum, a theatre or concert hall. (Bowman/Ball THEATRE)

odeum (Latin), **odeum**   See: *odeion.*

odogu (Japanese)   Literally: large articles. Stage scenery in *kabuki, bunraku,* modern theatre (and in films and television). See also: *tsukurimono.* (Scott KABUKI 152-156, Leiter ENCYCLOPEDIA 334-341) *Odogu kata* (scenery person) is a stage hand.

odori (Japanese)   Since the 17th C, folk and *kabuki* dance. From the verb *odoru,* to leap. The liveliness of *odori* is in marked contrast to *mai,* the floor-bound, older dance style of *no.* In *kyogen* performance, *odori* and *mai* are mixed. See also: *furi.* (Gunji BUYO 74-75, Brandon in Brandon/Malm/Shively STUDIES 77-78, Berberich "Rapture" 47)

odoriko (Japanese)   Literally: dance child. A female dancer, especially of *nihon buyo* and folk dance today, including professional dancers such as *geisha.*

oemboel-oemboel (Indonesian)   See: *umbul-umbul.*

off   1. Offstage. 2. Away from the center of the stage, as in: move off. 3. Not right, as when a performer fumbles lines or a performance does not run smoothly. 4. In acting, performers responding and playing 'off' one another rather than just with one another. 5. In vaudeville, not working (as opposed to 'on'—employed). See also: carry-off, go off, lock off, make off, open off, tie off. (Bowman/Ball THEATRE, Berrey/Van den Bark SLANG 587)

off Broadway   New York theatres located away from the Times Square/ Broadway area of the city. The off Broadway houses must seat fewer than 300 people and, as a consequence, are not bound by Actors' Equity minimum wage scales. (Cameron/Gillespie ENJOYMENT) Especially as an adjective, hyphenated. See also: off-off Broadway.

off-cast   To act a part, taking liberties with the script.

offer   1. To present a stage production. Hence, an offering. 2. In stage carpentry, the testing of a door or window and their frames to see if they fit: to offer a door to its frame. (Bowman/Ball THEATRE, Fay GLOSSARY)

offer up   In Britain, to show for approval before making final, e.g., a picture, a door shutter, a lighting set-up. "To offer up the blues" is to show the blue circuit as it will appear in production. The phrase is said to have begun as a carpenter's term. (Granville DICTIONARY, Baker THEATRECRAFT)

office act   An act owned by the circuit producing it. (Berrey/Van den Bark SLANG 582)

office actor   A performer who tries to get a part by behaving loftily while being interviewed by a producer. (Bowman/Ball THEATRE)

office keeper   In an 18th C theatre, an employee who sold tickets at the door, as opposed to the box bookkeeper, who took orders for places in the boxes. (Hogan LONDON xvi)

officium (Latin)   See: liturgical drama.

"Off, off!"   A traditional 18th C audience shout at a poor performer. (Hogan LONDON cxcviii)

off-off Broadway   New York theatres located away from the Times Square/ Broadway area that are generally non-traditional in their theatrical offerings, staging, and architectural space (some operate in coffee houses or churches, for example). Strictly limited in seating capacity, off-off Broadway theatres are exempt from many union regulations. (Cameron/Gillespie ENJOYMENT) See also: off Broadway.

off season   Summer in London and New York, when attendance is likely to be down. In Britain, also called the dead season.

offset   Said of scenery set at an angle to the center line of the stage or at an angle to another piece of scenery.

offstage   1. Not on stage in view of the audience. Short form: off. Hence, offstage action, offstage lines, offstage space, offstage speech. 2. Away from the center of the stage, as in "move offstage a bit."

offstage character   A character mentioned in the dialogue who never appears on stage.

offstage cue   A cue given by or for someone offstage. (Bowman/Ball THEATRE)

offstage effect   An effect such as the sound of battle or footsteps, made offstage.

offstage focus   In readers theatre, a technique of looking toward the audience and thus placing the action in the auditorium environment. See also: acoustic space.

off the nut   See: nut.

off to Buffalo   In vaudeville, a travelling step in dancing, used to make an exit. (Wilmeth LANGUAGE)

ofuku (Japanese)   The head of a *bunraku* puppet used for female clowns. (Keene BUNRAKU 59, 234)

ogi (Japanese)   A large folding fan used by a dancer in *bugaku, gigaku*, and *no*. See also: *sensu*.

ogiri (Japanese)   See: *kiri kyogen*.

oguchi (Japanese)   See: *okuchi*.

ogwangdae, o-gwande, okwangdae (Korean)   Literally: five performers. The generic term for humorous masked dance-dramas performed by folk troupes in the southwestern region of South Kyongsang Province, mainly the T'ongyong, Kosong, and Kasan areas. In five or six acts, it satirizes noblemen (*yangban*) and monks. The term is probably derived from the ritual of performing in 'five directions' to five deities. Also called *yaryu, yayu, tulnorum*, all meaning 'field play,' in the southeastern region of South Kyongsang. See also: *sandaeguk*. (Cho "Ogwangdae" 26, Cho "Suyong" 38, Korean MASKS 25-31)

oh-God-the-pain-of-it-school   Performers of serious roles. (Berrey/Van den Bark SLANG 572)

oiemono (Japanese)   Literally: clan play. A play in *kabuki* or *bunraku* that dramatizes a dispute, often over succession, within a samurai clan. Such a play includes both *jidai* and *sewa* scenes. Extremely popular in *kabuki* c. 1690-1750, *oiemono* is one type of history play (*jidaimono*). Also called *oiesodo* (family quarrel). (Gunji KABUKI 22, Leiter ENCYCLOPEDIA 285-286, Dunn EARLY 82-84)

oikomi (Japanese)   Literally: chase off. A conventional ending to a *kyogen* play in which an enraged master chases a fleeing servant down the bridgeway (*hashigakari*) and offstage. Illustrated in Keene NO 225.

oilcan   A failure.

oil-gas   A gas distilled from oil by a process perfected in the first quarter of the 19th C. Oil-gas was used in theatres alongside other illuminants through most of the century. (Rees GAS 17-19)

oiri (Japanese)   Literally: great entering. A full house. Primarily in 18th and 19th C *kabuki*, a sign proclaiming a full house was displayed prominently above the stage.

ojidai (Japanese)   See: *odaimono*.

ojuto (Japanese)   The head of a *bunraku* puppet used for characters of bad old men. (Keene BUNRAKU 59, 222)

okagura (Japanese)   See: *kagura*.

okawa (Japanese)   See: *otsuzumi*.

oki dogu (Japanese)   A 'placed property'; a small set prop in *no*, such as a spinning wheel, a bucket, a package, etc. that is placed on the bare stage. (Komparu NOH 255) *okina, Okina* (Japanese)   The smiling mask worn by the Old Man in the *no* play *Okina*, symbolizing longevity and prosperity. Among its unique features are its movable jaw (*kiri ago*) and ornamental eyebrows of white cotton. (Shimazaki NOH 63)

ok khaek (Thai)   The introductory song and dance that begins a *likay* performance; derived from Muslim prayer songs (*dikay*). (Virulrak "Likay" 222)

okribas (Greek)   1. About the beginning of the 5th C BC, perhaps a temporary platform on or near the stage; or possibly a synonym for *skene* (scene building), when the *skene* was wooden or temporary. By about the end of the century, an *okribas* was a temporary platform. 2. Some four centuries later, a synonym for *kothornos*. Compare Liddell/Scott LEXICON. (Haigh ATTIC 118; Arnott SCENIC 8; Pickard-Cambridge FESTIVALS 68, 205)

okubyo guchi (Japanese)   Literally: coward's door. 1. In the *kabuki* version of a *no* stage, the small sliding door upstage left. (Leiter ENCYCLOPEDIA 287) 2. Also in *kabuki*, a black-curtained door, one on each side of the inner proscenium, used primarily by acting assistants (*koken*) and stagehands (*kyogen kata*). 3. In *no*, see: *kirido guchi*.

okuchi, oguchi (Japanese)   Wide, stiff trousers worn in *no* and *kabuki*. (Togi GAGAKU 117, Nippon Gakujutsu JAPANESE xii-xiii)

okumkpa play (Ibo-English)   In Nigeria, songs, dances, and dramatic sketches presented annually by the local secret society. (Ottenberg in Fraser/Cole AFRICAN 101-116)

Okuni *kabuki* (Japanese)   1. The original style of *kabuki* performance, incorporating *no* musical instruments, popular dances (various types of *odori*), and sketches about urban life. Begun by the actress-dancer Okuni, hence the name. (Kincaid KABUKI 49-57) 2. The historical period of *kabuki* during which Okuni flourished. Scanty records suggest it began in 1586 (Bowers JAPANESE 39, Halford/Halford HANDBOOK 453), or 1596 (Ernst KABUKI 30, Scott KABUKI 35, Kincaid KABUKI 49), or 1603 (Toita KABUKI 11, Kawatake HISTORY 88, Gunji BUYO 115). The period ended 1610-1615 when Okuni disappeared, mysteriously, from the scene.

Okura *ryu* (Japanese)   Literally: Okura school. The oldest school of *kyogen* actors. The name Okura was taken from the name of a branch of the Komparu *no* house, to which the *kyogen* school was once attached. (Inoura HISTORY 92, 106)

okwangdai (Korean)   See: *ogwangdae*.

Old Comedy 1. The comedy of Aristophanes and his contemporaries in the 5th-4th C BC in Greece. 2. See: comedy of manners.

old makeup   Formerly, age makeup, character-creating makeup. (Bricker TODAY 355)

old man   1. An actor who specializes in elderly characters. 2. The elderly role itself.

old pro   1. A professional of long experience, often elderly. 2. Any veteran performer. Also called an old stager, stager, or old trouper.

old stager   See: old pro.

old trouper   See: old pro.

old woman   1. An actress who specializes in elderly characters. 2. The elderly role itself.

olio, oleo   1. A painted drop, often a roller drop, hanging just upstage of the first plane of the stage and serving as a backing for a scene played 'in one.' Hence, olio drop, olio curtain. Sometimes painted with advertisements; hence, ad curtain, ad drop, advertisement curtain (or drop). Also called a drop curtain or a roll curtain. The word may derive from the Latin *oleum*, oil, or *aulaeum*, curtain. 2. Especially in vaudeville, a specialty act performed in front of such a drop while a new scene is being set up backstage. Hence, an olio act, olio scene. 3. A medley of songs, sketches, dances, etc., especially in vaudeville, burlesque, revues, and minstrel shows. Thus olio in this meaning may derive from the Spanish *olla podrida*, miscellany or hodgepodge. (Bowman/Ball THEATRE, Stern MANAGEMENT, Wilmeth LANGUAGE)

olivette   Especially in the earlier decades of the 20th C, a simple floodlight. The typical olivette was box-like, with an open front and slanted sides. The usually white inside surfaces reflected the light of a large pear-shaped lamp; early in the century an arc light was sometimes used. The name may have come from the oval shape of the lamp bulb, or perhaps from the musical *Olivette*, said to mark the first use of the instrument. The spelling olivet is seen occasionally. Other designations: box light, open box, open box olivette, open-box light, and similar combinations. (Bellman LIGHTING 52, Wehlburg GLOSSARY, Bowman MODERN)

omang (Indonesian)   See: *jauk*.

ombres blanches (French)   See: white shadows.

ombres chinoises (French)   Literally: Chinese shadows. Asian shadow plays seen as early as Jacobean times in England. They enjoyed a vogue in London in the 1770s. (Speaight PUPPET 142) See also: *piyingxi*.

omies   British argot for incompetent actors. (Marsh VINTAGE 90)

omilia (Greek)   Literally: speech. Greek popular vernacular theatre of the later 17th C. Performances were given in public squares by actors and singers who improvised upon existing lyrics. They specialized in political satire. (Gassner/Quinn ENCYCLOPEDIA 393)

omi onna (Japanese)   Literally: woman of Omi Province. A mask worn by an evil spirit who is disguised as a charming young woman in the first part of a demon *no* play. (Shimazaki NOH 60-61)

Omi *sarugaku* (Japanese)   A family and a style of *sarugaku no* acting in the 14th C that emphasized elegant beauty of expression (*yugen*). The *no* of Kannami was greatly influenced by this style of *sarugaku*. (Inoura HISTORY 87)

omnes (Latin)   All, everyone—as in a group departure from the stage or a collective groan. See also: *exeunt omnes*. (Granville DICTIONARY)

omnibus box   In 19th C British theatres, a box seating a large number of people.

omo (Japanese)   See: *shite*.

omoiire, omoire (Japanese)   A silent moment in which a *kabuki* actor expresses an emotional reaction through physical action. Brandon, incorrectly, says a "thoughtful pose." (Brandon CHUSHINGURA 130)

omote (Japanese)   The standard term for mask in *no* and *kyogen*. Major *no* masks are described in Shimazaki NOH 57-65; they are illustrated in Nippon Gakujutsu JAPANESE xv-xxv and Keene NO 162-199. *Kyogen* masks are illustrated in Keene NO 200-205. See also: *men*.

omote kata (Japanese)   Literally: front person. Front-of-the-house or management staff of a theatre, in Japan responsible for tickets, publicity, ushering, finances, and other management functions. See also: *maku uchi, ura kata*. (Leiter ENCYCLOPEDIA 291)

omo zukai (Japanese)   Literally: chief manipulator. The head puppeteer of a three-man team. He moves the head and right arm of a *bunraku* puppet. (Adachi BUNRAKU 29-33)

on   1. On stage. 2. Toward the center of the stage, as in: move on. 3. Said of someone who is performing particularly well, as in: he is on. 4. Said of a performer who carries theatrical behavior into personal life. 5. In vaudeville, working (as opposed to off—not working). See also: open on, walk on. (Bowman/Ball THEATRE, Berrey/Van den Bark SLANG 587)

onadai (Japanese)   See: *nadai*.

onagori kyogen (Japanese)   Literally: farewell play. A *kabuki* play dedicated to a star actor who was not going to be with the troupe in the following season. It was staged on the autumn bill (*aki kyogen*) as the last play of the theatrical season. (Leiter ENCYCLOPEDIA 20)

on and off   Said of scenery set parallel to the curtain line, as in wing-and-shutter settings. (Parker/Smith DESIGN)

on-and-offer   A performer who appears intermittently. (Berrey/Van den Bark SLANG 572)

once-around   An act's first tour of a circuit. (Berrey/Van den Bark SLANG 590)

one   See: in one.

one acter   A one-act play.

one-act play   A dramatic work in one act. The term is applied loosely to short plays generally (playing time being from about 20 to 45 minutes). Also called a one acter.

one consecutive nighter   A show with a brief run.

one-eyed Connolly   A gate crasher, one who enters a theatre without a ticket. (Berrey/Van den Bark SLANG 574)

one-half peak angle   See: peak angle.

one-liner   A quick, short joke.

one-lunger   A one-set show.

one-night booker   A second-rate agent who gets his clients jobs for one night. (Berrey/Van den Bark SLANG 575)

one nighter   See: one-night stand.

one-night stand   1. A visit by a touring company that lasts only one night. Also called a night stand, one nighter, stand. 2. The town, or sometimes theatre, where such a performance is given. 3. In Britain, a portable theatre, set up for such a stand. (Granville DICTIONARY)

one-quarter position   A performer's position on stage one-quarter from a full front position. (Dean/Carra FUNDAMENTALS 35, McGaw ACTING 197)

one-scene show, one-set show   A production with a single stage setting.

one-sheet   1. The smallest theatrical poster, about 28'' x 42''. 2. Hence, especially in vaudeville and burlesque, to give an act minor billing, to one-sheet it. (Wilmeth LANGUAGE)

one spot   The first act on a bill.

one-step   A stair unit with one riser and one tread.

one-tenth peak angle   See: peak angle.

one to two bits   In the early 20th C U.S., a popular-price stock company, named for its ticket prices. (Krows AMERICA 241)

one-week house   A theatre booked for one week by a touring company. Also called a week-stand house.

one-week stand   A theatrical engagement lasting a week.

onfirer (Yiddish)   The director of a Polish Purim play. (Kirshenblatt-Gimblett ''Contraband'' 10)

ong dich (Vietnamese)   See: *sao*.

ongdongi ch'um (Korean)   See: *kungdungi ch'um*.

onintei (Japanese)   A *bugaku* mask with a white face, mustache, and goatee, perhaps representing a foreign ambassador. (Wolz BUGAKU 43)

onion at the end   Especially in Britain, a music hall expression for a theatrical gimmick which causes the audience to cry at the end of a performance.

onion ballad   A tearjerker. (Wilmeth LANGUAGE)

onion play   In Yiddish theatre, a melodrama which drew tears from overly-empathic audiences. (Sandrow VAGABOND 116)

on its dead   In Britain, a drop or piece of scenery which is in its exact position, that is, dead on. See also: dead.

oniwaka (Japanese)   The head of a *bunraku* puppet used for characters of good young men. (Keene BUNRAKU 59, 221)

onkos (Greek), **onkos**   Literally: bulk, mass. The high top of a mask. Characteristic of tragedy in both Greece and Rome, the *onkos* was used by the last third of the 4th C BC; there is no convincing evidence for its 5th C BC use. Some speak of the *onkos* as a high forehead, others as a high headdress. The size of the *onkos* varied with the character, and the type of character. The high-topped mask of men tended to be larger than that of women, that of a tyrant, largest of all. (Pickard-Cambridge FESTIVALS 189-190, 193-196; Webster PRODUCTION 43; Haigh ATTIC 244-245)

on lights   Especially in the non-professional theatre, working the stage lighting (as in "He's on lights.").

onnagata (Japanese)   Literally: woman-person. 1. The general term for female roles in *kabuki*. In the late 17th C there were two major divisions: young women (*waka onnagata*) and middle-aged and old women (*kashagata*) (Dunn/Torigoe ANALECTS 168). Numerous sub-types developed through the 19th C, see: *akuba, hime, katahazushi, musume, nyobo, tayu* (Gunji KABUKI 31-32). 2. A male actor, especially in *kabuki* but also in *shinpa*, who plays female roles. Female impersonation assumed artistic importance when the government banned actresses from public stages in 1629. (Hamamura et al KABUKI 101) Also called *oyama*. See also: *tate onnagata*. (Scott KABUKI 167-169, Kincaid KABUKI 132-134)

onna kabuki (Japanese)   See: *yujo kabuki*.

onna sarugaku (Japanese)   Literally: women's *sarugaku*. *Sarugaku* performed by professional women dancers, especially in the 16th and early 17th C. (Tsubaki "Performing" 306)

onoemon (Japanese)   The head of a *bunraku* puppet that is used for villainous clown characters. (Keene BUNRAKU 59, 246)

on one's card   In Britain, free admission to a theatre, primarily for members of the theatrical profession.

o nori (Japanese)   Literally: large rhythm. A *no* rhythmic pattern in which a syllable is sung on each beat of the eight-beat measure. One type of congruent (*hyoshi au*) rhythm. (Hoff/Flindt "Structure" 237)

on point   See: *sur les pointes.*

on spike   Said of furniture, properties, or scenery that is standing in its proper position on stage—on the 'spike' marks on the stage floor.

on stage, onstage   1. In the acting area; in that part of the stage visible to the audience. 2. Toward the center of the stage, as in "move onstage a bit." 3. A call to summon performers to the stage. See also: on. (Bowman/Ball THEATRE, McGaw ACTING)

onstage focus   In readers theatre, a technique of keeping focus onstage by having the readers establish eye contact with one another.

on the beach   Unemployed.

on the boards   On the stage.

on the book   Serving as prompter. See also: hold (the) book.

on the dead   See: dead.

on the dog   See: try it on the dog.

on the green   Especially in vaudeville, on the stage. A performer is said to be 'on the green' when performing, and the stage floor visible to the audience is 'the green.'

on the halls   In Britain, performing as a variety or vaudeville artist.

on the nut   See: nut.

on the plate   Formerly, on the electrical switchboard, that is, on duty there. See also: gas plate. (Granville DICTIONARY)

on the road   On tour.

on the sheet   See: sheet.

on the stage   1. In the theatrical profession. 2. Performing. (Granville DICTIONARY)

on the walk   Said of 'walk men' who sell tickets to a show on the sidewalk near the theatre. (Wilmeth LANGUAGE)

on tick   Upon tick—on credit.

on top of 'em   Said of a theatre with very little space between the first row of seats and the stage. (Granville DICTIONARY)

on tour   Said of a performer or company giving a series of performances in different towns.

on trim   See: trim.

on with others   Said of a performer with no lines. (Wilmeth LANGUAGE)

(the) o-o   The once-over, as when a stage manager checks the stage setting before curtain. (Granville DICTIONARY)

o otoshi (Japanese)   Literally: great conclusion. The emotional climax of a *bunraku* play. A major character, overwhelmed by grief, expresses his or her emotion in a torrential outpouring of tears. The scene is developed through music and chanting, as well as by actions of the puppets. (Brandon CLASSIC 17, Leiter ENCYCLOPEDIA 297)

OP   Opposite prompt—the side of the stage across from the prompter's position.

OPD   Opposite prompt door—a proscenium door opposite prompt side.

open   1. To begin the run of a show. Hence, opening night. 2. In acting, to open up—to turn the body toward the audience. 3. In theatres of the past with wing-and-shutter scenery, said of a pair of shutters that open (slide apart) to reveal another setting. 4. In playwriting, the beginning of a scene, as in "The first act opens in Rome." This use derives from meaning 3. (Bowman/Ball THEATRE)

open-air theatre   An unroofed theatre, such as a classic Greek theatre. Hence, open-air production, open-air stage. The term is often used interchangeably with outdoor theatre. See also: garden theatre.

open a show cold   See: open cold.

open box   1. A box for spectators that does not have enclosing curtains, partitions, or lattices. (Bowman/Ball THEATRE) 2. Said of a lighting instrument that has no lens. Also called open face.

open-box light   A simple floodlight. See also: olivette. (Fuchs LIGHTING 190)

open call   A professional audition open to performers without union cards.

open circuit   An electrical circuit in which current is not flowing, as when a switch is open. (Wehlburg GLOSSARY)

open cold   1. To open a Broadway show without an out-of-town tryout or invitational previews. Also called to bust cold, to crash cold, to open a show cold. 2. Especially in vaudeville, to be the first act, particularly at the first performance. (Berrey/Van den Bark SLANG 583)

open door   A term used by Lee, Sam, and Jack Shubert in opposing the Theatrical Syndicate in the early 20th C. The Shuberts wanted actors, producers, and managers to be able to put on presentations with no interference by the Syndicate. (Lippman "Monopoly" 68ff)

opened   Of a fuse, blown.

opener   The first act on a bill.

open face   See: open box.

open-faced, openfaced   See: open front.

open-flame oil lamp   An early form of oil lamp, often consisting of a wick floating in a saucer-like container of oil. Also called an open-wick oil lamp. Fuchs has illustrations. (Fuchs LIGHTING 35)

open front   In lighting, said of a unit such as a floodlight or striplight without a covering. Open-faced and openfaced also occur. (Bowman/Ball THEATRE 240)

open-front board   See: live-front board.

open full   To begin with all of the cast on stage.

opening   1. In the U.S., opening night, first performance. In Britain and the U.S., first night. 2. In Britain, an entertainment preceding the harlequinade in a pantomime performance. The opening in the 18th C was in dumbshow, but by 1814 dialogue was added (hence, the 'speaking opening'). Christmas pantomimes today consist chiefly of what was once just the opening. (Bowman/Ball THEATRE) 3. The proscenium opening.

opening chorus   The first chorus number in a musical.

opening glee   In Nigeria in Yoruba opera, the entrance song or curtain raiser in an operatic show, accompanied by music and dance. A closing glee ends the show. (Adedeji glossary)

opening light   Especially in Britain, the lighting on which the curtain rises. (Goffin LIGHTING 72)

opening night   The first performance of a production.

opening situation   The status quo at the beginning of a play.

opening spot, opening stanza   The first act on a bill.

open lights   See: open-trough striplight.

open lime   A limelight used as a floodlight. (Rees GAS 63, 202)

openly   In public. An Elizabethan term used of public performances of plays or interludes. (Wickham EARLY II, pt. 1, 194)

open off   See: open on.

open on, open off   Used to describe the swing of a door or hinged window: it opens toward the acting area (on) or away (off).

open on a blackout   To begin a scene with a darkened stage.

open out a speech   In acting, to vary tempo, rhythm, and the placement and length of pauses, and in other ways to enrich the meaning of a speech by taking the time necessary to focus on and convey its subtleties.

open rehearsal   A rehearsal to which visitors are admitted.

open scene   Formerly, a freestanding scenic unit, separate from the wings, borders, and backscene, with openings through which objects can be seen. Also called a pierced or cut scene.

open set   In vaudeville, a wing and drop setting, as opposed to a box set.

open stage   1. A thrust stage, open to the audience on three sides, having a permanent background and no proscenium or front curtain. Old and new examples are the Globe Theatre of Shakespeare's day and the Guthrie Theatre in Minneapolis, Minnesota. Hence, open staging. 2. A stage setting free from obstructions in the performing area, used for dance and some opera productions using large choruses. 3. Sometimes, experimental productions freed from the confinement of a script. (Baker THEATRECRAFT, Crampton HANDBOOK, Hatlen ORIENTATION)

open the show   1. To be the first act on a variety bill. 2. To be involved in the beginning of a show.

open time   Dates when a performer or a company is available for an engagement.

open-trough striplight   A row of lights in a trough-like metal container; a striplight without compartments. The other usual terms are open-trough border-light(s) and open-trough footlight(s). The phrase open lights is sometimes used for any of these.

open turn   A turn toward the audience by a performer. Also called a stage turn. The opposite of a closed turn.

open up   1. In acting, to turn the body toward the audience. 2. To give better visibility or emphasis to a property or scenic unit, sometimes by altering a performer's position, sometimes by rearranging furniture or scenery.

open white   Of a lighting instrument: without a color filter. Abbreviated O.W. (Bowman/Ball THEATRE)

open-wick oil lamp   See: open-flame oil lamp.

opera   1. Drama set to music, with most or all of the lines sung. Italian in origin, the earliest terms for opera were *favola tragedia* or *dramma*, often with a qualifying word: *favola in musica, favola pastorale, dramma per musica*, etc. *Melodramma* came to be much used, but the word *opera* was applied at least as early as the mid-17th C. 2. See: *xiqu*.

opera ballet   Originally, a dramatic form whose reason for being was the ballet which occurred in the opera, without the dance being in any way integrated into the opera. By the end of the 19th C, the ballet was of a piece with the opera plot, but it could also be eliminated without aesthetic damage to the opera's continuity. (Kersley/Sinclair BALLET)

opéra bouffe (French)   Comic opera.

opera buffa (Italian)   Comic opera.

opera chair   A fully upholstered theatre seat with its own arms, deep enough to accommodate a lady's bustle in the days when they were fashionable.

opéra comique (French)   Comic opera.

opera drape   See: tableau curtain.

opera eroica (Italian)   Literally: heroic work. A *commedia dell'arte* scenario or opera libretto using a mythological or tragic theme with a happy ending

opera glasses   Small binoculars used in large theatres.

opera hat   A man's formal top hat with an internal mechanism to make it collapsible. Also called a gibus. (Boucher FASHION)

opera house   1. A theatre especially designed for opera or other large-scale musical or dance productions requiring a full orchestra, chorus rooms, etc. Often built with the traditional horseshoe-shaped box and gallery seating. 2. In the 19th and early 20th C, a euphemism for theatre, implying high class entertainment.

opera mista (Italian)   See: *regiacomica.*

opera regia (Italian)   Literally: royal work. A type of elaborate and fantastic play involving kings and nobility, performed by *commedia dell' arte* troupes in the Renaissance. (Duchartre ITALIAN 51)

opera regiacomica (Italian)   See: *regiacomica.*

opera seria (Italian)   Serious opera.

operating crew   The stage crew running a performance.

operating gallery   See: fly gallery.

operating light   Usually, a carefully-shaded light which illuminates a control board. (Bellman SCENE, McCandless ''Glossary'' 637)

operating line   1. In a counterweight system, a rope line used to raise and lower a counterweight. 2. A rope line used to manage an act curtain or other curtain. Also called an endless, handling, hauling, overhaul, purchase, or working line.

operating on the nut   See: nut.

operating script   The stage manager's marked copy of a play.

operator   One who runs something during a performance, such as the curtain, lighting, or sound effects. Hence, floor operator (a crewman who works at floor level), bridge operator, control board operator, curtain operator, etc.

opera traps   Hand-operated elevators and trap doors. (Gassner/Barber PRODUCING 809)

operetta   A light musical drama with much song and dance.

op nut   Operating expenses.

opposite   See: play opposite.

opposite prompt   The side of the stage across from the prompter's position. Abbreviation: OP.

opposition   In dance, a position in which the entire arm is opposed to the active leg. (Grant TECHNICAL)

OP riots   Audience protests at Covent Garden Theatre, London, in 1809 against the raising of ticket prices in the new and larger theatre. The rioting went on for 67 nights, and the management finally restored the OP's (old prices).

opry house   1. A derogatory term for a run-down theatre used by touring companies. 2. A theatre specializing in country and western musical entertainments, such as the Grand Old Opry House in Nashville, Tennessee.

optical effect   1. In the U.S., a visual effect. (Bowman/Ball THEATRE) 2. See: optical effects machine.

optical effects machine   In Britain, a disc-shaped housing with an objective lens and a clockwork mechanism. The disc is designed to contain a circular glass slide and be mounted at the front of a projector; it permits moving visual effects such as snow, rain, clouds, flames, etc. Sometimes called an optical effect. (Bentham ART; Bax MANAGEMENT 187-188, fig. 53)

optical system   In stage lighting fixtures such as spotlights: the light source, the reflector, and the lens or lens system. (Bowman MODERN)

optique de théâtre (French)   Literally: theatre perspective. The proper attitude of a theatregoer, who is willing to accept such conventions as, for example, Hamlet speaking English verse rather than Danish prose.

oracle worker   In 19th C Britain, a press agent. (Wilmeth LANGUAGE 190)

orang darat (Malaysian)   Literally: up-country person, bumpkin. A puppet figure of a gardener, farmer, fisherman, or other unsophisticated character. (Sweeney RAMAYANA 291)

orange girl   See: orange wench.

orange wench, orange woman, orange girl   A seller of fruit in Restoration theatres and later. (Shadwell in Nagler SOURCES 212, Hogan LONDON xli)

orangewood stick   A slender wooden dowel formerly used by performers to line eyes and brows and to create wrinkles.

orang muda (Malaysian)   Literally: young person. The male lead, a prince, in *bangsawan*. (Yassin in Osman TRADITIONAL 149)

orateur (French)   In 17th C theatres, the person who announced the next day's bill at the end of a play and prepared the playbill or poster. (Chappuzeau in Nagler SOURCES 183)

orator   The manager (usually) of a 17th C French acting company, who at the end of a performance announced the next day's play. (Roberts STAGE)

oratorio   A sacred drama set to music and presented without action, scenery, or costumes. A typical oratorio, Handel's *Messiah* being an example, calls for solo voices, a chorus, and orchestra. (O'Hara/Bro INVITATION)

orchestes (Greek)   By the early 5th C BC, a dancer; in the 4th C BC, a pantomimic dancer. This came to be the word the Greeks used for the chief performer in a pantomime. The Romans used *pantomimus*.

orchestikoi (Greek)   In early mimes, dancers. (Nicoll MASKS 33)

orchestra   1. See: *orchestra* (Greek). 2. In Sebastiano Serlio's 1545 theatre, a semi-circular area in front of the stage, around which were rows of seats for spectators. 3. A seating area for the nobility, near the stage, in an Elizabethan theatre, according to the contemporary drawing of the Swan theatre. 4. In Cotgrave's *Dictionarie* of 1611, the seating space for senators and noblemen, between the stage and "common Seats," but Cotgrave also used the term for the stage itself. 5. The band of instrumentalists employed by the theatre management. ('Orchestra' was used in this sense as early as 1724 in *The Session of Musicians*). 6. The area in front of the stage where instrumentalists play; the orchestra pit. 7. In the U.S., the seating area on the main floor of the auditorium. Hence, orchestra floor, orchestra seat. Called in Britain the stalls. (Serlio in Hewitt RENAISSANCE 27, Bentley JACOBEAN VI 192, Cibber APOLOGY I 321, Avery LONDON cxxxvi, Cotgrave DICTIONARIE, Bowman/Ball THEATRE)

orchestra (Greek)   Literally: dancing-place. 1. In the Greek theatre, the circular area used by the chorus. The shape perhaps came from the circular threshing ground, a ready site for early choral performances. By the 4th C BC and after, a small segment of the circle was sometimes appropriated for the scene building (*skene*). 2. In later Graeco-Roman and Roman times, a similar area usually reduced to a semi-circle, or slightly larger. The Roman *orchestra*, however, was soon used as a seating place for honored spectators, and ultimately—before Christian times—was reserved for senators and members of the equestrian order; the practice is said to have been much resented by ordinary citizens. Surviving remains of Greek theatres including, for example, the theatre of Dionysus in Athens, were 'modernized' under Roman influence, and do not show the classic Greek circle.

Orchestra as dancing-place names the original purpose of the area, choral dancing and singing. *Choros* (chorus) appears to have been an early alternative term, perhaps preceding *orchestra*. In Latin times, *konistra* was used, especially after the *orchestra* had been walled in for gladiatorial and other purposes; *arena* was even more used in this signification. *Sigma* appears to have originated because of the similarity between the Romanized semi-circular *orchestra* and the semi-circular form adopted by the Romans for the Greek letter *sigma*. English orchestra has long been used for *orchestra*, whether Greek or Roman. (Bieber HISTORY 54, 59-64, 66-69, 172-174, figs. 223-230, 240, 254-256, 258-260, 272-274, 607, 641, 645, 650; Pickard-Cambridge DIONYSUS 5-9, 25-26, 146-147, 175, 257-259, 270-271)

orchestra bell   A bell in a theatre's band room, rung to warn musicians to enter the orchestra pit.

orchestra circle   A term, now rare, for parquet circle: that seating area on the main floor of an auditorium which is underneath a balcony. (Bowman/Ball THEATRE)

orchestra divan   A comfortable wide seat with folding arms, sometimes used in the front rows of an orchestra seating area. (Bowman/Ball THEATRE)

orchestra enclosure   See: orchestra shell.

orchestra leader   See: leader.

orchestra pit   The space for theatre musicians just in front of a stage or partly under it. Usually sunk below the auditorium floor level. Occasionally called the orchestra wall in Britain, and the pit in the U.S.

orchestra pit lift   See: forestage elevator.

orchestra rail   A barrier separating an orchestra pit from the audience.

orchestra seats   Seats on the floor of the auditorium. The modern British terms are the stalls (for upholstered seats) or the pit (for benches).

orchestra shell   An acoustical backing set behind an orchestra to reflect the sound into the auditorium. Also called an acoustical shell, concert set, concert shell, orchestra enclosure.

orchestra stalls   1. In Britain, seats in the front rows of the stalls. 2. Occasionally in the U.S., orchestra seats.

orchestra stands   Stands in orchestra pits for holding sheet music.

orchestra well   In Britain, the orchestra pit.

orchestrodidaskalos (Greek)   Literally: dancing master. Especially after the 5th C BC, the dance director of a chorus. See also: *coryphaeus*. (Mantzius HISTORY I 155)

order   In 18th C theatres, one of several forms of free admission. An order was written out on paper (hence, papering the house) and gave free admission to owners of certain renters' shares, to actors, and to other theatre employees for presentation to their friends. An order admitted up to seven people, but only for a given performance. See also: bones. (Hogan LONDON xxxiii)

ordinale (Latin)   In Cornwall, the authoritative text of a medieval play. (Chambers MEDIAEVAL II 143)

ordinary   A medieval prompter. (Carew in Nagler SOURCES 51-52)

ordo (Latin)   Literally: order, arrangement. Applied to liturgical plays sanctioned and adopted into the liturgy. (Tydeman THEATRE)

organic blocking   A system of planning the movement of a play in which the director allows the performers to move at will and then uses their movement as the basis for his or her blocking. (Stern MANAGEMENT)

organic dance   Dance which develops uniquely from a central core or source.

organ loft   A scene dock.

oribatae (Latin Roman)   An occasional term for the acrobatic rope dancers who were one of the types of performers attached to the mime. See also: *funambuli*. (Nicoll MASKS 85)

oriental dancer   U.S. slang for a striptease, belly, or cooch dancer. (Wilmeth LANGUAGE)

original, original book   The authoritative text of a medieval play. To bear the original was to prompt. Other spellings include orraginall, orygynal, rygynall. A French spelling is *origenall*. (Chambers MEDIAEVAL II 143; Frank MEDIEVAL 174)

original cast   A troupe which played in the first run of a show or the first run of a revival, as opposed to a touring company or company made up of new performers. Sometimes called the original company. (Bowman/Ball THEATRE)

original production   The first production of a work, as opposed to a revival of it. (Bowman/Ball THEATRE)

orixás (Portuguese)   A voodoo rite; a frequent element of Black Brazilian dramatic productions. (Fernández "Brazil" 10)

orizzonte (Italian)   Literally: horizon. In 17th C theatres, scenic shutters, closing off the perspective vista. (Troili in Craig MASK XIII 63)

Orlando puppet   A Sicilian marionette who represents a chivalric hero dating from the 16th C and possibly earlier. (Adler "Sicilian" 26)

ornamenta (Latin Roman)   Stage costumes. The word is literally trappings, equipment; hence, often decoration, embellishment. (Saunders COSTUME 17-20)

ornamental prop   A stage property used only for decoration.

orraginall   See: original.

orta oyunu, ortaoyunu (Turkish)   Literally: play in the middle. A *commedia dell'arte*-type drama still performed in the open air in Turkey. (Gassner/Quinn ENCYCLOPEDIA 865, And KARAGÖZ 12-14)

orum (Korean)   Rope walking. One of six acts in *namsadang*. *Orumsani* is the head tight-rope walker. (Kim "Namsadang" 13, Sim/Kim KOREAN 23)

orygynal   See: original.

osatsuma bushi, ozatsuma bushi (Japanese)   A *kabuki* style of *shamisen* music and singing established in the early 18th C by the singer Osatsuma Shusendayu. It is vigorous and lively and is used especially in bravura (*aragoto*) style plays. (Leiter ENCYCLOPEDIA 298-299)

Oscan farce, Oscan play   Terms for the *ludi Osci*, the name often used by the Romans for the Atellan play. See also: *fabula Atellana*. (Beare ROMAN 137-138)

Oscar Hammerstein   See: eleven forty-five.

Oscum ludicrum (Latin Roman)   A farce form which developed in Oscia in southern Italy in pre-Christian times. See also: *fabula Atellana*. (Chambers MEDIAEVAL I 2)

oshimodoshi (Japanese)   Literally: quelling. A *kabuki* scene in a bravura style (*aragoto*) play in which the hero physically quells a demon. (Leiter ENCYCLOPEDIA 299)

ospitii (Italian)   A term used by the Renaissance designer Antonio San Gallo for the facades on each side of a proscenium opening; on top of the *ospitii* he placed revolving *periaktoi* (Greek). (Nicoll DEVELOPMENT 81-82)

Osterspiel (German)   Literally: Easter play. The oldest German religious dramatic form, dating from the 9th C. (Gassner/Quinn ENCYCLOPEDIA 631)

ostium (Latin Roman)   On floor plans suggested by Beare for the staging of certain Roman comedies, a gate from a back street (*angiportum*). Such a gate ordinarily led to or from a garden which would ultimately give access to the back door of an onstage house. None of this but the house front was visible to the audience. (Beare ROMAN 258-260)

ostium horti (Latin Roman)   Garden gate (the literal meaning). See also: *ostium*. (Beare ROMAN 258)

ostium posticum (Latin Roman)   A gate permitting access to the back door of a house whose front is onstage in view of the audience. Compare *angiportum*. (Beare ROMAN 261)

otafuku (Japanese)   A *kyogen* mask or *bunraku* puppet head of a fat, smiling, comic woman. (Keene BUNRAKU 255)

otobide (Japanese)   A *no* mask with a gold face, round gold eyes, and a wide-open mouth. It is worn by powerful deities like the god of thunder and lightning. (Shimazaki NOH 62)

otokodate (Japanese)   1. The role of a dashing, chivalrous commoner in *kabuki*. An example is in Gunji KABUKI 183. It is one type of *tachiyaku* role. 2. An actor who plays this role.

otokokata (Japanese)   An actor in early *kabuki* who played male roles. The term became obsolete in the 18th C, being replaced by *tachiyaku*. (Leiter ENCYCLOPEDIA 389)

otsuzumi (Japanese)   The larger of the two hand-held drums used in *no* and *kabuki*. It is held at waist level and is struck with the fingers. Also called *okawa* (large skin). See also: *hayashi*. (Malm MUSIC 122-124)

ottam thullal (Malayalam)   A popular form of dance-drama in Kerala, south India, in which one performer narrates stories from epic literature. Taking the roles of all characters, he is accompanied by two musicians. Derived in part from *kutiyattam*.

out   In 17th C theatres in Britain: 1. Incorrect in one's lines or business. Bayes instructing an actor: "Pish, there you are out." 2. To set out on the stage, as a piece of furniture: "Two Chairs out." (Buckingham REHEARSAL 25, Belon MOCK 43) 3. A movement away from the center of a stage. 4. To make such a move.

outdoor theatre   An open-air theatre, sometimes partially roofed. See also: garden theatre.

outer stage   The forestage of an Elizabethan theatre. Also called the platform, it was the main acting area.

out front   The auditorium and other audience areas of a theatre. Also called front of house (FOH).

outlet   Any socket or other receptacle, whether in the floor, wall, or control board, which provides current for electrical equipment. (Sellman/Lessley ESSENTIALS, Wehlburg GLOSSARY)

outlet box   See: stage pocket.

outline scenery   Skeletal scenery, such as Jo Mielziner's design for *Death of a Salesman*. Brockett has illustrations. (Brockett HISTORY 651)

out of a shop   Unemployed. A British term for between plays, between engagements, or at leisure. (Marsh DOLPHIN 184)

out of scene   Said of a performer in readers theatre who remains on stage even though not in a scene being played. Being out of scene is indicated by such techniques as lowering the head and freezing, moving to another position, making a half-turn from the audience or a full turn with back to the audience. 'In scene' identifies a reader who is a participant in the scene being played.

out of type   Said of casting a performer in something outside his/her usual line, or of a performer so cast.

out on spec   Being considered for an engagement.

outrigger   A skeletal platform of irregular shape, mounted on casters, with scenery attached to one of its faces. (Gillette/Gillette SCENERY)

outsider theatre   See: theatre of the social outsider.

outstanding audience   A waiting line for tickets.

out with   Said of a British performer who is performing outside London with a touring company. (Granville DICTIONARY)

ouvert (French)   In ballet: 1. Use of open positions of the feet. 2. A position or direction of the body similar to *effacé* (q.v.). (Grant TECHNICAL)

oval beam (Fresnel) spotlight   A Fresnel spotlight with a lens which produces an oval rather than a round beam. Sometimes called simply oval beam. (Bellman LIGHTING 83-84, figs. 4-6a, 4-6b; Lounsbury THEATRE 93, 106)

Ovallaterne (German)   One of the types of lighting units which has been used in Germany to light the cyclorama. The instrument was a borderlight which used lamps which resembled fluorescent tubes in general shape; but their light came from a line-filament rather than a gas. The name *Ovallaterne* is from a semi-elliptical sheet of glass at the front of the fixture. The plural adds *-n*. (Fuchs LIGHTING 211)

overact   1. To overemphasize or exaggerate in acting. Also called overplay, ham, ham it, ham it up, tear a passion to tatters, etc. 2. In acting, to surpass; now obsolete. 3. To act over again; now obsolete. (Bowman/Ball THEATRE)

overcall   An assessment on financial backers of a theatrical production for additional money.

overcurve   In dance, a movement in which a part of the body or the center of weight describes a curve away from gravity.

overhang   See: nose.

overhaul line   1. A rope passing over a pulley and used to raise an object. 2. See: operating line.

overhead lighting   Lighting from above, ordinarily from the pipes above the visible stage. (Bowman/Ball THEATRE)

overlap   In acting, to move or speak before the cue is given. See also: clip a cue.

overload a circuit   To attach a load, such as a spotlight, greater than the rated capacity of any part of the circuit, i.e., greater than it can safely carry. (Lounsbury THEATRE)

overparted   In Britain: 1. Said of a performer not up to the major role he/she is performing. 2. Said of a repertory performer assigned too many leading roles. (Granville DICTIONARY)

overplay   See: overact.

overture   1. Music played before a performance or act begins. 2. A warning to performers that the music is to be played. The warning is sometimes "Overture and beginners!" (Bowman/Ball THEATRE)

ovoid auditorium   See: egg-shaped auditorium.

O.W.   See: open white.

Oxford bags   Early 1920s British trousers with flared bottoms. Also called *bracae* (Latin). (Chalmers CLOTHES 16, Wilcox DICTIONARY)

oxy-calcium lamp   In 19th C Britain, the early name for a variety of lime-light, and probably the first name in general use. In this lamp, oxygen was blown across an alcohol flame. The lamp was later adapted to use hydrogen mixed with oxygen. See also: safety jet. (Rees GAS 43)

oxy-gas jet   See: safety jet.

oxy-hydrogen blowpipe   See: Bude light.

oxy-hydrogen light   See: limelight.

oyama (Japanese)   See: *onnagata*.

oylem (Yiddish)   The audience. (Sandrow VAGABOND 94)

oylem goylem (Yiddish)   A catch phrase rhyming 'audience' with 'mindless giant' and referring to theatregoers, with whom Yiddish actors had a somewhat ambivalent relationship. See also: *Moyshe*. (Sandrow VAGABOND 94)

oyster part   In the 19th C, a role with one line. From a presumed habit of oysters, thought to open up just once.

ozatsuma bushi (Japanese)   See: *osatsuma bushi*.

ozone   See: sky border.

ozume (Japanese)   Literally: great conclusion. 1. In *kabuki*, the spectacular final scene of a history play (*jidaimono*), either at the end of an all-day play (*toshi kyogen*) or at the end of the first part (*ichibanme*) of a day's program. Examples are in Brandon CLASSIC 163-164, 348-349. See also: *ogiri*. 2. In modern drama (and also films and television), a grand finale.

P

P, PS, P.S. 1. Designations of pear-shaped lamps much used in stage lighting, mainly high-wattage sources used in floodlights. Sometimes called a P (or PS) lamp, P-S (now rare). (Philippi STAGECRAFT 398) 2. Prompt side—the side of the stage where the prompter is stationed. The term (and its opposite, OP—opposite prompt) were used as early as the 18th C in England.

PA Press agent.

pacca (Malayalam) Literally: green. A makeup type in *kathakali* and *kutiyattam* in which the face is painted a rich green. It is used for noble, virtuous, and heroic characters such as Rama or Krishna. (Jones/Jones KATHAKALI 25, Enros in Baumer/Brandon SANSKRIT 290)

pace 1. The overall speed of a scene, speech, or series of movements. 2. The effective speed of a performance, as in "The show lacks pace." Hence, pacing. Pace is usually understood to mean not only speed but the intensity or energy and, more subtly, a kind of rhythm brought to a production by the performers. (Canfield CRAFT, Cameron/Gillespie ENJOYMENT)

pacer A stripteaser who disrobes double-time to slow music. (Wilmeth LANGUAGE)

pa chiao ku (Chinese) See: *bajiaogu, danxian.*

pack 1. A scene pack—a group of flats. 2. To cluster flats or cloths in a pack, especially for storage. 3. To fill an auditorium. Hence, pack 'em in, pack the house, a packed house. 4. To send friends or spectators to applaud or hiss; to hire a claque. Hence, pack the audience. (Bowman/Ball THEATRE)

package 1. A prepared attraction—a star performer, a star and a few supporting players, a complete company—imported by (usually) a summer theatre. Hence, package company, package show, star package, packaged stars. (Bowman/Ball THEATRE) 2. One's place on a variety bill. (Berrey/Van den Bark SLANG 590)

package board   Any small, portable, preset control board. The usual elements are the power pack (dimmers, breakers, receptacles, etc.) and the console unit (controllers and shutoff devices, sometimes masters, faders, presets, etc.). Sometimes a third unit contains faders; these provide master control over a number of console units. Terms used of part or all of a package board include package dimmer, package console, package system, package unit, and dimmer pack. The last two terms are also used of small autotransformer boards. (Bellman LIGHTING 179, 219, 235–239, figs. 10–6a, b, c, d)

package console   See: package board.

package dimmer   See: package board.

packaged memory board   A portable control board with a memory.

package system, package unit   See: package board.

pack 'em in   To attract a capacity audience.

packer   A popular performer, one who packs a theatre.

packing-house cable   A fabric-covered electrical cable much used in the past as stage cable and so referred to even after rubber-covered cable had come into considerable use. See also: stage cable. (1967 Bellman LIGHTING 202)

packing rail   A length of steel projecting from a wall, against which flats can be stacked; several such rails form a scene dock.

pad   1. To add lines or business to a role, making it more important. Hence, pad a part. 2. To add stuffing to a costume to give the illusion of voluptuousness, fatness, a hump, etc. (Bowman/Ball THEATRE)

pada (Sanskrit)   Literally: a lyric. 1. The words of a song which together with notes (*svara*) and rhythm (*tala*), make up the three essential elements of classical Indian theatre music. (Bharata NATYASASTRA II 3) 2. In present-day regional theatre forms, especially in south India, a song form consisting of three verse segments (*pallavi*, *annupallavi*, and *caranam*). The song is accompanied by drums, and hence is set to a specific rhythmic pattern (*tala*). Also spelled *padam* (Telugu, Malayalam). See also: *sloka*. (Rajagopalan/Iyer "Aids" 205, Jones/Jones KATHAKALI 71, Gargi FOLK 134)

padalangan (Indonesian)   The art of the *wayang* puppeteer (*dalang*), including technical skills of performance, religious knowledge, and spiritual power. Lists of attributes are given in Holt ART 132 and in Brandon THRONES 68–69. Also spelled *pedhalangan*.

padam (Telugu, Malayalam)   See: *pada*.

paddle   1. A spade-shaped hinged device beneath a section of sliding stage floor. When the floor section is in its proper place, the paddle is swung 90 degrees to the vertical to bind the flooring into position. Paddles date from the 18th C and probably earlier. 2. A dance movement in which the shoulders rise and drop alternately and in opposition. (Schurman/Clark DANCE 138) 3. A turn in which the weight is on one foot while the other pushes.

paddock   See: *paletot.*

padjegan (Indonesian)   See: *pajegan.*

paegnia (Latin Roman)   Slight, plotless mimes, perhaps often vulgar; by contrast with *hypotheses* (mimes with plots). (Beare ROMAN 150, 152; Oxford CLASSICAL 688)

page   1. One who guides a draw or tab curtain to make sure the two halves overlap when they meet at center. Hence, to page the curtain, also called to walk the curtain. 2. To guide a curtain.

pageant   1. A wheeled scaffold or scenic unit used in medieval productions; each wagon was set for a different play in a cycle and moved from point to point in a town, the players repeating the performance for different audiences. The vehicle was also called a car, *edifizio* (Italian), karre, pageant car (or carriage), pageant wagon, wagon stage, etc., and was used for processional plays in England and on the Continent. 2. A play performed on such a wagon. (Rogers in Nagler SOURCES 49, Nicoll DEVELOPMENT 59). Among other forms of the word: pagenda, pagond, pagyn, paiande, paiaunt. (Chambers MEDIAEVAL II 137) 3. A wood and canvas structure used as a stage machine in Renaissance masques. 4. An entertainment produced (usually) outdoors, of an historical, patriotic, and usually spectacular nature, often presented by townspeople and involving tableaux and processions. (Bowman/Ball THEATRE, Purdom PRODUCING) 5. See: pageant lantern.

pageant house   A storage place for a medieval pageant wagon. (Chambers MEDIAEVAL II 360)

pageant lantern   Especially in the past in Britain, a lighting instrument consisting essentially of a high-wattage lamp, a reflector, and a housing. Producing a nearly parallel beam of light, the pageant lantern was in its time much favored for such effects as sunlight coming through a window. The name is from the instrument's first use for a pageant given in the moat of the Tower of London in 1935. Also called a pageant. (Bentham ART 43–44, 258; Stewart STAGECRAFT 129–130, fig. 93)

pageant master   The leader who organized the production of a medieval pageant-wagon play; he engaged the performers and technicians, arranged for rehearsal space, kept the accounts, etc. (Wickham EARLY I 297)

pageant pence, pageant silver   In medieval England, a tax levied by a guild on its members to defray the cost of producing a pageant-wagon play. (Chambers MEDIAEVAL II 116)

pageant stage, pageant wagon   See: pageant.

pagenda   See: pageant.

pagentes (Latin)   16th C stages. (Baxter/Johnson MEDIEVAL 327)

pagina (Latin)   Literally: plank. A pageant wagon on which medieval plays were performed.

pagoda sleeve   1. An 18th C man's coat sleeve with an elbow-deep cuff narrowed instead of flaring. 2. An 18th C woman's dress sleeve, flaring conically toward the wrist, and cuffed. This sleeve reappeared in France during the Second Empire.

pagond, pagyn   See: pageant.

pai, p'ai (Chinese)   1. Literally: school. See: *liupai*. 2. Literally: spoken. See: *nianbai*.

paiande, paiaunt   See: pageant.

pai chü (Chinese)   See: *baiju*.

pai hsi (Chinese)   See: *baixi*.

p'ai hsü (Chinese)   See: *daqu*.

pai mien (Chinese)   See: *baimian*.

paint bridge   A long, narrow platform hung from the gridiron near the back wall of a stage. From it one may paint a drop attached to a frame on the wall.

painted-face   See: *jing*.

painted on the drop   Especially in burlesque, said of a performer with no lines. (Wilmeth LANGUAGE)

paint frame   A large wooden frame on which a canvas drop is stretched for painting. In some theatres, the painter works on a paint bridge which can be raised and lowered, or on a boomerang (stepped platform), or on the floor, with the frame raised or lowered through a slot in the floor.

paint pallet   A metal-topped work table on which paints are mixed. The table can be fitted with casters and become a rolling paint pallet. (Gillette/Gillette SCENERY)

paircque (French)   A medieval term for auditorium. (Mantzius HISTORY II 54)

pair of bones player   See: Bones.

pair of flats   See: flat scene.

p'ai tzu (Chinese)   See: *paizi*.

p'ai tzu ch'ü (Chinese)   See: *danxian*.

paixu (Chinese)   See: *daqu*.

paizi, p'ai tzu (Chinese)   1. Literally: beat. In music: beat, time, meter. 2. Literally: tablet, name. See: *qupai*.

paiziqu (Chinese)   See: *danxian*.

pajamas   See: moghul breeches.

pajegan (Indonesian)   Literally: combination. Combining several types of performance in one form, common in Bali. Also spelled *padjegan*. See also: *topeng pajegan*. (de Zoete/Spies DANCE 165, 262) *pak ch'omji, bag cheomji, bag czonm-zi* (Korean)   Literally: gourd-headed official. 1. The main character in a puppet play (*kkoktu kaksi*). 2. The play narrator in *namsadang* or other puppet performance. He provides continuity between scenes and joins in repartee with an interlocutor (*sanbaji*). See also: *kkoktu kaksi*. (Cho KOREAN 17, Choe STUDY 18, Kim "Namsadang" 16)

pakem (Indonesian)   1. In Java, a scenario of a *wayang* play (*lakon*) or a "manual for the *dalang*" including production notes, music, and song lyrics. (Holt ART 138) *Pakem balungan* (bone guide) contains the barest outline of the plot. *Pakem gantjaran* (prose guide) is longer. *Pakem padalangan* (guide to performance) gives a complete play text. (Brandon THRONES 34) 2. In Sunda, the 'true' pool of materials from history and legend from which a play (*lakon*) is constructed. (Foley "Sundanese" 96–100)

pakhwaj (Hindi)   A double-faced drum used in old-style *jatra*. (Sarkar "Jatra" 98)

pak yong (Malaysian)   See: *pa'yong*.

pala (Bengali)   A *jatra* play. (Sarkar "Jatra" 87, Gargi FOLK 14)

palais à volonté (French)   1. A neutral setting used for tragedies in 17th C France. 2. An 18th C unlocalized palace and temple stage setting. (Brockett HISTORY 273, Roberts STAGE)

palatine   See: mousquetaire collar.

palatium (Latin)   Literally: palace. A medieval *mansion* (French) or scenic unit. (Sobel NEW 524)

palco (Italian)   Literally: floor or scaffold. In the theatre: 1. A stage. 2. A box in a theatre auditorium.

palco (Spanish)   A box in a modern theatre. See also: *aposento*.

palcos (Philippine)   A private box at a fiesta play. (Fernández ILOILO 26)

palemahan (Indonesian)   Literally: earth. The lower border of a Javanese shadow screen that represents the ground or floor on which the shadow puppet characters stand. It is part of a four to six inch colored border that surrounds the screen. (Long JAVANESE 18)

palenque (Spanish)   A passage, often a ramp, from the pit to the stage. (Shergold SPANISH)

paletot (French)   A 17th C French overcoat of silk, worn over armor. In the 19th C, a fabric overcoat, heavy for winter and light for summer, single-breasted with a sewn-on skirt. Also called a paddock. See also: *pardessus*.

pale week   A week of poor box-office receipts.

palin (Latin Roman)   Encore. The word, which is literally 'again,' is directly from Greek, where its theatrical use was identical. (Arnott ANCIENT 124)

palisade   See: commode.

palla (Latin Roman)   See: *himation*.

pallavi (Malayalam, Telugu)   The first line of a theatre song (*pada*), which may recur in whole or part in later sections of the song as a kind of refrain. (Jones/Jones KATHAKALI 111)

palliata (Latin Roman)   See: *fabula palliata*.

palliati (Latin Roman)   In at least one ancient source, comic actors. (Beare ROMAN 266)

pallium (Latin Roman)   See: *himation*.

palm   Applause.

paludamentum (Latin Roman)   Literally: military cloak. The Roman word for the Greek *chlamys* (q.v.). (Bieber HISTORY 242)

palwe (Burmese)   A bamboo flute used in theatre musical ensembles. Also spelled *pulway*. (Sein/Withey GREAT 47)

pam   See: panorama.

pamanhikan (Philippine)   A folk play describing the sacrifices expected of a bridegroom who must live with his wife's family. (Salazar in Cruz SHORT 65)

pan   1. Abbreviation for panorama. 2. See: panatrope. 3. See: dead pan. 4. See: tray. 5. To ridicule or criticize unfavorably a performer or production. 6. To move, e.g., a stage spotlight, right or left, or up and down.

pan (Chinese)   See: *ban*.

pan (Korean)   Literally: a board. A stage.

panah Arjuna (Malaysian)   See: *seligi kelir*.

panakawan (Indonesian)   See: *punakawan*.

pananapatan (Philippine)   Literally: street play. 1. A folk play depicting the travels of Mary and Joseph and the birth of Jesus, performed on Christmas eve in Tagalog-speaking areas. (Salazar in Cruz SHORT 78) 2. The folk *comedia* staged in Cuyo, Palawan Island. Also spelled *panawagan*, *panunuluyan*. (Mendoza COMEDIA 107).

panatrope   In Britain, a sound-mixing table or console designed to control, blend, and direct recorded sound effects.

panawagan (Philippine)   See: *pananapatan*.

pancanaka (Indonesian)   In Javanese *wayang*, the warrior Bima's large and razor-sharp thumbnail that he uses to disembowel his opponents. The thumbnail is a distinguishing feature of the descendants of the god Bayu. Also spelled *panchanaka*, *pantjanaka*. (Long JAVANESE 65, 92)

panchali (Bengali)   In eastern India, 16th–18th C, a monodrama that featured singing and dancing. (Gargi FOLK 15)

panchanaka (Indonesian)   See: *pancanaka*.

pan ch'iang (Chinese)   See: *banshi*.

pan ch'iang t'i (Chinese)   See: *banqiangti*.

pan chuang (Chinese)   See: *banxi*.

pandala (Assamese)   See: *rabha*.

pandanean pipe   See: panpipe.

pandita (Indonesian)   Literally: seer. The character or the puppet of a religious mystic in *wayang* drama. (Muljono in Osman TRADITIONAL 63, Foley ''Sundanese'' 37) In Java, *jejer pandita* (hermitage scene) is the second scene in the second part (*patet manyura*) of a *wayang* play, in which the hero gains advice from a seer. An example is in *The Reincarnation of Rama* in Brandon THRONES 124–128.

panel box   See: magazine panel.

panel dress, panel skirt   A piece of material used by strippers. It consists of two or more strips of cloth hanging from the waist and reaching the floor. It is worn over the G-string and used in disrobing. (Wilmeth LANGUAGE)

panes   See: slashings.

pang ch'iang (Chinese)   See: *bangqiang*.

panggong (Malaysian)   See: *panggung*.

panggung (Malaysian)   Literally: stage. Usually an enclosed shadow theatre stage. It is a raised platform about ten feet wide by twelve feet deep. Because the roof slopes from about twelve feet high in front to five feet at the rear, it is also called, in slang, *tenggong asu* (squatting dog). Also spelled *panggong*. (Yub in Osman TRADITIONAL 86)

pang hu (Chinese)   See: *banhu*.

pangotan (Indonesian)   Literally: a type of large machete. A large bulging nose found on robust *gagah* characters in Javanese shadow theatre. (Long JAVANESE 70)

pang ti (Chinese)   See: *di*.

pang tzu (Chinese)   See: *bangzi*.

pang tzu ch'iang (Chinese)   See: *bangziqiang*.

pan hsi, pan hsiang (Chinese)   See: *banxi*.

pan hu (Chinese)   See: *banhu*.

panic lighting system, panic system   In a power outage or similar emergency in the U.S., an automatic system which turns on house lights, exit lights, etc., regardless of dimmer settings. In a complete power outage, such a system is run by a battery or generator. Hence, panic switch. (Bellman LIGHTING 168–169, 220; Wehlburg GLOSSARY 42)

panic lights   In the U.S., emergency lights, primarily for the auditorium. The term is not merely apt, but is an outgrowth of theatre catastrophes, especially in the 19th C, in which the major loss of life was due to panic—often in darkness or near darkness. Compare: emergency lights, secondary lighting. (Bowman MODERN; Bellman LIGHTING 168–169, 220)

panic switch   A switch which, in an emergency, turns on the house lights at full intensity, bypassing the dimmer.

panic system   See: panic lighting system.

panic theatre   See: *théâtre panique*.

panjak (Malaysian)   A musician in a musical ensemble in traditional theatre. (Sweeney RAMAYANA 43)

pan ku (Chinese)   See: *danpigu*.

pannier, *panier* (French)   An 18th C underskirt stretched over a metal hoop to hold out an upper skirt at the sides, with a flat shape from front to back. Also called a *traquénard* or *janseniste*. See also: *guéridons*, farthingale, hoop-petticoat. (Barton COSTUME 312, Boucher FASHION)

panorama   1. A (usually) moving painted vista at the rear of a stage. Hence, panoramic cloth, panoramic. Also called a pam or pan. See also: diorama. 2. A 19th C theatrical form which aimed to use lighting, landscape painting, and the physical stage environment to permit the audience to forget they were in a theatre and to experience a sense of actually being in the stage environment. (Marsh "Williams" 289–90)

panorama floodlight   1. In Britain, a specially-shaped floodlight designed for cyclorama lighting. (Bax MANAGEMENT 184) 2. Any floodlight used in lighting a cyclorama. (Bowman/Ball THEATRE)

panorama groove   A channel in the stage floor in which the bottom of a panorama can be placed. (Bowman/Ball THEATRE)

panorama hinge   A hinge formed by two interlinked rings, each attached to a metal plate. (Win "Terms")

panoramic drama   See: epic.

panoramshchik (Russian)   A peep-show man in Russia in the 18th and 19th C. He had a large box containing crudely-drawn movable pictures which spectators could see through holes drilled in the box. Commentary was provided by the *raëshnik* (interpreter).

paños (Spanish)   Hangings in a *corral* theatre of the 17th C, presumably covering a doorway leading from backstage into the audience area. (Zabaleta in Nagler SOURCES 63)

panpipe   A musical instrument of ancient origin used to accompany all kinds of theatrical performances through the ages. Also called a pandanean pipe, syrinx. (Philpott DICTIONARY)

pan shih (Chinese)   See: *banshi*.

p'ansori (Korean)   Literally: *p'an*, stage; *sori*, voice. A narrative, sung and danced by a solo performer (usually male) to the accompaniment of a double-headed barrel drum (*puk*). It originated in the 18th C and is closely connected with shamanic performing style. (Korean KOREAN 27)

pansy, panz   1. A female impersonator. 2. A chorus boy. From the pejorative term for an effeminate man. (Berrey/Van den Bark SLANG 573)

pantalone (Italian), *pantalon* (French), **pantaloon**   A generic term for the usually wealthy and lecherous old man character in *commedia dell'arte*. The generic term was also the character's name. See also: *magnifico*.

pantie peeler   A strip-tease dancer.

pantin (French)   See: jumping jack.

pantjanaka (Indonesian)   See: *pancanaka*.

panto   A pantomime.

pantofle, *pantoufle* (French)   1. A 16th C backless overshoe. 2. Later, a house slipper or scuff. Also called a pianelle. (Boucher FASHION, Wilcox DICTIONARY)

pantograph   Primarily in television lighting but occasionally in theatres, an extendable hanger (for suspending lights) consisting mainly of a number of scissors-like parts. Wehlburg has an illustration. (Wehlburg GLOSSARY)

pantomima (Latin Roman)   A woman pantomimist. While men originally performed all roles, by the 1st C AD, women played women. Plural: *pantomimae*. See also: pantomime, *pantomimus*.

pantomime   1. From the late 1st C BC in Rome, a form of spectacular dance-theatre with a solo actor-dancer supported by musicians and a chorus. The plot of the pantomime was a brief version of a well-known heroic theme, Greek or Roman, mythical or historical. Occasionally comic, the performance was usually a remainder of or development from tragedy. The plot was sung or chanted by the chorus accompanied by the musicians while the pantomimist, using masks and perhaps changes of costume, presented a variety of characters, male or female as required. See also: *fabula saltica* (Latin Roman). 2. The solo actor-dancer. (Oxford CLASSICAL 776–777; Bieber HISTORY 165–166, 235–236, fig. 783; Beare ROMAN 234) 3. In 18th C France, a popular mime entertainment with music underscoring emotional scenes; by the mid-18th C dialogue was added. 4. A spectacle show that developed in 18th C Britain, first as a harlequinade in dumbshow and then as a spoken harlequinade, often with elements of burlesque, as in *Harlequin Doctor Faustus*. By the 19th C a pantomime (short form: panto) had become a mixed bag of acrobatics, clowning, tableaux, songs, dances, music, and dialogue, with spectacular scenery and effects. Pantomimes usually opened in late December; hence, Christmas Pantomime. 5. An 18th C British spectacular ballet afterpiece or dance drama. 6. Now, silent drama, mime, or dumbshow, either as an entire performance or part of a performance. 7. In acting, expressive movement of the face and body, called also stage business, action, or stage action. 8. To mime, to act without words. Hence, pantomimist, pantomime theatre. Marcel Marceau called pantomime "the art of expressing feelings by attitudes" (Gassner). (Brockett HISTORY 67, 326, 500; Bowman/Ball THEATRE; Wilmeth LANGUAGE; 1955 Gassner "Broadway" 319)

pantomime-arlequinade (French)   A short, simple 19th C boulevard skit with acrobatics, containing almost no plot but having some comic business. (Despot "Deburau" 364, 365)

pantomime business   In Britain, said of a show doing a brisk business, as pantomimes usually do.

pantomime dialoguée (French)   A form used by minor French theatres before the Revolution to circumvent legal restrictions on dramatic offerings. Pantomime was legal, so dialogued mime (the literal meaning) was lawful. The form was characterized by emphasis on the visual, with ballets and musical episodes interspersed throughout. (Carlson FRENCH 42ff)

pantomime director   In early 19th C London theatres, a person hired to oversee the preparation and performance of pantomimes.

pantomime the business   In rehearsing, before properties are available, to mime the use of properties, doors, etc. (Bowman/Ball THEATRE)

pantomimic dramatization   Mimed action that helps clarify character, situation, locale, and atmosphere. (Dean/Carra FUNDAMENTALS 250)

pantonnier (French)   See: minstrel.

pan torch   Formerly, a torch-like gasoline light used outdoors, occasionally for such popular entertainments as medicine shows. The torch was in reverse: a closed container at the top of a thin pipe fed a flaming open container below; the device was, of course, extremely dangerous. Sometimes called a banjo torch, from the general resemblance of the gasoline container and pipe to a banjo. (Noell in Matlaw AMERICAN 218)

panunuluyan (Philippine)   See: *pananapatan*.

pan yen (Chinese)   See: *banyan*.

pao erh (Chinese)   See: *baoer*.

pao hsiang (Chinese)   See: *guanzuo*.

pao i (Chinese)   See: *baoyi*.

pao t'iao (Chinese)   See: *baotiao*.

pao t'ou (Chinese)   See: *baotou*.

pap   A piece of paper, used as a stage property. An abbreviation found in old promptbooks. (Shattuck SHAKESPEARE 14)

papakha (Russian)   A high fur hat with a fabric top, worn by men of the Caucasus. From the mid-19th C it was the headgear of all cossack troops. See also: *kolpak*.

papel (Spanish)   Literally: paper. A performer's role.

paper   1. Theatrical advertising on outdoor billboards. 2. A complimentary ticket. Hence, papering a house. (Carrington THEATRICANA) See also: order.

paperer   One who gives out complimentary tickets.

paper house, papered house   An audience made up largely of people who had complimentary tickets. To paper the house is to give away free tickets in order to fill it up.

paper section   Seats occupied by holders of complimentary tickets. (Berrey/ Van den Bark SLANG 578)

paper set   A stage setting covered with wallpaper instead of paint. (Fay GLOSSARY)

Papposilenos*, *Papposilenus   In ancient Greece and Rome, the father of the satyrs. Bieber also gives Papa-Silenus and old Silenus, which latter she uses frequently. See also: *silenus*. (Bieber HISTORY 11–13, 339, fig. 38; Pickard-Cambridge DITHYRAMB 117)

Pappus (Latin Roman)   One of the types of stock clowns in Atellan farces. He seems to have been the elderly fool, an example being the old man with a young wife. The name is from the Greek for 'grandfather,' which Pollux includes among his comic masks. An ancient source says the Oscans called him Casnar. See also: *fabula Atellana*. (Beare ROMAN 138, 139; Pollux in Nagler SOURCES 13)

paprika   Drawing power.

PAR   1. See: reflector lamp. 2. See: PAR-can.

parabasis (Greek), **parabasis**   In Greek Old Comedy, the address to the audience by the chorus. The *parabasis* may be the earliest element of comedy, preserving the address to the audience of the older *komos*. The address itself was usually concerned with anything but the play: remarks by the playwright on himself or his public, on political questions, on rival playwrights, and so on, all in satirical fashion. Before the end of Aristophanes' career, the *parabasis* had become fragmentary, and after 338 BC, it disappeared completely. From *parabainein*, "to step across, to come forward, to turn around to the spectators instead of to the actors, and address the audience." (Flickinger GREEK 41, Liddell/Scott LEXICON)

parabolic aluminized reflector lamp   See: reflector lamp.

parabolic flood   A floodlight consisting of a parabolic reflector. See also: scoop. (Bellman LIGHTING 52–53)

parabolic reflector   In some floodlights and striplights, and in beam projectors and PAR lamps, a reflector with a paraboloid surface. If a small light source is placed at the reflector's single focus, the rays of the resulting beam are nearly parallel. Wehlburg has an illustration. (Bellman SCENE, Sellman/ Lessley ESSENTIALS, Wehlburg GLOSSARY)

parabolic spotlight   See: beam projector.

parachoregema (Greek)   A supernumerary, a fourth actor. The uses of the word suggest that it was applied to any added person(s) or character(s). When the three actors of ancient Greek drama could not handle all the roles in a play, one or more *parachoregemata* were added. Though often mute, such actors sometimes sang or had small speaking parts. The term was apparently used of any performer except one of the three chief actors or a member of the chorus. The origin of the word is obscure. (Haigh ATTIC 234–238, Flickinger GREEK 186, Pickard-Cambridge FESTIVALS 137)

parade   1. The balcony on the front of an English fair booth or concession. 2. In the U.S., the opening march of a burlesque cast across the stage. See also: eleven forty-five.

parade (French)   Especially in the 17th and 18th C, a brief farce or comic dialogue performed in front of a theatre to lure customers.

parade girl   A burlesque showgirl. (Wilmeth LANGUAGE)

parade one's wares   To perform.

parade strip   In burlesque, a showgirl who walks about, doing little dancing or acting, parading her sexuality but using few bumps and grinds. (Wilmeth LANGUAGE)

paradis (French)   Beginning in the 16th C, the top gallery in French theatres. Also called the *colombier* or *pouailler*. (Brockett HISTORY 255)

paradise   1. In medieval plays, either the heavenly or the earthly paradise. 2. The uppermost seating area in a multi-galleried theatre.

paradiso (Italian)   A Renaissance stage machine representing a heaven full of living figures and a quantity of lights which appeared and disappeared. (Larson "Vasari's" 287–288)

paradiso (Spanish)   The uppermost gallery in a theatre. Also called the *cazuela*.

paragammacist   In Britain, a performer who has difficulty pronouncing K or G. (Granville DICTIONARY)

parakataloge (Greek)   In tragedy and perhaps also comedy, a form of delivery between speech and song, often spoken of as recitative (sometimes as chant). *Parakataloge* is thought to have been accompanied by the *aulos* or the *klepsiambos*, and to have been used in drama along with speech and song. The accompaniment may have been pitched higher than the actor's voice. From *para*, beside, and *kataloge*, declamation. See also: *klepsiambos*. (Haigh ATTIC 268–270, Pickard-Cambridge FESTIVALS 157–158, 164, 257; Beare ROMAN 221)

parallel   1. In dance, a standing position with legs facing front and lined up directly under the hip joints. (Stodelle HUMPHREY 34) 2. A hinged trestle which, when unfolded, supports a platform. In Britain: a rostrum. (Bowman/ Ball THEATRE) For illustrations of the continental and the standard parallels, see Lounsbury THEATRE 111–112.

parallel action   1. Balanced stage movement by two performers or two groups of performers. 2. Two equally important plots in the same play. (Bowman/Ball THEATRE)

parallel beam projector   See: beam projector.

parallel top   A lid which fits on top of an opened parallel, with cleats to lock the parallel in its open position.

paralyze, paralyze the customers   To delight an audience. Hence, paralyzer—a successful show or performer.

parapet   A facing for the front of a stage, concealing the substage. (Sabbattini in Hewitt RENAISSANCE 84–85)

parascenia   See: *paraskenia*.

parasite   The shrewdly amusing hanger-on of ancient Greek and Roman comedy. Peniculus in Plautus' *Menaechmi* is an example. Always a lover of good food and of a free meal, he often makes jokes or runs errands to curry favor; sometimes he is a cynical flatterer. Bieber suggests three types: the coarse parasite popular in Latin comedy, first known in Sicily in the work of Epicharmus; the easy, worldly, hook-nosed parasite; and, between the two, the ordinary hanger-on, often a flatterer of the braggart. Similar types are frequent in later comedy. See also: *parasitus*. (Duckworth NATURE 265–267; Bieber HISTORY 99–100, figs. 372–377)

parasitus (Latin Roman)   1. One of the fools in the mime. (Allen ANTIQUITIES 26) 2. See: parasite.

paraskenia (Greek)   From probably the mid-5th C BC, the wings at either end of the *skene* (scene building). The *paraskenia* were contiguous with the scene building and usually projected toward the audience. The evidence for two-storied *paraskenia* by the 3rd C BC is substantial, in part because such side wings would have corresponded to a two-storied scene building. Especially in comedy, the *paraskenia* often represented houses.

Like *skene*, *paraskenia* has been used loosely in both singular and plural, so that the term may refer to the building, to part of it, or even to the panels (*pinakes*) which some think were near the side buildings and perhaps attached to them. The plural is seen much more often than the singular, *paraskenion*. When the wings had two stories, the floors were often designated upper *paraskenia* and lower *paraskenia*. The *versurae* (*versurae procurrentes*) of Rome were similar. Also called *parascenia* (Latin Roman), wings, side buildings, side wings, parascenia, parascenes (mainly British); all occur in the singular as well. (Bieber HISTORY 67–70, 111–112, 118–120, 216–217, figs. 253–266; Pickard-Cambridge DIONYSUS 46, 59–63, 66)

parastatae (Greek)   Literally: those who stand beside. The two assistants of the chorus leader in ancient drama. In the tragic chorus, they stood in the front file, nearest the audience, on either side of the leader. Also spelled *parastatai*. (Haigh ATTIC 301, Mantzius HISTORY I 156)

paratheatrical   A term used to refer to activities tangential to theatre, such as circus, parades, etc. (Cameron/Gillespie ENJOYMENT)

paratheatrics   In the theory of Jerzy Grotowski, a non-theatrical but theatre-related "clinic-workshop" in which participants put themselves into a retreat situation so as to explore their own values and how these detract from the creative theatrical process. It is a dangerous consciousness-raising ordeal with unpredictable psychological possibilities, and its reception has been mixed in theatrical training circles. (Argelander "Workshops" 17)

PAR border   A borderlight consisting of PAR lamps.

PAR-can   A lighting instrument using a PAR lamp. Also called PAR, sometimes PAR lamp.

pardessus (French)   A 19th C man's overcoat resembling a *paletot*. For a woman, the term encompassed any kind of top garment. (Boucher FASHION)

pardner   The player of drum and pipe preceding a 19th C English Punch and Judy show. He also served as interpreter of the show. See also: bottler, interpreter. (Speaight PUPPET 211)

parekan (Indonesian)   In Balinese theatre, the character or puppet of a retainer to a king, often a clown. See: *penasar*, *punakawan*. (Muljono in Osman TRADITIONAL 63)

pares (Latin Roman)   As used of the reed double-pipes which accompanied Roman plays, of equal length. If the pipes were unequal in length, they were called *impares*. See also: *tibicen*. (Beare ROMAN 168)

parfont (French)   The entrance to hell—a *mansion* in a medieval production. (Stuart DECORATION 178)

PAR head   A device designed to hold a PAR lamp. Similar to a PAR-can but with very little housing.

parikramana (Sanskrit)   Literally: walking around. A conventional acting technique in which an actor suggests traveling from one locale to another, within the same scene, through a stylized walk around the stage. (Gandhi in Baumer/Brandon SANSKRIT 133)

pariparshvika (Sanskrit)   In classical Indian theatre, an assistant to the stage manager (*sutradhara*). In regional folk theatres, also called *patak*, *sangi*. (Keith SANSKRIT 85, 340)

parisol (Italian)   An Italian Renaissance device recommended by Joseph Furttenbach for creating the illusion of a burning bush or other onstage fires. The *parisol*, which could be opened and shut and turned by an unseen operator, was a leather-covered parasol-umbrella whose twelve panels were painted with gilded flames. Both sources below have an illustration. (Furttenbach in Hewitt RENAISSANCE 232, 234, 235; Rosenthal/Wertenbaker MAGIC 50, 51)

PAR lamp   See: PAR–can, reflector lamp.

parlando (Italian)   Speaking in a declamatory manner, sometimes with a musical accompaniment, as in opera.

parley   In the Elizabethan theatre, a trumpet call.

parode   The first choral ode in ancient Greek drama. Rare. See also: *parodos*.

parodos (Greek)   1. One of the two open passages between the ends of the seating area and the *skene* (scene building) in an ancient Greek theatre. They were regularly used by the chorus, and by actors unless they were supposed to enter or leave by the scene building. There is evidence that by the time of New Comedy (late 4th C BC), the practice was that the stage right *parodos* led to areas outside the city, while the stage left *parodos* led to areas within the city, often the harbor or the *agora* (marketplace). In some theatres and at some times, the *parodoi* were also used by spectators. The Greeks used *eisodos* (plural *eisodoi*), not *parodos*, in the 5th C BC, but writers in English regularly use *parodos* for all periods. 2. The first choral ode in comedy and tragedy. In late Old Comedy the *parodos* sometimes included lines spoken by actors. English sometimes uses parode. 3. The chorus entrance accompanying or directly preceding the first choral ode. 4. Sometimes, in the developed stage building of Roman times, the entrance to the stage from one of the two *parascenia* (Latin Roman; Greek: *paraskenia*). This use seems clearly to have developed from meaning 1.

As noted above, the plural is *parodoi*. *Parodus* (plural *parodi*) is sometimes seen for any of these meanings, *paradus* occasionally; for meanings 1 and 2, U.S. English uses parodos and parodus (plurals parodoi, parodi). (Arnott SCENIC 27–31, 37–39; Flickinger GREEK 208, 233–234; Bieber HISTORY 29, 70, 72, figs. 238, 255, 258, 275; Pickard-Cambridge DIONYSUS 21)

parody   A song, dialogue, action, or play which imitates in order to ridicule or burlesque the original. Hence, parodist. (Bowman/Ball THEATRE)

par personnages (French)   By actors. In medieval times, almost any narrative might ultimately be turned into a play by telling it *par personnages*. (Frank MEDIEVAL 213–215, 266)

parq (French)   A bleacher-like stand for spectators. (Nagler MEDIEVAL 18)

parquet, parquette   1. Especially in the past, the main floor of an auditorium or part of it—sometimes the portion not overhung by balconies, or portions at the side or back. 2. The seats in such an area. (Bowman/Ball THEATRE)

parquet circle   See: *parterre*.

parquet stage cloth   A floor cloth painted to resemble parquet flooring; used for interior scenes.

part   1. A performer's role or character. 2. A performer's sides (lines for his character), with brief cues. 3. An individual musician's copy of his portion of a full score.

part actor   A performer who has a good but not leading role. (Berrey/Van den Bark SLANG 572)

partbook   In the past, a performer's part or sides—speeches and cues. (Shattuck SHAKESPEARE 5)

part d'auteur (French)   In 17th C France, the share of the box-office receipts received by the playwright. (Hawkins ANNALS I 187)

parte   An alternate medieval English term for pageant wagon. (Rogers in Nagler SOURCES 49)

parterre (French), **parterre**   1. In 17th and 18th C French theatres, a standing area in front of the benches of the *amphithéâtre*. From *par terre*, on the ground. In English: 2. The ground floor of a theatre, the pit. 3. That portion of the ground floor overhung by balconies. Also called the parquet circle or orchestra circle. 4. At the old Metropolitan Opera House in New York City, the lowest tier of boxes. (Bowman/Ball THEATRE, Granville DICTIONARY)

participation drama, participation theatre, participation play   A performance for young children, usually in the round, with directed opportunities for audience participation, such as by answering a direct question, or by physically becoming a character or object which is important to the plot. Audiences, usually from three to eight years old, are kept relatively small, typically from 100 to 250. Goldberg has an illustration. (Davis/Behm "Terminology" 10–11; Goldberg CHILDREN'S 52–53, 60–61, 104–105, 176)

parti-colored   Said of a costume with a distinctly marked line of color through the middle. One leg might thus be black and the other white. See also: harlequin. (Chalmers CLOTHES 17)

parting agent   A material—often a greasy substance—applied to a mold to prevent whatever is being cast from sticking to the mold. (Bellman SCENOGRAPHY)

partitura (Italian)   The dividing of a dramatic action into small units or bits, like phrases in music. See also: *kuski*. (Hobgood "Stanislavski's" 155)

partlet   See: guimpe.

partnering   Dancing done between partners. Also called double work. See also: *pas de deux*. (Kersley/Sinclair BALLET)

part of the pit laid into boxes   See: pit railed into boxes.

partures (French)   In medieval northern France, satirical dialogues used by wandering performers. (Ward LITERATURE I 21)

party claps   In 18th C theatres and later, friends of the author, used by him to applaud and counter any adverse audience response including heckling from rival authors' groups. See also: claque. (Sobel NEW)

parwa (Indonesian)   Literally: part or book. 1. Balinese for *purwa*, or original story. For example, in the shadow play, "*parwa* puppets are used." (McPhee in Belo TRADITIONAL 150) 2. A Balinese masked dance-drama based on the *Mahabharata* that uses the music and vocal style of the shadow play (*wayang kulit*). Also called *wayang parwa*. (de Zoete/Spies DANCE 160) *pas* (French)   In ballet, a step.

pas ballotté (French)   See: *ballotté*.

pas battu (French)   In ballet, a step embellished with a striking together of the legs. (Grant TECHNICAL)

pas ciseaux (French)   Literally: scissors step. In ballet, a movement in which the dancer's feet are thrown wide apart after springing into the air. Sometimes called a *pas de ciseaux*. Also called an *écart en l'air*. (Kersley/Sinclair BALLET)

pas couru (French)   In ballet, three running steps often used to gain momentum for a leap. (Grant TECHNICAL)

pas d'action (French)   A scene in a ballet that expresses emotion or tells a story by means of mime and dance. (Grant TECHNICAL)

pas de basque (French)   The characteristic step of the national dances of the Basques. In ballet, an alternating step in three counts, taken side to side. (Grant TECHNICAL)

pas de bourrée (French)   In ballet, a step consisting of a supposed glide on the toes in which the latter are, in quick succession, picked up precisely. There are more than twenty variations. The *bourrée* was a fashionable court dance of the 17th C, in duple time with an upbeat. (Kersley/Sinclair BALLET, Wilson BALLET)

pas de cheval (French)   Literally: horse step. In ballet, the pawing of the ground with one foot while the dancer hops on the other. (Kersley/Sinclair BALLET)

pas de cuisse (French)   See: *temps de cuisse*.

pas de deux (French)   In ballet, a dance for two performers. See also: partnering, *grand pas de deux*.

pas dégagé (French)   See: *dégagé*.

pasebanan (Indonesian)   See: *paseban djawi*.

paseban djawi (Indonesian)   Literally: outer audience. A standard scene in Javanese *wayang* in which generals and ministers gather in the outer audience hall to receive their king's orders. Also called *adegan paseban djawi* (outer audience scene). *Paseban djawi denawa* (ogres' outer audience) is an analogous scene set in an overseas kingdom. (Brandon THRONES 22–23) In Sundanese *wayang golek*, called *pasebanan*. (Foley "Sundanese" 112)

paseo (Philippine)   A parade of combatants before the tournament scene (*torneo*) in *comedia*. (Mendoza COMEDIA 54)

pash stuff   1. Passionate acting. 2. See: sob stuff.

pasinden (Indonesian)   See: *pesinden*.

pas marché (French)   1. The dignified, classical walk of a prima ballerina and the *premier danseur*. (Grant TECHNICAL) 2. Such a walk, whether done by one or more dancers. (Wilson BALLET) *paso* (Spanish)   1. In the 16th C and later, a dramatic interlude, usually a simple episode. 2. Now, a sketch, a curtain raiser. (Rennert SPANISH 14)

paso doble (Philippine)   Music in a brisk tempo used for an entrance or an exit in *comedia*. (Mendoza COMEDIA 53)

pass   A free ticket, though some passes require the payment of a service fee.

passacaille (French)   1. A lively, fashionable court dance of the late 17th C. (Perugini PAGEANT 109) 2. A Louis XIV cord which attached a muff to the waist; named after the fashionable dance. (Boucher FASHION)

passage at arms   Cut-and-thrust dialogue—a rapid emotional exchange of lines between two characters. Also called stichomythia.

pass check   In the U.S., a permit to readmit someone to a theatre; called in Britain a pass-out check. (Bowman/Ball THEATRE)

pass door   1. A door leading from backstage to the auditorium or front of the house. 2. In Fay, a fire door which must be kept locked. (Bowman/Ball THEATRE, Fay GLOSSARY)

passé (French)   Literally: passed. In ballet, movement in which the moving foot passes the knee of the other leg. (Grant TECHNICAL)

passementerie (French)   1. Fancy braid trimming. 2. Appliquéd embroidery. (Chalmers CLOTHES 242, Walkup DRESSING 270)

passepied (French)   A late 17th C fashionable court dance, minuet-like in style. (Perugini PAGEANT 109)

passer (French)   To mount (a production). (Moynet FRENCH 119)

pas seul (French)   A solo dance.

passing act   An act in which a Black performer plays a white role. (Berrey/Van den Bark SLANG 583)

passing at rear   Minor characters, such as guests, visitors, etc. making entrances and exits upstage, usually in a well-peopled scene.

passing link chain   A variety of chain especially resistant to kinking, often used to weight the bottom hem of draperies. Passing link trim chain, usually with a ring at one end and a snap hook at the other, serves to fasten scenery to pipe battens. See also: snatch chain, trim chain. (Lounsbury THEATRE 22)

Passion play   A play dealing with the life of Christ.

passive movement   1. In dance, the motion of a limb as the result of the motion of another limb, even if it moves independently. Example: an upper arm which, moving independently, can still be in passive movement because it is being carried by a separate movement of the shoulder. 2. Movement in dance in which muscle tension is released from a limb, and gravity is permitted to act upon it. (Eshkol/Wachmann NOTATION 165)

pass out   1. To fail to get applause. 2. Hyphenated, a spectator who leaves a theatre and returns.

pass-out check   In Britain, a ticket given to a patron who wishes to leave the theatre (during an interval—intermission—for example) but will return. In the U.S., pass check.

pasta (Spanish)   In the 17th C, pasteboard used to make properties for performances of sacred plays on pageant wagons. (Rennert SPANISH 311)

pasteboard   Ticket.

pasticcio (Italian)   Literally: a pie; figuratively, a mess. A patchwork of musical pieces by various composers, making up a musical theatre piece.

pastie, pasty   One of a pair of circular nipple caps affixed with adhesive and worn by a stripper or burlesque performer. (Wilmeth LANGUAGE)

pastoral   A romantic play in a rural setting, developed in the Italian Renaissance.

pastorale-comique (French)   A late 17th C play, often presented as a diversion for the members of the court at their country castles. It was essentially plotless and contained mythological figures in a rural setting, interspersed with music and dances. (Hawkins ANNALS I 350)

pastores (Latin)   Literally: shepherds. 1. Medieval liturgical plays dealing with the shepherds at the manger. (Tydeman THEATRE) 2. In the Philippines, folk plays depicting scenes of the Nativity and the lives of Saints, performed until the beginning of the 20th C in Sugbuanon. (Ramas in Bresnahan CROSS-CULTURAL 219)

pastourelle (French)   A lyrical narrative on a pastoral subject, sometimes a play on such a subject. Has been said to be a link between folk-song and drama. *Une pastourelle dramatique* (a dramatic pastoral) has been used of some medieval plays, as has *pastourelle par personnages* (a pastoral performed by actors). Compare *par personnages*. (Frank MEDIEVAL 215, 231, 232)

PA system   A public address (amplifying) system.

patadas (Spanish)   The stomping of an audience to show its displeasure.

patak (Assamese)   See: *pariparshvika*.

pataka (Sanskrit)   1. Episode. A subdivision of incidental actions of the subject-matter (*arthaprakrti*) of a classical Indian play. (Keith SANSKRIT 297) A "subsidiary plot" according to Byrski (Baumer/Brandon SANSKRIT 144). 2. The flat palm, or "flag hand" gesture (*hasta*) used in Indian classical acting and dance. (Bharata NATYASASTRA 174)

patch   A small piece of material worn by a stripper to cover the pubic area. It is sometimes worn under a G-string; hence, after the stripper removes the G-string, she is 'in the patch.' (Wilmeth LANGUAGE)

patch board, patch bay, patch panel   See: interconnecting panel.

patch cord   1. See: interconnecting panel. 2. In a stage sound system, a cord used to connect components.

patches   Small pieces of material shaped like flowers, diamonds, crescents, or occasionally human figures, placed on the face in the 17th C. By the 18th C such ornaments were called *mouches dans le lait* (French, literally: flies in the milk) because of the white powder upon which they rested, or simply *mouches*. Also called court patches or court plasters. (Walkup DRESSING 195)

patch panel   The unit in a stage lighting system where electrical circuits are connected to ('patched into') appropriate dimmer circuits.

patch sheet   See: interconnecting panel.

patent   In Britain, a grant: a royal act giving permission to erect a theatre and produce entertainments. (Hogan LONDON cxxviii)

patent automatic gas dip   In 19th C Britain, a term sometimes used for a patented water joint which allowed a connection to be made or unmade by a single movement of the operator. See also: water joint. (Rees GAS 112–113, fig. 71)

patentee   The owner or part-owner of a British royal theatre patent.

patent gas float   In British writing, patented gas footlights. So long as the float was patented, the phrase was and is used whether the burners were Argand lamps (patent lamps) or ordinary gas jets such as fishtail burners. (Rees GAS 25–28, figs. 9–11)

patent house   A theatre in Britain operating under a royal patent. Also called a Theatre Royal. (Hogan LONDON cxxviii)

patent lamp   A cylindrical wick and glass chimney controlling the portions of oxygen and oil and producing a bright, steady light. Also called an Argand lamp. Introduced into London theatres in 1785. (Brockett HISTORY 341)

patent theatre   A patent house.

patent tilter   19th C circles of light steel wire, graduated in size, taped to form a bell and worn under a skirt to hold it out. See also: farthingale. (Barton COSTUME 440)

patet (Indonesian)   Literally: mode or key. 1. A mode or key in Javanese *gamelan* music. When *gamelan* music accompanies a play (*wayang, ludruk, ketoprak*), the music progresses through three *patet*: *patet nem* or *enem*, *patet sanga*, and *patet manyura* or *manjura*. (Holt ART 137–138, Peacock RITES 65) 2. Any of three parts of a Javanese *wayang* play, each part named after the *patet* of music which is played during it. See examples of the three *patet* divisions in Brandon THRONES 20–27. (Muljono in Osman TRADITIONAL 59, Hood THEME 126–128) 3. Abbreviation for *patetan*.

patetan (Indonesian)   A mood song (*suluk*) in Javanese *wayang* which is descriptive. Use in Surakarta-style shadow theatre is given in Brandon THRONES 367–370. Commonly abbreviated *patet*.

pathetic drama   Restoration and 18th C plays, usually serious, designed to elicit an audience's pity. (Bowman/Ball THEATRE)

pathos   The quality or qualities which cause an audience to feel tender toward, to feel sorry for, or to empathize with a protagonist. Some Aristotelian scholars feel (others disagree) that the protagonist's irrational response to the situation in which he finds himself is what sets pathos in motion. The literal meaning of the Greek word (*pathos*) is suffering, deep feeling, or torment.

pati (Sanskrit)   See: *yavanika*.

patih (Indonesian)   The role of a prime minister in *wayang* and other traditional drama. (de Zoete/Spies DANCE 35)

patih (Malaysian)   Literally: minister. A shadow puppet of an officer or minister. (Sweeney MALAY 25, Sweeney RAMAYANA 55)

patio (Spanish)   The pit or ground viewing area in a *corral* theatre of the 17th C.

patma (Burmese)   A large drum used in the musical ensemble that accompanies traditional theatre performances. (Sein/Withey GREAT 48, Brandon SOUTHEAST 127)

patra (Sanskrit)   The generic term for role type in classical Indian drama. Major types are hero (*nayaka*), heroine (*nayika*), clown (*vidusaka*). (Keith SANSKRIT 310)

patra-pravesa (Sanskrit)   Literally: character entrance. The entry of the chief character in a *bhagavata mela* performance in Tamil Nadu state, south India. (Vatsyayan TRADITIONAL 60)

patriót (Russian, Yiddish)   In the Yiddish theatre, a fan of a performer or of a theatre. Fans were often wildly loyal, and the followers of one performer sometimes fought the devotees of another. In another kind of behavior, a fan at Jacob Adler's *Lear* was so overcome by the ingratitude of Lear's daughters that he wailed, "Mr. Adler. I'll give you bread. Come with me. Children are no good. To hell with them." Sometimes spelled *patriott*. The plural, *patriótn* or *patriotten*, sometimes means fans, and sometimes a fan club. English patriot also occurs. (Rosenfeld BRIGHT 183, 231, 336–337; Sandrow VAGABOND 101–102; Lifson YIDDISH 171, 172, 193)

patron   1. A theatregoer. 2. In Renaissance times and later, one who supported and protected an acting company. Hence, patronage. (Bowman/Ball THEATRE)

pat stuff   See: hoke.

patsy   1. An assistant who does all the work. 2. A performer on whom a director vents his anger.

pattala (Burmese)   A bamboo xylophone used in the musical ensemble that accompanies traditional theatre performances. (Sein/Withey GREAT 47, Brandon SOUTHEAST 127)

patte   See: guleron.

patten   1. A raised wooden clog worn in the 18th C to travel on cobblestone streets or in rough weather. (Wilcox DICTIONARY) 2. A medieval thick-soled leather or velvet over-slipper. 3. A medieval shoe with attached blade, for ice skating. (Boucher FASHION)

patter   1. Rapidly spoken or sung comic lines, usually in musical comedy, light opera (as in Gilbert and Sullivan), vaudeville, revues, and burlesque. 2. Occasionally, to deliver such lines. Hence, patterer, patterist (a very successful patterer), patter song. 3. Sometimes in vaudeville billings, jokes. (Bowman/Ball THEATRE, Wilmeth LANGUAGE)

pattern   1. Especially in ellipsoidal reflector spotlights, a drop-in metal cut-out whose shape can be projected. Also called a gobo. 2. See: play.

pattern control   See: counterpoint lighting.

pattern projector   An occasional term for an ellipsoidal reflector spotlight which will accept metal cutouts (patterns) for projection on a setting. (Bowman/Ball THEATRE)

patter song   See: patter.

patter specialist   A jokester.

patting juba   See: juba.

patting rabbit hash   In vaudeville, a brisk recitative accompanied by much patting and slapping of the hands on knees, hips, forearms, etc. in triple time. (Gilbert VAUDEVILLE 171)

pa tzu (Chinese)   See: *bazi*.

paudh (Gujarati)   See: *chachar*.

pause   1. A morality play performed during intervals in a mystery play. An interlude. (Ward LITERATURE I 108) In acting and directing: 2. A brief delay, usually to give emphasis, create suspense, etc. 3. To delay the action for such a purpose. (Bowman/Ball THEATRE)

pavane (French)   A 16th–17th C slow, stately, dignified court dance. (Perugini PAGEANT 69)

pavement   Stage floor.

pavilion   A curtained stage in an Elizabethan theatre, created by a portable structure placed on the platform stage between the two entrance doors; action could be discovered within the pavilion by drawing the curtains, or action could take place on the roof of the pavilion. This theory has been advanced in place of the inner stage or alcove theory, about which there has been considerable argument. Both methods of revealing chamber or study scenes could have been used, since physical features may have varied from theatre to theatre.

pawang (Malaysian)   A shaman, attached to or a member of a *bangsawan* troupe, responsible for reciting invocations to spirits to protect performances from mishap and, often, for providing protective holy water to cast members.

Called by Yassin a medicine man (in Osman TRADITIONAL 148–149). Generally synonymous with *bomoh*.

pawongan (Indonesian)   A clown-servant in Sundanese *wayang golek*. (Foley "Sundanese" 37)

paw payah (Lao)   An older male role, father or king, in a *mohlam* play. (Miller "Kaen" 222)

payat (Yiddish)   A clown in a Polish Purim play. *Payat* in Russian means solder; the *payat* did indeed hold the play together, since he often spoke the prologue, and he told performers when to enter and exit. (Kirshenblatt-Gimblett "Contraband" 10, Sandrow VAGABOND 10, 11)

pay box   1. In 18th C theatres and later, the box where receipts were kept. (Hogan LONDON xxix) 2. An office in a British theatre (and formerly some U.S. theatres) where patrons pay for tickets at the time of admission. (Bowman/Ball THEATRE)

paycheck   A theatrical sponsor or backer.

paying doors   In 18th C England, the theatre doors at which patrons purchased their tickets, as opposed to the doors leading to the various seating areas, where the tickets were given up to the keepers. (Hogan LONDON xxiii)

paying place   The place in an 18th C theatre where tickets could be obtained for the pit and galleries. (Hogan LONDON xxii)

paylist   In 18th C Britain and later, a payroll.

payoff   1. A punch line. 2. The end of an act. 3. The final performance of a show. 4. As two words, to pay production costs from the producer's pocket.

pa'yong (Malaysian)   The major male character, played by an actress, in *ma'yong*. Sometimes referred to as the *pa'yong tua* (old *pa'yong*) or *raja besar* (great king). A young hero or prince is called *pa'yong muda* (young *pa'yong*). Also spelled *pak yong*. (Malm in Osman TRADITIONAL 339, Sheppard TAMAN 64, Yousof "Kelantan" 91–92)

PB   Promptbook.

P.C.   1. Plano-convex, as in P.C. spotlight. 2. See: plano-convex spotlight.

P.C. light   See: plano-convex spotlight.

P.C. spot(light)   See: plano-convex spotlight.

PD   Prompt door, that is, a proscenium door on prompt side. (Shattuck SHAKESPEARE 16)

peach basket hat   A hat whose pleated ruffle or lace brim was formed from an extension of its oversized crown. (Chalmers CLOTHES 250)

peak angle   The angle at which a spotlight beam is at its maximum brightness. One-half (usually '1/2') peak angle notes the angle at which the spotlight beam is at one-half its maximum brightness, and one-tenth (usually '1/10') peak angle is that angle at which the beam reaches a tenth of its maximum brightness. The terms are used in describing the performance of modern spotlights.

peanut gallery   A U.S. term for the uppermost seating area in a theatre. Also called the gods, heavens, nigger heaven (now obsolete and offensive), or paradise.

peanuts   See: bubkas.

Pear Garden   See: *liyuan*.

pear-shaped   Of vocal tone, rounded.

pear-shaped lamp   A lamp with a pear-shaped bulb. Abbreviations: P, PS, P.S.

peasant actors   Non-professional rustics who appear in an indigenous production, as in the Passion Play at Oberammergau. (Sobel NEW)

peasants   In show business, unresponsive spectators. (Wilmeth LANGUAGE)

peccadillo   See: rabat(o).

pecking   A birdlike movement of the head in dancing.

pedal puppet   A puppet controlled from below the stage by strings and levers (pedals). Also called a piano puppet or key puppet. (Philpott DICTIONARY)

pedhalangan (Indonesian)   See: *padalangan*.

pedimental headdress   See: gable.

pee (Thai)   See: *pi*.

peek   To see past the masking of a set. (Parker/Smith DESIGN)

peekaboo waist   In minstrelsy, a woman's summer blouse with eyelet embroidery. (Wilmeth LANGUAGE)

Peel   A 19th C men's light jacket. (Boucher FASHION)

peel   To undress or do a striptease. Hence, peel act, peeler.

peep hole   1. An opening in a curtain through which people behind it on the stage can peek into the auditorium. 2. Said of a play which is realistic in style. 3. Said of a picture-frame or proscenium stage, as in peep-hole stage. Also called a peep-show theatre. (Bowman/Ball THEATRE)

peep show   1. A miniature theatre in a box, viewed through a single eyehole. Originating in the 15th C, some peep shows were very simple, showing a single scene, but others were fairly elaborate and involved changeable scenery and moving cardboard figures. 2. Especially in the 18th-19th C, portable entertainment consisting of a mounted box with a peep hole fitted with a magnifying glass. A small interior exhibition is thus seen, often depicting a historical event such as the battle of Waterloo. Also called a raree show. See also: *theatrum mundi*. 3. A term sometimes applied to shows involving striptease acts, lightly-clad chorus girls, etc. 4. A show supposedly providing a spectator with a peephole view of nude women or a sex act. (Wilmeth LANGUAGE)

peg　1. See: stage screw. 2. See: spike.

peglam　A person who, when leaving a theatre, wants the ticket price refunded. (Berrey/Van den Bark SLANG 574)

peg puppet　A miniature form of *marionnette à la planchette* (French). Also called a *tulukutu* (Hawaiian). (Philpott DICTIONARY)

peg-top, peg-top trousers　Early 20th C trousers with pleated fullness at the top, tapering in to the ankles. (Barton COSTUME 535)

peg-top skirt　An early 20th C skirt with fullness at the hips tapering to narrowness at the ankles. Also called a *tonneau* (French) or barrel skirt. (Wilcox DICTIONARY)

peg-top trousers　See: peg-top.

pei, p'ei (Chinese)　An outer garment with a low collar and center-front closure which is worn by high ranking characters in Beijing opera (*jingju*) and many other forms of music-drama (*xiqu*). The male version is full-length; the female is three-quarter, and worn over a skirt. (Halson PEKING 26, Scott CLASSICAL 148–149, Zung SECRETS 21)

pei ch'ü (Chinese)　See: *qu*.

pei kung (Chinese)　See: *beigong*.

peinture (French)　Literally: painting. Stage makeup. Also called *maquillage*.

Peiping opera　See: *jingju*.

pejah (Indonesian)　Literally: smashed or broken. In Javanese puppet theatre, a fall to the ground dead or in an unconscious state. (Long JAVANESE 67)

Peking opera　See: *jingju*.

pelawak (Indonesian)　A clown role in Javanese *ludruk*. Several clowns perform in the comic prologue and in the main play (*tjerita*). Also called *badut*, *punakawan*. (Peacock RITES 71)

pelepas niat, pelimau (Malaysian)　See: *berjamu*.

pelerine　See: *housse*.

pelisse (French)　1. An 18th C woman's cape, padded and trimmed with fur, sometimes hooded. 2. A 19th C formal evening cape for women. 3. A 19th-20th C man's fur coat, usually for evening wear. 4. A 19th-20th C child's long, hooded, padded coat. (Barton COSTUME 407, Boucher FASHION)

pelita (Malaysian)　The oil lamp that lights the shadow theatre screen. Today it is often replaced by a kerosene or pressure lamp, or by an electric lamp. (Yub in Osman TRADITIONAL 98)

pelmet　See: valance.

pelog (Indonesian)　A seven-note scale used in certain *gamelan* compositions. In Sunda, the music for *wayang golek cepak* and *topeng babakan* is played in *pelog* scale. See also: *slendro*.

pelokan (Indonesian)   In Javanese *wayang kulit*, the shape of an ogre's nose. The nose is fat and gross, resembling the inside of a mango. (Long JAVANESE 70)

peluca (Spanish)   Wig. Hence, *peluquero* (wig maker).

pemachak (Malaysian)   See: *mochok*.

pemangku dalang (Indonesian)   See: *mewinten dalang*.

pemetek (Malaysian)   A pair of wooden clappers used to provide sound effects and musical cues in shadow theatre. The clappers, separated by a spring, are struck by the puppeteer's right knee while he manipulates the puppets. Also spelled *pemintit*. (Sweeney RAMAYANA 59, Yub in Osman TRADITIONAL 101)

pemeting kelir (Malaysian)   Five-inch bamboo sticks that secure the Malaysian shadow theatre screen to the banana log stage. (Yub in Osman TRADITIONAL 96)

pemiat (Malaysian)   A slapstick, made of seven pieces of split bamboo, used in *ma'yong*. (Sheppard KITE ix)

pemintit (Malaysian)   See: *pemetek*.

pemungkah (Indonesian)   The opening music of a Balinese shadow play. Also called *gineman wayang*. See also: *talu*. (McPhee MUSIC 202)

penamprat (Indonesian)   See: *pengempat*.

penasar (Indonesian)   1. A generic term for clown-servants in Balinese theatre. (McPhee in Belo TRADITIONAL 155) Also called *parekan* by Holt in ART 128. 2. The haughty clown-attendant to the hero in Balinese dance plays. He assumes the role of a 'second minister,' and interprets into colloquial Balinese the archaic language spoken by his ruler. See also: *kartala*, *punakawan*. (de Zoete/Spies DANCE 35–37)

penché (French)   See: *baisse*.

pencilled date   An unconfirmed booking for a touring company.

pendya (Marathi)   In *tamasha*, the friend and confidant of a hero.

peng, p'eng (Chinese)   See: *goulan*.

pengalang (Indonesian)   A self-introduction by a character in a Balinese shadow play. (Moerdowo BALINESE II 122)

pengamprat (Indonesian)   See: *pengempat*.

pengempat (Indonesian)   A parade of masks, usually four, that opens a *topeng* performance. Also called *penglembar*, *penamprat*, *pengamprat*. (de Zoete/Spies DANCE 185)

penggantung kelir (Malaysian)   Literally: screen hanger. A rod across the top of a shadow theatre stage (*panggung*) from which the white cotton screen (*kelir*) hangs. (Yub in Osman TRADITIONAL 96) *pengipuk* (Indonesian)   A love scene in Balinese *gambuh*.

penglembar (Indonesian)   See: *pengempat*.

penglipur lara (Malaysian)   A generic term for story-tellers and storytelling. Sweeney identifies five major storytelling genres according to the name of their most popular hero: *tarik selampit*, *selampit* or *awang selampit*, *awang batil* or *awang belanga*, *jubang*, and *kaba*. Stories are sung or chanted, and some are accompanied by drums, a spike-fiddle, or a brass bowl (*batil*). (Sweeney in Malm/Sweeney STUDIES 52–53)

peng peng (Chinese)   1. See: *errenzhuan*. 2. See: *pingju*.

peng peng hsi (Chinese)   See: *pingju*.

penguin   Informally, a man in a tail coat, or less frequently, in a tuxedo or other formal dress.

penjepenging (Indonesian)   The techniques of holding a puppet for manipulation in Javanese shadow theatre. Long describes grips according to puppet size in JAVANESE 24–30. (Brandon THRONES 63)

penny   To throw pennies at a performer.

penny gaff, penny theatre   A 19th C London neighborhood theatre, usually illegal and operating on a subscription basis; often a fit-up (portable) theatre. The usual charge was a penny or twopence. Also called a dukey.

penny gallery   In an Elizabethan theatre, the upper of two galleries for spectators. Since a patron paid one penny at the main entrance and another to enter the top gallery, the area was also called the two-penny gallery. (Bowman/ Ball THEATRE)

penny plain or twopence coloured   In Britain, toy theatre scenes in black and white or color, popular in the 19th C.

penny stinkards   In Elizabethan times, groundlings: theatre patrons standing in the pit in a public playhouse. They paid a penny for admission. (Weiner Review 237)

penny theatre   See: penny gaff.

pen se (Chinese)   See: *bense*.

pensionnaire (French)   In the 17th C and later, a salaried, as opposed to sharing, member of the Comédie Française. (Brockett HISTORY 270)

penunjuk patung (Malaysian)   Assistants who sit beside the puppeteer (*dalang*), one on the left and one on the right, and hand him puppets during a shadow puppet performance. (Yub in Osman TRADITIONAL 100)

Pepper's ghost   An apparition effect achieved by reflecting the image of an actor onto the stage. Named for its 19th C English popularizer, John Henry Pepper. Originally called an aetheroscope. (Wilmeth LANGUAGE)

peran (Malaysian)   Literally: clown. A clown in *ma'yong* or the shadow theatre. *Peran tua* (old clown) is the role of a sacred character. (Yousof "Kelantan" 94–95, Sheppard TAMAN 64)

perang (Indonesian)   Literally: battle. A battle scene in a Javanese or Sundanese *wayang* play. Long describes specific fighting movements in JAVANESE 80–109 and gives 32 battle scenarios with fighting movements by puppet type in Appendix A.

perang ageng (Indonesian)   See: *perang amuk-amukan*.

perang ampyak (Indonesian)   The road-clearing scene in a Javanese shadow play, in which a marching army (*ampyak*) puppet clears away a forest, represented by the *kayon* puppet. See also: *prampogan*. (Brandon THRONES 22)

perang amuk-amukan (Indonesian)   Literally: running-amok battle. The final battle scene in a Javanese shadow play. Also called *perang ageng* (great battle). (Brandon THRONES 27)

perang barubuh (Indonesian)   Literally: concluding battle. The final battle scene in a Sundanese *wayang golek* play. (Foley "Sundanese" 114)

perang begal (Indonesian)   See: *perang kembang*.

perang gagal (Indonesian)   Literally: inconclusive battle. The first battle scene in a Javanese or Sundanese *wayang* play, occurring in part one (*patet nem*). An example is in *The Death of Karna* in Brandon THRONES 293–296. (Foley "Sundanese" 113, Holt ART 137)

perang kembang (Indonesian)   Literally: flower battle. A major battle scene, in part two (*patet sanga*) of a Javanese *wayang* play, in which a young knight kills three or four forest ogres. So named because of the beauty and grace of the hero's movements. Also called *perang begal* (battle with thieves) and *perang tuding* (arm-rod battle) because the rods of the hero are used as weapons in attacking the enemy. (Long JAVANESE 61–62) *Adegan perang kembang* is the scene in which the battle occurs. (Brandon THRONES 25–26)

perang lakon (Indonesian)   Literally: battle of the play. The major battle in a Javanese *wayang* play, in which the chief antagonist is killed. (Holt ART 138)

perang sampak (Indonesian)   A battle (*perang*) in a *wayang* play that is accompanied by the rapid melody *sampak*. It is a "subsidiary battle," following a major battle (*perang lakon*). (Holt ART 138) *Perang sampak sanga* is the major battle in part two (*patet sanga*). *Perang sampak manyura* (or *manjura*) occurs early in part three (*patet manyura*). Examples are in *The Death of Karna* in Brandon THRONES 320–329, 348–355.

perang tuding (Indonesian)   See: *perang kembang*.

peran hutan (Malaysian)   Literally: forest clown. The clown servants named Endeng and Epong who enter a forest at the beginning of a shadow play and engage a fierce tiger in battle. (Sheppard in Osman TRADITIONAL 31–32)

percentage basis   A financial arrangement which pays the theatre owner a percentage of the profits instead of a stipulated theatre rental fee.

perch   1. In Britain, a platform in the right or left wing (or both), just offstage of the proscenium arch, upstage of the house curtain, and well off the floor. The perch is used for spotlighting the downstage portions of the acting area; the term and the practice go back to the limelight era. Hence, perch lime and perch spot, now often shortened to perch. Some theatres had two perches on each side, an upper and a lower. The term is likely to be used for the position whether or not the platform is present. U.S. tormentor spot or torm spot are analogous. (Bentham ART, Rae/Southern INTERNATIONAL, Baker THEATRECRAFT) 2. The uppermost gallery. 3. A seat in the uppermost gallery. 4. See: control.

peretitala (Indonesian)   A fixed descriptive passage, sung to *gamelan* accompaniment in the Balinese shadow play. See also: *janturan*. (McPhee in Belo TRADITIONAL 154)

perezhivanie (Russian)   Literally: experience, feeling. Konstantin Stanislavsky's term for the authentic emotion experienced by a performer. (Slonim RUSSIAN 171)

(the) perfesh   The acting profession.

perform   To act, dance, sing, etc.; to take part in a theatrical performance. (Bowman/Ball THEATRE)

performance   1. A showing of a dramatic, dance, or musical entertainment. 2. A performer's execution of his or her acting assignment. (Bowman/Ball THEATRE)

performance theory   An hypothesis, such as Brecht's epic theatre theory, concerned with theatrical performance as well as playwriting.

performer   Any person appearing in any type of show. (Carrington THEATRICANA)

performing arts   Those arts, such as theatre, dance, and music, that result in a performance.

periacti (Latin Roman)   A variant of *periaktoi* (Greek). (Allen ANTIQUITIES 110, Sandys COMPANION 521)

periaktoi (Greek)   Literally: turning on a center or pivot. Prisms used to indicate a change of scene and to bring in certain characters. The primary sources are Pollux and Vitruvius. The prisms were three-sided (Vitruvius, 1st C BC) and fastened to doors right and left of the center door (Pollux, 2nd C AD). Both wrote of the prisms as able to revolve, and noted that each face was decorated differently. Vitruvius spoke of their use to accompany the entrance of gods, while Pollux specified sea gods and whatever was too heavy for the *mechane* (hoisting device). Vitruvius said each use was accompanied by thunder. Pollux reported that a turn in the right *periaktos* changed the scene locally, while the changing of both prisms changed the location to another area altogether. Those remarks, neither entirely clear nor completely consistent, have led to various interpretations. A common view is that the prisms were farther offstage than the two side doors, perhaps attached to the *paraskenia* (wings) of the *skene* (scene building). 5th C BC use of the prisms has been suggested, mainly because they are thought so simple, but it is a near certainty that they date no earlier than the later 4th C BC: no 5th C play requires them, and no early writer refers to them. In dealing with the evidence, which includes the plays and the remains of theatres, it should be noted that Pollux wrote two centuries after Vitruvius, that Pollux' work is known only from notes dating seven centuries after he wrote, and that the remarks on theatre in both writers are tiny portions of works devoted almost entirely to other matters. Singular *periaktos*. Also spelled *periacti* (Latin-Roman), singular *periactus*. See also: *katablemata*. (Arnott SCENIC 88–89; Pickard-Cambridge DIONYSUS 126–127; Oxford CLASSICAL 853, 1130)

periochi (Latin)   In 16th-18th C Jesuit drama, plot synopses given to spectators unfamiliar with the Latin used by the performers. (Schnitzler "Jesuit" 285)

period   Said of a play or production representing a past age. Hence, period acting, period play, period costume, period movement. (Bowman/Ball THEATRE)

period silhouette   The characteristic profile or outline of the costume of a particular period.

peripeteia (Greek)   In Aristotle's *Poetics*, a reversal in the dramatic situation. The term is often rendered in English as change of fortune, reversal of fortune, or simply reversal. A characteristic of plot, the change is often from good to bad, as in *Oedipus the King*, but Aristotle does not exclude a change from bad to good. U.S. English also uses peripeteia, peripetia, and peripety. (Vaughn DRAMA, Else ARISTOTLE'S 342–349, Lucas ARISTOTLE 291–297)

peripetia, peripety   See: *peripeteia*.

peripheral   1. In dance, body parts farthest from the upper and lower trunk: head, lower legs and feet, lower arms and hands. (Dell PRIMER 78) 2. Movement that occurs in the outer reaches of the kinesphere.

peripheral actor   A performer who develops his or her character from the outside. (Tynan "Olivier" 89)

permanent company   A troupe of players, whether resident or touring, which remains intact, as opposed to a group assembled for only one production. Hence, permanent stock company. (Bowman/Ball THEATRE)

permanent control   A stage lighting arrangement in which all circuits (typically footlights, borderlights, and floor pockets) are permanently connected to a control board. Essentially obsolete, such arrangements are still found in some older theatres. Derivative terms include permanent control system, permanent control switchboard, and permanent-control method. (Sellman/Lessley ESSENTIALS 117)

permanent cyclorama See: cyclorama, *Kuppelhorizont*.

permanent footlights Footlights fixed in position, usually in a footlight trough or trap.

permanent set See: unit set.

permissive direction A suggestion by a playwright or a director which allows a performer alternatives, including the right not to follow the suggestion.

per orchestram (Latin Roman) In the orchestra. (Flickinger GREEK 77)

peros See: startups.

perse A fashionable 18th-19th C painted fabric, possibly Persian in origin. (Boucher FASHION)

persona (Latin Roman) 1. A theatrical mask. 2. Especially in Terence, the character represented by a mask. The word may have come from Phersu, a masked figure in at least two Etruscan paintings. Plural *personae*. (Duckworth NATURE 92–94; Beare ROMAN 22, 192–195)

persona delusoris (Latin) A mime, an actor.

personae (Latin) See: *dramatis personae*.

personae Oscae (Latin Roman) Literally: Oscan masks, thence, Oscan characters. The stock characters of the Atellan plays. See also: *fabula Atellana*. (Duckworth NATURE 11–12)

personaje (Spanish) A character in a play. But in the 15th C, *juegos* (games) *y personajes* probably meant figures or actors in a tableau or simple disguising. (Shergold SPANISH)

personal app Personal appearance.

personales (Philippine) A cast of characters in a *zarzuela*. (Fernández ILO-ILO 124)

personal house seat See: house seats.

personality actor A performer who specializes in playing on his or her charm or magnetism. (Purdom PRODUCING)

personality boy A master of ceremonies.

personality puppet A 20th C puppet modeled after a real person, such as Charlie Chaplin, Fred Astaire, Ginger Rogers, etc. (Philpott DICTIONARY)

personal prop A property such as a pipe, eye glasses, or cane, often used by a performer to help establish character. See also: character prop.

personate To imitate, impersonate. Hence, personation, personator. (Bowman/Ball THEATRE)

personatus (Latin Roman) Literally: masked. Beare suggests the term may have meant masked actor. (Beare ROMAN 193)

personify   To characterize or to embody an abstract characteristic. Hence, personification. Examples are most of the characters in *Everyman*: Good Deeds, Knowledge, Fellowship, etc. (Bowman/Ball THEATRE)

perspective   1. In scene painting, the depiction of three dimensionality on a flat surface. 2. A view of such painting. 3. In Renaissance theatres and later, the backscene or back shutters on which a perspective scene was painted. (Vasari in Nagler SOURCES 72, Bowman/Ball THEATRE, Southern CHANGEABLE 156)

perspective glass   See: quizzing glass.

perspective lantern   A term used by Joseph Furttenbach for a Renaissance lighting instrument resembling a floodlight with sides, bottom, and top angled out from the light source. Furttenbach's 17th C standing light box is identical except that it has no top. (Furttenbach in Hewitt RENAISSANCE 237)

perspective setting   In Renaissance and later theatres, a setting, mainly architectural, painted according to the optical laws of diminution, foreshortening, and chiaroscuro. (Gorelik NEW)

pescante (Spanish)   1. A flying rig for sudden appearances or disappearances of characters. 2. A trap door.

pesinden (Indonesian)   A female singer in a Javanese *gamelan* ensemble that accompanies traditional theatre performances. (Brandon THRONES 37) In Sundanese, *pasinden*. (Foley "Sundanese" 86–87)

petaminarii (Latin Roman)   See: *petauristae*.

petasos (Greek)   1. In stage costuming, a wide-brimmed hat (the literal meaning). The wearers included the leader of a Greek satyr chorus and certain characters in Roman comedy. In the U.S., also called petasos or petasus. 2. An awning spread across the tops of some Roman theatres and amphitheatres. Also called in Latin a *velum* or *velarium*. (Bieber HISTORY 15, 154, 179)

petauristae (Latin Roman)   Tumblers, acrobats. These were among the performers attached to the mime. From *petaurum*, an acrobat's springboard, perhaps a trapeze. Also called *cernui* or *petaminarii*. (Nicoll MASKS 85, Chambers MEDIAEVAL I 7)

pet-en-l'air (French)   See: *caraco*.

petit draps (French)   See: *braies*.

petite batterie (French)   See: *batterie*.

petite logette (French)   In the 19th C, a control room for lighting; a light booth. (Moynet FRENCH 84)

petite pièce (French)   A late 18th C marionette show. (Speaight PUPPET 130)

petite théâtre (French)   In the 19th C, a room arranged for rehearsals, fitted up like a small theatre. (Moynet FRENCH 119) *petit jeté* (French)   In ballet, a small leap from one leg to the other in which the working leg appears to be thrown.

petits bonshommes (French)   18th C wrist frills worn with a gown à la Française. (Boucher FASHION)

petits-maîtres (French)   Young dandies in French theatres of the 18th C who liked to sit on stage at performances. (Nagler SOURCES 324)

petrushechnik (Russian)   A Russian puppeteer in the 18th and 19th C. Like some puppeteers in other countries, he spoke his mind on issues of the day. (Yershov SOVIET 10)

petrushka (Russian)   1. A kind of Punch and Judy puppet entertainment popular in the 18th and 19th C in Russia. 2. The name of the hero (Punch) of many of the comic and tragicomic plots in such shows. (Warner RUSSIAN 109–120)

petticoat breeches   17th C wide, flowing, loose upper stocks, heavily ornamented. Also called Rhinegrave breeches. (Boucher FASHION, Wilcox DICTIONARY)

petticoat interest   The female romantic element in a play.

petticôte (French)   A 15th C man's knee-length, wide-shouldered coat with a large fur collar and other fur trim. (Chalmers CLOTHES 141)

pettige (Kannada)   In *yaksagana*, a troupe member who carries and cares for cooking utensils, ornaments, food, the curtain, oil lamps, costumes, the harmonium, and firewood. (Ashton/Christie YAKSAGANA 53, 89, 93, 106)

peturan dalang (Malaysian)   Literally: bringing down the puppeteer. A ritual to bestow on a novice puppeteer (*dalang*) the capacity to learn from his teacher. The novice is brought into trance by his master to establish channels for future communication. (Sweeney RAMAYANA 43)

Pevear hood, Pevear tormentor hood   See: tormentor hood.

Pfifferling (German)   A small mushroom-shaped candle holder used in lighting devices described by Joseph Furttenbach in the 17th C. (Furttenbach in Hewitt RENAISSANCE 237–238)

phak samtra (Thai)   An old form of invocation, directed to the spirits of King Dasaratha and Rama, and chanted before a *nang yai* performance. (Dhaninivat NANG 9)

phalagama (Sanskrit)   In classical Indian dramaturgy, the attainment of the hero's desire, the last of five stages in the development of dramatic action (*avastha*) of a play. (Keith SANSKRIT 298)

phallika (Greek)   Phallic songs. The term is from Aristotle. (Pickard-Cambridge DITHYRAMB 157, 160)

phallophori (Greek), **phallophore**   See: *phallophoroi.*

phallophoroi (Greek)   Literally: phallus-wearers. In early Dionysian revels, phallus-wearing celebrants apparently with soot-covered faces and heads crowned with ivy and violets. Thus presumably disguised, even though not masked, the revelers were able to mock some of the well-known citizenry. The *phallophoroi* are thought to have been connected with early mimes and perhaps with the *parabasis* of Old Comedy. Singular *phallophoros*. In Latin, *phallophori* (singular *phallophorus*); in English, phallophore and attributive phallophoric. See also: *kaunakai*. (Pickard-Cambridge DITHYRAMB 76, 137–146, 151; 1927 Pickard-Cambridge DITHYRAMB 234; Nicoll MASKS 26–27; Duchartre ITALIAN 124, 135; Stuart DRAMATIC 106)

Phantasiestück (German)   A grotesque play. Sometimes spelled *Fantasiestück*.

phantom load   In circuits with resistance dimmers, the addition of resistance which serves no purpose other than to enable an onstage lamp to be dimmed to blackout; also, the resistance so used. A resistance dimmer must be loaded to near its capacity if it is to dim its load to blackout; such an extra "phantom" load is usually a light offstage or backstage that will not shine onstage. Heater coils can serve the same purpose. Also called a ghost load or loader. (Bellman LIGHTING 171, Wehlburg GLOSSARY, Cornberg/Gebauer CREW 172)

phleng lukthung (Thai)   Literally: field song. A popular song in a variety show (*luk thung*).

phlyakes (Greek)   1. Especially from the late 4th C BC, the name given the performers of rude mimes and farces in southern Italy, i.e., in the Greek portions of Italy. 2. From about the same time or slightly later, the plays so performed. The *phlyakes* parodied tragedy in plays mocking poets and great figures of the past, and in farces dealing with petty thievery, intrigue, and other subjects taken from daily life. Heracles was a favorite figure of the *phlyakes* farces. See also: *hilarotragodia*, which was at least a form of *phlyakes*; Liddell/Scott LEXICON says the two are synonymous. The source and meaning of the word are still uncertain; one suggestion is gossip, from a Greek word for chatter. Singular *phlyax*. Also called *phlyakes* farce and Italian mime; the latter is a translation of a phrase used by the Greeks to refer to the *phlyakes*. (Bieber HISTORY 129–146; Nicoll MASKS 50–53)

pho (Thai)   See: *phra*.

phonaskikon-organon (Greek)   A special instrument, apparently used in ancient Greece to indicate pitch and time in performances. (Mantzius HISTORY I 195)

phonaskos (Greek)   A professional voice teacher, perhaps serving in ancient Greece as a director of performances. (Mantzius HISTORY I 195)

phone in the act   See: "I think I'll phone in the act."

phony   1. A false beard. 2. A mask. Also called a phony face. 3. A hanger-on, often a monied amateur performer.

phortika (Greek)   Vulgar, tiresome jokes, characteristic of the Doric farces which preceded Old Comedy. Porters' jokes are typical, as with Xanthius in Aristophanes' *Frogs*. From *phortax* (porter), thence *phortikos* (a tiresome fool). (Bieber HISTORY 40, 45, 133)

photo call   Photograph call. A notice for performers and appropriate stage technicians to assemble for the photographing of scenes and characters. (Bowman/Ball THEATRE)

phra (Thai)   A male role in traditional dance theatre. *Phra ek* is the role of a hero, performed by either a male or female dancer in *lakon* performances. (Rutnin "Development" 13, Yupho PRELIMINARY 4) In *likay*, other male roles are *phra rong* (minor male role) and *pho* (father). (Virulrak "Likay" 188)

phran (Thai)   Literally: hunter. The clown character in *lakon jatri*, a hunter who finds Princess Manora in the forest. (Ginsberg in Rutnin SIAMESE 68)

phrase   In dance, a group of sequential movements that make a complete statement.

phruktorion (Greek)   A signal tower or beacon, a staging device mentioned by Pollux without explanation. (Nicoll DEVELOPMENT 22)

Phrygian bonnet   1. An ancient Greek chin-strapped cap or bonnet of leather or felt. 2. A French Revolution red bonnet emblematic of the struggle. Also called a liberty cap or mitra.

phrygium   A white wool cap worn by popes at medieval secular functions. It later evolved into the papal tiara. (Wilcox DICTIONARY)

phuong cheo boi (Vietnamese)   A professional or amateur troupe in the period before formal *hat cheo* troupes came into existence. Also called *cheo san dinh*. (Addiss "Theater" 132)

phuong nha tro (Vietnamese)   The official *hat boi* troupe attached to the imperial court from the 19th C to 1946. (Hauch "Study" 12, 15)

physical action memory   See: emotion memory.

physical actions   In the Stanislavsky system, external means of stimulating the emotional content of a role. (Stanislavsky OTHELLO 152–154)

physical style of acting   See: heroic acting style.

pi (Thai, Lao)   An oboe-like reed instrument (various sizes) used in the classical *pi phat* musical ensemble (Morton TRADITIONAL 80–90, 105) and in *likay*. Also spelled *pee*. (Virulrak "Likay" 168–170).

pianelle   See: pantofle.

piano act   A presentation using puppets and a live pianist (or sometimes a recording). The piano itself is occasionally a puppet. (Philpott DICTIONARY)

piano board   Early in the 20th C, a common portable control board usually containing switches and resistance dimmers. So named because of its resemblance in shape to an upright piano. Also called a piano box (switchboard), piano-case dimmer, piano-board dimmer, piano-box dimmer bank. Sometimes called a touring or road board. Lounsbury has an illustration. (Bowman MODERN, Lounsbury THEATRE 147, Bowman/Ball THEATRE, Wehlburg GLOSSARY)

piano dress   A rehearsal of a musical theatre piece with costumes and technical elements but a piano accompaniment instead of the full orchestra. The concentration is usually upon acting and technical matters rather than music.

piano puppet   See: pedal puppet.

piano wire   Steel wire used for flying an object when such a supporting wire needs to be virtually invisible. Also called music wire, trick wire. (Baker THEATRECRAFT)

piao mu (Chinese)   See: *jiamen*.

piaoyou, p'iao yu (Chinese)   An amateur performer of music-drama (*xiqu*), 18th C to present. Many professional performers began as amateurs, especially before 1949. See also: *keban*. (Mackerras MODERN 75; Mackerras RISE 191, 221; Scott CLASSICAL 59)

piazza della scena (Italian)   Sebastiano Serlio's 1566 term for the area directly in front of the stage. In the 1545 edition of his *Architettura* the term had been *proscenio*. (Serlio in Hewitt RENAISSANCE 22)

piccadilly   A 16th C deep ruff, trimmed with lace. (Chalmers CLOTHES 166)

pic-flesh   See: combo.

pichhvai (Hindi)   The backdrop or back curtain in a *raslila* performance. (Gargi FOLK 121)

pick 'em up and lay 'em down   To dance. (Berrey/Van den Bark SLANG 589)

pickout number   The final act in a burlesque show, when the comic appears with the chorus girls. He selects one of them and they do a number together. (Smith VAUDEVILLIANS 124–125)

picks   Pickaninnies—Black children who sang and danced with a female vaudeville performer at the end of her act, though she was billed as a single. The term is obsolete and offensive. (Laurie VAUDEVILLE 56)

pick up   1. To increase the amount of light, as in "Pick up the down right corner." Hence, a pick-up light. 2. During the travel of a master dimmer, to gather in one or more other dimmers. (Belasco DOOR 58) 3. In acting, to speed up, especially in response to cues. 4. A rope line used to hang or secure objects from above.

pick up a cue   To speak one's line immediately upon the previous speaker's final word.

pick up an audience   In the 19th C, to so absorb an audience that it wishes to break into the action. (Wilmeth LANGUAGE)

pick-up light   See: pick up.

pick-up rehearsal   See: brush-up rehearsal.

pick up the scene   To enliven the action.

picnic   A series of one-night stands that do not pay. (Berrey/Van den Bark SLANG 589)

pictorial dramatization   See: picturization.

pictorialism   Directorial use of the proscenium stage's potential for creating pictures. (Cameron/Gillespie ENJOYMENT)

pictorial scenery   See: picture setting.

picture   1. A grouping of performers to create a dramatic effect, as in a tableau. 2. The general composition of a stage setting as seen from the audience, that is, the stage picture. 3. A projection, such as a slide or film. (Cartmell HANDBOOK)

picture batten   See: picture rail.

picture-ending curtain   A tableau held by performers at the end of an act or play. It is sometimes held throughout the first curtain call.

picture frame hanger and socket   A metal hook and socket for hanging a picture on a stage wall, especially designed to avoid puncturing fabric when flats are stacked. Also called a Clancy or Clancy hook (after the manufacturer), picture hook and eye, or picture hanger.

picture-frame stage, picture stage   A feature of the theatre of realism in which the stage picture is conventionally set within the boundaries of a frame, the latter being provided by the proscenium arch. See also: peep hole. (Krows AMERICA 148)

picture rail   A wooden rail (toggle) fixed to the back of a flat so that a picture, mirror, etc. may be attached to the face of the flat at that level. Also called a picture batten. (Baker THEATRECRAFT)

picture scenery   See: picture setting.

picture setting   1. In the Renaissance, a stage setting showing distant perspective scenes. 2. A setting emphasizing the pictorial, as in Romantic and Symbolist settings. Hence, pictorial scenery, picture scenery. (Gorelik NEW)

picture sheet, picture screen   A drop curtain or motion picture screen upon which images can be projected.

picture stage   See: picture frame stage.

picturization   Directorial creation of stage groupings or pictures to help show character relationships or clarify the action. Sometimes called pictorial dramatization. (Cameron/Gillespie ENJOYMENT)

pie (Spanish)   A cue.

piece 1. A play. 2. A role. 3. A scenic unit, especially one that is three-dimensional. 4. A financial share in a production; hence, to own a piece of a show. (Bowman/Ball THEATRE)

pièce (French) 1. A play. 2. A 19th C play in which high comedy relief counterbalanced intense emotionality. Love was a standard theme. (Hennequin PLAYWRITING 45)

pièce à circonstance (French) A dramatic work on a subject of current interest.

pièce à écriteaux (French) In 18th C French open-air fair theatres, a play in which a canvas roll on a stick was lowered from the flies. On the scroll a couplet was written, together with the name of the person to sing it. An orchestra accompanied the couplet, and performers gestured as the audience joined in the singing. The plays were often political or social satire. (Striker "Protest" 56)

pièce à machine (French) A 17th C play calling for elaborate scenes and machines.

pièce à thèse (French) A dramatic work whose plot serves to make a point: political, religious, philosophical, etc.

pièce bien faite (French) See: well-made play.

pièce de résistance (French) A featured attraction; a principal number on a variety bill.

pièce noire (French) Literally: black play. A pessimistic play, devoid of villainy and persecution, with all characters, in their way, innocent. The guilt lies in the trap in which they are caught. (Clancy "Antigone" 253)

piece of the show Part ownership of a production. (Sobel NEW)

piece of white meat In the early 20th C, an actress. Offensive term. (Berrey/Van den Bark SLANG 571)

pièce rosse (French) See: *comédie rosse*.

pie cut A segment of a revolving stage. Such a stage is made up of several such wedges, bolted together.

pied-à-trois quarts (French) In ballet, a foot position three-fourths of the way to *sur les pointes* (on the toes).

pieds, cinq positions des (French) See: *cinq positions des pieds*.

pie formula See: West Virginia formula.

pie in the face A blackout routine in burlesque in which one performer throws a pie (or what looks like a pie) in another performer's face. (Wilmeth LANGUAGE)

pien tan (Chinese) See: *biandan*.

pien wen (Chinese) See: *bianwen*.

pierced scene See: open scene.

pierrot show   In Britain, a light entertainment consisting of songs, dances, and comic turns, usually performed by touring groups of actors (pierrots) and actresses (pierettes); hence, pierrot troupe. The performers usually followed the *commedia dell' arte* tradition of white clothes and makeup for the pierrot character. Popular in the late 19th and early 20th C. (Bowman/Ball THEATRE)

pie-throwing humor   See: knockabout.

pig   In the early 20th C, a chorus girl. Offensive term. (Berrey/Van den Bark SLANG 573)

pigache   A 12th C *poulaine* (French). (Boucher FASHION)

pigeon hole   1. In 18th C theatres and later, a small seating area between the slips and the stage at the top gallery level. Probably named for its alcove shape. (Avery LONDON lix, Leacroft DEVELOPMENT 179) 2. A seat in the top gallery.

pigeon roost   The uppermost gallery.

pigeon's wings   18th C loosely-coiled puffs over the ears of a man's powdered wig. (Wilcox DICTIONARY)

pigeonwing   In dancing, a fancy step in which the dancer jumps and strikes the legs together. (Berrey/Van den Bark SLANG 588)

pigtail, pigtails   In the U.S.: 1. The short length of cable or covered wire which protrudes from a lighting instrument. Also called a lead; in Britain, tail. 2. Any short piece of hanging or protruding cable, as from a batten or connector strip. Called a tail in Britain if the cable is heat-resisting. 3. A short piece of cable. A pigtail normally ends in a connector, but the term is likely to be used whether a connector is present or not. (Wehlburg GLOSSARY, Bowman MODERN, Rae/Southern INTERNATIONAL, Bentham ART)

pihuang, p'i huang (Chinese)   1. A musical system (*shengqiang xitong*) characterized by the use of *banqiangti* musical structure, the *jinghu* two-stringed spike fiddle, and the *ban* clapper. Its name comes from its two principal modes (*diaoshi*), *xipi* and *erhuang*. It developed in the 18th-early 19th C out of the mutual influence of a number of regional forms of music-drama (*xiqu*), including *hanju* and *huiju*. Today the major form which features *pihuang* music is Beijing opera (*jingju*); many other forms, such as *hanju*, also use music from this system. (Mackerras MODERN 19–20, Scott TRADITIONAL I 9–10) 2. See: *jingju*.

pilarii (Latin Roman)   See: *prestigiatores*.

pile-on   In control board design, an arrangement in which two or more controllers can feed voltage into a single dimmer at the same time. The controller at the higher voltage dominates; any lower setting has no effect on the light output. (Bellman LIGHTING 226–229, fig. 10–3; Wehlburg GLOSSARY)

pill   A large and difficult role (to swallow).

pillar stand   In the late 19th C in Britain, a light stand. (Rees GAS 205)

pilot   A director.

pilot board   A control board which operates an assembly of remotely-controlled electromagnetic switches. See also: contactor. (Fuchs LIGHTING 334–335)

pilot jet   A gas jet serving as a pilot light, as in some late 19th C footlights and borderlights. (Rees GAS 124–125)

pilot light   1. A small light which indicates whether a particular circuit is on or off. Such lights, often colored, are usually on control boards. 2. A naked lamp near center stage when the theatre is otherwise dark. This may be either on a light stand or hanging from the flies. Also called a ghost light. 3. A small working light which illuminates the face of a switchboard. 4. In gas lighting, a small burner permanently lit. These were used especially in footlights and borderlights so that they could be lighted from a central control point. For any of these meanings, one sometimes finds pilot or pilot lamp. (Bowman/Ball THEATRE, Bellman SCENE, Baker THEATRECRAFT, Fay GLOSSARY)

pilots   See: stage pilots.

pin   1. A metal or wood pin—a belaying pin to which rope lines from the gridiron are tied on the pin rail. 2. A pin holding together the two blades of a loose-pin backflap; a pin wire is a piece of wire used in the same way.

pinakes (Greek)   Literally: boards, planks. Especially from the early 3rd C BC, painted panels which provided a scenic background. The panels were used mainly between the columns of the *proskenion* (scenic facade of a theatre) but also, probably later, in the *thyromata* (openings) of the upper story of the *skene* (scene building). Some think they were sometimes used on the faces of the *periaktoi* (scenic prisms). While the materials and construction of the pinakes no doubt varied over time, they are thought to have been linen or wood early, and probably cloth-covered wood frames later. Singular *pinax*, for one meaning of which U.S. English accepts 'picture, especially one painted on a wooden tablet.' Sometimes called *scaena ductilis* (Latin), occasionally coulisse, both singular. (Pickard-Cambridge DIONYSUS 184–189, 208, 217–218, fig. 76; Bieber HISTORY 111, 115–116, 122–124, figs. 423–425)

pin-and-rail system   A hemp system (q.v.). (Parker/Smith DESIGN 294–296)

pinax (Greek)   See: *pinakes*.

pinch a call   To take up the curtain for a curtain call despite languid applause. See also: steal a bow. (Baker THEATRECRAFT)

pin connector   An older stage connector consisting of two insulating blocks, one with a pair of small split brass cylinders (pins), and the other with brass sleeves for the pins. (Modern versions have a third [grounding] pin.) The term is occasionally limited to the connector with the pins. Also called a pin plug (connector), slip connector, connector, or sometimes (stage) (cable) connector. (Wehlburg GLOSSARY, Bellman SCENE, Cornberg/Gebauer CREW 272–273)

ping   In acting, to speak softly, with little emphasis. (Bowman/Ball THEATRE)

p'ing chiang (Chinese)   See: *pingjiang*.

p'ing ch'iang pang tzu hsi (Chinese)   See: *pingju*.

p'ing chü (Chinese)   1. Literally: Beiping drama. See: *jingju*. 2. Literally: commentary drama. See: *pingju*.

p'ing hsi (Chinese)   See: *pingju*.

pinghua, p'ing hua (Chinese)   Literally: comment talk. A type of storytelling (*quyi*), usually presented by a single performer, which arose c. 7th C; today forms exist in a number of regions including Sichuan and Hubei Provinces, and parts of Jiangsu Province. Most forms are spoken, with little or no singing, in local dialect. The performer is usually seated behind a table, and strikes it with a block of wood at high points in the story. In some areas, called *pingshu* or *p'ing shu*, literally "comment book." (Howard CONTEMPORARY 30, Scott LITERATURE 62–63)

pingjiang, p'ing chiang (Chinese)   A form of music-drama (*xiqu*) popular in northeastern Fujian Province in the 19th C. It was originally a small-scale folk theatre form (*xiaoxi*) performed after harvests by itinerant troupes. It later adopted puppet-theatre scripts and finally developed its own scripts concerned with local stories. In the 20th C, *pingjiang* was absorbed by the developing *minju* drama. (Dolby HISTORY 224–225)

pingju, p'ing chü (Chinese)   1. Literally: commentary drama. A form of music-drama (*xiqu*) popular in Beijing, Tianjin, and throughout northern and northeastern China which originated in the *lianhualao* storytelling (*quyi*) form of eastern Hebei Province. It was influenced in the 19th C by Beijing opera (*jingju*), Hebei *bangzi*, and shadow theatre, and in the 1920s and 1930s by spoken drama (*huaju*). It uses *banqiangti* musical structure and features the *banhu* spike fiddle. In the past, also called *pingqiang bangzixi* or *p'ing ch'iang pang tzu hsi*, literally "level-tune clapper theatre," abbreviated *pingxi* or *p'ing hsi*; and *bengbengxi* or *peng peng hsi*, literally "bouncing theatre," abbreviated *bengbeng* or *peng peng*. (Halson PEKING 67–68, Howard CONTEMPORARY 16) 2. Literally: Beiping drama. See: *jingju*.

pingqiang bangzixi (Chinese)   See: *pingju*.

pingshu, p'ing shu (Chinese)   See: *pinghua*.

pingxi (Chinese)   See: *pingju*.

pin hinge   See: backflap.

pin matrix   See: matrix interconnection panel.

pinner   1. A 17th-18th C small apron pinned to the front of a gown, worn by ladies-in-waiting. 2. A 19th C parlormaid's apron. 3. An old term for a child's apron. 4. A sheer white lace-trimmed cap of the 17th-18th C, with two streamers in back. Also called a flandan. (Wilcox DICTIONARY) *pinpattu* (Tamil)   From *pin*, back; *pattu*, song. Musical accompaniment in *therukoothu* folk theatre in Tamil Nadu, south India. (Gargi FOLK 133)

pinpeat (Khmer)   The traditional musical ensemble that accompanies all classical Cambodian dance, *nang sbek*, and monastery ceremonies. Consists primarily of xylophones, gongs, and drums. See also: *pi phat*. (Brunet in Osman TRADITIONAL 216, Brandon SOUTHEAST 127)

pin plug, pin plug connector   See: pin connector.

pinpoint   1. To narrow a beam of light with an iris diaphragm. 2. To use such a beam.

pinrail, fly rail   A rail on a gallery, or at stage level, or on a wall, usually holding two rows of belaying pins or cleats, the upper being called the fly or working rail and the lower the tie-off or trim rail, to which flying lines are fastened. Some theatres have only one row, some have three. (Bowman/Ball THEATRE)

pin spot   1. A very narrow beam of light. 2. A spotlight which produces such a beam. 3. Sometimes as a verb: to light an actor or an area with a very narrow beam of light. 'Pin spot' suggests a narrower beam than 'head spot,' which is, however, more specific. Both terms were in use at least by the 1930s, but pin spot has for some years been used much more frequently than head spot, which is really an application of the general term. (Bowman MODERN, Wehlburg GLOSSARY, Carrington THEATRICANA)

pin wire   See: pin.

pipa, p'i p'a (Chinese)   A four-stringed, pear-shaped, fretted lute which is plucked with the fingers. It is an important instrument in the melodic orchestra (*wenchang*) in Beijing opera (*jingju*) and many other forms of music-drama (*xiqu*), and is also featured in many forms of storytelling (*quyi*). (Liu SIX 15, Mackerras PERFORMING 154, Scott CLASSICAL 45–46)

pipe   1. Short for pipe batten. A batten flown above the stage, to which can be attached lighting instruments, scenic units, draperies, etc. 2. Sometimes, a border—in the sense of a borderlight.

pipe arm   See: hanger.

pipe batten   In the U.S., a long pipe—about as long as the proscenium is wide—usually hung above the stage parallel to the proscenium wall. Scenery, lights, or anything else may hang from pipes, but their use for lights is frequent in the modern theatre. The first pipe is nearest the proscenium, the second pipe a few feet upstage of the first, and so on. Backstage, they are often called simply pipes, less often battens; but in Britain the latter and barrel or bar are the usual terms. A pipe used for lighting is sometimes called a light pipe, the British analogues being spot bar or spot batten, sometimes suspension barrel. (Baker THEATRECRAFT 264, Bowman MODERN)

pipe clamp   Any device used to fasten a lighting instrument to a batten or pipe. In Britain, barrel clamp, barrel clip, barrel grip, or hanging clip.

pipes   Said of a singer's vocal apparatus, especially of a vocalist with a powerful voice.

pipe stand   See: light stand.

pi phat (Thai)   Literally: music led by the *pi*. The musical ensemble that accompanies most types of classical theatre: *khon*, *nang yai*, and *lakon*. It consists of ten to fifteen instruments of five types: wooden xylophones (*ranad*), tuned bronze bowls (*gong*), hand drum (*tapone*), stick drums (*klong thad*), and oboe (*pi nai*), plus small metal percussion instruments (for example, *ching*). See also: *pinpeat*. Also spelled *piphat*. (Duriyanga THAI 13–36, Morton TRADITIONAL 105, Virulrak "Likay" 168–170)

pi phat khruang ha (Thai)   Literally: five-instrument *pi phat*. The basic classical theatre musical grouping, consisting of five types of instruments, plus a *ching* (pair of small cymbals). Abbreviated *khruang ha*. (Morton TRADITIONAL 105, Virulrak "Likay" 167)

pi phat likay (Thai)   Literally: *likay* musical ensemble. The small musical ensemble that accompanies a *likay* performance. It consists of one each of the five types of *pi phat* instruments, plus other instruments used in *likay*. (Virulrak "Likay" 167–170)

piqué (French)   In ballet, a direct stepping onto the toes of one foot without bending the knee; the other foot is raised in the air. (Grant TECHNICAL, Wilson BALLET)

piracy   1. Unauthorized publication or production of a play. Hence, to pirate, pirated edition, etc. 2. Plagiarism.

p'iri (Korean)   A bamboo, double reed musical instrument played for masked dance plays. See: *samhyon yukkak*. (Chang KOREAN 24, Cho "Hwanghae" 42)

pirouette, *pirouette* (French)   In ballet, a complete turn of the body on the toes or the ball of the foot, with the other foot between the ankle and the knee. (Wilson BALLET, Grant TECHNICAL)

pirutu (Quechua)   A pre-Colombian flute made of bone and used to accompany love songs and elegies in Incan drama. See also: *chayna*. (Karnis "Pre-Columbian" 42)

pit   1. In an Elizabethan public theatre, the audience area partly surrounding the platform stage, where playgoers could stand and watch the performance. 2. In Restoration theatres and later, the area in front of the stage, outfitted at first with backless benches. The area is now called the orchestra in U.S. theatres, the stalls in British theatres. 3. In Britain, and formerly in the U.S., an unreserved bench seating area at the back of the stalls or orchestra seating area. 4. The occupants of the pit.

pit and boxes laid together   See: pit railed into boxes.

pitch   1. The site where a showman's puppetry booth is put up. (Philpott DICTIONARY) 2. The highness or lowness of a sound, especially vocal sound in acting or singing. 3. To raise or lower the voice according to the musical scale. 4. A theatrical performance. 5. Ballyhoo.

pit circle   In Britain, a seating area above the pit in one of the galleries.

pit doorkeeper   In 18th C theatres and later, an employee who stood at the door to the pit and admitted playgoers to that seating area. (Stone LONDON 817)

pit entrance   In Britain, a door leading to the pit standing or seating area in a theatre.

pithamarda (Sanskrit)   In classical Indian drama, the role of a companion to the hero. (Keith SANSKRIT 308, 351)

pithamardika (Sanskrit)   In classical Indian drama, the role of a confidante to the heroine. (Keith SANSKRIT 308)

pit lift   See: forestage elevator.

pit man   A prompter stationed in the orchestra pit.

pitmen   Musicians in the orchestra pit of a theatre. (Wilmeth LANGUAGE)

pito (Spanish)   See: swazzle.

pit office keeper   In 18th C theatres and later, an employee who kept the accounts for the pit. (Stone LONDON 817)

pit orchestra   A theatre band playing in the orchestra pit (as opposed to on stage or in the wings).

pit passage   In Restoration theatres and later, a long passageway beneath the first tier of boxes, leading into the pit seating area. (Hogan LONDON xxiii)

pit public   Spectators in the pit.

pit railed into boxes   A practice in 18th C theatres on some benefit nights of railing off some benches in the pit (or all of them) and charging box prices. Also referred to as: throw boxes and pit together, pit and boxes laid together, part of the pit laid into boxes, railed, railing in. (Avery LONDON xlvi)

pit stall   In Britain, a seat in the front rows of the orchestra. (Bowman/Ball THEATRE)

pittites, pitites   Audience members who sat or stood in the pit in old theatres in Britain.

pity and fear   According to Aristotle, the two emotions aroused and then purged by tragedy. As a scientist, Aristotle was concerned with the primacy of objectivity over emotion and favored this purgation, which supposedly made the audience more rational, less emotional, and more in control of their actions. Pity is more than pathos and includes compassion and grief; fear is more than fright and includes awe and wonder. Not all translators use the terms pity and fear, but these are perhaps the most common. See also: *katharsis*. (Hatlen ORIENTATION)

pivetta   See: swazzle.

pivot jack   A support for a stage door or gate as it swings. (Carrington THEATRICANA)

pivot point   1. The center point of the curtain line. 2. The center around which a revolving stage rotates. 3. The fixed point of a jackknife stage.

piyingxi, p'i ying hsi (Chinese)   Literally: leather shadow plays, leather shadow theatre. A generic term for shadow theatre. The best known Chinese shadow puppets are silhouette cut outs with articulated arms, legs, and hands. They are translucent, and cast colored shadows on the screen. The heads are detachable, and may therefore be used with a variety of costumes. Performances include singing and musical accompaniment in the style of music-drama (*xiqu*). Abbreviated *yingxi* or *ying hsi*. See also: *kuileixi*. (Foreign FOLK 14–16; Liu INTRODUCTION 164–165; Obraztsov CHINESE 28–29, 44; Dolby HISTORY 33; Scott LITERATURE 57–58)

pizzicato   A failure. (Berrey/Van den Bark SLANG 585)

place   1. In Elizabethan public theatres, the platform stage. The term probably derived from the medieval *platea* (Latin)—an unlocalized acting area. 2. A sitting space in a Restoration theatre and later. The seat, except in the royal box, was probably a space on a backless bench—hence the term place instead of seat. Places, especially in the boxes, could be booked in advance, but they had to be occupied from the moment the doors were opened, or they would not be held. Servants were sent to the theatre to occupy the places until their masters or mistresses arrived. Hence, place keeper. (Hogan LONDON xxx–xxxii)

place (French)   1. In medieval productions, a generalized acting area. See also: *platea*. 2. The space reserved for a spectator. 3. See: *sur place*.

"Place au théâtre!" (French)   "Places, please!"

place keeper   Someone, usually a servant, sent to a Restoration or 18th C theatre to hold a seat or place for someone else—normally a member of the upper class. (Hogan LONDON xxxii)

placement   In dance, body alignment, whether in motion or at rest. (Stodelle HUMPHREY 37)

"Places!," "Places please!"   The call to performers to take positions for the opening of an act.

plafonds (French)   In 19th C theatres, borders which hid lighting apparatus and scene storage space. (Moynet FRENCH 3)

plain, playne   See: *platea*.

P lamp   See: P.

plan   1. See: floor plan. 2. See: seating plan.

plan (French)   In old theatres, a part or plane of the stage floor which runs parallel to the footlights and across the entire stage width. There were usually ten—less frequently, twelve or fifteen—the largest specifically designated for traps and called a *rue* (street). The others were called *trappilons*. (Moynet FRENCH 24)

plân an guare (Cornish)   Literally: place of the play. In medieval times, an auditorium, playhouse, theatre. (Peter CORNISH 11)

plane   A cross-stage area of a stage, bounded by wings. The first plane is the area downstage of the first wings, the second plane is the area between the first and second wings, etc. In French: *plan*.

plané (French)   Literally: hovered. In ballet, the illusion that a dancer is momentarily suspended in mid-air. (Kersley/Sinclair BALLET)

planipedes (Latin Roman)   Performers in the mime. The *planipedes* were apparently so named because they performed with feet and legs bare: the literal meaning is plain feet, flat feet, the latter presumably in the sense of without the support provided by footwear. Nicoll notes other explanations for the use of the term for mime performers. Singular *planipes*. (Nicoll MASKS 83; Allen ANTIQUITIES 26; Beare ROMAN 151, 154)

planipedia (Latin Roman)   The mime. Compare *planipedes*. (Nicoll MASKS 83)

plank-downer   In Britain, a spectator who paid for his or her seat—i.e., planked down money.

planks   The stage.

plano-convex   A shortening of plano-convex lens or plano-convex spotlight.

plano-convex lens   A lens with one plane and one convex surface. This was at one time—until about 1930—the basic lens used in stage spotlights. The resulting plano-convex spotlight is now uncommon, though the lens is sometimes used in combinations in other types of spotlights. Occasionally called a plano lens. (Wehlburg GLOSSARY, Lounsbury THEATRE 94)

plano-convex lens spotlight   See: plano-convex spotlight.

plano-convex spotlight   A spotlight with a plano-convex lens and a spherical reflector. The term is used of spotlights with no other lens, but not of spotlights which have one or more plano-convex lenses in combinations or a single lens with an ellipsoidal reflector. Sometimes simply plano-convex or P.C. light, P.C. spot(light), occasionally plano-convex lens spotlight or simply P.C. (Wehlburg GLOSSARY, Lounsbury THEATRE 94)

plano lens   See: plano-convex lens.

plano spotlight   See: plano-convex spotlight.

plant   1. To put a performer in the audience. 2. A performer so placed. 3. In playwriting, to introduce an idea or object which later in the play will become significant. Also used as a noun. 4. In acting, to introduce something—a gesture, mannerism, property, etc.—that will later become significant. 5. A theatre building. (Bowman/Ball THEATRE)

planter's hat   A panama hat.

plant show   A minstrel show. From plantation show. (Wilmeth LANGUAGE)

plaster cyclorama, plaster dome   See: cyclorama, *Kuppelhorizont*.

plastic   Three-dimensional. Said of scenic units such as practical steps, or of that which helps reveal that three-dimensionality. Hence, plasticity, plastic setting, plastic stage.

plastic lighting   Lighting which brings out the plasticity, or three dimensionality, of performers and objects on the stage. While color is involved, the characteristic of plastic lighting is the relation of light and shadow, as on the actor's face. Among other phrases: sculptural lighting, three-dimensional lighting and (occasionally) Rembrandt lighting. Compare: flat lighting. (Bellman SCENE 326, Bellman SCENE, Bowman MODERN)

plastron   See: cuirass.

plat   See: plot.

plate   1. In 19th C British theatres, the word used in various combinations to designate the control center for the gas lighting system. Gas plate ultimately became the official term in London. (Rees GAS 104) 2. See: keystone.

platea (Latin)   Literally: place. In medieval staging, the unlocalized, main performing area, between and around the mansions (localized scenic units). Other names include *campo* (Italian), *place* (French), plain (or playne), *zafaldo* (Italian).

platea (Spanish)   The orchestra or main floor of a theatre, facing the stage.

plate dimmer   A resistance dimmer built on a disk or plate-like core, originally of slate, later of cast iron, and still later of steel. These were the principal theatre dimmers of the period between the World Wars, and can still be seen occasionally. Two are named for their external shapes: round plate dimmer and rectangular plate dimmer. The interlocking plate dimmer permitted any of a number of individual dimmers to be locked into or unlocked from a shaft controlled by a master handle. Also called a disk (disc) dimmer. Fuchs has illustrations. (Fuchs LIGHTING 313–323, Bellman LIGHTING 176–177)

platform   1. In an Elizabethan or Restoration theatre, the forestage or main stage. Colley Cibber also called it the "Area." (Brockett HISTORY 204, Cibber APOLOGY I 84–85) 2. Any portable platform, collapsible or rigid, used to support actors or settings, such as a parallel and its top.

platform stage   A stage with an acting area extending into the auditorium, with the audience seating wrapped around the front and sides, and usually without a proscenium arch. See also: open stage, thrust stage.

platform theatre   1. A theatre with a platform stage. 2. See: readers theatre.

platok (Russian)   See: *babushka*.

platt   See: plot.

plaudite, "Plaudite!" (Latin Roman)   A request for applause at the end of a play. The word has been accepted in English for some time. (Beare ROMAN 268, Mantzius HISTORY I 213)

plausibility   Reasonableness and believability in the presentation of the plot and characters in a play.

play   1. A story written to be performed by actors. 2. A story so performed. 3. To act. 4. To be actable, as in "it played well." 5. To produce a dramatic composition. (Bowman/Ball THEATRE) 6. See: spontaneous drama. 7. In counterpoint lighting, to move patterns of light about, often melting the patterns into each other. The console operator's actions may be reminiscent of the playing of a piano or organ, and are sometimes almost as continuous. A pattern can vary from a spotlight or two to twenty or more instruments; there may be no color or a number of colors. See also: counterpoint lighting. (Bellman SCENE 357–358, Pilbrow LIGHTING 133)

play a call   In vaudeville in Britain, to give an encore to a well-received act, either by repeating it or by performing something else. (Granville DICTIONARY 28–29)

play-act   To perform.

play agent   One who helps a playwright find a producer. Hence, play agency. Also called a play broker.

playbill   1. A single-sheet printed notice of a theatrical performance, usually measuring about 8″ x 12″ and available at theatres from the 17th C on. Bills were also posted about the town; such bills date from the 1590s in England. (Hogan LONDON cxxxvii ff) 2. A theatre program containing a cast list and other information about a production.

play bits   To perform minor roles.

playboard   A shelf running across the top front edge of a hand-puppet booth. Used for stage properties. (Philpott DICTIONARY)

playbook   1. In medieval times, the authoritative ('original') text of a play. (Chambers MEDIAEVAL II 143) 2. The script of a play. 3. A book of plays.

play broker   An agent who helps playwrights find producers. Also called a play agent.

play carpenter   A playwright who makes plays out of non-dramatic sources or works changes on plays for different audiences—but with little originality. Also called a play doctor or play tinker. See also: *Dramaturg*.

play coach   A term sometimes used for a director of student productions.

play day   Benefit day. (Troubridge BENEFIT 55)

play doctor   One who rewrites, rearranges, or otherwise amends a play or musical to make it more suitable for performance. Also called a play carpenter or play tinker. (Purdom PRODUCING)

play down   1. In acting, to de-emphasize. 2. In acting, to be condescending to an audience not considered intelligent. (Bowman/Ball THEATRE)

player   From the mid-14th C, the general term for an actor or actress. Previously the term was probably equivalent to minstrel. (Chambers MEDIAEVAL II 185)

playerdom   In New York, anywhere theatre people congregate.

player-poet   Especially in the past, a performer who was also a playwright.

player's house   See: *mansion.*

playette   See: playlet.

play first spot, play second spot, etc.   To perform in the first position, second position, etc. on a variety bill.

play for a laugh, play for laughs   In acting, to stress lines or business that will bring laughter from an audience. (Bowman/Ball THEATRE)

play for apples   To work for a low salary.

play for a round   In acting, to seek applause, often by overacting or using tried-and-true tricks. See also: milk.

playgoer   One who goes to plays, usually frequently. Hence, playgoing. (Bowman/Ball THEATRE)

playhouse   A theatre.

playhouse copy   Formerly, a promptbook, or a printed acting version of a play based on a promptbook. (Hughes in Hume LONDON 121)

playing   1. Acting. 2. Said of a play or other entertainment currently being performed. (Bowman/Ball THEATRE)

playing a prize   See: trial of skill.

playing area   See: playing space.

playing 'em out   A practice introduced by producer Martin Beck on the Orpheum vaudeville circuit to close a performance. After the stereopticon slide picturing a child dressed in a nightgown and holding a candle with the caption "good night" was shown, the orchestra played an exit march. (Laurie VAUDEVILLE 63)

playing position   A performer's position on stage in relation to the audience, that is full front, profile, etc.

playing space   1. The area used by performers when in view of the audience. Also called playing area. 2. Sometimes, a portion of that area, e.g., that used for a particular scene.

playing time   1. Total days or weeks of employment for a performer. 2. The duration of a scene, act, or performance.

playing to the wings   In vaudeville, making jokes that only fellow performers could understand. (Gilbert VAUDEVILLE 277)

playitis   The ambition to write a play. (Granville DICTIONARY)

play it straight   To perform without exaggeration.

playlet   A short play. Especially in the past, sometimes called a playette.

playmaker   A playwright, a maker of plays.

playmaking   1. See: creative drama, story dramatization. 2. As two words, an occasional alternate for playwriting.

playne   See: *platea*.

play of atmosphere   A play in which an emotion, feeling, or mood dominates.

play of character   A play in which the study of character dominates. *The Lower Depths* and *The Glass Menagerie* are examples.

play off   See: play opposite.

play of ideas   A play in which social, moral, political, or philosophical ideas dominate. The plays of George Bernard Shaw are often so called. See also: *pièce à thèse*.

play of situation   A play in which events and plot dominate. Hence, situation comedy, situation play.

play on   To play music when a vaudeville or burlesque performer made an entrance. Hence, played on, to be played on. (Wilmeth LANGUAGE)

play opposite   Usually said of performers with equally important roles: the less-noted one appears opposite the more-noted one. One is usually male, the other female. But the term implies contrast and conflict and suggests how good performers play 'off' one another.

play out   1. To perform toward the auditorium. (Bowman/Ball THEATRE) 2. Especially in rehearsal: once begun, to complete a scene or act.

play package   A group of plays available for amateur production. (Bowman/Ball THEATRE)

playreader   A person who reads and evaluates scripts for a producing company or publisher. Often called simply reader.

play reading   1. The reading aloud of a script, usually for the purpose of convincing a producing company to accept the play for production. 2. The reading and evaluation of a play for possible production or publication. 3. A form of readers theatre restricted to plays as opposed to the narrative fiction of chamber theatre. 4. Such a reading.

play reviewer   A newspaper or magazine reporter who attends a play production and renders an opinion.

playright   In Britain, a copyright on a play.

play scout   A producer's representative who reports on productions of new plays.

playscript   See: script.

plays itself   Said of a good acting part.

play society   In Britain, a stage society or theatre club, usually private, which produces plays.

play the first spot   To be the first act, especially in vaudeville or a variety show. In Britain, play them in.

play the haylofts, play the tanks, play the sticks   To tour in small towns.

play the lead spot   To perform the leading role.

play the mask   In any theatre form in which performers wear masks, to supplement, augment, and enliven the qualities of the mask by the acting. (Duchartre ITALIAN 41–42)

play them in   See: play the first spot.

play the ponies   To court small chorus girls.

play tinker   See: play doctor.

play to capacity   To perform to a full house.

play to coppers   In Britain, to perform to a small house.

play to punks in hide-aways   In the early 20th C, to perform in small towns. (Berrey/Van den Bark SLANG 586)

play to the curtain   To build to a climax at the end of an act, especially in comedy. (Cartmell HANDBOOK)

play to the gallery   1. To cater to playgoers in the cheaper seats; to overact. 2. To seek applause.

play to the gas   Presumably since the 19th C, to perform to a very small audience. The source is perhaps from playing to little but the gas lighting, or (a 20th C interpretation) playing to an audience only sufficient to pay for the lighting. (Sobel HANDBOOK, Bowman/Ball THEATRE)

play up   To emphasize a line or piece of business.

play up the curtain   To play music preceding and sometimes through the rise of the curtain.

play up to   To support a fellow performer by giving him or her the focus of attention.

play West End   In Britain, to perform in the restrained, natural style used in London's West End theatres.

play-within-a-play   A dramatic performance that is part of a larger dramatic performance, such as the Murder of Gonzago in *Hamlet*.

play with music   A legitimate play with a considerable amount of music.

playwright   Literally: a maker of plays. A dramatist.

playwrightess   An old term for a female playwright.

playwrite   A frequent misspelling of playwright.

pleasure garden   In the 17th C and later, especially in Britain, an outdoor place of entertainment, featuring refreshments, pleasant landscaping, and performances ranging from tumbling to classical singing.

plebeian games   See: *ludi Plebeii*.

plega (Anglo-Saxon)   A play. (Wickham EARLY II, pt. 1, 166)

pleg-hús (Anglo-Saxon)   A playhouse. (Wickham EARLY II, pt. 1, 166)

pleg-stów (Anglo-Saxon)   A place for a play. (Wickham EARLY II, pt. 1, 166)

plelengan (Indonesian)   See: *telengan*.

pleureuses (French)   20th C ostrich feathers, each strand made longer with another strand. Also called amazones, weepers, willow plumes. (Boucher FASHION)

plié (French)   In ballet, an exercise involving bending of the knee or knees, often at the *barre*. (Wilson BALLET, Grant TECHNICAL)

plier (French)   See: movements in ballet.

Plinge   See: Walter Plinge.

(à) plis Gironées (French)   See: *robe Gironée*.

plomb (French)   See: *à plomb*.

plot   1. According to Aristotle, a selected sequence of significant events and situations in a play with a beginning, a middle, and an end. He said plot reveals human beings and their actions as they are in the real world, rather than as they should be. For more on Aristotle and plot see Vaughn DRAMA and Barnet/Berman/Burto ASPECTS. 2. A list of the furniture, properties, lighting, scenery, etc. for a production. Hence, light plot, property plot, scene plot etc. 3. The writing down of cues: to plot cues. (Purdom PRODUCING, Baker THEATRECRAFT) A prompter's abstract of a play, used backstage in Elizabethan theatres to remind performers of the sequence of the scenes. Sometimes spelled platt. (Chambers ELIZABETHAN II 125)

plot action   See: plot business.

plot business   Stage business or action necessary to the plot of a play. Also called point business, plot action. (Bowman/Ball THEATRE)

plot line   1. The story in a play. 2. Especially in the plural, dialogue essential to the plot of a play.

plot movement   The development of the dramatic action. (Bowman/Ball THEATRE)

plot play   A play in which the events of the story dominate.

plot scene   See: obligatory scene.

plot structure   See: dramatic structure.

plough the provinces   In Britain, to tour small towns.

plug   1. A 17th C hat halfway between a top hat and a derby. (Barton COSTUME 464) 2. A small flat used to fill an opening in a larger flat or between other scenic units. Hence, door plug, plain plug, window plug. 3. To use a small flat in such a way. 4. A unit built to cover any hole or gap, such as steps built into a thrust or platform. 5. In stage lighting, a male connector with an insulated handle. See also: stage plug. 6. In stage lighting, to connect, to plug in. 7. In acting, to give over-emphasis to a word, phrase, or line; to overplay, to plug a line, plug for laughs. 8. To promote a play, production, dance, song, etc. Hence, plugger, plugging. 9. A particular piece of such promotion. 10. To applaud.

plug box   See: plugging box.

pluggers' den, pluggers' paradise   See: Tin Pan Alley.

plugging box   Especially in the past in the U.S., a portable box containing a number of receptacles; such a box is fed by a single heavy cable which can be plugged into a current source on stage. Lighting people sometimes speak of such boxes as two-way, four-way, or six-way (for the number of receptacles per box). Also called a plug-in box. In Britain, shoe, connector box, sometimes plug box. (Bowman/Ball THEATRE, Gassner/Barber PRODUCING 804, Fay GLOSSARY)

plugging panel   See: interconnecting panel.

plugging schedule   In many types of interconnecting panels, a list of which load is connected to which circuit and when. See also: interconnecting panel.

plugging strip   See: connector strip.

plug-in box   See: plugging box.

plug socket   Early in the 20th C, a floor pocket. (Krows AMERICA 204)

plush family   See: bare-stall family.

plus-or-minus dimmer, plus-and-minus dimmer   See: variable load dimmer.

pneuma (Latin)   See: *neuma*.

pnigos (Greek)   See: *katakeleusmos*.

po (Chinese)   See: *bo*.

po, p'o (Chinese)   See: *daqu*.

pobutovyi theatre (Ukrainian-English)   Ukrainian theatre portraying manners and customs. (Hirniak in Bradshaw SOVIET 251–258)

POC   See: point of concentration.

pocapan (Indonesian)   See: *ginem*.

pochette (French)   An 18th C pocket-sized violin used by ballet masters to accompany themselves in classes and in rehearsals. Also called a kit. (Winter BALLET 261)

pocho (Spanish)   A mixture of Spanish and English, the language of Chicano theatre. Also called Spanglish. (Copelin "Chicano" 74)

pocket   1. A horizontal sleeve at the bottom of a drop, into which a batten can be slipped to make the drop taut. Also called a batten pocket. See also: chain pocket. 2. See: stage pocket.

pocket artist   A diminutive actress. (Berrey/Van den Bark SLANG 571)

pocket pannier   An 18th C pocket made by pulling skirt fabric through holes cut at the hip of the gown. (Wilcox DICTIONARY)

podium   See: lycopodium.

poeng mang (Thai)   See: *song na*.

poet   A playwright whose work is in verse. Formerly, any playwright. (Bowman/Ball THEATRE)

poetic drama   A play written in verse.

poetic justice   A condition in which a play, usually a melodrama, ends with good rewarded and evil punished. Sometimes called a dual-issue ending.

poet's collar   A 19th C soft shirt or blouse collar replacing the bulky cravat worn by writers and artists particularly. (Wilcox DICTIONARY)

poet's day   In Restoration theatres, the third performance of a new play, the profits of which went to the author. Also called the third day. If the run continued, the author also gained from the sixth and ninth days. (Van Lennep LONDON lxxxi)

pohon beringin (Malaysian)   Literally: banyan tree. A tree-shaped puppet that can represent a cave, mountain, tree, or forest in shadow theatre. (Sheppard TAMAN 74). Also spelled *pohon bringin*. Also called *gunongan* (mountain). (Sweeney MALAY 35)

poikilon (Greek)   Probably the long, ornate sleeved *chiton* of tragedy. The term is from Pollux. The literal meaning of the adjectival source is many-colored, dappled. See also: *chiton*. (Mantzius HISTORY I 185, Pickard-Cambridge FESTIVALS 203)

point   1. Formerly, a well-known passage in a play, eagerly awaited by playgoers, to which a performer would build, as when Hamlet first meets the Ghost. (Hogan LONDON cxiv) 2. A laugh or punch line. 3. In playwriting or performing, to give special emphasis to a word, phrase, line, or action. 4. In stage lighting, a specific portion of the travel of a dimmer. The arc in which a dimmer handle (controller) moves is almost always marked by the manufacturer with equally spaced numbers from 1 to 10. A movement from one number to the next is a point, from 3 to 5 (for example) two points, and so on. The language is standard in setting light intensity, so that a controlboard operator may be told, "Take out number 12 one point, and bring up 13 two points," etc.

point business   See: plot business.

pointer   In playwriting, a hint of what is to come, to create suspense. See also: foreshadowing.

pointes (French)   See: *sur les pointes.*

pointe **shoe** (French-English)   See: block shoe.

pointillage   A painting technique using small strokes or dots. Also called pointillism.

point line   A key line of dialogue.

point of attack   See: inciting action.

point of concentration   An agreed-upon object or event on which a performer can focus to achieve detachment. In Viola Spolin's vocabulary, the term is usually reduced to POC. (Spolin IMPROVISATION)

point of contraction   Formerly in scene painting, a vanishing point.

point of distance, point of sight   The viewing point in an old theatre auditorium corresponding to the vanishing point in the perspective scenery on the stage. From this point the perspective was supposed to look perfect. (Sabbattini in Hewitt RENAISSANCE 50)

point of focus   The place on stage where a director wants the audience to look.

points   1. Metal-tipped strings used to attach stockings to an upper garment. 2. A dancer's toes. See: *sur les pointes.*

point source   As used in theatre lighting terminology, the ideal source of light in a spotlight or any other lighting instrument with a lens (and/or a reflector). Since a point is theoretical, no lamp filament is a point. The filament of a spotlight lamp is designed to come as close as possible to providing a point source. The result is a concentrated filament, sometimes referred to as a point source; a point source is then defined as a very small light source (i.e., as small a filament as possible). (Wehlburg GLOSSARY, Bellman SCENE)

point up   To give emphasis.

poison at the box office   Said of a play, playwright, or performer unable to draw an audience. (Bowman/Ball THEATRE)

poix pilés (French)   In late medieval times, mixed performances in which farces followed serious plays. Also spelled *pois pilés.* (Chambers MEDIAEVAL II 182)

poke bonnet   See: capote.

poker-pan   A performer who maintains an expressionless face.

pokok (Indonesian)   See: *lakon*.

po lao (Chinese)   See: *bolao*.

polarity plug   In lighting, a plug or receptacle which will accept its mate in one way only. Three-pronged plugs and many twist-locks and interconnecting panels are polarized. (Lounsbury THEATRE 118)

pole-and-carriage system, pole-and-chariot system   See: chariot-and-pole system.

police lights   In Britain, lights which must by law be left burning during performance. Exit lights are an example. (Bax MANAGEMENT 194)

Polish gown   See: gown à la Polonaise.

polishing rehearsal   A rehearsal devoted to giving finishing touches to character, tempo, details of business, timing, etc.

Polish jests   A name for popular comic interludes performed at carnival time in Russia in the 17th C. The plays were derived from European mystery plays. (Fülöp-Miller/Gregor RUSSIAN 25)

polite comedy   See: genteel comedy.

political folk rhyme   A form of propagandist musical theatre used by the Communist Party in Russia in the 1920s, sung by its author, a chorus, or an accordion player. (Gorchakov RUSSIA 143)

political mysteries   Russian celebration spectacles showing Marxian struggles between masters and slaves. (Carter SPIRIT 143)

political theatre   Theatre devoted wholly or in part to productions dealing with current political questions. (Gorelik NEW)

polka piquée   In 1845 and later in the U.S., a high-kicking polka performed by chorus girls, and much appreciated by male audiences, especially when the dancers wore no knickers. (Parker/Parker CHORUS GIRL 29)

Polonaise, gown à la   See: gown à la Polonaise.

polychromatic stage   An occasional term for a stage lit so that performers move from one color to another. (Bellman LIGHTING 100)

pompa (Latin Roman)   The solemn procession which preceded some *ludi*. The procession for the *ludi Romani* moved from the Capitol through the forum and elsewhere to the Circus Maximus. Compare *pompe* (Greek). (Sandys COMPANION 504)

pompadour   1. An 18th C short cloak with slits for the arms, of black or another dark color, made of velvet or satin. (Walkup DRESSING 217). 2. A hairstyle in which the front hair is swept up high off the forehead.

pompe (Greek)   A procession at a Dionysian festival. Compare *pompa* (Latin Roman). (Bieber HISTORY 49)

pona (Korean)   See: *bona*.

pondo (Philippine)   The movements and formation of combatants before a battle in *comedia*. (Mendoza COMEDIA 65)

pong   1. In acting, to ad lib when a line is forgotten; to improvise. Hence, ponging it. 2. In acting, to speak a line with heavy emphasis. See also: ping. (Bowman/Ball THEATRE)

pong (Thai)   A *likay* actor's hand gesture that cues musicians to end a musical selection. (Virulrak "Likay" 233)

ponnani (Malayalam)   The lead singer in *kathakali* or *krishnanattam*. (Jones/ Jones KATHAKALI 77)

ponsandae (Korean)   See: *sandaeguk*.

pony   A short girl in a chorus line. Also called a broiler or cream puff.

pony chorus   A chorus of short girls.

Poochow *pang tzu* (Chinese)   See: *puju*.

pool   1. An area of the stage lit from vertically or almost vertically overhead. (Lounsbury THEATRE) 2. Any separately-lit area on a relatively dark stage.

pool lighting   An occasional term for spotlighting in which no illumination is used on the background. (Bellman LIGHTING 337)

poo rai (Lao)   An enemy or villain role in a *mohlam* play. Also called *dua gong*. (Miller "Kaen" 222)

poor man's spotlight   See: reflector lamp.

poor theatre   A dramatic concept of Jerzy Grotowski in the 1960s. Because the theatre, which has technical limitations, cannot be as lavish or spectacular as cinema or television or have their dazzling instantaneous shifts of locale, it should not attempt complex scenic or lighting effects but should rather be 'poor' in the sense of ascetic, thus retaining its unique, essential characteristic—a dedicated living performer in close proximity to spectators. Theatre should abolish frontiers, including a conventional stage, between performers and audience.

pop   1. Popular, as in popular prices. 2. Capitalized, a traditional nickname for a stage doorkeeper. In Britain, George. (Wilmeth LANGUAGE)

popet   A medieval spelling of puppet.

pop fast ones   To tell risqué jokes.

pop house   A popular-priced theatre.

poppet   1. An early spelling of puppet. An old word for doll.

pop price(s)   Popular price(s).

popular entertainment   Live amusements aimed at a broad audience. Examples are circus, the Italian *commedia dell'arte*, burlesque, vaudeville, pantomimes, melodrama, and farce. (McNamara "Introduction" 3)

popular prices   Relatively low admission charges.

porc-épic (French)   See: porcupine headdress.

porch comic   A comedian, usually working alone, who entertains tourists on the veranda of a resort hotel, as in the Catskills in the 1930s. (Alan King on the NBC TV Today Show 1983)

porcupine headdress   A late 18th C hairstyle with short hair sticking up like bristles. Also called a *porc-épic* (French). (Boucher FASHION)

port   An opening, usually in the auditorium ceiling, through which one or more spotlights may be directed to the stage. Such an opening is often called a ceiling port. Ports in the upper side walls near the front of the auditorium are side ports. See also: ceiling slot and sidewall slot. (Rubin/Watson LIGHTING 29, 34)

portable   1. In the U.S., movable to wherever needed, whether stage equipment, a stage, or a theatre. 2. In Britain, able to be carried by one or two men through a door of normal size. (Bowman/Ball THEATRE, Bentham ART)

portable board operator   In certain union contracts for stage electricians, the person who operates a portable control board. This operator is distinguished from the electrician and the assistant electrician, and is paid much less and by the day.

portable control board   In the U.S., a lighting control board designed to be moved about, especially from theatre to theatre. 'Portable board' has been used in the past in both Britain and the U.S. for a movable board, often on casters, used as an auxiliary to the main board in a theatre; but the U.S. use also included the piano board (q.v.) often carried by professional road companies. (Bellman SCENE, Corry PLANNING, Baker THEATRECRAFT, McCandless ''Glossary'' 638)

portable extension pipe stand   See: light stand.

portable footlights   Especially in the past, any of various types of footlights which could be set on the stage floor.

portable stage wiring   An occasional phrase for stage cable. Sometimes called portable wiring. (Bellman LIGHTING 156)

portable strip   A small striplight sometimes used for backings and other areas where undirected illumination is desirable.

portable (switch)board   A portable control board.

portable theatre   A fit-up theatre, prefabricated or a tent, with scenery, props, etc., used for touring.

portable wiring   See: portable stage wiring.

portal   1. Sometimes, short for light portal. See also: port. 2. An inner proscenium.

Portalbrücke (German)   A downstage light bridge. (Fuchs LIGHTING 211)

portal unit set   Scenery with a permanent frame, in front of and behind which units are changed to provide the various scenes. (Hewitt/Foster/Wolle PLAY) *portants* (French)   British 'lengths,' much like striplights hung vertically on the onstage upstage edges of wings. (Penzel LIGHTING 95, fig. 34)

porta regia (Latin Roman)   Literally: royal door. According to Vitruvius, the great central arch or door in the front of the *scaenae frons* (scenic facade). See also: *regia*. (Nicoll DEVELOPMENT 82)

port de bras, positions des bras (French)   In ballet, the carriage of the arms. 1. A movement (or series of movements) in which the arm or arms pass through various positions. 2. Special exercises whose purpose is to induce graceful movement of the arms. Wilson has illustrations. (Wilson BALLET 121, 234–235; Grant TECHNICAL)

porte de secours (French)   Literally: emergency door. Especially in the 19th and early 20th C, a private entrance to a theatre, reserved for members of claques. (Saxon "Claque" 18)

porter   See: call man.

porticus (Latin Roman)   Literally: colonnade, arcade. According to Vitruvius, a roofed colonnade directly behind a scene building and contiguous to it. The result was a rear portico, thought to have provided shelter when needed for nearby portions of the audience. (Bieber HISTORY fig. 680, Sandys COMPANION 518)

poscene   The back of the stage in 17th C theatres. (Southern CHANGEABLE 161–162)

pose plastique (French)   A novelty act of the penny showman John Richardson in the fairs of mid-19th C England. A young man, dressed as a statue, to a musical accompaniment, displayed a series of Greek attitudes: a gladiator, a listening slave, etc. Also called a living statue. (Rosenfeld in Mayer/Richards WESTERN 111)

poser   A stripper who moves little and poses while disrobing. (Wilmeth LANGUAGE)

poser (French)   In ballet, to place a foot on the ground. (Grant TECHNICAL)

position   See: stage position.

positions   1. Stage areas, such as: upstage, downstage, stage left, down right, center stage, right center, in one, in two, etc. 2. Actor positions, such as: full front, one quarter, profile, three-quarters, full back.

"Positions for curtain!"   A call to performers to take their places for the beginning of an act or for a curtain call.

positions of the body   In ballet, according to the Cecchetti method, there are eight body directions or positions, each a study in line and perspective: *croisé devant* (crossed in front), *à la quatrième devant* (to the fourth front), *écarté* (thrown wide apart), *effacé* (shaded, covered, oblique); *à la seconde* (to the second), *épaulé* (shouldered), *à la quatrième derrière* (to the fourth back), and *croisé derrière* (crossed in back). All are French terms and traditionally used.

The numbers refer to the ballet foot positions. See also: direction. (Grant TECHNICAL)

Posse (German)   Farce.

possession of parts   Mainly in the 19th C and earlier, the custom of a performer playing a line of roles through much of his or her career.

posticum (Latin Roman)   On floor plans for certain comedies, the unseen back door of a house whose front is onstage in view of the audience. See also: *angiportum*. (Beare ROMAN 258–260)

postillon   A 19th C piece of ruffled fabric at the back of the waist of a bodice. (Boucher FASHION)

postizo (Spanish)   Literally: artificial, false. Hairpiece, padding, or falsies. See also: *compostura*.

post-modern dance   A movement of the 1970s which sought to take the "danciness" out of dance. The emphasis tended to be on how movement was structured and organized, rather than on its particular style, demands on the dancer, emotional content, technique, etc. It was improvisational and invented rather than choreographed, and tried to be natural and simple. Also called anti-dance. (Kirby "Introduction" 115–116)

postscaenium (Latin Roman)   Literally: behind the scene. The backstage area of a scene building. Sometimes used for dressing, the *postscaenium* could, in some forms, have served as a waiting area for performers, as well as for small storage. Also spelled *postcaenium* (possibly an error); U.S. postscenium has the general meaning of backstage, behind the scenes; Britain has used parascene in this meaning. (Bieber HISTORY 203, 212, figs. 680, 712; Sandys COMPANION 518)

post scene   Sebastiano Serlio's term for the area in front of the stage, on the auditorium floor. (Campbell SCENES facing 34)

post siparium (Latin Roman)   A phrase used by Cicero to mean behind the scenes. See also: *siparium*. (Beare ROMAN 270)

post the bond   To provide the financial guarantee required of producers by the Actors' Equity Association. (Bowman/Ball THEATRE)

posture maker, posture master   Formerly, a contortionist.

posturer   1. A contortionist. 2. A juggler, especially one who lies prone on the stage and juggles children with his feet and hands. (Leavitt MANAGEMENT 473)

pot   1. Among stage lighting people, and especially control board crews, the usual term for a potentiometer. (Lounsbury THEATRE) 2. A shortening of pot dimmer.

potato Yiddish   Especially among Yiddish intellectuals in the days of vaudeville, a derogatory term for Yiddish intermixed with English. (Sandrow VAGABOND 294, Sandrow in Matlaw AMERICAN 95)

potboiler A play or performance designed primarily to make money. The implication is that the play has little intrinsic merit. (Wilmeth LANGUAGE)

potboiling Said of a talented performer working in a mediocre play.

pot dimmer See: salt water dimmer.

potentiometer A small, manually-operated variable resistor which controls a remotely placed dimmer; sometimes, a similar device used in sound control. Modern light control consoles often have a 'pot' for each circuit. Wehlburg has an electrical diagram. Compare controller, an older term with a slightly broader meaning. (Bellman LIGHTING 222, Wehlburg GLOSSARY, Lounsbury THEATRE)

po the hi (Indonesian) An Indonesian spelling of Chinese *pu tai hi*. An almost extinct glove-puppet theatre that depicts traditional Chinese stories and characters, performed in Indonesia, especially in major cities in Java. (Brandon SOUTHEAST 49)

potjapan (Indonesian) See: *ginem*.

po t'ou (Chinese) See: *botou*.

pot time The length of time a plastic material, such as resin, remains liquid in a heated container after the catalyst has been added.

poudrage (French) See: powdering.

poulailler (French) Literally: hen roost. The top gallery in a French theatre. Also called the *paradis* or *colombier*.

poulaine (French) A 14th C man's clog with a long, upturned toe, from Poland. See also: duckbill shoes, *solleret*. (Boucher FASHION, Chalmers CLOTHES 112)

pounce 1. The powder used in transferring a design to fabric by rubbing over thin perforated paper. (Wilcox DICTIONARY) 2. To prick leather into patterns and designs (16th C). (Chalmers CLOTHES 171)

pounce bag A cheesecloth bag filled with powdered charcoal. It is rubbed or tapped against holes punched in heavy paper, to mark scenery for painting a design motif.

pounce wheel A small wheel of spikes, with a handle, for punching patterns of holes in paper. Used for marking costume patterns or design motifs to be painted on scenery.

pounding In acting, heavily emphasizing line readings. (Dolman ACTING 109)

poupée à fil (French) Literally: doll on a string. A string puppet. Also called a *marionnette à fil*. (Philpott DICTIONARY)

pourpoint (French) A 14th C quilted doublet of leather or cloth, often sleeveless, worn under or without armor and by civilian men, women, and children.

It had a *carcaille* (flaring collar). Also called an acton or gambeson. See also: *hoqueton*. (Chalmers CLOTHES 112, Wilcox DICTIONARY)

powdering   Especially in the 18th C, the powdering of wigs. Also called *accomodage* or *poudrage*.

powder off   To tone down makeup and set it.

powder of vernis   Varnish, resin; ignited in Renaissance theatres for lightning effects. (Serlio in Hewitt RENAISSANCE 35)

powder puff   A makeup artist.

power equation   See: West Virginia formula.

power flying   The use of motorized winches or hydraulic devices to fly scenery, draperies, etc.

power formula   See: West Virginia formula.

power pack   See: package board.

ppiri (Korean)   Literally: the last person. Young or beginning members of a *namsadang* troupe. (Kim "Namsadang" 10)

prabu (Indonesian)   The role of a king.

practicable   See: practical.

practicable (French)   1. A set piece. 2. In 19th C French theatres, the frame which supported a platform used to vary the level of the stage floor, with access provided by ramps and stairs. (Moynet FRENCH 110)

practicables   The lines and contours of the body and limbs of a Russian performer. (Carter SPIRIT 63)

practical   Said of scenery or properties capable of being used in the action of a play, such as a window that can be opened. Sometimes called practicable.

praecinctio (Latin Roman)   A corridor in an auditorium. The typical such passageway separated one semi-circular tier of seats from another. There might also be a *praecinctio* between the seats of honor (*bisellia*) and the first tier of seats. (Bieber HISTORY xiii, 184, fig. 641; Allen ANTIQUITIES 91, fig. 15)

praecones (Latin Roman)   Literally: crier, herald. Public criers who announced plays. The *praecones* may have served also to silence the audience as the play was about to begin. Singular *praeco*. (Allen ANTIQUITIES 59, Sandys COMPANION 520, Beare ROMAN 169)

pra ek (Lao)   The leading male role, a prince, in a *mohlam* play. (Miller "Kaen" 222)

praetexta (Latin Roman)   See: *fabula praetexta*.

pragalbha (Sanskrit)   A bold heroine, one of three major types of heroine (*nayika*) roles in classical Indian plays. (Keith SANSKRIT 308)

prahasana (Sanskrit)   A one-act play which combines comedy and farce and deals with lowly, worldly characters. One of the ten major types (*rupaka*) of classical Indian plays. (Kale THEATRIC 166, Keith SANSKRIT 261–262)

prairie comedian In the U.S., an old term for an inadequate performer. (Wilmeth LANGUAGE)

prakarana (Sanskrit) A play of four or more acts in which the plot is the product of the playwright's imagination and the hero is not a god or royalty. Usually translated "social play." One of ten major types (*rupaka*) of classical Indian plays. An example is *The Little Clay Cart*. (Kale THEATRIC 162, Keith SANSKRIT 257–259)

prakari (Sanskrit) An episode, or a chain of episodes, the fourth element of plot or subject matter (*arthaprakrti*) in a classical Indian play. The result of an event is presented to further the main plot. (Byrski in Baumer/Brandon SANSKRIT 144) A plot "incident" according to Keith (SANSKRIT 298).

prakat khun khru (Thai) Literally: proclamation of the teacher's beneficence. An invocational prayer sung before many traditional theatre performances. See: *kat khru*.

praleng (Thai) A two-character dance, performed before a classical dance-drama (*lakon*) to exorcise misfortune. Danced in *rabam* style. One of several preliminaries to performance (*boek rong*). (Yupho in Rangthong SOUVENIR 113)

prampogan (Indonesian) In Java and Sunda, a puppet of a marching army. In the shadow theatre (*wayang kulit*) it appears in the *perang ampyak* scene, 'fighting' through a forest. Also called *rampogan, ampyak* or *ampjak*. It is illustrated in *Irawan's Wedding* in Brandon THRONES 191–192 and Scott-Kemball JAVANESE 53. (Foley "Sundanese" 45)

praptyasa (Sanskrit) In a classical Indian play, the point where success by the hero in achieving his goal seems possible. The fourth of five stages in the development of a play's action (*avastha*). (Keith SANSKRIT 297)

pra rawng (Lao) The secondary male role in a *mohlam* play. (Miller "Kaen" 222)

prarocana (Sanskrit) Literally: laudation. An appeal to the audience for the success of a performance. One of many preliminaries (*purvaranga*) which precede the performance of a classical play. (Keith SANSKRIT 340–341)

prasadiki dhruva (Sanskrit) See: *dhruva*.

prasanga (Kannada) The story of a play. (Ashton/Christie YAKSAGANA 27–32)

prasangika (Sanskrit) A subsidiary plot in a classical Indian drama. See also: *vatsu*. (Bharata NATYASASTRA 378)

prasnika (Sanskrit) An adjudicator who assessed the quality of a dramatic performance in ancient India and awarded prizes in a dramatic competition. (Raghavan in Baumer/Brandon SANSKRIT 42)

prastavana (Sanskrit) 1. A prologue in classical Indian drama in which the subject of the play is introduced. (Rangacharya NATYASASTRA 26) 2. In a puppet play in India, the introduction of the major puppet characters to the audience at the beginning of a performance. (ASIAN 20)

pratfall, prattfall   A comic fall on the rump. (Wilmeth LANGUAGE)

pratihari (Sanskrit)   The minor role of a doorkeeper in a classical Indian play. (Keith SANSKRIT 313)

pratimukha (Sanskrit)   Progression. The second of five junctures (*sandhi*) of dramatic action in a classical Indian play. (Keith SANSKRIT 298–299)

pratinayaka (Sanskrit)   In classical Indian drama, the role of the hero's enemy. (Keith SANSKRIT 307–308) In *yaksagana*, a villainous character.

pratisira (Sanskrit)   See: *yavanika*.

pratyahara (Sanskrit)   Arranging musical instruments on the stage, the first part of the preliminaries (*purvaranga*) which opened a classical theatre performance in India. (Keith SANSKRIT 339)

pravacan (Hindi)   Literally: elucidation. In *raslila*, a homily delivered by the actor playing Krishna, the last of seven elements of the *ras* portion of a performance. (Hein MIRACLE 151)

pravesagita (Sanskrit)   Literally: entrance song. An entrance song and dance of a chief character in *ankiya nat*. Also called *pravesa-daru* (entrance song) in other theatre forms. See also: *dhruva*. (Vatsyayan TRADITIONAL 103)

pravesaka (Sanskrit)   In classical Indian drama, an "introductory scene" to an act in which a minor character summarizes action that has occurred between acts. One of five types of introductory scene (*arthopaksepaka*). (Keith SANSKRIT 301, Byrski in Baumer/Brandon SANSKRIT 157) Called an "interlude" by Kale (THEATRIC 159).

pravesiki dhruva (Sanskrit)   See: *dhruva*.

pravrttaka (Sanskrit)   A sequence at the conclusion of the prologue to a classical Indian play in which a character, just described by the stage manager, makes his entrance. (Keith SANSKRIT 340)

praxis (Greek)   In Aristotle's *Poetics*, action, in the sense of a rational purpose or motivation which causes a character to act as he does. An example is Oedipus' action when he learns that the plague is caused by the slaying of Laius. (Fergusson POETICS 8–11)

prayatna (Sanskrit)   Determined effort by the hero to reach his goal, the second of the five stages of the development (*avastha*) of a plot in a classical Indian play. Also called *yatna*. (Keith SANSKRIT 297)

preacher play   In the past, a play in which the leading character is a preacher; or a piece with a strong moral message. (Wilmeth LANGUAGE)

pre-acting   An acting theory developed in the 1920s by Vsevelod Meyerhold in Russia: in pauses between speeches the performer tried to show in pantomime the transition from one situation to another. See also: fore-play. (Gorchakov RUSSIA 210)

precursor, prelocutor, presenter Medieval terms for the speaker of the prologue to a play. (Chambers MEDIAEVAL II 77, Mantzius HISTORY II 49)

prefocus base Especially in the U.S. and primarily in spotlight lamps, a smooth base whose top has two flanges of different sizes; as a result, when inserted in a receptacle, the lamp's filament bears a precise relation to the lighting instrument's reflector and lens system. Hence, prefocus lamp, prefocus receptacle. In Britain, prefocus cap. (Lounsbury THEATRE 80, Wehlburg GLOSSARY)

prefocus cap See: prefocus base.

prefocus lamp A lamp with a prefocus base.

prefocus socket An electrical receptacle which will accept only a prefocus base.

preksagrha (Sanskrit) Literally: a viewing house. The auditorium of a theatre in ancient India. (Kale THEATRIC 15)

preksaka (Sanskrit) A spectator in classical Indian theatre. Also spelled *prekshaka*. (Keith SANSKRIT 369–370)

preliminary tour David Belasco's term for an out-of-town tryout. (Belasco DOOR 87)

prelude A short preliminary performance.

prembon (Indonesian) An eclectic Balinese dance-drama form, incorporating elements from *gambuh* and *parwa* and adaptable to *Ramayana*, *Mahabharata*, and other story cycles. It was created in the 1940s. (Soedarsono DANCES 182–183)

premier (French) See: *jeune premier*.

premier danseur (French), **premier danseur** The principal male dancer in a ballet company.

première 1. The first public performance of a work. 2. To give a first performance. 3. The leading lady in a production. The word comes from the French, but even in English the accent mark is often kept. See also: *jeune premier*. (Bowman/Ball THEATRE)

première danseuse (French), **premiere danseuse** The principal female dancer in a ballet company. The phrase is used in English both with and without the accent.

premiere striptease A leading strip-tease dancer. (Berrey/Van den Bark SLANG 574)

premier garçon du théâtre (French) A 17th C stage manager. (Roberts STAGE) *prempah* (Indonesian)   A thick control rod for a large animal puppet or carriage in Javanese shadow theatre. (Long JAVANESE 118n, 120n)

prengesan (Indonesian)   The huge, gaping, wide-open mouth of a giant in Javanese shadow theatre. (Long JAVANESE 70)

preparation   See: foreshadowing.

preparation copy   Formerly, a director's annotated text of a play, reflecting his production ideas—cuts, changes, etc. (Shattuck SHAKESPEARE 5)

presence   Stage presence; a performer's onstage manner. A performer with presence attracts the attention of an audience. (Bowman/Ball THEATRE)

present   1. To produce and show an entertainment. 2. To introduce a new performer to the public.

presentation   1. A theatrical production. 2. An introduction, as when a performer is introduced to an audience. 3. A style of staging; see: presentational. (Bowman/Ball THEATRE)

presentational   Said of drama and theatre in which characters, plot, and dialogue are frankly fictitious, the stage is a space for acting (not an environment), the theatre remains a theatre, and the performer does not appear to lose his or her identity as a performer. Hence, presentationalism, presentational theatre, presentational acting, etc. See also: convention.

presentation house   A film theatre with vaudeville acts added to the picture bill.

presenter, presentor   In some medieval and Elizabethan plays, a sort of master of ceremonies, interlocutor, or speaker of inductions or prologues.

preset   1. In a light control console, an electrical device often called a controller or fader, which allows an operator to set a dimmer and switch well in advance of the need for that particular setting. The term usually refers to a row of such controllers, also called a preset bank; such banks often include other devices, such as pilot lights. A preset bank permits advance setting of the light for an entire scene, which may be faded in or out by a master controller, also called a preset master or master fader, sometimes a preset control. Two such banks make up a two-scene preset, five banks a five-scene preset, and so on. (Bellman LIGHTING 219; Sellman/Lessley ESSENTIALS 130–131, fig. 8.8; Wehlburg GLOSSARY) 2. Hyphenated, scenery, properties, or lighting arranged or set up in advance. 3. Unhyphenated, to arrange such elements.

preset-control selector switches   On a preset bank, a set of switches which tell the preset bank what to do. The set usually includes one control each for fader up, fader down, and 'on,' and sometimes a fourth for 'off' or blackout. (Bellman LIGHTING 220–221)

preset master   See: preset.

preset sheet   In the operation of a preset control system, a schedule of which circuits are used in each preset. See also: preset.

pre-set spot   In Britain, a term sometimes used for an FOH (front of house) spotlight with an automatic color-changing device. Also called 'auto.' (Bentham LIGHTING 343, 348–349)

press   See: efforts.

press agent   A publicity representative, as for a playwright or producer. Also called a flack, PA, rep, theatrical press agent, press representative, or theatrical representative. (Bowman/Ball THEATRE)

press book   A scrapbook with press clippings about a performer or a production. (Bowman/Ball THEATRE)

press list   A list of critics and reviewers who are to be given free tickets.

press matter   Publicity releases.

press pass   A complimentary ticket for a member of the press, usually a reviewer or someone who helps promote theatre through feature stories.

press release   A publicity story, prepared by a theatre or producing company's staff and given to the media.

press representative   See: press agent.

pressure board   A piece of wood used in compressing a limelight bag.

prestigiatores (Latin Roman)   Jugglers; they performed in the mime. Among the types were *pilarii*, who worked with balls, and *ventilatores*, who used daggers. See also: *acetabulum*. (Nicoll MASKS 85, Chambers MEDIAEVAL I 7)

pretend play   See: spontaneous drama.

prétintailles (French)   17th C printed materials appliquéd to a gown. (Boucher FASHION)

pretzel   See: artist's stump.

preventive puppetry   A performance before children which stresses preventive health (care of teeth, immunization, fire safety, etc.). Also sometimes used with children suffering from personality disorders, to head off even more serious mental problems in adulthood. (Philpott DICTIONARY)

preview   A performance given before the official opening of a production.

pride   See: *hubris*.

prima ballerina, *prima ballerina* (Italian)   The leading female dancer in a ballet company, a title bestowed on only the greatest dancers. The title in full is *prima ballerina assoluta*.

prima donna (Italian)   Literally: first woman. 1. The principal female singer in an opera company. 2. See: *innamorata*. 3. A leading actress whose temperamental outbursts present difficulties to directors and her fellow performers. 4. In burlesque, a female performer with a powerful soprano voice. 5. In minstrelsy, a female impersonator. Also called a wench role. (Sandberg "Mills" 341, Wilmeth LANGUAGE)

primal theatre   Enactment which stresses direct apprehension of a dramatic event at a deeply emotional level by performers and audiences. (Rubin "Primal" 55)

primarum partium actor (Latin Roman)   See: *protagonistes.*

prime   To treat new scenic canvas with size and pigment.

primera parte de barba (Spanish)   The first old man's part in a 17th C play. (Rennert SPANISH 187)

primera parte de galán (Spanish)   The first young man's part in a 17th C play. (Rennert SPANISH 187)

primitive theatre   A pejorative term, now obsolete, used in the early 20th C to describe ritual or religious performances in non-western, non-Judeo-Christian societies. According to Gorelik, tribal participation, masking, and spirit contact were the major performance elements. (Gorelik NEW)

primo uomo (Italian)   Literally: first man. The principal male singer in an opera company.

Prince Albert   See: frock coat.

princeps gregis (Latin Roman)   Literally: head of a theatre company. See also: *dominus gregis.* (O'Connor CHAPTERS 35)

prince's box, princess' box   See: royal box.

princess(e), princess(e) dress   1. A 19th C gown of one piece in front, with its fullness drawn to the back over a crinoline. (Boucher FASHION) 2. A 20th C silhouette using front and back seaming to draw the fabric close to the body from neck to hip, with a slight flare widening to the hem.

principal   1. In the Elizabethan theatre, an apprentice specializing in leading female roles. 2. In the Elizabethan theatre and later, a member of an acting troupe, as opposed to a hireling. 3. In the 18th C, a performer with a speaking part, as opposed to a walk-on. 4. A performer playing a leading role. Also called a principal actor or actress. (Bowman/Ball THEATRE)

principal boy   In British pantomimes, the role of the spirited hero, often played by a woman. Also called (the) boy. (Bowman/Ball THEATRE)

principales (Philippine)   Stage stars. (Fernández ILOILO 124)

principal girl   1. In British pantomimes, the role of the lovable heroine. 2. In vaudeville and burlesque, a female who plays major roles in skits or bits. (Bowman/Ball THEATRE, Wilmeth LANGUAGE)

printed flag   In Britain in the 19th C, a piece of information shown on stage in unlicensed theatres. (Bowman/Ball THEATRE)

prism stage   A Renaissance stage set with *periaktoi* (Greek). (Nagler SOURCES 87)

private   As a stage direction in the past, aside.

private box   In 18th and 19th C theatres, an enclosed box or one with partitions above eye level, for patrons wishing privacy. Sometimes called a lattice. Now it is called simply a box.

private house   See: private theatre.

private performance   1. A performance not open to the public but only to invited guests. 2. Formerly in Britain, a private theatre club's performance for its members. See also: coterie theatre.

private theatre   1. A theatre in Shakespeare's time, usually within the city of London proper and indoors; open to the public but with higher admission charges than the public theatres and hence a more sophisticated clientele. Sometimes called a private house. 2. A theatre not open to the public but only to members. Such theatres are usually used for amateur productions. Hence, private stage. (Bowman/Ball THEATRE)

private theatrical   A performance in a private home, usually by amateurs but sometimes involving professionals.

Proagon, proagon (Greek)   Literally: before the contest. From at least the mid-5th C BC, a ceremony preliminary to the City Dionysia and the Lenaea in which the competing poets announced the plays and their subjects, and introduced their actors; the actors were not masked or costumed. Pickard-Cambridge notes of a well-known Proagon: "A moving incident occurred at the Proagon of 406 BC, after the news of the death of Euripides had been received, when Sophocles appeared in mourning and brought in his chorus and actors without the customary garlands, and the audience burst into tears." (Pickard-Cambridge FESTIVALS 67–68, Allen ANTIQUITIES 42, Bieber HISTORY 53)

pro am   See: professional amateur.

probability   In playwriting, the establishment of credibility, or, as Aristotle postulated, making the action of a play seem necessary and probable. (Hatlen ORIENTATION)

problem play   See: social drama.

processe, procession   A medieval play or pageant. (Chambers MEDIAEVAL II 138, Ward LITERATURE I 104)

processio (Latin)   See: liturgical drama.

processional cycle, processional play, processional staging   Terms used for medieval plays performed on pageant wagons rather than on a stationary platform. Each episode in the story was presented on a separate wagon stage, which was wheeled to the places where audiences were gathered.

processus (Latin)   In medieval England, a play, especially one connected with a Corpus Christi festival. The term at first applied to the procession that was a part of the festival but in time came to mean the play itself. (Ward LITERATURE I 45) *procurator* (Latin Roman)   Apparently a person in charge of a kind of theatrical warehouse.

pro digs   In Britain, theatrical apartments—professional diggings.

pro-donna   A late 19th C music hall term for an actress.

produce   To stage a production.

producer   1. One who arranges for the staging of a production, including financing and management. Sometimes called, more specifically, a theatrical producer; sometimes also an impresario. In Britain, manager, formerly stage manager. 2. Formerly in Britain, a director. (Bowman/Ball THEATRE)

production   1. A completed stage presentation. (Carrington THEATRICANA) 2. In vaudeville, an act with a large cast and elaborate scenery. (Wilmeth LANGUAGE)

production account   Especially in Britain, a stage manager's record of all expenses incurred during the rehearsal period. (Baker THEATRECRAFT)

production book   The stage manager's copy of a play, complete with all types of cues and other notes on the staging of the work. Also called the promptbook.

production crew   Backstage personnel working on a show.

production manager   In Britain, the person who organizes and administers the backstage departments, including lighting, properties, and costumes.

production number   1. An elaborate ensemble routine. 2. The next to the last act on a bill.

production stage manager   A U.S. term for the stage manager of a production company, sometimes of a theatre frequently hosting production companies. Abbreviation: PSM. (Bowman/Ball THEATRE)

proedria (Greek)   1. From the 5th C BC, the right to a seat of honor in a theatre. 2. The section containing such seats. Depending upon the number needed at various times and in various theatres, the seats of honor might be limited to a portion of the front row of the auditorium, or they might extend through a number of rows. Often called in English seats of honor. See also: *tribunal*. (Haigh ATTIC 335–336, Pickard-Cambridge FESTIVALS 268–270, Allen ANTIQUITIES 65)

(the) profession   The theatre as a vocation and the people who practice it, particularly performers; sometimes restricted to exclude, for example, vaudeville. Hence, the theatrical profession, the dramatic profession, pro, professional actor, professional performance, professional production rights, professional theatre. (Bowman/Ball THEATRE)

professional amateur   A vaudevillian who made a career of performing in amateur nights. (Wilmeth LANGUAGE)

professional courtesy   See: courtesy.

professional matinee   An afternoon performance on a day not usually used for matinees, so that participants in other shows in town can attend. See also: midnight matinée. (Sobel NEW)

professor   1. In a Punch and Judy performance, the showman. Also called a Punch professor. (Crothers PUPPETEER'S 85) 2. In vaudeville, the leader of the house orchestra.

profile   1. The irregular edge of a flat piece of scenery representing rocks, trees, etc. Hence, profile board (plywood or hardboard, often used to create such scenery), profile flat, profile piece, profiling. In Britain, cut-out or fret piece. 2. See: profile position, profile spot.

profile board   Thin wood (such as plywood) covered with canvas and cut to give it an irregular edge—to simulate foliage, rocks, etc. Also called profiling.

profile position   The stance of a performer whose side is toward the audience.

profile spot   In Britain, the usual term for U.S. ellipsoidal reflector spot. The phrase is sometimes used more generally for any spotlight whose beam has a hard edge. Sometimes reduced to profile. (Bentham ART 68–69, 311; Baker THEATRECRAFT)

profiling   See: profile board.

profit and delight   The translation of a phrase, originally by the Roman theorist-critic Horace, for the enlightenment and entertainment which many accept as the double aim of drama.

program, programme (British)   1. The bill of a production—a printed folder or pamphlet containing information about the production: cast of characters, author, producing credits, notes on the play, sometimes biographies of the participants, and often advertising. Programs are sometimes given away and sometimes sold. See also: souvenir program. 2. The evening's entertainment, especially when it consists of more than one work. (Sobel NEW)

programma (Latin Roman)   Playbill, program. Plural *programmata*. See also: *praecones*. (Sandys COMPANION 520)

programming   Making up a season of productions or the sequence of acts on a variety bill.

programming panel   See: interconnecting panel.

progression   The forward movement of the plot of a play.

project   To make one's performance carry throughout an auditorium.

projected scenery   A scenic projection. An image (or images) in light used as part of the environment of a stage production. An element of the design produced by a variety of optical methods.

projecting platform stage   A thrust stage. (Miller "Factors" 89–90)

projection   1. The means by which a performer reaches an audience effectively, through speech, movement, or gesture. 2. An image thrown on the stage by light passing through a slide or other modifying object(s). 3. The throwing of such an image.

projection booth   1. A room, usually at the rear of an auditorium, where follow spots may be operated. 2. A specially-equipped room at the rear of an auditorium where film projectors are operated. One room may serve both the above purposes.

projection lantern, projector lantern   See: projector lamp, projector unit.

projection machine   An effects machine used for projecting still or moving pictures.

Projektionsapparat (German)   See: *Bildprojektionsapparat.*

projector   1. In the U.S., a frequent shortening of beam projector and of projector unit. Projector for slide projector, widespread outside the theatre, is often heard among backstage personnel. The meaning of projector in a particular theatre may vary with the theatre's stagecraft: slide projectors are more common in some theatres than beam projectors. (Bellman SCENE, Sellman/Lessley ESSENTIALS) 2. In Britain, any directional lighting instrument. (Corry PLANNING, Granville DICTIONARY, Bax MANAGEMENT 186)

projector lamp   1. A lamp used in a projector. 2. A reflector lamp. 3. In Britain, any lighting instrument which produces a narrow beam. Among other British terms: pageant lantern, projector lantern, projection lantern. (Bowman/Ball THEATRE)

projector lantern   See: projector lamp, projector unit.

projector spot   See: beam projector.

projector unit   A lighting instrument which will project scenery. Often shortened to projector. In Britain, projection or projector lantern. (McCandless "Glossary" 633, Bowman/Ball THEATRE)

proletarian opera   An opera dealing with the working class.

prologo (Italian)   Prologue: a speech preceding the performance of a play.

prologue   1. In some plays, an opening address to the audience. 2. The speaker of such an introduction. 3. In Aristotle's *Poetics*, the part of a play before the entrance of the chorus. Prologues were designed, even in classical times, to secure the attention of the audience and often to warm them for what was to follow. The main varieties of prologues were also developed in Greece and Rome: a prologue might begin the action of the play, report events which took place before it, explain the plot, or ask a fair hearing for the play or playwright. The speaker might be a character in the play, a character labeled Prologue (Prologus in some Latin plays), or a god. (Duckworth NATURE 29, 36–37, 61–65, 211–216) See also: induction. 4. An expository opening scene in a play. Sophocles' *Antigone* and *Oedipus the King* contain examples.

prologus (Latin)   In medieval productions: 1. The introduction to a play. 2. The speaker of that introduction.

(en) promenade (French)   Literally: in a walk. In ballet, a term indicating that a dancer turns slowly on one foot while holding a pose. (Grant TECHNICAL)

prompt   To give a performer his or her line or action, especially when it is forgotten. Also a noun. Hence, prompter, prompt corner, prompt side, opposite prompt, prompting, take a prompt, etc. (Bowman/Ball THEATRE)

prompt bell   In 17th C theatres and later, a bell rung by the prompter to signal performers, stage technicians, or musicians.

prompt board   A panel where cue signals, the house telephone, the act call bell, etc. are located. (Carrington THEATRICANA)

promptbook, prompt copy, prompt script   A play text containing the prompter's notes on entrances, scene shifts, music cues, etc.

prompt box, prompter's box   In opera houses and some older theatres, a small, hooded prompter's position downstage center, facing the stage. Here the prompter sits with his or her head just above stage level.

prompt copy   See: promptbook.

prompt corner   Especially in Britain, the prompter's position, on the working side (usually stage left) and offstage. Some theatres, especially opera houses, have prompt boxes downstage center.

prompt desk   The desk on the working side of the stage used by the prompter or stage manager.

prompt door   See: PD.

prompt entrance   In Britain, the way onto the stage from the prompter's corner.

prompter   The person who follows the script of the play during rehearsals and performances and assists performers when they forget lines. The use of a prompter is by no means universal in modern stage productions. The prompter in the 16th C and later was similar to a modern stage manager and was responsible for writing out sides for the performers and running rehearsals and performances. The prompter was also responsible for overseeing a company's library of play scripts. Some prompters filled in for absent performers. Also called the book-keeper or book holder, and, in medieval times, the ordinary.

prompter's bell   In Restoration theatres and later, a signal used to summon performers or cue music or dance. "By the tinkling of this bell, if a lady in Tragedy be in the spleen for the absence of her lover . . . [the prompter] can conjure up soft music to sooth [her] distress." (Hill/Popple PROMPTER 12 November 1734)

prompter's box   See: prompt box.

prompter's boy   An 18th C call boy; "a person (in all regular theatres) appointed to call the Performers from the Green-Room, when they are to go upon the stage." (Hughes in Hume London 130n, O'Keeffe RECOLLECTIONS II 422)

prompter's chalk   In the 18th C British theatre and later, a line drawn on the stage floor (now often a tape) behind each set of wings, beyond which people backstage are not to step lest they be seen by the audience. (Hogan LONDON cliii)

prompter's whistle   In 17th C theatres and later, a signal used to cue scene changes. "At the least blast of it I have seen houses move as it were upon wings, cities turned into forests. . . . " (Hill/Popple PROMPTER 12 November 1734)

prompt proper   In Britain, the usual position of the prompter, offstage down left. (Granville DICTIONARY)

prompt script   See: promptbook.

prompt side   Abbreviation: PS. The side of the stage where the prompter or stage manager is stationed; the working side of the stage, often stage left, but the side varies with the architecture of a theatre building.

prompt table   A table at the front of the stage during rehearsals, used by the stage manager for prompting.

prompt wing   The offstage space on the side where the prompter or stage manager is located.

prong connector   See: load connector.

pronuntiato tituli (Latin Roman)   An announcement of the title of a play as it was about to begin. (Sandys COMPANION 520)

prop   A property—any object used onstage that cannot be classified as scenery, costumes, or lights: furniture, ash trays, floor and table lamps, vases of flowers, etc. Plural: props. Properties are usually divided into personal (articles provided by or carried by a performer), character (articles used to aid characterization), hand or small (articles handled by performers), set or heavy (objects on the floor, such as furniture), and trim (hangings, pictures on a wall). Hence, prop basket, prop beard, prop box, prop list, prop plot, prop snow, prop table, prop truck, etc. A property required by the text of a play is sometimes called a functional prop.

propaganda play   A militant social or political play designed to agitate an audience, often to action. See also: agit-prop theatre.

propaganda trial   A form of theatre, partly prepared and partly improvised, presented by the Communist Party in Russia in the 1920s. Pseudo-leaders of the White Russian army, landed proprietors, drunkards, and historical figures who were out of favor were put on trial, with the audience serving as jurors and reaching a verdict by the end of the performance. (Gorchakov RUSSIA 142–143)

prop basket   In Britain, a hamper for small properties.

prop box   A container for stage properties. In Britain, property basket.

prop crew   Stagehands responsible for stage properties.

prop department   The unit within a theatre responsible for stage properties—the prop master/mistress and his/her prop crew.

property   See: prop.

property plot   See: prop list.

prop gag   A piece of comic business involving a property.

prop list   A schedule showing the required properties for a production and their placement. In Britain, property plot.

prop loft   A property room or storage area above stage level.

prop maker   Formerly, a theatre employee responsible for all light and heavy properties.

prop master, prop mistress   The person in charge of properties and the property crew (the clearers). The terms are usually shortened to prop master, prop mistress, or simply props; property person/prop person have recently come into use.

proportion   In directing, the relation of one part of the stage picture to another.

proportional dimming   Controlling a number of dimmers so that the relation between the brightness of the individual lights remains constant as all are faded up or down. Sometimes called differential dimming in Britain. (Bellman SCENE; Lounsbury THEATRE; Ridge/Aldred LIGHTING 56, 60, 76)

proportional mastering   Proportional dimming which uses a master control. (Bellman SCENE 353)

prop person   See: prop master.

prop rehearsal   In a production requiring many properties, a rehearsal concentrating on their placement and use.

proprietor   In a Restoration or 18th C theatre, the owner of a patent or license; in the 19th and early 20th C, the owner of a theatre (the owner of the license being the licensee, who might also be the proprietor).

prop room   A storage space for small properties.

props   The usual backstage term for: 1. Properties. 2. The person in charge of properties. 3. Sometimes, anyone on the property crew.

prop shop   A working area where properties are prepared. It is sometimes in the property room but is often part of a scene shop.

prop table   A table offstage where hand properties are laid out.

prop truck   An offstage wagon for laying out stage properties and sometimes for moving them.

pros   1. Abbreviation (usually followed by a period) for proscenium. 2. Short for professionals. (Bowman/Ball THEATRE) *prosa* (Latin)   A trope or addition to a medieval French church service using prose lines, particularly at the end of the Alleluia. (Frere WINCHESTER xxii)

pros. batten, pros batten   See: proscenium batten.

pros. border, pros border   In Britain, a shortening of proscenium border. See: teaser.

prosc   Proscenium.

proscaenium (Latin Roman)   1. The front wall of the low stage or *pulpitum*, which was the acting area. This use corresponds to the earlier use of *proskenion* for the much higher columned front of the Greek *skene* (scene building). In addition to being lower, the Roman front wall was closed, and did not necessarily have columns. 2. The stage—the *pulpitum* itself. 3. The theatre. 4. Occasionally, the colonnaded, highly decorated front of the scene building, behind the *pulpitum*. 5. See: *proskenion*. *Proscenium* is a variant spelling. (Arnott SCENIC 20; Arnott ANCIENT 85, 106, 108; Pickard-Cambridge DIONYSUS 216)

proscenio (Italian)   See: *piazza della scena*.

proscenio (Spanish)   Proscenium. See also: *embocadura*.

proscenium   1. In U.S. English, rarely, the stage of the ancient Greek and Roman theatre. 2. Formerly, the area in front of the 'scene.' 3. The wall which divides the stage from the auditorium. 4. The opening in that wall, through which the spectator views the stage, though that is more precisely called the proscenium arch or opening. See also: frontispiece. Proscenium is sometimes abbreviated to pros. or prosc.

proscenium (Latin Roman)   See: *proscaenium*.

proscenium arch, proscenium frame, proscenium opening   The opening in the proscenium wall through which the spectator views the stage.

proscenium balcony   In Restoration theatres and later, a small acting area (or sometimes spectator area) above a proscenium door, overlooking the forestage.

proscenium batten   In Britain, the first light pipe upstage of the proscenium. Also called the chamber batten, concert batten, number one batten (often written No. 1 or #1 batten), pros batten. (Granville DICTIONARY 154)

proscenium border   See: teaser.

proscenium box   A box for spectators next to or (formerly) in the proscenium. See also: stage box.

proscenium ceiling   In Restoration theatres and later, the ceiling of the proscenium arch.

proscenium closure   Any system—such as sliding panels or movable walls— capable of adjusting the size and shape of a proscenium opening or of closing it completely.

proscenium door   Formerly, a door in the proscenium wall, opening onto the forestage or apron, serving as a major entrance for performers. One door on each side of the stage was common, but some Restoration theatres had two.

proscenium frame   See: proscenium arch.

proscenium ladder   See: ladder lights.

proscenium length   Especially in Britain, a short striplight just upstage of the top or side of the proscenium. See also: proscenium strip. (Bowman/Ball THEATRE)

proscenium light(s)   Any light source just upstage of the sides of the proscenium. In the early decades of the 20th C in the U.S., the term meant proscenium striplight(s). Britain has used the phrase as an alternate for their 'ladder lights.' (McCandless "Glossary" 630)

proscenium opening   See: proscenium arch.

proscenium sides   In Restoration theatres and later, the side walls of the proscenium arch, into which proscenium doors were set.

proscenium slot   1. A vertical opening between the auditorium side wall and the side of the proscenium opening, for positioning spotlights. Also called a sidewall slot or port. 2. A similar but horizontal ceiling opening in the auditorium, close to the proscenium opening, for spotlights.

proscenium splay   A section of a proscenium arch which slants to meet the side wall of the auditorium. (Bowman/Ball THEATRE)

proscenium spot   A spotlight at the side of the proscenium, in the tormentor position. (Buerki STAGECRAFT, Rae/Southern INTERNATIONAL)

proscenium stage   A stage which is framed by a proscenium arch, as opposed to an arena stage or other form with no proscenium. (Bowman/Ball THEATRE)

proscenium strip, proscenium striplight   In the U.S., a vertical striplight on the stage side of the proscenium wall. See also: proscenium length. (McCandless "Glossary" 635)

proscenium theatre   A theatre with a stage framed by a proscenium arch.

proscenium thickness   The depth of a proscenium arch from front to back. In earlier theatres with proscenium doors, the depth was several feet. (Bowman/Ball THEATRE)

proscenium wall   The structural wall between the stage and auditorium. It is the front wall of the stage house, and in it is the proscenium arch or opening.

proscenium wing   See: tormentor.

proskenion (Greek)   1. At least by the late 4th C BC in some theatres, a colonnade just before the *skene* (scene building), contiguous to it, and as high as the first story of the *skene*. 2. The colonnade and its roof taken as a whole. 3. Sometimes, the roof alone. These uses are related to the term's literal meaning, which comes from *pro*, in front of, and *skene*. The word could therefore mean anything between the *skene* and the *orchestra*, whether simply space or what was in the space.

The use of the *proskenion* in production is disputed. The majority view is that the roof of the stone *proskenion* (2nd C BC?) was from the beginning used as the *logeion* (acting place). By the 1st C BC or perhaps somewhat earlier, *logeion* and possibly *theologeion* meant the roof, and perhaps the structure as a whole.

The word *proskenion* does not occur in any extant Greek play, nor in Greek at all until about 300 BC; some modern writers use the Latin spelling *proscaenium* (q.v.). (Pickard-Cambridge DIONYSUS 156–160, 172–190, 216–218; Arnott SCENIC 19; Arnott ANCIENT 84)

prospect   In theatres equipped with wing-and-shutter scenery, the view or vista painted in perspective on the scenery, especially on the shutters (or a drop).

prospective   Joseph Furttenbach's 17th C term for scenery; probably from Italian *prospettiva*: outlook, view, perspective. (Furttenbach in Hewitt RENAISSANCE 245)

prospettivo per angolo (Italian)   See: *scena per angolo*.

prosser   A pro, a professional.

prosthetics   See: makeup prosthetics.

prostitutes' *kabuki* (English-Japanese)   See: *yujo kabuki*.

pros. wings, pros wings   Especially in Britain and Australia, semi-permanent wings or returns used to mask the downstage extremities of a setting. (National TECHNICAL, Granville DICTIONARY)

Proszeniumsscheinwerfer (German)   Literally: proscenium spotlight. A spotlight used to light the stage apron or the stage area near the plane of the proscenium. In recent decades, these spotlights have evidently been used mainly in the tormentor position. Earlier in the century they were apparently used from the auditorium and covered more of the stage than its downstage portion. (Fuchs LIGHTING 210, Rae/Southern INTERNATIONAL 58)

protagonist   The principal character in a play. In some modern plays, such as Gerhart Hauptmann's *The Weavers*, the protagonist is a group of characters.

protagonistes (Greek)   Literally: first contestant. Protagonist, leading performer. The earliest known use, by Aristotle in the *Poetics*, is figurative: he says Aeschylus made the dialogue the protagonist in drama. The earliest known application of the word to an actor is after the end of the 1st C AD (when Latin *primarum partium actor* was an equivalent). In English, however, the temptation to speak of the leading actor of all periods as the protagonist has been irresistible; the sense of 'leading character' is also frequent. The occurrences of *deuteragonistes* as 'second actor' or 'secondary actor' are also late, and even rarer than theatre uses of *protagonistes*. The word *tritagonistes*, though relatively frequent, appears to have been coined by Demosthenes (4th C BC), who applied it scornfully (third-rate actor) in a political context; the word seems never to have become a general term for a third actor. By the 3rd C AD, the three Greek words distinguished three classes of actors into which the profession had by that time fallen. See also: deuteragonist, tritagonist. (Allen ANTIQUITIES 138–139, O'Connor CHAPTERS 31–36, Pickard-Cambridge FESTIVALS 132–135)

protasis   See: protatic character.

protatic character   One who, after taking part in the exposition of a play, sometimes silently, does not appear again. Such characters occur in classic Greek tragedy (for example, the watchman in *Agamemnon*, Hephaestus in *Prometheus Bound*) and are frequent in Terence. Since an explanation really intended for the audience is made instead to the protatic character, the technique replaces the monologue or an explanatory prologue; and the portion of the play in which it occurs, i.e., the beginning, is sometimes the protasis. (Stuart DRAMATIC 54, 144)

protean   1. A protean actor. (Bowman/Ball THEATRE) 2. Said of a performer able to assume various roles, a play requiring such a performer, etc.

protean actor   A variety performer of the 1890s who made quick changes of costume, makeup, and character, changing the song or monologue each time. Hence, protean artist, protean act, protean drama. Also called a transfigurator. (Sobel NEW)

protean drama   A play requiring a performer to play several roles and to make quick changes; usually a one-man show. Popular in the late 19th C. Hence, protean actor, protean act, etc. (Sobel HANDBOOK 32)

protestation   The prologue to a medieval play. (Chambers MEDIAEVAL II 360)

prothyron (Greek)   Probably the area directly before the *thyromata* (doors) in the *skene* (scene building). The literal meaning, front door, came to include the space before the door; this area was thought of as in the house, not on the street, and led to such meanings as porch, portico, and vestibule. Pickard-Cambridge does not believe a porch or even a vestibule is required by any 5th C BC play. Latin uses *vestibulum* for the same area; also seen are such phrases as *ante aedes*, *ante ianuam* (or *januam*), and *ante ostium*. (Pickard-Cambridge DIONYSUS 75–100, 230–234; Allen ANTIQUITIES 113–114)

proverbe (French)   1. A French dramatic fable with a general, frequently moral theme. These pieces were short, bright, and often funny. 2. In the 19th C, a dialogue with two or three characters on a very small, improvised stage. (Archer PLAY-MAKING 12, Moynet FRENCH 189)

(the) provinces   1. In Britain, theatres or towns outside the London area. 2. In the U.S., sometimes theatres or towns outside the New York area. Hence, provincial drama, provincial stage, etc. Also called Main Street. (Bowman/Ball THEATRE)

Prozessionsspiel (German)   A processional play. Also called an *Umgangspiel*.

prueba (Spanish)   Literally: proof. Try out. Hence, *hacer prueba*, to try out (for a role).

PS, P.S., P-S   See: P.

psaltria (Latin Roman)   A female lutenist, evidently not always just a lutenist: Chambers notes Macrobius' comment (5th C AD) on the "wanton motions" of the *psaltriae*. (Chambers MEDIAEVAL I 9–10)

pseudo-classic drama   Neo-classic drama imitating Greek and Roman models, but altered to satisfy current tastes. Popular in the 18th C in Europe. (Bowman/Ball THEATRE)

pshent   See: shenti.

P side   Prompt side.

PS lamp   See: P.

PSM   See: production stage manager.

psyche knot   A chignon: loops or braids of hair, worn high or low at the back of the neck. Also called a doorknocker. See also: waterfall.

psychodrama   A therapeutic technique in which the therapist (psychodramatist) seeks to mobilize the fantasy life of the patient(s) so that the latter can act out before their fellow patients their problems and fears. (Goodman/Prosperi "Therapies" 21) Others, especially patients and staff members, sometime take part as actors. (Bowman/Ball THEATRE)

psychological drama   A play dealing with psychological subject matter or emphasizing character psychology. (Bowman/Ball THEATRE)

psychological gesture   In acting, the physical equivalent of a psychological reaction; a truthful, expressive gesture used by a performer to externalize an emotion. (Cameron/Hoffman GUIDE)

psychological lighting   See: mood lighting.

psychological naturalism   Naturalism with a tendency to stress psychology in the characters and theme of a play. (Gorelik NEW)

psychological realism   Theatre based on a view of human behavior as defined by late 19th and early 20th C psychology. (Cameron/Gillespie ENJOYMENT)

publicity agent   A person in charge of promoting a stage production.

publicity chaser, publicity hog, publicity hound   A performer thirsty for public attention.

public performance   A theatrical performance before an audience.

public rehearsal   A rehearsal to which a limited number of people are invited; used to test audience reaction. David Belasco referred to this practice as "the French system." (Belasco DOOR 84–85)

public solitude   In the Actors' Studio method, absolute concentration.

public theatre   An open-air playhouse in Shakespeare's time—as opposed to the indoor private theatres and the court theatre.

p'u chü (Chinese)   See: *puju*.

pudding-basin cut   A 15th C hairstyle in which a skullcap of hair remained on the head, but the neck and temples were shaved. Widely seen in France, England, and Italy but not in Germany. (Boucher FASHION)

puddle   To pour small amounts of two or three different paint colors on a flat and then mix them, partially, with a brush. Hence, puddling.

puella (Latin Roman)   See: *virgo*.

pu erh (Chinese)   See: *buer*.

puff   Newspaper publicity, usually free. (Scouten LONDON civ)

pugutan (Philippine)   A beheading scene that appears in religious folk plays such as the *moriones*.

pui (French)   See: *puy*.

puja (Sanskrit, Hindi)   Literally: sacred offerings. In all traditional Indian theatre, the offerings presented before a play to various deities. Such offerings include flowers, incense, music, song, dance, and prayers asking for a successful performance. Bharata specifies in great detail elements of the *puja* in classical theatre (NATYASASTRA 16–17, 33–44). Also called *rangapuja* (stage offering).

puja pantai (Malaysian)   Literally: beach offering. A ceremonial offering to wind and sea spirits that incorporates elements of *ma'yong* performance. (Sheppard KITE x)

puju, p'u chü (Chinese)   A form of music-drama (*xiqu*) popular in southern Shanxi Province and parts of Shaanxi, Gansu, and Henan Provinces which developed c. 16th-17th C. It is the oldest form in Shanxi Province, and among the oldest anywhere, to use music from the *bangziqiang* musical system (*shengqiang xitong*). Also called Puzhou *bangzi* or Poochow *pang tzu*.

puk, bug (Korean)   A double-headed barrel drum used in masked dance plays and in *p'ansori*. (Cho "Ogwangdae" 29)

pull   1. Drawing power. 2. To attract an audience. Hence, pull 'em in, pull good, pull well. 3. To remove a piece of scenery, a costume, a property, etc. from storage. 4. See: jerk.

pull a beard, pull a whisker   To make a verbal blunder. (Berrey/Van den Bark SLANG 588)

pulled review   An advertisement which pulls out of context favorable words from a critic's unfavorable review so as to give the erroneous impression that a show is a hit.

puller   An attraction.

pulley   A grooved wheel in a frame, through which a rope is run. Often called a sheave, though sheave properly refers only to the grooved wheel.

pullim (Korean)   Literally: signal call. A short chant, usually of two or three lines, used in masked dance-drama as a musical cue to begin a dance. Often a Chinese poem and in archaic language. (Yi "Mask" 46)

pull in   A performer capable of attracting good audiences.

pull-off rigging   An operating line used to open and close a traverse curtain.

pull rod   An iron rod, 3/8″ in diameter, with a handle at one end and a hook at the other, used to pull wagons or revolving stages. (Gillette/Gillette SCENERY)

pull ropes   Short lengths of knotted ropes used to pull wagon stages. (Gillette/ Gillette SCENERY)

pulpitum (Latin Roman)   Especially in Vitruvius, the stage. The word is used of both the Greek and Roman theatre, but ordinarily of the Roman. The early Roman theatre of about the 4th to 2nd C BC was a small wooden platform, usually temporary; this was the characteristic performance place of the southern Italian farceurs through whom it reached Rome. It is the developed, permanent Roman stage, however, that is usually meant by the *pulpitum*. This was not usually more than five feet high and often had one or more short flights of steps leading down to the *orchestra*. The front of the *pulpitum* might be plain, or broken by recesses, niches, and perhaps panels. In some later Greek theatres, the front of the *pulpitum* had small doors, some of them not large enough for human use. Sometimes they led from the orchestra under the *pulpitum* to the basement of the scene building. Also called *bema*, occasionally *logeion*; Bieber sometimes uses podium, not clearly Latin or English and uncommon in writers on ancient theatre.(Pickard-Cambridge DIONYSUS 72, 212, 256–257; Arnott SCENIC 1–4, 6–18, 19; Bieber HISTORY 187–188, 202–205, 207–213, figs. 656, 695, 705, 721–722).

pulpitum (Latin)   Especially in medieval productions in Cornwall, a *mansion* (French) or locale. (Chambers MEDIAEVAL II 135–136)

pulpitum proscaenii (Latin Roman)   Literally: The stage of the proscenium. Occasionally, the stage, the *pulpitum*. (Sandys COMPANION 518)

pulp paint   Wet pigments—a paste form of scene paint.

pulse   In dance in its narrowest sense, equal phenomena recurring regularly; the strongest and the first part of a measure. (Turner/Grauert/Zallman DANCE 81)

pulway (Burmese)   See: *palwe*.

punakawan (Indonesian)   1. The collective term for the three, four, or five clown-servants who serve the Pandawa clan in *wayang* plays, most important of which is Semar, a god. In Bali, spelled *panakawan*. One group of *dagelan* characters. (Long JAVANESE 105, Brandon THRONES 13) 2. A clown role in *ludruk*. Also called *pelawak*, *badut*. (Peacock RITES 71) See also: *penasar*.

punch   1. In acting, to give improper emphasis to a word or line. (Carrington THEATRICANA) 2. See: efforts.

Punch and Judy show   A glove or hand puppet show featuring the hook-nosed, hunchback Punch and his wife Judy (originally Joan). Though English in origin (but influenced by Italian *commedia dell'arte* characters), Punch and Judy shows became popular in the U.S.

punched paper   A free ticket.

punch line   The climax of a joke, story, or plot. Also called a punch, payoff, or sock line. (Berrey/Van den Bark SLANG 581)

Punch man   A puppeteer specializing in Punch and Judy shows. (Baird PUPPET 16–17)

Punch professor   See: professor.

punch scene   A fight.

punebre (Philippine)   A funeral march that accompanies a sad scene in *comedia*. (Mendoza COMEDIA 53)

punggawa (Indonesian)   A strong, noble male puppet character in Sundanese *wayang golek*. One type of muscular character (*gagah*). See also: *angkara murka*. (Foley ''Sundanese'' 36)

p'ungmul (Korean)   In *namsadang*, the generic term for music and dances by a farmers' band, one of six acts in a performance. Specific numbers in the *p'ungmul* repertory are: salutation (*insakut*), acrobatics (*tollim-bopku*), a circling dance by groups (*obangjin*), dancing with a child standing on one's shoulders (*mudong-nori*), sideways movements (*kasaejin*), and a gong-player's dance (*sangsoe-nori*). Today, more often called *nongak* (farmers' music). (Kim ''Namsadang'' 11, 12; Sim/Kim KOREAN 23, Chang ''Farmers'' 29)

punk for   To act as a foil or feeder.

punks   Formerly, provincial U.S. audiences.

pupazzo (Italian)   A puppet. (Philpott DICTIONARY)

puppet   1. Usually, a three-dimensional approximation of a living being or animal which is moved by a human. 2. Slang for a performer.

puppet corner   A space, preferably removed from crowded areas and of sufficient size for a few children, where puppets can be made and put into dramatic play. (Hunt/Renfro PUPPETRY 27)

puppetalking   Employing puppets to encourage conversations related to social and emotional growth. (Hunt/Renfro PUPPETRY 121) The practice is especially appropriate with children. Also used in therapeutic situations with other age groups as well.

puppeteaching   A means by which a teacher imparts concepts and information to children, using puppets to capture and sustain interest. (Hunt/Renfro PUPPETRY 97)

puppeteer   An artist who manipulates puppets or marionettes.

puppetelling   Using puppets to tell stories. (Hunt/Renfro PUPPETRY 51)

puppetizing   Free-form enacting of children's ideas with puppets (which the children make themselves). It is informal, improvised, and has no audience.

Used to help children share ideas, stories, and experiences. (Hunt/Renfro PUP-PETRY 81)

puppetote   A device used to carry a puppet from place to place and/or to keep it concealed from view until the appropriate time. (Hunt/Renfro PUPPETRY 57)

puppet play   See: *bunraku, kaksi, kkoktu, kuileixi, nang, wayang, yokthe pwe.*

puppetucker   A place suitable for storing or displaying puppets. It may be a simple compartmented box or carton, or a more elaborate structure. (Hunt/Renfro PUPPETRY 41)

puppie, puppy show   In northern Britain and Scotland, a puppet show. (Philpott DICTIONARY)

purak-che (Korean)   See: *sonang-je.*

purappatu (Malayalam)   Literally: the going forth. In *kathakali*, a pure dance sequence, the third section of the preliminaries before a play. *Pakuti purappatu* is a short version of the dance; *mazhuva purappatu* is a long version. (Jones/Jones KATHAKALI 38)

purbawara (Malaysian)   Literally: old-style presentation. A type of *sandiwara* play in which historical materials are given a realistic presentation. Also called *drama sejarah* (history play).

purchase line   See: operating line.

purgation   See: *katharsis.*

purgos, pyrgos (Greek)   Pollux, the source of the term, says only that it is a tower (the literal meaning) which permits one to look down at the stage. Since *purgos* refers particularly to the towers on the walls of a city, Pollux may have meant a tower-like place on the wall of the theatre. See also: *teichos.* (Nicoll DEVELOPMENT 22)

purification   See: *katharsis.*

Purim King   In medieval Europe, a fat Bacchus on a wine cask; part of the procession leading up to the *Purimshpil* (Purim play). Analogous to a comic Pope, the King was often attended by students who wore goatlike horns and danced in the streets. (Sandrow VAGABOND 1, 3–4; Schauss FESTIVALS 268)

Purim plays   See: *Purimshpiln.*

Purim Rabbi   As part of the medieval *Purimshpil* celebration, a performer who, often with 'disciples,' was given complete freedom to parody prayers, customs, and institutions. (Sandrow VAGABOND 4, Schauss FESTIVALS 268)

Purimshpiln (Yiddish)   Literally: Purim plays. Folk plays given on, and sometimes before and after, the holiday of Purim, which celebrates the Biblical story of Esther (*megile*). The first presentation of the story has been dated 415

AD, the first play in the 9th C, the oldest published text in 1708. Over the centuries, the *Purimspil* acquired some of the characteristics of the medieval mystery: Jewish laws allowed plays at no other time, and as many as twenty Biblical tales have been played on Purim (early Spring). Also spelled *Purimspielen*. (Sandrow VAGABOND 1–20, Lifson YIDDISH 20–21, Kirshenblatt-Gimblett "Contraband" 5)

Purimspieler (Yiddish)   One who acts in a *Purimshpil*. (Lifson YIDDISH 36)

purl   16th C pleating in a ruff. (Chalmers CLOTHES 166)

puroguramu (Japanese)   The printed program sold in a theatre lobby. The term is a phonetic transcription of English 'program.' See also: *bangumi*.

purpose play   See: thesis play.

purvaranga (Sanskrit)   Literally: stage beginning. Preliminaries to the performance of a play in traditional Indian theatre. (Keith SANSKRIT 339–341, Enros in Baumer/Brandon SANSKRIT 277–280) Bharata enumerates 18 separate parts to the preliminaries for classical theatre that include various types of instrumental music, singing, and pure dance (*nritta*) in NATYASASTRA 76–99.

purwa (Indonesian, Malaysian)   Literally: old or original. Several repertories of classic plays based on ancient legends. See: *wayang golek purwa* and *wayang purwa*. (Ulbricht WAYANG 2, Moebirman WAYANG 21)

push   An easy engagement.

pusher   1. A wire device by which figures in a toy theatre are maneuvered into position. Also called a slider. (Philpott DICTIONARY) 2. A scene shifter.

push-on puppet   On a toy-theatre stage, a cutout figure pushed in from the wings via a wooden batten upon which the figure is mounted. (Philpott DICTIONARY)

push shutter   In ellipsoidal reflector spotlights, a built-in cut-off with a small external handle which permits the shutter to be pushed, pulled, or placed at an angle. Spotlights so equipped usually have four such shutters, at top, bottom, and each side. Often called simply shutter. Wehlburg GLOSSARY 52 has an illustration.

pusong (Philippine)   A clown stage assistant in *comedia*. He or she is a volunteer who serves onstage as penance for a favor received from God. See also: *bobo*. (Mendoza COMEDIA 54)

pusta (Sanskrit)   Stage properties. One of four types of spectacle (*aharya*). (Keith SANSKRIT 365)

pu tai hi (Chinese)   See: *po the hi*.

puteje (Philippine)   A puppet play presented by Chinese laborers in the Philippines from Spanish times into the early 20th C. A localized spelling of the Chinese *pu tai hi*. (Banas PILIPINO 182)

puteri ma'yong (Malaysian)   1. A princess role in *ma'yong*. 2. A special performance, lasting several days, in which a sick patient is first diagnosed through a shamanic ritual, and then exorcised by enactment of a *ma'yong* play featuring the character responsible for the patient's sickness. (Yousof "Kelantan" 255–260)

Püterschein system   A method of marionette construction in which the weight of the figure at rest resides in the headstrings. (Philpott DICTIONARY)

put in study   Formerly said of a play that has been cast and is being prepared for performance. (Dunlap in Nagler SOURCES 510)

put in the test tube   To try out a show in a provincial town. Also called try it on the dog. (Berrey/Van den Bark SLANG 583)

put it across, put it over   To impress an audience favorably; to put a performance "across the footlights."

put it up   To schedule a bill.

put on the war paint   To put on makeup.

put out   See: get out.

putran (Indonesian)   The generic term for characters or puppets of knights in Javanese *wayang*. (Muljono in Osman TRADITIONAL 62)

putren   (Indonesian)   The generic term for female characters or puppets in Javanese *wayang*. (Muljono in Osman TRADITIONAL 62)

putri (Indonesian)   Literally: woman. The role of a princess or queen in classical plays. The *jejer putri* (women's scene) in a shadow play is a scene set in the women's quarters or in which women play major roles. An example is in *The Death of Karna* in Brandon THRONES 315–320.

put the face on   1. To grimace. 2. To put on makeup.

put to bed   To take out of use permanently.

putty   A soft, pliable paste or viscous substance used by performers to fashion three-dimensional changes, especially of facial features (nose, chin, etc.). Also called nose putty.

putty nose   A low comedian.

"Put up your lights."   Especially in the professional theatre, a stage manager's direction to the electrician to increase the light. (Bowman/ Ball THEATRE)

"Put your hands together."   Especially in Britain, a call by a master of ceremonies for applause to welcome a performer to the stage. (PBS "Mystery" 1983)

puy (French)   A medieval religious-literary-dramatic club that produced plays. (Chambers MEDIAEVAL II 87)

Puzhou *bangzi* (Chinese)   See: *puju*.

pwe (Burmese)   The generic term for a show. See: *anyein pwe, yokthe pwe*.

pya zat (Burmese)   Literally: enacted story. Popular dramas, written during the 19th C, composed of prose and verse sections, and performed with songs and dances. Major playwrights were U Kyin U, U Pon Nya, and U Pok Ni. (Aung DRAMA 36, Pok Ni KONMARA 6)

pyjamas   See: moghul breeches.

pyolsandae (Korean)   See: *sandaeguk*.

pyolsin-kut (Korean)   Literally: shamanic ritual to a deity. A satirical masked dance-drama held every tenth year in Hahoe village, North Kyongsang Province, as part of *pyolsin* ritual observations. Its wooden masks are unique. (Cho KOREA 12, 49; Korean MASKS 9–10)

p'yonnom (Korean)   Performers of *sandaeguk*. (Cho ''Yangju'' 29)

pyrgos (Greek)   See: *purgos*.

pyrrhic dance   Originally a Spartan dance (6th C BC or earlier) using military movement; in Athens, a similar dance which emphasized graceful movement. After a time, the dance became distinctly Dionysian, using stories of the god and replacing spears with torches and *thrysi*. In Rome, the dance was apparently similar, but with greater emphasis on warlike movement. Also called a pyrrhic. In Greek: *pyrriche;* sometimes spelled *pyrrhiche* or *pyrricha*. (Lawler DANCE 106-108; Bieber HISTORY 50, 237; Chambers MEDIAEVAL I 7)

Q

Q   Short for light cue.

Q.I., Q.I. lamp   See: tungsten-halogen lamp.

qiang, ch'iang (Chinese)   Literally: tune. 1. A passage of music used to sing a single written character; one of the principal components of *banqiangti* musical structure. Sometimes translated as melodic-phrase. (Wichmann "Aural" 136–146) 2. More generally, a sung melodic passage of any length in music-drama (*xiqu*).

qiangdiao (Chinese)   See: *diaoshi*.

qianju, ch'ien chü (Chinese)   Guizhou (Kueichow) opera, a form of music-drama (*xiqu*) popular in Guizhou Province which developed out of story telling (*quyi*) in the 1950s; its principal accompanying instrument is the dulcimer. Also called *wenqinju* or *wen ch'in chü*.

qiantai (Chinese)   See: *wutai*.

qiba, ch'i pa (Chinese)   1. Literally: flags and handles. The collective name for stage properties (*qibao*) and stage weapons (*bazi*) in Beijing opera (*jingju*) and many other forms of music-drama (*xiqu*). 2. Written with different characters, literally: arising to dominance. A set of connected conventional movements, expressive of straightening a helmet and armor and preparing for battle, which are used in martial plays (*wuxi*) in Beijing opera (*jingju*) and many other forms of music-drama (*xiqu*). (Halson PEKING 50; Scott CLASSICAL 127, 129, 134, 226)

qibao, ch'i pao (Chinese)   Literally: flags and wraps, flags and parcels. The generic term for stage properties in Beijing opera (*jingju*) and many other forms of music-drama (*xiqu*). Frequently used stage properties are named and described in Halson PEKING 41–43, Scott CLASSICAL 172–175, and Zung SECRETS 23–27. See also: *qiba*.

qingchang, ch'ing ch'ang (Chinese)   Literally: pure singing. The singing of music-drama (*xiqu*) without makeup or costumes, to simple instrumental accompaniment. Most performances consist of excerpts from a number of plays, although one or two complete plays can make up a bill. (Mackerras RISE 79)

qingju, ch'ing chü (Chinese)   A form of music-drama (*xiqu*) popular in Hunan and Jiangxi Provinces which developed in the 17th C in the Qingyang region of Hunan. It uses both *lianquti* and *banqiangti* musical structure and includes music from three musical systems: *gaoqiang*, *kunshanqiang*, and a version of *bangziqiang*. Also called *qingyangxi* or *ch'ing yang hsi*. In Jiangxi Province, called *chu'nanxi* or *ch'u nan hsi*.

qingmingxi, ch'ing ming hsi (Chinese)   Plays performed during the fifth solar period (Qingming) festival, about two weeks after the spring equinox, in honor of the dead, c. 16th–18th C. (Mackerras RISE 22–23)

qingxi, ch'ing hsi (Chinese)   A form of music-drama (*xiqu*) which developed out of elements introduced into Hubei Province from Anhui Province in the 18th C. It featured music of the *gaoqiang* musical system (*shengqiang xitong*). *Qingxi* ceased to exist as a separate theatre form in the first half of the 20th C, but many of its techniques were absorbed by *chuju* in the 1950s. (Mackerras MODERN 156)

qingyangqiang, ch'ing yang ch'iang (Chinese)   A form of music-drama (*xiqu*) from Qingyang in Anhui Province, 15th–16th C and still extant. It developed from the combination of *yiyangqiang*, *yuyaoqiang*, and local folk music. (Mackerras RISE 4)

qingyangxi (Chinese)   See: *qingju*.

qingyi (Chinese)   See: *zhengdan*.

qinqiang, ch'in ch'iang (Chinese)   1. A regional form of music-drama (*xiqu*) which arose c. 15th C in Shaanxi and Gansu Provinces and is popular today throughout north and northwestern China. It is probably the earliest form of what came to be called the *bangziqiang* musical system; its music developed from Shaanxi and Gansu folk songs, utilizing the *bangzi* clapper for percussion accompaniment, and was later influenced by the *kunshanqiang* and *gaoqiang* musical systems. From the 16th to the 18th C it spread eastward, giving rise to a number of other forms which use *bangziqiang* music. Also called Shaanxi *bangzi* or Shensi *pang tzu*; in the 18th and 19th C, sometimes called 'jumbled plucking' (*luantan*). (Mackerras RISE 7–10, 81–115) 2. See: *bangziqiang*.

qiongju, ch'iung chü (Chinese)   A form of music drama (*xiqu*) popular today in the Hainan Island and Leizhou Peninsula regions of Guangdong Province. It arose in the 15th and 16th C, combining Jiangxi Province *yiyangqiang* and Hainan Island folk music, and was later influenced by southern *yueju* and civilized theatre (*wenmingxi*). Also called *hainanxi* or *hai nan hsi*.

qiongsheng, ch'iung sheng (Chinese)   Literally: poor male role. A poverty-stricken young male role, often that of a young scholar, which features dance-acting (*zuo*) and song (*chang*) skills; a major subdivision of the young male role (*xiaosheng*) in Beijing opera (*jingju*) and many other forms of music-drama (*xiqu*). See also: *xiepisheng*. (Dolby HISTORY 105, 180)

qizhuangtou, ch'i chuang t'ou (Chinese)   Literally: banner costume head. A female hairdressing style (*baotou*) featuring a wide, elaborate headdress called the *liangbatou* or *liang pa t'ou*, literally "two handle head." It is worn in Beijing opera (*jingju*) in the portrayal of Manchu court ladies. (Scott CLASSICAL 139, 166)

Qs   Cues.

qu, ch'ü (Chinese)   Literally: song, melody. A type of rhymed verse for singing, written in regulated lines of uneven length to fixed-melodies (*qupai*). It developed in the 10th-12th C and was widely used in the 13th-17th C. There were two main types, northern *qu* (*beiqu* or *pei ch'ü*) and southern *qu* (*nanqu* or *nan ch'ü*. The most important dramatic northern *qu* are the song lyrics of Yuan *zaju* plays; the major dramatic southern *qu* are the song lyrics of southern drama (*nanxi*) and *chuanqi* plays. See also: *chenzi*, *qupai*. (Dolby HISTORY 34–35, 54–58, 73–74)

quadro (Portuguese)   In Black Brazilian drama, a tableau. (Fernández "Brazil" 13)

Quaker bonnet   See: *calèche*.

quality   1. In dance, the manner in which a movement is performed—light, slow, free-flowing, etc.   2. In lighting, sometimes a synonym for color. (Sellman/Lessley ESSENTIALS)   3. In the plural (as qualities of light): intensity, color, direction, and movement.

quart d'heure (French)   Literally: quarter-of-an-hour. A one-act naturalistic tragedy with the suffering as brief as possible. (Strindberg in Cole/Chinoy PLAYWRITING 15, 21)

(the) quarter   In Britain, the warning call to cast and crew fifteen minutes before curtain.

"Quarter of an hour!"   In Britain, the official warning to performers 15 minutes before curtain time.

quarter position   In acting, a body position half way between full front (facing the audience) and profile.

quartz ellipsoidal   Among lighting personnel, an occasional term for an ellipsoidal reflector spotlight which takes a quartz lamp (now usually called a tungsten-halogen lamp). When the lamp is mounted along the optical axis of these instruments, they are now often called axial mounts.

quartz-halogen, quartz-halogen lamp, quartz-iodine, quartz lamp   See: tungsten-halogen lamp.

quartz light   A spotlight using a quartz lamp (now usually called a tungsten-halogen lamp). Among other terms are quartz-iodine spot and quartz-halogen spot. See also: tungsten-halogen lamp. (Lounsbury THEATRE 94)

quartzline   See: tungsten-halogen lamp.

(à la) quatrième devant, (à la) quatrième derrière (French)   See: positions of the body.

qudi (Chinese)   See: *di*.

qudiao (Chinese)   See: *banshi*.

queen it   Of a leading actress, to put on airs.

queen's box   See: royal box.

queer a manager's pitch   In Britain, to disappoint a manager. (Sobel HANDBOOK)

queer one's act, queer the act, queer the pitch   In Britain and the U.S., to spoil another performer's effect. (Berrey/Van den Bark SLANG 587)

"Que la fête commence!" (French)   Literally: "Let the festivities begin." In the 19th C, an announcement, just before the curtain rose, that the play was about to begin. (Moynet FRENCH 25)

Quem quaeritis? (Latin)   The opening line ("Whom seek ye?") in one of the earliest known tropes (9th C) or dramatic additions to the church service, spoken by the angel to the three Marys who came to the sepulchre on Easter morning. (Ethelwold in Nagler SOURCES 39) Later tropes began with the same words and were performed—always chanted, never spoken—on other religious occasions; Christmas is an example. (Chambers MEDIAEVAL II 9–17, 30–42)

questions   Cues. " . . . I read the questions to Knepp, while she answered me, through all her part of 'Flora's Figary's.' . . . " (Pepys DIARY 5 October 1667)

queue stool   See: stool.

quick change   A rapid costume or scene change. See also: *hayagawari*.

quick-change artist   A performer who specializes in an act requiring one or more fast changes of costumes. Also called a lightning change artist or transformist. See also: protean actor.

quick-change room   A room near the stage where performers can make rapid costume or makeup changes. Sometimes the room is a permanent feature of the building, but often it is a temporary booth created by flats. Also called a stage dressing room.

quick cue   In acting, a cue picked up without a pause.

quick curtain   See: fast curtain.

quick match   Formerly, a brew containing powdered sugar and potash as a base. When ignited, it flared to resemble an explosion. Used in vaudeville shows. (Gilbert VAUDEVILLE 30)

quick study   1. A performer who memorizes lines rapidly. 2. A hasty memorizing of lines. (Bowman/Ball THEATRE)

quintise   See: cointise.

quiver   In striptease, oscillating of the breasts and/or torso and—sometimes—wavelike movements of the abdomen. (Wilmeth LANGUAGE)

quizzing glass   A 19th C round magnifying lens, sometimes mounted in a jeweled fan or on a short or long metallic or tortoise-shell handle, or worn on a silk cord or metallic chain around the neck. Also called a perspective glass. (Wilcox DICTIONARY)

quju, ch'ü chü (Chinese)   A form of music-drama (*xiqu*) popular in Beijing which was developed in the 1950s by storytelling (*quyi*) performers such as Wei Xikui and Gu Rongfu. Its songs use fixed-melodies (*qupai*) derived primarily from popular folk songs.

qunkou (Chinese)   See: *xiangsheng*.

qupai, ch'ü p'ai (Chinese)   Literally: song tablet, song name. A fixed melody; each of the more than 1000 has its own identifying name. Most are derived from folk and popular music. The earliest were used in writing northern and southern song verse (*qu*); most extant fixed-melodies date from the 14th C or later. In those forms of music-drama (*xiqu*) which follow *lianquti* musical structure, a fixed-melody not only provides a melody, but also prescribes the number and placement of written characters within each musical line as well as the pattern of word tones to be followed in writing lyrics. In forms which follow *banqiangti* musical structure, fixed melodies are rarely used in songs, but frequently serve as instrumental music to accompany stage action and dance. Abbreviated *paizi* or *p'ai tzu*. See also: *qu*.

qupo, ch'ü p'o (Chinese)   Literally: song break. 1. A name given to the music and dance form used in the third section (*po*) of a 7th-13th C big song (*daqu*) when performed independently. Popular at palace banquets, 10th-13th C, and sometimes incorporated in 10th-14th C southern drama (*nanxi*) performances, usually as instrumental pieces unaccompanied by dance. (Dolby HISTORY 19) 2. More generally, a generic term for instrumental music used to accompany dance from the 10th to the 13th C. 3. See: *daqu*.

quyi, ch'ü i (Chinese)   Literally: song art. Since 1949, the generic term for all forms of performance in which stories are narrated through song and/or speech, and physical expression, often to musical accompaniment. Usually translated as storytelling. In most forms, one to three performers narrate in the third person, with some first person enactment or imitation of characters; in each such form, performers principally sit, stand, or dance. Forms with more performers emphasize first person enactment, and include only some connective third person narration; many of these forms involve stylized movement, and some are performed with makeup. There are currently more than 300 forms of storytelling in China; major types include *dagu, danxian, lianhualao, pinghua, tanci,* and *tanhuang*. See also: *shuochang*, *xiju*. (Howard CONTEMPORARY 29–31, Mackerras PERFORMING 101–104)

quzixi (Chinese)   See: *meihuju*.

R

R 1. Right—the stage right half of a proscenium stage. 2. At or toward stage right. All references to R or right are from the performer's point of view. 3. Ring—formerly, a prompter's signal to cue the curtain, music, the use of a trap-door, etc. Hence, ring down the curtain. (Shattuck SHAKESPEARE 21) 4. See: reflector lamp.

R1, R1E, R2, R2E, etc. Right first entrance, right second entrance, etc.

R20, R40, R56, R64, R-20, R-40, etc. Designations of the widest diameter of reflector lamps (q.v.) in eighths of an inch; for example, R40 has a five-inch diameter. (Bellman LIGHTING 56, 57)

RAB Ring act bell, that is, the bell used formerly to signal the end of an act, entr'acte music, a scene change, etc. (Shattuck SHAKESPEARE 22)

rabai (Thai) A border (q.v.). (Virulrak "Likay" 134)

rabam (Thai) Literally: group dance. Pure, non-mimetic dance, performed to instrumental music, often with a lyrical text. It is used in dance scenes in classical dance-dramas, in *likay*, during intervals of dramatic presentations, and in preliminaries to performances. See also: *tha lakhon*. (Anuman in Rangthong SOUVENIR 86, Virulrak "Likay" 181–182)

rabat(o), rabatine, rebato A 16th C rather wide, unadorned white collar, sometimes in three layers, sewn to a linen band. Also called a peccadillo. The 17th C woman's version was called a Tiffany whisk. See also: falling band. (Chalmers CLOTHES 166, Wilcox DICTIONARY)

rabbit hutch See: thunder run.

rabbit's foot See: hare's foot.

rabha (Assamese) A specially-constructed pavillion (*pandala*) for *ankiya nat* performances. Also called *namaghara*. (Vatsyayan TRADITIONAL 100)

raceway See: wire way.

racionista (Spanish)   A utility performer, a supernumerary. Also called a *supernumerario*. (Falk "Census" 86)

rack   1. An occasional designation for a framework which supports lights (for example, at the balcony front in some older theatres). See also: dimmer rack. (Bowman/Ball THEATRE) 2. A box office ticket rack.

racket row   See: Tin Pan Alley.

racking   In a box office, placing tickets for each performance in a specially-made rack and in the order of the auditorium's seating plan. (Crampton HANDBOOK)

RAD   Ring act drop—a bell signal used formerly to cue the lowering of a painted drop at the end of an act. (Shattuck SHAKESPEARE 22)

radial arm dimmer   See: stud contact dimmer. (Bowman/Ball THEATRE)

radical theatre   An alternative to traditional theatre, which it opposes. It usually stresses social and political subject matter and uses staging techniques that include *commedia*-like broad comedy, multi-media devices, Artaud-like sounds to convey atmosphere, etc. In the U.S., radical theatre goes back at least to the 1930s, though one associates the term more with the 1960s.

raëshnik (Russian)   The man who provided the commentary at peep shows presented by a *panoramshchik* or peep-show man in 18th-19th C Russia. (Yershov SOVIET 7)

rag   See: house curtain.

raga (Sanskrit)   The basic unit of organization of classical Indian music, combining mode and melodic pattern. A contemporary term. (Hawley KRISHNA 317) The musical system described by Bharata for ancient Indian theatre practice contains no mention of *raga*, and there appears to be a complete break in the melodic traditions of past and present in Indian theatre. See also: *tala*. (Raghavan in Baumer/Brandon SANSKRIT 38)

rag dolling   See: rolling.

rag oprie, rag opry   In early 20th C U.S., a farce with some pathos, presented under canvas. Also called a rag show. (Ashby in Matlaw AMERICAN 144–145)

rag-picture artist   A vaudeville performer whose act consisted of coming on stage with a pushcart full of rags, putting up an easel, and pinning the rags on it. Pictures were then painted on the rags, the last usually being the Statue of Liberty or the American flag. (Laurie VAUDEVILLE 212)

rag show   See: rag oprie.

ragtime   A musical form that originated in New Orleans and is marked by strong syncopation in the melody with a regularly accented accompaniment.

rai (Thai)   Various types of singing/chanting used in Thai classical dance drama, such as *rai chatri* in *lakon jatri*, *rai nai* in *lakon fai nai*, *rai nok* in *lakon nok*, and *ceraca* in *khon* or *nang yai*.

rail   1. A horizontal wooden member of a flat; the term is usually applied to the top and bottom pieces (top or head rail, bottom or sill rail), any intermediate rails being called toggles (short for toggle rails). 2. The horizontal side support of a legged platform, just under the platform top. 3. Pinrail. 4. Strap iron attached to the bottom of a door or French window to reduce friction when the scenic unit is slid along the floor. 5. A protective barrier on a rostrum or stairway, usually offstage. 6. A railing or barrier at the front of a stage. Restoration dandies '' . . . 'twixt Curtain and Rail . . . walk in Fop-alley. . . . '' (Davenant MAN'S 77) 7. Especially in older theatres, the balcony front lighting position, originally the rail at the front of a balcony. (Rubin/Watson LIGHTING 29)

railed, railing in   See: pit railed into boxes.

railing   1. A handrail separating seating areas, separating seating areas from cross aisles, or separating different parts of a theatre. 2. A safety rail at the edge of a balcony or gallery.

rail jump   A journey by train from one stand to the next.

rail lights   See: balcony rails. (Lounsbury THEATRE 9)

railroad   See: road.

rain and sea drum, rain box   An open drum, or a box open on one face, into which are poured dried peas or lead shot; when the container is swished, the sound of rain or the sea is simulated. (Collison SOUND 101)

rain barrel   See: rain pipe.

rainbow wheel   An effect(s) wheel whose rotation moves gelatines of a number of colors across the beam of a spotlight. See also: color wheel, effect wheel. (Bax MANAGEMENT 188, fig. 54; Bowman/Ball THEATRE)

rain box   See: rain and sea drum.

rain drum   A rotating drum containing buckshot or dried peas, for simulating rain.

rain machine   A rain box or rain drum.

rain pipe   A perforated pipe, closed at one end, hung above a stage; water pumped into the pipe escapes through the perforations and gives the effect of rain. Called in Britain a rain barrel or sparge pipe.

rain trough   A channel or pan to catch water dropping from a rain pipe hung above the stage when a rain effect is produced. (Collison SOUND 100)

rainy daisy   A late 19th C skirt whose hem reached a boot-top. Worn in inclement weather. (Barton COSTUME 512)

raise a palm   To receive applause.

raise the dead   In 19th C Britain, to announce to the audience the following week's bill.

raisonneur (French)   A character found in many French plays who serves as an adviser and sets matters straight. The *raisonneur* usually tells the main character and hence the audience what attitude to take toward the events in the play and is often considered the author's spokesman. A descendant of the Greek chorus. (Gallaway CONSTRUCTING 156, Krows PLAYWRITING 365)

rajah besar (Malaysian)   See: *pa'yong*.

rakandai (Japanese)   Literally: Buddhist statue shelf. A cheap, standing-room area located onstage, down right, in an 18th or 19th C *kabuki* theatre. People were crowded in like a row of statues in a temple, hence the name. See also: *yoshino*. (Ernst KABUKI 56, Leiter ENCYCLOPEDIA 309)

rake   Angle, as when the side walls of a stage setting are placed at an angle to the perpendicular, or when the stage or auditorium floor is sloped so that it is lower at the front than at the back.

raked stage   A stage floor that slopes upward from the front to the rear of the scenic area. Hence, downstage and upstage. Permanently raked stages, which developed with scenery painted in perspective, are no longer common.

raket   (Indonesian)   1. A court dance-drama performed at the court of the 14th C Javanese kingdom of Matjapahit. It may have been masked (Holt ART 151); Soedarsono believes it was (DANCES 124). 2. A masked dance-drama popular in the 17th C in Banten, West Java. (Soedarsono DANCES 123). *Raket* plays were based on *Panji* tales. See also: *wayang wong*.

raking flats   Side wings set at an angle instead of parallel to the curtain line. (Southern CHANGEABLE 237)

raking piece   1. A triangular flat used to cover the side of a ramp or sloping platform. 2. A wooden wedge placed under a flat on a raked stage floor, to level it.

raksasa (Indonesian, Malaysian)   In *wayang* drama, a generic term for huge, coarse 'foreign' ogres (Brandon THRONES 49, Sweeney RAMAYANA 55) and giants (Long JAVANESE 70, Ulbricht WAYANG 19). A "Hindu demon." (de Zoete/Spies DANCE 2) Also called *buta*, *danawa* or *denawa*, *sabrangan*. Holt, however, distinguishes between *raksasa*, a giant, and *buta*, a non-human monster (ART 137); a less firm distinction is also made by Foley for Sundanese *wayang golek* (Foley "Sundanese" 39). For Anderson *raksasa* is a "monstrous giant." (MYTHOLOGY 8) Also spelled *rakshasa*, *rasaksa*, *raseksa*.

raksasa (Sanskrit)   Literally: anti-God. The role of a male demon.

raksasi (Sanskrit)   The role of a demoness in *yaksagana*. *Raksasi vesa* is a male actor of the role. (Ashton/Christie YAKSAGANA 51, 93)

raksha (Thai)   See: *yak*.

rakshasa (Indonesian)   See: *raksasa*.

raksot (Thai)   See: *yak*.

rakugo (Japanese)   Comic storytelling. A solo performance lasting from 20 minutes to two hours. Usually performed as part of a commercial variety theatre (*yose*) program. *Rakugoka* or *rakugoshi* (*rakugo* person) is the raconteur. (Ernst KABUKI 116, Brandon GUIDE 88)

rally   In Britain: 1. To increase the tempo in a scene, especially in a farce or near the end of an act, for dramatic effect. 2. A chase in a pantomime. (Bowman/Ball THEATRE, Granville DICTIONARY)

ramlila (Hindi)   Literally: Rama's play. A generic term throughout north India for folk pageant-plays that draw on incidents in the *Ramayana* epic. They are performed in September and October by all-male troupes (boys playing the leading roles) for as many as 30 days. Various episodes are staged in city streets to immense throngs of worshippers. (Schechner ''Ramlila'' 67–98, Gargi FOLK 90–113, Hein MIRACLE 70–103)

rampe (French)   Footlights. (Penzel LIGHTING 95, fig. 27)

Rampe (German)   Literally: 'slope.' Originally, the stage apron, then the footlights. The recent preference among backstage people seems to be *Fuss-rampe*. See that entry and French *rampe*. (Fuchs LIGHTING 209)

rampe à gaz (French)   Gas footlights. Sometimes seen as *rampe au gaz*. (Penzel LIGHTING 95, fig. 27)

Rampenlicht (German)   Footlights.

ram phleng (Thai)   Literally: dance with song. A set dance piece, often excerpted from a dance-drama. Also spelled *ram pleng*. (Yupho TRAINING 4)

rampogan (Indonesian)   See: *prampogan*.

ranad (Thai)   A wooden xylophone played in classical theatre music. There are two types: large (*ranad thume* or *thume mai*) and small (*ranad ek*). Descriptions and illustrations are in Duriyanga THAI 17–25 and Morton TRADITIONAL 54–59. Also spelled *ranat*. See also: *roneat*.

ranat (Thai)   See: *ranad*.

ranbyoshi (Japanese)   A stamping dance performed in *ennen no* and in *no*. It probably derives from the religious ceremony of stamping to chastise evil spirits living underground. An example is in the *no* play *Dojoji*. (Inoura HISTORY 53, Shimazaki NOH 36)

randai (Indonesian)   A group story-telling dance from West Sumatra, in which tales of Minangkabau greatness are sung and danced. (Soedarsono DANCES 211, Holt ART 99)

random light   Especially in non-realistic or episodic plays, an occasional term for light which has no apparent source. See also arbitrary light, which is similar, and motivated light, which is the opposite. (Lounsbury THEATRE 85)

raneat (Khmer)   See: *roneat*.

ranga (Sanskrit)   1. Broadly, in ancient India any public place for presenting shows or performances. 2. A stage. (Hein MIRACLE 255–256) 3. In *nautanki*, a performing stage manager. See also: *sutradhara*. (Gargi FOLK 37) *ranga-bhumi* (Sanskrit)   Literally: stage ground. An outdoor stage or acting area. (Rangacharya NATYASASTRA 13)

rangalo (Gujarti)   The role of a clown in *bhavai*. See also: *vidusaka*. (Gargi FOLK 62–63)

rangamandapa (Sanskrit)   Literally: theatre hall. Auditorium. (Rangacharya INDIAN 44) Called *rangamantapam* in Kannada. See also: *rangasthala*.

rangapitha (Sanskrit)   In classical Indian theatre, the main acting area of the stage, located downstage. (Raghavan in Baumer/Brandon SANSKRIT 20)

rangaprasadhana (Sanskrit)   In *kutiyattam*, decoration of the stage with coconut palm leaves, bunches of coconuts, plantain trees and fruit, and red silk before a performance. (Raja KUTIYATTAM 10)

rangapuja (Hindi)   See: *puja*.

rangasala, rangashala (Sanskrit)   See: *natyasala*.

rangasirsa (Sanskrit)   Literally: Stage head. Upstage center. The head, or upper (*sirsa*) portion of a stage (*ranga*) in ancient India. Unclearly described by Bharata in NATYASASTRA 23, the term may have referred to a raised stage area (Raghavan in Baumer/Brandon SANSKRIT 20) or to the upstage part of the main acting area (Kale THEATRIC 21).

rangasthala (Sanskrit)   Stage. In *yaksagana*, a bamboo-frame structure that marks the acting area on the open ground and provides cover over the area. Originally called *rangamantapam*. (Ashton/Christie YAKSAGANA 7–8, 83–84, 93)

rangda (Indonesian)   Literally: widow. In Bali, a supernatural female whose mask is revered and feared and, in dance plays, can be worn only by a magically powerful person (*wong sakti*). Variously called ''witch'' (de Zoete/Spies DANCE 121), ''she-devil'' (Soedarsono DANCES 167), ''elaborated out of Durga worship'' (Belo BALI 32), and ''village protector'' (Bandem/deBoer BALINESE 122–123, 126–131). In theatre her role is that of antagonist. *Rangda* is a role type, and therefore her mask can be worn to portray various characters, for example Calonarang in the *barong*. See also: *barong, calonarang*. (McPhee in Belo TRADITIONAL 181; de Zoete/Spies DANCE 14, 132; Belo BALI 18)

range   1. The breadth of a performer's repertoire or talent. 2. The extent of a performer's vocal pitch.

rangmanc (Hindi)   A raised dais at one side of a *raslila* stage platform where Krishna watches the action. (Hein MIRACLE 137)

rankou, jan k'ou (Chinese)   Literally: whisker mouth. The generic term for stage beards in music-drama (*xiqu*). Most are made of hair bound to a wire frame which fits over the ears and rests on the upper lip. Also called mouth face (*koumian* or *k'ou mien*). Major styles of beards are described in detail in Halson PEKING 40–41 and Scott CLASSICAL 170–172; beard movements are described in Scott CLASSICAL 133–137.

rank theatre   A theatre with an auditorium that separated the various classes of theatregoers—the elite in the boxes, the poorer patrons in the gallery, etc. Typically, each seating section had its own entrance and was isolated from the other sections. This arrangement was typical in theatres from the Renaissance onward; in the 19th C more democratic seating developed, but there are still some ranked theatres. (Sobel NEW)

ranryoo (Japanese)   A *bugaku* mask with a ferocious face, surmounted by a golden dragon. (Wolz BUGAKU 38)

rant   To deliver lines in an extravagant and melodramatic manner. Hence, ranter, ranting.

ranting (Malaysian)   See: *cherita ranting.*

rappresentazione sacre (Italian)   See: *sacre rappresentazione.*

raras konda (Indonesian)   See: *capeng, ngibing.*

raree-show   An inexpensive street show, often presenting 'rarities;' a peep show. Also called a rarity show. (Bowman/Ball THEATRE)

ras (Hindi)   1. Broadly, a shortening of *raslila.* 2. More narrowly, see: *mangalacaran.* (Hein MIRACLE 129)

rasa (Sanskrit)   Flavor, color, residual essence, or the joyful consciousness which a spectator experiences while witnessing a dramatic performance. *Rasa* is the major aesthetic goal of classical Indian theatre as well as many regional theatre forms (*kathakali, kutiyattam, kuchipudi, raslila,* for example). Usually translated "sentiment," *rasa* is evoked by the actor's appropriate depiction of various fundamental emotions (*sthayibhava*), by means of a codified system of "determinants" (*vibhava*), "consequents" (*anubhava*) and transitory feelings (*vyabicari bhava*). Any one play should elicit one dominant and several sub-ordinate *rasa,* from among the eight described by Bharata—*srngara* (erotic), *vira* (heroic), *raudra* (furious), *hasya* (comic), *adbhuta* (marvellous), *bhyanaka* (terrible), *karuna* (pathetic), and *bibhasta* (odious). (NATYASASTRA 105–118). In theory, music or dance alone cannot elicit *rasa* in a spectator; only drama (*natya*) can produce this ultimate aesthetic experience. Today, *santa* (peace) is often described as the 'ninth *rasa.*' See also: *bhava.* (Keith SANSKRIT 323–324, Benegal PANORAMA 12, Deutsch in Baumer/Brandon SANSKRIT 216–219)

rasaksa (Indonesian)   See: *raksasa.*

ras asthan (Hindi)   In *raslila,* the down front acting area of a stage (*ras-mandal*). (Gargi FOLK 121)

rasdhari (Hindi)   In *raslila:* 1. A member of a professional troupe. 2. The leader (*svami*) of such a troupe. 3. A troupe. (Hein MIRACLE 135, 293)

raseksa (Indonesian)   See: *raksasa.*

raslila (Hindi)   A sacred musical theatre form in north India, celebrating the life of Krishna. It consists of two parts, a sacramental circle dance of Krishna with his milkmaid lovers, followed by the enactment of an episode (*lila*) in his life story. It is staged in a temple courtyard and major roles are taken by boys. (Hawley KRISHNA 317) Sometimes more formally called *raslilanukaran* (imitation of *raslila*). (Hein MIRACLE 129)

rasmandal (Hindi)   1. A round masonry platform, built on a site related to Krishna's life and used for performances of *raslila*. 2. The circle dance that appears in the first part of a *raslila* performance. 3. The circle of performers who execute the dance. (Hein MIRACLE 137)

ras mandali (Hindi)   A troupe that performs *raslila*, members of which are normally drawn from a single Brahmin family. (Hawley KRISHNA 317)

raspberry   Usually, a Bronx cheer, especially from the gallery, when a performer does badly. Hence, get the raspberry. Often shortened to razz or berry.

Rastus   In a minstrel show, an end man paired with Sambo. See also: Bones. (Sobel NEW)

rat   See: ticket scalper.

ratcatcher   A World War I flat sport cap for men. (Geen COSTUME 108)

rated voltage   The voltage at which an incandescent lamp is designed to be burned. If the actual voltage at which the lamp is burned varies from the rated voltage, the life of the lamp and the light it gives are affected, both in much greater proportion than the change in voltage. Occasionally called rated operating voltage. (Fuchs LIGHTING 160–161)

rates bends   Once said of a successful performance or show: it deserves bows.

rati (Sanskrit)   Literally: love. One of the eight fundamental emotions (*sthayibhava*) expressed by actors in a classical Indian play. See also: *srngara*. (Keith SANSKRIT 323)

rat-tail burner   In 19th C Britain, a gas outlet which produced a single flame. In its simplest form, the rat tail might be no more than the end of a gas pipe. The rat tail was one of the types of burners much used in the theatre. (Rees GAS 13, fig. 2)

rattling comedian   A performer who specializes in dashing, impudent parts. (Rowell in Donohue MANAGER 191)

ratu (Malaysian)   Literally: king. In the shadow theatre, a coarse and vulgar prince who is the antagonist in a play. (Sweeney MALAY 32)

raudra (Sanskrit)   Literally: furious. Fury is one of the eight principal sentiments (*rasa*) that, according to Bharata, spectators of classical Sanskrit plays could experience. It is aroused by the enactment on stage of the fundamental emotion (*sthayibhava*) of anger (*krodha*). (Bharata NATYASASTRA 113, 124; Keith SANSKRIT 323)

Raum (German)   A late 20th C development of German stage designers which places emphasis on strong visual qualities: deep, wide, luscious, colorful acting spaces so dominant that the director and performer must play to them rather than be supported by them. (Riddell "Raum" 43)

Raumgestaltung (German)   Literally: interior decoration. Adolphe Appia's term for the constructivistic shaping of space. (Stadler APPIA 15)

ravana chaya (Oriya)   Literally: shadow of Ravana. A shadow puppet theatre form in Orissa state, eastern India, that depicts episodes from the *Ramayana* epic in which the hero, Rama, defeats the demon king Ravana. (Vatsyayan TRADITIONAL 113)

ravanvadh (Hindi)   Literally: slaying of Ravana. An outdoor pageant which is the climax of a *ramlila* performance. Rama's final victory and the death of the demon king Ravana are enacted. (Hein MIRACLE 76–77)

rave   Extremely favorable criticism—though before about 1925 in the U.S., the term meant unfavorable criticism. Hence, rave notice. (Wilmeth LANGUAGE)

rayed   A 12th-13th C term for a material striped diagonally. (Barton COSTUME 130)

razz   See: raspberry.

RC   Right center.

RCE   Right center entrance.

reactance dimmer   A dimming device based on the use of magnetism to control voltage by moving a laminated iron core within the field created by transformer-like windings. Bulky and expensive, the reactance dimmer was never widely used in the theatre. Similar principles led to the reactor dimmer, whose highly saturable core of magnetic material produced such names as saturable core and saturable reactor; the British also used saturable choke. This dimmer led in turn to the magnetic amplifier dimmer or magamp, which massed a number of saturable cores electrically. All were superseded some time ago by the silicon-controlled rectifier. (Bellman LIGHTING 134, 190–192, 194–195; Lounsbury THEATRE 38; McCandless SYLLABUS 54)

reactor dimmer   See: reactance dimmer.

read   1. To audition for a play. 2. To read a play aloud in rehearsal but not go through the movements. 3. To evaluate a play script. 4. To register with the audience. A line 'reads' when it is effective with the spectators; a performer's makeup 'reads' when its purpose carries across the footlights. The angle of a scenic unit 'reads' when it can be perceived by the audience. The term is sometimes used in the negative sense, as when something onstage is satisfactory because it will *not* (i.e., is not supposed to) 'read' to the audience.

read a speech   To deliver a line of dialogue.

read downhill   In acting, to let a line of dialogue gradually lose force.

reader   1. A play reader—one who evaluates scripts. 2. A printed program. 3. See: card reader.

reader of plays   Formerly in Britain, a censor of plays.

readers theatre   A performance by a group of interpreters seeking by vocal and physical means to experience a text with an audience. Readers theatre is a flexible form which explores drama, fiction, non-fiction, and poetry. Scripts, which ordinarily include both dialogue and narration, are usually carried by the reader; costumes, props and settings, when present, are normally sparse. Though group reading of this sort goes back to the 19th C, the name probably began in New York in 1945 with a professional group called Readers Theatre, Inc. Also called interpreters theatre, staged reading, group reading, theatre of the mind, platform theatre, concert reading, and multiple reading. See also: chamber theatre, play reading. (Coger/White READERS 20)

read for a part   To audition.

reading   1. A rehearsal at which the performers hear the playwright (or a deputy) read the script aloud. 2. A rehearsal at which the performers read the script aloud, without movement or stage business. 3. A performer's interpretation of a line or character. 4. An evaluation of a script by a reader. 5. A performance at which a play is read by the actors but without any or much movement or business. Hence, readers theatre. 6. An audition. (Bowman/Ball THEATRE) 7. The number at which a control device is set. (Lounsbury THEATRE, McCandless SYLLABUS 54)

reading edition   A published play prepared for lay readers rather than performers. A reading edition differs from an acting edition.

reading fee   A fee charged by a playwright or agent for a play reading.

reading of the banes   In medieval England, announcing a play, usually by a messenger or herald, before the production date. (Ward LITERATURE I 59)

reading the questions   See: questions.

read-through   A rehearsal at which the script is read aloud by the cast, without movement or business, often for the first time.

realism   In playwriting and stage production, the effort to make a dramatic work look like real life. Realism was popular in the late 19th C and attracted such important writers as Henrik Ibsen and Anton Chekhov. Extreme realism, especially when the subject matter is the working man and social problems, is usually called naturalism. Despite many reactions against realism in the early 20th C because of its tendency to reproduce appearance rather than essence, realism remains the dominant mode in drama, theatre, and especially film and television.

realism of the soul   Konstantin Stanislavsky's term for psychological truth. (Markov SOVIET 63)

rear pit   In some 17th C German theatres, a cross-stage pit used for lighting instruments, to illuminate mid-stage backscenes or to manage a cross-stage movement of wagons and processions. (Furttenbach in Hewitt RENAISSANCE 195ff)

rear projection   1. See: back projection. 2. An image on the back of a translucent screen. (Wehlburg GLOSSARY)

rear screen projector   A projection device, usually with a wide-angle lens, which produces a rear projection. (Lounsbury THEATRE)

rear stage   1. In theatres of the 16th and 17th C, an acting area upstage which could be discovered by the drawing of a curtain or shutters. 2. A stage behind a main stage, often narrower and shallower, for the presentation of scenes requiring great depth. German: *Hinterbühne*.

rebab (Indonesian)   See: *gamelan*.

rebah (Indonesian)   See: *dhawah*.

rebato   See: rabat(o).

rebound   In dance, a counter movement at the bottom of a drop or fall which enables the body to spring back. (Stodelle HUMPHREY 20)

recall   1. The return of a performer or performers for an additional curtain call. 2. To request a performer to return for an additional audition. 3. Such a return. See also: call back.

receiver   In the 17th C, a theatre treasurer.

receptacle   See: outlet.

recinium (Latin Roman)   See: *fabula riciniata*.

reciprocating segment stage   An arc-shaped wagon stage capable of moving onstage and offstage and large enough to handle two full-stage settings. (Burris-Meyer/Cole THEATRES 208)

récit (French)   In neo-classic French drama, a lengthy set speech recounting past action. (Cameron/Hoffman GUIDE)

recitalist   A performer who gives dramatic recitals, usually with musical accompaniment. Also called a *diseur* or *diseuse* (French).

recitation   An old term for acting.

recitative   A form of utterance between speech and song. The word is often used of some forms of delivery on the classical stage. Compare *cantica*. Also, lines in operas and oratorios sung with the rhythmic patterns of natural speech and hence more easily understood than lines fully sung. Recitative was especially popular in Baroque opera and was narrative rather than reflective in character. In the late 18th and early 19th C, recitative was used in burlettas in Britain to avoid illegal use of spoken dialogue. (Donohue ''Burletta'' 43)

recitator (Latin)   A medieval reciter or declaimer. (Chambers MEDIAEVAL II 208)

recognition   The usual translation of the Greek *anagnorisis*: in a play, the finding of a previously undiscovered character trait or fact. Hence, recognition scene, as in *Oedipus the King*, when Oedipus discovers his true identity.

recognize the profession   To admit a member of the theatrical profession free to a performance.

recorder (French)   See: *répéter*.

recreational drama, recreational theatre   A production with children in which the emphasis is at least as much on the development of the child performer as on the enjoyment of the audience. See also: children's theatre, community theatre. (Goldberg CHILDREN'S 5, 9)

rectangular plate dimmer   See: plate dimmer.

Rederyker stage   A Renaissance outdoor stage in the Netherlands—a platform stage backed by an architectural facade, used for plays, songs, recitations, and other ceremonies. (Kernodle ART 117–118)

red-hot mama   In the U.S. in the 1920s, a spirited female singer. (Wilmeth LANGUAGE)

redingote   See: rotonne.

red-nosed comedian, red-nosed comic   1. A low comedian, common in burlesque, who used red makeup on his nose to indicate inebriation. Such performers often wore grotesque, clown-like clothing. 2. Such a role. (Bowman/Ball THEATRE, Wilmeth LANGUAGE, Granville DICTIONARY)

red one   A profitable engagement.

reeve   To pass a rope over a sheave (grooved wheel) in a block. (Gillette/Gillette SCENERY)

refined vaudeville   See: advanced vaudeville.

reflector   In lighting instruments, a surface which redirects light toward the opening in the instrument. The principal shapes are the spherical, the ellipsoidal, the parabolic, and the spherical parabolic. Reflectors are shiny in spotlights and projectors, dull in floodlights and borderlights. Lounsbury has illustrations. (Lounsbury THEATRE, Wehlburg GLOSSARY)

reflector (Spanish)   A spotlight.

reflector drop   See: bounce drop.

reflector lamp   1. A self-contained small floodlight or spotlight whose essential element is a funnel-shaped bulb which is both light source and reflector: the inside of the bulb's cone is silvered (with aluminum) so that it reflects much of the light "lost" in an ordinary lamp. 2. More specifically, a thin glass lamp of this type, often with inside frosting at the front. Also called R lamp, R-type, R, etc., and sometimes Birdseye (from Clarence Birdseye, the inventor) or bird's eye lamp, poor man's spotlight, or mushroom (from its shape). 3. A PAR (parabolic aluminized reflector) lamp, similar to the above, but of heavy, heat-treated glass. Some forms of the PAR resemble automobile headlights. Also called sealed-beam lamp, PAR, PAR-type lamp, etc. (Bellman LIGHTING 55–57; Bellman SCENE 347; Bowman MODERN; Bentham ART 78–79, fig. 43; Sellman/Lessley ESSENTIALS 65, fig. 4.20)

reflector strip   An occasional older term for a striplight consisting of individual reflector units. (McCandless "Glossary" 635)

(de) réflexion (French)   Premeditated performing, as opposed to instinctual *(d'âme)*.

regelling   Replacing a color filter, whether gelatine or not. Compare: gelling. (Bellman LIGHTING 34)

regenerative gas burner   A late 19th C round burner which produced a strong, steady light economically. The regenerative burner was used in large halls and was suited to theatre auditoriums. (Penzel LIGHTING 92–93)

regent   A medieval director and prompter. (Evans PASSION 1)

regia (Latin Roman)   Literally: palace, royal residence. The usual form of *aula regia*, Vitruvius' term for the central door (occasionally, doors) in the *scaenae frons* (scenic facade). Such doorways supposedly led to a royal palace. See also: *porta regia*, *valva*. Compare *hospitalia*, *thyromata*. (Bieber HISTORY 173, 187; Arnott ANCIENT 137)

regiacomica (Italian)   A variety of Renaissance elaborate and fantastic play, containing serious, comic, and pastoral elements. Also called an *opera regiacomica* or an *opera mista* (mixed work). In French, *comédie mixte*.

Regie (German)   Direction or stage management.

regie book   A promptbook. A German-English phrase used in English. Sometimes called *Regie-buch* (German), regie. (Bowman/Ball THEATRE)

Regie-buch (German)   Promptbook.

regieprotokol (Danish)   A document listing a play's setting, props, costumes, and characters. (Marker "Bloch" 91)

regional theatre   In the U.S., theatre or a theatre movement outside the New York City area or other major theatrical centers. (Cameron/Gillespie ENJOYMENT)

régisseur (French)   1. A stage director or manager. See also: *metteur en scène*. 2. In ballet, the stage manager of a company, responsible for re-staging and rehearsing the company's repertoire. (Wilson BALLET)

register   1. To portray by facial expression. 2. To project a line or gesture so that it is understood by spectators. 3. To impress an audience favorably. 4. The pitch of a performer's voice.

registrum (Latin)   Especially in medieval England, the approved transcript of a play, copied from the original. (Chambers MEDIAEVAL II 143)

régler une décoration (French)   To dress a stage. (Moynet FRENCH 101)

regös (Magyar)   A 13th C Hungarian itinerant story-teller-singer. He specialized in verse tales in mime. (Gassner/Quinn ENCYCLOPEDIA 437)

regular dancer   In burlesque, a dancer of ordinary size. (Wilmeth LANGUAGE)

regulation plate   See: gas plate.

rehearsal   1. The preparation of performers through repetition and practice. The term is usually used for a single practice period within the total preparation period. 2. Formerly, recitation, acting. Musician Roger North said the music lovers of the 17th and 18th C did not like music and drama mixed, for they "would not bear the interruption that so much rehearsall gave. . . . " (North MUSIC 354)

rehearsal book   Especially in Britain, an attendance register used by the stage manager to keep track of performers as they arrive for practice. (Bax MANAGEMENT 43)

rehearsal call   A notice to performers and other necessary theatre personnel to report for a practice period.

rehearsal copy   A performer's copy of a play, sometimes annotated, or a house copy, sometimes annotated but lacking warnings, cues, or other features of full promptbooks.

rehearsal light(s)   The lighting or lights used at a rehearsal in a theatre. The singular sometimes refers to a single light, usually a floodlight, used for this purpose. (Bowman/Ball THEATRE)

rehearsal promptbook   An annotated promptbook used during the rehearsals of a production; the same promptbook might serve for performances, or a cleaner, more readable copy might be made up. (Shattuck SHAKESPEARE 5)

rehearsal properties   Simulations of actual properties, for use in early rehearsals. Usually called rehearsal props.

rehearsal scene   A portion of a play, usually beginning with the entrance of a character or characters and ending with an exit of one or more of them or the entrance of a new character or characters. See also: French scene.

rehearsal system   In Britain, a special group of dimmer handles which control the lights used at a rehearsal. (Bentham ART)

rehearse   To practice. Hence, over-rehearse, under-rehearse, dress rehearsal, etc.

reherse   A medieval spelling of rehearse—to practice a play.

rejas (Spanish)   Grilled windows, through which spectators could look down on a 17th C *corral* theatre, as from a box. Also called *celosías*. (Rennert SPANISH 42)

relamp   To replace a lamp.

related tint system   A method of lighting the acting area spaces from either side (at the usual 45° angles) with tints which are closely related to each other. (Bellman LIGHTING 118–120)

relay switch   See: contactor.

release line   See: cut line.

relevé (French)   Literally: a lifted step. In ballet: 1. A raising of the body on the balls of one or both feet or on the toes. Also called *temps relevé*. 2. Sometimes, a lowering of the working foot to the ground and a re-raising of it. (Wilson BALLET, Grant TECHNICAL) 3. See: movements in ballet.

relief   1. A comic scene, role, or performer in a heavy drama. (Berrey/Van den Bark SLANG 572) 2. A scene built into a play to provide a relaxation of the emotional tension, often just before or after a scene of considerable strain. Hence, comic relief. 3. Cut-out pieces of scenery creating a vista in relief. See: relieve. (Bowman/Ball THEATRE)

relief stage   A staging theory of the early 20th C associated with the Munich Artists' Theatre. Performers were kept in the foreground, to throw them into relief against a flat scenic background.

relieve   1. In the 17th C, a cut-out scenic unit through which could be seen other scenery, further upstage. 2. A scenic unit built in three dimensions. A set piece. (Nicoll STUART 95, Roberts STAGE)

remanent (Latin)   In playwriting, primarily in the past, a stage direction for characters to remain on stage. Singular *remanet*.

Rembrandt lighting   See: plastic lighting.

remembered emotions   See: emotion memory.

remodador (Spanish)   Literally: imitator, mimic. In the 15th C, a mimic player. (Rennert SPANISH 254)

remote color changer   See: color boomerang.

remote color control   The capacity to change color filters with a remote color changer. See also: color boomerang. (Bowman/Ball THEATRE)

remote control board   See: remote control system.

remote control dimmer   A dimmer which can be placed at a considerable distance from the operator. Such dimmers have made it possible to place control boards in positions which provide a clear view of the scenic and acting areas. Among remotely controlled dimmers, in approximate order of their historical appearance in the theatre: reactance, reactor, magnetic amplifier, thyratron tube, silicon controlled rectifier. Remote control and remotely controlled occur both with and without hyphens.

remote control switchboard   See: remote control system.

remote control system   In lighting in the U.S., any arrangement which permits control of lighting equipment from a distance; called in Britain an all-electric dimmer system. Many modern control boards are remotely controlled; hence such terms as remote control (switch) board and remote control dimmers. The changing of color filters at a distance is usually called in the U.S. remote (control) color change(r) or color boomerang, and in Britain remotely operated colour change. The opposite of remote control is direct control, manual control, or local control. (Bellman LIGHTING 186–190, Wehlburg GLOSSARY)

remotely controlled dimmer   See: remote control dimmer.

remotely operated colour change   See: remote control system.

removable unit borderlight   A borderlight with compartments, each of which contains a lamp and reflector which can be removed as a unit. Hence, removable unit footlights.

renribiki (Japanese)   Literally: entwined-pulling. A *kabuki* scene in which a person fleeing from a ghost is pulled back by the ghost's eerie gestures, as if manipulated by strings. An example is in *The Scarlet Princess of Edo* in Brandon CLASSIC 330. (Leiter ENCYCLOPEDIA 310–311)

renter   1. In the 18th C, an investor in a theatrical venture. 2. Formerly, a theatre concessionaire. (Stone in Hume LONDON 184)

renversé (French)   In ballet, the bending of the body during a turn, in which the normal poise but not the equilibrium is disturbed. (Grant TECHNICAL)

renwu (Chinese)   See: *jiaose*.

reog (Indonesian)   A Sundanese street play performed by comedians accompanied by drums. (Foley "Sundanese" 22, Brandon SOUTHEAST 294)

reong (Indonesian)   See: *gamelan*.

reorientation   See: *Verfremdungseffekt*.

rep   1. Repertory. Hence, rep company, or a theatrical troupe with a schedule of prepared plays. 2. A representative, an agent. 3. To represent a performer or theatre. (Berrey/Van den Bark SLANG 594) 4. A heavy, ribbed, cotton fabric, sometimes used for making cycloramas or draperies. Also spelled repp.

repeater   A popular play in a company's repertory.

repertoire   1. The characters a performer is prepared to play. 2. The plays a company is prepared to perform. See: repertory.

repertorio (Italian)   Literally: repertory. A collection of set speeches (*concetti*) created or compiled and learned by a *commedia dell'arte* performer. (Mantzius HISTORY II 219)

repertory   1. Short form: rep. A group of productions (plays, dances, musical numbers, etc.) which a troupe can present, usually alternately; a system based on such productions. More properly the term should be repertoire, but repertory is widely used. Hence, repertory company, repertory theatre, repertory show. 2. A stock company. (Bowman/Ball THEATRE)

repertory company, repertory theatre   A performing troupe with a stock of productions which it can present.

repertory performance   In Britain, a derogatory phrase for an under-rehearsed production.

répéter (French)   To rehearse. Also called, less frequently, *recorder*.

répétiteur (French)   The pianist and vocal coach employed by an opera company.

répétition (French), **repetition**   A rehearsal.

répétition générale (French)   A private dress rehearsal, not open to the public, before opening night. (Bowman/Ball THEATRE)

repetitor   In 18th C theatres, a musician who trained the singing chorus; a choirmaster, and often a principal chorus singer. (Hogan LONDON clxiv)

réplique (French)   A cue.

repp   See: rep.

repping   Performing in repertory.

repraesentatio (Latin)   See: liturgical drama.

representación (Spanish)   A performance.

representación particular (Spanish)   In the 17th C, a private performance before the king or a nobleman. (Shergold SPANISH)

representatio (Latin)   1. A medieval dramatic performance. 2. A medieval mystery play. (Chambers MEDIAEVAL II 104)

representatio miraculi (Latin)   A medieval miracle play, dealing with the lives of the saints. (Chambers MEDIAEVAL II 104)

representation   1. A performance. Also called a theatrical representation. 2. Realism. Hence, representational, representationalism. The attempt to create on stage an illusion of real life. (Bowman/Ball THEATRE)

reprise   The repeat of all or a portion of a musical number, especially in a musical comedy.

reprise (French)   A revival.

rep show   A production playing in repertory.

repster   Anyone connected with a repertory company.

rescue opera   A play of the Romantic period in which the hero or heroine is liberated from a dungeon, tower, or other place or condition of confinement. (Roach ''Piranesi's'' 106)

reserve   1. A ticket for a reserved seat. 2. To order a seat or seats in advance. Hence, reserved seat.

resi (Lao)   See: *rusi*.

resident   Not touring; relatively permanent. Hence, resident company, resident manager. (Bowman/Ball THEATRE)

resident manager   In Britain, a theatre manager (as opposed to a company manager, who runs a touring troupe). Called in the U.S. a house manager. (Granville DICTIONARY)

resident s.m., resident stage manager   In British provincial theatres, the stage carpenter (or manager) in charge of the stage staff. (Baker THEATRECRAFT)

resin   See: rosin box.

resistance   In electricity, that quality of any material which opposes the passage of electric current. (Wehlburg GLOSSARY, Sellman/Lessley ESSENTIALS)

resistance board   A control board whose dimmers operate by electrical resistance. Also called a resistance dimmer board.

resistance dimmer   A device for changing the brightness of stage lights by altering the resistance in series with the circuit. The earliest type of electrical dimmer, the resistance dimmer may still be seen but is essentially obsolete. The principal types: plate dimmer, slider dimmer, salt water dimmer. See those entries for further information and alternate names. Also occasionally called a resistor, resistor dimmer, and rheostat. (Bellman LIGHTING 174–177, Lounsbury THEATRE 38–39, Wehlburg GLOSSARY, Philippi STAGECRAFT)

resistance dimmer board   See: resistance board.

resistor, resistor dimmer   See: resistance dimmer.

resolution   In playwriting, the point at which the major dramatic question is answered and the plot complications are resolved. (Rowe HEAD 113)

resonating chamber, reverberating chamber   A space beneath an orchestra pit to improve the orchestral sound. (Mullin PLAYHOUSE 78)

responsibles   In Britain, small but important parts in repertory or touring companies. Hence, responsible man, responsible woman, responsible player. (Bowman/Ball THEATRE)

resting   Unemployed. Also called at leisure, at liberty, available, between engagements, between plays.

rest light   See: work light.

retablo (Spanish)   A religious scene or play represented by wooden puppets; the term came to be a general one for puppet show. Derived from the *reredos* of the church—altar pieces with carved wooden figures. (Shergold SPANISH)

retardation   In playwriting, an occasional term for prolonging a pleasurable effect, withholding small surprises, giving essential facts time to establish themselves, or giving the plot time to develop. (Krows PLAYWRITING 158)

reticulated headdress   Hair contained in a jewelled net. See also: caul. (Wilcox DICTIONARY)

reticulation   Netting used in late Gothic headpieces. (Barton COSTUME 164)

reticule   A silk, beaded, plush or embroidered handbag of small proportions used for a handkerchief, perfume bottle, etc. Its inadequate size led to the term ridicule. Also called an *aumonière* (French) or ballantine. (Wilcox DICTIONARY)

retire   1. To withdraw from the main action of a performance without leaving the stage; to become a 'suspended' character. 2. To conclude a performing career.

retiré (French)   In ballet, a position in which the thigh is at right angles to the body and the toe is touching the knee of the supporting leg, either front or back. (Wilson BALLET, Grant TECHNICAL)

retiring room   1. A public rest room or lounge in a theatre. 2. A green room or performer's lounge backstage. (Bowman/Ball THEATRE)

retractable cord (interconnect) system   See: interconnecting panel.

retractatio (Latin Roman)   Literally: reconsideration. The process of re-working an old play for a revival. Such revivals of Roman comedy are thought to have taken place from about the middle of the 2nd C BC. In the later 19th C, many scholars blamed *retractatio* for the supposed imperfections in Plautus' comedies. By the early decades of the present century, much of this blame was shifted to *contaminatio* (using more than one Greek source for a Latin play). The more recent view is that *retractatio* (like *contaminatio*) had only a minor effect on the texts of revived plays. (Duckworth NATURE 66–68, 96, 119, 191, 197, 199–200, 208)

retractator (Latin Roman)   One who reworked old plays for revivals. (Duckworth NATURE 67, 94, 191)

(en) retraite (French)   Tied off. In the 19th C, said of fly lines fastened into bundles of ropes until they were needed. (Moynet FRENCH 45)

re-trim carbons   See: trim carbons.

return   1. A flat, usually painted black, attached to the downstage edge of a stage setting and running offstage behind the tormentor or the proscenium opening, to mask the backstage area. Also called a return piece, but in Britain that term is used for a jog or narrow flat. 2. See: thickness. 3. A ticket returned to the box office and offered for resale. (Baker THEATRECRAFT, Bellman SCENOGRAPHY)

return date, return engagement   An engagement for a performer or production to come back to the same theatre, usually to present the same program. (Fay GLOSSARY)

returns   1. The official list of all seats sold at a performance. 2. Unsold tickets returned by agencies. 3. Applause. (Fay GLOSSARY; Berrey/Van den Bark SLANG 591, 593) 4. The money taken in by a production.

reveal   See: thickness.

revels   A 16th C name for the lively, quick dances, such as the galliard and *coranto* (Italian), associated with masques, in which partners were selected from the audience.

revenge play   Especially in Elizabethan and Jacobean England, a play based on a struggle for vengeance. Many revenge plays were influenced by the works of Seneca, and some, like *Hamlet*, went well beyond being just thrillers.

reverberation   The persistence of reflected sound in an auditorium. (Burris-Meyer/Mallory SOUND 2)

reverberator   In late 17th C Britain, a lamp and reflector which lit the apron. (Bowman/Ball THEATRE)

révérence (French)   In ballet, an elaborate bow or curtsy at the end of a class, by male and female dancers respectively. The *révérence* is also used as an acknowledgement of audience applause in a curtain call. (Kersley/Sinclair BALLET)

reversal   The usual translation of the Greek *peripeteia*: a sudden change of direction in the action of a play, as when Oedipus, having heard that his father Polybus has died, is told that Polybus was not really his father.

reversed theatre   In Britain, a theatre with the prompter's corner offstage down right (instead of left).

reverse roller curtain   See: sinking curtain.

reversing the key   Brightening the key light and dimming fill light. (Bellman LIGHTING 341–343)

review   1. A published report on a stage production. Hence, dramatic review, reviewer, reviewing, etc. See also: criticism. 2. Sometimes, a revue, a variety show.

reviewer   A journalist who witnesses a theatrical event and writes of his response to it. A nice distinction is usually made between a reviewer and a critic—one who is a trained evaluator of theatrical productions and who works from a set of critical criteria rather than from personal responses.

revirement (French)   Reversal; *peripeteia* (Greek). (Strindberg in Cole/Chinoy PLAYWRITING 183)

revista (Portuguese)   Late 19th C sketches, politically satirical, with music. (Gassner/Quinn ENCYCLOPEDIA 76)

revival   A new production of a previously-produced theatrical work.

revolve   1. See: revolving stage. 2. Flats that can be turned on casters to reveal the scene painted on the back side. (Fay GLOSSARY)

revolver   1. In a limelight, the rod used to turn the calcium cylinder. Since the flame consumed the incandescent lime in a few minutes, a fresh lime surface had to be provided just as often. The revolver was geared to the pin on which the small lime cylinder was impaled. (Rees GAS 54–55, fig. 32) 2. See: revolving stage.

revolving gridiron   A scheme conceived by Harry Bishop in the early 1900s to revolve the gridiron of a theatre and everything hanging from it, so that hanging units would turn with a revolving stage. (Krows AMERICA 105)

revolving stage   1. A turntable set into or on a stage floor, on which scenery is placed so that as one setting turns out of sight, another comes into view; a stage or portion of a stage that can be revolved. Invented by the Japanese in the 18th C and again by the Germans in the 19th C; the basic idea of a revolve can be found in the Greek *periaktos* of the 5th C BC. 2. An annular revolving stage, used at the St. Louis World's Fair in the early 1900s: a revolving ring around the entire auditorium. A revolving stage is variously called a disc stage, revolve, revolver, revolving platform, table stage, turntable, etc. German: *Drehbühne.* Japanese: *mawari butai.*

revue   A mélange, often satiric, of songs, sketches, dances, and other light entertainments. (O'Hara/Bro INVITATION)

rewanda (Indonesian)   See: *wanara.*

rex (Latin)   See: minstrel.

rex gregis (Latin Roman)   Literally: king of the company. From at least the 3rd C BC, the head of a theatre company. See also: *dominus gregis.* (O'Connor CHAPTERS 4)

RH   Right hand (side of the stage).

RHD   Right hand door.

rheostat   A resistance dimmer. Originally any variable resistance, the word was early in the 20th C synonymous with the resistance dimmer used in the theatre. (Bellman LIGHTING 177; Sellman/Lessley ESSENTIALS 20–22, fig. 2.9)

rhetorick   The systematized study of voice and gesture in Elizabethan times. (Roberts STAGE)

Rhinegrave breeches   See: petticoat breeches.

Rhinthonica (Latin Roman)   See: *fabula Rhinthonica.*

rhodomontade (French), **rodomontade**   Especially in the Italian *commedia dell'arte*, a vainglorious boast. (Scott in Mayer/Richards WESTERN 25)

RHUE   Right hand upper entrance.

rhythm   1. In performance, the harmony of movement in all its ramifications. (Bowman/Ball THEATRE) 2. In dance, the organizing of strong and weak stresses. (Turner/Grauert/Zallman DANCE 81)

rhythm clacker bones   See: Bones.

rhythmic masks   A virtuoso acting technique used in Russia by Vsevelod Meyerhold in the early 20th C to reveal the social mask—the nature and psychology of a character—through individual speech rhythms, movements, and gestures; sociomechanics as opposed to biomechanics. (Gorchakov RUSSIA 210–211)

rhythmic pattern   In dance, the simple and complex manipulation of units of time, creating uniqueness and variety in a total dance composition. (Nahumck DANCE 33)

rhythmic space   In the designs of Adolphe Appia, the manipulation of line, form, mass, and lighting to create stage pictures.

rialto   A theatre area in a city; in the U.S., usually Broadway in New York City.

ribaud (French)   See: minstrel.

rice powder   In makeup, 19th C pulverized rice-based white powder used to avoid a shiny nose. (Wilcox DICTIONARY)

ricikan (Indonesian)   A generic term for small, minor puppets in Javanese *wayang* shadow theatre. Also spelled *ritjikan*. (Muljono in Osman TRADITIONAL 63)

ricinium (Latin Roman)   See: *fabula riciniata*.

rideau (French)   1. A curtain. 2. In 19th C French theatres, the drop at the back of the stage upon which landscapes, interiors, etc. were painted. (Moynet FRENCH 48)

ridicule   See: reticule.

ridiculous theatre   See: theatre of the ridiculous.

ridiculus (Latin Roman)   One who amuses, a buffoon. To be a *ridiculus* was the "art" of the parasite of Roman comedy. (Duckworth NATURE 266)

riding   A medieval processional show, pageant-like in character, often presented on the occasion of a royal visit. (Ward LITERATURE I 147)

rieur (French)   Especially in the 19th and early 20th C, a member of a claque hired to laugh at a comedy performance. Also called a *rigolard*. (Saxon "Claque" 19)

rig   Stiffness in performance. The term derives from *rigor mortis* (Latin). (Lees "Lexicon" 57)

rigaudon (French), **rigadoon**   A late 17th C fashionable court dance. (Perugini PAGEANT 76)

rigger   1. One who installs a theatrical rigging system. 2. A stagehand working on the fly gallery: a flyman.

rigging   1. The system of ropes, cables, battens, counterweights, etc. by which scenic units, lighting equipment, and draperies are flown. 2. The process of installing such a system.

rigging line   A rope or wire used for hanging scenery.

rigging loft   See: flies.

rigging plan, rigging plot   See: hanging plot.

right   1. The right half of a proscenium stage. 2. At or toward stage right. All references to R or right are from the performer's point of view.

right center   The area about half way between the center line and the far right side of a proscenium stage, from the performer's point of view. Abbreviation: RC.

right center entrance   A proscenium stage entrance part way upstage and to the right, from the performer's point of view. Abbreviation: RCE.

right dance   See: *umai*.

right first entrance, right second entrance, etc.   Entrances on the right side of a proscenium stage, from the performer's point of view, numbered from the farthest downstage to the farthest upstage. Abbreviations: R1, R1E, R2, R2E, etc.

right hand   See: RH.

right hand door   See: RHD.

right hand upper entrance   See: RHUE.

right second entrance   See: right first entrance.

right stage   The right side of a proscenium stage, from the performer's point of view. More often called stage right.

right theatre   One of three theatrical circles in Russia in the 1920s, the other two being politically left and center. Konstantin Stanislavsky was a leading figure in the right theatre. (Carter SPIRIT 115)

right upper entrance   The farthest upstage entrance on the right side of a proscenium stage, from the performer's point of view. Abbreviation: RUE.

rig lights   To put lighting instruments in their proper position.

rigolard (French)   See: *rieur*.

riken no ken (Japanese)   Literally: objective viewing. The prescription of Zeami that a *no* actor judge his own acting objectively, "as if seen from the audience." (Raz "Actor" 267)

rim lighting   See: back light.

ring   1. In lighting, a corona or candle hoop. 2. See: R.

ring act bell   See: RAB.

ring control   A method of marionette manipulation in which rings at the operator's end of the strings are slipped onto the fingers. (Philpott DICTIONARY)

ring down   To drop or close the main curtain. The term derives from the days when a bell was rung to signal the end of an act. By extension, it applied to lowering a trap mechanism to take a character or object down to the substage. The opposite: ring up.

ringgit (Indonesian)   Literally: puppet. The term used in Java as early as the 11th C for a shadow puppet made of flat leather, shaped, incised, and colored to represent either a specific character (e.g., Arjuna) or a character type (e.g., *gusen*). A set of *ringgit* makes up the cast of characters for a *wayang kulit* performance. Also called *wayang*. In Balinese spelled *ringit*. (Long JAVANESE 9, Holt ART 131, Hooykaas KAMA 320)

ring in, ring in the band   Especially in Britain, to cue the orchestra to play; the signal was a bell, activated by the stage manager. (Baker THEATRECRAFT)

ring music bell   See: RMB.

ring one in, ring one on   To schedule an act.

rings   In Restoration and 18th C London theatres, large chandeliers suspended over the stage. They were removed from view in 1765–66 at Drury Lane and Covent Garden theatres. (Hogan LONDON lxv)

ring trap bell   See: RTB.

ring up   See: ring down.

ring warning bell   See: RWB.

ripcord   See: zip cord.

ripple burner   A 19th C device for simulating ripples on water. This involved one or two cylinders whose metal or cloth covering contained many irregular transverse slits. When lit inside and turned, the device cast "ripples" of light on translucent portions of a painted drop in front of it. (Rees GAS 131, fig. 76, 132, 205)

(a) Rip van Winkle   A period when a performer has no engagement. See also: do a Joe Jefferson.

rise   To go up, as a curtain at the beginning of an act or scene. Hence, at rise (what is seen onstage when the curtain rises).

rise and sink   One scenic unit coming up through a cut in the stage floor and another descending from the flies to meet it. The two then part, one rising and the other sinking, to reveal a vision or other special effect. Also called a sink and fly. (Rees GAS 136)

riser   1. In lighting, a frequent shortening for the 'black riser' of step lenses. The longer name prevents possible confusion with the riser of a stair run, but the shortening is preferable in that not all lens risers are black. Wehlburg has an illustration. 2. In the 19th C British gas wing, the vertical pipe which supplied the gas jets. (Wehlburg GLOSSARY, Rees GAS 34) 3. The vertical portion of a step (the horizontal portion being the tread). 4. A platform on stage or in the auditorium.

rising action, rising movement   The dramatic action preceding the climax of a play. (Bowman/Ball THEATRE)

ritjikan (Indonesian)   See: *ricikan*.

ritournelle (French)   A 17th C instrumental refrain, interlude, or prelude in a vocal work; sometimes danced. (Winter BALLET 139)

Ritterdrama (German)   A late 18th C manifestation of the *Sturm und Drang* style: plays that are chivalric, heavy in pageantry, irregular in form, patriotic, and emotional. (Gassner/Quinn ENCYCLOPEDIA 712)

ritual   Performance on behalf of, but not necessarily by, a group or community, expressing and reinforcing some of its deepest values at a time (usually) of change in the seasonal cycle or the cycle of a person's life. (Graham-White "'Ritual'" 319–320).

ritual theatre   Broadly, any theatrical performance which has wholly or in part a ritual function. Ritual, which implies repetition of fixed actions, may be implied, as in the repeated act of inaction in *Waiting for Godot*, or expressed, as in the preliminary offerings to the gods which precede many traditional theatre performances in Asia. The *barong* dance-drama of Bali is a ritual performance because its aim is to mediate between the actual condition of villagers and the gods who are thought to affect their lives. In performances in which the spirit of a god being enacted is believed to manifest itself by entering the performer— as in *ramlila* in India, or numerous folk plays (*sato kagura*) in Japan—the performance is part of a larger ritual designed to honor or placate the gods; purification, appeasement, exorcism, or shamanic activities are often elements of the performance. In Africa, a cultic performance based on a dramatized enactment of past events uses dance, mime, music, song, and chant to evoke the supernatural presence. It is designed as a rite of passage for purposes of purification, appeasement, or exorcism, and has priests, worshippers, and novitiates playing roles in a dramatic conflict and resolution before a group of spectators. An example is the Ademuorisa play of Lagos, Nigeria. In other cases, a theatrical performance may be arranged as an offering of propitiation to a spirit or as part of a seasonal festival; though a performance may be secular, it takes on ritual overtones. Some plays are specifically reserved for ritual occasions, such as the exorcistic *Murwakala* play in Indonesian shadow theatre or the New Year's play *Okina* in Japanese *no* theatre. In the 20th C, Antonin Artaud became interested in a kind of total theatre with ritual as its base. See: theatre of cruelty.

R-lamp   See: reflector lamp.

RMB   In old promptbooks, ring music bell, that is, a bell to cue the musicians. (Shattuck SHAKESPEARE 22)

(the) road   The circuit of towns where a touring or road company performs. On the road: on tour. The term road is short for railroad, for the development of U.S. railroads made extensive touring possible. (Crampton HANDBOOK)

road apple   A performer on tour. (Wilmeth LANGUAGE)

road board   A lighting control board which travels with a touring company. The term, which has been much used of the portable—though by no means lightweight—resistance dimmer board known as a piano board, now often refers to package boards. (Bellman LIGHTING 238, fig. 10–6f; Wehlburg GLOSSARY 43)

road box   A shipping crate used when a show is on tour.

road card   An Actor's Equity certificate allowing a member to perform with a touring company.

road combination See: combination.

road company A troupe of performers on tour.

road house A theatre visited by touring companies, often without a resident company of its own.

road shoe A metal angle iron screwed to the corners of flats to protect them, especially on tour, when scenery receives much handling. Sometimes shortened to shoe.

road show 1. A show on tour. 2. To tour a show.

road-showing Going on tour.

robam nang sbek thom (Khmer) See: *nang sbek*.

robe A shortening of wardrobe. 1. Originally, all of a person's effects, including clothes and furniture. 2. Later, one's clothes. (Boucher FASHION)

robe à la créole (French) See: *caraco*.

robe à la Française (French) See: gown à la Française.

robe de chambre (French) 1. A 17th C man's bathrobe or woman's non-ceremonial gown at court. 2. A 19th C woman's bathrobe or negligée. (Boucher FASHION)

robe de commune (French) A 15th C designation for ordinary clothes, as opposed to a *robe déguisée*, for elegant occasions. Also called an *ancienne guise*.

robe déguisée (French) 15th C clothes for elegant occasions: daring and new fashions. See also: *robe de commune*. (Boucher FASHION)

robe Française (French) See: gown à la Française.

robe generiche (Italian) The body of business, tricks, set speeches, etc. used by the less talented *commedia dell'arte* performers who could not improvise effectively. French: *lieux communes*. (Mantzius HISTORY II 223)

robe Gironée (French) A 15th C loose-fitting gown with organ-pipe style pleats from waist to hem. Also called *à plis Gironée*. (Boucher FASHION)

robe longue (French) A 13th C long gown worn by academics and clerics.

robe Polonaise (French) See: gown à la Polonaise.

robe volante (French) See: sack gown.

Robinson Crusoe and Friday Two seats on the aisle. (Berrey/Van den Bark SLANG 578)

roca, rocha (Spanish) Literally: rock. The term was sometimes used for a medieval pageant wagon. (Shergold SPANISH)

rochet (French) 1. A Louis XIII short, collarless coat with elbow-length split sleeves worn at first by gentlemen, then by lackeys, and eventually by Italian comedy buffoons. (Boucher FASHION) 2. An Anglican bishop's full-length white lawn garment worn over a cassock. Also spelled *rochette*. See also: rocket. (Wilcox DICTIONARY)

rocker bar, rocking bar   On a marionette control, a crosspiece which enables walking or marking-time movement. (Philpott DICTIONARY)

rocker wheel   See: manual takeover.

rocket, roquet   1. From the Middle Ages to the present, a wool smock. Worn in the 15th C by pages and commoners, it had a shoulder cape with a hood. In the 18th C in Europe and the U.S., worn by men and women. 3. A 19th C ecclesiastical garment of linen with heavy lace from the waist down. See also: *rochet* (French). (Wilcox DICTIONARY)

rocking bar   See: rocker bar.

rodomontade   See: *rhodomontade.*

rod puppet   A two- or three-dimensional figure manipulated by means of rods of varying lengths, diameters, and materials. (Philpott DICTIONARY)

rod puppet play   See: *wayang golek, wayang kulit, zhangtou kuilei.*

rojaku (Japanese)   The aesthetic ideal in *no* of a performance redolent of ancient (*ro*) tranquility (*jaku*). According to Komparu it is an artistic aim beyond *yugen.* (Komparu NOH 14)

rokurin ichiro (Japanese)   Literally: six wheels one dew drop. Zenchiku's metaphysical, Buddhist interpretation of the aesthetic principle of *yugen* in *no.* It describes six progressively higher levels of attainment, culminating in the "level of the sublime" where "perfect enlightenment" is achieved in performance. See: *kabu isshin.* (Ortolani ZENCHIKU'S 8-24)

rokyoku (Japanese)   See: *naniwabushi.*

role   A character in a dramatic work or that character played on stage by a performer.

rôle accessoire (French)   See: *accessoire.*

rôle de niais (French)   The part of a simpleton.

role playing, role taking   See: sociodrama.

roll   1. To roll 'em in the aisles—to overcome an audience with laughter. 2. To clew—to fasten two or more rope lines together. 3. See: *bourrelet.*

roll ceiling   A large scenic unit serving as the ceiling of an interior set, framed and hung from battens attached to the downstage and upstage edges. When flown, the ceiling moves into a vertical position, often with the cloth rolled onto one of the battens.

roll curtain   A curtain that rolls itself around a batten as it is raised. A typical use is as a backing for a scene 'in one.' Hence it is also called an olio (or oleo) curtain. The term roll curtain is sometimes used interchangeably with roll drop or roller drop, but usually those two terms refer to a roll curtain hanging at any point on stage, not just downstage. Since a roll curtain is not a drapery with fullness, but rather a painted drop, it is sometimes called a drop curtain.

roll drop, roller drop   A roll curtain used at any point on stage rather than just as a backing for a scene 'in one.' A roll drop rolls itself around a batten as it is raised.

roll drop hook   A clamp used to fasten a partly rolled-up curtain to a batten, to shorten it. (Bowman/Ball THEATRE)

Rolle (German)   1. Role. 2. List of personnel.

roll 'em in the aisles   To delight an audience.

roller   1. A caster attached to the bottom of a scenic unit, such as a platform. 2. A wooden batten around which a curtain or drop can be rolled.

roller drop   See: roll drop.

rollers   Wheels on the bottoms of wings and shutters in 18th C theatres—though the more common practice in England was to slide the scenery in grooves. (Wilkinson WANDERING IV 42)

rolling   1. A painting technique in which a piece of canvas is dipped in paint, squeezed, and then rolled over the surface to be painted. Also called rag dolling. 2. Applying paint by this technique.

rolling cyclorama   A cyclorama which works like a panorama, rolling on or off a vertical cylinder at the side of the stage. Also called a rolling backcloth or a continental cyclorama.

rolling out, rolling in   The side of the foot (outer/inner) upon which the weight of a dancer's body rests when standing. (Kersley/Sinclair BALLET)

rolling scenery   Scenery mounted on casters for easy shifting.

rolling stage   See: wagon stage.

roll out   A hinged horizontal flap at the bottom of a flat, used in Britain in pantomimes to permit a performer to roll onto the stage suddenly.

roll tickets   Serially-numbered tickets in rolls, often used for performances when there is a general admission and no reserved seating. Also called sequence tickets.

(à la) Romaine (French)   See: *habit à la Romaine*.

roman (Indonesian)   Exotic European stories dramatized in popular theatre c. 1920-1940. (Brandon SOUTHEAST 51–52)

romance   1. A play dealing with love. 2. A play whose characters and events are somewhat fanciful, as in romantic drama.

Roman games   See: *ludi Romani*.

romantic acting   An acting style characterized by great emotional intensity, without the regard for studied gesture and line delivery found in classic acting. (Bowman/Ball THEATRE)

romantic actor   A performer who uses the florid romantic acting style or specializes in romantic roles.

romantic drama   Plays written in the period from c. 1790 to c. 1850 dealing with high adventure and romance. Settings were often exotic, characters stereotyped, and plots exciting. Romantic drama was idealized, emphasizing individualism and freedom from classical rules. Plays from the German *Sturm und Drang* school belong to this category and date from as early as Goethe's *Goetz von Berlichingen* in 1775; and the neo-romantic *Cyrano de Bergerac* of 1897 also belongs to the classification.

ronde de jambe (French)   In ballet, a circular movement of the leg. Grant and Wilson name and describe a number of types. (Grant TECHNICAL, Wilson BALLET)

rondel   See: roundel.

rondelle   A thin circle sliced from a jewel, or a bead with a hole bored in the center. Used for embroidering on fabric or for stringing in a necklace. (Wilcox DICTIONARY)

roneat (Khmer)   Several sizes of xylophone instruments used in the *pinpeat* musical ensemble. *Roneat dek* is a metalophone with 21 keys. *Roneat ek* is high-pitched, the lead melodic instrument in the ensemble. *Roneat thung* is a low toned xylophone. Also spelled *raneat*. (Brunet in Osman TRADITIONAL 216)

rong (Thai)   A stage. In *likay*, also called *na rong* (front of stage). (Virulrak "Likay" 122)

ronggeng (Indonesian)   A professional female street-dancer. In Java, street dancers are shown in 9th C temple sculpture and were popular through the 19th C. The dancer may be a female impersonator. (Soedarsono DANCES 23, 128; Holt ART 112) In Sunda, both a dancer and singer, the forerunner of the female singer (*pasinden*) in rod-puppet theatre (*wayang golek*). (Foley "Sundanese" 89–90)

rongi (Japanese)   Literally: debate. In a *no* play, a dialogue section written in verse and chanted in a style half-way between song (*fushi*) and speech (*kotoba*). The exchange is between the chorus (*ji*) and the protagonist (*shite*) and occasionally the secondary character (*waki*). A type of *shodan*. (Shimazaki NOH 46–47, Nippon Gakujutsu JAPANESE xii)

rong khon luang (Thai)   Literally: royal theatre. The dance theatre in the king's palace in Bangkok in the 19th and early 20th C. (Rutnin "Development" 7)

ronron tragique (French)   Literally: tragic purr. A style of delivering lines, especially evident in the performances of the actress Sarah Bernhardt as *Phèdre*. (Senelick "Trivial" 136)

roof   The uppermost gallery.

room   1. A medieval *mansion* (French) or locale in a stage production. 2. A seating area in an Elizabethan theatre, such as the lords' room, the two-penny room, etc. 3. A performer's position or place in the Restoration theatre.

roop naa bot (Thai)   Literally: figure before the text. The figure of a young prince in *nang talung* shadow theatre. (Smithies/Kerdchouay in Rutnin SIAMESE 134)

roost   The uppermost gallery.

rootitootoot   A multisyllable associated with Punch and his fellow puppets. Philpott says that in Russia a comparable nonsense word is *vanka-ru-tyu-tyu* and in China *u-dyu-dyu*. (Philpott DICTIONARY)

ropa (Spanish)   Literally: clothing. 16th-17th C women's outer clothing, open down the front, with sleeves puffed at the top and a straight collar. Called a *marlotte* in France and *simarra* in Italy. Also called a gamurra. (Boucher FASHION)

rope clamp   A rope lock.

rope house   See: hemp house.

rope-line system   See: hemp system.

rope lock   A clamping device on a lock (locking) rail. An operating line running to a counterweight passes through the clamp and is held in place when the lock is closed.

rope set   See: hemp system.

rope sheave   See: loft block.

ropes up   A capacity house.

rope system   See: hemp system

ropilla (Spanish)   A 16th C tight-fitting doublet with hanging sleeves. (Boucher FASHION)

roppo (Japanese)   In *kabuki*: 1. A bravura exit from the stage down the runway (*hanamichi*). Major types of *roppo* are given in Leiter ENCYCLOPEDIA 314, Gunji KABUKI 156–157, and Brandon in Brandon/Malm/Shively STUDIES 86–91. 2. Less often, an entrance on the *hanamichi*, as in *Sukeroku: Flower of Edo*. (Brandon CLASSIC 64) See also: *de, tanzen roppo, tobi roppo*.

Roquelaure, roquelo   An 18th C man's full coat or cape, frequently fur-trimmed and sometimes with a deep cape-collar. Named for the Duc de Roquelaure. (Boucher FASHION, Walkup DRESSING 212)

roquet   See: rocket.

Roscius   An actor, especially a fine actor. From the name of the Roman performer Quintus Roscius Gallus. Hence, Roscian, Roscian society. Several famous actors have been nicknamed Roscius: David Garrick, the British Roscius; John Henderson, the Bath Roscius; William H. W. Betty, the Young Roscius; Edwin Forrest, the Roscius of the Bowery. (Bowman/Ball THEATRE, Sobel NEW)

(the) rose   In the footlights of many 19th C theatres in Britain, a large cluster of lights in the center. (Brockett HISTORY 465)

rosin box   A small area, usually boxed off, where ballet dancers can apply rosin [*recte*: resin] to their shoes. See also: watering can.

Rosse **plays** (French-English)   Works of naturalistic playwrights who went to extremes in depicting depravity. (Rowe HEAD 190)

rosserie (French)   A 19th C realistic play which contained a note of harsh, cynical realism. Such works were often done at the Théâtre Libre. (Carlson FRENCH 183)

rostrum   In Britain, a collapsible platform. Called a parallel in the U.S. (Baker THEATRECRAFT)

rotai (Japanese)   See: *santai*.

rotating borderlight   In the 1920s and later in the U.S., a borderlight which could be turned toward the grid or the floor, thus providing a measure of control over where the light fell. (Fuchs LIGHTING 175)

rotation   In dance, the movement of a limb or the body around itself and around its up-down axis, the latter being the axis of movement. (Eshkol/Wachmann NOTATION 29–31)

rotonne   The lower collar of an 18th C man's redingote (riding coat). (Boucher FASHION)

rotten-apple   1. To throw rotten apples at a performer. 2. To hiss a performer. (Berrey/Van den Bark SLANG 592)

rough   A preliminary touring company box-office statement.

rough lamp   A late 19th C term for a calcium lamp. (Schuttler ''Sherlock'' 79)

rough out   1. To put up a stage setting to determine the positions of doors, windows, etc. 2. To work out the rudimentary movement of the performers.

rough soubrette   In a Toby show, an actress who played rustic parts. (Wilmeth LANGUAGE)

roukuilei, jou k'uei lei (Chinese)   Literally: flesh puppets. 10th-13th C puppets which were possibly hand or glove puppets but may in fact have been enacted by live performers, perhaps children, rather than manipulated. See also: *kuileixi*. (Dolby HISTORY 34, Liu INTRODUCTION 163, Obraztsov CHINESE 28)

rouleau (French)   A narrow cording of velvet or silk used in trimming. (Dreher HATMAKING)

round   1. Applause. Also called a round of applause. 2. A circular performing area in medieval times, such as the Cornish rounds. See also: *plân an guare*. 3. See: arena stage. (Bowman/Ball THEATRE)

round actor   A stage performer, as opposed to a film or TV performer; that is, one who appears in the flesh. See also: live. (Bowman/Ball THEATRE)

round batten   A wooden batten made up of two lengths of half-round, fastened together on their flat sides. (Bowman/Ball THEATRE)

round burner   See: Argand burner.

roundel, color roundel, glass roundel   A circular, convex glass color medium used primarily in footlights and borderlights. Occasionally spelled rondel. See also: color plate. (Wehlburg GLOSSARY)

roundel borderlight   See: borderlight.

roundel footlights   Footlights built with roundels as color filters. Lounsbury has illustrations. (Lounsbury THEATRE 89)

round figure   A three-dimensional puppet manipulated from above or below, or fitted over the hand as a glove puppet. (Speaight PUPPET 22)

round-flame burner   See: Argand burner.

round glass color plate   See: color plate.

round of parts   The roles played by a performer in repertory.

round plate dimmer   See: plate dimmer.

route   1. A series of bookings. 2. To book an act.

route sheet   The travel plan of a touring company. (Bowman/Ball THEATRE)

route the show   To schedule a company's playing dates.

routine   An act, especially in vaudeville or musical theatre, consisting of dance steps, dialogue, or (usually) comic business.

routining a show   In vaudeville, the planning of the running order of the (typically eight) acts. (Smith VAUDEVILLIANS)

row   1. A line of seats. 2. A low, free-standing scenic unit, such as a horizon row, sea row, etc.

rowlock   A bottleneck created in a row of auditorium seats when a spectator, in a panic, tries to squeeze ahead of other exiting patrons.

row spacing   The horizontal distance between rows of seats in an auditorium.

roy (French)   See: minstrel.

royal box   In Restoration theatres and later, the box or boxes reserved for the king, queen, prince, or princess. Hence, king's box, queen's box, etc. The royal box was at first located at the rear of the auditorium in the first tier of boxes and on the center line of the theatre, so that the view of the perspective scenery would be perfect. George II, who was near-sighted, had the box moved to near the stage, on the audience's left (the Prince of Wales' box was opposite, on the right). (Hogan LONDON xlviii)

royal circle   See: dress circle.

royalty   Compensation to authors and composers for permission to perform or publish their works. (Stern MANAGEMENT)

royberbande-shpil (Yiddish)   Purim plays about robbers, brigands, and high-waymen. Also called *gazin-shpil*. (Kirshenblatt/Gimblett "Contraband" 8)

rpf   Rigid plastic foam—styrofoam. (Parker/Smith DESIGN)

RSE   Right second entrance. See: right first entrance.

RTB   In old promptbooks, ring trap bell, that is, a bell signal to operate a trap door. (Shattuck SHAKESPEARE 22)

R-type lamp   See: reflector lamp.

ruan, juan (Chinese)   A three- or four-stringed lute with a round, flat body and a fairly long neck which is plucked with a plectrum, or with plectra. Often called a guitar in English translation. It is an important instrument in the melodic orchestra (*wenchang*) in Beijing opera (*jingju*) and many other forms of music-drama (*xiqu*), and is also featured in many forms of storytelling (*quyi*). (Wichmann "Aural" 450–451)

ruatan (Indonesian)   See: *ruwatan*.

rubashecka (Russian)   Literally: little shirt. A traditional embroidered smock, fastened at the left side from collar to waist. Worn tucked into trousers, or bloused with a leather belt. Also called a Russian blouse.

rube   1. A farmer character. 2. A rustic audience member or sucker.

rube up   To make up as a rustic. (Berrey/Van den Bark SLANG 588)

rubric   A stage direction in a medieval play.

rue (French)   Literally: street. A plane (q.v.) of the stage. The *rue* is the largest of the planes and is used for traps.

RUE   Right upper entrance.

ruf   Rigid (poly)urethane foam. (Parker/Smith DESIGN)

ruff   A kind of Elizabethan collar that rose from the top of a high neckband or, when wide, separate from the shirt, with a band which slipped inside the collar. Ruffs varied in width from about four inches to nine inches and were frequently three or more inches thick. Also called a *golilla* (Spanish), Medici collar, de Medici ruff. (Barton COSTUME 212, Walkup DRESSING 160, Wilcox DICTIONARY)

rug   Informally, a large wig.

ru-howzi (Iranian)   Literally: playing on the pond. Possibly pre-dating Greek classical theatre, a traditional comic form similar to the Italian *commedia dell'arte*. Using mime, music, and dance as well as the spoken word, it had its heyday in the 16th and 17th C. (P.R.R. "Ru-Howzi" 114)

Rührstück (German)   19th C sentimental drama.

ruido (Spanish)   See: *comedia de cuerpo*.

ruin the audience   In vaudeville, to stop the show, to be a hit—and spoil the audience for the act that followed. (Gilbert VAUDEVILLE 265–266) *rulin, ju lin* (Chinese)   A form of music-drama (*xiqu*), originally established as a single troupe in a private home in Fujian Province. It grew in popularity until some ten professional troupes existed in the 19th C. *Rulin* combined local folk music with elements from pre-existing forms, including *yiyangqiang*. In the early 20th C, *rulin* was absorbed by the developing *minju* drama. Also called *rulinban* or *ju lin pan*. (Dolby HISTORY 225, Mackerras MODERN 128)

ruling passion   A principal motivating force in the nature of a character. Othello's jealousy is an example. (Archer PLAY-MAKING 247)

rumble box   See: thunder run.

rumble cart   See: thunder cart.

run   1. The length of a stage engagement—the period during which a production continues to be performed. Hence, long run, short run, limited run. Also used as a verb. 2. The time it takes to perform an act or scene; a scene is said to run so many minutes. 3. To rehearse a scene or act without interruption. 4. To slide something along the floor, as when a stagehand runs a flat. 5. To operate or oversee something in the theatre, as, to run the light board, run a rehearsal, run the box office, etc. 6. A ramp or incline. (Stern MANAGEMENT, Bowman/Ball THEATRE) 7. In dance, a simple locomotor step in which weight is transferred from one foot to the other while contact with the ground is lost briefly during the transfer. (Hayes DANCE 47)

run a flat   To slide an upright flat along the floor, grasping it by its leading edge.

run a grind   To perform from 10 A.M. to 11 P.M. (Berrey/Van den Bark SLANG 583)

run away with the show   1. To be the best in a performance or production. 2. To steal the show from the star. Also called run off with the show.

Rundhorizont (German)   See: cyclorama.

run down   To forget one's lines.

runner   1. A slider. 2. A length of stage flooring that can be drawn offstage, leaving a narrow opening. Also called a cut. See also: slider. 3. Carpeting laid out backstage to dampen footsteps. 4. A narrow carpet for a hall or staircase. 5. A groove for a color frame at the front of a lighting instrument. 6. A ball sliding in a curtain track. 7. A curtain track. (Bowman/Ball THEATRE)

running account   A weekly tally of company salaries and petty cash expenses.

running gag   A comic line or piece of business that is repeated, usually with slight variations, throughout a scene or play.

running lights   Dim lights backstage during a performance. Also called safety lights. In Britain, pilots or stage pilots.

running order   A list of songs and/or scenes in playing order for a given performance of a revue or vaudeville.

running string, run-through string   In puppetry, a string running from one hand of a marionette, through the control, and to the other hand, thus facilitating movement of the marionette hands. (Philpott DICTIONARY)

running tabs   See: draw curtain.

running the pack   Moving a group of flats.

running time   The duration of a scene, act, or performance. (Crampton HANDBOOK)

run off with the show   See: run away with the show.

run-of-the-play contract   A contract with a performer assuring him or her of employment during the run of a play until the end of the season (usually 30 June in the U.S.).

run over   To rehearse lines.

run through   1. A rehearsal of a long section of a play, or the complete play, without interruption, often for a special purpose, such as a run through for lines. 2. To so rehearse.

run-through string   See: running string.

runway   A narrow platform projecting from the stage into the auditorium, used by the director during rehearsals or by actors in performance, especially in musicals, revues, vaudeville, or burlesque. Also called a catwalk; in Britain, a joy plank. See also: horseshoe runway, *hanamichi* (Japanese).

rupaka (Sanskrit)   1. In classical Indian dramatic theory, a generic term for the ten major dramatic forms. See: *bhana, dima, ihamrga, nataka, prahasana, prakarana, samavakara, utsrstikanka, vithi,* and *vyayoga*. They are distinguished from minor forms (*uparupaka*) by their ability to evoke in the spectator the *rasa* experience. (Keith SANSKRIT 296) 2. Drama in general. (Rangacharya INDIAN 10)

Rural Dionysia   Dionysian festivals held in city-states outside Athens. Tragedies, comedies, and dithyrambs were performed, but not necessarily all at one festival or in any one year, nor at every festival. Most productions were of old plays, often done by traveling troupes of actors. The greatest theatrical activity was in the 4th C BC; but at least one theatre existed in the later 5th C BC. The festivals themselves go back to prehistoric times, and fragmentary remains of one theatre seem to antedate the emergence of drama. Also called Rustic Dionysia or Lesser Dionysia. (Pickard-Cambridge FESTIVALS 42–56)

ruscus   Cut evergreen treated to retain its color indefinitely, used on stage for foliage. (Baker THEATRECRAFT)

rushes   Mats or individual rush stems put on the stage of an Elizabethan theatre, probably to protect the costumes of performers when they sank to the floor in a dying fall. Dekker spoke of "the very Rushes where the Commedy is to daunce" and of playgoers "spred either on the rushes, or on stooles. . . ." (Dekker in Nagler SOURCES 133–137)

rush seat   1. At late 19th and early 20th C matinees, a seat near the center of the front row, favored by young women who hurried to get one to watch their favorite matinée idol. (Carroll MATINEE 15) 2. In recent years, a seat made available at a reduced price shortly before curtain time. This is done with productions that are not selling out.

rush the show   To force one's way into a performance without paying.

rusi (Lao)   A hermit role in a *mohlam* play. (Miller "Kaen" 222)

Russian blouse   See: *rubashecka*.

rustic comedy   A play in a rural setting but with earthier subject matter than that of a pastoral.

rustic comic   A comedian specializing in farmer types.

Rustic Dionysia   See: Rural Dionysia.

rusty dusty   Formerly, a property gun. (Wilmeth LANGUAGE)

ruwatan (Indonesian)   An exorcistic performance of *wayang* shadow theatre that protects participants from the demon Kala's powers. Performed during the day in Javanese and Balinese *wayang kulit*, at night in Sundanese *wayang golek*. Also spelled *ngruwatan* in Java, *ruatan* in Sunda. See also: *wayang lemah*. (Holt ART 125; Foley "Sundanese" 235–238; Brandon THRONES 10, 14–15)

RWB   In old promptbooks, ring warning bell, that is, a warning signal for the end of an act, a coming scene shift, etc. (Shattuck SHAKESPEARE 22)

rybałt (Polish)   A 16th C wandering burgher minstrel. (Gassner/Quinn EN–CYCLOPEDIA 665)

rybałtowska **comedy** (Polish-English)   A 16th and 17th C farce deriving from Shrovetide interludes. The term derives from Latin *ribaldus*. (Csato POLISH 15)

rygynall   See: original.

ryu (Japanese)   1. A style of performing, especially in traditional dance and music. 2. The troupe or guild of performers of that style, for example, the Kanze *ryu* of *no* actors/acting. Often translated 'school,' because passing on the traditions of the style is an important function of the organization.

S

S   The designation of a low-wattage lamp with straight, slanting sides, now rarely seen in the theatre. Also called an S lamp, S-type, etc. (Gassner/Barber PRODUCING 802)

saajghar (Bengali)   Literally: decor-room. In *jatra*, a dressing room, often visible to the audience. Also spelled *shaj ghor*.

sabetan (Indonesian)   The generic term for puppet movement techniques in Javanese shadow theatre (*wayang kulit*). (Muljono in Osman TRADITIONAL 70, Brandon THRONES 63) Holt says "the art of puppetry." (ART 132) See: *penjepenging, bedolan, tantjeban, lampahan, perang.*

sabha (Sanskrit)   Literally: assembly. 1. A place where theatrical performances were held in ancient India. (Varadpande TRADITIONS 53) 2. In contemporary India, especially in Madras, a cultural group which sponsors theatrical and musical performances.

sabhapati (Sanskrit)   A patron or sponsor of a dramatic performance in ancient India, often a king or prince. (Keith SANSKRIT 370)

sablé (French)   Literally: covered with sand. An 18th C fabric woven from very tiny beads and used in ornaments, purses, shoes, etc. (Boucher FASHION)

sablière (French)   See: *mât.*

sabrangan (Indonesian)   Literally: overseas foreigner. In a *wayang* shadow play, a giant or ogre. (Soedarsono DANCES 83, Long JAVANESE 98) *Jejer sabrangan* (overseas scene) is a scene set in a foreign kingdom in a *wayang* play. (Brandon THRONES 22–23)

sabulo (Latin Roman)   During the decline of Rome, one of the types of comic entertainers. As the literal meaning of *sabulum* (coarse sand, gravel) may suggest, the *sabulo* is lumped with other entertainers characteristic of the decadence of the Empire. (Chambers MEDIAEVAL I 10)

saccularis (Latin)   See: minstrel.

sachek (Hebrew)   To play or to act. (Cherniack-Tzuriel "Omer" 12)

sack   See: chemise.

sack back   See: gown à la Française.

sack coat   Since the 18th C, a little boy's and adult's short shapeless jacket. See also: lounge. (Barton COSTUME 429)

sack gown   An 18th C loose-fitting dress, flared at the bottom. Also called a *robe volante* (French), Adrienne, Andrienne. (Boucher FASHION)

sack puppet   See: bag puppet.

SA come-on, SA stuff   A sex-appeal attraction.

sacque   See: chemise.

sacra rappresentazione (Italian)   A medieval religious play in Italy. (Nagler SOURCES 41) The order of the two words is sometimes reversed. The plural (*sacre rappresentazioni*) usually means mystery cycle, also called *rappresentazioni*. (Chambers MEDIAEVAL II 92–94)

sacristan   A 17th C five-or six-hoop wire farthingale worn in Spain. (Boucher FASHION)

sadang, satang (Korean)   Professional female singers and dancers. *Sadang pae (sandang* group) was an all-female troupe. When men (*nam*) joined such groups, the troupes were called *namsadang*. See also: *kosa* (Choe STUDY 28)

saddle   1. The charge made by a theatre manager for a performer's benefit night, evidently a fee in addition to the standard house charge. The term dates from as early as 1781. (Partridge TO-DAY 224) 2. A short rope or cable tied at both ends to a batten (or other object) with some slack; a lifting line is then tied to the center of the rope, forming a saddle and providing two points of support instead of one. Also called a bridle or becket. Lounsbury has an illustration. (Lounsbury THEATRE 15) 3. See: saddle iron.

saddle iron   A piece of strap iron screwed to the bottom of a door flat to give it rigidity. Two short, vertical parts are welded to the piece and screwed to the upright wood members that frame the door opening. Also called a saddle or door saddle. Burris-Meyer and Cole have an illustration. See also: sill iron. (Burris-Meyer/Cole SCENERY 415)

Sadler's Wells makeup   Especially in 19th C Britain, improvised makeup from found and unlikely substances: dust, chalk, paint and plaster from dressing-room walls, etc. (Bowman/Ball THEATRE)

sadanoshin (Japanese)   The head of a *bunraku* puppet used for characters of virtuous old men. (Keene BUNRAKU 59)

saeculares ludi (Latin Roman)   See: *ludi saeculares*.

safety cable, safety chain   A secondary suspension (and so-called in Britain) for a piece of lighting equipment. (Rae/Southern INTERNATIONAL, Bowman/Ball THEATRE)

safety curtain   See: fire curtain.

safety jet, blow-through jet, oxy-gas jet   A burner (gas jet) for the oxy-calcium light in which oxygen was blown through hydrogen at the end of the jet. In most forms, the oxygen and hydrogen met at the end of the jet. (Rees GAS 56–57, fig. 34)

safety lights   See: running lights.

safety rope clamp   A rope lock.

saga play   Norwegian author Paul Botten Hansen's synonym for historical drama, especially Henrik Ibsen's first major dramatic work, *The Pretenders*. (Meyer IBSEN 207)

sagayan (Philippine)   A war dance of the Maranaw and Magindanaos regions in which the exploits of a hero, Prince Bantugan, are enacted by a solo dancer, following an epic recitation. (Alejandro PHILIPPINE 179)

sage uta (Japanese)   Literally: low song. A song in *no* composed in verse, and sung in a low pitch to rhythmic musical accompaniment (*hyoshi au*). See: *shodan*. (Shimazaki NOH 45, Hoff/Flindt "Structure" 225)

sahrdaya (Sanskrit)   In classical Indian theatre, the ideal of a spectator becoming caught up in a performance until he becomes one with the play's story and characters. (Raghavan in Baumer/Brandon SANSKRIT 42)

saie   A 16th C sometimes-belted coat with regulation or cape sleeves, often worn by pages. Usually of luxurious fabric, sometimes long-waisted. See also: *hoqueton* (French). (Boucher FASHION)

sailalin (Sanskrit)   In ancient Indian theatre, one of two groups of actors, identified by their adherence to the school of Sailalin and described as early as the 5th C BC. Also spelled *sailalaka*. See also: *nata*. (Hein MIRACLE 258, Raghavan in Baumer/Brandon SANSKRIT 10)

sailusa (Sanskrit)   A term for actor used in India as early as 3000 BC. See also: *nata*. (Raghavan in Baumer/Brandon SANSKRIT 10)

sainete (Spanish)   In Spain, a short farce of the late 17th C, earlier called an *entremés*. Now, a short comedy or burlesque. Also spelled *saynete*. (Brockett HISTORY 197) In the Philippines, a one-act, spoken farce, inspired by Spanish models, popular during the late 19th C. Also called *entreme*. (Fernández ILOILO 33, Cruz in Cruz SHORT 125)

saing waing (Burmese)   1. A set of twenty-one tuned drums arranged in a circular configuration, used in theatre performances. (Sein/Withey GREAT 48, Brandon SOUTHEAST 129) 2. The percussion ensemble that accompanies traditional theatre performances, taking its name from the drum set in the ensemble. Also called *saing* and *kai waing*. (Malm CULTURES 93)

saint play   A medieval miracle play dealing with the life of a saint. (Chambers MEDIAEVAL II 132) *saisoro* (Japanese)   A *bugaku* mask of an old man. It is the prototype of the *okina* mask used in *no*. (Wolz BUGAKU 39)

saja (Korean)   Literally: lion. 1. The character of a lion (commonly a messenger of Buddha), acted by two men, that appears in a wide variety of masked dance-plays. 2. The mask of a lion character. (Korean MASKS 35; Yi "Mask" 54, 58, 67, 71)

sajiki (Japanese)   A gallery or balcony for spectators along the side of a *bunraku* or *kabuki* theatre in the 18th and 19th C. Considered better than floor-level (*doma* and *masu*) seating. A few theatres today retain some *sajiki*. (Ernst KABUKI 25)

sakara (Sanskrit)   The role of a strutting braggart in early Indian drama, for example, Samsthanaka in *The Little Clay Cart*. The role disappears in later plays. Also spelled *shakara*. (Keith SANSKRIT 65, 134)

sakhi (Sanskrit)   A milkmaid who appears in the opening of a *raslila* performance. (Swann "Braj" 22)

sakkos   1. An Eastern Orthodox seamless embroidered clerical vestment. 2. See: lounge. (Wilcox DICTIONARY)

sakusha (Japanese)   Playwright. In *kabuki*, see: *tate zakusha*.

sakusha beya (Japanese)   Literally: playwrights' room. A room backstage in 18th and 19th C *kabuki* theatres used by troupe playwrights. (Hamamura et al KABUKI 73)

sal   Salary.

salade (French)   See: sallet.

salad march, salad parade   In the late 19th and early 20th C, a parade of ballet girls in green, white and amber costumes. (Partridge TO-DAY 229)

salitan (Indonesian)   A mouth style for certain Javanese shadow puppets; distinguished by narrow lips pressed closely together. (Long JAVANESE 70)

salle (French)   Literally: room. The auditorium of a theatre; the house. (Hawkins ANNALS II 116)

salle de spectacle (French)   1. A small 16th–17th C theatre in the chateau of a French aristocrat. 2. More generally, any theatre. (Moynet FRENCH 186)

sallet, *salade* (French)   A 15th C helmet with a mail cape over the back of the neck, movable visor, and a separate chin piece. (Walkup DRESSING 129, Wilcox DICTIONARY)

Salome dancer   An old term for a cooch or belly dancer. (Wilmeth LANGUAGE)

salp'an (Korean)   An act consisting of acrobatics accompanied by music and dialogue between acrobats and a clown (*mehossi*). One of six acts in *namsadang*. (Kim "*Namsadang*" 11–12, Sim/Kim KOREAN 23) *saltatio* (Latin Roman)   Literally: dancing, dance. Gesture, the art of gesture. (Duchartre ITALIAN 25)

saltator (Latin Roman)   A mime actor, a meaning which continued into medieval times. Since the word is literally dancer, the presumption is that the mime began as dance, presumably mimic dance. See also: mime. (Nicoll MASKS 83)

salt box   1. A hollow wooden container upon which a spoon was drummed as musical accompaniment to 18th C Punch and Judy shows and other entertainments. (Speaight PUPPET 167) 2. A toy house, possibly containing the saltpeter used to simulate lightning. (Visser in Hume LONDON 110)

saltimbanque (French)   A buffoon, a mountebank. Also called a *bâtaleur*.

salt water dimmer   In the U.S., one of the more descriptive names of an early resistance dimmer, typically an earthenware pot containing salted water and two electrodes. One electrode was fixed to the bottom of the pot; the other moved upward through the water to dim the light. Other terms: water-barrel dimmer, water dimmer, water resistance dimmer (all U.S.); liquid dimmer, pot dimmer, liquid pot dimmer (all Britain). All books below have illustrations. (Lounsbury THEATRE 39–40; Bax MANAGEMENT 177–178, fig. 36; Goffin LIGHTING 49–52, figs. 21–22; Bentham ART 46–47; Fuchs LIGHTING 325–326, 485–486)

samai (Japanese)   Literally: left dance. A *bugaku* dance imported from India, China, or central Asia and identifiable by red-orange costuming. So named because the performers approached the stage from the left. See also: *bugaku, umai.* (Bowers JAPANESE 8, Wolz BUGAKU 36–42)

samaji (Hindi)   Adult members of a *raslila* troupe; they are musicians and singers. (Hawley KRISHNA 318, Swann "Braj" 22) Also called *samgit samaj.* (Hein MIRACLE 135)

samare, samarra, samarre, simar   1. See: *chamarre.* 2. A 17th C loose, full-sleeved, velvet jacket for women, often fur-trimmed, fastened only at the neck. Also called a Dutch jacket. (Walkup DRESSING 194)

samavakara (Sanskrit)   In classical Indian theatre, a three-act play with a well-known story. Gods and demons are heroes, and heroism (*vira*) is the principal *rasa.* (Rangacharya NATYASASTRA 53)

samban tsuzuki (Japanese)   See: *sanban tsuzuki.*

sambhoga (Sanskrit)   Literally: union. In classical Sanskrit drama, the subdivision of the erotic sentiment (*srngara rasa*) which emphasizes the union of lovers. (Keith SANSKRIT 323)

Sambo   In a minstrel show, an end man paired with Rastus. See also: Tambo.

samcari bhava (Sanskrit)   See: *vyabhicari bhava.*

samgit samaj (Hindi)   See: *samaji.*

samhyon yukkak (Korean)   Literally: three strings, six sounds. An ensemble of six musical instruments that accompanies masked dance-plays: one *chottae, haegum, changgo,* and *puk* and two *p'iri.* (Cho "Ogwangdae" 29)

Samoiloff effect   The use of complementary colors for trick effects. For example, under blue-green light a red object on a white background will appear as black on blue-green; under red light, the object will tend to disappear against the reddish background. The name is for Adrian Samoiloff, who created a stir in the British theatre in the 1920s by using these principles for trick effects. For at least a time thereafter, such color filters as Samoiloff Blue, Samoiloff Mauve, and Samoiloff Red were produced in England. (Bentham ART 38, 272; Ridge/ Aldred LIGHTING 92; Goffin LIGHTING 60)

samisen (Japanese)   See: *shamisen.*

samjin-samt'oe (Korean)   Literally: three steps forward, three steps backward. A military dance in masked dance-plays. (Cho "Yangju" 31)

samkhu (Sanskrit)   A conch shell, generally used in ritual, that sounds at important moments in *kathakali, kutiyattam,* and *krishnanattam.* It sounds as if it was "the very voice of the celestial beings" in the play. (Jones/Jones KATHAKALI 78)

sampak (Indonesian)   See: *perang sampak.*

sampho (Khmer)   A double-headed horizontal drum played with the fingers. It is part of the *pinpeat* musical ensemble that accompanies classical theatre. (Brandon SOUTHEAST 127)

sampur (Indonesian)   See: *ngibing.*

samvada (Sanskrit)   In *ramlila,* dialogue spoken in contemporary language. (Schechner "Ramlila" 67)

sanak paekhui (Korean)   Literally: hundred entertainments. A variety show of magic, tricks, games, and tumbling, introduced from China and popular in the northern kingdom of Koguryo c. 7th C. (Yi "Mask" 37, Sim/Kim KOREAN 8)

sanbaji, sanbadi (Korean)   In puppet plays and *namsadang,* a musician who takes the role of a villager, and as interlocutor engages in repartee with the puppeteers while playing a drum (*changgo*). See: *kkoktu kaksi.* (Choe STUDY 18, Sim/Kim KOREAN 66)

sanban, san pan (Chinese)   Literally: dispersed meter. The most basic free meter (*ziyouban*) metrical-type (*banshi*) used in the songs of Beijing opera (*jingju*). It occurs in both the *xipi* and *erhuang* modes (*diaoshi*), in a variety of dramatic situations. (Wichmann "Aural" 159–160)

sanbanmemono (Japanese)   See: *kazuramono.*

sanban tsuzuki, samban tsuzuki (Japanese)   Literally: three-parts-continuous. A three-act play in late 17th C *kabuki.* (Dunn/Torigoe ANALECTS 20) *sanchari bhava* (Sanskrit)   See: *vyabhicari bhava*.

san chiao hsi (Chinese)   See: *sanjiaoxi*.

sandae-chapkuk (Korean)   A type of dance-drama popular in the latter part of the Koryo dynasty, c. 13th–14th C. (Yi "Mask" 37)

sandae-dogam (Korean)   See: *sandae-togam*.

sandaeguk, sandae kuk (Korean)   Literally: mountain drama. The term may have derived from the tall stage once used. 1. A form of court masked dance-drama in the Choson dynasty (1392 AD to 1910 AD). It is believed that most existing folk masked dance-plays derived from this drama. 2. Abbreviated *sandae, santae, sande* (mountain), a generic term for several current types of folk masked-plays. In them noblemen (*yangban*) and monks are satirized. In Yangju and Kyonggi Provinces, also called *pyolsandae* (separate *sandae*), to distinguish the present form from its now extinct predecessor *ponsandae* (original *sandae*). In Hwanghae Province, also called *t'alch'um* (masked dance). Also called *sandae-nori* (mountain dance). See also: *ogwangdae*. (Cho "Hwanghae" 37, Cho "Yangju" 27–28, Korean MASKS 13–17)

sandae narye-hui (Korean)   A type of dance-drama performed in the latter part of the Koryo dynasty, c. 13th–14th C. (Yi "Mask" 37)

sandae-nori (Korean)   See: *sandaeguk*.

sandae-togam, sande-dogam (Korean)   Literally: bureau of mountain drama. 1. At the Choson court during the 16th and 17th C, the office which administered performances and players of all performing arts. (Cho "Yangju" 28) 2. A court masked dance play. See: *sandaeguk*.

sandan (Japanese)   Literally: three steps. 1. A three-step unit at the front of a *bugaku* or *no* stage. (Gunji KABUKI 45) 2. A three-step stair unit in *kabuki*. It may be free standing, but more often leads to an interior room (*niju butai*). (Scott KABUKI 155)

san dan no kiri (Japanese)   Literally: third-act-conclusion. The concluding section of the third act in a five-act *bunraku* history play (*jidaimono*). Typically a child or beloved family member is sacrificed for the sake of one's lord. The scene is considered the dramatic high point of the play. Keene CHIKAMATSU 240–246 has examples. (Brandon CLASSIC 17)

sandbag   A canvas bag filled with sand and used as a weight in a rope flying system.

sand cloth   A stage cloth painted to represent sand or a road.

s. and d.   In vaudeville, a term for song and dance.

sande (Korean)   See: *sandaeguk*.

sandhi (Sanskrit)   Literally: juncture. In classical Indian dramatic theory, the five divisions of a play's plot, or subject matter: *mukha, pratimukha, garbha, vimarsa,* and *nirvahna*. (Keith SANSKRIT 298) Byrski calls them "spans" and discusses the 64 "sub-spans" (*sandhyanga*) into which they can be divided (Baumer/Brandon SANSKRIT 145–160). Kale calls them "joints." (THEA-TRIC 157)

sandhima (Sanskrit)   One of four kinds of stage properties (*pusta*), made of bamboo and covered with skin or cloth. (Bharata NATYASASTRA 411, Keith SANSKRIT 365)

sandhyanga (Sanskrit)   See: *sandhi*.

sandiwara (Malaysian, Indonesian)   Literally: drama. The term originated in Indonesia c. 1926, where it initially meant modern spoken drama (namely, Western influenced), as distinct from traditional drama. 1. The general term in Indonesia for modern drama. 2. In Sunda (West Java), a popular, commercial Sundanese-language theatre form in which traditional dance-dramas and contemporary plays are performed in improvisatory style. (Brandon SOUTHEAST 50–51) 3. In Malaysia, associated with the first period of modern drama, c. 1930–1950, in which scripted plays, often on historical themes, were staged by amateurs. History plays of this period and style are also called *purbawara* (old-style presentation) or *drama sejarah* (history play).

sanduan (Chinese)   See: Song *zaju*.

sandwich batten   Two wooden battens screwed together with the top or bottom edge of a cloth drop sandwiched between them.

sandwich boards   Advertising boards hanging in front of and behind a person, forming a walking advertisement. Used by vaudevillians from the early 20th C in the U.S.

sang (Hindi)   A folk theatre of Haryana, north India, largely untouched by changes in contemporary India.

sangaku (Japanese)   Literally: miscellaneous entertainment. A Japanese reading of Chinese *sanyue*. The term encompasses a wide range of popular entertainments of the 8th and 9th C that had been imported from China. These include song, dance, acrobatics, juggling, magic, conjuring, and possibly dramatic sketches. (Araki BALLAD 199, Inoura HISTORY 40–41, Sakanishi KYOGEN 4)

sangeet bari (Marathi)   See: *tamasha*.

sanghyang (Indonesian)   Literally: revered divinities. In Bali: 1. A dancer, often a young girl, whom a deity possesses and through whom it dances. 2. A dance, concerned with ritual purification and exorcism, performed by such a dancer while in a state of possession or trance. Twenty-five types of *sanghyang* are described in Belo TRANCE 180–225, Soedarsono DANCES 164–166, and de Zoete/Spies DANCE 69–80. It is one type of 'sacred' (*wali*) dance. (Bandem/deBoer BALINESE 12–17) See also: *kecak*.

sangi (Assamese)   See: *pariparshrika*.

sangitaka (Sanskrit)   A form of ancient Indian theatre popular during the latter part of the classical period. (Vatsyayan TRADITIONAL 16)

sangita nataka (Sanskrit)   See: *sangitaka.*

sangjwa (Korean)   1. The character of a young monk in various types of masked dance-plays. He dances to bless the playing area. 2. The mask of the character. (Yi "Mask" 47, 51, 58)

sangkhit (Thai)   A general term for the arts of music, dance, and singing. (Anuman in Rangthong SOUVENIR 85)

sangsoe (Korean)   In *namsadang*, the first small gong player. (Kim "Namsadang" 12)

sangsoe-nori (Korean)   See: *p'ungmul.*

san hsien (Chinese)   See: *sanxian.*

san hsü (Chinese)   See: *daqu.*

sanhualian, san hua lien (Chinese)   See: *chou.*

san i, san i hsiang (Chinese)   See: *yixiang.*

sanjiaoxi, san chiao hsi (Chinese)   Literally: three-role play, theatre. A form of music-drama (*xiqu*) popular in Fujian Province which originated in Jiangxi Province, c. 17th C. So called because it initially included only three roles—a young male (*xiaosheng*), a flower female (*huadan*), and a painted-face (*jing*). It features percussion instruments and uses *lianquti* musical structure.

sanjiva (Sanskrit)   Literally: creature. One of four kinds of spectacle (*aharya*) in classical Indian theatre. Two possible meanings for this unclear term are an actor who impersonated an animal (Rangacharya NATYASASTRA 33) or "manipulation of effigies" on stage (Richmond in Baumer/Brandon SANSKRIT 102).

sanju (Japanese)   A type of *shamisen* melodic pattern in *nagauta* or *bunraku* music. (Malm in Brandon/Malm/Shively STUDIES 168)

san khau ca kich bai choi (Vietnamese)   See: *ca kich bai choi.*

sankiti (Malayalam)   The second singer, who also plays bronze cymbals (*ilattalam*), in *kathakali* and *krishnanattam*. (Jones/Jones KATHAKALI 77)

sanmaime (Japanese)   Literally: the third. A comic role in *kabuki* or the actor thereof. The name of the chief comic actor of a troupe appeared in third place on the marquee; hence the term. Also called *dokeyaku* (comic role) by Gunji (KABUKI 22, 188), and *dokegata* (comedian) by Scott (KABUKI 168–169). (Leiter ENCYCLOPEDIA 327)

sanmaime sakusha (Japanese)   See: *tate zakusha.*

sannio (Latin Roman)   One of the terms for the mime fool. The word has been related to Latin *sanna* (mocking grimace) but also to the *zanni* of the Italian *commedia dell'arte*. Despite the similarities between the *zanni* (other post-classical characters, too) and what is known of the *sannio*, the view of the *zanni* as a direct descendant of the *sannio* has been discarded. Plural *sanniones*. See also: *stupidus*. (Lea ITALIAN I 54, Nicoll MASKS 88–90)

sanniones (Latin Roman) See: *sannio*

san no kawari (Japanese) Literally: third change. In Kyoto-Osaka, the third production of the *kabuki* season. Analogous to *yayoi kyogen* in Edo (Tokyo) *kabuki*. (Dunn/Torigoe ANALECTS 19)

san no matsu (Japanese) Literally: third pine. 1. The third (and farthest from the stage) of three small pine trees that stand in front of the *no* bridgeway (*hashigakari*). 2. The acting area on the bridgeway marked by the third pine. (Berberich "Rapture" 64)

san pan (Chinese) See: *sanban*.

santa (Sanskrit) Literally: peace. 1. A hero (*nayaka*) of calm disposition, usually a Brahman or a merchant, in classical Indian drama. (Keith SANSKRIT 305–306) 2. The ninth sentiment (*rasa*), propounded by the 10th C scholar Abhinavagupta. It is not a part of classical Indian dramatic theory but appears in the aesthetic systems and performance styles of some later regional theatre forms, such as *kathakali*. Also spelled *shanta*. (Deutsch in Baumer/Brandon SANSKRIT 223–224, Kothari "Kathakali" 62)

santae (Korean) See: *sandaeguk*.

santai (Japanese) Literally: three bodies. In *no*, the three basic role types that an actor is called upon to portray: male warrior (*guntai*), woman (*nyotai*), and old person (*rotai*). See also: *monomane*. (Nearman "Kyui" 316)

san tso (Chinese) See: *sanzuo*.

san tuan (Chinese) See: Song *zaju*.

santuchu, san t'u ch'u (Chinese) Literally: three prominences. A theory of characterization found in the model plays (*yangbanxi*) of the Cultural Revolution period (1966–1976). It stipulates: among all characters, give prominence to positive characters; among positive characters, give prominence to heroic characters; and among heroic characters, give prominence to the main heroic characters.

sanwuqi, san wu ch'i (Chinese) See: *chuiqiang*.

sanxian, san hsien (Chinese) Literally: three strings. A long-necked, three-stringed lute without frets which is plucked with a plectrum. A small *sanxian* is an important instrument in the melodic orchestra (*wenchang*) in Beijing opera (*jingju*), *kunqu,* and many other forms of music-drama (*xiqu*); a large *sanxian* is used in many forms of storytelling (*quyi*). Also called *xianzi* or *hsien tzu*. (Scott CLASSICAL 45, 50; Scott TRADITIONAL I 163)

sanxu (Chinese) See: *daqu*.

san yaku (Japanese) Literally: three roles. In *no*, the three groups of performers who support the main actor (*shite*), namely *waki* and *kyogen* actors, and musicians. (Shimazaki NOH 83)

sanyi, sanyixiang (Chinese)   See: *yixiang*.

sanyue, san yüeh (Chinese)   Literally: diverse music. 1. A generic term for folk music and dance, c. 11th–3rd C BC. 2. The name given the hundred entertainments (*baixi*) when such performances were adopted by the imperial court of the Han dynasty (206 BC to 220 AD). Used to contrast these popular spectacles with the more formal, elegant music (*yayue*) indigenous to the court. See also: *suyue*. (Dolby HISTORY 3) 3. A type of performance which inherited certain features of 7th–10th C adjutant plays (*canjunxi*). It was very similar to Song *zaju*, and may have partly merged with that form. (Dolby HISTORY 19) 4. Since the 13th C, sometimes used as a generic term for folk performances.

sanzuo, san tso (Chinese)   Literally: scattered seats. In a tea-house theatre (*xiyuan*) of the 17th-early 20th C, the portion of ground-floor seating extending from the side and back edges of the pond (*chizi*) to beneath the second-story veranda on the sides and back of the auditorium. Seating in this area was on long benches and was inexpensive; only big wall (*daqiang*) seating was cheaper. Scattered seats underneath the veranda on the two sides of the auditorium were called the two corridors (*lianglang*) in the 19th and early 20th C. (Dolby HISTORY 191, Mackerras RISE 202–203, Scott CLASSICAL 221–222)

sao (Vietnamese)   A transverse flute played in *cai luong* and *hat boi*. Also called *ong dich*. (Addiss "Theater" 140, Brandon SOUTHEAST 128)

sap (Vietnamese)   A generic term for melodic patterns in *hat cheo*. Addiss gives five types in "Theater" 132–133.

sapak soder (Indonesian)   See: *ngibing*.

saphon (Thai)   See: *tapone*

saput (Indonesian)   An outer cloak, belted above the waist, worn by male characters in Balinese dance plays. Also spelled *sapoet*. (de Zoete/Spies DANCE 42)

sarafan (Russian)   A traditional female Russian peasant ensemble, still worn. It consists of a wool or brocade long, full skirt, with a sleeveless top worn over a loose, white blouse cuffed or ruffled at the wrists. With this ensemble, an embroidered bolero is often worn. (Wilcox DICTIONARY)

sardar (Hindi)   The director/manager of a *tamasha* troupe. See also: *sutradhara*. (Vatsyayan TRADITIONAL 174)

Sardoodledom   George Bernard Shaw's term ridiculing the French playwright Victorien Sardou, his well-made plays, and the general mindlessness of 19th C drama.

sarira (Sanskrit)   In classical Indian theatre, movement and gesture of limbs and hands in acting. One type of body movement (*angika*). (Raghavan in Baumer/Brandon SANSKRIT 32)

saron (Indonesian)   See: *gamelan*.

sarugaku (Japanese)   Literally: monkey entertainment. A term used inter-changeably with *sangaku* in the 10th C; *sangaku* later went out of use. (Araki BALLAD 52)   In the 11th and 12th C, *sarugaku* included juggling, dancing, singing, and probably trained monkeys. Later, dramatic pieces were added and during the time of the actor Kannami Kiyotsugu in the 14th C, *sarugaku* per-formances consisted solely of drama. These plays were called *sarugaku-no* (13th to 15th C) and then just *no* (beginning c. 17th C). See also: *no, onna sarugaku.* (O'Neill EARLY 4–6, Inoura HISTORY 66–67, Sakanishi KYOGEN 4–6)

saruwaka (Japanese)   1. In 17th C *nogaku* and *kabuki*, a comic role. 2. Especially in *kabuki*, an actor of that role. See also: *doke.* (Gunji KABUKI 19)

sashi (Japanese)   A unit of a *no* play written in arrhythmic language and chanted in a style between song (*utai*) and speech (*kobota*). A type of *shodan.* (Shimazaki NOH 48, Hoff/Flindt "Structure" 238)

sashidashi (Japanese)   Literally: held out. A candle on a long pole held out by a stage hand (*kurogo*) to light a *kabuki* actor's face. The technique is used today to create an antique effect. Also called *tsura akari* (face light). (Ernst KABUKI 110, Kincaid KABUKI 181, Scott KABUKI 78)

sashigane (Japanese)   Literally: thrust metal. In *kabuki* and occasionally *bun-raku*, a small prop fastened to the end of a thin flexible pole. A rat, butterfly, bird, or flaming cotton for a spirit fire (*shochobi*) comes to life when it is moved by a stage hand (*kurogo*). (Leiter ENCYCLOPEDIA 331)

sashikomi (Japanese)   A standard gesture (*kata*) in *no* in which the closed fan is lifted and thrust forward. It can suggest pointing or distance. Illustrated in Keene NO 220.

satang (Korean)   See: *sadang.*

satire   A form of comedy that ridicules human follies. Hence, satiric, satir-ical. Ben Jonson's *Volpone* and *The Alchemist* are examples.

satirical melodrama   A type of Russian comedy of the 1920s which ridiculed all negative characters and presented serious political ideas. (Slonim RUSSIAN 296)

sato kagura (Japanese)   Literally: village *kagura.* Folk dances and skits closely connected to the Shinto religion performed in villages on religious and festive occasions. Masked figures predominate. (Inoura HISTORY 17) Sadler ("O-Kagura" 276–277) emphasizes the inherent erotic and comic nature of these folk performances.

satsuki kyogen (Japanese)   Literally: fifth-month play. In *kabuki*: 1. A play performed on the fifth-month program in the 18th or 19th C. 2. The program of plays that opened on the fifth day of the fifth lunar month. (Leiter ENCY-CLOPEDIA 331)

sattvati (Sanskrit)   Literally: grand. One of four styles (*vrtti*) of writing and acting in classical Indian drama. Described as "encompassing an excess of passion'' (Kale THEATRIC 39) or as being ''grand and dynamic'' (Raghavan in Baumer/Brandon SANSKRIT 49). According to Bharata it is derived from the *Yajur Veda* (NATYASASTRA 404).

sattvikabhinaya (Sanskrit)   Literally: truth in acting. The rare and genuine quality of emotion which is projected by an actor through such involuntary states as blushing, fainting, weeping, and paralysis. It is one of four elements of acting (*abhinaya*). Abbreviated *sattvika*. (Bharata NATYASASTRA 102–106, 145–147)

satura (Latin Roman)   See: *fabula satura*.

saturable choke, saturable core, saturable reactor dimmer   See: reactance dimmer.

saturation lighting   When a performance in an outdoor theatre begins while daylight is still present, a brightening of the stage lighting as darkness approaches. (Rubin/Watson LIGHTING 68)

Saturnian verse   The verse form of the *satura* (q.v.). In Latin: *Saturninus*. (1939 Bieber HISTORY 301)

satyr   In Greek mythology, a horselike or goatlike figure, usually riotous and lascivious. Satyrs, who often attended Dionysus, were referred to by the 8th C BC and perhaps much earlier. They appeared first in phallic rituals and later in satyr plays and sometimes dithyrambs. Some satyrs were apparently smooth-skinned and some hairy; the chorus members in 5th BC satyr plays may normally have worn a shaggy loincloth, tail and phallus, mask with beard, and animal ears. Usually equine, they were sometimes a combination of the goatlike satyr and horselike *silenus*. The distinction between satyr and silenus is not made by all writers in English. They have reason: in 5th C BC Greek and later the words for satyr and silenus were interchangeable. See also: *silenus*. (Pickard-Cambridge DITHYRAMB 96, 116–118, 173; Flickinger GREEK 24–27; Allen ANTIQUITIES 10–11)

satyr choreut   A member of a satyr chorus. (Pickard-Cambridge DITHYRAMB 115)

satyr chorus   1. In classical Greece and Rome, the chorus of a satyr play or a dithyramb. 2. Before the emergence of Greek drama, a group of satyrs engaged in vigorous, often obscene dances or songs or both. Compare satyr, satyr play.

satyric   Having to do with satyrs or a satyr play. (Arnott SCENIC 105, Flickinger GREEK 22)

satyric drama   1. A satyr play. 2. Satyr plays as a genre.

satyrika (Greek)   Probably choral performances of satyrs. Singular: *satyricon*. (Pickard-Cambridge DITHYRAMB 96, 97)

satyrikos choros (Greek)   The chorus of a satyr play. (Mantzius HISTORY I 98) *satyroi* (Greek)   Satyr plays. (Pickard-Cambridge DITHYRAMB 65)

satyr play   A type of drama given literary form in the late 6th C BC. The satyr play which in the next century often followed a tragic trilogy, developed a superfical resemblance to tragedy: it had alternating episodes and choral odes, and its subject or theme might be similar to that of the trilogy which preceded it. But its tone was vastly different. Vigorous and phallic in both language and movement, the satyr play mocked gods and heroes in unrestrained dance and song. While there were occasional serious moments, the general effect was apparently that of a boisterous, licentious parody of tragedy. Satyrs (often followers of Dionysus) being wood sprites, the settings were pastoral. Characters and chorus were masked, most of them as satyrs, but some as the mythological figures being burlesqued. The plays continued to be performed through early Christian times. Greek plural: *satyroi*. English often uses satyr drama and satyric drama. Compare satyr, *silenus*. (Bieber HISTORY 9–12; Pickard-Cambridge DITHYRAMB 62–63, 96, 113–115, 124–126)

saubhika (Sanskrit)   See: *sobhanika*.

sauter (French)   See: movements in ballet.

sautoir (French)   A late 19th-early 20th C long metallic chain with an attached medallion, watch, small purse, etc., tucked into the belt. See also: *châtelaine*. (Wilcox DICTIONARY)

SA value   Sex-appeal value at the box office.

"Save your lights."   In Britain, a direction to the electrician to turn off the lights. (Baker THEATRECRAFT)

Savoyard   1. A regular performer in Gilbert and Sullivan operettas. 2. A devotee of Gilbert and Sullivan operettas. The term comes from the Savoy Theatre in London, built as the home of those works.

sawari (Japanese)   An emotional, melancholy type of *shamisen* music played during a *kudoki* scene in *kabuki* or *bunraku*. (Malm in Brandon CHUSHINGURA 68–69)

sawi (Korean)   A generic term for dance patterns in masked dance-plays. (Yi "Mask" 53)

sayap sandang (Malaysian)   Two curved 'wings' projecting to the rear of a heroic *wayang kulit* puppet figure. Believed by Sheppard to be an early 20th C borrowing from Thai theatrical costume. (Sheppard TAMAN 77)

sayaw (Philippine)   A folk play in which an army of Christian villagers confronts Muslim invaders. A possible antecedent of *comedia*. (Mendoza COMEDIA 81–83)

saynete (Spanish)   See: *sainete*.

sayu (Japanese)   Literally: left-right. In *no*, a standard movement pattern (*kata*) in which the actor pivots twice, raising first his left arm and then his right. Illustrated in Keene NO 220.

sbek thom (Khmer)   See: *nang sbek*.

Sbernia   1. At first, a coarse wool used for soldiers' blankets. The fabric came from Ireland (Hibernia). 2. By the 16th C, a long outer scarf draped from the left shoulder, where it was fastened. Also called a *berne* (French). (Boucher FASHION)

scab   See: dutchman.

scabellum (Latin Roman)   See: *scabillum*.

scabillarii (Latin Roman)   In a Roman pantomime, the time-keepers who signalled the rise or fall of the curtain (which hid the stage from view). The term is from *scabillum*, a clapper at the bottom of the foot. (Beare ROMAN 154, 169)

scabillum (Latin Roman)   In a Roman pantomime, a clapper (Mantzius: cymbal) fastened to the foot of the pantomimist. The *scabillum* aided in keeping performer, orchestra, and chorus together. Also appears as Latin *scabellum* and U.S. English scabelum. (Allen ANTIQUITIES 27, Mantzius HISTORY I 234)

scaena (Latin Roman)   The Latin transliteration of Greek *skene* (scene building). 1. See: *scaenae frons*. 2. The stage on which the actors perform, though *pulpitum* is the more common term. Sometimes spelled *scena*. (Duckworth NATURE 79; Arnott ANCIENT 13, 102, 137)

scaena ductilis (Latin Roman)   1. A movable scenic panel. The *scaena ductilis* is sometimes spoken of as if it were similar to a modern flat, and sometimes as if it were a large framed drop. 2. Not earlier than the 3rd C BC, a low stage (presumably containing a framed drop) rolled into view from its storage building alongside the stage. The literal meaning is approximately 'a scene drawn along.' See also: *pinakes*. (Bieber HISTORY 74–75, 255–256; Pickard-Cambridge DIONYSUS 199, 202, 227, fig. 66)

scaena ductilis (Latin)   A changeable scenic unit in the 16th C; the *scaena ductilis* became the sliding flat wing. (Nicoll DEVELOPMENT 105)

scaenae frons, frons scaenae (Latin Roman)   Literally: brow (hence, front) of the scene building. 1. In Vitruvius (1st C BC), the source of the phrase, the front of the second story of the Greek scene building. 2. In the Roman theatre, the front wall of the stage house, that is, the scenic wall or facade behind the actors. Sometimes called the *scaena*. For a discussion of the openings in the *scaenae frons*, see *thyromata*. Also called the facade and *Bühnenfassade* (German). (Bieber HISTORY Index, Arnott ANCIENT 102)

scaena versatilis (Latin Roman)   See: *scaena versilis*.

scaena versilis (Latin Roman)   According to a Renaissance commentary on Vitruvius, the *periaktoi*. There is ancient authority for the existence of the *scaena versilis*, but not all scholars accept the identification with the *periaktoi*. The phrase is literally turning scene, but *versilis* has the sense of turning often. Also called *scaena versatilis*. (Allen ANTIQUITIES 109–110, Beare ROMAN 284, Campbell SCENES 24, Pickard-Cambridge DIONYSUS 237)

scaffold   1. In the medieval theatre, a localizing structure—a pageant wagon or a *mansion* (French). Also spelled skaffold. 2. A construction on an 18th C stage to provide extra seating. A London playbill for 13 May 1731 stated that "Proper Accomodations will be made upon the Stage, by Seats and Scaffolding." The scaffold was also called "building" and was what we would call bleachers. (Scouten LONDON 139) 3. A raised platform used as a stage; hence scaffold stage, scaffolding. 4. A seating area for spectators; a gallery, hence, scaffolder for a patron seated there.

scala (Italian)   In medieval Italian productions, steps.

scaling the house   Fixing the prices to be charged for the different sections of an auditorium and for the rows within sections. (Krows AMERICA 338 ff)

scalp, scalp tickets   To resell tickets at an exorbitant price.

scalp doily   A wig.

scalper   See: ticket scalper.

scamna (Latin Roman)   The benches, as at a show. Compare *spectacula*. (Beare ROMAN 244)

Scandoll   A chorus girl in the *Scandals*, early 20th C revues in the U.S.

scapulary   1. A 3rd-5th C cowled or hooded monk's robe. 2. A long overcoat. (Chalmers CLOTHES 80)

scare wig   See: fright wig.

scarlet flush   In Britain, the financial loss of a failed production, the equivalent of the U.S. expression "in the red."

scarpino (Italian)   See: *solleret*.

scat singing   1. Performance using extemporaneous words to fill in parts of songs whose lyrics the singer has forgotten. 2. Jazz singing using nonsense words. (Mitchell VOICES 104–105)

scattering   In dance, a shaping movement away from the body. See also: gathering. (Dell PRIMER 56)

scena   1. Especially in the 18th and 19th C, the scene building of the ancient Greek theatre. See also: *skene* (Greek). 2. In the late 19th C, a short, farcical sketch with a story line and a distinct setting, using knockabout comedy and caricature. In time, the scena became a melodramatic playlet or pretentious social drama. (Senelick "Gagbooks" 10)

scena (Latin Roman)   See: *scaena*.

scena amorosa (Italian)   A love scene in *commedia dell'arte*. (Mantzius HISTORY II 243)

scena equivoca (Italian)   A scene in *commedia dell'arte* in which characters speak with double meanings. (Mantzius HISTORY II 228) *scena muta* (Latin)   In 16th–18th C Jesuit drama in Europe, dumb show.

scena parapettata (Italian)   A box set.

scena per angolo (Italian)   Angle or angular perspective. Instead of using a vanishing point upstage center, 18th C scene painters began using vanishing points, sometimes several, that ran off at an angle, creating the effect of greater complexity and grandeur. Ferdinando Bibiena introduced the *scena per angolo* in Italy in the 1690s. Also called *prospettivo per angolo*. (Burnim ''Notes'' 32)

scena pictura (Latin)   Perspective scenery; a term used by Sulpitius in 1486. (Campbell SCENES 44)

scenario, *scenario* (Italian)   The written outline of a *commedia dell'arte* presentation. Also called a *canavaccio* (or *canovaccio*) or *soggetto*. Now, the outline of the plot of any play.

scene, *scène* (French)   1. A division of a play that is shorter than an act and during which the locale does not usually change. 2. Especially in French neo-classic playwriting, a unit of a play marked by the entrance or exit of a character or characters. 3. A portion of a play containing a unit of action, such as a balcony scene, a mob scene, a love scene, etc. 4. The locale of the dramatic action, as in: the scene is Jack Absolute's lodgings. 5. The scenic area in Renaissance theatres and later. 6. Scenery, the stage setting. Hence, behind the scenes, scene construction, scene designer. 7. Formerly, the stage, the theatre, drama. (Bowman/Ball THEATRE)

scène à faire (French)   An obligatory scene. A scene late in a play that is required by the previous progress of the plot. (Hamilton THEORY 122–123)

scene barrel   In 19th C theatres and earlier, a cylinder in the substage to which ropes from the carriages carrying the wings were attached. See also: chariot-and-pole system. (Leacroft DEVELOPMENT 110)

scene bay, scenery bay   See: scene dock.

scene blind   See: blind.

scene board   A sign indicating the locale of a scene.

scene building   See: *skene*.

scene change   See: scene shift.

scene chewer   A performer who overacts. (Bowman/Ball THEATRE)

scene closes, scene shuts   A direction in a Restoration play for the shutters to draw onstage and close off the prospect.

scene cloth   A backdrop, usually painted.

scene curtain   1. A curtain closed between scenes to cover a change. 2. The fall or close of a curtain at the end of a scene.

scène de bataille (French)   See: battle scene.

scene designer   One who designs stage settings.

scene division   A division of an act.

scene dock, scenery dock   1. A space for storing scenery, fitted with partitions to simplify stacking. Also called a stacking rack, stacking space, scene bay, scenery bay. 2. The area below the stage of a spectacle theatre, containing the machinery for elevating scenery and space for scenery storage. (Krows AMERICA 74)

scene door   A door in the scenery, especially in a wing or shutter in 17th C theatres and later.

scene draws   A direction in a Restoration play for the shutters to slide offstage and reveal the prospect behind. Also called scene opens.

scene dressing   See: trim prop.

scène en boîte (French)   A box set.

scene frame   1. In a chariot-and-pole system, the vertical pole or ladder thrusting up through a slot in the stage floor, to which a scenic wing could be attached. Also called a scene ladder. The term was used in the 18th C London theatres, though the system was not regularly used in British playhouses. (Avery LONDON lxiv) 2. The wooden frame upon which cloth is attached to make a flat.

scene heading   A numerical designation at the beginning of a scene in a printed play, such as Act II, scene ii.

scene house   In the past, a storage building for scenery. (Campbell SCENES 242)

scene in one   A short scene played in the furthest downstage plane of the stage in front of a drop, usually while a new setting is being positioned behind the drop. Hence, scene in two, scene in three, etc. Often shortened to in one, in two, etc. Also called a carpenter's scene.

scene intermission   A break between scenes, usually brief. In Britain, a scene interval.

scenekeeper   In the past, a stagehand responsible for shifting the scenery. Also called a stagekeeper. (Wilson "Players' " 29)

scene ladder   See: scene frame.

scene master   A single switch or potentiometer controlling a number of circuits which have been set for a particular scene. (Baker THEATRECRAFT, Wehlburg GLOSSARY)

scenemen   In 18th C theatres, backstage employees who helped shift scenery, served as carpenters, and helped put out fires.

scene muslin   Heavy, unbleached cotton fabric used in place of canvas for covering flats.

scene opens   See: scene draws.

scene pack   A group of flats stacked in storage. Also called a pack. The pack is called live if it is to be used and dead if it has already been used and is not to be used again. Hence, to pack, to stack.

scene paint   A mixture of powder color, glue, and water. Hence, scene painter, one who paints scenery.

scene painting   See: *skenographia.*

scene picture   The stage picture; the visual effect a director achieves by placement of the performers on stage. The term often means the visual totality—actors, scenery, props, etc.

scene plan   See: floor plan.

scene plot   A list of all the scenes in a play, indicating what scenery is required for each scene. Such a plot was especially important in 19th C theatres and earlier, when theatres had wing-border-shutter/drop scenery and numerous changes.

scene projector   1. In the U.S., an early term sometimes used for a lensless projector. See also: Linnebach projector. 2. Now usually a slide projector with a lens system, a high wattage lamp, and often a blower to provide necessary cooling. The instrument thus named is not markedly different from the British effect projector. (Fuchs LIGHTING 151)

scene rehearsal   In Britain, a technical rehearsal, with special attention given to scenery, lighting, and other technical matters.

scene room   1. A room for the storage of scenery, though the usual term now is scene dock. 2. In 19th C theatres, the scene-painters' shop. 3. A room in Restoration theatres where actors lounged and practiced their lines—a space that came to be called the green room.

scenery   1. Formerly, a scenario, an outline. "I writ the first and Third Acts...and drew the Scenery of the whole Play..." (Dryden "Vindication" 203) 2. The elements of a stage setting, especially those made of wood and canvas, such as flats. (Bowman/Ball THEATRE) 3. The stage setting as a whole. See also: setting. 4. A minor performer with little or no dialogue. (Berrey/Van den Bark SLANG 572) 5. Sometimes, informally, a costume. (Berrey/Van den Bark SLANG 579)

scenery bay   See: scene dock.

scenery chewer   A performer who overacts.

scenery dock   See: scene dock.

scenery pusher   A scene shifter.

scenery store   In Britain, a storage area for flats.

scenery wagon   Short form: wagon. A low platform on large casters or small wheels, used to support scenery that needs to be shifted quickly. Also called a dolly or stage wagon. In Britain, a truck bogie or boat truck. See also: wagon stage. (Bowman/Ball THEATRE, Granville DICTIONARY 21)

scenes and machines   Scenery and stage spectacle, such as flying effects, sudden appearances or disappearances through trap doors, etc.

scene shift   A change from one stage setting to another. Also called a scene change. Hence, scene shifter.

scene shop   A space where scenery (and often properties) are constructed.

scene shop foreman   See: master carpenter.

scene shuts   See: scene closes.

scene sketch   1. A playwright's written outline of a scene from his play, designed to show the director what stage movement the playwright had in mind. (Sobel NEW) 2. A quick drawing of the appearance of a stage setting.

scene stealer   A performer in a secondary or tertiary role who commands the attention of the audience, either by calling attention to himself/herself unnecessarily or because of superior stage presence.

scene technician   One who makes or handles scenery. (Bowman/Ball THEATRE)

scenic   1. Of the classical Greek and Roman theatre, having to do with the stage, by contrast with the *orchestra*. Hence, scenic artist, scenic performance, etc. See also: thymelic. (Bieber HISTORY 126) 2. Pertaining to scenery, as in scenic artist (a scene designer), scenic design, scenic paint, scenic rock, etc. 3. Pertaining to theatrical productions, as in the scenic representation of a play. The term is usually intended to indicate a production using scenery. (Bowman/Ball THEATRE)

scenical dancing   In the 18th C, dances that explained "whole *Stories* by Action. . ." as in Roman pantomimes. (Weaver ESSAY 168)

scenic artist   A painter of scenery.

scenic background   The scenery in front of which players perform.

scenic color   See: scene paint.

scenic effect   The overall appearance of the visual elements in a production.

scenic effect machine   Lighting equipment which produces moving effects such as clouds in motion or rain. See also: effect machine.

scenic gauze   See: theatrical gauze.

scenici (Latin Roman)   Actors.

scenic image   See: dramatic metaphor.

scenic piece   Short form: piece. A unit of scenery, especially one built in three dimensions. (Bowman/Ball THEATRE)

scenic plug   A small flat used to fill an opening in a larger flat or between other scenic units. Hence, plug, door plug, fireplace plug, plain plug, etc.

scenic projection   See: projected scenery.

scenic theatre   A theatre that uses scenery and usually has a proscenium (picture-frame) stage.

scenic truth   Konstantin Stanislavsky's theory of the magic "if"—a performer believes that artificial surroundings and situations on stage are real. (Edward STANISLAVSKY 87–88)

scenic unit   An element of scenery, such as a flat.

scenographer   A scene designer. Hence, scenography. Also, in the broader sense, someone concerned with all the visual aspects of production other than acting and directing. Bellman notes various possible definitions of this developing concept, including the present differences between the European and the U.S. scenographer (SCENE 10–11).

scenography   1. Formerly, the art of painting scenery. See: *skenographia*. 2. See: scenographer.

Schäferei (Swedish)   A 17th C court masquerade with shepherds, shepherdesses, etc. Developed in Germany, it was soon seen in Denmark, Sweden, and France; in France it was known as a *bergerie*. (Carlson "Scandinavia's" 16)

Schalttafel (German)   After World War I, and perhaps for a time earlier, the lighting switchboard; this then consisted of switches and fuses only. After World War II, the term was used for any manually-operated board, including a dimmer board. Compare: *Bühnenregulator*. (Fuchs LIGHTING 367–369; Rae/Southern INTERNATIONAL 34, 36)

Schattenbildapparat (German)   See: Linnebach projector.

Schauspiel (German)   A play, a drama. Hence, *Schauspiel dichter* (playwright), *Schauspieler* (performer), *schauspielerisch* (theatrical), *schauspielern* (to act), *Schauspielhaus* (playhouse), *Schauspielkunst* (dramatic art), etc.

schauspieler (Yiddish)   From 1909, a dignified term for actor. See also: *Schauspiel*. (Lifson YIDDISH 127)

schedule   In lighting, a chart of equipment needed, circuits to be used, color filters required, dimmer assignments, etc.

Scheinwerfer (German)   A spotlight. (Fuchs LIGHTING 209, 210, 211, 212, 213; Rae/Southern INTERNATIONAL 72)

schematic   In lighting, a diagram of circuits, using electrical symbols. (Lounsbury THEATRE)

schematics   In makeup, outlines of the head with the face divided into planes or areas, showing the color or type of makeup to apply to each area. (Cassady/Cassady VIEW)

Schembartlaufen (German)   The Shrovetide procession of performers in Nürnberg, Germany, during the late Middle Ages.

Schicksalstragödie (German)   Literally: fate tragedy. A 19th C play involving an implacable, demonic, inescapable fate and a plot in which the sequence fatalistically links itself to particular places, days, and objects. The result is an inescapably unhappy outcome. (Gassner/Quinn ENCYCLOPEDIA 743)

Schiebebühne (German)   A sliding or rolling stage.

Schiebwiderstände (German)   Portable slider dimmers analogous to those used in the U.S. since well before World War II. Singular *Schiebwiderstand*. (Fuchs LIGHTING 369, Rae/Southern INTERNATIONAL 70)

schlager (Yiddish)   A show which is a hit. (Sandrow VAGABOND 311)

schlepitchka   A scene painting technique involving a large, broom-handled brush, its bristles tied into clumps; the result resembles chicken tracks. Burris-Meyer and Cole have an illustration (1938 SCENERY fig. IX-16).

Schlusszene (German)   The final scene in a play.

schmaltz, schmalz, schmalzy, schmaltzy, smaltz   Excessive sentiment, especially in music. Originally Yiddish.

schmegegge (Yiddish)   A disdainful term for an unlikable, untalented, inept person. The word has been popular among theatre people, in part because it sounds as unpleasant as the creature it identifies. (Rosten JOYS)

Schmelzsicherungen (German)   Perhaps chiefly before World War II, fuses. The singular drops *-en*. The literal meaning of the word approximates 'melting-safety.' The theatre now often uses simply *Sicherung* (singular). (Fuchs LIGHTING 367, Rae/Southern INTERNATIONAL 44)

Schnurramen (German)   Back shutters. (Furttenbach in Hewitt RENAISSANCE 210)

schoenobates (Latin Roman)   A Latin form of the Greek for rope dancers and acrobats, performers in the mime of both Greece and Rome. Schoenobatist and attributive schoenobatic are related. See also: *funambulus*. (Nicoll MASKS 84–85, Duchartre ITALIAN 24)

school act   A vaudeville skit with a harassed teacher, impossible students, ridiculous answers to questions, and slapstick turns. (Gilbert VAUDEVILLE 303)

school comedy   A play performed in a medieval university. (Mantzius HISTORY II 190)

school drama   Plays produced at an academy or school.

sciopticon   A spotlight equipped to produce lighting effects in motion, such as rain or rippling water. Sciopticons can also usually show slides. Occasional variants: sciop, scioptican (U.S.). (Bellman SCENOGRAPHY, Wehlburg GLOSSARY, McCandless "Glossary" 635, Gassner/Barber PRODUCING 804)

scissors cross   1. See: simultaneous cross. 2. An awkward movement when crossing the stage: beginning on the wrong foot, with legs crossing, like a pair of scissors. (Granville DICTIONARY)

scissor stage   See: jackknife stage.

scolder   In vaudeville, the straight man, who often scolded the comic. (Laurie VAUDEVILLE 87)

sconce bell   A prompter's bell located in the cellar of an 18th C theatre, apparently used to cue a lighting change. (Hughes in Hume LONDON 131)

scoop   A floodlight which consists of a scoop-shaped reflector, now usually finished in spun aluminum. Scoops are usually paraboloid or ellipsoidal; a sky pan is a shallow scoop with a wide beam spread, often used in lighting drops and cycs. The term is from television, but both word and instrument have been used in the theatre since the 1950s. Lounsbury and Wehlburg have illustrations. (Bellman SCENE, Lounsbury THEATRE 89, Wehlburg GLOSSARY)

scop   A traveling entertainer in Anglo-Saxon England; a scop was chiefly a singer and teller of tales. (Brockett HISTORY 106)

scorcher   An old term for a risqué play.

score   1. Box-office receipts. 2. To be a hit. Hence, score a knockout, score a smash, etc. 3. The music of a musical theatre work.

scorer   1. A successful production. 2. A popular performer.

scoring line   1. The point, normally at center stage, where sliding shutters meet to close off the prospect. (Southern CHANGEABLE 243) 2. The line where flats meet when lashed together. Also called a join. (Baker THEATRECRAFT)

scorpions   Restless children in an audience. (Granville DICTIONARY)

SCR, SCR dimmer   See: silicon controlled rectifier.

scraper   A cocked hat.

scratch company   1. A stock company. 2. A performing group gathered for the occasion.

scratch wig   A disordered, unkempt wig used by comedians. (Bowman/Ball THEATRE)

screamer   A highly successful performance of a comedy or farce.

screen   1. Apparently, a low partition in early 17th C court theatres in Britain, dividing the audience from the stage. (Nicoll STUART 57) 2. The surface on which a projected image falls, especially if essentially flat (for example, a drop).

screw   In Britain, salary.

screw base   The metal bottom of a lamp which is screwed into a socket to reach its electrical supply. The screw base is used in striplights, borderlights, and floodlights. In Britain: screwcap. (Wehlburg GLOSSARY)

screw body   See: socket.

screwcap   See: screw base.

screwed   Locked. London theatres in the 18th C had large screws on the pit doors; when the pit was full the occupants were locked in by screwing the doors shut. (Hogan LONDON xxiv)

screw plug   See: socket.

scribe   1. Modern slang for a playwright. 2. In earlier times, one who made a clean copy (called a fair copy) of a play.

scrim   1. A loose-weave, large-thread gauze material or netting used for disappearing and dissolving wall effects. When illuminated from the front and at a flat angle, it appears opaque. When only the object behind it is illuminated, it is transparent. It is also used in cut drops and borders. Scrim is less transparent than theatrical gauze. 2. To apply such a fabric to a cut drop or border. Hence, scrim an opening, scrimming, scrim drop, etc. (Lounsbury THEATRE, Bowman/Ball THEATRE)

scrimming   1. Covering an opening, such as a window, with scrim. 2. Covering any surface, such as plywood or lumber, with any fabric. (Lounsbury THEATRE)

script   1. The text of a play, sometimes, in the case of a new work, in manuscript but more often in typescript. But even after a play has been published, the text is referred to as the script. Hence, playscript, script reader, script girl, script holder (prompter). 2. In readers theatre, a production text, usually adapted or compiled or both. A compiled script consists of two or more pieces (short plays, poetry, fiction, etc.) arranged for performance.

scroll   In 19th C Britain, a piece of cloth which contains a line of dialogue. The scroll was carried onstage by a performer in lieu of spoken dialogue, in evasion of the licensing laws. (Bowman/Ball THEATRE)

scruto   A sheet of thin wooden strips with a canvas backing, used as a curtain or trap cover. (Bowman/Ball THEATRE)

scuffle   Show business struggle for survival. Hence scufflebread—a thin diet of nothing. (Lees ''Lexicon'' 57)

sculptural lighting   See: plastic lighting.

scumbling   A scene-painting technique in which two different colors are mingled by using two brushes simultaneously, or by dipping one brush first in one color and then in the other. Burris-Meyer and Cole have an illustration. (Burris-Meyer/Cole SCENERY 248)

scurra (Latin Roman)   A buffoon.

SD, S.D.   1. Stage director. 2. Stage door.

SE   Second entrance—that is, an entrance on the second plane of the stage.

sea cloth   A drop painted to represent the sea.

seal   See: *katakeleusmos*.

sealed-beam lamp   See: reflector lamp.

sealed set   Early in the 20th C, a box set. (Krows AMERICA 118)

sealed ticket   In the past, a benefit ticket purchased from the beneficiary and marked with his or her seal. (Avery LONDON xlvii)

sea plays   Russian plays of the 1920s dealing with the brotherly sailor type. (Orlovsky in Bradshaw SOVIET 30)

searchlight technique   On a relatively dark stage, spotlighting particular areas as needed. (Gorelik NEW)

sea row   A ground row shaped and painted to look like the sea.

season   1. The annual period when most theatrical activity takes place. Hence, theatrical season, summer season. (Bowman/Ball THEATRE) 2. A season ticket. (Berrey/Van den Bark SLANG 593)

seasonal shop, season shop   In Britain, an engagement for the summer season or for the pantomime season at and often after Christmas. (Granville DICTIONARY)

season ticket   A ticket or tickets for admission to a full season of performances.

seat   1. A place where a spectator may sit, now usually a chair with arms and a folding seat, fixed in place and part of a row; in boxes, a separate chair. In earlier theatres a seat was part of a bench, often backless. Hence theatre seat, seating area, seating capacity, seating chart or plan. 2. To usher a patron to a place. 3. To contain seats (as 'the auditorium seats 1000'). (Bowman/Ball THEATRE)

seat filler   An attraction.

seating chart, seating plan   A diagram of a theatre's auditorium, displayed at the box office for the convenience of ticket purchasers. Also called a box-office plan.

seats of honor   See: *proedria, bisellia.*

sebha (Thai)   A solo style of recitation used for local epics and romances, such as *The Story of Khun Chang Khun Phan*, in which chanted verse is followed by sung verse. Also spelled *sepa, sepha*. (Anuman THAI 8) *Sebha rom* (dance *sebha*) is a type of dance-drama that combines *sebha* recitation and *pi phat* music.

sebrakan (Indonesian)   A Sundanese mood song used as a bridge between scenes in rod-puppet theatre (*wayang golek*). Also called *pagedongan*. (Foley "Sundanese" 206)

second   1. See: second man. 2. See: first.

second account   In 18th C theatres, the accounting of the second (or half-price) money taken in after the third act of the mainpiece. Also called the latter account. (Hogan LONDON xxxix)

"Second act!"   The stage manager's warning to the company that the second act is about to begin.

seconda donna (Italian)   Literally: second woman. 1. The second leading actress in a *commedia dell' arte* troupe, playing roles similar to the *innamorata* but smaller. (Smith COMMEDIA 5) 2. An actress who plays the next most important parts to the leading roles in any company.

secondary emphasis   In directing, an arrangement of performers on stage that focuses the spectator's attention on one character or group of characters but gives some emphasis also to a second character or group.

secondary lighting   In Britain: 1. See: emergency lights. 2. Occasionally, lighting which augments the dominant lighting. See also: panic lights. (Bentham ART, Rae/Southern INTERNATIONAL, Baker THEATRECRAFT)

secondary mime   In the mimes of the 1st C BC, and perhaps earlier and later, the clown who was comically unsuccessful in trying to repeat the speech or actions of others. The secondary mime may occasionally have been the *archimimus* (Latin), the head of the mime company. Also called a mimic fool, perhaps at times *stupidus*. (Nicoll MASKS 87, 121–122)

secondary plot   See: subplot.

secondary suspension   See: safety chain.

second balcony   An upper balcony, called in Britain the second gallery or upper circle. (Rae/Southern INTERNATIONAL)

second banana   A supporting comedian in burlesque; the leading comedian is the top banana.

second border, second borderlight   See: first border, borderlight, border.

second boy   In Britain, a young actor who plays secondary roles, especially in pantomimes. The 'principal boy' takes the dashing hero roles, though they are sometimes played by women. (Bowman/Ball THEATRE)

second business   1. In a Toby show, an actress who can play either a soubrette or a heavy. (Wilmeth LANGUAGE) 2. See: second man.

second company   A troupe performing on tour or in a foreign country while the original troupe continues to perform the same work at the home theatre.

(*à la*) *seconde* (French)   See: positions of the body.

second entrance   See: SE.

second gallery   Especially in Britain, a second or upper balcony. See also: gallery.

second hand   Especially in the professional theatre, an assistant carpenter or assistant property man.

second juvenile   A young male performer who plays secondary youthful parts.

second lady lead   A woman who plays secondary but important roles.

second lead   1. The second most important part in a play. 2. The performer who plays such a role.

second man, second woman   Performers who play the roles second in importance to the leading parts. Also called second or second business. The second man was once the young actor who took juvenile roles, usually debonair but sometimes villainous. (Bowman/Ball THEATRE, Krows AMERICA 46)

second night list   A list of those who are to receive free tickets to a second performance of a work.

second old man   A performer who plays the less prominent of two older male characters.

second part   A secondary character in a production.

second position   In dance, the placement of the feet outward to the sides, in a line, with heels about twelve inches apart. (Rogers DANCE 259)

second price   See: half price.

second production   A production by a second company, usually on tour.

second-row vision   See: every-other-row vision.

second-run house   A theatre featuring revivals.

seconds   See: number two.

second stanza   The second act on a bill.·

(le) secret (French)   A foundation petticoat worn with a farthingale. (Wilcox DICTIONARY)

secretly   Especially in the past, aside.

secrets (French)   Medieval stage machines or special effects. Also called *feintes* (or *feyntes*) or *ingegni* (Italian).

section   1. In U.S. lighting, especially in the past, one of the segments into which footlights and borderlights were sometimes divided. Also called a footlight section or borderlight section. 2. In Britain, one of the color circuits in footlights or borderlights. 3. On a control board, a segment or grouping, such as of switches or dimmers. (McCandless "Glossary" 629, Fay GLOSSARY)

sectional   Compartmented, as in sectional footlights or borderlights. (Bowman/Ball THEATRE)

secular drama   A play that is not religious in purpose, that is, not liturgical, though it may contain religious subject matter. (Bowman/Ball THEATRE)

secular games   See: *ludi saeculares*.

se défendre (French)   Literally: to defend oneself. A French theatre concept, that the performer must effectively defend against an assumedly hostile audience through acting skill. (Gibson "Africa" 47)

sedes (Latin)   A *mansion* (French) or locale in a medieval production. (Chambers MEDIAEVAL II 83)

sedilia (Latin Roman)   Seats or rows, as at a show. See also: *spectacula*. (Beare ROMAN 244)

seditious drama   The term used by the American colonial government for Filipino plays (c. 1901–1912) that championed Philippine independence. Hence, seditious playwright. (Hernandez EMERGENCE 88)

see the ghost walk   To receive one's salary.

segment stage   A pie-shaped platform on casters, used in shifting scenery. (Gillette/Gillette SCENERY)

segue   In music, to make a transition from one piece of music to another.

segundo galán (Spanish)   The second leading man in a theatrical troupe. (Roberts STAGE)

seihon (Japanese)   See: *daihon*.

seilenos (Greek), **seilenos**   See: *silenus*.

Seilzüge (German)   Tracker wires (q.v.). (Fuchs LIGHTING 369–370, Rae/Southern INTERNATIONAL 78)

Seilzuglaterne (German)   Lighting instruments with tracker wires for remotely-controlled color boomerangs. (Fuchs LIGHTING 370)

Seilzugstellwerk (German)   A special controlboard for the tracker wires (q.v.) used in some remote control systems. (Fuchs LIGHTING 370)

sekai (Japanese)   Literally: world. A known historical period and the characters from that period around which a play is written. Zeami wrote that a *no* play should be written about familiar people and events (KADENSHO 68–71). *Kabuki* and *bunraku* plays are based on 275 *jidai* and *sewa* worlds. See also: *shuko*. (Brandon CLASSIC 25–26, Gunji KABUKI 35, Leiter ENCYCLOPEDIA 343)

sekkyo bushi (Japanese)   A narrative style of singing and *shamisen* music that originated in the late 17th C to accompany a puppet performance. Now it is performed mainly on isolated Sado Island. Abbreviated *sekkyo*. (Keene BUNRAKU 33, 35, 45; Malm in Brandon CHUSHINGURA 115)

selampit (Malaysian)   See: *penglipur lara*.

Selby   See: Harry Selby.

selective realism   A style in stage production that uses realistic elements but does not attempt a fully realistic stage setting. Epic theatre usually makes use of selective realism.

self-release board   Especially in Britain, a mechanical arrangement in older manual switchboards by which an interlocked dimmer releases itself at the end of its travel or at a predetermined earlier point. (Corry PLANNING)

seligi kelir (Malaysian)   Two vertical rods or sticks, on the right and left sides of the shadow theatre stage (*panggung*), to which the screen is tautly lashed. Also called *panah Arjuna* (Arjuna's arrows). (Yub in Osman TRADITIONAL 96) *selingan* (Indonesian)   In Javanese *ludruk*, a song that functions as an interlude between scenes of the main play (*cerita*). It is sung by a transvestite. (Peacock RITES 167)

sell   To impress an audience favorably.

selling a bargain   In Elizabethan England, catch questions in clowns' dialogue, as in that of the two Dromios of *A Comedy of Errors*; a possible ancestor of the gags of end men in minstrel shows. (Paskman GENTLEMEN 25)

selling plan   The sequence in which a computer system will select and sell tickets, designed to dress a house and make the best seats available on a first-come, first-served basis.

sell-out   1. A performance or production for which all seats have been sold or otherwise disposed of. 2. A show that is highly successful.

selupsupan (Indonesian)   In Bali, a theatre troupe. Also spelled *seloepsoepan*. (de Zoete/Spies DANCE 199)

sem (Indonesian)   A peaceful atmosphere (Muljono in Osman TRADITIONAL 71) or a romantic meeting (Humardani in Osman TRADITIONAL 83) in a *wayang* performance.

sembah (Indonesian, Malaysian)   A gesture of respect, by a character in a puppet play or dance-drama. One or both hands are raised toward the face or chest. *Sembah* types in Javanese *wayang kulit* are *biasa* (usual), *jaya* (chest), *karna* (ear), *ratu* (king), and *suwunan* (overhead). (Long JAVANESE 71, 78, 106)

sembah guru (Malaysian)   Literally: honoring one's teacher. A confirmation ceremony for a performer in traditional theatre. Usually administered by a master teacher and/or a shaman. Trance states, ritual bathing with holy water and limes, and reciting of invocations are part of the ceremony, which varies in length and content depending on the particular theatre form. (Yousof "Kelantan" 206–209, Sweeney RAMAYANA 48)

seme ba (Japanese)   Literally: bullying scene. A scene of torture or oppression in *kabuki* or *bunraku*, particularly common in 19th C plays. Abbreviated *seme*. (Gunji KABUKI 171)

semi-arena theatre   A theatre in which the audience partly surrounds the stage. See also: thrust stage.

semi-chorus   See: chorus.

semicircle   A low, castered, semi-circular platform, pivoted at the center of the straight side. (Gillette/Gillette SCENERY)

semi-direct light   An occasional term for light softened by a diffusing filter, such as frost.

semiopera   The Restoration musician Roger North's term for operas, which were then part music and part drama. (North MUSIC 306)

semi-permanent set   See: unit set.

semi-windup   The next to the last act on a bill.

sempalan (Indonesian)   See: *lakon.*

senah (Lao)   A servant role in a *mohlam* play. (Miller "Kaen" 222)

sendon (Indonesian)   In Java, a gentle, highly emotional type of mood song (*suluk*) sung by the puppeteer in *wayang kulit.* Examples are given in Brandon THRONES 367–370. *Sesendon* in Sundanese *wayang golek* is a mood song (*kakawen*) sung by the puppeteer in moments of extreme sadness. (Foley "Sundanese" 206)

sendratari (Indonesian)   Literally: art-drama-dance. Since c. 1960, a dance-ballet based on classical dance-drama in which dialogue and most narration is eliminated. Performed for popular audiences on large, open-air stages in Java, Sunda, and Bali. (Soedarsono DANCES 56–60, 186–187; Brandon GUIDE 68)

Senecan tragedy   Plays influenced by works of the Roman playwright Seneca; the plays usually contain lofty language, little comic relief, and gory plots.

senex (Latin Roman)   The old man in comedy. The term is really limited to the older male members (usually either side of sixty) of a household. An elderly character outside the household is not called a *senex*. Plural: *senes.* (Duckworth NATURE 242–249)

sennet   A fanfare. In Elizabethan times a distinction was made between a flourish and a sennet, the sennet being a piece played after a flourish or fanfare. The term may have derived from *sonata* (Italian: loud ringing).

sensation drama   A 19th C term for melodrama.

sensation scene   1. In 19th C British melodrama, a stage setting for a particularly exciting scene. 2. The scene itself.

sense memory, sensory memory   In the Stanislavsky system of acting, a performer's remembrance of emotions, physical sensations, etc. See also: emotion memory. (McGaw ACTING 70–71)

sensu (Japanese)   A folding fan used in *kabuki* dance. See also: *ogi.*

sentimental comedy   Tearful comedy. A dramatic form popular in the 18th C which favored pathos rather than laughter. See also: *comédie larmoyante.*

sentimental drama   Plays stressing pathos and sensibility, popular in the 18th C. The comedies showed the virtues more than the foibles of characters, while the tragedies appealed to the audience's pity and similar emotional responses.

sepa (Thai)   See: *sebha.*

separate the palms   See: stretch.

seperit (Malaysian)   The arm stick of a shadow puppet. Most puppets have only one articulated arm and, therefore, one *seperit.* (Sweeney RAMAYANA 59) *sepha, sepha rom* (Thai)   See: *sebha*.

seppo (Japanese)   Literally: preaching. A comic scene of preaching by a Buddhist priest or acolyte in a *kyogen* play. (Berberich "Rapture" 124)

sequence   1. A series of scenes without breaks in the action. 2. In playwriting, the linking of scenes to provide continuity. 3. In directing, the spatial relationship of elements in the stage picture. (Bowman/Ball THEATRE)

sequence play, sequence player   In memory lighting systems, an arrangement which calls up a cue automatically as soon as its predecessor has ended. Also called a sequencer. (Bellman LIGHTING 245, 253)

sequence tickets   See: roll tickets.

sequentia (Latin)   A wordless melody at the end of a medieval Alleluia; a variety of trope. (Roberts STAGE)

sequential staging   Processional staging, using a series of pageant wagons.

seri (Japanese)   A stage elevator. First used in *bunraku* in 1727. By the early 19th C the main stage of a *kabuki* theatre was equipped with a variety of traps (*seriage*) for the appearance and disappearance of characters and scenery elevators (*seridashi*). See also: *suppon*. (Ernst KABUKI 29)

serial play   In the 19th C, a play performed in installments.

serifu (Japanese)   Literally: stage speech. 1. Dialogue. The term originated in *kabuki*, but is also used for modern drama. In *kabuki*, also called *taihaku*. In *no* and *bunraku*, the equivalent term is *kotoba*. 2. By extension, the speaking of dialogue. More properly, *serifu mawashi* (speaking dialogue). (Scott KABUKI 117–119, Leiter ART 258, Leiter ENCYCLOPEDIA 345)

serimpi (Indonesian)   See: *srimpi*.

seriocomic   An old vaudeville term for a soubrette who could sing either tearful or comic songs. (Wilmeth LANGUAGE)

serious dancing   In 18th C theatres, said of dances that were genteel and graceful, and sometimes dealt with a character from an ancient fable. The dances could be either brisk or grave.

serious drama   A play, whether comedy or tragedy, containing important ideas and depth of characterization, as opposed to a trivial entertainment or melodrama.

seri panggong (Malaysian)   The role of a heroine in *bangsawan*. (Yassin in Osman TRADITIONAL 149)

serk   See: berserk.

Serlian wing   An angle wing, built and painted in perspective, named for the Italian Renaissance architect and designer Sebastiano Serlio, who used such scenic pieces. (Cameron/Hoffman GUIDE)

sermons joyeux (French)   Medieval burlesque sermons. (Frank MEDIEVAL 246–247, Brockett HISTORY 137) *serpentaux* (French)   A Louis XIII woman's hairstyle consisting of hanging, barely-curled tresses. (Boucher FASHION)

serpette (French)   Literally: sickle, pruning knife. In the leg of a ballet dancer, an angle occurring in what should be the unbroken line from hip to ankle; a fault in which a foot is turned in or out in relation to the leg, like a sickle. Also called sickly foot or sickling. (Kersley/Sinclair BALLET)

serre-tête (French)   A skullcap of black velvet, worn by some pierrots. (Mantzius HISTORY II 225)

serte   See: *justaucorps*.

serunai (Malaysian)   See: *gamelan*.

serva (Italian)   See: *servetta*.

serve corn on the cob   To tell a trite joke. (Berrey/Van den Bark SLANG 587)

servetta (Italian)   A serving maid in *commedia dell'arte*, usually waiting on the *innamorata*. She was ususally named Colombina, Corallina, Diamantina, Franceschina, Lisetta, Nespola, Oliva, Pierette, Ricciolina, Spinetta, etc. Also called a *fantesca* (or fantesch), *serva*, or in the early days of *commedia*, a *zagna*. See also: soubrette. (Smith COMMEDIA 5, Oreglia COMMEDIA 123)

servette birichina (Italian)   Literally: naughty maid-servant. In *commedia dell'arte*, a crafty confidante, rarely a maiden. (Duchartre ITALIAN 278)

service   In 19th C theatres, a gas pipe of small diameter which ran directly to gas burners. But gas service and main service, and sometimes service, seem to have been used of the somewhat larger pipes which fed the theatre or a major portion thereof (auditorium, stage, and backstage). (Penzel LIGHTING 80, 81, 83)

service-charge ticket   A theatre ticket, usually a pass or a complimentary ticket, for which the patron must pay a handling fee.

sesendon (Indonesian)   See: *sendon*.

set   1. A stage setting or a set of scenery. Hence, box set, chamber set, exterior set, garden set, etc. 2. A three-dimensional scenic unit, such as a set tree; a set piece that can stand by itself. 3. To set the stage; to put up the scenery and properties. 4. To position a lighting instrument. 5. To arrange the intensity and color of the lighting. 6. In playwriting, to establish the locale and mood, to set the scene. 7. To establish a routine, as in a duel, dance number, or stage movements. (Bowman/Ball THEATRE, Canfield CRAFT)

set-back   See: thickness.

set dressing   See: trim prop.

set-in   To move a show into a theatre and set it up. (Lounsbury THEATRE)

set lights   In preparing a production, to angle and focus the lights to be used. (Lounsbury THEATRE)

set line   1. Especially in Britain, a line marked on the floor indicating to performers and crew the boundaries of the stage setting, to prevent anyone from inadvertently coming into the view of the audience. See also: sight lines. 2. An imaginary line marking the downstage limit of a stage setting. Also called a front set line.

set of lines   A group of lines, usually three to five, used in a rigging system to suspend a single batten to which scenery, draperies, lighting instruments, etc. may be attached. The lines are named for their length: short, short center, center, long center, and long (or end). A set of lines is sometimes called a line set.

set of press matter   A group of publicity releases.

set of scenes   Formerly, a full complement of wings, borders, and shutters. (Cibber APOLOGY II 85)

set of tickets   Reserved-seat tickets for each seat in the house for one performance.

set out   To place on stage.

set piece   1. A scenic unit, usually three-dimensional, which can stand by itself. Sometimes shortened to piece, or called a set unit. 2. See: relieve.

set prop   See: trim prop.

set scene   In 18th C theatres, a discovered stage setting, revealed by opening the shutters or curtain. (Visser in Hume LONDON 87)

set scenery   Formerly, scenic units or pieces which could be placed wherever needed on stage (as opposed to wings and shutters).

set speech   See: *concetto*.

set the scene   1. To determine what the scenery will be. 2. To put the scenery in its place on stage.

set the stage   To put scenic units and properties in place.

setting   The scenery and properties for a play or some part of a play.

setting line   An imaginary line, parallel to the curtain line, marking the downstage limit of a stage setting.

settle   Formerly, green room; a performer's lounge.

settled   Said of an 18th C performer who forgot his lines. An actor "had not delivered above ten lines, out of sixty, when he 'settled,' and looked to me for assistance...." (Bernard RETROSPECTIONS II, 74)

set unit   See: set piece.

set-up, setup, set up   1. In lighting, the planned arrangement of the equipment. The principal use of the term is for the board set-up, which means the proper positions of switches and dimmers on the control board, but the term is also used of scenery and properties. 2. To put up such elements. (Bricker TODAY 325) 3. In burlesque, a female performer's body. (Wilmeth LANGUAGE)

set water   1. In a seashore setting, a space between profile strips in which scenic ships can be seen to glide. (Krows AMERICA 128) 2. In the plural, the profile strips depicting the sea. (Southern CHANGEABLE 259)

seven movements in ballet   See: movements in ballet.

sewa kyogen (Japanese)   See: *sewamono.*

sewamono (Japanese)   Literally: scandal play. In *kabuki* and *bunraku*, a play about a recent event or scandal among townsmen, in contrast to a history play (*jidaimono*). Usually translated 'domestic play.' The first *kabuki* examples were Okuni's prostitute-buying plays (*keiseikai*) as early as 1603 (Brandon CLASSIC 5–8). Chikamatsu Monzaemon wrote the first domestic *bunraku* play in 1703, *The Love Suicides at Sonezaki* (Keene CHIKAMATSU 39–56). Also called *sewa kyogen* (scandal play) in *kabuki* and *sewa joruri* (scandal piece) in *bunraku*. See also: *shinjumono, kizewamono, ninbanme, zangirimono.* (Kincaid KABUKI 255–260, Ernst KABUKI 231–232, Kawatake KABUKI 11)

sex act   A girl act.

sex appeal   In the U.S. in the 1940s, a showgirl's term for falsies or a padded bra. (Wilmeth LANGUAGE)

Shaanxi *bangzi* (Chinese)   See: *qinqiang.*

shackle   In Britain, a U-shaped iron with a threaded pin passing through the ends of the U, used at the end of a grid line for suspending a scenic piece or lighting instrument. (Corry PLANNING)

shade   A mask.

shading colors   Colored creme or grease makeup in small cases, pots, jars, or sticks, used by performers for highlights, shadows, wrinkles, eye makeup, and painting designs on the face. Also called lining colors.

shadow   1. In makeup, a sunken area or deep wrinkle created with shading colors. 2. The partial roof over an Elizabethan stage. Also called the heavens.

shadow box   A cutoff sometimes used on borderlights to control light spread. The shadow box, which runs the length of the borderlights, has spill shields on each side of the individual lamps. (McCandless METHOD 27, Bowman/Ball THEATRE)

shadow-box projector   See: Linnebach projector.

shadowgraph   See: shadow play.

shadowgraph projector   See: Linnebach projector.

shadowgraphs   In vaudeville, animated silhouettes made by skillful contortions of the fingers, hands, arms, and even feet of the performer and projected on the back of a white screen. (Gilbert VAUDEVILLE 173)

shadow pantomime   See: shadow play.

shadow picture machine   See: Linnebach projector.

shadow play   A performance in which the audience sees the shadows of the players on a translucent screen. The shadows may be of performers or of rounded or flat figures. Sometimes called shadow theatre or shadow show, *ombres chinoises* (French), occasionally shadowgraph; a shadow pantomime is, of course, a wordless shadow play. (Bowman/Ball THEATRE, Wilmeth LANGUAGE)   For related Asian terms see: *bommalata, carillo, chaya nataka, nang, piyingxi, tholapavukoothu,* and *wayang kulit.*

shadow projection   A projected image, essentially black and white, produced by a large slide or silhouette in a lensless projector. See also: Linnebach projector. (Burris-Meyer/Cole THEATRES 191)

shadow projector, shadowgraph projector   Two of the descriptive names for a Linnebach projector (q.v.). Shadow projector, which may have begun in the professional theatre, goes back at least to the 1950s; the longer term may have originated in Britain. (Bowman/Ball THEATRE, Sellman/Lessley ESSENTIALS 82, 187)

shadow puppet   Typically, a flat, two-dimensional puppet that is played between a cloth screen and a lamp. Shadow puppets of varying sizes may be opaque or transluscent, articulated or non-articulated, and are usually manipulated by one or more rods. Sophisticated shadow puppet traditions are most commonly found in Asia, but Turkish and Greek examples also exist.

shadow show, shadow theatre   See: shadow play.

shaft and drum   See: drum and shaft.

shahir (Urdu)   Literally: poet. The composer/proprietor of a *khel-tamasha* troupe.

shaj ghor (Bengali)   See: *saajghar.*

shakara (Sanskrit)   See: *sakara.*

shake   1. Vibrato in singing. (Burney GENERAL II 745)   2. A percentage of the box-office receipts.

shake artist, shaker   A cooch dancer. (Berrey/Van den Bark SLANG 573)

(The) Shakespeare   A box seating 200 to 300 people in the center of the second tier of a 19th C U.S. theatre. (Hewitt U.S.A. 66)

shakubyoshi (Japanese)   In *gagaku,* a pair of wooden sticks, one held in each hand, struck together to produce a thin, dry tone. (Wolz BUGAKU 19)

shakumi (Japanese)   See: *fukai.*

shal' (Russian)   See: *babushka.*

shallaballa   See: Jim Crow.

shamam (Sanskrit)   See: *bhava.*

shamisen (Japanese)   A three-stringed, sharp-sounding lute, played with a large ivory plectrum. Introduced from China by way of Okinawa in the late 16th

C, it soon became the most important musical instrument in urban performing arts, especially *kabuki* and *bunraku*. Usually spelled and pronounced *samisen* in the Kyoto-Osaka region. See also: *nagauta, gidaya*. (Malm MUSIC 185–222)

Shandong *bangzi*, Shantung *pang tzu* (Chinese)   A form of music-drama (*xiqu*) popular in parts of Shandong, Henan, and Hebei Provinces which arose in the 17th C out of the influence of *qinqiang* and/or *jinju*. It features music from the *bangziqiang* musical system.

shangban, shang pan (Chinese)   Literally: to be on an accented beat. To follow a pattern of metrical organization (*banyan*); descriptive of the majority of metrical-types (*banshi*) in music-drama (*xiqu*). Sometimes translated as "regulated" or "metered." In Beijing opera (*jingju*), the principal regulated metrical-types include: *erliuban, huilong, kuaiban, kuaisanyan, liushuiban, manban,* and *yuanban*. See also: *ziyouban*. (Wichmann "Aural" 146–158, 167)

shangchang, shang ch'ang (Chinese)   1. To enter the playing area. 2. The entry of a performer or performers. Conventional types of song and speech (*changbai*) and movement (*dongzuo*) used for entrances in Beijing opera (*jingju*) are described in detail in Scott CLASSICAL 93–96 and 178–184. See also: *xiachang*.

shangchangbai, shang ch'ang pai (Chinese)   Literally: entrance speech. A simplified, combined version of the set-the-scene poem (*dingchangshi*) and set-the-scene speech (*dingchangbai*); it is spoken by a supporting character upon his or her first entrance in Beijing opera (*jingju*) and many other forms of music-drama (*xiqu*). It often consists of a single couplet in which the character speaking is identified; it may also be broken into segments and delivered in succession by two or more characters. Sometimes called entrance poem (*shangchangshi* or *shang ch'ang shih*). See also: *zibao jiamen*.

shangchang duilian (Chinese)   See: *duilian*.

shangchangmen, shang ch'ang men (Chinese)   Entrance door. 1. A permanent curtained doorway upstage right on a traditional stage in music-drama (*xiqu*); characters conventionally entered through this doorway. See also: *xiachangmen*. 2. In contemporary proscenium theatres, stage right.

shang ch'ang pai, shangchangshi, shang ch'ang shih, (Chinese)   See: *shangchangbai*.

shang ch'ang tui lien (Chinese)   See: *duilian*.

shang chü (Chinese)   See: *lian*.

Shanghai opera   See: *huju*.

shangju (Chinese)   See: *lian*.

shang pan (Chinese)   See: *shangban*.

shangwuse, shang wu se (Chinese)   Literally: upper five colors. The five principal colors used in stage costuming in Beijing opera (*jingju*) and many other forms of music-drama (*xiqu*): red, green, yellow, white, and black. Each color signifies a particular age, rank, and/or character trait. See also: *xiawuse*. (Scott CLASSICAL 139–140)

Shansi opera, Shansi *pang tzu* (Chinese)   See: *jinju*.

shanta (Sanskrit)   See: *santa*.

Shantung *pang tzu* (Chinese)   See Shandong *bangzi*.

shan tzu sheng (Chinese)   See: *shanzisheng*.

Shanxi *bangzi* (Chinese)   See: *jinju*.

shanzisheng, shan tzu sheng (Chinese)   Literally: fan male role. A role category which includes young men about town and young scholars, who frequently carry and manipulate a fan; a major subdivision of the young male role (*xiaosheng*) in Beijing opera (*jingju*) and many other forms of music-drama (*xiqu*). It is essentially the same as the cloth-cap male role (*jinsheng*) in *kunqu* drama. (Dolby HISTORY 180, Scott CLASSICAL 67–68)

shao chü (Chinese)   See: *shaoju*.

shao hsing hsi (Chinese)   1. See: *shaoju*. 2. See: *yueju*, meaning 2.

Shaohsing *luan t'an* (Chinese)   See: *shaoju*.

shaoju, shao chü (Chinese)   A form of music-drama (*xiqu*) popular in the Shaoxing, Ningbo, and Hangzhou regions of Zhejiang Province which developed in the late 16th and early 17th C. Its plays are derived from a number of forms including *qinqiang* and *kunqu*; both civil plays (*wenxi*) and martial plays (*wuxi*) are performed, the latter utilizing ancient martial techniques which are unique to *shaoju*. Its music is primarily derived from the *gaoqiang* and *bangziqiang* musical systems. Called Shaoxing theatre (*shaoxingxi* or *shao hsing hsi*) in the early 20th C; also called Shaoxing *luantan* or Shaohsing *luan t'an* because in Shaoxing that was the name given music from the *bangziqiang* musical system. (Mackerras MODERN 115–117)

Shaoxing *luantan* (Chinese)   See: *shaoju*.

shaoxingxi (Chinese)   1. See: *shaoju*. 2. See: *yueju*, meaning 2.

shape   1. In the 17th C, a costume, probably a form-concealing outer garb. ". . . [H]is shape flyes off, and he appears dressed like a cupid." Also called a habit or dress. (Duffett PSYCHE 36) 2. A hat form or foundation, without trim or cover. (Dreher HATMAKING) 3. In dance, a correlate of effort, to which it has affinities in stipulated measurements in space. It involves the adjustment of a dancer to the three-dimensionality of objects in the space in which movement is made. (Dell PRIMER 6, 55)

shapes and shirts   In the late 19th and early 20th C, a term used by young actors to describe old actors. The latter preferred Elizabethan drama and costuming. (Partridge TO-DAY 229)

share   1. A part interest in a theatre or a performing troupe. 2. To participate as a sharer in such a troupe. Hence, shareholder, sharing actor, sharing system, sharer (also called an adventurer). 3. In acting, to take a stage position equal in importance with another performer, such as two actors in one-quarter or in profile positions. (Bowman/Ball THEATRE)

shareholder, sharer   A member of a theatrical company in Shakespeare's time and later who owned part of the troupe's stock of costumes, properties, plays, etc. and whose income came from the division of the profits. Also called an actor-sharer. (Cameron/Gillespie ENJOYMENT, Roberts STAGE)

sharing system   A financial arrangement going back at least to Elizabethan times (but seldom found today) in which members of a theatrical company shared in the profits and losses. Sharers were the principal members of a troupe, having invested in the theatrical venture; other members of the company were on straight salary.

sharing table   In the 17th C, a table, probably in a theatre office, where shares were distributed or collected. "To prevent the Disorders of the sharing Table. . . " sharers were called in one by one. (Nicoll HISTORY I 324)

sharp edge, sharp-edged   See: hard edge(d).

shatter prices   To reduce ticket prices when a show is not doing well.

sheath   See: chemise.

sheave   A grooved wheel in a frame or casing; a pulley wheel.

"She came from the back row of the chorus."   A performer who has risen in the acting ranks from a modest beginning.

sheet   1. A plan of the seating in a theatre, used to mark off seats that have been sold. Hence, on the sheet. 2. A standard size for a lithographed theatrical poster (litho); a sheet measures 20'' x 30'' and is called a double crown. Thus, a six-sheet is the size of six such sheets.

sheik ham   A well-dressed ham actor.

sheng (Chinese)   1. Male role. A basically serious, dignified role portrayed in stylized but fundamentally realistic makeup; a major role category (*hangdang*) in many forms of music-drama (*xiqu*). In *kunqu* drama, major subcategories of the male role include older male (*laosheng*) and young male (*xiaosheng*); in Beijing opera (*jingju*), older male (*laosheng*), martial male (*wusheng*), and young male (*xiaosheng*). (Dolby HISTORY 105, 180; Scott CLASSICAL 31, 66–68) 2. Written with a different character, a multiple reed-pipe instrument, sometimes called a mouth-organ or reed-organ in translation. Each pipe is equipped with a single free reed. The *sheng* is used in the melodic orchestra (*wenchang*) in *kunqu*, and in music derived from the *kunshangqiang* musical system in Beijing opera (*jingju*) and other forms of music-drama (*xiqu*). (Dolby HISTORY 147, Mackerras RISE 107, Wichmann "Aural" 440–441)

shengqiang xitong, sheng ch'iang hsi tung (Chinese)   Literally: vocal tune system. 1. The music of two or more forms of music-drama (*xiqu*) with related or mutually influencing development producing resemblances in melody, singing styles, and musical accompaniment. Often translated as musical system. The principal musical systems include *gaoqiang* and *kunshanqiang*, which follow *lianquti* musical structure, and *bangziqiang* and *pihuang*, which follow *banqiangti* musical structure. (Dolby HISTORY 222–223, Mackerras RISE 4–11) 2. Two or more related modes (*diaoshi*) in the music of each form of music-drama which follows *banqiangti* musical structure; one of the principal musical components of such structure. Sometimes translated as modal system. There are standard procedures for modulating between the modes of each modal system; the music of every form of music-drama which follows *banqiangti* musical structure includes at least one modal system. (Wichmann "Aural" 167–261)

Shensi *pang tzu* (Chinese)   See: *qinqiang*.

shenti   An Egyptian loincloth, often seen in pictures of the Pharoahs. Also called a pshent. (Boucher FASHION)

shepherd   1. A character type in *commedia dell'arte,* usually named Corinto, Selvaggio, or Sireno. 2. A standard character type in pastoral plays. (Kennard MASKS 39)

she-tragedy   A 17th–18th C tragedy with a love-and-honor theme and a woman as the central character.

shewes   An early 17th C term, evidently meaning scenery. (Campbell SCENES 209)

shibai (Japanese)   Literally: on-the-grass. 1. The ground area in front of an early *no* or *kabuki* stage where the audience sat. (Komparu NOH 141, Ernst KABUKI 30) 2. Later in an enclosed *kabuki* or *bunraku* theatre, the pit area (*doma* and *masu*), as opposed to raised boxes (*sajiki*) along the sides. (Gunji KABUKI 43) 3. More broadly, especially in the 18th and 19th C, a *kabuki* or *bunraku* theatre building. *Gekijo* is now the more usual term for this meaning. (Gunji KABUKI 43) 4. A theatre performance or the theatre as an institution, as in "the customs of *shibai*". (Kincaid KABUKI 169, Gunji KABUKI 43). 5. A play or drama in *kabuki*. (Hamamura et al KABUKI 95–96). The term is never used for *shingeki*. See also: *kage shibai, kami shibai, ningyo shibai.*

shibai chaya (Japanese)   See: *shibai jaya.*

shibai e (Japanese)   Literally: theatre picture. 1. A woodblock print that uses a *kabuki* performance or actors as subject matter. Thousands of such prints were made by such artists as Shunsho, Sharaku, Toyokuni, and members of the Torii family between the late 17th and the mid-19th C. They are a source of invaluable information. In this meaning *shibai e* is a type of *ukiyo e* (floating world picture). (Leiter ENCYCLOPEDIA 347–349) 2. In Kyoto-Osaka, a painting of an actor or a scene from a *kabuki* or *bunraku* play posted in front of the theatre as advertising. Also called *e kanban.* See: *kanban.* (Scott KABUKI 279)

shibai goya (Japanese)   See: *ko shibai.*

shibai jaya, shibai chaya (Japanese)   Literally: theatre teahouse. A teahouse adjoining a large *kabuki* or *bunraku* theatre, c 1700–1920s. It provided tickets, food and drink between acts, and a place to meet actors after a performance. (Hamamura et al KABUKI 58, Kincaid KABUKI 179–180, Shively in Brandon/ Malm/Shively STUDIES 24–26, Leiter ENCYCLOPEDIA 349)

shibuxian, shih pu hsien (Chinese)   A form of storytelling (*quyi*), popular in Beijing in the 17th–18th C, which was frequently performed by *dangziban* story tellers. Performances involved two main performers, one of female (*dan*) and one of clown (*chou*) roles. Occasionally still seen in Beijing.

shichi go cho (Japanese)   Literally: seven-five melody. A passage in a *kabuki* play written in alternating phrases of seven and five syllables, the standard meter of Japanese poetry. It is delivered in a rhythmic and melodic manner. (Bowers JAPANESE 61, Brandon CLASSIC 23–24)

shichi san (Japanese)   Literally: seven three. The area of the *kabuki* runway (*hanamichi*) seven units from one end and three units from the other end. It is considered the most effective acting position on stage. (Ernst KABUKI 50, 95–98) Before the 20th C, the position was seven-tenths of the distance away from the stage. When Western-style balconies covered that position in modern *kabuki* theatres, it was moved forward to three-tenths of the distance away from the stage. (Brandon in Brandon/Malm/Shively STUDIES 93–94, 128 n. 79)

shidai (Japanese)   1. The entrance song of the secondary character (*waki*) in *no*. It contains three lines, of 7 + 5, 7 + 5, and 7 + 4 syllables and is sung in rhythmic fashion (*hyoshi au*). (Keene NO 55, Inoura HISTORY 116, Hoff/ Flindt "Structure" 241) 2. A similar song in a *kyogen* play. (Berberich "Rapture" 47)

shift   1. A Restoration dressing room: "she took us up into the tiring-rooms: and to the women's shift, where Nell [Gwyn] was dressing herself." The shift was evidently a common dressing room, while a tiring room was an individual performer's room. (Pepys DIARY 5 October 1667) 2. See: chemise. 3. A change in costume. 4. See: scene shift.

shih pu hsien (Chinese)   See: *shibuxian*.

shih san che (Chinese)   See: *shisanzhe*.

shikami (Japanese)   A *no* mask with angry eyes, worn by a devil or demon in a demon play. (Shimazaki NOH 62–63)

shikata banashi (Japanese)   Literally: gesture story. A story narrated with gestures in a *kyogen* or *kabuki* play. (Berberich "Rapture" 113–115, Scott KABUKI 114, Brandon CLASSIC 29)

shiki gaku (Japanese)   Literally: ceremonial entertainment. A performing art supported and sanctioned by the government for state and ceremonial occasions: *bugaku* in the Imperial court and, at the Shogun's court, 17th–19th C, *no* and *kyogen*. (Berberich "Rapture" 20)

shimai (Japanese)   A dance in *no* accompanied by song, sung either by the performer and the chorus (*ji*) or by the chorus alone. Many *no* plays have two *shimai*, one in the middle of the play (commonly the *kuse*) and one in the finale. One type of *mai*. (Shimazaki NOH 34)

shimboyaku (Japanese)   Literally: silent-suffering role. 1. A role in *kabuki* or *bunraku* of a man who silently accepts great suffering. Examples are given in Gunji KABUKI 183. One type of *tachiyaku* role. 2. An actor of this role.

shimmy, shimmy shaking   A frenetic striptease dance in which the entire body quivers, said to have been performed originally by Little Egypt at the 1893 Chicago World's Fair. (Wilmeth LANGUAGE)

shimogakari za (Japanese)   Literally: lower troupes. Among the five schools of *no*, the Komparu, Kongo, and Kita schools were based in Nara. Since Nara is south of Kyoto, they were the 'lower troupes.' See also: *kamigakari za*. (Inoura HISTORY 108; Keene NO 44, 67; Shimazaki NOH 84)

shimote (Japanese)   Literally: lower hand. Stage right in *kabuki* and other commercial theatres. Also called *nishi* (west). (Leiter ENCYCLOPEDIA 354)

shimpa (Japanese)   See: *shinpa*.

shingeki (Japanese)   Literally: new theatre. 1. Broadly, theatre in the 'spoken' style of the West that began in the 1910s and continues today as one of the main streams of Japanese theatre. Shakespeare and Greek tragedy as well as Ibsen or Shaw, and modern Japanese plays and productions, are part of *shingeki*. Important playwrights include Kinoshita Junji, Tanaka Chikao, Kishida Kunio, Abe Kobo. (Ortolani in Shively MODERNIZATION 483–499, Rimer MODERN 3–6) 2. Increasingly today, more narrowly, serious or literary realistic drama, as opposed both to traditional theatre and to more modern experiments. See also: *angura, shogyoshugi engeki*.

shinjumono (Japanese)   Literally: lovers' suicide play. A *kabuki* or *bunraku* play, often based on an actual event, in which young lovers commit suicide. The term was apparently first used in 1662 for a *kabuki* play. Usually written in two or three acts, the final scene features a beautiful journey (*michiyuki*) to the scene of death, usually a Buddhist temple. It is one type of domestic play (*sewamono*). (Keene CHIKAMATSU 15–16, Brandon CLASSIC 7–8)

shin kabuki (Japanese)   Literally: new *kabuki*. A *kabuki* play written in modern times. The first *shin kabuki* play was Tsubouchi Shoyo's *The Paulownia Leaf*, staged in 1904. Although they are included in standard *kabuki* programs, they are not acted or staged in *kabuki* style. (Gunji KABUKI 29–30)

shinpa, shimpa (Japanese)   Literally: new school. The first Western-influenced theatre form in Japan, *shinpa* was started as a political theatre in the 1890s by Kawakami Otojiro. Today plays depict urban, middle-class life, in a sentimental fashion, and are usually set in the Meiji and Taisho periods (1868–1925). (Komiya MEIJI 39, 40) Also called *shinpa geki* (new school drama). (Kawatake KABUKI 11)

shin sarugaku (Japanese)   Literally: new *sarugaku*. A popular variety theatre, 9th–11th C, that emphasized mimicry and comic gesture. The term was replaced by *sarugaku* in the 13th C, when the form changed to include further dramatic elements. See also: *no*. (Inoura HISTORY 40–45)

shintoriso (Japanese)   A male *bugaku* mask with a stylized curvilinear face that has bright red circles painted on the cheeks. (Wolz BUGAKU 42)

shiny back   A pit musician, so called from the shine on the seat of his pants from constant sitting. (Wilmeth LANGUAGE)

shiori (Japanese)   In *no*, a standard gesture (*kata*) in which one open hand is raised to the eyes, suggesting weeping or grief. Illustrated in Keene NO 221 and Komparu NOH 218.

shirabyoshi (Japanese)   1. A professional female dancer of the 12th and 13th C. 2. The dances she performed. The dances were accompanied by mace or fan beating and occasionally by drum, flute, and cymbal music. (Inoura HISTORY 53)

shiragigaku (Japanese)   In *gagaku*, music of Shiragi, or Silla (a Korean kingdom), a subdivision of *komagaku* music. (Inoura HISTORY 31)

shirasu (Japanese)   Literally: white sand bar. The narrow white sand or pebble border surrounding an indoor *no* stage, a reminder of the fact that *no* stages prior to the 20th C were set up in the open air. *Shirasu hashigo* (or *bashigo*), pebble bridge, is a three-step stair unit at the front of the stage, crossing over the border. (Berberich "Rapture" 5, Komparu NOH 141)

shisanzhe, shih san che (Chinese)   Literally: thirteen rhymes. The thirteen categories of rhymes used in the composition of song lyrics and spoken poetry in Beijing opera (*jingju*); all the sounds in each category are considered to rhyme with one another. Also called the *jingju zhekou* or *ching chü che k'ou*. (Scott CLASSICAL 93, Wichmann "Aural" 104–108)

shishiguchi (Japanese)   A *no* mask with a wide-open mouth (*guchi*) showing sharp tusks, worn by a lion (*shishi*) character. (Keene NO 269, Shimazaki NOH 63)

shishi mai (Japanese)   Literally: lion dance. 1. Perhaps the only remaining type of *gigaku* dance. The pug-faced mask and mane of hair suggest a mythological animal popularly thought to be a lion. 2. A dance of a *shishi* character in *no, kabuki*, and folk plays of many kinds. (Inoura HISTORY 79)

shitai (Japanese)   In *no*, the standard position (*kata*), kneeling with one knee on the floor, that indicates sitting. Illustrated in Keene NO 219.

shitamenmono (Japanese)   See: *hitamenmono*.

shite (Japanese)   Literally: doer. 1. The principal role in a *no* play. In a typical play the *shite* is the only performer who dances. The major song-dance scenes (*kuse* and *shimai*) are about the life of the character played by the *shite* actor. Paul Claudel's observation that Western "drama is something that happens, *no* is someone that happens" is wonderfully apt. (Komparu NOH 8). See also: *waki*. (Inoura HISTORY 112, 127; Keene NO 62–63; Shimazaki NOH 3–

7) 2. The principal role in a *kyogen* play. Also called *omo*. See also: *ado*. (Keene NO 62, Berberich "Rapture" 54) 3. The secondary role in *kowakamai*. See also: *tayu*. (Araki BALLAD 92)

shite bashira (Japanese)   Literally: protagonist pillar. The upstage right pillar of a *no* stage. So named because the protagonist (*shite*) takes a position beside it on his first entrance. (Shimazaki NOH 12)

shite kata (Japanese)   Literally: *shite* people. Performers within a *shite* school (for example, Kanze) who play related roles in a play: *shite, shite tsure, tomo, kokata,* and *jiutai*. (Komparu NOH 155)

shite tsure (Japanese)   See: *tsure*.

shite za (Japanese)   See: *nanori*.

shite zure (Japanese)   See: *tsure*.

shiwajo (Japanese)   A *no* mask of a wrinkled old man, worn by an aged deity or a spirit in the second part of a god play. Also called *maijo* or *ishiojo*. (Shimazaki NOH 58)

***shkil'nyi* theatre** (Ukrainian-English)   Ukrainian school theatre. (Hirniak in Bradshaw SOVIET 251)

sho (Japanese)   A wind instrument made of seventeen bamboo pipes arranged in a circle and set in a cup-like windchest. Of Chinese origin, it is used in *gagaku*. (Wolz BUGAKU 18)

shochobi (Japanese)   See: *sashigane*.

shochu (Japanese)   See: *shonaka*.

shock troops, shock troupes   See: *Agit-truppe*.

shodan (Japanese)   Literally: small scene. A named unit within a *no* play, identifiable by dramatic function, rhythmic structure, language type, musical accompaniment, and vocal style. It is the basic unit of *no* play construction. Major *shodan* are given in Shimazaki NOH 44–54, Keene NO 55–57, Hoff/ Flindt "Structure" 225–228, Nippon Gakujutsu JAPANESE xii–xiii. The most important of these is the *kuse*. Dance units (*mai*) without verbal accompaniment usually are not called *shodan*, even though they function as analogous units of play structure.

shodanmemono (Japanese)   See: *kami no*.

shoe   1. See: brush. 2. In stage lighting in Britain, a box or "board" with a number of receptacles, similar to a U.S. plugging box. Compare connector box. (Baker THEATRECRAFT, Rae/Southern INTERNATIONAL, Granville DICTIONARY)

shoe plot   In costumes, a list of the shoes and the characters they are designed for.

shoestring production   A stage presentation done with little or no capital. Hence, shoestringer: an inexpensive theatrical operation or one who performs in such an operation.

shogyoshugi engeki (Japanese)   Literally: commercial theatre. Popular modern theatre that aims at a mass audience. The term includes boulevard comedies, historical romances (*roman*), musicals, variety shows, and similar entertainments. Broadly speaking, one type of modern theatre (*shingeki*).

shohon (Japanese)   Literally: true text. A handwritten play script: 1. The text of the song lyrics that comprise a *kabuki* dance play, usually in *takemoto*, *tokiwazu*, *tomimoto*, or *kiyomoto* styles. (Leiter ENCYCLOPEDIA 366–367) 2. The text of a *joruri* puppet play. (Dunn EARLY 70–71) 3. A *kabuki* text, a synonym for *daihon*. See also: *gikyoku*, *kyakuhon*.

shoka (Sanskrit)   See: *soka*.

shokher jatra (Bengali)   Literally: amateur *jatra*. New secular *jatra* plays, first performed in the 18th C by wealthy amateur Bengalis; hence the name. They were a marked departure from older religious *jatra* plays that had been the province of professional troupes. (Sarkar ''Jatra'' 88)

shoko (Japanese)   A small suspended gong played in *gagaku*.

shomen (Japanese)   Downstage center.

shomyomono (Japanese)   Literally: small landowner play. A *kyogen* play in which a small landowner appears. Also called *shomyo kyogen* (small landowner play) and *tarokajamono* (Tarokaja play), after the chief servant role. (Berberich ''Rapture'' 21)

shonaka (Japanese)   Literally: true center. The dead center position on a *no* stage. Also called *shochu*. (Komparu NOH 130)

S-hook   1. In the U.S., a piece of S-shaped hardware, usually about 2″ from top to bottom and made of metal ³⁄₁₆″ or ¼″ in diameter. 2. See: keeper hook.

shook on the pros   In Britain, a term for stagestruck. (Marsh VINTAGE 21)

shooting   Planing the edges of adjoining flats so they will join without gaps. (Bax MANAGEMENT)

shop   1. A place where scenery, properties, costumes, lighting equipment, etc. are worked on. 2. In Britain, a theatrical engagement; hence, season or seasonal shop. (Bowman/Ball THEATRE, Granville DICTIONARY)

shop grade   Said of medium-grade lumber used in general construction in scene shops.

shop manager   The person who supervises the making of costumes for a play, and is often also in charge of the maintenance and storage of the wardrobe collection.

short   Sometimes among lighting personnel, a short circuit (an uncontrolled flow of electrons). (Wehlburg GLOSSARY)

short-arc lamp   A special type of gaseous discharge lamp which produces a brilliant point of light used as a substitute for a carbon arc and in projecting scenery. One type is the xenon lamp (also called a xenon arc lamp), which uses the rare gas under great pressure to produce a white light used in some follow spots. The newer HMI (hygerium metallic iodide) lamp replaces the xenon gas with a special combination of gases under lower pressure. In addition to being much safer, an HMI is more than twice as bright per watt as a xenon lamp, which is more than twice as bright per watt as an incandescent lamp. (Bellman SCENE 311, fig. 30.3)

short center line   See: set of lines.

shortening side   In a Renaissance theatre, the perspective (onstage, angled) face of an angle wing. (Serlio in Nagler SOURCES 79)

short line   See: set of lines.

short scene   A shallow scene in Restoration theatres. See also: carpenter's scene, in one, scene in one. (Visser in Hume LONDON 83)

short throw   See: throw.

shosa (Japanese)   See: *shosagoto.*

shosa butai (Japanese)   Literally: dance stage. A temporary dance floor laid on top of the main *kabuki* stage for dance and bravura (*aragoto*) style plays. It is made of a number of eight-inch high, polished cyprus-wood platform units, placed side-by-side. (Ernst KABUKI 127–128)

shosagoto (Japanese)   Literally: posture play. An inclusive term for *kabuki* dance plays, regardless of type, including *michiyuki, hengemono,* and *buyogeki.* Also called *keigoto* in Kyoto-Osaka. (Brandon in Brandon/Malm/Shively STUDIES 76–82, Scott KABUKI 84, Gunji BUYO 118–119) Abbreviated *shosa.* (Dunn/Torigoe ANALECTS 170)

shosaki (Japanese)   Literally: true front. Downstage center on a *no* stage. (Berberich "Rapture" 64, Komparu NOH 130)

shot   Planed. See: shooting.

shot bag   A small bag filled with lead shot, used as a weight.

shoujiu, shou chiu (Chinese)   See: *dazhang.*

show   1. A work intended for stage production. 2. A stage production. 3. A performance of a stage production. 4. To produce, to exhibit a production. (Bowman/Ball THEATRE)

show biz   See: show business.

showboat   A U.S. theatre on a boat, usually on a river or lake rather than salt water. Hence, showboater, showboating, to show off. Also called a floating theatre. See also: floating stage. (Wilmeth LANGUAGE, Bowman/Ball THEATRE)

show box   A storage box which can be opened up into a stage for a marionette show.

show business, show biz   From the late 19th C, the professional theatre, often in the broadest sense but sometimes limited to musical theatre.

showcase   1. A production designed to display the talents of playwrights, directors, performers, etc. Hence, showcase stage, showcase theatre. 2. To perform in such a production. (Bowman/Ball THEATRE)

showcloth   1. A show curtain, hung well downstage. Also called a frontcloth. (National TECHNICAL) 2. In puppetry, a curtain painted and captioned to publicize a show. (Philpott DICTIONARY)

show curtain   A special front curtain designed for a particular production.

show folk   Professional theatre people.

showgirl   A young woman who appears in an ensemble, usually in an elaborate costume in a musical theatre piece, but who does little or no acting. Also called a clothes horse. (Bowman/Ball THEATRE)

showman   Anyone connected with a stage production—a performer, author, and especially a highly successful producer. Hence, showmanship. (Bowman/Ball THEATRE)

"(The) show must go on."   A theatrical statement that, whatever the difficulties, if an audience is present, a scheduled performance must be given.

show people   Members of the theatrical profession; by extension, all those who participate in theatrical productions.

show portal   A special adjustable inner proscenium.

showroom theatre   See: dinner theatre.

show-stopper   A piece of business, a song, a speech, etc., so effective that the applause momentarily stops the performance.

show tape   A sound tape with cue tapes added, for use during performances.

show the act   Give an audition.

show town   A town where productions (often on tour) are presented. Hence, a good show town, a bad show town.

show wise   Said of sophisticated audiences.

shozoku (Japanese)   See: *isho*.

shredded wheat   See: breakfast food.

shroud   See: surround.

Shrovetide play   In medieval Germany, a short, earthy farce in verse, performed during the carnival season. (Sobel NEW)

shrubbery   A false beard.

shtik (Yiddish), **shtick**   1. Stage business, usually comic. 2. A performer's trademark idiosyncrasies. The two meanings are close: the term has the sense of studied or calculated and sometimes moves over into overdone or tricky, as in Rosten's "Play it straight: no *shtiklech*," *shtiklech* being the plural. Both the term and its source, German *Stück*, mean piece. (Rosten JOYS, Sandrow VAG-ABOND 63, Picon/Grillo MOLLY 26, Wentworth/Flexner SLANG)

shuaifa, shuai fa (Chinese)   In Beijing opera (*jingju*) and many other forms of music-drama (*xiqu*), a long, thick switch of black hair worn atop the head by a male character who is in distress. It is swung and flicked by controlled head movements to express consternation or anger. (Halson PEKING 36, Scott CLASSICAL 163)

shuangwanyier, shuang wan i erh (Chinese)   1. Literally: double amusement intention. See: *errentai*. 2. Literally: double amusement art. See : *errenzhuan*.

shuban, shu pan (Chinese)   Rhymed poetry, rhythmically delivered, which is accompanied by a percussion orchestra; a type of stage speech (*nianbai*), usually delivered by clown role (*chou*) actors upon entrance, in many forms of music-drama (*xiqu*) and storytelling (*quyi*). In Beijing opera (*jingju*), it is some-times considered a metrical-type (*banshi*); accompaniment features the *ban* clap-per. See also: *zibao jiamen*. (Scott CLASSICAL 93)

shuck   To fail to give one's best.

shucker   In the U.S., a stripper. (Wilmeth LANGUAGE)

shugen (Japanese)   1. A congratulatory passage, or a section containing the passage, in a god *no* play. (O'Neill EARLY 86, 116–117) 2. A drama developed in the late 13th C by mountain monks (*yamabushi*) to disseminate *shugendo*, a religion born out of the union of Shinto mountain worship and Buddhism. A performance consisted of rituals and prayers, pieces containing droll humor, and a warrior dance. It declined in the 20th C when Shinto and Buddhism were separated by government decree. (Inoura HISTORY 10, 12, 77–79)

shuhui, shu hui (Chinese)   Literally: writing society. A writers' guild or cooperative association which wrote *yuanben* and other plays in the 13th C, and perhaps earlier. (Dolby HISTORY 16)

shui hsiu (Chinese)   See: *shuixiu*.

shuikuilei, shui k'uei lei (Chinese)   Literally: water puppets. Wooden figures seemingly operated by water, probably automata; they were made and performed for the emperor and court. Described in the 3rd, 6th, 7th, and 10th–13th C. (Dolby HISTORY 5, 261–262, 265; Obraztsov CHINESE 28)

shuimodiao, shui mo tiao (Chinese)   See: *kunqu*.

shuixiu, shui hsiu (Chinese)   Literally: water sleeves. A white silk cuff, between one-and-a-half and two feet long, left open at the seam and attached to the end of the sleeve of a traditional costume in Beijing opera (*jingju*) and many other forms of music-drama (*xiqu*). Water sleeves are manipulated in a number of conventional and interpretive ways, described in detail in Scott CLASSICAL 96–101 and Zung SECRETS 77–95. They are worn with *mang, pei, guanyi, xuezi*, and numerous other types of costumes. (Halson PEKING 20, Scott TRA-DITIONAL II 17)

shukke mono (Japanese)   Literally: priest play. A *kyogen* play that contains songs and dances, and parodies the form and Buddhist content of a *no* play. Also called *mai kyogen* (dance play). One type of *shukke zato kyogen*. (Berberich "Rapture" 185)

shukke zato kyogen (Japanese)   Literally: priest-handicapped play. A category of *kyogen* plays in which the principal role (*shite*) is either a feckless Buddhist priest (see: *shukke mono*) or a blind or crippled person (*zato*). (Inoura HISTORY 129)

shuko (Japanese)   The plot of a play, especially *kabuki* and *bunraku*. A playwright began with characters and circumstances from known worlds (*sekai*) and then imaginatively combined them (*mitate*) to create original and often bizarre plots. (Brandon CLASSIC 30–31, Gunji KABUKI 35)

shumei (Japanese)   Literally: name succession. Succession by a *kabuki* actor to a new acting name, marking achievement of higher artistic status. For example, the heir to the Ichikawa Danjuro acting name would successively take the names of Natsu, Shinnosuke, and Ebizo before becoming Danjuro. *Shumei hiro* is the announcement of the name change to the audience. (Leiter ENCYCLOPEDIA 369–370, Scott KABUKI 161–162)

shund (Yiddish)   Literally: trash. Productions aiming at mass appeal and relying on double entendre, sentiment, topical humor, puns, thrills, and a mixed bag of escapist comedy and melodrama. The concept is broad and elastic and encompasses some very good and some very bad theatre. Sandrow notes that soap opera, cowboy movies, and many Broadway plays are *shund*. Occasionally called *shund*ism. Sometimes used as an adjective, as in *shund* musical. High *shund* has been used lightly to describe melodrama-operettas, usually on exotic historical subjects. (Sandrow VAGABOND 109–112, 114; Rosenfeld BRIGHT 332–333; Lifson YIDDISH 60, 223, 277)

shunkan (Japanese)   A *no* mask with a bitter expression, worn by Shunkan, a priest who was exiled to a remote island for conspiracy. (Shimazaki NOH 64)

shunt circuit   See: multiple circuit.

shuochang, shuo ch'ang (Chinese)   Literally: talk and song. A general term for various forms of popular entertainment which consist mainly of talking and/or singing; first described in the 7th C. Usually translated as storytelling. See also: *quyi*.

shuoshu, shuo shu (Chinese)   Literally: talk book. The generic term for story-telling (*shuochang*) performances in which one or two long stories, rather than several short ones, are related through song and/or speech.

shu pan (Chinese)   See: *shuban*.

shura ba (Japanese)   Literally: carnage scene. A bloody battle scene in history plays, especially in *bunraku* but also in *kabuki*. (Brandon CLASSIC 28)

shuramono (Japanese)   Literally: hell piece. A *no* play in which the protagonist (*shite*) is a warrior. It appears second on a bill of five plays. So named because the warrior suffers in hell after his death in battle. An example is *Kiyotsune* in Nippon Gakujutsu JAPANESE 59–73. Also called: *shura no* (hell *no*) and *nibanmemono* (second piece play). (Shimazaki NOH 23–24)

shut, shutdown   The last act on a bill.

shuto (Japanese)   A *bunraku* puppet head used for bad old men, such as a cruel father-in-law. (Keene BUNRAKU 59, 223)

shutter   1. In Renaissance theatres and later, a flat, normally one of a pair, sliding on and off stage in a groove; two shutters, when closed, formed a prospect and also concealed scenic units further upstage. The pair were also called the backscene. (Southern CHANGEABLE 34) 2. In or on a spotlight, a mechanical means of modifying the size or shape (or both) of the beam of light. The term often refers to the four-piece shutter in the gate of an ellipsoidal reflector spotlight. Other terms include the iris shutter, framing shutter, and curtain shutter. (Wehlburg GLOSSARY) 3. To close a theatre.

Sicherung (German)   See: *Schmelzsicherungen*.

Sichuan opera   See: *chuanju*.

sicinnis   See: *sikinnis*.

sickle foot, sickling   See: *serpette*.

sidaw (Burmese)   A small drum used in the musical ensemble that accompanies traditional theatre performances.

side   A page of a performer's part, containing lines and cues. Sides are usually written or typed on half sheets (about 6'' × 9'') though some surviving in manuscript from the 17th and 18th C are full sheets. A side was also called a length, and the importance of a performer's role was often indicated by the number of sides or lengths, a role of 30 typed sides or more being considered major. When sides were written out, a major role came to about 10 full-page sides or more.

side arm   See: boom arm.

side boxes   In Renaissance theatres and later, expensive seating sections at the sides of the auditorium, divided by partitions. (Hogan LONDON xlviii)

side buildings   See: *paraskenia, versurae*.

side coaching   During an improvisation or theatre game with young people, an assist given by the leader to help the participants keep focus.

side lights   1. In 18th C theatres, lighting instruments situated behind the wings and capable of being rotated to increase or reduce illumination. See also: blind. (Visser in Hume LONDON 114) 2. See: wing lights.

side port   See: port.

side scene   1. See: side scenes. 2. Occasionally, a scene performed at the side of the stage. (Bowman/Ball THEATRE)

side scenes, side shutters, side wings   Formerly, flats painted in perspective, arranged from front to back along the sides of the stage, spaced a few feet apart, often sliding onstage and off in grooves.

side shutter   A side wing.

side stage   A performing area at the side of the auditorium, close to and usually connected with the main stage. When the main stage and side stages are used together, the form is called an extended stage or multi-proscenium stage. See also: caliper stage. (Burris-Meyer/Cole THEATRES 130)

side stringer   See: stringer.

sidewalk actor   A performer who discourses about how he would interpret a role but is a failure onstage. (Bowman/Ball THEATRE, Berrey/Van den Bark SLANG 572)

sidewalk conversation   In vaudeville and variety shows, a comic scene by a pair of wisecracking comedians, playing 'in one' (downstage) in front of a street drop. (Wilmeth LANGUAGE)

sidewall slide   A counterweight track attached vertically to the side wall of a stage house. (Bowman/Ball THEATRE)

sidewall slot   A vertical opening for spotlights in a side auditorium wall, usually near the front.

side wing   See: wing and drop.

side wings   1. See: *paraskenia, versurae.* 2. See: side scenes.

siège (French)   A *mansion* or locale in a medieval production. (Nicoll DEVELOPMENT 52)

siesta   A period when a performer has no engagement.

sifflet pratique (French)   See: swazzle.

sight act   See: dumb act.

sight comedian   A comic who relies heavily on his appearance, movement, and sight gags.

sight comedy   Comic business, as opposed to dialogue. Hence, sight comedian.

sight cue   1. A non-verbal signal backstage such as the pointing of a finger. Used when a verbal cue might be heard by the audience. 2. A piece of business onstage which serves as a visual cue for lights, sound, curtain, a performer's line, etc.

sight gag   A visual joke such as a pratfall, a pie in the face, or a green fright wig.

sightlines, sight lines   What audience members can see of the stage from their seats. Seating charts sometimes indicate to patrons which seats have poor sightlines. Also called lines of sight. Often used in the singular. See also: deadline and set line.

siglaton   14th C and later gold brocade. (Boucher FASHION)

sigma (Greek)   Orchestra. The word was used in later times because of the similarity between the Romanized semi-circular orchestra and the semi-circular form adopted in the 4th C BC for the Greek letter *sigma*. See also: *orchestra*. (Haigh ATTIC 101, Flickinger GREEK 72)

signal light   A small light that can be turned on or off by a stage manager to cue the orchestra, stage technicians, etc. The light is usually turned on as a warning and off as a cue.

signature music   A musical theme associated with a particular character, usually in opera but also in melodramas of the 19th C. See also: *Leitmotiv* (German). (Cameron/Gillespie ENJOYMENT)

signed   Booked, engaged.

sigong (Chinese)   See: *jiben gongfu*.

sigu, ssu ku (Chinese)   Literally: drum manager. The conductor of the orchestra (*changmian*) in music-drama (*xiqu*); he is a member of the percussion ensemble (*wuchang*). In Beijing opera (*jingju*), he conducts by his use of the *ban* clapper and the single-skin drum (*danpigu*). Also called drum master (*gushi* or *ku shih*). See also: *guban*. (Wichmann "Aural" 452–460)

sikinnis (Greek)   The characteristic dance of the satyr play. Often accompanied by shouting, the *sikinnis* is said to have been "lively, vigorous, and lewd, with horseplay and acrobatics, and at times, an affected, mincing gait, together with exaggerated movements of the hips and shaking of the whole body" (Lawler). The dance probably originated in Crete. Also called in U.S. English sikinnis, sicinnis; hence, sicinnian. All are rare. (Lawler DANCE 91–92, Pickard-Cambridge FESTIVALS 254)

silbo (Spanish)   In 17th C theatres and later, a whistle used by the dandies (*mosqueteros*) when they were displeased with a performance. (Sobel NEW)

silence   In the Renaissance and later, to close a theatre by law; to silence the players.

silent cue   A visual cue, as opposed to a cue by a line of dialogue, a bell, a whistle, etc.

silenus, Silenus (Latin)   1. In theatre literature, the leader of the satyrs and the satyr chorus in ancient Greece. Often referred to as the father of the satyrs and the companion of Dionysus, *Silenus* is in mythology a forest god who is the foster father of Dionysus and his mentor and follower; he is usually represented as hairy and white-bearded, often as snub-nosed and drunken. Also called *Papposilenus*, sometimes spelled *Papposilenos* (Greek). 2. A satyr. The distinction between a satyr and a *silenus* is not always made. Plural: *sileni*. Also called *seilenos* (archaic Greek), *silenos* (Greek), silen, U.S. silenus, seilenos. See also: satyr. (Pickard-Cambridge DITHYRAMB 114–118, 167; Pickard-Cambridge FESTIVALS 186; Bieber HISTORY figs. 37, 38; Flickinger GREEK 341)

silete (French)   In medieval play manuscripts, usually an indication that musicians are to play, typically to quiet the audience, introduce important characters, etc. (Frank MEDIEVAL 173)

silicon-controlled rectifier   A semiconductor (solid state) device which has for some years been the principal theatre dimmer, especially for remote control. Each of two SCRs uses a ''gate'' to control half the AC cycle, thus controlling the voltage which reaches the lamp. SCR (strictly, the device) and SCR dimmer are the principal theatre terms. Also called a silicon rectifier or thyristor (thyrister) dimmer (mainly British). The Triac (occasionally TRIAC or triac) dimmer, superficially similar, is a patented device which has come into use for smaller loads: a single Triac replaces the two SCRs. (Sellman/Lessley ESSENTIALS 127–129, fig. 8.7; Bellman LIGHTING 196–198; Wehlburg GLOSSARY; Bentham ART 127–130, figs. 77–79, 81)

sill   The bottom edge or ledge of a scenic piece. (Corry PLANNING)

sillas (Spanish)   Seats in a 17th C *corral* theatre. (Rennert SPANISH 51)

sillas de respaldo (Spanish)   Seats with backs in a 17th C *corral* theatre. (Rennert SPANISH 51)

sill iron   A piece of strap iron screwed to the bottom of a door flat to give it rigidity. Also called a floor iron. See also: saddle iron.

sill rail   The bottom rail of a flat.

silo circuit   A summer stock circuit of small country towns. (Wilmeth LANGUAGE)

silo operator   The manager of a summer theatre.

silver tickets   In 18th C theatres, opera tickets; actually silver discs. Also called checks. See also: gold tickets. (Avery LONDON lxii, Hogan LONDON xxvii)

simar   See: samare.

simarra (Italian)   See: *ropa*.

similitudo (Latin)   See: liturgical drama.

simodi (Greek)   Probably singers of indecent songs. Duchartre groups *simodi* with other farce performers of ancient Greece and Rome. (Duchartre ITALIAN 24)

simodia (Greek)   Probably a form of early lyric mime thought to be one of the varieties of *mimodia*. The term is from Simus (or Simon), the name of a supposed figure in the satyr play, or of the first writer of *simodia*. (Nicoll MASKS 34)

Simon Legree   1. A villain character. 2. An actor who plays such parts. 3. One who overworks performers. (Berrey/Van den Bark SLANG 576) *simpingan* (Indonesian)   Literally: tapered ornament. An ornamental display of c. 150 puppets arranged at the two sides of a Javanese *wayang kulit* screen. The arrangement 'tapers' toward the screen, hence the name. Illustrated in Long JAVANESE 4. Also spelled *sumpingan*. (Brandon THRONES 38–39) *Wayang simpingan* are the puppets in this display. (Long JAVANESE 69)

simulation   See: sociodrama.

simultaneous cross   Two performers moving across the stage simultaneously in opposite directions. Also called a scissors cross.

simultaneous setting, simultaneous staging   A medieval system of staging in which several different locales were represented on stage at the same time. Also called multiple setting, multiple simultaneous staging, and *décor simultané* (French). Sometimes used of more recent settings which show two or more locations simultaneously.

sinakulo (Philippine)   See: *cenaculo*.

sinden (Indonesian)   In Javanese *wayang*, the singing of female singers (*pesinden*) seated with the *gamelan* ensemble. (Brandon THRONES 54) In Java, *sindenan* is the song they sing. Also spelled *nyinder* in Sunda. (Muljono in Osman TRADITIONAL 71, Foley ''Sundanese'' 211–215)

singing-actor   A term applied by the Moscow Art Theatre's co-founder Vladimir Nemirovitch-Danchenko to the perfect performer—one whose voice, movements, and rhythmic acting would express the inner essence of the character. (Markov SOVIET 126)

singing ensemble   The vocal chorus of a musical theatre piece.

single   1. One who performs alone. To perform alone is to do a single. 2. An act with one performer. 3. A flat one foot wide. 4. A ticket for one seat at one performance.

single bill   A program consisting of a single dramatic work. (Bowman/Ball THEATRE)

single-color system   A method of lighting the acting area spaces from either side (at the usual 45° angles) with the same tint in all instruments. Compare: complementary-tint system, related-tint system. (Bellman LIGHTING 120–121)

single end   See: lamp base.

single purchase   Said of a counterweight system in which the weight travels the same distance as the scenery. See also: double purchase.

single-row footlights   The usual type of footlights, with a single line of lamps. Double-row footlights have two such lines. Lounsbury has illustrations. (Lounsbury THEATRE 89)

sing-sing   In New Guinea, pidgin for drama-music-dance.

sing-song   In the early 20th C, a Chinese theatre in the U.S.

Singspiel (German)   Literally: sing-play. A comic opera.

sinhasan (Hindi)   Literally: throne. In *raslila*, a throne mounted on a dais (*rangmanc*) for seating important characters. (Hein MIRACLE 137)

sink and fly   See: rise and sink.

sinking   A stage effect using trapdoors: "with all the Musick, Songs, Sinkings, Flyings, and other decorations." (Southern CHANGEABLE 214)

sinking curtain   A curtain which drops into a slot in the stage floor or rolls onto a cylinder in the stage floor. Also called a reverse roller curtain.

sinking stage   See: elevator stage.

Sink T   Sink Trap—that is, to lower the trapdoor elevator mechanism. Used in David Garrick's promptbook for *Macbeth* for the disappearance of the ghost of Banquo. Also written ST. (Burnim GARRICK 118)

sinpa (Korean)   Literally: new school theatre. A form of melodrama influenced by Western models, written by Korean playwrights, c. 1911–1920. Also call *sinpa* were Japanese *shinpa* plays translated into Korean. (Korean KOREAN 50–53, Kim "Development" 26–29)

siparium (Latin Roman)   Usually, an inner curtain, a lesser curtain smaller than the main curtain (*aulaeum*) and upstage of it. Analysis of a number of ancient monuments and references suggests that the *siparium* may first have been a folding screen or screens, perhaps at times a small portable curtain, used by early itinerant mime players. By the late 4th C BC (Bieber), a *siparium* may sometimes have been used to conceal parts of the permanent stage facade such as one of the doors or openings not used or not appropriate in a particular scene or play. In such a use the curtain seems to have been hung. Later, depending upon the period and the theatre, it was sometimes hung and drawn, or raised and lowered. About the 1st C BC, the term appears to have been interchangeable with the *aulaeum*. Still later, the *aulaeum* and the *siparium* were again distinct from one another. The occasional *siparii* is an error for the plural, *siparia*. Compare *instrumenta*. (Beare ROMAN 154, 270–274; Bieber HISTORY 180, figs. 324, 831)

siphon light   See: inverted float.

siping (Chinese)   See: *sipingdiao*.

sipingdiao, ssu p'ing tiao (Chinese)   1. A musical mode (*diaoshi*) in the music of Beijing opera (*jingju*) expressive of a wide variety of emotional states, including relaxed lightness, remembrance, impelling indignation, and sorrowful desolation. Abbreviated *siping* or *ssu p'ing*; also called *erhuang pingban* or *erh huang p'ing pan*. (Wichman "Aural" 244–253) 2. A contemporary form of music-drama (*xiqu* popular today in the region where Henan, Jiangsu, and Anjui Provinces share borders; it developed out of the flower drum plays (*huanguxi*) of this region. It was probably influenced early in its development by *yiyangqiang* music-drama, and by the music of the *bangziqiang* musical system; in the 20th C it was influenced by the *pingju, quju,* and *yuju* forms.

sipingqiang (Chinese)   See: *sipingdiao*.

Sis Hopkins   The female counterpart of Toby in a Toby show. Also called Susie. (Wilmeth LANGUAGE)

sisias (Indonesian)   In Bali, the role of a disciple of the witch Calonarang. (de Zoete/Spies DANCE 118)

sisinderan (Indonesian)   In Sundanese *wayang golek*, a poetic form in which many of the lyrics of the female singer (*pasindeni*) are sung. See also: *kakawen*. (Foley ''Sundanese'' 212–215)

sissone (French)   A ballet step named for its originator. There are over three dozen different forms of *sissone*. Grant describes them. It is basically a spring into the air from both feet and a landing on one foot. (Grant TECHNICAL)

sister act   In vaudeville, burlesque, or revues, an act by two women, often billed as sisters whether they were or not. (Wilmeth LANGUAGE)

sister circuit   See: twofer.

sitting on their hands   Said of an audience that is not responding (that is, not applauding).

situation   1. Dramatic situation, the state of events in a play. 2. In Britain, the position of the performers on the stage at any particular moment. 3. In Britain, the main event to which the action of a play is pointed. (Downs THEATRE II 1139)

situation play   See: play of situation.

Sitzprobe (German)   Especially in Australia, a first rehearsal of opera singers and the orchestra together. No staging is attempted. (National TECHNICAL)

six-sheet   1. A theatrical poster consisting of six double-crown (20″ × 30″) sheets. 2. To advertise prominently, originally in vaudeville. 3. To exaggerate. (Wilmeth LANGUAGE, Bowman/Ball THEATRE)

six-way   1. See: plugging box. 2. See: two-way.

size   1. A thin solution of glue used to fill the pores in surfaces, in preparation for a coat of paint. Now usually a synthetic resin paint. A size coating on cloth-covered flats tightens the cloth on the frame. Also called sizing, size water. 2. To apply such a solution.

sizhouxi, ssu chou hsi (Chinese)   A form of music-drama (*xiqu*) popular in Anhui Province; the Anhui version of *liuqinxi*. It is greatly influenced by the music of local storytelling (*shuochang*) and by local forms of small-scale folk theatre (*xiaoxi*). See also: *lahunqiang*.

skaffold   See: scaffold.

skate   A piece of scenery that can be slid on the stage. (Berrey/Van den Bark SLANG 579)

skate a flat   To slide a flat along the floor.

sked   A program, a bill; the schedule of a performance.

skeleton   1. Especially in Britain, a single figure giving the total receipts for a performance. (Baker THEATRECRAFT) 2. See: dissecting skeleton.

skeleton play   A scenario or set form upon which an improvisation can be built. (Spolin IMPROVISATION)

skeleton script   An actor's term for a manuscript of a play that omits the part of the protagonist. (Foust LIFE 441)

skeleton set   See: unit set, constructivism.

skeleton strip   A line of household-size electrical sockets (medium screw base) mounted on a length of wood or metal. (McCandless "Glossary" 635)

skene (Greek)   Literally: hut, tent. The scene building of the ancient Greek theatre. The *skene* may originally have been a small hut or tent used as a dressing and waiting room by the performers. In Latin: *scaena*, sometimes *scena*. English commonly uses scene building; stage building is less frequent, and scena is found mainly in 18th and 19th C writers. (Arnott SCENIC 4–6, 9–14, 17–18, 19, 117–119, 146–147; Bieber HISTORY figs. 223, 232, 238–240, 271, 451–459)

skenographia (Greek)   Literally: scene painting. Decoration of the *skene*. This may have been an architectural facade painted (possibly in perspective) on the wooden *skene*. On the basis of ancient evidence, including Aristotle's statement in the *Poetics* that *skenographia* was introduced by Sophocles, this earliest known scene painting dates between 468 and 458 BC. Also called, occasionally, scenography. (Arnott SCENIC 93–96, Beare ROMAN 275–276, Pickard-Cambridge DIONYSUS 124–126)

skenotheke (Greek)   A storeroom for stage properties, probably also often used as a dressing area. The size and placement of the *skenotheke* varied with the theatre and the period. Some reconstructions show a warehouse abutting the *scaenae frons* and almost co-extensive with it. (Bieber HISTORY 57, 59, 122, 217, figs. 233, 236, 255, 276)

sketch   1. A playlet with few characters and a single incident, usually humorous and lasting a few minutes. 2. A brief, usually comic, scene or skit in a revue. In Britain, called a turn. 3. An outline or scenario of a play. 4. A rough drawing of a stage design. (Bowman/Ball THEATRE)

skin   1. A dust cover for a piece of furniture or a rolled-up drop. 2. An animal costume in pantomimes and children's plays. (Baker THEATRECRAFT)

skins   Tights. (Bowman/Ball THEATRE)

skin show   Occasionally, a striptease or burlesque show. (Wilmeth LANGUAGE)

skip   In Britain: 1. A performer's traveling basket or hamper, also used for wardrobe and properties. 2. To dance. Hence, skippers (stage dancers). (Granville DICTIONARY) 3. In dance, a compound locomotor step consisting of a first step followed by a hop, the step needing twice the amount of time of the hop. (Hayes DANCE 47)

skirts part   A role in which an actor dresses as a woman, as in *Charley's Aunt*.

skit   See: sketch.

skomorokhi (Russian)   Strolling semi-professional performers in Russia from the 11th to the 17th C; they provided a wide variety of entertainments—acrobatics, juggling, conjuring, and the like. They became the puppeteers, bear-trainers, and clowns of later centuries. See also: *petrushechnik, medvezhatnik, ded-balagur*, and *raëshnik*. (Yershov SOVIET 7)

skope (Greek)   According to Pollux, a device "made for those who view the action." Nicoll suggests that this was a vantage point for the person who served the function of director. Possibly the *skope* was akin to the prompter's box in opera. (Nicoll DEVELOPMENT 22)

skor thom (Khmer)   A large, buffalo-hide kettle-drum which provides rhythmic patterns for classical dance music. Also called *thom*. (Brunet in Osman TRADITIONAL 216, Anonymous ROYAL 22)

skuespil (Norwegian)   Drama.

skull   1. A complimentary ticket. 2. See: take.

sky backing   See: backing.

sky batten   See: back batten.

sky border   A hanging strip of cloth above the stage, painted to represent the sky. Also called a sky piece, sky strip, ozone.

sky cloth   1. A border; a horizontal strip of cloth hanging above the stage, representing the sky. (Hogan LONDON 1x) 2. See: sky drop.

sky cyclorama   See: cyclorama.

sky dome   See: cyclorama.

sky drop   A drop painted to simulate the sky. In Britain: a sky cloth.

sky foots   An occasional term for footlights used to light a sky, whether cyc, drop, or other scenic piece. (Bowman MODERN)

skylight   See: smoke hatch.

sky pan   See: scoop.

sky piece, sky strip   See: sky border.

SL   Stage left.

slack off, slack out   To loosen ropes.

slammerkin   See: gown à la Polonaise.

S lamp   See: S.

slang   1. In the 18th C, to exhibit anything at an English fair or market. 2. A 19th C British traveling show. 3. In 19th C Britain, the wires of a marionette. (Speaight PUPPET 234, 307)

slanted scenes   In 17th C theatres and later, side wings set obliquely instead of parallel to the front of the stage. (Scouten LONDON cxxi)

slap-around   See: knockabout.

slapstick   1. Originally, and often still, a pair of lath paddles fastened together at one end, used by low comedians to slap one another noisily, especially in vaudeville and circus. In France, *batte*. See also: whip. 2. Comic stage business that depends on physical activity (pratfalls, for example). (Wilmeth LANGUAGE) 3. A noisy or broadly-played comic entertainment, as in slapstick comedy. See also: knockabout. 4. To engage in slapstick comedy. (Wilmeth LANGUAGE, Bowman/Ball THEATRE)

slash   See: efforts.

slashings   In the Renaissance and later, slits in sleeves, gloves, and shoes which showed the lining of the item, the latter usually of a contrasting color. Also called *acuchillados* (Spanish), *crevés* (French), *chiquetades, mouchetures* (the smallest of slashings), panes. (Boucher FASHION)

slate   1. A program, a bill. 2. In Britain, to condemn a production. Also called go for.

slaughter 'em, slay 'em   To delight an audience.

sleeper   A modest theatrical offering which achieves unexpected success.

sleeper jump   1. Originally, a distance for a touring company requiring an overnight railroad trip. 2. In show business generally, any great distance, as a hotel room far from the theatre or a long railroad platform. 3. In burlesque, a dressing room far from the stage. (Wilmeth LANGUAGE)

sleep producer   A poor show.

slendro (Indonesian)   A five-interval *gamelan* tuning system (as opposed to *pelog*, using seven intervals). The instruments of a *slendro gamelan* are permanently tuned to this scale and are used to accompany Javanese *wayang kulit* (Holt ART 137), *wayang wong* and *wayang golek* (Brandon THRONES 52), and *ludruk* (Peacock RITES 53–54).

slëznaia **drama** (Russian-English)   A Russian adaptation of the French *comédie larmoyante*—tearful comedy or sentimental drama. Also called *meshchanskaia komediia* or *meshchanskaia tragediia*. (*Meshchanskii* means philistine, vulgar, narrow-minded.) (Welsh RUSSIAN 110–113)

slice of life   An extreme form of late 19th C naturalism in which the play appears to be an accidental segment of life. Characteristic is an apparent lack of plot or structure, resulting in an effect of aimlessness marked by non-essential detail; curtains are unemphatic, with the play simply stopping at the final curtain. The plays tend to deal with the underside of life, showing people earlier thought unsuitable subjects for drama. A typical example is Maxim Gorki's *The Lower Depths*, set in a dank cellar peopled by starving derelicts and near-derelicts. Also called *tranche de vie* (French), of which slice of life is a translation.

slide   1. In lighting, a cutout, or a translucent photograph, painting, or drawing used for projection. In Britain, diapositive. 2. Short for gelatine slide. 3. The electrical brush in a slider dimmer. Also called a slider. 4. See: sloat. (Bowman/Ball THEATRE, Wehlburg GLOSSARY) 5. In dance, a compound locomotor step consisting of a first step (usually to the side) plus a second (a leap), which closes to the first, the latter needing twice the amount of time of the leap. (Hayes DANCE 47)

slide dimmer, slider dimmer   Especially in the past, a non-interlocking resistance dimmer whose electrical brush was manually moved in a straight line. 'Spotlight dimmer' has also been used, since the device was constructed so that it could be fastened to a pipe (as on a light stand) for control of an individual fixture. Also occasionally called a slide resistance dimmer. In Britain, wire dimmer or wire resistance dimmer. (McCandless SYLLABUS 58, Bowman/Ball THEATRE, Gassner/Barber PRODUCING 794)

slide frame   Especially in Britain, an occasional term for a color-frame holder. (Goffin LIGHTING 25)

slide holder   In projectors, an accessory consisting of a small frame which will accept a projection slide. (Bowman/Ball THEATRE)

slider   1. In Britain, a section of a stage floor that is movable, sliding in grooves and covering a cut in the stage floor. Also called a filling or runner. When a slider is unlocked and slid offstage, a bridge is brought up through the space thus created. (Bowman/Ball THEATRE) 2. See: pusher. 3. An electrical brush on a dimmer. (Bellman LIGHTING 177, Bax MANAGEMENT 178)

slider cut   See: cut.

slider dimmer board   Especially in Britain, a light control board which uses slider dimmers. (Corry PLANNING 62, fig. 32)

slide resistance dimmer   See: slide dimmer.

slider interconnection panel   See: interconnecting panel.

sliding stage   See: wagon stage.

sliding trap   See: sloat.

slim   See: swazzle.

slim take   Poor box-office receipts.

slinger   1. In the U.S., a stripper. 2. In Britain, a prompter.

sling in   To perform, especially to dance. Now obsolete. (Wilmeth LANGUAGE)

slip a programme   In Britain, to insert a sheet into a theatre program, usually to announce a change, such as the substitution of an understudy for the regular performer. (Marsh DOLPHIN 234)

slip box   In 19th C Britain, a box at the end of an amphitheatre slip or top side gallery. See also: slips.

slip connector   See: pin connector.

slip counterweight   See: counterweight.

slips   1. Side seating in the top gallery in Britain, above the side boxes. Also called amphitheatre slips, as at Covent Garden Theatre. Found in some 18th and 19th C theatres, but rarely in more recent houses. 2. The wings of a theatre.

slip stage   See: wagon stage.

slittamento (Italian)   Literally: side-step. A term coined by Ettore Petrolini and now in Italian theatre jargon: a sudden break in character by an actor, in which he comments on something outside his role—a non-functioning light, a colleague who has dropped a cue, an audience heckler, etc. (Longman "Petrolini" 378)

sloat, slote   In Britain, a device for raising or lowering a performer or scenery through an opening in the stage floor. It consists of grooved parallel rails, vertical or sloping, in which slide bearers or tongues attached to a platform or a piece of scenery. Also called a boot, slide, sliding trap. In the U.S.: hoist. See also: Corsican trap. (Granville DICTIONARY)

sloat box   1. A wooden curtain track. 2. In Britain, a long wooden box containing a roller on which a curtain may be wound. Used for lowering or raising a curtain or cloth when it is impossible to do so through a cut in the stage floor. But Bowman and Ball call it a stage cut into which a curtain can be rolled. (Baker THEATRECRAFT, Bowman/Ball THEATRE)

sloka (Sanskrit)   A Sanskrit verse within the text of a play. A *sloka* is chanted, rather than sung, and is delivered in a free rhythm (drums do not accompany *sloka*, hence there is no guiding rhythm, or *tala*). See Gandhi in Baumer/Brandon SANSKRIT for *sloka* in the classic play *The Vision of Vasavadatta* (167–207) and the syllable count and accents of eleven meters used in *sloka* composition (138–140). Examples used in present-day regional theatre are given in Rajagopalan/Iyer "Aids" 206–209 and Varyyar "Nala" 216–247. In vernacular languages spelled *slokam*. See also: *pada*.

slot   See: ceiling slot.

sloughed joint   A theatre at which no show is being given. (Berrey/Van den Bark SLANG 577)

sloughed off   Said of an act that is cut off short. (Berrey/Van den Bark SLANG 588)

slow burn   In acting, a reaction showing slowly mounting exasperation, often followed by an outburst. (Bowman/Ball THEATRE)

slow clap, slow handclap   Since at least the first half of the 20th C, slow rhythmic applause by a dissatisfied audience. See also: Colonial clap.

slow curtain   A curtain lowered or closed slowly at the end of an act or scene.

slow handclap   See: slow clap.

slow-motion wheel   Especially on some older dimmer boards, a hand-operated wheel geared so that it provides close control over one or more dimmers. (McCandless "Glossary" 638, Bowman/Ball THEATRE)

slow night   1. A night of the week (for example, Monday) when business at a theatre is poor. 2. A performance for which tickets are not selling.

slow study   A performer who does not learn lines easily.

slow take   See: take.

slumming   Formerly, acting, including the "acting" seen in 19th C Punch and Judy shows. (Partridge TO-DAY 225)

SM, S.M.   Stage manager.

smacko   See: smash.

small group work   In creative drama, improvisational activities with participants in small groups which work/perform simultaneously. (O'Neill/Lambert DRAMA 26)

small part   A minor role, though sometimes an important one. Hence, small-part player, small-part man, small-part woman. 'Small parts and understudies' means a small-role performer who also understudies major roles. (Bowman/Ball THEATRE, Granville DICTIONARY)

small people   Minor members of a British theatrical company. (Troubridge BENEFIT 127)

small prop   See: prop.

smalls   1. Theatres showing small-time vaudeville. 2. In Britain, small towns visited by touring companies. (Granville DICTIONARY)

small time   A vaudeville theatre or circuit of vaudeville theatres offering at least three shows daily. The fare was usually low-salaried acts, sometimes mixed with movies. By extension, a theatre that was not very successful. Hence, small-time performer, small-time act, etc. See also: big time. (Wilmeth LANGUAGE)

small timer   1. A performer on a minor theatre circuit. 2. A minor circuit vaudeville theatre.

smart   A character in a play who is a fop, a dandy. (Wilkinson WANDERING I 209)

smash   Very successful. Hence, smash act, smash biz, smash hit, smash show, smasherino, smacko. (Berrey/Van den Bark SLANG 584, 592)

smear   Greasepaint.

smell of the greasepaint   A metaphor for the supposed glamour and excitement of the stage.

smoke box, smoke case   In Britain, a bucket, pot, box, or other container for creating smoke effects by heating a sheet of mica on which a pinch of smoke powder has been placed. Generally fired electrically from an offstage control point. In the U.S., smoke pot.

smoke boxes   See: smoke pockets.

smoke case   See: smoke box.

smoke door   Smoke hatch.

smoke hatch   A door in the stage roof, above the gridiron, designed to open in case of fire. The draft thus created draws smoke upward. Also called a skylight or smoke door. In Britain: lantern light or lantern, smoke outlet, ventilator.

smoke pockets   Vertical channels backstage on each side of the proscenium opening which enclose the guides for the side of the asbestos safety curtain. Their purpose is to prevent smoke from passing from stage to auditorium in case of fire when the fire curtain is down. Also called smoke slots, smoke traps. In Britain, smoke boxes.

smoke pot   See: smoke box.

smoke slots, smoke traps   Smoke pockets.

smut   Especially in the past, burnt cork used in minstrel makeup.

snake type   A more-than-usually seductive stripper. (Wilmeth LANGUAGE)

snap   In a 19th C oxy-calcium light, a miniature explosion which sometimes occurred in certain types of gas jets which mixed oxygen and hydrogen at the end of an open tube. (Rees GAS 56–57, fig. 34)

snap cue   In lighting, a signal to turn a light off or on, as by opening or closing a switch. (Bellman LIGHTING 213)

snap hook   A metal hook with a spring trigger that closes its throat. When attached to the end of a snatch line, it eliminates the need for rope knots. (Gillette/Gillette SCENERY 84)

snap line   1. A string rubbed with chalk, charcoal, or scenic pigment, then held against a surface and snapped to make a straight line for painting or carpentry. 2. A shortening of bow snap line.

snapper line   The concluding line in a (usually) comic play.

snatch block   A pulley block (such as a loft block) with a removable side so that it can be inserted into a rigging system without having to rethread all the lines. (Parker/Smith DESIGN)

snatch chain   A chain three feet long hanging from a counterweighted batten. It is used to fasten a flown object to the batten.

snatching   Hooking and unhooking a flown scenic unit during a scene shift.

snatch line   1. A rope used to tie a flown object to a counterweighted batten. See also: snatch chain. 2. A light rope attached to a piece of scenery to permit operators to swing the scenery while it is suspended. (Stern MANAGEMENT, Bellman SCENOGRAPHY)

sneak   1. To operate a dimmer so that the change in light intensity is not perceptible. Also called cheat or steal. To sneak in is to increase intensity; to sneak out is to decrease intensity. 2. In sound effects, to bring in (or fade out) music, sound, or voices slowly. 3. In acting, to change one's stage position unobtrusively.

sneak in the business   To improvise without warning fellow performers. (Berrey/Van den Bark SLANG 588)

sneak thief   A scene stealer.

snipe plant   A company that owns and services billboards locally. (Wilmeth LANGUAGE)

sniper   One who posts theatrical bills where they would not normally be seen, such as on trash barrels, shanties, etc. A sniper usually works surreptitiously and delights in posting a bill over a notice saying "Post No Bills." Hence, sniping. Also called fly posting. (Krows AMERICA 326)

snipe the town   To post bills around a town. (Wilmeth LANGUAGE)

snoot, snout   See: funnel.

snow   1. Free admission passes. 2. Theatregoers admitted on such passes.

snow bag   In Britain, the term for the old but still frequent method of producing stage snow: a shallow, horizontal, cylindrical bag open at the sides and hung on two parallel battens. When appropriately loaded, often with bits of confetti-sized white paper, movement of the battens causes the paper to fall through the many small holes in the lower part of the bag. Also called a snow box, snow cradle, or snow trough. (Pilbrow LIGHTING 171)

snowing   In a Punch and Judy show, said of a good collection of money from the audience. (Crothers PUPPETEER'S 85)

snow trough   See: snow bag.

snub line   A line tied to the operating line of an out-of-balance counterweight and secured to the locking rail to prevent the operating line from slipping. Hence, to snub, snub off. (Bellman SCENOGRAPHY)

snuff boy   Formerly, a lighting assistant who clipped the wicks of theatre candles. As a tallow or wax candle burned and its charred wick lengthened, the candle burned more rapidly and smokily. The snuff boy was trained to clip wicks during performance without extinguishing the candle. Though he was supposed to be invisible, a particularly skillful boy sometimes drew applause. (Rosenthal/Wertenbaker MAGIC 46)

snuffer   The tool used by snuff boys. Rosenthal/Wertenbaker have an illustration. (MAGIC 46)

soap, soap over   To cover a reflecting surface, such as a mirror, with soap, dulling spray, grease, thick size, or thin gauze to prevent a reflection into the audience.

sobhanika (Sanskrit)   A pantomimist or dancer-actor in ancient Indian theatre. Also called *saubhika*. See also: *granthika*. (Raghavan in Baumer/Brandon SANSKRIT 12–13)

sobojan (Mande tan)   In Guinea, a rod-and-string puppet theatre in which animal and human figures perform solo or in pairs to the music of drummers and a chorus of women. The performance developed as a court entertainment. (Adedeji glossary)

sobresaliente (Spanish)   In 18th C provincial Spain, an understudy. See also: *suplente*. (Falk "Census" 86)

sob stuff   1. An element in a play which appeals to the emotions. Also called HI, human interest, human interest stuff, and pash stuff. (Berrey/Van den Bark SLANG 581)   2. Sentimental acting. Hence, sob sister.

soccus (Latin Roman)   1. A soft shoe or slipper worn by actors in comedy. The Romans adopted the *soccus* from the Greeks. It was the comic counterpart of the *kothornos* of tragedy, and was, like a *kothornos*, quite colorful. Characteristically Roman comedies such as the *fabulae togatae* used sandals rather than the *soccus*. 2. By association, comedy. Also called a sock. See also: *embas*. (Allen ANTIQUITIES 141–142, Bieber HISTORY 154)

social comedy   A drawing-room comedy, dealing with the life of high society.

social drama   A play dealing with current social problems but not necessarily the solution of them. Examples are such plays of Henrik Ibsen and George Bernard Shaw as *An Enemy of the People* and *Major Barbara*. Also called a drama of ideas or problem play.

socialist realism   The official Soviet style for a theatrical (and other art) work in the 1930s—showing that which not only could happen in real life but would be useful to the socialist cause. (Orlovsky in Bradshaw SOVIET 57–58)

social theatre   Theatre which takes an active interest in the sociological problems of its day. (Gorelik NEW)

sociétaire (French)   In the 17th C and later, a shareholder of the Comédie Française. (Brockett HISTORY 270)

société joyeuse (French)   See: *compagnie joyeuse*.

society drama   A play dealing with upper-class society.

sociodrama   Dramatic activities and games that focus on interpersonal relations and social values. Usually held in classes in social studies. Also called role playing, role taking, or simulation.

sociodramatic play   See: spontaneous drama.

sock   1. A successful production. Also called socker, sockerino, socko. 2. Very successful. Hence, sock biz, sock show, etc. 3. The low slipper or shoe traditionally associated with comedy—as opposed to the high boot or buskin used in tragedy. (Chetwood HISTORY 37) See also: *soccus.*

sock and buskin   1. Nicknames for comedy and tragedy, deriving from the low shoes and high boots worn by classic performers. 2. The drama; the acting profession. (Bowman/Ball THEATRE)

socket   In the U.S., a support in which the base of a lamp can make electrical contact. Screw body, screw plug, and cord connector body are devices which can be screwed into a socket; they will accept a pronged connector such as an appliance cap. (Cornberg/Gebauer CREW 274, Wehlburg GLOSSARY)

socket adaptor   See: adaptor.

sock line   See: punch line.

socko   Said of a very good performance or show. See also: boffo, whammo.

sock puppet   A puppet made of a sock pulled over the operator's hand, forming the head, with the thumb providing lower-jaw mobility. Eyes, hair, and other features made of various materials are added. (Philpott DICTIONARY)

sock vaudeville   A fast-moving, riotous variety show. (Wilmeth LANGUAGE)

soffit   1. A hanging border. 2. A thickness piece added to the bottom edge of an architectural border, to give it apparent solidity.

Soffitten (German)   Strictly, flies. But the word is also used for 'borders,' and thence sometimes extended to 'borderlights;' the latter sense is presumably a shortening of *Soffittenlampen*, just as English borderlight is often simply borders. (Fuchs LIGHTING 210, Rae/Southern INTERNATIONAL 24)

soft   Of lighting, somewhat diffuse or dim, or both. Thus, a soft-edge(d) spotlight is one whose beam edge is diffuse rather than sharply defined. A soft shadow is one which does not stand out sharply. The contrast in both instances is with 'hard.' (Bowman/Ball THEATRE, Bellman SCENE)

soft-edge(d) spot   1. Especially in Britain, an alternate name for a Fresnel spotlight. (Bentham ART 65)   2. See: soft.

soft goods   Fabrics; theatrical goods not using lumber, such as drapery borders, curtains, or drops; a soft inner proscenium, soft portals, or soft scenery. Hence, soft show, soft stuff.

softlight   Primarily in Britain, a light source which is diffuse enough to produce relatively shadowless lighting. Typical is a striplight such as a borderlight. Sometimes spelled soft-light. Hence, soft lighting. (Bentham ART)

soft-shoe   A nearly noiseless style of tap or clog dancing, with no taps. Hence, soft-shoeing. (Berrey/Van den Bark SLANG 588)

soft sugar   A wealthy person who invests in a theatrical venture. (Berrey/Van den Bark SLANG 574)

soggetto (Italian)   See: scenario.

sogo (Korean) Literally: little drum. In *namsadang* and masked dance-plays, a hand-held drum played with a small wooden stick. (Kim "Namsadang" 11)

soka (Sanskrit) Literally: sorrow. One of the eight fundamental emotions (*sthayibhava*) expressed by actors in a Sanskrit play. Also spelled *shoka*. See also: *karuna*. (Gandhi in Baumer/Brandon SANSKRIT 120)

sola (Latin) A stage direction used by Elizabethan playwrights when a female character enters or is on stage alone.

sold out A performance for which all tickets have been sold or distributed. Also called a full house or (in Britain) house full.

solers Slippers. (Boucher FASHION)

solette See: *soulette*.

solid borne noise Noise carried through a structure.

soliloquy A speech, usually lengthy, delivered by a performer on stage alone, giving the audience the character's thoughts. Hence, soliloquize. See also: interior monologue.

solleret (French) A piece of armor for the foot. See also: *poulaine*. Also called a bear's paw or *scarpino* (Italian). (Boucher FASHION)

solo See: manual takeover.

solo button In stage lighting, a switch on a computer-assisted control board which kills all but the selected dimmer channel.

solus (Latin) A term used by Elizabethan playwrights when a male character enters or is on stage alone.

somation (Greek) The padding often worn by Greek actors under their costumes. The padded upper body of comic figures is characteristic. Plural: *somatia*. (Nicoll DEVELOPMENT 30; Bieber HISTORY 40–43, figs. 160–165)

somerset A frequent Elizabethan spelling of somersault; the spelling lasted into the 19th C. The term was used in connection with acrobats performing in theatres.

so mudang (Korean) Literally: little shaman. The character of a young female shaman in a puppet play (*kkoktu kaksi*). (Choe STUDY 18) In masked dance-plays, called *somu*. (Korean MASKS 6, 27)

sona (Vietnamese) See *ken*.

so na (Chinese) See: *suona*.

sonang-je (Korean) A seasonal, ritual performance of masked dance-drama at a village shrine ceremony, as distinct from court-derived masked plays (*sandaeguk*). Also called *purak-che*. (Yi "Mask" 36)

songadya (Marathi) Literally: player with many faces. A type of stock comic character in *tamasha*. (Mukherjee in Mukhopadhyay LESSER 55)

song-and-dance carnival A musical comedy.

song-and-dance man   1. An old vaudeville term for a performer who sang a few songs, told some jokes, danced (usually tap or soft shoe), and concluded with some complicated dance tricks. 2. From about 1920, a leading man in musical comedy. (Wilmeth LANGUAGE)

song-and-dance stage   The musical comedy stage.

songbird   In show business, a female vocalist.

song na (Thai)   A horizontal, double-faced drum, similar to but smaller than the *tapone*, that may be found in a *pi phat* musical ensemble in addition to its basic five instruments. Also called *poeng mang* when used for song accompaniment. (Duriyanga THAI 31)

song plugger   In the early 20th C, an entertainer who promoted songs by singing them in stores, ice cream parlors, cafes, producers' offices, etc. He was often a vaudevillian who used such songs in his act.

songster's avenue   See: Tin Pan Alley.

Song *zaju*, Sung *tsa chü* (Chinese)   Literally: Song dynasty variety drama. A type of entertainment including farce, song, dance, and acrobatics popular from the late 11th to the early 15th C; during and after the Jin (or Chin) dynasty (1115–1234), called *yuanben* or *yüan pen*. It developed in the Song (or Sung) dynasty (960–1279) from adjutant plays (*canjunxi*) and various other forms of song, dance, and entertainment. Roles in Song *zaju* performances included two major role categories (*hangdang*), male clown (*fujing*) and dominant male (*fumo*); two main stage functionaries, the actor-director (*moni*), and the play leader (*yinxi*); as well as supporting roles (e.g. *zhuanggu* and *zhuangdan*) and stock characters (e.g. *baoer* and *suan*). By the 12th C, performances had three main sections: an introduction (*yanduan* or *yen tuan*) which was either a complete short play or a one-man comic act; the *zaju* play itself; and a dispersal section (*sanduan* or *san tuan*) consisting of another comic act or a *zaban* play. Song *zaju* of southern China contributed to the development of southern drama (*nanxi*); those of northern China, the *yuanben*, were instrumental in the development of Yuan *zaju*, and continued to be performed as an independent form into the 15th C. See also: *zaju*. (Dolby HISTORY 18–33, Liu INTRODUCTION 166)

so odori (Japanese)   Literally: group dance. In early *kabuki*, a dance, usually a grand finale, performed by the entire company.

sopana (Malayalam)   Literally: stairs. In Kerala, south India, the style of singing heard in ritual and drama. (Jones/Jones KATHAKALI 77)

sophistai (Greek)   Literally: experts. Possibly a variety of early mime players. Compare *ethelontai*. (Nicoll MASKS 26–27)

soplador (Spanish)   Prompter. See also: *apuntador*.

sori (Korean)   Literally: voice. Song in *p'ansori*. (Korean KOREAN 27)

sori-pan (Korean)   Literally: voice stage. A stage for *p'ansori*.

sorquenie, soucanie   1. A 13th–19th C woman's tight-fitting tunic. 2. A coachman's smock. (Boucher FASHION)

sortie (French)   1. An exit speech. 2. The exit itself. 3. The receipt sometimes given spectators at intermissions to allow them back into the theatre.

sot (French)   A medieval fool or buffoon. Also called a *fou* or *fol*. (Mantzius HISTORY II 184)

sotie, sottie (French)   In medieval times, a short, comic curtain-raiser performed by *sots* (traditional fools). (Frank MEDIEVAL 243-245, Tydeman THEATRE)

sottana (Italian)   A 12th-13th C tunic underdress, sometimes made of colored bands of cloth, sometimes in plain fabric. Girls wore it as an outer tunic. (Boucher FASHION)

sotternyen (Flemish)   14th C crude satirical farces. Also called *boerden* or *kluchten*. (Gassner/Quinn ENCYCLOPEDIA 60)

sottie (French)   See: *sotie*.

soubresaut (French)   A sudden bound. In ballet, a springing jump, upward and forward, with the feet fully pointed. (Grant TECHNICAL)

soubrette   1. A lively and intelligent type of female role which has thrived since the 17th C. She is often a servant of not overly-conscious virtue, secure in the family constellation and often speaking her piece via lively repartee. The term is from the French. In the Italian *commedia dell'arte* she was the *servetta* or *fantesca*. 2. An actress who plays such a role. 3. A soprano who sings such a role in comic opera. 4. In burlesque, the head chorus girl. 5. In a Toby show, an actress who specialized in teenage parts. (Wilmeth LANGUAGE)

soubreveste   A waistcoat or vest worn with a short-sleeved gown à la Polonaise. (Boucher FASHION)

soucanie   See: sorquenie.

souffle   See: modesty.

souffler (French)   To prompt. Hence, *souffleur* (prompter).

soulette (French), **solette**   In the 18th C, a strap which held a patten to a boot.

soundboard   A board at the rear of a theatre gallery, designed to absorb and distribute sound from the stage. (Granville DICTIONARY)

sound booth   See: sound control.

sound console   The desk-like control board of a theatre's sound system. Also called a sound mixing table. In Britain: panatrope.

sound control, sound control booth   The place in a theatre, usually enclosed, where the control console for sound effects is located. The same place often serves also for lighting control and sometimes for stage management.

sound cue   A signal to begin a sound effect. Hence, sound-cue sheet—a list of sound effects cues.

sound effect   A stage effect, live or recorded, involving sound—such as a doorbell, door slam, music, rain, etc.

sound effects system   Theatrical equipment used to create such sounds as rain, thunder, traffic, etc., usually by means of recordings and speakers. More broadly, the term includes doorbells, offstage door slams, thunder sheets, wind machines, etc.

sound horn   Formerly, a large speaker suspended above the stage or fixed to a stage truck on the stage floor.

sounding board   In the 18th C, the ceiling of an auditorium. (PUBLIC ADVERTISER 30 September 1775)

sound lock   A vestibule at the entrance to a theatre seating area consisting of two sets of doors separated by a space—to minimize the transmission of unwanted sound (and often light).

sound mixing table   See: sound console.

sound operator, sound technician   The theatre worker who runs sound effects.

sound plot   A list of sound effects cues.

soured   Said of a town that lost a Toby show money: by extension, said of a company that failed. (Wilmeth LANGUAGE)

sous-sus (French)   Literally: under-over. In ballet, a term indicating that a dancer springs onto the *pointes*, drawing the legs and feet tightly together. Also found as *sus-sous* (over-under). (Grant TECHNICAL)

soutane (French)   See: cassock.

soutenu (French)   See: sustained.

Souvaroff boot   See: Hessian boot.

souvenir program   A usually lavish special program for a show, much more complete than the regular program, sold at a premium price.

souvenir promptbook   Especially in the past, a perfected copy of a promptbook of a famous production, made up as a record or a model for future reproduction. (Shattuck SHAKESPEAREAN 5)

space   In dance, the nature of volume which a movement's shape, symmetry, or asymmetry defines or creates. (Turner/Grauert/Zallman DANCE 29)

space grabber   A performer who courts publicity. (Berrey/Van den Bark SLANG 571)

space stage   An abstract stage setting, sometimes consisting only of platforms and steps, seen in a void. Through lighting, the focus is kept on the performers, so that the background is barely discernible.

spaghetti   Among stage lighting people in the U.S., a tangle of stage cable. See also: tripe.

Spanglish   See: *pocho*.

spare   An understudy.

sparge pipe   See: rain pipe.

Sparks   In British stage parlance, an electrician. (Baker THEATRECRAFT)

sparsiones (Latin Roman)   1. From about the 1st C AD, sprays sometimes used to cool an auditorium. 2. Sprays which both cooled and perfumed an auditorium by using scented water. The scent was presumably *crocus* (saffron), which is known to have been used for this purpose. (Bieber HISTORY 190, Sandys COMPANION 518–519)

spats, spatterdashes   See: gamashes.

spattering   A painting technique in which the brush is snapped to throw flecks of paint onto the surface of scenery. Used to provide texture.

speak at concert pitch   To increase vocal projection in order to be heard effectively by the audience.

speak-in   See: *Sprechstück*.

speaking opening   See: opening.

speaking part, speaking role   A role with dialogue.

spear bearer, spear carrier   A player of walk-on parts, such as soldiers. See also: super.

spec   A spectacle.

special   A spotlight used for a particular purpose, often to emphasize a particular area, person, or mood. Hence such terms as desk special, door special, etc. Occasionally called a special light. (Dean/Carra FUNDAMENTALS 375; Rubin/Watson LIGHTING 11, 35, 37)

special effect   See: effect.

special effects board   In Britain, an auxiliary switchboard. (Corry PLANNING, Rae/Southern INTERNATIONAL)

specialist lead   A performer who plays leading roles of a special kind, such as older men or older women.

special light   See: special.

special performance   A performance given at some time other than the normal early evening or matinee hours or on the normal day off.

specialty   1. A performer's line, or usual character type. 2. An act or turn, such as songs, dances, comic sketches, especially in vaudeville. Hence, specialty act, specialty artist, specialty actor, etc. (Bowman/Ball THEATRE)

specialty artist   A vaudeville performer who specializes in impersonations, juggling, or a musical instrument.

specialty number   In a musical comedy, a song that is not an integral part of the show. (Wilmeth LANGUAGE)

specific illumination, specific instrument, specific light, specific lighting   See: general ilumination.

spectacle, spec   1. A stage production that is visually dazzling. 2. The visual aspects of a stage production.

spectacle d'enseignement (French)   Drama seeking to show truth through emotion and feeling rather than persuasion and abstraction; a brainchild of the 19th C novelist Louis Lumet. (White "Lumet" 37)

spectacula (Latin Roman)   Literally: the places from which one sees. 1. Shows, spectacles. *Spectacula* included plays of all sorts as well as chariot races, gladiatorial combats, and other entertainments. In late uses, *spectacula theatri* may have distinguished dramatic forms, however attenuated, from other *spectacula*. 2. By the late 3rd C BC, the spectators' seats or stands at a show. Beare notes that *spectacula* is the most precise word for this meaning; the others (*subsellia, scamna*, and *sedilia*) being no more specific than 'seating places.' *Subsellia* is most frequently seen in theatre literature in English. 3. By extension, the seating area, the auditorium. (Beare ROMAN 242–247, 375; Chambers MEDIAEVAL I 2–21; Sandys COMPANION 518)

spectacular extravaganza   An early U.S. musical theatre piece, usually with lavish production numbers and exotic settings. (Wilmeth LANGUAGE)

spectacula theatri (Latin Roman)   See: *spectacula*.

spectatory   A pseudo-Latin term, now rare, for an auditorium or similar place for spectators, or for an audience in an auditorium. (Bowman/Ball THEATRE)

specular reflection   The technical name of mirror reflection, characteristic of reflectors in spotlights.

speculator   See: scalper.

speech   1. A unit of stage dialogue completed before another performer speaks. 2. In Britain, such a unit if more than six lines in length. (Granville DICTIONARY)

speech ascription   See: speech prefix.

speech cue   1. A verbal cue, whether for a line, action, or effect. 2. A cue of any kind (e.g., a line, a shot, a lightning flash) for a performer to speak.

speech prefix   In a play text, the character's name preceding a speech. Also called a speech ascription or speech title.

speech tag   The final words in a speech. See also: tag.

speech title   See: speech prefix.

speira (Greek)   Literally: something wrapped around. A coiffure marked by a coil around the head just above the brow. The sole source is Pollux, who used the word in describing one of the comic masks. (Nicoll MASKS 29, figs. 14, 15)

spelen van zinne (Dutch)   Literally: plays of the senses. 16th C dramatic productions which were didactic, allegorical, rhetorical, and critical of society. (Gassner/Quinn ENCYCLOPEDIA 194)

Spelvin   See: George Spelvin.

spencer   A 19th C small jacket usually darker than the dress it covered, worn indoors or out. Often sleeveless, but added sleeves were long and tight. (Barton COSTUME 374)

spherical aberration   The failure of a lens or mirror to bring light rays to a single focal point. In a stage spotlight, when the light starts at or near a focal point, spherical aberration may cause some of the rays to appear outside the main pool of light cast by the spotlight. (Lounsbury THEATRE, Wehlburg GLOSSARY)

spherical mirror reflector   See: spherical reflector.

spherical-parabolic reflector   In some older footlights and borderlights, a reflector which is spherical at the back and parabolic in front. The focal points of the sphere and the parabola are the same. Lounsbury has an illustration. (Lounsbury THEATRE 126–127)

spherical reflector   A highly polished segment of a hollow sphere, usually metal, in Fresnel and plano-convex spotlights. If the filament of a spotlight lamp is at the reflector's center of curvature, the reflected rays will return to the filament and thus add to the light produced by the spotlight. A spherical mirror reflector is of silvered glass. (Bellman SCENE, Philippi STAGECRAFT)

sphon (Thai)   See: *tapone.*

sphragis (Greek)   See: *katakeleusmos.*

spider   An occasional term for a multiple connector, used especially for the wiring for orchestra pit lights. (Lounsbury THEATRE)

Spiel (German)   Acting, playing, performing. Hence, *spielen* (to perform), *Spieler* (performer), *Spieloper* (comic opera), *Spielplan* (program, repertory), etc. See also: *Schauspiel.*

Spielflächenbeleuchtung (German)   Acting area lighting. (Fuchs LIGHTING 370)

Spielflächenbeleuchtungskörper (German)   An earlier name for the *Spielflächenleuchte. Körper* is literally 'body'; here it means 'housing.' See: *Spielflächenlaterne.* (Bentham ART 320)

Spielflächenlaterne (German)   Acting area lighting instrument: a fixture used to light the acting area. The plural adds *-n.* Also used for the same broad meaning is *Spielflächenleuchte (leuchte* means light). *Spielfläch* is 'acting area.' (Fuchs LIGHTING 209, 210–211)

Spielflächenleuchte (German)   See: *Spielflächenlaterne*.

Spielleute (German)   Medieval strolling players who acted, sang, performed acrobatics, etc. (Mantzius HISTORY II 179)

spike   To mark on the stage floor the position of furniture, properties, and scenery. By extension, the mark itself. Also called peg.

spikes   A row of vertical metal pointed irons at the front edge of a Restoration theatre's acting area, designed to prevent members of the audience from climbing onto the stage. In time these evolved into ornamental ironwork at each end of the footlights, but they were still called spikes. (Hogan LONDON lvi)

spill   Light which falls outside the area intended. But light may also spill onstage, as from a worklight in an offstage area. In the earlier decades of the 20th C, some British stage managers used spill in an opposite sense: the stage area in which the light of a lamp is effective; but it is not clear in what sense they were using 'lamp.' Also called light spill, spill light, stray light, and spilled light. The last two are used only occasionally. (Wehlburg GLOSSARY, Fay GLOSSARY)

spilled light, spill light   See: spill.

spill rings, spill shields   Concentric rings or strips of lightweight metal designed to keep light from falling outside the main beam thrown by a lighting instrument. Such beam protectors, also called baffles or louvers (British: louvres) are in front of the light source within the instrument housing. Some spill shields are not louvers, but a flat piece of metal which blocks off direct light which would fall outside the main beam. (Bax MANAGEMENT 186, Fuchs LIGHT-ING 206–207, Heffner et al MODERN 607, Wehlburg GLOSSARY)

spine   The acting teacher Richard Boleslavsky's term for the basic line or action of a play. The term is also used for the consistent line that connects all elements of a character throughout a play—the dominant trait or unconscious driving need motivating a character's actions. Also called a through line. See also: superobjective. (Clurman in Gassner/Barber PRODUCING 277, Bowman/Ball THEATRE)

spiral   In dance, a fall or turn incorporating a whirlpool image, with increasingly rapid pulls around an imaginary center. (Stodelle HUMPHREY 152)

spirit cotton   In 19th C Britain, an alcohol-soaked cotton ball. Such balls (not always cotton) were often used in lighting gas jets in theatres. Also called a spirit wad. (Rees GAS 124–125).

spirit gum   An adhesive in varnish-like liquid form used by a performer to attach beards, moustaches, hairpieces, latex appliances, etc. to the skin.

spirit gum part   A role requiring a false beard or moustache.

spirit wad   See: spirit cotton.

spirit wine   In 19th C Britain, alcohol. For a time, as at Covent Garden Theatre through mid-century, the gas jets in auditorium chandeliers were lighted by a wire-encased cotton-like ball which had been soaked in 'spirit of wine.' Since the flaming ball was at the end of a long bamboo pole, and hundreds of jets were lit by this means, it will not be surprising that the gas man was accompanied by a fireman. (Rees GAS 114–115)

splashing   In scene painting, allowing dye or very thin paint to dribble off the brush onto the surface to be painted.

splay   See: proscenium splay.

splicing clamp   A metal sleeve used to join two traveler-curtain tracks.

split autofader   See: split fader.

split fader, split-handle fader   In some lighting consoles, a two-handled fader which permits individual control of the up and down portions of a cross-fade. A split autofader (or split-handle autofader) will automatically operate such a cross-fade on a time schedule previously set. (Bellman LIGHTING 246, 253)

split-handle autofader, split-handle fader   See: split fader.

split plug   See: half-plug.

split-service footlights   In the late 19th C, footlights in two halves, split and fed at the center. (Penzel LIGHTING 97, fig. 27)

split stage   A stage setting showing two different locales.

split week   An engagement for part of the week at one theatre and the rest of the week at another. Hence, split weeker (a theatre which changes shows twice a week.) Also called split time. (Berrey/Van den Bark SLANG 577, 589)

sponge stippling, sponging   In painting, the use of a sponge, sliced in half to give it a flat surface; the sponge is then dipped in paint, squeezed, and pressed lightly against the surface to be painted.

spontaneous drama   Unguided or lightly guided experiences in drama growing out of a situation established by a trained person working with young children. Also called dramatic play, imaginative play, pretend play, sociodramatic play, and sometimes simply play.

spot   1. In vaudeville, the place of an act on the bill. To play the first spot is to open the show. (Wilmeth LANGUAGE) 2. To schedule an act—to 'spot' it. 3. A play within a play. 4. Limelight, prominence. 5. Backstage, the usual term for a spotlight.

spot bar, spotbar, spot batten   In Britain, a pipe hung from the grid, to which lighting instruments can be attached.

spot block, spot sheave   A loft block specially positioned on the gridiron, as for hanging a chandelier.

spot border(light)   Especially in the U.S in the past, a pipe or frame, usually in the position of the first borderlight, containing a number of individual spotlights. Sometimes called a cradle or spotlight cradle. (Bowman MODERN)

spot broker   A booking agent, especially for individual acts. (Berrey/Van den Bark SLANG 575)

spot frost   In stage lighting, a translucent color medium whose center has been treated, as with a drop of oil or vaseline. Such a frost produces a relatively bright center with a soft edge. A star frost is one with a jagged circle cut out of its center. (Bowman/Ball THEATRE)

spot lamp   Especially in the U.S., an occasional term for a lamp designed for use in a spotlight.

spot lantern   In Britain, a spotlight. (Corry LIGHTING)

spotlight   1. Primarily in the U.S., a lighting instrument capable of producing a strong, well-defined beam of light. A spotlight is often defined as a lighting instrument with a lens or lens system which produces a concentrated beam of light; indeed, the presence of a converging lens or lens system is characteristic of spotlights. The principal types are the Fresnel, the ellipsoidal reflector, the now less common plano-convex, and the baby. Spotlights are sometimes identified by their placement (balcony spot, beam spot) or their use (follow spot, sun spot). 'Spot' is the usual term among backstage people, but lens hood, an older term, occurs occasionally. Terms formerly used include lens, lens lamp, and lens light. All these are primarily or solely U.S.; for British usage, see lantern, focus lamp, and focussing lamp. Spot and spotlight are sometimes used as transitive verbs. 2. Limelight, prominence.

spotlight booth   An enclosure, usually above and behind the seating area, from which spotlights are directed. Sometimes reduced to 'booth.' (Bowman/Ball THEATRE)

spotlight chaser, spotlight hog, spotlight hound, spotlight hunter, spotlight louse, spotlight stealer   A scene stealer. A vain performer who seeks center stage. (Berrey/Van den Bark SLANG 573)

spotlight chorus   See: lighting by chorus.

spotlight cradle   Especially in the past, a term sometimes used for a horizontal pipe containing a spotlight, or for a small group of spotlights, often in a framework. Sometimes shortened to cradle. See also: spotlight strip.

spotlight dimmer   See: slide(r) dimmer.

spotlight strip   An occasional term for a group of baby spots hung from a batten, sometimes in a framework. See also: spotlight cradle. (McCandless "Glossary" 635)

spotlight tower   See: light tower.

spot line   A single line positioned directly over its working position, such as a line for a chandelier.

spotlit, spot-lit   Occasionally in Britain, picked out by one or two spotlights. (Rees GAS 196, 202)

spot man, spot woman   One who directs theatre patrons to the proper aisles. (Berrey/Van den Bark SLANG 576)

spot sheave   A pulley and block placed for a special purpose such as holding a chandelier or hanging a drop askew. Parker/Smith have an illustration. (Parker/Smith DESIGN 294–295)

spotted   Booked, engaged.

spotted on the program   To be given a place on a variety bill.

spotting   In ballet, a movement during a quick body rotation in which the dancer's head faces front until the last possible moment and is then quickly swiveled and turned forward again. (Kersley/Sinclair BALLET)

spotting attachment   In Britain, a lens added to a spotlight to narrow and sharpen its beam. (Bowman/Ball THEATRE)

spouting   1. A 19th C term for unnatural, overprecise speaking by a performer. (Nichols "Glover" 520) 2. Reciting, acting.

spouting club   An amateur dramatic club. The term goes back at least as far as 1756.

spray curtain   A suggested improvement on the light curtain used in some outdoor theatres: a water curtain on which colored lights are played. (Rubin/Watson LIGHTING 68)

sprayed lamp   A ready-made lamp, now rare, with relatively permanent sprayed color.

spread   See: beam spread.

spread a part   To play a role more broadly.

spreader   A brace between the long battens on a ceiling frame, corresponding to a toggle on a flat. (Bowman/Ball THEATRE)

spread lens   A fluted lens, designed to widen the beam of a lighting instrument. (Bowman/Ball THEATRE)

spread of spotlight   The area covered by the beam of a spotlight. (Lounsbury THEATRE, Wehlburg GLOSSARY)

spread reflection   A mixture of diffuse (non-directional) and specular (mirror-like) reflection, with much of the reflection mirror-like. Spread reflection is usual in borderlights and footlights. (Bellman LIGHTING 49–51)

Sprechstimme (German)   Speaking voice.

Sprechstück (German)   A "talk-happening" or "speak-in." A modern German theatre form of Peter Handke, exemplified by his *Offending the Audience*. (Arnold "German" 51)

spring foot iron   A spring hinge screwed to the bottom of a scenic unit, for securing it to the floor. The spring foot iron closes itself against the scenic unit when the unit is not in use. (Win "Terms")

spur leathers   Large four-leafed shapes worn at the boot instep to conceal spur fastenings. (Wilcox DICTIONARY)

square cut   An 18th C man's skirted coat worn in plays. (Fay GLOSSARY)

square law projector   See: Linnebach projector.

squeaker   See: swazzle.

squib   1. A last-minute insertion in a newspaper advertisement or program. 2. A sky rocket; a firework used in Renaissance theatres to simulate lightning. (Serlio in Nagler SOURCES 81)

SR   Stage right.

sralay (Khmer)   An oboe-like reed instrument used in a classical theatre musical ensemble (*pinpeat*). (Anonymous ROYAL 22, Brandon SOUTHEAST 127)

srimpi (Indonesian)   1. A Javanese female court dance. (Soedarsono DANCES 43)   2. A dancer of *srimpi*, until the 20th C exclusively girls of noble birth. (Holt ART 117–118)   3. A special *wayang* shadow puppet, jointed at the neck and waist, that imitates *srimpi* dance movements. Also spelled *serimpi*. (Long JAVANESE 121n)

srngara (Sanskrit)   Literally: love. In classical Indian dramatic theory, the erotic or romantic sentiment (*rasa*) which is aroused in the spectator by experiencing the enacted emotion (*sthayibhava*) of love (*rati*) in the play. The most important of the eight sentiments. It has three subdivisions; see also: *sambhoga*, *vipralambha*, *ayoga*. (Keith SANSKRIT 323)

srngari (Sanskrit)   A costumer and makeup man in a *raslila* troupe. (Hein MIRACLE 135)

SRO   Standing room only. But the term is sometimes misapplied to mean merely capacity business. (Lees "Lexicon" 57)

srutigara (Kannada)   A harmonium player in *yaksagana*. (Ashton/Christie YAKSAGANA 62)

ssu chou hsi (Chinese)   See: *sizhouxi*.

ssu ku (Chinese)   See: *sigu*.

ssu kung (Chinese)   See: *jiben gongfu*.

ssu p'ing, ssu p'ing ch'iang, ssu p'ing tiao (Chinese)   See: *sipingdiao*.

ST   See: Sink T.

Staatsaktion (German)   An 18th C production with spectacular scenery and a plot dealing with state affairs.

stab   The low trim for tying off on the bottom rail of a double pinrail. (Parker/Smith DESIGN)

staccato words   Words delivered by a performer in a short, clear-cut manner.

stack   See: scene pack.

stacking rack, stacking space   See: scene dock.

stacking rail   See: packing rail.

stadium   A balcony seating area in an auditorium. Hence, stadium seating.

stage   1. In Restoration theatres, the area extending from the front of the stage to the shutters. Also called the theatre. (Behn MARRIAGE 18, Visser in Hume LONDON 73)   2. A platform or floor for performances, and, by extension, the working spaces above, below, and alongside the stage proper.   3. A theatre building, the theatre, acted drama, the theatrical profession. The word is used in connection with things related to the theatre, such as stage carpenter, stage crew, stage fright, stage meal, stage sailor, etc.   4. To produce a show on stage; hence, stageable, unstageable. (Bowman/Ball THEATRE)

stage a comeback   To return to the stage.

stage action   1. The physical movement of a performer on the stage.   2. Such movements collectively.   3. Sometimes, collectively, such movements and the speaking of lines.   4. Pantomime. (Bowman/Ball THEATRE)

stage actor   One who performs live on stage, as opposed to a film or TV actor.

stage area   1. The performance space.   2. A specific portion of the performance space, such as down right or up center.   3. The entire stage space, including the wings.   4. See also: acting area.

stage art   1. The arts and skills involved in presenting theatrical productions.   2. Often, acting.

stage audience   Spectators watching a performance from onstage—as in an Elizabethan or 18th C theatre.

stage balance   A stage picture that is in balance.

stage board   Occasionally in Britain, a stage switchboard. (Corry PLANNING 62)

stage box   A semi-private, partly-enclosed seating area next to the stage. In the Restoration and later, some stage boxes were actually on the stage, beside the proscenium doors.

stage brace   A stick attached to the back of a flat and to the stage floor, to hold the flat upright. The standard manufactured brace is in two parts and adjustable in length. Typically, the brace is hooked to a brace cleat on the back of a flat, and secured to the stage floor by a stage screw. Usually called simply a brace. Also called an adjustable, extending, or extension brace.

stage building   See: *skene*.

stage business   Often shortened to business or, less often, bus.: a performer's gestures and movements, especially minor physical actions used to make a character more lifelike or add flavor to the general action of a performance, such as lighting a cigarette, reading a book, adjusting one's costume. (Bowman/Ball THEATRE)

stage cable, cable   Heavily insulated electrical conductors which are nevertheless flexible. Most stage cable contains two or three—now almost always three—separately insulated conductors encased in a thick outer insulation. The cable is designed to withstand the rough usage of the stage. The usual backstage term is cable; this shortening in particular also serves for borderlight cable. The British sometimes use stage flex or flexible cable. See also: packing-house cable. (Bellman SCENE, Bowman/Ball THEATRE, Fay GLOSSARY)

stage cable connector   See: stage connector.

stage call   1. An act call or warning, bringing performers to their positions for the beginning of an act. 2. A meeting of the cast and director on stage.

stage carpenter   Especially in the professional theatre, the person in charge of scenery in a play production. Also called a master carpenter.

stage carpet   A carpet covering all or most of the acting area of a stage.

stage ceiling   The ceiling of the stage house, above the gridiron.

stage center   The middle of the acting area. Abbreviation: C.

stage children   Child performers. In the 18th C and later they were called Lilliputians.

stage clamp   A metal device, like a C clamp, used to hold two flats tightly together.

stage cloth   See: floor cloth.

stage clothes   Clothes worn only onstage, as opposed to street clothes.

stage connector   A pin connector (q.v.). Sometimes called a stage cable connector, cable connector, or simply connector. (Fuchs LIGHTING 69, Bowman/Ball THEATRE)

stage convention   See: convention.

stage copy   As early as Elizabethan times, the prompter's copy.

stage costume   See: costume.

stage cover   See: heavens.

stagecraft   A general term covering skill in preparing a stage production, including the writing of the play. But the term usually concerns the technical aspects of theatre work—especially scene construction.

stage crew   The backstage production staff—those who handle scenery, properties, lighting, sound effects, etc. in rehearsal and performance.

stage cut   See: cut.

stage decoration   An old term for a stage setting—the décor or design.

stage depth   The distance from the setting line (or sometimes the house curtain) to the back wall of the stage. (Baker THEATRECRAFT)

stage designer   One who designs stage settings and, sometimes, stage lighting and costumes.

stage dip   1. See: lamp dip. 2. In Britain, a stage floor pocket. (Bowman/ Ball THEATRE, Rae/Southern INTERNATIONAL 34)

stage direction   1. A script's instructions to performers or others, often simple exits and entrances but sometimes extensive character descriptions or details of stage business, along with indications of other production elements, such as scenery, lighting, and properties.   2. The work of a director in preparing a play for performance. Hence, stage directing. (Bowman/Ball THEATRE)

stage director, director   1. In the U.S., the person responsible for the interpretation of a play text and the artistic unity of a stage production. In the non-professional theatre the stage director also coaches the performers in movements, gestures, and lines.   2. Formerly, a stage manager—the person who ran performances from backstage.   3. In Britain until some years after World War II, a stage manager; at that time a British producer was the equivalent of a U.S. director.

stage door   1. An exterior door for theatre personnel, usually at the back or side of a theatre, leading backstage. The door sometimes serves also as a loading door, at least for small properties and costumes, but a loading door for scenery is much larger.   2. A door used on the stage as part of the stage setting.   3. In Restoration theatres and later, a proscenium door.

stage-door Johnny   An old term for an admirer of female performers who sent a woman flirtatious notes and waited at the stage door, hoping for a date. Sometimes shortened to John or Johnny. (Sobel NEW)

stage doorkeeper   Especially in the professional theatre, an employee responsible for security at the stage door. He usually handles the theatre telephone switchboard and the company mail. Also called a stage doorman.

stage doorman   A stage door attendant. In Britain, a hall keeper.

staged reading   See: readers theatre.

stage dressing room   See: quick-change room.

stage duchess   An actress with airs.

stage effect, effect   1. Something visual or aural, such as lightning or thunder, created by a manual, mechanical, electrical, or chemical device.   2. Sometimes, a striking bit of acting. (Bowman/Ball THEATRE)

stage electrical circuit   A formal phrase for stage circuit, usually called simply circuit.

stage electrician   The head of the electrical crew.

stage elevator   See: elevator stage.

stage English   An unaffected and unlocalized English pronunciation resembling the educated English of southern England; considered standard stage pronunciation. Also called stage speech or theatrical speech. (Bowman/Ball THEATRE)

stage entrance   1. A door leading to the stage from another part of the theatre, usually not directly from the outside of the building. See also: stage door.   2. Any access to the acting area to be used by performers, and consequently, a stage exit as well.

stage exit   See: stage entrance.

stage fall   A performer's drop or tumble to the stage floor in a way which avoids injury. (Bowman/Ball THEATRE)

stage flex   See: flex.

stage flood   In Britain, an occasional term for a floodlight. (Corry PLANNING 99)

stage floor   The surface of the stage, normally made of a soft wood. The surface is usually the floor on which performers work, but many designers create an acting surface on top of the stage floor, and some theatres have wagon stages which are stage floors riding on the basic stage floor.

stage floor pocket   See: floor pocket.

stage fright   The nervousness often experienced by performers before, sometimes during, a stage appearance. While common among performers making a first appearance in public, the phenomenon is frequent even among performers of long experience.

stage grip   A stagehand.

stage grouping   The picture created by a director through the arrangement of performers on the stage.

stagehand   One who handles scenery and properties on the stage floor. Also called a grip, grip hand, stage grip. Stagehand is also used generally to encompass all backstage workers in a theatre.

stage history   The record over the years of productions of a particular play. See also: theatre history.

stage hog   A scene stealer.

stage house   1. The part of a theatre building housing the stage and the space above it.   2. An obsolete term for a theatre.

stage imagery   The portrayal of the ideas in a play through the acting, scenery, lighting, etc.

stage intake   See: intake.

stage jubilee   A celebration of a performer's 50th year on stage.

stagekeeper, stage keeper   1. In Elizabethan times, a custodian charged with sweeping the stage. Also called a theatrekeeper.   2. In Restoration times, a scenekeeper, chiefly responsible for shifting scenery. (Chambers ELIZABETHAN II 541, Wilson ''Players' '' 28)

stage left   The left side of a proscenium stage, from the performer's point of view. Abbreviation: SL.

stage level   Usually, the distance from the stage floor to the auditorium floor, in modern theatres typically about three feet.

stage lighting computer   See: computer-assisted lighting system.

stage loft   See: flies.

stage machinery   Short form: machinery. The various mechanical devices used on, below, or above the stage, such as the counterweight system, elevators, and wagon stages. Hence, in early days, stage machinist. The machinist was responsible for the scene shifting, which was often done mechanically, and for flying devices and special effects. (Bowman/Ball THEATRE)

stage main   See: main.

stage makeup   Makeup used onstage, as opposed to the lighter street makeup.

stage manager   1. The director's deputy during the run of a play, in charge of performances from backstage. Before the opening of a play, the stage manager often serves as a coordinator between the director and the performers and technical and business crews. Sometimes abbreviated SM. Hence, stage management.   2. See: acting manager.

stage manager's desk   A desk backstage from which a stage manager can run a performance.

stage money   Fake money used on stage.

stage mother   A woman whose child is a performer and who, often annoyingly, lingers backstage.

stage movement, movement   The moves of performers about the stage.

stage name   A name taken by a performer for professional purposes. (Bowman/Ball THEATRE)

stage nursery   A place, usually a small theatre without elaborate equipment, used for the training of young actors. The term dates from the later 17th C.

stage peg   See: stage peg and plug, stage screw.

stage peg and plug   A bolt-threaded peg which fits into an inside-threaded plug. (Parker/Smith DESIGN)

stage picture   What is seen by the audience at any given moment in a stage performance—the position of the performers as well as the scenery, properties, lighting, etc.

stage pilots, pilots   In Britain, dim lighting used in scene shifts and for moving about backstage. In the U.S., running or safety lights.

stage play   A play intended for stage production (as opposed to radio, film, TV, etc.).

stage plug   An electrical connector consisting of a relatively large fiber block with a heavy copper strip on one side and, on the other side, a similar strip with a spring. These were formerly much used in stage floor pockets and in some switchboards but are now obsolete and illegal, because the pockets into which they fit were too large, open, and dangerous. Also called a floor plug, sometimes plug. (Wehlburg GLOSSARY)

stage pocket   Short form: pocket. A metal box set into the stage floor (usually) outside the acting area, containing receptacles into which stage cables can be plugged to connect lighting instruments to the lighting control system. Sometimes called an outlet box. In Britain: dip. Also called a floor pocket, to distinguish it from a wall pocket, which is set into the stage wall. Pockets in mid-air, on lines coming from the gridiron: drop boxes, or hanging or drop pockets. (Bowman/Ball THEATRE)

stage position, position   The place onstage where a performer stands at any given moment in a performance or rehearsal. For the designations of the parts of a stage, see: acting area. (Bowman/Ball THEATRE)

stage presence   A performer's bearing; the ability to take stage and hold an audience.

stage prop, stage property   See: prop.

stager   An old term for a performer.

stage regulator   See: gas table.

stage rehearsal   A rehearsal held on stage rather than in a rehearsal room or other area. (Bowman/Ball THEATRE)

stage right   1. The right side of a proscenium stage, from the performer's point of view. Abbreviation: SR. 2. In the plural, permission to perform a work under copyright.

stage roof   The roof of the stage house, over the gridiron.

stage screw   A large, winged screw used to secure stage braces, foot irons, etc. to the stage floor. Also called a stage peg. See also: stage peg and plug.

stage seat   A seat onstage for a spectator.

stage setting   The scenery for a production or a portion of a production.

stage society   In Britain, a private theatre club that produces plays. Before the censorship rules were relaxed in the 20th C, many plays that could not be presented in the commercial theatres were done by stage societies.

stage space   1. The cubic volume of the stage area.   2. The area of the stage floor. (Gorelik NEW)

stage spectators   In Renaissance and Baroque theatres, audience members seated on the stage, especially in England and France. Garrick in England and Voltaire in France banished stage spectators in the 18th C.

stage speech   See: stage English.

stage staff   Theatre workers, especially those working backstage.

stage stay   See: stay.

stage step   A portable step unit, often called a one-step, two-step, etc. In Britain, tread.

stage stool   A stool onstage for a spectator.

stage stride   See: stage walk.

stagestruck   Addicted to the theatre. The term is used of young performers or others fascinated by the apparent glamour of theatre life.

stage technician   A theatre worker, such as a carpenter, electrician, etc. involved in backstage duties.

stage technique   1. Stagecraft, including the various elements of technical theatre.   2. Acting skill. (Bowman/Ball THEATRE)

stage trap   See: trap.

stage trick   1. A means for effecting some illusion, often to surprise the audience, such as a sudden appearance through a trap. See also: *truc* (French). (Bowman/Ball THEATRE) 2. The illusion created.

stage turn   See: open turn.

stage upholstery   An old term for furnishings used in a stage setting. (Bowman/Ball THEATRE)

stage version   1. An acting edition of a play, based on the production book.   2. A play derived from a novel or some other non-dramatic form.

stage wagon   See: scenery wagon.

stage wait   1. An unintended delay during a performance.   2. Sometimes, an inferior performance.

stage walk, stage stride   A performer's steps on stage that give the impression of a long walk. (Bowman/Ball THEATRE)

stage wandering   A performer's shift of his position on stage for no good reason.

stage weight   See: counterweight.

stage whisper   A quietly spoken line that can be heard throughout the auditorium. In some instances, the line is not supposed to be heard by certain characters onstage. (Baker THEATRECRAFT)

stage width   The distance between the side walls of a stage.

stagey   Theatrical, in an unflattering sense. (Bowman/Ball THEATRE)

staggered seating   An arrangement of auditorium seats that, as seen from above, avoids placing one seat directly behind another.

stag mag   1. A stage manager.   2. To stage manage.

staircase cut   An opening in the stage floor (plugged when not in use) for a staircase descending to the substage.

stakeman, stakesman   A theatrical sponsor or backer.

stall   1. A *mansion* (French) or locale in a medieval production. (Mantzius HISTORY II 61)   2. A seat in a theatre in Britain, usually with arm rests, on the main auditorium floor between the orchestra pit and the unreserved seating area at the back of the auditorium, called the pit. See also: balcony stall, dress stall, pit stall.   3. In the plural in Britain, the occupants of such seats. Hence, that seating area. See also: orchestra stalls.   4. In acting, to spar for time by improvising during an unforeseen delay in the stage action. (Bowman/Ball THEATRE, Cartmell HANDBOOK)

stall-pots   In Britain, those sitting in the stalls in a theatre. (Partridge TODAY 229)

stalls circle bar   In Britain, a refreshment room serving spectators with seats in the stalls or circle. The room is sometimes used as a rehearsal space.

stamboel (Indonesian)   See: *stambul*.

stambouline   A Turkish sultan's lavish ensemble: a satin, velvet, or brocade robe with gold and jeweled buttons down its center front, a sleeveless robe (doliman) over it, and a flower-pot hat with a white silk turban draped around it. (Wilcox DICTIONARY)

stambul (Indonesian)   A form of operetta influenced by Malaysian *bangsawan* and performed in large cities by commercial troupes in the late 19th and early 20th C. Also spelled *stamboel*. (Peacock RITES 57)

stamp   In Restoration theatres, a signal for a scene change or special effect: "Stamps, Sir Arthur and Bramble are let down under the Stage. . . ." (Leanerd RAMBLING 43)

stand   1. A poster (or a place for a poster) advertising a theatrical event. The size of the poster is indicated by the number of 20'' x 30'' (double crown) sheets used. Hence, a six-sheet stand, a 24-sheet stand.   2. An engagement by a theatrical troupe, such as a one-night stand, a two-night stand, a two-week stand.   3. The theatre in which the stand takes place.   4. See: light stand.   5. A dressmaker's dummy. (Bowman/Ball THEATRE)

standard   1. See: light stand. 2. In Britain, a lighting instrument on a pipe stand. This use goes back at least to the 19th C. (Bowman/Ball THEATRE, Fay GLOSSARY)

standard act   A vaudeville act familiar to managers and bookers. (Smith VAUDEVILLIANS)

standard base   The usual household lamp base.

standard drama   Said of plays of merit and popularity that have held the stage.

standard flood   In Britain, a floodlight on a pipe stand. (Rae/Southern INTERNATIONAL)

standard lamp   In Britain, a stage lighting instrument on a pipe stand. (Bowman/Ball THEATRE 355)

standard rep   A Toby show term for the larger and better Toby companies. (Wilmeth LANGUAGE)

stand by   1. An order to be ready.   2. As one word, an understudy.   3. An established performer engaged to be on call in case a replacement for a principal performer is needed.

stand-by table   Especially in Britain, a table in the wings where performers pick up their hand properties. (Baker THEATRECRAFT)

standee, stander   A theatregoer who has a ticket for standing room only. See also: groundling.

stander-upper   1. A performance that draws more than a seated capacity audience.   2. A popular performer. (Berrey/Van den Bark SLANG 580)

standing floodlight   Especially in the U.S., a floodlight on a pipe stand. (Bowman/Ball THEATRE)

standing light box   See: perspective lantern.

standing play   A medieval term, apparently for a play using multiple simultaneous staging rather than pageant wagons. (Chambers MEDIAEVAL II 134, 379)

standing room, standing room section   Space, usually at the back of an auditorium, for standing spectators. Hence, standees.

standing room only   Abbreviation: SRO. A notice at a theatre that all seats are taken but that one may buy a ticket to stand and watch the show—usually at the back of the orchestra or stalls seating section.

standings   Viewing places at medieval performances, such as the pavement or roofs. (Wickham EARLY I 61)

standing scene   Especially in the 19th C, a scenic unit separate from the wings, borders, and backscene, representing something (such as a tree or arch) detached from the rest of the design.

standing set   A stage setting that remains in place during the run of a show.

standout part, standout role   A leading role.

Stanislavsky System   A set of techniques and theories about acting which promote a natural style and inner truth, as opposed to conventional theatricality. Sometimes called the Stanislavsky Method or, especially in the U.S., simply the Method.

stanza   1. An act.   2. A week's engagement.

star   1. A performer prominent in the theatrical world whose name takes priority in the billing. The term was used as early as 1795 in Britain by the manager Tate Wilkinson, who did not open his summer season "unless with a star . . . unless a Siddonian comet appeared. . . ." The term seems at first to have been used for a luminary out of his or her normal sphere, making a guest appearance, usually in a provincial theatre. Hence, the star system. In time the term was applied to stellar performers at their home theatres. (Wilkinson WANDERING I 84) Hence, star billing, stardom, star dressing room, star room, star entrance, star part, star play, starring, star turn. 2. To cast a performer in a leading role—to star him or her. 3. A triangular segment, one of six forming the cover of a star trap. (Bowman/Ball THEATRE, Baker THEATRECRAFT)

star billing   Advertising that gives special attention to the leading performer or act, through placement on the bill or size of type or both. Also called top billing or top of the bill.

star cloth   A hanging drop pierced with holes, through which small lights shine to produce a star effect. (Bowman/Ball THEATRE)

star complex   An affectation of superiority in an ordinary or inferior performer.

star dressing room, star room   A private dressing room for a leading performer, usually identified by a star on the door.

star entrance   The first appearance of the leading performer, usually staged to give it special focus.

star frost   See: spot frost.

star in a night   Said of a performer who achieves fame through an outstanding first-night performance.

star letters   The large type on an advertisement, used for the name of the leading performer. See also: star billing.

star maker   A 19th and 20th C producer or manager, such as Augustin Daly, who developed star performers. (Brockett HISTORY 523)

star package   See: package.

star part, star role   A role given to (sometimes written for) a leading performer.

star play   A play written to emphasize the star performer at the expense of the rest of the cast. (Hennequin PLAYWRITING 74)

star quality   The stage presence or magnetism which sets an actor or actress above the run-of-the-mill performer. (Marsh DOLPHIN 75)

star queller   A performer whose bad acting worries the leading performer.

starring vehicle   1. A play rich in acting opportunities for a leading performer. Also called a star play or star vehicle. 2. A play successful only because it features a star performer. (Bowman/Ball THEATRE)

star role   See: star part.

star room   A star's dressing room.

stars and sticks   Leading performers and their supporting casts. (Hudson ENGLISH 19)

star system   1. The practice of attracting an audience by placing great emphasis on the leading performer. Sometimes called the starring system. 2. Especially in opera and summer theatres, a company organization where performers hired for the season play secondary parts, with principal roles taken by leading performers brought in for each production. (Bowman/Ball THEATRE, Cameron/Gillespie ENJOYMENT)

start   In acting, a sudden, surprised, or frightened movement ending in a frozen position, as when Hamlet first sees the Ghost. (Hogan LONDON cxiv)

start cue   In a gradual change in lighting, the cue on which the board operator begins the change. The change must be completed on the 'stop cue.' (Bellman LIGHTING 369–370)

starter   See: catch line.

star theatre   A theatre using the star system.

star the road, star the stands, star the sticks   To tour as a star performer. (Berrey/Van den Bark SLANG 590)

star trap   A trap in the stage floor, usually circular, with a star-shaped lid consisting of six wooden triangles hinged to the circumference. A performer standing on a counterweighted platform or elevator can thus appear suddenly. When one steps away from the trap, the triangles fall and the floor appears to be solid. See also: bristle trap, vampire trap. (Bowman/Ball THEATRE)

startups   13th C peasant high shoes. Also called bagging shoes or peros. (Chalmers CLOTHES 104)

star turn   A music hall act by a favorite comedian.

starvation jaunt   A series of one-night engagements with pay on a percentage basis. (Berrey/Van den Bark SLANG 590)

stasimon (Greek)   A choral ode sung between dramatic episodes in ancient tragedies and, later, comedies. In the 6th C BC, the odes were the important part of the play; the actors' dialogues (episodes, *epeisodia*) between them were considered interruptions, a view which was later reversed. It was characteristic of a *stasimon* that any necessary amount of time might be conceived as passing during its recital. The old view that the term implied that the chorus was stationary during the *stasimon* has been discarded: the source, *stasis* (station), means to modern scholars that the chorus had arrived at its 'station' in the orchestra. Plural *stasima*. Occasionally seen are *chorikon* (plural *chorika*) and *stasimum*. Also called a choral ode or ode. U.S. English has long used stasimon and stasima; the plural stasimons is relatively recent. (Pickard-Cambridge FESTIVALS 251–252, 256; Pickard-Cambridge DITHYRAMB 11–12; Allen ANTIQUITIES 119–120; Arnott ANCIENT 35; Nicoll DEVELOPMENT 25)

state   In the Renaissance and later, a dais or platform. In a court theatre auditorium it was used as a place for the king (or ranking nobleman) to sit and watch the performance; on stage it was similarly used for royal characters in court scenes.

state theatre   A theatre subsidized by the government.

static play   1. A play with no marked change in characters or situation. 2. A play with little stage movement. (Bowman/Ball THEATRE)

station   In medieval productions: 1. A place at which the pageant wagons of a processional play stopped for a performance. 2. A *mansion* (French) or locale. (Chambers MEDIAEVAL II 133, 138; Davidson STUDIES 73)

stationary setting   A permanent stage setting.

stationery   Complimentary tickets.

statuesqueness   The Russian director Vsevelod Meyerhold's idea of the pictorial appeal of a performer on stage. (Bakshy RUSSIAN 64)

status cap   See: city flat cap.

stay   1. Abbreviation for stage stay, or stay rod—a stage brace used to hold a scenic unit in position. 2. A wooden wedge used to make a flat secure on a stage having an uneven floor. 3. A piece of wood or metal used to keep flats firm when they are cleated together. 4. In costumes, a piece of boning or plastic used to keep the bodice of a costume in place.

stay in character   In acting, to remain in a role and not resume one's own personality, as when the audience interrupts the action with laughter. (Bowman/Ball THEATRE)

steal   1. To attract the audience's attention and destroy the proper focus. Hence, steal the limelight, steal a scene. 2. To change position on stage without drawing the attention of the audience. 3. To fake; to use an imitation of a real object on stage. 4. To cheat, as when a performer turns slightly toward the audience in order to be better seen and heard, while appearing to be in profile. 5. In lighting, to alter brightness so slowly that the change is not perceived by the audience. 6. See: sneak.

steal a bow   To take an undeserved bow or encore. See also: pinch a call.

stealer   A scene stealer.

stealing   A term used by Elizabethan playwrights to indicate a furtive entrance, exit, or movement.

steal the show   To attract more attention than the star or other performers. Also called: steal thunder.

steal the spot, steal the spotlight   To seek the center of attention.

steal thunder   1. To get more applause in a secondary part than a leading performer, to steal the show. 2. To appropriate an effect achieved by another performer.

steam barrel   See: steam pipe.

steam curtain   Especially in outdoor theatres, a wall of steam serving in place of a curtain during scene changes. A perforated pipe is laid at the front of the stage to create the effect. See also: water curtain.

steam pipe   A perforated pipe through which steam can be forced to simulate fog or mist. In Britain, steam barrel.

Stecherkupplungen (German)   Connectors. Sometimes called *Kupplung* (singular). (Fuchs LIGHTING 367, Rae/Southern INTERNATIONAL 30)

Steckdose (German)   See: *Anschlussdose*.

Stecker (German)   Electrical plug. (Fuchs LIGHTING 367, Rae/Southern INTERNATIONAL 60)

steeple headdress   See: hennin.

steerer   One who directs to a ticket speculator theatregoers who have been unable to get tickets at the box office. (Wilmeth LANGUAGE)

Steigerung (German)   Growing tension in the second act of a play. (Sobel NEW)

stella (Latin)   A term applied to a medieval play dealing with the Nativity. (Tydeman THEATRE)

stellar attraction   A featured entertainer or act.

stellardom   Stardom.

stellar role   A leading part.

(the) Stem   Broadway. Also called the Main Stem.

stencil   A cut-out piece of cardboard, once used like a slide in a projection machine to make such effects as lightning, the moon, etc.

stenochoreography   See: movement notation.

step   1. In lighting, the change between adjacent elements, such as the contact points on a resistance or autotransformer dimmer. As applied to a memory lighting system, a step becomes the smallest unit into which a dimmer's action can be broken. Thus, a dimmer channel with 100 steps can put into memory any of 100 brightness settings. Such capacities are stated as stops per channel. 2. The space between the adjacent elements. (McCandless SYLLABUS 55, Bellman LIGHTING 242–243)

step dance   Especially in vaudeville, a type of dance, such as a clog or tap dance. (Wilmeth LANGUAGE)

step lens, stepped lens   1. A plano-convex lens thinned by reducing the plane side to a series of steps. Lounsbury has an illustration. (Lounsbury THEATRE, Bellman LIGHTING 84) 2. Sometimes, a Fresnel lens. (Philippi STAGECRAFT, Bentham ART 312) 3. Any lens with ridges. (Bowman/Ball THEATRE)

step lights   See: aisle and step lights.

step on a laugh   To speak a line before the audience has had enough time to laugh at the previous line, thus squelching the laughter.

step on a line   To speak one's line before another performer has finished his. See also: cue bite, step on a laugh, clip a cue.

stepped lens   See: step lens.

stepper   A dancer. Hence, stepping.

stepping sister, stepsister   A chorus girl.

steps per channel   See: step.

step unit   A set of stairs (one-step, two-step, etc.), movable and built to stand alone. Used in stage settings, especially backstage as access steps.

stereopticon   A lens projector for slides. A pair is sometimes used for dissolving one image into another. (Bowman MODERN, Philippi STAGECRAFT)

stet finale   A final scene that goes back to the opening scene. (Berrey/Van den Bark SLANG 582)

sthapaka (Sanskrit)   A member of an Indian theatre troupe in ancient times, variously described as an assistant to a troupe manager (*sutradhara*), a performer, a person who introduces the play, or a puppeteer. (Keith SANSKRIT 52, 126, 265, 340; Hein MIRACLE 248)

sthapana (Sanskrit)   An early form of prologue (*prastavana*) used in the classical Indian dramas written by Bhasa about 350 AD. (Keith SANSKRIT 111)

sthayibhava (Sanskrit)   See: *bhava*.

stichomythia (Greek)   Rapid-fire dialogue in which each of two speakers replies to the other in a single line, often using some of his opponent's words in reversing the opponent's meaning. Archer's phrase, cut-and-thrust dialogue, suggests the tone and technique of a stichomythic exchange. Also called cat-and-mouse or cut-and-parry dialogue, or passage at arms. Also found, especially in U.S. English, stichomythia and stichomythy. See also: crossfire. (Pickard-Cambridge FESTIVALS 158–160, Archer PLAY-MAKING 33)

stick   1. A supporting actor. See also: stars and sticks. 2. In acting, to pause because of a forgotten line or piece of business.

stick puppet   See: rod puppet.

(the) sticks   See: country.

stick town   A provincial town.

Stiefel (German)   See: *stivale*.

stiffener   A batten secured to the back of scenery to strengthen it.

stile   One of the long vertical side members in the frame of a flat.

still date   A period when a performer has no engagement.

still music   Background mood music in the Elizabethan theatre. (Bowman/Ball THEATRE)

stippling   In painting, touching the surface to be painted with the relatively dry bristles of a brush held at right angles to the surface. By extension, a similar treatment of a surface, using a sponge.

stivale (Italian)   A 12th–14th C high, light summer boot, black or red, in a soft fabric. Also called a *Stiefel* (German) or *estival* (French). (Boucher FASHION)

stock   1. Stock company; a troupe with its own theatre and a series of plays it can present. Hence, stock actor, stock rights, summer stock. 2. A company or performer's repertory. Hence, stock plays, stock roles. 3. Typical or frequently recurring. Hence, stock character, stock costumes, stock drama, stock gag, stock line, stock setting, stock situation. (Bowman/Ball THEATRE) 4. See: cravat. 5. A stocking. The wider, upper portion is called the upper stock. The lower portion is called the netherstock. If the term is not qualified, it is understood to mean the lower or netherstock.

stock burlesque   A burlesque company that does not travel but is based at a specific theatre. (Wilmeth LANGUAGE)

stock company   See: stock.

stock debt   In Britain in the 18th C, the amount owed by a theatre management. (Bowman/Ball THEATRE)

stock dramatist   In Britain in the 19th C, a house playwright—a writer regularly hired by a theatre manager to furnish plays to order. (Bowman/Ball THEATRE)

stock play   A standard play kept in a company's repertoire, usually to serve as a substitute when a scheduled play cannot be performed.

stock response   The predictable reaction of an uncritical reader or playgoer to the conventional appeal of a stereotyped character, situation, or emotion. (Brooks/Heilman UNDERSTANDING)

stock role   Especially in old plays, a standard character, such as the handsome hero, the villain, the fair damsel, the confidante, the clever servant. Performers specializing in such stereotyped characters are often classified as leading man, leading woman, juvenile, ingenue, soubrette, etc.

stock setting   A standard stage setting, usable for a variety of plays—such as a drawing room, a garden, a street, etc.

stock star system   Especially in the 19th C U.S., a theatrical arrangement centering on prominent performers who traveled from one town to another, appearing with resident companies.

stock theatre   Especially in the past, a playhouse with a regular company, which changed its shows frequently.

stomp   See: artist's stump.

stood 'em up   Pleased the audience.

stooge   1. A subordinate performer or foil who feeds lines to a comedian. 2. A performer placed in the audience to heckle an on-stage comedian. Also called a straight man. (Josefsberg BENNY 97)

stool   1. A small seat which in Britain a theatre patron may mark with his or her name and put in a queue for the pit or gallery. The patron may then leave and return without losing the place in line. Also called a queue stool. (Granville DICTIONARY)   2. A theatre seat without arms or back, as on Elizabethan stages.

stool holder   In the 18th C and earlier, a spectator occupying a stage seat or stool.

stop   1. In 18th C acting, a pause. (Stone/Kahrl GARRICK 543)   2. See: knuckle buster.

stop block   See: stop cleat.

stop chain   A chain attached to the gridiron and to the batten of a flown curtain—especially the asbestos safety curtain—to stop the curtain when its lower edge reaches the floor.

stop clause   In U.S. booking arrangements, a provision in a theatre owner's contract with a producer by which a show can be given notice if its receipts fall below a stated sum. (Bowman/Ball THEATRE, Gibson SEASAW 26)

stop cleat   A metal plate fastened to the back of a flat, protruding over the edge, or to doors and hinged windows. Used to insure good joins and to prevent hinged units from opening in the wrong direction. Also called a flat cleat. A similar wooden piece is called a stop block. Lounsbury has an illustration. (Lounsbury THEATRE 54)

stop cue   See: start cue.

stop gap   A revival of an old play, put on between the end of one production and the opening of another, to keep the theatre open.

stopper   An insert placed in the neck of a hand puppet to keep the operator's fingers from going too far into the puppet's head. (Philpott DICTIONARY)

stopper line   A rope used to secure a counterweight operating line to the locking rail.

stop the show, stop the show cold   To so delight an audience that the performance stops briefly for laughter or applause or both.

storefront theatre   Theatre performed in a store with a glass window, so that the play has two audiences: the one inside the store, which has paid, and the one which has gathered to look in from the sidewalk. The term has been used primarily of the Squat Theatre, which has performed in Hungary, Rotterdam, and New York.

store show   Before WW I, a cheap version of a dime museum, one set up only for a few months, weeks, or even days. (Wilmeth LANGUAGE) *storia* (Italian)   A medieval mystery play. (Mantzius HISTORY II 2)

storm and stress   See: *Sturm und Drang*.

storm troops   1. See: agit brigades. 2. See: *Agit-truppe*.

story   1. The narrative element in a play from which the plot develops. 2. Sometimes, the plot. (Bowman/Ball THEATRE)

story dramatization   A form of creative drama in which children improvise a playlet from a story, often developing one part of the story at a time. Also called playmaking. See also: creative drama. (Viola "Children" 140)

story glove   A glove with adhesive fingers to which various puppet characters can be attached. The fingers can also be colored to represent trees, flowers, snow, water, etc. (Hunt/Renfro PUPPETRY 71)

story line   The narrative thread or plot of a play.

story theatre   1. A dramatization of a story which remains mainly narrative. The performer functions as storyteller, with portions of the tale using dramatic action and dialogue. The performer must therefore portray many characters (including animals and objects). (Davis/Evans CHILDREN'S 38)   2. In Africa, performances by raconteurs and *griots* (Wolof, Fulani, Songhai), who lead musicians, troubadours, or a chorus of singers and dancers. Performances may involve masquerades, puppets, or other means of impersonation, but the core of the show is the dramatization of a story by playing, and thus illustrating, its plot, character, and locale. An example is the *kwagh-hir* (Tiv) story theatre in the *kwagh-hir* puppet theatre in Nigeria. (Adedeji glossary)

stovepipe   See: funnel.

stovepipe spotlight   A term sometimes used to describe a simple lighting instrument which consists of a light source in a cylindrical housing. (Bellman LIGHTING 49, 73–74)

straight   1. Normal, not eccentric. Hence, straight makeup, play it straight. 2. Having to do with legitimate drama, as opposed to vaudeville, musical comedy, etc. Hence, straight actor, straight part. (Bowman/Ball THEATRE)   3. Especially in the days of vaudeville, a program with only a stage performance and no film showing (or vice versa). (Berrey/Van den Bark SLANG 590)   In dance: 4. Any movement in one plane which describes a straight line. 5. A description of the vertical alignment of a number of parts of the body. (Love DANCE, Eshkol/Wachmann NOTATION 165)

straightaway   A continuous program.

straight cross   A stage movement in a straight line by a performer.

straight foot iron   See: foot iron.

straight line   A feeder line: a line of dialogue spoken by a stooge or straight man, upon which a comedian plays for a laugh.

straight makeup   Makeup which emphasizes the performer's natural features, with enough color to compensate for the draining effect of stage lighting.

straight man   A performer who has a normal rather than an eccentric role and often feeds lines upon which the main comedian can play for laughs; a stooge. (Bowman/Ball THEATRE)

straight man lectures on   In burlesque, said of the talk of a straight man. (Wilmeth LANGUAGE)

straight part   A role without eccentricities.

straight play   A drama, comedy, or farce, as opposed to a musical.

strain   In Britain, to cover a framework with canvas. (Southern CHANGE-ABLE 19)

strainer   A piece of perforated sheet metal which fits into the color frame grooves at the front of a spotlight. A strainer reduces the amount of light without altering its color (as dimming would). (Lounsbury THEATRE)

strain relief   A coupling designed to prevent tension on a stage cable which might be subject to pull. Similar in function to a cable cradle.

stranded cable, stranded conductor   See: stranded wire.

stranded wire   An electrical conductor made up of thin strands of wire twisted together. Also called a stranded conductor. Most stage cable uses such wire and is sometimes called stranded cable. In Britain: flex. (Lounsbury THE-ATRE 162, Wehlburg GLOSSARY, Bowman MODERN, Bentham ART 338)

strap   A flat piece of wood or metal used, in the manner of a keystone, to hold two pieces of wood together. Hence, to strap.

strap iron   A strip of flat steel, wider than it is thick. Most strap iron used in the theatre is ¾″ wide by ⅛″ thick and is used, for example, for sills on door flats.

straw hat   A summer stock theatre. Hence, straw hat circuit.

stray light   See: spill.

(the) Street   Broadway.

street backing   A flat or drop painted to look like a street; used behind window or door openings.

street-sweeper   See: *balayeuse*.

street theatre   1. From Renaissance times on, temporary booth theatres at fairs. 2. In the late 20th C, a propagandist form, typically consisting of a small group of itinerant actors in an urban setting and working in improvised acting areas, on portable stages, on flatbed trucks, etc. Their material usually takes the form of short skits portraying current social or political problems. It is largely unstructured, with simple technical effects, and encourages audience participation. Also called guerilla theatre. (Wright UNDERSTANDING 91)

stremlenie (Russian)   In the Stanislavsky system, aspiration; striving to fulfill tasks which lie ahead for the character. (Hobgood "Stanislavski's" 156)

stretch   To prolong a scene or act, especially in burlesque in its later days, when there were fewer chorus members, and comics had to fill in time. The cue to stretch (a separating of the palms) came from the stage manager in the wings; it is still used in radio and television.

stretcher   1. A horizontal crosspiece in a flat frame. Also called a toggle rail.   2. Any of the center supports of a ceiling (analogous to the toggles in a flat).   3. A brace in a structure, as from a stair stringer to a leg. (Lounsbury THEATRE)

stretches   In dance, exercises for body suppleness and flexibility.

strif (French)   See: flyting.

strike   1. A 17th C prompter's cue for music—that is, strike up the band. 2. To take down, dismantle, or take away to storage—as scenery, properties, lights, costumes, etc. Hence, the work period when a production is dismantled. 3. To delete or remove from use in a show; to kill or pull.

strike night   After an evening performance, the dismantling of scenery, properties, and (often) lights. In a stock company, when the strike is finished, the new setting for the next day's performance is put up.

striker   1. A scene shifter.   2. One who takes down a stage setting.

string   A chain of theatres under one management.

stringer   A board supporting a platform top, stair tread, etc. Hence, cross stringer, side stringer. (Bowman/Ball THEATRE)

stringing stand   A device used to hold a marionette in a stationary position while its strings are placed and adjusted. (Philpott DICTIONARY)

string of talk   In the early 20th C, a monologue. Also called junk. (Wilmeth LANGUAGE)

strings   Tackle; theatrical rigging. (Berrey/Van den Bark SLANG 579)

strip   1. To take off one's clothes. 2. An act in which one does so. 3. See: striplight.

strip-and-shake artist   A strip-tease dancer who does a hip dance. (Berrey/Van den Bark SLANG 574)

striplight, strip light, strip   1. In the U.S., a group of lamps set in a line, usually in a trough-like metal container which may have compartments. Borderlights and footlights are striplights, though striplights are sometimes said to "resemble" borderlights. Some older backing strips had as few as two lamps, while a modern borderlight may be a single strip with 30 or 40 lamps. Striplight has largely replaced strip light, and strip is the usual backstage word. (Wehlburg GLOSSARY) 2. In Britain, a fluorescent tube, or a low-wattage lamp with a line filament.

strip out   To widen the beam of a follow spot so that it covers most of the stage. (Lounsbury THEATRE)

stripper   1. A piece of fabric glued over a crack between two flats. More often called a dutchman.   2. A performer who specializes in gradually disrobing. (Bowman/Ball THEATRE)

strip sister   A striptease dancer.

striptease   An act in which a performer, usually a woman, slowly and seductively disrobes.

strip the flat   To cover the crack between two adjoining flats with a strip of canvas (a dutchman).

strip well   In costumes, to have a good physique. (Berrey/Van den Bark SLANG 588)

Strode float   See: inverted float.

stroller   A touring performer. In Elizabethan times, some mediocre actors would "strowle (thats to say trauell) with some notorious wicked floundring company abroad." Hence, strolling, strolling player, strolling company. (Chambers ELIZABETHAN I 332n)

strolling players   1. A traveling company. 2. See: stroller.

strong actor   In Britain, an actor with a broad and somewhat old-fashioned technique. (Granville DICTIONARY)

strong back   A headblock beam.

strong city   Among strippers, a city whose obscenity laws or their enforcement are lenient. (Wilmeth LANGUAGE)

strong curtain   In playwriting, a line or lines which bring an act or play to a powerful, moving conclusion. (Macgowan "Vital" 28)

strong performance   A striptease with more than the usual complement of nudity and related erotica. (Wilmeth LANGUAGE)

strong play   In Britain, a heavy domestic or controversial sex play.

stropheion (Greek)   A device mentioned only by Pollux as showing men dying at sea or in battle, or (and?) joining the gods. Since Pollux gave no details, the *stropheion*, whose meaning has to do with turning, may have been a revolving machine which showed (a representation of?) one or more of the scenes noted. Arnott assigns the effect to the 4th C BC or later. (Pollux in Nagler SOURCES 9, Arnott SCENIC 90, Haigh ATTIC 218, Pickard-Cambridge DIONYSUS 238)

struck   Said of a scenic unit or property which has been removed from the stage.

structuralism   In drama and theatre, an analytical approach which sees the essence of a play in the relationship between its parts and not in the parts taken piece by piece. Thus, a character would not be examined in isolation but only in relation to other characters. Such relations are said to form patterns (structures) through which a play can be seen for what it is. In this view, structuralism is not so much doctrine as it is attitude—an attitude toward what a play is. The term began to be used of the theatre in the 1960s, and remains controversial. (Hornby SCRIPT 10–39, Kirby "Manifesto" 82–83)

structural scene   A rehearsal scene consisting of a segment of the action. Such a scene usually begins with the entrance and ends with the exit of one or more major characters. See also: French scene. (Bowman/Ball THEATRE)

structural setting   A fixed, three-dimensional stage setting. (Gascoigne WORLD 243)

structure   See: dramatic structure.

strut   1. A wooden brace used to support a flat; a stage brace. 2. In dance, to lift the knee with a proud gait and erect head. Hence, strut your stuff. (Berrey/ Van den Bark SLANG 589)

strut the boards   To perform.

stub   1. A portion of a ticket. 2. A counterfeit ticket.

Stück (German)   Literally: piece. A play.

Stückeschreiber (German)   Playwright.

stud contact dimmer   An occasional term for a resistance dimmer with a radial arm which moves across individual studs connected to the resistance wire. Also called a radial arm dimmer. (Bowman/Ball THEATRE)

student drama   Medieval and Renaissance dramatic productions by university students.

student rush   A brief period shortly before curtain time when any remaining tickets are sold at minimal prices to students.

studio   An old term for a theatre workroom where scenery is built.

studio production   1. A tryout of a production, with little preparation. 2. A laboratory theatre production. (Bowman/Ball THEATRE)

studio theatre   A theatre which functions as a laboratory for the training of performers, directors, playwrights, designers, technicians, etc. and often for experiments and research. Sometimes called a laboratory theatre. (Bowman/Ball THEATRE)

study   1. An understudy or substitute. 2. To learn one's lines in a play. See also: quick study. 3. The conjectural inner acting area or alcove in an Elizabethan theatre. See: inner stage.

studybook   Especially in the past, a performer's copy of a play, sometimes annotated. (Shattuck SHAKESPEARE 5)

stuff   1. A performer's stock-in-trade, such as a comedian's jokes. (Wilmeth LANGUAGE) 2. Stage business, a dance routine, etc.

stultus (Latin)   The fool in a medieval mystery play. (Mantzius HISTORY II 44)

stump   See: artist's stump.

stump speech   A monologue in vaudeville and minstrel shows involving much misuse of language for comic effect. (Wilmeth LANGUAGE)

stunt   A performance, especially an unusual feat in a performance. (Berrey/ Van den Bark SLANG 580)

stupidus (Latin Roman)   Literally: foolish one, dunce. Especially in Roman mimes, a dull-witted clown, probably often a foil to the leading character. Such a role also apparently occurred in the early *phlyakes* (Greek) and *fabula Atellana* (Latin Roman). He is thought to have been dull, often talkative, fat-cheeked or bald-headed or both. But he has also been identified in Roman bronzes wearing what we might call a dunce cap; because of this he was called (perhaps only when so hatted) *apiciosus*, one whose hat rises to a point at the top. He might, indeed, have sometimes removed his hat to reveal a bald pate, but the likelihood is that the *stupidus* was not a single physical or character type beyond the common characteristic of dull-wittedness. See also: *calvi mimici, alapus, momos phalakros* (Greek), mimic fool, secondary mime. (Nicoll MASKS 87–88, 406; Allen ANTIQUITIES 26; 1939 Bieber HISTORY 307)

Sturm und Drang (German)   Storm and stress. The term given the period in German playwriting from 1767 to 1787, characterized by rhapsodic emotionalism and a revolt against traditional drama. Goethe's *Goetz von Berlichingen* is an example. (Brockett HISTORY 398)

style   1. A theory or practice in staging, acting, etc. The manner in which a thing is done. Examples: arena style, illusionistic style, realistic style, Epic Theatre style, presentational style, representational style. 2. In dance, the posture, carriage, and control of the body, peculiar to a given tradition.

stylization   1. A theory and practice in production and occasionally in playwriting that breaks away to some degree from the realistic depiction of everyday life by means of exaggeration, formalism, selectivity, abstraction, etc. Hence, stylistic, stylize, stylized, etc. The aim of stylization is usually to emphasize inner reality rather than the surface of life. 2. A Russian idea subjecting all the elements or ideas in a work of art to the control of one guiding or principal sentiment. (Bakshy RUSSIAN 60–61)

S-type, S-type lamp   See: S-lamp.

styteler   A 15th-16th C prompter's assistant who would (if necessary) intervene between audience and actors to assure the progress of a performance. (Tribby "Prompter" 74)

suan (Chinese)   Literally: sour, pedantic. A scholar role; a type of stock character in Song *zaju* and Jin *yuanben*. (Dolby HISTORY 26–27)

suara ghaib (Malaysia)   Literally: voice outside. An omniscient, offstage voice, especially in *bangsawan*, that comments on a character's action. In *sandiwara*, called *suara latar* (voice backstage).

sub   1. An understudy. 2. To substitute, to serve as an understudy. 3. In Britain, part of a performer's salary, paid in advance. (Baker THEATRECRAFT) *suban, su pan* (Chinese)   Literally: Suzhou troupe. A company which performed *kunqu* in Beijing, 17th–19th C, so named because many were from Suzhou (Soochow). (Scott CLASSICAL 34)

sub-main   In stage lighting, a circuit which supplies current to two or more circuits (sub-circuits) but is itself controlled by a main, such as a color main. Fuchs LIGHTING 62 has a diagram.

sub-master   A switch or dimmer which operates a portion of the switches or dimmers on a lighting control board.

sub-master control   Any arrangement on a lighting control board which provides for sub-masters. See also: grand master. (Bowman/Ball THEATRE)

subplot   A shortening of subordinate plot. A minor or secondary plot or a subordinate action, such as the Gloucester plot in *King Lear*.

subscription   Tickets for a series (usually a season) of theatrical performances. Hence, subscriber, subscription audience, etc.

subsellia (Latin Roman)   The rows of seats in an auditorium; the bench-like seats themselves. (Mantzius HISTORY I 225, Sandys COMPANION 519)

substage   The area below a stage; the cellar, basement.

subtext   In Stanislavskian terms, meanings that lie beneath the surface of the lines and dramatic action, giving a play an extra dimension.

subway circuit   New York theatre beyond Broadway. (Wilmeth LANGUAGE)

succès de scandale (French)   A show that succeeds because of its sensational subject matter.

succès d'estime (French)   A critical success but one that brings the author little more than esteem.

succession   In dance, the movement of all body parts either simultaneously or in sequence, spreading through adjacent parts of the body in succession. See also: wave. (Dell PRIMER 79)

su chu (Vietnamese)   See: *noi su*.

su chü (Chinese)   See: *suju*.

sudden death   In British stage management, a term for the "go" signal in a cue system with one light. The cue light is switched on at the warning, and switched off at "go." (Baker THEATRECRAFT)

suddha maddalam (Malayalam)   A barrel-shaped, double-headed drum played with the palms and fingers in *kathakali*. Similar to the *mridangam*. (Jones/Jones KATHAKALI 77)

sue dogu (Japanese)   A large set prop in *no*, such as a gate, a pavilion, or a hut, which is placed on the bare stage. (Komparu NOH 255)

suitcase opera   A show whose performers travel with little baggage. (Berrey/Van den Bark SLANG 580) *suivante* (French)   Literally: female follower. An actress in the 18th C theatre whose roles supported the leading lady. (Arnott FRENCH 34)

sujet (French)   See: *ballerina*.

suju, su chü (Chinese)   A form of music-drama (*xiqu*) popular in the Suzhou region of Jiangsu Province which developed in the early 20th C from the form of *tanhuang* storytelling popular in Suzhou. It is strongly influenced by *kunqu*.

suling (Indonesian)   See: *gamelan*.

sultana gown   See: gown à la sultane.

suluk (Indonesian)   A generic term for a mood song, sung by the *dalang*, in Javanese and Sundanese *wayang* theatre. (Holt ART 138–139) There are three types in Surakarta-style performance: *patet(an)*, *sendon*, and *ada-ada*. See also: *kakawen*. (Brandon THRONES 55–57)

sumbar (Indonesian)   Pointing a finger at an opponent as a warning or admonishment in Javanese *wayang kulit* puppet theatre. Also called *suraweyan*. (Long JAVANESE 47)

sumbu (Malaysian)   See: *benang mentah*.

sumi (Japanese)   Literally: corner. The acting area of a *no* stage down right beside the eye-fixing pillar (*metsuke bashira*). (Berberich ''Rapture'' 64–65)

summa cavea (Latin Roman)   See: *maenianum primum*.

summer stock   A summer theatrical operation away from major cities, usually presenting a play a week and sometimes booking in stars to play leading roles. Hence, summer stock theatre, summer stock company.

summer theatre   A theatre and company operating only in the summer.

summer tour   In Britain, a provincial tour from May or June to September or October.

summer tryout   A test of a new play by a summer stock company.

sumpingan (Indonesian)   See: *simpingan*.

sunburner, sun-burner, sun burner   Especially in the latter half of the 19th C, the principal fixture used in lighting theatre auditoriums. Sunburners varied a good deal in design and appearance, but the characteristic feature was a large circle of gas jets so closely spaced that they produced an essentially solid circle of relatively brilliant light; by the end of the century, electricity sometimes replaced gas. A chandelier-like fixture, the sunburner was at or not far below the auditorium ceiling. The much-used alternate name 'sunlight' perhaps suggests the general effect. Rees has illustrations. (Rees GAS 95–102, 214–215; Penzel LIGHTING 104–105)

sunday   1. A knot used to bind (clew) a set of rope lines together and allow a sandbag to be attached. 2. A knot used to fasten two ends of a cable or wire rope together without putting a kink in the wire. (Lounsbury THEATRE 77)

Sunday run   A long journey from one engagement to another.

Sunday school circuit   The nickname of the old Keith vaudeville circuit, which catered to family audiences. (Wilmeth LANGUAGE)

Sunday theatre club   A stage group in Britain operating privately and thus not subject to interference by a censor. Performances are often on Sundays. The Stage Society, founded in 1899, was the earliest. (Sobel NEW)

Sung *tsa chü* (Chinese)   See: Song *zaju*.

sunlight   In the 19th C, a frequent name for the sunburner. There were occasional attempts to distinguish the two, especially by those who designed or installed a new version, but usage ignored such attempts.

sun spot, sunspot   1. A strong light, usually a spotlight or beam projector, which creates the effect of sunlight (for example, by pouring through a window). 2. In the U.S., a name for a beam projector. (Bowman/Ball THEATRE, Philippi STAGECRAFT)

su odori (Japanese)   Literally: uncostumed dance. In *no*, a solo dance excerpt (*shimai*), performed unmasked and in rehearsal costume to singing without musical accompaniment. (Wolz "Spirit" 56)

suona, so na (Chinese)   A double reed instrument with a conical wooden body and a movable flared metal bell. It is important in the melodic orchestra (*wenchang*) in Beijing opera (*jingju*), *kunqu*, and many other forms of music-drama (*xiqu*), and it is often the only melodic instrument to play celebratory or martial fixed-melodies (*qupai*) in conjunction with the percussion orchestra (*wuchang*). The *suona* is also used for sound effects. (Mackerras MODERN 23, Mackerras PERFORMING 155, Scott CLASSICAL 49–50)

su pan (Chinese)   See: *suban*.

super, supernumerary   An extra; a player of a role with no lines. Also called a walk on, walker-on, camel driver, *gagiste* (French), spear bearer, and occasionally, supe.

super master   A person in charge of supernumeraries. Also called the head of the supers.

supernumerario (Spanish)   An extra, a supernumerary. Also called a *racionista*.

supernumerary   See: super.

superobjective   In the Stanislavsky system of acting, the main theme or meaning of a play, contributed to by all the play's characters. "In a play the whole stream of individual, minor objectives, all the imaginative thoughts, feelings, and actions of an actor, should converge to carry out the *super-objective* of the plot." The term has also been applied to the life goal of an individual character. Sometimes called the superproblem. See also: spine. (Stanislavski ACTOR 256)

suplente (Spanish)   A substitute, an understudy.

supper room   In 19th C Britain, a place where patrons could have supper while watching music-hall shows, as in a modern dinner theatre. (Bowman/Ball THEATRE)

supper show, supper turn   In a continuous vaudeville show, an act that went on about 6 p.m., when the audience was smallest. (Wilmeth LANGUAGE)

suppon (Japanese)   Literally: snapping turtle. A small trap in the runway (*hanamichi*) of a *kabuki* theatre. Used primarily for the appearance and disappearance of a spirit. It is a specialized type of *seri*. (Ernst KABUKI 100, Gunji KABUKI 217)

support   To play a secondary role in a cast with a star. Hence, supporting actor, supporting role, supporting cast, to be supported by, etc. By extension, the theatrical company supporting a star.

supporting cast   Performers other than the star or stars.

supporting leg   In conventional ballet usage, the limb last to leave the ground. In certain movements, a misnomer, since this leg may actually be doing the work. See: working leg. (Kersley/Sinclair BALLET)

suraweyan (Indonesian)   See: *sumbar*.

surcoat, surcôte   A 12th–13th C floor-length sleeveless tunic, quite full and belted. It became shorter as time went on, particularly its front. Shorter versions were worn by men when riding. The female versions were worn into the Renaissance. (Boucher FASHION, Walkup DRESSING 99)

sure fire   1. A vaudeville act that was certain of success. 2. See: hoke.

surf   In Britain, a minor performer or other theatre employee who does some outside work during the day. Possibly a pun on serf. (Partridge UNCONVENTIONAL)

surface image   A stage image readily perceived by the audience.

surf box   A device for creating the sound of surf. It is a long container, covered top and bottom with window screen and filled with dried peas or shot, such as BBs.

(the) surge   About the beginning of the 20th C, a movement away from the sight-gag, surprise-laughter, trickster style of puppetry toward a goal of high creativity and artistic/aesthetic effort in both puppets and shows. (Baird PUPPET 181)

suri ashi (Japanese)   In *kabuki* dance, a sliding step in which the foot is not lifted from the floor. It is based on the standard *no* walking movement (*hakobi*).

sur les pointes (French)   Literally: on the toes. In ballet, the raising of the body so that its weight is on the ends of the toes. Also occurs as *sur la pointe*. (Grant TECHNICAL 82)

surpied (French)   A piece of leather which trimmed the instep of a boot. The *soulette* fitted over it. (Boucher FASHION) *sur place* (French)   In ballet, a step or steps performed in place. (Kersley/ Sinclair BALLET)

surprise pink   A light lavender color medium. This filter, which casts a flattering orchid-pink light, has been a favorite of performers for many decades. The popular name may originate in the difference between the apparent color of the gelatine and the effect of its light. (Rubin/Watson LIGHTING 57, Bowman MODERN)

surrealism   A literary and theatrical movement that insisted that reality is grasped by the unconscious rather than the conscious. The movement was strong in the 1920s and 1930s, but forerunners go back as early as Alfred Jarry's *Ubu Roi* in 1896. (Barnet/Berman/Burto ASPECTS)

surround   1. A drapery cyclorama. 2. Removable platforms surrounding a turntable or revolving stage. Also called a shroud. (Baker THEATRECRAFT, Parker/Smith DESIGN)

Susie   See: Sis Hopkins.

suspended   Said of a character in a play who for a considerable time is not involved in the dialogue or action. (Bowman/Ball THEATRE)

suspense   See: dramatic suspense.

suspension   In dance, a moment when the body supports itself while off balance, before returning to equilibrium. (Stodelle HUMPHREY 20)

suspension arm   See: hanger.

suspension barrel   See: pipe batten.

sus-sous (French)   See: *sous-sus*.

sustained   In dance, prolonged, lingering, slow, smooth, or gradually changing movement. In French, *soutenu*. (Preston-Dunlop DANCE 14–16)

sutdongmu (Korean)   Literally: male comrade. Actors of male roles in a *namsadang* troupe. See also: *yodongmu*. (Kim ''Namsadang'' 10)

sutezerifu (Japanese)   Literally: throw-away dialogue. 1. In *kabuki*, dialogue that is ad-libbed by the actor during performance, a practice common in the late 17th and 18th C but rare today. 2. A dialogue passage that may be changed during rehearsal if an actor wishes. Such sections are indicated in *kabuki* play texts. See also: *kuchidate*. (Brandon CLASSIC 77–79, Brandon CHUSHIN-GURA 137, Gunji KABUKI 34)

sutradhara (Sanskrit), *sutradhar* (Hindi)   Literally: string holder. 1. Possibly a puppeteer in ancient Indian shadow theatre. (Keith SANSKRIT 52) 2. In present-day Rajasthan state in northwest India, the chief puppeteer of a troupe (ASIAN 18). 3. In classical Indian theatre, the director/manager of a theatre troupe. Described by Bharata as the person responsible for all aspects of performances—forming the troupe, training actors, casting, directing, producing, making offerings to the gods (*puja*), supervising the building of a theatre, and appearing before the audience in preliminaries (*purvaranga*) to the play. (NATYASASTRA I 10, 84–98, 404–405; II 4–99, 232–234) Also called *natyacarya* (teacher of actors), *natagamani* (head of a troupe of actors). (Keith SANSKRIT 360; Raghavan in Baumer/Brandon SANSKRIT 11, 41) 4. In most extant regional theatre forms, the director/manager of a troupe, who also functions as a narrator or singer guiding the performance or assumes a role in the play. He is called by various regional names: *adhikari, bhagavata, kattiakaran, naik, ranga, sardar, svami (swami), vyas,* and others.

su utai (Japanese)   Literally: only song. The singing of a *no* play text without musical accompaniment or dance, especially at an amateur performance. *Su utai* books intended for study were first published in Kyoto in the 15th C. (Bethe/Brazell NO 41, Nakamura NOH 137)

suyue, su yüeh (Chinese)   Literally: common music. A generic term for folk music and dance from c. 11th C BC to 9th C AD. It referred especially to performances of the hundred entertainments (*baixi*) and other popular forms given at palace banquets, as opposed to elegant music (*yayue*) performances. See also: *sanyue*.

svagatam (Sanskrit)   See: *atmagatam*.

svami (Hindi)   Literally: master. A performing stage manager or director of a professional *raslila* company. Also spelled *swami*. See also: *sutradhara*. (Gargi FOLK 120–121, Swann "Braj" 21)

svang, svanga (Hindi)   An operatic folk theatre form in Punjab, north India. (Hein MIRACLE 2, Vatsyayan TRADITIONAL 159)

svara (Sanskrit)   1. In ancient Indian dramatic theory, the musical notes out of which melody was composed. *Svara* together with rhythm (*tala*) and lyrics (*pada*) are the three essential elements of theatre music. (Bharata NATYASASTRA II 3) 2. The tonal system used in *kutiyattam*.

svarup (Hindi), *svarupa* (Sanskrit)   Literally: the very form. A boy actor in *raslila* who plays the role of Krishna or Radha and in whom the god manifests himself. (Hawley KRISHNA 319, Hein MIRACLE 230)

svis'kyi theatre (Ukrainian-English)   Ukrainian civil theatre. (Hirniak in Bradshaw SOVIET 251)

swab   To wipe over with thin glue and hot water a patch of canvas covering a hole in a cloth or flat. (Fay GLOSSARY)

swag   1. A festooned or looped-up curtain. Hence, swag border, swag curtain, to swag, etc. 2. A decoration, usually painted, representing a festoon of drapery, leaves, flowers, ribbons, etc.

swallow   In Britain: 1. Memory. 2. To memorize readily. (Bowman/Ball THEATRE)

swami (Hindi)   See: *svami*.

swan song   A performer's last appearance or a playwright's last play.

swazzle   A reed or tin whistle put into the mouth of a puppeteer which enables him or her to effect a variety of vocal sounds. Also called a call, *pito* (Spanish), pivetta, *sifflet pratique* (French), slim, squeaker, swatchel. (Speaight PUPPET 173, Jacobus "Puppets" 111)

Swedish hat   A large felt hat with a feather, frequently seen on musketeers. Also called a cavalier's hat. (Boucher FASHION)

sweep   The curved structural members of an arch flat which give it its shape. Also called an arch sweep. (Gillette/Gillette SCENERY)

sweeper   In 18th C theatres, an employee apparently responsible for cleaning the chimneys (for company lists also cited charwomen to clean the floors). (Stone LONDON 817)

swifter   In Britain, a steel line along which scenery, lights, properties, etc., are carried swiftly into position during a fast shift. (Granville DICTIONARY)

swing   In dance, a movement which initiates a falling motion, but also incorporates its rebound and subsequent suspension. (Stodelle HUMPHREY 61)

swing girl   1. A chorus singer or dancer who can take any one of the other chorus parts and thus relieve girls who are absent. 2. In burlesque which played every night, one who relieved other chorines on their nights off. (Wilmeth LANGUAGE)

swing joint   A flat circular metal device which allows a lighting instrument on a stand to turn. (Bowman/Ball THEATRE)

swing stage, swinging stage   See: jackknife stage.

Swiss bodice   See: *chemisette*.

switchboard   1. In stage lighting, originally a case whose principal elements were the switches which controlled the lights. 2. Later, a case which included both switches and dimmers. 3. Now sometimes called a control board, and even console. In its strict sense as a stage lighting term, switchboard is obsolescent if not obsolete, but its use persists. (Bellman SCENE, Sellman/Lessley ESSENTIALS, Wehlburg GLOSSARY)

switchboard operator   See: control board operator.

switched only   See: non-dim.

swivel   A loft block (grooved wheel or sheave in a frame) which can be hung under a grid and turned to any point in a complete circle.

swivel arm   A movable batten allowing a leg to hang at an angle to the setting line. Also called a swivel and hook. (Baker THEATRECRAFT)

sword dance   Especially in medieval times, a dance entertainment involving intricate maneuvers with swords.

syl slinger   In Britain, a performer whose speech is over-precise, tending to make each syllable an entity. (Granville DICTIONARY)

symbolic gesture, symbolic movement   A movement so familiar that its significance is recognized at once by the audience, such as scratching the head or stroking the chin. (Dolman ACTING 37)

symbolism   A movement in literature and theatre in the late 19th and early 20th C stressing mood, myth, symbol and legend—especially symbols in scenography, often isolated against a relatively plain background. In playwriting, Maurice Maeterlinck was one of the more successful exponents.

symmetricals   Tights with padding inside, called hearts, which improve the shape of the tights and of the wearer. In Britain, false calves. (Carrington THEATRICANA)

symmetry   In dance, the transposition of a movement on one side of the body to the corresponding limb on the other side, mirror fashion. (Eshkol/Wachmann NOTATION 162)

symphonic drama   An historical pageant with music and spectacle, usually performed out-of-doors. (Green in Stevens TALENTS 253, 261)

symphony   Especially in Britain, a term sometimes applied to music played at curtain time. (Bax MANAGEMENT 227)

synagonistes (Greek), **synagonist**   After about the 3rd C BC, a subordinate or assistant actor. The non-theatrical meaning is helper, and this suggests the theatrical use: in the production of old plays, the word could be applied to any actor but the protagonist. Unsurprisingly, the synagonists were so numerous that they had their own organization within the Artists of Dionysus (the theatrical guild). (O'Connor CHAPTERS 28–31; Pickard-Cambridge FESTIVALS 135, 155, 297–298)

synchoregia (Greek)   The service rendered by wealthy citizens in bearing financial responsibility for the production of a play or plays at the Dionysian festivals. This division of the costs of play production among two or three citizens was a temporary expedient caused by the financial distress of the Peloponnesian War (late 5th C BC). Plural *synchoregiae*. (Allen ANTIQUITIES 46, Pickard-Cambridge FESTIVALS 87)

synchoregus, synchoregos (Greek)   A citizen who rendered the service of *synchoregia*. Plurals *synchoregi, synchoregoi*. (Allen ANTIQUITIES 46, Flickinger GREEK 271, Pickard-Cambridge FESTIVALS 87)

synchronous winch system   A rigging system consisting of individual lines running to electronic winches on the gridiron. The winches can be ganged and their movement synchronized electronically.

(the) Syndicate   The Theatrical Syndicate (also called the Theatre Trust, or the Trust), an organization that flourished from 1896 to 1916 and had a virtual monopoly on U.S. theatrical bookings by controlling the best theatres in the country. (Bowman/Ball THEATRE)

synthesis   In staging, the principle advocated by Richard Wagner, Gordon Craig, Adolphe Appia, and others, that the art of the theatre is made up of the harmoniously fused elements of acting, painting, lighting, music, dance, etc. (Gorelik NEW)

syntheticalism The unification of a variety of production elements in a performance. The word emphasizes not only the presence, but also the synthesis of such differing elements as song, dance, mime, costumes, and the varying appearance of even a single setting under changes in lighting. The creation of a European director (from synthesis, via synthetical), the term was apparently not created for children's theatre, but its sense has been thought especially important there. (Goldberg CHILDREN'S 142–144)

syrinx See: panpipe.

syrmata (Latin Roman) 1. The long sweeping robes of tragedy. 2. By extension, tragedy. Also called in U.S. English, syrma (singular). (Nicoll DEVELOPMENT 47)

syrtos (Greek) The long trailing robe often worn by actors playing female characters in tragedy. The Greek *chiton syrtos* is similar to the *syrmata* of Rome. (Haigh ATTIC 250)

(the) System Short for the Stanislavsky System.

Szechwan opera See: *chuanju*.

Szene (German) Scene. Hence, *Szenerie* (scenery, decor), *szenisch* (scenic).

szopka, szupka (Polish) Literally: manger. A medieval Christmas puppet play. The *szopka* still survives. See also: *crèche parlante*. Called *bertep* (Bethlehem) in Byelorussia. (Baird PUPPET 67)

T

T Tubular, the designation of the bulb shape of a relatively high-wattage lamp much used in spotlights.

ta (Chinese) See: *da*.

tab 1. A narrow, masking drop, like a leg, normally hung at the side of the stage to mask the offstage area. The masking function is like that of the side wings in theatres of the 19th C and earlier. 2. See: tableau curtain. 3. See: tabloid.

tab backing Tableau backing—a drop, usually of velour, lowered behind a tableau curtain to mask the backstage area.

tabby An 18th C woman's loose gown, worn around the house. Especially popular in the American colonies. (Walkup DRESSING 217)

tab company A touring group competing with vaudeville and motion pictures by presenting condensed versions (Tabloids) of successful musicals. Such companies thrived in the early 20th C in the U.S. (Wilmeth LANGUAGE)

tab curtain See: tableau curtain.

taberes A variety of medieval minstrels; in the 14th C they were drummers. (Chadwick PLOWMAN 29)

tabernaria (Latin Roman) See: *fabula togata*.

tab hook A spring hook holding a running tableau curtain.

tab house A theatre specializing in condensed (tabloid) shows. (Wilmeth LANGUAGE)

tabik (Malaysian) A pre-performance greeting, sung or chanted, welcoming both audience and members of the spirit world, used by some storytellers (*penglipur lara*). (Sweeney in Malm/Sweeney STUDIES 60).

tabla (Hindi) Two small drums of different pitches that are played with the hands. They are used in many forms of rural and urban Indian theatre. (Hawley KRISHNA 319) *tablado* (Spanish)   A 16th C stage or platform. (Rennert SPANISH 8).

tableau   1. A medieval spectacle show with religious, allegorical, and mythological figures. 2. A frozen stage picture at the end of an act.

tableau (French)   1. A call sheet. A notice posted inside a theatre to tell cast and crew the work to be done that day, including rehearsals and performances. 2. A new scene division.

tableau curtain   1. A curtain that parts in the center and gathers upward and to the sides, forming an ornamental festoon. Short forms: tab curtain, tabs. Also called an opera drape. A tableau curtain is used behind or in place of an act curtain. The term derives from the use of a curtain which parted in the middle and drew upward to reveal a tableau held by performers. When a tableau curtain is used to end an act, it may be called an act drop. The term has been sometimes loosely applied to the main or house curtain; hence, grand tab, house tab. (Bowman/Ball THEATRE, Corry PLANNING, Bentham ART) 2. A curtain raised to reveal a tableau. 3. The resulting tableau.

tableau vivant (French)   A medieval and Renaissance tableau in which the figures move; a silent, living, picture. The subject matter was usually biblical, allegorical, historical, or fanciful. Often presented to celebrate the visit of an important personage. (Davidson STUDIES 88)

table base   A device resembling the base of a floor stand, so that a fixture such as a spotlight can be mounted close to the horizontal surface on which the base rests. (Bowman MODERN)

table part   A role played from behind a table by an entertainer or quick-change artist.

tablero de iluminación (Spanish)   A control board for stage lighting.

table stage   A revolving stage.

tablier (French)   Apron. (Boucher FASHION)

tabloid, tab   A shortened version of a full-length show, especially a burlesque or musical production. Hence, tab house, tab show.

tabster   A performer in a tabloid or condensed play. (Berrey/Van den Bark SLANG 571)

taburetes (Spanish)   Leather-covered benches with upholstered backs, in a theatre pit.

ta chang (Chinese)   See: *dazhang*.

tachi ai (Japanese)   A contest between rival *no* troupes, 14th–19th C. (Zeami KADENSHO 40)

ta ch'iang (Chinese)   See: *daqiang*.

tachi geiko (Japanese)   Literally: standing rehearsal. A rehearsal involving movement as well as lines, as distinguished from reading rehearsals. (Hamamura et al KABUKI 102) Originally used in *kabuki*, the term is used in modern theatre as well.

tachikata (Japanese)   See: *tachiyaku*.

tachimawari (Japanese)   Literally: standing-moving about. 1. In *no*, large crossing movements by the protagonist (*shite*). One type of dance (*hatarikigoto*). 2. In *kabuki*, fighting scenes of all types. See also: *tate*. (Brandon in Brandon/ Malm/Shively STUDIES 91–93, Gunji KABUKI 176–178)

tachimi (Japanese)   Literally: standing-seeing. 1. To watch a performance while standing. 2. The standing room area, especially in a *kabuki* theatre. (Scott KABUKI 288)

tachishu (Japanese)   In *kyogen*, a minor role without lines, a walk-on. (Kenny GUIDE 12, Berberich "Rapture" 59)

tachiyaku (Japanese)   Literally: standing role. In *kabuki*: 1. In early 17th C troupes, actors (who stood) as distinguished from other performers, such as musicians, who sat on stage. Also called *tachikata* (standing person). (Dunn/ Torigoe ANALECTS 171) 2. Since the late 17th C, a leading male role. Sub-types include *aragotoshi, jitsugoto, nimaime, otokodate, shimboyaku, wakashu-gata,* and others. (Gunji KABUKI 182–183, 186; Leiter ENCYCLOPEDIA 389) 3. An actor who plays such a role. (Hamamura et al KABUKI 101) 4. Less often, any male role. See also: *otokokata*.

ta chou tzu (Chinese)   See: *zhouzi*.

ta ch'ü (Chinese)   See: *daqu*.

tacite (Latin)   In Elizabethan plays, aside.

tacker   See: modesty.

tackle the calfskin   To play the banjo. (Wilmeth LANGUAGE)

tack-up   An old term for a poster advertising a theatrical event, placed in a shop window. Complimentary tickets were given to the shopkeepers. (Krows AMERICA 324)

ta-da   A musical fanfare introducing a performer.

Tad comic   An Irish comedian, especially in vaudeville. From Irish versions of Thaddeus. (Wilmeth LANGUAGE)

taegwangdae-p'ae (Korean)   An early theatre troupe, the probable progenitor of *ogwangdae* and *yaryu* masked theatre. In addition to a masked dance-drama, the repertory is believed to have consisted of dancing with a child on one's shoulders (*mudong-ch'um*), acrobatic dancing (*chikpangul–patki*), and tumbling (*ttangjaeju*). (Cho "Ogwangdae" 27)

taejabi (Korean)   See: *daejabi*.

taep'osu (Korean)   A male actor in the *p'ungmul* section of a *namsadang* performance. (Yi "Mask" 53) *t'aep'yongso* (Korean)   Literally: pacifying musical instrument. A type of oboe used in traditional theatrical performances. Also called *nalnari, nallari, hojok*. (Cho KOREAN 38, Kim "Namsadang" 11)

ta fa (Chinese)   See: *datou*.

tag   1. In Elizabethan plays, the last lines (usually a rhymed couplet) of a scene. The tag and the performer's exit, leaving a clear stage, meant the end of the scene and a change of locale. In later periods the tag was usually used only at the end of the play—a final couplet, often moral in tone. (Hogan LONDON lxxxix) 2. The last line in a scene, act, or play. Also called a curtain line. Hence, tag line, speech tag. There is an old superstition that the tag at the end of the play should not be spoken until opening night. (Stern MANAGEMENT, Baker THEATRECRAFT) 3. The last act on a variety bill.

tagulaylay (Philippine)   A dirge-like singing style used by leading characters in early *comedia*. It evolved into the present stylized delivery called *dicho* or *loa*. (Mendoza COMEDIA 45)

ta hsi (Chinese)   See: *daxi*.

ta hsing hsi ch'ü (Chinese)   See: *daxi*.

ta hua lien (Chinese)   See: *dahualian*.

ta i (Chinese)   See: *yixiang*.

taihaku (Japanese)   See: *serifu*.

ta i hsiang (Chinese)   See: *yixiang*.

taiko (Japanese)   A small stick drum that is part of the instrumental ensemble (*hayashi*) in *no* and *kabuki*.

tail   1. A border or short piece of canvas hung from the fly gallery to mask the backstage area. 2. In Britain, a leg. 3. A line dropped from a batten to hold a scenic unit several feet below the batten. 4. In stage lighting, a pigtail. 5. A queen's train in 18th C tragedy. (Roberts STAGE) 6. A waiting line for tickets. Also called a queue (from the French, meaning tail). (Berrey/Van den Bark SLANG 575)

tail batten   Especially in Australia, a length of timber, or a pipe, inserted in the horizontal pocket or sleeve at the bottom of a flown cloth to make it taut. (National TECHNICAL)

taisotoku (Japanese)   A *bugaku* mask of an old man. (Wolz BUGAKU 42)

tajungan (Indonesian)   See: *tayungan*.

take   1. A comic reaction to a line or piece of business, consisting of snapping the head and looking at another performer. There are four basic kinds of takes: a skull (a sudden look; hence, skull a line, give him the skull), a double take (two looks, the second more definite), a body take (a double take using the whole body), and a slow take (a delayed reaction) (Wilmeth LANGUAGE) 2. To draw audience attention, often by moving to a dominant position on stage.

Hence, to take the stage, take a scene. (Bowman/Ball THEATRE) 3. To impress an audience favorably. 4. In the drama of the Federal Theatre, a short sequence—pantomime, skit, radio broadcast—which depicted social problems of the 1930s. (Mathews FEDERAL 71) 5. Box-office receipts. 6. Of a dimmer control, to move, as in "Take 4 to half."

take a bend, take a bow, take a call, take a hand   To acknowledge the applause of the audience with a bow, usually at the end of a performance—though in opera, often after each act. To take a curtain call.

take a break   See: break.

take a Brodie   See: Brodie.

take a call   See: take a bend.

take a count   In performing, to time a pause, a reaction, a bit of business. The count can be fast or slow and take as many beats or seconds as a director or performer thinks will be effective.

take a hand   See: take a bend.

take an encore   To repeat something the audience has loudly applauded, usually a song.

take a powder, take a run-out, take a run-out powder   To evade an engagement.

take a prompt   To receive a whispered correct line from a prompter when one has forgotten a line.

take it away   1. To open the curtain. 2. To remove.

take down   1. Of a light, to decrease the brightness by dimming. To take up is to increase brightness. 2. To strike (dismantle) a show. (Stern MANAGEMENT)

take down and put up   See: comic up in all.

take five, take ten, etc.   Permission to stop a rehearsal and relax for five minutes, ten minutes, etc.

take in   1. To move scenery into a theatre. The term is also used as a noun. In Britain: get in. 2. To lower something from the flies. Also called bring in. 3. Hyphenated, box-office receipts.

"Take it away!"   In variety shows, the master of ceremonies' verbal signal to a performer to begin his act.

takemoto (Japanese)   The common name given to *gidayu bushi* music when played in *kabuki*. From the name of the music's creator, Takemoto Gidayu (1651–1714).

take out   1. To move scenery out of a theatre. The term is also used as a noun. In Britain: get out. 2. To raise something into the flies. 3. In lighting, to dim out or turn off.

take stage   In performing, to move to a dominant position on stage, such as upstage center, in order to force other performers to yield focus. A term of opprobrium usually, but some performers can figuratively take stage or take a scene through the strength of their performance or their stage presence, without resorting to tricks.

take the boards   To perform.

take the cake   To win a cakewalk contest.

take the corner   Especially in Britain: 1. In acting, to move to either the right or left corner of a proscenium stage, usually downstage. 2. To serve as the prompter or stage manager. (Bowman/Ball THEATRE)

take the nap   Especially in Britain, to clap hands to simulate a blow struck onstage. (Baker THEATRECRAFT)

take the owl   See: make a sleeper jump.

take the road   To tour.

take the scene   See: take stage.

take the veil   To leave show business.

take three bends and an encore   To be well received—that is, to bow thrice and repeat a number, or a direction to do so, as from the stage manager.

take up   See: take down.

take up a cue   To respond.

take-up block   A block with a sheave at the bottom of a counterweight unit, through which the operating line runs. The sheave is in tension to keep the operating line taut. Also called an idler, tension block, tension idler, tension pulley.

takigi no (Japanese)   Literally: firelight *no*. From as early as the 12th C, a religious festival performance of *no*, held at night and lighted by hanging baskets filled with burning kindling. (O'Neill EARLY 60–62)

takilya (Philippine)   Box office. (Fernández ILOILO 132)

taking date   In the rental of lighting equipment for the professional theatre, especially for out-of-town tryouts, the day the equipment is taken from the renter. (Rubin/Watson LIGHTING 21)

takings   Box-office receipts.

tako tsukami (Japanese)   Literally: octopus grab. A type of puppet's grasping hand (*tsukamite*) used for strong male warriors in *bunraku*. Its wrist and fingers are jointed and movable. (Keene BUNRAKU 60, 174)

ta ku (Chinese)   1. A type of storytelling. See: *dagu*. 2. A kind of drum. See: *tanggu*.

ta kuo men (Chinese)   See: *guomen*.

t'al (Korean)   A generic term for mask. (Korean MASKS 5)

tala (Sanskrit)   Literally: palm. Hence, drum beats which are counted on the hand. A rhythmic pattern (of 2, 3, 4, 5, 7, 9, 10, 11, or 14 beats) that controls the beat of drums, cymbals, songs (*pada*), and dances (*nritta* and *nritya*) in all types of Indian theatre. The dancer's footwork especially is tied to the *tala* being used. One of three elements of theatre music. See also: *svara, pada.*

tala maddale (Kannada)   1. A *yaksagana* performance without costumes, makeup or dance, where musicians are seated center-stage and actors are in the rear. 2. A story sung in *yaksagana* style with emphasis on vocal aspects rather than makeup, costumes, or dance. See: *arthadhari.* (Ashton/Christie YAKSA-GANA 21–22, 68; Gargi FOLK 163)

talami (Italian)   Platforms on which medieval liturgical plays were presented. (Chambers MEDIAEVAL II 85)

t'alch'um (Korean)   See: *sandaeguk.*

taledek (Indonesian)   A transvestite who sings, and occasionally dances, between scenes (*selingan*) in a *ludruk* troupe. (Peacock RITES 292)

t'alje (Korean)   Literally: mask ritual. A sacrificial ceremony to pray for a safe performance. It is held prior to a performance of masked dance-drama in the presence of a display of masks. (Cho "Suyong" 36)

talkers   A vaudevillian's term for talking pictures. (Wilmeth LANGUAGE)

talk green room   To gossip about theatre matters.

talk-happening   See: *Sprechstück.*

talking single   A vaudeville act consisting of a single performer who tells jokes and stories. (Wilmeth LANGUAGE)

talking woman   In burlesque, a woman who assisted the comedian by delivering lines in brief skits or scenes; she was often a former stripper. (Wilmeth LANGUAGE)

tall grass   The locale of an especially remote town where a touring company is scheduled to play a one-night stand.

tall timber   The provinces.

tally   See: mimic.

ta lo (Chinese)   See: *daluo.*

t'al pan (Korean)   Literally: mask stage. The outdoor playing area for a masked play. (Korean KOREAN 75)

talu (Indonesian)   Introductory *gamelan* music played before a performance of Javanese *wayang* or *ludruk*. In Bali, called *pemungkah.* (Peacock RITES 65) In Sunda, *tatalu.*

tamasha (Marathi)   Literally: noisy happening. A traditional, free-wheeling theatre form, dating from c. 18th C, popular in rural areas of Maharashtra, northwest India. The singing of a narrative poem expressing vigor and love and the songs of actresses are chief attractions. Two styles are *dholki bari*, emphasizing drumming, and *sangeet bari*, emphasizing music. (Gargi FOLK 72–90)

Tambo, Brudder Tambo   One of the end men in a minstrel show, so named because he usually played a tambourine. His partner at the other end of the semicircle of performers was called Bones. See also: Sambo. (Wilmeth LANGUAGE, Toll BLACKING 54)

tambour (French)   In the 19th C, a one-drum winch with attached ropes which turned in one direction or the other to raise or lower scenery. It could be installed in the substage, in the galleries, in the flies, or on the grid. (Moynet FRENCH 42)

ta mien (Chinese)   See: *damian*.

tamra fon ram (Thai)   A dance training text or treatise. The first such text was commissioned by King Rama I in the late 18th C. See also: *mae bot, tha ram*. (Rutnin ''Development'' 11)

tam-tam (French)   Drums, especially those struck three times in a 19th C theatre to signal the audience that the performance was about to begin. (Moynet FRENCH 118)

tan (Chinese)   See: *dan*.

tanangipun cakot (Indonesian)   Literally: to bite one's hands. In Javanese shadow theatre, a movement by a frenzied ogre that indicates his uncontrolled and vicious anger. (Long JAVANESE 67)

tanceban (Indonesian)   See: *tanceb kayon*.

tanceb kayon (Indonesian)   Literally: planting the *kayon*. In Java and Sunda, placing the *kayon* puppet in the center of the screen to close a performance of *wayang kulit* or *wayang golek*. Also spelled *tantjeb kayon, tanjep kajon*. (Holt ART 135, Foley ''Sundanese'' 114) *Tanceban* or *tantjeban* is to place the *kayon* in the center of the screen between scenes. Illustrations are in Brandon THRONES 114, 170, 359.

t'an ch'iang (Chinese)   See: *chuanju*.

tanci, t'an tz'u (Chinese)   A type of storytelling (*quyi*) which developed c. 14th–16th C; currently popular forms exist in a number of regions throughout China, including portions of Jiangsu, Zhejiang, Shandong, and Hunan Provinces and the Guangxi Zhuang Autonomous Region. They are performed in regional dialect by one to four seated performers who usually sing, speak, and play musical instruments. The three-string lute (*sanxian*), lute (*pipa*), or moon guitar (*yueqin*) is usually the principal instrument. (Howard CONTEMPORARY 30)

tanda (Spanish)   A Chicano term for all or part of a theatrical performance.

tandava (Sanskrit)   Vigorous, rhythmic dance style. Often described as masculine, in contrast to the feminine (*lasya*) style.

tandem lead block   See: head block.

tane (Japanese)   Literally: seed. In Zeami's writings, the subject matter or germ of a *no* play. (O'Neill EARLY 118)

tañer (Spanish)   To play a musical instrument, such as a trumpet or drum, to attract attention.

tang (Thai)   Literally: bed. Typically a low, flat, wooden bench that is used as a throne, bed, city wall, etc. in Thai dance-drama (*lakon ram*). Invariably the only set property used. Also called *tiang* (bench). (Virulrak "Likay" 142)

t'ang chü (Chinese)   See: *tangju*.

tanggu, t'ang ku (Chinese)   Literally: hall drum. A barrel-shaped drum with two ox-hide heads; its various sizes are usually as tall as their greatest diameter. It is used in the percussion orchestra (*wuchang*) in Beijing opera (*jingju*) and many other forms of music-drama (*xiqu*), usually for martial or formal occasions. Also called big drum (*dagu* or *ta ku*). (Scott CLASSICAL 47)

tanghui, t'ang hui (Chinese)   Literally: hall meeting. A type of celebratory banquet prevalent from the 17th to the early 20th C; an important performance occasion. Such banquets were given by the wealthy, either in a private home or a play establishment (*xizhuang*), and featured theatrical entertainment, usually music-drama (*xiqu*) performances by major performers and companies. Some performers specialized in playing at hall meetings. (Mackerras MODERN 83–85, 90–91; Mackerras RISE 198–199, 214)

tangju, t'ang chü (Chinese)   A form of music-drama (*xiqu*) popular in the area of Hebei around Tangshan which began developing in 1959 from shadow theatre (*piyingxi*). It uses *banqiangti* musical structure. Called shadow tunes drama (*yingdiaoju* or *ying tiao chü*) from 1970–1979.

t'ang ku (Chinese)   See: *tanggu*.

tangma, t'ang ma (Chinese)   A set of connected, conventionalized dance movements expressive of riding a horse which are used in Beijing opera (*jingju*) and many other forms of music-drama (*xiqu*). These movements all involve the use of an ornate, tassled riding whip (*mabian* or *ma pien*). (Halson PEKING 41–42, 50–51; Scott CLASSICAL 114, 176–177, 183; Zung SECRETS 24, 138–141)

tangmu, t'ang mu (Chinese)   See: *dazhang*.

tango   A Latin-American dance in 4/4 time with a pattern of step-step-step-step-close, with long pauses and stylized body positions.

tang tzu pan (Chinese)   See: *dangziban*.

tan hsien (Chinese)   See: *danxian*.

tanhuang, t'an huang (Chinese)   A type of storytelling (*quyi*) which arose in Zhejiang and Jiangsu Provinces and Shanghai in the 18th–19th C. Most forms feature one to six performers who speak, sing, and provide simple musical accompaniment. In a number of areas, *tanhuang* forms began developing into regional theatre forms (*difangxi*) after 1912. See also: *huju, suju, xiju* (meaning 2), yongju. (Mackerras MODERN 108–111)

tanjep kayon (Indonesian)   See: *tanceb kayon.*

tank, tank town   A remote small town, far from the major performing locations. Also called a jerkwater or filling-station town. (Wilmeth LANGUAGE)

tank circuit   A circuit of small towns.

tank drama   1. A spectacular play. 2. A play performed in small towns. (Berrey/Van den Bark SLANG 581) 3. An aquatic drama, featuring real water in a tank. Also called a tank spectacle. See also: aqua drama.

tank opera   A show performing in small towns. (Berrey/Van den Bark SLANG 580)

tan k'ou (Chinese)   See: *xiangsheng.*

tank spectacle   See: tank drama.

tank town   See: tank.

tan p'i ku (Chinese)   See: *danpigu.*

tanqiang (Chinese)   See: *chuanju.*

tantjeban, tantjeb kayon (Indonesian)   See: *tanceb kayon.*

t'an tz'u (Chinese)   See: *tanci.*

Tanz (German)   Dance.

tanzen roppo (Japanese)   A swaggering entrance walk by a young male character in *kabuki*. An example is the hero's entrance in *Sukeroku: the Flower of Edo* in Brandon CLASSIC 64–65. In Kyoto-Osaka, the same as *deha.* (Dunn/Torigoe ANALECTS 138) See also: *roppo.*

tao ch'i hsi (Chinese)   See: *luju.*

tao kuan tso (Chinese)   See: *daoguanzuo.*

tao ma tan (Chinese)   See: *daomadan.*

tao pan (Chinese)   See: *daoban.*

tap cue   Among professional stage electricians, a dimming technique in which the board operator unobtrusively increases or decreases the light on stage by tapping the handles of resistance dimmers.

tap dien (Vietnamese)   See: *kich.*

tape fuse   In Renaissance theatres, an inflammable tape running from candle to candle on a chandelier, making it possible to light them without using long poles or tapers. (Sabbattini in Hewitt RENAISSANCE 97)

tap for coda   In Britain: 1. A two-tap signal from the musical director to the stage manager that it is curtain time. 2. Behavior on the part of a performer which can lead to dismissal from a play or a company. (Granville DICTIONARY)

tap mat   A mat or runner made of wooden slats glued to a strip of canvas. It can be rolled up when not needed. Used by tap dancers. (Bax MANAGEMENT 146)

tap-off   1. See: twofer. 2. See: branch-off connector.

tapone (Thai)   A horizontal, double-faced drum played with the fingers in a classical *pi phat* musical ensemble. Also called *saphon, sphon*. Also spelled *taphone*. (Duriyanga THAI 27–30, Morton TRADITIONAL 68–70)

tapped transformer dimmer   In Britain, an autotransformer dimmer. (Bowman/Ball THEATRE)

taps   A drummer in a minstrel show. (Wilmeth LANGUAGE)

taquilla (Spanish)   1. A box office. 2. A ticket rack. 3. Box-office receipts.

taquillera, taquillero (Spanish)   A (female, male) ticket taker.

tarantella   A lively folk dance from southern Italy in 6/8 time.

Tarentini   (Latin Roman)   See: *ludi saeculares*.

tarik selampit (Malaysian)   See: *penglipur lara*.

tarima (Spanish)   A bench, bleacher, or seat in a public theatre. (Shergold SPANISH)

Tarokaja (Japanese)   The name given the chief servant in all *kyogen* plays.

tarokajamono (Japanese)   See: *shomyomono*.

tarras   In Elizabethan theatres that had an inner above (upper curtained stage), the space in front of the curtain. Also spelled terrace.

tarsos (Philippine)   Clowns in *zarzuela* plays. (Fernández ILOILO 138)

t'aryong (Korean)   A 12/8 beat rhythmic pattern commonly used to accompany dances in masked plays. See: *kkaeki-chu'm*. (Yi "Mask" 46)

ta sang tzu (Chinese)   See: *dasangzi*.

ta san t'ung (Chinese)   See: *dasantong*.

tassel   A bunch of thin strands, usually silver or gold in color, attached to the bra or pastie covering a stripper's nipple—to be twirled as the stripper gyrated; tassels were also on occasion attached to the panties, one on each buttock. Hence, tassel twirler. (Wilmeth LANGUAGE)

tassette (French)   1. Medieval thigh armor. 2. In the 17th C, the top of a doublet. (Boucher FASHION)

tat   In Britain, a piece of shoddy scenery or costume—something tattered. Hence, tatty. (Granville DICTIONARY)

tatalu (Indonesian)   See: *talu*.

tatas (French)   See: leading strings.

tate (Japanese)   1. A highly choreographed group fighting scene in *kabuki*. It is one type of battle (*tachimawari*). 2. The one-hundred-plus fighting movements used in such scenes. Leiter ENCYCLOPEDIA 385–386 has examples. 3. Similar kinds of fighting techniques used in film and television history plays. *Tateshi* is a choreographer of fight scenes, normally not the same person as the dance choreographer (*furitsukeshi*). (Brandon in Brandon/Malm/Shively STUDIES 93)

tate onnagata (Japanese)   Literally: lead *onnagata*. The leading female impersonator in a *kabuki* troupe and the troupe's second ranking member. This actor could play a number of different female role types. See: *onnagata*. Also called *tate oyama*. (Gunji KABUKI 184–185)

tate oyama (Japanese)   See: *tate onnagata*.

tate sakusha (Japanese)   See: *tate zakusha*.

tateyaku (Japanese)   A term erroneously used for a male actor in some Western books. The term does not exist in Japanese. (Dunn/Torigoe ANALECTS 171)

tate zakusha, tate sakusha (Japanese)   Literally: lead playwright. The chief playwright of a *kabuki* troupe, early 18th-late 19th C. He was assisted by a second rank playwright (*nimaime sakusha*), a third rank playwright (*sanmaime sakusha*), and half a dozen apprentice playwrights (*kyogen sakusha* or *kyogen kata*) and beginners (*minarai*). He was responsible for the main play (*hon kyogen*), in part writing it himself and in part directing the writing of his assistants. He also supervised rehearsals. Also called *tate tsukuri* (chief maker). (Kincaid KABUKI 225, Leiter ENCYCLOPEDIA 392–393, Gunji KABUKI 36)

tati (Malayalam)   Literally: beard. In *kathakali*, red, black, and white bearded characters are distinguished as major role types. See: *cukannattati, vellattati, karuttatati*. (Jones/Jones KATHAKALI 29–32)

ta t'ou (Chinese)   See: *datou*.

tatterman   A medieval earth-sprite puppet. Also called a kobold. (Baird PUPPET 65–66)

ta t'ung (Chinese)   See: *dasantong*.

tau ma (Vietnamese)   A song sung in *hat boi* and *cai luong* when pantomiming riding a horse. (Addiss "Theater" 148)

ta uta (Japanese)   Literally: field song. A folk dance associated with *dengaku*. (Hoff SONG 121)

tawajuh (Indonesian)   An initiation ceremony for a young puppeteer in Sundanese *wayang golek*. (Foley "Sundanese" 72–73)

tawak-tawak (Malaysian)   See: *gamelan*.

ta ying hsi (Chinese)   See: *dayingxi*.

Taylor trunk   A standard theatrical trunk made by the Taylor Trunk Company. Considered by touring performers a sign of their professional status. (Wilmeth LANGUAGE)

tayu (Japanese)   Literally: master. 1. Originally a court rank, and by extension in theatre a leading performer, a star. 2. A *sarugaku no* troupe leader in the 13th C. (Nakamura NOH 158) 3. The star *onnagata* actor of a *kabuki* troupe. The name is from the courtesan role (*tayu*) often played by the actor. An example is Agemaki in *Sukeroku: The Flower of Edo* in Brandon CLASSIC 55–92. 4. A chanter of narrative music, including in *bunraku*. Often the term becomes the chanter's personal name suffix, for example, Takemoto Ujitayu. (Ernst KABUKI 113, Kawatake HISTORY 57) 5. The major role in *kowakamai*. (Araki BALLAD 8)

tayumoto (Japanese)   In the 17th and 18th C, a *kabuki* theatre manager, the person holding the government license (*yagura*) to produce *kabuki* plays. Also called *zamoto*. (Leiter ENCYCLOPEDIA 442–443)

tayungan (Indonesian)   A victory dance by the winner, usually Bima or Hanuman, of the final battle in a Javanese *wayang* shadow play. Also spelled *tajungan*. (Humardani in Osman TRADITIONAL 85, Brandon THRONES 27)

ta'zia, taziyeh, ta'ziya (Iranian)   Literally: consolation. An Iranian ritual drama enacting the martyrdom of Husain, youngest son of Ali, the latter the son-in-law of Mohammed. (Gassner/Quinn ENCYCLOPEDIA 647)

T bar, T bar track, T track   A counterweight track secured vertically to the wall behind a counterweight set. The track guides a counterweight arbor.

T box   A container with hinged sides which fold like a parallel. (Carrington THEATRICANA)

TC   Abbreviation for tragicomedy or for theatre of cruelty.

TD   Technical director.

teaching plays   See: *Lehrstücke*.

teacup-and-saucer   See: cup-and-saucer.

tea-house theatre   See: *xiyuan*.

team   Two or more performers who work together, usually regularly.

tea party   In 18th C Britain, a morning performance, given to avoid licensing laws.

teapot acting style   A formal acting style of the 19th C which used a rising and falling vocal delivery and stances in which the performer put one hand on the hip and gestured with the other, creating a teapot image.

tear a passion to tatters   To overact. See also: chew the scenery.

tear down   To remove one's costume.

tear 'em out of their chairs   To delight an audience. (Berrey/Van den Bark SLANG 584)

tearful comedy   See: sentimental comedy.

tearjerker   1. A play or performance designed to make the audience weep. Also called an onion ballad, weeper, or weepie. See also: onion at the end. 2. An actor who employs gimmicks for the same purpose.

tear the house down   To receive liberal applause.

teaser   1. A border which hangs behind the act (main) curtain and in front of the tormentors, setting the height of the proscenium opening just as the tormentors set its width. The teaser also masks the first light pipe. In Britain: proscenium border, pros. border, pros border, house border. In France: *manteau d'Arlequin* (Harlequin's cloak) or *frise du manteau*. See also: grand drape, valance. 2. An advertisement designed to lure an audience into a theatre, as by not revealing the title of a forthcoming play. 3. Stage business used in 19th C melodrama to create suspense. (Bowman/Ball THEATRE)

teaser batten   See: first electric.

teaser position   See: bridge position.

teaser spot(light)   A spotlight on the teaser (first electric) batten. (Bowman MODERN, Philippi STAGECRAFT)

teaser strip   A striplight in the teaser position. The term sometimes means first border.

teaser thickness   See: box teaser.

teater (Yiddish)   Theatre.

teater kontemporari (Malaysian)   Malaysian for 'contemporary theatre.' Non-realistic, avant garde drama and theatre, established during the 1970s. Contrasted to realistic *drama moden*.

teater rakyat (Malaysian)   Literally: people's theatre. Theatre for the working class, as opposed to the middle class audiences.

teatr (Russian)   Theatre. The term is used for the theatre building, the troupe of performers and supporting personnel, or a training school. (Bowers ENTERTAINMENT 74)

teatro (Spanish and Italian)   1. A playhouse. 2. The stage. 3. The drama, plays.

teatro dei pupi (Italian)   A 19th–20th C Sicilian popular marionette theatre. The stories came from medieval legends of Charlemagne and the *Song of Roland*. (Gassner/Quinn ENCYCLOPEDIA 484)

teatro del grottesco (Italian)   See: theatre of the grotesque.

teatro di prosa (Italian)   Literally: prose theatre. In the 19th C, a dramatic genre characterized by stock characters and trivial plots. The term was also used to differentiate between spoken drama and opera (*teatro lirico*). (Archer in Matthews PAPERS 95–97)

teatro lirico (Italian)   Opera. See also: *teatro di prosa*.

techie   See: technician.

technical   Those aspects of a stage production other than the acting, directing, and business management: scenery, properties, lighting, sound effects, etc.

technical director   The person in charge of the preparation of scenery, properties, lighting, sound effects, etc., especially in a non-commercial theatre. See also: master carpenter.

technical rehearsal   A rehearsal focusing on all the technical cues in a show—curtain, light, scene shift, sound, etc. In Britain: scene rehearsal.

technician   A theatre worker chiefly concerned with lighting, scenery, sound effects, stagecraft, etc. A common nickname is techie, tekkie.

technique   1. A general method or specific application of it in any area of theatre, as acting technique, dramatic technique, stage technique, theatrical technique. (Bowman/Ball THEATRE) 2. In acting and dance, discipline: technical and mechanical skills, as opposed to such matters as interpretation and emotional expression.

technitae (Latin Roman), *technitai* (Greek)   See: Artists of Dionysus.

tedai gataki (Japanese)   1. The role of a villainous clerk in *kabuki*, usually in a gangster play (*kizewamono*). It is one type of villain role (*katakiyaku*). 2. An actor who plays this role. (Gunji KABUKI 188)

Ted Lewis   See: funnel.

tee-piece   In 19th C theatres, a gas bracket in the shape of a T, whether upright or inverted. As a kind of elementary chandelier, the T was inverted, with at least one light at either end of the crosspiece. As a worklight for rehearsals, the T was upright, with a number of burners on the crosspiece. The term was also used of gas supply pipes which formed a T. T light is a variant. (Rees GAS 94, 109, 118, 205, 208, figs. 69, 72)

teichos (Greek)   Literally: wall. Supposedly a raised place from which one might look down at the stage. Nicoll suggests that this and the *purgos* (tower) might have been high platforms. Since *teichos* means especially a wall around a city, perhaps the sole source (Pollux) meant the wall around the theatre. (Nicoll DEVELOPMENT 22)

tekkie   See: technician.

telaro (Italian)   Wing. (Plural: *telari*.) In the 17th C, Joseph Furttenbach and Nicola Sabbattini used the term to refer to any canvas-covered wooden frame— a *periaktos* (Greek), an angle wing, even a curved cloud border. (Furttenbach in Hewitt RENAISSANCE 186, Sabbattini in Nagler SOURCES 91)

telegraph   In performing, to anticipate in such a way that the audience can tell what will be said or done. Hence, telegraphing.

telengan (Indonesian)   1. The rounded eye style of many robust (*gagah*) and ogre (*raksasa*) puppet characters in Javanese *wayang*. Also spelled *thelengan*. Also called *plelengan*. (Long JAVANESE 70) 2. A shadow puppet with that eye style. (Brandon THRONES 48)

telephone board interconnector, telephone-type interconnecting system   See: interconnecting panel.

telescope   In acting, to quicken the tempo by overlapping speeches or business.

telescope pipe   The movable pipe in an extension pipe stand. (Bowman MODERN)

telescopic floor stand, telescopic pipe stand   See: light stand.

telescopic puppet   A collapsible and stretchable puppet. (Philpott DICTIONARY)

telinga kelir (Malaysian)   Literally: screen ears. Loops at the bottom of a shadow screen (*kelir*) that are fastened to a banana log to hold the screen taut. (Sheppard TAMAN 70, Yub in Osman TRADITIONAL 96)

telling the play   In Restoration theatres, announcing the next bill at the end of a performance. In the 18th C the announcement was called giving out the play. (Pepys DIARY 7 March 1667)

Tellspiel (Swiss-German)   A play dramatizing the deeds of the folk-hero William Tell. Such plays date from as early as 1512. (Matlaw MODERN 742)

telon (Philippine)   A painted backdrop used in *comedia* or *zarzuela*. (Mendoza COMEDIA 52, Fernández ILOILO 128) *Telon de boca* is a front curtain, closed between scenes or acts, and *telon de fondo* is a back curtain. (Fernández ILOILO 128) *Telon de calle* or *telon corto* is a street drop. (Hernandez EMERGENCE 143)

telón (Spanish)   A drop or curtain. *Cae el telón* means the drop curtain falls. (Rennert SPANISH 97)

tembang (Indonesian)   1. A type of classical song lyric, in a number of set meters. A *tembang* song can be sung in Javanese *wayang* shadow theatre by a puppet character (Brandon THRONES 55), and in *ludruk* by a transvestite singer (Peacock RITES 54). 2. In Sundanese *wayang golek*, also a style of singing that is not bound by the regular multiple-of-eight musical structure. (Foley "Sundanese" 153–156) See also: *kawih, langen driya, selingan.*

template   See: cookie, gobo.

template, template bench, template table   A special workbench used for constructing flats. It is carefully squared and has metal plates embedded in its surface at the proper places for turning clout nails when keystones and corner blocks are nailed to the frame of a flat. The table also has flanges, so that the stiles and rails of a flat can quickly be aligned.

templet   A 15th C metal ornament used as a hair roller. (Boucher FASHION)

temple theatre   A theory of the Russian symbolist Viacheslav Ivanov that the modern theatre should be brought back to its religious origins and express national and spiritual culture, involving spectators and performers in a common ecstasy. (Slonim RUSSIAN 191)

tempo   1. Pace; the speed at which a performance or any part of it moves. Also, the speed at which a performer speaks. 2. In dance, the pulse's speed. (Turner/Grauert/Zallman DANCE 81)

temps (French)   In ballet, a part of a step or movement in which there is no transfer of weight. A *temps* is a section of a *pas* (step). (Grant TECHNICAL)

temps de cuisse (French)   Literally: thigh step. In ballet, a term indicating that one foot is picked up and quickly replaced in preparation for a small *sissone* (a spring into the air). Also called a *pas de cuisse*. (Grant TECHNICAL, Wilson BALLET)

temps de flèche (French)   Literally: arrow step. In ballet, a man's step in which the left leg acts as a kind of bow and the right leg an arrow. (Grant TECHNICAL, Wilson BALLET)

temps de l'ange (French)   Literally: angel's step. In ballet, a step similar to the *temps de poisson* but with the legs bent as in attitude (q.v.) and the legs slightly open. (Grant TECHNICAL)

temps de poisson (French)   Literally: fish's step. In ballet, a jump with the back arched, forming a curve. The legs are extended and the feet are crossed to look like a fishtail. (Grant TECHNICAL)

temps levé (French)   In ballet, the holding of one foot in position while the dancer hops on the other. (Kersley/Sinclair BALLET)

temps lié (French)   Connected movement. In ballet, an exercise used in center practice, composed of a series of steps and arm movements based on the second, fourth, and fifth positions (q.v.). (Grant TECHNICAL)

ten-center   In early 20th C U.S., a theatre with a 10 cent admission charge. (Berrey/Van den Bark SLANG 577)

tendencies   In the Stanislavsky system, aspects of a performer's work that (incorrectly) digress from the spine or through line of a character. (Cameron/Gillespie ENJOYMENT 325)

tendu (French)   In ballet, stretched or held.

tenggong asu (Malaysian)   See: *panggung*.

teng hsi (Chinese)   See: *dengxi*.

tenjikugaku (Japanese)   Music of Tenjiku (India) played in *gagaku*. (Wolz BUGAKU 169)

tenkutittu (Kannada)   See: *yaksagana tenkutittu*.

"Ten minutes!"   A warning to performers and crew before the beginning of an act.

tennis-court theatre   In Baroque times, a roofed tennis court converted into a theatre.

tenor's farewell   A farewell performance designed to be repeated often. (Berrey/Van den Bark SLANG 580)

ten per and cakes   The salary of a mediocre performer. (Wilmeth LANGUAGE)

ten percenter   A performer's agent.

ten-shilling squat   In Britain, a seat in the stalls or dress circle. Obsolete, since ticket prices are now much higher. (Granville DICTIONARY)

tension   In dance, the restriction of movement flow. (Dell PRIMER 14)

tension block, tension idler, tension pulley   See: take-up block.

tensons (French)   In the 12th C, satirical dialogues between *trouvères* (troubadours) which dealt with the fine points of gallantry. Also called *jeux-partis*. (Hawkins ANNALS I 7)

tenti (Latin)   *Mansions* (French) or acting platforms in medieval Cornish productions. (Chambers MEDIAEVAL II 135)

tent rep op   The operator of a tent show presenting stock or repertory shows. (Berrey/Van den Bark SLANG 575)

tent show   Any entertainment given under canvas. Though tent shows were regular fare in the 19th C, by the 1920s they were the most popular form of village and small town entertainment. (In 1927 the editor of *Billboard* estimated in the *New York Times* that tent shows outdrew Broadway and all other U.S. legitimate theatre by about 76 million spectators to 48 million.) Often Toby shows with vaudeville interspersed, they were done by traveling companies which usually played a different show each night except Sunday (when they traveled). See Ashby/May for a treatment of this period. Other terms included repertoire (never repertory) and tent rep. (Ashby/May TROUPING 1-2; Wilmeth LANGUAGE 219, 271)

tent theatre   A theatre under canvas, often used for musical theatre performances. Hence, musical tent theatre.

ten-twent'-thirt'   1. Popular melodramas of the 19th C in the U.S., so named for the ticket prices of 10, 20, or 30 cents. 2. By extension, a touring company that played such melodramas. (Wilmeth LANGUAGE)

teoigoto (Japanese)   Literally: wounded business. 1. A scene in *kabuki* in which a major character is slowly, cruelly killed. It focuses on his or her suffering. 2. The acting of such a role. Abbreviated *teoi*. (Dunn/Torigoe ANALECTS 88) *Teoi no jukkai* is a confession (*jukkai*) by the dying character in such a scene. (Scott KABUKI 115)

teppu (Malayalam)   Literally: painted. A group of special characters in *kathakali*, including animals, whose makeup is descriptive, in contrast to characters who wear *pacca* or *katti* symbolic makeup. (Jones/Jones KATHAKALI 33)

Terence stage   A simple platform stage backed by a facade with four or five doorways for the characters; used at Renaissance Italian academies for revivals of plays by Terence. (Nicoll DEVELOPMENT 71)

Terentini (Latin Roman)   See: *ludi saeculares.*

termer   A long-term contract.

terp, terper, terpsichorean   A dancer. Hence, terping. From the Greek muse of dancing and choral song, Terpsichore.

terpsichorienne, terpsichorine   A chorus girl. (Berrey/Van den Bark SLANG 573)

terrace   See: tarras.

terre (French)   Literally: earth. A ground row. A long, low masking piece across the rear of the stage, painted to represent land. (Carlson "Inventory" 48)

(à) terre (French)   In ballet: 1. With the entire base of the foot touching the ground. 2. A direction to keep on the ground a foot usually raised in a certain position. (Grant TECHNICAL)

tertulia (Spanish)   1. That part of a public theatre occupied by priests and members of religious orders. 2. A gallery in the highest part of old theatres. (Shergold SPANISH)

tesserae (Latin Roman)   Tickets. The word was used for theatre tickets as well as many other types of tickets, tiles, and cubes. The literal meaning is thought to be 'four-cornered,' implying squares or cubes, though most surviving tickets, whether Greek or Roman, are circular. *Tessera theatralis* (ticket of the theatre) is specific for theatre ticket. (Sandys COMPANION 519; Bieber HISTORY 71, 186, 247, figs. 270, 811–816)

testa (Latin)   See: heavens.

tetep (Indonesian)   A noble giant in Sundanese *wayang golek.* (Foley "Sundanese" 39)

tetimimes   In later Roman times (c. 1st C AD and after), choreographed mimes in honor of the Titan goddess Tethys. Since 3,000 of the children of Tethys and Oceanus were rivers, it will be no surprise that the tetimimes were performed in the flooded orchestras of theatres. The term, evidently from Tethys and mime, is rare and may be a coinage. (Bieber HISTORY 237, Larousse MYTHOLOGY 93)

tetralogy   A series of four related plays by the same playwright.

text   The written or printed words and stage directions of a play.

text appeal   A loosely structured dramatic presentation of the *malé divadla* (small theatres) in Prague in the 1960s. The entertainment consisted of somewhat literary sketches, poetry readings, some improvisation, and light-hearted clowning. (Burian "Prague" 232)

texture   In dance, an aspect of style referring to the inner tensions in all movement. (Love DANCE)

T-H   See: tungsten-halogen lamp.

tha lakhon (Thai)   Dramatic or mimetic gesture in classical dance plays. See also: *rabam*. (Virulrak "Likay" 179–180)

than (Vietnamese)   A type of song composed in lines of seven syllables sung in *hat boi*. Used for exceptionally sad situations. (Addiss "Theater" 141)

than lwin (Burmese)   Small bell-cymbals used to mark time in theatrical musical ensembles. (Brandon SOUTHEAST 127)

thapone (Thai)   See: *tapone*.

tha ram (Thai)   Literally: dance movements. Beginning in the late 18th C, classical dance movements (*tha ram*) were arranged into 'alphabets' of movement (*mae bot*) and preserved in teaching treatises (*tamra fon ram*) at the Thai court. (Rutnin "Development" 12)

thaumatopoios (Greek)   A magician, one of the entertainers in mimes by at least the 3rd C BC. His work may have included tumbling and acrobatics. (Nicoll MASKS 35, 85)

theatarian, theaterian   An obsolete term for a performer. (Bowman/Ball THEATRE)

theater   See: theatre.

Theaterforschung (German)   Theatre research.

Theaterwissenschaft (German)   The science of the theatre arts. *Theatergeschichte* is theatre history

theatral   Of or pertaining to theatre.

theatrales operae (Latin Roman)   A claque, paid applauders. Plural of *theatralis opera*, theatre worker. Also called *fautores*. (Sandys COMPANION 520)

theatrama   See: multi-proscenium stage.

theatre, theater   1. Broadly, performance before an audience. In this sense, theatre includes everything from musical performance through circus and night clubs to plays of all kinds. See the front matter for information on the limits of the present work. 2. In Restoration times, the forestage or apron: "the Clouds descend to the Stage: then the Women and Men enter upon the Theater, and dance. . . ." Also called the stage. Later called the area or platform. (Boyle PRINCE 12, Stone/Kahrl GARRICK 131) 3. A building housing a stage for play, dance, and musical productions, or a substitute for such a building, such as a floating theatre, tent theatre, outdoor theatre, etc. 4. Things pertaining to or used in a theatre, such as plays, a stage, productions, a performing company, the audience. 5. Stageworthiness, as in good or bad theatre. 6. A word used in a variety of compound terms such as theatrecraft, theatregoer, theatro-, etc. (Bowman/Ball THEATRE).

Theatre and theater are U.S. spellings of this word. Although both endings were used in Shakespeare's day and so appear in early English dictionaries, Samuel Johnson prescribed the *-re* ending in his dictionary (1755) for the official English spelling used since his time. Merriam-Webster used the *-er* ending (to make it conform to other words said to be in that class) in the 1852 edition of Noah Webster's dictionary for Americans. Both spellings are recognized in Webster. (*Webster's Third New International Dictionary* 24a at -er/-re) Most U.S. editors prefer -er and the theatrical profession -re. It would appear an emotional context surrounds this word, making it difficult to shift completely from -re, because that spelling symbolizes a distinctive art form closely related to English and French/Italian traditions and remains usual in the profession in the U.S. The *New York Times* continues (1983) to use both spellings, with -er (since 9/16/62) for editorial columns and -re in the advertising copy (names of playhouses, etc.). The same practice is widespread in U.S. newspapers and other publications which carry theatrical advertising. See Hodge "Theat-*re*" 36–44 for a history of the two uses.

théâtre (French)   1. The stage. 2. A playhouse. 3. Plays. 4. The place of action.

theatre by children and youth   See: recreational drama, theatre for young audiences.

theatre club   See: stage society.

theatre critic   One who writes commentaries and passes judgment on the-atrical productions.

theatre Dame   In Britain, an actress who has been knighted.

théâtre de fauteuil (French)   Literally: armchair theatre. Plays written for reading rather than performance. Also called closet drama. (Matlaw MODERN 621)

théâtre de la foire (French)   In the Renaissance and later, an open-air stage and its productions at the fairs in France and Italy. See also: *forain*. (Roberts STAGE)

theatre education   See: children's drama.

theatre family, theatrical family   A family with several members, usually performers, in theatre work.

theatre folk   People involved in theatrical productions.

théâtre forain (French)   See: *forain*.

theatre for young audiences   The term for plays performed by adults for audiences ranging in age from early childhood to early adolescence. This term includes: theatre for children (typically, 12 years and under), theatre for youth (typically, adolescents), and participation theatre. Theatre organizations often call themselves a Theatre for Children or a Theatre for Youth although each may produce plays for both child and adolescent audiences. A variant of theatre for young audiences is 'theatre by children and youth,' the term for performances by young people, usually 10 years or older, playing for younger children. See also: theatre for youth. (Davis/Evans CHILDREN'S 37)

theatre for youth   1. See: theatre for young audiences. 2. In the U.S., performances directed primarily at audiences 13 through 15. In Europe, the age range sometimes goes into the mid-twenties. (Davis/Behm "Terminology" 10–11)

theatre games   In creative drama, improvisational activities with a game structure, designed to increase drama skills.

theatregoer   One who attends theatrical performances.

theatre group   An acting or producing company, often amateur. (Bowman/Ball THEATRE)

theatre history   The record of the development of the theatre (in the broadest sense—theatre architecture, acting, management, scenery, etc.)

theatre in education   1. See educational drama. 2. A comprehensive in-school approach to children's drama which always includes creative drama, integrated arts, and the use of local cultural resources to provide children's theatre. 3. In Britain (as Theatre in Education or TIE), the creation of theatre by artists-in-residence working with children in schools. Both the process and the end product involve participation by children; objectives often include political or social reform. (Goldberg CHILDREN'S 61)

theatre-in-the-round   See: arena theatre.

théâtre intime (French)   Intimate theatre.

theatrekeeper   See: stagekeeper.

theatre Knight   In Britain, an actor who has been knighted.

theatre laboratory   A workshop for training in one or more aspects of theatre.

theatreland   The theatre district in any large city.

théâtre libre (French)   In the late 19th C, free theatre, a form of French naturalistic theatre in which "all prohibitive laws have been cancelled, and only the demands of taste and of the modern spirit are allowed to determine the artistic form. . . ." The name derives from André Antoine's Théâtre Libre in Paris. (Strindberg in Cole/Chinoy PLAYWRITING 21)

théâtre mixte (French)   In partly Romanized western Europe, including northern France, a theatre intended for both amphitheatrical and theatrical use. Also called a *demi-amphithéâtre*. (Bieber HISTORY 202)

theatre of actualism   The realistic or naturalistic theatre of the late 19th C which tried to create a slice of life on stage.

theatre of cruelty   Antonin Artaud's visionary concept of a theatre based on magic and ritual which would liberate deep, violent, and erotic impulses; he wanted to integrate spectators and performers and bombard the audience with light, color, movement, and sound.

theatre of dreams   Jerzy Szaniawski's term for anti-naturalistic, poetic theatre in Poland. (Syzdtowski POLAND 41)

theatre of fact   A mid-20th C radical dramatic form resembling agit-prop theatre but less strident. It relied on the dialectic of courtroom argument and the weight of fact as the basis of feeling and movement. (Isaac "Fact" 109)

theatre of sources   According to the Polish director Jerzy Grotowski, the wellsprings of celebration, healing, and meditation in the here-and-now which the actor seeks out as sources of ongoing discovery. (Grimes "Sources" 68)

theatre of the absurd   A term coined by Martin Esslin to describe a post-World War II kind of drama that viewed existence as meaningless and treated language as an inadequate means of communication. Action becomes senseless, useless, absurd; hence, absurdist plays often convey their ideas by poetic images rather than standard plot. The chief practitioners were Samuel Beckett and Eugene Ionesco, and the classic absurdist play is Beckett's *Waiting for Godot*. (Cameron/Gillespie ENJOYMENT, Esslin ABSURD 1–10)

theatre of theatricality   In late 20th C German drama, plays whose preoccupation is with a basic mistrust of traditional dramatic performance and convention and with audience responses to them. The aim is to clarify and heighten awareness of what underlies the theatrical experience, so as to pave the way for innovative theatrical forms. (Arnold "German" 51)

theatre of the Bauhaus   A theatre movement of the 1920s in Germany that stressed mechanization and abstraction and tried to create total theatre—the mobile or immobile body in space, light in motion, and architecture. The Bauhaus, based at Weimar, was led by the architect Walter Gropius, and the chief figures in the Bauhaus theatre were Oskar Schlemmer and Laszlo Moholy-Nagy. (Schlemmer/Moholy-Nagy/Molnar BAUHAUS 7–14)

theatre of the grotesque   A World War I dramatic movement that stressed the paradoxical and contradictory aspects of life, especially the conflict between illusion and reality. Luigi Pirandello was closely associated with the movement. In Italian: *teatro del grottesco*.

theatre of the mind   See: readers theatre.

theatre of the ridiculous   Late 20th C plays written in a wildly farcical manner, postulating among other ideas that man mocks his own ideals, his weaknesses lie in what he is most serious about, paradoxes stop mental processes, and theatre is event, not object. The theatre of the ridiculous uses bizarre clowning, grotesque makeup, nudity, burlesque, melodrama, and sado-masochistic properties. (Ludlam "Ridiculous" 70, Brecht "Family" 117–119)

theatre of the social outsider   A late 20th C German theatre form concerned with the suffering of working-class people. (Arnold "German" 48)

théâtre panique (French), **panic theatre**   Playwright Fernando Arrabal's term (c. 1962) for what he called "a ceremony—partly sacrilegious, partly sacred, erotic, and mystic, a putting to death and exaltation of life, part Don Quixote and part Alice in Wonderland." Brockett comments that Arrabal, at least in his later plays, "not only challenges all [i.e. pan] values, he ferrets out all the hidden corners of the human psyche.'' (Brockett HISTORY 689, Arrabal ''Arrabal'' 73–76)

theatre party   1. A special performance, such as a benefit. 2. A group of theatregoers who attend a performance in a group, sitting together. (Bowman/Ball THEATRE)

theatre plant   A theatre building and its equipment, particularly such production facilities as a scene shop, costume shop, etc.

theatre proprietor   In Britain, a theatre owner.

theatre restaurant   See: dinner theatre.

Theatre Royal   See: patent house.

théâtres de la foire (French)   Theatres at the fairs, popular in medieval times and later.

theatre ship   In Britain, a merchantman converted into a theatre. (Granville DICTIONARY)

théâtre subventioné (French)   A subsidized theatrical company.

théâtre supérieure (French)   In the 17th C, a second stage, raised 13 feet above the main platform stage. (Brockett HISTORY 255)

theatre theatrical   Theatricalism.

(the) Theatre Trust   See: Syndicate.

theatre workshop   See: theatre laboratory.

theatric   Having to do with theatre.

theatrical   1. Belonging to the theatre. The term is often complimentary but can also be used in a derogatory sense, indicating something affected or extravagant. 2. Having to do with theatricalism. Hence, theatrically, theatricality, theatricalness, theatricals, etc. 3. In the past, a performer. (Bowman/Ball THEATRE)

theatrical agent   An agent serving as a play agent, talent scout, etc.

theatrical art   The arts and skills involved in dramatic representation, especially acting and playwriting and often design. (Bowman/Ball THEATRE)

theatrical bobbinet(te)   See: theatrical gauze.

theatrical circuit   A chain of theatres operated or controlled by a single person or company. In the early 20th C some circuits stretched across the U.S. Theatrical circuits go back at least to the 18th C in Britain.

theatrical coach   A person who trains performers. (Bowman/Ball THEATRE)

theatrical cold cream   A special cold cream used by performers and characterized by ease of removal.

theatrical company   See: acting company.

theatrical convention   See: convention.

theatrical costume   See: costume.

theatrical costumer   See: costume designer.

theatrical criticism   Serious analysis and judgment of a theatrical production.

theatrical face powder   A special substance used by performers in making up, characterized by special adhesive qualities.

theatrical family   See: theatre family.

theatrical gauze   A thin, open-weave fabric, semi-transparent but not as opaque as scrim, used for drops to create dream or hazy effects, for transparencies, on cut drops and borders, etc. Also called bobbinet(te), scenic gauze. (Bowman/Ball THEATRE)

theatrical hardware   Specialized hardware used in the theatre, such as stage braces, brace cleats, stage screws, etc.

theatricalism   A style of playwriting and stage production which emphasizes theatricality for its own sake and uses the artifice of the stage without attempting to create an illusion of real life on stage. (Most plays or productions incorporate a certain amount of theatricality, however.) Also called theatre theatrical and theatricism.

theatricality   See: theatrical.

theatricalize   To make dramatic or theatrical.

theatrical lamp dip   See: lamp dip.

theatrical maid   An actress's dresser.

theatrical net   An open-weave fabric used in foliage borders. Not to be confused with theatrical gauze or scrim.

theatrical press agent, theatrical representative   See: press agent.

theatricals   Especially in the past, stage productions, usually amateur.

theatrical speech   See: stage English.

theatrical stores   Warehouses for scenery and properties.

Theatrical Syndicate   See: Syndicate.

theatrical technique   Stage skill, especially in technical theatre; but the term is also applied to one with skill in the technical (as opposed to interpretive and emotional) side of performing.

theatrical trunk babies   Children of performers, brought up to perform. See also: born in a trunk.

theatrical world   1. The domain of the theatre. 2. The people connected with the theatre.

theatrician   An old term for a person specializing in dramatic production. (Bowman/Ball THEATRE)

theatricism   Theatricalism.

theatricize   1. To make dramatic, theatrical. 2. To perform. (Bowman/Ball THEATRE)

theatrics   1. The arts and skills of stage production. 2. Histrionics; extravagant performing. 3. Extravagant behavior. (Bowman/Ball THEATRE)

theatromania   A rare term for a passion for theatre.

theatron (Greek)   Literally: place for seeing. 1. Audience, group of spectators. 2. The space for the audience, the auditorium. 3. The theatre taken as a whole. 4. Performance in a theatre. 5. Any performance place. The order of meanings is about the order in which they grew up; even meaning 3, the commonest, is 5th C BC, though most examples are after the middle of the following century; it is sometimes used figuratively. Meaning 4, though perhaps next after meaning 3 in frequency of use, is late: no example can certainly be dated earlier than the 1st C AD. Meaning 5 is rare. See also: *cavea, koilon.*

theatrones (Greek)   At least in the 5th C BC, the lessee of a theatre. The money received from ticket sales was his; in exchange, he was obligated to keep the theatre in good repair. Also called an *architecton.* (Allen ANTIQUITIES 40)

theatrophone   A device to assist audience members who are hearing impaired or who are in acoustically poor seats. Earphones bring them the sound of a performance. The device can also be used to bring a translation of the dialogue of a play to those unfamiliar with its language.

theatrum (Latin Roman)   Literally: place for seeing. 1. The theatre, the theatre building. 2. The seating area of the theatre. (Duckworth NATURE 79, Beare ROMAN 171, Sandys COMPANION 514–515, 518)

Theatrum Graecorum (Latin Roman)   A Greek theatre. (Flickinger GREEK 76, fig. 43)

Theatrum Latinum (Latin Roman)   A Roman theatre. (Flickinger GREEK 75, fig. 42)

theatrum mundi (Latin)   From as early as the 16th C, an itinerant marionette theatre in which small, intricately-designed figures moved on rails. A wide variety of scenes and remarkable dexterity were displayed. In the 18th C, called *titirimundi* (Spanish). See also: peep show. (Malkin PUPPETS 23, 24)

theatrum tectum (Latin Roman)   A roofed theatre. (Beare ROMAN 273)

theayter   A misspelling of theatre which suggests its (usually) comic pronunciation.

the hung (Vietnamese)   In *hat cheo*, a poetic passage expressing love. (Pham-Duy MUSICS 136)

thelengan (Indonesian)   See: *telengan.*

them   The audience. (Berrey/Van den Bark SLANG 574)

theme   1. The meaning of a work; the thesis or main idea. Hence, thematic. 2. An Elizabethan actor's improvisation in verse on a subject provided by a member of the audience, presented at the end of a performance. (Bowman/Ball THEATRE)

theologeion (Greek)   Literally: speaking place for the gods, from *theos*, god, and *logeion*, speaking place. There seems to be no doubt that the *theologeion*, whatever and wherever it was, designated the place from which the gods spoke. The word occurs in Pollux, who speaks of it as high above the stage. Scholars have argued for the roof of the *proskenion*, the second story of the *skene*, the roof of the *skene*, and a special platform above the *skene*. Also called in U.S. English theologium, with theologeion as a variant. (Arnott SCENIC 42–43, 76, 104, 118–120; Arnott ANCIENT 24–25; Pickard-Cambridge DIONYSUS 46, 48, 55–56, 157, 172, 184, 267; Pollux in Nagler SOURCES 9)

theoric fund, theoricon   See: *theorikon*.

theorikon (Greek)   Money given full citizens for attending the theatre. Ancient sources lay the introduction of the theoric fund to Pericles, who established the fund on behalf of the poor. While little is known of the *theorikon*, it was apparently used for the Dionysia and at least one other festival. Pickard-Cambridge believes that it was paid in cash and included not only the cost of a ticket but also other of the citizen's festival expenses. The meaning of U.S. English theoricon is similar. (Pickard-Cambridge FESTIVALS 265–268, 270)

theory   In criticism, a coherent idea of dramatic literature or theatrical production or both. An example is Bertolt Brecht's epic theatre theory.

the phu (Vietnamese)   The poetic form used in *hat cheo* when referring directly to a person, scene, or situation. (Pham-Duy MUSICS 136)

Thérèse   See: *calèche*.

therukoothu (Tamil)   Literally: street play. A folk dance-drama, based on epic and legendary stories, that is performed in Tamil Nadu state, southeast India, by an all-male troupe. (Gargi FOLK 132–143)

thesis play   A drama of ideas; a play designed to set forth problems and sometimes their solution. Occasionally called a purpose play.

thespian   1. A performer. 2. Having to do with the theatre. From the 6th C BC actor-playwright Thespis. Hence, thespian art, thespic, children of Thespis, thesp, etc. (Bowman/Ball THEATRE)

thespian rage   Simulated anger.

the ty (Vietnamese)   The poetic form used for comparing one thing to another in *hat cheo*. (Pham-Duy MUSICS 136)

they threw the babies out of the balcony   A vaudeville and burlesque description of a successful act or show. (Wilmeth LANGUAGE 273)

thiasos (Greek)   A group of worshipers, especially of Dionysus. The *thiasos* ultimately became the chorus of ancient Greek drama. *Thiasarch*, the leader of a *thiasos*, occurs in the 19th C in Britain. In U.S. English: thiasos, thiasus. (Harrison RITUAL 241, Bieber HISTORY 16)

thiasote, thiasite   An individual member of a *thiasos*. The entry is U.S. English. The Greek source is *thiasotes*. (Bieber HISTORY 16)

thickness   Thickness piece—a narrow flat, board, or other stiff material set at right angles to a door or window opening in a flat, to give the appearance of solidity. Also called a reveal, return, or (in Britain) set back.

thief   A scene stealer.

thief of bad gags   A comic who steals jokes from other comics. (Berrey/ Van den Bark SLANG 572)

thimble   A grooved, usually tear-shaped metal ring used to keep a loop of rope or wire from chafing. (Bowman/Ball THEATRE)

Thingplatz (German)   One of about 40 multi-purpose theatres in Nazi Germany. See also: *Thingspiel*. (Gadberry "Thingspiel" 104–105)

Thingspiel (German)   Nazi pageant drama of 1933–1937: open-air performances whose underlying principle was National Socialism. Large in scale, the pageant form was derived from Reformation and medieval drama. The performances consisted largely of courtroom debates with choruses and sub-choruses of the people delivering judgment and glorifying the "new order." (Gadberry "Thingspiel" 103, 104; Gassner/Quinn ENCYCLOPEDIA 353)

thinking part   A role with no lines.

thirai cheelai (Tamil)   A white hand-held curtain in *therukoothu*. Principal characters sing and dance their introduction while half-concealed behind it. (Gargi FOLK 135)

third banana   The fall guy in burlesque; the comic stooge who takes most of the falls and is mauled by the other performers. (Wilmeth LANGUAGE)

third border   See: first border.

third business   Tertiary roles.

third company   A troupe performing a production on tour while the first and second companies are performing elsewhere.

third day   In Restoration and 18th C British theatres, the third performance of a new play, the profits of which went to the author. Also called the poet's day. (Anonymous in Nagler SOURCES 231)

third position   In dance, the placement of the feet so that the heel of one foot touches the other foot at or near the instep. (Rogers DANCE 259)

thirds   See: number three.

third sex   Formerly in show business, a homosexual. (Wilmeth LANGUAGE)

third sound   The third piece of music before the beginning of a performance in an Elizabethan theatre, the last to be played before the play began. (Dekker in Nagler SOURCES 137)

third stanza   The third act on a bill.

thissahta (Burmese)   An engagement scene in *zat*, featuring songs and dances performed by the prince-hero and one or more prospective wives.

tholapavu koothu (Malayalam)   Literally: leather puppet play. A shadow play in Kerala state, southwest India, that uses small leather puppets to perform episodes from the 12th C Tamil language version of the *Ramayana* epic, written by the poet Kamban. Also spelled: *tholpavai kuthu*. (Vatsyayan TRADITIONAL 114)

tholu bommalattam (Telugu)   See: *tolu bommalu kattu*.

thom (Khmer)   See: *skor thom*.

three   See: in one.

three-a-day   Especially in vaudeville, a production that is performed thrice daily. See also: two-a-day, four-a-day.

three-decker   A three-act play.

three-dimensional lighting   See: plastic lighting.

three-dimensional trim   Molding, scrollwork, etc. that is built rather than painted.

threefer, three-in-one   Especially among U.S. professional stage electricians, a single circuit with three outlets in parallel. Also called a W.

three-fold   Three flats hinged together and capable of being folded for storage.

three-in-one   See: threefer.

three-legged stool   In playwriting, a device in which the author reveals two facts to the audience, and then a third. The last fact causes the preceding events to be viewed in a new, different, and often surprising context. (Macgowan "Vital" 28)

three-light system   In lighting the acting space of an arena theatre, a method which uses three instruments in each area. Seen from above, each instrument is separated from its neighbor by 120°. In the four-light system, the additional instrument results in a spacing of 90°. (Rubin/Watson LIGHTING 52–55)

three-line clew   See: clew.

three-quarter position   A performer's position on stage in which he or she faces one of the upstage corners, that is, one-quarter from a full back position. (Dean/Carra FUNDAMENTALS 35, McGaw ACTING 197)

three-riser   A platform with three levels, or three platforms of different levels placed together.

three-sheet   To exaggerate.

three-sheet an act   To play a leading role in an act.

threesome   A scene for three performers.

three-step   A stair unit with three risers and three treads. In Britain: three-tread. (Bowman/Ball THEATRE)

(the) three unities   See: unities.

three-way connector   See: multiple connector.

threnos (Greek)   A dirge, which was one type of choral ode (*stasimon*) used in ancient tragedy. (Webster CHORUS 147, 149)

through line   See: spine.

throw   1. The distance from a light source to the area or object it illuminates. Hence: long throw, short throw, and (occasionally) medium throw. The term is usually used of spotlights, but also of the distance from a projector to a screen. 2. The working distance or range of distances at which a lighting instrument is effective. 3. As a verb, sometimes followed by 'in' or 'out': to turn on or off, to throw a switch. (Wehlburg GLOSSARY, Bellman SCENE, Bowman MODERN)

throw a cleat, throw a line   To join two flats by lacing them together with a lash line. (Granville DICTIONARY)

throw a life line, throw a line, throw a prompt   To prompt, to give a cue.

throw a performance   To perform.

throwaway   1. A reduced-price ticket. 2. An incidental joke or witty remark sandwiched between major jokes. Originally vaudeville. 3. A brochure, flier, or other printed matter used for advertising a production. See also: throw away. (Wilmeth LANGUAGE)

throw away   To speak a line indifferently, rendering it unimportant. This is usually done as a way of putting the focus of attention on another line or piece of business, or with lines offering little opportunity to a performer. Sometimes a performer will throw away lines (yet make them heard) as a character trait (such as showing boredom or weariness). And sometimes an unskilled performer will throw away a line without realizing it. Hence, throw away one's lines, throw it away, a throw-away line. See also: throwaway.

throw boxes and pit together   See: pit railed into boxes.

throw distance   See: throw, meanings 1 and 2.

"Throw him a fish!"   Formerly, a call of derision at an unsatisfactory performer. (Berrey/Van den Bark SLANG 592)

throwing it from the velvet   Especially in pre-microphone vaudeville, belting out a song. The velvet was the house curtain. See also: blues shouter. (Hughes/Meltzer MAGIC 97, 99)

throw in, throw out   See: throw.

throw line   See: lash line.

throw out the voice   To project; to make oneself heard and understood by all members of the audience.

thrust   See: thrust stage.

thrust out   In an Elizabethan performance, to push a heavy property onstage.

thrust stage, thrust   An open stage, thrusting into the audience, with seats on three sides, as in Shakespeare's Globe Theatre or the Guthrie Theatre in Minneapolis, Minnesota.

thud and blunder   Crude, noisy, melodramatic acting.

thume mai (Thai)   See: *ranad*.

thunder barrel   See: thunder crash.

thunder bell   In 18th C theatres, a prompter's bell used to cue thunder. (Hughes in Hume LONDON 131)

thunder box   See: thunder run.

thunder cart   A heavy cart with irregularly shaped wheels; when pushed it produces the sound of thunder. Also called a rumble cart.

thunder channel   See: thunder run.

thunder crash   A suspended barrel from which stones are dropped onto iron sheets to simulate thunder. Also called a thunder barrel. (Bowman/Ball THEATRE)

thunder curtain   See: thunder sheet.

thunder drum   A wooden drum or barrel containing rocks or iron balls. When rotated, it simulates thunder.

thunder pipe   An 18th C device for simulating thunder: "like the bullets. . . when they roll *down the thunder-pipe . . .*" The device must have been similar to a thunder channel or thunder run. (Hill/Popple PROMPTER 23 May 1735)

thunder roller   See: thunder run.

thunder run   In Renaissance theatres, a stepped channel down which a cannonball was rolled to give the effect of thunder. The thunder run was usually over the front of the stage or in a room above the auditorium. Also called a thunder box, thunder channel, thunder roller, hutch, rabbit hutch, or rumble box.

thunder sheet   A hanging strip of sheet iron which simulates thunder when shaken or struck. Also called a thunder curtain.

thunder tank   A suspended galvanized iron tank which is struck to simulate thunder. (Bowman/Ball THEATRE)

thymele (Greek)   Literally: altar. 1. The sacrificial altar. In archaic Greece and perhaps also in the 5th C BC, the *thymele* was ordinarily in the center of the circular *orchestra*. There is evidence, however, that it was sometimes placed at the circumference of the *orchestra*, opposite the *skene* (scene building). Other altars could be used as properties, and might then be placed anywhere in the actors' area; *thymele* is used of such altars, but references to the sacrificial altar are much more frequent. 2. By extension, the *orchestra*. 3. That which takes place in the *orchestra*. 4. The platform or foundation of the sacrificial altar, also known as the *bema*. (Both terms are also used for any platform.) 5. In Rome and Asia minor, a stage. This is a late use. By the time of Plutarch, *thymele* and derivatives had become very broad in meaning. As part of this broadening, the distinction between *thymele* and derivatives, and *skene* and derivatives, had been pretty thoroughly blurred in the minds of some writers. (Arnott SCENIC 43–46, 51–54; Pickard-Cambridge DIONYSUS 129–132, 168)

thymelic   In the ancient Greek theatre, having to do with the *orchestra*. Hence such phrases as thymelic artist, thymelic performance, and other combinations. The meanings are various and may include choral dance, song, and instrumental performances, in various combinations at different times. A major use contrasts thymelic artist or performance with scenic artist or performance, the latter referring to what is done on the stage by contrast with the *orchestra* area. See also: scenic. (Bieber HISTORY 126)

thymelicae (Latin Roman)   In the later Eastern Roman Empire (c. 3rd–4th C AD), female dancers of the lowest class. They were virtually slaves until Justinian, influenced by his wife Theodora, a former *thymelica*, freed them and in other ways assisted their rehabilitation. The purpose of this and similar actions affecting other entertainers was to remove most of the vulgar varieties of performance for the benefit of regular comedy and tragedy. (Tunison TRADITIONS 95–98)

thymelic artist   See: thymelic.

thymelici (Latin Roman)   In the Greek theatre, thymelic performers, that is, those who performed in the *orchestra* rather than on the stage. U.S. English thymelici is limited to the Greek chorus. See also: thymelic. (Bieber HISTORY 187)

thyratron tube dimmer   A remote control electronic device which, by a process known as gating, controls the pulses of alternating current. Because a thyratron tube passes only half of each AC cycle, George Izenour developed the first pure thyratron dimmer by matching two tubes; the arrangement has been known by the trade name Izenour dimmer. Among other names: thyratron dimmer, tube dimmer, electronic tube dimmer. Control boards based on the thyratron were early known as Izenour switchboards and ultimately as tube boards. (Bellman LIGHTING 192–194, Lounsbury THEATRE 41)

thyristor dimmer, thyrister dimmer   See: silicon controlled rectifier.

thyromata (Greek)   Literally: doorways. In the 4th C BC theatre and after, the wide openings in the second story of the *skene* (scene building). Three or five such openings were usual, but there are examples of one and seven.

The term is sometimes used for folding doors within the opening, sometimes for the space behind the openings (which thus formed rear or inner stage areas), and sometimes for large, painted panels placed behind the openings. Singular: *thyroma*. See also: *regia*. (Bieber HISTORY 111, 114–115, 124, 125, figs. 469, 470; Webster PRODUCTION 140, 162–163) *thyrsos* (Greek), *thyrsus* (Latin), **thyrsus**   The Bacchic wand, originally wrapped in ivy and vine leaves and topped by a pine cone. The *thyrsos* was characteristic of Dionysian revels. Plural: *thyrsi*.

ti (Chinese)   See: *di*.

tiada (Philippine)   An interlude between combat sequences in the tournament (*torneo*) scene in *comedia*. (Mendoza COMEDIA 194)

tiang (Thai)   See: *tang*.

tiang seri (Malaysian)   The center post of a *ma'yong* theatre. (Yousof "Kelantan" 74)

tiao ch'ang   See: *diaochang*.

tiao shih (Chinese)   See: *diaoshi*.

tiao yü t'ai (Chinese)   See: *diaoyutai*.

tibag (Philippine)   A folk dramatization of St. Helena's "search for the Cross on which Christ died," enacted during April and May. (Tonogbanua SURVEY 81–82, Salazar in Cruz SHORT 81)

tibia (Latin Roman)   A flute, clarinet, double pipe. Flute is the usual English. *Tibia* originally meant shin-bone, and the first pipes were of bone. See also: *tibicen*. (Bieber HISTORY 148, 151)

tibicen (Latin Roman)   A flute player, piper. He used two pipes (*tibiae*) bound to his mouth in such fashion that both hands were free. He was probably onstage, where his accompaniment was a major element in most plays. (Beare ROMAN 168–169, 219)

ti bot (Thai)   Literally: to interpret text. 1. To learn a new role in classical dance theatre. (Rutnin "Development" 14) 2. In Thai dance-drama, the use of bodily movement and hand gesture appropriate to the text.

tick   Ticket. Playgoers entering a theatre 'on tick' enter free or on credit.

ticket   1. An admission slip to a theatre. 2. The admission fee. Among the many combinations: ticket stub, ticket buyer, ticket holder, ticket agency, ticket agent, ticket broker, ticket box, ticket rack, ticket office, ticket window.

ticket agency   An office serving as a ticket broker. In Britain, booking office or library.

ticket checker   In Britain, a ticket taker.

ticket gouger, ticket hustler   A ticket scalper.

ticket hustling   Speculation on theatre tickets.

ticket night   In 18th C theatres in Britain, a performance for which house servants and minor performers were allowed to sell as many tickets as they could, sharing their sales with the management. (Troubridge BENEFIT 28)

ticket rack   See: rack.

ticket scalper   A ticket speculator; one who buys tickets at box-office prices and sells them for a profit. Also called a digger, gyp, rat, speculator, ticket gouger, or ticket hustler.

ticket speculator   See: ticket scalper.

ticket stub   The portion of a theatre ticket kept by the ticket taker.

ticket taker   A theatre employee who takes theatregoers' tickets at the playhouse door. In Britain, called a ticket checker, check taker, or checker.

ticket window   A box-office window where tickets are sold. In Britain: wicket. (Bowman/Ball THEATRE)

tie   1. A strip of canvas or woven cotton used in place of a rope to tie around a rolled drop. Also called a tyer. 2. In lighting, to put on the same circuit (to gang), as in "Let's tie the baby spotlight to the chandelier in Act I."

TIE   See: theatre in education.

tie (Chinese)   See: *tiedan*.

tie cord   A piece of cord, a flat woven strip, or a shoestring used to tie a drapery to a batten. Also called tie line.

tiedan, t'ieh tan (Chinese)   Secondary female role. 1. A young supporting female role, such as a maidservant; a major subcategory of the female role (*dan*) in *kunqu* and many other forms of music-drama (*xiqu*). Abbreviated *tie* or *t'ieh*. (Dolby HISTORY 105, Mackerras RISE 2, Scott CLASSICAL 32) 2. See: *huadan*.

t'ieh, t'ieh tan (Chinese)   See: *tiedan*.

tieh tzu (Chinese)   See: *xuezi*.

tie-in system   A requirement by a ticket broker that a buyer must purchase tickets for a second performance in order to get the tickets of his or her choice. (Bowman/Ball THEATRE)

tie line   A cord (often a shoelace) used to tie a curtain to a batten.

tien chü (Chinese)   See: *dianju*.

tie off   To fasten, as when the lash line holding two flats together is secured, or when a line from the gridiron is secured to the pinrail. In Britain: make off.

tie-off cleat   Usually, the lowest cleat on the back of a flat. The lash line holding two flats together is secured to the cleat.

tie-off hitch   A knot used to tie off a lash line when two flats are lashed together. The knot secures the line, but a downward pull on the end of the line releases it completely.

tie-off pin   A metal or wooden rod, like a belaying pin, to which lines from the gridiron are tied off at the pinrail.

tie-off rail   See: trim rail.

tie-off screw   A long screw used in place of a tie-off cleat on a flat. (A nail is sometimes used instead of a screw.)

tier   1. A balcony or gallery. 2. One of a group of rows of theatre seats or boxes, especially when such groups rise behind or above one another. 3. In either sense, to arrange or to be arranged (tiered) in such a manner. (Bowman/ Ball THEATRE)

tier man   See: tire man.

tie-tack   A milliner's sewing stitch used to secure light trimmings to headgear permanently, lightly, and gracefully. (Dreher HATMAKING)

tie wig   A 17th–18th C wig tied in back with silk ribbon bows. (Fay GLOSSARY)

ti fang hsi (Chinese)   See: *difangxi*.

Tiffany whisk   See: rabat(o).

tight-pin backflap   See: backflap.

tights   Close-fitting costumes, like leotards, though sometimes worn only from the waist down.

tights play   A 19th C entertainment using chorus girls in tights. (Leslie ACT 27)

tilter   A bustle which tilted when its wearer walked. (Wilcox DICTIONARY)

tilting fork   See: yoke.

tilting yoke   See: bracket.

tilt jack   See: tip jack

timber   A stock forest drop carried by touring companies in the early 20th C. See also: back room, front room, town. (McNamara "Scenography" 20)

timber and town   See: front and back.

(the) timbers   The provinces.

time   1. In a play text or program, the indication of the time of the action of a scene, act, or play, such as the time of day, the year or period, etc. 2. In the plural, the dates of a touring engagement. (Bowman/Ball THEATRE) 3. A vaudeville engagement, the importance of which was indicated by whether it was big time or small time. (Wilmeth LANGUAGE) 4. In dance, the relative duration of movements and their accents, rhythm, pauses, meter, or non-meter. (Turner/Grauert/Zallman DANCE 29)

time book   See: time sheet.

time cue   A cue of some duration, as when a spotlight is dimmed to blackout over several seconds.

time sheet   The stage manager's notes on the running time of each act, the length of the intermissions (in Britain: intervals), the length of the full performance, audience response, etc. The time sheet also concerns the work time of the stage crews, to avoid overtime charges. Also called in Britain a time book.

timing 1. In performing and directing, the selection of the precise moment for saying or doing something. Timing involves tempo, rhythm, and pauses. 2. In dance, the patterns of release of energy, performed within time limitations. (Turner/Grauert/Zallman DANCE 24)

timing tape See: cue tape.

tin beard Formerly, an actor's crêpe-hair beard not well smoothed into the makeup. (Bowman/Ball THEATRE)

ting ch'ang pai (Chinese) See: *dingchangbai*.

ting ch'ang shih (Chinese) See: *dingchangshi*.

tin hat See: funnel.

tin-pan alley, Tin Pan Alley The nickname given to 28th Street between 5th and 6th Avenues in New York City, the location of many popular music publishers in the early 20th C. (Later, around Broadway and 50th Street.) Also called racket row, songsters' avenue, pluggers' den, pluggers' paradise, etc. The name stems from the practice of putting paper behind the steel strings of an upright piano, creating a tinny, wheezy, guitar-like sound. The name came to be associated with the song-writing and -selling business generally. (Bowman/Ball THEATRE, Ewen MUSICAL 45, Wilmeth LANGUAGE)

tip 1. A usually curled, short ostrich feather. 2. The top of a hat's crown. Also called the lid. (Dreher HATMAKING) 3. In 19th C theatres, the fitting at the end of a gas burner which determined the shape of the flame. Tips were either batwing or fishtail; otherwise, Argand burners were used. (Rees GAS 204; figs. 15, 16)

tipi fissi (Italian) Literally: stock types. The masks of the *commedia dell'arte*. (Erenstein in Mayer/Richards WESTERN 34)

tip jack A triangular lifting mechanism on casters, used for shifting large scenic units. Two or more such jacks create a rolling platform for the scenic unit when it is tipped backward until the casters touch the floor. The uprights of the jack can be made adjustable to control the angle of the tip. Lounsbury has an illustration. Also called a tilt jack. (Lounsbury THEATRE 133)

tipsy A toe dancer. (Berrey/Van den Bark SLANG 573)

tirade (French) A lengthy, impassioned speech. (Hamilton THEORY 87)

tiranokku (Malayalam) Literally: curtain-look. An entrance sequence in *kathakali* in which a powerful character gradually appears from behind a hand-held curtain while dancing to instrumental music. (Jones/Jones KATHAKALI 75–76)

tirassila (Malayalam) See: *yavanika*.

tirate (Italian) Soliloquies. See: *bravura*.

tire   Attire, costume. The term is obsolete, but is the root of such other old terms as tireman, tirewoman, tiring house, tiring room, etc.

tired businessman   The theatrical description of a theatre patron who prefers light entertainment.

tire house   See: tiring house.

tireman, tirewoman   1. In the Restoration theatre and later, the rough equivalent of the modern wardrobe master or mistress. (Roberts STAGE) Also called a tiring-man, tiring-woman. 2. A dresser.

tire man, tier man   An all-purpose backstage worker in an Elizabethan theatre. He fitted costumes and beards, furnished stools, and, in private indoor theatres, was in charge of the lights. (Chambers ELIZABETHAN II 541)

tirer le rideau (French)   To draw the curtain.

tire room   See: tiring room.

tireynge house   See: tiring house.

tiring house   In Shakespearean theatres and later, the backstage area, used for dressing, storage, etc. Also found as attiring house, tire house, tireying house, tireynge house, tyreing howse.

tiring-man   See: tireman.

tiring room, attiring room   A dressing room in early English theatres. See also shift, which was evidently a common dressing room, as opposed to the more private tiring room. (Pepys DIARY 5 October 1667)

tiring-woman   See: tireman.

tiroir (French)   Literally: drawer. In the 19th C, offstage space under the stage floor equal to half the width of the acting area. Trap covers were slipped into it. See also: *levées*. (Moynet FRENCH 31)

títere (Spanish)   1. In 17th C Spain and later, a puppet, puppet show, or pantomime. Hence, *titerero* (puppeteer). Also called a *muñeco*. (Philpott DICTIONARY, McPharlin PUPPET 73) 2. See also: *carillo*.

titire(s) (Philippine)   See: *carillo*.

titirimundi (Spanish)   See: *theatrum mundi*.

title board   See: locality board.

title role   The character whose name appears in the title of a play—usually the most important role. (Stern MANAGEMENT)

ti tzu (Chinese)   See: *di*.

tiubeteika (Russian)   A Central Asian and Russian pillbox-style hat with a flat or beaked crown decorated with embroidery in many colors. Also called an Uzbek cap.

tjak (Indonesian)   See: *kecak*.

tjalonarang (Indonesian)   See: *calonarang*.

tjarangan (Indonesian)   See: *lakon.*

tjarijos (Indonesian)   See: *cariyos.*

tjelempung (Indonesian)   See: *celemung.*

tjempala (Indonesian)   See: *cempala.*

tjempurit (Indonesian)   See: *cempurit.*

tjerita (Indonesian)   See: *cerita.*

tjoepak (Indonesian)   See: *cupak.*

tjondong (Indonesian)   See: *condong.*

tjupak (Indonesian)   See: *cupak.*

T lamp   A lamp with a tubular (T) bulb.

T light   See: tee-piece.

toa talok (Thai)   A clown or comic puppet figure in *nang talung* shadow theatre. (Smithies/Kerdchouay in Rutnin SIAMESE 134)

tobi roppo (Japanese)   Literally: leaping in six-directions. A vigorous, leaping exit by a bravura (*aragoto*) character in a *kabuki* play. An example is Benkei's exit in *The Subscription List* in Brandon TRADITIONAL 235–236. See: *roppo.*

toby   1. In melodrama, a patsy, a sucker. 2. Capitalized, the trained dog in a Punch and Judy show. 3. Capitalized, the light comedy part in a Toby show—usually a young rustic. See also: Sis Hopkins. (Wilmeth LANGUAGE)

Toby boob and blackface   See: up in all and make them go.

Toby show   A popular U.S. rural theatre form in the early 20th C, often performed in tents for family audiences and featuring the stock rural comic character Toby. Hence, Toby play. (Wilmeth LANGUAGE)

todori (Japanese)   In *kabuki*: 1. In the 17th C, a minor actor. 2. From the 18th C, an assistant stage manager or doorkeeper. (Hamamura et al KABUKI 109)

toe   To brace with the toe, as when holding a flat in position on the floor as another person raises it to an upright position by walking it up.

toe-and-heeler   A dancer.

toe dance   To dance on point—on the toes.

toe shoe   See: block shoe.

toesmiths   Dancers.

toe terpery   Tap dancing.

togaki (Japanese)   Written stage directions in a script. When they are set down (*gaki*) they are always preceded by the word "thus" (*to*), hence the name.

togaku (Japanese)   Chinese-derived music in *gagaku*. See also: *komagaku.* (Inoura HISTORY 132)

toga play   A drama on a classical theme. (Partridge TO-DAY 229) *togata* (Latin Roman)   See: *fabula togata*.

togatarius (Latin Roman)   Strictly, an actor in a *fabula togata*. Beare believes a 2nd C AD use refers to the first actor who wore a toga in a pantomime. See also: *fabula togata*. (Beare ROMAN 136)

toggle   1. In Australia, to cleat two flats together.   2. See: toggle bar, toggle iron. (National TECHNICAL 7)

toggle bar   A crosspiece in a flat frame. Also called a toggle rail. It is attached to the stiles (upright framing pieces) with a keystone and/or a toggle iron (socket).

toggle iron   A metal shoe or socket used to secure a toggle bar to the stile of a flat. Sometimes shortened to toggle, though the latter is usually used to refer to the toggle bar itself. Also called a shoe.

toggle rail   See: toggle bar.

toggle shoe   See: toggle iron.

to have line   An old phrase used of an actress with a graceful figure. (Granville DICTIONARY 97)

toile, *toile* (French)   1. Cloth, fabric. 2. A working sample made up in temporary material. Also called a mock-up, muslin fitting, muslin mock-up, muslin model, tryout. (Wilcox DICTIONARY) 3. A curtain.

tojung (Korean)   In *sandaeguk* court masked plays, the performers' guild, usually made up of eleven members of three different ranks. (Cho "Yangju" 29)

tok dalang muda (Malaysian)   Literally: young *dalang*. A shadow play prologue, named after the assistant puppeteer who performs it. It contains several sections: a ritual recitation of invocations, followed by a brief battle and a procession to pay obeisance to Prince Rama. (Sweeney in Osman TRADITIONAL 15)

tokiwazu bushi (Japanese)   A style of narrative singing (*joruri*), accompanied by *shamisen*, created for *kabuki* dance plays about 1740 by Tokiwazu Mojidayu. (Malm MUSIC 191–192)

tokoyama (Japanese)   A wig dresser, especially in *kabuki*. (Scott KABUKI 127, 128)

tok wak (Malaysian)   The role of an old man in *ma'yong*. (Yousof "Kelantan" 101)

tollin-bopku (Korean)   See: *p'ungmul*.

tolmi, dolmi (Korean)   Literally: puppet nape. In *namsadang*, the common term for a puppet play. (Sim/Kim KOREAN 66)

tolu bomma (Kannada, Tamil, Telugu)   A leather puppet used in shadow theatre in south India.

tolu bommalu kattu (Telugu)   A shadow play using leather puppets, in Andhra Pradesh state, south India. Also spelled *tholu bomalattam*.

Tom   In a limited tour, to travel to a small town for a one-night stand. The term derives from troupes performing *Uncle Tom's Cabin*. (Wilmeth LANGUAGE)

tombé (French)   Literally: fallen. In ballet, a fall on a leg from a position in which the other leg is straight. The "fallen" leg remains bent at the end of the maneuver. (Kersley/Sinclair BALLET)

tombo (Japanese)   See: *tonbo*.

Tom company   A 19th C troupe presenting *Uncle Tom's Cabin*, usually on tour.

Tom dogs   In the early 1900s, Great Danes used by some producers of *Uncle Tom's Cabin* because they looked fiercer and more frightening than the bloodhounds called for in the play. (Laurie VAUDEVILLE 358)

tome (Japanese)   Literally: end, ending. In *kyogen*, the concluding section of a play. Conventional endings include *oikomi dome* (chasing-off ending), *shikari dome* (scolding ending), *kusame dome* (sneezing ending), *warai dome* (laughing ending), *serifu dome* (dialogue ending), *utai dome* (singing ending), *hayashi dome* (musical ending), *mai dome* (dance ending), among others. (Berberich "Rapture" 61)

tome byoshi (Japanese)   Literally: end stamp. Two stamps of the foot by the major character (*shite*) that conclude a *no* or *kyogen* play. (Berberich "Rapture" 167)

tome kyogen (Japanese)   Literally: end *kyogen*. The last *kyogen* play on a multi-play bill, usually celebratory in tone. (Berberich "Rapture" 181)

tome no (Japanese)   Literally: end *no*. The final *no* play on a day's program. The same as *kiri no*. (Komparu NOH 39)

Tommer   1. Originally, a 19th C performer in *Uncle Tom's Cabin*, usually on tour. 2. Later a performer in similar touring melodramas. (Wilmeth LANGUAGE)

tomo (Japanese)   Literally: companion. A minor role in a *no* play. If a companion of the main character, the role is performed by an actor from one of the schools of *shite* actors; if a companion of the supporting character, the role is played by an actor from one of the *waki* schools. (Komparu NOH 155)

Tom show   1. A 19th C production of *Uncle Tom's Cabin*, usually by a troupe on tour. 2. The company of such a show. Hence, Tom company, Tomming, Tomming the tanks (small towns), etc. (Bowman/Ball THEATRE)

tomu (Korean)   A dance of joy and exultation in masked plays. (Yi "Mask" 53)

ton (Thai)   A section, scene, or act of a play in most Thai theatre forms other than masked ballet (*khon*). See also: *chud*. (Dhaninivat KHON 16, Yupho KHON 52) *tonadilla* (Spanish)   1. In the 18th C, a short sketch, with music, song, and dance. 2. A musical interlude.

tonal light   Lighting, as from a borderlight, which illuminates a setting, sometimes avoiding the acting area as far as possible. The purpose is to provide the performers with a background of the desired color and brightness. See also: toning. (Bellman LIGHTING 361)

tonbo, tombo (Japanese)   A flip or somersault in a *kabuki* fight scene. (Leiter "Depiction" 152)

tone   1. A 17th and 18th C term for rhetorical affectation—giving cadence to words when speaking. (Aston in Nagler SOURCES 228) 2. Short for voice tone—the sensuous, emotionally affective sound of speech when spoken by a skilled performer. (Selden ACTING 76) 3. The general effect produced by a playwright's selection and treatment of materials. Similar to atmosphere. (Brooks/ Heilman UNDERSTANDING)

toneel (Indonesian)   From Dutch. Western-style spoken drama performed in Indonesia in the 1920s in Jakarta and Bandung. (Brandon SOUTHEAST 51)

tonglüe (Chinese)   See: *jiamen*.

tongming, t'ung ming (Chinese)   Literally: name announcing. 1. The first portion of a set-the-scene speech (*dingchangbai*) in Beijing opera (*jingju*) and many other forms of music-drama (*xiqu*); the portion in which a character gives his or her full name. 2. More generally, the entire set-the-scene speech. (Scott CLASSICAL 93, Scott TRADITIONAL I 150)

toning lights   An occasional term for borderlights or other lights used to smooth the lighting or enhance its mood or color tone. The singular is also used for the result of such lighting. See also: blending light. (Lounsbury THEATRE, Bellman SCENE)

tonkaram (Malayalam)   In *kathakali*, a dance sequence, often with song, that is added to a standard pure dance section (*kalasam*). (Jones/Jones KA-THAKALI 72)

tonneau (French)   See: peg-top skirt.

tonnelet   An 18th C short, bell-like skirt over a wicker frame, cloth-covered and fringe-decorated, worn by actors and dancers. (Noverre in Nagler SOURCES 334, Roberts STAGE)

tonsil test   A voice audition.

tonsure wig   A grey wig with a bald crown surrounded by a circular fringe of hair. (Wilcox DICTIONARY)

tontillo (Spanish)   A 17th C steel-hooped farthingale. (Boucher FASHION)

Tony Lumpkin part   A comic country character. From the role in Oliver Goldsmith's *She Stoops to Conquer*.

took   Succeeded, as in a production that 'took' an audience in Restoration London.

toomler, Toomler   In the early 20th C, the chief entertainer, often also entertainment director, in a hotel in the Catskill mountains in New York. The toomler was a boisterous comedian and often a singer and dancer. He was sometimes also called the Social Director or Social. The word was originally a corruption of tumulter, for tumult-maker. Hence the verbs toomle and Toomling (behaving as a toomler). (Adams/Tobias BORSCHT 9, 40–58)

tooth enamel   A special liquid makeup used by actors to block out, whiten, color, or discolor teeth.

top   1. To build a line higher than the one that preceded it—by means of volume, tempo, intensity, or higher pitch. Hence, top it, topping. 2. The highest price asked for tickets; hence, top prices, $10.00 top, $20.00 top. 3. Upstage— the top of the stage. 4. In scenery, short for parallel top—the wooden platform that fits on top of a parallel (folding supporting frame). 5. See: top one's part. (Bowman/Ball THEATRE, Burnim GARRICK 124) 6. Of a script or an act or scene, the beginning.

top a laugh   1. To outdo a preceding joke. 2. To come in high on a cue after a laugh has passed its peak.

top banana   The best or senior comic in a burlesque or vaudeville show.

top billing   See: star billing.

top box   See: box.

top drop   A border. (Southern CHANGEABLE 258-259)

topeng (Indonesian)   Literally: mask. 1. A generic term for a theatrical mask in Indonesia. 2. A generic term for a classical masked play. 3. In Bali, a partially comic masked dance-play based on Balinese chronicles performed by a small all-male troupe. See also: *wayang topeng.* (de Zoete/Spies DANCE 178–195)

topeng babakan (Indonesian)   In Sunda, a masked street play, performed by professional actors. Also called *topeng dalang.* See: *wayang wong.* (Soedarsono DANCES 124–125)

topeng padjegan (Indonesian)   Literally: combination *topeng.* In Bali, a style of dance-drama in which a single actor wears many masks in quick succession. (de Zoete/Spies DANCE 178–195).

top flies   The upper fly gallery in an 18th C London theatre. (Highfill "Rich's" 28)

top hat   See: funnel.

topho (Thai)   See: *chaopo.*

topical dramatist   1. A playwright who is currently fashionable. 2. A playwright who writes about contemporary subject matter which is fashionable, faddish, or current and/or controversial.

topka (Oriya)   Basic dance steps in the *chhau* dance-drama of eastern India.

top lighting   1. Light which reaches the performer from directly above. Also called top light or downlight. (Wehlburg GLOSSARY, Rubin/Watson LIGHTING 34) 2. The light on the upper portion of a setting. (Bowman/Ball THEATRE) 3. In Britain, any lighting instruments hung ''higher than the top of the setting.'' Baker includes virtually all front-of-house lighting and much of the onstage lighting. (Baker THEATRECRAFT)

top lights   In Richard D'Oyly Carte's prospectus for the new Savoy theatre in 1881 (the first in which carbon filament lamps lit every part of the theatre), light battens. D'Oyly Carte spoke of footlights and side lights but not battens; it is possible that his 'top lights' also included lights on the grid, and perhaps the fly gallery. (Rees GAS 169)

top line   Star billing; at the top in advertisements. Hence, top liner, top lining (though top lining is sometimes used in the sense of a top-line play, a good work).

top-line vaudeville   See: advanced vaudeville.

top of the bill   See: star billing.

top one's part   To outdo oneself in a performance.

topper   A star performer.

topping   See: top.

topping and tailing   Especially in Australian technical rehearsals, skipping the dialogue and action between technical cues. (National TECHNICAL)

topping the bill   In Britain, being the leading act—headlining, especially in music-hall performances. (Bowman/Ball THEATRE)

top rail   The uppermost horizontal wooden member of a flat. Also called a head rail.

top scene   See: hanging scene.

top shelf   The uppermost gallery.

torao (Japanese)   A *bunraku* puppet head used for characters of bad old men. (Keene BUNRAKU 59)

torcher, torch singer   A blues singer with a deep, passionate voice. (Wilmeth LANGUAGE)

tordion   A French 15th C variation of the galliard, with the same 6/8 rhythm and step pattern. Also spelled tourdion.

torm   A shortening of tormentor, tormentor light, tormentor lighting, etc.

tormentor   See: tormentors.

tormentor boom, tormentor batten   See: tormentor pipe.

tormentor entrance   A side entranceway just upstage of the tormentor.

tormentor flipper   A narrow flat attached to a tormentor wing, often at a right angle, to make the wing self-supporting.

tormentor hood   A special spotlight developed in the early part of the 20th C by Monroe R. Pevear and marketed at the time by Color Specialty Company. Intended for use in the tormentor position, the spotlight was approximately square, with a fixed spherical reflector, a plano-convex lens, and built-on barn doors and vertical shutters. Its special vogue was in the 1930s; both the term and the instrument are now rare. Also called a Pevear hood, Pevear tormentor hood, hood; most variations were sometimes capitalized. (1940 Selden/Sellman SCENERY Part II figs. 12, 13)

tormentor light   In the U.S., any lighting unit mounted just upstage of the tormentor at either side of the stage. (Bellman SCENE, McCandless "Glossary" 630)

tormentor pipe   A vertical light pipe just upstage of the tormentor. Sometimes called a tormentor boom or tormentor batten.

tormentors, torms   1. Wings or curtains at the sides of a stage just behind the teaser, determining the width of the stage opening. The teaser and tormentors form an inner proscenium just upstage of the main curtain. A tormentor is also called a proscenium wing or simply torm. 2. Shortenings of tormentor lights, tormentor spotlights, tormentor lighting.

tormentor spot(light)   In the U.S., a spotlight mounted just upstage of the tormentor at the side of the stage. (Philippi STAGECRAFT, Baker THEATRECRAFT)

tormentor tower   A light tower in the tormentor position. (Bowman/Ball THEATRE)

tormentor wing   1. A flat used as a tormentor. 2. The offstage space behind a tormentor.

torms   See: tormentors.

torneo (Philippine)   The tournament scene in *comedia*. (Mendoza COMEDIA 54)

torniskos (Greek)   In an early 3rd C BC inscription, perhaps a hoisting machine (*mechane*). (Webster PRODUCTION 147–148)

torso tosser   A cooch dancer.

toshi kyogen (Japanese)   Literally: through play. An all-day play in *kabuki* and, less commonly, in *bunraku*, written in the 18th or 19th C. It would last between nine and twelve hours, from dawn to near sunset and included history (*jidai*), domestic (*sewa*), and dance (*shosa*) sections. See also: *hon kyogen*. (Brandon CLASSIC 24–25).

totaka (Sanskrit)   See: *trotaka*.

total blank   An unprofitable engagement.

tough number   In 20th C U.S. burlesque, a very suggestive song and dance by a soubrette, with choral and band accompaniment. (Allen in Matlaw AMERICAN 48)

toupee tape   Double-faced adhesive used in securing false hair. (Bowman/Ball THEATRE)

toupee wig   See: campaign wig.

tour   1. A trip made by a performing company to provincial towns. Hence, on tour, touring company, to tour, etc. (Bowman/Ball THEATRE) 2. Front-of-the-head false hair. Also called *tour de cheveux* (French). (Boucher FASHION)

tour de cheveux (French)   See: tour.

tourdion   See: tordion.

tour en l'air (French)   In ballet, a turn made in mid-air.

touret (French)   1. A 13th–15th C woman's headdress: a veil covering the forehead. 2. In the 16th C, the edge of that veil and the decorated portion of a woman's coiffure. The *touret de nez* was a winter headdress attached to the ear-flaps of a hood and covered the nose. It was the forerunner of the *cache-nez* (muffler) and the *loup* (loo mask). (Boucher FASHION)

touret de col (French)   See: *gorget*.

touret de nez (French)   See: *touret*.

touring board   See: road board.

touring cast   The performers in a production on tour.

touring rights   The permission to tour a show.

touring staff   The front-of-house and backstage workers carried by a company on tour.

tour in stock   To tour with a stock company.

tour list   A schedule of the towns and theatres where a touring company will appear.

tourner (French)   See: movements in ballet.

tournure (French)   A bustle. (Wilcox DICTIONARY)

tovaglia (Italian)   See: *bavolet*.

towel   To close a theatre.

towel trunk   Formerly, one of two trunks often carried by touring performers who stayed in the better hotels; the towel trunk contained many stolen hotel towels. (Wilmeth LANGUAGE)

tower   See: light tower.

tower flood   Especially in Britain, a floodlight mounted on a light tower.

tower headdress   See: Fontanges.

tower operator   A crew member who works on a light tower during a show. He or she might change gelatines, or occasionally, run a follow spot. (Halstead MANAGEMENT 163–164)

town   A stock exterior drop carried by touring companies in the early 20th C. See also: back room, front room, timber. (McNamara ''Scenography'' 20)

(the) town   To theatre people in England, London.

town hall   A term sometimes applied to small-town theatres to give them an air of respectability. (Wilmeth LANGUAGE)

toy theatre   A 19th C children's pasteboard model of a theatre, kits for which may still be purchased. The kits were advertised as ''penny plain and twopence colored.''

toy toy toy   A mild adaptation of a raspberry or Bronx cheer; a traditional good-luck wish from one performer to another before going on stage.

tozai (Japanese)   Literally: east-west. A stock phrase, equivalent to 'hear ye.' It is loudly intoned to gain audience attention at the beginning of a stage announcement (*kojo*) in *kabuki* or *bunraku*. (Ando BUNRAKU 82, 91)

T-plate   A T-shaped metal plate sometimes used to secure a toggle to a stile.

trabeata (Latin Roman)   A special type of Latin comedy modeled after New Comedy, but treating middle class life. The *trabeata* is thus a form of the *fabula togata*. The word is from *trabea*, the robe of the squires, a privileged class between the ordinary citizen and the senator. (Beare ROMAN 136)

track   See: counterweight track, curtain track.

track bracket   See: curtain track bracket.

tracker lines   See: tracker wires.

tracker wire board   A remote control board which uses tracker wires.

tracker wires, tracker lines   Especially in Britain, steel wires (or cables) which run over pulleys for control of remotely placed equipment such as dimmers or color booms. Sometimes called track wires. (Rae/Southern INTERNATIONAL, Bowman/Ball THEATRE)

tracking   A technique in playwriting, directing, acting, and/or mime in which the composites of these (for example in acting—dialogue, movement, gesture, etc.) are both organized and separated so as to control and mix them. The term derives from film and music recording; visuals and musical elements are recorded separately, then played together for a layering, contrapuntal, or whatever other effect is desired. (Argelander ''Workshops'' 13)

track wires   See: tracker wires.

trades   Newspapers and magazines devoted to some special interest, such as theatre. Example: *Variety*. (Stern MANAGEMENT)

tragedian   1. An actor who specializes in tragic roles. 2. One who writes tragedies.

tragédie à machine (French)   A huge stage spectacle, with music. An outgrowth of ballet, with frequent use of classical subjects and choruses of singers and dancers. (Hawkins ANNALS I 237, Arnott FRENCH 55) *tragédie bourgeois* (French)   18th C "tragedy" which concerned itself with the lives of the middle class. (Sobel HANDBOOK)

tragédie du peuple (French)   An alternative term for *mélodrame*.

tragédie lyrique (French)   Grand opera.

tragedienne   An actress who specializes in tragic roles.

tragedy   A great spirit meeting calamity greatly. (Hamilton GREEK 243) A form of drama distinguished from plays of mere violence and disaster by the close relationships established between character and fate and the fitness of its means to its ends.   (Preminger/Warnke/Hardison ENCYCLOPEDIA 860) Some critics have said that character *is* fate. Another recent definition: a basic form of drama treating in a serious style the misfortune and misery that human beings suffer as a result of conflicts within themselves, with other human beings, or with the inescapable and uncontrollable forces of fate. (McGraw-Hill ENCY-CLOPEDIA V 259-260) For a discussion which focuses on Aristotle's views, see Hatlen ORIENTATION 59ff.

tragedy queen   A leading actress specializing in tragic roles. The term often applies to those who perform in the grand tradition of the 19th C.

tragic   Pertaining to tragedy. Hence, tragic actor, tragic actress, tragical, etc.

tragic carpet   See: green.

tragic flaw   A traditional but perhaps incorrect (and inadequate) translation of Aristotle's *hamartia*, a quality in the protagonist in a tragedy which leads to his downfall. An alternate interpretation for *hamartia* is an error in judgment.

tragic irony   Most often the result of a plot mechanism in tragedy in which the protagonist acts, or has insights, that he or she believes will effect good fortune, when in actuality the reverse occurs.

tragic muse   Melpomene, the Greek muse of tragedy.

tragicomedy   A play that tends toward tragedy but ends happily. In French, *tragi-comédie*.

tragicomoedia (Latin Roman)   See: *hilarotragodia*.

tragic rhythm   The pattern of a life that grows, flourishes, and declines as translated into dramatic action; this rhythm takes on the aspect of the rhythm of a lifetime, but is presented as a single action. (Langer FEELING 356)

tragikon drama (Greek)   Probably the choral song of the dithyramb. (Pickard-Cambridge DITHYRAMB 100)

tragitour   A term for a variety of medieval minstrel; in the 14th C the term meant juggler. (Ward LITERATURE I 50)

tragoedian   A variant early spelling of tragedian.

tragoidia, tragoedia, tragodia (Greek)   Literally: goat song. 1. Tragedy. 2. Sometimes, satyr play. The second meaning is a 19th C hypothesis which derived tragedy from the dithyramb through the satyr play; this evolution has been widely disputed. Pickard-Cambridge, for example, has argued that there is no evidence for the meaning satyr play in Aristotle or earlier. (Flickinger GREEK 1–4; 1927 Pickard-Cambridge DITHYRAMB 13, 130–131)

tragoidos (Greek)   Literally: goat singer, singer of a goat song. 1. In the 4th C BC, the protagonist in tragedy. From the early 3rd C BC, festival records used *tragoidos* for the protagonist of old plays and *hypokrites* for the other actors; but *hypokrites* could also be used for the protagonist, and was apparently always used for the protagonist of a new play. By Christian times (for example in Plutarch) and perhaps somewhat earlier, *tragoidos* was regularly used for the protagonist, *hypokrites* for the other two actors. 2. Hence, especially from the 3rd C BC, the head of a tragic company. 3. From at least the later 5th C BC for more than a century, in the plural (*tragoidoi*), members of the tragic chorus; but sometimes tragic performers without distinction between actors and members of the chorus. 4. From the mid-4th C BC (also in the plural), the performance, the contest, or the entire festival. Except in late writers, the use—singular or plural—for the poet, is rare.

As the meanings above may suggest, there is a long history of disagreement over the origin and meaning of *tragoidos* and related words. Latin *tragoedus* is perhaps the commonest of a number of readily recognizable variant spellings; but writers in English often use the Greek rather than any Romanization.

The uses of *komoidos* and *komoidoi* are parallel to those given here for *tragoidos* and *tragoidoi*. (Pickard-Cambridge FESTIVALS 127–132, Pickard-Cambridge DITHYRAMB 112–124)

trailer   1. A narrow wing suspended from a track, trailing a curtain behind it. Also called a trailer wing. (Bowman/Ball THEATRE) 2. In Britain, a single curtain drawn across the stage. Also called a French tab, or draw tab. (Corry PLANNING 106) 3. In striptease, the introductory strut before the strip, designed to stir audience interest. (Wilmeth LANGUAGE)

trailing tab   A tableau curtain suspended from a curtain track. (Bowman/Ball THEATRE)

train call   Especially in the past, a notice on a touring company's call board giving the departure and arrival times of the train that would take the players to their next town. (Fay GLOSSARY)

traînées (French)   Movable lights, such as striplights (e.g., used behind a ground row). (Moynet FRENCH 82)

train machine   A rotating drum used to simulate the sound of a train or cart. (Collison SOUND 100)

tramoya (Spanish)   Stage machinery.

tramoyista (Spanish)   A stagehand or theatre machinist. Also called a *maquinista*. *Tramoyista* has also been adopted as a Philippine term. (Fernández ILOILO 128)

tramp comedian   In the early 20th C, an itinerant actor who often stole rides on trains and lived like a hobo or tramp.

tramplin act   In Britain, a vaudeville or variety number on stilts. (Granville DICTIONARY 206)

trampoline, trampolin   A safety net or a mat with springs to break a performer's fall. Also spelled tramplin. (Bowman/Ball THEATRE)

trance-dance   1. A term applied to a variety of dances, especially in India and Southeast Asia, in which the performer enters a state of trance. 2. Frequently, the trance or dagger (*kris*) dance in Balinese *barong*.

tranche de vie (French)   Slice of life (q.v.).

transfer contract   An agreement for transporting scenery and baggage when a company goes on tour. (Krows AMERICA 339)

transfigurator   See: protean actor.

transformation   1. A change by a performer from one character to another in full view of the audience and with changes in costume, makeup, or mask. 2. In medieval and Renaissance theatre, the change of men into beasts, wives into salt, etc. 3. See: transformation scene. (Cameron/Gillespie ENJOYMENT, Bowman/Ball THEATRE) 4. A small wig or hairpiece which alters a hairstyle. (Wilcox DICTIONARY) 5. A Russian theatrical concept: revealing reality as profoundly as possible in a stage production.

transformational acting   In story theatre, a method of performance in which the actor plays (is transformed into) an object, an animal, or an element of the environment such as wind, water, air, fire, etc. (Davis/Evans CHILDREN'S 38)

transformation puppet   A puppet from the bottom of which another puppet can be dropped.

transformation scene   A moment in an entertainment when the setting is changed as if by magic through the use of scrim, lighting effects, etc. Popular in pantomimes when characters in the opening scene are changed into those of the harlequinade. (Bowman/Ball THEATRE)

transformed gesture   A Russian expressionistic acting style used in the Les' Kurbas production of Georg Kaiser's *Gas* in 1923. It demanded great physical endurance on the part of performers. (Hirniak in Bradshaw SOVIET 287)

transformer vault   See: intake.

transformist   A quick-change artist. (Leslie ACT 122)

transition   In playwriting, the material used between major scenes to blend or to isolate them. (Gallaway CONSTRUCTING 318)

transitory emotion   See: *vyabhicari bhava* (Sanskrit).

translucency   A drop or curtain through which lighted objects can be seen.

transolene   A color medium used for a time (from the 1920s) as an alternate to gelatine. Chemically different, transolene was superior to gelatine in most ways—more durable and more resistant to fading, cracking, and moisture. (Fuchs LIGHTING 413–414)

transparency   Scenery with cut-out areas covered by translucent material. Used in England as early as 1675. Probably similar to the modern scrim (q.v.). (Southern CHANGEABLE 206)

transpontine melodrama   In 19th C London, sensational melodramas produced at theatres on the south bank of the Thames.

transverse   In dance, subtle, transitional, complex movement across the kinesphere between the body and its periphery. (Preston-Dunlop DANCE 129-130)

transverse stage   A performing area with the spectators seated on two sides, facing each other.

trap   An opening in the stage floor or a piece of scenery through which performers, scenery, objects, etc. may pass. When not in use, it is concealed by a flap or door. Hence, bristle trap, Corsican trap, English trap, Macbeth trap, ghost trap, stage trap, star trap, trap cellar, trap door, trap room, trapped area, trapped floor, trapped stage. (Bowman/Ball THEATRE)

trap bell   In the past, a prompter's bell to cue the use of a trap door. (Visser in Hume LONDON 131)

trap box   See: dip.

trap cellar   The space in a substage below the trapped area.

trap door   See: trap.

trap lights   In 18th C Britain, footlights raised and lowered through a stage floor trap. (Bowman/Ball THEATRE)

trap man   A stagehand responsible for the operation of trap doors.

trappe anglaise (French)   A trap the French call an English trap; the British call it a bristle trap. It consists of bristles or twigs the color of the stage floor, projecting inward from the edge. The arrangement permits a surprise appearance or disappearance. In principle, similar to a star trap. (Bowman/Ball THEATRE, Crampton HANDBOOK)

trapped area   That portion of a stage floor fitted with traps.

trapped floor, trapped stage   A stage floor containing trap doors.

trappillons (French)   Divisions of the stage floor: two and sometimes three long, narrow, cross-stage traps which can be opened to allow large backings to pass through from the substage. See also: *plan*. (Moynet FRENCH 24)

trap room   The area beneath the stage floor where trap mechanisms are operated.

traquénard (French)   See: pannier.

trasponte (Philippine)   In *zarzuela*, prompting, by the prompter-director (*apuntador*). (Fernández ILOILO 128)

traveler, traveler curtain   1. A draw or traverse curtain.   2. The track on which a draw curtain operates.   3. A device for simulating aerial flight. See also: trailer.

traveler ball, traveler block   A ball or block in a traveler track from which the traveler curtain is suspended.

traveler track   See: curtain track.

traveling company, traveling theatre   A touring company.

traveling cyclorama   See: arm cyclorama.

traveling stage   A portable stage.

travel on one's props   In Britain, to leave one's luggage with the railroad company as security. Also called travel in one's trunks. (Granville DICTIONARY)

travel scene   See: *michiyuki.*

travel the boards   To tour.

traverse curtain   See: traveler.

travesti (Italian)   A part in which an actor or actress of the 16th–17th C was costumed and enacted the role of a member of the opposite sex. (Winter BALLET 3)

travesty   A burlesque imitation, a parody. (Carrington THEATRICANA)

travodore (Spanish)   See: *troubadour.*

tray   A metal pan under a spotlight, especially in an audience area. The primary purpose is to prevent injury to anyone below the spotlight, typically from a metal color frame which might slip out of its slot. An example is the balcony tray sometimes used under spotlights at the front edge of a balcony. Trays have also been used under spotlights in auditorium boxes in older theatres and in arc follow spots. Also called a pan.

treadmill, treadmill stage   An endless belt or runner on which actors may appear to be moving while remaining in view of the audience. Used in concert with a moving diorama in 19th C melodramas. Also called moving tracks. (Bowman/Ball THEATRE)

tread plate   The metal top, flush with the floor, of a stage floor pocket.

tread the boards   See: boards.

treasurer   See: box-office manager.

treasury   In Britain, salary payment time.

treasury call   An announcement on the theatre call board indicating when company members will be paid.

treasury day   Payday.

tree   See: light tree.

tree border   A short hanging cloth simulating leaves.

tree of hope   For Black actors, a good-luck tree which stood near 131st Street and 7th Avenue in New York City. (Mitchell VOICES 128–129)

tree tab   A short leg or short, narrow drop representing the top of a tree, used in conjunction with a scenic unit representing the tree trunk. (Bowman/ Ball THEATRE)

trench unionist   A member of the pit orchestra in a theatre. (Sobel HAND-BOOK 825)

tressour, tressure   See: caul.

trestle stage   A simple stage floor mounted on a braced frame; a portable stage used by strolling players.

tréteaux (French)   Literally: boards. The stage.

trey spot   The third place on a variety bill.

Triac, triac   A patented solid-state device (General Electric), the basis of a theatre dimmer resembling the silicon controlled rectifier. (Wehlburg GLOSSARY)

trial of skill   In Restoration times and later, a term for a fencing match. Some matches took place in legitimate theatres as part of the bill or as special events. Also called playing a prize. (Adams HERBERT 81-82)

trial setup   The assembling of the various parts of a stage setting for the first time. (Gillette/Gillette SCENERY)

triangle   See: corner block.

triangle play   A drama dealing with two men in love with the same woman, or two women in love with the same man. (Sobel NEW)

triangular movement   Stage movement in which three or more performers move to positions which conform to the points of a triangle. (Bowman/Ball THEATRE)

triangular theatre   The Russian director Vsevelod Meyerhold's theory of the hegemony of the director. The audience and the performers are at the base angles of the triangle and the director is its apex. (Gorchakov RUSSIA 59)

tribunal (Latin Roman)   In the early temporary wooden theatres, a platform for honored spectators; hence, an auditorium box. In the later stone theatres, there were usually two *tribunalia*, one at each end of the semi-circular auditorium; these boxes were therefore above the vaulted side entrances between the auditorium and the stage. A special box was occasionally created among the seats of honor (*bisellia*) in the auditorium. From *tribunus*, commander, tribune. (Bieber HISTORY 172–173, Allen ANTIQUITIES 86, 92)

tribunus voluptatum (Latin Roman)   Literally: the chief of pleasure or entertainment. By the 5th C AD, and perhaps earlier, the city official in charge of shows (*spectacula*). (Chambers MEDIAEVAL II 229)

tributary theatre   Especially in mid-20th C. U.S., the professional and amateur theatre outside New York City.

trick   See: stage trick.

trick line   A strong black (hence invisible) string or wire used to pull an object off the stage or to trigger a breakaway or trick device.

trick puppet   A puppet built and designed for a special type of use in performance. Examples are the dissecting skeleton, the transformation puppet, and the Grand Turk (q.v.). (Philpott DICTIONARY)

trick wire   Wire, often piano wire, used for trick effects or flying.

tried-and-true clap trap   See: hoke.

trigata (Sanskrit)   In classical Indian theatre, a discussion among the troupe manager (*sutradhara*), the clown (*vidusaka*), and an attendant that is one part of the preliminaries (*purvaranga*) described by Bharata in the *Natyasastra*. (Bharata NATYASASTRA 94, Keith SANSKRIT 328, 340)

trigger   In Britain, a handle under the stage which controls the movement of a slider. (Bowman/Ball THEATRE)

Trilby heart   A late 19th C locket of silver or gold on a long chain. (Chalmers CLOTHES 246)

Trilby shoe   Late 19th C woman's cloth footwear with buttons or laces and a knit top. (Walkup DRESSING 325)

trilogy   A series of three related plays by the same playwright.

trim   1. The decorative facing around a door or window. 2. See: trim prop. 3. To adjust hanging scenic units, making them level. Hence, the trim of a piece, on trim, in trim (in Britain: on the dead). (Cornberg/Gebauer CREW 276, Bowman/Ball THEATRE) 4. In a carbon arc light, to adjust the carbons so that they burn properly.

trim block   See: trim clamp.

trim carbons   To adjust the position of carbons in an arc spotlight. The term sometimes means to replace the carbons. Also called re-trim carbons. (Lounsbury THEATRE, Rae/Southern INTERNATIONAL)

trim chain   A short length of chain used to attach a scenic unit to a batten. Also called a trimming chain, batten trim chain.

trim clamp   A metal device used to attach rope lines to a counterweight arbor or a sandbag. The lines pass through the clamp individually, and each can be adjusted. Also called a trimmer, trimming clamp, trim block.

trim mark   On the operating line of a curtain or flown batten, an indication (piece of masking tape, strip of cloth, etc.) of the point at which the line should be stopped so that the flown object will be at its correct level.

trimmer   See: knuckle buster, trim clamp.

trimming   See: trim.

trimming chain   See: trim chain.

trimming clamp   See: trim clamp.

trim of carbons   A set of carbons in an arc light. (Bellman SCENE 346)

trim prop   1. A property which hangs, as a picture on a wall. 2. A property which is used to dress a setting but is not necessarily handled by a performer. Also called trim.

trim rail   The lower of two rows of pins in a pinrail. It is used for tying off lines when scenic units are in trim. Also called the bottom or tie-off rail. (Bowman/Ball THEATRE)

tringle (French)   A single-rod control mechanism for a marionette. (Malkin PUPPETS 27) See also: *marionnette à tringle.*

trionfo (Italian)   An elaborate Renaissance allegorical procession. (Brockett HISTORY 176)

trios   See: concert party.

trip   1. A rope used to trim a piece of scenery. Also called a trip line. 2. To raise the lower edge of a drop so that it is level with the upper edge—a practice used in theatres with little fly space. Also called tumble. 3. To clew a cloth. (Bowman/Ball THEATRE)

trip border   A rare alternate term for teaser. (Carrington THEATRICANA)

trip cyclorama   A cyclorama rigged to fold as it is raised, thus needing less grid height. (Gillette/Gillette SCENERY)

tripe   In Britain, flexible stage cable. This is an extension of what appears to have been the original use: asbestos- or canvas-covered borderlight cable. British stage manager Bax, noting that meaning, adds that the term is also used for ". . . any loose cable trailing about, and was probably first applied by a tidy-minded stage manager." As this suggests, tripe is similar to U.S. 'spaghetti.' (Bentham ART; Bax MANAGEMENT 182; Ridge/Aldred LIGHTING 3, 32; Rae/Southern INTERNATIONAL)

triple bill   A program with three dramatic works.

triple block   See: block.

triple booking   See: double booking.

triple connector   See: multiple connector.

triple lantern   See: dissolving view.

triplet   In dance, a three-beat pattern executed with the feet: a step down, up, up, with weight falling on the first step, with the knee bent as the entire foot is on the floor. The second and third steps are on half toe with knees straight. (Stodelle HUMPHREY 225, 227)

trip line   See: trip.

tripper   A dancer.

trips   Lines supporting the arms of a cyclorama.

tritagonistes (Greek)   Literally: third contestant. There is no evidence for the application of this word to actors until early Christian times, and its use to mean 'third-rate actor' has been disputed, notably by Pickard-Cambridge. The English word (tritagonist) has long been used for the third actor of all periods of the Greek theatre. See also: *protagonistes*. (Pickard-Cambridge FESTIVALS 132–135).

triumph   In late medieval times, a play or pageant. (Chambers MEDIAE-VAL II 176)

tri-unial lantern   See: dissolving view.

tro he (Vietnamese)   Literally: clown character. A 10th C theatre form believed to be a precursor of *hat boi*. (Pham-Duy MUSICS 114)

trollopée (French)   See: gown à la Polonaise.

trombenick   An inferior or amateur actor. (Berrey/Van den Bark SLANG 571)

trompong (Indonesian)   See: *gamelan*.

trong (Vietnamese)   Literally: drum. Generically, instrumental music accompanying action, fights, and songs in *hat boi*. The term indicates the importance of the large drum (*trong chien*) in the ensemble. (Pham-Duy MUSICS 123)

trong chau (Vietnamese)   Literally: critic's drum. A large drum, placed at the side of the stage during a ceremonial *hat boi* performance. An expert member of the audience beats the drum in one of five patterns to indicate the degree of his approval or disapproval of the performance. (Pham-Duy MUSICS 123, Hauch "Study" 83–84)

trong chien (Vietnamese)   Literally: battle drum. A large drum played in *hat boi*. By striking it in various ways, six different sounds can be produced. (Pham-Duy MUSICS 122, Addiss "Theater" 139)

troparium (Latin)   A collection of medieval tropes—dramatic additions to the church service. Also called a troper. (Chambers MEDIAEVAL II 8, 10)

trope   In medieval times, a dramatic addition to the church service. In Latin: *tropus*.

troper   See: *troparium*.

tropus (Latin)   A trope.

trotaka (Sanskrit)   1. A type of drama with divine and mortal characters, containing seven to nine acts, with a jester (*vidusaka*) appearing in each act. It is a derivative of the major dramatic types (*rupaka*). Also called *totaka*. (Keith SANSKRIT 151, 350–351; Shastri LAWS 27)   2. A metrical pattern used within the text of a classical Indian drama. (Bharata NATYASASTRA 272)

trotteur (French)   An early 20th C ankle-length rain skirt. (Chalmers CLOTHES 251) *tro u* (Khmer)   A two-stringed fiddle with coconut-shell sounding box used in *lokhon bassac*. (Brandon SOUTHEAST 128)

troubadour (French)   A medieval singer-poet in Provence specializing in songs of courtly love. In Spain: *travodore*. In Italy: *trovatore*. In England: troubadour. See also: *trouvère*.

trou de memoire (French)   Literally: gap in the memory. In acting, forgetting one's line or lines. (Gershman "Mesguich's" 19)

trough   1. The long metal container much used in the past for footlights and some borderlights, now primarily for cyclorama footlights. 2. The break in a stage floor containing footlights. Hence, footlight trough. 3. Toning lights in open trough reflectors. All uses appear to be U.S. (Bowman/Ball THEATRE, Carrington THEATRICANA, Lounsbury THEATRE)

troupe   1. A performing company, especially one on tour. 2. To tour. Hence, trouper, trouping, etc. 3. To perform like a veteran. Hence, old trouper.

trousers part, trousers role   See: breeches part.

trousses (French)   See: breeches.

troussoire (French)   See: châtelaine.

trouvère (French)   A medieval poet-composer-performer of northern France, equivalent to the *troubadour* of Provence, in the south.

trovatore (Italian)   See: *troubadour*.

truc (French)   Literally: knack, trick.   1. An apparently inexplicable stage effect, such as a sudden appearance or disappearance, a transformation scene, or an abrupt physical change in an object or person. By extension, the stage machinery often used for such effects, and stage machinery generally.   2. A mechanism used to move scenic units.

truc d'accessoires (French)   Trick properties.

truck   A term, chiefly in Britain, for: 1. A scenery wagon to move heavy scenic units quickly. Also called a truck bogie, boat truck. See also: scenery wagon, wagon stage. 2. A cyclorama floodlight on casters.

truck full of quits   In burlesque, said of a temperamental performer who was always leaving the show. (Wilmeth LANGUAGE)

truffe, truffeau (French)   1. 15th C gold thread and leaves hanging from a necklace. 2. False hair worn on the temples. 3. Coiffure pads used in the tall styles of the 15th C. (Boucher FASHION)

trunk hose   See: upper hose.

trunkline of action   A Konstantin Stanislavsky theory that there is a mainstream of action in a play, with tributaries for the individual characters. (Gorchakov RUSSIA 37–38)

trunnions   Projections on each side of some spotlights. Used for attaching a yoke. (Bowman/Ball THEATRE)

(the) Trust   See: Syndicate.

tryasra (Sanskrit)   In ancient India, a playhouse of triangular shape which had a triangular acting area. Scantily described by Bharata (NATYASASTRA 19, 32), playhouses of this shape may never have existed.

try back   Especially in Britain, a direction to repeat a scene or part of a scene. In the U.S., often, go back. (Granville DICTIONARY)

trygoidia (Greek)   1. Comedy. 2. According to some ancient writers, a mixture of the comic and the serious which was the ancestor of both comedy and tragedy. Pickard-Cambridge argues that the term is simply a comic version of *tragoidia*. There seems no doubt that the word is related to Greek *tryx*, new wine. (Pickard-Cambridge DITHYRAMB 74–76, 186)

trygoidos (Greek)   Probably a comic version of *tragoidos*. Pickard-Cambridge believes that if the word is not such a coinage, it may mean singer stained with wine lees, or (his preference) singer at the vintage. Greek *tryx* means new wine. See also: *trygoidia*. (Pickard-Cambridge DITHYRAMB 123)

try it on the dog   To test a play on an out-of-town audience. Hence, dog town, dog house, dog show. (Bowman/Ball THEATRE)

try out, tryout, try-out   1. Test performance(s) of a production out of town. Hence, tryout-theatre, try-out tour, try-out town. 2. An audition. 3. A theatrical experiment, especially during a rehearsal. Also used as a verb: to experiment. (Bowman/Ball THEATRE) 4. See: costume fitting, muslin mock-up.

tsa chü (Chinese)   See: *zaju*.

ts'ai ch'a hsi (Chinese)   See: *caichaxi*.

ts'ai ch'iao (Chinese)   See: *caiqiao*.

ts'ai tan (Chinese)   See: *choudan*.

ts'an chün, ts'an chün chuang, ts'an chün hsi, ts'ang ku, ts'ang t'ou (Chinese)   See: *canjunxi*.

tsao chou tzu (Chinese)   See: *zhouzi*.

tsa pan (Chinese)   See: *zaban*.

tsarouchi (Greek)   The trademark pompommed sabots worn by Greek resistance fighter-actors (*andartes*) in World War II. (Myrsiades "Resistance" 102)

tsa shua kuan (Chinese)   See: *zashuaguan*.

tsaytbilder (Yiddish)   Literally: pictures of the times. Sensational, semi-documentary plays of the late 19th C Yiddish theatre, based on current events. Also spelled *zeit bilder*. (Rosenfeld BRIGHT 229, Sandrow VAGABOND 114)

T-shaped lamp   See: tubular lamp.

tso (Chinese)   See: *zuo*.

tso ch'ang pai (Chinese)   See: *dingchangbai*.

tso ch'ang shih (Chinese)   See: *dingchangshi*.

tso erh ch'ien (Chinese)   See: *zuoerqian*.

tso tan (Chinese)   See: *zuodan*.

tsou pien (Chinese)   See: *zoubian*.

tsukamite (Japanese)   Literally: grab hand. A special grasping hand of a male *bunraku* puppet, the finger joints of which are all movable. See also: *tako tsukami*. (Keene BUNRAKU 60)

tsuke (Japanese)   Two cherry-wood clappers that are beaten on a flat board (*tsuke ita*) to highlight important moments of acting in *kabuki*. Offstage beating (*kage o utsu*) was used c. 1700. (Dunn/Torigoe ANALECTS 116) Today *tsukeuchi* (*tsuke* beating) occurs in view of the audience, stage left by the proscenium arch. Major patterns are given in Leiter ENCYCLOPEDIA 409–410 and Brandon CLASSIC 354–356. See: *batan, batabata, battari, uchiage*.

tsuke butai (Japanese)   Literally: attached stage. The forestage of an 18th C *kabuki* theatre and a principal acting area. (Ernst KABUKI 51)

tsuke cho (Japanese)   A production book, in outline form, of some aspect of *kabuki*, used as a cuing book during performance. 1. A list, by acts, of wigs, properties, sets, or costumes. (Leiter ENCYCLOPEDIA 410). 2. A cue book for offstage musicians (*geza*). (Brandon CLASSIC 357–359)

tsuki no ogi (Japanese)   Literally: moon fan. In *no* and *kyogen* dance, the standard gesture (*kata*) to indicate looking at the moon. An open fan is held horizontally against the left shoulder. Illustrated in Keene NO 220, 223.

tsuki zerifu (Japanese)   A short speech (*serifu*) by the secondary character in a *no* play announcing his arrival (*tsuki*) at his destination. A type of *shodan*. (Shimazaki NOH 48)

tsukurimono (Japanese)   Literally: built things. A large, constructed set prop in *no* and early *kabuki*. From about the 18th C the term *odogu* (scenery) replaced this word in *kabuki*. (Ernst KABUKI 52, Nippon Gakujutsu JAPANESE xxv)

tsura akari (Japanese)   See: *sashidashi*.

tsurane (Japanese)   A powerful, declamatory type of speech by a male hero in a *kabuki* play. The name-saying speeches (*nanori*) in Leiter ART 41–42 are examples. See also: *yakuharai*. (Gunji KABUKI 34, Scott KABUKI 117, Brandon in Brandon/Malm/Shively STUDIES 104)

tsure (Japanese)   The role of an attendant, friend or companion who appears in a *no* play together with the *shite* (then called *shite zure*) or the *waki* (then called *waki zure*). There may be as many *tsure* characters as the plot demands.

tsuri eda (Japanese)   Literally: hanging branches. A hanging border of maple leaves, cherry blossoms, or other natural objects identifying the season of a scene. Used primarily in *kabuki* but also in *bunraku*. (Ernst KABUKI 54, Scott KABUKI 155) *tsurimono* (Japanese)   Literally: hanging things. Scenery that can be flown, especially in *kabuki*. (Leiter ENCYCLOPEDIA 412)

tsuyogin (Japanese)   Literally: strong singing. In *no*, the dynamic mode of singing (*utai*), analogous to the "minor" key in Western music. (Konishi "Approaches" 13) Its scale is described by Shimazaki as having five pitches (NOH 45) and by Bethe/Brazell as having two approximate pitches (NO 43). See also: *yowagin*.

tsuzuki kyogen (Japanese)   Literally: continuous play. A multi-act play in *kabuki*. The first use of the term is c. 1664, to indicate a continuous play rather than the usual variety program of unrelated plays (*hanare kyogen*). (Leiter ENCYCLOPEDIA 415)

ttangjaeju (Korean)   See: *taegwangdae-p'ae*.

T track   See: T bar.

ttunsoe, ddunsoe (Korean)   Veteran performers and supervisors of a *namsadang* troupe. (Kim "Namsadang" 10)

T-type (lamp)   See: tubular lamp.

tua likay (Thai)   Literally: *likay* actor. (Virulrak "Likay" 273)

tuan kerja (Malaysian)   Literally: work person. The sponsor or host of a performance, often a sick patient who hires a performance such as *puteri ma'yong* as a curing ritual. (Yousof "Kelantan" 259)

tuan ta (Chinese)   See: *duanda*.

tuanzi, t'uan tzu (Chinese)   Literally: round written-character. A sound whose pronunciation requires that the tongue be rounded in the mouth, or actually curved back; such sounds are particularly stressed in Beijing opera (*jingju*). See also: *jianzi*. (Wichmann "Aural" 363–370)

tube   In stage lighting in the U.S., a thyratron tube.

tube board, tube dimmer   See: thyratron tube dimmer.

tubular lamp   An incandescent lamp of tubular shape, much used in modern spotlights. In the U.S., also called T, T-lamp, T-shaped lamp, T-type (lamp), and similar combinations.

tucker   See: modesty.

tucket   A trumpet call announcing the arrival of an important character in an Elizabethan play. The word was probably an anglicization of the Italian *toccata* (a thing touched).

tuding (Indonesian)   The rod controlling a movable arm of a Javanese *wayang kulit* puppet. Human characters have two, ogres usually one, *tuding*. See also: *cempurit*. (Long JAVANESE 15–17)

tui k'ou (Chinese)   See: *xiangsheng*.

tui lien (Chinese)   See: *duilian*.

tulnorum (Korean)   See: *ogwangdae*.

tulukutu (Hawaiian)   See: peg puppet.

tumble   1. A thin round batten around which drops are rolled either for storage or for flying when there is little fly space. Also called a tumbler, tumbler batten.   2. To roll a drop onto a batten.   3. See: trip, meaning 2.

tumbler   1. A narrow wooden spacer hinged between two sections of a three-fold or four-fold flat to allow the folded unit to lie flat in storage. Also called a dutchman, compensating strip, jigger.   2. See: tumble.

tumbler batten   A batten upon which drops are rolled for storage in the flies.

tung hsiao (Chinese)   See: *xiao*.

t'ung lüeh (Chinese)   See: *jiamen*.

t'ung ming (Chinese)   See: *tongming*.

tungsten-halogen lamp, quartz-halogen lamp   An incandescent lamp whose heat-resisting bulb, containing iodine and other halogens, is made of quartz. These lamps are now widely used in stage lighting instruments because the light is near-white, the lamp and filament last longer, and the lamps are small; in recent years hard glass has replaced quartz in some lamps. Among other terms are T-H, quartz-iodine lamp, quartzline, quartz lamp, Q.I. lamp, Q.I., and halogen lamp. (Bellman SCENE 314–315, Wehlburg GLOSSARY, Sellman/Lessley ESSENTIALS 66–67)

tung tso (Chinese)   See: *dongzuo*.

tunic à la mameluck   A 19th C half-length tunic with short or long sleeves. Later called a *Juive* or *tunique à la Juive* (French). (Boucher FASHION)

tunic à la Romaine   A Directoire period long tunic with wrist-length sleeves and a high waist, in a gauzy or linen fabric.

tunique à la Juive (French)   See: tunic à la mameluck.

tuntuna (Marathi)   A one-stringed melodic instrument played in *tamasha*. (Gargi FOLK 73, 77, 80)

tuong (Vietnamese)   Literally: a play. 1. See: *tuong do, tuong thay*. 2. The earliest name for *hat boi*, first used in the 11th C (Hauch "Study" 7) or the 13th C (Pham-Duy MUSICS 124, Addiss "Theater" 137). 3. The role of a warrior.

tuong do (Vietnamese)   One of two major categories of *hat boi* drama: a play drawn from a novel or poem, often comic and satiric. See also: *tuong thay*. (Hauch "Study" 23–24)

tuong kiem hiep la ma (Vietnamese)   A type of *cai luong* that specializes in "Roman-swashbuckler" plays. Chinese sword fighting stories are transferred to Roman times. (Pham-Duy MUSICS 146)

tuong Phat (Vietnamese)   A type of *cai luong* popular in the 1930s that used Buddhist story content. (Pham-Duy MUSICS 146)

tuong tau (Vietnamese)   Literally: Chinese drama. 1. A generic term for theatre that uses Chinese story material. A predecessor of *cai luong*. (Pham-Duy MUSICS 145) 2. A form of modernized, popularized *hat boi*. (Addiss "Theater" 144, Brandon SOUTHEAST 76)

tuong tay (Vietnamese)   Literally: Western play. An early variation of *cai luong* that drew upon Western stories or modern Vietnamese social problems for its dramatic content. Also called *tuong xa hoi*. (Pham-Duy MUSICS 145)

tuong thay (Vietnamese)   Literally: plays of the masters. One of two major categories of *hat boi* drama: a play set in the imperial court of China, Vietnam, or a legendary kingdom, usually concerning the struggle of a king to remain in power. See also: *tuong do*. (Hauch "Study" 21–23)

tuong tien (Vietnamese)   A type of *cai luong* that uses fairy tales as its primary subject material. (Pham-Duy MUSICS 146)

tuong xa hoi (Vietnamese)   See: *tuong tay*.

tuo tzu (Chinese)   See: *chenzi*.

turk   A small show in which the performers take potluck with the management. Also called a turkey. (Berrey/Van den Bark SLANG 580)

turkey   In the U.S., a poor production that fails. The term has been said to derive from bad American productions that opened on Thanksgiving Day, with the hope of making expenses on performances during the holiday season. Hence, turkey actors. There are other explanations of the origin. See also: turk. (Stern MANAGEMENT)

turkey show   Especially in the early days of burlesque, a touring one-night-stand show, usually obscene. (Wilmeth LANGUAGE)

Turkish gown   See: gown à la Turque.

turn   1. Especially in Britain, an act, usually in a variety show, where each act gets its turn. 2. One's place on a variety bill. 3. In dance, a revolution of the entire body around a vertical axis.

turn a riot into an oilcan   To allow a good play to fail. (Berrey/Van den Bark SLANG 585)

turnaround   A change from the stage setting for one show to the setting for another.

turnaway   1. A sold-out performance or production. Hence, turnaway business, turnaway crowds, etc. 2. A person who is turned away from a theatre because a performance is sold out.

turned down   Denied professional courtesies by a manager. (Wilmeth LANGUAGE)

turner   An acrobat in 18th C England.

turn in   To turn toward center stage. (Canfield CRAFT)

turning point   In playwriting, a crisis.

turnip control   An 18th C Venetian wood marionette control shaped like a turnip. (Philpott DICTIONARY)

turnips   Provincial British audiences.

turnout   Attendance.

turn out   1. In dance, the out-rotation of the legs from the hip joint, resulting in the toes pointing to the side. 2. In performing, to turn away from center stage, toward the audience.

turn over   To go through a pack of flats, turning each one around and inspecting it.

turntable   See: revolving stage.

turret   1. A 12th C open-crown, white linen toque worn with a *barbette* (French). Sometimes worn over a chignon, flowing coiffure, or a wimple. (Wilcox DICTIONARY) 2. In Elizabethan theatres, the upper part of the tiring house, containing the music room. (Bowman/Ball THEATRE)

tutu   A short, very full tulle or net calf-length skirt worn by a female ballet dancer. If made ankle length it is called *juponnage* (French). (Kersley/Sinclair BALLET)

twelve-penny rooms   See: lords' rooms.

twelve-sheet, twenty-four sheet   See: sheet.

twenty-pound actor   A baby born into the theatrical profession. (Granville DICTIONARY)

twice-nightly cuts   Omissions made in a play text when the running time has to be reduced so that two performances can be given nightly. (Granville DICTIONARY)

Twist-lock connector   A patented connector (Harvey Hubbell, Inc.) which has been widely used in the theatre for many years. The connector is a small hard cylinder whose functional heart is its hooked prongs; they are twisted into the line (female) connector with the result that even rough stage use does not separate them. Often called simply Twist-lock, sometimes spelled Twist Lock or Twistlock, and not always capitalized. (Bellman LIGHTING 287, 288, fig. 11–3b; Wehlburg GLOSSARY)

two   See: in one.

two-act   A vaudeville act with two performers. (Gilbert VAUDEVILLE 294–295)

two-a-day   A production that was performed twice daily, as in big-time vaudeville (whereas small-time vaudeville usually ran four shows daily). (Smith VAUDEVILLIANS)

two-bottle jump, two-quart jump   Especially in traveling burlesque, an indication of the distance between engagements. A train ride of 200 miles equalled two consumed bottles of liquor. (Wilmeth LANGUAGE)

two by   A 2''×4'' piece of lumber.

2^{ce}, 3^{ce}, etc.   A 19th C prompter's note for the number of times a given performer goes onstage in an act (twice, thrice). (Shattuck SHAKESPEARE 15)

two-dimensional scenery   Framed or unframed scenery having height and width but no more depth than the material from which it is made. (Gillette/Gillette SCENERY)

two-faced door   A stage door, both sides of which can be seen by the audience; consequently, both faces must be finished.

twofer   1. Especially among U.S. stage electricians, a device with a single load (male) connector and two line (female) connectors. Also called a Y, double connector, tap-off, two-in-one, two-to-one, multiple; sometimes spelled twofor. Two outlets permanently wired in parallel on a single circuit are known as sister circuits. A device with a single load connector and three line connectors is a threefer or a W. 2. See: two-for-one. (Wehlburg GLOSSARY, Lounsbury THEATRE 118)

two-fold   Two flats hinged to fold together. When open, a twofold can be free-standing. Also called a book, a book flat, a wing.

twofor   See: twofer.

two-for-one   Two tickets for the price of one or a card authorizing such a sale. Also called twofer. (Bowman/Ball THEATRE)

two-for-one deal   See: half-price deal.

two-handed scene, three-handed scene, etc.   In Britain, a scene for two performers, three performers, etc. (Baker THEATRECRAFT)

two hander   See: duodrama.

two-in-one   See: twofer.

two-leaf ceiling   A book ceiling.

two-line gag   A joke in two parts: a cue and a response. (Wilmeth LANGUAGE)

two lines and a spit   A very small role.

two on the aisle   Two adjacent aisle theatre seats, one on the aisle.

two-penny gaff   See: penny gaff.

two-penny gallery   See: penny gallery.

two-penny room   A room or box in the gallery of an Elizabethan theatre. (Bowman/Ball THEATRE)

two-preset board, two-scene preset board   A control board (light console) which provides two complete sets of controls for the stage lights. Both can be prepared in advance to make possible a nearly instantaneous change from one setting to the other. Other phrases include two-scene preset, two-scene console, etc. So also five-scene preset, infinite preset, etc. Lounsbury has illustrations. (Lounsbury THEATRE 147, Bowman/Ball THEATRE 271)

two-riser   A platform with two levels, or two platforms of different heights set together.

two-scene console, two-scene preset   See: two-preset board.

two-shilling gallery   In early 19th C theatres in Britain, the first gallery, above the boxes. (Wyatt in Nagler SOURCES 451)

twosome, twosome scene   A scene for two performers. See also: two-handed scene. (Bowman/Ball THEATRE)

two spot   The second act on a bill.

two-step   1. A stair unit with two risers and two treads. 2. A dance in 2/4 or 4/4 time with a pattern of step-close-step.

two-to-one   See: twofer.

two tread   In Britain, a two-step unit.

two-way, four-way, six-way   Terms used attributively by stage electricians to indicate a number of actions, paths, or other possibilities. A two-way switch is one which can go in either of two opposed directions, while two-way barn doors are barn doors with two hinged leaves. See also: plugging box.

two-week stand   See: stand.

two weeks under, one week out   In contracts, a theatre owner's right to give one week's notice to a show whose receipts have fallen below a stated figure. (Bowman/Ball THEATRE)

tyer   See: tie.

type   1. A stock role, such as the handsome young hero, the fair damsel, the villain, etc. 2. A performer who specializes in one kind of role. 3. To categorize such a performer. Hence, type casting, cast to type, typing, etc. 4. Genre—such as comedy, tragedy, melodrama, etc.

Type C   See: C-lamp.

type cast   1. To cast a performer in a part that is close to his/her own personality or line (specialization). Hence, typing. 2. A performer so cast.

tyrbasia (Greek)   A dance in a dithyramb. (Pickard-Cambridge DITHY-RAMB 33)

tyreing howse   See: tiring house.

tyreman, tyrewoman   See: tireman, tirewoman.

tzanga   See: zancha.

tzu pao chia men (Chinese)   See: *zibao jiamen*.

tz'u sha tan (Chinese)   See: *cishadan*.

tz'u ta mien (Chinese)   See: *zhengdan*.

tzu yu pan (Chinese)   See: *ziyouban*.

U

U   Upstage.

uba (Japanese)   The mask and role of an old woman in *no*. (Shimazaki NOH 61, Komparu NOH 58)

Übermarionette (German)   1. A super puppet. Suggested by the designer Gordon Craig as what a master artist needed in place of a living actor, since actors have egos and emotions and cannot be so totally controlled as the inanimate elements in a stage production. The theory stirred much controversy when Craig set it forth in a 1909 issue of his periodical *The Mask*, since many took him literally. 2. A nearly life-sized (four to five foot) marionette of the 18th C, probably manipulated by string or wire, and vying for public favor with the traditionally smaller version. (Speaight PUPPET 163)

UC   Up center.

ucap (Malaysian)   Prose dialogue or speeches in *ma'yong*, usually of a conventional nature. Also spelled *uchap*. (Yousof "Kelantan" 75) See also: *bilangan*.

uchap (Malaysian)   See: *ucap*.

uchiage (Japanese)   Literally: beating-lifting. A complex and extended pattern of beating the wooden clappers (*tsuke*). The beating accompanies the final pose (*mie*) in a *kabuki* performance. It softens, rises to a furious crescendo, and terminates with a loud final pattern (*battari*). (Brandon CLASSIC 355)

uchikake (Japanese)   An outer robe worn open over a kimono, by a high ranking female character in *kabuki* or *bunraku*. See also: *isho*. (Shaver COSTUMES 178–179)

udatta (Sanskrit)   Literally: exalted. In classical Indian drama, the role of a hero (*nayaka*) who is self-controlled and gallant, usually a king's minister or general. One of four types of hero. (Shastri LAWS 205–206, Keith SANSKRIT 305–306) *uddhata* (Sanskrit)   Literally: arrogance. In classical Indian drama, the role of a hero (*nayaka*) who is proud, assertive, and adept in magic. One of four types of hero. (Keith SANSKRIT 305–306)

uddipana (Sanskrit)   Usually translated "excitant determinants." In classical Indian dramatic theory, the place, time, and given circumstances of a scene and its attendant atmosphere which 'excite' the desired emotional state (*bhava*). One category of determinant (*vibhava*). See also: *alambana*. (Keith SANSKRIT 315, Raghavan in Baumer/Brandon SANSKRIT 22)

UDOP, UDPS   Upper door opposite prompt, upper door prompt side. Found in some 18th C London promptbooks to indicate which proscenium door or wing passageway was to be used for an entrance. The upper door was probably a wing entrance. Sometimes printed VDOP, VDPS.

u-dyu-dyu (Chinese)   See: rootitootoot.

UE   Upper entrance.

ufli (Oriya)   A basic gait used to depict character in the *chhau* dance-drama of eastern India.

ujung (Indonesian)   The upper portion of the main control rod of a Javanese shadow puppet. The upper section of the rod is split and the puppet is held securely between the two parts. (Long JAVANESE 14)

UL   Up left.

ulan muchir (Mongolian)   See: *wulanmuqi*.

ulap-ulap (Indonesian)   Shadow puppet movements such as rolling frantically along the ground or spinning around in the air. Used for comic effect by Javanese *wayang* characters such as ogres and apes. (Long JAVANESE 67)

ULC   Up left center.

ulek bandar (Malaysian)   A trance-dance ritual in which a young woman encircled by a ring of female and male dancers communicates with 'spirits of the rice field'. (Sheppard TAMAN 88)

ullapya (Sanskrit)   A type of minor dramatic form (*uparupaka*) in ancient India, of which almost nothing is known. (Keith SANSKRIT 351)

ultra-realism   Naturalism excessively given to the doctrine of replica or facsimile. (Gorelik NEW)

ultra-symbolism   The tendency to overstress symbolic, mystic, or obscurantist ideas. Examples are dadaism, expressionism, surrealism. (Gorelik NEW)

ultraviolet light   See: black light.

umai (Japanese)   Literally: right dance. In *bugaku*, a dance imported from Korea or Manchuria and costumed predominantly in green. So named because performers approach the stage from the right. See also: *samai*. (Bowers JAPANESE 7, Wolz BUGAKU 42–47)

Umbhang (German)   A 17th C stage drapery. (Furttenbach in Hewitt REN-AISSANCE 215)

umbi cherita (Malaysian)   Literally: root of the story. In the shadow theatre, the title of a play. By implication, the specific content of a play, since different plays may have the same title or a single play may be known by several titles. (Sweeney RAMAYANA 267)

umbrator   In Steele Mackaye's description of his Cloud Creator, a semi-transparent cloth containing clouds or cloud shadows, the whole on a sliding frame. The light source above the cloth was to cast cloud shadows on set pieces representing a distant landscape. The word appears to have been an invention of Mackaye. (Mackaye EPOCH II lxxviii)

umbul-umbul (Indonesian)   Tall, curved banners that accompany the witch Rangda in the Balinese *barong* play. Also spelled *oemboel-oemboel*. (de Zoete/Spies DANCE 13)

Umgangspiel (German)   See: *Prozessionsspiel.*

ummanteltes Kabel (German)   See: *Biegsameskabel.*

Umwelt (German)   The self-contained unit or world of the performer, especially including effective interaction with other performers and with the environment. (Wepner "Orientation" 82–83)

uncover   Unmask, as when a performer alters position so as not to block the audience's view of another performer.

underact   To perform weakly, underemphasizing lines and business. The term is not always pejorative. Hence, underacting. See also: weak. (Bowman/Ball THEATRE)

under curve   In dance, movement in which a part of the body, or the center of weight, describes a curve toward gravity.

underdress   1. A second costume worn under another which is needed first and can be removed quickly. 2. To wear such a second costume. (Crampton HANDBOOK)

underhung block   A loft or head block secured to the underside of a gridiron.

underhung grid, underhung system   In a theatre with little space above the gridiron, a system of clamping head and loft blocks to the underside of the grid beams.

under image   A stage image, suggested or evoked rather than visibly or orally stated, which supports the inner meaning of the play and the inner action of the characters. (Selden ACTING)

underlighting   An occasional term for dim stage lighting. This use is not necessarily pejorative. (Lounsbury THEATRE)

underline   A small advertisement placed at the bottom of a regular theatre ad, announcing a coming attraction, such as: Next week: *East Lynne.* (Krows AMERICA 320)

underling   A groundling or standee in the pit of an Elizabethan theatre.

underpart   A role unworthy of a performer's talent and reputation.

underplay   To underemphasize lines or business. The term is not necessarily pejorative.

underplot   See: subplot.

under prompter, underprompter   In 18th C theatres, a deputy prompter who could take over whenever the prompter was ill or was needed onstage to substitute for a missing actor. (Hogan LONDON clxiv)

underrehearsed   A production not fully prepared.

under-rouge   In makeup, wet rouge.

understrapper   In 18th C theatres, a minor performer. (Hogan LONDON lxxvii)

understudy, study   A performer who stands by, prepared to substitute in a part in the absence of the regular performer. Hence, to understudy, understudying, understudy rehearsal. Understudies also usually fill minor roles. See also: walking understudy.

understudy list   A posted roster of understudy assignments.

understudy rehearsal   A rehearsal with the understudies taking the roles in which they must be prepared to substitute.

understudy's chance   The opportunity for an understudy to play the part he/she has understudied.

undertaker   A producer or one who undertakes to supervise a production. (Bowman/Ball THEATRE)

under treasurer   An assistant treasurer in 18th and 19th C London theatres. (Folger MS T.6.1.)

underwriter's knot   See: electrician's knot.

undressing room   Dressing room.

undress parade   A chorus show.

undulatory movement   See: wave.

unemphatic   1. Said of something, such as a property, which is not essential to the dramatic action but may have incidental value, as in characterization. 2. Said of an ending or curtain that is deliberately casual or anti-climactic. (Bowman/Ball THEATRE)

unfocussed limelight   Occasionally in British discussions of 19th C stagecraft, the light produced by one or more "bare" limelights—limelights without lenses. (Rees GAS 186)

union   Jocularly, or waggishly, the orchestra in a vaudeville house. See also: trench unionist. (Wilmeth LANGUAGE)

union grid   A gridiron with a permanently counterweighted rigging system, using wire ropes, as opposed to a loose grid, using rope lines and a pinrail.

union jet, union burner   See: fishtail burner.

uniplate   An occasional term for a projector designed to hold a single slide. A multiplate is a projector which will hold several remotely controlled slides. (Lounsbury THEATRE 121–122)

unit   A division of a play, usually labeled a scene or act.

unitard   A one-piece leotard; a body stocking.

unit batten   Occasionally in Britain, especially in the past, a pipe batten containing a number of individually controlled lighting instruments, often floodlights, but sometimes floods and spots. The term dates from the early use of individual fixtures as an improvement upon the flat lighting produced by borderlights. (Ridge/Aldred LIGHTING 72, fig. 19)

unities   A Renaissance belief that classic rules of playwriting required a play to have unity of time, place, and action. Aristotle, in fact, had observed only that Greek tragedies had unified plots—that is, unity of action. Until this century, however, the Renaissance misconception had considerable influence, perhaps most notably in French neoclassicism. Also called the three unities. See also: unity. (Vaughn DRAMA 198-199, 207-208; Barnet/Berman/Burto ASPECTS 269)

unit set   A stage setting made up of a number of units—such as flats, drapes, platforms, steps, etc. It can be used in a variety of combinations or kept unchanged. Also called a convertible set, flexible set, key set, permanent set, semi-permanent set, skeleton set. (Carrington THEATRICANA, Gorelik NEW)

unity   1. In playwriting and stage production, cohesion, consistency, oneness. (Cameron/Gillespie ENJOYMENT) 2. See: unities.

unity of action, unity of place   See: unities.

unity of production   As defined by Rene Pixérécourt early in the 19th C, a theatre piece well-constructed, well-written, well-rehearsed, and well-played under the auspices and care of one person alone, having one taste, one judgment, one mind, one heart, and one opinion. (Brockett "Pixérécourt" 181)

unity of time   See: unities.

universal burning   A phrase which indicates a lamp may be burned in any position. This is true of most PS (pear-shaped) lamps.

unlicensed theatre   In Britain before 1843, a theatre not licensed to produce legitimate drama.

unlocalized scene   A scene in a play that does not take place in a specific location; there are many such scenes in plays written for the sceneryless Elizabethan public stage.

unmodified light   The light given off by the filament of a lamp, by a candle flame, etc.

unrealized character   A character left undeveloped by a playwright.

unspoken subtext   See: subtext.

unsympathetic part   An unflattering role which may affect the popularity of its performer.

unwind the stanza   To finish a week's engagement.

up   1. Upstage—away from the audience. 2. To forget one's lines, to go up. 3. To know one's part, to be up. (Bowman/Ball THEATRE) 4. In stage lighting, above blackout. A light or lights may be part way up, or up to 'full.'

up and down   Said of a scenic unit that is perpendicular to the curtain line.

uparakon (Thai)   See: *natadontri*.

uparupaka (Sanskrit)   Minor or 'near drama' forms in ancient India. They emphasized dance and music but, lacking in drama (*natya*), they were not capable of arousing sentiment (*rasa*). They are a more probable link to present-day regional dance-drama forms than are the major forms of drama (*rupaka*). (Swann in Baumer/Brandon SANSKRIT 265–266)

upasthayika (Sanskrit)   See: *varsadhara*.

up center   The area in the middle and to the rear of a proscenium stage. Abbreviation: UC.

upholstery drama   In 19th C Britain, melodramas staged with realism in dress and furniture. (Bowman/Ball THEATRE)

up in all and make them go   Said of an actor who knew all of the comic roles in a Toby show and could make audiences laugh. Also called 'Toby boob and blackface.' (Wilmeth LANGUAGE 275)

up in a part   Said of a performer who has a role memorized.

up left   The left rear corner of a proscenium stage, from the performer's point of view. Abbreviation UL.

up left center   The area at the rear and between the center and the left corner of a proscenium stage, from the performer's point of view. Abbreviation: ULC.

upon tick   On credit. Sometimes shortened to on tick. The term may have derived from the bloodsucking tick, a parasite.

upper backscene, upper shutters   Sliding flat scenic units at mid-stage, above the regular shutters. Used in London by Inigo Jones as early as 1640. The system permitted opening either the lower or the upper shutters or both, to reveal the deeper reaches of the scenic area. (Southern CHANGEABLE 180)

upper balcony   Especially in the U.S., the uppermost separate seating area in an auditorium. In Britain: the upper circle. (Bowman/Ball THEATRE)

upper boxes   In Renaissance theatres and later, box seats on upper levels at the back of the auditorium. See also side boxes.

upper circle   See: upper balcony.

upper door opposite prompt, upper door prompt side   See: UDOP, UDPS.

upper entrance   See: UE.

upper gallery   Especially in Britain, a balcony seating area, usually the uppermost. (Bowman/Ball THEATRE)

upper grooves   In 17th C theatres and later, channels, often attached to the underside of the fly galleries on each side of the stage, to steady the tops of sliding wings and shutters. The grooves were in two sections; the section extending out over the stage was hinged and could be drawn up and back to the side of the stage when not needed.

upper hose   Stockings covering the lower trunk and upper leg. Also called upper stocks or trunk hose. See also: breeches, petticoat breeches. (Boucher FASHION)

upper *paraskenia* (English-Greek)   Of the Greek theatre, the upper floors of the wings of the *skene* (scene building) when there were two stories. See also: *paraskenia*.

upper perch   See: perch.

upper prompt wing   See: UPW.

upper shutters   See: upper backscene.

upper stage   A second story acting area in an Elizabethan theatre.

upper stocks   See: upper hose.

upptag (Swedish)   17th C Swedish court entertainments containing masquerade elements and featuring knights in mythological or historic costumes, fighting in tournaments. Songs and dances were frequently included. (Carlson "Scandinavia's" 15)

up right   The right rear corner of a proscenium stage, from the performer's point of view. Abbreviation: UR.

up right center   The area at the rear and between the center and the right corner of a proscenium stage, from the performer's point of view. Abbreviation: URC.

uproar   Grand opera.

upstage   In a proscenium theatre: 1. The rear half of the performing area and, indeed, of the entire stage area. Hence, upstage wall. Abbreviation: U. 2. Any position on stage that is behind something or someone. 3. To move toward the rear of the stage, sometimes forcing other performers to turn away from the audience while speaking. Hence, upstaging. See also: steal. 4. Vain, snobbish, haughty. (Bowman/Ball THEATRE, Berrey/Van den Bark SLANG 594)

upstage and county   In Britain, said of an aloof performer. (Granville DICTIONARY)

upstage left, upstage right   See: up left, up right.

UPW   Upper prompt wing—that is, an upstage side wing in old theatres, on the prompter's side of the stage. (Burnim GARRICK 124)

UR   Up right.

ura kata (Japanese)   Literally: backstage person. Costumers, wig makers, hair dressers, property people, and stage and lighting crews. See also: *omote kata*. (Leiter ENCYCLOPEDIA 419)

ura kido (Japanese)   Literally: rear door. The stage door of a *kabuki* theatre. (Scott KABUKI 286) A more general term is *gakuya guchi* (stage door).

urbanae cantilenae (Latin)   9th C historical scenes dealing with the lives of the saints, acted by *jongleurs* (French). (Sobel NEW)

URC   Up right center.

uscita (Italian)   Literally: exit. A memorized set speech used just before an exit in *commedia dell'arte*. Also called a *concetto* or conceit.

U-shaped auditorium   An auditorium in which tiers of boxes and galleries form a U around the auditorium floor seating area. Typical of many 17th C theatres. In later centuries, an egg- or horseshoe-shape was favored. (Mullin PLAYHOUSE 48)

usher   A theatre worker who shows spectators to their seats and (in many theatres) hands them programs.

ushiro o tsukeru (Japanese)   Literally: stick behind. To prompt a *kabuki* actor. If an actor is unsure of his lines a prompter (*kyogen kata*) crouches close behind the actor to do the prompting. (Leiter ENCYCLOPEDIA 419–420)

utai (Japanese)   Literally: song. In *no*, those portions of a play which are sung in a melodic fashion (*fushi*). The vocal line may be in the dynamic mode (*tsuyogin*) or melodic mode (*yowagin*). Accompanying instrumental music (*hayashi*) is in congruent rhythm (*hyoshi au*) or non-congruent rhythm (*hyoshi awazu*). See also: *kotoba*. (Bethe/Brazell NO 42–43, 50; Hoff/Flindt ''Structure'' 234)

utai bon (Japanese)   Literally: song book. The printed text of a *no* play. Texts were first published in the 15th C for the use of amateurs, including townsmen, studying *no* singing. The texts include partial musical notation. (Nakamura NOH 120–121)

utaimono (Japanese)   Literally: sung piece. A lyric piece of *kabuki* vocal music, the most important style of which is *nagauta*. See also: *katarimono*. (Malm MUSIC 203–205)

UTC company   Especially in the past, a troupe performing *Uncle Tom's Cabin*, usually on tour.

util   See: utility.

utilera, utilero (Spanish)   One in charge of properties.

utileria (Spanish)   Properties.

utility   1. Formerly, a person capable of performing a variety of minor roles and backstage tasks. 2. Any player of small parts. Also called a utility actor, utility actress, utility man, utility woman, util, or general utility.

utility character, utility role   A character in a play who is used to aid the exposition but is not integral to the main plot.

utility man   See: utility.

utility outlet   See: convenience outlet.

utility role   See: utility character.

utility truck   A wheeled platform for moving scenery and other stage equipment.

utility woman   See: utility.

utsaha (Sanskrit)   Literally: energy. One of the eight fundamental emotions (*sthayibhava*) expressed by actors in classical Indian theatre. See also: *vira*.

utsrstikanka (Sanskrit)   One of ten major forms of drama (*rupaka*) mentioned by Bharata in the *Natyasastra*: a one-act play based on legend that emphasized the emotion of pathos (*soka*). Also called *anka*. (Bharata NATYASASTRA 368, Kale THEATRIC 165)

UV, UV light   See: black light.

Uzbek cap   See: *tiubeteika*.

V

vacana (Kannada)   Literally: speech. In *yaksagana*, a quiet, prose introduction to a play spoken by the troupe manager (*bhagavata*). (Ashton/Christie YAKSAGANA 32, 37, 67, 95)

vacika (Sanskrit)   The spoken words of a play. In classical Indian theatre, one of four elements of acting (*abhinaya*). (Raghavan in Baumer/Brandon SANSKRIT 24) "Speech" according to Kale THEATRIC 125–136.

vacuum lamp   See: B.

vag (Marathi)   The main play in a *tamasha* performance, usually based on mythological themes, and consisting of a mixture of satire, farce, and ribaldry. (Nadkarni in Mukhopadhyay LESSER 52–54)

vairagi (Sanskrit)   See: *bhada*.

valance   1. A border, often hanging in front of the act (main) curtain, setting the height of the proscenium opening. Sometimes called a grand drape or a grand drapery border (but that border is more often the teaser) and, in Britain, a pelmet. 2. A short horizontal curtain at the top of a window, used to conceal the curtain rod or pole.

valva (Latin Roman)   The royal door, usually in the center of the *scaenae frons* (scenic facade). The term is an infrequent alternate for *regia*, perhaps a shortening of the occasional *valva regia*. The plural *valvae*, very rare in theatre literature, is literally a pair of door leaves. See also: *regia*. (Bieber HISTORY 187, fig. 680)

valve dimmer   In Britain, a tube dimmer. Hence, valve bank and other combinations. See also: thyratron tube dimmer. (Bowman/Ball THEATRE, Rae/Southern INTERNATIONAL)

vamp   1. Especially in vaudeville, introductory music that can be repeated again and again until a performer is ready to begin the song. During the vamp the performer often tells jokes. Hence, vamp till ready. 2. To improvise. To substitute a makeshift for a scenic unit, property, etc. Hence, vamped up. 3.

Short for vampire. 4. To vampire—to play a vampire character. 5. Short for vampire trap. (Bowman/Ball THEATRE)

vampire, vamp   1. A seductive character, usually a woman who debases her lover. Hence, vamp part, vampire part. 2. An actress who plays such a role. (Bowman/Ball THEATRE)

vampire door   See: vampire trap.

vampire trap   A trap with two spring flaps or leaves that parted under pressure and reclosed. Such traps might have been in the stage floor or in the scenery. Also called a vamp, vamp trap, vampire door. Named for the 19th C play *The Vampire*. See also: bristle trap, star trap. (Bowman/Ball THEATRE, Brockett HISTORY 513)

vamps   Double doors with springs, used in British pantomimes for quick appearances of performers.

vamp up   1. To remake, as when an old scenic unit is rebuilt into a new and different one. 2. See: vamp, meaning 2.

vandana (Hindi)   The opening prayer song in *ramlila*. (Gargi FOLK 122)

Van Dyck   See: falling band.

vanka-ru-tyu-tyu (Russian)   See: rootitootoot.

Värdskap (Swedish)   17th C Swedish court masquerades in which "hosts" or "innkeepers" and "guests" enjoyed a party. Prepared texts/scripts were not used, dancing was included, and mythological characters were frequently portrayed. The form emigrated either from Germany (where it was called *Wirtschaft*) or from France (where it was known as *hôtellerie*). (Carlson "Scandinavia's" 16)

variable dimmer   See: variable-load dimmer.

variable-load dimmer   A dimmer able to handle a range of electrical loads satisfactorily. All such dimmers can dim to blackout loads well below their capacity, and most can take any low load to blackout; some can take loads somewhat beyond their capacity. The auto transformer dimmer is a type of variable-load dimmer which is sometimes called a variable transformer dimmer. Used similarly are flexible dimmer, multi-capacity (resistance) dimmer, dual rated dimmer, dual capacity dimmer, and variable dimmer. In Britain, plus-or-minus dimmer, plus-and-minus dimmer. (Corry PLANNING 98, Bowman/Ball THEATRE)

variable transformer dimmer   See: autotransformer dimmer.

variation (French)   In classic ballet, a solo dance. (Grant TECHNICAL)

varicose alley   The runway in a burlesque theatre. (Wilmeth LANGUAGE)

variety   1. An entertainment made up of a number of acts, as in U.S. vaudeville and British music hall. Hence, variety show. The term was used in the U.S. in the late 19th C, faded, and has recently come back into use. 2. Capitalized, the name of the professional U.S. theatre periodical, sometimes called the actors' bible. 3. In children's theatre, technical changes of focus used by a director to keep children interested by compensating for their short attention spans. See also: syntheticalism. (Goldberg CHILDREN'S 142)

variety public   Fans of London music halls.

variety stage   A music hall, devoted to popular variety entertainment.

variety turn   A song-and-dance routine, acrobat act, animal act, comic skit, or specialty performance used as a filler or interlude in a puppet or other theatrical program. (Philpott DICTIONARY)

varsadhara (Sanskrit)   The role of a eunuch in classical Indian drama. Also called *nirmunda*, *upasthayika*. (Keith SANSKRIT 313)

vatsu (Sanskrit)   Plot in a classical Indian play. Bharata discusses plot elaborately, in terms of five "stages of development" (*avastha*), five "elements" (*arthaprakrti*), five "junctures" (*sandhi*), and five "explanatory devices" (*arthopaksepaka*) as well as "principal plot" (*adhikarika*) and "subsidiary plot" (*prasangika*). Also called *itivrtta*. (NATYASASTRA 378–400, Keith SANSKRIT 297–299, Byrski in Baumer/Brandon SANSKRIT 143)

vaudevillain   A vaudeville villain character.

vaudeville   In the U.S. in the late 19th and early 20th C, a popular entertainment made up of varied, usually unrelated acts: skits, songs and dances, comic routines, magic acts, etc. Hence, vaudevillian. In Britain, music hall, variety. (Cameron/Gillespie ENJOYMENT)

vaudeville (French)   1. Before Napoléon, satirical plays with lyrics set to familiar tunes; frequently based on social issues, class questions, and political concerns. The form may have begun its development as early as the 15th C. 2. After 1804, programs which were less political and social and more intellectual, rounded out with broad depictions of the lower classes, parodies, etc. 3. Eugene Scribe's sketches of contemporary life, with witty dialogue and graceful verse. (Carlson FRENCH 49)

vaudeville house   A theatre featuring variety entertainments.

vaudeville-revue   In the Russian theatre, an episodic series of skits with song, dance, and music. (Bowers ENTERTAINMENT 66)

vaudevillian   A performer in vaudeville.

vaudfilm   See: combo.

vaulting   Acrobatic feats on horseback at old equestrian theatres.

VDOP, VDPS   See: UDOP, UDPS.

vedette (French)   A star performer.

veethinatakam (Telugu)   A folk or street theatre form acted by members of the Yenadi tribe in Andhra Pradesh state, southeast India. It draws its repertory from the Brahmanic plays of the *yaksagana* tradition (meaning 3). (Vatsyayan TRADITIONAL 59)

vegetable actor   A performer who acted behind a net so that audiences could throw vegetables, eggs, and other perishables at him if they wished to. As early as the 1870s, some Shakespearean actors worked behind such screens and prospered: the audiences enjoyed the throwing. (Laurie VAUDEVILLE 272)

vehicle   A play or other entertainment, especially one that shows off a particular performer's abilities.

veladas (Philippine)   Songs and piano pieces played between short *zarzuelas*, or between acts of long ones. (Fernández ILOILO 41)

velarium   1. In Britain, a canvas canopy used in place of a battened ceiling cloth. The term comes from ancient Roman practice. (Bowman/Ball THEATRE) 2. See: *velum*.

vellattati (Malayalam)   In *kathakali*, a white-bearded role type such as the monkey general Hanuman of the *Ramayana*. One type of bearded (*tati*) role. (Jones/Jones KATHAKALI 30)

velours   A set of stage draperies consisting of legs (wings), borders, and at least one drop, all of velour.

velum, velarium (Latin Roman)   From the 1st C BC, an awning across the top of an amphitheatre and some theatres. The awning was controlled by ropes stretched from masts or poles (*mali*). Since the smaller theatres tended to be roofed, the *velum* was used especially in the larger theatres. Its material was canvas or linen, usually brightly colored, its purpose the protection of spectators from sun or rain. In U.S. English: velarium. See also: *petasos*. (Bieber HISTORY 179, Allen ANTIQUITIES 91, Sandys COMPANION 518)

velvets   Legs, drops, and borders of velvet or velour.

venationes (Latin Roman)   Animal shows. These spectacles may at first have been primarily exhibitions. Fights were introduced not later than 79 BC. In addition to exhibitions of tame animals, the *venationes* included fights between trained men or condemned criminals and wild animals, and between wild animals of different kinds.

venatores (Latin Roman)   Literally: hunters. The animal fighters in the *venationes*. See also: *bestiarii*. (Sandys COMPANION 509)

venerable hood   See: French hood.

vent   See: ventro.

ventilator   1. In Britain, a play or performance that empties the house, leaving no chance for the theatre to become overheated. (Granville DICTIONARY) 2. See: smoke hatch.

ventilatores (Latin Roman)   See: *prestigiatores*.

ventriloquist's guy   The doll with whom a ventriloquist works.

ventro, vent   In show business, a ventriloquist.

verba (Latin)   A trope—words added to the church service.

verdingale   See: farthingale.

verdugo (Spanish)   Literally: rod, wand. A 15th C supple tree limb used for the frames supporting the fullness of a gown. Predecessor of the farthingale. (Boucher FASHION)

Verfremdungseffekt (German)   In Bertolt Brecht's epic theatre theory, a distancing or reorientation, sometimes translated as alienation (hence, A-effect). It is achieved (theoretically) by showing a legend or screen projection, by changing spoken dialogue to song, etc.; such devices are designed to force the spectator to consider objectively a play's social implications. From the verb meaning ''to make strange.''

verismo (Italian)   Realism. Hence, the verist school of naturalistic writing.

veritism   Occasionally, realism, in the sense of breaking down all artificial theatricalism. Associated with the actor-director Konstantin Stanislavsky. (Sobel NEW)

Versatzständer (German)   Floodlights on stands. The term is broad, having in the past included bunchlights and open-box olivettes. Singular *Versatzstand*.

Versenkung (German)   Trap door.

verses   Formerly, lines of dialogue.

version   A play altered in translation from one language to another. Also called an adaptation.

verso (Philippine)   Lines of a verse in *comedia*. (Mendoza COMEDIA 99)

Versöhnungsdrama (German)   Literally: reconciliation drama. Tragi-comedy. (Hennequin PLAYWRITING 41)

versurae (Latin Roman)   According to Vitruvius, the side wings or side buildings which projected from either end of the stage building. These wings were analogous to the *paraskenia* of the Greek theatre. The literal meaning, turnings jutting forward, leads to the theatre meaning: the side buildings turned forward from the ends of the scene building. Sometimes called *versurae procurrentes*. (Bieber HISTORY xiv, 194; Sandys COMPANION 518)

versus (Latin)   A 9th C trope—an addition to the Kyrie of the Mass. (Frere WINCHESTER ix)

versus Fescennini (Latin Roman)   See: Fescennine verses.

vertical sight line   An imaginary line drawn from the eye of a seated spectator upward or downward to determine what needs to be done to mask the flies or to assure good visibility. Also called elevation sight line.

vertugadin   See: farthingale.

vesa (Malayalam)   Roles in *kathakali*. Also spelled *vesam*, *vesha*. Major role types are: *katti*, *pacca*, *tati*, *kari*, *teppu*, *minukku*.

veshadhari (Sanskrit)   Literally: one wearing costume and makeup. A performer of *yaksagana* who acts out his character, using all the theatrical devices, as opposed to a recitalist (*arthadhari*). (Gargi FOLK 163)

vestibule   1. A passageway between the exterior of a theatre and the foyer, needed especially in areas with extremes of hot and cold weather. 2. In Britain, a theatre lobby. (Burris-Meyer/Cole THEATRES 50, Bowman/Ball THEATRE)

vestibulum (Latin Roman)   The area in front of the entrance to an onstage house. The *vestibulum* was viewed as part of the house, not the street. (Pickard-Cambridge DIONYSUS 75–76, 78–79, 81; Allen ANTIQUITIES 113)

vestido (Spanish)   A costume.

vestuario (Spanish)   A dressing room.

vesuvian   Especially in the 19th C, a large match sometimes called for in Britain in stage directions involving colored fire. (Rees GAS 155)

vet   In Britain, to fix up a bad play; to doctor it.

vexillatores (Latin)   Medieval heralds who advertised a forthcoming play by carrying banners about the countryside; sometimes they delivered prologues. (Chambers MEDIAEVAL II 140–141, 156)

via negativa (Latin)   The negative path in Jerzy Grotowski's actor training: the necessity to strip away all disguises, masks, or other protections of a performer in order to work at a basic, truthful level. (Cameron/Gillespie ENJOYMENT)

vibhava (Sanskrit)   A "determinant" or "emotive situation" which underlies or helps express emotion (*bhava*) in classical Indian theatre. *Vibhava* are of two types, character and setting. See: *alambana*, *uddipana*. (Bharata NATYA-SASTRA 105–125, Benegal PANORAMA 13) Called "indicator" by Kale (THEATRIC 83).

vidusaka (Sanskrit), *vidusak* (Hindi)   A jester or fool. A traditional character type that appears in most classical Indian plays. Portrayed as fat, ugly, uncouth, and greedy but always a Brahman and always witty. (Benegal PANORAMA 16) Equivalent comic character types in rural theatre are: *behowa*, *bhand*, *hanumanayaka*, *kodangis*, *komali*, *maskhara*, *rangalo*, and others.

vignette   1. See: cut-down scenery. 2. A room beyond the main stage setting, seen only partially. 3. A short scene in a play.

vikrsta (Sanskrit)   A rectangular playhouse, described in detail by Bharata (NATYASASTRA 18–30) as the appropriate theatre for the major types of drama (*nataka*, *prakarana*). (Richmond in Baumer/Brandon SANSKRIT 76–79)

vilasika (Sanskrit)   A minor form (*uparupaka*) of ancient Indian drama: a one-act play in which the hero is supported by a parasite and a friend. The chief sentiment is the erotic (*srngara*). (Keith SANSKRIT 351)

village blacksmith   An actor who seldom gets long engagements; a failure.

villain   The antagonist in a play, especially an old-fashioned melodrama; the character who opposes the hero, or protagonist.

villancico (Spanish)   A medieval pastoral song, dramatic in character. (Ticknor SPANISH I 291)

villyun   An occasional comic misspelling of villain which suggests its (comic) pronunciation.

vimarsa (Sanskrit)   Literally: deliberation. The fourth of five junctures (*sandhi*) in the dramatic action of a classical Indian play. The attainment of the super-objective (*artha*) is obscured because of complications, but the scene ends with hope of its attainment. Also spelled *vimarsha*. (Bharata NATYASASTRA 384; Shastri LAWS 89–96, 130–140; Keith SANSKRIT 299)

vipralambha (Sanskrit)   Literally: separation. In classical Indian theatre, the depiction of the erotic sentiment (*srngara rasa*) in which lovers are separated from each other. (Bharata NATYASASTRA 108–110, Varadpande KRISHNA 27)

vira (Sanskrit)   Literally: heroism. One of eight principal sentiments (*rasa*) to be experienced by spectators of classical Indian theatre. It is aroused by the enacted fundamental emotion (*sthayibhava*) of energy (*utsaha*). (Keith SANSKRIT 323, Bharata NATYASASTRA 114–115)

virgo (Latin Roman)   A virtuous young woman, a virgin. A minor character in comedy, the *virgo* is more talked about than seen. Also called a *puella*. (Duckworth NATURE 253–254).

Virtuose (German)   A star.

visagière (French)   A hood opening, around the face. (Boucher FASHION)

vis comica (Latin)   Strong comedy.

vision cloth   A hanging cloth with a portion cut out and covered with theatrical gauze. Through the gauze an illuminated object or person can be seen, giving the effect of a vision.

visite   A 19th C large printed shawl-cloak with slits in front for the arms. (Boucher FASHION)

viskambha, viskambhaka (Sanskrit)   In classical Indian theatre: 1. Pure dance movements (*angahara, karana*) performed during the preliminaries to a play. (Bharata NATYASASTRA 47–61) 2. An "introductory scene" or "interlude" between acts that explains past or future events. One of five "explanatory devices" (*arthopaksepaka*). (Shastri LAWS 64–65, Kale THEATRIC 159–160, Keith SANSKRIT 301)

vismaya (Sanskrit)   Literally: astonishment. One of the eight fundamental emotions (*sthayibhava*) expressed by actors in classical Indian theatre. See also *adbhuta*. (Keith SANSKRIT 323)

vista   A 19th C term for a scene in perspective. See also: *a vista*.

visual effect   A special effect produced primarily by light. Examples are a starlit sky, a moon, falling snow. Sometimes called an optical effect in the U.S. (Bowman/Ball THEATRE)

visualization   In children's theatre, visual language: anything which makes it easy for a child to see plot, character, or other elements necessary to an understanding of a play. (Goldberg CHILDREN'S 141)

visual scenario, visual script   A graphic pattern (not representational) which a performer must find the means to enact. Also called a graphic score. (Cole ''Visual'' 28)

visus (Latin)   In medieval England, a play. (Chambers MEDIAEVAL II 138)

vita (Sanskrit)   The stock character of a parasite in classic Indian drama. Described by Bharata in the *Natyasastra* but not commonly found in extant plays. (Keith SANSKRIT 311)

vithi (Sanskrit)   Literally: way. In classical Indian theatre: 1. One of ten major dramatic forms (*rupaka*). It contains one act and two junctures (*sandhi*); graceful dance (*lasya*) can be used. It was performed by one or two actors, possibly as a street play. (Shastri LAWS 24–25, Kale THEATRIC 166–167) 2. One of four types of verbal style (*bharati vrtti*), used especially in the prologue (*sthapana*). (Shastri LAWS 44–45)

vítor (Spanish)   1. A shout of approval in a 17th C *corral* theatre. 2. A triumphal pageant.

vivek (Bengali)   Literally: conscience. A stock figure in *jatra* plays, c. 1911–1960, who could appear in any scene to admonish an erring character in song. (Gargi FOLK 28–30, Mukherjee in Mukhopadhyay LESSER 35)

vizard   1. A 14th C mummer's mask. 2. In the 17th C, a mask worn for protection or as a disguise, usually by women attending the theatre. 3. A woman wearing such a mask.

vlieger   A 17th C Low Country version of the *ropa* (Spanish). (Boucher FASHION)

vocatores (Latin)   Two singing characters in an early medieval dialogue who introduce the prophets and comment on their predictions. (Chambers MEDIAE-VAL II 54)

voci (Italian)   Young men who performed in liturgical plays.

vodavil (Philippine)   American-style vaudeville, introduced in 1916. (Fernández ILOILO 151)

voice tone   See: tone.

voix du sang (French)   Literally: voice of the blood. A theatrical convention in which filial affection and/or recognition brings a play to a happy end. Also called *cri du sang*. (Archer PLAY-MAKING 230)

volant   1. An 18th C lightweight, unlined jerkin without pockets, and no buttons except at the neck. 2. A flounce or ruffle. (Boucher FASHION) *(de) volée* (French)   In ballet, aerial: performed with a flying or soaring movement. (Grant TECHNICAL)

volet   1. See: cointise. 2. A short, full veil attached to a medieval woman's headdress. (Wilcox DICTIONARY)

Volksbühne (German)   People's theatre.

Volkstück (German)   A popular play, a folk play dealing with ordinary people.

volta (Italian)   The European forerunner of the modern waltz. In the Renaissance it was danced by a couple, with the woman lifted and swung around by the man as she executed a leap from the ground. Also called a *coranto*. (Perugini PAGEANT 69)

vomedy   Vaudeville comedy.

vomitoria (Latin Roman)   The great doors which opened into the seating area, often from covered corridors in the auditorium. English vomitory means the entrance rather than the door(s). The word is ultimately from *vomo*, to throw up, throw forth. (Bieber HISTORY 172, 185, 194; Allen ANTIQUITIES 91)

vomitory   1. A passageway for spectators, opening into a bank of seats, as in an athletic stadium but also in some theatres. 2. A passageway for performers to enter or leave the performing area through a bank of seats. Often found in arena theatres or theatres with thrust stages.

Vong Co (Vietnamese)   Literally: remembrances. A sentimental melody sung several times during a *cai luong* performance to stir audience emotions.

Vorspiel (German)   A curtain-raiser, a prologue.

Vorstellung (German)   Performance. Hence, *Erstevorstellung* (first performance).

vote with your feet   To walk out of a show. (Wilmeth LANGUAGE)

votive games   See: *ludi votivi.*

voyagé (French)   In ballet, a "suffix" to a given position in which the position is kept as the dancer moves, leg bent, in small, quick hops. (Kersley/Sinclair BALLET)

vrtti (Sanskrit)   In classical Indian drama: 1. A dramatic style, a style of writing a play. The four styles described in the *Natyasastra* are: *arabhati*, *bharati*, *kaisiki*, and *sattvati*. (Keith SANSKRIT 326–329) 2. Methods used in production. (Rangacharya NATYASASTRA 41) 3. The bearing or mode of behavior of a character. (Shastri LAWS 318–320)

V-shaped set   A triangular stage setting, showing the corner of a room.

vulture   Feathers from a vulture. Theatrical costumers find them durable, soft, and inexpensive. (Dreher HATMAKING)

vyabhicari bhava (Sanskrit)   Transitory states or emotions. The fleeting feelings of a character that an actor must express in order to convey the fundamental emotions (*sthayibhava*) of the play. Bharata describes 33 (joy, agitation, envy, despondency, etc.) but later writers mention others as well. (NATYASASTRA 126–145) Kale THEATRIC 94–103 charts the connection between the 33 transitory emotions and their corresponding "determinants" (*vibhava*) and "consequents" (*anubhava*). Also called *samcari bhava*.

vyas (Hindi)   1. A professional Brahman reciter of the Hindu epics. 2. A specialist in the *Ramayana* epic who directs and prompts a *ramlila* drama. See also: *sutradhara*. (Hein MIRACLE 97, Gargi FOLK 96–97)

vyayoga (Sanskrit)   One of ten major types of classical drama (*rupaka*) described by Bharata in the *Natyasastra*. It is a one-act play with a well-known story. A divine being or sage is hero and any *rasa* can be used except humor (*hasya*) and love (*srngara*). (Rangacharya NATYASASTRA 52)

W

W   1. Whistle—formerly a prompter's signal to shift the scenery. 2. Written—a property paper with writing on it. 3. Wing. (Shattuck SHAKESPEARE 14, 19) 4. See: threefer.

wa (Chinese)   See: *wazi*.

WAD   Warn act drop—formerly, a prompter's note to prepare for the lowering of a drop at the end of an act. (Shattuck SHAKESPEARE 22)

waffle   In acting, to fluff lines.

Wagenbühne (German)   Wagon stage.

wagon   See: scenery wagon.

wagon (Japanese)   A six-stringed zither used in *gagaku*. (Wolz BUGAKU 19)

wagon stage   1. A (usually mechanized) floor on wheels and in guide tracks, on top of the regular stage floor. It is capable of carrying a full stage setting and bringing it from offstage to center stage. Sometimes called a sliding stage or slip stage. 2. A medieval stage on a cart—a pageant wagon. (Bowman/Ball THEATRE)

wagoto (Japanese)   Literally: soft style. A romantic, humorous male style of *kabuki* acting, popularized by the Kyoto actor Sakata Tojuro in the period c. 1678–1704. It is used especially for comic leading men roles (*nimaime*) in plays set in the licensed quarters. An example is Izaemon in *Love Letters From the Licensed Quarter* in Brandon CLASSIC 217–237. *Wagotoshi* is an actor who plays this type of role. See also: *aragoto*. (Brandon in Brandon/Malm/Shively STUDIES 70–74, Gunji KABUKI 22)

Wahltafel (German)   Literally: selection board, selection table. In early 20th C electrical control, an auxiliary which permitted a particular lighting circuit to be connected to a selected control circuit. This was analogous to a plugging panel. (Fuchs LIGHTING 369)

Wahrhaftigkeit (German)   Truth; fidelity to reality in acting and scene design.

wai (Chinese)   Literally: secondary. A supporting older male role (*laosheng*) in many forms of music-drama (*xiqu*) including Beijing opera (*jingju*) and *kunqu*. Similar to *mo*. Also called *laowai* or *lao wai*. (Dolby HISTORY 105, 180)

waichuan, wai ch'uan (Chinese)   1. The custom whereby a distinguished actor performed with actors of a company other than his own for music-drama (*xiqu*) performances at large-scale celebratory events; prevalent in the 19th C. (Mackerras RISE 182) 2. Today, any music-drama performer participating in a performance given by a company other than his or her own.

waidan (Chinese)   See: *dan*.

wai khru (Thai)   A ceremony in which *lakon* or *khon* performers pay respect (*wai*) to their teachers (*khru*). (Yupho CUSTOM 3)

waimo, wai mo (Chinese)   See: *mo*.

waistcoat   1. A Louis XVI man's garment, in many styles but always with a front in fine fabric and a back in a lining fabric. In the 19th C, waistcoats were worn layered on top of each other. 2. A front-buttoning trim for a very low-cut gown. Also called a *compère* (French). See also: soubreveste. (Boucher FASHION)

wait   1. The time between a performer's appearances in a show. 2. The time between a performer's engagements. 3. An intermission, interval. See also: stage wait. 4. In Britain, a public musician who plays in processions or public entertainments. The tradition goes back to medieval times, as does the term.

wai tan (Chinese)   See: *dan*.

waiter girl   At a concert saloon, a female employee who sometimes performed in specialty acts, skits, and other entertainments provided by the management. (Zellers "Saloon" 582)

wajang (Indonesian, Malaysian)   See: *wayang*.

waka (Japanese)   A poem of thirty-one syllables which is used as a structural unit (*shodan*) in a *no* play. It is sung to non-rhythmic musical accompaniment (*hyoshi awazu*). (Shimazaki NOH 48)

waka onna (Japanese)   A *no* mask of a young woman, used primarily by the Kanze school. (Shimazaki NOH 60)

waka onnagata (Japanese)   Literally: young female role. In 17th C *kabuki*, a general term for young female roles in *kabuki* and the actors of such roles. See also: *kashagata*. (Dunn/Torigoe ANALECTS 168, Kawatake KABUKI 35) Now it is often replaced by terms for specific sub-types. See: *onnagata*.

wakashu kabuki (Japanese)   Literally: adolescent *kabuki*. 1. The style of *kabuki* performed by troupes of boys, between 10 and 15 years old, who depended upon their sexual attractiveness to draw an audience. 2. The historical period of *kabuki*, c. 1629–1652, when these troupes flourished. (Gunji KABUKI 20–21, Kincaid KABUKI 64–73)

wakashukata, wakashugata (Japanese)   1. An adolescent male role in *kabuki*, emphasizing gentleness and sensuous appeal. (Gunji KABUKI 180, 186) In the 17th C it was a role type separate from leading men (*tachiyaku*); today it is a sub-type of *tachiyaku*. (Dunn/Torigoe ANALECTS 172) 2. An actor who plays such a role. (Leiter ENCYCLOPEDIA 423) Abbreviated: *wakashu*.

waki (Japanese)   Literally: beside. A secondary, or supporting, role: 1. In *no*, the role, typically, of a traveling priest who meets and questions the protagonist (*shite*), thus initiating the dramatic action. (Inoura HISTORY 105, Shimazaki NOH 3–7) 2. In *bunraku*, a second chanter, who performs along with a chief chanter (*tayu*). 3. The supporting role in *kowakamai*. (Araki BALLAD 8) See also: *ado*.

waki bashira (Japanese)   See: *daijin bashira*.

waki kata (Japanese)   Literally: supporting people. A collective term for all the roles and the performers of the roles associated with the *waki* in *no*. This includes the *waki* role itself, *waki zure*, and *tomo*. (Komparu NOH 155)

waki kyogen (Japanese)   Literally: next-to play. 1. In a joint performance of *no* and *kyogen*, the *kyogen* comedy which is performed immediately after, that is, 'next to' (*waki*), the first *no* play. It is auspicious in tone. Examples are *The God of Wealth* and *The Treasure Mallet*. (Inoura HISTORY 127) 2. In 18th and 19th C *kabuki*, the play which appeared second on a day's program, and hence 'next to' the opening ceremonial dance play, *Sanbaso*. A theatre had several such plays in its repertory but since no scripts have survived, their nature is unclear. (Dunn/Torigoe ANALECTS 20, Brandon CLASSIC 24, 30)

waki no (Japanese)   See: *kami no*.

waki shomen (Japanese)   In a *no* theatre, seating which faces the side of the stage, hence the cheapest seats. (Komparu NOH 140)

waki za (Japanese)   In *no*: 1. The supporting character's (*waki*'s) standard position (*za*) on stage. It is beside the supporting character's pillar (*waki bashira*), down left. 2. The side stage, abutting the left side of the main stage (*hon butai*), on which the chorus sits. (Komparu NOH 129, 130)

waki zure (Japanese)   See: *tsure*.

wa le kot (Burmese)   Two long bamboo clappers used in theatrical musical ensembles. Also called *wa let kyong*. (Sein/Withey GREAT 48, Malm CULTURES 93)

wali (Indonesian)   Sacred ritual dances in Bali, usually nondramatic. An essential part of worship, in which the gods directly participate. See: *sanghyang*. See also: *bali-balihan*, *bebali*. (Bandem/deBoer BALINESE 1–2)

wali miring (Indonesian)   The small, thin, and sharply pointed nose shape of a very refined *wayang* shadow puppet. (Long JAVANESE 70)

walk   1. In 18th C Britain, a performer's line or specialty. 2. In dance, a simple locomotor step in which weight is transferred from one foot to the other while contact with the ground is maintained. (Hayes DANCE 47) 3. In checking the look of a lighted area, to move about in: "John, walk that spot."

walk across   In burlesque, a girl walking across the stage during a comedian's skit and delivering one or two lines followed by a grind and bump. (Wilmeth LANGUAGE)

walk a flat   See: run a flat.

walk a part   To go through one's role below performance level.

walk-around   In minstrel shows: 1. A danced walk around the stage by the full company, accompanied by much cane-twirling and hand-clapping. 2. The music for the walk.

walk a scene   To go through a scene mechanically, without attempting to act it fully.

walkaway   1. A successful production. Hence, a walkaway hit. 2. Change left by a ticket buyer. (Berrey/Van den Bark SLANG 584, 592)

walk down   To ease a scenic unit, such as a flat, from the vertical to the horizontal by having one stagehand hold the bottom in place while another lets the unit fall and supports it, walking backward until the top reaches the floor.

walker   1. A stripper who performs while walking to music. (Wilmeth LANGUAGE) 2. An unflattering term for an unused musician who is required (by contract) only to appear once a week to pick up his or her salary.

walker-on   A performer in a role with no lines; a performer who regularly plays such roles; a supernumerary, extra. See also: walk on. (Bowman/Ball THEATRE)

walk-in business   Money taken in at the box office from tickets sold to walk-up patrons without advance reservations.

walking coat   See: frock coat.

walking gentleman, walking lady   1. In the 19th C and earlier, a performer playing third-line parts. (Brockett HISTORY 345) 2. Performers in minor roles, usually walk-ons. 3. In Britain, lady or gentlemen supers (supernumeraries). (Granville DICTIONARY)

walking part   A non-speaking role, often in a procession. See also: walk on.

walking suit   An early 20th C woman's jacket and skirt, the latter barely clearing the ground; it was later shortened slightly. (Boucher FASHION)

walking through   Rehearsing without using much energy, without "acting." (Brockett HISTORY 546)

walking understudy   A performer who is prepared to substitute in walk-on parts.

walk men   Men who sell tickets to a show on the sidewalk near the theatre. They are said to be 'on the walk.' (Wilmeth LANGUAGE)

walk off with the show   To steal the show, to receive the greatest applause.

walk on   1. A minor role without lines. 2. One who plays such a role. Hence, walk-on part, walking part, walker on, walking on, walk ons, etc. 3. Hyphenated, an entrance without lines. 4. To make an entrance without lines.

walk on and understudy   A performer who plays a minor role without lines and also understudies a larger part.

walkout assignment   The last act on a bill.

walk the boards   See: boards.

walk the curtain   To walk behind a draw or tab curtain as it closes to make certain the two halves overlap when they meet at center. See also: page.

walk through   1. A rehearsal with stage movement, often the first such rehearsal. 2. A rehearsal with complicated movement or business, worked through slowly. 3. A pick-up rehearsal, well below concert pitch in both speech and movement, usually before a performance which follows a break of a few days. 4. Hyphenated, a walk-on part. 5. To read one's lines perfunctorily. Hence, walking through. 6. A minor performer with few or no lines. (Bowman/Ball THEATRE)

walk up   1. To raise a flat or scenic unit to a vertical position by having one stagehand hold the bottom in position while a second raises the top from the floor and pushes the unit up as he walks toward it. Also called edge up. 2. To walk upstage, toward the rear of the stage. 3. See: walk-in business.

wall box   See: wall pocket.

wall bracket   A device designed to be fastened to a wall to hold a lighting fixture. The phrase is used of fixtures fastened to the wall of a setting to provide motivating light and suggest a particular period or style. Especially in the U.S., also called a bracket, bracket light, or bracket fixture. (Bowman MODERN, Lounsbury THEATRE, Rae/Southern INTERNATIONAL, Cornberg/Gebauer CREW 157)

wall connector   See: wall pocket.

wall pocket, wall outlet   A stage pocket in or on a wall of the stage and containing one or more receptacles for lighting equipment. Also called a wall box or wall connector. See also: floor pocket, stage pocket. (Bowman MODERN, Corry PLANNING, Wehlburg GLOSSARY)

Walter Plinge   Since about 1900, a fictitious name used in British theatre programs to conceal the identity of an actor doubling in a second role. The U.S. equivalent is George Spelvin. (Granville DICTIONARY)

wanara (Indonesian)   Literally: monkey. A monkey character in a Javanese or Sundanese puppet or dance play. Body type is similar to a muscular (*gagah*) character. Also called *rewanda*. (Long JAVANESE 103–105, Foley "Sundanese" 36)

wanda (Indonesian)   The 'expression' or mood of a Javanese or Sundanese *wayang* puppet, indicated by coloring and a particular set of body features. (Brandon THRONES 50–51, Muljono in Osman TRADITIONAL 63–64, Foley "Sundanese" 43–44)

Wandeldekoration (German)   A rolling panorama.

wangsalan (Indonesian)   Literally: riddle. A word cue to musicians to call for a specific instrumental selection in a Javanese *wayang* performance. The cue is integrated into the puppeteer's speech or song. (Brandon THRONES 59–60)

wangsul nimblis (Indonesian)   A movement used by refined *wayang* characters in Javanese shadow theatre during battle scenes. A character returns after having been thrown away and strikes from above with an outstretched arm. (Long JAVANESE 84–85)

waraba (Kankan)   In Guinea, a form of theatre using musicians, a chorus of female singers, and life-size puppets in the shape of lions. (Adedeji glossary)

waraijo (Japanese)   A mask of a smiling old man, worn in the first part of a *no* play by a deity disguised as a humble fisherman or rustic. Also called *sankojo* or *asakurajo*. (Shimazaki NOH 58)

wardrobe   1. Stage costumes and accessories collected for a production or stored in a theatre. 2. The room in which they are fitted or stored.

wardrobe keeper, wardrobe master, wardrobe mistress   A theatre employee responsible for the maintenance and storage of a theatre's stock of costumes. Also called a costume mistress, costume master, mistress of costumes, master of costumes.

warizerifu (Japanese)   Literally: divided dialogue. A major stylized dialogue sequence in *kabuki* in which two characters speak alternately. Each speech is shorter than the last and the final phrase is spoken in unison. It indicates parallel actions by the two characters. It is often written in seven-five meter (*shichi go cho*). Examples are in Brandon CLASSIC 307–308.

warm   1. Said of a responsive audience. 2. To narrow the focus of a spotlight and thus increase the intensity of the light. 3. To move color toward the warm end of the spectrum, as in lighting, painting, etc.

warm color   Of light or pigment, in or toward the yellow-orange-red range. (Wehlburg GLOSSARY)

warmers   See: curtain warmers.

warm key   Key light in one or more warm colors. (Bellman LIGHTING 228)

warm them up   1. To please an audience, especially at the beginning of a show, so that they will respond readily to what follows. 2. In a variety show, to entertain an audience before the main attraction begins.

warm up   1. Generally, to add warm color(s), to increase the light level, or both. 2. Especially in Britain, to narrow the beam of a spotlight and increase its brightness. (Stewart STAGECRAFT) 3. To exercise the voice and/or body in preparation for a rehearsal or performance. 4. The exercise itself.

warn   To signal by voice, bell, or light for a performer or crew member to be ready for a coming cue. (Bowman/Ball THEATRE)

warn act drop   See: WAD.

warn and go   Paired signals used by prompters or stage managers, the first to prepare a performer or stage technician and the second to execute the cue.

warn curtain   See: WC.

warn drop   See: WD.

warning cue   A signal to prepare for a coming cue.

warning signal   A warning to members of the audience that the performance is about to begin. The signal is usually a bell, chime, buzzer, or blinking light. Hence, warning bell, warning light.

war paint   Greasepaint.

warrior play   See: *shuramono*.

wart   See: dutchman.

wasan bori (Hausa)   See: *bori*.

wash   1. A spread of light which covers much or all of the acting area. The purpose is to tone and smooth the lighting. Sometimes called a color wash. 2. As a verb, to use such light.

wash-and-key   An occasional phrase for lighting which combines wash light and key light. (Bellman LIGHTING 350–351, Bellman SCENE)

washe, wa she, washi, wa shih (Chinese)   See: *wazi*.

wash light   1. A broadly-focused lighting instrument which provides fill light over a fairly large area. 2. The result of using such light. (Wehlburg GLOSSARY, Lounsbury THEATRE)

washtub   See: beam projector.

watarizerifu (Japanese)   Literally: passed-along dialogue. A major stylized dialogue sequence in *kabuki* in which a single thought is 'passed along' from one character to the next in linked speeches. The final line is often spoken in unison. (Dunn/Torigoe ANALECTS 38, Brandon in Brandon/Malm/Shively STUDIES 101) Leiter applies the term to a series of name-saying speeches (*nanori*) in *Benten the Thief* (ART 11).

water-barrel dimmer   See: salt water dimmer.

water black   Mascara.

water curtain   1. A sprinkler system in front of or behind a theatre's fire curtain. See also: deluge curtain. 2. A pipe or hose pierced with holes, suspended over the stage near the curtain line, to simulate rain or, in an outdoor theatre, to create a curtain of water behind which scenery can be changed. See also: steam curtain.

water dimmer   See: salt water dimmer.

waterfall   A 19th C headdress with a knot atop the head, from which the hair cascaded to the nape of the neck. See also: psyche knot. (Chalmers CLOTHES 240, Wilcox DICTIONARY)

watering can   In ballet, the generic term for the rosin used by dancers to keep from slipping on a stage with insufficient traction. In earlier times, water stored in a can was used to counteract the slipperiness of the floor. See also: rosin box. (Kersley/Sinclair BALLET)

water joint   In 19th C lighting, a safety device in gas outlets for the stage floor. A gas pipe in the stage floor, with another gas pipe outside it (the latter becoming a floor outlet) were inside a larger brass pipe connected to a water supply. Water in the brass pipe created a leak-proof joint; the gas pressure was equal to about two inches of water while the brass tube held some twelve inches of water. Sometimes called a hydraulic joint. See also: patent automatic gas dip. (Rees GAS 112–113, 231, figs. 70–71)

water joint slide   In a gas supply for the stage in 19th C Britain, the coupling pipe which fitted over the central gas pipe in the water joint in the stage floor. See also: dip. (Rees GAS 204, figs. 70–71)

watermelon man   A blackface act based on a black watermelon vendor's sales pitch played for four decades by G. Swaine Buckley. (Toll BLACKING 45)

water resistance dimmer   See: salt water dimmer.

Watteau gown   An 18th C French Regency sack dress worn over a closely-fitted bodice and full underskirt. Loose folds fell from the shoulders in the back and became part of the skirt. The front neckline was low with a ribbon-orna-mented stomacher. Forerunner of the gown à la Française. The *robe volante* (French) was a variation of this style. See also: gown à l'Anglaise. (Wilcox DICTIONARY)

Watteau pleat   An 18th C French Regency box pleat sweeping from the back of the shoulder to the floor. The gown itself was fitted at front and sides. See also: gown à la Française. (Barton COSTUME 313, Boucher FASHION)

wa tzu (Chinese)   See: *wazi*.

wave   In dance, the result of a curved movement of an arm or leg in a regular sequence of a certain series. Also called an undulatory movement. Similar to a succession. (Eshkol/Wachmann NOTATION 103)

wave movement   As seen and used by Isadora Duncan, the undulation and cadence of the sea as the source of maximum psychic satisfaction and therefore the logical basis of the natural rhythm of modern dance. (Love DANCE 94)

wax   Wax candles, as in a 19th C Covent Garden announcement that "The Circles of Boxes will be illuminated with wax." (Rees GAS 19)

wax light   In some 19th C British writing on the theatre, a candle. (Rees GAS 12–13)

way   Primarily in Britain, an electrical circuit, especially a control-board circuit with provision for a dimmer. (Corry PLANNING, Bentham ART)

wayang (Indonesian, Malaysian)   Derived from *bayang* (shadow). 1. A flat leather puppet used to represent a character in a shadow play (*wayang kulit*). (Ulbricht WAYANG 43) The word was used as early as the 9th C in Java. (Holt ART 283) In Java also called *ringgit*. Muljono lists major puppet groupings in Osman TRADITIONAL 62–63. 2. By extension, a play or performance in which shadow puppets are used and, therefore, an abbreviation of *wayang kulit*. 3. By further extension, a play or performance derived from *wayang kulit*, but differing from it either in dramatic repertory or medium of performance. For example, "listening to *wayang* on the radio," when *wayang golek* doll-puppet theatre is meant. (Foley "Sundanese" 14) See the following sources for some of the c. 50 *wayang* genres that are, or were, performed. Extensive lists are in Sweeney RAMAYANA 3–6; Muljono in Osman TRADITIONAL 65–69, 79–81; Holt ART 123–128; and Brandon THRONES 5–10, 396. 4. Until recently in Indonesia and still in Malaysia a generic term for a play or performance, encompassing movies, Chinese opera, and most stage presentations. Also spelled *wajang*. (Holt ART 123)

wayang beber (Indonesian)   Literally: scroll *wayang*. A Javanese theatre form in which a performer (*dalang*) recites an episode from the *Panji* tales while unrolling a scroll painted with the episode being narrated. *Wayang beber* probably originated in prehistoric times but is now rarely performed. (Rassers PANJI 119–124, Holt ART 127, Brandon SOUTHEAST 45)

wayang calonarang (Indonesian)   A Balinese shadow play performance of the Calonarang story, featuring the demon witch-widow *rangda*. (Moerdowo BALINESE II 116)

wayang cepak (Indonesian)   See: *wayang golek cepak*.

wayang cupak (Indonesian)   The Balinese story of Cupak and his brother, performed in *wayang kulit*. (Moerdowo BALINESE II 116)

wayang dhudhahan (Indonesian)   See: *wayang dudahan*.

wayang djawa (Indonesian)   See: *wayang jawa*.

wayang dudahan (Indonesian)   Literally: taken-out puppets. In Javanese *wayang kulit*, those puppets taken and placed in stacks beside the puppeteer for use in performance. Also spelled *wayang dhudhahan*. Also called *wayang dugangan* (kicking puppets). (Muljono in Osman TRADITIONAL 63, Long JAVANESE 69, Brandon THRONES 39)

wayang dugangan (Indonesian)   See: *wayang dudahan*.

wayang gambuh (Indonesian)   In Bali, the *Panji* tales performed as shadow theatre. (McPhee in Belo TRADITIONAL 150, Moerdowo BALINESE II 116)

wayang gedek (Malaysian)   The Malaysian term for Thai *nang talung* shadow theatre, performed by Thais in Thailand and occasionally in northern Malaysia. Also spelled *wayang kedek*. (Sweeney in Osman TRADITIONAL 5)

wayang gedog (Indonesian)   A Javanese shadow theatre form based primarily on the *Panji* tales. It is said to have been created in the 16th C. (Muljono in Osman TRADITIONAL 66, Brandon SOUTHEAST 44) In East Java, Damar Wulan legends are also staged occasionally. (Holt ART 124)

wayang golek (Indonesian)   Literally: doll-puppet *wayang*. A Sundanese and Javanese puppet theatre using rod-doll puppets, said to have been created by the Sunan of Kudus in the 16th C (Brandon THRONES 6) and closely related to, perhaps derived from, *wayang kulit*. (Brandon SOUTHEAST 44, 50) In Sunda, two different repertories are performed: *purwa* plays in *wayang golek purwa*, and chronicles based on Javanese, Sundanese or Islamic history in *wayang golek cepak*. In a recent innovation, *wayang golek modern* (modern *wayang golek*) puppets are played on a small stage within movable sets. (Foley "Sundanese" 25–29, 262; Muljono in Osman TRADITIONAL 65) In Central and East Java, the *wayang golek* repertory is based on Islamic *Menak* stories. (Holt ART 125)

wayang jawa (Indonesian, Malaysian)   1. In Malaysia, a localized adaptation of Javanese shadow theatre, using *Mahabharata* characters and puppets patterned after Javanese models. (Sweeney RAMAYANA 3, Brandon SOUTHEAST 56) 2. In Java, a shadow play dramatizing events from 19th C Javanese history, with Prince Diponegoro as the hero. Also spelled *wayang djawa*. (Holt ART 124, Brandon SOUTHEAST 44)

wayang kedek (Malaysian)   See: *wayang gedek*.

wayang kerutjil (Indonesian)   See: *wayang klitik*.

wayang kiwa (Indonesian)   Literally: left *wayang*. In Java, puppets that appear on the left side of the screen when confronted by *wayang* heroes. See also: *wayang tengen*. (Rassers PANJI 134, 151; van de Kroef "Roots" 322)

wayang klitik (Indonesian)   Literally: small *wayang*. In Java, a rarely seen daytime puppet play that uses small, flat, wooden puppet figures and no screen. Its repertory is drawn from the stories of Damar Wulan of the Majapahit kingdom, 13th-16th C (Muljono in Osman TRADITIONAL 66, Ulbricht WAYANG 2, Brandon SOUTHEAST 44) and from the east Javanese Panji tales (Holt ART 125). Also called *wayang karucil* or *karutjil*, *wayang kerucil* or *kerutjil*, and *wayang krucil* or *krutjil*.

wayang krutjil (Indonesian)   See: *wayang klitik*.

wayang kulit (Indonesian, Malaysian)   Literally: shadow of leather. Derives from *bayang* (shadow) and *kulit* (hide). 1. A shadow puppet. 2. The generic term for shadow theatre, often abbreviated *wayang*. Rassers argues the shadow aspect of performance is coincidental, and that in origin it was a puppet play. (Rassers PANJI 124–132, 210–214) 3. In Java, nearly synonymous with *wayang purwa*, the vast majority of shadow play performances being of that repertory and using those puppets. (Holt ART 123, Ulbricht WAYANG 1–3, Sweeney RAMAYANA 3, Long JAVANESE 5–7, McPhee in Belo TRADITIONAL 146–150) 4. For Malaysian forms, see: *wayang jawa, wayang siam*.

wayang lemah (Indonesian)   A Balinese ritual performance of shadow theatre "occasioned by either personal or community disaster," and directed to the gods rather than a human audience. Performed during the day without a screen by a priest-puppeteer (*pemangku dalang*). See: *wayang sudamala*. (Moerdowo BALINESE II 110–111, McPhee in Belo TRADITIONAL 150)

wayang madya (Indonesian)   Literally: middle *wayang*. A type of Javanese shadow theatre (*wayang kulit*), rarely performed, created in the 19th C in Surakarta to stage plays about the Javanese prophet-king Djayabaya. Also spelled *wayang madiya*. (Muljono in Osman TRADITIONAL 66, Holt ART 124, Ulbricht WAYANG 2)

wayang makau (Malaysian)   See: *mendu*.

wayang melayu (Malaysian)   Malaysian-style shadow puppets.

wayang orang (Indonesian)   See: *wayang wong*.

wayang panca sila (Indonesian)   Literally: Five Principles *wayang*. A c. 1950s adaptation of Javanese *wayang kulit*, in which the five Pandawa brothers are called the Five Principles of the Nation (for example, Arjuna is 'Nationalism'). Also spelled *wayang pantja sila*. (Muljono is Osman TRADITIONAL 66, Holt ART 125, Brandon SOUTHEAST 287–288)

wayang parsi (Malaysian)   Literally: Parsee theatre. A popular, commercial theatre form (flourished c. 1870–1905), initially performed by Parsee (Persian-descent) troupes from Bombay and transformed by local Malaysian troupes into a Malay-language theatre.

wayang parwa (Indonesian)   See: *sayang purwa*

wayang purwa (Indonesian)   Literally: old or original *wayang*. 1. In Java and Sunda, a *wayang* play based on one of the four ancient dramatic cycles: the animistic, the *Ardjuna Sasra Bau*, the *Rama*, or the *Pandawa* (*Mahabharata*). The last cycle is the most popular by far. (Foley "Sundanese" 25–27, Ulbricht WAYANG 50–51, Holt ART 124) Since the great majority of shadow play performances in Java are *purwa* plays, *wayang purwa* in Java is virtually synonymous with *wayang kulit*. Also spelled *wayang poerwa*. (Long JAVANESE 1, Brandon THRONES 2, 17) 2. In Bali, a shadow play based on the *Ramayana* or the *Mahabharata*. (Moerdowo BALINESE II 115, Soedarsono DANCES 180) 3. See: *parwa*. See also: *wayang wong*.

wayang siam (Malaysian)   Literally: Siamese *wayang*. The most common form of shadow theatre in Malaysia. The flat, leather, rod-puppets are usually between one and two feet high, with one movable arm. Iconography of the puppet figures draws heavily on Thai dance, puppet, and costume styles; hence, probably, the name. Widely performed in northern Malaysia. The majority of its repertory is based on the Malaysian version of the *Ramayana* epic. (Sweeney in Osman TRADITIOINAL 8, Sweeney RAMAYANA 3–6)

wayang simpingan (Indonesian)   See: *simpingan*.

wayang sudamala (Indonesian)   Literally: free-from-curse *wayang*. A Balinese shadow play of the Kala story, performed to exorcise his evil influence. See also: *mewinten dalang, ruwatan*. (McPhee in Belo TRADITIONAL 188–190, Moerdowo BALINESE II 111-115)

wayang suluh (Indonesian)   Literally: torch or information *wayang*. A type of shadow play created in 1947 to stage contemporary stories designed to support the Indonesian independence movement. (Holt ART 124–125, Brandon SOUTHEAST 287)

wayang technik (Indonesian)   Literally: technical *wayang*. A contemporary form of *wayang golek* in Sunda that uses devices such as smoke and lights for stage effects. (Foley "Sundanese" 262)

wayang tengen (Indonesian)   Literally: right *wayang*. In Javanese *wayang kulit*, puppets that stand on the stage right side of the screen to face their opponents. They are the heroes, the positive side, the "forces of light and goodness," as van der Kroef says in "Roots" 322. See also: *wayang kiwa*. (Rassers PANJI 135, Brandon THRONES 18, 20)

wayang topeng (Indonesian)   Literally: masked *wayang*. A classical and folk masked dance-drama dating from the 12th C and still popular in Central and East Java. Only *Panji* stories are enacted. Abbreviated *topeng* (mask). *Klana topeng* is a masked dance-play about Panji's opponent, King Klana. See also: *topeng*. (Holt ART 153–155, Soedarsono DANCES 50, 92)

wayang wong (Indonesian)   Literally: human *wayang*. A classical dance-drama that melds dialogue, narrative (by a *dalang*), dance, and *gamelan* music. 1. In Central Java, an unmasked dance-drama based on *Ramayana* and *Mahabharata* stories. Staged at court, 18th to early 20th C (Soedarsono DANCES 36, Holt ART 151–167), and by professional troupes in commercial proscenium theatres in the 20th C (Brandon GUIDE 67–68). Females usually play refined male roles. Also called *wayang orang* (human *wayang*). (Brandon SOUTHEAST 47) 2. In Cirebon (West Java), a masked dance play primarily presenting *Mahabharata* stories. Also called *topeng dalang* (masked-drama with a narrator). (Soedarsono DANCES 124) 3. In Bali, a ceremonial all-male masked dance-drama dating from the 16th C enacting *Ramayana* stories. Emphasis is on narrative rather than dance. (Soedarsono DANCES 179, Brandon SOUTHEAST 53–54). See also: *langen, raket, parwa, sendratari*.

wazi, wa tzu (Chinese)   Literally: tiles. An amusement quarter in a major city, c. 10th-14th C. Each contained shops such as restaurants, pharmacies, and tailors, as well as a number of hook balustrade (*goulan*) theatres where Song and Yuan *zaju* and Jin *yuanben*, storytelling (*shuochang*), acrobatics, and the hundred entertainments (*baixi*) were performed. Also called *wa, washi* or *wa shih*, and *washe* or *wa she*. (Dolby HISTORY 17, 67; Mackerras RISE 193–194, 213)

WC   Warn curtain—formerly, a prompter's note to prepare for the lowering of a curtain. (Shattuck SHAKESPEARE 22)

WD   Warn drop—formerly, a prompter's note to prepare for the lowering of a drop. (Shattuck SHAKESPEARE 22)

weak   Said of apparently unemphatic actions or line readings which, when purposeful, underline a dramatic point. (Bowman/Ball THEATRE)

wedge, wedge act   See: *xiezi*.

weed   To distribute a small audience over the house; to dress the house. (Berrey/Van den Bark SLANG 591)

weekly rep   In Britain, a repertory company performing one play a week.

week out   In Britain, a week during which a touring company has no engagement.

week stand   A theatrical engagement one week long.

week-stand house   See: one week house.

weenie   In playwriting, a gimmick or plot manipulation which brings about a happy ending; a script whose ending is not organic to the organization of the plot. (Herzel "Anagnorisis" 504)

weeper   See: tearjerker.

weepers   See: *pleureuses*.

weepie   A tearjerker.

weight   See: counterweight.

weighting empty lines   Attaching a small weight—a sandbag, for example—to a line or lines not attached to a batten or scenic unit, so that the line(s) will drop to the stage floor when untied at the pinrail.

weiyang daban, wei yang ta pan (Chinese)   Literally: Weiyang big troupe. A form of small-scale folk theatre (*xiaoxi*) accompanied by percussion instruments, performed c. 18th-early 20th C in Yangzhou (formerly called Weiyang), Jiangsu Province at religious festivals and events; the themes of plays were frequently religious as well. In 1935 it combined with Weiyang civil theatre (*weiyang wenxi*) to become *yangju*.

weiyang wenxi, wei yang wen hsi (Chinese)   Literally: Weiyang civil plays, Weiyang civil theatre. A form of flower drum play (*huaguxi*) accompanied by wind and string instruments which was originally performed at the Chinese New Year Lantern Festival in Yangzhou, Jiangsu Province c. 18th-early 20th C. It took the name Weiyang (an old name for Yangzhou) civil theatre in 1919, when Yangzhou flower drum play troupes began performing in Hangzhou and Shanghai. In 1935 it combined with Weiyang big troupe (*weiyang daban*) to become *yangju*.

wekasan (Indonesian)   The concluding scene of a Sundanese *wayang golek* puppet play. (Foley "Sundanese" 114)

well   1. A theatre subcellar, used for machinery which works traps, elevators, etc. 2. Short for orchestra well—a variant of orchestra pit. 3. A wide gap in the gridiron structure to accommodate loft blocks and hoisting lines. Also called a grid or loft well. (Bowman/Ball THEATRE)

(to be) well firmed   To know one's part.

Wellington half boot, Wellington   A 19th C round, low-heeled boot, ankle-high and fastened with a strap or gaiter under the sole. (Chalmers CLOTHES 232, Wilcox DICTIONARY)

well-made play   From the French, *pièce bien faite*. A term applied to the plays of Eugène Scribe and Victorien Sardou in 19th C France; the plays had carefully-formulated plots and stereotyped characters. Despite the derogatory connotation of the basic meaning, the term is sometimes used loosely to refer to any play with a strong cause-and-effect structure and a tendency to conform to the unities of time, place, and action—such as Henrik Ibsen's *A Doll's House* or Lillian Hellman's *The Little Foxes*.

Welsbach burner   A late 19th C gas mantle widely used in theatres without electricity. The most successful of gas mantles, the Welsbach was a gauze-like cotton mesh impregnated with oxides of cerium and thorium. A Bunsen burner inside the mesh consumed the cotton and left a delicate, brightly-glowing cylindrical web which gave more than three times the light of ordinary gas jets. Also called a Welsbach gas mantle, mantle, or incandescent burner. (Penzel LIGHTING 93)

wen (Chinese)   Literally: civil. See: *wenxi, wenchang*.

wench   In white black-face minstrel shows, a female impersonator. Also called a prima donna. Hence, wench role. See also: yaller girl. (Wilmeth LANGUAGE)

wenchang, wen ch'ang (Chinese)   Literally: civil orchestra. The collective name for the melodic instruments in a music-drama (*xiqu*) orchestra (*changmian*). Important instruments in many forms of music-drama include various types of two-stringed spike fiddles (*huqin*), the moon guitar (*yueqin*), *ruan* guitar, lute (*pipa*), three-string lute (*sanxian*), horizontal bamboo flute (*di*), mouth-organ (*sheng*), and the *guan* and *suona* reed wind instruments. See also: *wuchang*. (Wichmann "Aural" 433–441, 449–452, 464–478)

wen ch'in chü (Chinese)   See: *qianju*.

wenchou, wen ch'ou (Chinese)   Civil clown role. The type of comic male role found in civil plays (*wenxi*); includes both good and evil characters from all levels of society. It is a major subcategory of the clown role (*chou*) in Beijing opera (*jingju*) and many other forms of music-drama (*xiqu*). (Dolby HISTORY 181, Scott CLASSICAL 76–78)

Wenchow *tsa chü* (Chinese)   See: *nanxi*.

wen hsi (Chinese)   See *wenxi*.

wenlaosheng, wen lao sheng (Chinese)   Civil older male role. An older male role featuring song (*chang*), speech (*nian*), and/or dance-acting (*zuo*) skills; a major subdivision of the older male role (*laosheng*) in Beijing opera (*jingju*). Abbreviated *laosheng*. (Dolby HISTORY 180)

wen ming hsi, *wen ming hsin hsi* (Chinese)   See: *wenmingxi*.

wenmingxi, wen ming hsi (Chinese)   Literally: civilized plays, civilized theatre. Western-style plays performed in the 1910s and 1920s. They included translations of Western plays, adaptations of Western novels and plays, translations of Japanese *shinpa* and *shingeki* plays, and original Chinese spoken dramas (*huaju*) with both ancient and modern content; the majority were fully written-out scripts, but some were act-outline plays (*mubiaoxi*). Also called civilized new plays (*wenming xinxi* or *wen ming hsin hsi*) and enlightened plays (*kaimingxi* or *k'ai ming hsi*). Before 1910, such plays were included among those referred to by the term new plays (*xinxi*). In the 1920s, the term civilized plays came to connote low quality; by the latter part of that decade, all Western-style plays were called spoken drama (*huaju*). (Dolby HISTORY 203–206, 279; Hu TS'AU 15–21; Scott LITERATURE 36)

wenming xinxi (Chinese)   See: *wenmingxi*.

wenqinju (Chinese)   See: *qianju*.

wensheng, wen sheng (Chinese)   Civil male role. A generic term for all male roles (*sheng*) which engage in civil (*wen*) rather than martial (*wu*) activity in Beijing opera (*jingju*) and many other forms of music-drama (*xiqu*). The term includes all older male (*laosheng*) and young male (*xiaosheng*) roles other than martial older male (*wulaosheng*) and martial young male (*wuxiaosheng*). (Dolby HISTORY 180, Scott CLASSICAL 66–67)

went up   Forgot lines.

wenxi, wen hsi (Chinese)   Literally: civil play. A play whose plot involves personal, social, domestic, and/or romantic situations in Beijing opera (*jingju*) and many other forms of music-drama (*xiqu*). Such plays emphasize song (*chang*), speech (*nian*), and/or dance-acting (*zuo*) skills, and feature performers who specialize in these civil techniques. See also: *wuxi*. (Scott CLASSICAL 20, 185; Wichmann "Aural" 50–53)

Wenzhou *zaju* (Chinese)   See: *nanxi*.

West End   The theatrical district of London.

western roarers   In early minstrel shows, frontier folk stories and heroes. (Wilmeth LANGUAGE)

West Virginia formula   W = VA (watts equals volts times amperes), the simple equation by which stage electricians may be certain they are not over-loading dimmers. The 'pie formula' (P = IE) is the same: power (watts) equals intensity (amperes) times electromotive force (volts). The terms power formula and power equation are also sometimes used. (Lounsbury THEATRE 49–50, Bowman MODERN)

wethi (Thai)   Literally: stage. An acting space.

wethi pi phat (Thai)   Literally: music stage. In *likay*, a sidestage at stage right where *pi phat* musicians sit. (Virulrak "Likay" 122)

wet meter   See: dry meter.

wet rouge   In makeup, under-rouge.

wet white   Formerly, white liquid makeup.

wham   A striptease in which the stripper disrobes completely. (Wilmeth LANGUAGE)

whammo   A smash hit. See also: boffo, socko.

wheel   1. A circuit, a tour route. 2. A theatre in a circuit.

wheeled stage   See: chariot stage.

wheeze   In Britain, a music hall gag.

whip   Two thin plywood strips strapped together with a handle which keeps the strips about a quarter of an inch apart. Smacking the plywood whip against a solid surface makes a cracking sound. See also: slapstick. (Collison SOUND 102)

whipped off   Taken offstage rapidly.

whisker   A slip of the tongue.

whiskey seats   In Britain, end seats in the stalls or dress circle, close to the bar.

whisperer   A prompter.

whispering tube   In 19th C British theatres, a tube to carry the prompter's voice cues to backstage workers.

whistle   In Restoration theatres and later, a signal for a scene shift.

Whistler   See: do a Whistler.

white   1. In an electrical cable, the color of the insulation of the neutral wire. 2. See: open white. (Bellman LIGHTING 167)

white cake makeup, white creme makeup, white greasepaint, white liquid makeup   Various types of makeup that whiten the face.

white elephant   A piece of scenery hung over the forestage. (Berrey/Van den Bark SLANG 579)

white face powder   In makeup, a powder used on the face and, when there is no practical alternative, for greying hair.

white-light district   A theatrical district.

white meat   From about 1930, a white woman hired as a singer or actress. Now rare. (Wilmeth LANGUAGE)

white minstrel   A white man who performed in minstrel shows, wearing burnt-cork makeup. (Hughes/Meltzer MAGIC 18)

whitening   An old term for makeup that whitens the face, such as clown white, white cake makeup, white liquid makeup, white creme makeup, or white greasepaint.

white shadows   The effect created by light coming through shapes cut from black cards, the reverse of the usual silhouette. French: *ombres blanches*. (Philpott DICTIONARY)

white way   A theatrical district.

whiting   1. Powdered chalk used in scene painting. 2. White makeup. (Bowman/Ball THEATRE)

whole-group drama   In creative drama, improvisational activities in which all participants assume a role and join the playing. (O'Neill/Lambert DRAMA 27)

wicket   Primarily in Britain, a ticket window, especially in a box office. (Bowman/Ball THEATRE)

wide-angle floodlight   See: broad.

wide-open   Of spotlights, focused to provide the maximum beam spread.

widow's peak   1. See: attifet. 2. A hairstyle having a dipping point of hair at mid-forehead. (Wilcox DICTIONARY)

wig band   A strip of adhesive cloth used to hold a wig against the forehead. (Bowman/Ball THEATRE)

wig block   A block of wood with a rounded top, for dressing or making wigs. (Wilcox DICTIONARY)

wiggle-stick   A device sometimes placed next to a theatre seat for purposes of determining a playgoer's response to a play. The person sitting in the seat moves the lever in response to specific events on stage, enabling researchers to gauge responses to the performance. Unfortunately, playgoers often become so absorbed in the stage goings-on that they forget to move the lever. The research was tried in the 1940s in the U.S. (Addington "Audience" 483)

wig lace   A fine-gauge, flesh-colored lace used to let air into a hairpiece, or to fasten a hat when there is insufficient hair to anchor a hatpin. (Dreher HATMAKING)

wig line   The rim of a wig, where it joins the face. (Bowman/Ball THEATRE)

wig paste   A material used to fasten a wig and to blend in the wig line. Loosely referred to as greasepaint. (Bowman/Ball THEATRE)

wig play   See: *kazuramono*.

wig plot   A schedule indicating the scenes in a play in which a wig or wigs will be worn. (Bowman/Ball THEATRE)

wik (Thai)   A *likay* or *lakon* theatre building.

wild   Said of the hinged part of a stage setting that is free to move. (Parker/Smith DESIGN)

wildcatting   In vaudeville, making one's way across large parts of the country playing unscheduled, no-contract engagements. (Smith VAUDEVILLIANS 90)

(a) William Winter   Formerly, a critic. After the U.S. 19th-20th C critic, William Winter. (Wilmeth LANGUAGE)

willing suspension of disbelief   An observation made by the critic Samuel Taylor Coleridge in the 19th C of the conscious willingness of a Western play reader or audience member to go along with the make-believe of a play or a stage production.

willow plumes   See: *pleureuses*.

wimple   A medieval hood-like veil which covered the entire head, concealing the hair but not the face. Also called a *couvre-chef* (French) or coverchief. See also: gable, guimp(e), headrail, mitra. (Barton COSTUME 111, 121; Boucher FASHION; Chalmers CLOTHES 88)

winder   1. In marionette storage and travel, a device used to prevent the tangling of strings. (Philpott DICTIONARY) 2. A wind machine.

winding in   In 19th C theatres, admitting playgoers. The "door-keepers . . . kept *winding* in their late arrivals. . . . " (Boaden INCHBALD 237)

windjammer   A trombonist in a minstrel show. (Wilmeth LANGUAGE)

wind machine   A device for simulating the sound of wind. In one type, a piece of canvas is pulled over a revolving ribbed wooden drum.

window backing   See: backing.

window card   A poster advertising a theatrical event, placed wherever it might attract attention, as in a store window. Also called a day bill.

window flat   A flat with a window opening in it.

window sale   A ticket sale at the box office, as opposed to a sale at an auxiliary outlet.

window stage   The acting space at a gallery window above an entrance door in an Elizabethan theatre.

window stiles   The vertical members of a flat which form the sides of a window opening. (Gillette/Gillette SCENERY)

window unit   A solid wooden window, operable if necessary, made to fit into a window flat.

windup, windupper   The last act on a bill.

wine-room girls   Waitresses at vaudeville performances who occasionally appeared on stage. (Gilbert VAUDEVILLE 33–36)

wing   1. Short for wing flat, as in a wing-and-drop setting. 2. Two or three flats hinged together, or a leg drop, used to mask the side of the stage. 3. The offstage space on either side of the stage setting (usually stated in the plural). 4. To play a part without memorizing it, to 'wing it,' relying on the prompter in the wings or pages of the text fastened in a convenient place such as the back of a wing flat. Hence, wing 2 part, wing 2 side. 5. One who learns a part while waiting in the wings. 6. See: buck and wing. (Bowman/Ball THEATRE, Cartmell HANDBOOK)

wing-and-drop, wing-and-shutter   Obsolete scenic systems consisting of sliding side wings painted and arranged in perspective, with a painted drop or shutters providing the vista. (Hanging above each of the wing positions were painted borders). Hence, wing-and-drop setting, wing or winged setting, wing set, wing flat, etc.

wing a part, wing a side   See: wing.

wing bell   In 18th C theatres in Britain, a prompter's bell for cuing changes in wings. (Hughes in Hume LONDON 131)

wing carriage   See: chariot-and-pole system.

wing cuts   Cutouts in a scenic wing.

winged setting, wing set   See: wing-and-drop.

wing flat   See: wing

wing flood   1. A floodlight used from a wing of the stage, especially when mounted on a light stand. 2. A floodlight designed for use from a wing of the stage. (Goffin LIGHTING 73; Ridge/Aldred LIGHTING 26, fig. 18; Bowman/Ball THEATRE)

wing ladders   See: wing lights.

wing lights   Lights at the side of the stage, especially when behind vertical wings which mask the offstage space. Also called side lights or wing ladders (19th C). Other terms used in 19th C Britain: gas wings, gas ladders. (Rees GAS 31–34, Penzel LIGHTING 88)

wing men   Stagehands who attend the wing flats or who handle properties taken on and off through the wings. (Granville DICTIONARY)

wings   1. See: *paraskenia* (Greek), *versurae* (Latin Roman). 2. In Renaissance theatres and later, scenic units at the sides of the stage, usually painted in perspective. There were normally four or more wings on each side of the stage, usually set parallel to the curtain line, with spaces between the wing positions for entrances. At first the units were angle wings, usually immovable; later they were sliding flat wings in pairs or packs. In some theatres the wings were set at an angle. See also: slanted scenes. 3. See: wing space.

wing setting   See: wing-and-drop.

wing space   The area offstage and to the sides of the acting area. Also called the wings.

winking ghost   A hand puppet containing a small bulb which lights up the head. (Philpott DICTIONARY)

winter theatre   A playhouse or company normally in operation from Fall through Spring.

wire act   Especially in vaudeville, a balancing act. (Wilmeth LANGUAGE)

wire cable, wire rope   Strong, heavy, multi-strand wire used in a counter-weight system to connect battens and their counterweight arbors.

wire dimmer, wire resistance dimmer   See: slide dimmer.

wire grip   See: grip.

wire-guide counterweight set   A set of lines attached to a counterweight arbor that is guided by two wires stretching from the gridiron to the floor (as opposed to an arbor running on a track).

wire leads   See: asbestos leads.

wire resistance   In Britain, a rheostat. (Bowman/Ball THEATRE)

wire rope   A strong rope made of wire. Hence, wire rope clip, wire guide, etc. (Bowman/Ball THEATRE)

wire way   Especially in the U.S., a sheet metal trough designed to carry and protect a number of circuits. Also called a gutter or raceway. (Lounsbury THEATRE)

Wirtschaft (German)   See: *Värdskap*.

with   A preposition used in advertisements and programs just below the production title, naming a featured but not leading performer, as "*Hamlet*, with John Smith as Claudius." (Bowman/Ball THEATRE)

with books, without books   Of a rehearsal, with or without scripts in hand. Synonyms of 'without books' include books down and off book.

within   Offstage in an Elizabethan theatre. Then also called in stage directions 'without.'

without books   See: with books.

w^n   Written—a property paper with writing on it. The manuscript note can be found in old promptbooks. (Shattuck SHAKESPEARE 14)

woffle   In British music-hall performances, to evade adroitly a difficult note or passage. (Partridge TO-DAY 229)

wolak-walik (Indonesian)   To reverse positions. In Javanese shadow theatre, the technique of flipping the arm rods forward and backward during the major battle (*perang kembang*) between a heroic knight and a group of attacking giants. (Long JAVANESE 86)

Wolkenapparat (German)   Literally: cloud apparatus. Cloud projector, cloud machine. As early as the 1920s, some German cloud projectors used a 3000-watt lamp with a number of sets of condenser and objective lenses, each with its own photographic slide of clouds. These could be moved at various speeds and in various combinations to produce intricate cloud effects. The projectors were available in a number of sizes and types. Unruh has illustrations. The plural adds −*e*. (Fuchs LIGHTING 212–213; Unruh THEATERTECHNIK 222-223)

woman of parts   A versatile actress.

woman play   See: *kazuramono*.

women's *kabuki* (English-Japanese)   See: *yujo kabuki*.

women's shift   The women's dressing room in a Restoration theatre. The room was apparently a general one; the private dressing rooms were called tiring rooms.

wood border   See: foliage border.

wood cuts   In a framed drop or side wing painted to represent a forest, openings or cuts through which the deeper reaches of the stage setting can be seen.

wooden arm   See: hook.

wooden heads   18th C puppets. (Jacobus "Puppets" 111, 117)

wooden O   Shakespeare's metaphor in *Henry V* for an Elizabethan public theatre, supposedly descriptive of its shape.

wood family   See: bare-stall family.

wood graining   See: graining.

wood up   To applaud with the feet. (Berrey/Van den Bark SLANG 591)

woodwing   A small stage. (Berrey/Van den Bark SLANG 578)

wood wing   A side wing with irregular onstage edges, painted to resemble a forest.

Woolworth circuit   See: fish-and-chip tour.

(the) word   A prompt.

word rehearsal   A rehearsal concentrating chiefly or exclusively on lines.

words   Lines, as in "Do you know your words?"

work   1. To be effective, as a gel in a lighting instrument or a piece of stage business that will 'work' or be satisfactory. 2. To assist in a production or performance, as in 'to work a show.' 3. To move unobtrusively to a better stage position, as in: to work upstage or work left. 4. To perform.

work a show   To participate in a production.

workbook   A stage manager's copy of a play. (Shattuck SHAKESPEARE 5)

work boy   A local boy who helped pitch the tent for a traveling show, such as a Toby show, in return for a pass to the performance. (Wilmeth LANGUAGE)

work downstage   See: work upstage.

workers' theatre   Theatre concerning itself with the laboring class. (Bowman/Ball THEATRE)

work for cakes, work for peanuts   To work for a low salary.

working   1. Said of scenery, costumes, properties, etc. that are in use or to be used. Hence, working border, working props, etc. Also called live. 2. Said of a door, window, etc. that is practical, that will operate—as opposed to the same thing inoperable or even painted.

working area   The stage space outside the acting area.

working border   See: border.

working curtain   See: house curtain.

working distance   Especially of spotlights, an occasional term for the distance at which the instrument is designed to be effective. Also called throw.

working drawing   A scaled drawing showing a carpenter what to build and how to build it.

working flies   A fly gallery which is in use. (Bowman/Ball THEATRE)

working hot   In burlesque, emphasizing the number of bumps and grinds a stripper can do during the chorus of a popular song. (Green in Mayer/Richards WESTERN 165)

working in one   See: in one.

working leg   In conventional ballet usage, the limb first to leave the ground. In certain movements it is a misnomer, since the other leg may actually be doing the work. (Kersley/Sinclair BALLET)

working light   See: work light.

working line   1. A rope line used throughout a performance. 2. The operating line of a counterweight set. 3. The line in a mechanical shop drawing representing a movement pattern or extension line, as opposed to one representing the edge of an object.

working men   Men, usually local, who pitched the tent of a traveling show, such as a Toby show. (Wilmeth LANGUAGE)

working rail   See: pinrail.

working script   The prompter's copy of the play, with notes on movement, business, etc.

working side   The side of the stage where the prompter sits, which should also be the side where the curtain pull is located and the stage manager is positioned. Also called prompt side. Often stage left, but varying with the architecture of a theatre building.

working title   A usually temporary title for a play.

work left   See: work upstage.

work light, work lights   Usually, the light provided on the stage when the stage is not in view of the audience. This may be when a curtain is down; more often, work light is used for rehearsals and other such work sessions as construction, painting, and set-up. Work lights are ordinarily independent of the stage lighting in a separate switch or group of switches. The term is sometimes used of the working lights in other areas of the theatre, including very dim offstage light needed by crews or actors during a performance, called in Britain stage pilots. U.S. technical personnel sometimes say 'works,' and Britain's 'working light' has been used in the U.S., especially in the past. The British also use 'rest light.' (Bellman SCENE, Wehlburg GLOSSARY, Bowman MODERN, Baker THEATRECRAFT, McCandless ''Glossary'' 629)

work opposite another   In vaudeville, to appear with another performer who had most of the lines. (Wilmeth LANGUAGE) Work opposite has since been used similarly to mean play opposite a better-known performer.

workout   An audition.

work right   See: work upstage.

works   In the U.S., work lights.

workshop   1. A drama or theatre workshop—a practical and usually short and concentrated course in some aspect or aspects of theatre. 2. A space where scenery and properties are prepared, a scene shop. 3. A costume shop. (Bowman/Ball THEATRE)

workshop flex   See: flex.

work straight   To act without assuming a special character, to play a straight role.

work strong   In striptease, to almost disrobe: the more clothes a stripper took off, the stronger the act. (Wilmeth LANGUAGE)

work tech   To participate in a production in a technical capacity.

work the come-in   To entertain an audience before the main attraction begins. (Berrey/Van den Bark SLANG 572)

work upstage   In acting, to move upstage unobtrusively. Also: work downstage, work left, work right.

worrier   A performer's agent.

Wort-Tondrama (German)   Literally: word-tone drama. A type of drama envisioned by Adolphe Appia which sought to bring together the separate elements of actor, setting, music, lighting, and language by mutually subordinating them in a hierarchy of expression. (Rogers ''Appia's'' 468)

wow   1. A very successful show. 2. A surprising and successful ending to an act or show. 3. To cause spectators to applaud wildly, to 'wow' them. (Bowman/Ball THEATRE, Krows PLAYWRITING 409)

wower   A good comedian.

wrap   To take in money at the box office.

wrap it up and take it away   To steal the show. (Berrey/Van den Bark SLANG 588)

wring   See: efforts.

"Write it."   A direction to record a light setting. 'Write' is no longer always to be taken literally: in memory lighting systems, for example, the press of a button will record an entire light setting. (Bellman SCENOGRAPHY 501)

wrot, wrt, w^t   In old promptbooks, written—a property paper with writing on it. (Shattuck SHAKESPEARE 14)

wu (Chinese)   Literally: martial. See: *wuxi, wuchang*.

wuchang, wu ch'ang (Chinese)   Literally: martial orchestra. The collective name for the percussion instruments in a music-drama (*xiqu*) orchestra (*changmian*). Important instruments in many forms include the *ban* clapper, *bangzi* clapper, single-skin drum (*danpigu*), hall drum (*tanggu*), small gong (*xiaoluo*), large gong (*daluo*), cloud gong (*yunluo*), cymbals (*bo*), and castanets (*xiangban*). Also called gongs and drums (*luogu* or *lo ku*). See also: *wenchang*. (Wichmann "Aural" 433–434, 442–449, 452–460, 478–497)

wu ching (Chinese)   See: *wujing*.

wuchou, wu ch'ou (Chinese)   Martial clown role. The type of comic male role found in martial plays (*wuxi*); emphasizes combat (*da*) skill and strong, clear speech. It is a major subcategory of the clown role (*chou*) in Beijing opera (*jingju*) and many other forms of music-drama (*xiqu*). (Dolby HISTORY 181, Scott CLASSICAL 76–78)

wu chü (Chinese)   See: *wuju*.

wudan, wu tan (Chinese)   1. Literally: martial female role. A fairly young female role which features martial arts and emphasizes combat (*da*) skill; a major subcategory of the female role (*dan*) in Beijing opera (*jingju*) and many other forms of music-drama (*xiqu*). (Dolby HISTORY 180, Scott CLASSICAL 73) 2. Literally: fifth female role. See: *guimendan*.

wu hsi (Chinese)   See: *wuxi*.

wu hsiao sheng (Chinese)   See: *wuxiaosheng*.

wuhualian, wu hua lien (Chinese)   See: *wujing*.

wujing, wu ching (Chinese)   Martial painted face role. A vigorous, powerful male role which features combat (*da*) skill; a major subcategory of the painted-face role (*jing*) in Beijing opera (*jingju*). Also called martial flower-face (*wuhualian* or *wu hua lien*). (Dolby HISTORY 181, Scott CLASSICAL 75–76)

wuju, wu chü (Chinese)   1. Literally: dance drama. A type of theatrical performance which features dance but is not performed exclusively in the style of either music-drama (*xiqu*) or ballet. Such a performance may consist of an original Chinese composition, or of a minority nationality or non-Chinese piece. Performances of this type were much encouraged in the 1950s and early 1960s, and are now being actively developed. See also: *xiju*. (Mackerras PERFORMING 112–114) 2. A form of music-drama (*xiqu*) popular in parts of Zhejiang Province which includes music from six musical systems (*shengqiang xitong*): *gaoqiang*, *kunshanqiang*, *pihuang*, *luantan* (i.e., *bangziqiang*), *tanhuang*, and local folk music. The form takes its name from the River Wu in Jiangxi Province, where the *gaoqiang* music in *wuju* originated. See also: *chuiqiang*. (Dolby HISTORY 229, Halson PEKING 69)

wulanmuqi, wu lan mu ch'i (Chinese)   A Chinese transcription of the Mongolian phrase ''red culture troupe'' (*ulan muchir*); a mobile performing arts troupe especially appropriate to the vast grasslands of the Inner Mongolian Autonomous Region, where such troupes arose in 1957; they were highly encouraged during the Cultural Revolution period (1966–1976). They are among the few cultural phenomena of that period which have remained in favor since the fall of the ''gang of four'' in 1976. Sometimes called ''caravan troupe'' in English. (Mackerras PERFORMING 57–58, Mackerras MODERN 185–186)

wulaosheng, wu lao sheng (Chinese)   Martial older male role. An elderly, white-bearded, older male role featuring combat (*da*), dance-acting (*zuo*), and song (*chang*) skills; a major subdivision of the older male role (*laosheng*) in Beijing opera (*jingju*). Sometimes considered a subdivision of the martial male role (*wusheng*). (Dolby HISTORY 180, Scott CLASSICAL 66)

wungyi ka (Burmese)   Literally: minister's style. A walking style in the puppet theatre that mimics the ceremonious gait of a court official. (Tilakasiri PUPPET 38)

wusheng, wu sheng (Chinese)   Martial male role. A fairly youthful male role which requires combat (*da*) skills, and in some forms acrobatics; a major subcategory of the male role (*sheng*) in many forms of music-drama (*xiqu*). In Beijing opera (*jingju*), many martial male characters are unbearded, but all speak and sing in the ''natural'' voice (*dasangzi*). Two major subdivisions of the martial male role in Beijing opera are ''long armor'' (*changkao*) and ''short fighting'' (*duanda*). See also: *wulaosheng*. (Dolby HISTORY 180, Scott CLASSICAL 66)

wutai, wu t'ai (Chinese)   Literally: dance platform. A stage. Also called front platform (*qiantai* or *ch'ien t'ai*) and play platform (*xitai* or *hsi t'ai*). The principal type of 18th and 19th C stage is described in detail in Dolby HISTORY 191, Mackerras RISE 203–204, and Scott CLASSICAL 221. Most contemporary stages are proscenium-style, and usually quite wide; the orchestra is generally seated downstage left for music-drama (*xiqu*) performances, and in the orchestra pit or offstage when used in other types of performances.

wu tan (Chinese)   1. Literally: martial female role. See: *wudan*. 2. Literally: fifth female role. See: *guimendan*.

wuxi, wu hsi (Chinese)   Literally: martial play. A play whose plot involves war, military encounters, the activities of bandits, or other situations which emphasize heroic, martial activity in Beijing opera (*jingju*) and many other forms of music-drama (*xiqu*). Such plays emphasize acrobatics, combat (*da*), and dance-acting (*zuo*) skills and feature performers who specialize in these martial techniques. See also: *wenxi*. (Scott CLASSICAL 20, 185; Wichmann "Aural" 50–53)

wuxiaosheng, wu hsiao sheng (Chinese)   Martial young male role. Usually the role of a young military hero, featuring four performance skills: song (*chang*), speech (*nian*), dance-acting (*zuo*) and combat (*da*). It is a major subdivision of the young male role (*xiaosheng*) in Beijing opera (*jingju*) and many other forms of music-drama (*xiqu*). Also called pheasant-tail male role (*zhiweixiaosheng*). (Dolby HISTORY 180, Scott CLASSICAL 67–68)

X

X Cross, as when a performer moves across the stage. The abbreviation is found in promptbooks and in acting editions based on promptbooks.

xenon lamp, xenon arc lamp   See: short-arc lamp.

xi, hsi (Chinese)   1. To play. 2. A game, a show, an entertainment. 3. A play, a drama, a theatrical work. 4. The concept of theatre.

xiachang, hsia ch'ang (Chinese)   1. To exit the playing area. 2. The exit of a performer or performers. Conventional types of song and speech (*changbai*) and movement (*dongzuo*) used for exits in Beijing opera (*jingju*) are described in detail in Scott CLASSICAL 93–96 and 178–184. See also: *shangchang*.

xiachang duilian (Chinese)   See: *duilian*.

xiachangmen, hsia ch'ang men (Chinese)   Exit door. 1. A permanent curtained doorway upstage left on a traditional stage for music-drama (*xiqu*) performances; characters conventionally exited through this doorway. See also: *shangchangmen*. 2. In contemporary proscenium theatres, stage left.

xiaju (Chinese)   See: *lian*.

xiandaiju, hsien tai chü (Chinese)   Literally: contemporary play. Since 1949, a music-drama (*xiqu*) play with a contemporary theme, plot, and characters. In performance, such plays require adapting traditional skills and techniques and developing new ones. Also called *xiandaixi* or *hsien tai hsi*. See also: *chuantongju, xinbiande lishiju*. (Mackerras ORIGINS 189)

xiandaixi (Chinese)   See: *xiandaiju*.

xiangban, hsiang pan (Chinese)   Castanets, a type of clapper used in the percussion orchestra (*wuchang*) in some forms of music-drama (*xiqu*), including those derived from the *haiyanqiang* musical system (*shengqiang xitong*). (Dolby HISTORY 91).

xiangju, hsiang chü (Chinese)   Hunan opera, a form of music-drama (*xiqu*) popular in the Changsha and Xiangtan region of Hunan Province with origins in the 15th-16th C. It includes music from the *gaoqiang*, *kunshanqiang*, and *pihuang* musical systems. See also: *chuiqiang*.

xiangsheng, hsiang sheng (Chinese)   A form of storytelling (*quyi*) which developed in the mid-19th C in Beijing and is popular today throughout China; often translated as comedy act, comic duo, comic dialogue, or cross-talk. Most performances are in Beijing dialect, although a regional dialect is sometimes used. There are three main styles of performance: one in which a single comedian tells jokes (*dankou* or *tan k'ou*), one in which a comedian plays off a straight man (*duikou* or *tui k'ou*), and one which features three or more performers (*qunkou* or *chün kou*). Performances in many respects resemble those of clown role (*chou*) actors in Beijing opera (*jingju*) and many other forms of music-drama (*xiqu*). (Dolby HISTORY 7, 21; Howard CONTEMPORARY 23, 30; Mackerras PERFORMING 102–104)

xiansheng (Chinese)   See: *jiamen*.

xianzi (Chinese)   See: *sanxian*.

xianzixi (Chinese)   1. See: *meihuju*. 2. See: *liuzixi*.

xiao, hsiao (Chinese)   The generic term for vertical bamboo flutes which are used in the melodic orchestra (*wenchang*) in *kunqu*, Beijing opera (*jingju*), and other forms of music-drama (*xiqu*). They are technically called *dongxiao* or *tung hsiao*. (Mackerras MODERN 23, Mackerras RISE 7)

xiaochizi (Chinese)   See: *diaoyutai*.

xiaochou, hsiao ch'ou (Chinese)   Literally: small clown role. A term frequently used for the clown role (*chou*) in small-scale folk theatre forms (*xiaoxi*). (Dolby HISTORY 227)

xiaodan, hsiao tan (Chinese)   Literally: young female role. 1. A young, supporting female role; a major subcategory of the female role (*dan*) in Yuan *zaju*. (Dolby HISTORY 60) 2. A generic term for all supporting young female roles in Beijing opera (*jingju*). Also called secondary female role (*tiedan* or *t'ieh tan*). 3. A popular generic term for all female roles (*dan*) except the old female role (*laodan*); the term can be applied to characters in most forms of music-drama (*xiqu*). 4. See: *guimendan*.

xiaogu (Chinese)   See: *danpigu*.

xiaoguomen (Chinese)   See: *guomen*.

xiaohualian (Chinese)   See: *chou*.

xiaoluo, hsiao lo (Chinese)   Literally: small gong. A brass gong about 6 inches in diameter which is held in the left hand and is struck with a flat, tapered piece of wood. It is featured in the percussion orchestra (*wuchang*) in Beijing opera (*jingju*) and many other forms of music-drama (*xiqu*). (Scott CLASSICAL 48–50; Wichmann ''Aural'' 446, 453–460)

xiaomian, hsiao mien (Chinese)   Literally: small face. An agreeable, noble, or admirable comic character; a major subcategory of the clown role (*chou*) in *kunqu* drama. (Dolby HISTORY 105–106)

xiaomo, hsiao mo (Chinese)   A young, supporting male role; one of the main subcategories of the male role (*mo*) in Yuan *zaju*. (Dolby HISTORY 60)

xiaosangzi, hsiao sang tzu (Chinese)   Literally: small voice. Falsetto. One of two basic types of vocal production in many forms of music-drama (*xiqu*). Also called ''false'' voice (*jiasangzi* or *chia sang tzu*), as opposed to ''natural'' voice (*dasangzi*). In Beijing opera (*jingju*), falsetto vocal production is used for all young male roles (*xiaosheng*), and all female roles (*dan*) except the old female role (*laodan*).

xiaosheng, hsiao sheng (Chinese)   Young male role. A beardless young male role portrayed with a blend of masculine and feminine characteristics to indicate youth; a major subcategory of the male role (*sheng*) in many forms of music-drama (*xiqu*). In *kunqu* and Beijing opera (*jingju*), the young male role is spoken and sung in a combination of falsetto (*xiaosangzi*) and ''natural'' voice (*dasangzi*). Major subdivisions of the young male role include headdress male (*guansheng*), cloth-cap male (*jinsheng*), pheasant-tail male (*zhiweisheng*), and shoe-leather male (*xiepisheng*) in *kunqu*; and fan male (*shanzisheng*), poor male (*qiongsheng*), and martial young male (*wuxiaosheng*) in Beijing opera. (Dolby HISTORY 105, 180; Scott CLASSICAL 31, 67–68)

xiaoxi, hsiao hsi (Chinese)   Literally: small theatre, small plays. 1. Any form of music-drama (*xiqu*) which comes directly from folk songs and dances. Such forms use few role categories, usually only young male (*xiaosheng*), young female (*xiaodan*), and small clown (*xiaochou*); they are most often performed by amateurs or part-time professionals, who usually have no permanent theatre buildings. The plays are few in number, structurally rudimentary, and concerned primarily with local life and love stories. The range of performance skills is relatively restricted, usually limited to song and dance, with simple music, using only a few instruments. Often translated as ''small-scale folk theatre form,'' as opposed to large-scale theatre form (*daxi*). Representative small-scale folk theatre forms include flower drum plays (*huaguxi*), flower lantern plays (*huadengxi*), and rice-seedling songs (*yangge*). Also called small folk play, small folk theatre (*minjian xiaoxi* or *min chien hsiao hsi*). (Dolby HISTORY 220–229) 2. A one-act music-drama play, as opposed to a full-length play (*daxi*). Also called *zhezixi*. 3. A light or comic music-drama play, as opposed to a serious play (*daxi*).

xiaoxing duoyang, hsiao hsing to yang (Chinese)   Literally: small-scale many kinds. A slogan that calls for performance pieces which are short, simple, frugally produced, and rich in variety of form and content; it is applied to amateur theatre and amateur theatre troupes in the People's Republic of China.

xiaozhouzi (Chinese)   See: *zhouzi*.

xiawuse, hsia wu se (Chinese)   Literally: lower five colors. The five secondary colors used in stage costuming in Beijing opera (*jingju*) and many other forms of music-drama (*xiqu*); purple, sapphire blue, pink, turquoise, and dark crimson or bronze. Each color signifies a particular age, rank, and/or character trait. See also: *shangwuse*. (Scott CLASSICAL 139–140)

xieer (Chinese)   See: *xiezi*.

xiepisheng, hsieh p'i sheng (Chinese)   Literally: shoe-leather male role. A poverty-stricken young male scholar role featuring dance-acting (*zuo*) and song (*chang*) skills; a major subdivision of the young male role (*xiaosheng*) in *kunqu* and many other forms of music-drama (*xiqu*). Essentially the same as the poor male role (*qiongsheng*) in Beijing opera (*jingju*), and sometimes called by that name. Also called suffering male role (*kusheng* or *k'u sheng*). (Dolby HISTORY 105)

xiezi, hsieh tzu (Chinese)   Literally: wedge. A short act. Often translated as "wedge act." One, and sometimes two, were frequently included in Yuan *zaju* plays in addition to the four main acts (*zhe*). Wedge acts gave background information, sometimes functioning as prologues, and sometimes bridging leaps in time and/or space between main acts. Also called *xieer* or *hsieh erh*. (Dolby HISTORY 54, Liu INTRODUCTION 170, Liu SIX 13)

xifang (Chinese)   See: *houtai*.

xiju, hsi chü (Chinese)   1. Literally: theatre drama. The generic term for all forms of theatre. It includes music-drama (*xiqu*), spoken drama (*huaju*), dance drama (*geju*), song drama (*wuju*), song and dance drama (*gewuju*), puppet theatre (*kuileixi*), storytelling (*quyi*), and all forms of theatre foreign to China as well. 2. Literally: Wuxi theatre. A form of music-drama (*xiqu*) popular in southern Jiangsu Province and Shanghai. It originated in folk songs popular in Changzhou and Wuxi counties in Jiangsu Province c. 18th-19th C; these developed into Wuxi and Changzhou *tanhuang* storytelling, which were then influenced by local small-scale folk theatre (*xiaoxi*) forms. In the early 20th C troupes from these two areas began to perform together in Shanghai, and the resultant form was called Changzhou and Wuxi civil theatre (*changxi wenxi* or *ch'ang hsi wen hsi*), or sometimes Changzhou and Wuxi drama (*changxiju* or *ch'ang hsi chü*). As the Wuxi influence came to dominate after 1949, the name was simplified to *xiju*. (Dolby HISTORY 229, Mackerras MODERN 110)

xilou (Chinese)   See: *xiyuan*.

xilu huagu (Chinese)   See: *chuju*.

xinbiande lishiju, hsin pien te li shih chü (Chinese)   Literally: newly-written historical play. Since 1949, a newly or recently written music-drama (*xiqu*) play which is set in the 19th C or earlier. Traditional skills and techniques are used in performance, but most plays are not fixed musically or choreographically, and must be composed and choreographed in rehearsal. See also: *chuantongju, xiandaiju*. (Mackerras ORIGINS 188–189)

xingeju, hsin ko chü (Chinese)   Literally: new song drama. A type of performance influenced by both spoken drama (*huaju*) and music-drama (*xiqu*) which developed and was popular in the 1940s. Such performances had contemporary plots and themes and contained much spoken dialogue, but also included songs and poetic matter, and often used music from traditional music-drama and folk music. A well-known example is *The White-haired Girl*. After 1949, this type of performance was subsumed by a larger category, the song drama (*geju*). (Dolby HISTORY 214)

xingtou, hsing t'ou (Chinese)   The generic term for theatrical costumes worn in music-drama (*xiqu*). Differences in style and color are indicative of age, economic and social position, and situation. Principal types of traditional costumes are described in detail in Halson PEKING 19–31, Scott CLASSICAL 137–160, and Zung SECRETS 17–23. See also: *yixiang, shangwuse, xiawuse*.

xinju (Chinese)   See: *xinxi*.

xinxi, hsin hsi (Chinese)   Literally: new plays, new theatre. Reformist and revolutionary plays written and performed between 1895 and c. 1910, some of which used Western subject matter. Most were music-drama (*xiqu*) plays, but some were translations from Western or modern Western-style Japanese plays (i.e., *shinpa* and *shingeki*), and others were Chinese plays written in Western realistic style. Also called new drama (*xinju* or *hsin chü*). See also: *wenmingxi, huaju*. (Dolby HISTORY 201, Mackerras MODERN 65–68)

xipi, hsi p'i (Chinese)   In music-drama (*xiqu*), the musical mode (*diaoshi*) considered best suited for expressing joy, delight, and vehemence. It developed in the 17th and 18th C in Hubei Province from the combination of Shaanxi Province *qinqiang* and local folk music. It is now one of the two principal modes (*zheng diaoshi*) in the *pihuang* musical system (*shengqiang xitong*). See also: *erhuang*. (Mackerras MODERN 19, Wichmann "Aural" 167–227)

xiqu, hsi chü (Chinese)   Literally: song theatre. Chinese traditional theatre, sometimes translated as music-drama (Crump/Malm CHINESE) or as opera. It is performed by stage entertainers, each of whom portrays an individual character as presented in a script. Performance is stylized and conventionalized, and synthesizes story, music, song, speech, dance and pantomime, and frequently martial arts and acrobatics as well. Characters are conceived of as each belonging to one of several role categories (*hangdang*); each role category has its own patterns of stylized basic performance skills (*jiben gongfu*). The song, speech, and movement of stage performers are all supported and accompanied by the musicians of the orchestra (*changmian*). Music-drama is believed to have originated in 3rd C BC-3rd C AD forms of performance such as the hundred entertainments (*baixi*). Early historical development is usually measured by the increasing synthesis of performance elements; Song *zaju* and Jin *yuanben* are seen as leading to the first fully mature music-drama forms, southern drama (*nanxi*), c. 10th-15th C, and Yuan *zaju*, c. 12th-15th C. *Kunqu* is regarded as the most important 16th-18th C form, and Beijing opera (*jingju*) as the principal form of the late 18th–20th

C. Forms are differentiated primarily by their musical structure (either *banqiangti* or *lianquti*), by the musical system (*shengqiang xitong*) from which they are derived, and by the region and regional language of their origin. There are currently more than three hundred forms of music-drama; the great majority originated and are popular in only one region of the country, and are therefore known as regional theatre forms (*difangxi*). See also: *daxi, xiaoxi, xiju*.

xitai (Chinese)   See: *wutai*.

xiwen (Chinese)   See: *nanxi*.

xiyuan, hsi yüan (Chinese)   Literally: theatre garden, play garden. A type of fixed public theatre which served tea and refreshments rather than wine and full meals; usually called tea-house theatre in translation. Tea-house theatres were the most popular and prevalent of the three main types of fixed public theatres in the 17th-early 20th C; they were open to all social classes without prior booking, and presented performances by both major and lesser music-drama (*xiqu*) troupes. The audience was seated on three sides of a raised stage which jutted out into the auditorium. Two-story tea-house theatres had four main types of second-floor veranda seating: officials' seats (*guanzuo*), tables (*zhuozi*), backwards officials' seats (*daoguanzuo*), and principal upstairs (*zhenglou*). Seating in these sections was more prestigious and expensive than in the four main types of ground-floor seating: pond (*chizi*), fishing platform (*diaoyutai*), scattered seats (*sanzuo*), and big wall (*daqiang*). Since 1976, modified tea-house theatres designed primarily for story-telling (*quyi*) performances have begun to reappear in China. Also called tea garden (*chayuan* or *ch'a yüan*), tea bower (*chalou* or *ch'a lou*), and play bower (*xilou* or *hsi lou*). See also: *xizhuang, zashuaguan*. (Dolby HISTORY 189–193, Mackerras MODERN 83–91, Mackerras PERFORMING 194–196, Mackerras RISE 200–211, Scott CLASSICAL 220–224)

xizhuang, hsi chuang (Chinese)   Literally: play establishment. A type of theatre-restaurant booked in entirety by wealthy, elite customers for banquets accompanied by theatrical performances; one of three main types of fixed public theatres, 17th-early 20th C. These establishments were usually equipped with a permanent stage, and presented music-drama (*xiqu*) performances by major troupes. See also: *tanghui, zashuaguan, xiyuan*. (Mackerras MODERN 83–88, Mackerras RISE 197–199)

X-Rays, X-Ray border (light)   1. Formerly in the U.S., a borderlight. "X-Ray" was originally the trade name of an open striplight with individual glass reflectors used in store window lighting about 1918. Before 1920 the name had come to be used of all theatre borderlights. (McCandless "Glossary" 635) 2. For a time, borderlights with the ribbed reflectors characteristic of the original X-ray reflectors. 3. The first border. This became the principal meaning and is still used occasionally. X-ray occurs in other combinations, such as X-ray reflector and even X-ray light. All uses are U.S. Compare: concert border. (Bellman SCENE, Lounsbury THEATRE 90)

xuansi kuilei (Chinese)   See: *mu'ou.*

xuan xe (Vietnamese)   A *cai luong* song sung accompanying the retreat of a hero in battle. (Addiss "Theater" 148, Brandon SOUTHEAST 133)

xuezi, hsüeh tzu (Chinese)   A soft robe which serves as informal dress or as an under-robe worn with other types of costumes in Beijing opera (*jingju*) and many other forms of music-drama (*xiqu*). Most have wide collars and fasten on the right, although female versions may fasten down the front instead. Some English language works use the non-theatrical pronunciations and romanizations of this term, *zhezi* or *che tzu*, and *diezi* or *tieh tzu.* (Halson PEKING 21–22, Scott CLASSICAL 149–153, Zung SECRETS 19)

xusheng (Chinese)   See: *laosheng.*

Y

Y See: twofer.

yabu, ya pu (Chinese)   Literally: elegant part. A term of approbation used by the elite in the 17th-19th C to refer to the classical *kunqu* drama. See also: *huabu*. (Dolby HISTORY 274; Mackerras RISE 6–7, 53)

ya chou tzu (Chinese)   See: *zhouzi*.

yack   See: yock.

yago (Japanese)   The guild name of a *kabuki* acting family (i.e., Naritaya for Ichikawa Danjuro). The name is often called out during performance as a shout of praise (*kakegoe*). (Halford/Halford HANDBOOK 396–398)

yagura (Japanese)   Literally: tower. 1. A turret-like platform built above the entrance to a professional theatre. In medieval times it was a place for the gods to descend to protect the performance. (Hoff SONG 204) In the 18th and 19th C it held doorkeepers' weapons and a large drum (*odaiko*) to advertise a performance. Today, it has only a decorative function. (Ernst KABUKI 31, Kincaid KABUKI 221) 2. From the 17th through the 19th C, the symbol of a government license to operate a *kabuki* or *bunraku* theatre. See also: *hikae yagura*. (Gunji KABUKI 44, Scott KABUKI 276)

yak   See: yock.

yak (Khmer, Thai)   A demonic, ogre-like character in traditional theatre, especially in plays based on the *Ramayana* epic. Lustful and violent, these characters are the enemies of the hero. In Khmer, also called *yaksas*. (Brunet in Osman TRADITIONAL 4) In Thai, also spelled *yaksa* or *yaksha, raksha*, and *raksot*. (Rutnin "Development" 13, Smithies/Kerdchouay in Rutnin SIAMESE 133)

yaksagana (Kannada)   Literally: god-song. 1. A vigorous regional dance-drama form in South Kanara (Mysore), India. 2. The style of music in these plays. (Ashton/Christie YAKSAGANA 17, 19; Ranganath KARNATAK 63) 3. A generic term encompassing a variety of rural forms of drama performed throughout south India. Also spelled *yakshagana*. (Vatsyayan TRADITIONAL 34–36)

yaksagana badagatittu bayalata (Kannada)   Literally: *badaga*, north; *tittu*, style; *bayal*, open space; *ata*, play. The outdoor style of performing *yaksagana*, popular around Udipi, Mysore state, southwest India. (Ashton/Christie YAKSAGANA 17, 19) Shortened, *yaksagana badagutittu* (Ranganath KARNATAK 63) and *bayalata* (Gargi FOLK 163). Also called *doddata* (big play).

yaksagana tenkutittu (Kannada)   A style of performing *yaksagana*, in which music and costumes are similar to *kathakali*, popular in the southern part of Mysore state, around Mangalore city, southwest India. Abbreviated *tenkutittu*. (Ashton/Christie YAKSAGANA 17, 19, 94)

yaksas (Khmer)   See: *yak*.

yaksha (Thai)   See: *yak*.

yakshagana (Kannada)   See: *yaksagana*.

yaku (Japanese)   Literally: function. Role.

yakubarai (Japanese)   See: *yakuharai*.

yakugara (Japanese)   Literally: role types. In *kabuki* and *bunraku*, the classification system of major acting roles—first into male and female, then into hero, heroine, villain, youth, comic, child and other roles, and finally into subtypes of these. More than 30 named role types were common in the Edo period (1600–1868). They are systematically illustrated in Gunji KABUKI 179–192 and Keene BUNRAKU 209–256. See: *katakiyaku, onnagata, tachiyaku, dokeyaku*. (Leiter ENCYCLOPEDIA 313, Brandon CLASSIC 31–32)

yakuharai (Japanese)   In *kabuki*, a highly musicalized style of speaking *shichi go cho* (seven-five) dialogue that is believed to derive from Buddhist religious chanting. Used, for example, by the five thieves in *Benten the Thief* in Leiter ART 41–42. (Hamamura et al KABUKI 80)

yakusha (Japanese)   Literally: task-person. The traditional term for an actor in *no* or *kabuki*. See also: *haiyu*. (Gunji KABUKI 31, Kincaid KABUKI 153–156)

yakusha hyobanki (Japanese)   Literally: actor critique. A book of descriptions of *kabuki* actors popular during one theatre season. Such books were published annually from 1656 (Shively in Brandon/Malm/Shively STUDIES 49) or from 1659 (Leiter ENCYCLOPEDIA 429) until 1877.

yaller gal   In minstrel shows, a beautiful female character (a male in skirts) with the features of a Caucasian and exoticism of a Black. Popular in the U.S. in the 1840s. See also: wench. (Wilmeth LANGUAGE)

yamamba (Japanese)   Literally: old woman of the mountain. A *no* mask of an aged female demon who wanders in the mountains, symbolizing the chain of Buddhist rebirth. (Shimazaki NOH 64)

Yamato *sarugaku* (Japanese)   The type of *sarugaku* performed in the Yamato area (Kyoto-Nara) in the 14th C. This style, practiced by four troupes attached to Kofukuji Temple in Nara, evolved in time into *no*. See: Hosho, Kanze, Kongo, Konparu. (Immoss/Mayer JAPANESE 69–70, O'Neill EARLY 11–15)

yan (Chinese)   See: *banyan*.

yanduan (Chinese)   See: Song *zaju*.

yangban (Korean)   The role of an official or nobleman who is the butt of merciless ridicule in all forms of traditional theatre. (Korean MASKS 11, 16, 26)

yangbanxi, yang pan hsi (Chinese)   Literally: model plays. A term applied to a theatrical work which satisfied the criteria proposed by Jiang Qing, the wife of Mao Zedong. Eight works were so named in 1967: five revolutionary modern Beijing operas (*geming xiandai jingju*), two revolutionary modern ballets (*geming xiandai wuju*), and one symphony; the number of model plays was increased during the latter part of the Cultural Revolution period (1966–1976), but remained less than twenty. (Mowry NEW)

Yangchow opera, *yang chü* (Chinese)   See: *yangju*.

yangge, yang ko (Chinese)   Literally: rice-seedling songs. The generic term for a number of small-scale folk theatre forms (*xiaoxi*) popular in northern China which arose c. 18th C out of labor folk songs, particularly rice-seedling planting songs. Performances in most forms consist of three parts: the first and third are large-scale group dances, and the second, central part is a small play with a simple plot presented primarily through song or dance by two or three performers. In the early 20th C, *yangge* performances were usually given by semiprofessional groups of villagers during religious and other festivals; such groups continue to give performances at holidays and large meetings, but full-time professional troupes have been established for a number of forms as well. Also called *yanggexi* or *yang ko hsi*. (Dolby HISTORY 220–222; Howard CONTEMPORARY 5, 7–8, 65; Mackerras MODERN 165)

yangju, yang chü (Chinese)   Yangzhou (Yangchow) opera, a form of music-drama (*xiqu*) popular in southern Jiangsu Province, Shanghai, and parts of Anhui Province; developed in 1935 out of two types of small-scale folk theatre (*xiaoxi*), *weiyang wenxi* and *weiyang daban*. It uses combat (*da*) skills absorbed from Beijing opera (*jingju*), follows *lianquti* musical structure, and features *erhu* spike fiddle accompaniment. (Mackerras RISE 67)

yang ko, yang ko hsi (Chinese)   See: *yangge*.

yang pan hsi (Chinese)   See: *yangbanxi*.

yangsawi (Korean)   A hopping dance step used in the scene of eight Buddhist monks in masked plays of the Pongsan area. (Yi "Mask" 53)

Yangzhou opera   See: *yangju*.

yank   See: jerk.

yankamanci (Hausa)   In Nigeria, an entertainment by minstrels who sing satirical sketches and comedies to drum accompaniment. The form was popularized by Haji Katsina. (Adedeji glossary)

Yankee   A native U.S. character, typically a shrewd farmer, popular in many comedies of the late 18th and early 19th C and then in melodrama. (Wilmeth LANGUAGE)

yanyuan, yan yüan (Chinese)   See: *you*.

yaoban, yao pan (Chinese)   Literally: shaking meter. A free meter (*ziyouban*) metrical-type (*banshi*) used in the songs of many forms of music-drama (*xiqu*) to express exterior calm and interior tension. Although the singing is free of metrical organization and is fairly slow, the accompaniment is in single-beat meter and is quite rapid. In Beijing opera (*jingju*), *yaoban* occurs in both the *xipi* and *erhuang* modes (*diaoshi*). (Scott TRADITIONAL I 164, Wichmann "Aural" 164–165)

yaodan (Chinese)   See: *choudan*.

yaokuilei, yao k'uei lei (Chinese)   Literally: herb puppets, powder puppets. Puppets whose manipulation probably involved the use of gunpowder and fireworks; described in the 10th-13th C. (Dolby HISTORY 265, Obraztsov CHINESE 27–28)

yao pan (Chinese)   See: *yaoban*.

yao tan (Chinese)   See: *choudan*.

ya pu (Chinese)   See: *yabu*.

yard, yarde   The pit or standing area around the stage platform in an Elizabethan theatre. (Gosson in Nagler SOURCES 130)

yaro kabuki (Japanese)   1. The style of *kabuki* in which adult males (*yaro*) first performed all roles. The plays are characterized by virile plots, sword play, and the art of female impersonation (*onnagata*). 2. The historical period in *kabuki*'s development, c. 1652–1688, when troupes of adult males replaced troupes of boys (*wakashu*). (Brandon CLASSIC 2–3, Scott KABUKI 36, Shively in Brandon/Malm/Shively STUDIES 9–10)

yaryu, yayu (Korean)   See: *ogwangdae*.

yase onna (Japanese)   Literally: emaciated woman. A *no* mask of a haggard woman, worn by a ghost of a woman who has fallen into hell because of her "worldly passion." (Shimazaki NOH 61)

yase otoko (Japanese)   Literally: emaciated man. A *no* mask of a haggard man, worn by a ghost of a man who has fallen into hell because of his "worldly attachment." (Shimazaki NOH 60)

yatna (Sanskrit)   See: *prayatna*.

yatra (Sanskrit)   See: *jatra*.

yatsushi (Japanese)   Literally: in disguise. A playwriting convention, basic to *kabuki*, in which the hero assumes another identity for dramatic purposes. The convention is related to the techniques of joining history and domestic plots (*mitate*). Examples are the characters Sukeroku and Izaemon (Brandon CLASSIC 5, 7). See also: *keiseikai, nochi jite. Yatsushimono* (disguise play) is a play based on this convention. (Gunji KABUKI 16–17)

yavanika (Sanskrit)   1. A curtain which covered the tiring room and formed the background of the Indian stage in ancient times. Also called *pratisira.* (Keith SANSKRIT 61, 359–360) 2. In many existing regional theatres in India, a cloth held in front of an actor and then pulled aside when he is to appear before the audience. Also called *apati, pati,* or *tirassila.* (Mathur DRAMA 19–21)

yayako odori (Japanese)   Literally: child's dance. A predecessor of *kabuki* dance. (Hoff SONG 131) It is supposed to have been danced by Okuni, the founder of *kabuki*, as early as 1600. (Tsubaki ''Performing'' 307–308)

yayoi kyogen (Japanese)   Literally: spring play. In *kabuki*: 1. In the 18th and 19th C, a play performed during the spring production. It featured a romantic theme, in keeping with the season (Brandon CLASSIC 55–92) or the activities of noble women (Leiter ENCYCLOPEDIA 375). 2. The spring production in the 18th and 19th C, consisting of one or more *yayoi* plays. Traditionally it opened on Girls' Day, the third day of the third lunar month (usually mid-April).

yayu (Korean)   See: *ogwangdae.*

yayue, ya yüeh (Chinese)   Literally: elegant music. The generic term for music and dances used by the imperial court for religious and filial rites, and for important formal occasions. Such music and dances emphasized form and elegance, and were not popularized. Each dynasty from c. 11th C BC to the 9th C AD developed its own *yayue.* See also: *sanyue, suyue.* (Dolby HISTORY 3)

yazhouzi (Chinese)   See: *zhouzi.*

yeekay (Thai)   See: *likay.*

yein (Burmese)   A group dance, modeled after dances of the Royal Court, introduced into popular Burmese theatre performances in the 1930s. (Sein/Withey GREAT 104)

yellow card   A card sent by a stage carpenter to the local union of the next town on a tour, containing information about the requirements of the production, especially how many stagehands will be needed. (Bowman/Ball THEATRE)

yellow handkerchief bit   Distracting movement by one performer during another performer's speech or movement: scene stealing.

yell play   A farce with a weak plot but many jokes. (Partridge TO-DAY 229)

yen (Chinese)   See: *banyan.*

yen tuan (Chinese)   See: Song *zaju.*

yen yüan (Chinese)   See: *you*.

yeondung, yondung (Korean)   Literally: burning of lanterns. A court cere-mony of the 10th–14th C during which puppets appeared. (Cho KOREAN 8)

yibansanxiang (Chinese)   See: *banxi*.

Yid   About the beginning of the 20th C, a Hebrew or Yiddish impersonator. Also called a goose. See also: Hebe comic. (Wilmeth LANGUAGE)

yi i (Khmer)   A two-stringed fiddle with a small, cylindrical sounding box, derived from the Chinese *hu qin*. It is used in *lokhon bassac*. (Brandon SOUTH-EAST 128)

yi ke (Khmer)   A popular theatre form melding dance, song, mime, and music that parodies classical dance, legend, and tradition. The form evolved as a kind of variety show drawing upon segments of theatre forms from throughout Southeast Asia. Especially popular at the end of the 19th C, it was revived in the mid-20th C. (Anonymous ROYAL 12)

yingdiaoju (Chinese)   See: *tangju*.

ying hsi (Chinese)   See: *piyingxi*.

ying hsiung i (Chinese)   See: *baoyi*.

ying tiao chü (Chinese)   See: *tangju*.

yingxi (Chinese)   See: *piyingxi*.

yingxiongyi (Chinese)   See: *baoyi*.

yin hsi (Chinese)   See: *yinxi*.

yin tzu (Chinese)   See: *yinzi*.

yinxi, yin hsi (Chinese)   Literally: play leader. A stage functionary in Song *zaju* and Jin *yuanben* who led the central, main play section of the standard three-section performance. The play leader sang and danced but generally did not perform specific roles. (Dolby HISTORY 19, 26–27)

yinzi, yin tzu (Chinese)   Literally: lead-in. 1. A short verse which establishes the general atmosphere of the scene which is to follow; a type of self-introductory material (*zibao jiamen*) in Beijing opera (*jingju*) and many other forms of music-drama (*xiqu*) delivered by a major character immediately upon entrance and followed by a set-the-scene poem (*dingchangshi*). Lead-in poems are partly spoken and partly sung, and are without orchestral accompaniment. See also: *dingchangbai*. (Scott CLASSICAL 93, Scott TRADITIONAL I 149–150) 2. In southern drama (*nanxi*) and *chuanqi* plays, a fairly long introductory verse which was written to a fixed-melody (*qupai*) and sung to orchestral accompaniment during the prologue (*jiamen*).

yixiang, i hsiang (Chinese)   The collective name for the chests in which music-drama (*xiqu*) costumes (*xingtou*) are kept. Costumes for civil (*wen*) roles are called "big costumes" (*dayi* or *ta i*) and are kept in a "big costume" chest (*dayixiang* or *ta i hsiang*); such costumes include the *guanyi, mang, pei,* and *xuezi*. Costumes for martial (*wu*) roles are called secondary costumes (*eryi* or *erh i*) and are kept in a secondary costume chest (*eryixiang* or *erh i hsiang*); they include the *jianyi*, *kao*, *kuayi*, and *baoyi*. Undergarments, trousers, and boots are termed tertiary costumes (*sanyi* or *san i*) and are kept in a tertiary costume chest (*sanyixiang* or *san i hsiang*). (Scott CLASSICAL 137)

yiyangqiang, i yang ch'iang (Chinese)   A form of music-drama (*xiqu*) which arose c. 14th C in Yiyang, Jiangxi Province. It is characterized by solo singing supported by offstage choral backing (*bangqiang*) on the closing line(s) of songs, and by musical accompaniment consisting entirely of percussion instruments. A number of new forms of regional theatre developed from *yiyangqiang* c. 16th C in Nanjing and Beijing, and throughout southern and southeastern China, giving rise to one of the principal musical systems (*shengqiang xitong*) of music-drama, sometimes referred to as *yiyangqiang*, but more frequently called *gao-qiang*. (Mackerras MODERN 15–16, Mackerras RISE 4–6, Mackerras "Growth" 67–73)

yobanme kyogen (Japanese)   Literally: fourth place play. A *kyogen* play that appears fourth on a multi-play bill consisting of *no* and *kyogen* plays in alternation.

yobidashi (Japanese)   Literally: call in. A standard sequence early in a *kyogen* play in which a character is called on stage. (Berberich "Rapture" 60)

yobikake (Japanese)   Literally: call off. To call to someone offstage, a standard sequence that appears early in a *no* or a *kyogen* play. (Berberich "Rapture" 60)

yock   Formerly, an uproarious laugh. Variants include yack, yak, yuck, yuk.

yodaji-ch'um (Korean)   A type of pantomimic dance in various masked dance-drama forms. (Cho "Yangju" 31)

yodongmu (Korean)   Literally: female comrade. Female impersonators in an all-male *namsadang* troupe. See also: *sutdongmu*. (Kim "Namsadang" 10)

yogam (Malayalam)   Literally: an assembly. A *kathakali* troupe. (Jones/Jones KATHAKALI 115)

yoke   A U-shaped device much used in hanging spotlights. Each end of the U is fastened to a side of the spotlight; a bracket clamp is used to attach the U to a pipe. In Britain, tilting fork, fork. (Lounsbury THEATRE, Wehlburg GLOSSARY, Philippi STAGECRAFT, Bax MANAGEMENT 185, fig. 48)

yoke clamp   See: bracket clamp.

yokel, yokey   An out-of-town theatre patron.

yokthe pwe (Burmese)   Stringed-marionette theatre. The two and one-half to three foot puppets may need up to sixty different strings for the most complex movements. All-night performances typically feature Buddhist birth stories (*Jataka* tales), although more recent material may be woven into the plays. Also called *yoke thay*. (Sein/Withey GREAT 17, ASIAN 93) *yokyoku* (Japanese)   1. A text of a *no* play. (Kawatake KABUKI 13) 2. A concert of *no* singing or recitation. (Inoura HISTORY 105, 114)

yombul (Korean)   A slow, heavy, six-beat rhythmic pattern which accompanies traditional theatre performances, perhaps derived from Buddhist invocation music. (Yi "Mask" 46, Cho "Yangju" 31)

yomi awase (Japanese)   Literally: reading together. A reading rehearsal in *kabuki*. (Hamamura et al KABUKI 102)

yonbanmemono (Japanese)   See: *kyoranmono*.

yondung (Japanese)   See: *yeondung*.

Yongjia *zaju* (Chinese)   See: *nanxi*.

yongju, yung chü (Chinese)   Literally: Yong drama. A form of music-drama (*xiqu*) popular in Shanghai and the Ningbo region of Zhejiang Province which originated in folk labor songs. As professional troupes emerged in the late 19th C, they were given the name "roving guests" (*chuanke* or *ch'uan k'e*). In the 1920s, the developing form was influenced by the *tanhuang* storytelling popular in Ningbo, as well as by several forms of small-scale folk theatre (*xiaoxi*) such as horse lantern plays (*madengxi*); the name Yong (another name for Ningbo) drama was given to the resulting, more complex form.

yongsanhoesang-gok (Korean)   Music accompanying the *t'alch'um* masked play in Pongsan, consisting of approximately ten different tunes. (Cho "Hwanghae" 69)

Yonkel Schnorer (Yiddish)   Literally: Jacob Beggar. In Yiddish theatre, a stock character who was a humpbacked, popeyed scrounger. (Lifson YIDDISH 50)

yorimasa (Japanese)   A *no* mask originated for the role of the aged warrior and poet, Yorimasa. (Shimazaki NOH 64)

Yoruba opera   Nigerian musical and dramatic plays, almost always comic and moralistic, mixing Western and Yoruba musical instruments. The texts are in Yoruba. Also known as (Yoruba) folk operas, they developed from entertainments put on in the 1930s by separatist African churches and were popularized in the 1930s and 1940s by traveling troupes. (Adedeji "Yoruba" 263)

yose (Japanese)   Literally: gathering place. An intimate variety theatre. Several dozen exist in Tokyo, Osaka, and Kyoto today. A bill consists of twelve to fifteen acts: storytelling, singing, comedy skits, juggling. See: *engei*, *kodan*, *rakugo*. (Brandon GUIDE 88)

yoshino (Japanese)   An on-stage audience seating area in 18th and 19th C *kabuki* theatres. They were the cheapest seats in the house, raised above the stage, up right. The name is from Mt. Yoshino. See also: *rakandai*. (Gunji KABUKI 50, Leiter ENCYCLOPEDIA 434)

yoten (Japanese)   1. In *kabuki* and *bunraku*, a thigh-length costume with slits in the sides to allow vigorous movement. (Shaver COSTUME 134–137) 2. A character in a *kabuki* play who wears such a costume, either a solo role (*go-chushin*) or a member of a group of constables or minor soldiers, dressed alike. Group *yoten* serve as foils to the hero in fighting scenes (*tate*). *Kuro* (black) *yoten* are costumed completely in black; *hana* (flower) *yoten* wear flowered costumes and carry cherry branches. (Brandon in Brandon/Malm/Shively STUD-IES 93)

you, yu (Chinese)   1. A professional singer, dancer, acrobat, or performer of farcical skits, c. 8th-5th C BC; usually translated jester. 2. The term later came to mean an actor in music-drama (*xiqu*). It is still sometimes used in this sense, although today the common word for actor and actress is *yanyuan* or *yen yüan*. (Dolby HISTORY 2)

young men's *kabuki* (English-Japanese)   See: *wakashu kabuki*.

"You take 'em!"   Sometimes said by a performer leaving the stage to one going on. (Berrey/Van den Bark SLANG 587)

yowagin (Japanese)   Literally: weak singing. The soft mode of singing (*utai*) in *no*, analogous to the minor key in Western music. (Konishi "Approaches" 13) Its scale is described by Shimazaki as having eight pitches (NOH 45) and by Bethe/Brazell as "composed primarily of fourths," sounding like Gregorian chant (NO 43). See also: *tsuyogin*.

yu (Chinese)   See: *you*.

yuanban, yüan pan (Chinese)   Literally: primary meter. The most basic regulated (*shangban*) metrical-type (*banshi*), used in the songs of many forms of music-drama (*xiqu*) for narrating events or setting forth facts and explanations in relatively straightforward, unemotional situations. It is in duple meter. In Beijing opera (*jingju*), it is used in both the *xipi* and *erhuang* modes (*diaoshi*). See also: *banyan*. (Wichmann "Aural" 147–148)

yuanben (Chinese)   See: Song *zaju*.

Yüan *ch'ü* (Chinese)   See: *qu*, Yuan *zaju*.

yüan pan (Chinese)   See: *yuanban*.

yüan pen (Chinese)   See: Song *zaju*.

Yuan *qu* (Chinese)   See: *qu*, Yuan *zaju*.

Yuan *zaju*, Yüan *tsa chü* (Chinese)   Literally: Yuan dynasty variety drama. A form of music-drama (*xiqu*), usually considered the first fully developed and synthesized such form. It developed in northern China during the 12th and 13th C out of *yuanben* and other then-contemporary poetic and musical forms, and flourished during the Yuan dynasty (1271–1368). It was originally centered in Beijing (then Dadu); Hangzhou became its center in the mid-14th C. Yuan *zaju* included three major role categories (*hangdang*), male (*mo*), female (*dan*), and clown or villain (*jing*), and numerous types of stock characters, including soub-rette (*meixiang*), elderly female (*buer*), monarch (*jia*), minister (*qu*), and elderly male (*bolao*). Its scripts featured *qu* poetry as song lyrics, and were written in four acts (*zhe*), often with one and sometimes two wedge acts (*xiezi*). Each act was in a single musical key and consisted of a song set; the principal male role (*zhengmo*) or the principal female role (*zhengdan*) did all the singing in a given act, and sometimes in an entire play. The character of Yuan *zaju* changed greatly in the late 14th and early 15th C, and its popularity waned; during that period it was ultimately supplanted by southern drama (*nanxi*). Some play excerpts (*zhezixi*) are still performed in contemporary forms of music-drama. Also called Yuan *qu* or Yüan *ch'ü*; in the 13th-early 15th C, sometimes also called *chuanqi*. See also: *zaju*. (Dolby HISTORY 40–59, Shih GOLDEN)

yü chü (Chinese)   See: *yuju.*

yuck   See: yock.

yudai, yü tai (Chinese)   Literally: jade belt. A stiff, hoop-like belt worn by both male and female characters dressed in ceremonial or official costumes, including the *guanyi* and *mang*, in Beijing opera (*jingju*) and many other forms of music-drama (*xiqu*). (Halson PEKING 20, Scott CLASSICAL 145)

yuedui (Chinese)   See: *changmian.*

yueguan (Chinese)   See: *lingren.*

yüeh ch'in (Chinese)   See: *yueqin.*

yüeh chü (Chinese)   See: *yueju.*

yüeh kuan (Chinese)   See: *lingren.*

yüeh tui (Chinese)   See: *changmian.*

yueju, yüeh chü (Chinese)   1. A major southern form of music-drama (*xiqu*) popular in Guangdong Province and the Guangxi Zhuang Autonomous Region as well as in overseas Chinese communities. It developed in the 17th C under the influence of touring companies representing at least four major musical systems (*gaoqiang, bangziqiang, kunshanqiang,* and *pihuang*); it also absorbed Guangdong folk and popular music. Its songs blend *banqiangti* and *lianquti* musical structures; its musical accompaniment features both Chinese and Western instruments, including the violin and saxophone. In translation, often called Guangdong (Kwangtung, Cantonese) opera. (Howard CONTEMPORARY 16, Mackerras MODERN 145–152, Scott INTRODUCTION 5–7) 2. Written with a different initial character, a major eastern form of music-drama (*xiqu*) popular in Shanghai and Zhejiang, Jiangsu, Jiangxi, and Anhui Provinces, with influence in northern and central China as well. It originated c. 1910 in Sheng County, Zhejiang Province, under the influence of Yuyao *yangge* and local folk ballads and songs, and was later influenced by *shaoju* music, Beijing opera (*jingju*) dance and movement conventions, *kunqu* music and dance, and spoken drama (*huaju*) acting and staging. Between the 1930s and 1960, the most successful *yueju* troupes were composed entirely of women; since 1960 men have been included as well. Called Shaoxing theatre (*shaoxingxi* or *shao hsing hsi*) in the 1930s and 1940s. Also called Sheng County theatre (*shengxianxi* or *sheng hsien hsi).* (Foreign FOLK 41–43; Halson PEKING 66–67; Howard CONTEMPO-RARY 17; Mackerras MODERN 111–113, 205)

yueqin, yüeh ch'in (Chinese)   Literally: moon-shaped stringed instrument. A fretted lute with a round, flat body and a short neck which is plucked with a plectrum; it may be constructed with two pairs of strings or with three or four independent strings. Often called moon guitar in translation. It is an important instrument in the melodic orchestra (*wenchang*) in Beijing opera (*jingju*) and many other forms of music-drama (*xiqu*) and is also used in many forms of story-telling (*quyi*). (Scott CLASSICAL 44, 50; Wichmann ''Aural'' 450)

yugen (Japanese)   A changing Japanese aesthetic ideal applied to *no* acting by Zeami Motokiyo (1363-1443). In Zeami's writings it means ''subdued splen-dor'' (Nippon Gakujutsu JAPANESE III xx), ''hidden appeal'' (Shimazaki NOH 1), or ''subtle mystery'' (Nakamura NOH 82). Ueda says it is the ''beauty of seeing . . . an ideal person go through an intense suffering'' thus touching on ''cosmic truth.'' (Ortolani ''Zeami's'' 114–115) To suggest *yugen*, Zeami uses the image ''white snow piled within a silver bowl'' (Keene NO 30–31). In acting, outer gentleness (*yu*) together with inner strength (*mu*) produces the desired *yugen* effect in the audience. (Nearman ''Kyui'' 324) Or, by melding together in a *no* play aristocratic, ancient magnificence (*yu*) with warrior-like and rural nothingness (*mu*), the resulting effect is called *yugen*. (Tsubaki ''Zeami'' 63)

yujo kabuki (Japanese)   Literally: prostitutes' *kabuki*. 1. The style of *kabuki* performed by troupes of female prostitutes, featuring the new *shamisen* music, sensuous dances and songs, skits about the licensed quarters, and luxurious costuming. 2. The period in *kabuki* history, c. 1615–1629, during which pros-titutes performed. Also called *onna* (women's) *kabuki*. (Gunji KABUKI 20, Kincaid KABUKI 58–63)

yuju, yü chü (Chinese)   Henan (Honan) opera, a form of music-drama (*xiqu*) popular in Henan Province and many areas throughout west, north, central, and east China. It probably arose c. 17th C through a number of influences, including the *bangziqiang* musical system (*shengqiang xitong*) and Henan folk music. Its music uses both *banqiangti* and *lianquti* musical structures, and features the *banhu* spike fiddle. Also called Henan *bangzi* or Honan *pang tzu*.

yuk   See: yock.

yuka (Japanese)   The place, near the stage left side of the proscenium arch in a *kabuki* theatre, where the puppet-derived chanter (*tayu*) and *shamisen* player sit when plays adapted from *bunraku* are performed. It may either be at stage level and open to view or in a second floor alcove and closed off from the audience by a bamboo blind. (Leiter ENCYCLOPEDIA 439–440, Malm in Brandon/Malm/Shively STUDIES 139)

yuken ogi (Japanese)   In *no* dance, a standard gesture (*kata*) expressing joy. The open fan is moved outward from the chest, usually twice. Illustrated in Keene NO 221.

yukiko (Japanese)   Literally: snow clothes. A white costume and hood worn by a stage assistant in a snow scene in *kabuki*. See also: *koken*.

yuki nuno   See: *jigasuri*.

Yungchia *tsa chü* (Chinese)   See: *nanxi*.

yung chü (Chinese)   See: *yongju*.

yunluo, yün lo (Chinese)   Literally: cloud gong. A musical instrument consisting of nine or ten small tuned gongs, each about 2 1/2 inches in diameter, which are suspended from a wooden frame and struck with a small wooden hammer. It is used in the percussion orchestra (*wuchang*) in Beijing opera (*jingju*) and other forms of music-drama (*xiqu*), usually for special effects and ceremonial scenes. Also called the nine-tone gong (*jiuyinluo* or *chiu yin lo*). (Scott CLASSICAL 49; Wichmann "Aural" 448–449, 454–455)

yusuriba (Japanese)   Literally: extortion scene. A scene in a gangster play (*kizewamono*) in 19th C *kabuki*, in which a hero extorts money by means of a daring ruse. An example is in *Benten the Thief* in Ernst THREE 173–185 and Leiter ART 13–36. It is one type of *miseba*. (Hamamura et al KABUKI 77)

yü tai (Chinese)   See: *yudai*.

yuyaoqiang, yü yao ch'iang (Chinese)   1. A form of music-drama (*xiqu*) native to Yuyao in north central Zhejiang Province which began its development in the 14th C and was quite influential in the 15th and 16th C. Its music may have derived at least in part from that of southern drama (*nanxi*); it possibly included some choral backing (*bangqiang*), and was probably accompanied only by the rhythmical punctuation of percussive instruments. 2. A musical system which arose in the mid-16th C as the influence of the *yuyaoqiang* form spread to various areas in Jiangsu and Anhui Provinces. It ceased to exist as a discrete system in the 17th C, although some elements are preserved today in at least one form of music-drama in Zhejiang Province. (Dolby HISTORY 90–91)

Z

za (Japanese)   1. Originally, to sit or a seat. Hence, by extension, a sitting place within a theatre, as in the *no* "musicians' seat" (*hayashi za*). 2. An early (13th-15th C) term for a theatre troupe; for example, in *no*, the Kanzeza. (Komparu NOH 135) 3. After the 17th C, especially in *kabuki* and *bunraku*, a theatre building, such as the Meijiza. (Gunji KABUKI 44)

zaban, tsa pan (Chinese)   Literally: miscellaneous playing. A type of play which originated as a comic entertainment in the 12th-13th C and was later associated with Song *zaju*, frequently comprising the concluding, "dispersal section" of a Song *zaju* performance. It remained comic, including a story or sketch and probably dance and song, and was slighter and briefer than the main *zaju* play. (Dolby HISTORY 19)

zacho (Japanese)   The head of a traditional theatre troupe. (Komparu NOH 135)

zadacha (Russian)   In the Stanislavsky system of acting, the performer's momentary task: the work to be done within each phrase or bit of his role. See also: *kuski partitura*, (Italian). (Hobgood "Stanislavski's" 155)

zafaldo (Italian)   See: *platea*.

zagashira (Japanese)   Literally: troupe head. 1. In *kabuki*, the leading actor of a troupe. Also called *tayumoto*. See also: *nadai*, *zamoto*. (Dunn/Torigoe ANALECTS 16, Gunji KABUKI 31, Leiter ENCYCLOPEDIA 392) 2. In *bunraku*, the leader of the puppet handlers (*ningyo tsukai*) in the troupe. (Scott KABUKI 63–64)

zagna (Italian)   An alternate term for the *servetta* or maidservant in *commedia dell'arte*. *Zagna* was evidently an early term; *servetta* and *fantesca* were more common for the saucy serving maid. (Oreglia COMMEDIA 123)

zaju, tsa chü (Chinese)   Literally: variety drama. Various types of entertainment and drama have been termed *zaju* since at least 832 (Dolby HISTORY 15). The two principal forms of music-drama (*xiqu*) bearing this name are Song dynasty *zaju* (Song *zaju*) and Yuan dynasty *zaju* (Yuan *zaju*). Other forms include southern *zaju* (*nanzaju*) and southern drama (*nanzi*, sometimes called Wenzhou *zaju* and Yongjia *zaju*). The term is most frequently used to refer to Yuan *zaju*.

zamoto (Japanese)   Literally: theatre head. 1. In Kyoto-Osaka *kabuki* in the early 17th C, the manager of a theatre or the person holding a government license to produce plays. Later, the star actor who headed a troupe and who functioned as artistic director. (Dunn/Torigoe ANALECTS 16) 2. In Edo (Tokyo) *kabuki*, and written with different ideographs, a theatre manager or the person holding the government license to stage productions. Also called *tayumoto*. See: *yagura*. (Leiter ENCYCLOPEDIA 442–443)

zancha   A very high, close-fitting boot of supple, black leather. Also called a tzanga, zanga. (Boucher FASHION)

zangirimono (Japanese)   Literally: cropped-hair play. A *kabuki* play written between 1879 and 1889 in which male characters wore their hair cut short in the new European fashion. Hence, a *kabuki* play set in post-feudal Japan. Most were commissioned and performed by the star actor Onoe Kikugoro V. Also called *zangiri kyogen* (cropped-hair play). (Komiya MEIJI 204–205, Tsubouchi/Yamamoto KABUKI 69)

zanni, zani (Italian)   The stock comic male servant characters in *commedia dell'arte*. The term is usually used to include such characters as Arlecchino, Brighella, Pulcinella, Scaramuccia, and others. Though the word seems at first to have referred only to the two servant types from Bergamo (Arlecchino and Brighella), it appears in time to have been reserved for comic male servant characters other than these major ones. (Duchartre ITALIAN 29, Oreglia COMMEDIA 17, Brockett HISTORY 181)

zany   1. A 16th C doll's head at the end of a stick, used by jesters. (Barton COSTUME 221) 2. A comic character or clown.

zaozhouzi (Chinese)   See: *zhouzi*.

zarabanda (Spanish)   A stately dance introduced in Spanish theatres about 1588, considered voluptuous by some critics. (Brockett HISTORY 237)

zarzuela (Philippine)   An operetta. First brought from Spain in 1878 and by 1899 written and acted in vernacular languages. It was a popular, commercial theatre form through the 1920s. It is occasionally staged today. *Zarzuela grande* is a three-act tragi-comic operetta. *Zarzuela chica*, *genero chica*, or *genero chico* designate a one-act comedy. (Fernández ILOILO 33, Hernandez EMERGENCE 58-59, Banas PILIPINO 187-200, Tonogbanua SURVEY 86-89)

zarzuela (Spanish)   Spanish musical comedy; developed in the 17th C. (Brockett HISTORY 231)

zashuaguan, tsa shua kuan (Chinese)   Literally: variety house. A type of theatre-restaurant similar to but much less formal than a play establishment (*xizhuang*); one of three types of fixed public theatres in the 17th-early 20th C.

Variety houses were open to individuals from all social classes without prior booking and offered smaller-scale entertainment than did play establishments, usually presenting groups of storytellers (*dangziban*) rather than music-drama (*xiqu*) troupes. See also: *xiyuan, xizhuang.* (Mackerras RISE 199–200)

zat (Burmese)   A traditional theatre form, with much song and dance, using *Jataka* tales (Buddha birth-stories) as its basic dramatic subject matter. The term derives from the word *Jataka* and was used at least as early as the mid-18th C. Also called *zat pwe.* See also: *hto zat, nan dwin zat.* (Aung DRAMA 35)

zat ok (Burmese)   The business manager of a *zat* troupe.

zat pwe (Burmese)   See: *zat.*

zatsumono (Japanese)   See: *kyoranmono.*

zatsu no (Japanese)   See: *kyoranmono.*

zawgyi (Burmese)   The character of a juggler, magician, or alchemist in Burmese marionette theatre. The *zawgyi* appears in the opening section of the two-part entertainment. (Aung DRAMA 148, ASIAN 93)

zeit bilder (Yiddish)   See: *tsaytbilder.*

zenei engeki (Japanese)   A direct translation of the Western term 'avant garde theatre.' Widely used since the 1950s.

zenna (Turkish)   Any female character in a *Karagöz* puppet play. (Malkin PUPPETS 57)

zhangtou kuilei, chang t'ou k'uei lei (Chinese)   Rod puppets, popular at least as early as the 10th C. See also: *kuileixi.* (Dolby HISTORY 33, Liu INTRODUCTION 163, Obraztsov CHINESE 22–23)

zhe, che (Chinese)   1. An act in a Yuan *zaju* play; most plays included four acts. All lyrics in one act were sung by a single character. See also: *xiezi, zhezixi.* 2. See: *chu.*

zhekou (Chinese)   See: *shisanzhe.*

zhengben daxi, cheng pen ta hsi (Chinese)   A type of c. 18th C play written for palace performances of music-drama (*xiqu*). Many such plays consisted of 240 acts, divided into 10 sections of 24 acts each; a full play required ten days to perform. Sometimes translated as bumper play. (Dolby HISTORY 142–143)

zhengdan, cheng tan (Chinese)   Principal female role, generally young or middle-aged. 1. A virtuous, respectable, serious female role which features song (*chang*) skill; a major subcategory of the female role (*dan*) in many forms of music-drama (*xiqu*). Popularly called female big face (*cidamian* or *tz'u ta mien*) in *kunqu*, and blue/black clothing (*qingyi* or *ch'ing i*) in Beijing opera (*jingju*). (Dolby HISTORY 105, 180; Scott CLASSICAL 31–32, 71–74) 2. In Yuan *zaju*, also a major subcategory of the female role, but inclusive of a wider range of characters, "from maidservants and singing girls to noble ladies." Abbreviated *dan.* (Dolby HISTORY 60)

zheng diaoshi, cheng tiao shih (Chinese)   Literally: principal modes. The most important, basic modes (*diaoshi*) by which the music of each form of music-drama (*xiqu*) which uses *banqiangti* musical structure may be identified. The term is used most frequently in Beijing opera (*jingju*), to contrast each such mode with its inverse counterpart (*fandiaoshi*). Abbreviated *zhengdiao* or *cheng tiao*. (Scott CLASSICAL 51; Wichmann "Aural" 168, 228)

zhengjing, cheng ching (Chinese)   Principal painted-face role. 1. An important, upright, forceful male role which features song (*chang*) skill; a major subcategory of the painted-face role (*jing*) in Beijing opera (*jingju*). (Dolby HISTORY 181, Scott CLASSICAL 75) 2. See: *damian*.

zhenglou, cheng lou (Chinese)   Literally: principal upstairs. In a tea-house theatre of the 17th-early 20th C, the portion of second-floor veranda seating at the back of the auditorium facing the stage. Originally this area was without seats; possibly it was held for the sudden appearance of an important dignitary. It was later partitioned into boxes like the officials' seats (*guanzuo*). (Dolby HISTORY 190–191)

zhengmo, cheng mo (Chinese)   Principal male role; a major subcategory of the male role (*mo*) in Yuan *zaju*. Inclusive of a wide range of characters, both young and old, serious and comic, and dignified and ignoble. Sometimes called *moni*. Abbreviated *mo*. (Dolby HISTORY 60)

zhengsheng, cheng sheng (Chinese)   Principal male role. The term has been used in some periods and forms of music-drama (*xiqu*) to refer to the older male role (*laosheng*), and in others to indicate the young male role (*xiaosheng*); today the former use is most prevalent in the majority of forms.

zhensangzi (Chinese)   See: *dasangzi*.

zhezi (Chinese)   See: *xuezi*.

zhezixi, che tzu hsi (Chinese)   One-act plays, often scenes (*chu*) or acts (*zhe*) from full-length plays whose plots are familiar to the audience. In music-drama (*xiqu*), a bill frequently consists of several different *zhezixi*. See also: *zhe, zhouzi*. (Howard CONTEMPORARY 14, Wichmann "Aural" 58–59)

zhiwei, chih wei (Chinese)   Literally: pheasant tail. Usually translated as pheasant feather. A long feather; two are worn in the headdress of a general or commanding officer in Beijing opera (*jingju*) and many other forms of music-drama (*xiqu*). The feathers are manipulated in a number of conventional and interpretive ways described in detail in Scott CLASSICAL 131–133 and Zung SECRETS 129–133. Also called plume (*lingzi* or *ling tzu*).

zhiweisheng, chih wei sheng (Chinese)   Literally: pheasant-tail male role. 1. A role category which includes young princes and young male warriors and features dance-acting (*zuo*) skill; a major subdivision of the young male role (*xiaosheng*) in *kunqu* and many other forms of music-drama (*xiqu*). The name is derived from the pheasant-tail feathers (*zhiwei*) often worn in the headdresses of such characters. Also called plume male role (*lingzisheng* or *ling tzu sheng*). (Dolby HISTORY 105) 2. See: *wuxiaosheng*.

zhonglu bangzi (Chinese)   See: *jinju*.

zhongxu (Chinese)   See: *daqu*.

zhongzhouzi (Chinese)   See: *zhouzi*.

zhougun, chou kun (Chinese)   Literally: axle rod. A horizontal bar running across the entire width of a traditional stage, especially in a tea-house theatre (*xiyuan*), 17th-early 20th C. It was about ten feet above the stage floor, attached at either end to the two downstage pillars, and was used to assist in combat (*da*) and acrobatic movements in martial plays (*wuxi*). (Dolby HISTORY 191)

zhouzi, chou tzu (Chinese)   Literally: axle. One-act plays (*zhezixi*) given featured positions in a bill of several one-acts, especially in 19th C programs. A performance—usually five or six hours long—included approximately ten one-act plays, of which four were featured: the second or third (*zaozhouzi* or *tsao chou tzu*, literally "early featured piece", or *xiaozhouzi* or *hsiao chou tzu*, literally "small featured piece"), the fifth or sixth (*zhongzhouzi* or *chung chou tzu*, literally "central featured piece"), the next-to-last (*yazhouzi* or *ya chou tzu*, literally "approaching featured piece"), and the last, most important piece (*dazhouzi* or *ta chou tzu*, literally "big featured piece"). All but the next-to-last were generally martial plays (*wuxi*); the next-to-last was usually a civil play (*wenxi*) emphasizing song (*chang*) skill.

zhuangdan, chuang tan (Chinese)   Literally: impersonated female role. A young, graceful female role; a type of supporting role in Song *zaju* and Jin *yuanben*. (Dolby HISTORY 26–27, 107)

zhuanggu, chuang ku (Chinese)   Literally: impersonated official role. A dignified government official or member of the gentry; a type of supporting role in Song *zaju* and Jin *yuanben*. (Dolby HISTORY 26–27)

zhuangju, chuang chü (Chinese)   The drama of the Zhuang people, the most populous of China's fifty-five minority nationalities, who inhabit the Guangxi Zhuang Autonomous Region and a portion of Yunnan Province. There are several distinct forms. The oldest, the *zhuangju* of Longlin, goes back 200 years. It began as a form of small-scale folk theatre (*xiaoxi*); semiprofessional troupes arose in the 19th C. All forms of *zhuangju* are based on the dancer, and include religious dances and folk songs. (Howard CONTEMPORARY 116)

zhugongdiao, chu kung tiao (Chinese)   A form of storytelling (*shuochang*) prevalent in the 11th-15th C. A performance related one long story presented in several suites, or song sets, each in one rhyming scheme and mode throughout and interspersed with speech. Musical accompaniment featured the lute (*pipa*). See also: *guzici*. (Dolby HISTORY 35, Dolezelova–Velingerova/Crump BALLAD 3–28, Kuan SELECTED 6)

zhuozi, cho tzu (Chinese)   Literally: tables. In a tea-house theatre (*xiyuan*) of the 17th-early 20th C, the portion of second-floor veranda seating on the two sides of the house between the officials' seats (*guanzuo*) near the stage and the principal upstairs (*zhenglou*) section at the back of the auditorium. Seating in these two *zhuozi* areas was at tables or benches, and was fairly expensive, though less so than in the officials' seats. (Dolby HISTORY 190, Mackerras MODERN 86, Mackerras RISE 202)

zibaldone (Italian)   1. A commonplace book kept by a *commedia dell'arte* performer—a collection of jests, conceits, etc. 2. A collection of scenarios by one author, constituting the repertory of a company.

zibao jiamen, tzu pao chia men (Chinese)   Literally: self-delivered background. The generic term for conventional self-introductory materials delivered by major characters upon their first entrances. Such materials probably originated in oral literature, and were featured in Yuan *zaju* plays. Since the 18th C they have been widely used in most forms of music-drama (*xiqu*), including Beijing opera (*jingju*), and have included the lead-in poem (*yinzi*), set-the-scene poem (*dingchangshi*), and set-the-scene speech (*dingchangbai*), delivered in that order. They are related to the prologue (*jiamen*) of southern drama (*nanxi*) and *chuanqi* plays. See also: *shangchangbai, shuban*. (Shih GOLDEN 24–27)

zikir (Malaysian)   See: *likay*.

zill-i hayal (Turkish)   See: *hayali zil*.

zimarra (Italian)   A cloak, usually black, worn by the *commedia dell'arte* character Pantalone and others. It has been used into the 20th C. (Duchartre ITALIAN 188)

zinc white   Formerly, white greasepaint used in makeup; now an oxide of zinc used in paint pigment.

zip cord   A common name for household electric cord, sometimes used on stage for practical lamps and for low voltage applications. Often called a lamp cord, sometimes a ripcord. In Britain: domestic twisted flex, sometimes flex or lead. (Lounsbury THEATRE)

zits   A false beard.

ziyouban, tzu yu pan (Chinese)   Literally: free accented-beat. In music-drama (*xiqu*), any metrical-type (*banshi*) which is free of a pattern of metrical organization (*banyan*); sometimes translated as free metrical-type. In Beijing opera (*jingju*), the principal free metrical-types include: *daoban, sanban*, and *yaoban*. See also: *shangban*. (Wichmann "Aural" 146, 159–167)

zo (Japanese)   See: *zo no onna*.

zoned scene   A puppet stage action which is divided into side-by-side areas. Into these separate areas, the action moves and lighting follows, maintaining visual continuity in the performance. (Philpott DICTIONARY)

zo no onna (Japanese)   A *no* mask of a mature young woman, used for a goddess or a heavenly maiden in a god play. Abbreviated *zo onna* or *zo*. (Shimazaki NOH 60)

zoom lens   A lens with a variable focal length.

zo onna (Japanese)   See: *zo no onna*.

Zouave jacket   A 19th C bolero-like garment with three-quarter sleeves either loose or tight, trimmed with braid in military style. Worn by women and the members of some regiments. (Barton COSTUME 438)

Zouave pantaloons   Late 19th C wide trousers gathered into a tight band below the knee and trimmed with frills. (Boucher FASHION)

zoubian, tsou pien (Chinese)   Literally: walking on the edge. A set of connected, conventional dance movements used in martial plays (*wuxi*) in Beijing opera (*jingju*) and many other forms of music-drama (*xiqu*), usually to portray tense, rapid night travel along the edge of country roads. The movements may be performed by one character alone or by two or more simultaneously. (Halson PEKING 50)

zucchetto (Italian)   See: *calotte*.

zuo, tzo (Chinese)   Literally: do, act, engage in. The physical, visible results of 'acting,' including pure dance, pantomime, and all interpretive movements, gestures, and facial expressions; one of the basic performance skills (*jiben gongfu*) in Beijing opera (*jingju*) and many other forms of music-drama (*xiqu*). Sometimes translated as dance-acting. See also: *dongzuo*. (Wichmann ''Aural'' 25)

zuochangbai (Chinese)   See: *dingchangbai*.

zuochangshi (Chinese)   See: *dingchangshi*.

zuodan, tso tan (Chinese)   Literally: action female role. A young or middle-aged female role emphasizing dance-acting (*zuo*) skill; a major subcategory of the female role (*dan*) in *kunqu* drama. When dance-acting skill is called for, performers of the action female role may play young boys, as well as characters otherwise played by performers of the principal female (*zhengdan*), stabbing and killing female (*cishadan*), and secondary female (*tiedan*) roles. (Dolby HISTORY 105, Scott CLASSICAL 32)

zuoerqian, tso erh ch'ien (Chinese)   Literally: seat money. Money paid for seating at a performance in a tea-house theatre (*xiyuan*), 17th-early 20th C; it covered seating only, and did not include tea. See also: *chapiao*. (Dolby HISTORY 191)

BIBLIOGRAPHY

Most of the works listed here are cited in the body of the *Dictionary*; others provide useful background, often on a range of subjects. Information on how to find a cited work in the bibliography is in the Guide to the Dictionary, especially in the segment labelled Citations (pp. xxviii-xxix); that passage also notes the range of material to which citations lead—sometimes considerable and sometimes merely an example of the use of the term defined.

The bibliography includes many theatre glossaries and dictionaries. Further details on the most extensive of these can be found in A Brief History of Theatre Glossaries and Dictionaries listed in the Contents.

Abe, Kobo. *Friends*. Translated by Donald Keene. New York: Grove Press, Evergreen, 1969.

———. *The Man Who Turned Into a Stick: Three Related Plays*. Translated by Donald Keene. Tokyo: University of Tokyo Press, 1975.

Adachi, Barbara. *The Voices and Hands of Bunraku*. New York: Harper & Row, 1978.

Adams, Joey, and Tobias, Henry. *The Borscht Belt*. New York: Bobbs-Merrill, 1966.

Adams, Joseph Quincy, ed. *The Dramatic Records of Sir Henry Herbert*. New Haven: Yale University Press, 1917.

Addington, David W. "Varieties of Audience Research: Some Prospects for the Future." *Educational Theatre Journal* 26 (December 1974): 482-487.

Addison, Michael, and Harrop, John. "Actor Training in Australia." *Educational Theatre Journal* 22 (May 1971): 178-186.

Addiss, Stephen. "Theater Music of Vietnam." *Southeast Asia, An International Quarterly* 1 (Winter-Spring 1971): 129-152.

Adedeji, Joel A. Glossary of terms. Typescript, 1983.

———. "The Origin and Form of the Yoruba Masque Theatre." *Cahiers d'études Africaines* 12 (1972): 254-276.

Adler, Lois. "Sicilian Puppets." *The Drama Review* 20 (June 1976): 25-30.

Adler, Thomas P. Review of *Metafictional Characters in Modern Drama*, by June Schlueter. New York: Columbia University Press, 1979. *Theatre Journal* 32 (May 1980): 272-273.

Albertson, Chris. *Bessie*. New York: Stein and Day, 1974.

Albright, H.D.; Halstead, William P.; and Mitchell, Lee. *Principles of Theatre Art*, 2d ed. Boston: Houghton Mifflin, 1969.

Alejandro, Reynald G. *Philippine Dance: Mainstream and Crosscurrents*. Quezon City: Vera-Reyes, 1978.

———. *Sayaw Silingan: The Dance in the Philippines*. New York: Dance Perspectives Foundation, 1972.

Allen, James Turney. *The Greek Theater of the Fifth Century Before Christ*. 1920. Reprint. New York: Haskell House, 1966.

———. "On the Program of the City Dionysia During the Peloponnesian War." *University of California Publications in Classical Philology* 12 (1935): 35-42.

———. *Stage Antiquities of the Greeks and Romans and Their Influence*. New York: Longmans, Green, 1927.

All-Russian Theatrical Society. *The Soviet Theatre*. Moscow: n.p., 1973.

Altman, George. "Good Advice From the 'Bad' *Hamlet* Quarto." *Educational Theatre Journal* 2 (December 1950): 308-318.

And, Metin. *Karagöz. The Turkish Shadow Theatre*, rev. ed. Istanbul: Dost, 1979.

———. "Mevlana Ceremony." *The Drama Review* 21 (Summer 1977): 83-94.

Anderson, Benedict R. O'G. *Mythology and the Tolerance of the Javanese*. Monograph Series, Modern Indonesia Project. Ithaca: Cornell University, 1965.

Anderson, Michelle. "Authentic Voodoo is Synthetic." *The Drama Review* 26 (Summer 1982): 89-110.

Ando, Tsuruo. *Bunraku: The Puppet Theatre*. Translated by Don Kenny. New York: Walker/Weatherhill, 1970.

Angotti, Vincent L., and Herr, Judie L. "Étienne Decroux and the Advent of Modern Mime." *Theatre Survey* 15 (May 1974): 1-17.

Anonymous. *Bayanihan*. New York: Dunetz & Lovett, 1970.

———. *A Comparison Between the Two Stages*. Edited by Staring B. Wells. Princeton: Princeton University Press, 1942.

———. *Folk Arts of New China*. Peking: Foreign Languages Press, 1954.

———. "Names in the News." *Pomona College Bulletin*, October 1982, p. 7.

———. *Royal Cambodian Ballet*. Phnom Penh: Information Department, 1963.

———. *Secret History of the Green Room*, 2d ed. London: 1792.

———. *The Session of Musicians*, May, 1724.

Anuman, Rajadhon Phya. *A Brief Survey of Cultural Thailand*. Thailand Culture Series, no. 2. Bangkok: National Culture Institute, 1956.

———. *Chat Thi and Some Traditions of Thai*. Thailand Culture Series, no. 6. Bangkok: National Culture Institute, 1955.

———. *Thai Literature in Relation to the Diffusion of Her Cultures*, 3d edition. Thailand Culture New Series no. 9. Bangkok: Fine Arts Department, 1963.

Appia, Adolphe. *Music and the Art of the Theatre*. Translated by Robert W. Corrigan and Mary Douglas Dirks. Edited by Barnard Hewitt. Coral Gables: University of Florida Press, 1962.

———. *The Work of Living Art* and *Man Is the Measure of All Things*. *The Work of Living Art* translated by H.D. Albright. *Man Is the Measure of All Things* translated and edited by Barnard Hewitt. Coral Gables: University of Miami Press, 1960.

Aquino, Francisca Reyes. *Fundamental Dance Steps and Music*. Manila: n.p., 1957.

———. *Philippine Folk Dance*, 3. Manila: n.p., 1956.

Araki, James T. *The Ballad-Drama of Medieval Japan*. Berkeley: University of California Press, 1964.

Arce, Hector. *Groucho*. New York: G.P. Putnam's Sons, 1979.

Archer, William. *Play-Making*. 1912. Reprint. New York: Dover, 1960.

Argelander, Ron. "Performance Workshops: Three Types." *The Drama Review* 22 (December 1978): 3-18.

Aristotle: *Poetics*. Translated by Gerald Else. Ann Arbor: University of Michigan Press, 1967.

Aristotle. *Poetics*. Introduction, Commentary, and appendixes by D.W. Lucas. Oxford: Clarendon, 1968.

Aristotle's *Poetics*. Translated by S.H. Butcher. Introduction by Francis Fergusson. New York: Hill & Wang, 1961.

Arjona, Doris K. "The Spanish Theatre of Today." *Educational Theatre Journal* 11 (December 1959): 265-270.

Armstrong, Margaret Wilson. *Fanny Kemble, A Passionate Victorian*. New York: Macmillan, 1938.

Arnold, Herbert A. "The Other Tradition: A Brief Anatomy of Modern German Drama." *Theatre Journal* 32 (March 1980): 43-53.

Arnott, James Fullarton, and Robinson, John William. *English Theatrical Literature 1559-1900*. London: Society for Theatre Research, 1970.

Arnott, Peter D. *The Ancient Greek and Roman Theatre*. New York: Random House, 1971.

————. *Greek Scenic Conventions in the Fifth Century, B. C.* Oxford: Clarendon, 1962.

————. *An Introduction to the French Theatre*. Totowa, N.J.: Rowman and Littlefield, 1977.

————. *An Introduction to the Greek Theatre*. London: Macmillan, 1959.

————. *Plays Without People*. Bloomington: Indiana University Press, 1964.

————. *The Theatres of Japan*. New York: St. Martin's, 1969.

Arnott, W. Geoffrey. *Menander, Plautus, Terence*. In *New Surveys in the Classics*, no. 9: Greece & Rome. Oxford: Clarendon, 1975.

Aronson, Arnold. *The History & Theory of Environmental Scenography*. Ann Arbor: UMI Research Press, 1981.

Arrabal, Fernando. "Arrabal: Auto-Interview." *The Drama Review* 13 (Fall 1968): 73-76.

Artaud, Antonin. *The Theatre and its Double*. Translated by Mary Caroline Richards. New York: Grove, 1958.

Arthur, Douglas. Review of a performance of *Oedipus the King* [by Sophocles]. Munich, Germany: Muenchener Kammerspiele, Schauspielhaus, 11 December 1977. *Educational Theatre Journal* 30 (October 1978): 410-411.

Ashby, Clifford, and May, Suzanne DePauw. *Trouping Through Texas: Harley Sadler and His Tent Show*. Bowling Green, Ohio: Bowling Green University Popular Press, 1982.

Ashton, Martha Bush. "The Ritual of Yaksagana Badagatittu Bayalata." *Journal of South Asian Literature* 10 (Winter, Spring, Summer 1975): 249-274.

Ashton, Martha Bush, and Christie, Bruce. *Yaksagana, A Dance Drama of India*. New Delhi: Abhinav, 1977.

Asian Puppets: Wall of the World. An exhibition catalogue, UCLA Museum of Cultural History. Los Angeles: University of California, 1979.

Aung, Maung Htin. *Burmese Drama*. London: Oxford University Press, 1957.
————. *A History of Burma*. New York: Columbia University Press, 1967.
Avery, Emmett L., ed. *The London Stage, 1660-1800*. Part 2: 1700-1729, 2 vols. Carbondale: Southern Illinois University Press, 1960.
Azari, Fedele. "Futurist Aerial Theatre." *The Drama Review* 15 (Fall 1970): 128-130.
Bailey, Richard W., and Burton, Dolores M. *English Stylistics; A Bibliography*. Cambridge: M.I.T. Press, 1968.
Bailey, Richard W., and Doložel, Lubomír, eds. *Stylistics and Style*. New York: American Elsevier, 1969.
Baird, Bil. *The Art of the Puppet*. New York: Macmillan, 1965.
Baker, Blanch M. *Theatre and Allied Arts*. New York: Wilson, 1952.
Baker, Hendrik. *Stage Management and Theatrecraft*. New York: Theatre Arts Books, 1968.
Baker, Henry Barton. *History of the London Stage and Its Famous Players, (1576-1903)*, 1st ed. in 2 vols., 1889. 2d ed. (rewritten) in 1 vol. London: George Routledge and Sons, 1904.
Bakshy, Alexander. *The Path of the Modern Russian Stage and Other Essays*. London: C. Palmer & Hayward, 1916.
Balandier, Georges, and Maquet, Jacques. *Dictionary of Black African Civilization*. New York: Leon Amiel, 1974.
Baldry, H.C. *The Greek Tragic Theatre*. New York: Norton, 1971.
Bañas, Raymondo. *Pilipino Music and Theater*. Quezon City: Munlapaz, 1969.
Bandem, I. Madé, and deBoer, Frederik Eugene. *Kaja and Kelod; Balinese Dance in Transition*. Kuala Lumpur: Oxford University Press, 1982.
Band-Kuzmany, Karin R.M. *Glossary of the Theatre: In English, French, Italian, and German*. Amsterdam: Elsevier, 1969.
Baral, Robert. *Revue, the Great Broadway Period*, rev. ed. London: Fleet, 1962.
Barber, Philip. *Scene Technician's Handbook*. New Haven: Whitlock's Book Store, 1928.
Barlow, Anthony D. "Lighting Control and Concepts of Theatre Activity." *Educational Theatre Journal* 25 (May 1973): 135-146.
Barnet, Sylvan; Berman, Morton; and Burto, William, eds. *Aspects of the Drama*. Boston: Little, Brown, 1962.
————. *Types of Drama*. Boston: Little, Brown, 1977.
Barton, Lucy. *Historic Costume for the Stage*. Boston: Walter H. Baker, 1938.
Baumer, Rachel Van M., and Brandon, James, eds. *Sanskrit Drama in Performance*. Honolulu: University Press of Hawaii, 1981.
Bax, Peter. *Stage Management*. 1936. Reprint. New York: Benjamin Blom, 1971.
Baxter, J.H., and Johnson, Charles. *Medieval Latin Word-List From British and Irish Sources*. London: Oxford University Press, 1934.
Bayanihan. See: Anonymous, *Bayanihan*.
Beare, W. *The Roman Stage*, 3d ed. rev. New York: Barnes and Noble, 1964.
Beaumont, Cyril W. *The History of Harlequin*, 1926. Reprint. New York: Benjamin Blom, 1967.
Beckerman, Bernard. *Dynamics of Drama*. New York: Alfred A Knopf, 1970.
————. "The Globe Playhouse at Hofstra College, II: Notes on Direction." *Educational Theatre Journal* 5 (March 1953): 6-11.
————. *Shakespeare at the Globe, 1599-1609*. New York: Macmillan, 1962.
Behn, Aphra. *The Forc'd Marriage*. London: 1671.

Belasco, David. *The Theatre Through its Stage Door*. Edited by Louis V. Defoe. New York: Harper, 1919.

Bell, Morlin. "Platform Staging in a Proscenium Theatre." *Educational Theatre Journal* 22 (May 1968): 152-156.

Bellman, Willard F. "Aesthetics for the Designer." *Educational Theatre Journal* 5 (May 1953): 117-124.

———. *Lighting the Stage: Art and Practice*, 2d ed. New York: Chandler, 1974.

———. *Scene Design, Stage Lighting, Sound, Costume & Makeup: A Scenographic Approach*. Rev. ed. of *Scenography and Stage Technology*. New York: Harper & Row, 1983.

———. *Scenography and Stage Technology*. New York: Thomas Y. Crowell, 1977.

Belo, Jane. *Bali: Rangda and Barong*. Monograph no. 16, American Ethnological Society. Edited by Marian W. Smith. Seattle: University of Washington Press, 1949.

———. *Bali: Temple Festival*. Monograph no. 22, American Ethnological Society. Edited by Marian W. Smith. Seattle: University of Washington Press, 1949.

———, ed. *Traditional Balinese Culture*. New York: Columbia University Press, 1970.

———. *Trance in Bali*. New York: Columbia University Press, 1960.

Belon, P[eter]. *The Mock-Duellist*. London: 1675.

Benegal, Som. *A Panorama of Theatre in India*. New Delhi: Indian Council for Cultural Relations, 1967.

Bender, J.E. "The Criterion Independent Theatre." *Educational Theatre Journal* 18 (October 1966): 197-209.

Bentham, Frederick. *The Art of Stage Lighting*. New York: Taplinger, 1969.

———. *The Art of Stage Lighting*, 3d ed. London: Pitman House, 1980.

———. *Stage Lighting*, 2d ed., rev. and reprinted. London: Pitman, 1957.

Bentley, Eric., ed. *The Theory of the Modern Stage*. Baltimore: Penguin Books, 1968.

Bentley, Gerald Eades. *The Jacobean and Caroline Stage*. 7 vols. Oxford: Clarendon, 1941-1968.

Berberich, Junko. "Rapture in Kyogen." Ph.D. dissertation, University of Hawaii, 1982.

Bergman, Gösta M. *Lighting in the Theatre*. Totowa, N.J.: Rowman and Littlefield, 1977.

Bernard, John. *Retrospections of the Stage*. 2 vols. London: Colburn and Bentley, 1830.

Berrey, Lester, and Van den Bark, Melvin. *The American Thesaurus of Slang*, 2d ed. New York: Crowell, 1947.

Berval, Rene. *Kingdom of Laos, The Land of the Million Elephants*. Saigon: France-Asie, 1959.

Bethe, Monica, trans. *Bugaku Masks*. Tokyo: Kodansha and Shibundo, 1978.

Bethe, Monica, and Brazell, Karen. *No As Performance: An Analysis of the Kuse Scene of "Yamamba."* Ithaca: Cornell University China-Japan Program, 1978.

Betterton, Thomas. *The Prophetess*. London: 1690.

Bharata (Bharata-Muni). *The Natyasastra: A Treatise on Ancient Indian Dramaturgy and Histrionics*, 2d rev. ed. 2 vols. Translated by Manomohan Ghosh. Calcutta: Granthalaya, 1967.

Bhasa. *Thirteen Trivandrum Plays Attributed to Bhasa*. Translated by A.C. Woolner and Lakshman Sarup. London: Oxford University Press, 1930-31.

Bieber, Margarete. *The History of the Greek and Roman Theater*, 1st ed. Princeton: University Press, 1939. 2d rev. ed. 1961.

Bills, Bing D. "The 'Suppression Theory' and the English Corpus Christi Play: A Re-Examination." *Theatre Journal* 32 (May 1980): 157-168.

Birch, Cyril. Introduction to *The Peach Blossom Fan*, by K'ung Shang-jen, edited and translated by Chen Shih-hsiang and Harold Acton. Berkeley: University of California Press, 1976.

Boaden, James. *The Life of Mrs. Jordan*. 2 vols. London: Edward Bull, 1831.

————. *Memoirs of Mrs. Inchbald*. 2 vols. London: Richard Bentley, 1833.

Bogard, Travis, and Oliver, William, eds. *Modern Drama: Essays in Criticism*. New York: Oxford University Press, 1965.

Bond, Edward. *The Sea*. London: Eyre Methuen, 1973.

Bordman, Gerald. *American Musical Theatre: A Chronicle*. New York: Oxford University Press, 1978.

Boswell, Eleanore. *The Restoration Court Stage*. Cambridge: Harvard University Press, 1932.

Bouchard, Alfred. *La Langue Théâtrale*. Paris: Arnaud et Labat, 1878.

Boucher, François. *20,000 Years of Fashion*. New York: Harry N. Abrams, 1967.

Bowers, Faubion. *Entertainment in Russia; Ballet, Theatre, and Entertainment in Russia Today*. Edinburg, N.Y.: T. Nelson, 1959.

————. *The Japanese Theatre*. 1952. Reprint. Rutland, Vt.: Tuttle, 1974.

————. *Theatre in the East: A Survey of Asian Dance and Drama*. New York: Grove, 1956.

Bowman, Ned Alan. *Handbook of Technical Practice for the Performing Arts*. Wilkinsburg, Pa.: Scenographic Media, 1972.

Bowman, Walter Parker, and Ball, Robert Hamilton. *Theatre Language*. New York: Theatre Arts Books, 1961.

Bowman, Wayne. *Modern Theatre Lighting*. New York: Harper & Brothers, 1957.

Boyd, Lou. "Just Checking." *Honolulu Advertiser*, 25 May 1983.

Boyle, Roger. *The Black Prince*. London: 1669.

————. *Guzman*. London: 1693.

Boyle, Walden Philip. *Central and Flexible Staging*. Berkeley: University of California Press, 1956.

Bradshaw, Martha, ed. *Soviet Theatres, 1917-1941*. New York: Research Program on the U.S.S.R., 1954.

Brandon, James R. *Brandon's Guide to Theater in Asia*. Honolulu: University Press of Hawaii, 1976.

————, ed. *Chūshingura: Studies in Kabuki and the Puppet Theater*. Honolulu: University of Hawaii Press, 1982.

————, trans. *Kabuki: Five Classic Plays*. Cambridge: Harvard University Press, 1975.

————, ed. *On Thrones of Gold*. Cambridge: Harvard University Press, 1970.

————. *Theater in Southeast Asia*. Cambridge: Harvard University Press, 1967.

————, ed. *Traditional Asian Plays*. New York: Hill and Wang, 1972.

————. "Training at the Waseda Little Theater: The Suzuki Method." *The Drama Review* 22 (December 1978): 29-42.

————. "Types of Indonesian Professional Theatre." *Quarterly Journal of Speech* 45 (February 1959): 51-58.

Brandon, James R.; Malm, William P.; and Shively, Donald M. *Studies in Kabuki: Its Acting, Music, and Historical Context*. Honolulu: University Press of Hawaii, 1978.

Braun, Edward. *The Theatre of Meyerhold*. New York: Drama Book Specialists, 1979.

Brecht, Bertolt. *Brecht on Theatre*. Edited and translated by John Willett. New York: Hill and Wang, 1964.

———. "A Short Organum for the Theatre." In *Brecht on Theatre*. Edited and translated by John Willett. New York, Hill & Wang, 1964.

Brecht, Stefan. "Family of the f.p." *The Drama Review* 12 (Fall 1968): 117-141.

———. "Peter Schumann's Bread and Puppet Theatre." *The Drama Review* 14 (1970): 44-51.

Bresnahan, Roger J., ed. *Literature and Society: Cross-cultural Perspectives*. n.p.: n.p., n.d.

Bretz, Rudolf C. *Techniques of Television Production*, 2d ed. New York: McGraw Hill, 1962.

Bricker, Herschel, ed. *Our Theatre Today*. New York: Samuel French, 1936.

British Library. Additional MS. 12, 201, f.30, 1743. Inventory of Stage Properties and Scenery at Covent Garden Theatre.

Broadbent, R.J. *A History of Pantomime*. 1901. Reprint. New York: Benjamin Blom, 1964.

Brockett, Oscar C. *History of the Theatre*, 4th ed. Boston: Allyn and Bacon, 1982.

———. "Pixérécourt and Unified Production." *Educational Theatre Journal* 11 (October 1959): 181-187.

———. *The Theatre: an Introduction*, 4th ed. New York: Holt, Rinehart & Winston, 1979.

Brooke, Iris. *Costume in Greek Classic Drama*. London: Methuen, 1962.

Brooks, Cleanth, and Heilman, Robert B. *Understanding Drama*. New York: Henry Holt, 1948.

Brown, Benjamin Williams. *Theatre at the Left*. Providence, R.I.: The Book Shop, 1938.

Brown, Gilmor, and Garwood, Alice. *General Principles of Play Direction*. New York: Samuel French, 1936.

Brown, John Russell. "Marlowe and the Actors." *Tulane Drama Review* 8 (Summer 1964): 155-173.

Browne, Van Dyke. *Secrets of Scene Painting and Stage Effects*, 6th ed. London: George Routledge & Sons, n.d.

Brownsmith, John. *The Theatrical Alphabet*. London: 1767.

Bruford, W.H. *Theatre Drama and Audience in Goethe's Germany*. London: Routledge and Kegan Paul, 1950.

Brunet, Jacques. "Nang Sbek." *The World of Music* 11 (1969): 19-34.

Buckingham, Duke of (George Villiers), et al. Edited by Montague Summers. *The Rehearsal*. Stratford-Upon-Avon: Shakespeare Head Press, 1914.

Buckle, J.G. *Theatre Construction and Maintenance*. London: "The Stage" Office, 1888.

Buerki, F.A. *Stagecraft for Non-Professionals*, 3d ed. Madison: The University of Wisconsin Press, 1972.

Bullins, Ed. "A Short Statement on Street Theatre." *The Drama Review* 12 (Summer 1968): 93.

Burian, Jarka M. "Alfred Radok's Contribution to Post-War Czech Theatre." *Theatre Survey* 22 (November 1981): 213-228.

———. "Art and Relevance: The Small Theatres of Prague, 1958-1970." *Educational Theatre Journal* 23 (October 1971): 229-257.

———. "The Liberated Theatre of Voskovec and Werich." *Educational Theatre Journal* 29 (May 1971): 153-177.

————. *The Scenography of Josef Svoboda.* Middletown, Conn.: Wesleyan University Press, 1974.

Burney, Charles. *A General History of Music*, 2 vols. 1789. Reprint. New York: Dover 1957.

Burnim, Kalman. *David Garrick, Director.* Pittsburgh: University of Pittsburgh Press, 1961.

————. "La Scena Per Angolo—Magic By the Bibienas?" *Theatre Survey* 2 (1961): 67-76.

————. "Some Notes on Aaron Hill and Stage Scenery." *Theatre Notebook* 12 (Autumn 1957): 29-33.

Burns, George. Johnny Carson Show, 1980.

Burris-Meyer, Harold, and Cole, Edward C. *Scenery for the Theatre.* 1938. Reprint. Boston: Little, Brown, 1949.

————. *Scenery for the Theatre*, rev. ed. Boston: Little, Brown, 1971.

————. *Theatres and Auditoriums*, 2d ed. 1964. Reprint with supplement. Huntington, N.Y.: R.E. Krieger, 1975.

Burris-Meyer, Harold, and Mallory, Vincent. *Sound in the Theatre.* Mineola, N.Y.: Radio Magazines, 1959.

Burris-Meyer, Harold; Mallory, Vincent; and Goodfriend, Lewis S. *Sound in the Theatre*, rev. ed. New York: Theatre Arts Books, 1979.

Butcher, S.H., *Aristotle's Theory of Poetry and Fine Art*, 4th ed. with critical text and translation of the Poetics, and a Prefatory essay by John Gassner. New York: Dover, 1951.

Bywater, Ingram, trans. *Aristotle on the Art of Poetry*, revised. Oxford: Clarendon, 1909.

Calandra, Denis. "Terror Rote Rübe." *The Drama Review* 19 (June 1975): 114-118.

Cameron, Kenneth M., and Gillespie, Patti P. *The Enjoyment of Theatre.* New York: Macmillan, 1980.

Cameron, Kenneth M., and Hoffman, Theodore. *A Guide to Theatre Study.* New York: Macmillan, 1974.

Campbell, Lily B. *Scenes and Machines on the English Stage During the Renaissance.* Cambridge: University Press, 1923.

Canfield, Curtis. *The Craft of Play Directing.* New York: Holt, Rinehart and Winston, 1963.

Capps, Edward. *Vitruvius and the Greek Stage.* Chicago: University of Chicago Press, 1893.

Carlson, Marvin. *The French Stage in the 19th Century.* Metuchen, N.J.: Scarecrow, 1972.

————. *The German Stage in the Nineteenth Century.* Metuchen, N.J.: Scarecrow, 1972.

————. "The Golden Age of the Boulevard." *The Drama Review* 18 (March 1974): 25-33.

————. "*Hernani*'s Revolt from the Tradition of French Stage Composition." *Theatre Survey* 13 (May 1972): 1-27.

————. "Renaissance Theatre in Scandinavia." *Theatre Survey* 14 (May 1973): 22-54.

————. "Scandinavia's International Baroque Theatre." *Educational Theatre Journal* 28 (March 1976): 5-34.

————. "A Theatre Inventory of the First Empire." *Theatre Survey* 11 (May 1970): 36-49.

Carnegie, David. "Theatre in New Zealand." *Canadian Theatre Review* (Spring 1977): 15-32.

Carpenter, Mark. *An Illustrated Glossary of Stage Lighting*, 3d ed., n.p., 1st ed. publ. by National Institute of Dramatic Art (Australia), 1978.

Carrington, Ken. *Theatricana*. Chicago: Ken Carrington, 1939.

Carroll, David. *The Matinee Idols*. New York: Arbor House, 1972.

Carroll, Dennis. "The United States in Recent Australian Drama." *Educational Theatre Journal* 25 (October 1973): 344-352.

———, ed. *Kumu Kahua Plays*. Honolulu: University of Hawaii Press, 1983.

Carroll, Dennis, and Carroll, Elsa. "Contemporary Finnish Theatre: National Myths and Beyond." *The Drama Review* 26 (Fall 1982): 35-50.

———. "Hawaiian Pidgin Theatre." *Educational Theatre Journal* 28 (March 1976): 57-68.

Carroll, Noel. "Air Dancing." *The Drama Review* 19 (March 1975): 5-12.

Carter, Huntly. *The New Spirit in the Russian Theatre, 1917-1928*. London: Brentano's, 1929.

Cartmell, Van. *A Handbook for the Amateur Actor*. Garden City, N.Y.: Doubleday Doran, 1936.

Cassady, Marshall, and Cassady, Pat. *Theatre: A View of Life*. New York: Holt, Rinehart and Winston, 1982.

del Castillo y Tuazon, Teofilo, and Medina, Buenaventura S., Jr. *Philippine Literature from Ancient Times to the Present*. Quezon City: Del Castillo & Sons, n.d.

Cavett, Dick. Interview with John Gielgud. PBS 1981.

Chadwick, D. *Social Life in the Days of Piers Plowman*. Cambridge: Cambridge University Press, 1922.

Chalmers, Helena. *Clothes, On and Off the Stage*. New York: D. Appleton, 1928.

Chambers, Edmund K. *The Elizabethan Stage*, corrected edition. 4 vols. Oxford: Clarendon, 1951.

———. *The Mediaeval Stage*. 2 vols. Oxford: Clarendon, 1903.

———. *William Shakespeare, A Study of Facts and Problems*. 2 vols. Oxford: Clarendon Press, 1930.

Chang, Sa-hun. "Farmers' Band Music." In *Traditional Performing Arts of Korea*. Seoul: Korean National Commission for UNESCO, 1975.

———. *Korean Music*. Seoul: Korean Musicological Society, 1972.

Charters, Ann. *Nobody: The Story of Bert Williams*. New York: Macmillan, 1970.

Cheney, Sheldon. *The New Movement in Theatre*. New York: M. Kennerly, 1914.

———. *Stage Decoration*. New York: John Day, 1928.

———. *The Theatre*, 4th ed. New York: McKay, 1972.

Cherniack-Tzuriel, Abba. "The Omer Festival of Kibbutz Ramat Yochanan (Israel)." *The Drama Review* 21 (September 1977): 11-20.

Chetwood, William Rufus. *A General History of the Stage*. London: 1749.

Chinoy, Helen Krich. "Reunion: A Self-Portrait of the Group Theatre." *Educational Theatre Journal* 28 (December 1976): 445-552.

———. Review of *Bright Star of Exile* by Lulla Rosenfeld. *Educational Theatre Journal* 30 (December 1978): 563-564.

Chinoy, Helen Krich, and Jenkins, Linda Walsh, eds. *Women in the American Theatre*. New York: Crown, 1981.

Cho, Oh-kon. *Korean Puppet Theatre: Kkoktu Kaksi*. East Lansing: Michigan State University Asian Studies Center, 1979.

————. "The Mask-Dance Theatre from Hwanghae Province." *Korea Journal* 22 (May 1982): 36-45.

————. "Ogwangdae: A Traditional Mask-Dance Theatre of South Kyongsang Province." *Korea Journal* 21 (July 1981): 26-31.

————. "On the Traditional Korean Puppet Theatre." *Korea Journal* 21 (January 1981): 27-34.

————. "Suyong Yayu: A Mask-Dance Theatre of Southeastern Korea." *Korea Journal* 21 (October 1981): 34-38.

————. "The Theatrical Presentation at the Hahoe Village Festival." *Korea Journal* 20 (October 1980): 49-53.

————. "Yangju Pyolsandae: A Theatre of Traditional Korean Mask-Dance Drama." *Korea Journal* 21 (April 1981): 27-34.

Choe, Sang-su. *A Study of the Korean Puppet Play*. Korean Folklore Series, 4. Seoul: Korean Books, 1961.

Choe, Suk Hee. "*Yangju Byol Sandae Nori:* A Translation and Critical Introduction." M.A. Thesis, University of Kansas, 1969.

Chou, Prudence Sui-ning. "Lao She: An Intellectual's Role and Dilemma in Modern China." Ph.D. Dissertation, University of California at Berkeley, n.d.

Chujoy, Anatole, and Manchester, P.W., eds. *The Dance Encyclopedia*, rev. ed. New York: Simon and Schuster, 1967.

Cibber, Colley. *An Apology for the Life of Colley Cibber*. 2 vols. Edited by Robert W. Lowe. London: John C. Nimmo, 1889.

Clancy, James H. "The American *Antigone.*" *Educational Theatre Journal* 6 (October 1954): 249-253.

Clancy, J.D. Inc. *Catalog #52*. Syracuse, N.Y.: n.d.

Clark, Barrett, ed. *European Theories of the Drama*. Revised by Henry Popkin. New York: Crown, 1965.

Clark, Ebun. *Hubert Ogunde and His Theatre*. Lagos, Nigeria: Oxford University Press, 1978.

Clark, William Smith. *The Early Irish Stage*. Oxford: University Press, 1955.

————. *The Irish Stage in the County Towns*. Oxford: University Press, 1965.

Clurman, Harold. *The Fervent Years*. New York: Hill and Wang, 1957. New York: Harcourt, Brace, Jovanovich, 1975. Reprint of 1945, with Foreword and Epilogue of 1957 and a new Afterword by the author.

Cobin, Martin. "Traditional Theater and Modern Television in Japan." *Educational Theatre Journal* 21 (May 1969): 156-170.

Coger, Leslie Irene, and White, Melvin R. *Readers Theatre Handbook*, 3d ed. Glenview, Ill.: Scott, Foresman, 1981.

Cole, David. "The Visual Script: Theory and Technique." *The Drama Review* 20 (December 1976): 27-50.

Cole, Toby, and Chinoy, Helen Krich, eds. *Actors on Acting*, rev. ed. New York: Crown, 1970.

————. *Directors on Directing*, rev. ed. New York: Bobbs Merrill, 1963.

————. *Playwrights on Playwriting*. New York: Hill & Wang, 1961.

Cole, Wendell. "Current Trends in European Scene Design." *Educational Theatre Journal* 5 (March 1953): 27-32.

————. "The Triple Stage." *Educational Theatre Journal* 14 (December 1962): 302-311.

Collins, E.J. "Comic Opera in Ghana." *African Arts* 9 (January 1976): 50-57.

Collins, Fletcher, Jr. *The Production of Medieval Church Music-Drama*. Charlottesville: University Press of Virginia, 1972.

Collison, David. *Stage Sound*. 2d ed. London: Cassell, 1982.

Congreve, William. *Works*. 4 vols. Edited by Montague Summers. London: Nonesuch, 1923.

Conolly, Leonard W. *A Directory of British Theatre Research Resources in North America*. London: British Theatre Institute, 1978.

Conolly, Leonard W., and Wearing, J.P. *English Drama and Theatre, 1800-1900: A Guide to Information Sources*. Detroit: Gale Research, 1978.

Cooper, Lane. *Aristotle on the Art of Poetry*, rev. ed. Ithaca: Cornell University Press, 1947.

Copelin, David. "Chicano Theatre: *El Festival de los Teatros Chicanos.*" *The Drama Review* 17 (December 1973): 73-89.

Cornberg, Sol, and Gebauer, Emanuel L. *A Stage Crew Handbook*, 2d rev. ed. New York: Harper and Row, 1957.

Cornford, Francis Macdonald. *The Origin of Attic Comedy*. Edited by Theodor H. Gaster. Garden City, N.Y.: Anchor, Doubleday, 1961.

Corrigan, Robert W. "Some Aspects of Chekov's Dramaturgy." *Educational Theatre Journal* 7 (May 1955): 107-114.

Corrigan, Robert W., and Rosenberg, James L., eds. *The Context and Craft of Drama*. Boston: Little, Brown, 1972.

Corry, Percy. *Lighting the Stage*, 3d ed. London: Pitman, 1961.

————. *Stage Planning and Equipment for Multi-Purpose Halls, in Schools, Colleges, Little Theatres, Civic Theatres, Etc*. London: Strand Electric and Engineering Company, 1949.

Corson, Richard. *Stage Makeup*, 6th ed. New York: Prentice-Hall, 1981.

Cotgrave, Randle. *A Dictionarie of the French and English Tongues*. London: 1611.

Courtney, Richard. *Play, Drama & Thought: The Intellectual Background of Drama in Education*, 3d rev. ed. New York: Drama Book Specialists, 1974.

————. *Re-Play*. Toronto: Ontario Institute for Studies in Education, 1982.

Covarrubias, Miguel. *Island of Bali*. New York: Alfred A. Knopf, 1950.

Cowan, Suzanne. "The Throw-Away Theatre of Dario Fo." *The Drama Review* 19 (June 1975): 102-113.

Craftsman. London: 1727.

Craig, Edward Gordon. *Books and Theatres*. London: J.M. Dent, 1925.

————, ed. *The Mask: A Journal of the Art of the Theatre*, 15 vols. 1908-1929. Reprint. 13 vols. New York: Benjamin Blom, 1967.

————. *The Theatre-Advancing*. Boston: Little, Brown, 1919.

Cramptom, Esmé. *A Handbook of the Theatre*, 2d ed. Toronto: Gage, 1972.

Cravath, Paul. "Earth in Flower: An Historical and Descriptive Study of the Classical Dance Drama of Cambodia." Ph.D. dissertation, University of Hawaii, 1985.

Crawford, Ann Caddell. *Customs and Culture of Vietnam*. Rutland, Vt.: Tuttle, 1966.

Creese, Robb. "The Theatre of Mistakes." *The Drama Review* 23 (September 1979): 67-76.

Crothers, J. Francis. *The Puppeteer's Library Guide: The Bibliographic Index to the Literature of the World Puppet Theatre*. Metuchen, N.J.: Scarecrow, 1971.

Crump, J.I., and Malm, William P., eds. *Chinese and Japanese Music-Dramas*. Ann Arbor: Center for Chinese Studies, University of Michigan, 1975.

Cruz, Isagani R., ed. *A Short History of Theater in the Philippines*. n.p.: Philippine Educational Theatre Association, 1971.

Csato, Edward. *The Polish Theatre*. Translated by Christina Cenkalska. Warsaw: Polonia, 1963.

Cunningham, Peter; Planché, J.R.; and Collier, J. Payne. *Inigo Jones*. London: Shakespeare Society, 1848.

Dace, Wallace. "The Dramatic Structure of Schönberg's *Erwartung*." *Educational Theatre Journal* 5 (December 1953): 322-327.

Daily Advertiser. London: 1733 and 1744.

Daily Post. London: 1733.

Daily Post and General Advertiser. London: 1736.

Dale, Amy Marjorie. *Collected Papers of A.M. Dale*. Edited by T.B.L. Webster and E.G. Turner. London: Cambridge University Press, 1969.

Dana, Henry Wadsworth Longfellow. *Drama in Wartime Russia*. New York: National Council of American-Soviet Friendship, 1943.

Dancing Times. Edited by Philip J.S. Richardson. London: n.p., 1927.

Darnutzer, Don, and Hemsley, Gilbert. "Cinegel Diffusion Media." Edited by Ned A. Bowman and Nick Bryson. *Technotes 4*. Port Chester, N.Y.: Rosco, 1981.

Davenant, William. *The Works of Sir William Davenant*. 2 vols. 1673. Reprint. New York: Benjamin Blom, 1968.

Davidow, Mike. *People's Theatre: From the Box Office to the Stage*. Moscow: Progress Publishers, 1977.

Davidson, Charles. *Studies in the English Mystery Plays*. 1909. Reprint. New York: Haskell House, 1965.

Davies, Robertson. *The Fifth Business*. New York: Viking, 1970.

Davies, Thomas. *Dramatic Miscellanies*. 3 vols. London: 1784.

Davis, Eugene C. *Amateur Theater Handbook*. New York: Greenberg, 1945.

Davis, Jed, and Behm, Tom. "Terminology of Drama/Theatre With and For Children: A Redefinition." *Children's Theatre Review* 27 (1978), 10-11.

Davis, Jed, and Evans, Mary Jane. *Theatre, Children and Youth*. New Orleans: Anchorage Press, 1982.

Davis, Norman, ed. *Non-Cycle Plays and Fragments*. London: Oxford University Press, 1970.

Davy, Kate. "An Interview with George Burns." *Educational Theatre Journal* 27 (October 1975): 345-355.

Deák, František. "Structuralism in Theatre: The Prague School Contribution." *The Drama Review* 20 (December 1970): 83-94.

———. "*Théâtre du Grand Guignol*." *The Drama Review* 18 (March 1974): 34-43.

———. "Two Manifestos: The Influence of Italian Futurism in Russia." *The Drama Review* 19 (December 1975): 88-94.

Dean, Alexander. *Fundamentals of Play Directing*. New York: Farrar, 1941.

Dean, Alexander, and Carra, Lawrence. *Fundamentals of Play Directing*, 4th ed. New York: Holt, Rinehart and Winston, 1980.

Dell, Cecily. *A Primer for Movement Description*. New York: Dance Notation Bureau, 1970.

Dent, Edward Joseph. *Opera*. 1949. Reprint. Westport, Conn.: Greenwood, 1978.

Despot, Adriane. "Jean-Gaspard Deburau and the Pantomime at the Théâtre des Funambules." *Educational Theatre Journal* 27 (October 1975): 364-376.

de Zoete, Beryl, and Spies, Walter. *Dance and Drama in Bali*. 1938. Reprint. Kuala Lumpur: Oxford University Press, 1973.

Dhaninivat, H.H. Prince. *The Nang*, 3d ed. Thai Culture New Series 3. Bangkok: Fine Arts Department, 1962.

Dhaninivat, H.H. Prince, and Yupho, Dhanit. *The Khon*, 3d ed. Thai Culture New Series 6. Bangkok: The Fine Arts Department, 1962

Dietrich, John E., with Ralph Duckwall. *Play Direction*, 2d ed. New York: Prentice-Hall, 1983.

Digby, George. *Elvira*. London: 1667.

Disher, Maurice. *Blood and Thunder*. London: Muller, 1949.

Dolby, William, ed. and trans. *Eight Chinese Plays: From the Thirteenth Century to the Present*. New York: Columbia University Press, 1978.

―――. *A History of Chinese Drama*. New York: Barnes & Noble, 1976.

Dolezelova-Velingerova, M., and Crump, J.I., trans. *Ballad of the Hidden Dragon*. London: Oxford University Press, 1971.

Dolman, John, Jr. *The Art of Acting*. New York: Harper & Brothers, 1949.

Dolman, John, Jr., and Knaub, Richard K. *The Art of Play Production*, 3d ed. New York: Harper and Row, 1973.

Donohue, Joseph. "Burletta and the Early Nineteenth-Century English Theatre." *Nineteenth Century Theatre Research* 1 (Spring 1973): 29-51.

―――. *Dramatic Character in the English Romantic Age*. Princeton: Princeton University Press, 1970.

―――. *Theatre in the Age of Kean*. Totowa, N.J.: Rowman and Littlefield, 1975.

―――, ed. *The Theatrical Manager in England and America*. Princeton: Princeton University Press, 1971.

Downs, Harold. *Theatre and Stage*, 2 vols. London: Pitman, 1934.

Dreher, Denise. *From the Neck Up: An Illustrated Guide to Hatmaking*. Minneapolis: Madhatter, 1981.

Drummond, A.M. *Play Production for the Country Theatre*. Ithaca: Cornell University Extension Service, 1924.

Dryden, Deborah. *Fabric Painting and Dyeing for the Theatre*. New York: Drama Book Publishers, 1981.

Dryden, John. *The Works of John Dryden*. Berkeley: University of California Press, 1962—. In progress.

―――. "The Vindication of the Duke of Guise." In *The Works of John Dryden*, vol. 7. Edited by Sir Walter Scott and George Saintsbury. Edinburgh: William Patterson, 1883.

Dryden, John, and Lee, Nathaniel. *Oedipus*. London: 1679.

Duchartre, Pierre Louis. *The Italian Comedy*. Translated by Randolph T. Weaver. 1929. Reprint. New York: Dover, 1966.

Duckworth, George, ed. *The Complete Roman Drama*, 2d ed. rev. 2 vols. New York: Random House, 1967.

―――. *The Nature of Roman Comedy*. Princeton: University Press, 1957.

Duerr, Edwin. *The Length and Breadth of Acting.* New York: Holt, Rinehart and Winston, 1962.

Duffett, Thomas. *Psyche Debauched.* London: 1678.

Duffy, Charles, and Pettit, H.J. *A Dictionary of Literary Terms,* rev. ed. Denver: University of Denver Press, 1952.

Dukore, Bernard F., ed. *Dramatic Theory and Criticism: Greeks to Grotowski.* New York: Holt, Rinehart Winston, 1974.

Dunham, Katherine. "Open Letter to Black Theaters." *The Black Scholar* 10 (July-August 1979): 3-6.

Dunn, Charles J. *The Early Japanese Puppet Drama.* London: Luzac, 1966.

Dunn, Charles J., and Torigoe, Bunzo, editors and translators. *The Actor's Analects: Yakusha Rongo.* New York: Columbia University Press, 1969.

Durham, Weldon B. "The Tightening Rein: Relations Between the Federal Government and the American Theatre Industry During World War One." *Educational Theatre Journal* 30 (October 1978): 387-397.

Duriyanga, Phra Chen. *Thai Music in Western Notation.* Thai Culture New Series no. 16. Bangkok: The Fine Arts Department, 1962.

Dye, William S., Jr. *A Study of Melodrama in England from 1800 to 1840.* State College, Pa.: Nittany, 1919.

Ebon, Martin, ed. *Five Chinese Communist Plays.* New York: John Day, 1975.

Eccles, Mark. *Christopher Marlowe in London.* Cambridge: Harvard University Press, 1934.

Edwards, Christine. *The Stanislavsky Heritage: Its Contribution to the Russian and American Theatre.* New York: New York University Press, 1965.

Ellis, Frank H., ed. *Poems on Affairs of State.* vol. VI, 1697-1704. New Haven: Yale University Press, 1970.

Else, Gerald. *Aristotle: Poetics.* See: Aristotle.

———. *Aristotle's Poetics: The Argument.* Cambridge: Harvard University Press 1957.

Endicott, K.M. *An Analysis of Malay Magic.* Oxford: Clarendon, 1970.

Ernst, Earle. *The Kabuki Theatre.* New York: Oxford University Press, 1956.

———, ed. *Three Japanese Plays from the Traditional Theatre.* 1959. Reprint. Westport, Conn.: Greenwood, 1976.

Eshkol, Noa, and Wachmann, Abraham. *Movement Notation.* London: Weidenfeld and Nicolson, 1958.

Esslin, Martin. *Brecht: The Man and His Work,* rev. ed. Garden City, N.Y.: Anchor, 1971.

———. "Max Reinhardt: High Priest of Theatricality." *The Drama Review* 21 (June 1977): 3-24.

———. *The Theatre of the Absurd,* rev. ed. New York: Anchor, 1969.

Evans, M. Blakemore. *The Passion Play of Lucerne.* New York: The Modern Language Association of America, 1943.

Everard, Edward Cape. *Memoirs of an Unfortunate Son of Thespis.* Edinburgh: James Ballantyne, 1818.

Ewen, David. *Complete Book of the American Musical Theater,* rev. ed. New York: Henry Holt, 1959.

Fairbanks, Douglas, Jr. "The Amazing Years of Cinema." PBS, 1983.

Falk, Florence. "Cosmic Mass." *The Drama Review* 20 (March 1976): 90-98.

———. "Physics and the Theatre: Richard Foreman's *Particle Theory.*" *Educational Theatre Journal* 29 (October 1977): 395-404.

Falk, Heinrich Richard. "Actors, Audiences and Theatrical *Sainetes*: A Formula for Success on the Eighteenth-Century Stage." *Educational Theatre Journal* 28 (October 1976): 299-311.

———. "A Census of the Provincial Theatre in Eighteenth-Century Spain." *Theatre Survey* 20 (May 1979): 75-123.

Fane, Francis. *Love in the Dark.* London: 1675.

Fay, William G. *A Short Glossary of Theatrical Terms.* New York: Samuel French, 1930.

Feldenkrais, Moshe. "Image, Movement and Actor: Restoration of Potentiality." Translated and edited by Kelly Morris. *Tulane Drama Review* 10 (Spring 1966): 112-126.

Fergusson, Francis. *The Idea of a Theater.* Princeton: University Press, 1968.

Fernández, Doreen G. *The Iloilo Zarzuela: 1903-1930.* Quezon City: Ateneo de Manila University Press, 1978.

Fernández, Oscar. "Black Theatre in Brazil." *Educational Theatre Journal* 29 (March 1977): 5-17.

Ferraro, Susan. "The Clamor for Klezmer." *American Way* (American Airlines magazine), July 1983, pp. 54-57.

Findlay, Robert R., and Filipowicz-Findlay, Halina. "The 'Other Theatre' of Wroclaw: Henryk Tomaszewski and the Pantomima." *Educational Theatre Journal* 27 (December 1975): 453-465.

Flecknoe, Richard. *Love's Kingdom.* London: 1664.

———. *Miscellania.* London: 1653.

Flickinger, Roy C. *The Greek Theater and its Drama,* 4th ed. Chicago: University of Chicago Press, 1936.

———. *Plutarch as a Source of Information on the Greek Theater.* Chicago: University of Chicago Press, 1904.

Flying Post. London: 1700.

Foley, Mary Kathleen. "Sundanese Wayang Golek." Ph.D. Dissertation, University of Hawaii, 1979.

Folger Shakespeare Library, Washington, D.C., manuscripts.

Foregger, Nikolai. "Experiments in the Art of Drama." Translated by D. Miller. *The Drama Review* 19 (March 1975): 74-77.

Foreign Languages Press. *China: Folk Arts of the New China.* Peking, 1954.

Foust, Clement. *The Life and Dramatic Works of Robert Montgomery Bird.* New York: Knickerbocker, 1919.

Frank, Grace. *The Medieval French Drama.* Oxford: Clarendon, 1954.

Fraser, Douglas, and Cole, Herbert M., eds. *African Art and Leadership.* Madison: University of Wisconsin Press, 1972.

Frazer, James George. *The Golden Bough,* 3d ed., 12 vols. London: Macmillan, 1919-1920.

Frere, Walter. *The Winchester Troper.* London: Harrison and Sons, 1894.

Frick, John, and Johnson, Stephen. "'Tricks and Treats' on Coney Island." *The Drama Review* 26 (Spring 1982): 132-136.

Friederich, Willard J., and Fraser, John H. *Scenery Design for the Amateur Stage.* New York: Macmillan, 1950.

Fuchs, Georg. *The Revolution In the Theater*. Translated by Constance Conner Kuhn. Ithaca: Cornell University Press, 1959.

Fuchs, J.W. *Classics Illustrated Dictionary*. Translated by Livia Visser-Fuchs. New York: Oxford University Press, 1974.

Fuchs, Theodore. *Stage Lighting*, 1929. Reprint. New York: Benjamin Blom, 1963.

Fuegi, John. *The Essential Brecht*. Los Angeles: Hennessey & Ingalls, 1972.

Fuerst, Walter René, and Hume, Samuel J. *Twentieth Century Stage Decoration*. 2 vols. London: Alfred A. Knopf, 1928.

Fülöp-Miller, René, and Gregor, Joseph. *The Russian Theatre; Its Character and History with Especial Reference to the Revolutionary Period*. Translated by Paul England. London: G.G. Harrap, 1930.

von Furer-Haimendorf, Elizabeth. *An Anthropological Bibliography of South Asia Together with a Directory of Recent Anthropological Field Work*. Paris: Mouton, 1958.

Gadberry, Glen. "The *Thingspiel* and *Das Frankenberger Wurfelspiel*." *The Drama Review* 24 (March 1980): 103-114.

Gallaway, Marian. *Constructing a Play*, 1950. Reprint. Philadelphia: Century Bookbinders, 1981.

Gamble, Sidney D., ed. *Chinese Village Plays from the Ting Hsien Region: A Collection of 48 Rural Plays as Staged by Villagers from Ting Hsien in Northern China*. New York: Abner Schram, 1972.

Gamble, William Burt. *Development of Scenic Art and Stage Machinery*. New York: New York Public Library, 1928.

Gargi, Balwant. *Folk Theatre of India*. Seattle: University of Washington Press, 1966.

———. *Theatre in India*. New York: Theatre Arts Books, 1962.

Garrick, David. *Letters*. Edited by David M. Little and George M. Kahrl. 3 vols. Cambridge, Mass.: Belknap Press of Harvard University Press, 1963.

Gascoigne, Bamber. *World Theatre*. Boston: Little, Brown, 1968.

Gassner, John. "Broadway in Review." *Educational Theatre Journal* 7 (December 1955), 315–323.

———. ed. *A Treasury of the Theatre; From Aeschuylus to Ostrowsky*. 3d ed. New York: Simon & Schuster, 1967.

Gassner, John, and Allen, Ralph G., eds. *Theatre and Drama in the Making*. 2 vols. Boston: Houghton Mifflin, 1964.

Gassner, John, and Barber, Philip. *Producing the Play*, with *The New Scene Technician's Handbook*, rev. ed. New York: Holt, Rinehart and Winston, 1953.

Gassner, John, and Quinn, Edward, eds. *The Reader's Encyclopedia of World Drama*. New York: Crowell, 1969.

Geen, Michael. *Theatrical Costume and the Amateur Stage*. London: Arco, 1968.

Gerard, Albert. "The Birth of Theatre in Madagascar." Translated by Anthony Graham-White. *Educational Theatre Journal* 25 (October 1973): 362-365.

Gerould, Daniel. "Bim-Bom and the Afanasjew Family Circus." *The Drama Review* 18 (March 1974): 99-103.

———. "Eisenstein's *Wiseman*." *The Drama Review* 18 (March 1974): 71-76.

———, ed. *20th Century Polish Avant-Garde Drama*. Ithaca: Cornell University Press, 1977.

Gershman, Judith. "Daniel Mesguich's Shakespeare's *Hamlet*." *The Drama Review* 25 (Summer 1981): 17-28.

Gibson, Michael. "Brook's Africa." *The Drama Review* 17 (September 1973): 37-51.

Gibson, William. *The Seasaw Log.* New York: Knopf, 1959.

Gidley, C.G.B. "Yankamanci—The Craft of the Hausa Comedians." *African Language Studies* 8 (1967): 52-81.

Gilbert, Douglas. *American Vaudeville; Its Life and Times.* New York: Dover, 1940.

Gildon, Charles. *The Life of Mr. Thomas Betterton.* London: 1710.

Gillespie, Patti, and Cameron, Kenneth. *Western Theatre.* New York: Macmillan, 1984.

Gillette, Arnold S. *Stage Scenery: Its Construction and Rigging,* 2d ed., New York: Harper and Row, 1972.

Gillette, Arnold S., and Gillette, J. Michael. *Stage Scenery,* 3rd ed. New York: Harper and Row, 1981.

Godard, Colette. "Sören Brunen's *Figurer.*" *The Drama Review* 14 (Fall 1969): 86-91.

Goff, Lewin. "The Owen Davis-Al Woods Melodrama Factory." *Educational Theatre Journal* 11 (October 1959): 200-207.

Goffin, Peter. *Stage Lighting for Amateurs,* 4th ed. Chicago: Coach House, 1955.

Goldberg, Moses. *Children's Theatre, A Philosophy and a Method.* Englewood Cliffs, N.J.: Prentice-Hall, 1974.

Golden, John, and Shore, Viola Brothers. *Stage-Struck.* New York: Samuel French, 1930.

Golden, Leon, translator, and Hardison, O.B., commentator. *Aristotle's Poetics: A Translation and Commentary for Students of Literature.* Englewood Cliffs, N.J.: Prentice-Hall, 1968.

Goodman, Judith, and Prosperi, Mario. "Drama Therapies in Hospitals." *The Drama Review* 20 (March 1976): 20-30.

Gorchakov, Nikolaï Aleksandrovich. *The Theater in Soviet Russia.* Translated by Edgar Lehrman. New York: Columbia University Press, 1957.

Gordon, Mel. "German Expressionist Acting." *The Drama Review* 19 (September 1975): 34-50.

Gorelik, Mordecai. *New Theatres for Old.* 1940. Reprint. New York: E.P. Dutton, 1962.

Gougerot, Abbé Jean. *Lettre sur la Peinture, la Sculpture et l'Architecture a M***.* Amsterdam: 1749.

Gove, Philip Babcock, Editor in chief. *Webster's Third New International Dictionary.* Springfield, Mass.: G. & C. Merriam, 1979.

Graham-White, Anthony. *The Drama of Black Africa.* New York: Samuel French, 1974.

———. Review of *The Reader's Encyclopedia of World Drama.* Edited by John Gassner and Edward Quinn. *Educational Theatre Journal* 22 (May 1980): 230-232.

———. "'Ritual' in Contemporary Theatre and Criticism." *Educational Theatre Journal* 28 (October 1976): 318-324.

Grant, Gail. *Technical Manual and Dictionary of Classical Ballet,* 2d rev. ed. New York: Dover, 1967.

Granville, Wilfred. *The Theater Dictionary: British and American Terms in the Drama, Opera, and Ballet.* New York: Philosophical Library, 1952.

Grebanier, Bernard. *Playwriting.* 1961. Reprint. New York: Barnes and Noble, 1979.

Greg, W.W. "Act-Divisions in Shakespeare." *Review of English Studies* 4 (April 1928): 152-158.

———. *Dramatic Documents from the Elizabethan Playhouses.* 2 vols. 1931. Reprint. Oxford: Clarendon, 1969.

Gregersen, Edgar A. *Language in Africa.* New York: Gordon and Breach, 1977.

Grimes, Ron. "The Theatre of Sources." *The Drama Review* 25 (Fall 1981): 67-74.

Grossman, Manuel L. "Alfred Jarry and the Theatre of the Absurd." *Educational Theatre Journal* 19 (December 1967): 473-477.

Grotowski, Jerzy. *Towards a Poor Theatre*. New York: Clarion, 1968.

Grove's Dictionary of Music and Musicians, 5th ed. Edited by Eric Blom. New York: St. Martins, 1954. See also: *New Grove Dictionary*.

Gründ-Khaznader [*recte*:-Khaznadar], Francoise. "Masked Dances and Ritual in Tanzania, Mozambique and Zambia." *The Drama Review* 25 (Winter 1981): 25-38.

Gruver, Elbert. *A Stage Manager's Handbook*. Revised by Frank Hamilton. New York: Drama Book Specialists, 1972.

GTE Sylvania, Inc. *Sylvania Lighting Handbook*, 6th ed. Danvers, Mass.: GTE Sylvania, Inc., 1977.

Gunji, Masakatsu. *Buyo: The Classical Dance*. Translated by Don Kenny. New York: Weatherhill/Tankosha, 1971.

———. *Kabuki*. Translated by John Bester. Palo Alto: Kodansha International, 1970.

Haigh, Arthur E. *The Attic Theatre*. Revised by A.W. Pickard-Cambridge. Oxford: Clarendon Press, 1907.

———. *The Tragic Drama of the Greeks*. 1896. Reprint. Oxford: Clarendon, 1938.

Haight, Elizabeth H. *The Symbolism of the House Door in Classical Poetry*. New York: Longmans, Green, 1950.

Haims, Lynn. "First American Theatre Contracts: Wall and Lindsay's Maryland Company of Comedians, and the Annapolis, Fells Point and Baltimore Theatres, 1781-1783." *Theatre Survey* 17 (November 1976): 179-194.

Halford, Aubrey S., and Halford, Giovanna M. *The Kabuki Handbook: A Guide to Understanding and Appreciation, With Summaries of Favorite Plays, Explanatory Notes, and Illustrations*. Rutland, Vt.: Tuttle, 1956.

Hall, John Whitney, and Toyoda, Takeshi, eds. *Japan in the Muromachi Age*. Berkeley: University of California Press, 1977.

Halson, Elizabeth. *Peking Opera: A Short Guide*. Hong Kong: Oxford University Press, 1966.

Halstead, William Perdue. *Stage Management for the Amateur Theatre*. New York: F.S. Crofts, 1937.

Hamamura, Yonezo, et al. *Kabuki*. Edited and Translated by Fumio Takano. Tokyo: Hokuseido, 1956.

Hamilton, Clayton. *So You're Writing a Play!* Boston: Little, Brown, 1935.

———. *Studies in Stagecraft*. New York: Henry Holt, 1914.

———. *The Theory of the Theatre*. 1913. Reprint. New York: Henry Holt, 1939.

Hamilton, Henry, and Legros, E. *Dictionnaire International Français-Anglais*, vol. 2. Paris: A. Fouraut, 1901.

Harcourt, Robertson. *Burmese Vignettes, 24 Sketches of Burmese Life and Character*. London: Luzac, 1949.

Hardingham, Martin. *The Fabric Catalog*. New York: Pocket Books, 1978.

Hardison, Felicia. "Valle-Inclán and Artaud: Brothers Under the Skin." *Educational Theatre Journal* 19 (December 1967): 455-466.

Hare, W.B. *The Minstrel Encyclopedia*. Boston: Walter H. Baker, 1926.

Harris, Jessica. "Toward a New Senegalese Theatre." *The Drama Review* 25 (Winter 1981): 13-18.

Harrison, Jane Ellen. *Ancient Art and Ritual*. (Home University Library of Modern Knowledge, no. 70). New York: Holt, 1913.

————. *Themis*. Cambridge: University Press, 1927.

Harsh, Philip W. "Angiportum, Platea and Vicus." *Classical Philology* 32 (1937): 44-58.

————. *A Handbook of Classical Drama*. Stanford: University Press, 1944.

Hartmann, Louis. *Theatre Lighting; A Manual of the Stage Switchboard*. New York: D. Appleton, 1930.

Hartnoll, Phyllis, ed. *The Oxford Companion to the Theatre*. Oxford: Oxford University Press, 3d ed.1967, 4th ed.1983.

Hase, Karl. *Miracle Plays and Sacred Dramas*. Boston: Houghton, Mifflin, 1880.

Haslewood, Joseph. *The Secret History of the Green Room*, 2d ed. London: 1792.

Hatlen, Theodore W. *Orientation to the Theatre*, 3d ed. Englewood Cliffs, N.J.: Prentice-Hall, 1981.

Hauch, Duane Ernie. "A Descriptive Study of Hat Boi, the Classical Theatre of Viet Nam." Master's Thesis, University of Hawaii, 1970.

Hawkins, Frederick. *Annals of the French Stage*. 2 vols. 1884. Reprint. New York: Greenwood, 1969.

————. *The French Stage in the 18th Century*. 2 vols. 1888. Reprint. New York: Haskell House, 1969.

Hawley, John Stratton. *A Play with Krishna*. Princeton: University Press, 1981.

Hayashiya, Tatsusaburo. "Ancient History and Performing Arts." *Acta Asiatica* 33 (1977): 1-14.

Hayden, George A., ed. and trans. *Crime and Punishment in Medieval Chinese Drama: Three Judge Pao Plays*. Cambridge: Harvard University Press, 1978.

Hayes, Elizabeth R. *An Introduction to the Teaching of Dance*. New York: Ronald Press, 1964.

Hayes, Helen, and Sandford, Dody. *On Reflection; An Autobiography*. New York: M. Evans, 1968.

Hebel, John William, and Hudson, Hoyt H., eds. *Poetry of the English Renaissance, 1509-1660*. c. 1929. Reprint. New York: F.S. Crofts, 1940.

Heffner, Hubert C., et al. *Modern Theatre Practice*, 5th ed. New York: Appleton-Century Crofts, 1973.

Hein, Norvin. *The Miracle Plays of Mathura*. New Haven: Yale University Press, 1972.

Heinig, Ruth Beall, and Stillwell, Lyda. *Creative Drama for the Classroom Teacher*. Englewood Cliffs, N.J.: Prentice-Hall, 1974.

Helbing, Terry. "Gay Plays, Gay Theatre, Gay Performance." *The Drama Review* 25 (March 1981): 35-46.

Helvenston, Harold. *Scenery*. Stanford: Stanford University Press, 1931.

Hemsley, Gilbert, and Darnutzer, Don. "Using Light Diffusion Media." Edited by Ned A. Bowman and Nick Bryson. *Technotes 3*. Port Chester, N.Y.: Rosco, 1980.

Hennequin, Alfred. *The Art of Playwriting*. Boston: Houghton, Mifflin, 1890.

Henshaw, N.W. "Graphic Sources for a Modern Approach to the Acting of Restoration Comedy." *Educational Theatre Journal* 20 (May 1968): 156-170.

Henshaw, Wandalie. "The 'Open Scene' as a Directing Exercise." *Educational Theatre Journal* 21 (October 1969): 275-284.

Henslowe, Philip. *Henslowe's Diary*. Edited by R.A. Foakes and R.T. Rickert. Cambridge: University Press, 1961.

————. *Henslowe's Diary*. Edited by W.W. Greg. 2 vols. London: A.H. Bullen, 1904-1908.

Hernandez, Tomas Capatan. *The Emergence of Modern Drama in the Philippines (1898-1912)*. Philippine Studies Working Paper no. 1. Honolulu: University of Hawaii Asian Studies Program, 1976.

Herzel, Roger W. "Anagnorisis and Peripeteia in Comedy." *Educational Theatre Journal* 26 (December 1974): 495-505.

Hesler, Richard. "A New Look at the Theatre of Lope de Rueda." *Educational Theatre Journal* 16 (March 1964): 47-54.

Hewes, Henry. "Total Theatre." *The Saturday Review*, 26 January 1957, pp. 22-23.

Hewitt, Barnard W. *Art and Craft of Play Production*. Philadelphia: Lippincott, 1940.

———, ed. *The Renaissance Stage*. Translated by Allardyce Nicoll, John H. McDowell, and George Kernodle. Coral Gables: University of Miami Press, 1958.

———. *Theatre U.S.A. 1668 to 1957*. New York: McGraw-Hill, 1959.

Hewitt, Barnard; Foster, J.F.; and Wolle, Muriel S. *Play Production; Theory and Practice*. Chicago: J.B. Lippincott, 1959.

Highfill, Philip. "Rich's 1744 Inventory of Covent Garden Properties." *Restoration and 18th Century Theatre Research* 5 (May 1966): 7-17; 5 (November 1966): 17-26; 6 (May 1967): 28-35.

Highfill, Philip; Burnim, Kalman A.; and Langhans, Edward A. *A Biographical Dictionary of Actors, Actresses, Musicians, Dancers, Managers, and Other Stage Personnel in London, 1660-1800*. Carbondale: Southern Illinois University Press, 1973—. In progress.

Hill, Aaron, and Popple, William. *The Prompter*. Edited by William W. Appleton and Kalman A. Burnim. New York: Benjamin Blom, 1966.

Hill, Errol. "Calypso Drama." *Theatre Survey* 9 (November 1968): 45-64.

———, ed. *The Theater of Black Americans*. 2 vols. Englewood Cliffs, N.J.: Prentice-Hall, 1980.

———. *The Trinidad Carnival*. Austin: University of Texas Press, 1972.

Hobgood, Burnet M. "Central Conceptions in Stanislavski's System." *Educational Theatre Journal* 25 (May 1973): 147-159.

Hodge, Francis. *Play Directing: Analysis, Communication & Style*, 2d ed. Englewood Cliffs, N.J.: Prentice-Hall, 1982.

———. "Theatre and Its Developing Audience." *Educational Theatre Journal*. International Conference on Theatre Education and Development, 20 (August 1968): 269-290.

———. "Theat-*re* or Theat-*er*: Samuel Johnson or Noah/Merriam Webster?" *Theatre Survey* 9 (May 1968): 36-44.

Hoff, Frank. *Song, Dance, Storytelling: Aspects of the Performing Arts in Japan*. Ithaca: Cornell University China-Japan Program, 1978.

Hoff, Frank, and Flindt, Willi. "The Life Structure of Noh: An English Version of Yokomichi Mario's Analysis of the Structure of Noh." *Concerned Theatre Japan* 2, 3, 4 (Spring 1973): 209-256.

Hogan, Charles Beecher, ed. *The London Stage, 1660-1800*. Part 5: 1776-1800. 3 vols. Carbondale: Southern Illinois University Press, 1968.

Holmberg, Arthur. Review of a performance of *Coquelico*, by Josef Svoboda. New York: Laterna Magika, The Twenty-Two Steps Theater. 4 March 1979. *Theatre Journal* 31 (October 1979): 416-417.

Holt, Claire. *Art in Indonesia: Continuities and Change*. Ithaca: Cornell University Press, 1967.

Honolulu Advertiser.

Hood, Mantle. "The Enduring Tradition: Music and Theatre in Java and Bali." In *Indonesia*, edited by Ruth T. McVey. New Haven: Human Relations Area Files Press, 1963.

————. *The Nuclear Theme as a Determinant of Patet in Javanese Music*. Groningen, The Netherlands: J.B. Wolters, 1954.

Hooykaas, Christiaan. *Kama and Kala: Materials for the Study of Shadow Theatre in Bali*. Amsterdam: North Holland, 1973.

Hopi Indian Calendar. Phoenix, Ariz.: Pelley Studios, 1981.

Horiguchi, Yasuo. "Literature and Performing Arts in the Medieval Age—Kan'ami's Dramaturgy." *Acta Asiatica* 33 (1977): 15-31.

Hornby, Richard. *Script into Performance*. Austin: University of Texas Press, 1977.

Horton, Robin. "The Kalabari Ekine Society: A Borderland of Religion and Art." *Africa* 33 (April 1963): 94-114.

Hosley, Richard. "The Origins of the So-called Elizabethan Multiple Stage." *The Drama Review* 12 (Winter 1968): 28–50.

————, ed. *Shakespeare's Holinshed*. New York: Putnam, 1968.

Hotson, Leslie. *The Commonwealth and Restoration Stage*. Cambridge, Mass.: Harvard University Press, 1928.

————. *Shakespeare's Wooden O*. New York: Macmillan, 1960.

Houghton, Norris. *Moscow Rehearsals: The Golden Age of the Soviet Theatre*. 2d ed. New York: Grove, 1962.

————. *Return Engagement: A Postscript to "Moscow Rehearsals"*. New York: Holt, Rinehart and Winston, 1962.

Howard, Roger. *Contemporary Chinese Theatre*. Hong Kong: Heinemann, 1978.

Howells, William Dean. *Complete Plays*. Edited by Walter J. Meserve. New York: New York University Press, 1960.

Hu, John Yaw-herng. *Ts'ao Yu*. New York: Twayne, 1972.

Hu, Qiaomu, ed. *Zhongguo Da Baike Quanshu: Xiqu Quyi*. Beijing: Zhongguo Da Baike Quanshu Chubanshe, 1983.

Hudson, Lynton. *The English Stage, 1850-1950*. London: G.G. Harrap, 1951.

Huerta, Jorge A. *"El Teatro de la Esperanza"*. *The Drama Review* 21 (March 1977): 37-46.

Hughes, Alan. "Henry Irving's Tragedy of Shylock." *Educational Theatre Journal* 24 (October 1972): 249-268.

Hughes, Langston, and Meltzer, Milton. *Black Magic: A Pictorial History of Black Entertainers in America*. New York: Bonanza Books, 1967.

Hume, Robert, ed. *The London Theatre World, 1660-1800*. Carbondale: Southern Illinois University Press, 1980.

Hume, Samuel J., and Foster, Lois. *Theatre and School*. New York: Samuel French, 1932.

Hunt, Hugh. *The Live Theatre*. London: Oxford University Press, 1962.

Hunt, Tamara, and Renfro, Nancy. *Pocketful of Puppets: Mother Goose*. Austin, Texas: Nancy Renfro Studios, 1982.

————. *Puppetry in Early Childhood Education*. Austin, Texas: Nancy Renfro Studios, 1982.

Huston, Hollis. "Dimensions of Mime Space." *Educational Theatre Journal* 30 (March 1978): 63-72.

Idema, Wilt, and West, Stephen. *Chinese Theater, 1100-1450: A Source Book*. Weisbaden: Franz Steiner, 1982.

Immoss, Thomas, and Mayer, Fred. *Japanese Theatre*. New York: Macmillan, 1977.

Ingersoll, Fern S., trans. *Sang Thong. A Dance-Drama from Thailand*. Written by King Rama II and the poets of his court. Rutland, Vt.: Tuttle, 1973.

Ingham, Rosemary, and Covey, Elizabeth. *The Costumer's Handbook: How to Make All Kinds of Costumes*. Englewood Cliffs, N.J.: Prentice-Hall, 1980.

Innes, R.A. *Costumes of Upper Burma and the Shan States in the Collections of Bankfield Museum*. Halifax: Halifax Museums, 1957.

Inoura, Yoshinobu. *A History of Japanese Theatre I: Up to Noh and Kyogen*. Tokyo: Kokusai Bunka Shinkokai, 1971.

Irwin, Vera R., ed. *Four Classical Asian Plays in Modern Translation*. Harmondsworth, Essex: Penguin Books, 1972.

Isaac, Dan. "Theatre of Fact." *The Drama Review* 15 (Summer 1971): 109-135.

Isaacs, Edith J.R., ed. *Theatre, Essays on the Arts of the Theatre*. Boston: Little, Brown, 1927.

Izenour, George C. *Theater Design*. New York: McGraw-Hill, 1977.

Jablonski, Edward, and Stewart, Lawrence D. *The Gershwin Years*, 2d ed. Garden City, N.Y.: Doubleday, 1973.

Jackson, Arthur. *The Book of Musicals, from Showboat to Evita*, rev. ed. London: Mitchell Beazley, 1979.

Jacobus, Marion. "Puppets at Parisian Fairs 1649-1742." *Educational Theatre Journal* 18 (May 1966): 110-121.

Japanese Tradition: Search and Research. Conference Journal, Asian Performing Arts Summer Institute. Los Angeles: University of California, 1981.

Jenkins, Linda Walsh, and Wapp, Ed, Jr. "Native American Performance." *The Drama Review* 20 (June 1976): 5-12.

Jerstad, Luther. *Mani-Rimdu: Sherpa Dance-Drama*. Seattle: University of Washington Press, 1969.

Johnson, Samuel, ed. *The Plays of William Shakespeare*, vol. I. London: 1765.

Johnson, Steven Mark. "Using LEDs." *Theatre Crafts* (April 1982): 35, 38–39.

Johnston, Mary. *Exits and Entrances in Roman Comedy*. Geneva, N.Y.: Humphrey Press, 1933.

Jones, Clifford R., and Jones, Betty True. *Kathakali: An Introduction to the Dance-Drama of Kerala*. San Francisco: The American Society for Eastern Arts and Theatre Arts Books, 1970.

Jonson, Ben. *Three Masques*. New York: Robert Grier Cook, 1903.

Josefsberg, Milt. *The Jack Benny Show*. New Rochelle, N.Y.: Arlington House, 1977.

Kale, Pramod. *The Theatric Universe*. Bombay: Popular Prakashan, 1974.

Kalvodova, Dana, and Vanis, Sis. "The Origin and Structure of the Szechwan Theatre." *Archiv Orientalni* 34, (1966): 505-523.

Kamlongera, Christopher F. "Theatre for Development: The Case of Malawi." *Theatre Research International* 7 (Autumn 1982): 207-221.

Karanth, K. Shivarama. *Yaksagana*. Manasagangotra, Mysore: The Institute of Kannada Studies, University of Mysore, 1975.

Kardoss, John. *An Outline History of Korean Drama*. Greenvale, N.Y.: Long Island University Press, 1966.

Karnis, Michael V. "The Crisis in the Argentine Theatre." *Educational Theatre Journal* 5 (December 1953): 306-312.

————. "The Role of the River Plate in Colonial Hispanic American Drama." *Educational Theatre Journal* 7 (May 1955): 102-106.

————. "Surviving Pre-Columbian Drama." *Educational Theatre Journal* 4 (March 1952): 39-45.

Kawatake, Shigetoshi. *Kabuki, Japanese Drama*. Tokyo: Foreign Affairs Association of Japan, 1958.

Kawatake, Toshio. *A History of Japanese Theatre II: Bunraku and Kabuki*. Tokyo: Kokusai Bunka Shinkokai, 1971.

Keene, Donald. *Bunraku: The Art of the Japanese Puppet Theatre*. Tokyo: Kodansha International, 1965.

————, ed. *Major Plays of Chikamatsu*. New York: Columbia University Press, 1961.

————. *No: The Classical Theatre of Japan*. Palo Alto, Calif.: Kodansha International, 1966.

————, ed. *Twenty Plays of the No Theatre*. New York: Columbia University Press, 1970.

Keith, Arthur Berriedale. *The Sanskrit Drama in its Origin, Development, Theory and Practice*. London: Oxford University Press, 1924.

Kennard, Joseph Spencer. *The Italian Theatre from its Beginning to the Close of the Seventeenth Century*. 2 vols. 1932. Reprint. New York: Benjamin Blom, 1964.

————. *Masks and Marionettes*. Port Washington, N.Y.: Kennikat Press, 1967.

Kenny, Don. *A Guide to Kyogen*. Tokyo: Hinoki Shoten, 1968.

Kernodle, George R. *From Art to Theatre*. Chicago: University of Chicago Press, 1944.

————. *Invitation to the Theatre*. New York: Harcourt Brace & World, 1967.

————. "Style, Stylization and Styles of Acting." *Educational Theatre Journal* 12 (December 1960): 251-261.

Kerr, Walter. *How Not to Write a Play*. New York: Simon & Schuster, 1955.

Kersley, Leo, and Sinclair, Janet. *A Dictionary of Ballet Terms*, 3d ed. London: Adam & Charles Black, 1977.

Khaing, Mi Mi. *Burmese Family*. London: Longmans, Green, 1946.

Khaznadar, Chérif. "Tendencies and Prospects for Third World Theatre." Translated by Norma Jean Deák. *The Drama Review* 17 (December 1973): 33-35.

Kim, Chŏng-hŭng, and Heyman, Alan. "Chinju Kŏmmu and T'ongyŏng Sŭngjŏnmu." *Korea Journal* 15 (1975): 51-55.

Kim, Ho Soon. "The Development of Modern Korean Theatre in South Korea." Ph.D. dissertation, University of Kansas, 1974.

Kim, Lai An-Quan. *The Vietnamese Theatre*. Saigon: Horizons, n.d.

Kim, Tong-uk. "On P'ansori." *Korea Journal* 13 (March 1973): 10-17.

Kim, Young Ja. "The Korean *Namsadang*". *The Drama Review* 25 (March 1981): 9-16.

Kincaid, Zoe. *Kabuki, the Popular Stage of Japan*. 1935. Reprint. New York: Arno Press, 1977.

King, T.J. *Shakespearean Staging, 1599-1642*. Cambridge: Harvard University Press, 1971.

Kirby, E.T. "Introduction: The New Dance." *The Drama Review* 16 (September 1972): 115-116.

Kirby, Michael. "Indigenous African Theatre." *The Drama Review* 18 (December 1974): 22-36.

――――. "Introduction" (to "Futurist Performance"). *The Drama Review* 15 (Fall 1970): 127-146.

――――. "Manifesto of Structuralism." *The Drama Review* 19 (December 1975): 82-83.

――――. "On Literary Theatre." *The Drama Review* 18 (June 1974): 103-113.

――――, ed. "Theatre in Asia." *The Drama Review* 15 (Spring 1971 issue).

Kirshenblatt-Gimblett, Barbara. "Contraband: Performance, Text and Analysis of a *Purim-shpil.*" *The Drama Reivew* 24 (September 1980): 5-16.

Kitto, H.D.F. *Greek Tragedy, A Literary Study*, 3d ed. London: Methuen, 1961.

Kleinau, Marion L., and McHughes, Janet L. *Theatres for Literature: A Practical Aesthetics for Group Interpretations.* Sherman Oaks, Calif.: Alfred Publishing, 1980.

Kliegl Theatrical-Decorative Spectacular Lighting. Catalog no. 40, 40th Anniversary Issue, n.d.

Komissarzhevskii, V. *Moscow Theatres.* Translated by Vic Schneierson and W. Perelman. Moscow: Foreign Language Publishing House, 1959.

Kommissarzhevskii, Fedor F. *Myself and the Theatre.* London: W. Heinemann, 1929.

Komiya, Toyotaka. *Japanese Culture in the Meiji Era.* Vol. 3. Translated and Adapted by Edward G. Seidensticker and Donald Keene. Tokyo: Obunsha, 1956.

Komparu, Kunio. *The Noh Theater: Principles and Perspectives.* New York: Weatherhill/ Tankosha, 1983.

Kongo, Iwao. *Noh Costumes.* Translated by Chitose Kuroha. Kyoto: Korinsha, 1949.

Konishi, Jinichi. "New Approaches to the Study of the No Drama." *The Bulletin of the Tokyo Kyoku University Literature Department* 27 (1960): 1-31.

Korean Center of ITI. *The Korean Theatre: Past and Present.* Seoul: Korean Center of ITI, n.d.

Korean National Commission for UNESCO. *Traditional Performing Arts of Korea.* Seoul: Korean National Commission for UNESCO, 1975.

Korean Overseas Information Service. *Masks of Korea.* Seoul: Ministry of Culture and Information, 1981.

Kothari, Sunil. "Kathakali, the Sacred Dance-Drama of Kerala." *Marg: A Magazine of the Arts* 32 (1979): 55-64.

Kourilsky, Françoise. "Dada and Circus: Bread and Puppet Theatre." *The Drama Review* 18 (March 1974): 104-109.

Kroll, Jack "An Electronic Cassandra." *Newsweek*, 21 February 1983, p. 77.

Krows, Arthur Edwin. *Equipment for Stage Production.* New York: D. Appleton-Century, 1928.

――――. *Play Production in America.* New York: Holt, 1916.

――――. *Playwriting for Profit.* New York: Longmans, Green, 1928.

Kuan, Han-ch'ing. *Selected Plays of Kuan Han-ch'ing.* Translated by Yang Hsien-yi and Gladys Yang. Peking: Foreign Languages Press, 1958.

Kubly, Herbert. "The Outdoor People's Theatre of Europe." *Educational Theatre Journal* 4 (May 1952): 97-103.

Kuhlke, William. "Vakhtangov and the American Theatre of the 1960's." *Educational Theatre Journal* 19 (May 1967): 179-187.

Kumakura, Isao. "Traditional Performing Arts and the Modern Age." *Acta Asiatica.* 33 (November 1977): 55-73.

LaCasse, Don. "Edwin Booth on Dion Boucicault, Playwriting, and Play Production—A Previously Unpublished Letter." *Theatre Survey* 21 (November 1980): 181-184.

Lal, P., ed. and trans. *Great Sanskrit Plays in Modern Translation*, Norfolk, Conn.: New Directions, 1964.

Langer, Susanne. *Feeling and Form*. New York: Charles Scribner's Sons, 1953.

Langhans, Edward A. *Restoration Promptbooks*. Carbondale: Southern Illinois University Press, 1981.

———. "Staging Practices in the Restoration Theatres 1660-1682." Ph.D. dissertation, Yale University, 1955.

———. "Three Early 18th Century Manuscript Promptbooks." *Modern Philology* 65 (November 1967): 114-129.

de Laporte, Joseph, and Chamfort, S.R.N. *Dictionnaire Dramatique*. 1776. Reprint. Geneva, Switzerland: Slatkine, 1967.

Larlham, Peter. "Festivals of the Nazareth Baptist Church." *The Drama Review* 25 (Winter 1981): 59-74.

———. "Isicathamia Competition in South Africa." *The Drama Review* 25 (March 1981): 108-112.

Laroon, Marcellus. *Cryes of the City of London Drawne at the Tide*. London: 1688.

Larousse Encyclopedia of Mythology. Translated by Richard Aldington and Delano Ames. Revised by a panel of editorial advisers. New York: Prometheus, 1960.

Larson, Orville K. "Giacomo Torelli, Sir Philip Skippon, and Stage Machinery for the Venetian Opera." *Theatre Journal* 32 (December 1980): 448-458.

———. "New Evidence on the Origins of the Box Set." *Theatre Survey* 21 (November 1980): 79-91.

———. "Vasari's Descriptions of Stage Machinery." *Educational Theatre Journal* 9 (December 1957): 287-299.

Laurie, Joe, Jr. *Vaudeville: From the Honky-Tonks to the Palace*. New York: Henry Holt, 1953.

Law, Alma H. "Meyerhold's *Woe to Wit*, 1928." *The Drama Review* 18 (September 1974): 89-107.

Lawler, Lillian Beatrice. *The Dance in Ancient Greece*. Middletown, Conn.: Wesleyan University Press, 1964.

Lawrence, William J. *The Elizabethan Playhouse and Other Studies*, 2 vols. 1912-1913. Reprint. New York: Russell and Russell, 1963.

———. *Pre-Restoration Stage Studies*. Cambridge: Harvard University Press, 1927.

Lea, K.M. *Italian Popular Comedy*, 2 vols. 1934. Reprint. New York: Russell and Russell, 1962.

Leacroft, Richard. *The Development of the English Playhouse*. Ithaca: Cornell University Press, 1973.

Leacroft, Helen, and Leacroft, Richard. *The Theatre*. New York: Roy, 1958.

Leanerd, John. *The Rambling Justice*. London: 1678.

Leavitt, Michael B. *Fifty Years in Theatrical Management*. New York: Broadway, 1912.

Lee, Briant Hamor. "The Origins of the Box Set in the late 18th Century." *Theatre Survey* 18 (November 1977): 44-59.

Lees, C. Lowell. *Play Production and Direction*. New York: Prentice-Hall, 1948.

Lees, Gene. "A Show Business Lexicon." *Show Business Illustrated*, 23 January 1962, p. 57.

Leiter, Samuel, trans. and commentator. *The Art of Kabuki*. Berkeley: University of California Press, 1979.
————. "The Depiction of Violence on the Kabuki Stage." *Educational Theatre Journal* 21 (May 1969): 147-155.
————. *Kabuki Encyclopedia: An English-Language Adaptation of Kabuki-jiten*. Westport, Conn.: Greenwood, 1979.
————. "*Keren*: Spectacle and Trickery in Kabuki Acting." *Educational Theatre Journal* 28 (May 1976): 175-188.
Lenhoff, Gail. "The Theatre of Okhlopkov." *The Drama Review* 17 (March 1973): 90-105.
Leslie, Peter. *A Hard Act to Follow; A Music Hall Review*. New York: Paddington, 1978.
Levin, R.E., and Lemons, T.M. *Sylvania Lighting Handbook*. Danvers, Mass.: Sylvania Electrical Products, 1978.
Lewis, Charlton T., and Short, Charles. *Harper's Latin Dictionary*. New York: American Book Company, 1907.
Lewis, Norman. *Golden Earth; Travels in Burma*. London: Cape, 1952.
Lewis, Sinclair. *Bethel Merriday*. New York: Doubleday Doran, 1940.
Liddell, Henry George, and Scott, Robert. *A Greek-English Lexicon*, rev. 2 vols. Oxford: Clarendon, 1925-1940.
Lifson, David S. *The Yiddish Theatre in America*. New York: Thomas Yoseloff, 1965.
Lindfors, Bernth. "Ogunde on Ogunde: Two Autobiographical Statements." *Educational Theatre Journal* 28 (May 1976): 239-246.
Lippman, Monroe. "Death of the Salesmen's Monopoly." *Theatre Survey* 1 (1960): 65-81.
Liu, Jung-en, ed. and trans. *Six Yuan Plays*. Harmondsworth, Essex: Penguin, 1972.
Liu, Wu-chi. *An Introduction to Chinese Literature*. Bloomington: Indiana University Press, 1966.
Locke, Matthew. *The English Opera; Or the Vocal Musick in Psyche, With...the Instrumental Musick in The Tempest*. London: 1675.
Locke, Stephen. "Klaus Michael Grüber." *The Drama Review* 21 (June 1977): 45-58.
Lokko, Sophia D. "Hunger-Hooting Festival in Ghana." *The Drama Review* 25 (Winter 1981): 43-50.
Lombard, Frank Alanson. *An Outline History of the Japanese Drama*. Boston: Houghton Mifflin, 1929.
Long, Roger. *Javanese Shadow Theatre: Movement and Characterization in Ngayogyakarta Wayang Kulit*. Ann Arbor: UMI Research Press Theatre and Drama Series no. 11, 1982.
Longman, Stanley Vincent. "Eleanora Duse's Second Career." *Theatre Survey* 21 (November 1980): 165-180.
————. "The Modern *Maschere* of Ettore Petrolini." *Educational Theatre Journal* 27 (October 1975): 377-386.
Lord Chamberlain's Warrant, Public Record Office. *Company Personnel and Supply List*. Probably c. 1703.
Lounsbury, Warren C. *Theatre Backstage from A to Z*, rev. ed. Seattle: University of Washington Press, 1972.
Loup, Alfred J. "Vienna's Burgtheater in the 1970's." *Theatre Journal* 32 (March 1980): 55-70.
Love, Paul D. *Modern Dance Terminology*. New York: Kamin Dance Publishers, 1953.

Lucas, Donald William, ed. *Aristotle Poetics*. Oxford: Clarendon, 1968.

Lucas, Newton Ivory. *A Dictionary of the English and German and German and English Languages*. 2 vols. Bremen: C. Schunemann, 1868.

Lucier, Mary. "Industrials: The Theatre of Persuasion." *Theatre Crafts* January 1981, pp. 13-15, 81.

Ludlam, Charles. "Ridiculous Theatre, Scourge of Human Folly." *The Drama Review* 19 (December 1975): 70.

Luterkort, Ingrid, et al, eds. *Theatre Words*, 3d ed. Stockholm: Nordiska Teaterunionen, 1980.

Mabesa, Antonio. "The Philippine Komedya: An Introduction." Typescript, University of Hawaii, n.d.

MacEwan, Elias J., ed. *Freytag's Technique of the Drama*. Translated from the 6th German edition. Chicago: Scott, Foresman, 1898.

Macgowan, Kenneth. "The Vital Principal in Playwriting." *Educational Theatre Journal* 3 (March 1951): 25-31.

MacKay, Patricia, and Loney, Glenn. *The Shakespeare Complex: A Guide to Summer Festivals and Year-Round Repertory in North America*. New York: Drama Book Specialists, 1975.

Mackaye, Percy. *Epoch*. 2 vols. New York: Boni & Liveright, 1927.

Mackerras, Colin P. *Amateur Theatre in China, 1949-1966*. Canberra: Australian National University Press, 1973.

―――, ed. *Chinese Theatre: From its Origins to the Present Day*. Honolulu: University of Hawaii Press, 1983.

―――. *The Chinese Theatre in Modern Times: From 1840 to the Present Day*. Amherst: University of Massachusetts Press, 1975.

―――. "The Growth of the Chinese Regional Drama in the Ming and Ch'ing." *Journal of Oriental Studies* 9 (January 1971): 58-91.

―――. *The Performing Arts in Contemporary China*. London: Routledge & Kegan Paul, 1981.

―――. *The Rise of the Peking Opera, 1770-1870: Social Aspects of the Theatre in Manchu China*. Oxford: Clarendon, 1972.

Macklin, Charles. *An Apology for the Conduct of C. Macklin, Comedian*. London: 1773.

Macleod, Joseph Todd Gordon. *Actors Cross the Volga; a Study of the 19th Century Russian Theatre and of Soviet Theatres in War*. London: Allen and Unwin, 1946.

―――. *The New Soviet Theatre*. London: Allen & Unwin, 1943.

―――. *A Soviet Theatre Sketch Book*. London: Allen & Unwin, 1951.

Malkin, Michael R. *Traditional and Folk Puppets of the World*. South Brunswick, N.J.: A.S. Barnes, 1977.

Malm, William P. *Japanese Music and Musical Instruments*. Rutland, Vt.: Tuttle, 1959.

―――. *Music Cultures of the Pacific, the Near East, and Asia*. Englewood Cliffs, N.J.: Prentice-Hall, 1967.

―――. *Nagauta: The Heart of Kabuki Music*. Rutland, Vt.: Tuttle, 1963.

Malm, William P., and Sweeney, Amin. *Studies in Malaysian Oral and Musical Traditions*. Ann Arbor: University of Michigan Center for South and Southeast Asian Studies, 1974.

Mander, Raymond, and Mitchenson, Joe. *Musical Comedy*. New York: Taplinger, 1969.

Mantzius, Karl. *A History of Theatrical Art in Ancient and Modern Times*. 6 vols. Translated by Louise von Cossel. New York: Peter Smith, 1937.

Manuel, E. Arsenio. *The Maiden of the Buhong Sky*. Quezon City: University of the Philippines, 1958.

Manuud, Antonio G. *Brown Heritage: Essays on Philippine Cultural Tradition and Literature*. Quezon City: Ateneo de Manila University Press, 1967.

Mao, Tse-tung. *Talks at the Yenan Forum on Art and Literature*. n.p.: Foreign Languages Press, 1967.

Mara, Thalia. *The Language of Ballet*. Cleveland: World, 1966.

Marinetti, Filippo Tomasso. "Marinetti's Short Plays." *The Drama Review* 17 (December 1973): 116-125.

Marker, Frederick J. "Negation in the Blond Kingdom: The Theatre Criticism of Eduard Brandes." *Educational Theatre Journal* 20 (December 1968): 506-515.

Marker, Frederick J., and Marker, Lise-Lone. "Thalia in the Welfare State: Art and Politics in Contemporary Danish Theatre." *The Drama Review* 26 (Fall 1982): 3-14.

Marker, Lise-Lone. "William Bloch and Naturalism in the Scandinavian Theatre." *Theatre Survey* 15 (November 1974): 85-104.

Markov, Pavel Aleksandrovich. *The Soviet Theatre*. New York: G.P. Putnam's Sons, 1935.

Marsh, John L. "Captain E.C. Williams and the Panoramic School of Acting." *Educational Theatre Journal* 23 (October 1971): 289-297.

Marsh, Ngaio. *Black Beech and Honeydew*. Boston: Little, Brown, 1965.

———. *Colour Scheme*. Boston: Little, Brown, 1978.

———. *Killer Dolphin*. New York: Little, Brown, 1966.

———. *Last Ditch*. New York: Berkeley, 1978.

———. *Light Thickens*. New York: Little, Brown, 1982.

———. *Overture to Death*. New York: Jove, 1978.

———. *Vintage Murders*. New York: Jove, 1978.

Marshall, Herbert. *The Pictorial History of the Russian Theatre*. New York: Crown, 1977.

Massinger, Philip. *Believe as You List*. Edited by W.W. Greg. Malone Society Reprints. London: Oxford University Press, 1928.

Mathews, Jane DeHart. *The Federal Theatre, 1935-1939; Plays, Relief, and Politics*. Princeton: University Press, 1967.

Mathur, J.C. *Drama in Rural India*. Delhi: Indian Council for Cultural Relations, 1964.

Matlaw, Myron, ed. *American Popular Entertainment: Papers and Proceedings of the Conference on the History of American Popular Entertainment*. Westport, Conn.: Greenwood, 1979.

———. *Modern World Drama*. New York: E.P. Dutton, 1972.

Matley, Bruce. "West Germany's Systematic Approach to Actor Training." *Theatre Journal* 32 (October 1980): 329-335.

Matson, Lowell. "Theatre for the Armed Forces in World War II." *Educational Theatre Journal* 6 (March 1954): 2-11.

Matthews, Brander. *A Book About the Theater*. New York: Charles Scribner's Sons, 1916.

———. *Development of the Drama*. New York: Charles Scribner's Sons, 1926.

———, ed., *Papers on Playmaking 1: 1914-1926*. Reprint. New York: Hill & Wang, 1957.

———. *The Principles of Playmaking*. New York: Charles Scribner's Sons, 1919.

Mayer, David, and Richards, Kenneth, eds. *Western Popular Theatre*. London: Methuen, 1977.

Mazzone-Clementi, Carlo. "*Commedia* and the Actor." *The Drama Review* 18 (March 1974): 59-64.

McCaffrey, Oona. "The Nyau Dance." *The Drama Review* 25 (Winter 1981): 39-42.

McCandless, Stanley R. "A Floor Plan of a Typical Stage of Moderate Size." *Theatre Arts Monthly*, September 1926, p. 626.

———. "Glossary of Stage Lighting." *Theatre Arts Monthly*, September 1926, pp. 627-642.

———. *A Method of Lighting the Stage*. New York: Theatre Arts Books, 1939.

———. *A Syllabus of Stage Lighting*, 11th ed. New York: Drama Book Publishers, 1964.

McCaslin, Nellie. *Creative Dramatics in the Classroom*. New York: Longman, 1974.

McCollum, John I., Jr., ed. *The Restoration Stage*. Boston: Houghton Mifflin, 1961.

McDermott, Douglas. "Agitprop: Production Practices in the Workers' Theatre, 1932-1942." *Theatre Survey* 7 (November 1966): 115-124.

McGaw, Charles. *Acting is Believing*, 4th ed. prepared by Gary Blake. New York: Holt, Rinehart and Winston, 1980.

McGraw-Hill Encyclopedia of World Drama. 2d ed. Edited by Stanley Hochman. 5 vols. New York: McGraw-Hill, 1984.

McKinnon, Richard N. *Selected Plays of Kyogen*. Tokyo: Uniprint, 1968.

———. "Zeami on the Art of Training." *Harvard Journal of Asiatic Studies* 16 (June 1953): 200-225.

McNamara, Brooks. "An Interview with Percy Press and a Portfolio of Buskers." *Educational Theatre Journal* 27 (October 1975): 313-322.

———. "Introduction" (to "Popular Entertainments Issue"). *The Drama Review* 18 (March 1974): 3-4.

———. "The Scenography of Popular Entertainment." *The Drama Review* 18 (March 1974): 17-24.

McPharlin, Paul. *The Puppet Theatre in America*. Boston: Plays, 1969.

McPhee, Colin. *Music in Bali*. New Haven: Yale University Press, 1966.

Medina, Buenaventura S., Jr., and del Castillo y Tuazon, Teofilo. *Philippine Literature: From Ancient Times to the Present*. Quezon City: del Castillo and Sons, n.d.

Meillasoux, Claude. "The 'Koteba' of Bamake." *Présence Africaine*, English ed. 24 (1964): 28-62.

Melchinger, Siegfried. *The Concise Encyclopedia of Modern Drama*. New York: Horizon, 1964.

Melvill, Harald. *Magic of Make-up*, 2d ed. London: Barrie & Rockliff, 1965.

———. *Theatrecraft*. London: Rockliff, 1954.

Mencken, H.L. *The American Language*, New York: Alfred A. Knopf, 1919. 4th ed. 1936. Reprint 1980.

Mendoza, Felicidad M. *The Comedia (Moro-Moro) Re-Discovered*. Manila: Society of St. Paul Makati, 1976.

Mendoza, Liwayway. "Lenten Rites and Practices (The Philippines)." *The Drama Review* 21 (September 1977): 21-32.

Mennen, Richard. "Jerzy Grotowski's Paratheatrical Projects." *The Drama Review* 19 (December 1975): 58-69.

Meserve, Walter J. *An Emerging Entertainment: The Drama of the American People to 1828*. Bloomington: Indiana University Press, 1977.

Meserve, Walter J., and Meserve, Ruth I., eds. *Modern Drama from Communist China*. New York: New York University Press, 1970.

Meserve, Walter J., and Reardon, William R., eds. *Satiric Comedies*. Bloomington: Indiana University Press, 1969.

Messenger, John C. "Ibibio Drama." *Africa* 41 (July 1971): 208-221.

Meyer, Michael. *Ibsen: A Biography*. Garden City, N.Y.: Doubleday, 1971.

Milhous, Judith, and Hume, Robert D. "The Silencing of Drury Lane in 1709." *Theatre Journal* 32 (December 1980): 427-447.

————, eds. *Vice Chamberlain Coke's Theatrical Papers 1706-1715*. Carbondale: Southern Illinois University Press, 1982.

Miller, James Hull. "Initial Factors in Theatre Planning." *Educational Theatre Journal* 8 (May 1956): 89-96.

Miller, Judith. "The Festival of Avignon." *Educational Theatre Journal* 27 (December 1975): 541-542.

————. "Théâtre Populaire de Lorraine: Regional Theatre." *Educational Theatre Journal* 26 (October 1974): 352-364.

Miller, Terry Ellis. "Kaen Playing and Mawlum Singing in Northeast Thailand." Ph.D. Dissertation, Indiana University, 1977.

Miller, Walter. *Daedalus and Thespis*. 3 vols. New York: Macmillan, 1929-1932.

Millett, Fred Benjamin. *Reading Drama*. New York: Harper & Brothers, 1950.

Millett, Fred Benjamin, and Bentley, Gerald Eades. *The Art of the Drama*. New York: D. Appleton-Century, 1935.

Mishima, Yukio. *Five Modern No Plays*. Translated by Donald Keene. New York: Alfred A. Knopf, 1957.

————. *Madame de Sade*. Translated by Donald Keene. New York: Grove, 1967.

Mitchell, Loften. *Black Drama; The Story of the American Negro in the Theatre*. New York: Hawthorn Books, 1967.

————. *Voices of the Black Theatre*. Clifton, N.J.: James T. White, 1975.

Mitosz, Czestaw. *The History of Polish Literature*. London: Macmillan, 1969.

Mlama, Penina O. "Digubi: A Tanzanian Indigenous Theatre Form." *The Drama Review* 25 (Winter 1981): 3-12.

Moebirman. *Wayang Purwa: The Shadow Play of Indonesia*, rev. ed. Jakarta: Yayasan Pelita Wisata, 1973.

Moerdowo, R.M. *Reflections on Balinese Traditional and Modern Arts*. Two parts in one volume. Den pasar, Bali: Udayana University, 1977.

Mongrédien, Georges. *Daily Life in the French Theatre at the Time of Molière*. Translated by Claire Elaine Engel. London: George Allen and Unwin, 1969.

Monthly Mirror. London: November 1798, November 1800.

Moody, Richard. *The Astor Place Riot*. Bloomington: Indiana University Press, 1958.

Morley, Sheridan. *Gertrude Lawrence: A Biography*. New York: McGraw-Hill, 1981.

Morrison, Jack. "Paper World: AETA's Administrative Structure." *Educational Theatre Journal* 3 (December 1951): 335-337.

Morton, Carlos. "Nuyorican Theatre." *The Drama Review* 20 (March 1976): 43-49.

Morton, David. *The Traditional Music of Thailand*. Berkeley: University of California Press, 1976.

Mosel, Tad, and Macy, Gertrude. *Leading Lady: The World and Theatre of Katharine Cornell*. Boston: Little, Brown, 1978.

Moses, Montrose J., and Brown, John Mason, eds. *The American Theatre as Seen by its Critics*. New York: W.W. Norton, 1934.

Moss, Arnold. "The Language of Show Business." *American Speech* 11 (October 1936): 219-222.

Mossman, Harry. "Dissonance Between an Acting Role and an Actor's Personal Beliefs." *Educational Theatre Journal* 27 (December 1975): 535-539.

Motofuji, Frank, trans. *The Love of Izayoi and Seishin: A Kabuki Play by Kawatake Mokuami*. Rutland, Vt.: Tuttle, 1966.

Mowry, Hua-yuan Li. *Yang-pan Hsi—New Theater in China*. Berkeley: University of California Press, 1976.

Moynet, J. *French Theatre Production in the Nineteenth Century*. Translated and augmented by Allen S. Jackson, with M. Geen Wilson. Edited by Marvin Carlson. Binghamton, N.Y.: Max Reinhardt Foundation with the Center for Modern Theatre Research, 1976.

Mukhopadhyay, Durgadas, ed. *Lesser Known Forms of Performing Arts in India*. New Delhi: Sterling, 1978.

Mullin, Donald C. *The Development of the Playhouse*. Berkeley: University of California Press, 1970.

———. "Lighting on the 18th Century London Stage: A Reconsideration." *Theatre Notebook* 34 (1980): 73-85.

Murray, Christopher. "Elliston's Productions of Shakespeare." *Theatre Survey* 11 (November 1970): 99-123.

Murray, Gilbert. *Five Stages of Greek Religion*, 2d ed. New York: Columbia University Press, 1925.

Murrie, Eleanore. See: Boswell, Eleanore.

Myers, Henry Alonzo. *Tragedy: A View of Life*. Ithaca: Cornell University Press, c.1956.

Myrsiades, Linda Suny. "Greek Resistance Theatre in World War II." *The Drama Review* 21 (March 1977): 99-107.

———. "Nation and Class in the Karaghiözis History Performance." *Theatre Survey* 19 (May 1978): 49-62.

Nagler, Alois M. *The Medieval Religious Stage*. New Haven: Yale University Press, 1976.

———. *Sources of Theatrical History*. New York: Theatre Annual, 1952. Paperback ed.: *A Source Book in Theatrical History*. New York: Dover, 1959.

Nahshon, Edna, et al. "With Foreman on Broadway: Five Actors' Views." *The Drama Review* 20 (September 1976): 83-100.

Nahumck, Nadia Chilkovsky. *Introduction to Dance Literacy*. Transvaal, S.A.: International Library of African Music, 1978.

Nakamura, Yasuo. *Noh: The Classical Theatre*. Translated by Don Kenny. New York: Walker/Weatherhill, 1971.

Nalbach, Daniel. *The King's Theatre 1704-1867*. London: The Society for Theatre Research, 1972.

Napier, Frank. *Curtains for Stage Settings*, 2d ed. London: Frederick Muller, 1949.

———. *Noises Off*, 4th ed. Edited by Christopher Ede. London: J. Garnet Miller, 1962.

National Institute of Dramatic Art (Australia). "Technical Production Course." Mimeograph, 1981.

Naxon, Lenore. "Learning the Wigmaker's Process." *Theatre Crafts*, January 1981, pp. 40-41, 88.

Neal, Larry. "The Black Arts Movement." *The Drama Review* 12 (Summer 1968): 29-39.

Nearman, Mark J. "Zeami's *Kyui*: A Pedagogical Guide for Teachers of Acting." *Monumenta Nipponica* 33 (Autumn 1978): 229-332.

Nelms, Henning. *Play Production*, rev. ed. New York: Barnes & Noble, 1958.

———. *A Primer of Stagecraft*, 1941. Reprint. New York: Dramatists Play Service, 1955.

Nelson, Alan. *The Medieval English Stage*. Chicago: University of Chicago Press, 1974.

Neog, Maheswar. *Sankaradeva and His Times*. Gauhati: Department of Publication, Gauhati University, 1965.

Neto, Jose Possi. "The Bumba-meu-Boi." *The Drama Review* 21 (September 1977): 5-10.

Nettleton, George H., and Case, Arthur E., eds. *British Dramatists from Dryden to Sheridan*. Boston: Houghton Mifflin, 1939.

New Grove Dictionary of Music and Musicians. Edited by Stanley Sadie. 20 vols. London: Macmillan, 1980.

Nichols, Harold J. "Julia Glover and the 'Old School' of Comic Acting." *Educational Theatre Journal* 29 (December 1977): 517-525.

Nicklaus, Thelma. *Harlequin*. New York: George Braziller, 1956.

Nickolich, Barbara E. "Alwin Nikolais' Uses of Light." *The Drama Review* 17 (June 1973): 80-91.

Nicoll, Allardyce. *The Development of the Theatre*, 5th ed. rev. New York: Harcourt Brace, 1966.

———. *A History of English Drama 1660-1900*. 6 vols. Cambridge: University Press, 1952-1959.

———. *Masks, Mimes and Miracles*. 1931. Reprint. New York: Cooper Square, 1963.

———. *Stuart Masques and the Renaissance Stage*. London: George C. Harrap, 1937.

———. *The Theory of Drama*. 1931. Reprint. New York: Thomas Y. Crowell, 1967.

———. *The World of Harlequin*. Cambridge: University Press, 1963.

Nippon Gakujutsu Shinkokai. *Japanese Noh Drama*. 3 vols., Tokyo: 1955, 1959, 1960.

Noma, Seiroku. *Masks*. Translated and adapted by Meredith Weatherby. Rutland, Vt.: Tuttle, 1957.

Norrish, Peter John. *Drama of the Group*. Cambridge: University Press, 1958.

North, Roger. *Roger North on Music*. Edited by John Wilson. London: Novello, 1959.

Norton, Dan S., and Rushton, Peters. *Classical Myths in English Literature*. New York: Rinehart, 1952.

Norvelle, Lee. "Stanislavski Revisted." *Educational Theatre Journal* 14 (March 1962): 29-37.

Norwood, Gilbert. *Greek Tragedy*, 2d ed. London: Methuen, 1928.

Obraztsov, Sergei Vladmirovich. *The Chinese Puppet Theatre*. Translated by J.T. MacDermott. London: Faber and Faber, 1961.

O'Connor, Donald. James Cagney PBS Special, 1982.

O'Connor, John Bartholomew. *Chapters in the History of Actors and Acting in Ancient Greece*. New York: Haskell House, 1966.

Odell, George C.D. *Annals of the New York Stage*, 15 vols. New York: Columbia University Press, 1927-1949.

————. *Shakespeare from Betterton to Irving.* 2 vols. New York: Charles Scribner's Sons, 1920.

Odom, Maggie. "Mary Wigman: The Early Years 1913-1925." *The Drama Review* 24 (December 1980): 81-92.

OED. See: *Oxford English Dictionary.*

O'Hara, Frank Hurburt, and Bro, Margueritte Harmon. *Invitation to the Theater.* New York: Harper & Brothers, 1951.

O'Keeffe, John. *Recollections of the Life of John O'Keeffe.* 2 vols. London: Henry Colburn, 1826.

Olf, Julian. "Acting and Being: Some Thoughts About Metaphysics and Modern Performance Theory." *Theatre Journal* 33 (March 1981): 34-45.

————. "The Man/Marionette Debate in Modern Theatre." *Educational Theatre Journal* 26 (December 1974): 488-494.

Oliver, Donald, comp. and ed. *The Greatest Revue Sketches.* New York: Avon, 1982.

Oliver, William I. "Between Absurdity and the Playwright." *Educational Theatre Journal* 15 (October 1963): 224-235.

————. *Voices of Change in Spanish-American Theater.* Austin: University of Texas Press, 1971.

Oman, Carola Mary. *David Garrick.* London: Hodder and Stoughton, [1958].

O'Neill, Cecily, and Lambert, Alan. *Drama Structures.* London: Hutchinson, 1982.

O'Neill, P.G. *Early No Drama: Its Background, Character, and Development, 1300-1450.* London: Lund Humphries, 1959.

————. *A Guide to Noh.* Tokyo: Hinoki Shoten, 1954.

Oreglia, Giacomo. *The Commedia dell' Arte.* Translated by Lovett F. Edwards. New York: Hill & Wang, 1968.

Ortolani, Benito. "Iemoto." *Japan Quarterly* 16 (July-September 1969): 297-306.

————. "Zeami's Aesthetics of the No and Audience Participation." *Educational Theatre Journal* 24 (May 1972): 109-117.

————. *Zenchiku's Aesthetics of the No Theatre.* New York: Riverdale Center for Religious Research, 1976.

Orwell, George. *Down and Out in Paris and London.* New York: Harcourt, Brace & World, 1961.

Osman, Mohd. Taib, ed. *Traditional Drama and Music of Southeast Asia.* Kuala Lumpur: Dewan Bhasa Dan Pustaka, 1974.

Owen, Arthur S., ed. *Euripides Ion.* Oxford: Clarendon, 1939.

Oxford Classical Dictionary, 2d ed. Edited by N.G.L. Hammond and H.H. Scullard. Oxford: Clarendon, 1978.

Oxford English Dictionary, Compact Edition. 2 vols. New York: Oxford University Press, 1971.

Oxford Latin Dictionary. 8 fascicles. London: Clarendon, 1968–1976.

Parker, Derek, and Parker, Julia. *The Natural History of the Chorus Girl.* New York: Bobbs-Merrill, 1975.

Parker, W. Oren, and Smith, Harvey K. *Scene Design and Stage Lighting,* 4th ed. New York: Holt, Rinehart, and Winston, 1979.

Parsons, Charles S. *Amateur Stage Management and Production.* London: Sir Isaac Pitman and Sons, 1931.

Partridge, Eric. *A Dictionary of Slang and Unconventional English,* 5th ed. New York: Macmillan, 1961.

————. *Origins: A Short Etymological Dictionary of Modern English*, 2d ed. New York: Macmillan, 1959.

————. *Slang To-Day and Yesterday*, 4th ed. New York: Barnes & Noble, 1970.

Paskman, Dailey. *"Gentlemen, Be Seated" A Parade of the American Minstrels*, rev. ed. New York: Clarkson N. Potter, 1976.

Peacock, James L. *Rites of Modernization*. Chicago: University of Chicago Press, 1968.

Penzel, Frederick. *Theatre Lighting Before Electricity*. Middletown, Conn.: Wesleyan University Press, 1978.

Pepys, Samuel. *The Diary of Samuel Pepys*. Edited by Robert Latham and William Matthews. 11 vols. Berkeley: University of California Press, 1970-1983.

Perugini, Mark Edward. *A Pageant of the Dance and Ballet*. London: Jarrolds, 1935.

Peter, Thurston C. *The Old Cornish Drama*. London: Elliot Stock, 1906.

Petit de Julleville, Louis. *Histoire du Théâtre en France. La Comédie et les Moeurs en France au Moyen Age*. Paris: Librairie Leopold Cerf, 1886.

Pettet, Edwin Burr. "Report on the Irish Theatre." *Educational Theatre Journal* 8 (May 1956): 109-114.

Pettys, Rebecca Ansary. "The Ta'zieh: Ritual Enactment of Persian Renewal." *Theatre Journal* 33 (October 1981): 341-354.

Pham-Duy. *Musics of Viet Nam*. Carbondale: Southern Illinois University Press, 1975.

Philippi, Herbert. *Stagecraft and Scene Design*. Boston: Houghton-Mifflin, 1953.

Philpott, Alexis R. *Dictionary of Puppetry*. Boston: Plays, 1969.

Pickard-Cambridge, A.W. *Dithyramb, Tragedy and Comedy*. 1927. 2d rev. ed. edited by T.B.L. Webster. Oxford: Clarendon, 1962.

————. *The Dramatic Festivals of Athens*. Oxford: Clarendon, 1953. 2d ed. rev. by J. Gould and D.M. Lewis, 1968.

————. *The Theatre of Dionysus in Athens*. Oxford: Clarendon, 1946.

Pickering, Jerry V. *Theatre. A History of the Art*. St. Paul, Minn.: West, 1978.

Picon, Molly, and Grillo, Jean. *Molly*. New York: Simon and Schuster, 1980.

Pilbrow, Richard. *Stage Lighting*, rev. ed. New York: Drama Book Specialists, 1979.

Planché, James Robinson. *A Cyclopedia of Costume*. 2 vols. London: Chatto and Windus, 1877-1879.

Platnauer, Maurice, ed. *Iphigenia in Tauris*. [by Euripides]. Oxford: Clarendon, 1938.

Pluggé, Domis E. *History of Greek Play Production in American Colleges and Universities from 1881 to 1936*. New York: Columbia University Press, 1938.

Pok Ni, U. *Konmara Pya Zat: An Example of Popular Burmese Drama in the XIX Century*, vol. 1. Translated by Hla Pe. London: Luzac, 1952.

Pollard, Alfred William, ed. *English Miracle Plays, Moralities and Interludes*, 8th ed. rev. Oxford: Clarendon, 1927.

Post Man., London, 1696.

Pougin, Arthur. *Dictionnaire Historique et Pittoresque du Théâtre*. Paris: Librarie de Firmin (Didot), 1885.

Powell, Jocelyn. "Marlowe's Spectacle." *Tulane Drama Review* 8 (Summer 1964): 195-210.

Preminger, Alex; Warnke, Frank J.; and Hardison, O.B., eds. *Princeton Encyclopedia of Poetry and Poetics*. Enlarged Edition. Princeton: Princeton University Press, 1974.

Press, David R. "Autocrat or Collaborator? The Stanislavsky Method of Acting." *Educational Theatre Journal* 18 (October 1966): 264-270.

Preston-Dunlop, Valerie. *A Handbook for Modern Educational Dance*, rev. ed. Boston: Plays, 1980.

Pronko, Leonard C. *Theater East and West: Perspectives Toward a Total Theater*. Berkeley: University of California Press, 1974.

P.R.R. "A Ru-howzi Evening." *The Drama Review* 18 (December 1974): 114-115.

Public Advertiser. London: 1784.

Public Record Office documents, London.

Purdom, Charles Benjamin. *Producing Plays: A Handbook for Producers and Players*. Reprint of 1951 3d enlarged ed. London: J.M. Dent, 1975.

Radcliffe, Alexander. *The Ramble, an Anti-Heroick Poem*. London: 1692.

Rae, Kenneth, and Southern, Richard. *An International Vocabulary of Technical Theatre Terms*. New York: Theatre Arts Books, 1959.

Raghavan, V. "Music in Ancient Indian Drama." *Sangeet Natak Akademi Bulletin*, 4 (March 1956): 5-12.

Raja, K. Kunjunni. *Kutiyattam, An Introduction*. New Delhi: Sangeet Natak Akademi, 1964.

Rajadhon, Phya. See: Anuman, Rajadhon Phya.

Rajagopalan, L.S., and Iyer, V. Sabramanya. "Aids to the Appreciation of Kathakali." *Journal of South Asian Literature* 10 (Winter, Spring, Summer 1975): 205-210.

Rajathon, Phraya Anuman. See: Anuman, Rajadhon Phya.

Ralph, James. *The Taste of the Town* (reissue of *The Touch-Stone*, 1728). London: 1731.

Rama II, H.R.H. *Sang Thong. A Dance-Drama from Thailand*. Translated by Fern Ingersoll. Rutland, Vt.: Tuttle, 1973.

"Ramker (Ramayana Khmer)." *Kambuja* (October 1969): 142–147, (November 1969): n.p., (December 1969): 176–190.

Ramsey, Charles George, and Sleeper, Harold Reeve. *Architectural Graphic Standards*, 7th ed. Edited by Robert T. Packard. New York: John Wiley, 1981.

Rangacharya, Adya. *The Indian Theatre*. New Delhi: National Book Trust, 1971.

―――. *Introduction to Bharata's Natya-Sastra*. Bombay: Popular Prakashan, 1966.

Ranganath, H. K. *The Karnatak Theatre*. Dharwar: Karnatak University, 1960.

Ranganathan, Edwina. "Krsnanattam: A Traditional Dance-Drama Concerning the Life of Lord Krishna." *Journal of South Asian Literature* 10 (Winter, Spring, Summer 1975): 275-287.

Rangthong, Jaivid, ed. *A Souvenir of Siam*. Bangkok: Hatha Dhip, 1954.

Rassers, W. H. *Pañji, The Culture Hero. A Structural Study of Religion in Java*. The Hague: Martinus Nijhoff, 1959.

Raz, Jacob. "The Actor and His audience. Zeami's Views on the Audience of the Noh." *Monumenta Nipponica* 31 (Autumn 1976): 251-274.

Reed, Daphne. "LeRoi Jones: High Priest of the Black Arts Movement." *Theatre Journal* 31 (March 1979): 53-59.

Rees, Abraham. *The Cyclopaedia*. 45 vols. London: Longmans, 1802-1820.

Rees, Terence. *Theatre Lighting in the Age of Gas*. London: Society for Theatre Research, 1978.

Reinhardt, Paul D. "Movement in Period Costume." *Educational Theatre Journal* 14 (March 1962): 50-55.

Rennert, Hugo. *The Spanish Stage in the Time of Lope de Vega*. New York: Hispanic Society of America, 1909.

The Revels History of Drama in English. London: Methuen, 1975―. In progress.

Rhodes, R. Crompton. *Shakespeare's First Folio*. New York: D. Appleton, 1923.

―――. *The Stagery of Shakespeare*. Birmingham: Cornish Brothers, 1922.

Richards, Kenneth, and Thomson, Peter, eds. *Essays on Nineteenth Century British Theatre*. London: Methuen, 1971.

Richardson, Philip J.S., ed. *Dancing Times*. London: n.p., 1927.

Richey, Robert L. "Theatre Management Practices." *Educational Theatre Journal* 8 (December 1956): 311-315.

Richmond, Farley. "The Vaisnava Drama of Assam." *Educational Theatre Journal* 26 (May 1974): 145-163.

―――. *Vanio and Zanda Zulan: Two Gujarati Plays By Asaita Thakar*. Calcutta: Writers' Workshop, 1971.

Riddell, Richard. "The German Raum." *The Drama Review* 24 (March 1980): 39-52.

Ridge, C. Harold, and Aldred, F.S. *Stage Lighting*. London: Pitman, 1935.

Rimer, J. Thomas. "Four Plays by Tanaka Chikao." *Monumenta Nipponica* 31 (Autumn 1976): 275-298.

―――. *Toward a Modern Japanese Theater: Kishida Kunio*. Princeton: University Press, 1974.

Roach, Joseph R., Jr. "From Baroque to Romantic: Piranesi's Contribution to Stage Design." *Theatre Survey* 19 (November 1978): 91-118.

Roberts, Vera Mowry. "New Viewpoints on Nineteenth Century Scene Design." *Educational Theatre Journal* 18 (March 1966): 41-46.

―――. *On Stage: A History of Theatre*, 2d ed. New York: Harper and Row, 1974.

Roebuck, Carl. *The World of Ancient Times*. New York: Charles Scribner's Sons, 1966.

Rogers, Clark M. "Appia's Theory of Acting: Eurhythmics for the Stage." *Educational Theatre Journal* 19 (December 1967): 467-472.

Rogers, Frederick Rand, ed. *Dance: A Basic Educational Technique*. New York: Macmillan, 1941.

Roggendorf, Joseph, ed. *Studies in Japanese Culture*. Tokyo: Sophia University, 1963.

Rose, A. *Stage Effects*. London: George Routledge & Sons, n.d.

Rose, Al. *Eubie Blake*. New York: Schirmer Books, 1979.

Rosenberg, Helane S., and Prendergast, Christine. *Theatre for Young People*. New York: Holt, Rinehart and Winston, 1983.

Rosenberg, Merrill A. "Vichy's Theatrical Venture." *Theatre Survey* 2 (November 1970): 124-150.

Rosenfeld, Lulla. *Bright Star of Exile: Jacob Adler and the Yiddish Theatre*. New York: T.Y. Crowell, 1977.

Rosenfeld, Sybil. *Strolling Players and Drama in the Provinces 1660-1765*. Cambridge: University Press, 1939.

―――. *Temples of Thespis*. London: Society for Theatre Research, 1978.

Rosenmeyer, Thomas G. *The Masks of Tragedy*. Austin: University of Texas Press, 1963.

Rosenstein, Sophie; Haydon, Larrae A; and Sparrow, Wilbur. *Modern Acting: A Manual*. New York: Samuel French, 1936.

Rosenthal, Jean, and Wertenbaker, Lael. *The Magic of Light*. Boston: Little, Brown, 1972.

Rosten, Leo. *The Joys of Yiddish*. New York: McGraw-Hill, 1968.

Rowe, Kenneth Thorpe. *A Theater in Your Head*. New York: Funk & Wagnalls, 1960.

Royal Cambodian Ballet. Phnom Penh: Information Department, 1963.

Rubin, Alec. "Primal Theatre." *The Drama Review* 20 (March 1976): 55-63.

Rubin, Joel, and Watson, Leland H. *Theatrical Lighting Practice.* New York: Theatre Arts Books, 1954.

Rudnitsky, Konstantin. *Meyerhold the Director.* Translated by George Petrov and edited by Sidney Schultze. Ann Arbor, Mich.: Ardis, 1981.

Russell, Douglas A. "Mannerism and Shakespearean Costume." *Educational Theatre Journal* 16 (December 1964): 324-332.

―――. "Shakespearean Costume: Contemporary or Fancy Dress." *Educational Theatre Journal* 10 (May 1958); 105-112.

―――. *Stage Costume Design: Theory, Technique, and Style.* New York: Appleton-Century-Crofts, 1973.

Rutnin, Mattani. "The Development of Theatre Studies at the University Level." *Journal of the National Research Council of Thailand* 14 (1982): 1-19.

―――, ed. *The Siamese Theatre.* Bangkok: Siam Society, 1975.

Ryan, Paul Ryder. "The Living Theatre's Money Tower." *The Drama Review* 18 (June 1974): 9-19.

―――. "Theatre as Prison Therapy." *The Drama Review* 20 (March 1976): 31-42.

Sadler, A. W. "O-Kagura: Field Notes on the Festival Drama in Modern Tokyo." *Asian Folklore Studies* 29 (1970): 275-300.

Saito, Seijiro, et al, eds. *Masterpieces of Japanese Puppetry: Sculptured Heads of the Bunraku Theater.* Rutland, Vt.: Tuttle, 1958.

Sakanishi, Shio, trans. *Kyogen, Comic Interludes of Japan.* 1938. Reprint. Rutland, Vt.: Tuttle, 1960.

Salerno, Henry F., trans. *Scenarios of the Commedia dell' Arte: Flaminio Scala's Il Teatro della favole rappresentative.* New York: New York University Press, 1967.

Sandberg, Trish. "An Interview with Steve Mills." *Educational Theatre Journal* 27 (October 1975): 331-341.

Sandrow, Nahma. *Vagabond Stars, A World History of Yiddish Theater.* New York: Harper & Row, 1977.

Sandys, John Edwin. *A Companion to Latin Studies.* New York: Hafner, 1968.

Santiago, Francisco. *The Development of Music in the Philippine Islands.* Quezon City: University of the Philippines, 1957.

Sarhan, Samir. "The Zar Beat." *The Drama Review* 25 (Winter 1981): 19-24.

Sarkar, Pabitra. "Jatra: The Popular Traditional Theatre of Bengal." *Journal of South Asian Literature* 10 (Winter, Spring, Summer 1975): 87-107.

Saunders, Catherine. *Costume in Roman Comedy.* 1909. Reprint. New York: AMS Press, 1966.

Saxon, A. H. "A Brief History of the Claque." *Theatre Survey* 5 (May 1964): 10-26.

―――. "The Circus as Theatre: Astley's and its Actors in the Age of Romanticism." *Educational Theatre Journal* 27 (October 1975): 299-312.

Sayler, Oliver M. *Inside the Moscow Art Theatre.* New York: Brentano's, 1925.

―――, ed. *Max Reinhardt and His Theatre.* New York: Brentano's, 1926.

―――. *The Russian Theatre.* New York: Brentano's, 1922.

Schauss, Chayyim. *The Jewish Festivals.* Translated by Samuel Jaffe. New York: Union of American Hebrew Congregations, 1938.

Schechner, Richard. "Approaches to Theory/Criticism." *Tulane Drama Review* 10 (Summer 1966): 20-53.

―――. "From Ritual to Theatre and Back: The Structure/Process of the Efficacy-Entertainment Dyad." *Educational Theatre Journal* 26 (December 1974): 455-481.

————. "Guerilla Theatre: May 1970." *The Drama Review* 14 (1970): 163-167.

————. "Ramlila of Ramnagar: An Introduction." *National Centre for the Performing Arts Quarterly Journal* 11 (September and December 1982): 66-98.

Schlemmer, Oskar; Moholy-Nagy, Lazlo; and Molnar, Farkas. *The Theater of the Bauhaus.* Translated by Arthur S. Wensinger. Middletown, Conn.: Wesleyan University Press, 1961.

Schnitzler, Henry. "The Jesuit Contribution to the Theatre." *Educational Theatre Journal* 4 (December 1952): 283-292.

————. "World Theatre: A Mid-Century Appraisal." *Educational Theatre Journal* 6 (December 1954): 289-302.

Schurman, Nona, and Clark, Sharon Leigh. *Modern Dance Fundamentals.* New York: Macmillan, 1972.

Schuttler, Georg W. "Sherlock Holmes as Hamlet?" *Theatre Survey* 18 (November 1977): 72-85.

Scott, Adolphe Clarence. *The Classical Theatre of China.* London: Allen & Unwin, 1957.

————, trans. *Genyadana: A Japanese Kabuki Play.* Tokyo: Hokuseido, 1953.

————. *An Introduction to the Chinese Theatre.* Singapore: Donald Moore, 1958.

————. *The Kabuki Theatre of Japan.* London: Allen & Unwin, 1955.

————, trans. *Kanjincho: A Japanese Kabuki Play.* Tokyo: Hokuseido, 1953.

————. *Literature and the Arts in Twentieth Century China.* New York: Doubleday, 1963.

————. *The Puppet Theatre of Japan.* Rutland, Vt.: Tuttle, 1963.

————. *The Theatre in Asia.* New York: Macmillan, 1972.

————, ed. and trans. *Traditional Chinese Plays.* 3 vols. Madison: University of Wisconsin Press, 1967-1975.

Scott, George. *Burma, A Handbook of Practical Commercial and Political Information.* London: A. Moring, 1921.

Scott, Virginia P. "The Infancy of English Pantomime: 1716-1723." *Educational Theatre Journal* 24 (May 1972): 125-134.

Scott-Kemball, Jeune. *Javanese Shadow Puppets.* London: The Trustees of the British Museum, 1970.

Scouten, Arthur H., ed. *The London Stage, 1660–1800.* Part 3: 1729–1747, 2 vols. Carbondale: Southern Illinois University Press, 1961.

Secret History of the Green Room. See: Anonymous.

Seduro, Vladimir. *The Byelorussian Theater and Drama.* Edited by Edgar H. Lehrman. New York: Research Program on the U.S.S.R., 1955.

Segal, Harold B. *Twentieth Century Russian Drama: From Gorky to the Present.* New York: Columbia University Press, 1979.

Sein, Kenneth (Maung Khe), and Withey, Joseph A. *The Great Po Sein: A Chronicle of Burmese Theatre.* Bloomington: Indiana University Press, 1966.

Selden, Samuel. *First Steps in Acting,* 1964. Reprint. New York: Appleton-Century-Crofts, 1980.

Selden, Samuel, and Sellman, Hunton D. *Stage Scenery and Lighting,* rev. ed. New York: F.S. Crofts, 1940.

————, *Stage Scenery and Lighting,* 3d ed. New York: Appleton-Century-Crofts, 1959.

Seller, Maxine. "Antonietta Pisanelli Alessandro and the Italian Theatre of San Francisco: Entertainment, Education, and Americanization." *Educational Theatre Journal*, 28 (May 1976): 206-219.

Sellman, Hunton D. *Essentials of Stage Lighting*. New York: Appleton-Century-Crofts, 1972.

Sellman, Hunton D., and Lessley, Merrill. *Essentials of Stage Lighting*. Englewood Cliffs, N.J.: Prentice-Hall, 1982.

Senelick, Laurence. "All Trivial Fond Records: On the Uses of Early Recordings of British Music-Hall Performers." *Theatre Survey* 16 (November 1975): 135-149.

———. Review of Bernard Dukore's *Dramatic Theory and Criticism: Greeks to Grotowski*. *Educational Theatre Journal* 28 (May 1976): 271-275.

———, trans. and ed. *Russian Dramatic Theory from Pushkin to the Symbolists*. Austin: University of Texas Press, 1981.

———. "Variety into Vaudeville, the Process Observed in Two Manuscript Gagbooks." *Theatre Survey*, 19 (May 1978), 1-15.

Sergel, Sherman Louis, ed. *The Language of Show Biz*. Chicago: Dramatic Publishing, 1973.

Seyffert, Oskar. *Dictionary of Classical Antiquities, Mythology, Religion, Literature and Art*. Revised and edited by Henry Nettleship and J.E. Sandys. New York: Meridian, 1964.

Seyler, Athene, and Haggard, Stephen. *The Craft of Comedy*. New York: Theatre Arts Books, 1946.

Seymour, Victor. "Theater Keeps PACE in Secondary Education." *Educational Theatre Journal*, 20 (October 1968), 389-397.

Shadwell, Thomas. *The Complete Works of Thomas Shadwell*. 5 vols. Edited by Montague Summers. London: Fortune Press, 1927.

———. *Psyche*. London: 1675.

———. *The Tempest*. London: 1674.

Shafteland, Fannie R., and Shaftel, George. *Role-Playing for Social Values*. Englewood Cliffs, N.J.: Prentice-Hall, 1967.

Shakespeare, William. *Hamlet*. London: 1604.

Shanghai Yishu Yanjiusuo, and Zhongguo Xijujia Xiehui Shanghai Fenhui, eds. *Zhongguo Xiqu Quyi Cidian*. Shanghai: Shanghai Cishu Chubanshe, 1981.

Shastri, Surendra Nath. *The Laws and Practice of Sanskrit Drama*. Varanasi: Chowkhamba Sanskrit Series, 1961.

Shattuck, Charles H., ed. *John Philip Kemble Promptbooks*. 11 vols. Charlottesville: University Press of Virginia, 1974.

———. *The Shakespeare Promptbooks*. Urbana: University of Illinois Press, 1965.

Shaver, Ruth M. *Kabuki Costumes*. Rutland, Vt.: Tuttle, 1966.

Sheppard, Mubin. "Joget Gamelan." *Journal of the Malaysian Branch, Royal Asiatic Society (JMBRAS)* (1967): 149-152.

———. "The Khmer Shadow Play and its Links With Ancient India: A Possible Source of the Malay Shadow Play of Kelantan and Trengganu." *Journal of the Malaysian Branch, Royal Asiatic Society (JMBRAS)* (July 1968): 199-204.

———. *The Magic Kite and Other Ma'yong Stories*. Kuala Lumpur: Federal Publications, 1960.

———. "Pa Dogol and Wa Long." *Journal of the Malaysian Branch, Royal Asiatic Society (JMBRAS)* (1965): 1-5.

———. *Taman Indera*. Kuala Lumpur: Oxford University Press, 1972.

Shergold, N.D. *A History of the Spanish Stage*. Oxford: Clarendon, 1967.

Shih, Chung-wen. *The Golden Age of Chinese Drama: Yuan Tsa-chu*. Princeton: University Press, 1976.

Shimazaki, Chifumi. *The Noh*, vol. 1, *God Noh*. Tokyo: Hinoki Shoten, 1972.

Shively, Donald H. *The Love Suicide at Amijima (Shinju Ten no Amijima), A Study of a Japanese Domestic Tragedy by Chikamatsu Monzaemon*. Cambridge: Harvard University Press, 1953.

————, ed. *Studies in the Modernization of Japan*. Princeton: University Press, 1971.

Siks, Geraldine Brain. "An Appraisal of Creative Dramatics." *Educational Theatre Journal* 17 (December 1965): 328-334.

————. *Drama with Children*. New York: Harper & Row, 1977.

Silapabanleng, Prasidh. "Thai Music at the Court of Cambodia—A Personal Souvenir of Luang Pradit Phairoh's Visit in 1930." *Journal of the Siam Society* 58 (January 1970): 121-124.

Sim, Woo-sung, and Kim, Se-chung. *Introduction to Korean Folk Drama*. Seoul: Korean Folk Theatre Troupe "Namsadang," 1970.

Simonson, Lee. *The Stage is Set*. New York: Harcourt, Brace, 1932.

Skeat, Walter William. *Malay Magic*. 1900. Reprint. New York: Dover, 1967.

Sledd, James H., and Ebbitt, Wilma R., eds. *Dictionaries and That Dictionary*. Glenview, Ill.: Scott, Foresman, 1962.

Sledd, James H., and Kolb, Gwin J. *Dr. Johnson's Dictionary; Essays in the Biography of a Book*. Chicago: University of Chicago Press, 1955.

Slonim, Mark L'vovich. *Russian Theatre, from the Empire to the Soviet*. Cleveland: World, 1961.

Smiley, Sam. *Playwriting: The Structure of Action*. Englewood Cliffs, N.J.: Prentice-Hall, 1971.

Smith, Bill. *The Vaudevillians*. New York: Macmillan, 1976.

Smith, Harvey, et al. *Area Handbook for South Vietnam*, rev. ed. Washington: American University Foreign Areas Studies Division, 1967.

Smith, O. "Persons Employed in the Theatres Royal at Drury Lane and Covent Garden." Folger Shakespeare Library, MS. t.6.1., c. 1810.

Smith, William Charles. *The Italian Opera and Contemporary Ballet in London 1789-1820*. London: Society for Theatre Research, 1955.

Smith, Winifred. *The Commedia dell' Arte*. New York: Columbia University Press, 1912.

————. *Italian Actors of the Renaissance*. 1930. Reprint. New York: Benjamin Blom, 1968.

Sobel, Bernard. *Burleycue*. New York: Farrar & Rinehart, 1931.

————, ed. *The New Theatre Handbook and Digest of Plays*, 8th ed. New York: Crown, 1959.

————. *Pictorial History of Vaudeville*. New York: Citadel, 1961.

————, ed. *The Theatre Handbook and Digest of Plays*. New York: Crown, 1940.

Soedarsono. *Dances in Indonesia*. Jakarta: Gunung Agung, 1974.

Sogliuzzo, A. Richard. "Notes for a History of the Italian-American Theatre of New York." *Theatre Survey* 14 (November 1973): 59-75.

Song-Ban. *The Vietnamese Theatre*. Hanoi: Foreign Language Publishing House, 1960.

Sorensen, Neils Roed. "Tolu Bommalu Kattu: Shadow Theatre in Andhra Pradesh." *Journal of South Asian Literature* 10 (Winter, Spring, Summer 1975): 1-19.

Southern, Richard. *Changeable Scenery*. London: Faber & Faber, 1952.

————. *The Medieval Theatre in the Round*. London: Faber & Faber, 1957.

————. *The Seven Ages of the Theatre*. New York: Hill & Wang, 1961.

————. *The Staging of Plays Before Shakespeare*. London: Faber & Faber, 1973.

Spatharis, Sotiris. *Behind the White Screen*. New York: Red Dust, 1976.

Speaight, George. *The History of the English Puppet Theatre*. London: George G. Harrap, 1955.

Spolin, Viola. *Improvisation for the Theater*. Evanston: Northwestern University Press, 1963.

Stadler, Edmund. *Adolphe Appia*. London: Victoria and Albert Museum, 1970.

Stalberg, Roberta Helmer. *China's Puppets*. San Francisco: China Books, 1984.

Stanislavski, Constantin. *An Actor Prepares*. Translated by Elizabeth R. Hapgood. New York: Theatre Arts Books, 1948.

————. *Building a Character*. Translated by Elizabeth R. Hapgood. New York: Theatre Arts Books, [1949].

————. *Creating a Role*. Translated by Elizabeth R. Hapgood. Edited by Hermine I. Popper. New York: Theatre Arts Books, 1965.

————. *My Life in Art*. Translated by J.J. Robbins. New York: Theatre Arts Books, 1948.

————. *Stanislavsky Produces Othello*. Translated by Helen Nowak. London: Geoffrey Bles, 1948.

States, Bert O. "Servandoni's Successors at the French Opera: Boucher, Boquet, Algieri, Girault." *Theatre Survey* 3 (1962): 40-58.

Steinberg, David, et al. *Cambodia: Its People, Its Society, Its Culture*, rev. ed. New Haven: Herbert H. Vreeland, 1959.

Stern, Lawrence. *Stage Management*. Boston: Allyn & Bacon, 1974.

Stevens, David H., ed. *Ten Talents in the American Theatre*. Norman: University of Oklahoma Press, 1957.

Stewart, David C. "Recent Developments in the Theatre of Turkey." *Educational Theatre Journal* 6 (October 1954): 213-216.

Stewart, Hal D. *Stagecraft*. London: Pitman, 1957.

Stock, William H. "The Method of Multi-Vanishing Point Perspective." *Educational Theatre Journal* 17 (December 1965): 346-353.

Stockwell, La Tourette. *Dublin Theatres and Theatre Customs (1637-1828)*. 1938. Reprint. New York: Benjamin Blom, 1968.

Stoddard, Richard. "Aqueduct and Iron Curtain at the Federal Street Theatre, Boston." *Theatre Survey* 8 (November 1967): 106-111.

Stodelle, Ernestine. *The Dance Technique of Doris Humphrey and Its Creative Potential*. Princeton: Princeton Book Co., 1978.

Stone, Donald, Jr. "French Renaissance Tragedy: New Light on the Sixteenth Century." *Educational Theatre Journal* 26 (October 1974): 287-290.

Stone, George Winchester, Jr. "Lag and Change: Standards of Taste in Early American Drama." *Educational Theatre Journal* 28 (October 1976): 338-346.

————, ed. *The London Stage 1660-1800, Part 4: 1747-1776*. 3 vols. Carbondale: Southern Illinois University Press, 1962.

Stone, George Winchester, Jr., and Kahrl, George. *David Garrick*. Carbondale: Southern Illinois University Press, 1979.

Strand Electric and Engineering Company. *A Completely New Glossary of Technical Theatrical Terms*. London: Strand Electric and Engineering Co., 1947.

Striker, Ardelle. "A Curious Form of Protest Theatre: The *Pièce a Écriteaux*." *Theatre Survey* 14 (May 1973): 55-71.

Stuart, Donald Clive. *The Development of Dramatic Art*. New York: D. Appleton, 1928.

———. *Stage Decoration in France in the Middle Ages*. New York: Columbia University Press, 1910.

Survey of London, XXXV: *The Theatre Royal Drury Lane and the Royal Opera House Covent Garden*. Edited by F.H.W. Sheppard. London: Athlone, 1970.

Suvin, Darko. "Reflections on Happenings." *The Drama Review* 14 (1970): 125-144.

Suzuki, Beatrice Lane, trans. *Nogaku, Japanese No Plays*. London: J. Murray, 1932.

Swann, Darius. "The Braj Ras Lila." *Journal of South Asian Literature* 10 (Winter, Spring, Summer 1975): 21-44.

———. "Three Forms of Traditional Theatre of Uttar Pradesh, North India." Ph.D. dissertation, University of Hawaii, 1974.

Sweeney, Amin. *Malay Shadow Puppets: The Wayang Siam of Kelantan*. London: Trustees of the British Museum, 1972.

———. *The Ramayana and the Malay Shadow Play*. Kuala Lumpur: National University of Malaysia Press, 1972.

Szydtowski, Roman. *The Theatre in Poland*. Warsaw: Interpress Publishers, 1972.

Takaya, Ted T., ed. and trans. *Modern Japanese Drama*. New York: Columbia University Press, 1979.

Takeda, Izumo; Miyoshi, Shoraku; and Namiki, Senyru. *Chushingura*. Translated by Donald Keene. New York: Columbia University Press, 1971.

Talma, François Joseph. *Reflexions on the Actor's Art*. With an Introduction by Sir Henry Irving. New York: Dramatic Museum of Columbia University, 1915.

Taplin, Oliver Paul. *Greek Tragedy in Action*. Berkeley: University of California Press, 1978.

Taylor, Aline. *Next to Shakespeare*. Durham: Duke University Press, 1950.

Taylor, John Russell. *The Penguin Dictionary of the Theatre*. Harmondsworth, England: Penguin, 1966.

Taylor, Theodore. *Jule: The Story of Composer Jule Styne*. New York: Random House, 1979.

———. *The Street Where I Live*. New York: W.W. Norton, 1978.

Telford, Kenneth A., trans. *Aristotle's Poetics*. South Bend, Ind.: Gateway Editions, 1961.

Thailand Government Tourist Bureau. *Aspects & Facts of Thailand*. Bangkok: Public Relations Department, n.d.

Thaler, Alwin. *Shakespere to Sheridan*. 1922. Reprint. New York: Benjamin Blom, 1963.

Thompson, L.F. *Kotzbue. A Survey of His Progress in France and England*. Paris: Champion, 1928.

Ticknor, George. *History of Spanish Literature*, 4th ed. 3 vols. Boston: Houghton Mifflin, 1891.

Tilakasiri, J. *The Puppet Theatre of Asia*. Colombo, Sri Lanka: Department of Cultural Affairs, 1968.

Togi, Masataro. *Gagaku: Court Music and Dance*. Translated by Don Kenny. Tokyo: Weatherhill/Tankosha, 1971.

Toita, Yasuji. *Kabuki: The Popular Theatre*. Translated by Don Kenny. New York: Weatherhill/Tankosha, 1970.

Toll, Robert C. *Blacking Up: The Minstrel Show in Nineteenth-Century America*. New York: Oxford University Press, 1974.

Tonogbanua, Francisco J. *A Survey of Filipino Literature*. Manila: n.p., 1959.

Trapido, Joel. "The Atellan Plays." *Educational Theatre Journal* 18 (September 1966): 381–390.

———. "An Encyclopaedic Glossary of the Classical and Mediaeval Theatres and of the *Commedia dell'Arte*." Ph.D. dissertation, Cornell University, 1942.

———. "A Handlist Of Dictionaries on Technical Theatre." *Theatre Design and Technology*, May 1968, pp. 30–33; October 1968, pp. 23–27.

———. "The Language of the Theatre: I. The Greeks and Romans." *Educational Theatre Journal* 1 (October 1949): 18–26.

———. "Theatre Dictionaries: A View from Inside." *Dictionaries* 2–3 (1980–81): 106–115.

Tribby, William L. "The Medieval Prompter: A Reinterpretation." *Theatre Survey* 5 (May 1964): 71-78.

Trivedi, K. H. *The Natyadarpana of Ramacandra and Gunacandra: A Critical Study*. Ahmedabad: L.D. Institute of Indology, 1966.

Troubridge, St. Vincent. *The Benefit System in the British Theatre*. London: Society for Theatre Research, 1967.

Tsubaki, Andrew T. "The Performing Arts of Sixteenth Century Japan: A Prelude to Kabuki." *Educational Theatre Journal* 29 (October 1977): 299-309.

———. "Zeami and the Concept of Yugen: A Note on Japanese Aesthetics." *The Journal of Aesthetics and Art Criticism* 30 (Fall 1971): 55-67.

Tsubouchi, Shoyo, and Yamamoto, Jiro. *History and Characteristics of Kabuki: The Japanese Classical Drama*. Translated and edited by Ryozo Matsumoto. Yokohama: Heiji Yamagata, 1960.

Tunison, Joseph Salathiel. *Dramatic Traditions of the Dark Ages*. Chicago: University of Chicago Press, 1907.

Turner, Darwin T. "Jazz-Vaudeville Drama in the Twenties." *Educational Theatre Journal* 9 (May 1959): 110-116.

Turner, Margery J; Grauert, Ruth; and Zallman, Arlene. *New Dance*. Pittsburgh: University Press, 1971.

Turner, Victor, and Turner, Ruth. "Performing Ethnography." *The Drama Review* 26 (Summer 1982): 33-50.

Tydeman, William. *The Theatre in the Middle Ages*. Cambridge: University Press, 1978.

Tyler, Royall, trans. *Granny Mountains: A Second Cycle of No Plays*. Ithaca: Cornell University China-Japan Program, 1978.

———. *Pining Wind: A Cycle of No Plays*. Ithaca: Cornell University China-Japan Program, 1978.

Tynan, Kenneth. "The Actor: Tynan Interviews Olivier." *Tulane Drama Review* 11 (Winter 1966): 71-101.

Ueda, Makoto, trans. *The Old Pine Tree and Other Noh Plays*. Lincoln: University of Nebraska Press, 1962.

———. *Zeami, Basho, Yeats, Pound: A Study in Japanese and English Poetics*. The Hague: Mouton, 1965.

Ulbricht, H. *Wayang Purwa: Shadows of the Past*. Kuala Lumpur: Oxford University Press, 1970.

Unruh, Walther. *ABC der Theatertechnik*. Berlin: Carl Marhold Verlagsbuchhandlung, 1950.

———. *Theatertechnik*. Berlin: Bickfeld, Klasing, 1969.

Van der Kroef, Justus M. "The Roots of the Javanese Drama." *Journal of Aesthetics and Art Criticism* 12 (March 1954): 318-327.

Van, Giang. *The Vietnamese Traditional Music in Brief*. Saigon: Ministry of State in Charge of Cultural Affairs, n.d.

Van Gyseghem, Andre. *Theatre in Soviet Russia*. London: Faber and Faber, 1943.

Van Lennep, William, ed. *The London Stage, 1660-1800*. Part 1: 1660-1700. Carbondale: Southern Illinois University Press, 1965.

Varadpande, M. L. *Krishna Theatre in India*. New Delhi: Abhinav, 1982.

———. *Traditions of Indian Theatre*. New Delhi: Abhinav, 1979.

Varneke, Boris Vasil'evich. *History of the Russian Theatre, Seventeenth Century Through Nineteenth Century*. Edited by Belle Martin, translated by Boris Brasol. New York: Macmillan, 1951.

Varyyar, Unnayi. "*Nala Caritam Attakatha*." *Journal of South Asian Literature* 10 (Winter, Spring, Summer 1975): 211-248.

Vatsyayan, Kapila. *Traditional Indian Theatre: Multiple Streams*. New Delhi: National Book Trust, 1980.

Vaughn, Jack A. *Drama A to Z*. New York: Ungar, 1978.

Verma, K.M. *Natya, Nrtta and Nrtya: Their Meaning and Relation*. Bombay: Oriental Longmans, 1957.

Vincent, L.M. *The Dancer's Book of Health*. Kansas City, Kansas: Sheed, Andrews and McMeel, 1978.

Viola, Ann. "Drama With or For Children: An Interpretation of Terms." *Educational Theatre Journal* 8 (May 1956): 139-142.

Virulrak, Surapone. "Likay: A Popular Theatre in Thailand." Ph.D. dissertation, University of Hawaii, 1980.

Visser, Colin. "Garrick's Palace of Armida: A Neglected Document." *Theatre Notebook* 34 (1980): 104-112.

Vitruvius, Pollio. *The Ten Books on Architecture*. Translated by Morris Hicky Morgan. 1914. Reprint. New York: Dover, 1960.

Voss, Lawrence Jensby. "The Theory and Practice of Change of Place in the Drama and Scene-Shifting in the Theatre." Ph.D. dissertation, Cornell University, 1932.

Walcot, Peter. *Greek Theatre in its Theatrical and Social Context*. Cardiff: University of Wales Press, 1976.

Walkup, Fairfax D. *Dressing the Part*, rev. ed. New York: Appleton-Century Crofts, 1950.

Wang, Chi-ssu. Foreword to *Selected Plays of Kuan Han-ch'ing*. Edited and translated by Hsien-yi Yang and Gladys Yang. Shanghai: New Art and Literature Publishing House, 1958.

Wang, Peilun. *Xiqu Cidian*. Taipei: Zhonghua Shuju, 1969.

Ward, A.W. *A History of English Dramatic Literature*, 2d rev. ed. 3 vols. London: Macmillan, 1899.

Ward, A.W., and Waller, A.R., eds. *The Cambridge History of English Literature*. 15 vols. London: G.P. Putnam's, 1907-1917.

Waren, Stanley A. "Theatre in South Africa." *Educational Theatre Journal* 20 (October 1968): 408-414.

Warner, Elizabeth A. *The Russian Folk Theatre*. The Hague: Mouton, 1977.

Washburn, John N. *Soviet Theatre: Its Distortion of America's Image, 1921 to 1973*. Chicago: American Bar Association, 1973.

Watson, Ernest Bradlee. *Sheridan to Robertson. A Study of the Nineteenth Century London Stage*. Cambridge: Harvard University Press, 1926.

Watson, Lee. "Color Concepts in Lighting Design." *Educational Theatre Journal* 10 (October 1958): 254-258.

Waxman, Samuel Montefiore. *Antoine and the Théâtre Libre*. Cambridge: Harvard University Press, 1926.

Wearing, J.P. *American & British Theatrical Biography: A Directory*. Metuchen, N.J.: Scarecrow, 1979.

———. *The London Stage 1890-1899: A Calendar of Plays and Players*. Metuchen, N.J.: Scarecrow, 1976.

Weaver, John. *An Essay Towards An History of Dancing*. London: 1712.

Webster, Glenn, and Wetzel, William. *Scenery Simplified*. Franklin, Ohio: Eldridge Entertainment House, 1934.

Webster, T.B.L. *The Greek Chorus*. London: Methuen, 1970.

———. *Greek Theatre Production*. London: Methuen, 1956.

Webster's New Collegiate Dictionary. Springfield, Mass.: G. & C. Merriam, 1979.

Wedd, Nathaniel, ed. *Euripides: The Orestes*. Cambridge: University Press, 1942.

Weekly Packet. London, 1714.

Wehlburg, Albert F.C. *Theatre Lighting: An Illustrated Glossary*. New York: Drama Book Specialists, 1975.

Weiner, Albert B. Review of Leslie Hotson's *Shakespeare's Wooden O*. *Educational Theatre Journal* 12 (October 1960): 237-238.

Weiner, Jack. *Mantillas in Muscovy: The Spanish Golden Age Theatre in Tsarist Russia, 1672-1917*. Lawrence: University of Kansas Publications, 1970.

Weiner, Leo. *The Contemporary Drama of Russia*. 1924. Reprint. New York: AMS Press, 1971.

Weinreich, Uriel. *Modern English-Yiddish Yiddish-English Dictionary*. New York: McGraw-Hill, 1968.

Welsh, David J. *Russian Comedy 1765-1823*. The Hague: Mouton, 1966.

Wentworth, Harold, and Flexner, Stuart Berg, eds. *Dictionary of American Slang*, 2d ed. New York: Crowell, 1975.

Wepner, Franklin. "The Theory and Practice of Orientation Therapy." *The Drama Review* 17 (September 1973): 81-101.

West, E.J. "Revolution in American Theatre: Glimpses of Acting Conditions on the American Stage 1855-1870." *Theatre Survey* 1 (1960): 43-64.

Westermann, Diedrich, and Bryan, M. A. *The Languages of West Africa* (Part II of *Handbook of African Languages*). Folkestone: Dawsons of Pall Mall, 1970.

White, Robert. "Democracy in the Theatre: Louis Lumet's Théâtre Civique." *Theatre Journal* 31 (March 1979): 35-46.

Wichmann, Elizabeth. "They Sing Theatre: The Aural Performance of Beijing Opera." Ph.D. dissertation, University of Hawaii, 1983.

Wickham, Glynne. *Early English Stages 1300 to 1660*. London: Routledge & Kegan Paul, 1959—. In progress.

———. *The Medieval Theatre*. New York: St. Martin's, 1974.

Wilcox, Ruth Turner. *The Dictionary of Costume*. New York: Charles Scribner's Sons, 1969.

Wiley, Autrey Nell, ed. *Rare Prologues and Epilogues, 1642-1700*. London: George Allen & Unwin, 1940.

Wilkes, Thomas. *A General View of the Stage*. London: 1759.

Wilkinson, Tate. *The Wandering Patentee*. 4 vols. York: 1795.

Willett, John. *The Theatre of Bertolt Brecht*, rev. ed. New York: New Directions, 1968.

————. *The Theatre of Erwin Piscator*. London: Eyre Methuen, 1978.

Williams, Jay. *Stage Left*. New York: Charles Scribner's Sons: 1974.

Wilmeth, Don B. *George Frederick Cooke*. Westport, Conn.: Greenwood, 1980.

————. *The Language of American Popular Entertainment*. Westport, Conn.: Greenwood, 1981.

Wilson, Albert Edward. *Edwardian Theatre*. London: Arthur Barker, 1951.

Wilson, Edwin, and Goldfarb, Alvin. *Living Theatre*. New York: McGraw-Hill, 1983.

Wilson, Garff B. "Achievement in the Acting of Comedy." *Educational Theatre Journal* 5 (December 1953): 328-332.

————. *Three Hundred Years of American Drama and Theatre*, 2d ed. Englewood Cliffs, N.J.: Prentice-Hall, 1982.

Wilson, G.B.L. *A Dictionary of Ballet*, 3d ed. New York: Theatre Arts Books, 1974.

Wilson, John Harold. "Players' Lists in the Lord Chamberlain's *Registers*." *Theatre Notebook* 18 (Autumn 1963): 25-30.

Win, Run. "Theatre Terms." Mimeographed, n.d.

Winstedt, Richard. *History of Classical Malay Literature*. 1940. Reprint. New York: Oxford University Press, 1969.

————. *The Malay Magician; Being Shaman, Saiva and Sufi*, rev. London: Routledge and Kegan Paul, 1951.

————. *The Malays, A Cultural History*. London: Routledge and Kegan Paul, 1961.

Winter, Marian Hannah. *The Pre-Romantic Ballet*. London: Pitman, 1974.

Winters, Shelley. *Shelley Also Known as Shirley*. New York: William Morrow, 1980.

Wirth, Andrzej. "Brecht's Fatzer: Experiments in Discourse Making." *The Drama Review* 22 (December 1978): 55-66.

Witham, Barry B. "The Play Jury." *Educational Theatre Journal* 24 (December 1972): 430-435.

Withey, Joseph A. "An Annotated Bibliography of the Theatre of Southeast Asia to 1971." *Educational Theatre Journal* 26 (May 1974): 209-220.

Wolz, Carl. *Bugaku: Japanese Court Dance*. Providence, R.I.: Asian Music Publications, 1971.

————. "The Spirit of Zen in Noh Dance." *Dance Research Annual VIII. Asian and Pacific Dance: Selected Papers from the 1974 CORD-SEM Conference*. New York: New York University Committee on Dance Research, (1977): 55-64.

Wong, Yen Lu. "Chinese-American Theatre." *The Drama Review* 20 (June 1976): 13-18.

Wouk, Herman. *Youngblood Hawke*. Garden City, N.Y.: Doubleday, 1962.

Wright, Edward A., and Downs, Lenthiel. *A Primer for Playgoers*, 2d ed. Englewood Cliffs, N.J.: Prentice-Hall, 1969.

————. *Understanding Today's Theatre*, 2d edition. Englewood Cliffs, N.J.: Prentice-Hall, 1972.

Wright, James. *Historia Histrionica*. London, 1699.

Wyndham, Henry Saxe. *The Annals of Covent Garden Theatre from 1732 to 1897.* 2 vols. London: Chatto & Windus, 1906.

Yajnik, R.K. *The Indian Theatre.* London: George Allen & Unwin, 1933.

Yamashita, Hiroaki. "The Structure of 'Story-telling' (*Katari*) in Japanese War Tales." *Acta Asiatica* 37 (September 1979): 47-69.

Yamazaki, Masakazu. *Mask and Sword.* Translated by Thomas Rimer. New York: Columbia University Press, 1980.

Yang, Daniel S.P. *An Annotated Bibliography of Materials for the Study of the Peking Theatre.* Madison: University of Wisconsin Press China Series 2, 1967.

———. "Peking Drama with Contemporary Themes." *The Drama Review* 13 (Summer 1969): 167-172.

Yao, Hsin-nung. "The Rise and Fall of the *K'un Ch'u* (Quinsan Drama)." *T'ien Hsia Monthly* 2, no. 1 (1936): 63-84.

Yershov, Peter. *Comedy in the Soviet Theater.* New York: Frederik A. Praeger, 1956.

Yi, Tu-hyŏn. "Mask Dance Dramas." In *Traditional Performing Arts of Korea.* Seoul: Korean National Commission for UNESCO, 1975.

Young, Marjorie. "Performance in Polish Villages." *The Drama Review* 18 (December 1974): 5-21.

Young, William C. *Documents of American Theatrical History,* 2 vols. Chicago: American Library Association, 1973.

Yousof, Ghulam-Sarwar. "The Kelantan Mak Yong Dance Theatre: a Study of Performance Structure." Ph.D. dissertation, University of Hawaii, 1976.

Yupho, Dhanit. *Classical Siamese Theatre.* Translated by P.S. Sastri. Bangkok: Hatha Dhip, 1952.

———. *The Custom and Rite of Paying Homage to Teachers of Khon, Lakon and Piphat.* Thai Culture New Series, no. 11. Bangkok: Fine Arts Department, 1961. Bangkok: Hatha Dhip, 1952.

———. *The Khon,* 2d ed. Thai Culture New Series, no. 6. Bangkok: Fine Arts Department, 1958.

———. *The Khon and Lakon.* Bangkok: The Dept. of Fine Arts, 1963.

———. *Khon Masks.* Thai Culture New Series, no. 7. Bangkok: Fine Arts Dept., 1960.

———. *The Preliminary Course of Training in Thai Theatrical Art,* 4th ed. Thailand Culture Series, no. 15. Bangkok: National Culture Institute, 1956.

———. *Thai Musical Instruments,* 2d ed. Translated by David Morton. [Bangkok]: Fine Arts Department, 1971.

Zaide, Gregorio. *Philippine Political and Cultural History,* vol. 1., rev. ed. Manila: Philippine Education Co., 1957.

Zangwill, Israel. *Children of the Ghetto.* New York: Macmillan, 1906.

Zeami. *Kadensho.* Translated by Chuichi Sakurai, et al. Kyoto: Sumiya-Shinobe, 1968.

Zellers, Parker R. "The Cradle of Variety: The Concert Saloon." *Educational Theatre Journal* 20 (December 1968): 578-585.

———. *Tony Pastor: Dean of the Vaudeville Stage.* Ypsilanti: Eastern Michigan University Press, 1971.

Zhongguo Xiju Nianjian Bianjibu, eds. *Zhongguo Xiju Nianjian, 1982.* Beijing: Zhongguo Xiju Chubanshe, 1982.

Zimbardo, Rose A. "Comic Mockery of the Sacred: *The Frogs* and *The Second Shepherd's Play.*" *Educational Theatre Journal* 30 (October 1978): 398-406.

de Zoete, Beryl, and Spies, Walter. *Dance and Drama in Bali*. 1938. Reprint. Kuala
    Lumpur: Oxford University Press, 1973.
Zolotow, Maurice. *Stagestruck*. New York: Harcourt, Brace, 1965.
Zung, Cecelia S.L. *Secrets of the Chinese Drama: A Complete Explanatory Guide to
    Actions and Symbols as Seen in the Performance of Chinese Dramas*. 1937. Reprint.
    New York: Benjamin Blom, 1964.